Lecture Notes in Computer Science 1141

Edited by G. Goos, J. Hartmanis and J. van Leeuwen

Springer
Berlin
Heidelberg
New York
Barcelona
Budapest
Hong Kong
London
Milan
Paris
Santa Clara
Singapore
Tokyo

Hans-Michael Voigt Werner Ebeling
Ingo Rechenberg Hans-Paul Schwefel (Eds.)

Parallel Problem Solving from Nature – PPSN IV

International Conference on Evolutionary Computation – The 4th International Conference on Parallel Problem Solving from Nature
Berlin, Germany, September 22-26, 1996
Proceedings

Springer

Volume Editors

Hans-Michael Voigt
Technische Universität Berlin
Ackerstraße 71-76, D-13355 Berlin, Germany
E-mail: voigt@fb10.tu-berlin.de
and: GFaI Berlin
Rudower Chaussee 5, D-12484 Berlin, Germany
E-mail: voigt@gfai.fta-berlin.de

Werner Ebeling
Humboldt Universität zu Berlin
Unter den Linden 6, D-10099 Berlin, Germany
E-mail: werner@summa.physik.hu-berlin.de

Ingo Rechenberg
Technische Universität Berlin
Ackerstraße 71-76, D-13355 Berlin, Germany
E-mail: rechenberg@fb10.tu-berlin.de

Hans-Paul Schwefel
Universität Dortmund
D-44221 Dortmund, Germany
E-mail: schwefel@evol.informatik.uni.dortmund.de

Cataloging-in-Publication data applied for

Die Deutsche Bibliothek - CIP-Einheitsaufnahme

Parallel problem solving from nature : proceedings / PPSN IV, International Conference on Evolutionary Computation, The 4th Conference on Parallel Problem Solving from Nature, Berlin, Germany, September 22 - 26, 1996. Werner Ebeling ... (ed.). - Berlin ; Heidelberg ; New York ; Barcelona ; Budapest ; Hong Kong ; London ; Paris ; Santa Clara ; Singapore ; Tokyo : Springer, 1996
(Lecture notes in computer science ; Vol. 1141)
ISBN 3-540-61723-X
NE: Ebeling, Werner [Hrsg.]; PPSN <4, 1996, Berlin>; GT

CR Subject Classification (1991): C.1.2, D.1.3, F.1-2, I.2.6, I.2.8, I.2.11, J.3

ISSN 0302-9743
ISBN 3-540-61723-X Springer-Verlag Berlin Heidelberg New York

Typesetting: Camera-ready by author
SPIN 10513631   06/3142 – 5 4 3 2 1 0   Printed on acid-free paper

Preface

All life is problem solving.

Karl R. Popper

These proceedings contain the written record of the International Conference on Evolutionary Computation – The Fourth International Conference on Parallel Problem Solving from Nature, held in Berlin, Germany, September 22 through 26, 1996.

The conference was jointly organized by the Technical University of Berlin and the Humboldt University at Berlin. It was a great pleasure for the organizers to bring this conference to the place where the evolution strategies were born some thirty years ago.

The unifying theme of the PPSN conference is natural computation, i.e., the design, the theoretical and empirical understanding, and the comparison of algorithms gleaned from nature together with their application to real-world problems in science and technology. Quite dominant is the subject called evolutionary computation, a synonym for evolutionary approaches to problem solving as evolution strategies, genetic algorithms, evolutionary programming, and genetic programming.

We have tried to arrange the papers in thematically coherent sections. The first section on basic concepts of evolutionary computation contains papers which emphasize such topics like hardware evolution, evolution of multiple agent systems, and speciation and symbiogenesis in evolutionary computation.

The second section describes new developments for the theoretical understanding of evolutionary computation. This concerns for example the asymptotic behavior and the statistical description of evolutionary algorithms, the connection between evolutionary algorithms and probabilistic data bases as well as between interactive evolutionary computation and stochastic automata.

The third section shows several extensions of evolutionary algorithms. This concerns problem representation issues and the design of genetic operators, the implications of adaptation, niching, and isolation in evolutionary computation and further modifications.

The next section contains comparative studies which are necessary to grasp the advantages and disadvantages of evolutionary approaches in diverse applications.

Evolutionary algorithms are not the only biological metaphor for computation and problem solving. Other sources of inspiration which are investigated in the fifth section are collective and cooperative behavior, pattern formation, and the immune system.

Evolutionary algorithms have been applied to many domains. The sixth section has been subdivided in applications in machine learning, neural networks, and fuzzy systems, in applications in electrical, electronics, and communications engineering especially for VLSI design and testing, in applications in computer science and operations research, and finally, in applications in such distinct fields like mechanical, chemical, and optical engineering.

Just like during the former PPSN conferences, most of the emphasis is on poster presentations. This promotes active interaction between presenters and the interested people. Only few papers have been selected for oral presentation based on how well they could stimulate the following discussion. Again, this has been done to promote active participation of the attendees.

The papers of these proceedings have been carefully selected from more than 160 submitted papers based on a peer review process. Each paper has been rated independently by, in general, three leading researchers in the field. Each reviewer provided each author with recommendations for the improvement of her/his paper which led to high quality contributions. The effort of these volunteering reviewers is gratefully acknowledged.

We would like to personally thank all the volunteers from the Technical University of Berlin and the Humboldt University at Berlin who have spent many late hours and long weekends on organizing this conference.

Finally, we acknowledge the financial support of the several organizations and companies that made the conference possible.

July 1996

Hans–Michael Voigt
Werner Ebeling
Ingo Rechenberg
Hans–Paul Schwefel

Organization

Steering Committee

Yuval Davidor (Israel)
Hiroaki Kitano (Japan)
Reinhard Männer (Germany)
Hans-Michael Voigt (Germany)
Kenneth DeJong (USA)
Bernard Manderick (Belgium)
Hans-Paul Schwefel (Germany)

Conference Committee

Ingo Rechenberg
Conference Co-Chair
Technical University of Berlin

Hans-Michael Voigt
Conference Co-Chair
Technical University of Berlin
and GFaI Berlin

Werner Ebeling
Program Co-Chair
Humboldt-University at Berlin

Hans-Paul Schwefel
Program Co-Chair
University of Dortmund

Program Committee

Jarmo Alander (Finland)
Thomas Bäck (Germany)
Dmitry I. Batishchev (Russia)
Yuval Davidor (Israel)
Marco Dorigo (Belgium)
Terence C. Fogarty (UK)
Martina Gorges-Schleuter (Germany)
Tetsuya Higuchi (Japan)
Phil Husbands (UK)
Mark Jelasity (Hungary)
Cornelia Kappler (Germany)
Bernard Manderick (Belgium)
J.J. Merelo Guervos (Spain)
Zbigniew Michalewicz (USA)
Mukesh Patel (UK)
Günter Rudolph (Germany)
Lutz Schimansky-Geier (Germany)
Franciszek Seredynski (Poland)
J.L. Verdegay (Spain)
L. Darrell Whitley (USA)
Torsten Asselmeyer (Germany)
Wolfgang Banzhaf (Germany)
Joachim Born (Germany)
Kenneth DeJong (USA)
Agoston E. Eiben (The Netherlands)
David Fogel (USA)
Michael Herdy (Germany)
Robert Hinterding (Australia)
Hitoshi Iba (Japan)
Terry Jones (USA)
Hiroaki Kitano (Japan)
Reinhard Männer (Germany)
Jean-Arcady Meyer (France)
Heinz Mühlenbein (Germany)
Nicholas J. Radcliffe (UK)
J. Dave Schaffer (USA)
Marc Schoenauer (France)
William Spears (USA)
Gunter P. Wagner (USA)

Organization Committee

Michael Herdy
Technical University of Berlin

Cornelia Kappler
Humboldt-University at Berlin

Hans-Michael Voigt
Technical University of Berlin
and GFaI Berlin

Acknowledgments

Invited Speakers

We thank the invited speakers for their talks given at the conference.

Michael Conrad
Wayne State University, Detroit, USA

Manfred Eigen
Max-Planck-Institute for Biophysical Chemistry, Göttingen, Germany

Leonard A. Rastrigin
Technical University of Riga, Riga, Latvia

Ulrich Witt
Max-Planck-Institute for Economic Systems Research, Jena, Germany

Sponsors

The financial support by the following organizations and companies is gratefully acknowledged.

Deutsche Forschungsgemeinschaft (DFG)
European Network of Excellence on Evolutionary Computing (EvoNet)
Parsytec EE GmbH
Daimler-Benz AG
Siemens AG
Center for Applied Computer Science (GFaI)

Contents

Basic Concepts of Evolutionary Computation

Theoretical Foundations of Evolutionary Computation

Modifications and Extensions of Evolutionary Algorithms

Genetic Operators and Problem Representation

Comparison of Methods

Other Metaphors

Applications of Evolutionary Computation

Evolutionary Computation in Machine Learning, Neural Networks, and Fuzzy Systems

Evolutionary Computation in Electrical, Electronics, and Communications Engineering

Evolutionary Computation in Computer Science and Operations Research

Evolutionary Computation in Mechanical, Chemical, Biological, and Optical Engineering

Basic Concepts of Evolutionary Computation

Computational Brittleness and the Evolution of Computer Viruses

Paul–Michael Agapow

Computer Science, La Trobe University, Melbourne, V. 3083, Australia*

Abstract. In recent years computer viruses have grown to be of great concern. They have also been proposed as prototypical artificial life, but the possibility of their evolution has been dismissed due to modern computer programs being computationally brittle (i.e. a random change to a functional program will almost certainly render it non–functional) and the series of steps required for the evolution of a new virus being improbable. These allegations are examined by studying homology between functional program sequences. It is concluded that programs are far less brittle than expected. While the evolution of viruses de novo is still unlikely, evolution of pre–existing viruses and programs is feasible. This has significant implications for computer security and evolutionary computation.

1 Introduction

> A hypercard can carry a virtually infinite amount of information — all the books in the Library of Congress, every episode of *Hawaii Five-O* ... or more likely a wide variety of nasty computer viruses. If Hiro reaches out and takes the hypercard, then the data will be transferred from this guy's system into Hiro's computer. Hiro, naturally, would not touch it any more than you would take a free syringe from a stranger in Times Square and jab it in your neck.
>
> (Neal Stephenson, *Snow Crash*)

Computer viruses have existed as an idea for a quarter of a century and as real entities loose "in the wild" for half that time. That short period has seen explosive development amongst viruses. One work traces the developments in the field on a month by month basis [19]. Defence against viruses has become a lively industry with some major viral outbreaks being assessed at millions of dollars due to lost time or corrupt data. Asides from economic impact, viruses are a major concern for sensitive or critical systems [10, 17].

Besides these issues, there is another more theoretical but perhaps no less important aspect to computer viruses — the idea of viruses as lifeforms. In a sense viruses are prototypically alive, as they can be said to reproduce, metabolise,

* Email: agapow@latcs1.oz.au, current address for correspondence: Infocalypse, GPO Box 964 G, Melbourne, V. 3001, Australia.

sense and adapt. It has also been asked whether, like other life, viruses can evolve. Although this possibility has previously been regarded as remote, there are significant reasons for doubting this.

2 The Biology and Ecology of Computer Viruses

A computer virus may be defined as [9] :

> a program that can "infect" other programs by modifying them to include a possibly evolved copy of itself

Viruses are a member of a class of software entities called *malicious logic* [6] which have the attribute of hiding potentially harmful computations from human operators. Although borderlines between members of this class are indistinct, viruses are held to have certain behaviours. Firstly, viral replication is not simply automatic but involves the expenditure of resources to affect reproduction in a specific fashion to ensure survival. Secondly, the actions of a virus are triggered and modified by its environment. Finally viruses are parasitic upon other programs — they "hijack" the execution resources of other processes.

Functionally, a virus masquerades as part of the code of a larger program so as to be executed when the "host" is. When run, the viral code typically tests for a particular condition. If this condition (a particular time or date, the existence of certain files etc.) is met the virus will attempt to replicate. This can be just the simple appending of the virus code onto another program's code, although the virus may replace, shift or overwrite some of the host code entirely. Other activity may then take place, for the purpose of concealing the viruses presence (e.g. altering the file system records on its volume) or inflicting damage (e.g. deleting files).

A variety of abilities can be found in viruses (for a detailed list see [19]). Some even deliberately mutate, although in most cases this mutation does not result in functional change, serving simply as a form of disguise. Amongst recent discoveries are viruses that are multi–platform, written in high–level languages or word–processor macros, that can infect spreadsheets and even Prolog source files [21]. It should be stressed that not all viruses are harmful per se. While deliberately malicious ones that corrupt data abound, such overt symptoms tend to work against the replicative success of the virus. Many viruses are nominally benign, with any harmful effects usually being the result of faulty programming, memory consumption and other problems caused by viral replication.

It could be argued that any study of viruses is largely academic because developments will surely soon render them a thing of the past. While it is possible that a revolutionary invention in hardware or software may cause the extinction of viruses, the regular repetition and failure of such predictions should be regarded as evidential of their value. By and large, "hard" schemes that rely upon detecting and destroying every virus are imperfect, may inhibit use of any system they guard [12] and are subject to abuse and misuse [14]. There are also good grounds for concluding that perfect detection of viruses may be a logical impossibility [9, 1] and that any computer system has covert channels of data transmission that may be exploited by viruses [27]. Although the growth in the number of virus strains (currently in the thousands [22]) may be plateauing [24], it seems unlikely that the viruses will disappear in the near future.

3 The Evolution of Viruses

Named as they are after their terrestrial (protein/DNA) counterparts, it is unsurprising that computer viruses have been suggested as a prototypical electronic lifeform [19, 38, 29, 13]. Although there is no "Turing Test" for life, one can compare the properties of a computer virus to those which are generally possessed by living organisms [38, 2]. A computer virus obviously reproduces and in some ways can be said to sense its environment, adapt and metabolise. It is a fairly natural step therefore to ask whether computer viruses share other properties of living organisms. Some have argued argued that evolution is an inherent and even inevitable property of living things [7, 18]. Can viruses be said to evolve?

Accepting evolution as [4] :

> ... [the] process by which organisms come to differ from generation to generation ... change in the gene pool of a population.

it is clear virus evolution exists on a number of trivial levels. For example there is a great deal of human–mediated evolution in that old virus designs are often modified and rereleased, not always by the original designer. More significantly, viruses exercise natural selection amongst themselves. "Unfit" individuals are easily detected by anti–viral software or advertise their presence and are thus intercepted and selected against. "Fit" individuals exert their influence in a subtle manner and attempt to escape detection. Each generation of anti–viral techniques introduces new selection pressures, shaping the composition of the surviving viral population. Viruses may even compete amongst each other, with there being several instances of established viruses being displaced and made extinct by newcomers. This "genetic takeover" has been used deliberately on occasion to wipe out an undesired strain of virus.

Diversity may also appear in a viral population due to the computing environment. Some viral strains are thought to have arisen due to the effect different compilers had on identical source code. Alternatively, due to the intricate way in which viruses are constructed, subtly different computing environments may bring about vastly different behaviours. Further changes that result from the accidental disruption (mutation) of virus code. There are plentiful opportunities for data corruption in the modern computing environment, from faults or failures in hardware and storage media, through stray electromagnetic radiation to buggy software. While it is reasoned that most changes will be non–functional (see below) several strains of viruses apparently created by such events have been seen in the wild. Their modifications vary from single (and silent) instruction substitution, to multi–instruction changes resulting in vast behavioural aberrations [19, 38].

Many might argue that, excepting human–mediated evolution and despite the number of mutants noted above, spontaneous "real" evolution is unlikely to occur to any significant degree. Although rarely stated explicitly the grounds for this argument are :

1. Modern computer programs are computationally brittle.
2. Modern machine language is unsuitable for evolutionary processes.
3. The level of noise required for supplying diversity for evolution is inadequate.
4. The modern structured computing environment is hostile to any minor and evolving rogue computations.
5. The series of steps required for the evolution of a computer virus is highly improbable.

The second point is debatable and perhaps largely a matter of opinion [16, 3] and there is possible grounds for argument on the third as well. This work however will only examine the first of these propositions leading to a reassessment of the last.

4 Computational "Brittleness" and Program Homology

When it is alleged that von Neumann computer programs are computationally brittle [18, 34], this is to say that the ratio of viable programs to the total number of possible programs is minuscule, and thus any random mutant of a functional program is almost certain to be non–functional. It follows therefore that evolution is unlikely as "successful" mutations (those that give rise to a functional program) are improbable. Although several successful computational ecosystems are based on a von Neumann machine language design (for example [32, 16, 34] and many, many others) with one showing "biogenesis" from random, disorganised code [31], it is difficult to derive any lessons about computational brittleness from these. In all cases the machine language of the system has been simplified and shored up against the effects of mutation. Brittleness, if it exists, has been greatly suppressed in these cases.

There are other grounds for doubt. First, if one accepts that computational brittleness is a barrier to evolution, this implies that biological evolutionary systems (i.e. living things) have genetic systems that are not brittle. This is a debatable point [3]. Secondly, this implies that functional programs are dissimilar to each other. It is obvious that any bit–sequence should be on average 50% homologous to any other bit sequence of the same length (i.e half the bits are identical). Further, it seems intuitive that functional programs should share sequences with other functional programs. This is consistent with the not infrequent false positive alarms made by anti–viral software scanning for viral code sequences [37].

To examine homology between real world program sequences, a series of executable binaries on a Unix workstation were converted into hexadecimal code. (Note that thus each byte of the binary was translated into 2 hexadecimal numbers.) The binaries (15 in total including *env*, *tty*, *sleep*, *zcat* et al., adding up to 4 megabytes in total) were selected for their ubiquity and representation of a variety of functions. Binaries that obviously shared common functions (e.g. *mosaic* subsumes the functionality of *gopher*) or contained a great deal of ASCII string data were not used.

Searching for homologous sequences was performed by a modified version of *agrep* (approximate grep [39]), which may scan text sequences and report the number of matches for a sequence within a given limit of substitutions, insertions and deletions. This software was chosen over specialised DNA/protein sequence searchers for the ease of preparing the data, the minor modifications necessary to the search engine and the ability to weight certain types of matches. Note that this approach, matching on the half-byte ("nybble") level, will actually underestimate homology. For example the hex values 9 and 8 will be seen as a mismatch, despite sharing 3 out of 4 bits in common.

Sequences were randomly extracted from each of the executable's hexdumps and matches of varying degrees of homology were searched for in other hexdumps. The pattern of homology was complex but generally high, with virtually all short (64 bytes or less) sequences finding multiple matches within a moderate stringency, some finding literally thousands of matches This decreased with longer sequences (which computational demands limited to 128 bytes, comparable to simple viruses, see below) but not as sharply as might be expected (see Fig. 1). Quite surprising was the large number of sequences that were perfect matches even at long sequence lengths.

In order to test that the matches seen were significantly above the background level, 30 random sequences of the length of the shortest hex pattern were generated and matches searched for. No matches were found at all within the the least stringent homology used (30%). To check that this effect was not caused by a bias in the actual bytes used (i.e. perhaps functional programs are have a non-random frequency of byte usage) another 30 sequences were assembled with random bytes (pairs of hexadecimal characters) from the executable hexdumps. Once again no matches were seen within the most lenient stringency.

It can be reasoned that in a computing environment most random mutations should be substitution / point mutations rather than insertion or deletion. Searches were therefore made for matches allowing only substitutions. However this resulted in only a slight lowering of homology (see Fig. 2). It is also possible the homology might be the result of code from libraries included at program compilation. Testing this hypothesis is difficult due to the lack of non-trivial programs that don't use common libraries. Nonetheless a small number (5) were obtained and treated as above. Again there was only a small lowering in homology (see Fig. 2) although due to the small sample size this result should be treated cautiously. So given a sufficiently large body of code, one should expect good matches for quite substantial lengths of machine code.

The level to which the homology seen is above background (i.e. simple coincidence) may be assessed thus : a 64 byte sequence is 512 bits. Therefore it will perfectly match other randomly generated 64 byte sequences 1 in every 2^{512} trials. From the homology data above (using the search with substitution only and

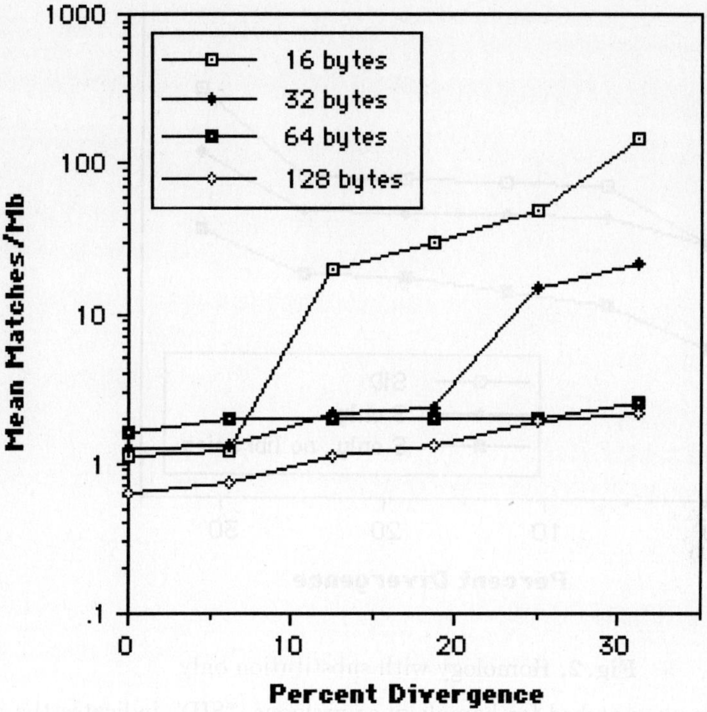

Fig. 1. Sequence homology

Each plot represents the mean success rate for finding matches for 15 search sequences within the given divergence over 4 megabytes of data. A divergence of x% means that the target sequence differed by only x% or less from the search sequence.

without included libraries) a perfect match is found about once every megabyte. As matching is done on the nybble level, there are nearly 2^{21} sequences of 64 bytes that can serve as possible matches. Thus 64 byte sequences show a homology of 1 in 2^{21}, or 2^{491} times more than expected.

5 The (Im)Probability of Evolution

Several investigators have attempted to calculate the likelihood of viruses evolving from "inanimate code" by random mutation [8, 11], concluding that such an event was vastly improbable. For example, Burger [8] asserts the probability as $500!/1000^{500}$, assuming the code in question is 1000 bits long and half the bits are already in the desired state. These odds may be expressed as 1.22×10^{-366}.

Most computer viruses have a length of around 1000 bytes and so the length

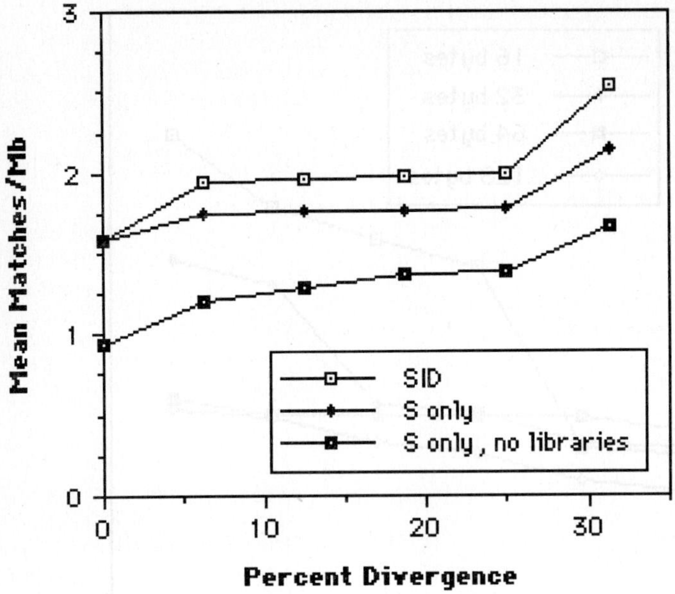

Fig. 2. Homology with substitution only

64 byte sequences matched for homology as previous. "SID" indicates the previously curve, with substitutions, deletions and insertions allowed. "S only" indicates only substitutions were allowed. "No libraries" indicates matches over programs that did not include library code.

of 1000 bits used for this calculation is, if anything, generous. However it would be more accurate to base this calculation on the smallest possible viable virus. Calculations based on a longer length (and more sophisticated viruses) are akin to saying terrestrial life is unlikely since it is improbable that a chimp will spontaneously assemble from a polynucleotides soup. As infectious agents have been reliably reported at 70 bytes (and there are isolated reports of even smaller ones [15]), a length of 500 bits for the primordial computer virus does not seem unreasonable and may be significantly longer than the minimal infectious sequences. Further, the data above has shown there is reason to expect functional programs to resemble each other. A similarity of 60% is feasible and clearly we can expect higher homologies at lower frequencies. Performing the calculations again, we find that the probability of evolution for a 500 bit, 60% homologous sequence is 1.27×10^{-165}. Assuming 80% homology the result is 1.18×10^{-112}.

These are still extremely poor odds, but far removed from the original figure. The spontaneous evolution of an infectious agent is still unlikely, but there are other factors that may significantly alter this probability. For example these calculations neglect any selection effect, that initial mutations may favour the survival of the sequence and its further evolution. Also the bit by bit mutation assumed in the calculation does not allow for "correct" bits being flipped and restored by later mutations, nor for insertion or deletion, or whole segments of functional code being gained by accidental over–writing. The most significant flaw is that the calculation is based on a specific single instance of a random sequence of code evolving into a specific single virus of the same length, on par with watching a particular dog, in the hope it will turn into a specific species of cat. More accurate, but more difficult to calculate, is the idea of any code segment on all of the computers in the world mutating into any virus. From the homology results above it is clear some legitimate code sequences will be extremely similar to functional virus sequences, which is consistent with reports of legitimate programs that are 1 byte different from infectious programs [15, 29].

6 Discussion and Future Work

Assessing the possibility of computer viruses evolving is in many ways akin to the Drake equation (the famous rule–of–thumb calculation of the prevalence of intelligent life in the universe). In order to reach any conclusion, many of the variables involved can only be roughly estimated or guessed. This does not mean that the calculations involved are meaningless, but their results should be accepted cautiously and with all the assumptions in mind.

With this caveat, it would seem that the evolution of computer viruses "in the wild" is not nearly as improbable as has been previously judged. The chance of a wholly new computer virus evolving de novo from legitimate code is still highly improbable. Far more probable is the "mutation" of pre–existing viruses and legitimate programs, with homology serving to explain those mutant viruses and rogue programs that have already been seen. It is a natural (and glamorous) thought that "mutant" software poses a deadly threat to this planet's computing resources. At this stage however it is more realistic to say that rogue programs and the evolvability of machine code (whether under human direction or not) may present a substantial security problem. This is especially worrying with reference to platform–independent mobile programs such as Java and Telescript agents. The other objections listed above to the evolution of computer viruses may still be significant and investigation of these is obviously called for. Nonetheless there is a clear need for more flexible and general mechanism to defeat malicious logic and damaged software, one that is capable to fighting attacks and agents that that have not been seen before or even anticipated. Given that a perfect defence is unlikely if not impossible, the best technique may be a biology–inspired one. Systems may be quarantined to contain the "disease" and a diversity of computation may have to be encouraged so that viral attacks will be defeated by "hybrid vigour" (Hillis quoted in [5]) or an adaptive "immune system" [25]. Indeed, machine language evolution may prove to be a valuable component in an anti-viral immune response.

This leads to a final point — evolutionary computation on the machine instruction level. Although it may not have widespread applicability, such a powerful (albeit very "grainy") evolutionary device may prove useful for program optimisation for specific platforms. It also has another benefit, avoiding the sufficiency problem [26] where an EC alphabet must contain "sufficient" symbols to solve a problem. Machine language contains a very low–level but universal and powerful set. Further study along these lines is sure to reveal important data, useful in the design of EC languages.

Thanks is extended to Joan McGalliard (Infocalypse / Telstra) and Tom Richards (Qualitative Solutions and Research) for their comments. Experimentation was carried out with Perl 5.0 and agrep 2.03 on a SPARCstation running SunOS 4.01. Data was analysed and visualised using Mathematica (Wolfram Research) and Cricket Graph (Cricket Software) on a Macintosh LC III.

References

1. L. M. Adleman. An abstract theory of computer viruses. In S. Goldwasser, editor, *Lecture Notes in Computer Science 403 : Advances in Cryptography — CRYPTO '88 Proceedings*, pages 354–374, New York, 1990. Springer–Verlag.
2. P.-M. Agapow. Computer viruses: the inevitability of evolution? In D. Green and T. Bossomaier, editors, *Complex Systems: From Biology to Computation*, pages 46–54, Amsterdam, 1993. Ios Press.
3. P.-M. Agapow. Computational brittleness and evolution in machine language, 1996. To be presented at *Complexity 96*, Albury, July 1996.
4. K. Arms and P. S. Camp. *Biology.* Holt, Reinhard and Winston, New York, 1979.
5. R. K. Belew. Alife–2 : The second Artificial Life conference. *IEEE Expert*, 6(2):53–59, Apr. 1991.
6. M. Bishop. An overview of computer viruses in a research environment. Technical report, Department of Mathematics and Computer Science, Dartmouth College, 1990.
7. D. Brooks and E. Wiley. *Evolution as Entropy.* University of Chicago Press, Chicago, 1988.
8. R. Burger. *Computer Viruses — a High Tech Disease.* Abacus Software, San Francisco, 1988.
9. F. Cohen. Computer viruses: Theory and experiment. *Computers & Security*, 6(1):22–35, 1987.
10. F. Cohen. On the implications of computer viruses and methods of defense. *Computers & Security*, 7(2):167–184, 1988.
11. F. Cohen. Computational aspects of computer viruses. *Computers & Security*, 8(4):325–344, 1989.
12. F. Cohen. *A Short Course on Computer Viruses.* ASP Press, Pittsburgh, 1990.
13. F. Cohen. *It's Alive! The New Breed of Living Computer Programs.* John Wiley & Sons, New York, 1995.
14. R. Courtney. Comment on biometrics program. *Computers & Security*, 14(5):373–375, 1995.
15. J. Croall and I. C. MacKay. Computer viruses. *British Medical Journal*, 297(41):981–982, Oct. 15, 1988.
16. R. Davidge. Processors as organisms. Cognitive Science CSRP 250, University of Sussex, 1992.

17. T. Durham. The perils of polluted software. *Datamation*, pages 26–27, Feb. 11, 1988.
18. J. D. Farmer and A. Belin. Artificial Life: the coming evolution. In Langton et al. [28], pages 815–840.
19. D. Ferbrache. *A Pathology of Computer Viruses.* Springer–Verlag, Berlin, 1992.
20. S. Gordon. The generic virus writer. In *Virus Bulletin '94 Proceedings*, pages 24–31, Abingdon (Oxfordshire), 1994. Virus Bulletin.
21. H. J. Highland. Random bits and bytes. *Computers & Security*, 14(5):365–371, 1995.
22. P. Hoffman. VSUM — virus information list, 1996.
23. M. Hypponen. F–PROT professional update bulletin 2.13, 1994. Internet resource found at `<http://www.datafellows.fi/bulletin/bull-213.htm>`.
24. M. Hypponen. F–PROT professional update bulletin 2.19, 1995. Internet resource found at `<http://www.datafellows.fi/bulletin/bull-219.htm>`.
25. J. O. Kephart. A biologically inspired immune system for computers. In R. Brooks and P. Maes, editors, *Artificial Life IV*, pages 131–139. MIT Press, 1994.
26. J. Koza. *Genetic Programming.* MIT Press, Cambridge (Massachusetts), 1992.
27. B. Lampson. A note on the confinement problem. *Communications of the ACM*, 16(10):613–615, 1973.
28. C. G. Langton, C. Taylor, J. D. Farmer, and S. Rasmussen, editors. *Artificial Life II*, Menlo Park (California), 1992. Addison–Wesley.
29. M. A. Ludwig. *Computer Viruses, Artificial Life and Evolution.* American Eagle Publications, Tucson (Arizona), 1994.
30. J. Norstad. *Disinfectant On–Line Documentation.* Northwestern University, Framingham (Massachusetts), 1996.
31. A. Pargellis. The spontaneous generation of digital "life". *Physica D*, 91:86–96, 1996.
32. S. Rasmussen, C. Knudsen, R. Feldberg, and M. Hindsholm. The Coreworld : emergence and evolution of cooperative structures in a computational chemistry. *Physica D*, 42:111–134, 1990.
33. T. S. Ray. An approach to the synthesis of life. In Langton et al. [28], pages 371–408.
34. T. S. Ray. An evolutionary approach to synthetic biology: Zen and the art of creating life. *Artificial Life*, 1(1):179–210, 1993.
35. E. S. Raymond. *The New Hackers Dictionary.* MIT Press, 1991.
36. J. Skipper. The computer zoo — evolution in a box. In F. J. Varela and P. Bourgine, editors, *Towards a Practice of Autonomous Systems*, pages 355–364, Cambridge (Massachusetts), 1992. MIT Press.
37. A. Solomon. False alarms. *Virus News International*, pages 50–52, Feb. 1993.
38. E. H. Spafford. Computer viruses — a form of artificial life? In Langton et al. [28].
39. S. Wu and U. Manber. Fast text searching with errors. Technical Report 91–11, Department of Computer Science, University of Arizona, June 1991.

Evolutionary Computing in Multi-Agent Environments: Speciation and Symbiogenesis

Lawrence Bull and Terence C Fogarty

Faculty of Computer Studies and Mathematics
University of the West of England,
Bristol, BS16 1QY, England
E-mail: {l_bull, tcf}@btc.uwe.ac.uk

Abstract. In this paper we introduce two macro-level operators to enhance the use of population-based evolutionary computing techniques in multi-agent environments: speciation and symbiogenesis. We describe their use in conjunction with the genetic algorithm to evolve Pittsburgh-style classifier systems, where each classifier system represents an agent in a cooperative multi-agent system. The reasons for implementing these kinds of operators are discussed and we then examine their performance in developing a controller for the gait of a wall-climbing quadrupedal robot, where each leg of the quadruped is controlled by a classifier system. We find that the use of such operators can give improved performance over static population/agent configurations.

1 Introduction

Darwinism describes evolution by the differentiation of species, like the branching of a river [6]. The inverse process [13] - the bringing together of species to provide evolutionary innovation - has been termed "symbiogenesis" [11]. In this paper we implement both processes as a way of exploiting the capabilities of population-based evolutionary computing techniques in multi-agent environments; we evolve the gait of a simulated wall-climbing quadruped by evolving the controllers of each leg. These processes are termed macro-level operators since they work at the population level, thereby distinguishing them from the usual micro-level operators such as allele mutation and recombination.

Previously [e.g. 2] we have examined the application of the genetic algorithm (GA) [7] in both heterogeneous and homogeneous multi-agent systems. That is, we have used the GA to evolve a number of separate populations for a multi-agent system, one for each aspect (heterogeneous), and used it to evolve a single population for a multi-agent system, where an individual can be responsible for any aspect of the problem (homogeneous). However a large multi-agent system will typically consist of both heterogeneous and homogeneous aspects. By adding the process of speciation to an initial homogeneous configuration for a multi-agent system it becomes possible to allow the most efficient assignment of populations to agents (system aspects) to emerge over evolutionary time, rather than being prescribed a priori; members from a given population configuration can form a new configuration which then competes for existence in an overall fixed population space via the macro-level mutation operator.

Within multi-agent systems it can also be the case that some agents are highly interdependent. Under these conditions the configuration of one agent has a large, often derogatory [8], effect on the performance of one or more other agents in the system. By adding the process of symbiogenesis to multi-agent systems with some heterogeneity it becomes possible to allow agents to join together forming a new super-agent responsible for both (all) interdependent aspects. That is, the effects of inefficient divisions in the overall system's search space - the identification of highly interdependent aspects - can be reduced by allowing agents to join together over evolutionary time; again members from a given population configuration can form a new configuration which then competes for existence in an overall fixed population space via the macro-level mutation operator.

We will now demonstrate the use of these processes. The paper is arranged as follows: the next section firstly describes the details of the wall-climbing quadruped on which we aim to implement our evolved controller and then describes the simulation used in this paper. Section 3 describes the use of the speciation macro-level operator on the task. Section 4 describes the use of the symbiogenesis operator on the task. Finally we discuss our findings.

2 Wall-Climbing Quadruped

The control of walking in natural systems is known to be distributed among a number of parallel sub-systems - "flexible control appears to arise from the cooperation of several autonomous control centres"[5]. This type of system therefore represents an ideal platform on which to examine the use of evolutionary computing techniques in multi-agent systems.

2.1 The Robot

We are developing the control system of a wall-climbing robot for the inspection and maintenance of buildings. The robot is built on a framework of steel tube and measures approximately 400mm x 400mm x 150mm. It consists of four vacuum feet, one on each corner of its chassis, and a central assembly, also consisting of four vacuum feet. The corner feet are each connected to a leg consisting of two pneumatic cylinders allowing vertical and lateral movement, i.e. each foot is connected to a leg consisting of two pistons which enables overall backwards/forwards movement by the robot. The central assembly of four feet is able to move vertically and rotate enabling the robot to alter its path. The robot also carries a distance sensor which can return the robot's distance to some fixed point (e.g. the ground); forward/backward movement is detectable. For this paper we are concerned with the evolution of gait in the qaudruped - the evolution of a complete control system will be presented in the future.

2.2 The Simulation

To examine the performance of the macro-level operators on this system we use Pittsburgh-style classifier systems [Smith 1980] to control the movement of each leg. The robot's pneumatic leg joints lend themselves nicely to digital control as they represent an almost discrete system. Therefore in the simulation each leg controller can return one of three actions for each of the two pistons - move forward or backward, or do nothing - which are coded for by two two-bit pairs. Actions such as move forward when a piston is already in the forward position are simply said to have no effect. For this paper we assume a stable gait to consist of at least two opposite corner feet being down. Feet in contact with a surface are said to have enough contact for a vacuum to have (automatically) formed. Failure to satisfy this stability constraint on a given time step means that all outputs are ignored and the system remains in its previous state. The legs also fail to execute their outputs if any two or more legs try to give a power stroke in opposing directions, or if any legs would effectively be dragged, since they are attached to the surface by their vacuum feet.

Each leg receives its own environmental input message (detector), which contains a unique address for each leg in order that an agent can identify which leg it is currently responsible for. This detector string contains information as to whether or not the robot moved on the previous time step, which would be available from the distance sensor.

The robot scores on every one of the twenty discrete time step it moves forward, that is every time at least two legs give the correct power stroke (front to back) in a stable gait. All agents receive this fitness. We have also found it necessary to reward individual legs for executing either a power or return stroke to obtain walking systems from experiments with populations of reasonable size. The maximum achievable fitness for each leg is therefore (2x20) 40.

We use roulette wheel selection at both levels (as will be explained), allele mutation (rate 0.001 per bit), and multi-point crossover (rate 0.01 per bit) with the GA(s) operating over the genomes of concatenated rules. The classifier systems are a simplified version of the Pitt-style in that they have fixed length genomes and it should also be noted that we don't make any of Smith's level distinctions over the rules when using the crossover operator. Effectively we turn a normal fixed length GA string into a classifier system for evaluation. The internal matching/firing is the same, with all satisfied rules posting actions onto the message list and the highest bidder taken as the effector (conflict resolution is arbitrary when strengths match). All classifier systems contain six bi-conditional rules resulting in a genome length of 132 bits for each agent.

The simulation starts with all four feet being on the ground and with diagonally opposite legs in the same horizontal position, as Cruse et al. [5] point out "the start is particularly difficult when [opposite corner] legs begin from the same x-position". We now examine the use of our operators within this simulation.

3 Speciation

The two suggested mechanisms for speciation are termed allopatric and sympatric. Allopatric speciation [10] - speciation through the geographic separation of a parent species - is the most widely accepted explanation for the phenomenon. That is, such separation stops or severely restricts the flow of genetic material between individuals in the different populations which, combined with their obviously different environments, leads to differentiation. Sympatric speciation is the divergence of individuals in the same environment. A number of causes are suggested for this form of speciation such as the emergence of phenotypic characteristics which affect breeding (shape of genitalia, breeding times), the infertility of particular gene combinations, reproductive events such as polyploidy, etc. Therefore allopatric speciation can be viewed as a stochastic process due to separation events, whereas sympatric speciation is possibly due to the active selection of traits.

Allopatric speciation was also the inspiration for the "Island-model" parallel GA [4]. Here a given population P is divided into N sub-populations of P/N individuals, with each typically evolved on a separate node of an N-dimensional hypercube. Each node

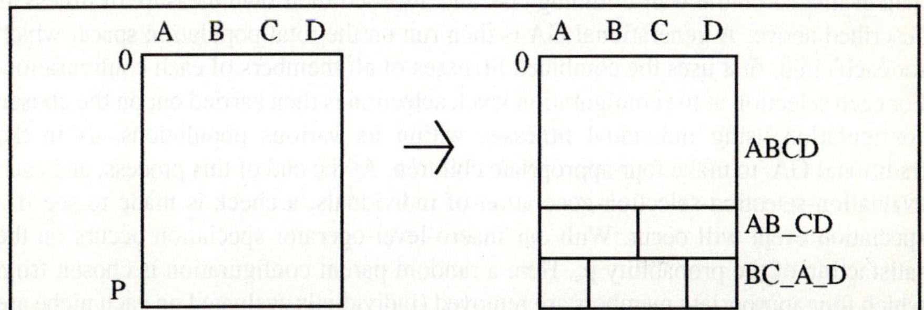

Fig. 1. During evolutionary time the population space of the homogeneous species can be invaded by configurations containing two or more species.

runs a normal GA on the sub-population but periodically, at the end of an "epoch", selected members from each node "migrate" to connected nodes. These migrators then compete against the node's sub-population for survival into the next epoch. The idea here is that each node may evolve into its own niche and hence the migration allows discovered specialist genes to compete and flow around the hypercube, thus improving the GA's overall search. However in these models populations always solve the same (homogeneous) task and their existence is predetermined. We now describe how the speciation process can be exploited in the application of population-based evolutionary computing approaches to mixed multi-agent systems by decreasing the amount of a priori knowledge required.

3.1 Speciation Macro-Level Operator

In this model there are four niches, one for each leg of the quadruped (A, B, C and D).

For four nodes there are fifteen different population configurations for the assignment of individuals to niches. For example there is the completely heterogenous configuration of one population per niche/leg (labelled A_B_C_D), there is the configuration of one population for the front legs and one for each of the rear legs (labelled AB_C_D), up to the completely homogeneous configuration of one population providing individuals for all niches (labelled ABCD). We start with the homogeneous configuration ABCD, initially set to size P, but during the course of a simulation individuals can move from one configuration to another via the speciation operator (hence there is always effectively P individuals overall). Over evolutionary time the most appropriate configuration of populations to niches - be it ABCD or A_B_C_D or AC_B_D, etc. - will emerge rather than being prescribed by a designer; various population configurations can emerge from the other (parent) configurations and compete against all others for population "space" (figure 1).

The individuals of the populations supplying agents to more than one niche are chosen for evaluation simply in blocks, so for example in the configuration AB_C_D the next two members in the list of members of population AB would be evaluated with the next members of populations C and D which had also not been evaluated. Individuals are then evaluated on the wall-climbing task and awarded their own measure of fitness as described above. A generational GA is then run on the total population space, which for each child, first uses the combined fitnesses of all members of each configuration. For each selection at the configuration level, selection is then carried out on the chosen configuration using individual fitnesses within its various populations, as in the traditional GA, to make four appropriate children. At the end of this process, and each evaluation-selection-selection-generation of individuals, a check is made to see if a speciation event will occur. With our macro-level operator speciation occurs on the satisfaction of the probability p_s. Here a random parent configuration is chosen from which four appropriate members are removed (individuals evaluated on each niche are taken, e.g. four are simply taken when ABCD is chosen). A second random configuration is then chosen from all possible configurations (fifteen here) and the appropriate members are moved into it (e.g. ABCD to AB_CD involves putting two members randomly chosen from ABCD into population AB and another two into CD).

3.2 Results

For this implementation we used an initial homogeneous population (ABCD) containing 8000 members (P=8000) and set the speciation rate p_s at 1/5, i.e. on average a speciation event occurs once every five generations.

Figure 2 shows the typical (20 runs) dynamics of the fixed population space for the four niches/aspects. On the task legs A and C are diagonally opposite each other which means they are in effect doing the same thing; they must give power and return strokes on the same time steps for the optimal gait, as must the controllers on legs B and D. That is, in the four node multi-agent system there is symmetry diagonally across the robot. It can be seen from figure 2 that the homogeneous configuration quickly loses its share of the population and that the completely heterogenous configuration (A_B_C_D) and symmetry configuration (AC_BD) come to dominate the population equally, sharing 60% of the total space. The emergence of the configuration AC_BD is

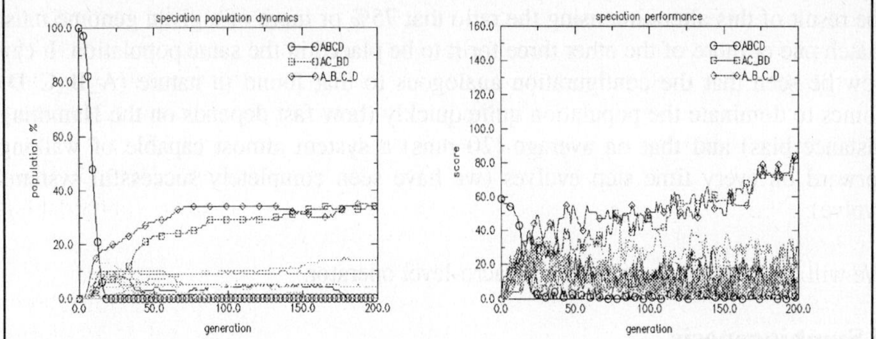

Fig. 2. Showing the evolution of the various configurations under speciation.

not unexpected therefore and shows that it is possible, through the use of the speciation operator, for the obvious assignment of populations to aspects/niches to evolve. The emergence of the configuration A_B_C_D was also not unexpected since a fully distributed configuration appears to have evolved in natural quadrupedal walking

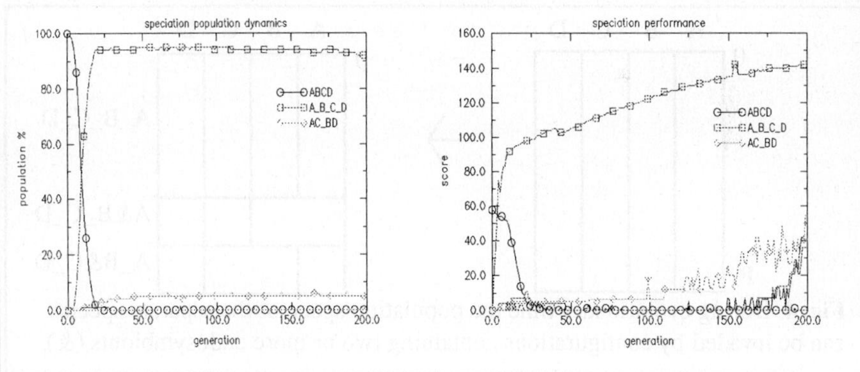

Fig. 3. Showing the effect of using Hamming distances in speciation events.

"[there are] several autonomous control centres ... each of which controls the movement of one leg" [5].

When we examine the corresponding performance of these various configurations (figure 2 - only the scores of best individuals are shown for clarity) we find that a successful gait capable of making a move on every time step has not evolved. In the above model the choice of population configuration for a group of speciating individuals was selected randomly from any of the possible set (fifteen). To improve the functional performance of our multi-agent system we altered this mechanism to include a bias based on the Hamming distance of the members involved. That is, we introduced the ability of genetically similar agents to go into the same population resulting in a more "intelligent" speciation event; like is put with like. Figure 3 shows the result of this alteration using the ratio that 75% or more of a given genome must match one or more of the other three for it to be placed in the same population. It can now be seen that the configuration analogous to that found in nature (A_B_C_D) comes to dominate the population quite quickly (how fast depends on the Hamming distance bias) and that on average (20 runs) a system almost capable of walking forward on every time step evolves (we have seen completely successful systems evolve).

We will now introduce our second macro-level operator.

4 Symbiogenesis

Symbiogenesis is the name given to evolutionary innovation through the establishment of symbiotic associations. Symbiosis is the phenomenon in which organisms of different species live together, resulting in a raised level of fitness for one or more of the organisms, i.e. heterogeneous cooperation. Endosymbiosis is the name given to symbiotic relationships in which partners are contained within a host partner. A large number of endosymbioses are hereditary, wherein the host's endosymbionts are passed

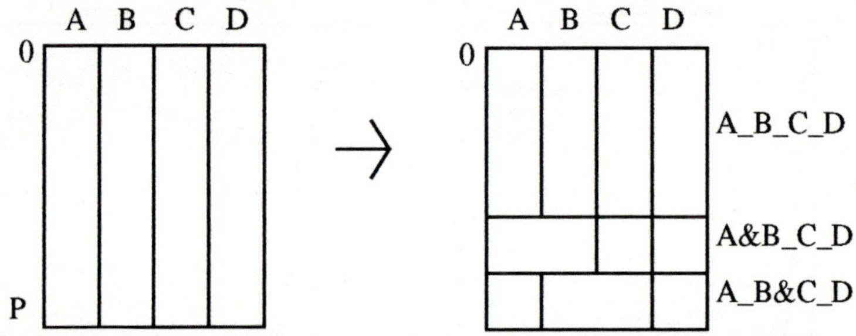

Fig. 4. During evolutionary time the population space of the separate species can be invaded by configurations containing two or more endosymbionts (&).

directly to its offspring, e.g. through transmission in the egg cytoplasm, as seen in insects. This mechanism has been described as "twice as efficient in the case of symbiosis than Mendelian hereditary, since half the [hosts] (the females) transmit [endosymbionts] to all progeny" [12] and even Lamarckian-like in that it represents the perpetuation of acquired characteristics, "What is an [endosymbiont] from a genetic point of view? A new cluster of genes!"[ibid.]. This joining together of heterogeneous organisms can be viewed as resulting in a new supra-organism [1] with the combined abilities of the partners involved. This phenomenon is now widely accepted as the mechanism by which eukaryotic cells evolved [9].

4.1 Symbiogenesis Macro-Level Operator

We suggest that artificial multi-agent systems will also benefit from such a joining process. *Note that symbiogenesis effects the identification of nodes within a system, whereas speciation effects the assignment of populations to the nodes.* To implement symbiogenesis as a macro-level mutation operator we alter the standard GA in a similar way to that described above. We say that at anytime two or more heterogeneous agents can join together to form a new population configuration in which an agent (super-agent) carries genomes for each of the originally existing nodes (e.g. if C and D join, A_B_C_D -> A_B_C&D). In the evaluation of such an individual all genomes are expressed as if they had come from their original separate heterogeneous populations. During the application of the GA the genomes of the chosen parents are also treated as if they were separate during recombination; each carried genome of a child is a mix of the corresponding genomes carried by its parents. The difference

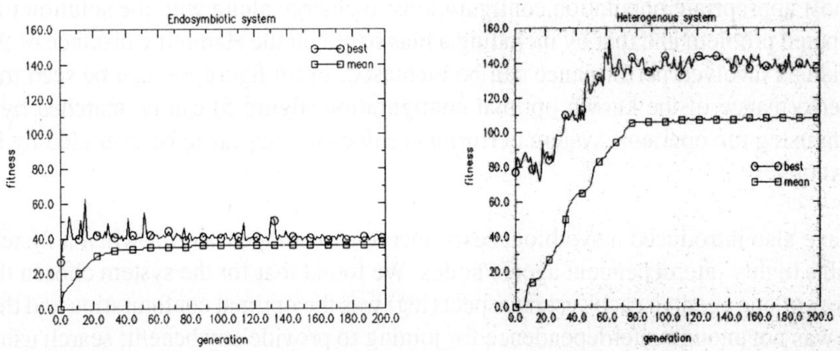

Fig. 5. Showing the progress of a system under the two extreme configurations.

comes in that the carried genomes are kept together during selection rather than evolving in separate populations where they can suffer from the oscillatory dynamics of selfish selection [8]. We note that the operator assumes the predefined nodes to be of the finest granularity for the task; predefined aspects cannot split.

To demonstrate this operator we start with the populations in the completely heterogeneous configuration A_B_C_D (figure 4) and do not allow speciation (for clarity). Selection is again done at the population configuration level first, before being done within the populations. All other parameters remain the same as those above.

4.2 Results

We tried various rates for the operator but were unable to get any population configuration containing an hereditary endosymbiosis to establish itself. Other initial species configurations were also tried (e.g. AC_BD) to no avail. Figure 5 shows the typical progress of a fixed population configuration in which all members contain genomes for each agent (complete symbiogenesis). It can be seen that on average (20 runs) the configuration has been able to evolve controllers which can individually make power or return strokes but the evolution of the necessary coordination has yet to emerge. When this is compared to the separate, completely heterogeneous, configuration it can be seen that on average (20 runs) the latter performs much better. This explains why we were unable to successfully evolve any super-agent configurations; it is more efficient in this system for the agents to stay separated.

5 Conclusion

We suggest that population-based evolutionary computing techniques can be expanded to enhance their performance in multi-agent environments. In this paper we have introduced two macro-level mutation operators: speciation and symbiogenesis. It was shown that the process of speciation (population differentiation) can be used to allow the most appropriate population configurations to emerge along with the solution to a distributed problem and that by including a bias based on the Hamming distance of the individuals involved performance can be increased. From figure 3 it can be seen that the performance of the known optimal configuration (figure 5) can be matched by a system using the operator; system performance does not appear to be degraded by its inclusion.

We have also introduced a symbiogenesis operator to compensate for when a system contains highly interdependent agents/nodes. We found that for the system chosen the division of one agent to each system aspect (leg) was the optimal configuration and that there was not enough interdependence for joining to provide any benefit; search using nodes at the task's finest granularity proved optimal here. The conditions under which symbiogenesis represents an advanced multi-agent configuration was recently examined in [3] and was shown to be a small sub-set of the total space of possibilities. However we maintain that the operator should be included in the evolution of multi-agent systems since it has proved so significant in natural evolution [9].

Therefore, with both operators, it is our intention that an initial homogeneous population should be specified for a multi-agent system containing predetermined (user or task) niches at the finest level of granularity for the task. Over the course of evolutionary time the speciation operator will cause a varying number of heterogeneous (and so more specialised) populations to form within the system. If these represent a more efficient configuration for the given system they will begin to establish themselves (they too may find themselves being broken-up of course, and so on). The symbiogenesis operator allows for any of the populations/niches to join should they be highly interdependent; identified nodes can become one. Again, if these prove more efficient they will be able to establish themselves as a more optimal configuration. We have shown that these two processes are easily implemented in the population-based search technique that is the GA. Both operators will be used together in the application of evolutionary computing on larger multi-agent systems in future work.

6 Acknowledgments

This work was supported by a Hewlett Packard External Research Program.

7 References

1. *Allee W C, Emerson A E, Schmidt K P, Park T & Park O* (1949), "Principles of Animal Ecology", Saunders Company.
2. *Bull L & Fogarty T C* (1994), "Evolving Cooperative Communicating Classifier Systems", Third Conference on Evolutionary Programming, World Scientific.
3. *Bull L, Fogarty T C, & Pipe A G* (1995), "Artificial Endosymbiosis", Proceedings of the Third European Conference on Artificial Life, Springer-Verlag, pp273-289.
4. *Cohoon J P, Hegde S U, Martin W N & Richards D* (1987), "Punctuated Equilibria; A Parallel Genetic Algorithm", Proceedings of the Second International Conference on Genetic Algorithms, Lawrence Erlbaum Associates, pp148-154.
5. *Cruse H, Muller-Wilm U & Dean J* (1992), "Artificial Neural Nets for Controlling a 6-legged Walking System", Animals to Animats 2, MIT Press.
6. *Dawkins R* (1995), "River Out of Eden", Weidenfeld & Nicholson.
7. *Holland J H* (1975), "Adaption in Natural and Artificial Systems", Univ. of Michigan Press, Ann Arbor.
8. *Kauffman S A* (1993), "The Origins of Order: Self-organisation and Selection in Evolution", Oxford University Press.
9. *Margulis L* (1970), "Origin of Eukaryotic Cells", Yale University Press.
10. *Mayr E* (1942), "Systematics and the Origin of Species", Columbia Press, New York.
11. *Merezhkovsky* (1920) in Khakhina L N (1992), "Concepts of Symbiogenesis: History of Symbiogenesis as an Evolutionary Mechanism", Yale University Press.
12. *Nardon P & Grenier M* (1991), "Serial Endosymbiosis Theory and Weevil Evolution: The Role of Symbiosis", Symbiosis as a Source of Evolutionary Innovation, MIT Press, pp155-169.
13. *Rosen R* (1994), "Cooperation and Chimera", Cooperation and Conflict in General Evolutionary Processes, John Wiley & Sons, pp 343-358.
14. *Smith S F* (1980), "A Learning System Based on Genetic Adaptive Algorithms", PhD Dissertation, University of Pittsburgh.

Evolution Strategies with Subjective Selection

Michael Herdy

Technische Universität Berlin, Bionik und Evolutionstechnik,
Ackerstr.71-76, Sekr.Ack1, D-13355 Berlin ,
email: herdy@fb10.tu-berlin.d400.de

Abstract. Evolution strategies with subjective selection of the offspring can be applied to optimization problems, when no objective evaluation of the offspring is possible. For this class of optimization problems, strategies with insensitivity towards incorrect selection decisions are necessary. With subjective selection, incorrect decisions are unavoidable and have the effect of noise being overlaid onto the fitness value. Three examples of different evolution strategies (ES) are presented which are resistant against wrong selection decisions.

The convergence of an ES with manually controlled stepsize for the adaptation of a mixture of colored liquid components towards a target color is shown. This first example can be regarded as a real world experiment. In two computer experiments an ES with automatically adapted stepsize has been applied for the first time to this type of optimization problems. The color and shape of a rectangle will be adapted towards a target rectangle, and the adaptation of the shape of a polygon towards a symmetric dodecagon will be shown. With these two test problems the convergence of different strategy variants with and without recombination is examined.

1 Introduction

In most cases where evolution strategies are being used for optimization, the mutated objects can be evaluated objectively with a numerically defined fitness function or with a fitness function that uses measurements of an experiment. A definite objective order of rank among the individuals of the population can be given. However, there are optimization problems where such a fitness function does not exist and where it can only be decided by subjective decision of an experimentator, which of the offspring have the best quality and become parents of the next generation.

In the literature, the optimization with evolutionary algorithms like evolution strategy or genetic algorithms is called "interactive evolution", if the experimentator manually intervenes in the optimization process. The way of intervention should be apparent in the name of the strategy. If the experimentator simply selects the offspring to be used as parents of the next generation, the appendix "with subjective selection" should be added. In this case, no fitness values are being assigned to the offspring and no ranking takes place. If a (subjectively determined) fitness value is being assigned to the offspring, the appendix should be "with subjective evaluation".

The evolution of mixtures of color components towards a target color [Rechenberg, 1978], the evolution of "biomorphs" towards the letters of the alphabet [Dawkins, 1991], the optimization of the mixture of components for an optimal blue chromium plating [Riedel, 1984], the tracking of a criminal suspect through "face space" [Caldwell and Johnston, 1991], evolving of line drawings [Baker, 1993] and other applications have successfully been carried out with means of subjective selection.

In the present paper, the application of an evolution strategy with subjective selection for the adaptation of a mixture of liquid color components towards a target color is demonstrated. The accuracy of the adaptation and the way this strategy converges towards the target color is shown for this real world problem. Here, no adaptive stepsize control has been used but stepsize was controlled manually. In addition, two computer experiments are introduced, in which the color and shape of a rectangle is adapted towards a target rectangle and a polygon is adapted towards a target polygon. In both cases, optimal strategy parameter settings for maximum convergence rate and convergence certainty have been found and an effective adaptive stepsize control has been applied for the first time to this class of problems. This damped stepsize control was first proposed by OSTERMEIER (1994).

2 Evolution of a mixture of colors - the Cherry-Brandy problem

With the three liquid primary food colors cyan-blue, magenta-red and yellow and with clear water, a mixture has to be found, that is identical in color with the liqueur "Cherry Brandy" (BOLS). Originally this experiment has been designed by RECHENBERG (1978) for his practical seminar to the lecture *Evolutionsstrategie I,* but it is also a useful practical test experiment for the efficiencies of different evolution strategy variants with subjective selection.

The strategy. The (1,λ)-ES has been used for this optimization problem. No adaptive stepsize control has been applied because there are only very few generations necessary for reaching the optimum (no more than 20 generations as a maximum). The parent has a norm stepsize, which can only be changed by the operator. Nevertheless, there are individuals with different stepsizes: One third of the offspring gets a smaller stepsize than the parent, one third has the same stepsize and the last third gets a bigger stepsize than the parent. However, the stepsize of the selected offspring is not being transferred to the next generation, but the norm stepsize is assigned to the parent again.
The optimization process works as follows

- The optimization initially starts with a given parent mixture of color components; the color of this start mixture is blue-purple.
- With the computer the dispensing of λ offspring mixtures is generated. Each mixture is standardized to a quantity of 30 ml, the volume of a standard test-tube.
- Each 'offspring'-student takes his/her test-tube and produces the mixture according to the generated dispensing of the computer.

- All offspring test-tubes are positioned in front of an illuminated surface. Together the students decide, which offspring mixture is the best (closest to the target color) and is taken as the parent mixture of the next generation.
- The number of the best offspring is being entered in the computer, which starts the next generation.

Experiments and results. The following **figure 1a** shows a typical plot of the course of the amount of the four liquids with a (1,8)-ES with start color blue-purple and the reddish target color of Cherry Brandy:

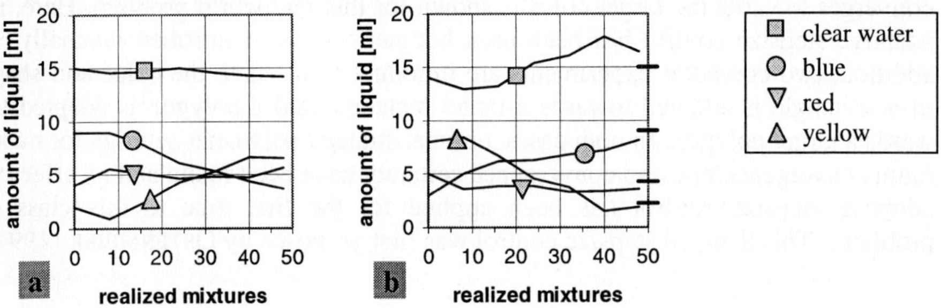

Figure 1: Amount of the four liquids in the standard test-tube with 30 ml during the optimization from blue-purple towards reddish (a) and during the optimization from reddish towards blue-purple (b)

The convergence of the different color components is clearly seen, but the difference between the color of the mixture at the end of the optimization and the true color of the Cherry Brandy is unknown. Therefore, the experiment was started in reversed order: The optimization was started with a mixture of the liquids being similar to that at the end of the optimization in **figure 1a** and it was adapted towards the start color of **figure 1a**. The mixture of this color is known and the error between the two colors is calculable. **Figure 1b** shows the results of this optimization with a (1,8)-ES. The markers at the right side of the plot give the target of the four liquids (from top to bottom: clear water, blue, red, yellow).
The target mixture of colors was found with a maximum difference of 1.3 ml (clear water: 1.3 ml, blue: 0.8 ml, red: 0.4 ml, yellow: 0.1 ml). The reading errors of the pipettes for filling in the colors have been estimated to be 1 ml. Taking this into account, the target mixture of colors was found with high precision.

3 Evolution of Color and Shape

By means of subjective selection, a rectangle is to be found that is identical in color and shape to a randomly generated rectangle on the screen of the computer (see **figure 2**). Both two features, *color* and *shape*, have to be considered for the selection at the same time. The shape of the rectangle is determined by the parameters length and width and its color is determined by the RGB (red, green, blue) color

components. Therefore, the optimization problem has five dimensions. All object variables are adjustable between 0 and 63.
This problem is not really a problem where subjective selection is necessary, but it is a test problem for evolving optimum strategies; an objective fitness function can be formulated. The least square error between target figure and parental figure as the objective fitness has been used.

The strategy. The ($\mu/\mu,\lambda$)-ES with discrete recombination (see i.e.: [RECHENBERG, 1994] and [SCHWEFEL, 1995]) and the damped stepsize control as described by OSTERMEIER (1994) and RECHENBERG (1994) has been applied to this problem. RECHENBERG understands the stepsize control as a disturbed optimization process and he regards the role of stepsize control with damping as an instrument to reduce the noise effect of the adaptation process. The principle of the damped stepsize control is easy to explain: the stepsize variations passed from one generation to the next are made much smaller than the variations within one generation [OSTERMEIER, 1994]. The following parts of a PASCAL computer program show the implemented stepsize control:

```
{ for one quarter of the offspring the stepsize factor szfac is set to 2.0, for one
  quarter it is set to 4.0, for the third quarter it is set to 1/2.0 and for the last
  quarter it is set to 1/4.0.}
choice:=random
if choice < 0.25 then szfac:= 2    else
if choice < 0.5  then szfac:= 4    else
if choice < 0.75 then szfac:= 1/2  else szfac:=1 /4

{ for all npar parameters of the offspring the new offspring parameters ov[i]
  result from adding (0,1)-normal distributed random numbers normdist[i],
  multiplied by the stepsize factor szfac and the parental stepsize sz^g, to the
  parental parameters pv[i] :}
for i :=1 to npar do
  ov[i] :=pv[i] + szfac·sz^g·normdist[i]

{ the stepsize sz^(g+1) being transferred to the next generation g+1 is not the effec
  tive stepsize szfac·sz^g  with which the parental parameters have been mutated
  but a largely reduced stepsize. The damping exponent depends on the dimen
  sion of the problem and has been found by some experiments to be 0.1: }
sz^(g+1) :=sz^g·szfac^0.1
```

Starting out from μ randomly generated parents, the λ offspring are generated and then the optimization process works as follows:

- On the screen of the computer, λ offspring rectangles are presented to the experimentator according to the (μ/μ, λ)-ES used for the optimization.

- All offspring rectangles differ in color and shape and the experimentator has to select μ of them to be parent rectangles of the next generation. It is decided by means of subjective selection, which offspring are closest to the target figure and become parents of the next generation. In the case of more than one selected offspring, no ranking takes place. The selected offspring are marked by clicking with the mouse and the next cycle begins. Again, λ offspring are generated and the process is repeated until the experimentator stops.

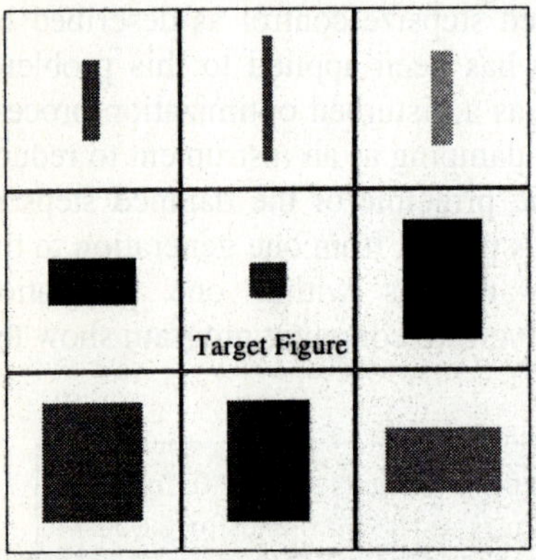

Figure 2: Screen copy of the initial situation of the color and shape example. The original colors have been converted to grey colors for this copy but the principle features are still visible. The target figure is drawn in the middle of the picture, the offspring figures are arranged around it.

Experiments and results. With the color and shape problem two different evolution strategies have been compared, a (1,8)-ES and a (2/2,8)-ES with discrete recombination. In both strategies the damped mutative stepsize control has been applied to one global stepsize for all parameters. Without damped stepsize control these strategies did not converge: either the stepsize became too small in a few generations or it became too large and no reasonable selection was possible.

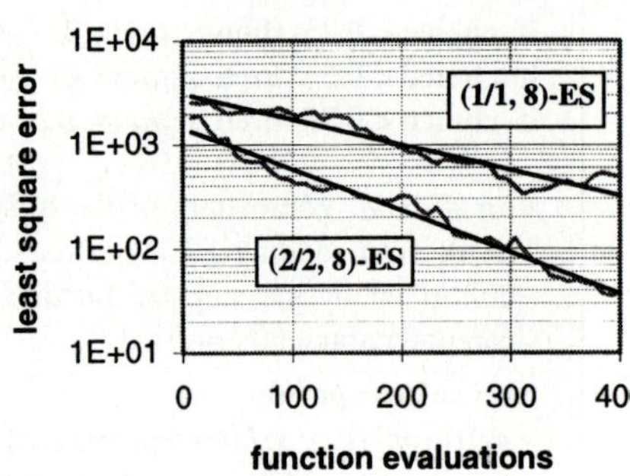

Figure 3: Course of the quality over function evaluations for a (1,8)-ES without recombination and a (2/2,8)-ES with discrete recombination. Each curve results as the mean of 20 runs.

Both strategies have been tested by 20 untrained subjects. **Figure 3** shows the course of the (numerically calculated) quality over the function evaluations, which results from the sum of the least square errors between parental figure and target figure. The gradient of the regression line is a measure of the rate of convergence: The (2/2,8)-ES with discrete recombination shows a significant higher rate of convergence than the (1,8)-ES.

4 Evolution of a polygon - the dodecagon problem

By means of subjective selection, a polygon is to be found, that is identical in shape with a target polygon on the screen of the computer. The shape of the polygon is determined by the length of 12 lines which lead off radially from the origin of the coordinate system (**figure 4**). The lines are arranged symmetrically with angles of $2*\pi/12$ between two neighboured radial lines. The connecting lines between the endpoints of the radial lines form the polygon. The target polygon has the shape of a dodecagon. Thus, the optimization problem has 12 dimensions; all object variables are adjustable between 0 and 63.

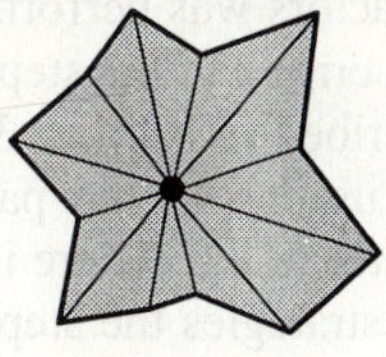

Figure 4: The shape of the polygon is defined by the length of the 12 lines.

This problem like the color and shape example in **section 3** is also a test problem designed for evolving optimum strategies. As well as in **section 3**, an objective fitness function can be formulated as the least square error between target figure and parental figure. However, in contrast to the afore mentioned example, the dodecagon problem has only one feature, shape, to be considered during selection. Furthermore, the number of variables is easily adjustable because for changing the number of variables only the number of radial lines has to be changed.

With the 12 dimensions of the dodecagon problem, the validity of the results of the example in **section 3** can be verified, namely that the strategies with recombination show a higher convergence rate than those without recombination.

The strategy. The variation and selection procedures are the same as in the color and shape example. Again the damped stepsize control has been applied.

Figure 5 shows a screen copy of the initial situation of the optimization. The target figure is in the middle of the picture, the offspring figures are arranged around it. The set of equidistant circles serves as an aid for the selection process.

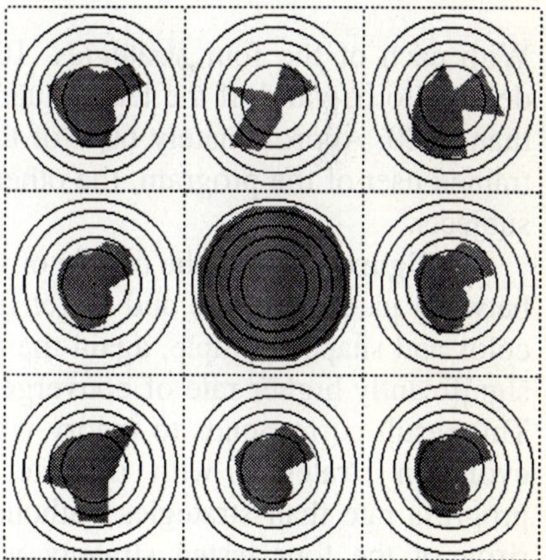

Figure 5: Screen copy of the initial situation in generation 1. The target figure, a symmetric dodecagon, is in the middle of the figure, the 8 offspring are arranged around it.

Experiments and results. Four different evolution strategies have been compared, a (1,8)-ES, a (2,8)-ES without recombination, a (2/2,8)-ES with intermediate recombination, and a (2/2,8)-ES with discrete recombination. For all strategies, the damped mutative stepsize control has been applied to one global stepsize for all parameters.

Representative for all four strategies, the following **figure 6** shows the (2/2,8)-ES with discrete recombination when the damping of the stepsize is switched off. The stepsize gets stuck and with this no more visible variation takes place, a sensible selection is no longer possible. In order to test, whether the extreme stepsize factors of 4 and ¼ respectively, are responsible for the failure of the stepsize control, a run with only two moderate stepsize factors was performed. The left part of **figure 6** shows the courses of the least square error and the stepsize with four different stepsize factors in the population as described in **section 3**. In the right part of **figure 6,** only two stepsize factors were used with the parent stepsize being increased and decreased, respectively, by a factor of 2.0. There is no essential difference between the two runs to be seen, in both strategies the stepsize control fails.

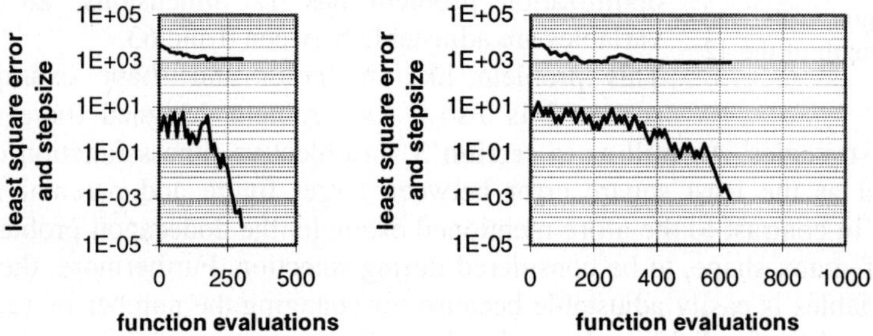

Figure 6: The (2/2,8)-ES without damping of the global stepsize. The strategy in the left figure uses 4 different stepsize factors (2, 4, 0.5, 0.25), the strategy in the right figure uses only 2 different stepsize factors (2, 0.5). The upper curve shows the least square error, the lower curve shows the stepsize.

With each of the four strategies, 10 valid runs have been carried out. A run is defined to be valid, if the least square error after 1000 function evaluations is less than 5000. Approximately 60% of the runs have been performed by the author, a trained user of the program, the other runs have been performed by inexperienced subjects.

Figure 7 shows the course of the (numerically calculated) least square errors between parental figure and target figure over the function evaluations. As in the color and shape example, again the (2/2)-ES with discrete recombination shows a significantly higher rate of convergence than the (1,8)-ES without recombination. This result corresponds to theory where it is found that, in the presence of noise, evolution strategies with discrete recombination have a significantly higher progress rate than strategies without recombination [HERDY, 1995]. The comparison of the four tested strategy variants shows a similar rate of convergence between the two strategies without recombination and the two strategies with recombination. Obviously, the probability to select the objectively best individual out of the 8 offspring is higher, if two individuals are selected in each generation. The percentage of cases where the best individual is among the selected individuals is 25.9% with the (1,8)-ES, 48% with the (2,8)-ES, 44.3% with the (2/2,8)-ES with intermediate recombination and 48.9% with the (2/2,8)-ES with discrete recombination. By means of recombination, information of each of the two individuals is transferred to each of the offspring in the next generation.

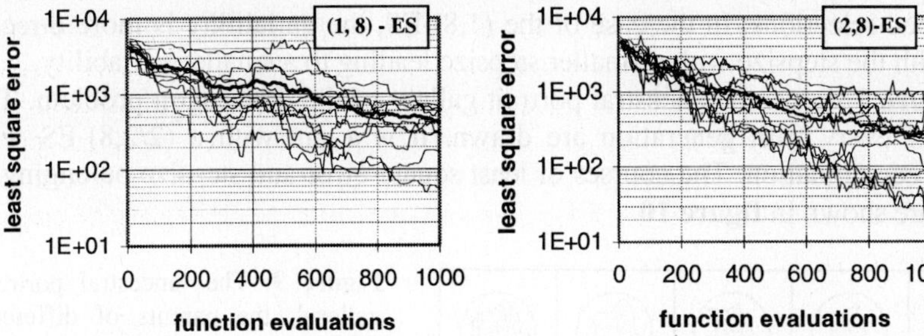

Figure 7a: Least square error over function evaluations for strategies without recombination. For each strategy 10 runs have been performed, the bold lines represent the mean curve.

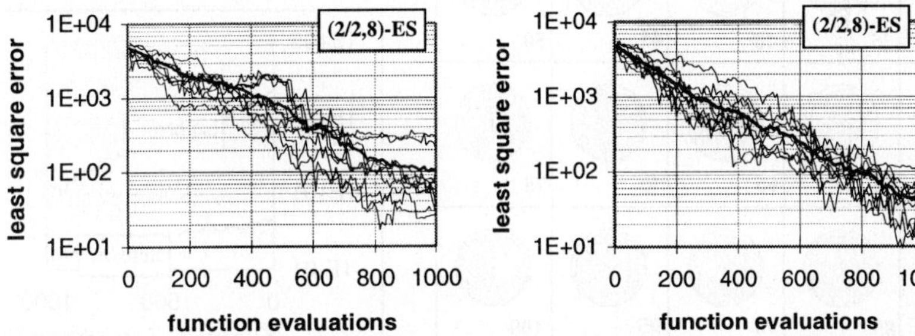

Figure 7b: Least square error over function evaluations for strategies with recombination (left: intermediate recombination, right: discrete recombination). For each strategy 10 runs have been performed, the bold lines represent the mean curve.

For better clarity, the following **figure 8** again shows the mean curves of each strategy in one diagram. The difference of a factor of ten between the (1,8)-ES and the (2/2,8)-ES with discrete recombination at the end of the simulation (after 1000 function evaluations) is statistically significant. The difference between the two strategies with recombination has to be examined with further simulations.

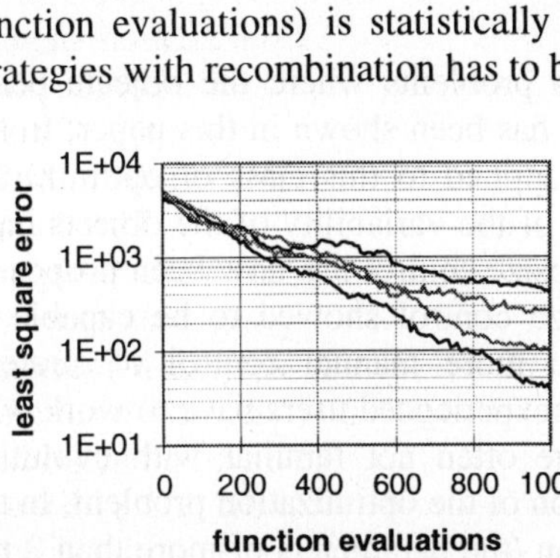

Figure 8: Mean curves of the four different strategies applied to the evolution of a polygon. From top to bottom at function evaluation 1000: (1,8)-ES, (2,8)-ES without recombination, (2/2,8)-ES with intermediate recombination. and (2/2,8)-ES with discrete recombination.

The high convergence rate of the (2/2,8)-ES with discrete recombination may depend on the fact that even if the stepsize has already become small, there is still a rather high variability because of the discrete recombination. This leads to more undisturbed selections. In the case of the (1,8)-ES, the variability is more directly linked with the stepsize with a smaller stepsize leading to a smaller variability.

Figure 9 shows the ancestral portrait gallery of the dodecagon problem. The parents of every fifth generation are drawn. It is a run with a (2/2,8)-ES with discrete recombination. The courses of least square error and stepsize belonging to this run are shown in **figure 10**.

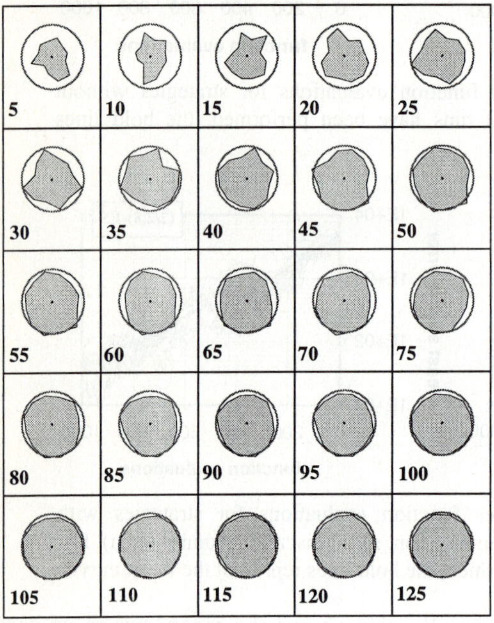

Figure 9: The 'ancestral portrait gallery', the parents of different generations, for the evolution of a polygon towards a symmetric dodecagon. The numbers indicate the generation number.

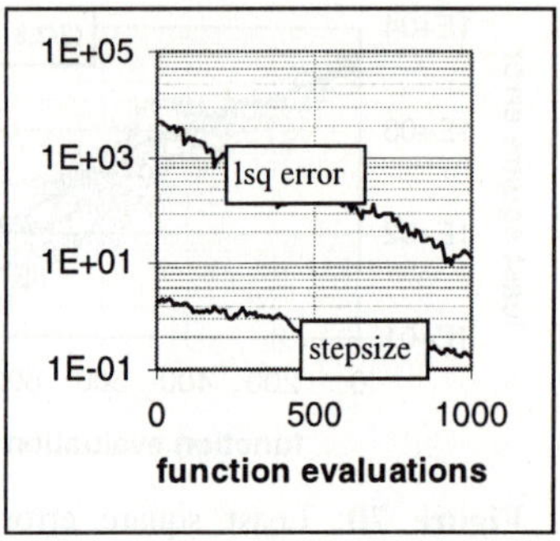

Figure 10: Courses of least square error and stepsize for a run with the (2/2,8)-ES.

5 Conclusions

The application of the evolution strategy to problems where the objects being optimized can be evaluated only subjectively has been shown in this paper. In the past, no adaptive stepsize control has been applied to this class of optimization problems. Only manually controlled changes of the variability of the objects have been performed. A strategy with adaptive stepsize control has now been proposed: the (2/2,8)-ES with adaptive damped stepsize control showed to be capable of solving subjective evaluation problems. No more manual control of strategy parameters is necessary. This is essential, if inexperienced users have to work with such optimization programs. These users are often not familiar with evolution strategies but only with their area of application of the optimization problem. In the near future, strategies with multirecombination (the parameters of more than 2 parents are involved during recombination) will be investigated with test functions.

The application of the presented algorithms to an industrial optimization problem with no possibility of objective evaluation has been started recently. In the coffee industry it is an everyday task to find out the ratio of different coffee types to obtain the taste of a special target mixture. Mostly, this is the taste of a proprietary article which shall always be distinctively consistent, but this may also be the taste of a mixture the bulk purchaser provides as a model to the coffee roaster. Last but not least it may be the taste of a new blended coffee, where no physical model exists. The taste of the model exists only in the mind of the coffee taster.

Commonly sold coffee brands consist of up to ten different types of coffee beans, the quality of which vary year after year. Like wine, coffee is an agricultural product and its taste is therefore dependent on weather conditions, condition of the soil and of course of the idiosyncrasies of the plant itself.

In a first simple test, the taste of a mixture of two coffee types had to be adapted to the taste of a target mixture. A (1, 5)-ES with subjective selection was applied and the ratio of the two components was found with less than 5 % error. At present, tests with more than two components are being performed.

6 References

E. Baker. Evolving line drawings. In: *Proceedings Of The Fifth International Conference On Genetic Algorithms*, ed. S. Forrest. San Mateo, California: Morgan Kaufmann Publishers, 1993. pp. 627

C. Caldwell and V. S. Johnston. Tracking a criminal suspect through "face-space" with a genetic algorithm. In: *Proceedings Of The Fourth International Conference On Genetic Algorithms*, eds. R. K. Belew and L. B. Booker. San Mateo, California: Morgan Kaufmann Publishers, 1991.pp. 416-421.

R. Dawkins. *The Blind Watchmaker*. London: Penguin books, 1991, first published by Longman, 1986

M. Herdy. *Beitrag zur Theorie der Evolutionsstrategie mit Rekombination bei ungestörten und gestörten Qualitätsfunktionen*. Technical Report TR-04-95. Berlin: Technische Universität, 1995

I. Rechenberg. *Evolutionsstrategie ' 94*, Stuttgart-Bad Cannstatt: frommann-holzboog, 1994.

I. Rechenberg. *Practical seminar to the lecture Evolutionsstrategie 1, 1978,* unpublished manuscript. Berlin: 1978

H. Riedel, *Einsatz rechnergestützter Optimierung mittels der Evolutionsstrategie zur Lösung galvanotechnischer Probleme*. Dissertation. Berlin: Technische Universität, 1984.

A. Ostermeier, A. Gawelczyk, and N. Hansen. Step-size Adaptation Based on Nonlocal Use of Selection Information. In: *Parallel Problem Solving from Nature - PPSN III, Proceedings* (Davidor, Y., Schwefel, H.-P., and Männer, R. Eds.). Berlin: Springer, 1994. pp. 189-198

H. Schwefel. *Evolution And Optimum Seeking*, New York-Chichester-Brisbane-Toronto-Singapore: John Wiley&Sons, 1995.

Emergent Cooperation for Multiple Agents Using Genetic Programming

Hitoshi IBA

Machine Inference Section, Electrotechnical Laboratory (ETL),
1-1-4 Umezono, Tsukuba Science City, Ibaraki, 305, Japan.,
email. iba@etl.go.jp

Abstract. This paper presents the emergence of the cooperative behavior for the multiple agents by means of Genetic Programming (GP). Our experimental domain is the Tile World, a multi-agent test bed [Pollack90]. The world consists of a simulated robot agent and a simulated environment which is both dynamic and unpredictable. For the purpose of evolving the cooperative behavior, we propose three types of strategies, i.e, homogeneous breeding, heterogeneous breeding, and co-evolutionary breeding. The effectiveness of these three types of GP-based multi-agent learning is discussed with comparative experiments.

1 Introduction

Recently intelligent agents and multi-agent systems have garnered much interest in Distributed Artificial Intelligence (DAI) [Wooldrige96]. The research has suggested that it would be worthwhile to study "aspects of cooperative behavior", i.e. general rules that cause agents to act in ways conducive to cooperation [Goldman94]. This is because some tasks can be solved easily or can only be solved by separating them into subtasks among multiple agents. Behavior is cooperative when agents independently altering the environment make it easier for other agents to perform effectively. An example of this behavior is a soccer player kicking the ball towards the goal area in order for another player to make a goal. Another example is observed in the pheromone trail of foraging ants, i.e. the dropped pheromones aid other ants in efficiently locating the food source.

This paper presents the emergence of the cooperative behavior for multiple agents by means of Genetic Programming (GP). GP and its variants have been applied to multi-agent learning. For instance, Koza used GP to evolve sets of seemingly simple rules that exhibit an emergent behavior. The goal was to genetically breed a common computer program, when simultaneous executed by all the individuals in a group of independent agent, i.e. the homogeneous breeding, that causes the emergence of beneficial and interesting higher-level collective behavior [Koza92,ch.12]. Haynes proposed an approach to the construction of cooperation strategies based on GP for a group of agents [Haynes95]. He experimented in the predator-prey domain, i.e. the pursuit game, and showed that the GP paradigm could be effectively used to generate apparently complex cooperation strategies without any deep domain knowledge. Luke examined three breeding strategies (clones, free and restricted) and three coordination mechanisms (none, deictic sensing, and named-based sensing) for evolving teams of agents in the Serengeti world, a simple predator/prey environment [Luke96].

This paper is motivated by the previous studies mentioned above and focuses on the following points:–

1. Applying GP to a multi-agent test bed, i.e. the Tile World.
2. Confirming the emergence of the cooperative behavior by means of GP.
3. Comparing different types of strategies for GP-based multi-agent learning.

The proposed strategies are as follows:

1. Homogeneous breeding (Fig.1(a)).
   All agents use the same program evolved by GP. Individuals breed as in an ordinary GP.
2. Heterogeneous breeding (Fig.1(b)).
   Each agent uses a distinct program. A GP individual maintains multiple branches, each of which serves as a specialized program for a distinct agent. The breeding proceeds in the same way as the ADF (Automatic Defining Function) version of GP [Koza94], i.e. crossover operations are restricted to correspondent branch pairs.
3. Co-evolutionary breeding (Fig.6).
   Subpopulations of GP individuals are distributed. Breeding is performed in the same way as in a distributed GP [Iba96a]. As generations proceed, some individuals are expected to perform specialized tasks for different agents.

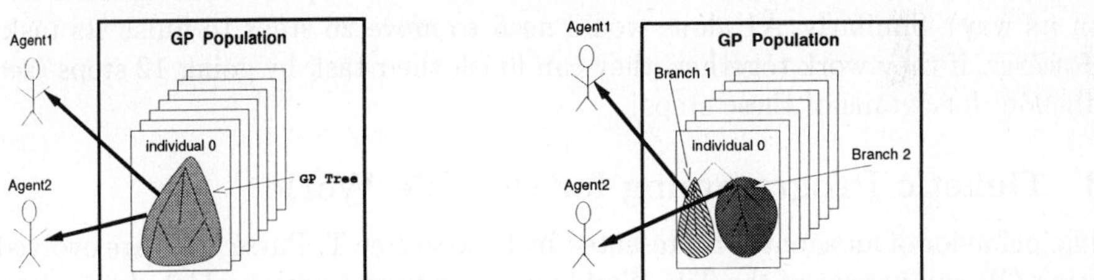

(a) Homogeneous Strategy. (b) Heterogeneous Strategy.

Fig. 1. Homo-/Heterogeneous Strategies.

In Sections 4 and 5, we show how each breeding strategy works for GP-based multi-agent learning by the experiments in evolving a cooperative behavior in the Tile World.

The rest of this paper is structured as follows. Section 2 describes the Tile World and the cooperative behavior in the world. Section 3 describes the experimental set–up of the Tile World. Section 4 shows some experimental results for homogeneous and heterogeneous strategies. In Section 5, we extend these strategies to co-evolutionary breeding. Section 6 discusses the results, followed by some conclusions in Section 7.

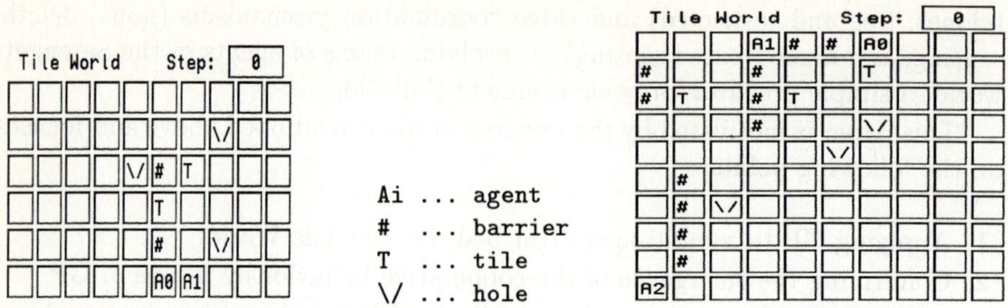

(a) Tile World 1 (TW1). (b) Tile World 2 (TW2).

Fig. 2. The Tile World.

2 The Tile World and Multi-Agent Learning

Our experimental domain is the Tile World, a multi-agent test bed that consists of simulated robot agents and a simulated environment which is both dynamic and unpredictable [Pollack90, Hanks93]. The world consists of a rectangular grid on which agents (denoted as Ai, $i = 0, 1, \cdots$), some tiles (T), some obstacles (#), and some holes (\/) can be placed (see Fig.2). Each object occupies one cell of the grid. The agent can move up, down, left, and right unless doing so would cause it to run into the world's boundaries or an obstacle. When a tile is in a cell adjacent to the agent, the agent can push the tile by moving in its direction. The agents their goal is to push all tiles into the holes[1].

Consider the simple interaction shown in Fig.2(a). This is an example of strongly-coupled interactions (i.e. the constraints on movement are so severe) [Goldman94]. For either agent to accomplish its goal, it would need to carry out a large number of movements to perform its own task. For example, for A0 alone to fill holes with two tiles, it needs to move 17 steps (assuming A1 is not on its way). Similarly, A1 alone would need to move 26 steps to finish its task. However, if they work together, they can finish their task by going 12 steps (see [Iba96b] for details of these steps).

3 Genetic Programming for the Tile World

The behavior of an agent is represented by a parse tree T. Parse trees are evolved using GP and in case of the Tile World always output a vector which determines the action to be taken. The actions are STAY or move RIGHT, UP, LEFT or DOWN. In order to apply GP to evolving an agent's program in the Tile World, we use the terminal and nonterminal sets shown in Table 1[2]. In the table, a symbol without arguments is a terminal symbol.

We have chosen vector operations for the GP tree representation. This is aimed at incorporating more precise directional information as to the environment surrounding the agents. For instance, assuming that x and y axes are

[1] For the sake of simplicity, this paper omits the hole's capacity and score, which were introduced in the original Tile World.

[2] The usage of these symbols is motivated by the study reported by [Luke96]. Luke studied evolving teamwork by GP for a pursuit game, in which the world is a continuous 2-dimensional one.

Table 1. GP Terminals and Functions.

Name	#Args.	Description
Tile	0	The vector from the agent to the nearest tile.
Hole	0	The vector from the agent to the nearest hole.
last	0	The last output vector of the GP tree for the agent. If this is the first move, then returns a random vector.
Ag0	0	The vector from the agent to Agent0.
Ag1	0	The vector from the agent to Agent1.
Rand	0	A random vector.
+	2	Add two vectors.
-	2	Subtract two vectors.
*2	1	Multiply the magnitude of a vector by 2.
/2	1	Divide a vector by 2.
->90	1	Rotate a vector clockwise 90 degrees.
inv	1	Invert a vector, i.e. if the input is **v**, then return −**v**.
if_dot	4	Evaluate the first and second arguments. If their dot product is greater than 0, then evaluate and return the third argument, else evaluate and return the fourth argument.
if>=	4	Evaluate the first and second arguments. If the magnitude of the first argument is greater than the magnitude of the second argument, then evaluate and return the third argument, else evaluate and return the fourth argument.

$$Wrapper(\mathbf{v}) = \begin{cases} \text{STAY, if } \parallel \mathbf{v} \parallel < Radius \\ \text{RIGHT, if } \parallel \mathbf{v} \parallel \geq Radius, \theta_{\mathbf{v}} \in [-\frac{\pi}{4}, +\frac{\pi}{4}] \\ \text{UP, if } \parallel \mathbf{v} \parallel \geq Radius, \theta_{\mathbf{v}} \in [+\frac{\pi}{4}, +\frac{3\pi}{4}] \\ \text{LEFT, if } \parallel \mathbf{v} \parallel \geq Radius, \theta_{\mathbf{v}} \in [+\frac{3\pi}{4}, +\frac{5\pi}{4}] \\ \text{DOWN, if } \parallel \mathbf{v} \parallel \geq Radius, \theta_{\mathbf{v}} \in [+\frac{5\pi}{4}, +\frac{7\pi}{4}] \end{cases}$$

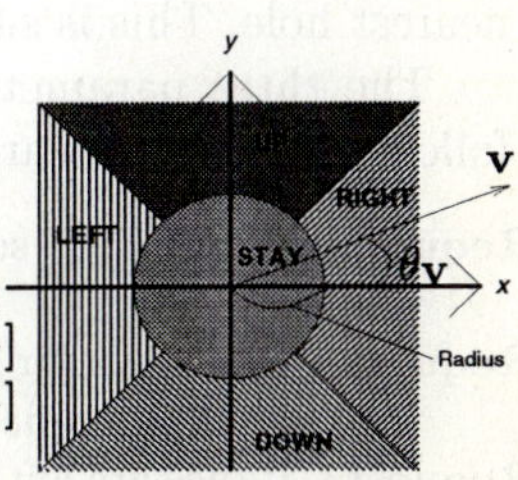

Fig. 3. Wrapper, i.e. mapping between the output of a parse tree and the action to be taken.

rightwards and upwards as usual, the Hole terminal returns a vector $\binom{2}{1}$ for the agent A0 and $\binom{1}{1}$ for A1, in the initial Tile World TW1 (Fig.2(a)). What is required from a GP tree program is to tell how to move an agent, i.e. right, left, up, down and stay. Thus, the wrapper (i.e. the mapping between the output of a parse tree and the action to be taken) is applied to the output of the GP tree so as to decide the agent's move. The mapping between vectors and actions is determined as follows: If the norm of the vector **v** is less than or equal to the parameter Radius, then STAY where you are. Otherwise, move 1 step RIGHT, UP, LEFT or DOWN depending on the direction of **v**, i.e. when **v** is between $[-\frac{\pi}{4}, +\frac{\pi}{4}]$, $[+\frac{\pi}{4}, +\frac{3\pi}{4}]$, $[+\frac{3\pi}{4}, +\frac{5\pi}{4}]$ and $[+\frac{5\pi}{4}, +\frac{7\pi}{4}]$, respectively. This mapping is shown in Fig.3.

Each time step, an agent is executing an action according to the above mapping and gets a fixed number of time steps *Eval*. During this period, the agents can either complete the task, i.e. all tiles are pushed in one of the holes, or some tiles are left.

In order to assign a fitness f to an agent's behavior, we have to take into account 3 factors:

1. the number of tiles pushed into the holes,
2. the number of time steps left, when the task is completed during the considered time period,
3. the distances to the closest hole of the tiles left, when the task could not be completed.

These three factors are weighted by the parameters *Bonus*, *Speed_Up* and C_T, respectively. Thus, the fitness f is given as follows:-

$$f = Bonus \times ft + Speed\_UP \times (Evals - t_F) + C_T \times \sum_{t \in LT} \{D(og(t), nr(t)) - D(cr(t), nr(t))\}, \tag{1}$$

where ft is the number of tiles pushed into the holes after the execution. t_F is the steps required to push all tiles into the holes. If the task is not completed, then t_F is equal to $Evals$. LT is the set of remained tiles. $D(x, y)$ means the distance of x and y. $og(t)$, $cr(t)$, and $nr(t)$ are the original position, the current position, and the position of the nearest hole for a tile t. Thus, $\{D(og(t), nr(t)) - D(cr(t), nr(t))\}$ equals to the movement of a tile t toward the nearest hole. This is summed over all remained tiles (i.e. LT).

The three parameters *Bonus*, *Speed_Up* and C_T are chosen such that the following conditions are met:

Request1 Give a high score to a GP program which moves the agents to push a tile into a hole.
Request2 Give a higher score to a GP program which finishes the tasks (i.e. pushes all tiles into holes) quickly.
Request3 If tiles are left after the execution of a GP program, give a higher score when tiles have been moved nearer to some holes.

In the experiments, the parameter values used are $Bonus = 3000$, $Speed\_Up = 80$ and $C_T = 100$ to meet the conditions above. The number of time steps $Eval = 50$ and $Radius = 1$.

GP is using the fitness of an agent's behavior to evolve new and possibly better behaviors. The implementation used is sgpc1.1 with the parameters shown in Table 2.

4 Homo-/Heterogeneous Breeding Strategies

In the homogeneous breeding, all agents use the same algorithm (Fig.1(a)). Thus, in evaluating a GP tree, each agent decides its movement according to the result of the wrapper for the GP tree. Of course, since each agent is situated in a different environment, the output of the wrapper may vary from agent to agent. For instance, the nearest tile (i.e. Tile terminal in Table 2) might not be the same for all agents.

Table 2. GP Parameters for sgpc1.1.

max_generation	100	steady_state	0
population_size	1024	max_depth_for_new_trees	5
max_depth_after_crossover	17	max_mutant_depth	4
grow_method	GROW	selection_method	TOURNAMENT
tournament_K	6	crossover_func_pt_fraction	0.1
crossover_any_pt_fraction	0.7	fitness_prop_repro_fraction	0.1

The acquired GP trees and the evolved behaviors of multiple agents for two Tile Worlds TW1 and TW2 are shown in [Iba96b]. As mentioned in Section 1, the number of steps (i.e. 12) taken for TW1 is optimal and only possible by the cooperation of both agents. Fig.4 shows the emergence of cooperation, i.e. the job specialization, which was observed in the typical run. As can be seen in the figure, A1 is going ahead and waiting for A0 with a tile to come (Fig.4(a)). In step 9, A0 pushes a tile in front of A1, so that A1 can fill a the hole with the tile in one step. This behavior is reminiscent of the cooperation between soccer players.

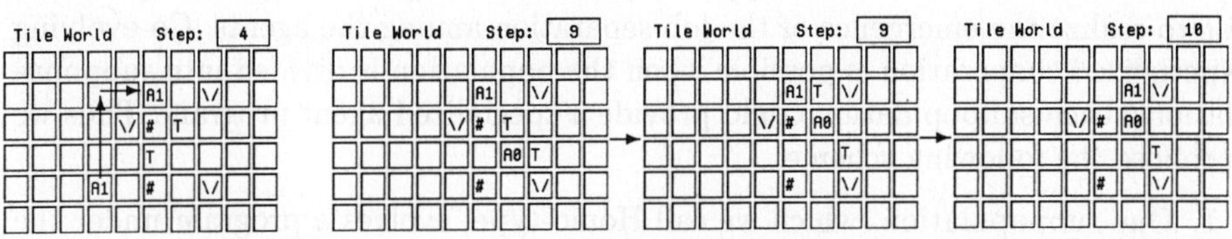

(a) A1 Waiting for A0. (b) Assistance of A0.

Fig. 4. Emergence of Cooperation Observed in TW1.

In the heterogeneous model, each agent uses a distinct specialized program, which is evolved by GP (Fig.1(b)). According to [Haynes95], the heterogeneous strategy is realized by means of a multiple-branch tree as follows. Each branch of the multiple-branch tree corresponds to a different agent's program. In case of evaluating the fitness of the tree, an agent moves according to the wrapper result of the output of the correspondent branch. Breeding proceeds in the same way as the ADF version of GP, i.e. crossover operations restricted to the correspondent branch pairs.

Fig.5 shows the result of experiments for the heterogeneous strategy. The figure plots the best fitness value with generations averaged over 20 runs. For the sake of comparison, the curve for the homogeneous strategy is also shown in the graph. As can be seen, the performance of the heterogeneous strategy is superior to the homogeneous strategy. Note that in TW1, the fitness value of $2 \times Bonus (= 6000.0)$ is given to a GP tree which completes the task i.e. pushes the two tiles into the holes. Thus, GP reaches a solution around 20 generations on average by the homogeneous strategy, whereas about 6 generations by the heterogeneous strategy were needed. The maximum fitness value for TW1 is $6000.0 + 80.0 \times (50 - 12) = 9040.0$, because 6000.0 is the bonus fitness value,

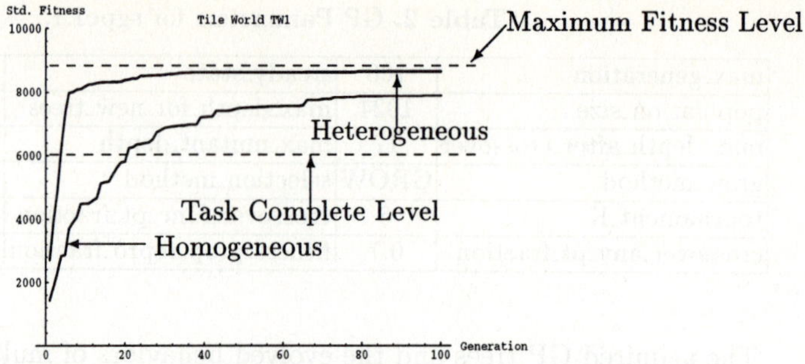

Fig. 5. Averaged Performance (Homogeneous vs. Heterogeneous)

the optimal step is 12 and the *Speed_UP* parameter was set to 80.0 (see eq.(1)). The difference between the two fitness curves at later generations means that the agents by the heterogeneous method complete the task more rapidly, i.e. establish effective cooperation.

5 Co-evolutionary Strategy

This section describes a new approach to co-evolving multi-agent cooperation, i.e to realize the emergence of the job separation among the agents. Co-evolving specialized cooperation is possible when the population is divided into subpopulations; each subpopulation could provide a specialized agent program. Thus we propose the following scheme:

1. One subpopulation, which we call Homo-type, evolves a program under the homogeneous strategy.
2. Each subpopulation (except the above subpopulation), which we call Agent-type, provides a program specialized for a particular agent.
3. Migration occurs from the Homo-type subpopulation to all Agent-type subpopulations.

Fig.6(a) shows the proposed scheme for TW1, i.e. the two-agent cooperation. The Homo-type subpopulation is aimed at evolving a common program for all agents. It might maintain useful building-blocks which could be commonly used for all agents. Thus, in this co-evolutionary scheme, the Homo-type subpopulation emigrates M individuals to other Agent-type subpopulations, intending to provide building-blocks for them. We set M to 10 in our experiment.

Selecting an agent's program from the subpopulation complicates the evolution process with the credit assignment problem [Hanks96]. That is, when evaluating the fitness of a program specialized for a particular agent, how to choose other agents' programs? To solve this difficulty, we evaluate the fitness of individuals in an Agent-type subpopulation as follows: Initially, i.e. at generation 0, the other agents' programs are chosen randomly. At later generations, we choose as the other agents' program the best programs evolved so far in the other Agent-type subpopulations.

Fig.6(b) shows the result of the experiment in TW1. This figure plots the evolution of the standard fitness averaged over 20 runs. The three curves represent the performances achieved by the above three subpopulation. For the sake

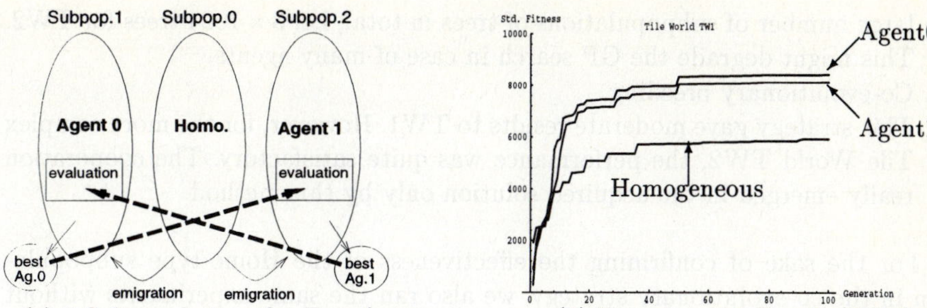

(a) 3 Subpopulations for Two Agents. (b) Experimental Result (TW1).

Fig. 6. Co-evolutionary Strategy.

of comparison, we set the total number of subpopulations to be equal to that used in the previous experiments, i.e. 1,024. That is, for TW1, each subpopulation (i.e. one Homo-type and two Agent-types) consists of 340 individuals, and for TW2 it consists of 256 individuals. Note that the Agent-type subpopulations gave better results than the Homo-type subpopulation. However, the overall performance was poorer than the previous two strategies. The difference of the two curves for Agent0 and Agent1 was caused by the fact that each subpopulation was processed asynchronously.

6 Discussions

6.1 Summary of Experiments

The previous sections described the three different strategies for GP-based multi-agent learning. The performance comparison is summarized in Table 3. The table shows the number of steps required for the agents to complete the task according to the acquired GP program, averaged over 20 runs. The number in the bracket is the average of the standard fitness values acquired at the final generation. From the table, the following points should be emphasized:

1. Homogeneous breeding.
   This strategy gave satisfactory results for both experiments. However, the acquired solutions were not necessarily optimal, i.e. the agents did not always work together.
2. Heterogeneous breeding.
   The optimal solution was often acquired for TW1. However, it gave poor performance on TW2. The reason seems to be that this strategy requires a

Table 3. Performance Comparison. Averaged time steps to complete the task is shown. The number in the bracket is the average of the standard fitness values acquired at the final generation.

Strategy	Homogeneous	Heterogeneous	Co-evolutionary	
			w Homo-type	w/o Homo-type
Tile World TW1	27.35 (7892.00)	17.81 (8655.0)	20.66 (8427.14)	36.16 (7187.00)
Tile World TW2	39.89 (9889.00)	49.98 (6081.09)	20.19 (11465.0)	48.93 (9165.00)

large number of subpopulations of trees in total, i.e. 3×1024 trees for TW2. This might degrade the GP search in case of many agents.
3. Co-evolutionary breeding.
This strategy gave moderate results to TW1. However, for the more complex Tile World TW2, the performance was quite satisfactory. The cooperation really emerged in the acquired solution only by this method.

For the sake of confirming the effectiveness of the Homo-type subpopulation in the co-evolutionary strategy, we also ran the same experiments without any migration (the w/o Homo-type column in Table 3). The results were much poorer than those with Homo-type. Thus, we have confirmed the role of the Homo-type subpopulation in providing useful building-blocks to the Agent-type subpopulations.

For the co-evolutionary strategy, the total number of trees is as small as in the homogeneous strategy. Therefore, we can conclude that the co-evolutionary strategy seems to be promising for GP-based multi-agent learning. We are currently working on the extension of this co-evolutionary scheme based on our distributed GP [Iba96a].

6.2 Future Research

Terminal and functional symbols chosen in this paper are based on name-based sensing coordination described in [Luke96]. Luke showed that the name-based sensing consistently outperforms the other two (i.e. none and deictic sensing) for his experiment. The effect of the agent view range for the pursuit game has been discussed in many DAI papers [Gasser89,Levy92]. We are also working on comparative studies of different coordination mechanisms for the Tile World.

The robustness is an important feature of a program evolved by GP [Ito96]. The robustness is defined as the ability of agents to cope with noisy or unknown situations. In the Tile World, the robustness could be examined by testing an evolved program for another Tile World. We have conducted several experiments so as to ascertain that the evolved programs for a certain Tile World could give a good performance for another Tile World. These programs are expected to keep useful building-blocks, which could be used as general subroutines. The subroutine discovery based on GP is our current research concern [Hondo96].

7 Conclusion

This paper described the emergence of cooperative behavior based on GP. We have confirmed the following points by experiments:

1. GP was successfully applied to a multi-agent test bed, i.e. the Tile World.
2. The emergence of the cooperative behavior was observed as the result of GP-based multi-agent learning (Fig.4).
3. Three different types of evolving strategies, i.e. homogeneous, heterogeneous, and co-evolutionary strategies, were compared empirically.

Our goal was to realize the emergence of the jobs separation among multiple agents. For this purpose, the co-evolutionary strategy seems to be ideal for GP-based multi-agent learning. This scheme was derived from our previous research result of a distributed GP, a parallel implementation of GP [Iba96a]. We are in pursuit of a more general way to show the effectiveness of this co-evolutionary scheme.

Acknowledgments.
We have profited from many suggestions and discussions with Bernard Manderick. We are also grateful to Walter Alden Tackett, for providing his Simple Genetic Programming in C ("sgpc1.1"), which we used to conduct our comparative experiments.

References

[Gasser *et al.*89] Gasser,L., Rouquette,N.F., Hill,R.W., and Lieb,J., Representing and Using Organizational Knowledge in Distributed AI Systems, in *Distributed Artificial Intelligence*, Gasser,L. and Huhns,M.N. (eds.), vol.2, Morgan Kaufmann, 1989

[Goldman *et al.*94] Goldman,C.V. and Rosenshein,J.S. Emergent Coordination through the use of Cooperative State-Changing Rules, in *Proceedings of the 12th National Conference on Artificial Intelligence*, 1994

[Hanks *et al.*93] Hanks,S., Pollack,M.E., and Cohen,P.R., Benchmarks, Test Beds, Controlled Experimentation, and the Design of Agent Architectures, In *AI Magazine*, Winter, 1993

[Haynes *et al.*95] Haynes, T., Wainwright,R., and Sen,S., Evolving a Team, In *Working Notes of the AAAI-95 Fall Symp. on Genetic Programming*, AAAI Press, 1995

[Hondo *et al.*96] Hondo,N, Iba,H. and Kzkazu,Y., COAST: An Approach to Robustness and Reusability in Genetic Programming, in *PPSN96*, (this volume), 1996

[Iba *et al.*96a] Iba,H. and Niwa, T., Distributed Genetic Programming, Empirical Study and Analysis, ETL-TR-96-1, in *Genetic Programming 96*, 1996

[Iba96b] Iba,H., Emergent Cooperation for Multiple Agents using Genetic Programming, ETL-TR-96-8, 1996

[Ito *et al.*96] Ito,T., Iba,H. and Kimura,M., Robot Programs Generated by Genetic Programming, in *Genetic Programming 96*,1996

[Koza 92] Koza, J., Genetic Programming, On the Programming of Computers by means of Natural Selection, MIT Press, 1992

[Koza94] Koza, J. Genetic Programming II: Automatic Discovery of Reusable Subprograms, MIT Press, 1994

[Levy *et al.*92] Levy,R. and Rosenschein,J., A Game Theoretic Approach to Distributed Artificial Intelligence and the Pursuit Problem, in *Decentralized A.I.*, Werner,E. and Demazeau,Y. (eds.), Elsevier Science Pub., 1992

[Luke *et al.*96] Luke,S. and Spector,L., Evolving Teamwork and Coordination with Genetic Programming, in Genetic Programming 96, MIT Press, 1996

[Pollack *et al.*90] Pollack,M.E. and Ringuette,M., Introducing the Tileworld: Experimentally Evaluating Agent Architectures, in *Proceedings of the 8th National Conference on Artificial Intelligence*, 1990

[Wooldrige *et al.*96] Wooldridge,M., Müller,J.P., and Tambe,M. (eds.), Intelligent Agents II, Springer, 1996

Evolution Programs Evolved

Christian Jacob

University of Erlangen-Nürnberg, Lehrstuhl für Programmiersprachen,
Martensstr. 3, D-91058 ERLANGEN, Germany
email: jacob@informatik.uni-erlangen.de
http://www2.informatik.uni-erlangen.de/IMMD-II/Persons/jacob

Abstract. Growth grammars in the form of parallel rewrite systems (L-systems) are used to model morphogenetic processes of plant structures. With the help of evolutionary programming techniques developmental programs are bred which encode plants that exhibit characteristic growth patterns advantageous in competitive environments.
Program evolution is demonstrated on the basis of extended genetic programming on symbolic expressions with genetic operators and expression generation strongly relying on templates and pattern matching.

1 Introduction: Why model morphogenesis?

One reason for attempting to model nature is to gain more and more detailed insight into natural processes. Computer simulations have turned out to provide excellent means to explore phenomena observed in nature. One crucial characteristic of natural organisms is their ability to grow and form new structures, these processes being subsumed as *structure formation* or *morphogenesis*. Such structure formation can be interpreted as the execution of »developmental programs«, there is no blueprint for an organism, instead, complex »rule systems« encode how to build organels and how to combine diversified parts to form a complete and functioning organism. However, these »programs« are highly complex and parametrized with diverse influence from organism-internal signals (genes mutually switching on and off by activator and repressor mechanisms) as well as from the environment in which development takes place.

There is a special area of morphogenesis which is being studied extensively: the morphological modeling of plant growth in 3-dimensional space, an area that turns out to me of more and more importance for realistic simulations of botanical ecosystems, such as forests, thus gaining new insight into natural interaction processes and understanding how environmental factors influence those ecosystems. The creation of plant models in 3D space is required for being able to model interfaces between a plant and its environment, like light interception, its mechanic and hydraulic architecture, or interaction with neighboring plants.

In the sequel, we will focus on modeling growth processes of plant structures in three dimensions. Chapter 2 will briefly mention different approaches used for modeling plant morphology. We will discuss parallel rewrite systems, commmonly termed L-systems, in more detail, as these will serve as our preferred formalization of developmental programs. In chapter 3, combining those L-systems with evolutionary programming techniques will lead to a first step in being able to model evolution in ecosystems, or at least, to help design L-systems encoding plants that exhibit characteristic growth patterns, as will be shown in detail by several example evolution experiments in chapter 4. Finally, in chapter 5, we will conclude with an outlook towards a simulation system for coevolutionary plant development.

2 Morphological modeling of plant growth

Quite a lot of diverse approaches for modeling plant morphology have been developped within the last decade (with some being extensions of techniques dating back more than 20 years): iterated function systems [Peitgen et al., 1993], cellular automata or voxel space growth [Green, 1989], Lindenmayer systems [Lindenmayer, 1975; Prusinkiewicz and Lindenmayer, 1990], or stochastic growth grammars [Kurth, 1994].

In the scope of this article we focus on Lindenmayer systems (L-systems), a special type of string based rewrite systems, named after the biologist Aristid Lindenmayer (1925-1989). L-systems are successfully being used in theoretical biology for describing and simulating all different kinds of natural growth processes (for a great number of examples see e.g. Prusinkiewicz and Lindenmayer, 1990). With L-systems all letters in a given word are replaced in parallel and simultaneously. This feature makes Lindenmayer systems especially suitable for describing fractal structures, cell divisions in multicellular organisms [Jacob, 1995b], or flowering stages of herbaceous plants [Prusinkiewicz and Lindenmayer, 1990, Jacob, 1995a and 1996], as we will demonstrate in the sequel.

D0L-systems (D0 meaning: deterministic with no context) are the simplest type of L-systems. Formally a D0L-system $L = (\Sigma, \alpha, P, T)$, capable of encoding geometrical structures, consists of the following ingredients:

- an *alphabet* $\Sigma = \{\sigma_1, \ldots, \sigma_n\}$, each symbol of which stands for a morphological unit, like a cell, an internode, a sprout, or a leaf,
- a start string α, referred to as the *axiom*, which is an element of Σ^*, the set of all finite words over the alphabet Σ,
- $P = \{p_1, \ldots, p_k\}$, a set of productions or *rewrite rules* $p_i : \Sigma \to \Sigma^*$ with $\sigma \to p_i(\sigma)$ for each $\sigma \in \Sigma$, which replaces a symbol by a (possibly empty) string of symbols, and which are to be applied in parallel to all symbols of a string,
- a *geometrical interpretation* T, a 3D semantics, for some of the symbols from Σ, translating a string into a spatial structure, i.e. special symbols represent commands to draw graphic objects like points, lines, polygons etc; this translation is commonly known as *turtle geometry* interpretation.

Whenever there is no explicit rewriting rule for a symbol σ, the identity mapping is assumed. Iterated application of an L-system $L = (\Sigma, \alpha, P, T)$ generates a (potentially infinite) sequence of words $\alpha^{(0)}\alpha^{(1)}\alpha^{(2)}\ldots$ as exemplified in fig 1, where P^k denotes k-fold parallel application of the productions in P, and each string $\alpha^{(i+1)}$ is generated from the preceding string $\alpha^{(i)} = \alpha_1^{(i)}\alpha_2^{(i)}\ldots\alpha_{n_i}^{(i)}$ with $\alpha_m^{(i)} \in \Sigma$ the following way ($p_{i_j} \in P$):

$$\alpha^{(i+1)} = P(\alpha^{(i)}) = p_{i_1}(\alpha_1^{(i)})\, p_{i_2}(\alpha_2^{(i)}) \ldots p_{i_{n_i}}(\alpha_{n_i}^{(i)}) .$$

Fig. 2 shows an example L-system describing growth sequences of sprouts, leaves and blooms of an artificial flower, together with its graphical interpretation. The D0L-system encodes turtle geometry macros for generating graphical representations of the leaves, blooms and stalks. All the non-italic, bold terms (**f**, **pu**, **pd**, **rl**, **rr**, **yl**, **yr**) represent commands to move the turtle (**f**: forward, **b**: backward) and change the drawing tool´s orientation by rotation around its longitudinal, lateral, and vertical axes (**rl/rr**: roll left/right, **pu/pd**: pitch up/down, **yl/yr**: yaw left/right), thus translating a one-dimensional string into a 3D geometrical object resembling a plant (some of these commands do not occur in the example L-system). In order to be able to generate branching structures a kind of stacking mechanism for the turtle´s position and orientation is necessary. For each string of the form $s_1\,[s_2]\,s_3$ the strings s_1, s_2, and s_3 are interpreted in sequence, however, before starting the interpre-tation of s_2 the current turtle position and orientation are pushed on a stack, so that, having finished interpreting s_2, the turtle is reset to its prior coordinates and orientation.

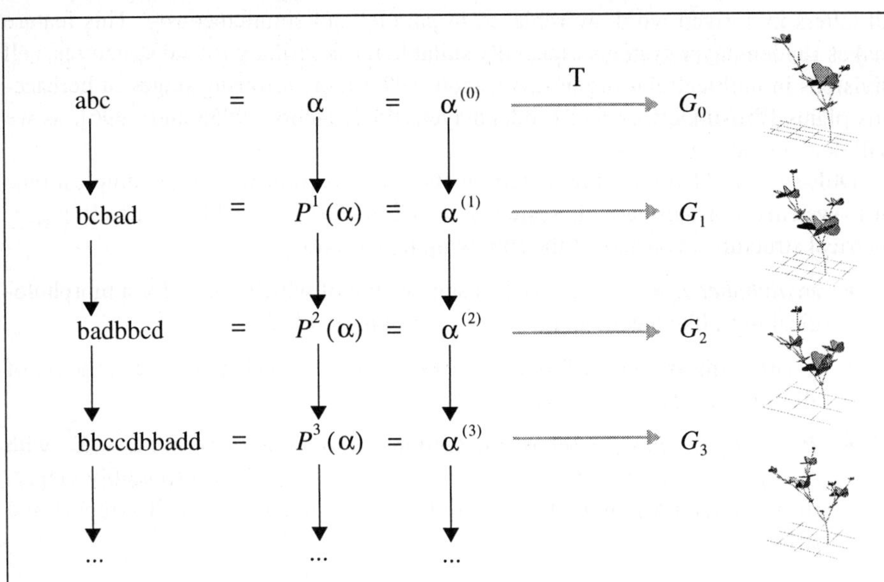

Fig. 1. Rewriting with D0L-systems and geometrical interpretation for an axiom *abc* and productions $a \to bc$ and $c \to ad$.

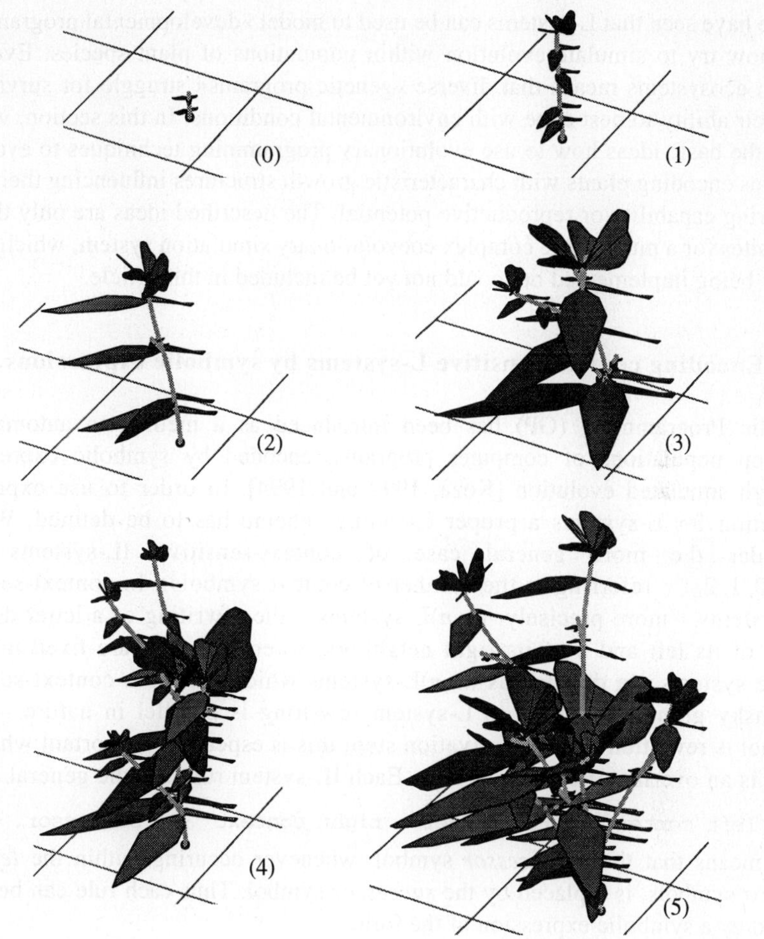

Initial start word: *sprout*(4)

Sprout developing leaves and flower:

p_1 : *sprout*(4) → **f** *stalk*(2) [**pu(20)** *sprout*(2)] **pu(20)** [**pu(25)** *sprout*(0)] ... [**pu(60)** *leaf*(0)] **rr(90)** [**pu(20)** *sprout(3)*] **rr(90)** [**pu(20)** *sprout*(2)]**f** stalk(1) *bloom*(0)

Riping sprout:

p_2 : *sprout*(t < 4) → *sprout*(t+1)

Stalk elongation:

p_3 : *stalk*(t > 0) → **f f** *stalk*(t-1)

Changing leaf sizes:

p_4 : *leaf*(t) → *leaf*(t + 1.5)
p_5 : *leaf*(t > 7) → *Leaf*(7)
p_6 : *Leaf*(t) → *Leaf*(t - 1.5)
p_7 : *Leaf*(t < 2) → *leaf*(0)

Growing bloom:

p_8 : *bloom*(t) → *bloom*(t + 1)

Fig. 2. Example of a growth grammar (L-system) modeling plantlike geometrical structures

3 Growth grammars and evolution

As we have seen that L-systems can be used to model »developmental programs« we will now try to simulate evolution within populations of plant species. Evolution within ecosystems means that diverse »genetic programs« struggle for survival, or for their ability to best cope with environmental conditions. In this section, we describe the basic ideas how to use evolutionary programming techniques to evolve L-systems encoding plants with characteristic growth structures influencing their light-gathering capability or reproductive potential. The described ideas are only the prerequisites for a much more complex coevolutionary simulation system, which is currently being implemented but could not yet be included in this article.

3.1 Encoding context-sensitive L-systems by symbolic expressions

Genetic Programming (GP) has been introduced as a method to automatically develop populations of computer programs, encoded by symbolic expressions, through simulated evolution [Koza, 1992 and 1994]. In order to use expression evolution for L-systems a proper encoding scheme has to be defined. We will consider the more general case of context-sensitive IL-systems (with $I = 0, 1, 2, \dots$ referring to the number of context symbols). In context-sensitive IL-systems – more precisely: (m,n)L-systems – the rewriting of a letter depends on m of its left and n of its right neighbors, where m and n are fixed integers. These systems are denoted as (m,n)L-systems which resemble context-sensitive Chomsky grammars, but – as L-system rewriting is parallel in nature – every symbol is rewritten in each derivation step; this is especially important whenever there is an overlap of context strings. Each IL-system rule has the general form

```
left context < predecessor > right context  →  successor.
```

This means that the *predecessor* symbol, whenever occuring within the *left/right context* symbols, is replaced by the *successor* symbol. Thus each rule can be represented by a symbolic expression of the form

```
LRule[ LEFT[ leftContext ], PRED[ predecessor ]
       RIGHT[ rightContext ], SUCC[ successor] ].
```

Accordingly, an L-system with its axiom and rule set is encoded by an expression of the form

```
LSystem[ □ AXIOM, LRULES[ □□ LRule] ],
```

where we use a pattern notation with □ F denoting a term of the form F[...], and □□ F representing a non-empty sequence of □ F expressions. So our example L-system of the previous section would be represented as follows:

```
LSystem[AXIOM[sprout[4]],
  LRULES[
    LRule[LEFT[],PRED[sprout[4]],RIGHT[],
      SUCC[f,stalk[2],STACK[pu[20],...],bloom[0]]],
    LRule[LEFT[],PRED[sprout[t<4]],RIGHT[],SUCC[sprout[t+1]]],
    LRule[LEFT[],PRED[stalk[t>0]],RIGHT[],SUCC[f,f,stalk[t-1]]],
```

where L-system bracketing of the form [s] is now represented as `STACK[s]`.

3.2 Stochastic generation of L-system encodings by templates

One of the main differences of our GP approach to the GP paradigm introduced by Koza (1992) is the use of high-level building blocks for generating expression as well as modifying expressions. Instead of just defining a set of function symbols together with their arities, each expression from a template pool, as depicted in figure 2, serves as a possibly partial description of a genotype, encoding an L-system in our case. Each of these templates (marked with 1., 2., 3., ...) is associated with a set of attributes like, e.g., predicates constraining the set of subexpressions that can be plugged in. Thus the encoded L-system productions are restricted to contextfree forms (4., LEFT[], RIGHT[]) with their left-hand sides (4., □ PRED) constrained to *sprout[i]*, with *i* replaced by an integer number from the interval, say, *[0,4]* (5.), and their right-hand sides (4., □ SUCC) defined either as a sequence (SEQ) of expressions (6., 7. and 8.) or a bracketed expression sequence (6., □ STACK) for which the productions are omitted here. Each expression is constructed from a start pattern (here: LSystem[□ AXIOM,□ LRULES]) by recursively inserting matching expressions from the expression pool until all pattern blanks – marked by □ – have been replaced by according subexpressions. Of course, one has to take care that this construction loop eventually comes to an end.

```
1.    LSystem[□ AXIOM,□ LRULES],                                          (1)
2.    AXIOM[sprout[4]],                                                   (1)
3.    LRULES[
        LRule[LEFT[], PRED[ sprout[4] ], RIGHT[],
              SUCC[SEQ[SEQ[f],SEQ[stalk[2]], STACK[PD[60],leaf[0]], ...,
              □□ SEQ,
              SEQ[f],SEQ[stalk[1]], bloom[0]]]],
        LRule[LEFT[], PRED[ sprout[t<4] ], RIGHT[], SUCC[sprout[t+1]]],
        ...
        LRule[LEFT[], PRED[ bloom[6] ], RIGHT[], SUCC[ bloom[1]]],
       □□□ LRule
      ],                                                                  (1)
4.    LRule[LEFT[],□ PRED,RIGHT[],□ SUCC],                                (1)
5.    PRED[sprout[i]],                                                    (1)
6.    SUCC[□ SEQ | □ STACK],                                              (1)
7.    SEQ[□□ [□ sprout | □ stalk | □ leaf | □ bloom | f |
          □ YL | □ YR | □ PU | □ PD | □ RL | □ RR | □ SEQ]],              (1)
8.    SEQ[□□ [□ sprout | □ stalk | □ leaf | □ bloom | f |
          □ YL | □ YR | □ PU | □ PD | □ RL | □ RR ]],                      (4)
      ...
      sprout[sproutIndex], ..., bloom[bloomIndex]                   (1,...,3)
```

Fig. 3. A typical set of templates used for generating L-system encodings

Some further remarks should be made about the encoding scheme of figure 3. The templates basically describe a D0L-system as exemplified in figure 2. However, the □□ SEQ pattern within the first LRule expression (3.) enables the generation system to create rule variants by inserting new expression sequences, i.e. one or more expressions of the form SEQ[...]. Accordingly, the L-system encoding might be enhanced by additional rules by replacing the □□□ LRule pattern with a (possibly empty) sequence of LRule[...] expressions. Each sequence of expressions is constructable via alternative templates (7. and 8.), where SEQ[□□ [a|b|c]] denotes an arbitrary sequence of expressions taken from the set {a,b,c} as, e.g., SEQ[a,a,c,b] or SEQ[c,c,c,a,b,a] with the sequence length restricted to, say, between 4 and 6.

Whenever there are several templates matching one pattern the expressions are selected with probabilities proportional to their weights (see the bracketed numbers right from the expressions in figure 2, serving as fitness values for the templates) leading to a kind of fitness proportionate selection among templates. The pattern matching is not unique for the □ SEQ pattern (6.) for which there are two matching templates (7. and 8.), a recursive (SEQ[.... □ SEQ]) and non-recursive version which will be selected with a probability of 0.8, thus implicitly restricting the nesting of expressions. For further details on expression templates see [Jacob, 1994 and 1996].

3.3 Changing evolution program genes

Principally, we want to be able to change any subexpression within the developmental programs which should not be considered as parametrized modules encoding some fixed L-system in a black box fashion [Niklas, 1986]. As with the expression generating operators the basic idea is, again, to use templates for controling which subexpressions should be in the scope of each operator:

- *Mutation* replaces a randomly selected subexpression by an expression – with the same head expression – generated from the template pool.
- *Crossover* is a recombination operator between two or more expressions. Subexpressions with the same head are selected within the expressions and interchanged.
- *Deletion* erases expression arguments whenever this is possible according to restrictions of the number of arguments for the selected expression.
- *Duplication* inserts a copy of a randomly selected argument as an additional subexpression.
- *Permutation* interchanges the sequence of arguments of an expression.

These operators are defined for general expressions and are not especially tailored to L-system encodings. Subexpressions are chosen according to operator specific selection schemes based on pattern matching mechanisms. Thus it is, e.g., possible to restrict recombinations to subexpressions with head SUCC, i.e. expressions of the form SUCC[...], which allows to interchange right-hand sides of L-system productions, or permute only LRule expressions thus changing the ordering of rules. With a set of templates defined for each operator the effects of genetic operators can be constrained in a problem specific way. A more detailed description of a general scheme for the application of genetic operators on expressions can be found in [Jacob, 1996].

4 Breeding evolution programs

In order to demonstrate by a simple example how plantlike structures with specific characteristics could be developed by L-system evolution, we will consider the following influential factors important in ecosystem competition: a plant´s insemination and light gathering capability, and its ability to shed shadow on neighboring plants. We try to incorporate these factors with the following fitness function.

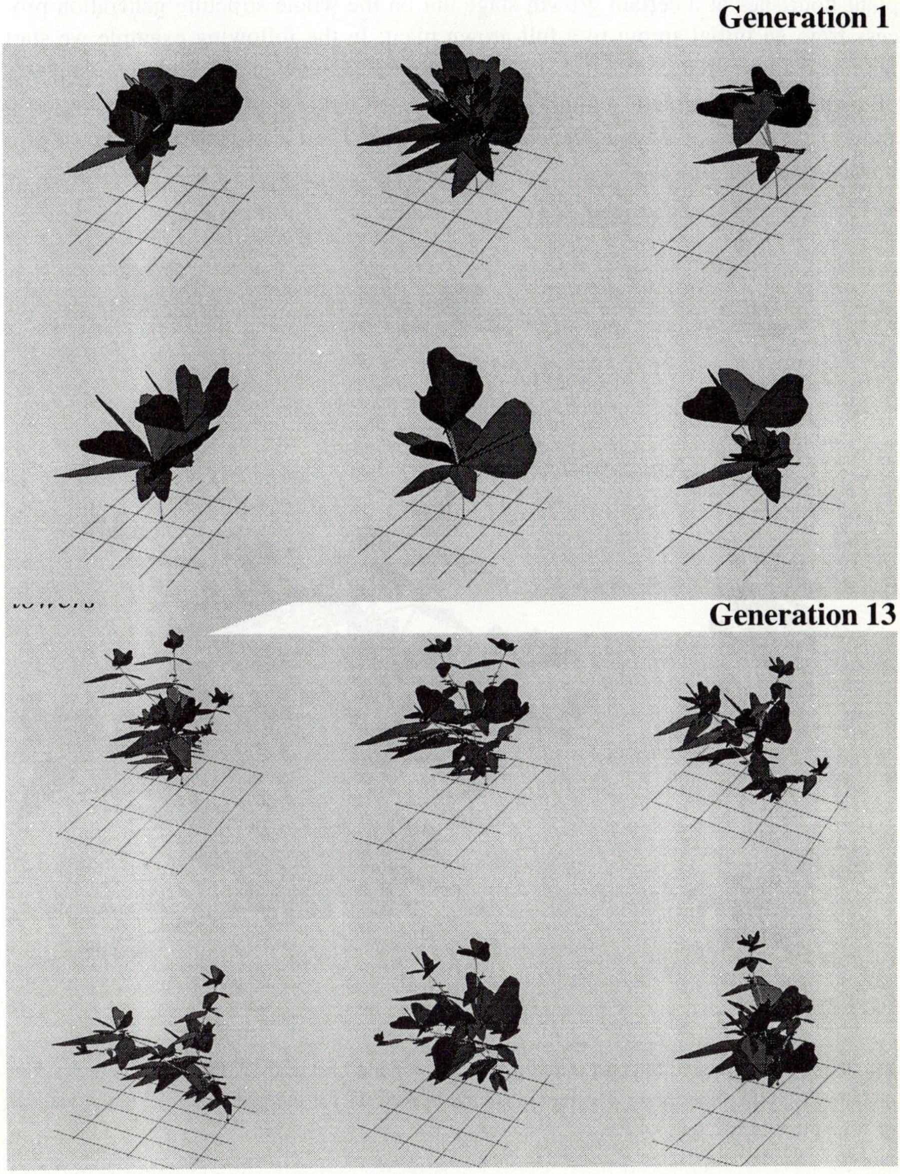

Fig. 4. Snapshots of the phenotypes from an evolution of plant encoding development programs. The plants are depicted with different scales in order to show most of their details

$$fitness\,(plant) = \sum_{i=0}^{m} \Delta x_i \cdot \Delta y_i \cdot \Delta z_i + 2 \cdot B_i + L_i$$

Δx, Δy, Δz: extension of the geometric plant structure in x-, y-, and z-dimension

B, : the number of blooms blossoming; L: the number of leaves the plant carries

m: the maximum number of L-system iterations

The total fitness is computed as the sum of the plant´s extension, blooms, and leaves for each L-system iteration. This means that fitness does not only depend on how the plant flourishes at a certain growth stage but on the whole structure generation process from an initial sprout to a full-grown plant. In the following example we start with a small population of six L-system genomes each generated with the templates of figure 3. A maximum number of $m = 6$ L-system iterations is used. Figure 4 shows two stages of a typical evolution sequence. The individuals are selected proportional to their fitness.

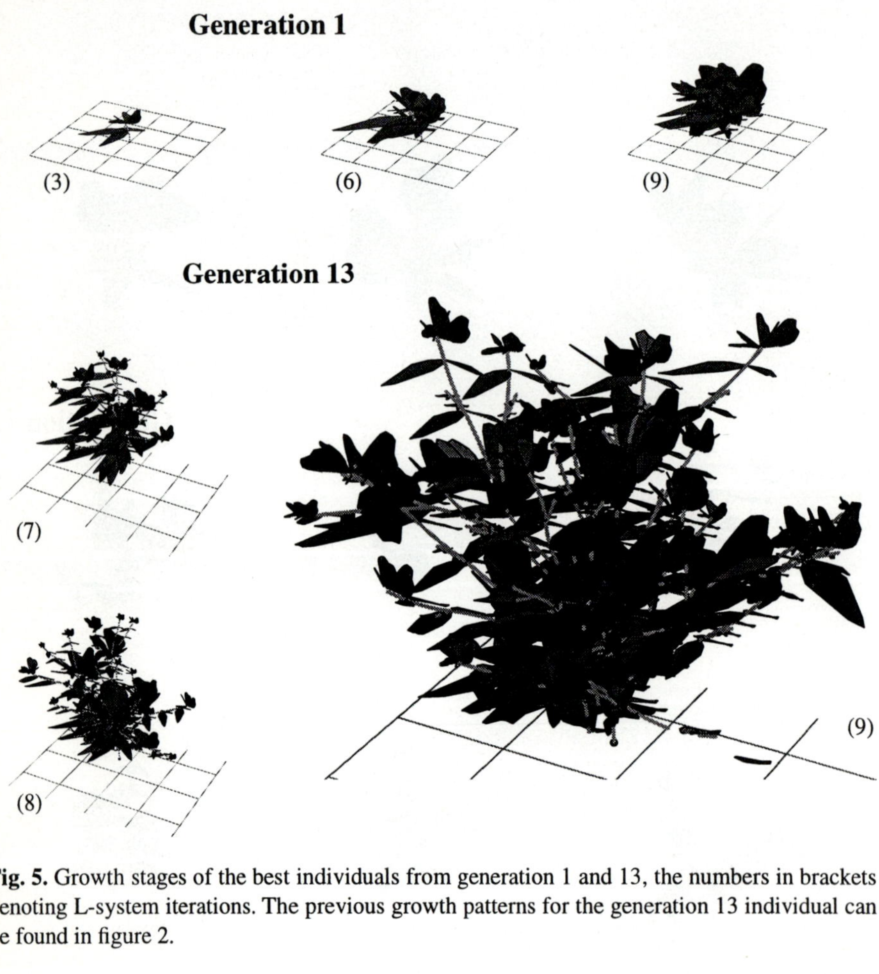

Fig. 5. Growth stages of the best individuals from generation 1 and 13, the numbers in brackets denoting L-system iterations. The previous growth patterns for the generation 13 individual can be found in figure 2.

All individuals of generation 13 encode for complex growth patterns which is on the one side due to the property of non-causality of L-systems which means that small changes within the rewrite rules can have dramatic effects on the encoded phenotypic appearance. On the other side, evolutionary selection and variation applied to sets of L-systems drive the evolution process to ever more competitive encodings of development programs. Figure 5 shows growth stages of the best individual of the initial population (indiv. 2) compared to the best individual after 13 generations (indiv. 1). This best evolved L-system encodes a plantlike structure that grows rapidly, widespread, and with a bunch of blooms and leaves.

5 Steps towards realistic development and coevolution

Of course, there are many more factors that influence an organism´s development in a natural competitive environment. With our simple example we only intended to show the feasibility of inferring L-systems encoding morphogenetic processes exhibiting specific characteristics. The described evolutionary programming techniques are currently being incorporated into a coevolutonary system for simulating plants growing in competition for resources like nutrients, sunlight, or space. Finally, on a more microscopic level, our L-system based developmental programs will be extended by functional genome structures like operons, promoters, and regulators in order to include intra-gene interaction into evolution processes.

References

1. Green, N., *Voxel space automata: Modeling with stochastic growth processes in voxel space*, Computer Graphics, ACM SIGGRAPH, 23(3), 1989, pp. 175-184.
2. Jacob, C., *Genetic L-System Programming*, Parallel Problem Solving from Nature - PPSN III, LNCS 866, Springer, Berlin, 1994, pp. 334-343.
3. Jacob, C., *MathEvolvica - Simulierte Evolution von Entwicklungsprogrammen der Natur*, Dissertation, Arbeitsberichte des Instituts für mathematische Maschinen und Datenverarbeitung, Band 28, Nummer 10, Erlangen, 1995.
4. Jacob, C., *Modeling Growth with L-Systems & Mathematica, Mathematica* in Education and Research, Vol. 4, No. 3, TELOS Springer, 1995.
5. Jacob, C., *Evolving Evolution Programs: Genetic Programming and L-Systems*, in: Koza, J.R., Goldberg, D.E., Fogel, D.B., and Riolo, R.L. (eds.), Genetic Programming 1996, MIT Press, Cambridge, MA, 1996.
6. Koza, J., *Genetic Programming*, MIT-Press, Cambridge, MA, 1992.
7. Koza, J., *Discovery of rewrite rules in Lindenmayer systems and state transition rules in cellular automata via genetic programming*, Symposium on Pattern Formation - SPF-93, Claramont, CA, 1993.
8. Koza, J., *Genetic Programming II*, MIT-Press, Cambridge, MA, 1994.
9. Kurth, W., *Growth Grammar Interpreter GROGRA 2.4*, Berichte des Forschungszentrums Waldökosysteme, Universität Göttingen, Reihe B, Band 38, 1994.
10. Lindenmayer, A., and Rozenberg, G. (eds.), *Automata, Languages, Development*, North-Holland, 1975.
11. Niklas, K.J., *Computer-simulated Plant Evolution*, in: Scientific American, 254 (March), 1986, pp. 68-75.
12. Peitgen, H.-O., Jürgens, H., Saupe, D., *Chaos and Fractals*, New Frontiers of Science, Springer-Verlag, 1993.
13. Prusinkiewicz, P., and Lindenmayer, A., *The Algorithmic Beauty of Plants*, Springer, New York, 1990.

Encoding Scheme Issues for Open-Ended Artificial Evolution

Nick Jakobi

School of Cognitive and Computing Sciences
University of Sussex, Brighton BN1 9QH, England
email: nickja@cogs.susx.ac.uk
tel: (UK) 01273 678061
fax: (UK) 01273 671320

Abstract. This paper examines the ways in which the encoding scheme that governs how phenotypes develop from genotypes may be used to improve the performance of open-ended artificial evolution for design. If an open-ended framework involving variable complexity genetic algorithms is adopted, then the vast majority of the evolutionary effort is spent exploring neutral flat areas of the search space. Domain-specific heuristics may be employed to reduce the time spent on searching these neutral areas, however, and the ways in which domain knowledge may be incorporated into the encoding scheme are examined. Experiments are reported in which different categories of scheme were tested against each other, and conclusions are offered as to the most promising type of encoding scheme for a viable open-ended artificial evolution.

1 Introduction

Genetic Algorithms (GAs) are primarily employed as optimization techniques on problems which involve finding satisfactory values for a given, fixed number of parameters. However, GAs are one of the few techniques that may also be used on design problems, where the size of the optimal parameter set, and the complexity of satisfactory solutions, is not known beforehand. In these situations, the size (and sometimes structure) of the genotype is put under evolutionary control resulting in what shall be referred to throughout this paper as variable complexity GAs [4, 3]. Areas in which these have been tried include aircraft wing design [2], computer programming [6], and the design of control architectures for autonomous agents [5]. Although some success has been reported in all of these fields, an artificial evolution that is a general alternative to human design ingenuity has not yet been achieved. This paper looks at the form that such an open-ended evolutionary process would have to possess, and compares and contrasts ways in which domain-specific heuristics may be applied using the encoding scheme to ensure that the time periods involved remain within sensible limits.

2 Open-ended artificial evolution

There is nothing magic about an evolutionary process capable of producing better designs than a human. What is hard, is to produce better designs than a human within a reasonable period of time. This section examines the basic form of open-ended evolutionary process we will be dealing with in this paper, and section 3 and 4 look at how the performance of this process may be improved.

The term 'open-ended' is here used to refer to a necessary feature of a viable evolutionary design alternative, namely that the process will continue to produce better and better solutions as long as there are better solutions to produce. Thus, in an open-ended evolutionary scenario, if greater or lesser complexity is *required* for fitter solutions, then it *will* evolve. Eventually and inevitably, such a process will evolve better designs than a human designer.

Although at first sight it may seem miraculous, there are in fact many simple methods by which the open-endedness of the evolutionary process may be ensured [1]. The one considered in this paper, however, seems the most amenable to performance improvements [8]. In its simplest form, restrictions on the way in which genotypes code for phenotypes ensures that the search space upon which a variable-complexity GA operates contains no *local* fitness maxima. Since there are no local fitness maxima in the search space, the GA will only come to rest on a global maxima if there is one, or not at all if there isn't one (in a coevolutionary situation for example). To understand how this is possible, a brief analysis of the nature of variable complexity search spaces is given below, and then a simple example encoding scheme is put forward that ensures an open-ended evolutionary process.

The way in which genotypes are represented and the nature of the genetic operators determines the (potentially infinite) set of possible genotypes upon which a particular GA operates. If a GA is employed to optimize a fixed number n parameters, then the set of possible genotypes can be, and usually is, visualized for explanatory purposes as an n dimensional Euclidean space. This is normally referred to in the optimization literature as 'genotype space'. The set of possible genotypes searched by a variable complexity GA, however, is best thought of for the purposes of this paper as a graph or network (i.e. a set of interconnected nodes) rather than a fixed dimensionality space. Each node on such a graph corresponds to a possible genotype and each connection between nodes corresponds to a single application of a genetic operator.

In order to make this more explicit, consider as an example a stripped down version of a variable complexity GA acting upon genotypes of finite cardinality. It involves two genetic operators: mutation, as normally conceived, and a 'change size' operator which adds and/or subtracts material to and/or from the genotype, thus changing the size of the genotype and the complexity of the solution it encodes. Two genotypes, under such a GA, are maximally similar, though not identical, if they differ by a single genetic base unit (bit, character, nucleic acid

[1] The most trivial of these involves the creation of a totally random genotype at regular time intervals.

etc.). This is the case if *either* they are the same size and shape but differ by a single genetic base unit (the mutation operator) *or* one genotype contains exactly one more genetic base unit than the other but in all other respects they are identical (the 'change size' operator). A connection is defined to exist between two nodes on the graph of possible genotypes if and only if their corresponding genotypes are maximally similar. The more similar two genotypes are to each other, the shorter the direct path between their corresponding nodes.

A variable-complexity GA, then, is regarded here as searching a graph of possible genotypes, rather than a Euclidean genotype space, for nodes that correspond to phenotypes of high fitness. A local fitness maximum on such a graph is constituted either by a single node or by a subnetwork of inter-connected nodes that are all of the same corresponding fitness, and may be recognised by the fact that *all* the nodes directly connected to it are of lower corresponding fitness. If there are no local fitness maxima on the graph of possible genotypes then the evolutionary process may be considered open-ended. Encoding schemes that ensure this may take many forms and, in fact, open-endedness of this nature turns out to be trivial. An example encoding scheme is outlined below.

A simple encoding scheme that precludes local fitness maxima

Consider a scheme in which it is always possible to add extra genetic material (in the form of extra bits, characters etc) to the genotype without effecting the phenotype, and it is always possible to switch segments of the genotype 'on' or 'off' by way of single point mutations. These restrictions may seem strange but they are in fact true of the encoding scheme behind natural development. Now consider a worst case scenario - the genotype coding for a particular phenotype cannot undergo any normal single point mutation anywhere without suffering a loss in fitness. Extra genetic material that is 'off' can always be added to the genotype without effecting the phenotype, however, and this will eventually lead, after a monkeys-typing-Shakespeare length of time, to the evolution of a stretch of 'off' genotype that codes for a fitter phenotype (if there is one) than that expressed by the current 'on' stretch of genotype. Since a single-point mutation can always switch an 'on' stretch of genotype to 'off' and an 'off' stretch of genotype to 'on', we may expect that *eventually* 'junk DNA' that produces a fitter phenotype is switched 'on' while the rest of the genome is switched 'off'.

Under this or any number of more subtle domain-specific encoding schemes that display similar properties, we can guarantee that no node or set of nodes on the graph of possible genotypes constitutes a local fitness maximum. All nodes will connect to at least a few other nodes of the same corresponding fitness thus forming large *neutral networks* (see [9]). In every neutral network there will be one or more nodes that also has a connection to a node in a neutral network of higher fitness (if there is one). It is always possible, therefore, to find a path from *any* node through the graph of possible genotypes that monotonically increases[2], with respect to corresponding fitness, ad infinitum.

[2] monotonically increasing means never going down, not always going up.

3 Applying domain-specific heuristics to neutral network search

What is immediately obvious, if one excepts the basic open-ended framework laid out above, is that by far the largest proportion of the computational effort will be spent on blindly searching neutral networks as opposed to climbing hills. This is not only because hill-climbing type search *is* directed, but also because nodes on the graph of possible genotypes that are directly connected to nodes of greater fitness will be in the vast minority. Thus although other techniques (such as simulated annealing) may out-perform artificial evolution at hill-climbing type search, there is a certain amount of evidence [1, 7] that artificial evolution is better suited to neutral network search than these other techniques, and should therefore constitute the search method of choice on the sort of open-ended design problems this paper is concerned with. Neutral network search is, however, non-directed by definition, and if open-ended artificial evolution is to be a viable alternative to human design then all attention must be focused on ways to speed up the efficiency of neutral network search from the unacceptable monkeys-typing-Shakespeare levels reported above. This section looks at what it would mean to apply domain-specific heuristics to this search and general ways in which this can be accomplished using the encoding scheme.

As an example of what it means to apply a heuristic to open-ended artificial evolution, we shall consider a certain property p of phenotypes in a particular design domain such that *in general* successful phenotypes display p rather than p' (i.e. not p). The property p could be symmetry, for example, or large amounts of repeated structure, or even the existence of specific configurations of elements within the phenotype. In addition, we notice that the instantiation of p in a *random* phenotype is very unlikely and are thus lead to suspect that the success of phenotypes that display p is somehow causally related to p. By concentrating the evolutionary search on genotypes that code for p (i.e. which correspond to phenotypes that display p), therefore, we are employing the hypothesis that p contributes to phenotypic success as a heuristic. If the heuristic is well-founded then we may expect to decrease the time taken to evolve satisfactory results.

There are two ways in which the encoding scheme can be employed to achieve this (both of which are explained below) by increasing the relative frequency of nodes that code for p throughout the *entire* graph of possible genotypes. First though, it is important to understand exactly why increasing the relative frequency of p genotypes should improve the performance of neutral network search. The heuristic implies that for any particular neutral network, the nearest area of higher fitness is more likely to be constituted by nodes that code for p than nodes that code for p'. This is true both in the case where the neutral network is itself constituted wholly by nodes that code for p, and in the case where it is constituted by a mixture of nodes that code for p and nodes that code for p'. In both of these two cases, increasing the relative frequency of p nodes throughout the entire graph of possible genotypes will increase the proportion of new offspring that are p, thus increasing the rate at which p genotypes are sampled and decreasing the time taken to find the area of higher fitness. Furthermore, in the latter case, increasing the relative frequency of p nodes will also increase the proportion of individuals in the population that code for p rather than p', thus increasing the likelihood of p genotypes being picked as parents in offspring events, and thus again increasing the proportion of new offspring that are p. Therefore, whether at the beginning of the evolutionary process with a mixture of p and p' individuals in the population, or at an advanced stage where only primarily p individuals remain, an increased relative frequency of p nodes throughout the graph of possible genotypes will continue to do work in improving the performance of neutral network search.

A simple *direct* encoding scheme (where phenotype space is mapped evenly onto the graph of possible genotypes) may be altered to increase the relative frequency of nodes that code for a certain property p in only one of two distinct ways. Either the encoding scheme is *biased* so that there are lots of ways in which genotypes may code for p but only a few ways in which a genotype may code for p', or it is *restricted* so that genotypes are incapable of coding for some or all of the phenotypes that display p'. The first method uniformly increases the proportion of nodes on the graph of possible genotypes that code for p, and the second method uniformly decreases the number of nodes on the graph of possible genotypes that code for p'. In what follows, the encoding schemes that fall into each of these two categories shall be referred to as biased and restricted encoding schemes respectively. There is of course a third category that involves both biasing the search in favour of phenotypes that display p and restricting the ways in which phenotypes may display p' and this will be referred to as a *hybrid* encoding scheme.

4 Testing the different categories of encoding scheme against each other

This section reports the results of experiments designed to compare the relative abilities of the four different categories of encoding. Two different sets of experiments were performed, the first designed to see just what sort of performance improvements we can expect from applying heuristics to neutral network search, and the second designed to see what happens if the heuristic that is applied is not well-founded. In the first set of experiments specifically devised direct, restricted, biased and hybrid encoding schemes were tested against each other on their ability to apply a heuristic, namely that fit phenotypes were symmetrical, to a certain symmetrical evolutionary task. In the second set of experiments only the biased and direct encoding schemes were tested against each other, but this time on an asymmetrical evolutionary task. In both experiments, schemes were judged on the average time taken by a GA to search a neutral network of a particular fitness for nodes in a second fitter network. Precise details of the neutral networks and encoding schemes are given below.

Phenotypes consisted of the pattern of filled squares on an eight by eight grid. Their fitnesses were assigned according to the templates shown in figure 2. As can be seen from the diagrams, in both experiments the templates of fitness

0	2	4	6	7	5	3	1
16	18	20	22	23	21	19	17
24	26	28	30	31	29	27	25
8	10	12	14	15	13	11	9
40	42	44	46	47	45	43	41
56	58	60	62	63	61	59	57
48	50	52	54	55	53	51	49
32	34	36	38	39	37	35	33

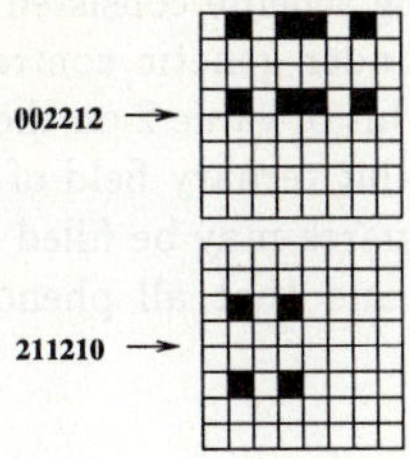

Fig. 1. The numbering system used to fill in squares on the phenotypic grid. On the right are two example genotype fields from the biased encoding scheme, and their corresponding phenotypic effect

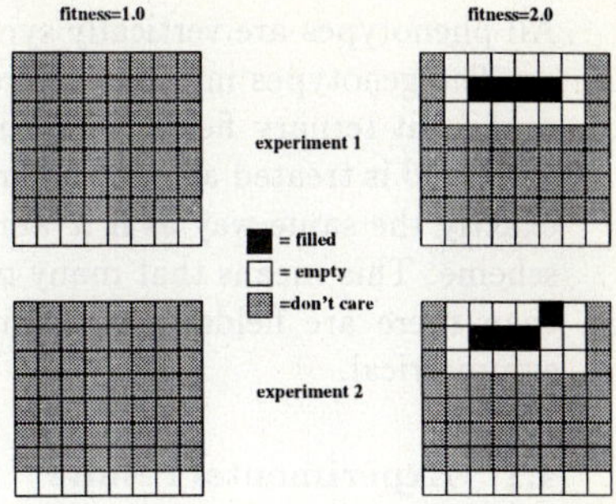

Fig. 2. This figure shows the phenotypic templates that were used to define neutral networks on the graph of possible genotypes.

2.0 are special cases of the templates of fitness 1.0. This means that the two neutral networks formed by nodes which correspond to phenotypes that match the templates of fitness 2.0 are both sub-networks of the huge neutral network formed by the nodes which correspond to phenotypes that match the templates of fitness 1.0. In experiment 1, the template of fitness 2.0 is symmetrical and in experiment 2, the corresponding template is not.

The genotypes in the direct encoding scheme consisted of a precise number n of 6-bit binary fields joined together to make a string, where n was under genetic control. In order to decode a phenotype from a genotype, a decimal value is calculated from the binary value of each field, and the relevant square filled in on the grid according to the special numbering shown in figure 1. Thus each phenotype has as many squares filled in as there are fields on the genotype.

The genotypes in the biased encoding scheme consisted of a precise number n of 6-bit *ternary* fields, where n was under genetic control. Of the three possible bit values, 0 represents 0, 1 represents 1, but 2 is a wild card character. Therefore each 6-bit ternary field maps to 2^k 6-bit binary numbers, where k is the number of 2s in the ternary field. When decoding a ternary field, a square is filled in on the grid (according to the special numbering shown in figure 1) for every binary number that matches. Two examples of decoded fields are given in figure 1. It is important to note that although the biased encoding scheme is capable of encoding any phenotype, genotypes that code for a high degree of symmetry and order will be much more common than those that don't.

The genotypes in the restricted encoding scheme consisted of a precise number n of 5-bit binary fields, where n was under genetic control. During decoding, each field is treated as if it had an extra bit of value 2 on the end, and decoded in the same way as for the biased encoding scheme. This means that for each field on the genotype a symmetrical pair of squares is filled in on the phenotype.

All phenotypes are vertically symmetrical.

The genotypes in the hybrid encoding scheme consisted of a precise number n of 5-bit ternary fields, where n was under genetic control. During decoding, each field is treated as if it had an extra bit of value 2 on the end and decoded in exactly the same way as if it were a six-bit ternary field of the biased encoding scheme. This means that many more squares may be filled in on the phenotype than there are fields on the genotype and that all phenotypes are vertically symmetrical.

4.1 Experimental results

In both experiments, the GA[3] was run 500 times for each encoding scheme. On every run the population was started from the same point on the first neutral network, namely the node that corresponds to a genotype of length 0 (which represents a blank grid under every encoding scheme). On each run, the number of fitness evaluations performed before the GA found the second neutral network was counted and assigned as the score for that run.

A table of the average scores per five hundred runs per encoding scheme per experiment is given in Table 1. Because the distributions underlying the numbers of evaluations taken approximate a Poisson distribution, the variances of the scores are of the same order of magnitude as the means, and conventional graphical representations are largely uninformative. To produce Figures 3 and 4, the scores from each set of five hundred runs were sorted in order of magnitude and plots were made of rank against value (i.e. the number of evaluations taken to find the neutral networks of fitness 2.0 on each run). This give a fairly good picture of the abilities of each encoding scheme to apply heuristics to neutral network search. The shallower the gradient, the better.

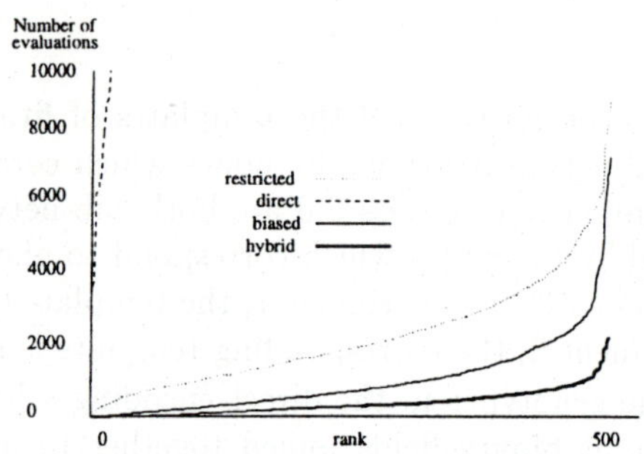

Fig. 3. Results of experiment 1 (see text).

The first thing to say about these results is that they prove quite conclusively that the choice of an appropriate encoding scheme which exploits domain knowledge in a heuristic way, does indeed significantly speed up neutral network search. Of the four encoding schemes tested in experiment 1 only the direct encoding scheme does *not* employ symmetry as a heuristic and this makes it two orders of magnitude worse than its nearest rival. The hybrid encoding scheme, which employs the heuristic in a dual way, seemed to work the best.

In experiment 2, an asymmetrical template defines the neutral network of fitness 2. Only the biased and the direct encoding schemes are capable of rep-

[3] Population 100. Steady state. Tournament selection. Genetic operators included a mutation operator and a 'change size' operator capable of adding or subtracting a random genotype field. These operators were applied at a rate of *one* (of the two operators) applications per offspring event in the of ratio 4:1, respectively. A modified form of single-point crossover was employed at all offspring events.

encoding scheme	*experiment 1*	*experiment 2*
direct	175220	133700
biased	1054.1	1650600
restricted	2312.4	
hybrid	404.5	

Table 1. The average number of evaluations for each encoding scheme, taken over a series of 500 runs, that the GA took to find the neutral network of fitness 2.

resenting a phenotype of this type, and the experiment was performed in order to test the biased scheme's ability to search for asymmetrical phenotypes when it is biased in favour of symmetrical ones. As can be seen, the biased encoding scheme performs an order of magnitude *worse* than the direct encoding scheme on this task. This is not surprising if one considers that increasing the relative frequency of nodes that code for symmetry on the graph of possible genotypes decreases the relative frequency of nodes that code for asymmetry.

4.2 A hybrid restricted scheme is advocated

No definite conclusions can be drawn from these results as to which type of encoding scheme is the most promising for a viable open-ended evolutionary design alternative. Filling in squares on a grid is not the same as evolving complex designs for real world problems. The results are, however, extremely suggestive. Even though the performance difference between the hybrid encoding scheme and the biased encoding scheme seem slight, it is nevertheless some sort of (biased) restricted encoding scheme rather than a pure biased encoding scheme that is advocated here.

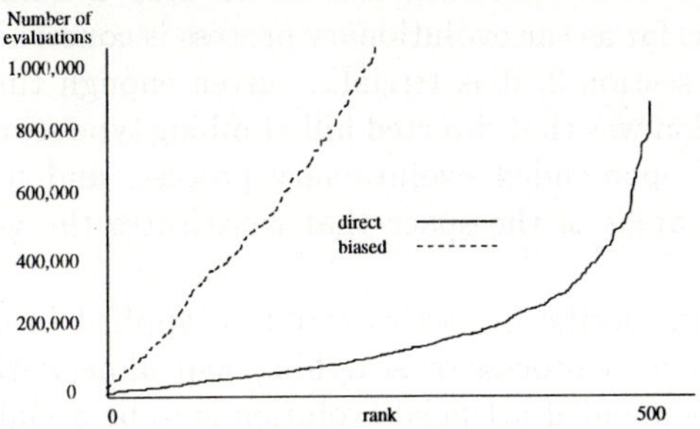

Fig. 4. Results of experiment 2 (see text).

To appreciate why, consider how each encoding scheme could apply heuristics to the task of evolving the design for something that displayed a great deal of repeated structure such as a millipede, for example. A hybrid restricted scheme could encode the design for a single leg once on a genotype and reuse this code 1000 times. Perhaps it would also code for a small number of position dependent operators, such that the front legs differed from the back legs according to some spatial transformation (see [10] for examples of this sort of thing occurring in nature). A true biased encoding scheme, on the other hand, would have to safeguard the possibility that any leg may evolve independently to any other, since every phenotype is potentially representable. Thus, although it could encode the design for a millipede in a similar way to the hybrid restricted scheme (by repeating the code for 1 leg 1000 times), it would also have to be able, at least in principle, to code for each of the 1000 legs individually. However it is done, this will involve a longer or higher cardinality genotype resulting in a larger search space with a lower relative frequency of nodes that code for the sort of repeated structure we are after.

Many researchers will feel uneasy about the idea of adopting encoding schemes for open-ended artificial evolution that are unable to encode all possible phenotypes. They may feel that, even if this does lead to performance increases, it amounts to pre-judging the problem and prevents the evolution of unexpected solutions - precisely the reason evolution is being used in the first place. There is one further thing to be said, however, that may quell these fears. An encoding scheme that is heuristically biased for the evolution of certain traits, is biased *against* the evolution of other traits. This is clear from experiment 2. Therefore in order for a biased scheme to even come close to competing with a hybrid restricted scheme at evolving complex phenotypes (such as in the millipede example above), the level of bias would be such that the evolution of a particular phenotype which the scheme is biased *against* would take a totally impractical length of time. In fact, as can be seen from experiment 2, it would actually take many, many orders of magnitude longer to evolve than if a simple direct encoding scheme was used. Thus, by removing the possibility of representing such phenotypes, we are actually losing very little.

5 Conclusions

The open-ended artificial evolution of designs that are better than a human designer could produce *is*, at least as far as the evolutionary process is concerned, possible. In fact, as was shown in section 2, it is trivial..... given enough time. What also became clear in this section was that directed hill-climbing type search plays a minor role in this sort of open-ended evolutionary process, and it is the non-directed search of neutral areas of the space that constitutes the vast majority of the evolutionary effort.

Section 3 explained how domain-specific heuristics could be applied to decrease the time spent by the evolutionary process on searching neutral networks. This is a pressing requirement if open-ended artificial evolution is to be a viable alternative to human design. The four different categories of encoding scheme were introduced, and broad explanations were given as to how each category incorporates domain knowledge to speed up the process.

Finally, in section 4, specially devised instances of the different categories of encoding scheme were tested against each other. Although the three types of encoding scheme that employed heuristics out-performed a simple direct encoding scheme (by several orders of magnitude) on a task where the heuristics were well-founded, it was shown that the direct encoding scheme was in fact the best performer on a task where the heuristics were *not* well-founded.

Since the time taken by a direct encoding scheme to evolve anything really complicated is assumed to be totally impractical, it seems that the only scenario in which open-ended artificial evolution can ever be a viable alternative to human design is if domain-specific heuristics are employed *and* these heuristics are well-founded. There is no point in making allowances for the scenario in which the heuristics are not well-founded, since if this is the case then evolution will take even longer than a direct encoding scheme to evolve anything complex or useful. The type of encoding scheme that is advocated for open-ended artificial evolution, therefore, is one that heuristically restricts the evolutionary search space.

Acknowledgements

I would like to thank Phil Husbands, Inman Harvey and others at the School of Cognitive and Computer Sciences for various crucial discussions. Thanks also to the school of COGS itself for the bursary that allows me to undertake this work.

References

1. M. Eigen, J. McCaskill, and P. Schuster. Molecular quasi-species. *Journal of Physical Chemistry*, 92:6881–6891, 1988.
2. P.J. Gage and I.M. Kroo. A role for genetic algorithms in a preliminary design environment. *A.I.A.A.*, 1993.
3. P.J. Gage, I.M. Kroo, and I.P. Sobieski. A variable-complexity genetic algorithm for topological design. *A.I.A.A.*, 33(11), 1995.
4. I. Harvey. Species adaptation genetic algorithms: the basis for a continuing saga. In F. J. Varela and P. Bourgine, editors, *Toward a Practice of Autonomous Systems: Proceedings of the First European Conference on Artificial Life*, pages 346–354, Cambridge, Massachusetts, 1992. M.I.T. Press / Bradford Books.
5. I. Harvey, P. Husbands, and D. Cliff. Seeing the light: Artificial evolution, real vision. In *Proceedings of the Third International Conference on Simulation of Adaptive Behavior*, 1994.
6. J. Koza. *Genetic Programming: on the programming of computers by means of natural selection*. MIT Press, Cambridge, Massachusetts, 1992.
7. Phil Husbands Malcolm McIlhagga and Robert Ives. A comparison of search techniques on a wing-box optimisation problem. In *Proceedings of Parallel Problem Solving in Nature*, Berlin, Germany, 1996. Springer-Verlag.
8. N.Jakobi. Facing the facts: Necessary requirements for the artificial evolution of *complex* behaviour. Cognitive Science Research Paper CSRP422, University of Sussex, 1996.
9. P. Schuster. Artificial life and molecular evolutionary biology. In *Proceedings of the European Conference on Artificial Life*, pages 3–19. Springer-Verlag, 1995.
10. D.W. Thompson. *On Growth and Form*. Cambride University Press, 1942.

Hardware Evolution at Function Level

Masahiro Murakawa[1] Shuji Yoshizawa[1] Isamu Kajitani[2]
Tatsumi Furuya[3] Masaya Iwata[4] Tetsuya Higuchi[4]

[1] 7-3-1,Hongo,Bunkyo,Tokyo,Japan,University of Tokyo
e-mail : murakawa@bios.t.u-tokyo.ac.jp
[2] 1-1-1,Tennoudai,Tsukuba,Ibaraki,Japan,University of Tsukuba
[3] 2-2-1,Miyama,Funabashi,Chiba,Japan,Toho University
[4] 1-1-4,Umezono,Tsukuba,Ibaraki,Japan,Electrotechnical Laboratory

Abstract. This paper describes a function-level Evolvable Hardware (EHW). EHW is hardware which is built on programmable logic devices (e.g. PLD and FPGA) and whose architecture can be reconfigured by using a genetic learning to adapt to new unknown environments in real time. It is demonstrated that the function-level hardware evolution can attain much higher performances than the gate-level evolution , in neural network applications (e.g. two-spiral). VLSI architecture of the function-based FPGA dedicated to function level evolution is also described.

1 Introduction

Recently, the idea of evolving hardware itself has attracted a rapidly increasing interest of the researchers. Evolvable Hardware (EHW) is a hardware which is built on software-reconfigurable logic devices (e.g. PLD (Programmable Logic Device) and FPGA (Field Programmable Gate Array)) and whose architecture can be reconfigured by using a genetic learning to adapt to new unknown environments. If hardware errors occur, or if new hardware functions are required, EHW can alter its own hardware structure rapidly and accommodates such changes in real-time.

In order to design the conventional hardware , it is necessary to prepare all specifications of hardware functions in advance. In contrast to this , EHW can reconfigure itself without such specifications. In other words, EHW is most suitable for applications where no hardware specification can be given in advance. Applications solved by artificial neural network (ANN) are such examples because pattern classifier functions can not be obtained until learning is complete.

Research on EHW was initiated independently in Japan and in Switzerland around 1992 (for recent overviews, see [Higuchi94] and [Marchal94]). Since then, the interest is growing rapidly (e.g., EVOLVE95, the first international workshop on evolvable hardware was held in Lausanne in 1995).

Most of researches on EHW, however, have a common problem that the evolved circuit size is small. The hardware evolutions are based on primitive gates such as AND-gate and OR-gate; we call the evolution at this level *gate-level* evolution. The gate-level evolutions are not powerful for the use in industrial applications.

In order to solve this problem, we propose a new type of hardware evolution, *function-level* evolution, and a new FPGA architecture dedicated to the function-level evolution. We demonstrate that ANN applications such as two-spiral are solved by the function-level EHW. Actually EHW can synthesize a non-linear function genetically. This suggests that EHW may substitute ANN in industrial applications because EHW enables faster and more compact implementation than ANN.

In section 2, the basic idea of EHW is described. Section 3 introduces the functional-level evolution. Its advantage is demonstrated in section 4 by ANN applications. Section 5 proposes the FPGA architecture for the function-level evolution. Section 6 describes future EHW applications and concludes this paper.

2 Evolvable Hardware (EHW)

Function-level evolution, the theme of this paper, is a natural extension of the *gate-level* evolution. So, here we describe a basic idea of the gate-level EHW.

EHW changes its hardware structure to adapt itself to the environment in which it is embeded. To attain this goal, EHW utilizes PLDs and Genetic Algorithms (GAs) [Goldberg89]. PLDs are hardware devices whose architecture can be determined by downloading binary strings, called *architecture bits*. Architecture bits are the compilation result of higher level hardware description such as boolean functions and truth tables. On the other hand, GAs are robust search algorithms which use multiple chromosomes (usually represented as binary strings) and apply the natural selection-like operation to them to find out better solutions.

The basic idea of EHW is to regard the architecture bits of PLDs as chromosomes of GAs and to find out better hardware structure by GAs, as shown in Figure 1. Every chromosome is downloaded for evaluation while learning.

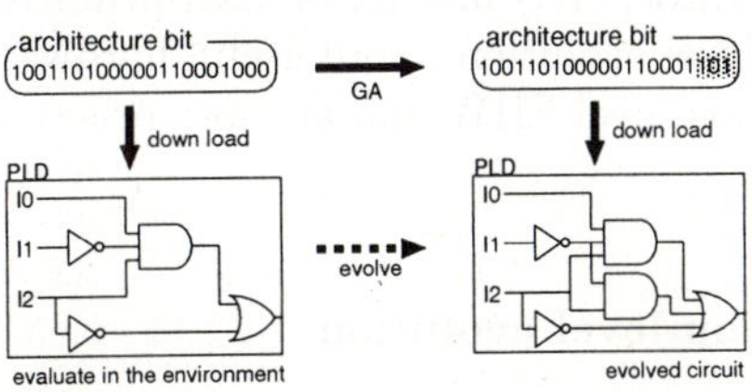

Fig. 1. Evolvable Hardware(EHW)

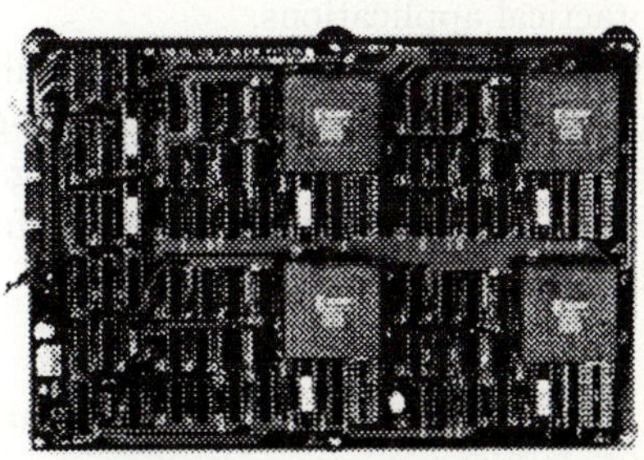

Fig. 2. The EHW-board

3 Function-level Evolution

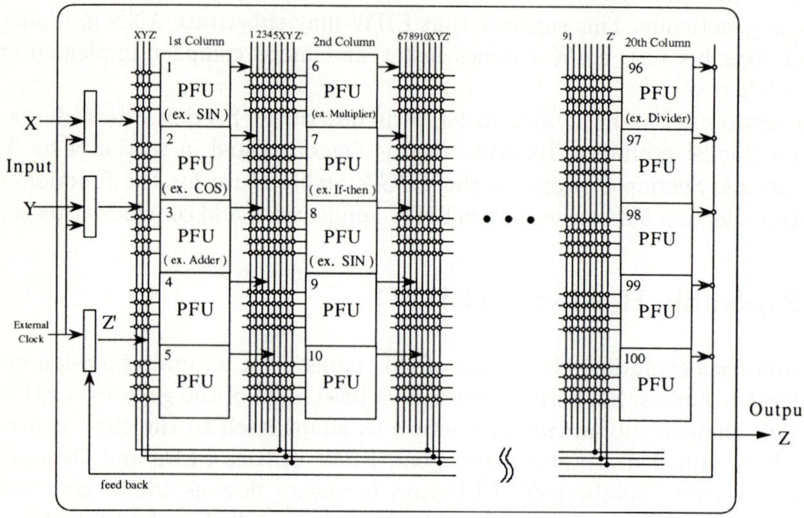

PFU : Programmable Floating processing Unit

Fig. 3. The FPGA model for function level evolutions

At Present , EHW researches are all based on the gate-level evolution. Figure 2 is such an example of the EHW board implemented with four Xilinx FPGAs [Iwata95] which is designed as a pattern recognition system. The size of a circuit available to the gate-level evolution is not so large because of the limitation of GA execution time. So the gate-level EHW can not gain strong enough functions for practical applications.

However, if hardware is genetically synthesized from high-level hardware functions (e.g. adder, subtracter, sine generator, etc.) instead of such primitive gates (e.g. AND,OR gates) as in the gate-level evolution, more useful hardware functions can be obtained. Thus, the function-level EHW aim at more practical applications than the gate-level EHW.

3.1 The FPGA model for the function-level evolution

We use the FPGA model in Figure 3 to realize the function-level evolution. The FPGA model consists of 20 columns, each containing five Programmable Floating processing Units (PFUs). Each PFU can implement one of the following seven functions: an adder, a subtracter, an if-then, a sine generator, a cosine generator, a multiplier, and a divider. The selection of the function to be implemented by a PFU is determined by chromosome genes given to the PFU.

Constant generators are also included in each PFU. Columns are interconnected by crossbar switches. The crossbars determine inputs to PFUs.

In addition to these columns, a state register holding a past output is prepared for applications which deal with time-continuous data. This FPGA model assumes two inputs and one output. Data handled in the FPGA are floating point numbers.

3.2 Genetic Learning

Genetic learning in the function level evolution determines PFU functions and the interconnection among PFUs. In short, hardware function which is more suitable for the environment is found out by the Genetic learning. Genetic operators used in the function-level evolution are the reproduction and the mutation; the crossover is not used.

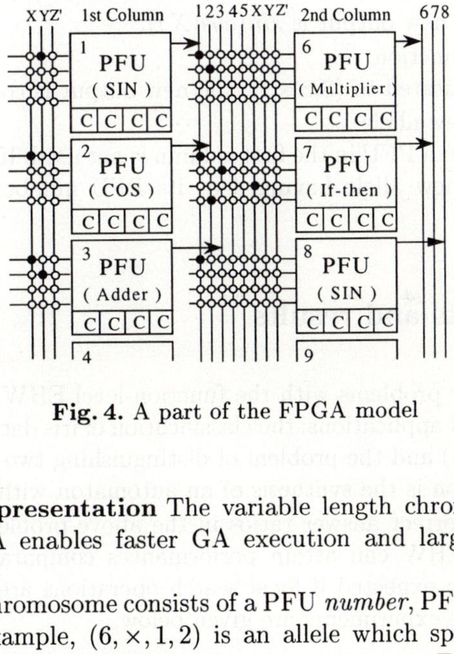

Fig. 4. A part of the FPGA model

Chromosome representation The variable length chromosome GA (VGA) is used here. VGA enables faster GA execution and larger circuit evolution [Kajitani95].

An allele in a chromosome consists of a PFU *number*, PFU *function* and *input operand(s)*. For example, $(6, \times, 1, 2)$ is an allele which specifies the hardware function executed at the 6th PFU in the second column in Figure 4. The function is a multiplication using operands coming from the first PFU (i.e. sine) and the second PFU (i.e. cosine) in the first column, respectively. The output of the 6th PFU will be $sin(Y) \times cos(X)$.

A chromosome looks like;

$$(1, sin, Y), (2, cos, X), \cdots, (6, \times, 1, 2), \cdots, (96, \div, 90, 91)$$

representing a hardware function implemented by a whole FPGA in Figure 3.

Multiple chromosomes are prepared as a population for GA. By repeating GA operations to the population, the most desirable hardware function is gradually synthesized.

Reproduction The roulette wheel reproduction rule is used. The chromosome with the best fitness value is always reproduced by the elitist strategy.

When EHW is used for ANN applications, the fitness value of each chromosome is determined by n/N , where N is the number of training patterns and n is the number of correct answers of the EHW.

Mutation After the reproduction, every chromosome undergoes one mutation. There are three kinds of mutations.

1. Mutation of an operand
   In Figure 4, the output of the 8th PFU is $sin(sin(Y))$. If (8,sin,1) is mutated to (8,sin,2), the new output is $sin(cos(X))$.
2. Mutation of a function
   If (8,sin,1) is mutated to (8,cos,1), the new output is $cos(sin(Y))$.
3. Insertion of a new allele
   Suppose the fourth PFU in the first column is not used. If (8,sin,1) is mutated to (8,sin,4), a new allele having 4 as its PFU number is inserted in the chromosome.

4 Experiments and results

We have tested four problems with the function-level EHW. Three of them are the well known ANN applications: the classification of iris data, transformation of 2D images (rotation) and the problem of distinguishing two intertwined spirals. The other application is the synthesis of an automaton with 4-state.

Table 1 shows correct answer ratios in the above problems. It is clear that the function-level EHW can attain performances comparable to ANN. More improvement can be expected if local search operations are introduced. Detail descriptions of these experiments are given below.

4.1 Two-Spiral Problem

The two-spiral problem is to learn a mapping function (two inputs and one output) which distinguishes points on two intertwined spirals. This is one of the typical difficult problem due to its extreme nonlinearity.

In the experiments, the X-Y coordinates of 97 points from each spiral are given as a training data set. The fitness is the correct output ratio. The population size is 900. A run terminates at 1000 generations.

Table 1. Simulation results

	Correct Answer Ratio			
	Average(30 runs)	Std. Dev.	Max.	Min.
Iris(training)	100.0%	0.0	100.0%	100.0%
Iris(test)	93.1%	5.4	97.3%	90.7%
Two Spirals	92.1%	4.8	100.0%	84.0%
Automata	100.0%	0.0	100.0%	100.0%
	Mean Square Error			
	Average(30 runs)	Std. Dev.	Max.	Min.
Rotation(test)	0.00269	0.00268	0.0135	0.0005

Fig. 4. Classification for the two-spiral problem obtained by the best-of-generation individual

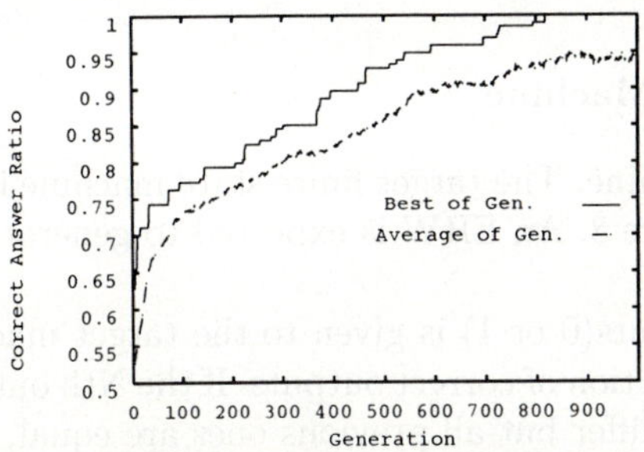

Fig. 5. Fitness curves for the two-spiral problem

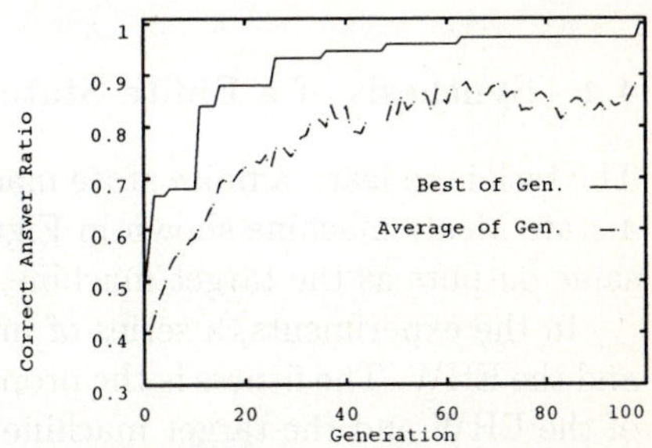

Fig. 6. Fitness curves for the Classification of Iris Data

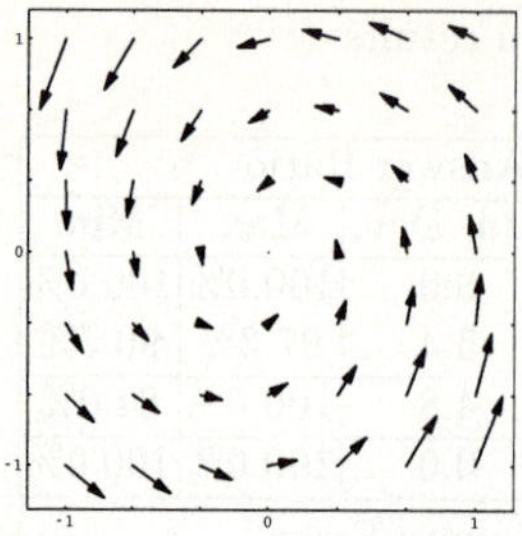

Fig. 7. The vector field of transformation of 2D images

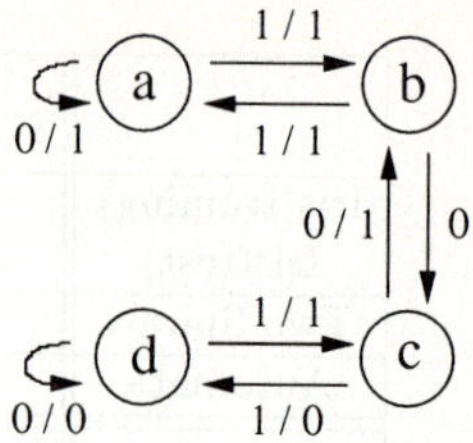

Fig. 8. The target 4-state automaton

Figure 4 shows the best-of-generation individual in the final population at a run. This individual properly classifies not only all 194 training points but also some never learned points. Figure 5 shows one of the successful evolutions.

4.2 Classification of Isis Data

The task is to learn a classification function (four inputs and three outputs) which distinguishes whether a given flower is iris or not.

In the experiments, we train the EHW using 75 training data. The fitness is the correct output ratio. The population size is 50. Figure 6 shows the fitness curves of a run. New 75 data are tested after the EHW is trained to classify all the training data correctly.

4.3 Rotation of 2D images

The problem is to learn a function(two inputs and two outputs) which rotates the 2D images. In the experiments , 10 training data sets are given. The fitness is the inverse of the mean square error and the population size is 100. Figure 7 shows the vector field of the transformation which is obtained at a run. It is observed that the points without training data are also rotated as we expected.

4.4 Synthesis of a Finite State Machine

The task is to learn a finite state machine. The target finite state machine is the 4-state Mealy machine shown in Figure 8. An EHW is expected to generate the same outputs as the target machine.

In the experiments, a series of inputs(0 or 1) is given to the target machine and the EHW. The fitness is the proportion of correct outputs. If the Nth outputs of the EHW and the target machine differ but all previous ones are equal, then the fitness is N/M (M is the total number of inputs).The population size is set at 1000.

Thirty all runs were successful. The structure of the obtained EHW shows clearly that the state registers and if-then functions work effectively.

5 Hardware Implementation

The purpose of the hardware implementation is to demonstrate that the function-level EHW can realize most of the adaptation problems in *real-time* with present state of technology. We are developing a prototype system and an ASIC VLSI chip. The chip ,F^2PGA (Function-based FPGA) ,is designed for the hardware evolution at function level.

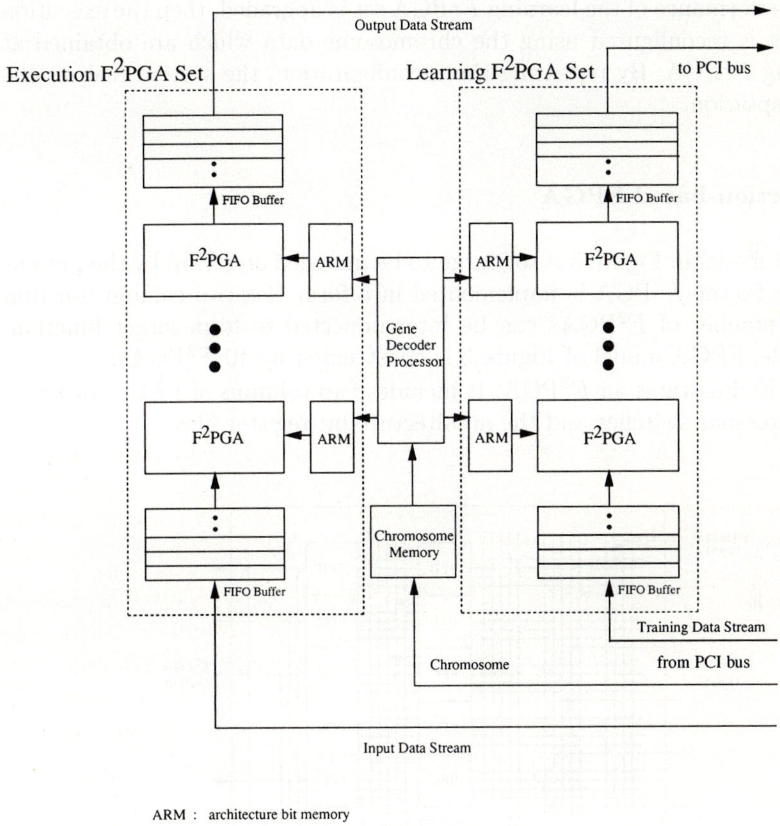

Fig. 9. The prototype board

5.1 The prototype system

The prototype board is designed to be connected with PCI bus of a personal computer. The system is used in applications to adaptive digital signal processing, which require quick response.

As shown in Figure 9, the prototype board includes chromosome memories, a gene decoding processor, FIFO I/O buffers, architecture bit memories and two columns of F^2PGA. The GA calculation is performed outside the board, by a personal computer.

One of the two F^2PGA columns is the *execution* F^2PGA set which actually processes the incoming data. The other column is the *learning* F^2PGA set which is always used to find a better hardware structure by GA while the execution F^2PGA is processing the confronting work. The training data are updated with a regular interval to reflect the change of the environment.

If the performance of the learning F^2PGA set is upgraded, then the execution F^2PGA set is reconfigured using the chromosome data which are obtained at the learning F^2PGA. By repeating the reconfiguration, the system realizes the *on-line* adaptation.

5.2 Function-based FPGA

The FPGA model in Figure 3 is too large to be included on a chip by the present technology. So,the F^2PGA is implemented in a form of a two-column function slice. Any number of F^2PGAs can be interconnected to form larger function. For example, FPGA model of Figure 3 is constructed by 10 F^2PGAs.

Figure 10 illustrates an F^2PGA. It includes two columns of PFUs (10 PFUs in total), crossbar switches and the architecture-bit register files.

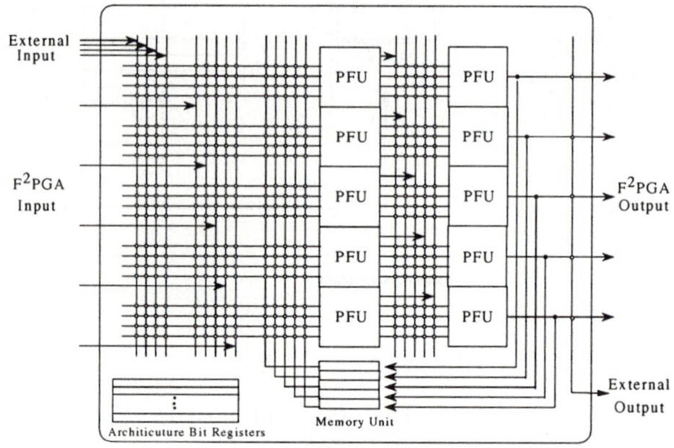

Fig. 10. Function-based FPGA

The PFU includes a floating ALU (about 3000 gates; 16-bit floating numbers), a floating multiplier (about 2000 gates) to attain comparable performances to a DSP (Digital Signal Processing) chip. Trigonometrical functions are implemented with ROM tables and the multiplier. PFU has a nano-sequencer and a nano-memory to control these functions.

6 Conclusion

Two proposals are described in this paper. The first is the hardware evolution at function level. The function-level EHW can attain comparable performances as ANN even in ANN applications.

The second is the function-based FPGA architecture designed for the hardware evolution at function level. This is a quite new type of FPGA which directly implements a dedicated hardware function to an application problem. The important point of this implementation is that it is hard-wired and leads to a high performance as in DSP chips. But, different from DSP chips, there is no need of programming; genetic algorithms can automatically synthesize the best hardware function dedicated to the application.

This indicates that EHWs can be used in many kinds of applications where hardware specifications to implement are not known. EHWs may take the place of ANN in industrial applications because they can response in real-time and easily deal with time-continuous data. We are developing a prototype system board to demonstrate that the on-line evolution of a hardware is really realizable.

We are now investigating on crossover and local search strategies to attain faster convergence. The F^2PGA is designed in Verilog HDL environment. The F^2PGA chip is scheduled to appear in the third quarter of 1996.

References

[Fisher36] Fisher R., "The use of Multiple Measurements in Taxonomic Problems" , Ann. Eugenics.,vol.7, 1936.

[Goldberg89] Goldberg D., "Genetic Algorithms in Search, Optimization, and Machine Learning" ,Addison Wesley, 1989.

[Higuchi94] Higuchi T. et al., "Evolvable Hardware with Genetic Learning" ,Massively Parallel Artificial Intelligence (eds. H. Kitano), MIT Press, 1994.

[Iwata95] Iwata M. et al., "Consideration on pattern recognition system based on evolvable hardware" , ETL technical report, 1995.

[Kajitani95] Kajitani I. et al., "Variable Length Chromosome GA for Evolvable Hardware", ETL technical report, Oct. 1995.

[Marchal94] Marchal P. et al., "Embryological Development on Silicon" ,Artificial Life IV, 1994.

Coevolutionary Life-Time Learning

Jan Paredis

Research Institute for Knowledge Systems
University of Limburg
Postbus 463, NL-6200 AL Maastricht, The Netherlands
e-mail: jan@riks.nl

Abstract. This work studies the interaction of evolution and learning. It starts from the coevolutionary genetic algorithm (CGA) introduced earlier. Two techniques - life-time fitness evaluation (LTFE) and predator-prey coevolution - boost the genetic search of a CGA. The partial but continuous nature of LTFE allows for an elegant incorporation of life-time learning (LTL) within CGAs. This way, not only the genetic search but also the LTL component focuses on "not yet solved" problems. The performance of the new algorithm is compared with various other algorithms.

1 Introduction

The combination of evolutionary learning and life-time learning (LTL) in genetic algorithms (GAs) is an active field of research nowadays. The rise of interest in the combination of both types of learning has several reasons.

First of all, it is clear that nature combines both types of learning. Hence, it is of interest to gather a better understanding of the interaction between, and the advantages of, both types of learning. A crucial question is: which type of learning is needed when? An answer to this question might provide important insight in the optimal computational use of the different types of learning.

Secondly, most of the research has concentrated on the combination of genetic search with a local search method, such as gradient descent. A local search method iteratively improves its estimate of the optimum by searching for better solutions in the neighbourhood of the current solution. In this context, the local search methods implement LTL. Both types of algorithms nicely complement each other. Local search methods are typically fast but are prone to get stuck in local minima. GAs, on the other hand, are better in avoiding local minima. One drawback of GAs is that they are slow in fine-tuning solutions. A local search method like back-propagation (BP) - which is used here - is much faster at fine-tuning [7]. Hence, one wants to combine the advantages of both: genetic and local search. A good overview of past research on this combination can, for example, be found in [5].

The biological study of the interaction between life-time learning and evolutionary learning has a long history. Molecular biology has firmly rejected the Lamarckian idea that individual adaptation (life-time learning) can alter information in an individual's gametes. Or, in other words, the characteristics acquired during a life-time cannot be communicated genetically to offspring.

The biological rejection of Lamarckian evolution does not necessarily have a consequence on evolutionary computation. If the use of Lamarckian principles increases the performance of an evolutionary algorithm then there is no reason to reject it. At the moment there is, however, no consensus on this topic. Some work, e.g. [1], found that Lamarckian learning outperformed non-Lamarckian local search. Whitley et al [16], on the other hand, report that non-Lamarckian learning can sometimes be more effective than Lamarckian learning. They hypothesize that problem complexity might play an important role. In the work presented here, Lamarckian learning is used. It is however straightforward to change this aspect of the algorithm. This is actually an important point for future research.

The work presented here starts from earlier research on Coevolutionary Genetic Algorithms (CGAs). A CGA combines life-time fitness evaluation (LTFE; see later) and coevolution. In contrast with traditional "single population" GAs, a CGA operates on two or more coevolving populations. Just as in the case of predator-prey interactions in nature, there is a *inverse fitness interaction* between both populations: one side's success is the other side's failure. This typically results in an arms race in which the complexity of both populations increases in a stepwise manner. Predator-prey coevolution is the main motor behind the first two - completely unrelated - CGA applications: the search for good classification neural networks [9] and the search for solutions of constraint satisfaction problems [10]. Both applications have demonstrated the power of the CGA.

As far as the author is aware of, Hillis [6] was the first to propose the computational use of predator-prey coevolution. The combination of LTFE and coevolution is an important difference with Hillis' work, it makes a CGA more robust and fine-grained ([9], [10]). In addition to this, the coevolution in a CGA is not restricted to predator-prey systems. Obviously, many other mechanisms exist in nature. Symbiosis is such an important and widely occurring counterexample. A symbiotic variant of the CGA algorithm has been used to search for good genetic representations for a given problem ([11], [12]).

The next section of this paper introduces the classification problem on which the approach is tested. Section three and four briefly describe a traditional single population GA and a CGA, respectively. Section 5 provides an empirical comparison between both algorithms. Next, section 6 incorporates LTL in these algorithms. The paper closes with conclusions and a discussion of the proposed framework.

2 The Test Problem

Figure 1 depicts the classification task used in our experiments. A neural net (NN) has to learn a correct mapping from $[-1,1] \times [-1,1]$ to the set of classes {A, B, C, D} given 200 pre-classified, randomly selected, examples. The triple (-0.6, 0.9, D) is such an example. It indicates that the point with coordinates (-0.6, 0.9) belongs to the class D (cf. figure 1).

Here, a standard layered feed-forward network with one hidden layer is used. The two inputs to this network are the coordinates of the point to be classified. Each output node is associated with one class.

A correct NN should classify, for example, the point (0.2,0.1) as belonging to class A. This classification proceeds as follows: 1) the coordinates 0.2 and 0.1 are clamped on the associated input nodes of the NN, 2) feed-forward propagation is executed - here the standard sigmoidal activation function is used, 3) the result of the classification is the class corresponding to the output node with the highest activity level. Hence, the NN is said to classify the example above correctly when the output node associated with class A is the most active one. The goal of the genetic algorithm is to determine the weights of the NN such that it correctly classifies the examples. But first, we turn to a traditional GA for this task.

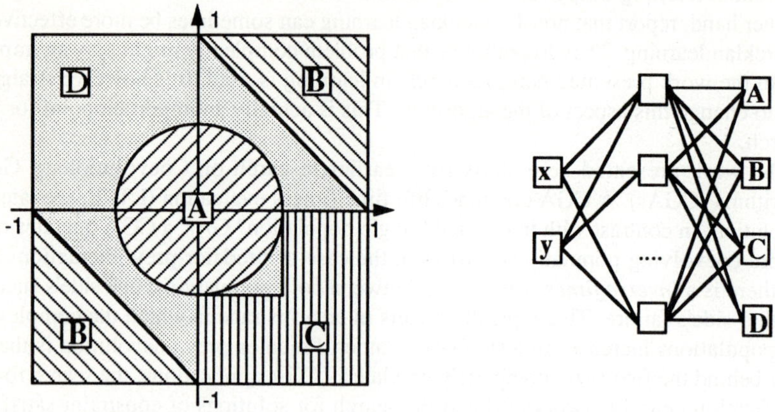

Fig. 1. Left: classification problem; Right: neural net classifier

3 The Traditional GA

The traditional evolutionary approach generates an initial population of NNs with randomly assigned weights. We use a simple genetic representation of a NN: a linear string of its weights, with weights belonging to links feeding into the same node located next to each other. In accordance with [8] and [15] the weights are encoded directly as real numbers. Their value is in the interval [-100,100]. The FITNESS of a NN is equal to the number of the 200 examples it classifies correctly. After the creation of the initial population, the reproduction gives higher chances to good NNs to reproduce. The particular algorithm used here is based on GENITOR ([14], [15]). At each cycle it executes the following steps: 1) two parents are SELECTed. This selection is biased towards the fitter individuals, 2) a child is generated (here, two-point crossover and adaptive mutation [14] is used), 3) its FITNESS is calculated, 4) if this fitness is higher than the minimum fitness in the population then the child is INSERTed into the appropriate rank location in the NN population. At the same time, the individual with the least fitness is removed. In this way, the population remains sorted on fitness. The code below describes the basic cycle of this algorithm, called TRAD:

```
nn1:= SELECT(nn-pop)    ; parent1
nn2:= SELECT(nn-pop)    ; parent2
child:= MUTATE-CROSSOVER(nn1,nn2)
f:= FITNESS(child)
INSERT(child,f,nn-pop)
```

As we will see below, this algorithm performs extremely poor on our classification task. The computational effort needed to obtain good solutions is unexpectedly large. This is because most time is spent on fitness evaluation: each child is tested on all 200 examples.

Most of these tests are uninformative: in the beginning of a run the majority of examples is wrongly classified, at later stages most of them are correctly classified. Hence, the individual tests have a relatively low discriminative power: only a few of the 200 examples are relevant.

4 The CGA

The alternative approach, inspired by biological arms races, operates on two populations which interact through their fitness. The first population contains NNs. The second population, however, consists of the 200 pre-classified examples with an - initially identical - (low) fitness. In the strictest sense, the examples do not form a real population because they are never replaced. The population consists all the time of the same 200 pre-classified examples, only their ranking changes during a run. In general, this need not be the case. It depends on the characteristics of the problem. In some of the other CGA applications ([11], [12]) all populations truly evolve.

In order to reduce the time spent on fitness evaluation, both types of *objects* - NNs and examples - get a continuous, but partial, feedback about their fitness. Examples and NNs continuously meet each other in pairs. Each such *encounter* results in updating the fitness of the involved example and NN. The *fitness of an object* is defined as the average of the results of the last twenty encounters it was involved in. If the NN classification is wrong (right) then the result of this encounter for the NN is zero (one). Analogous to biological arms races, the success of one entails failure for the other one. Hence, an example which is (in)correctly classified during an encounter results in a fitness feedback of zero (one). We use the term *life-time fitness evaluation* (LTFE) for the continuous fitness feedback discussed above.

The fitness of examples now allows for a biased selection of examples as well. Similar to fit NNs, fit examples are more often involved in an encounter. Or, in other words, the more difficult an example is, the more often it will be presented to the NNs. Now, CGA's basic cycle can be described (see also the code given below). The do-loop in this code below ensures that the fitnesses keep up with the changing populations - or the ranking within them. The algorithm first executes 20 encounters between examples and NNs. The function TOGGLE in this basic cycle implements the inverse fitness interaction between examples and NNs. It changes a 1 into a 0 and vice versa. The call to the procedure UPDATE-FITNESS updates the fitness (moving average) of the NN or example after each encounter. Finally, new offspring is created and INSERTed in the neural net population. The FITNESS of the new NN-offspring is the average result of twenty encounters of the NN with SELECTed examples. This same procedure is also used to calculate the fitness of the members of the initial NN population.

```
DO 20 TIMES
    nn:= SELECT(nn-pop)
    ex:= SELECT(ex-pop)
    res:= ENCOUNTER(nn,ex)
    UPDATE-FITNESS(nn,res)
    UPDATE-FITNESS(ex,TOGGLE(res))
nn1:= SELECT(nn-pop)     ; parent1
nn2:= SELECT(nn-pop)     ; parent2
child:= MUTATE-CROSSOVER(nn1,nn2)
f:= FITNESS(child)
INSERT(child,f,nn-pop)
```

In the code above, two parameters are introduced: the number of encounters before each reproduction and the number of most recent encounters used to calculate the fitness of the NNs and examples. In the code above, in all experiments in the rest of this paper, and in all other CGA applications, both parameters are - rather arbitrarily - set to 20.

Because of the fitness interaction between examples and NNs both populations are kept in constant flux. As soon as the NNs are becoming successful on a certain set of examples then these examples get a lower fitness and other, not yet solved examples will be selected more often. This process forces the NN to concentrate now on these examples too (because of fitness proportional SELECTion of the pairs of individuals involved in an encounter). In this way, fitness testing becomes much more efficient: one mainly focuses on not yet solved examples. During a run, examples situated near the boundaries between different classes rapidly get a high fitness and move up in the population.

Both algorithms - TRAD and CGA - spend, by and large, most of their time on NN propagation. Each propagation involves the calculation of the activation value of the output nodes for a given example. Hence, one NN propagation is executed every time a NN is tested on an example. The number of propagations needed to reach a given accuracy level allow to compare the computation demand of the algorithms. It is good to emphasize the difference in computation demand of CGA and TRAD. The basic cycle of TRAD involves 200 propagations (to calculate the fitness of the new-born NN). The basic cycle of a CGA, on the other hand, involves only 40 propagations (one for each of the 20 encounters and 20 to calculate the fitness of the new-born NN). This data will be used in the empirical comparison of both algorithms presented in the next section.

5 TRAD versus CGA: Empirical Comparison

For each algorithm used in the experiments below, 10 runs were executed. The best-so-far was averaged over these 10 runs. TRAD used a population size of 100 NNs and generated a total of 50000 offspring. CGA used the same population size of NNs, its example population contains the 200 pre-classified examples. The CGA was allowed to run for 100000 basic cycles, which is only double the number allocated to TRAD. Given the difference in computation demand between both algorithms (as discussed at the end of the previous section), this means that CGA is allowed to run about half as long as TRAD.

The empirical results given in table 1 confirm the superior performance of the CGA in comparison with TRAD. It shows the number of propagations (in thousands) executed before a NN with a given level of classification accuracy (i.e.: 70%, 80%, 85%, 90%, and 95% of the 200 examples are correctly classified. Or, in other words, the calculation of the accuracy is based on all 200 examples) is obtained. The last column gives the average accuracy (and its standard deviation) of the best NN found during each of the 10 runs. This way, not only the progress during a run but also the final solution quality is given. The table shows, for example, that - on average - TRAD reaches a solution which correctly classifies 85% of the examples after executing 1320000 propagations. In order to reach the 90% accuracy level, for example, CGA needs less than a third of the propagations needed by TRAD. Note also that TRAD does not reach an average best-so-far of 95% of correct classifications within the allowed 50000 offspring.

Table 1 clearly shows the superiority of CGA over TRAD. This in terms of solution quality as well as computation demand. The CGA not only reaches a better final solution in less time. Also intermediate levels of solution quality are reached substantially quicker. As a matter of fact, CGA needs (far) less time to reach an accuracy of 95% than TRAD needs to reach an accuracy of 90%! In addition to this, the standard deviation of the solution quality of the CGA (0.99) is considerably smaller than that of TRAD (3.4). Paredis [9] provides much more empirical evidence, including the performance increase resulting from LTFE and coevolution separately. The performance data given in table 1 will be used to compare the performance of TRAD and CGA with their counterparts which learn during their life-time. But first, the incorporation of LTL in these algorithms is explained.

	>70	>80	>85	>90	>95	final accuracy
TRAD	520	920	1320	2420	-	93 (3.4)
CGA	162	342	502	762	1902	96.45 (0.99)

Table 1: Number of propagations (in thousands) needed to reach a given accuracy level. The rightmost column gives the average accuracy (and the standard deviation) of the best-so-far (TRAD: 50K cycles; CGA: 100K cycles)

6 Introducing Learning

The variants of TRAD and CGA which include BP learning [3] are called: TRAD-LAM and CGA-LAM, respectively. The postfix 'LAM' reminds us that Lamarckian learning is used here, i.e. BP acts directly on the genes (weights). Each time a NN is confronted with an example which it classifies incorrectly, BP is applied on that example-NN pair. Hence, the number of back-propagations per cycle is - at most - equal to the number of propagations per cycle. As a consequence, TRAD-LAM involves, at most, 200 back-propagations per cycle (as was discussed at the end of section 4 this occurs during the fitness calculation of the new offspring). In CGA-LAM, a cycle consists of 20 encounters (each involving at most one back-propagation) and the fitness calculation of the new offspring (at most 20 back-propagations).

The following BP parameter settings are used: learning rate = 0.35, momentum term = 0.9. Two points remain to be discussed here. In CGA and TRAD the weights of the initial NN population were randomly drawn from the interval [-100,100]. BP works best when starting from relatively small weights. Hence, the weights of the NNs belonging to the initial population in TRAD-LAM and CGA-LAM are drawn from the interval [-1,1]. Secondly, a standard momentum term is used to stabilize weight updates. This way a change to a weight depends partially on the previous changes of this weight. Now, the genetic code of a NN also includes, for each weight, the previous weight change. Hence, in comparison with TRAD and CGA, the genetic code is doubled in size. The "previous weight changes" of offspring have an initial value equal to the average of the weight changes of their parents.

In the experiments, TRAD-LAM was, again, allowed to generate 50000 offspring. CGA-LAM was allowed 75000 offspring (instead of 100000 before). Hence, in comparison with TRAD-LAM, CGA-LAM was allowed even less CPU-time than before. Table 2 allows to compare the performance of TRAD-LAM and CGA-LAM. It gives the number of propagations needed to reach the accuracy levels. Now, the number of propagations includes forward as well as (error) backward propagations. The computational cost of the error back-propagation process is assumed about equal to that of a forward propagation

[7]. In comparison with table 1 the algorithms clearly need less propagations to reach the respective accuracy levels than their counterparts without LTL. Table 2 also shows that the final performance of CGA-LAM has improved substantially . It is almost 98%! This is a clear improvement over TRAD-LAM (91.3%). Here, the fact that a CGA(-LAM) SELECTs more often difficult examples - i.e. examples not yet solved by the NNs - plays an important role . It ensures that these "not yet solved" examples are used more often to test (and train) the NNs. In this way, the genetic as well as the LTL component of CGA-LAM concentrate their effort where it is needed most.

Furthermore, after 75K cycles the performance increase of CGA-LAM had not yet totally stopped. TRAD-LAM, on the other hand, was not improving anymore after its 50K cycles. It is important to note that BP rapidly steers the NNs towards regions in the weight space with low error. This way, genetic diversity decreases fast. This is probably why the final solution quality obtained by TRAD-LAM is lower than that of TRAD. CGA-LAM, on the other hand, benefits from its partial fitness evaluation: LTFE allows to track, with some delay, the influence of the weight changes on the fitness of the NN. This short delay probably helps to keep up the genetic diversity. Hence, CGA-LAM can use more BP than TRAD-LAM without losing too quickly its genetic diversity.

	>70	>80	>85	>90	>95	final accuracy
TRAD-LAM	152	171	296	1258	-	91.3 (0.4)
CGA-LAM	133	162	217	321	1139	97.95 (1.49)

Table 2: Number of forward and backward propagations (in thousands) needed to reach a given accuracy level. The rightmost column gives the average accuracy (and the standard deviation) of the best-so-far (TRAD-LAM: 50K cycles; CGA-LAM: 75K cycles)

Fahlman [4] noted that with BP "units were being turned off hard during the early stages of the learning, and they were getting stuck in the zero state". In order to avoid this, Fahlman added a constant 0.1 to the derivative of the sigmoid function before multiplying it with the error. We also made this change to CGA-LAM. As a result of this change, CGA-LAM converges quicker towards the accuracy levels of 70%, 80%, 85%, 90%. Only the 95% accuracy level is reached later. In addition to this, the average best-so-far at the end of a run was lower as well: 95.55. It looks as if the larger weight changes now cause a rapid loss of genetic diversity for CGA-LAM as well. As a result, CGA-LAM starts to converge prematurely. Or, in other words too much or too quick learning results in too much exploitation at the expense of exploration.

7 Conclusions and Discussion

This paper describes some initial experiments with coevolutionary LTL. The use of LTFE in a CGA, as opposed to the "once and for all" fitness evaluation of traditional GAs, enables the use of real life-time learning in which the NNs (and their fitness) change during their life-time. It is really the partial but continuous nature of LTFE which allows for an elegant introduction of LTL in CGAs. The experiments described here show that CGA-LAM clearly outperforms CGA, TRAD, and TRAD-LAM. This in terms of final solution quality as well as computation demand. An important advantage of the CGA-LTL combination is that LTFE forces both learning mechanisms (genetic and life-time) to concentrate on "not yet correctly trained" examples. This way, the fine-tuning capabilities of BP are exploited in an optimal manner. The current paper also shows the robustness of CGAs. LTFE allows the fitness to track changes in the environment or in the individual itself. Here, the latter changes are incurred by LTL.

We think, however, that a lot of parameters could be improved further such that an even better balance between exploration and exploitation is obtained. Unfortunately, this balance not only depends on the problem to be solved it also depends on the type of LTL which is used. Some interesting questions are: How much LTL should there be for a given problem? What is the right size of (weight) changes resulting from LTL? Should one use Lamarckian or "Baldwinian" learning? Hart [5] has investigated some of these issues and their interaction for different types of single population GAs. His work clearly shows the complexity of the interactions between evolutionary learning and LTL. Hence, we suggest to let evolution itself solve these questions (as was done in nature). Our CGAs might prove instrumental for this as well. One promising attempt is to use a symbiotic CGA ([11], [12]) in which solutions and learning algorithms symbiotically coevolve. Here, one can start from the research of Chalmers [2] who evolved learning algorithms for single-layer feedforward networks. Such a learning algorithm is represented as a linear function of 4 variables. For a given connection between input unit i and output unit j these variables are: the activation of i, the activation of the j, the training signal on j and the current weight of the connection. Given variables for these four variables the linear function calculates the size of the weight change. In our approach we would not only like to calculate the weight changes during the learning process. In addition, we would like to calculate answers (values) to the questions above (probability-of-learning, Lamarck-or-Baldwin). An encounter would now involve a triple consisting of an example, a NN, and a learning algorithm. Probably, the most difficult problem would be to define a reliable fitness feedback for the learning algorithms. To be continued.

Acknowledgements

This research is sponsored by the European Union as Brite/Euram Project No. BE-7686 (PSYCHO). The author is indebted to Roos-Marie Bal for proof-reading this paper.

References

1. Belew, R.K., McInerney, J., Schraudolph, N. N., (1992), *Evolving Networks: Using the Genetic Algorithm with Connectionist Learning*, in Artificial Life III, C.G. Langton, C. Taylor, J.D. Farmer, S. Rasmussen (eds.), Addison-Wesley.
2. Chalmers, D. J., (1991), *The Evolution of Learning: an Experiment in Genetic Connectionism*, in Connectionist Models, Proceedings of the 1990 Summer School, Morgan Kaufmann.
3. Fahlman, S. E., Hinton, G. E., (1987), *Connectionist Architectures for Artificial Intelligence*, IEEE Computer 20(1), IEEE Computer Society Press
4. Fahlman, S. E., (1988), *An Empirical Study of Learning Speed in Back-Propagation Networks*, CMU Technical Report CMU-CS-88-162, Carnegie Mellon University, Pittsburgh.
5. Hart, W. E. H., (1994), Adaptive Global Optimization with Local Search, PhD Dissertation University of California, San Diego.
6. Hillis, W. D., (1992), *Co-evolving Parasites Improve Simulated Evolution as an Optimization Procedure*, in Artificial Life II, Langton, C.G.; Taylor, C.; Farmer, J.D., and Rasmussen, S., (eds), Addison-Wesley, California.

7. Kitano, H., (1990), Empirical Studies on the Speed of Convergence of Neural Network Training using Genetic Algorithms, Proceedings of the Eight National Conference on Artificial Intelligence, AAAI Press.
8. Paredis, J., (1991), *The Evolution of Behavior: Some Experiments*, Proceedings of Simulation of Adaptive Behavior: From Animals to Animats, Meyer, and Wilson (eds.), MIT Press / Bradford Books.
9. Paredis, J., (1994), *Steps towards Coevolutionary Classification Neural Networks,* Proceedings Artificial Life IV, R. Brooks, P. Maes (eds), MIT Press / Bradford Books.
10. Paredis, J., (1994), *Coevolutionary Constraint Satisfaction*, Proceedings PPSN-III, Lecture Notes in Computer Science, vol. 866, Davidor, Y., Schwefel, H-P., Manner, R. (eds.), Springer Verlag.
11. Paredis, J., (1995), *The Symbiotic Evolution of Solutions and their Representations*, Proceedings of the Sixth International Conference on Genetic Algorithms (ICGA 95), Eshelman, L. (ed.), Morgan Kaufmann Publishers.
12. Paredis, J., (1996), *Symbiotic Coevolution for Epistatic Problems*, Proceedings of the European Conference on Artificial Intelligence 1996 (ECAI 96), John Wiley & Sons (in press).
13. Paredis, J., (1996), *Coevolutionary Computation,* Artificial Life Journal, Vol. 2, nr. 4, Langton, C. (ed.), MIT Press / Bradford Books (in press).
14. Whitley, D., (1989), *Optimizing Neural Networks using Faster, more Accurate Genetic Search.* Proc. Third Int. Conf. on Genetic Algorithms, Morgan Kaufmann.
15. Whitley, D., (1993), *Genetic Reinforcement Learning for Neurocontrol Problems*, Machine Learning, 13: p. 259-284, Kluwer Academic Publishers.
16. Whitley, D., Gordon, V. S., Mathias, K., (1994), *Lamarckian Evolution, The Baldwin Effect and Function Optimization*, Proceedings PPSN-III, Lecture Notes in Computer Science, vol. 866, Davidor, Y., Schwefel, H-P., Manner, R. (eds.), Springer Verlag.

Genetic Programs and Co-Evolution

Developing robust general purpose controllers using local mating in two 2-dimensional populations

Andreas Ronge[1,2] and Mats G. Nordahl[2,3]

[1] Studies of Artificial Neural Systems, Dept. of Numerical Analysis and Computing Science, Royal Institute of Technology, S–100 44 Stockholm, Sweden

[2] Institute of Theoretical Physics, Chalmers University of Technology, S–412 96 Gothenburg, Sweden

[3] Santa Fe Institute, 1399 Hyde Park Road, Santa Fe, NM 87501, USA

Abstract. A co-evolutionary approach for developing programs for controlling a very simple "robot-like" simulated vehicle is presented. The main goal is to find programs that can generalize and solve other similar problems. Good results are achieved by coevolving the test cases and the simulated vehicles and using locality in both the reproduction and evaluation phases. The fitness of a controller is determined by its performance in competition with its neighbours in the test case population. The fitness of a test case is similarly determined through competition with its neighbours in the controller population. The co-evolved controllers are more robust and general than a simple hand-designed algorithm or controllers evolved using a fixed training set.

1 Introduction

In machine learning it is frequently desirable to minimize heavy dependence on trainers. One way to reduce this dependence is by using co-evolution. In co-evolution there are two (or more) populations of individuals. The environment for the first population consist of the second population, and conversely, the environment for the second population consists of the first population. The most successful (and thus most numerous) species at a certain instant will be targeted for attacks by future generations of the second population, which could cause rapid never-ending evolution in the system (the Red Queen effect [12]).

One example of such a co-evolutionary feedback mechanism in nature could occur in the predator–prey relation, where it may lead to a coevolutionary arms race: strong evolutionary pressure for prey to defend themselves in response to which future generations of predators develop better attacking strategies.

In complex software engineering applications the construction of appropriate test suites to demonstrate the reliability of software is considered almost as important as the development of the software itself. By viewing the software solutions as one population and the test suites as another, competitive co-evolution allows the simultaneous search for both.

Competitive co-evolution among many species has been explored in the context of co-evolution of strategies for games such as the Iterated Prisoner's Dilemma (e.g., [9, 6, 7]). It is also used in a wide range of ecological simulations studied in Artificial Life (see, e.g., [8]). The use of co-evolution of solutions and training set in a machine learning application was introduced by Hillis [3], who showed that the addition of co-evolving parasites can considerably improve the performance of a genetic algorithm in finding a minimal sorting network.

Our goal for an implementation of competitive co-evolution is to automatically discover robust and general controllers for a particular problem by simultaneously evolving the test cases. This approach stands in contrast to evolving controllers by pitting them against a static, predetermined training set.

2 The Problem

The problem is how to create a robust, general purpose controller for navigating a robot-like simulated vehicle attempting to find all the food pellets on a trail in a square $m \times n$ toroidal grid. Each site of trail initially contains one food pellet, which an ant "eats" as soon it steps on it. The ant has a trail–sensor that only senses the single immediately adjacent cell in the direction the ant is currently facing (it only senses the trail and not food pellets). Its success is measured by the number of distinct trail cells traversed, i.e., the number of food pellets eaten. The food trail must not have any gaps but there are no restrictions on the width of the trail (the problem is then essentially that of searching a finite region of the plane, which can be solved by a 2-d finite automaton using 4 pebbles [1]). In this implementation, a trail is defined by an "anti-ant", which lays a trail site by site by moving around on the grid.

3 Methods

The technique used to evolve computer programs in this paper is known as Genetic Programming (GP) [5]. GP is an the extension of the conventional genetic algorithm [4] in which each individual in the population is a computer program. The size, shape, and content of these programs can change dynamically during the simulated evolution.

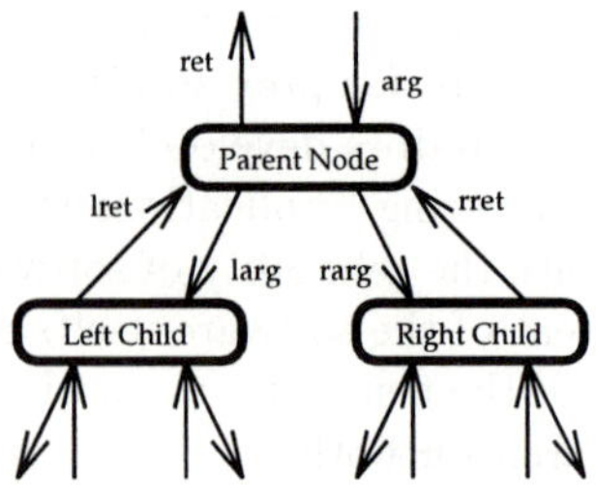

Fig. 1. Arguments and return values (unsigned bytes) from and to nodes.

We have implemented a C based version of GP, using a simple fixed sized linear array in which the program's binary tree is stored. Values (unsigned chars) are passed in both directions (up and down) between a parent and its two children nodes as shown in figure 1. In this paper we are using 10 levels for the main tree and 7 levels for the ADF.

An ant has no knowledge of where it is and where it has been unless it keeps track of that information. We have provided the programs with the capability of using an indexed memory [11]. Each individual has not only two functional trees (one for the main tree, one for its ADF), but also an array of elements (unsigned bytes) indexed from 0 to 255. During a run, an individual can read and write from this array. The initial state of this array is evolved (like a GA string).

The following 14 terminals and 16 functions were used (note that in this implementation, there are no pre-defined constant terminals):

terminal	*action*
Move	Move ant; *ret* :=0
Input	IF food-ahead THEN *ret*=1 ELSE *ret* :=0
TurnL	Turn left; *ret* :=1
TurnR	Turn right; *ret* :=2
Nop1	*ret* := adfLeaf1
Nop2	*ret* := adfLeaf2
IncM	mem[*arg*] := mem[*arg*] −1; *ret* :=mem[*arg*]
DecM	mem[*arg*] := mem[*arg*] +1; *ret* :=mem[*arg*]
Inc	*ret* := *arg* + 1
Dec	*ret* := *arg* − 1
Not	IF *arg*=0 THEN *ret*:=1 ELSE *ret*:=0
ExecI	*x* := *arg* (mod 4); *x* = 0 ⇒ **Move**; *x* = 1 ⇒ **TurnL**; *x* = 2 ⇒ **TurnR**; *x* = 3 ⇒ **Input**
ExecM	*x* := mem[*arg*] (mod 4); *x* = 0 ⇒ **Move**; *x* = 1 ⇒ **TurnL**; *x* = 2 ⇒ **TurnR**; *x* = 3 ⇒ **Input**
Read	*ret*:=mem[*arg*]

function	*action*
ADF	adfLeaf1 := *lret*; adfLeaf2 := *rret*
Prog	*larg* := *arg*; *rarg* := *lret*; *ret* := *rret*
DoWhile	DO *larg* := *arg*; *rarg* := *lret*; WHILE *rret* = 0
WhileTrue	x := *larg* := *arg*; WHILE *lret* ≠ 0 ⇒ [*rarg* := *x*; *x* := *larg* := *rret*;] *ret* := *rret*;
If	*larg* := *arg*; IF *arg* ≠ 0 THEN *ret* := *lret* ELSE *ret* := *rret*
IfElse	IF *arg* = 0 THEN *ret* := *rret* ELSE *ret* := *lret*
EQ	*larg* := *arg*; *rarg* := *arg*; *lret* = *rret* ⇒ *ret* := 1 ELSE *ret*:=0
Less	*larg* := *arg*; *rarg* := *arg*; *lret* < *rret* ⇒ *ret* := 1 ELSE *ret* := 0;
Max	*larg* := *arg*; *rarg* := *arg*; *ret* := max(*lret*, *rret*)
Add	*larg* := *arg*; *rarg* := *arg*; *ret* := *lret* + *rret*
Sub	*larg* := *arg*; *rarg* := *arg*; *ret* := *lret* − *rret*
Write1	*larg* := *arg*; *rarg* := *arg*; mem[*lret*] := *rret* *ret* :=*rret*
Write2	*larg* := *arg*; mem[*lret*] := *arg*; *rarg* := *lret*; *ret*:=*rret*
Write3	*larg* := *arg*; mem[arg] := *lret*; *rarg* := *lret*; *ret*:=*rret*
Read1	*larg* := *arg*; *rarg* := mem[*lret*]; *ret* := *rret*;
Read2	*larg* := *arg*; *rarg* := mem[mem[*lret*]]; *ret* := *rret*;

The crossover operator can be guided by a bit field for each node in the tree, which is evolved together with the parse tree. Better performance was achieved in the experiments by using *guided crossover*. An agent starts each interaction with a fixed amount of energy, in this case 20000 units. When the agent's energy level drops below zero, the simulation ends. There are no costs for using functions, only for using terminals.

	cost A		*cost B*	
terminal	*ant*	*anti-ant*	*ant*	*anti-ant*
Move	100	100	100	200
Input	10	10	5	10
TurnL	10	10	5	10
TurnR	10	10	5	10
Other	1	1	1	1

3.1 Breeding Policy

With the standard population model used in GA and GP a new population is created all at once, in contrast to most real populations in which births and deaths occur continuously at random intervals. The standard GP also uses the same fitness function across the entire population, and there is no locality in reproduction. The introduction of geographical separation tends to improve population diversity. Evolution pushes individuals toward fitness with respect to their immediate environment rather than the population as a whole. We have introduced locality in both the evaluation and reproduction phases.

Fitness Evaluation In this paper the second population consists of anti-ants, which create food-pellets by moving around in the 128x128 grid. The two populations are organized into two 32x32 lattices. A site always contains one individual. An individual only dies when it is replaced by a child. Fitness is defined in terms of the worst performance among the five interactions with neighbouring opponents (and also previous interactions with neighbouring opponents).

$$Fitness_t(a_i) = \min_{j \in N_i} \{f(a_i,\ b_j),\ Fitness_{t-1}(a_i)\}$$

f the score from the interaction between two individuals
N_i the neighbourhood of five individuals

An interaction gives a score to both combatants. The ant score is defined as the percentage of food pellets eaten; the anti-ant score is defined as the percentage of food pellets left by the ant. Children start their life with a fitness value of 100%. Each interaction could reduce this value (fitness is never increased).

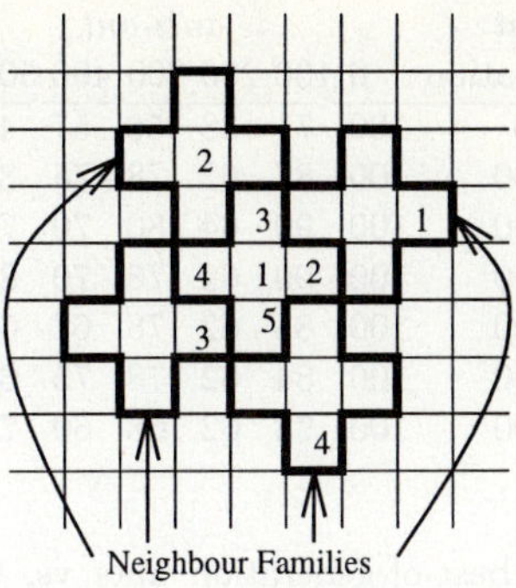

Fig. 2. A family and its four neighbouring families. In each of the neighbouring families a random individual is selected as a potential parent. The best of these will breed with the best of the five individuals in the middle.

Reproduction Our method for implementing locality in the reproduction phase is based on the steady-state K-tournament selection technique. A generation corresponds to the birth of 1024 children. Mating is done by selecting the best two individuals from two neighbouring families. Each family consists of five members. The procedure works as follows:

1. Randomly pick one location on the grid. Select the five individuals from population A around this location as the central family (see figure 2).
2. Randomly pick one individual from each neighbouring family.
3. Select one individual from step 1 and one from step 2, with maximum fitness values. Let the two winners breed.
4. Replace the worst individual from central family with the new child.
5. Evaluate new fitness values for both the child and its neighbours in the other population.
6. Repeat step 1–6 but with alternating populations.

4 Results

By using co-evolution there is no pre-determined "fitness landscape" against which progress can be measured. The fitness landscape of one population is determined by the current opponent population. One possible technique for monitoring co-evolutionary progress is to evaluate individuals from generation x against individuals from generation y from the other population [2].

Seven generations of ant and anti-ant populations were selected from a run. Each ant/anti-ant population pair was compared by testing each ant in the population on ten random tracks from the anti-ant population. Terminal costs A were used. The best ants from this comparison are summarized in the following table.

ant	*anti-ant*						
Generation	0	100	200	300	400	500	600
0	100	71	38	50	57	41	52
100	100	87	62	78	75	81	80
200	100	90	64	80	70	70	78
300	100	90	62	78	70	82	81
400	100	85	62	78	67	68	80
500	100	84	62	78	75	69	83
600	100	73	62	68	60	73	71

Table 1. Fitness scores of best-of-generation ants vs. ten random tracks from the anti-ant population.

As shown in this table, the fitness of one population depends on the current opponent population. The movement of one population over a fitness landscape significantly alters the fitness landscape of the other population.

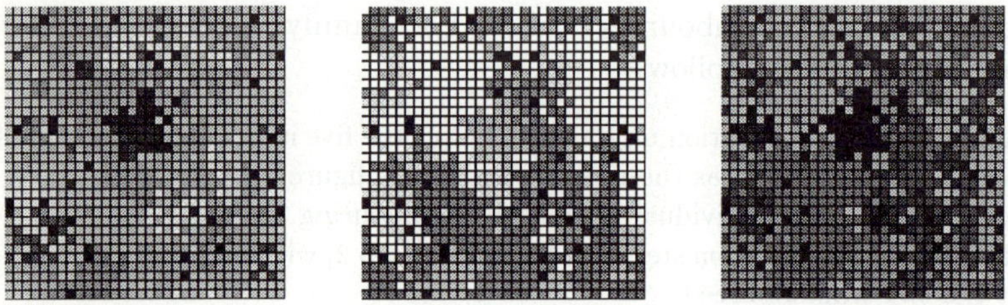

Track 1. Track 6. Track 9.

Fig. 3. Fitness distribution of a co-evolved ant population evaluated on three test tracks. Dark sites represent low fitness.

Figure 3 shows the spatial structure of a co-evolved ant population after 200 generations, and illustrates similarities in the behaviour signatures between close individuals.

In order to compare performance and measure generality of ants we have selected ten tracks from different generations and runs. Each ant is tested on each of these tracks. The results are combined to form a *behaviour signature* of ten fitness values. One way of defining generality of an individual is in terms of the uniformity of its behaviour signature. An individual with wildly varying fitness values in its behaviour signature is said to be less general (more specialized) than an individual with a smooth behaviour signature, even though the two may have the same average fitness.

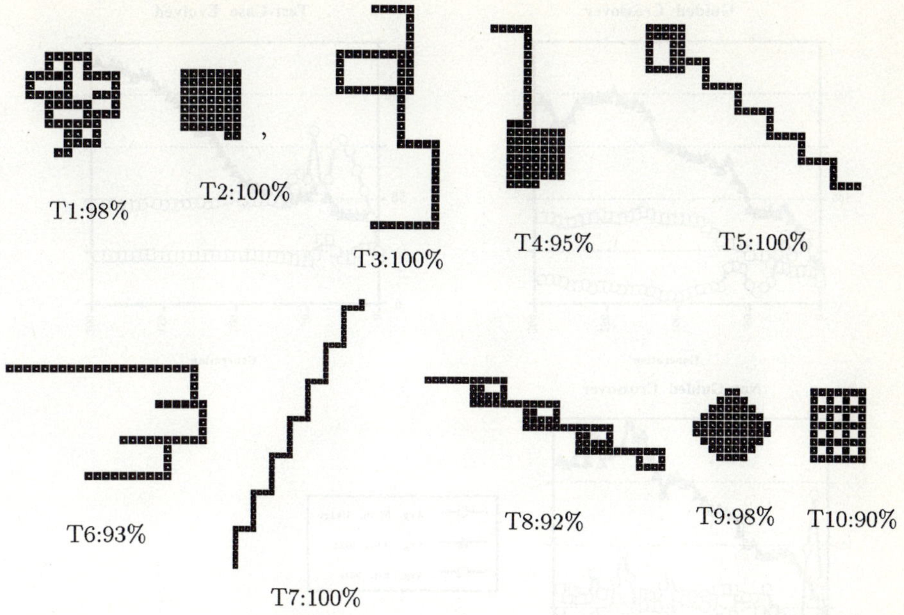

Fig. 4. The ten test-cases and one good co-evolved ant with its behaviour signature

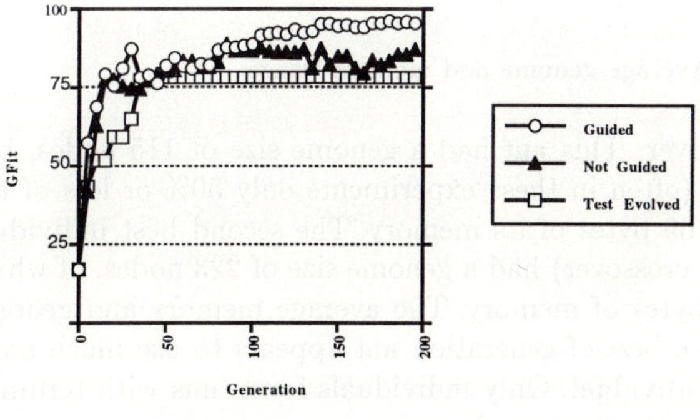

Fig. 5. The GFit value of best individual in the population.

The test tracks in figure 4 were used to produce behaviour signatures. The black squares represent the tracks, and the white dots depict a walk by a good co-evolved ant. We now define the *Generalization Fitness* (GFit) as the average of the behaviour signature. Figure 5 shows the development of the GFit value of the best individual over 200 generations. The worst performing curve was from a run with a fixed training set, where the system tends to stick in a non-optimal local maximum. Even when the non-coevolved (test-case evolved) ants were trained on the ten test tracks used for measuring the GFit value, the two co-evolved runs showed better performance.

The best individual had a GFit value of 96% and was found by using co-

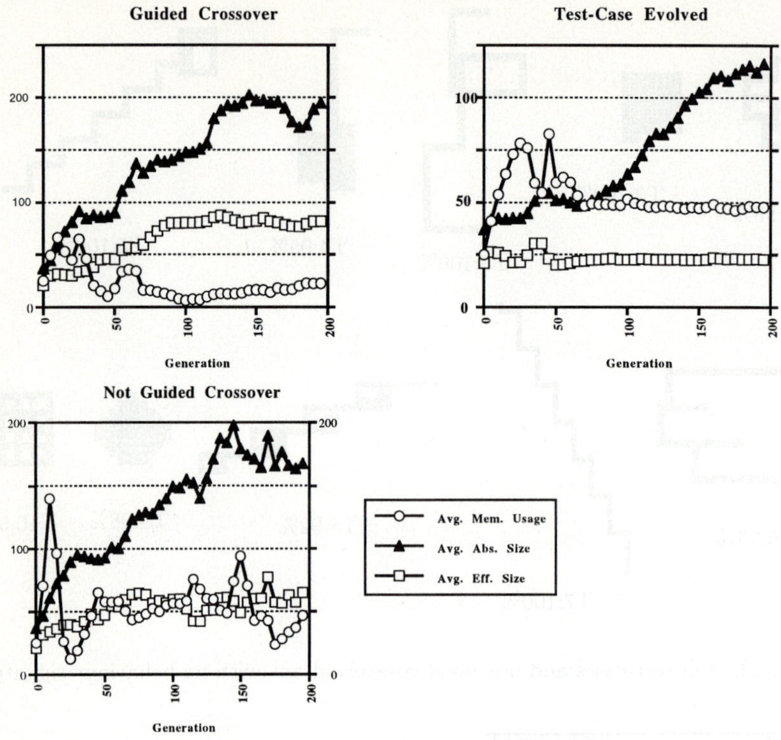

Fig. 6. Average genome and memory usage.

evolution and guided crossover. This ant had a genome size of 115 nodes, but only 74 were actually used (often in these experiments only 50% or less of the genome was used). It used 69 bytes of its memory. The second best individual (from a run without guided crossover) had a genome size of 223 nodes, of which 149 were used. It used 14 bytes of memory. The average memory and genome use is shown in figure 6. The best-of-generation ant appears to use much more memory than the average individual. Only individuals from runs with terminal cost B used their ADF.

In order to judge the effectiveness of co-evolution we compared the best co-evolved ant (terminal cost B) with a simple hand-designed algorithm and a test-case-evolved ant. The following algorithm was used:

> **IF** food trail ahead **AND** not been in next site **THEN** move **ELSE** **IF** not turned left four times **THEN** turn left **ELSE** move to one of the sites which are part of the trail.

This simple algorithm achieved a GFit value of 75% with wildly varying scores. This is not a general and robust controller. A fitness comparison between this algorithm, a test-case-evolved ant and a co-evolved ant is shown below:

track	*simple algorithm*	*co-evolved*	*test-evolved*
1.	56 (14 – 66)	81	81
2.	86 (76 – 100)	96	74
3.	95 (58 – 100)	100	90
4.	87 (75 – 100)	95	87
5.	80 (75 – 100)	100	75
6.	33 (33 – 33)	100	100
7.	100 (100 – 100)	100	98
8.	50 (50 – 50)	97	77
9.	53 (53 – 53)	100	70
10.	88 (74 – 92)	98	70
GFit:	75	97	82

Table 2. Fitness scores of a hand-designed algorithm, a co-evolved ant, and an evolved ant which was trained on these ten tracks.

Terminals used on track 9.

Move	156	Input	216	Turn Left	113
TurnR	73	IncrM	31	DecrM	62
Not	31	Read	11	ExecI	194

Functions used on track 9.

Prog	64	DoWhile	106	WhileT	22
If	53	If Else	53	Equal	53
Less	88	Add	106	Sub	124
Write3	42				

Table 3. The best co-evolved ant (from table 2) used these 1729 terminals and functions and had a genome size of 115 nodes (74 used).

5 Discussion

Evolving robust general purpose programs is a difficult task. The co-evolutionary approach described here provides a promising approach towards this goal. The benefits of allowing the test cases to co-evolve are twofold. First, it helps in preventing the population from becoming stuck in local optima. The second advantage is that testing becomes more efficient. Since only test-case sets that expose weaknesses are widely represented in the population, fewer tests per individual are necessary in each generation.

This approach can be applied to a range of problems, for example the corridor-following problem (e.g., [10]). In this task, this would mean the co-evolution of corridor-followers and corridors.

It is often hard to find natural ways of using co-evolution in a problem. For example, the training set may restricted to be an already given finite set, e.g., in predicting currency exchange rates. One interesting possibility for coevolutionary problem solving is to co-evolve teachers. A teacher would be rewarded depending on the quality of its pupils. This is a positive fitness feedback (symbiosis) relation as opposed to the predator-prey relation. Instead of having a fixed fitness function, the teacher could also evaluate its pupils.

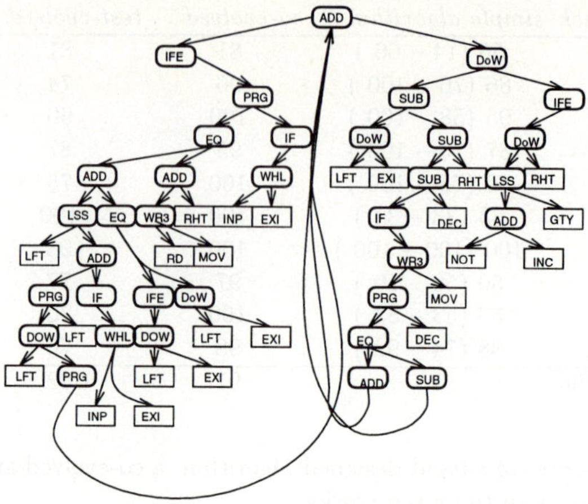

Fig. 7. Genome of the co-evolved ant from table 2 (only nodes used on a certain test trail are shown).

References

1. Blum, M., Sakoda, W. J.: On the capability of finite automata in 2 and 3 dimensional space, in Proceedings of 18th IEEE Conference on Foundations of Computer Science, pp. 147–161, (1977).
2. Cliff, D., Miller, G.: Tracking the Red Queen: Measurements of adaptive progress in co-evolutionary simulations, in F. Moran, A. Moreno, J. J. Merelo and P. Cachon (eds.), Advances in Artificial Life: Proceedings of the Third European Conference on Artificial Life, pp. 200–218, Springer-Verlag (1995).
3. Hillis, W. D.: Co-evolving parasites improves simulated evolution as an optimization procedure, in C. G. Langton, C. Taylor, J. D. Farmer, and S. Rasmussen (eds.), Artificial Life II, pp. 313–323, Addison-Wesley (1992).
4. Holland, J. H.: Adaptation in Natural and Artificial Systems, University of Michigan Press (1975).
5. Koza, J. R.: Genetic Programming: On the Programming of Computers by Natural Selection, MIT Press (1992).
6. Lindgren, K.: Evolutionary phenomena in simple dynamics, in C. G. Langton, C. Taylor, J. D. Farmer, and S. Rasmussen (eds.), Artificial Life II, pp. 295–312, Addison-Wesley (1992).
7. Lindgren, K., Nordahl, M. G.: Cooperation and community structure in artificial ecosystems, Artificial Life **1** (1994) 15–38.
8. Lindgren, K., Nordahl, M. G.: Evolutionary dynamics of spatial games, Physica D **75** (1994) 292–309.
9. Miller, J. H.: The coevolution of automata in the repeated Prisoner's Dilemma, Santa Fe Institute working paper 89-003 (1989).
10. Reynolds, C. W.: Evolution of corridor following in a noisy world, in From Animals to Animats 3, D. Cliff, P. Husbands, J.-A. Meyer, S. W. Wilson (eds.), pp. 402–410, MIT Press (1994).
11. Teller, A.: The evolution of mental models, in K. E. Kinnear Jr. (ed.), Advances in Genetic Programming, pp. 199–219, MIT Press (1994).
12. Van Valen, L.: A new evolutionary law, Evolutionary Theory **1** (1973) 1-30.

Self-Assemblage of Gene Nets in Evolution via Recruiting of New Netters

Alexander V. Spirov

I.M.Sechenov Institute of Evolutionary Physiology and Biochemistry, 44, Thorez Prospect, S.-Petersburg,194223, Russia

e- mail: spirov@iephb.ru; WWW http://avs.iephb.ru

Abstract. The fundamental dynamical processes of evolution are connected to processes based on sequences - the genetic messages coded by DNA. In biological evolution we can discover stages of the *emergence* of novel features. Nature apparently explores some unknown mechanisms of complexification of nets of replicating strings.

It is known that genetic changes are not directly manifested in phenotypic changes. Rather, a complex developmental machinery mediates between genetic information and phenotypic characteristics. It provides a certain *robustness* by filtering out genetic changes.

Such degree of freedom allows the species to accumulate appropriate mutations without interruption of the development. When the volume of heritable changes achieving critical threshold, this can force out the development to a new higher-level trajectory.

I intend to overview here some findings on the way of searching and exploitation of the rules for evolutionary complexification. I hope these algorithms could find applications in the presentation problem of evolutionary computations.

1. Introduction

Understanding the conditions under which mutations and selection can lead to rising levels of organisation is of importance for evolutionary biology as well as for evolutionary computations. The fundamental dynamical processes of evolution are connected to processes based on sequences - the genetic messages coded by DNA.

Considering detaily evolutionary pathways, we can discover stages of the emergence of novel features as well as stages of slow-scale change of existing ones. To model the origin of new features, we require a mechanism for how complex, higher-level behavior emerges from low-level interactions (*Kaneko, 1994*). Nature apparently explores some unknown mechanisms of evolutionary complexification of the replicating strings nets.

According to classic point of view evolutionary complexification of the living beings apparently requires the co-ordinate change of several phenotypic characters to produce adaptive variants. However this requires *simultaneous* mutations at several genes. But it is impossible, of course!

On the other hand, genetic changes are not directly manifested in phenotypic changes. Rather, a complex developmental machinery mediates between genetic information and phenotypic characteristics. It provides a certain *robustness* by filtering out genetic changes. Some genetic changes make little or no difference to the final phenotype. In other words, *robustness* is a way to escape the requirement of *simultaneous* mutations at several genes for evolutionary complexification.

Such degree of freedom allows the species to accumulate appropriate mutations without interruption of the development. When the volume of heritable changes achieving critical threshold, this can force out the development to a new higher-level trajectory.

Our computer simulations of evolution of the gene networks governing the morphogenesis of early embryos shows the possibility for self-organisation or self-assemblage (or "outgrowth") of gene networks during evolution. This self-assemblage proceeds by means of recruiting of a new gene via closing up of new cascades of interactions between new and old members of the network. (These new genes could appear by way of duplication of the members of this net or another one.) The recruiting of new "netters" does not need to be forced by selection; stabilising selection is quite enough for this. However, if these newly formed gene systems prove to be good for raising the morphological or functional level of organisation, then these Goldschmidt's "hopeful monsters" (Wallace, 1985) can be caught up by driving selection.

Following Dellaert and Beer (1994), Kitano (1994), Wagner and Altenberg (1995), we will study, from the point of view of self-organisation, the evolution of the genotype to phenotype map via the creation of new genes. The fundamental dynamical processes of evolution are connected to dynamical processes based on sequences. Nature apparently explores some unknown mechanisms of strings nets self-complexification. In the paper we present our findings on the way of searching and exploitation of the algorithms for the self-complexification of the regulatory nets of replicating strings. We think these complexification algorithms are not trivial result and it could find applications in the presentation problem of evolutionary computations.

2. Networks of Genes-Controllers and Their Evolution

The identification of controller genes has been a significant recent finding in developmental biology. Networks and cascades of controller genes serve to orchestrate expression of the genome during embryo development. Now we have a lot of knowledge about mechanisms of appearance and maintenance of patterns of the controller genes expression. The networks activity as kind of self-organising mechanisms of morphogenesis allows the conditions of the selection effectiveness to be better understood. Stabilising and driving selection applied to these self-organising mechanisms can dramatically accelerate evolutionary complexification of developmental processes. According to this, self-organisation become apparent in evolution as self-assemblage of the gene nets and cascades.

My approach exploits the following essential characters of gene networks. Each gene-member of the network encodes a peptide-product whose function is activation or repression of another gene (its so called target gene). These transcription factors recognise specific sequences of DNA in regulatory domains of the target genes and tightly bind to the target sites. A given member of the network produces transcription factors that specifically activate or repress other netters, and vice versa. A complex network of autoregulatory and cross-regulatory actions functionally connects the genes thereby forming gene networks and cascades. The result of action of the network or cascade is a particular spatial pattern of activity (expression) of the network members. Down-activated members, in turn, switch on structural genes at the appropriate time and place. These genes, in turn, produce enzymes for the subsequent differentiation and morphogenesis of embryo rudiments. We preferably assume the concentration-dependent action of the peptide-regulator on the targeting gene. Namely, at low concentrations it acts as activator, while at high concentrations it acts as repressor (See Jackle et al., 1992).

We may be considering the space of all possible length sequences of DNA composed of four types of bases. Our genotypes consist of set of **N** sequences of length **L,** forming a certain region in the sequence space. The majority of possible sequences are *forbidden* in biological reality, leaving only a subset of **N** allowed ones for participation in the evolution (See Asselmeyer et al., 1995).

Let us include in consideration a mutation that takes place in a sequence. To measure the strength of the change we can use a metric on the sequence space introduced by means of the Hamming prescription. The Hamming distance between two sequences is defined as the number of non-coincidences. Two sequences with Hamming distance equal to one are neighbours.

Discussing the problem of the complexification of living beings we really bringing in mind following picture. Neighbourhood structure of the sequence space of ancestor and its advanced offspring are generally two unconnected graphs, as is the case of Fig.1a. Evolutionary pathway from lower to higher level of organisation needs connection between the graphs. It is impossible to jump from real ancestor to potential offspring graph. All appropriate sequences formally connecting two graphs are forbidden because they give abnormal phenotypes.

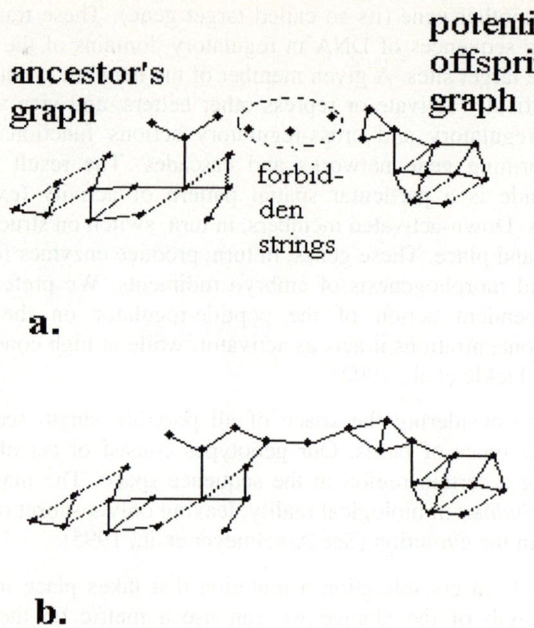

Fig.1. Complicated topology of the neighbourhood structure of the sequence space (a) and its change in evolution (b).

It is strict definition of above mentioned evolutionary complexification scheme via simultaneous mutations in several points of the DNA-string.

Apparently to achieve the higher level, the evolutionary process must have chance to get over the gap. In principle, we can imagine some ways to achieve this. The simplest one consists in decreasing of adaptive role of the traits under consideration. This leads to broadening of variability the traits. In such a case, previously forbidden sequences determining phenotypes with deviations will get chance for reproduction. As a result, connection between actual and potential graph forms, as in the case of Fig.1b.

3. Mechanisms for Jumping Over the Gaps: Conflicting Gene Systems

Complicated topology of the neighbourhood structure of the sequence space (Fig.1a) is ensured by intrinsic potential for complexification of the string regulatory networks. Meanwhile connections between isolated actual and potential graphs might be facilitated by the robustness of the developmental mechanisms. Appearance of such connections between diverged levels of organisation is assumed to be achieved by exploitation of *canalization* schemes of development.

In our simulations of the “emergence of novel features” the host genome initially consists of functionally coupled pair of gene regulatory elements (***O***-gene +

A-gene): O → A (the ***O***-gene product activates ***A***-gene). The ***A***-gene contains **CATAAT** sequences that belong to targeting sequences for ***O***-product binding.

For the purpose of an oversimplified but indirect implementation of the driving force, I assume the appearance of a "virus". The virus is randomly transmitted from "carriers" to healthy genomes. By definition, the virus is successfully transmitted if the host genome has in the ***A***-gene an ***O***-binding site. I assume it inserts in the ***A***-gene by cutting of the ***O***-binding site and becomes silent. With a predetermined probability the virus wakes up and with time gradually decreases the host's reproductive potential, finally killing the host, thus eliminating the affected genome from evolution.

Point mutations in the ***O***-binding sites lead to insensitivity to virus. However, the "wild" type of our genome could not lack the ***O***-binding sites in ***A***-gene, because it would consequently lack the normal phenotype (the ***A***-product concentration profile). Hence, in the case of a genome with absence of the wild-type ***O***-binding site in the ***A***-gene (but with a normal pattern of ***A***-gene expression), this prospective mutant will be insensitive to the virus and obtain a selective advantage. In time, the mutant genome will exclude the wild type. This is, of course, a model example of host-parasite evolution.

I must emphasize that such selection by parasite pressure is effective only if the design of the wild genome allows appropriate reorganization in principle. The virus acts as a catalyst of the process. It does not produce but catches new forms. If the wild-type genome does not have an appropriate potential for reorganization (testable in calculations), a virus will not help. In this I imply a broad interpretation of "virus", that is, it may be plasmid or transposable element (Daniels et al., 1990).

4. Regulatory Nets with High Potential for Complexification

Evolutionary outgrowth of gene networks is possible if only the design of the wild genome allows appropriate reorganizations in principle. If testable in calculations wild-type genome have not appropriate potential for complexification, selection will not help. Impressive outgrowth of the Drosophila' *pair-rule* network on the way from primitive to higher insects are inspired us to search simple regulatory networks with high potential for complexification.

Recruiting of new netters depends upon plasticity of regulatory pathways inside the network. Firstly, each transcription factor can recognize not unique DNA sequence (say, CATAAT), but family of similar sequences (say, *CATAAT, CATAAC, AATAAT, AATAAC*).

Then, the sequence families for binding of different transcription factors can be very similar or overlap each other. In other words, the same target sequence can be recognized by two factors, especially if they have antagonistic action on the same targeting gene. These two characteristics are necessary and sufficient to ensure the recruiting phenomenon.

Consider following simple gene cascade having potential for complexification. Each genome initially consists of functionally coupled pair of gene regulatory elements (***O***-gene + ***A***-gene): $\mathrm{M} \Rightarrow \mathrm{O} \rightarrow \mathrm{A}$.

M is site-specific transcription factor and its target is gene ***O***. It forms exponentially decaying gradient like *Drosophila*'s bicoid morphogen. ***M*** has affinity to the *CATAAT*-like family of sequences and regulatory region of the ***O*** has two such sites. The exponential-in-distance morphogen gradient activates ***O***-gene in concentration dependent manner. In its turn, ***O***-product will activate ***A***-gene in concentration-dependent manner also. Concentration profiles of the ***O***- and ***A***-products for wild species have following simple view:

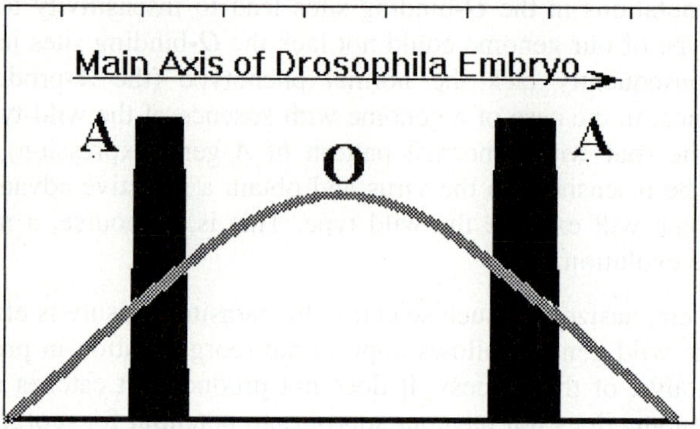

and correspond to the early embryo phenotype with two bands of ***A***-gene expression:

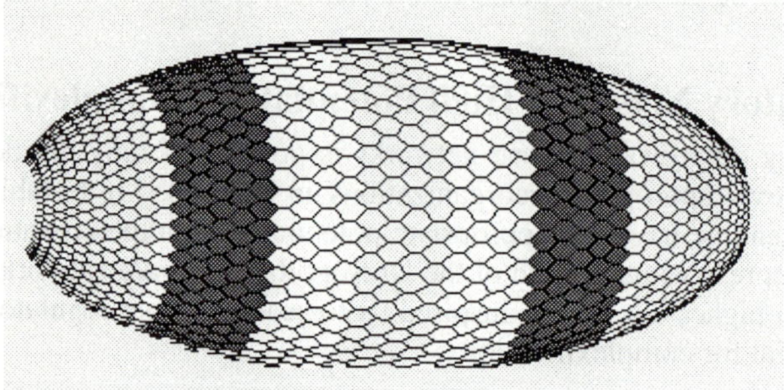

The wild-type genomes are two-string variables. Initially the **A**-gene string is **CATAATnCATAATnCATAATn**, where A, T, G, C is four-letter DNA code and ***n*** is spacer. The ***O***-gene string has a similar form. A fixed probability for point mutations, that is for substitution of one of the simbols by another, is prescribed before the first run. When the computations begin, each genome is tested for "governing of development". This genotype-phenotype presentation is achieved by "translation" of the strings into coupled ordinary differential eqs.

The overall view of the eqs. set depends not only upon the number of genes-strings in a given genome, but also upon sequences of targeting sites. Special subroutine ('ODE_Set') analyses the sequences and choses equations of adequate structure (See next section).

After evaluation of the eqs. set the program finds the phenotype of the tested species. Namely, the values of ***A***-product (and products of other genes) are calculated for each of 50 points of the exponentially decaying ***M***-gradient. The results are used for graphic presentation of the phenotypes and for the Scoring procedure.

The Scoring procedure compares the calculated set of the ***A***-values with the prescribed canonical ***A***-pattern. The sum of square deviations in each of 50 points of the ***M***-gradient is calculated. If the sum is above threshold, then the species genome are eliminated.

Then assume, that two new genes ***O'*** and ***A'*** appear in the genome as a result of duplication of initial ***O*** + ***A*** pair: $O \rightarrow A\ (O' \rightarrow A')$.

Initial duplication of the ***O+A*** gene pair is followed by multiple point mutations in these ***O'*** and ***A'*** gene regulatory sites. Functionally useless duplicates ***O'*** and ***A'*** are lost over time with a prescribed probability. However, before this happens, the silent genes accumulate point mutations. With time appear, by chance, first example of genome consisting of four genes, including proper to recruitment of a new gene pair, ***B*** + ***C***. $O \rightarrow A\ (B' \rightarrow C')$.

The silent ***O'*** and ***A'*** extra-copies accumulate point mutations and there is possibility for shifting the target site specificity compared with the wild-type ***O*** and ***A*** pair. Only unique combinations of nucleotide substitutions in the silent pair of duplicates facilitate following recruiting of newly modified genes in the growing cascade:

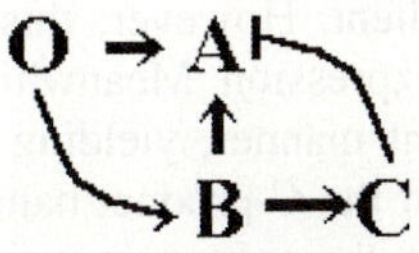

The recruiting of new genes via closing of new regulatory pathways really includes step-by-step "handing of steerage" from an old gene-regulator to a new one. Intermediate mutant genes regulated by both regulators represent a bottleneck for evolution of the net. A rare combination of kinetic parameters of gene activation will facilitate passing through the "bottleneck" to a new structure of the net.

In our computations, for example, the ***A***-gene has three ***O***-binding sites: CCTAAT...CATAAT...AATAAT. In the example discussed, the ***O***-product recognizes CATAAT sequence family. Hence, the change of the ***B***-gene product recognition specificity to CAGAAT sequence would be appropriate for subsequent evolution. However, this must coincide also with shifting of the ***C***-gene product specificity to the AGAAT sequence. I assume that "waking up" of the appropriate ***B*** + ***C*** pair coincides with appropriate point mutations in the ***A***- and ***C***-genes. There is a very low but finite probability of the triple coincidence. Thus the first intermediate mutant has the following ***A***-gene sequence (two "old" binding sites for the ***O***-product and one site for ***B***-binding overlapping with ***C***-binding site): CCTAAT...<u>CAGAAT</u>...AATAAT.

Apparently the intermediate forms with doubly regulated ***A***-gene have weaken fitness and will be eliminated by selection. However, if the mutant has selective advantages, say partial tolerance to the virus, then the "intermediates" will accumulate in population.

In the future, the number of the new mutants will grow and eventually a complete mutant with absence of the ***O***-binding sites and tolerance to the virus will appear. In our case it will have the gene ***A***: CAGAAT...CAGAAT...CAGAAT.

The 4-gene cascades escape infection pressure but curry out morphogenesis successfully (the ***A***-product concentration pattern produces the morphology of the wild type). This hopeful monster shows additional four bands of the ***C***-expression as compared with the wild type early embryo:

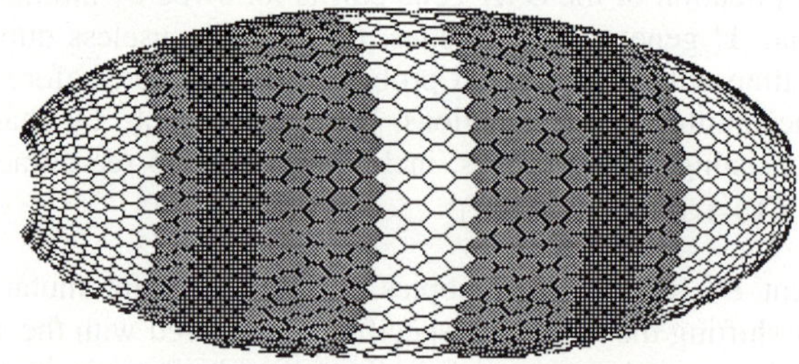

Now main idea became clear: action of the activator ***B***-product and the repressor ***C***-product mimics action of the ***O***. Namely, ***B***-product gives two-wave gradient, similar to the ***A***-concentration profile. The ***B***-gradient activate ***A***-gene by pure activation mechanism giving rise similar two-wave ***A***-gradient. However, this pure activation mechanism gives too broad bands of the ***A***-gene expression. Meanwhile the ***C***-product is activated by the ***B*** in concentration-dependent manner, yielding four-wave ***C***-concentration profile. It is essential that each pair of the ***C***-product bands set boundaries for ***A***-bands, narrowing them. Finally we obtain the same two-waive ***A***-concentration profile, as in the case of the wild type genome.

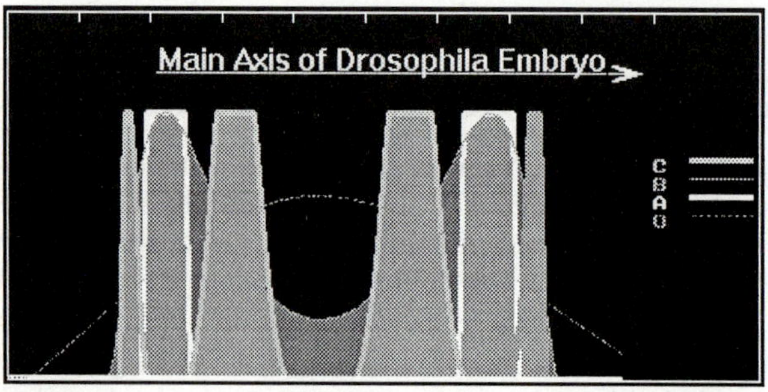

Hence we achieve the recruitment of a pair of new members into simple cascade. As we can see, the same pattern of ***A***-gene expression is achieved by action of more complicated gene network. Apparently it is a kind of evolutionary game with strings, but it remains some essential features in organization of Drosophila segmentation network.

5. Computer Evolution

The overall organisation of the program is similar to many known simple programs in GA's approach. Depending upon RAM volume, up to 12,000 of strings-genomes could treat in this example of computational evolution. There are 'Mutation', 'Scoring' and 'Reproduction' subprograms. The Mutation subprogram includes a 'Point_Mutation' subroutine, as well as 'Crossover' one. The Scoring subprogram begins treatment of each genome with reconstruction of an ODE set describing genotype to phenotype transformation procedure. Then calculated profiles of the genes' expression are compare with a "canonical" picture. Finally, the Reproduction subprogram completes reproduction of the winner-genomes in accordance with truncated or proportional strategies. Results of each Mutation-Scoring-Reproduction round are displayed as a horizontal multicoloured line. Each pixel of the line corresponds to one (or 2 or 4) genome, and the genomes are arranged by score. Addition line by line gives, with time, a "live" tree of the computer evolution.

When the program starts, a population of wild-type genomes is created. Probabilities for random point nucleotide substitutions as well as for $\boldsymbol{O} + \boldsymbol{A}$ gene pair duplication are predetermined before first run. The genes encode patterns of their expression that are scored. I prefer to use truncation strategy of stabilizing selection, namely, those which score above threshold are preferentially reproduced for the next generation, with the mutation operators applied. Losers are eliminated. I performed simulations both with and without recombination. In this case, recombination turned out not to have a major influence on computational evolution.

Our computations reveal simple but impressive examples of rising of structural and functional redundancy in evolutionary computation. Namely, the pair of wild-type genes ***O*** & ***A*** and the four-gene cascade really perform the same task: maintenance two-waive pattern of the ***A***-gene expression. Such redundancy is ensured by known features of kinetics of gene expression.

Drosophila has rapid establishment of its body plan, in comparison with primitive insects. The segments in long germ-band insect embryos, like the fruit fly, are all determined at syncytial blastoderm stage. This is in contrast to short germ-band insects (such as grasshopper) which show an early determination of only the anterior head segments, whereas the more posterior thoracic and abdominal segments are sequentially added after formation of a primary germ anlage (Patel et al., 1992). Segment formation in Drosophila involves the pair-rule genes network which defines double segmental periodicities and which has been considered to represent a special adaptation to the long germ-band type of development.

My computational experiments allow an evolutionary appearance of the Drosophila segmentation mechanism to be simulated and tested. I suggest that the evolutionarily fast formation of the fly segmentation scheme is facilitated by self-enlargement of the initial segmentation cascade via recruiting of new gene members.

Acknowledgements. Supported by Russian Foundation for Basic Researches (Grant No 96-04-49350). I thank Richard Gordon, Denis Thieffry and anonymous reviewers for critical comments.

References

1. Asselmeyer, T., W.Ebeling amd H.Rose, (1995). Smoothing representation of fitness landscapes - the genotype-phenotype map of evolution, *BioSystems*.
2. Daniels SB; Peterson KR; Strausbaugh LD; Kidwell MG; Chovnick A (1990). Evidence for horizontal transmission of the P transposable element between Drosophila species. *Genetics* 124, 339-55.
3. Dellaert, F. and R.D. Beer (1994). Toward an evolvable model of development for autonomous agent synthesis. In: Artificial Life IV: Proceedings of the Fourth International Workshop on the Synthesis and Simulation of Living Systems. R. Brooks and P. Maes (Eds.). MIT Press.
4. Jackle H; Hoch M; Pankratz MJ; Gerwin N; Sauer F; Bronner G. (1992). Transcriptional control by Drosophila gap genes. *J Cell Sci* Suppl 16, 39-51.
5. Kaneko, K (1994). Chaos as source of complexity and diversity in evolution, *ALife*, 1, 163-177.
6. Kitano, H. (1994). Evolution of Metabolism for Morphogenesis. In: Artificial Life IV: proceedings of the fourth international workshop on the synthesis and simulation of living systems. R. Brooks and P. Maes (Eds.). MIT Press.
7. Patel NH; Ball EE; Goodman CS (1992). Changing role of even-skipped during the evolution of insect pattern formation. *Nature* 357: 339-342.
8. G.P. Wagner and L. Altenberg. (1995). Complex Adaptations and the Evolution of Evolvability. WWW http://peaplant.biology.yale.edu:8001/papers/CompAdapt/compadapt.html
9. Wallace, B. (1985). Reflections on the still "hopeful monster". *Quart. Rev. Biol.* 60, 31-42.

A Survey of Intron Research in Genetics

Annie S. Wu[1] and Robert K. Lindsay[2]

[1] Artificial Intelligence Laboratory, University of Michigan, Ann Arbor, MI 48109-2110, aswu@eecs.umich.edu

[2] Mental Health Research Institute, University of Michigan, Ann Arbor, MI 48109-0720, lindsay@umich.edu

Abstract. A brief survey of biological research on non-coding DNA is presented here. There has been growing interest in the effects of non-coding segments in evolutionary algorithms (EAs). To better understand and conduct research on non-coding segments and EAs, it is important to understand the biological background of such work. This paper begins with a review of basic genetics and terminology, describes the different types of non-coding DNA, and then surveys recent intron research.

1 Introduction

There has been growing interest in the effects of non-coding segments in evolutionary algorithms (EAs). Non-coding segments, also called non-coding material or introns in the literature, is a computational model of what is known as non-coding DNA in biological systems. Simply put, non-coding segments refer to the portions of an individual that make no contribution to its fitness value. In genetic programming (GP) systems, non-coding material is a natural by-product of the evolutionary process [19] [26] [29] [30] [28]. In genetic algorithm (GA) systems, studies have included both manually inserted non-coding segments and evolved segments [8] [17] [21] [23] [38] [39] [37]. Both theoretical and empirical studies suggest that non-coding segments may encourage the recombination of and discourage the destruction of existing building blocks in EAs. Evidence indicates that non-coding segments have a stabilizing effect, improving the EA's ability to preserve good building blocks. All of these qualities are desirable in an EA.

Interestingly, there seem to be many parallels between the computational arguments for non-coding segments and the biological hypotheses and explanations for non-coding DNA. To better understand and conduct research on non-coding segments and EAs, it is necessary to understand the biological inspirations of such work. The goal of this paper is to present a brief survey of the research on biological non-coding DNA and introns. This paper begins with a review of basic genetics and terminology, describes the different types of non-coding DNA, and then surveys recent research on non-coding DNA.

2 Basic Genetics

The study of genetics is the study of how living organisms reproduce and evolve. In trying to understand how entire organisms reproduce, biologists have had to

...AATCGAGGTCCTCGGA...
...TTAGCTCCAGGAGCCT...

Fig. 1. Chromosomes consist of complementary strands of DNA nucleotides.

study the cellular and molecular biology of organisms. There are two fundamentally distinct types of cells, eukaryotes and prokaryotes. *Eukaryotes* are cells that have membrane bound organelles, a membrane bound nucleus containing the genetic material of the cell, and introns in the genome. *Prokaryotes* are cells which lack a membrane bound nucleus and membrane bound organelles and store genetic material in a large single molecule of DNA. All prokaryotic organisms are single celled; eukaryotic organisms may be single or multi celled.

Proteins, which are considered the building blocks of life, are the most abundant type of organic molecule in living organisms. A *protein* is made up of one or more polypeptide chains. A *polypeptide chain* is a chain of amino acids. An *amino acid* is an organic molecule consisting of a carbon atom bonded to one hydrogen atom, to a carboxyl group, to an amino group, and to a side group which varies from amino acid to amino acid. There are 20 different amino acids of genetic importance. The order of the amino acids in the polypeptide chains and the folding structure of the polypeptide chains are what give a protein its structural or functional capabilities.

When an organism reproduces, it is imperative that the instructions for building its proteins are reproduced accurately and completely. These instructions are largely maintained by a second type of organic molecule. *Nucleotides* are organic molecules that consist of a five carbon sugar, a phosphate group, and a nitrogenous base. Nucleotides are joined together to form large molecules called *nucleic acids.* The two most common types of nucleic acids are deoxyribonucleic acid (DNA) and ribonucleic acid (RNA). DNA is made up of four different nucleotides: adenine, guanine, cytosine, and thymine, abbreviated A, G, C, T. A and T are complementary; G and C are complementary. A molecule of DNA is organized in the form of two complementary chains of nucleotides (see figure 1) wound in a double helix. In eukaryotes, DNA combines with proteins to form *chromosomes.* Chromosomes are found in the nucleus of a cell and the complete set of chromosomes of an organism is called its *genome.* DNA is the genetic material that is propagated from generation to generation, and contains the instructions on how to build the proteins necessary for a particular organism. Though all genetic information is stored in the ordering of the nucleotides in the DNA, DNA is not directly involved in protein synthesis. DNA directs protein synthesis by sending instructions in the form of RNA. RNA is a nucleic acid similar to DNA and is also made up of four types of nucleotides: adenine, guanine, cytosine, and uracil, abbreviated A, G, C, U. In RNA, thymine is replaced by uracil and A and U are complementary. RNA carries out the synthesis of proteins from the DNA instructions.

A *gene* is a segment of DNA that codes for an RNA product. The different

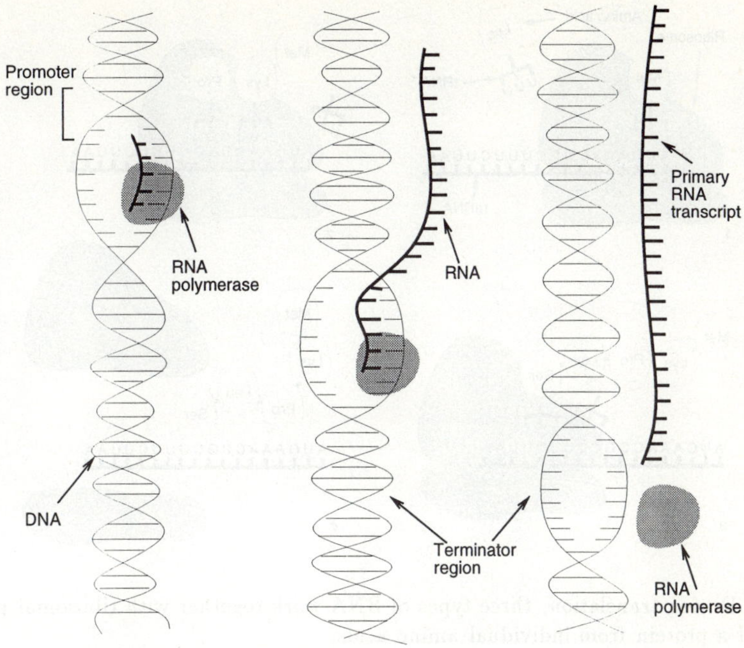

Fig. 2. During transcription, one strand of DNA of a gene is copied into RNA. This figure was adapted from figure 13.3 of [35].

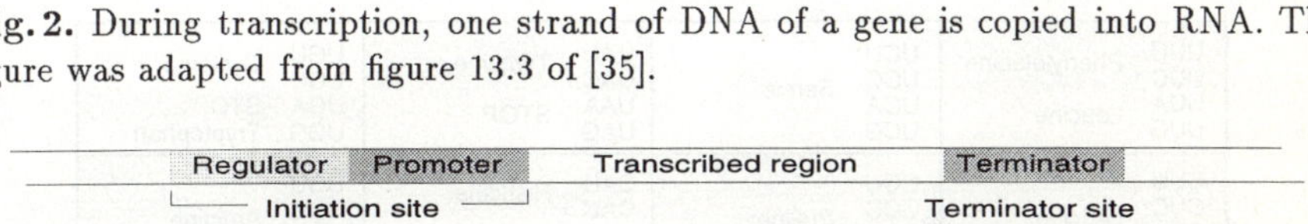

Fig. 3. A gene is bound by initiation and terminator sites.

values of a gene are called *alleles*. The synthesis of proteins from DNA occurs in two steps: transcription and translation. During *transcription*, the DNA of a gene is copied into RNA (see figure 2). Only one strand of the DNA in a chromosome is transcribed. A gene is bounded by its initiation and terminator sites as shown in figure 3. Initiation sites contain zero or more regulator regions and a promoter region. Regulator regions inhibit or allow the expression of a gene. The promoter regions are recognized by an enzyme called RNA polymerase as starting points for transcription. Transcription of the gene continues until the RNA polymerase encounters the terminator site. At this point, transciption ends and the RNA transcript and RNA polymerase are released from the DNA.

There are several types of RNA products. Three of these types — messenger RNA (mRNA), transfer RNA (tRNA), and ribosomal RNA (rRNA) — have specific functions in the translation step of protein synthesis. During *translation*, mRNA, tRNA, and ribosomes, which are made up of rRNA and proteins, work together to build a protein (see Figure 4). The mRNA contains the ordering of the amino acids, as copied from the DNA, for the protein to be created. This

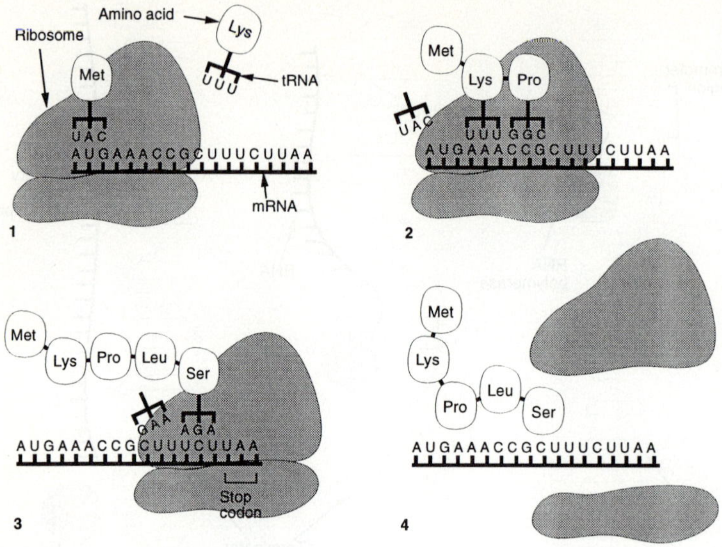

Fig. 4. During translation, three types of RNA work together with ribosomal proteins to build a protein from individual amino acids.

UUU UUC Phenylalanine UUA UUG Leucine	UCU UCC UCA UCG Serine	UAU UAC Tyrosine UAA UAG STOP	UGU UGC Cysteine UGA STOP UGG Tryptophan
CUU CUC CUA CUG Leucine	CCU CCC CCA CCG Proline	CAU CAC Histidine CAA CAG Glutamine	CGU CGC CGA CGG Arginine
AUU AUC Isoleucine AUA AUG Methionine	ACU ACC ACA ACG Threonine	AAU AAC Asparagine AAA AAG Lysine	SGU AGC Serine AGA AGG Arginine
GUU GUC GUA GUG Valine	GCU GCC GCA GCG Alanine	GAU GAC Aspartic acid GAA GAG Glutamic acid	GGU GGC GGA GGG Glycine

Fig. 5. The genetic code. Each codon represents one amino acid or termination sequence.

ordering is stored in the form of *codons*, triplets of nucleotides that represent either an amino acid or a termination signal. Since each codon is three nucleotides long and there are four possible nucleotides for each location, there are a total of $4^3 = 64$ different codons: 61 representing amino acids and three that terminate protein synthesis. Figure 5 shows the entire genetic code. The tRNA "reads" the mRNA three nucleotides at a time and retrieves the correct amino acid from the cytoplasm. The ribosome attaches to the mRNA and moves sequentially down the mRNA chain. As the tRNA retrieve amino acids in the correct order, the

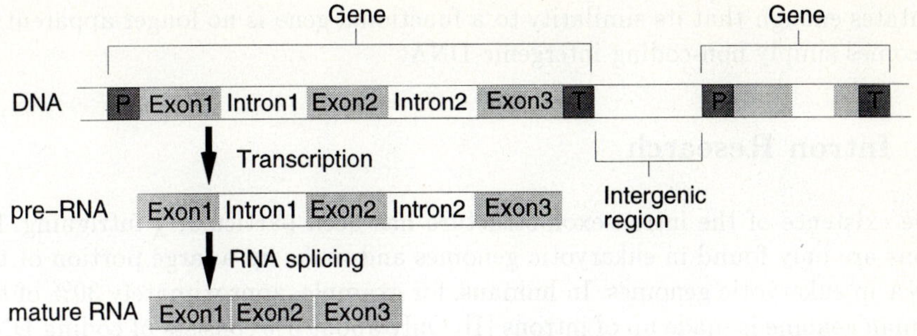

Fig. 6. Non-coding DNA: intragenic regions and introns.

ribosome attaches each new amino acid to the growing polypeptide chain. When the end of the mRNA chain is reached, the ribosome separates from the mRNA and releases a complete polypeptide chain. [4] [22] [35] [36].

3 Non-coding DNA

The term non-coding DNA refers to all DNA that is not involved in the coding of a mature RNA product. Though non-coding DNA is prevalent in biological systems, its origin and function are as yet uncertain. Because a great deal of extra energy is required to sustain and process non-coding DNA, it must not contribute negatively to the genetic process or it would most likely have been eliminated by natural selection long ago. There are three types of non-coding DNA: intergenic regions, intragenic regions, and pseudogenes [27] [22].

Though genes lie linearly along chromosomes, they are not necessarily contiguous. *Intergenic regions* are the regions of DNA in between genes. These regions are not transcribed into RNA. Some portions of intergenic regions are known to regulate the expression of adjacent genes; other portions have no known function. *Intragenic regions*, also called *introns*, are segments of DNA found within genes. Introns are transcribed into RNA along with the rest of the gene but must be removed from the RNA before the mature RNA product is complete. RNA that still contains the intron regions is often called *pre-RNA*. After the introns are spliced out of the pre-RNA, the remaining segments of RNA, the *exons* or *expressed regions*, are joined together to become the mature RNA product. Figure 6 shows an example of intergenic regions, introns, and exons.

The third type of non-coding DNA is the pseudogene. A *pseudogene* is a segment of DNA that is similar to a functional gene, but contains nucleotide changes that prevent its transcription or translation. Pseudogenes are believed to arise from gene duplication or reverse RNA transcription. Reverse RNA transcription refers to the transcription of RNA into DNA. Interestingly, pseudogenes produced from reverse transcription do not contain introns. Since pseudogenes are not expressed, they are not subject to selection pressure from the environment. As a result, pseudogenes accumulate mutations quickly. When a pseudogene mutates enough that its similarity to a functional gene is no longer apparent, it becomes simply non-coding intergenic DNA.

4 Intron Research

The existence of the intron-exon structure has been particularly intriguing. Introns are only found in eukaryotic genomes and make up a large portion of the DNA in eukaryotic genomes. In humans, for example, approximately 30% of the human genome is made up of introns [1]. Only about 3% consists of coding DNA and the rest of the genome consists of other non-coding DNA, repetitive sequences, and regulatory regions. The unusual placement of introns, interrupting the coding regions of genes, and the fact that extra energy is needed to maintain and process these structures that have no apparent function, have made introns an important topic of study since their discovery in the 1970's. Intron research has focused for the most part on three questions: (1) how are they removed from the RNA, (2) what do they do, and (3) what is their origin?

Of these three issues, the first one is probably the most well understood. Introns are removed from RNA by a process called *RNA splicing* which occurs in the nucleus of a cell [22] [31] [32]. There are many different methods of RNA splicing [22] [3] [7]. Most of the splicing processes require the aid of proteins. Proteins recognize specific sequences in the pre-RNA to catalyze the splicing process. The majority of introns in this group follow the GT-AG rule: the intron begins with the dinucleotide GT and ends with the dinucleotide AG. Certain genes also allow for *alternative splicing*, a situation where one gene codes for more than one RNA sequence depending on how many pre-RNA segments are spliced out. Other splicing processes such as that of fungal mitochondria introns involve self-splicing RNA [22] [11]. Though proteins assist in these self-splicing processes, all information necessary for the reaction resides in the intron sequence.

The second question — what do introns do? — continues to be studied. The *exon theory of genes* [2] suggested that exons are the building blocks of proteins, and genes are created from combinations of these building blocks. This theory lead to the *exon shuffling hypothesis* [9] [10] [12] [13] which states that introns increase the rate of recombination of exons and make it easier to move exons around and create new genes. Statistically, "...introns represent hot spots for recombination: by their mere presence and length they increase the rate of recombination, and hence the shuffling of exons, by factors of the order of 10^6 or 10^8 [12, pg. 901]." Evidence suggests that exons may correspond to both structural and functional subunits of proteins [2] [16] [18] including specific examples of the same exon existing in different genes where the same structure or function is required by two different proteins [10]. According to this theory then, the intron-exon structure of eukaryotic genes encourages the formation of new genes from structural and functional subunits of existing genes. This process would certainly be more efficient than building new genes one nucleotide at a time.

If introns are so useful for recombination, why are they found only in eukaryotes and not in prokaryotes? This difference raises the third question: what is the

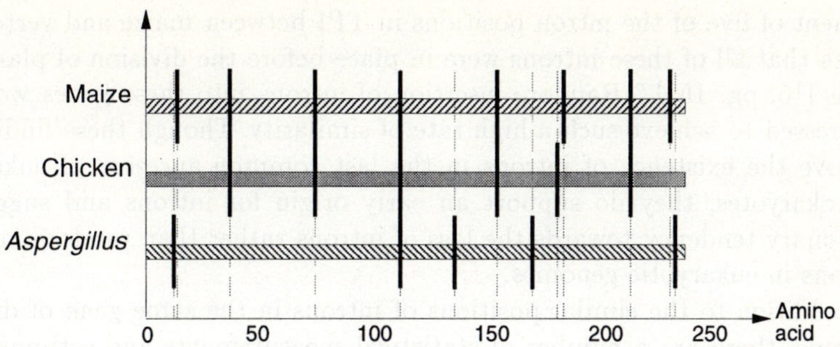

Fig. 7. A comparison of the introns locations in three different TPI genes. Each horizontal shaded bar represents the amino acid sequence created by one TPI gene. The bold vertical lines show the approximate locations of the introns in the RNA templates that coded for the amino acid sequences shown.

origin of introns? There are two main schools of thought. The "introns-early" theory asserts that the ancestral organisms of both eukaryotes and prokaryotes possessed introns and that prokaryotes lost introns in the evolutionary process. The "introns-late" theory asserts that ancestral organisms did not possess introns and that eukaryotes gained introns in the evolutionary process.

The introns-early theory suggests that the last common ancestor of prokaryotes and eukaryotes had introns in its genome [5] [6]. To accommodate their short reproductive and life cycles, prokaryotes subsequently lost the introns from their genomes due to selection for increased efficiency in gene expression and for a reduction in genome size. The price paid for this increased efficiency was a decreased potential for future evolution due to the loss of the introns' assistance in exon shuffling. Eukaryotes, on the other hand, continued to evolve with the assistance of introns and have been able to develop much more complex and diverse organisms. Accordingly, we currently find much less complexity and variation in prokaryotes than in eukaryotes.

Research on the gene for the protein triosephosphate isomerase (TPI) has pushed the known existence of the intron structure back before the divergence of plants and animals [25] [15] [14]. TPI is an extremely old protein whose gene sequence is relatively conserved across all organisms. Studies on the introns of this gene found five introns in *Aspergillis*, six introns in chickens and humans, and eight introns in maize. Five of the introns from the chicken and maize genes were found at identical locations in the corresponding genes; one intron occurred at similar locations on the two genes, differing by only three amino acid positions; and the maize gene had two additional introns. The similarity between *Aspergillis* and maize was less apparent, but still substantial. One intron was found at the same location in both genes. Two others were found at similar locations, and two introns in the *Aspergillis* gene occurred at completely novel locations compared to the chicken and maize genes. Figure 7 shows the approximate locations of the introns in the amino acid sequences of these three TPI genes. "The striking agreement of five of the intron positions in TPI between maize and vertebrates suggests that all of these introns were in place before the division of plants and animals [15, pg. 151]." Random insertion of introns into these genes would be hard pressed to achieve such a high rate of similarity. Though these findings do not prove the existence of introns in the last common ancestor of eukaryotes and prokaryotes, they do support an early origin for introns and suggest an evolutionary tendency towards the loss of introns rather than random insertion of introns in eukaryotic genomes.

In addition to the similar positions of introns in the same gene of different organisms, there are a number of statistical measurements and estimations of introns and exons that discourage the belief of random insertion of introns into genes. Among these measurements are the distribution of the lengths of introns and exons [22] [14] and the positions of introns with respect to the codons [24]. In addition, from known exon sizes and intron positions, it has been possible to predict the positions of introns that have been lost from one species but may still exist in another [14] [16].

The introns-late theory suggests that introns developed in the eukaryotic evolutionary process. [3] [33] [7]. Since prokaryotes have traditionally been considered more primitive than eukaryotes, the even-more-primitive genome of the common ancestor of prokaryotes and eukaryotes is often assumed to resemble the tightly organized prokaryotic genome. The introns-late theory contends that introns were inserted into eukaryotic genomes some time after the division of the prokaryotic and eukaryotic lines of evolution. Proponents of a late insertional origin of introns argue that the data supporting the exon theory of genes is intermittent and thus not solid enough to favor an early origin of introns [34]. There is a growing interest in the different classes of introns and the appearance and distribution of these classes in the genomes of organisms. A study of the different classes of introns showed that the relationship between the classes is related to the phylogenetic organization of the organisms in which they appear [3]. This suggests that introns arose and evolved in eukaryotic genomes. It has been speculated that introns could have arisen from gene duplication, transposable elements, or self insertion [22] [33].

5 Summary

EAs have successfully incorporated many ideas from biological systems into computational search algorithms, including that of non-coding material. This paper reviews the basics of genetics and surveys recent research on biological non-coding DNA. Though the function of introns is not completely understood and the benefits of non-coding segments are not yet certain, a number of parallels exist between biological hypotheses on introns and computational hypotheses on non-coding segments.

First of all, both introns and non-coding segments are thought to separate building blocks of what is being evolved. Introns (and intergenic regions) separate a segment of DNA into exons which are thought to code for functional or structural subunits of proteins. Building or modifying proteins from such subunits is expected to be easier and faster than building proteins one nucleotide at a time. The discovery and exchange of building blocks or partial solutions is one of the unique aspects of evolutionary search algorithms. According to the *building block hypothesis* [20] such algorithms are expected to search for multiple building blocks in parallel and recursively combine these building blocks to form a complete solution.

Secondly, both introns and non-coding segments are thought to increase the rate of recombination during evolution. Combined with the first point above, the extra material in a genome or individual is expected to increase the chance of crossover combining existing building blocks and decrease the chance of crossover destroying any useful material. Specifically, the exon shuffling hypothesis theorizes that introns increase the recombination rate of exons and assist in the creation of new genes from exon building blocks. The exact same argument may be made for the building blocks of an EA system.

Third, the ability to dynamically evolve the placement of introns and non-coding segments appears to be important. Biological organisms with the same gene have been found to have similar but not identical collections of introns. There is also the issue of why prokaryotes do not have introns. A number of computational systems have investigated the evolution of non-coding segments [17] [30] [38] allowing the EA to determine both the placement and arrangement of information on an individual.

Acknowledgements

This research was supported by NASA grant NGT-51057. The authors would like to thank John Holland for many interesting discussions relating to this work.

References

1. G. I. Bell and T. G. Marr, editors. *Computers and DNA*. Addison-Wesley, 1988.
2. C. C. F. Blake. Do genes-in-pieces imply proteins-in-pieces? *Nature*, 273:267, 1978.
3. T. Cavalier-Smith. Intron phylogeny: a new hypothesis. *Trends in Genetics*, 7(5):145–148, May 1991.
4. H. Curtis. *Biology*. Worth Publishers, 1983.
5. W. F. Doolittle. Genes in pieces: were they ever together? *Nature*, 272:581, 1978.
6. W. F. Doolittle. What introns have to tell us: Hierarchy in genome evolution. *Cold Spring Harbor Symposia on Quantitative Biology*, 52:907–913, 1987.
7. A. Flavell. Introns continue to amaze. *Nature*, 316:574–575, August 1985.
8. S. Forrest and M. Mitchell. Relative building-block fitness and the building-block hypothesis. In *FOGA*, 1992.
9. W. Gilbert. Why genes in pieces? *Nature*, 271:501, February 1978.
10. W. Gilbert. Genes-in-pieces revisited. *Science*, 228:823–824, May 1985.
11. W. Gilbert. The RNA world. *Nature*, 319:618, February 1986.
12. W. Gilbert. The exon theory of genes. *Cold Spring Harbor Symposia on Quantitative Biology*, 52:901–905, 1987.

13. W. Gilbert. Gene structure and evolutionary theory. In *New perspectives on evolution*, pages 155–163. Wiley-Liss, 1991.
14. W. Gilbert and M. Glynias. On the ancient nature of introns. *Gene*, 135, 1993.
15. W. Gilbert, M. Marchionni, and G. McKnight. On the antiquity of introns. *Cell*, 46:151–153, July 1986.
16. M. Go. Correlation of DNA exonic regions with protein structural units in haemoglobin. *Nature*, 291:90–92, May 1981.
17. D. E. Goldberg, B. Korb, and K. Deb. Messy genetic algorithms: Motivation, analysis, and first results. *Complex Systems*, 3:493–530, 1989.
18. D. L. Hartl. New perspectives on the molecular evolution of genes and genomes. In *New perspectives on evolution*, pages 123–137. Wiley-Liss, 1991.
19. T. Haynes. Duplication of coding segments in genetic programming. In *13th AAAI*, 1996.
20. J. H. Holland. *Adaptation in Natural and Artificial Systems.* University of Michigan Press, 1975.
21. J. R. Levenick. Inserting introns improves genetic algorithm success rate: Taking a cue from biology. In *ICGA-4*, pages 123–127, 1991.
22. B. Lewin. *Genes 5.* John Wiley & Sons, 1994.
23. R. K. Lindsay and A. S. Wu. Testing the robustness of the genetic algorithm on the floating building block representation. In *13th AAAI*, 1996.
24. M. Long, C. Rosenberg, and W. Gilbert. Intron phase correlations and the evolution of the intron/exon structure of genes, 1995. Under review.
25. M. Marchionni and W. Gilbert. The triosephosphate isomerase gene from maize: introns antedate the plant-animal divergence. *Cell*, 46:133–141, July 1986.
26. N. F. McPhee and J. D. Miller. Accurate replication in genetic programming. In *ICGA-6*, 1995.
27. M. Nei. *Molecular Evolutionary Genetics.* Columbia University Press, 1987.
28. P. Nordin and W. Banzhaf. Complexity compression and evolution. In *ICGA-6*, 1995.
29. P. Nordin and W. Banzhaf. Evolving turing-complete programs for a register machine with self modifying code. In *ICGA-6*, 1995.
30. P. Nordin, F. Francone, and W. Banzhaf. Explicitly defined introns and destructive crossover in genetic programming. Workshop on GP, ML, 1995.
31. B. Patrusky. The intron story. *MOSAIC*, 23(3):22–33, Fall 1992.
32. M. Robertson. The post-RNA world. *Nature*, 335:16–18, September 1988.
33. J. H. Rogers. How were introns inserted into nuclear genes? *Trends in Genetics*, 5(7):213–216, July 1989.
34. A. Stoltzfus, D. F. Spencer, M. Zuker, J. M. Logsdon, Jr., and W. F. Doolittle. Testing the exon theory of genes: the evidence from protein structure. *Science*, 265:202–207, July 1994.
35. R. A. Wallace, G. Sanders, and R. Ferl. *Biology: The Science of Life.* Harper College, 3rd edition, 1991.
36. J. D. Watson. *Molecular Biology of the Gene.* W. A. Benjamin, 2nd edition, 1970.
37. A. S. Wu. *Non-coding DNA and floating building blocks for the genetic algorithm.* PhD thesis, University of Michigan, 1995.
38. A. S. Wu and R. K. Lindsay. A comparison of the fixed and floating building block representation in the genetic algorithm, 1995. Submitted to *Evol. Comp.*
39. A. S. Wu and R. K. Lindsay. Empirical studies of the genetic algorithm with non-coding segments. *Evolutionary Computation*, 3(2), 1995.

Theoretical Foundations of Evolutionary Computation

Analytical and Numerical Investigations of Evolutionary Algorithms in Continuous Spaces

T. Asselmeyer, W. Ebeling and H. Rosé

Institut of Physics, Humboldt University Berlin
Invalidenstr. 110
D - 10115 Berlin
Germany

Abstract. We investigate the biologically motivated selfreproduction strategies by numerical and analytical calculations. In the analytical part we show that each of these strategies can be reduced to an eigenvalue problem of Sturm-Liouville-type. The properties of the landscape and the dynamics of the optimization are encoded in the spectrum of the Hamiltonian, which is different in both cases. We discuss some model cases with exact solutions and compare them with simulations.

1 Introduction

The optimization problem appears in several fields of physics and mathematics. It is known from mathematics that every local minimum of a convex function defined over a convex set is also the global minimum of the function. But the main problem is to find this optimum. From the physical point of view, every dynamical process can be considered in terms of finding the optimum of the action functional. The best example is the trajectory of the free point mass in mechanics which follows the shortest way between two points.

Let us assume one has successfully set up a mathematical model for the optimization problem under consideration in the form

$$F(x_1, x_2, \ldots, x_d) \longrightarrow \text{Min} \tag{1}$$

where F is a scalar potential function (fitness function) defined over a d-dimensional vector space $X = \text{Lin}\{x_1, \ldots, x_d\}$. Let $x^{(0)}$ be the absolute minimum of F which is the search target. Problems of this type are called parameter optimization. Typically the search space is high-dimensional ($d \gg 1$).

Next we follow the idea to consider an ensemble of searchers which move through the search space. We will be concerned with the time evolution of an ensemble of searchers defined by a density $P(\vec{x}, t)$. The search process defines a dynamics

$$P(\vec{x}, t + \Delta t) = \mathbf{T}[P(\vec{x}, t); \Delta t] \tag{2}$$

with continuous or discrete time steps. A dynamics $\mathbf{T}$ is considered as an optimization dynamics, if any (or nearly any) initial density $P(\vec{x}, 0)$ converges to a target density $\lim\limits_{\tau \to \infty} P(\vec{x}, \tau)$ which is concentrated around the minimum $x^{(0)}$ of

$F(\vec{x})$. Next we restrict to the case of second order partial differential equation as dynamics **T**. Among the most successful strategies are the class of thermodynamic oriented [1, 2, 3] and the class of biological oriented strategies [4, 5, 6]). Our aim is to compare on the basis of a PDE-model biologically motivated strategies with different methods of simulations.

2 Biological strategy

In the following we will deal with a simple model known as Fisher-Eigen model. To illustrate this model we switch to the chemical reaction picture. A searcher with fixed fitness can be seen as a species A and another searcher with a different fitness is species C. So the process of mutation is the reaction $A \to C$ and is described by a diffusion term. Then the reproduction process is given by $A \xrightarrow{F} 2A$ with the fitness F of A as transition rate. The simplest model with a similar behaviour was introduced by Fisher [7] and Eigen [8] known as the Fisher-Eigen equation defined by

$$\frac{\partial}{\partial t}P(\vec{x},t) = [F(\vec{x}) - \langle F\rangle]P(\vec{x},t) + D\Delta P(\vec{x},t) \tag{3}$$

$$\langle F\rangle(t) = \frac{\int F(x)P(\vec{x},t)dx}{\int P(\vec{x},t)dx} \quad .$$

By using the ansatz

$$P(\vec{x},t) = \exp\left[-\int_0^t \langle F\rangle(t')dt'\right] y(\vec{x},t) \tag{4}$$

one obtains

$$\frac{\partial}{\partial t}y(\vec{x},t) = -Hy(\vec{x},t) = (D\Delta + F(\vec{x}))y(\vec{x},t) \tag{5}$$

and the separation of time and space variables reduces the dynamic to the Sturm-Liouville type eigenvalue equation

$$-\epsilon_i\psi_i(\vec{x}) = D\Delta\psi_i(\vec{x}) + F(\vec{x})\psi_i(\vec{x}) \tag{6}$$

where ϵ_i are the eigenvalues and $\psi_i(\vec{x})$ are the eigenfunctions. This leads to the complete solution

$$y(\vec{x},t) = \sum_i a_i e^{-\epsilon_i t}\psi_i(\vec{x}) \quad . \tag{7}$$

For the quadratic fitness

$$F(x) = F_{max} - \frac{1}{2}\sum_{i=1}^{d} a_i(\vec{x}_i - \vec{x}_i^{(0)})^2 \quad . \tag{8}$$

the problem is exactly solvable for any dimension d and the solution is very similar to the thermodynamical strategy for $a_i > 0$. In the other case $a_i < 0$ we obtain a different problem known from scattering theory. If the search space is unbounded the spectrum of the operator H is continuous. But we are interested in positive values of the fitness function (8). This leads to the restriction to a compact search space given by the interval $[-b, b]$ in each direction with $b = \sqrt{2F_{max}/|a_i|}$. Now we have to introduce boundary conditions. The most natural choice is to let the solution vanish on the boundary. As a result an additional restriction appears and the spectrum of the operator H is now discrete.

Most important for the decision, which algorithm is faster than an other algorithm, is the calculation of the velocity. Here we define only one velocity $v^{(1)}$ on the fitness landscape. The measure of the velocity is given by the time-like change of the expectation values of the fitness $F(\vec{x})$. With respect to the Fisher-Eigen equation (3) one obtains

$$v^{(1)} = \frac{d}{dt}\langle F\rangle = \langle F^2\rangle - \langle F\rangle^2 + D\langle\Delta F\rangle \quad . \tag{9}$$

We are interested in the condition of positive velocity $v^{(1)}$. A sufficient condition for that is

$$\left(\frac{F}{\langle F\rangle}\right)^2 > 1 - \frac{D}{\langle F\rangle}\Delta\left(\frac{F}{\langle F\rangle}\right) \tag{10}$$

For the case of a quadratic fitness the velocity can be calculated from the solution. In the case of $a_i > 0$ and with the initial distribution $P(x,0) = \delta(x - x_0)$ one can calculate the velocity to get

$$v^{(1)} = \sum_{i=1}^{d} \sqrt{Da_i}\, \frac{\sqrt{2}a_i\,(x_0)_i^2 \sinh(t\sqrt{2Da_i}) - \sqrt{a_i D}\cosh(t\sqrt{2Da_i})}{\cosh^3(t\sqrt{2Da_i})} \quad , \tag{11}$$

and for the expectation value of the fitness (8) one obtains

$$\langle F\rangle(t) = F_{max} - \sum_{i=1}^{d}\left(\frac{1}{2}\sqrt{2a_i D}\tanh(t\sqrt{2a_i D}) - \frac{a_i(x_0)_i^2}{2\cosh^2(t\sqrt{2a_i D})}\right) \quad . \tag{12}$$

The comparison with the numerical results will be discussed below. On the basis of this velocity one can compare the biological strategy with the thermodynamical strategy also known as annealing as done in [9].

3 Simulation and Comparison

In this section we try to simulate the Fisher-Eigen equation (3) with an stochastic algorithm to compare the theoretical method with an algorithm accessible for optimization. Furthermore we discuss the mutation/selection ratio in detail.

Similar to the discussion in the beginning of section 2 we introduce species x_i and x_j with fitnesses $F(x_i)$ and $F(x_j)$, respectively. To realize the reproduction and selection processes we consider the following transitions $(x_i, x_j) \rightarrow (x_i, x_i)$ if $F(x_i) > F(x_j)$ and $(x_i, x_j) \rightarrow (x_j, x_j)$ if $F(x_i) < F(x_j)$ with the obvious property of population size conservation. The solution of equation (3) is a distribution of searchers over the continuous search space. To compare the algorithm and the partial differential equation (PDE) (3) one has to introduce the time evolution of the density $P(x_i)$ of the species x_i with respect to the transitions known as master equation. In the following we consider only reactions of a pair of species used in the computer algorithm later on. To establish the master equation one has to divide the transitions into parts, i.e. in loss W^- and gain W^+. We express the transition rates W^- and W^+ by $W^+(x, \acute{x}; y) := W((\acute{x}, y) \to (x, y))$ and $W^-(\acute{x}, x; y) := W((x, y) \to (\acute{x}, y))$ leading to the master equation for the two species x_i and x_j

$$\frac{\partial}{\partial t} P(x_i, x_j, t) = \int [W^+(x_i, \acute{x}_i; x_j)\, P(\acute{x}_i, x_j) - W^-(\acute{x}_i, x_i; x_j)\, P(x_i, x_j)]\, d\acute{x}_i$$
$$+ \int [W^+(x_j, \acute{x}_j; x_i)\, P(x_i, \acute{x}_j) - W^-(\acute{x}_j, x_j; x_i)\, P(x_i, x_j)]\, d\acute{x}_j \quad (13)$$

This two-particle picture of the selection and reproduction processes was developed by Schimansky-Geier [10] and we thank for many discussions to clarify the questions. The problem is now to determine the transition rates with respect to the processes "reproduction" and "selection". To this end we introduce intermediate steps denoted by $\acute{x}$. By integration over these steps we get back the correct processes. As abbreviation we use $\Delta F(x_i)$ instead of $F(x_i) - \langle F \rangle$ with the expectation value or mean fitness $\langle F \rangle$. For the gain rate one obtains

$$W^+(x_i, \acute{x}_i; x_j) = k(\Delta F(x_i)\Theta(\Delta F(x_i)) + |\Delta F(\acute{x}_i)|\Theta(-\Delta F(x_i)))\delta(x_i - x_j) \quad (14)$$
$$W^+(x_j, \acute{x}_j; x_i) = k(\Delta F(x_j)\Theta(\Delta F(x_j)) + |\Delta F(\acute{x}_j)|\Theta(-\Delta F(x_j)))\delta(x_i - x_j)$$

whereas the loss is given by

$$W^-(\acute{x}_i, x_i; x_j) = k(\Delta F(\acute{x}_i)\Theta(\Delta F(\acute{x}_i)) + |\Delta F(x_j)|\Theta(-\Delta F(x_j)))\delta(\acute{x}_i - x_j) \quad (15)$$
$$W^-(\acute{x}_j, x_j; x_i) = k(\Delta F(\acute{x}_j)\Theta(\Delta F(\acute{x}_j)) + |\Delta F(x_i)|\Theta(-\Delta F(x_i)))\delta(\acute{x}_j - x_i) \quad .$$

With the gain (14), loss (15), and the one-particle distribution $P(x) = \int P(x, y) dy$ one obtains a Masterequation. Then we integrate the master equation with respect to the variable x_j to get the one-particle distribution. Without fluctuation the two-particle distribution factorizes $P(x_i, x_j) = P(x_i)\, P(x_j)$ and the mean fitness is given by $\langle F \rangle = \int F(x)\, P(x)\, dx$. After these calculations the Masterequation reduces to the Fisher-Eigen equation

$$\frac{\partial}{\partial t} P(x_i, t) = k\, \Delta F(x_i)\, P(x_i) = k\, (F(x_i) - \langle F \rangle)\, P(x_i)\,. \quad (16)$$

So we obtain the reproduction and selection schema of our evolutionary algorithm, but without mutation. To get the mutation process leading to the Laplacian term in the equation (3) one has to add a symmetric transition rate W_D with

$$W_D(x_i, x_j) = W_D(x_j, x_i) = W_D(x_j; r) \qquad r = x_i - x_j$$

to the loss and gain terms given above. To visualize the equation we consider only this rate to get the following Masterequation ([11] p.214):

$$\frac{\partial}{\partial t} P(x_i, t) = \int W_D(x_i - r; r) P(x_i - r, t) dr - P(x_i, t) \int W_D(x_i; -r) dr \quad . \tag{17}$$

If we following the argumentation in[11] then one obtains

$$\frac{\partial}{\partial t} P(x_i, t) = \frac{1}{2} \int r^2 \frac{\partial^2}{\partial x_i^2} (W_D(x_i; r) P(x_i, t)) dr \quad . \tag{18}$$

where the term with the first derivative is neglected by the symmetry of W_D. If we set

$$2D = \int r^2 W_D(x_i; r) dr = \text{const.}$$

then the diffusion equation is obtained. So with respect to the assumption of sufficiently small steps r we unify the mutation and the reaction processes (reproduction and selection) in one equation. But we note the important difference between mutation and the other processes given by the small steps r leading to a different realization in the algorithm. Furthermore we remark that the diagonal term $W(x, x)$ of the rates can be chosen arbitrarily.

The simulation of the Masterequaton is a well known problem in the theory of stochastic processes. We use the waiting time distribution of (13) to realize a stable and effective algorithm of the evolutionary process [12]. The main idea of the algorithm is very simple. The dynamics of the process can be split in two parts. At first: The population remains a certain time - the waiting time τ - at the current state. And second: After this time the population is changed into a new state. Knowing the distribution of the random time interval τ one has to simulate the changes of the system only. Indeed, this is exactly the method of the evolutionary algorithms to execute the evolutionary process. But the common simulation scheme of evolutionary algorithms pays no attention to the time scale of the process, resulting in the inability to compare the dynamical behaviour of the evolutionary algorithm with analytical results of the Fisher-Eigen equation.

In fact, it is easy to extend the common simulation scheme to an algorithm respecting the real time scale of the evolutionary process. Solving the *first passage time* problem of (13) with initial and boundary condition

$$P(x, 0) = \delta_{x\acute{x}}, \; P(x, t) = 0 \; : \; x \neq \acute{x} \, , \tag{19}$$

we get the waiting time distribution [13, 14, 15, 12]

$$\begin{aligned} p(\tau) &= \frac{\partial}{\partial \tau} (1 - P(x, \tau)) \\ &= \frac{1}{\langle \tau \rangle} \exp\left(-\frac{\tau}{\langle \tau \rangle} \right) . \end{aligned} \tag{20}$$

The waiting time between two changes is exponential distributed and $\langle \tau \rangle$ is the mean waiting time.

The mutation term of the Fisher-Eigen equation describes a diffusion process. To simulate such a process we have to guarantee that one mutation step Δx is small in comparison with the size of $P(x,t) > 0$. The mean value of a diffusion step is $\langle x \rangle = \sqrt{2\,D\,\Delta t}$; thus we must choose the time scale $\Delta t < \Delta t_{max}$ of the mutation step in such a manner that Δx is sufficiently small. Diffusion is a continuous process whereas selection is discrete. Thus we execute every step a mutation and the selection with the rate $F(x) - \langle F \rangle$. To guarantee that the diffusion step Δx is small we set the mean waiting time between two steps $\langle \tau \rangle < \Delta t_{max}$. The stochastic dynamics of diffusion is given by Gaussian mutation

$$x(t') = x(t) + \sqrt{2\,D\,(t-t')}\,\xi\,, \tag{21}$$

with the normal distributed random accession ξ. The selection process can be modelled by a birth-death process. A randomly chosen individual x_i dies if the rate $W_s = F(x) - \langle F \rangle$ is negative and will be reduplicated if W_s is positive. To keep the population size N constant an other randomly chosen opponent x_j must be reduplicated or die. This process can be considered as tournament selection with the rate $|W_s|$.

The selection step will be executed if a uniform random number is

$$z < W_s,\; z \in (0, \frac{1}{\langle \tau \rangle}),$$

with a mean waiting time $\langle \tau \rangle$ fulfilling

$$\langle \tau \rangle < min(\frac{1}{max(W_s)}, \Delta t_{max}).$$

The choice of $max(W_s)$ instead of W_s synchronizes both time scales $1/max(W_s)$ and Δt_{max}. In the Masterequation such choice is equivalent to the introduction of diagonal terms in the rates which leave the Masterequation unchanged. Let us summarize one generation of the algorithm by the following scheme with uniform random numbers z, the exponentially distributed number τ and the normally distributed number ξ:

for N steps:
  $t' = t + \frac{\langle \tau \rangle}{N}\,\tau$
    $i = z_1 \in \{1, ..., N\}$
    $x(t') = x(t) + \sqrt{2\,D\,(t-t')}\,\xi$
    $z_2 \in \left(0, \frac{1}{\langle \tau \rangle}\right)$
    if $z_2 < W_s = |F(x_i) - \langle F \rangle|$
      $j = z_3 \in \{1, ..., i-1, i+1, ..., N\}$
      $x_j = x_i \;:\; W_s > 0$
      $x_i = x_j \;:\; W_s < 0.$

The selection process in the algorithm was developed by Fricke [16] in his PhD-thesis and we thank for the explanation of the algorithm.

We compare the dynamics of this algorithm with the analytical solution of the Fisher-Eigen equation (3) for two different fitness functions: the parabola $f(x) = 100 - x^2$ and the double hill $f(x) = 0.84 - 0.0278\,x^2\,(0.16667\,x - 0.9)\,(0.16667\,x + 0.8)$. Fig. 1 shows the time evolution of the probability distribution of the population. The exact solution of the Fisher-Eigen equation (PDE) is drawn by the solid line. The circles, diamonds and squares represent the density of the population ($N = 10000$) at different times. Without any doubt, the evolutionary algorithm realizes nearly exactly the dynamics of the Fisher-Eigen equation. Also, Fig. 2 emphasizes this fact for the time dependence of the mean fitness of the population. For small population size ($N < 1000$) the stochastic fluctuations are still visible and go to zero for larger populations. The Fisher-Eigen equation describes the dynamics of the population without taking into account fluctuations, but we can see already that a population of $N = 10$ individuals shows a quite similar behaviour like the Fisher-Eigen equation in the case of a parabolic fitness function. For the multimodal fitness landscape

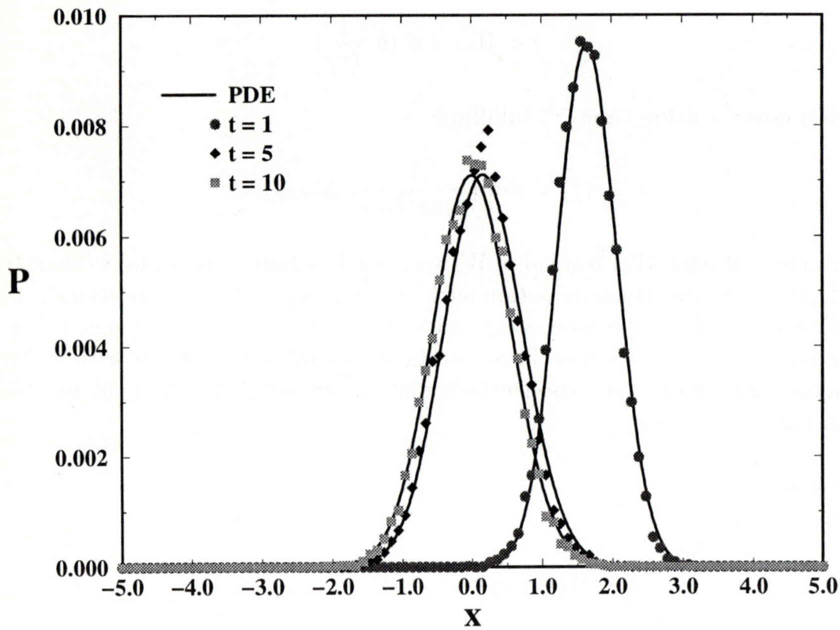

Fig. 1. Time evolution of distribution, parabola.

of the double hill we found also a good agreement between the solution of the

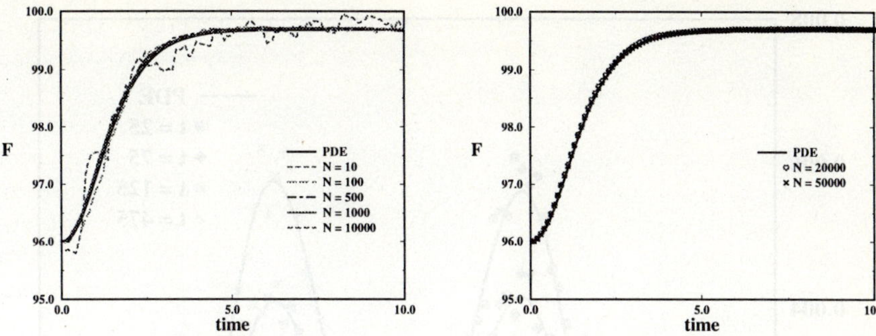

Fig. 2. Time evolution of mean fitness, parabola.

Fisher-Eigen equation (PDE) [1] and simulation of $N = 10000$ individuals, Fig. 3. The mean fitness, Fig. 4, shows slightly more fluctuations, but the main feature of PDE and evolutionary algorithm are still the same. The parabola and double hill represent the main features of a general fitness landscape: the existence of local optima and the transition between two optima. For both cases we could find a good agreement between the dynamics of the Fisher-Eigen equation and its stochastic realization - the evolutionary algorithm. Within the range of this agreement we can say: That the analytical results found for the Fisher-Eigen equation remains still valid for the evolutionary algorithm and in this sense the Fisher-Eigen equation become an important tool for the analytical investigation of evolutionary algorithms.

4 Conclusion

In this paper we investigated an evolutionary algorithm by analytical and numerical calculations. For the analytical model we chose a non-linear partial differential equation (3) of parabolic type to describe the "reproduction", "selection" and "mutation" process as a dynamical process of the distribution of the searcher. For the problem (8) of the parabola the PDE can be solved exactly to calculate the velocity of the algorithm as the time derivative of the mean fitness $\langle F \rangle$. With the help of the stochastic simulation of the PDE (3) we developed such stochastic algorithm to simulate the PDE and compare the numerical results with the analytical one. This comparison shows a very good agreement between the stochastic algorithm and the integration of the PDE (3).

[1] The exact solution was found by numerical integration of the PDE.

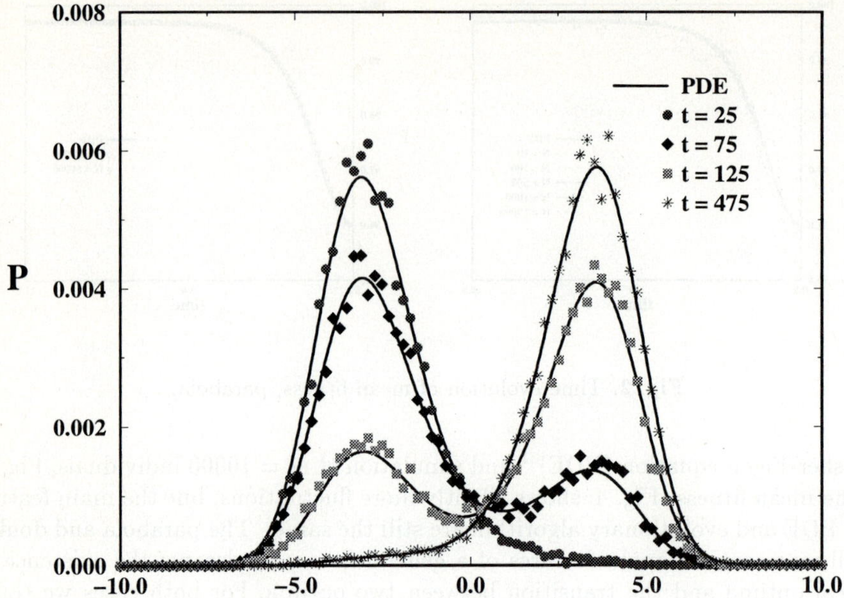

Fig. 3. Time evolution of distribution, double hill.

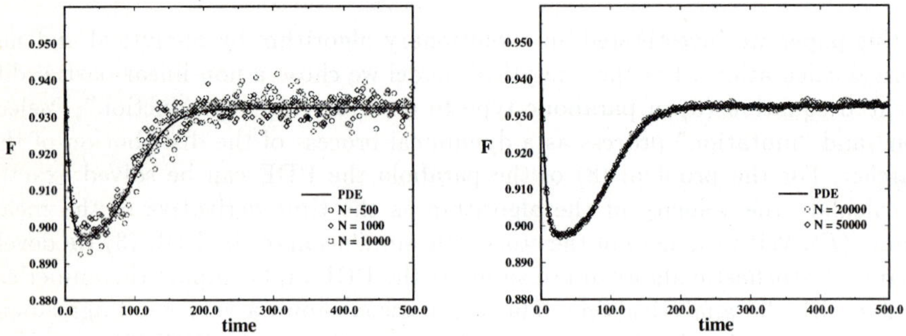

Fig. 4. Time evolution of mean fitness, double hill.

5 Acknowledgement

This work is supported by the BMBF in the frame of the project EVOALG. We thank Prof. L. Schimansky-Geier and Dr. T. Fricke for useful discussions.

References

1. J.D. Nulton and P. Salamon. Statistical mechanics of combinatorical optimization. *Phys. Rev.*, **A 37**:1351, 1988.
2. B. Andresen. Finite-time thermodynamics and simulated annealing. In *Proceedings of the Fourth International Conference on Irreversible Processes and Selforganization*, Rostock, 1989.
3. P. Sibiani, K.M. Pedersen, K.H. Hoffmann, and P. Salamon. Monte carlo dynamics of optimization: A scaling description. *Phys. Rev.*, **A 42**:7080, 1990.
4. H.P. Schwefel. *Evolution and optimum seeking.* Wiley, New York, 1995.
5. I. Rechenberg. *Evolutionsstrategien - Optimierung technischer Systeme nach Principien der biologischen Information.* Friedrich Frommann Verlag (Günther Holzboog K.G.), Stuttgart - Bad Cannstatt, 1995.
6. R. Feistel and W. Ebeling. *Evolution of Complex Systems.* Kluwer Academic Publ., Dordrecht, 1989.
7. R.A. Fisher. *The Genetical Theory of Natural Selection.* Oxford University Press, Oxford, 1930.
8. M. Eigen. The selforganization of matter and the evolution of biological macromolecules. *Naturwiss.*, **58**:465, 1971.
9. T. Asselmeyer and W. Ebeling. Unified description of evolutionary strategies over continous parameter spaces. *submitted to BioSystems*, 1996.
10. L. Schimansky-Geier. Beschreibung evolutionärer Algorithmen durch 2-Teilchenreaktionen. private communication, 1996.
11. N.G. van Kampen. *Stochastic processe in physics and chemistry.* North-Holland Publishing Company, Amsterdam-New York-Oxford, 1981.
12. R.L. Stratonovich. *Topics in the theory of random noise*, volume 1. Gordon & Breach, New York, 1963.
13. D.T. Gillespie. A general method for numerically simulating the stochastic time evolution of coupled chem. reactions. *J. Comp. Phys.*, **22**:403–434, 1976.
14. R. Feistel. Betrachtung der Realsierung stochastischer Prozesse aus automatentheoretischer Sicht. *Wiss. Z. W. Pieck Univ. Rostock*, **26**:663, 1977.
15. D.T. Gillespie. Monte carlo simulation of random walks with residence time dependent transition probability rates. *J. of Comp. Phys.*, **28**:435–450, 1978.
16. T. Fricke. *Neue Algorithmen zur Simulation von Zufallsprozessen.* PhD thesis, University AAchen, 1994.

On the Asymptotic Behavior of Multirecombinant Evolution Strategies

Hans-Georg Beyer*

University of Dortmund, Department of Computer Science,
Systems Analysis Research Group,
D-44221 Dortmund, Germany

Abstract. The performance of $(\mu/\mu, \lambda)$-ESs (Evolution Strategies) in the asymptotic limit for $N \to \infty$ and $\lambda \to \infty$ is investigated. The conjecture made by Schwefel that the maximum performance of such strategies scales like $\mu \ln(\lambda/\mu)$ will be proved. Furthermore, it will be shown that an optimally tuned $(\mu/\mu, \lambda)$-ES performs exactly λ times faster than an optimally tuned $(1+1)$-ES, if the hyper-sphere is taken as the fitness model (using the number of generations as the performance measure). The notion of fitness efficiency will be introduced and will be used to derive the ES time complexity. The results are compared to the non-recombinant (μ, λ)-ES.

1 Introduction

The performance of Evolution Strategies (ES) can be investigated by experiments and by theoretical analysis. Both approaches have their advantages and disadvantages. Usually it is much easier to perform ES runs and present the results by graphs. This method can be applied to each fitness function $F(\mathbf{x})$. However, there remains always an uncertainty as to the significance of such results with respect to its generality. The question is what can we learn from those very special ES results as to the ES performance in general? For example, what would we expect if the size N (dimension of the parameter vector $\mathbf{x}$ to be optimized) of the optimization problem is increased?

Indeed, it is really difficult to estimate the computational complexity of the ES algorithms by experiments. The same holds for the influence of the strategy parameters like the mutation strength σ, the number of parents μ and offspring λ used, etc. Even for the simplest fitness functions, as e. g. the inclined hyperplane or the sphere model, the ES time complexity G (for the definition, see Sec. 3 below) becomes a multidimensional function of these exogenous parameters (N, μ, $\lambda, \ldots$). Deriving (better: estimating) this function from empirical data and by ES simulations is almost excluded if there is not any clue from the theory. Actually, *the theory determines what we will measure* (after Einstein).

The second approach to the ES performance analysis is by theory. Such analysis is necessarily restricted to simple fitness models and special ES variants.

* e-mail: beyer@LS11.informatik.uni-dortmund.de

However, one hopes that the results obtained can be applied as approximations to real world fitness functions. That is, if one derives results from the sphere model, for example, one expects that "similar" fitness landscapes exhibit a similar behavior. Thus, the result of the sphere model analysis can be extended to more complicated fitness functions. The predictions made from such extensions should be the starting point for ES experiments (and not the other way around). From this point of view ES experiments should serve first of all as *tests* to verify the approximations made and to investigate the application limits of the model(s) used.

This paper deals mainly with the asymptotic performance behavior of multirecombinant $(\mu/\mu, \lambda)$-ESs, i. e., with the question how the ES does work for $N \to \infty$, $\lambda \to \infty$, and $\mu \to \infty$. It is the goal to derive formulae that describe the ES performance in a rather simple fashion than the more accurate results provided in [3]. Note, this is a good example for which the experimental approach is almost excluded.

The paper is divided in two parts dealing with the microscopic and the macroscopic aspects, respectively, of the ES performance. The microscopic aspect of the ES performance can be measured by the progress rate φ. In the first part we will investigate the asymptotic behavior of the *normalized* progress rate $\varphi^\star$ on the sphere model. This comprises the analysis of the progress rate formula for $N \to \infty$ and the investigation of the *progress coefficients* $c_{\mu/\mu,\lambda}$ for $\lambda \to \infty$. This result will be used to prove Schwefel's $\varphi^* \approx \mu \ln(\lambda/\mu)$-conjecture [10]. Furthermore, the *fitness efficiency* η will be introduced and it will be shown that in the asymptotic limit the $(\mu/\mu, \lambda)$-ES performs exactly λ-times faster than the simple $(1+1)$-ES.

The shorter second part is devoted to the ES dynamics and the (local) ES time complexity, again for the asymptotic case.

It is assumed that the reader is familiar with the recent results of the ES theory. Because of the page limitation, the readers are to refer to the article of Beyer [3] where the $(\mu/\mu, \lambda)$-algorithms are defined, the basic theory is developed, and the benefit of recombination is explained by the *genetic repair principle.* Here, we can give only a very rough overview, aiming first of all as a reminder.

The $(\mu/\mu, \lambda)$-ES. The mutations used are in accordance with those from [3]. The mutation strength is denoted by σ, the progress rate by φ. The normalizations $\varphi^\star := \varphi\ N/R$ and $\sigma^\star := \sigma\ N/R$ use N as the dimension of the object parameter vector $\mathbf{x}$ to be optimized (with respect to a fitness function $F(\mathbf{x})$) and R is the distance of the *center of mass parent* to the center of the spherical model at generation (g).

There are two variants of "μ/μ"-recombination which have been investigated by theoretical analysis: the *intermediate* version, denoted by $(\mu/\mu_I, \lambda)$, and the *dominant* version, often called *global discrete recombination* [9], denoted by $(\mu/\mu_D, \lambda)$.

In $(\mu/\mu_I, \lambda)$-strategies the λ offspring $\mathbf{y}_l$ are generated from the μ parents $\mathbf{x}_m$ by mutation of the center of mass parent $\langle\mathbf{x}\rangle_\mu := \frac{1}{\mu}\sum_{m=1}^{\mu} \mathbf{x}_m$, i. e. $\mathbf{y}_l := \langle\mathbf{x}\rangle_\mu + \mathbf{z}$, where $\mathbf{z}$ is a random vector with N iid normal variates $z_i = \mathcal{N}(0, \sigma^2)$.

The dominant recombination $(\mu/\mu_D, \lambda)$ produces each vector component $(\mathbf{y}_l)_i$ of the offspring $\mathbf{y}_l$ by randomly choosing *one* of the ith components from the μ parents $\mathbf{x}_m$ and subsequent addition of a $\mathcal{N}(0, \sigma^2)$ normally distributed random number. As in the $(\mu/\mu_I, \lambda)$ case as well as for (μ, λ)-strategies the new parents are produced by (μ, λ)-selection, sometimes called *truncation selection*, i. e. the μ best offspring are chosen.

2 The Asymptotic Progress Law of the $(\mu/\mu, \lambda)$-ES

2.1 The Limit $N \to \infty$ Progress Rate Formulae

The progress rate φ measures - roughly speaking - the expected distance change (in the parameter space) of the parent's center of mass from generation (g) to $(g+1)$. For the $(\mu/\mu_I, \lambda)$-ES on the hyper-sphere one finds [3, p. 90] the normalized progress rate

$$\varphi^{\star}_{\mu/\mu_I,\lambda}(\sigma^{\star}) = N\left(1 - \sqrt{1 + \frac{\sigma^{\star 2}}{\mu N}}\right) + \sigma^{\star}\, c_{\mu/\mu,\lambda}\, \frac{1 + \frac{\sigma^{\star 2}}{2\mu N}}{\sqrt{1 + \frac{\sigma^{\star 2}}{2N}}\,\sqrt{1 + \frac{\sigma^{\star 2}}{\mu N}}} + \ldots \quad (1)$$

and for the $(\mu/\mu_D, \lambda)$ dominant case [3, p. 101]

$$\varphi^{\star}_{\mu/\mu_D,\lambda} = N\left(1 - \sqrt{1 + \frac{\sigma^{\star 2}}{N}}\right) + \frac{\sqrt{\mu}\, c_{\mu/\mu,\lambda}\, \sigma^{\star}}{\sqrt{1 + \frac{\sigma^{\star 2}}{N}}} + \ldots, \quad (2)$$

with the $c_{\mu/\mu,\lambda}$-progress coefficient having an integral representation [3]

$$c_{\mu/\mu,\lambda} = \frac{\lambda - \mu}{2\pi}\binom{\lambda}{\mu}\int_{-\infty}^{\infty} \mathrm{e}^{-t^2}\, (\Phi(t))^{\lambda-\mu-1}\, (1 - \Phi(t))^{\mu-1}\, dt \quad (3)$$

where Φ is the cdf (cumulative distribution function) of the standard normal variate

$$\Phi(t) := \frac{1}{\sqrt{2\pi}}\int_{-\infty}^{z=t} \mathrm{e}^{-\frac{1}{2}z^2}\, dz. \quad (4)$$

From the N-dependent progress rate (1) and (2) the asymptotic $N \to \infty$ formulae are easily obtained by Taylor expansion using $\sqrt{1+x} = 1 + \frac{x}{2} + \mathcal{O}(x^2)$ and $(1+x)^{-\frac{1}{2}} = 1 - \frac{x}{2} + \mathcal{O}(x^2)$. Thus one gets $\varphi^{\star}$ formulae which are *independent* of N (for $N \to \infty$; also obtained by Rechenberg [7])

$$\varphi^{\star}_{\mu/\mu_I,\lambda}(\sigma^{\star}) = c_{\mu/\mu,\lambda}\sigma^{\star} - \frac{\sigma^{\star 2}}{2\mu} \quad (5)$$

and

$$\varphi^{\star}_{\mu/\mu_D,\lambda}(\sigma^{\star}) = \sqrt{\mu}\, c_{\mu/\mu,\lambda}\sigma^{\star} - \frac{\sigma^{\star 2}}{2}. \quad (6)$$

These expressions can be used as approximations for the case $N < \infty$, if the conditions

$$\sigma^{\star 2} \ll N \qquad \text{and} \qquad \mu^2 \ll N \tag{7}$$

are fulfilled. Furthermore, they allow for an analytical calculation of the maximal achievable (normalized) progress rate $\hat{\varphi}^\star = \varphi^\star(\hat{\sigma}^\star) = \max_{\sigma^\star}[\varphi^\star(\sigma^\star)]$. By maximizing (5) and (6) one finds

$$\hat{\varphi}^\star_{\mu/\mu_I,\lambda} = \mu \frac{c^2_{\mu/\mu,\lambda}}{2} \qquad \text{at} \qquad \hat{\sigma}^\star_{\mu/\mu_I,\lambda} = \mu c_{\mu/\mu,\lambda} \tag{8}$$

and

$$\hat{\varphi}^\star_{\mu/\mu_D,\lambda} = \mu \frac{c^2_{\mu/\mu,\lambda}}{2} \quad \text{at} \quad \hat{\sigma}^\star_{\mu/\mu_D,\lambda} = \sqrt{\mu}\, c_{\mu/\mu,\lambda}. \tag{9}$$

As can be seen, in the asymptotic $N \to \infty$ limit both strategies have the same maximal achievable progress rate, however, the corresponding mutation strengths are different.

2.2 The $\lambda \to \infty$ Asymptotic of the $c_{\mu/\mu,\lambda}$ Progress Coefficient

Though the formulae (5), (6) and (8), (9) are rather simple, they contain the $c_{\mu/\mu,\lambda}$ coefficient which is the complicated integral (3). To see the influence of λ and μ on the ES performance the $\lambda \to \infty$ is investigated. In [3] an asymptotically *exact* $c_{\mu/\mu,\lambda}$ expression has been derived

$$c_{\mu/\mu,\lambda} \simeq \frac{1}{\vartheta} \frac{1}{\sqrt{2\pi}} \exp\left\{ -\frac{1}{2} \left[\Phi^{-1}(1-\vartheta)\right]^2 \right\} \qquad \text{with} \qquad \vartheta := \frac{\mu}{\lambda} \tag{10}$$

which depends on the truncation ratio $\vartheta := \mu/\lambda$ only.[2] In this paper we will even go further and ask for the λ, μ order of (10). To derive this (new) order expression we resolve (10) for ϑ in $\Phi^{-1}(1-\vartheta)$

$$\vartheta \simeq 1 - \Phi\left(\sqrt{-\ln\left(2\pi\vartheta^2 c^2_{\mu/\mu,\lambda}\right)} \right). \tag{11}$$

For small ϑ ($\vartheta \to 0$) $\Phi(\cdots) \to 1$ does hold, therefore one can apply the asymptotic expansion of $\Phi(t)$ (see, e. g. [1, p. 85]) $\Phi(t) \simeq 1 - \exp(-t^2/2)/\sqrt{2\pi}\, t$ with the result

$$\begin{aligned} c_{\mu/\mu,\lambda} &\simeq \sqrt{-\ln\left(2\pi\vartheta^2 c^2_{\mu/\mu,\lambda}\right)} \\ c^2_{\mu/\mu,\lambda} &\simeq -\ln(2\pi) - 2\ln\vartheta - 2\ln c_{\mu/\mu,\lambda}. \end{aligned} \tag{12}$$

[2] N. B., $\Phi^{-1}(y)$ is the quantile of the standard normal variate, i. e., $\Phi^{-1}(y)$ is the inverse to $\Phi(t)$, equation (4).

Thus, we obtain for sufficiently large $c_{\mu/\mu,\lambda}$

$$c_{\mu/\mu,\lambda} \sim \sqrt{-2\ln\vartheta}, \qquad \text{that is,} \qquad c_{\mu/\mu,\lambda} = \mathcal{O}\left(\sqrt{\ln\frac{\lambda}{\mu}}\right). \tag{13}$$

This result is in accordance with the order relation of the $(1,\lambda)$-ES from [2, p. 171] $c_{1,\lambda} = \mathcal{O}(\sqrt{\ln\lambda})$, if $\mu = 1$ is chosen.

2.3 The Asymptotic Progress Law

Now we are able to ask for the scaling law of the $(\mu/\mu,\lambda)$-ES working in the vicinity of its performance optimum.[3] This question has gained some attention. Schwefel [10] conjectures:

> Based upon the observation that in the linear theory the convergence rate mainly depends on the ratio λ/μ if the population size is not too small, one might speculate about putting together what we know so far to the rather simple formula[4]
>
> $$\varphi^* \approx \mu\ln\frac{\lambda}{\mu}$$
>
> A proof is still missing, however.

His conjecture can be easily proved by the use of (13) and (8), (9). If we insert the asymptotic $c_{\mu/\mu,\lambda}$ (the left formula from (13)) into (8), (9), then we obtain

$$\boxed{\hat{\varphi}^\star \sim \mu\ln\frac{\lambda}{\mu},} \qquad \text{that is,} \qquad \boxed{\hat{\varphi}^\star = \mathcal{O}\left(\mu\ln\frac{\lambda}{\mu}\right).} \tag{14}$$

As can be seen, the progress rate increases logarithmically with λ whereas the μ influence can be decomposed in a linearly increasing part $\mu\ln\lambda$ and a nonlinear loss part $-\mu\ln\mu$. For small μ (let $\lambda = \text{const.}$) the linear part dominates. Therefore, for small μ the function $\hat{\varphi}^\star(\mu,\lambda)$ increases with μ, however, for $\mu \to \lambda$ it approaches zero. There must be an optimal $\hat{\vartheta} = \mu/\lambda$ ratio for which the $(\mu/\mu,\lambda)$-ES works with maximal efficiency. This is the question on the most efficient $(\mu/\mu,\lambda)$-ES. They cannot be answered by maximizing (14) directly, because (14) was obtained by neglecting terms in (12), i. e., for $\mu \ll \lambda$. If one ignores this fact and maximizes the left formula in (14) with respect to μ, then one finds $\lambda/\mu = \mathrm{e} \approx 2.718$, or for the truncation ratio $\hat{\vartheta} \approx 0.368$. This value is not so far from the exact result $\hat{\vartheta} \approx 0.270$ that will be derived in the next section.

[3] This requires the control of σ in such a way that the optimal $\hat{\sigma}^\star$, given by (8) and (9), respectively, is roughly realized. Usually this is attained by σ-self-adaptation developed by Schwefel [9] or statistical inference methods (see Ostermeier et al. [6]).

[4] N. B., Schwefel uses the φ^* to indicate the maximum of the normalized φ, whereas the author uses $(\cdot)^\star$ to label normalized quantities. Therefore $\hat{\varphi}^\star = \varphi^*$ holds.

2.4 The Fitness Efficiency η and the Optimal ϑ-Choice

Motivation and Definition of η. Besides the main goal of maximal progress towards the optimum there remains the question how efficient an ES algorithm performs the generational change. In order to have a "fair" measure, the progress rate $\varphi^\star$ is to be normalized with respect to the number of fitness evaluations within one generation. Since there are λ offspring there are λ fitness computations, thus the *progress rate per offspring* $\varphi^\star/\lambda$ is that "fair" performance measure.

As an example the $\varphi^\star/\lambda = f_\lambda(\sigma^\star)$ curves of the $(1,\lambda)$- and $(1+\lambda)$-ES (see Beyer [2]) are displayed in Figure 1. It is obvious that there is always an optimal

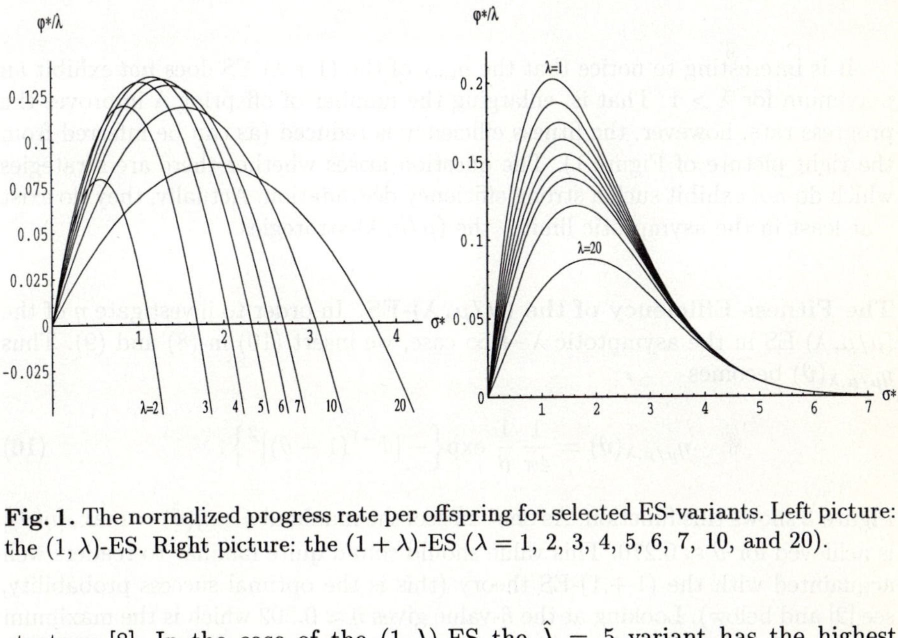

Fig. 1. The normalized progress rate per offspring for selected ES-variants. Left picture: the $(1,\lambda)$-ES. Right picture: the $(1+\lambda)$-ES ($\lambda = 1$, 2, 3, 4, 5, 6, 7, 10, and 20).

strategy [8]. In the case of the $(1,\lambda)$-ES the $\hat{\lambda} = 5$ variant has the highest maximum, whereas for the $(1+\lambda)$-ES $\hat{\lambda} = 1$ provides the largest progress per offspring.

In order to have a measure that quantifies this observation for each algorithm, the *fitness efficiency* η is defined

$$\text{FITNESS EFFICIENCY:} \qquad \eta := \frac{\max_{\sigma^\star}[\varphi^\star(\sigma^\star)]}{\lambda} = \frac{\hat{\varphi^\star}}{\lambda}. \tag{15}$$

In the case of the $(1,\lambda)$-ES, for example, one easily finds $\eta_{1,\lambda} = \eta(\lambda) = c_{1,\lambda}^2/2\lambda = c_{1/1,\lambda}^2/2\lambda$. This function is plotted in Figure 2. As can be seen, the most efficient strategy is obtained for $\hat{\lambda} \approx 5.02$.

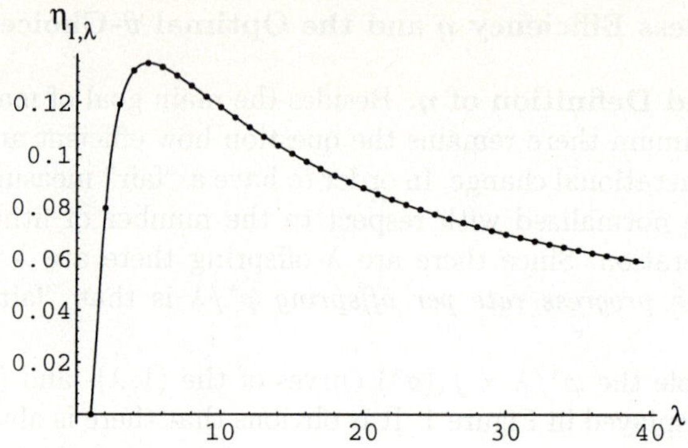

Fig. 2. The fitness efficiency of the $(1, \lambda)$-ES. One observes a maximum at $\lambda \approx 5$.

It is interesting to notice that the $\eta_{1+\lambda}$ of the $(1 + \lambda)$-ES does *not* exhibit an maximum for $\lambda > 1$. That is, enlarging the number of offspring λ improves the progress rate, however, the fitness efficiency is reduced (as can be inferred from the right picture of Figure 1). The question arises whether there are strategies which do *not* exhibit such a strong efficiency degradation. Actually, they do exist – at least in the asymptotic limit – the $(\mu/\mu, \lambda)$-strategies.

The Fitness Efficiency of the $(\mu/\mu, \lambda)$-ES. In order to investigate η of the $(\mu/\mu, \lambda)$-ES in the asymptotic $\lambda \to \infty$ case, we insert (10) in (8) and (9). Thus $\eta_{\mu/\mu,\lambda}(\vartheta)$ becomes

$$\eta_{\mu/\mu,\lambda}(\vartheta) = \frac{1}{4\pi} \frac{1}{\vartheta} \exp\Big\{ - \left[\Phi^{-1}(1-\vartheta)\right]^2 \Big\} . \tag{16}$$

Figure 3 shows this function. As one can see, the maximal $\hat{\eta} = \eta(\hat{\vartheta}) = \max_\vartheta[\eta(\vartheta)]$ is achieved for $\hat{\vartheta} \approx 0.270$. This value should sound quite familiar to readers well acquainted with the $(1 + 1)$-ES theory (this is the optimal success probability, see [2] and below). Looking at the $\hat{\eta}$-value gives $\hat{\eta} \approx 0.202$ which is the maximum of $\varphi^\star_{1+1}$ (cf. Figure 1, right picture). This is *not* merely an incidence, but a deep connection that can be formally proved.

In order to uncover the connection, we first derive the equation for $\hat{\vartheta}$ from (16) by solving $\left.\frac{d\eta}{d\vartheta}\right|_{\vartheta=\hat{\vartheta}} = 0$ for $\hat{\vartheta}$

$$\frac{d\eta}{d\vartheta} \stackrel{!}{=} 0 \qquad \Rightarrow \qquad 1 = 2\hat{\vartheta}\sqrt{2\pi}\,\Phi^{-1}(1-\hat{\vartheta}) \exp\Big\{ \frac{1}{2} \left[\Phi^{-1}(1-\hat{\vartheta})\right]^2 \Big\} . \tag{17}$$

If one substitutes $x := \Phi^{-1}(1 - \hat{\vartheta})$, i. e.,

$$\hat{\vartheta} = 1 - \Phi(x) \tag{18}$$

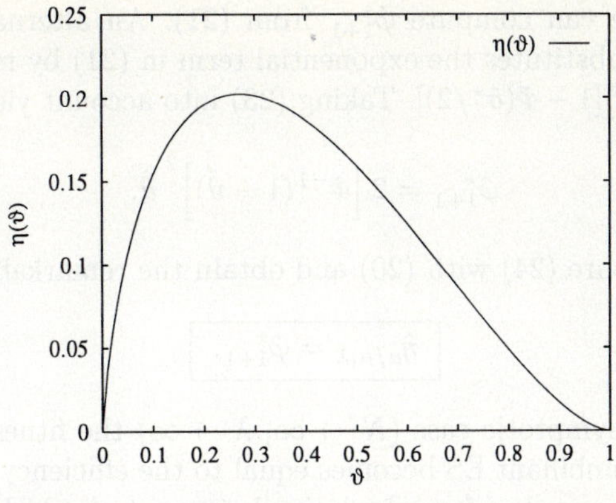

Fig. 3. The fitness efficiency $\eta_{\mu/\mu,\lambda}(\vartheta)$ in the asymptotic limit case as a function of the truncation ratio $\vartheta = \mu/\lambda$.

in (17), then one obtains after a simple re-arrangement the nonlinear equation

$$0 = \frac{1}{\sqrt{2\pi}} \exp\left(-\frac{1}{2}x^2\right) - 2x\left[1 - \Phi(x)\right]. \tag{19}$$

This equation could be solved numerically for x yielding $\hat{\vartheta}$ by (18). Provided that x and therefore $\hat{\vartheta}$ are known, then $\hat{\eta}$ can be calculated. One can get an alternative $\hat{\eta}$ formula (needed below) if the exponential in (16) is expressed by (17)

$$\hat{\eta}_{\mu/\mu,\lambda} = 2\left[\Phi^{-1}(1-\hat{\vartheta})\right]^2 \hat{\vartheta}. \tag{20}$$

In a second step we maximize the (1 + 1)-ES progress rate formula [2, 7]

$$\varphi^{\star}_{1+1}(\sigma^{\star}) = \frac{\sigma^{\star}}{\sqrt{2\pi}} \exp\left(-\frac{1}{8}\sigma^{\star 2}\right) - \frac{\sigma^{\star 2}}{2}\left[1 - \Phi\left(\frac{\sigma^{\star}}{2}\right)\right]. \tag{21}$$

By differentiation one obtains

$$\frac{d\varphi^{\star}}{d\sigma^{\star}} \stackrel{!}{=} 0 \quad \Rightarrow \quad 0 = \frac{1}{\sqrt{2\pi}} \exp\left(-\frac{1}{8}\hat{\sigma}^{\star 2}\right) - \hat{\sigma}^{\star}\left[1 - \Phi\left(\frac{\hat{\sigma}^{\star}}{2}\right)\right]. \tag{22}$$

Here $\hat{\sigma}^{\star}$ is the mutation strength which maximizes $\varphi^{\star}_{1+1}$. Now, let us compare (22) with (19). Both equations become equivalent, if one substitutes $x = \frac{\hat{\sigma}^{\star}}{2}$ in (22). For (18) one gets

$$\hat{\vartheta} = 1 - \Phi\left(\frac{\hat{\sigma}^{\star}}{2}\right). \tag{23}$$

Given the $\hat{\sigma}^\star$ one can compute $\hat{\varphi}^\star_{1+1}$ from (21). An alternative expression is obtained, if one substitutes the exponential term in (21) by means of (22). This gives $\hat{\varphi}^\star_{1+1} = \frac{1}{2}\hat{\sigma}^{\star 2}\left[1 - \Phi(\hat{\sigma}^\star/2)\right]$. Taking (23) into account yields finally[5]

$$\hat{\varphi}^\star_{1+1} = 2\left[\Phi^{-1}(1-\hat{\vartheta})\right]^2 \hat{\vartheta}. \tag{24}$$

Now we can compare (24) with (20) and obtain the remarkable result

$$\boxed{\hat{\eta}_{\mu/\mu,\lambda} = \hat{\varphi}^\star_{1+1}.} \tag{25}$$

That is, for the asymptotic case ($N \to \infty$, $\lambda \to \infty$) the fitness efficiency of the $(\mu/\mu, \lambda)$ multirecombinant ES becomes equal to the efficiency of the $(1+1)$-ES.

Besides this more or less formal relation between $(\mu/\mu, \lambda)$-ESs and the $(1+1)$-ES there is another remarkable connection. In the theory of the $(1+1)$-ES the *success probability*[6] $P_s(\sigma^\star)$ is given by the expression $P_s(\sigma^\star) = 1 - \Phi(\sigma^\star/2)$. Therefore, an optimally performing $(1+1)$-ES, i. e. $\sigma^\star = \hat{\sigma}^\star$, exhibits an optimal success probability $\hat{P}_s = P_s(\hat{\sigma}^\star)$

$$\boxed{\hat{P}_{s1+1} = 1 - \Phi\left(\frac{\hat{\sigma}^\star}{2}\right) = \hat{\vartheta},} \qquad \hat{P}_{s1+1} \approx 0.27027, \tag{26}$$

which is equal to the optimal truncation ratio $\hat{\vartheta} = \mu/\lambda$ of the $(\mu/\mu, \lambda)$-ES. This holds because of equation (23). Thus, the $\hat{\vartheta}$ value has an interesting interpretation. To obtain optimal performance for the $(1+1)$-ES the mutation strength σ has to be tuned in such a way that in average each $1/0.27 \approx 3.7$th offspring replaces the parent (this holds exactly for the sphere model). That is, *one* parent has to produce 3.7 offspring in order to get optimally replaced. In $(\mu/\mu, \lambda)$ strategies μ parents have to produce $\hat{\lambda} = \mu/\hat{\vartheta} \approx 3.7\mu$ offspring. It is as if the $(1+1)$-ES has get its "natural continuation" in the realm of multi-membered strategies. Note, the $(1+\lambda)$-ES cannot do the continuation (without performance degradation), because $\eta_{1+\lambda}$ is a decreasing function of λ. If we switch back to the maximum progress rate $\hat{\varphi}^\star$ using (15) we will find $\hat{\varphi}^\star_{1+\lambda}(\lambda)$ as a sub-linearly increasing function of λ, however, as to the multirecombinant strategies one finds

$$\hat{\varphi}^\star_{\mu/\mu,\lambda} = \lambda \hat{\eta}_{\mu/\mu,\lambda} \approx \lambda \cdot 0.20245. \tag{27}$$

3 The Dynamics of the Evolution Process and the ES Time Complexity

A prime goal of theoretical computer science concerns the computational complexity of the algorithms. Since this measure depends also on the complexity of

---

[5] N. B., this $\hat{\varphi}^\star_{1+1}$-formula must not be applied for values $\vartheta \neq \hat{\vartheta}$. The same holds for (20).

[6] The P_s is defined as the probability by which the parent is replaced by the offspring.

the fitness function (as far as optimization is considered), it is not well suited for comparing optimization algorithms with respect to their performance. A better measure for EAs (Evolutionary Algorithms) is usually the number of generations G needed to obtain a certain improvement under the assumption of an optimally working EA. The author will call this G the *EA* or *ES time complexity.*[7] Alternatively one can consider the number of fitness evaluation ν^F given by

$$\nu^F = \lambda G. \tag{28}$$

In order to compute G it is necessary to investigate the *macroscopic* behavior of the ES, i. e., the dynamics of the R change over the generations g. For large N this evolution is governed by the differential equation [2, 5] $\frac{dR(g)}{dg} = -R(g)\,\varphi^\star(g)/N$ which must be solved for $R(g)$. If we assume that there is a σ-control mechanism (see also footnote 3) which drives the ES into its optimal working regime,[8] then one can expect that $\varphi^\star(g) \approx$ const. $\approx \hat{\varphi}^\star$ roughly holds. For this case the differential equation has the simple solution

$$R(g) = R(0)\exp\left(-\frac{\hat{\varphi}^\star}{N}\,g\right), \tag{29}$$

with the distance R to the optimum at generation g starting from an initial distance $R(0)$. If one asks for a certain relative improvement $R(g)/R(0)$, then one can determine the number of generations expected to reach this objective. From (29) we obtain with (15)

$$g = \frac{\lg(R(0)/R(g))}{\lg(e)}\frac{N}{\hat{\varphi}^\star} = \frac{\lg(R(0)/R(g))}{\lg(e)}\frac{N}{\lambda\eta}. \tag{30}$$

Applying this to the optimal $(\mu/\mu, \lambda)$-ES yields with (27)

$$G_{\mu/\mu,\lambda} = \hat{g}_{\mu/\mu,\lambda} = \frac{\lg(R(0)/R(g))}{\lg(e)\,\hat{\eta}_{\mu/\mu,\lambda}}\frac{N}{\lambda}. \tag{31}$$

Thus one obtains for the

$$(\mu/\mu, \lambda)\text{-ES TIME COMPLEXITY:} \qquad G_{\mu/\mu,\lambda} = \mathcal{O}\left(\frac{N}{\lambda}\right). \tag{32}$$

That is, in multirecombinant ESs the (average) time complexity is of order N and inversely proportional to the population size λ. Equation (32) is a strong

[7] One might argue that such a measure neglects those parts of the ES-algorithm which are due to the selection, mutation, and the recombination operators. Furthermore, if parallel computers are under investigation, the communication overhead is to be taken into account. However, if the fitness calculation time is sufficiently large, then the other parts of the algorithm can be neglected. Developing more realistic performance models remains as a future task.

[8] This has been proved for the $(1, \lambda)$-σ-self-adaptation in [5] and it is observed in multi-parent strategies, too.

argument for parallelizing $(\mu/\mu, \lambda)$-ESs provided that the fitness calculation time does sufficiently exceed the communication time in the multiprocessor system under consideration.

The number of fitness evaluations ν^F becomes by virtue of (28) $\nu^F = \mathcal{O}(N)$. That is, in the asymptotic limit ($N \to \infty$, $\lambda \to \infty$, and assuming the validity of the sphere approximation) ν^F *cannot* be reduced by the multi-recombination, it is of the same order as for the $(1+1)$-ES.

It is interesting to compare these results with non-recombinant (μ, λ)-strategies. For the progress rate one finds [7, 4] $\varphi^\star = c_{\mu,\lambda}\sigma^\star - \sigma^{\star 2}/2$. The asymptotic behavior of the progress coefficient $c_{\mu,\lambda}$ can be obtained from the solution of an integral equation constituting some kind of nonlinear eigenvalue problem for the offspring distribution. Due to the space limitations the derivation must be omitted here, they will be published elsewhere. One finds for $\lambda \to \infty$ $c_{\mu,\lambda} \sim \sqrt{2\ln(\lambda/\mu)}$. Thus one obtains for the expected number of generations (30)

$$g = \frac{\lg(R(0)/R(g))}{\lg(\mathrm{e})} \frac{N}{\ln(\lambda/\mu)}. \tag{33}$$

As one can see, maximal performance (i. e. minimal g) is achieved for $\mu = 1$, therefore we get the

$$\boxed{(\mu, \lambda)\text{-ES TIME COMPLEXITY:} \qquad G_{\mu,\lambda} = \mathcal{O}\left(\frac{N}{\ln\lambda}\right).} \tag{34}$$

Again the complexity scales linearly with the problem size N, however, increasing λ decreases $G_{\mu,\lambda}$ only logarithmically. Furthermore, due to (33) the $\mu = 1$ strategy is the fastest (μ, λ) variant,[9] its ν^F scales sub-linearly with the population size $\nu^F = \mathcal{O}(\frac{\lambda N}{\ln\lambda})$.

4 Conclusions and Outlook

This paper has dealt with the asymptotic properties of $(\mu/\mu, \lambda)$-strategies. The advantage of such an analysis is that it yields simple analytical formulae which can be much better interpreted than the bulky results from the N-dependent theory presented in [3]. Of course, this is bought at the price of lower accuracy, if one tries to use these results as *approximations* for the real world case $N < \infty$, $\lambda < \infty$. For example, the optimal truncation ratio $\hat{\vartheta} \approx 0.27$ becomes a function $\hat{\vartheta} = f(N, \mu, \lambda)$, however, this function can only be computed numerically (a table for the optimal μ-choice has been presented in [3, p. 97]).

Having a theory on the ES time complexity, we are able to determine what to measure (cf. the introduction). Now it is the ES-experimenter's turn to look at their algorithms for the scaling laws described by (30) – (34). The question is,

---

[9] Note, this statement concerns the local performance of the ES. It does *nothing* say about the ES's ability to locate the global optimum in multi-modal fitness landscapes.

whether one can observe the scaling laws in (continuous) *real world optimization problems*, too.

In ES-experiments it is common practice to display the evolutionary progress by $\lg(R)$ vs. g plots. This allows for the comparison with (29). If (29) is fulfilled, i. e., if there is linear convergence the $\lg(R)$ vs. g plot should exhibit nearly straight lines. Indeed, this is often observed. However, the scaling behavior with respect to N and λ as indicated by (32) and (34) are up until now *not* common subjects of investigation. This will hopefully change with this article.

The analysis presented can be extended to other strategies. Results for the (μ, λ)-ES have been already obtained. They are to be published in a forthcoming paper. Furthermore, one might think about the behavior of $(\mu+\lambda)$- and $(\mu/\mu+\lambda)$-ESs. This is a task for future research.

5 Acknowledgement

The author is grateful to the anonymous referee # 13 for his helpful comments. This work was funded by the DFG, grant Be 1578/1-2.

References

1. M. Abramowitz and I. A. Stegun. *Pocketbook of Mathematical Functions.* Verlag Harri Deutsch, Thun, 1984.
2. H.-G. Beyer. Toward a Theory of Evolution Strategies: Some Asymptotical Results from the $(1,^{+} \lambda)$-Theory. *Evolutionary Computation*, 1(2):165–188, 1993.
3. H.-G. Beyer. Toward a Theory of Evolution Strategies: On the Benefit of Sex - the $(\mu/\mu, \lambda)$-Theory. *Evolutionary Computation*, 3(1):81–111, 1995.
4. H.-G. Beyer. Toward a Theory of Evolution Strategies: The (μ, λ)-Theory. *Evolutionary Computation*, 2(4):381–407, 1995.
5. H.-G. Beyer. Toward a Theory of Evolution Strategies: Self-Adaptation. *Evolutionary Computation*, 3(3):311–347, 1996.
6. A. Ostermeier, A. Gawelczyk, and N. Hansen. A Derandomized Approach to Self-Adaptation of Evolution Strategies. *Evolutionary Computation*, 2(4):369–380, 1995.
7. I. Rechenberg. *Evolutionsstrategie '94.* Frommann–Holzboog Verlag, Stuttgart, 1994.
8. H.-P. Schwefel. Adaptive Mechanismen in der biologischen Evolution und ihr Einfluß auf die Evolutionsgeschwindigkeit. Technical report, Technical University of Berlin, 1974. Abschlußbericht zum DFG-Vorhaben Re 215/2.
9. H.-P. Schwefel. *Evolution and Optimum Seeking.* Wiley, New York, NY, 1995.
10. H.-P. Schwefel and G. Rudolph. Contemporary Evolution Strategies. In F. Morana, A. Moreno, J. J. Merelo, and P. Chacon, editors, *Advances in Artificial Life. Third ECAL Proceedings*, pages 893–907, Berlin, 1995. Springer-Verlag.

Are Long Path Problems Hard for Genetic Algorithms?

Christian Höhn*[1] and Colin Reeves[2]

[1] Institut für Grundlagen Elektrotechnik/Elektronik, TU Dresden, Germany
[2] School of Mathematical and Information Sciences, Coventry University, UK

Abstract. Long path problems have been introduced into GA literature as problems that are hard for hill-climbers but empirical results suggest they can easily be solved by GAs. However, no formal analysis has been carried out which would explain this apparent success. The paper shows that the *Root2path* problem resembles a *Royal Road* function which allows the GA to exploit short cuts in the crossover landscape.
To fully understand the GA behaviour the original problem as introduced by Horn *et.al.* has been decomposed into its components: the *Root2path* and the slope function. Although both functions may be classified as GA-easy, they impose different requirements on the constitution of the population. These requirements are shown to be incompatible, so that the combination of *Root2path* and slope function results in a problem that is hard for a GA.

1 Introduction

Genetic algorithms (GAs) can be considered as fairly robust search algorithms that work with few assumptions made about the problem to be solved. This advantage clearly has costs and GAs usually require longer execution times than those algorithms that are specialized for a given problem. Consequently, when looking for applications it is natural to turn to those problems that do not fulfil the requirements made by alternative search algorithms and thus are likely to be difficult to solve for the latter.

Probably, one of the simplest search strategies is employed by the so called "hill-climbing" algorithms. Hill-climbing algorithms make a fairly strong assumption about their landscapes, namely that they provide monotonic increasing paths leading to the global optimum. Thus a hill-climbing strategy is endangered from two sides. One one hand, to solve a given problem a hill-climber requires a feasible initial point that sits on a strictly monotonic increasing path to the global optimum. Now there exist landscapes where finding such a point is almost as difficult than finding the global optimum. For example, such a condition is often given in multimodal landscapes.

On the other hand, there exists the class of *long path problems.* Although plenty of feasible initial points are available it is the sheer length of the paths that renders the use of a hill-climber inefficient. The hardness of these problems for hill-climbers has been recently pointed out in [1]. Moreover, the experiments

---

* This work was undertaken when the first author was with the Control Theory and Appplications Centre, Coventry University, UK

carried out by Horn *et.al.* suggest that long path problems are instances where GAs are likely to outperform hill-climbing algorithms. The question still remains, however, whether such problems are intrinsically hard or easy for a GA.

2 Landscapes and operators

The search algorithms we consider conduct a search over some finite *search space*, denoted by S, to maximize some real-valued *objective function* $f : S \to \mathbb{R}$. Furthermore, the order relation $\leq$ defined on $\mathbb{R}$ can be extended over the subsets of the search space through the function f. For two non-empty sets $U, V \subseteq S$ we say $U \leq V$ if $f(u) \leq f(v)$ for all $u \in U$ and for all $v \in V$.

In this paper, the search space will be identified with the set of binary strings of fixed length l represented by the binary vector space $\mathbb{Z}_2^l$. The elements of $\mathbb{Z}_2^l$ are the vectors (or binary strings) $\mathbf{z} = (z_1, z_2, \cdots, z_l)$.

A *landscape* Λ is a triple (S, f, d) where S is a search space, f an objective function defined on S and d a distance measure $d : S \times S \to \mathbb{R} \cup \{\infty\}$ for which we require that

$$d(s,t) \geq 0, \;\; d(s,t) = 0 \Leftrightarrow s = t, \;\; d(s,u) \leq d(s,t) + d(t,u),$$

for all $s, t, u \in S$. The distance d can be extended to define a distance between subsets of S. For two non-empty sets $U, V \in S$ we define

$$d(U,V) = \min_{u \in U, v \in V} d(u,v).$$

Landscapes over the binary space are often defined relative to the Hamming distance $H(\mathbf{x}, \mathbf{y})$ between two vectors $\mathbf{x}, \mathbf{y}$. During this paper we will have occasion to consider different landscapes generated by the same objective function. The landscape $\Lambda = (\mathbb{Z}_2^l, f, H)$ will be therefore referred to as the *Hamming landscape* of f.

A sequence $s_0, \cdots, s_n$ of points in the search space S defines a *path* of length n in the landscape $\Lambda = (S, f, d)$ if $d(s_i, s_{i+1}) = 1$, $i = 0, \cdots, n-1$. Furthermore, a path $s_0, \cdots, s_n$ in the landscape Λ is *strictly monotonic increasing* if $f(s_i) < f(s_{i+1})$, $i = 0, \cdots, n-1$.

Clearly, it is the landscape rather than the objective function that defines a long path problem but landscapes can be defined relative to any distance measure. However, the link between landscape and search algorithm is given by the *neighbourhood search* (NS) operators used in the algorithm. NS operators generate new points in the search space relative to a given point. Hence they define a distance $d(s,t)$ on the search space given by the minimum number of applications required to obtain the element t from the element s.

For example, the distance determined on the binary vector space by the 'bit-flipping' operator or *Hamming cube operator* which flips a single bit at a time, just corresponds to the Hamming distance. Hence a hill-climbing algorithm that uses the Hamming cube operator, in the following called *Hamming cube* (HC) *hill-climber*, is associated with the Hamming landscape. Conversely, if a hill-climbing algorithm performs a search in the Hamming landscape, it is valid to assume that the algorithm uses the Hamming cube operator.

3 Horn's long path problem

3.1 Construction of the *Root2path*

The long path problem we are going to consider in detail is the *Root2path* introduced by Horn *et.al.* As described in [1] the l-dimensional *Root2path* can be iteratively constructed in the binary space $\mathbb{Z}_2^l$. The one-dimensional path is given by the sequence $(0 \quad 1)$ where 0 is the starting point and 1 the end point of the path. To construct the $(l+2)$-dimensional path one takes two copies of the l-dimensional path. Whereas the pair 00 is attached in front of all elements of the first copy the pair 11 is attached to those in the second. In this manner, it is ensured that the Hamming distance between both paths is two. Finally, the end points of both copies are connected through a *bridge point* which naturally reverses the order of the elements in the second subpath. At this stage of the construction bridge points start with the tuple (10) followed by the string of the end point of the l-dimensional path. So the 3-dimensional Root2path is given by the sequence

$$(000 \quad 001 \quad 101 \quad 111 \quad 110).$$

Following this construction, the size of the path, i.e. the number of elements, more than doubles every iteration. More precisely, let n_l denote the size of the l-dimensional *Root2path*. Then

$$n_l = 2n_{l-2} + 1 \text{ or explicitly } n_l = 3 \cdot 2^{(l-1)/2} - 1. \tag{1}$$

Let R denote the set of all binary strings in $\mathbb{Z}_2^l$ that belong to the *Root2path*. Then the function $g : R \to \mathbb{N}$ that returns the position of each element in the path defines a strictly monotonic increasing function on the path and will serve as an objective function.

Although the size of the path increases exponentially in l it does so at a slower rate than the size of the binary vector space. Thus as pointed out by Horn *et.al.*, the *Root2path* becomes a 'Needle-in-a-haystack' problem for higher values of l. To direct the search towards the path they introduced a *slope function*. In particular, they use the *unitation* function that returns the sum of the coordinates of a vector in $\mathbb{Z}_2^l$ and has a minimum at the zero vector which is the starting point of the *Root2path*. Hence while searching for the minimum of the slope function the search algorithms will be guided towards the beginning of the path. The resulting objective function of the *extended Root2path* is given by

$$f(\mathbf{z}) = \begin{cases} g(\mathbf{z}) & \text{if } \mathbf{z} \in R \\ \sum_{i=1}^{l} z_i & \text{otherwise} \end{cases} \tag{2}$$

which has the maximum for the string $1100 \cdots 000$.

3.2 Performance of a genetic algorithm

The *Root2path* clearly imposes a long path problem on HC hill-climbers. After having optimized the slope function they have no choice but to follow the entire path. Although they will eventually solve the problem the number of function evaluations required is a multiple of the size of the path and increases exponentially in the problem size. By contrast, experiments carried out by Horn *et.al.*

show that GAs find the optimum in significantly shorter times. We have repeated these experiments with an algorithm we shall term here a *standard GA*. This is a generational GA using binary tournament selection and one-point crossover with crossover rate $\mu_X = 1$. The population size will be maintained at 200. As in [1] our GA does not use mutation. Likewise, it is restarted with a new initial population whenever the GA converges prematurely. The results in Table

l	Size n_l	Function eval. MIN	MAX	MEAN	SEMEAN	Generations MIN	MAX	MEAN	SEMEAN	Restarts MEAN
9	47	200	800	441	29	0	4	1.5	0.19	0.0
19	1535	1062	16144	5505	770	5	169	52.1	8.44	2.2
29	49151	3866	106814	29583	4577	27	997	272.1	43.90	11.3
39	1572863	2808	246990	73673	10124	17	2054	603.2	82.75	23.4
49	50331647	11378	1442224	349207	61449	90	10950	2645.1	464.78	95.4

Table 1. Performance of the standard GA on the long path problem. The number of function evaluations required to solve the problem grows exponentially but at a slower rate than the size of the path. A linear regression analysis yields a grows rate of $\approx 1.17^l$. As all subsequent statistics these data have been derived from 30 runs.

1 show indeed that the number of function evaluations required by the GA to solve the problem is only a fraction of the size of the path. Hence, the GA clearly outperforms a HC hill-climber but does this imply that the long path problem is GA-easy? Or does it merely reflects the fact that the long path problem is extremely hard for HC hill-climbers? In the latter case one would expect to find other search algorithms that do better on the *Root2path* than HC hill-climbers.

There are two possible explanations. First, GAs do not follow a hill-climbing strategy and therefore do not require a strictly monotonic increasing path to the global optimum. To rule out this case we added a point-based selection scheme where offspring first have to compete against their parents before the winner is passed on to the population-based selection scheme. However, under this condition the GA performed even better[3], which proves that a departure from a hill-climbing strategy is not essential for outperforming a HC hill-climber.

On the other hand, it is very likely that the *Root2path* defines a long path problem only relative to the Hamming distances. The care required in constructing the path almost prohibits the introduction of another distance without introducing 'short cuts' into the path. Consequently, search algorithms that use landscapes other than the Hamming landscape have a fair chance to find shorter paths leading to the global optimum. In particular, it is not too difficult to imagine that the landscape relevant for the GA significantly differs from the Hamming landscape and admits several 'short cuts'. Since crossover is the only operator in our standard GA this is the same as to say that the long path problems contains *building blocks* exploitable by crossover as suspected by the authors in [1].

In searching for possible short paths we will first decompose the long path problem into its components, the slope function and the *Root2path*. Therefore, we introduce the *Root2path problem* as the problem of finding the top of the *Root2path* when the search starts already on the path. This in contrast to Horn's original problem where the search could start at any point in $\mathbb{Z}_2^l$. The latter will be referred to as the *extended Root2path problem* and considered at the end of the paper.

[3] These results are not included in the paper.

4 The Royal Road in the *Root2path*

Before we start the analysis some more definitions are required. We will define $\lambda = (l+1)/2$ where l is the dimension of the *Root2path*. Already defined is the set $R \subset \mathbb{Z}_2^l$ which contains all binary strings that belong to the *Root2path*. The complement of R will be denoted by O and contains all strings that lie outside the path. Under the objective function (2) we have $O \leq R$.

Furthermore, the set R is composed of two types of elements. On one hand we find the bridge points, which connect two lower-dimensional paths during the construction of the path. Therefore, all bridge-points have a pair (10) at the $(2i+1)$st and $(2i+2)$nd position, $i = 0, \cdots, \lambda - 2$. *Non-bridge points*, by contrast, are made up from tuples (00) or (11) up to the lth position. The set of all bridge points will be denote by B and that of all non-bridge points by N. From equation (1) follows $|B|/|N| \approx 1/2$.

The set of non-bridge points is of particular interest for our analysis and therefore will be further structured. Consider the schemata

$$\begin{array}{lcccccccc} H_0 & = & * & 0 & * & * & * & * & \cdots & * \\ H_1 & = & 1 & 1 & 1 & * & * & * & \cdots & * \\ H_2 & = & 1 & 1 & 0 & 0 & 1 & * & \cdots & * \\ \vdots & & & & & & & & & \\ H_\lambda & = & 1 & 1 & 0 & 0 & 0 & 0 & \cdots & 0 \end{array}$$

where $*$ denotes the *don't care* symbol. First observe that all schemata listed above are mutually disjoint. Secondly, apart from H_0 and H_λ, all binary strings in schema H_i share exactly the first $2i$ positions with the optimum of the *Root2path* which is the only element in H_λ. Then define the sets $N_i = N \cap H_i$, $i = 0, \cdots, \lambda$ which are all non-empty and form a partition of the set N. Furthermore, consider the schemata

$$\begin{array}{cccccccccc} 1 & 1 & * & * & * & * & \cdots & * & * & * \\ * & * & 0 & 0 & * & * & \cdots & * & * & * \\ * & * & * & * & 0 & 0 & \cdots & * & * & * \\ & & & & & & & & & \\ * & * & * & * & * & * & \cdots & 0 & 0 & * \\ * & * & * & * & * & * & \cdots & * & * & 0 \end{array}$$

which all define ***building blocks***, i.e. partial solutions, for the optimum of the *Root2path*. Apart from N_0, all sets N_i are subsets of at least one of these schemata and therefore contain partial solutions. Moreover, it is not difficult to see how crossover can assemble the optimal string from the elements in the sets N_i. In addition, under the objective function (2) we have $i \leq j \Leftrightarrow N_i \leq N_j$ so that the set $\{N_0, \cdots, N_\lambda\}$ is totally ordered. Hence not only do non-bridge points offer partial solutions they also provide suitable stepping stones for a strictly monotonic increasing path to the global optimum. In all these aspects the *Root2path* shares the structure of the *Royal Road* functions by Mitchell *et al.* [2, 3]. In particular, it is fair to say that the sets $N_0, N_1, \cdots, N_\lambda$ lay out a 'royal road' in the *Root2path* that leads quickly to the top of the path.

4.1 The CX landscape and CX hill-climber

The presence of a 'royal road' supports our hypothesis that the GA exploits 'short cuts' in the crossover landscape, but this requires some firm proof. Before investigating the crossover landscape it is worthwhile to consider the far simpler landscape generated by the *complementary crossover* [4, 5]. Complementary crossover (CX) can be thought of as a crossover performed over two complementary binary strings. If the cross point falls in front of the ith position one-point CX "flips" all bits from the ith position onwards. Unlike normal crossover, we will admit cross points in front of the first position.

Let d_{CX} denote the distance induced by the one-point CX. Then for any objective function f the landscape $\Lambda = (\mathbb{Z}_2^l, f, d_{CX})$ will be called the *CX landscape* of f. Likewise a hill-climbing algorithm searching in this landscape may be referred to as *CX hill-climber.* Complementary crossover involves only one parent; the CX-landscape is therefore static and easier to analyse. Nevertheless, through the close relation between CX and normal crossover one may hope that the CX landscape reasonably approximates the crossover landscape.

Under CX every element in N_i has a neighbour in some set $N_j > N_i$, $0 \le i < j \le \lambda$ which will be generated when the cross point falls in front of $(2i+1)$th position. For example, for $l = 7$ the sequence

$$0011001\ 1100110\ 1100001\ 1100000$$

defines a strictly monotonic increasing path in the CX landscape stepping through the sets N_0, N_2, N_3 and N_4.

Hence to make efficient use of the 'royal road' the task of a CX hill-climber reduces to finding the right cross point. The latter is not too difficult. An inspection of the neighbourhood of non-bridge points reveals that the neighbour which sits higher up at the 'royal road' is also the one having the highest objective function value. Hence a steepest ascent search is bound to find the right cross point. Therefore, when the search starts at a non-bridge point a steepest ascent hill-climber requires less than $\lambda = (l+1)/2$ moves or equivalently less than $l(l+3)/2$ function evaluations. It can also be shown that the performance is still bounded by $O(l^2)$ when the search starts at any point of the path. Although it can be shown that there is an exponentially increasing number of local optima in the CX landscape (every second bridge point forms a local optimum under CX), the *Root2path* qualifies as an easy problem for CX hill-climbers. Consequently, not only is the *Root2path* an exception to the rule that unimodal landscapes are easy but also to the rule that landscapes where the number of local optima increases exponentially are hard for hill-climbers. Table 2 summarizes the performance of two CX hill-climbers. For both cases the results confirm the simplicity of the *Root2path* problem for CX hill-climber.

4.2 Genetic algorithms

Walking up the 'royal road' using crossover is more difficult than it may seem at the first glance. Normal crossover involves two parents. Hence not only the choice of the right cross point but also the selection of the proper second parent is important. Consider some non-bridge point $\mathbf{x} \in N_i$, $i < \lambda - 1$. Then the

	STEEPEST ASCENT						NEXT ASCENT					
	Optima		Moves		Func. eval.		Optima		Moves		Func. eval.	
l	global	local	mean	semean	mean	semean	global	local	mean	semean	mean	semean
9	889	111	2.5	0.05	33	0.4	846	154	2.8	0.06	22	0.2
19	853	147	4.2	0.07	100	1.4	804	196	6.5	0.13	62	0.8
29	850	150	6.1	0.10	207	3.0	779	221	11.1	0.22	121	1.8
39	840	160	8.0	0.14	350	5.3	760	240	16.5	0.33	198	3.0
49	835	165	9.9	0.17	534	8.2	736	264	21.8	0.44	289	4.7

Table 2. Performance of CX hill-climbers on the *Root2path*. For both cases the number of moves required is below the predicted upper bound $\lambda = (l+1)/2$. Likewise the number of function evaluations increases quadratically in l. These data have been obtained for 1000 initial points.

probability that crossover will produce an offspring in some set $N_j > N_i$ can be shown to be

$$p(i) = \frac{2^{2i+1} - 1}{l 2^{\lambda+i}}, \quad i = 0, \cdots, \lambda - 2.$$

Although increasing in i, if $\mathbf{x} \in N_0$ we have $p(0) = \frac{1}{l}\frac{1}{2^\lambda}$ which decreases exponentially in l. Hence a GA that selects the second parent for crossover randomly from the entire search space, as for example in Jones' 'Headless chicken' experiments [6], would not even get off the ground.

By contrast, the probability to achieve some improvement on the 'royal road' is significantly higher if the second parent is a non-bridge point too, provided that the first and second parents do not belong to the same subset. If the latter is the case no improvement can be made because both parents share the value at the $(2i+1)$st and $(2i+2)$nd positions. Therefore, once the population has converged into any of the subsets N_i the search of the GA terminates.

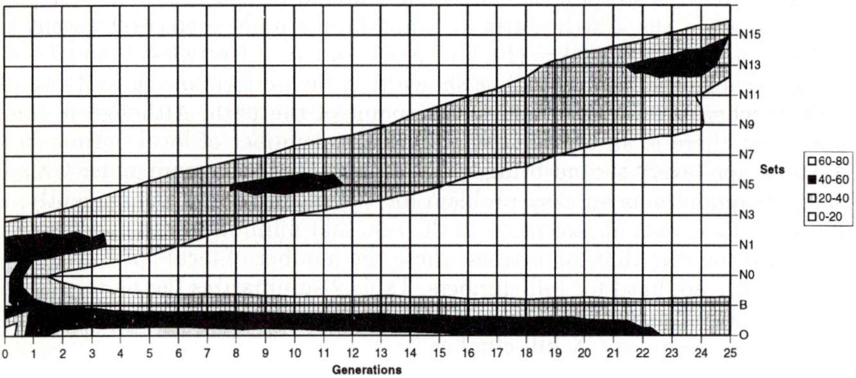

Fig. 1. Density plot of the population of the standard GA while solving the *Root2path* problem for $l = 29$. The population is seeded on the path. Whereas one part of the population leaves the path in the first generation the other climbs up the 'royal road' towards the global optimum in the right upper corner.

When solving the *Root2path* problem we have assumed that the search starts on the path, i.e. the initial population is seeded on the path. Provided that the population is sufficiently large the GA will be able to exploit the 'royal

l	Function eval. MIN	MAX	MEAN	SEMEAN	Generations MIN	MAX	MEAN	SEMEAN	Restarts MEAN
9	336	502	365	8.1	1	2	1.1	0.06	0.0
19	374	2552	906	95.7	1	16	4.1	0.60	0.0
29	394	5120	2532	198.0	1	28	13.2	1.19	0.0
39	1878	39094	9296	1484.6	9	285	59.7	10.84	0.9
49	3230	52498	14862	2391.5	16	373	95.1	16.70	1.4
59	17320	2588734	626040	102321.3	117	18608	4483.2	733.69	149.3

Table 3. Performance of the standard GA when applied to the Root2path. The performance of the GA depends strongly on the population size.

road' that leads to the global optimum. Figure 1 shows a density plot of the population of the standard GA as it evolves through time. Apparently, for $l = 29$ a population size of 200 is sufficient to let the GA walk the 'royal road' up to the global optimum. By contrast, as shown in Table 3, for $l = 59$ the GA requires a substantial number of restarts. The population size is much too small for the problem size and the GA converges most of the time on the 'royal road' before it reaches the global optimum.

5 The slope function and the extended *Root2path* problem

Having studied the *Root2path* we now turn our attention to the slope function. The slope function used by Horn corresponds to the *Onemax* function introduced by Ackley [7] which has been widely studied in the literature and requires no further analysis here. The Hamming landscape of the *Onemax* function is unimodal and accommodates an easy problem for a hill-climbing algorithm. By contrast, as shown by Culberson [4], the number of local optima in the CX landscape increases exponentially in the problem size.

l	Function eval. MIN	MAX	MEAN	SEMEAN	Generations MIN	MAX	MEAN	SEMEAN	Restarts MEAN
9	200	592	372	24.4	0	3	1.1	0.16	0.0
19	912	1656	1284	33.2	4	9	6.4	0.22	0.0
29	1120	2406	2005	46.9	5	13	10.4	0.32	0.0
39	2294	5948	2889	138.8	12	35	16.1	0.88	0.1
49	2868	14282	4386	429.4	16	89	25.8	2.76	0.3

Table 4. Performance of the standard GA. The effort, measured in terms of both, function evaluations and generations, required to solve the *Onemax* problem grows linearly in the string length.

The *Onemax* problem has been commonly regarded as a GA-easy problem. Indeed, the GA solves the problem with moderate effort (Table 4); generations and function evaluations required to solve the problem increase linearly in the string length.

Nevertheless, to circumvent the local optima present in the crossover landscape of the *Onemax* function it is essential that the population of the GA has sufficiently converged so that crossover takes place between fairly close parents [8]. However, this requirement is incompatible with the need for a diverse population for solving the *Root2path* problem subsequently. Indeed, what happens in the extended *Root2path* is that after having solved the *Onemax* problem the majority of the population moves straight into the set N_0 where the algorithm eventually terminates (Figure 2). In other words, the 'royal road', so beneficial for solving the *Root2path* problem, cannot be taken by the GA when solving the extended *Root2path* problem. Thus Horn's original long path problem has a less favourable structure than one would have expected in the first place. Under

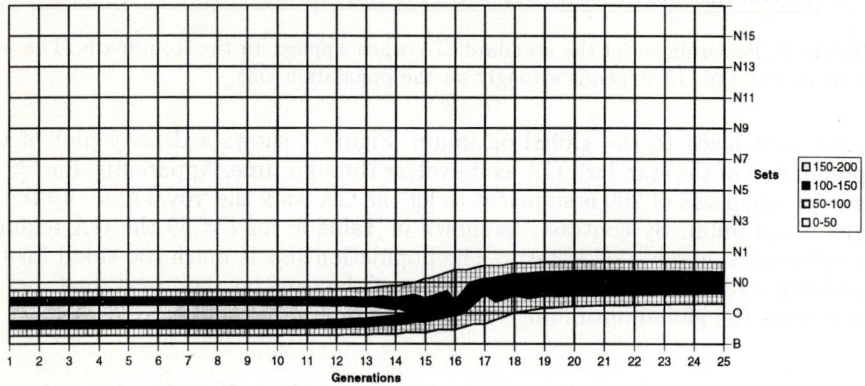

Fig. 2. Density plot of the population of the standard GA when solving the extended *Root2path* problem for $l = 29$. The population changes gradually from the set O into the set N_0 which contains the minimum of the *Onemax* function and where the algorithm eventually terminates.

these circumstances one may wonder that the GA solves the extended *Root2path* problem after all. However, the reason is that the Hamming distance between the optimum of the *Root2path* and the minimum of the *Onemax* function is two. Hence the GA most of the time hits the top of the *Root2path* while attempting to solve the *Onemax* problem. Table 5 shows the origin of the parents that generated the optimal solution. If the GA were walking up the 'royal road' in

	First parent			Second parent		
l	Off-path	Non-bridge	Bridge	Off-path	Non-bridge	Bridge
9	0.27	0.47	0.13	0.73	0.13	0.00
19	0.80	0.13	0.07	0.93	0.07	0.00
29	0.87	0.10	0.03	0.83	0.17	0.00
39	1.00	0.00	0.00	0.90	0.10	0.00
49	0.90	0.10	0.00	0.93	0.07	0.00

Table 5. When solving the extended *Root2path* problem the majority of optimal solutions are formed by crossover between elements that lie off the path. The share of non-bridge points is too small to attribute the success of the GA to the 'royal road' in the *Root2path*. The values are averaged over 30 experiments.

the *Root2path* the first parent at least would have been an instance of the path. Instead the figures show that the majority of parents lie outside the path. Thus the GA hits the optimum more by chance than by exploiting building-block structures. Nevertheless, it remains true that the GA take advantage of 'short cuts' not available to Hamming cube hill-climbers. However these 'short cuts' are not properties of the *Onemax* function nor of the *Root2path* but arise from the way that the functions are linked.

6 Summary

When investigating Horn's long path problem we have distinguished between the *Root2path* problem and the *extended Root2path* problem. The latter includes the minimization of the *Onemax* function.

As for the *Root2path* problem the GA takes advantage of the 'royal road' structure present in the *Root2path* which admits short paths to the global optimum. In essence, the GA solves the *Root2path* in a landscape where it does not show up as a long path problem. However, if we want to solve the *Root2path* problem in a landscape other than the Hamming landscape then a CX hill-climber solves the problem more efficiently than the GA does. This begs the question can we construct a long path problem for GAs and if how long could it be?

On the other hand, the GA is able to solve the *extended Root2path* problem faster than neither CX nor HC hill-climber could do alone. But again, a hybrid hill-climber using both landscapes would outperform the GA.

Finally, the investigation of the *Root2path* has brought up another phenomena that causes difficulties for a GA. The extended *Root2path* contains two problems that impose incompatible requirements on the GA. Solving the *Onemax* problems requires fairly similar binary strings for performing crossover. This significantly reduces the diversity in the population needed for solving the *Root2path* problem. Since this condition causes considerable difficulties for the GA it is reasonable to label the extended *Root2path* problem as GA-hard.

References

1. J.Horn, D.E. Goldberg, and K. Deb. Long path problems. In Yuval Davidor, Hans-Paul Schwefel, and Reinhard Männer, editors, *Parallel Problem Solving from Nature*, volume 3. Springer-Verlag, Berlin, 1994.
2. M. Mitchell, S. Forrest, and J.H. Holland. The royal road for genetic algorithms: Fitness landscapes and genetic algorithm performance. In F.J. Varela and P. Bourgine, editors, *Toward A Practice of Autonomous Systems: Proceeding of the First European Conference on Artificial Life.* MIT Press, Cambridge, MA, 1991.
3. Melanie Mitchell, John H. Holland, and Stephanie Forrest. When will a genetic algorithm outperform hill-climbing? In J.D.Cowan, G.Tesauro, and J.Alspector, editors, *Advances in Neural Information Processing Systems 6.* Morgan Kaufmann, San Mateo, CA, 1994.
4. J.C. Culberson. Mutation-crossover isomorphisms and the construction of discriminating functions. *Evolutionary Computation*, 2(3), 1995.
5. C.R. Reeves and C. Höhn. Integrating local search into genetic algorithms. In *Applied Decision Technologies.*, volume 2, London, 1995.
6. T. Jones. Crossover, macromutation, and population-based search. In Larry J. Eshelman, editor, *Proceedings of the Sixth International Conference on Genetic Algorithms.* Morgan Kaufmann, San Mateo, 1995.
7. D.H. Ackley. *A Connectionist Machine for Genetic Hillclimbing.* Kluwer Academic Publishers, Boston, 1987.
8. C. Höhn and C.R. Reeves. The genetic algorithm landscape for the *onemax* problem. Submitted to *Second Nordic Workshop on Genetic Algorithms*, 1996.

Random Tree Generation for Genetic Programming

Hitoshi IBA

Machine Inference Section, Electrotechnical Laboratory (ETL),
1-1-4 Umezono, Tsukuba Science City, Ibaraki, 305, Japan.,
email. iba@etl.go.jp

Abstract. This paper introduces a random tree generation algorithm for GP (Genetic Programming). Generating random trees is an essential part of GP. However, the recursive method commonly used in GP does not necessarily generate random trees, i.e the standard GP initialization procedure does not sample the space of possible initial trees uniformly. This paper proposes a truly random tree generation procedure for GP. Our approach is grounded upon a bijection method, i.e., a 1–1 correspondence between a tree with n nodes and some simple word composed by letters x and y. We show how to use this correspondence to generate a GP tree and how GP search is improved by using this "randomness".

1 Introduction

Generating random trees is an essential part of Genetic Programming (i.e., GP). It plays an important role both in the initialization process and in the mutation. However, the recursive method commonly used in GP does not necessarily generate random trees. We suspect that biased tree generation degrades the GP search performance.

[Koza92] defines two different ways of generating a member of the initial population, the "full" method and the "grow" method. For both methods, each tree is generated recursively using the following algorithm described in pseudo-code [Montana95, p.201]:–

```
Recursive_Tree(max_depth, generation_method)
begin
 if max_depth=0 then
    set the root of the tree to a randomly selected terminal;
 else if generation_method=full then
    set the root of the tree to a randomly selected nonterminal;
 else
    set the root to a randomly selected node
            which is either terminal or nonterminal;
 for each argument of the root, generate a subtree with the call
    Generate_Tree(max_depth - 1,generation_method);
end;
```

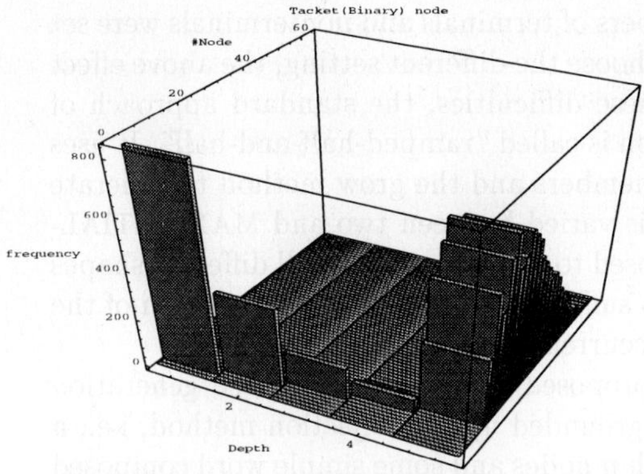

(a) Frequencies of Different Trees.

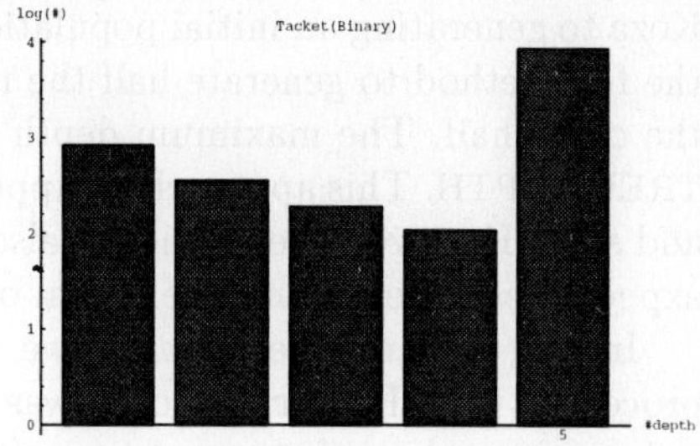

(b) Log-Scale Frequencies of Generated Trees.

Fig. 1. Tree Generation by Recursive Method.

We call the above algorithm Recursive_Tree. For a parse tree generated by the full method, the length along any path from the root to a leaf is the same no matter which path is taken, i.e., the tree is of full depth along any path. Thus, we often use the grow method for the sake of generating random trees. Therefore, this paper focuses on the above Recursive_Tree with generation_method=GROW.

Trees generated by the above recursion are not necessarily random. For instance, consider generating a tree for the following terminal set (T) and nonterminal set (F):–

$$T = \{D_0,\ D_1,\ D_2,\ D_3\} \tag{1}$$
$$F = \{AND_2,\ OR_2,\ NAND_2,\ NOR_2\} \tag{2}$$

The subscript of a nonterminal (i.e., 2) represents the number of its arity. Fig. 1 shows the generation result, in which trees are generated 10,000 times by the above Recursive_Tree with max_depth=5 and generation_method=GROW. Fig. 1(a) shows the frequencies of generated trees of different depths and node sizes. Fig. 1(b) plots the log-scale frequencies for different depths.

This experiment shows that generated trees are not random in the following senses:–

1. Trees of depth 5 (i.e. maximum depth) are generated most often. Although this seems to be natural because of the tree distribution, yet its frequency deviates from the actual number of trees.
2. Trees of depth 1 (i.e. minimum depth) are generated more often[1]. This is not expected because the following single tree topology exists for depth 1:–

3. The trees of depths between 2 and 5 are generated less often and the frequencies are decreasing with depths. This is unexpected because the numbers of distinct trees are increasing with their depths.

[1] Note that a tree of depth 0 is a terminal node.

For the sake of simplicity, the numbers of terminals and nonterminals were set to be equal for this experiment. If we choose the different setting, the above effect will be more remarkable. To avoid these difficulties, the standard approach of Koza to generating an initial population is called "ramped-half-and-half". It uses the full method to generate half the members and the grow method to generate the other half. The maximum depth is varied between two and MAX-INITIAL-TREE-DEPTH. This approach is supposed to generate trees of all different shapes and sizes. However, the method is also suffering from the salient deviation of the expected occurrence and the actual occurrence.

In our earlier paper [Iba95], we proposed a truly random tree generation procedure for GP. Our approach was grounded upon a bijection method, i.e., a 1–1 correspondence between a tree with n nodes and some simple word composed by letters x and y. This paper presents experimental results to show that GP search is improved by using this truly random tree generation. Thereafter we discuss our experimental results and how to use this randomness in order to investigate a GP efficiency criterion.

2 Tree Generation for Genetic Programming

This section briefly describes a random tree generation process for GP. The detailed description of this process is given in Appendix and [Iba95].

There exists a 1–1 correspondence between a tree with n nodes and a set of Dyck words[2] with n letters x and $n-1$ letters y. Given a 1-dominated word[3] v that has n letters x and $n-1$ letters y, we can build a tree $g(v)$ of size n as follows [Alonso95,p.47]:–

Algorithm Tree_by_Dyck:

Step1 We initialize an empty stack.

Step2 We read the letters of v from the left to the right and each time we find a letter x followed by k letters y, we take from the stack the last k trees that we have added, the trees $T_1, \cdots, T_k$, and we put into the stack the tree formed by a root that has for children the roots of the trees $T_1, \cdots, T_k$. The tree $g(v)$ is the unique tree that remains in the stack.

For instance,suppose that we have generated the word $xxyxxxxyyxyyy$, then the tree generation is shown in Fig. ??. Fig. 2(a).

Now we can introduce an efficient algorithm that builds a random tree with n nodes. This method generates a random permutation of size $2n-1$, then a random word with n letters x and $n-1$ letters y, and next a random 1-dominated

[2] w is a Dyck word if w is either an empty word or a word $xuyv$ where u and v are some Dyck words. If we denote by D the language of the Dyck words, we obtain:–

$$D = \epsilon + xDyD. \tag{3}$$

[3] w is a 1-dominated sequence if and only if there exists a Dyck left factor u such that $w = xu$.

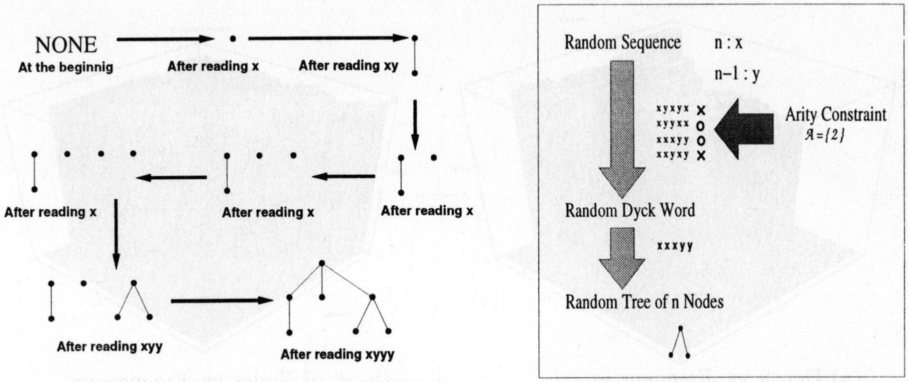

(a) Generating a Tree from a Dyck Word. (b) Generating a Random Tree.

Fig. 2. Generation Process of a Random GP Tree from a Dyck Word.

word v with n letters x and $n-1$ letters y. Finally, we compute $g(v)$ so as to obtain a random tree with n nodes. All these steps have a complexity in $O(n)$. Thus, we have obtained a linear algorithm that builds a random trees with n nodes as desired (see [Alonso95,p.41] for details).

GP trees should follow the constraints of the nodes' arities. For instance, there should be no nonterminal nodes other than 2-arity for the nonterminals given in Eq.(2). Thus we have to modify the previous tree generation method in order to generate legal trees according to the arity constraint. We have built an efficient algorithm **Algorithm RAND_Tree (node_min, node_max)** to generate a random tree of nodes between node_min and node_max under an arity constraint. Fig. 2(b) shows the revised generation process of a 1-dominated Dyck word. See Appendix or [Iba95] for the details.

Fig. 3 shows the result of generating trees of sizes up to 6. This figure plots the frequencies of distinct trees (i.e., id.) for different depths (Fig. 3(a)) and for different node sizes (Fig. 3(b)). The trees were generated 10,000 times. The arity constraint chosen was Eq.(7). Tree identity (id.) is the natural ordering of a tree (see [Er85] for details). As can be seen, all trees are generated uniformly.

3 Experimental Results

It is well-known that "randomness" is important for stochastic algorithms. If the random generator is wrongly designed, i.e., the randomizer is biased, the search performance will deteriorate. This is supposed to be true of the tree generation in GP. Thus, we expect that the random tree generation process we have described will improve the GP search. We have conducted several experiments to confirm the effectiveness of the "randomness" introduced.

For the sake of the page limitation, we only show the effectiveness of RAND_Tree with experiments on the problem of predicting the Mackey-Glass time series. The Mackey-Glass time series is generated by integrating the following delay differential equation and is used as a standard benchmark for prediction algorithms:–

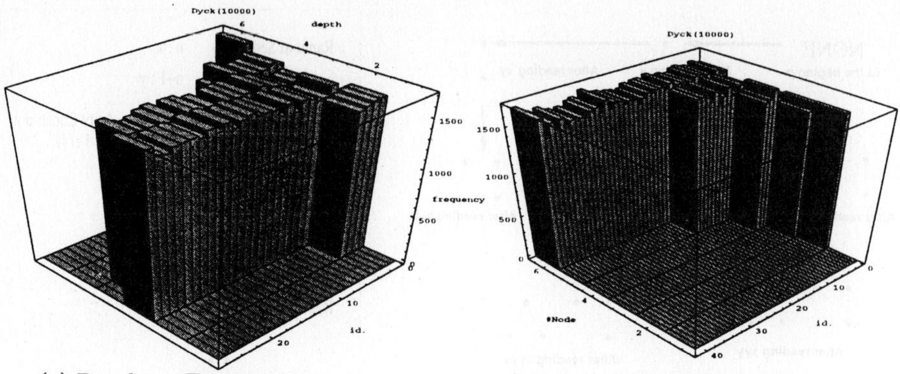

(a) Depth vs. Frequencies. (b) # of Nodes vs. Frequencies.

Fig. 3. Frequencies of Different Trees Generated by Bijective Method.

Table 1. Tree Generation Parameters for GP.

RAND_Tree	min_node	1
	max_node	30
Recursive_Tree	max_depth_for_new_trees	6
	max_depth_after_crossover	17
	max_mutant_depth	4
	grow_method	GROW

$$\frac{dx(t)}{dt} = \frac{ax(t-\tau)}{1+x^{10}(t-\tau)} - bx(t), \tag{4}$$

with a=0.2, b= 0.1 and τ=17. The trajectory is chaotic and lies on an approximately 2.1-dimensional strange attractor.

For the sake of comparison, all the parameters chosen were the same as those used in the previous study [Oakley94, p.380, Table17.3], except that the terminal set consisted of ten past data for the short-term prediction. We use the GP parameters[4] shown in Table 1.

Fig. 4 shows the results of experiments. This figure shows the best raw fitness (i.e. mean square error, MSE) by generation for training data (Fig. 4(a)) and for test data (Fig. 4(b)). The mean square errors were averaged over 20 runs. Note the superiority of RAND_Tree over the usual recursive method, not only for training data but also for test data.

Table 2 summaries the experimental results for various problems. The table shows the averages (i.e., avg.) and the standard deviations (i.e., std.) of best performances (i.e. best raw fitnesses) over 20 runs. Table 3 shows the number of successes (i.e. some expression equivalent to the target expression is acquired) for 20 runs within a maximum of 200 generations. The tables clearly show the

[4] The parameters for Recursive_Tree are those used in a GP system called "sgpc1.1", i.e., a Simple Genetic Programming in C written by Walter Alden Tackett.

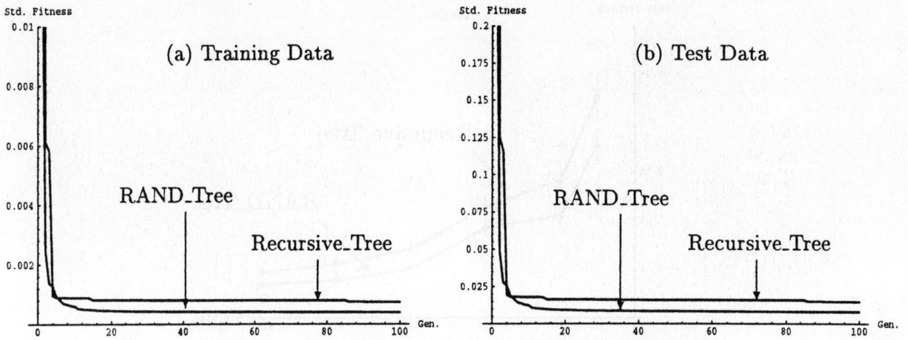

Fig. 4. Predicting the Mackey–Glass equation

Table 2. Summary of Experimental Results.

Problem	RAND_Tree avg.	RAND_Tree std.	Recursive_Tree avg.	Recursive_Tree std.
Regression ($y = \frac{1}{2}x^2$)	1.33×10^{-2}	2.38×10^{-4}	1.72×10^{-2}	3.18×10^{-4}
Trigonometric Identities	1.03×10^{-1}	9.41×10^{-3}	1.57×10^{-1}	3.82×10^{-2}
Chaotic Time Series (training)	3.95×10^{-4}	1.00×10^{-7}	8.97×10^{-4}	1.10×10^{-7}
Chaotic Time Series (test)	8.29×10^{-3}	4.00×10^{-5}	1.84×10^{-2}	5.81×10^{-5}

superiority of the random tree process we have proposed over the usual recursive method. The details of the above experiments are described in [Iba95].

4 Discussion

For the above experiments, the population size we chose was relatively small, compared to that chosen by [Koza92]. This is because we expect the randomness effect to be much more remarkable in a smaller population. To confirm this, we have repeated the same experiment (i.e. trigonometric identities) for various sizes of populations. Fig. 5 shows the result, which plots the averaged best performances over 20 runs with standard deviation bars. As expected, the figure shows that the greater the population size is, the smaller the difference of performances. However, the difference is statistically significant for greater population sizes, which was confirmed by statistical t-test. Thus, we have provided the evidence for the superiority of RAND_Tree over the recursive method.

[Koza92,Ch.9] showed by experiments that GP is more efficient than random generate–and–test on a Boolean circuit synthesis task. [Lang92] also compared

Table 3. Number of successes (i.e. some expression equivalent to the target is acquired) for 20 runs.

Method	$y = \frac{1}{2}x^2$	$\cos 2x = 1 - \sin^2 x$
Recursive_Tree	2	1
RAND_Tree	7	5

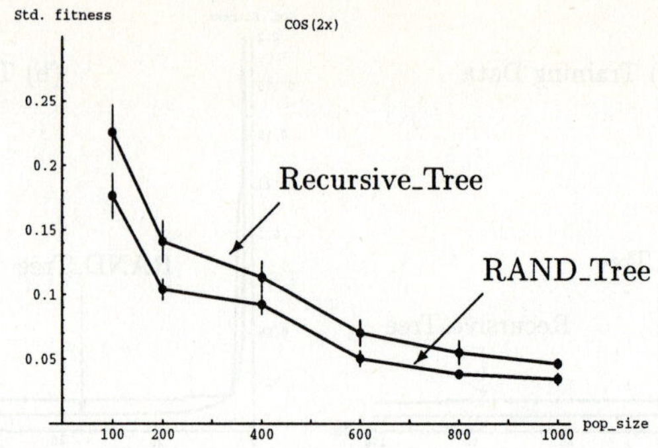

Fig. 5. Best Standard Fitness Found for Various Population Sizes

GP with the hill climbing method for this task. The benchmark problem was the task of finding logic circuits (i.e., Boolean functions) to compute the various functions of 3 inputs. Koza compared GP with the process of selecting an S-expression at random. He enumerated the total number of possible trees of node size 41 and generated 10,000,000 random integers, each between 1 and the total number. For each of the selected integers, he constructed the corresponding rooted, point-labeled tree with ordered branches for that integer. He did not explain this constructive process. We used our RAND_Tree process for this benchmark and conducted an experiment in comparing the following three methods; i.e., 1) Random Tree Selection, 2) GP (Recursive_Tree), and 3) GP (RAND_Tree). For the random tree selection, we have only to call RAND_Tree for a given node size (i.e., 41). Thus we need not conduct the enumeration as [Koza92] did. As expected, the experiment gave almost the same result as [Koza92,ch.12,Table9.3,9.4]. Through this experimental, we have confirmed the following efficiency ordering of three methods:–

$$\text{Random Tree Selection} \preceq \text{GP (Recursive\_Tree)} \preceq \text{GP (RAND\_Tree)} \quad (5)$$

Koza proposed an efficiency criterion called "computational effort" [Koza92, p.194]. This experiment showed that RAND_Tree gives a relatively precise performance criterion without the enumeration as Koza did. Thus we think RAND_Tree process is used as another criterion for computational efforts (see [Iba95] for details of this experiment). We are working on this topic for the sake of the mathematical analysis of GP performance.

5 Conclusion

This paper introduced a random tree generation procedure for GP. Our approach was based upon a bijection method. We extended the bijective method for tree generation so that generated trees follow the arity constraint. We showed the GP search was improved by introducing this "randomness" in the generation process. The "randomness" proposed in this paper will lead to a suitable performance criterion for GP search.

Acknowledgments.
We are grateful to Walter Alden Tackett, for providing his Simple Genetic Programming in C ("sgpc1.1"), which we used to conduct our comparative experiments.

References

[Alonso95] Alonso,L. and Schott,R., Random Generation of Trees, Kluwer Academic Publishers, 1995

[Er85] Er,M.C., Enumerating Ordered Trees Lexicographically, in *The Computer Journal*, vol.28, no.5, pp.538–543, 1985

[Iba95] Iba,H., Generating Random Trees for Genetic Programming, Computers ETL-TR-95-35, 1995

[Koza92] Koza, J. Genetic Programming, On the Programming of Computers by means of Natural Selection, MIT Press, 1992

[Lang95] Lang,K.J., Hill Climbing Beats Genetic Search on a Boolean Circuit Synthesis Problem of Koza's, in *Proc. of 12th Machine Learning Workshop*, pp.340–344, 1995

[Lovasz79] Lovasz, L. Combinational problem and exercises, Akademiai Kiado, Budapest, 1979

[Montana95] Montana, D.J., Strongly Typed Genetic Programming, in *Evolutionary Computation*, vol.3, no.2, pp.199–230, 1995

[Oakley94] Oakley, H. Two Scientific Applications of Genetic Programming: Stack Filters and Non-Linear Equation Fitting to Chaotic Data, in *Advances in Genetic Programming*, (ed. Kenneth E. Kinnear, Jr.), MIT Press, 1994

Appendix: Generating Random GP Trees

The appendix briefly overviews the generation process of GP trees. See [Iba95] for the details.

First, we define the following notions:–

Definition 1 Arity Constraint. An arity constraint $\mathcal{A}$ is the set of numbers of arities of nonterminal (i.e. functional) nodes.
For instance, $\mathcal{A} = \{2\}$ for Eq.(2).

Consider generating a random tree of n nodes according to an arity constraint $\mathcal{A}$. Let l_i be the number of nodes whose arity is i. Generated trees should satisfy the following equation:–

$$\sum_{i \in \mathcal{A}} i \times l_i = n - 1 \tag{6}$$

Definition 2 Arity Equation. We call the above equation the "arity equation" for $\mathcal{A}$ and denote it as $AE(\mathcal{A})$. We represent the solutions to this arity equation as $SL_n(AE(\mathcal{A})) = \{(l_{i1}, l_{i2}, \cdots, l_{ik})\}$. We call $s \in SL_n(AE(\mathcal{A}))$ the "node constraint" of $AE(\mathcal{A})$.

Example Let n be 5 and $\mathcal{A}$={1,2,3,4}. Then we get

$$AE(\mathcal{A}) : l_1 + 2l_2 + 3l_3 + 4l_4 = 4, \tag{7}$$

and we can derive

$$SL_5(AE(\mathcal{A})) = \{(4,0,0,0), (2,1,0,0), (1,0,1,0), (0,2,0,0), (0,0,0,1)\}. \tag{8}$$

Definition 3 Residue. For $s = (l_{i1}, l_{i2}, \cdots, l_{ik}) \in SL_n(E)$, let $r(s) = n - l_{i1} - l_{i2} - \cdots - l_{ik}$. $r(s)$ is called the "residue" of s.

Example Consider the previous example. We get the residues shown in Table 4.

Definition 4. For $s = (l_{i1}, l_{i2}, \cdots, l_{ik}) \in SL_n(E)$, let $\overline{Cn(s)}$ be as follows:-

$$\overline{Cn(s)} = \frac{n!}{l_{i1}! \times l_{i2}! \times \cdots \times l_{ik}! \times r(s)!} \times \frac{1}{n}, \tag{9}$$

where $r(s) = n - l_{i1} - l_{i2} - \cdots - l_{ik}$.

$\overline{Cn(s)}$ is the number of distinct trees according to a node constraint s, in which the number of nonterminal nodes of i-arity is l_i and the number of terminal nodes is $r(s)$. For instance, consider the tree generation for $n = 5$ under the arity constraint $\mathcal{A} = \{1, 2, 3, 4\}$. Generating of a Dyck word of 5 letters of x and (5-1) letters of y is regarded as putting y letters into the 5 slots (i.e._) described below:–

x _ x _ x _ x _ x _

Let us take the following solution:–

$$s2 = (l_1, l_2, l_3, l_4) = (2, 1, 0, 0) \in SL_5(E). \tag{10}$$

Remember that $r(s2) = 2$. In this case, the Dyck word under the node constraint $s2$ is the one given by filling the 5 slots with y twice ($= l_1$), yy once ($= l_2$), and null strings (denoted as $*$) twice($= r(s)$), without overlapping. For instance,

```
  x y x y y x * x * x y
= x y x y y x x x y
```

is a legal word. The number of the different strings under the node constraint $s2$ is derived from the polynomial theorem in the following way:–

$$\frac{5!}{l_1! \times l_2! \times l_3! \times l_4! \times r(s)!} = \frac{5!}{2! \times 1! \times 0! \times 0! \times 2!} = 30 \tag{11}$$

Transforming a 1-dominated word by the cyclic permutation gives us the equivalent classes of 1-dominated words. For instance, the following two words belong to the same class:–

```
x y x y y x x x y
x y y x x x y x y
```

Thus, the number of distinct 1-dominated Dyck words under the node constraint $s2$ is $\frac{30}{5} = 6$, which means that there exist five distinct trees of six nodes with two 1-arity nonterminal nodes, one 2-arity nonterminal node, and two terminals (see Table 4 and Fig. 6(b)).

In the same way, the numbers of trees under the other node constraints are derived as shown in Table 4.

With these preparations, we can build a random tree of nodes between node_min and node_max under an arity constraint $\mathcal{A}$ as follows:–

Algorithm RAND_Tree (node_min, node_max):

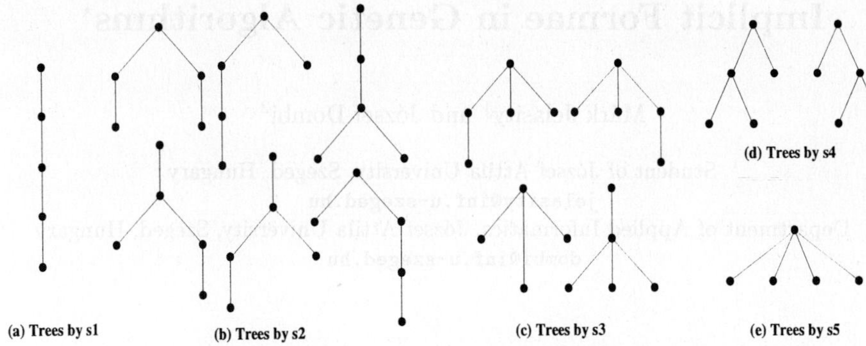

Fig. 6. Different Trees Generated by Various Solutions.

Table 4. Generating GP Trees of Five Nodes.

Solution	l_1 l_2 l_3 l_4	residue	$\overline{Cn}$
s1	4 0 0 0	1	$\frac{5!}{4!\,0!\,0!\,0!\,1!} \cdot \frac{1}{5} = 1$
s2	2 1 0 0	2	$\frac{5!}{2!\,1!\,0!\,0!\,2!} \cdot \frac{1}{5} = 6$
s3	1 0 1 0	3	$\frac{5!}{1!\,0!\,1!\,0!\,3!} \cdot \frac{1}{5} = 4$
s4	0 2 0 0	3	$\frac{5!}{0!\,2!\,0!\,0!\,3!} \cdot \frac{1}{5} = 2$
s5	0 0 0 1	4	$\frac{5!}{0!\,0!\,0!\,1!\,4!} \cdot \frac{1}{5} = 1$
$l_1 + 2l_2 + 3l_3 + 4l_4 = 4$		$5 - l_1 - l_2 - l_3 - l_4$	$\frac{5!}{l_1! \times l_2! \times l_3! \times l_4! \times r(s)!} \cdot \frac{1}{5}$

Step1 According to the probability distribution proportionate to Catalan number $Cn(n)$[5] or more precisely the following $N(n)$, pick an integer n from node_min to node_max.
Step2 Derive the number of different trees of n node sizes for each solution s of the arity equation $AE(\mathcal{A})$. Let the number be $\overline{Cn(s)}$ and $N(n) = \sum_{s \in SL_n(AE(\mathcal{A}))} \overline{Cn(s)}$.
Step3 According to the probability proportionate to $\overline{Cn(s)}$, pick a solution s.
Step4 Generate a Dyck word w following the node constraint of s.
Step5 Translate w into a 1-dominate word and generate a tree as shown in Fig. 2(a).

We call the above algorithm **RAND_Tree** (see also Fig. 2)(b). Considering $\overline{Cn(s)}$ and $N(n)$ are derived off-line or before the tree generation process of GP, the computational complexity of this algorithm with GP run is $O(n)$. **Step4** is executed straightforwardly by filling the slots between x by y letters. For instance, in case of $s2$ in Table 4, all we have to do is to choose two slots for y and one slot for yy.

[5] The number of distinct trees with n nodes. Cn is given as follows [Lovasz,ch.1.4]:–

$$Cn(n) = \frac{1}{n}\binom{2n-2}{n-1}. \tag{12}$$

Implicit Formae in Genetic Algorithms*

Márk Jelasity[1] and József Dombi[2]

[1] Student of József Attila University, Szeged, Hungary
jelasity@inf.u-szeged.hu
[2] Department of Applied Informatics, József Attila University, Szeged, Hungary
dombi@inf.u-szeged.hu

Abstract. This paper discusses the term *implicit forma*, which is useful for explaining the behaviour of genetic algorithms. Implicit formae are predicates over the chromosome space that are not strongly connected to the representation at hand but are capable of directing the search. After a short theoretical discussion, three examples are given for illustration, including the subset sum problem which is NP-complete.

1 Introduction

An understanding of how genetic algorithms (GAs) work is of major importance from the point of view of both theory and application. For a long time, the concept of schemata played the central role in GA theory [1]. However, it is now clear that this concept is itself not enough for a prediction of the behaviour of the GA [11]; at least some generalization of the concept is necessary for both binary and general representations.

For general representations, the concept of formae (e.g. [4]) has been introduced. This approach is especially useful in the design of genetic operators, but it should be mentioned that formae are very similar to schemata in the sense that they are strongly connected to the representation at hand (though the representation is normally designed using the previously chosen formae).

This paper shows that besides the carefully designed formae there are other factors capable of directing or even misleading the search. These factors seem to be treated as properties of formae in the literature, e.g. the variance of fitness [7, 9] or noise [10]. While understanding that these are useful tools for gaining information about the quality of a given representation of the problem at hand, we try to provide a deeper insight into the search process by introducing the term *implicit forma*.

In section 2, we give a brief introduction to forma analysis, restricting ourselves only to the basic definitions, and implicit formae are then discussed. In section 3, the new term is illustrated through three case studies. One of the examples is the subset sum problem, an NP-complete combinatorial problem. The relation of the GA and the bit-hillclimber algorithm is also discussed on the basis of implicit formae.

* This work was supported by the OTKA grant T 020150

2 Formae and Implicit Formae

2.1 Formae

A discussion of formae is needed only to make it clear why the name *implicit forma* has been used to denote the properties discussed in the paper. Thus, a very basic knowledge suffices. A detailed description can be found in [4].

A representation maps the solution space S to a chromosome space C. Usually, every $x \in C$ can be regarded as an intersection of a set of predicates over C. If $C = \{0,1\}^n$, then these predicates are the schemata of order 1. If C is the chromosome space of the permutation representation of the traveling salesman problem, then these predicates are the subsets of the set of all permutations with a fixed town at a given position. Thus, a set of *alleles* (i.e. predicates that a chromosome may contain) can be assigned to every representation. A *forma* is simply the intersection of a subset of the alleles. The empty set is not a forma. It is clear that if $C = \{0,1\}^n$, then formae reduce to schemata, so a forma is a generalization of the concept of a schema.

From our point of view, the essence of the above definitions is that formae are predicates over the chromosome space C that are used to design representations and operators.

2.2 Implicit Formae

It has already been shown [2, 3] that every predicate over the space of all chromosomes C behaves according to the schema theorem for some appropriate genetic operators; in other words, its proportion is approximately determined by its observed fitness provided that the appropriate operators are used. The forma analysis is connected to this result, i.e. representation-independent operators are designed [9] to be "friendly" with the formae given by the representation. However, it is possible that these operators are also "friendly" with other (previously unknown) subsets of C so these subsets are also capable of directing the search. Examples of this phenomenon will be given in section 3. The existence of such predicates motivates our central definitions.

First, let us fix the main GA components; the chromosome space C, a set of genetic operators (selection, crossover, mutation) and their parameters designed not to be too disruptive (this assumption will be clarified later). We will refer to these components later as *fixed GA components.* The following definitions are independent of the objective function.

Notation 1. Let $\mathcal{P}(C)$ be the set of all predicates over C.

Definition 2 has a central role.

Definition 2. The *degree of relevance* of a given predicate $P \in \mathcal{P}(C)$ with respect to the fixed GA components is $r(= r(P))$ iff during the successive iterations of the GA (given by the fixed GA components and P as the objective function), starting from an infinite uniformly distributed random population, the proportion of P goes to r as the number of generations goes to infinity, where

$$P(x) = \begin{cases} 1 \text{ if } x \in P \\ 0 \text{ otherwise} \end{cases}$$

If the above limit does not exist[3], let $r = 0$.

Note that the degree of relevance of a predicate is a more general feature than the disruption of the operators in the sense that it takes into account all the GA components.

Definition 3. A given predicate $P \in \mathcal{P}(C)$ is *relevant* iff $r(P) > p_0$ and is *neutral* iff $r(P) = p_0$, where $p_0 = |P|/|C|$.

The rate of relevance is also important and would be worth discussing in more detail, but for our present purposes Definition 3 suffices.

Though this paper focuses on the experimental results, for illustration we give an analysis of predicate EVEN without the straightforward technical details.

Definition 4. $C = \{0,1\}^n$, EVEN $\in \mathcal{P}(C)$; EVEN(x) iff the number of 1s in x is even.

Through this simple example, we would like to emphasize an advantage of Definition 2: due to the very simple objective function, an *exact* dynamic analysis of the relevance level can be given even for realistic problems and predicates.

Theorem 5. *Let the GA components be $C = \{0,1\}^n$, 1-point crossover with a probability P_c, generational and proportional selection without the transformation of the objective function (i.e. the fitness function equals the objective function) and no mutation. Then, for a large enough n,*

$$r(EVEN) \approx (1 - P_c) + \frac{1}{2}P_c \tag{1}$$

Proof. If n is large enough, then for any $x \in C$ the probability that a randomly chosen half of x contains an even number of 1s is $1/2$.

Let p_t be the proportion of EVEN in the tth generation, and let $g(p_t)$ be the expected proportion in generation $t+1$ without the effect of the genetic operators. Here, $g(p_t) = 1$.

The disruption of the genetic operators under the above assumptions is

$$p_{t+1} = \mathrm{dr}(g(p_t)) = g(p_t)(1 - P_c) + \frac{1}{2}P_c$$

It is trivial that $\mathrm{dr} \circ g$ has a unique fixpoint x_0 in $(0,1]$ which is given by the equation $\mathrm{dr}(g(x_0)) = x_0$ and equals (1).

[3] For instance, consider the GA components given in Theorem 5 but with $P_c = 0$ and a mutation operator that flips one random bit with a probability 1. Then, the proportion of predicate EVEN (see Definition 4) will show an oscillating behaviour.

Theorem 6. *Let the GA components be the same as in Theorem 5 except that the fitness function is the objective function incremented by 1. Then, for a large enough n,*

$$r(EVEN) \approx \frac{1}{2}\left(1 - \frac{3}{2}P_c + \sqrt{(\frac{3}{2}P_c)^2 - P_c + 1}\right) \qquad (2)$$

Proof. The same as the proof of Theorem 5, except that $g(p_t) = 2p_t/(p_t + 1)$.

A trivial corollary immediately follows from Theorems 5 and 6.

Corollary 7. *Under the assumptions of Theorem 5 or 6, if $P_c = 1$, then EVEN is neutral, and if $P_c \neq 1$, then EVEN is relevant with the relevance level given by (1) and (2), respectively.*

Now we can clarify the assumption that the operators in the fixed GA components are designed not to be too disruptive. This simply means that we want the members of F to have a high degree of relevance (preferably around 1). In our terms, this is what applying representation-independent genetic operators provides [9].

Finally, the implicit formae can be defined:

Definition 8. $F \in \mathcal{P}(C)$ is the set of all formae given by the fixed GA components. The formae will also be called *explicit formae* if emphasis of the difference from the implicit formae is necessary. The predicate $P \in \mathcal{P}(C)$ is an *implicit forma* iff it is not an explicit forma (i.e. $P \notin F$).

The term *implicit* means that these predicates are *not* related to the given representation (e.g. because they have not been considered important by the designer). Note that the majority of the elements of $\mathcal{P}(C)$ is an implicit forma.

Finally, it should be emphasized that a relevant predicate is not necessarily a useful predicate, in the sense that it is not necessarily capable of directing the search. Its usefulness depends on the particular objective function f, e.g. the variance of f in it and the properties of its "building blocks". Recall that the above definitions are independent of f.

3 Implicit Formae at Work

In this section, three case studies will be presented. The first illustrates how (rather exotic) implicit formae can direct the search process. The second is the subset sum problem, where we analyze the GA from the basis of implicit formae. The third offers a possible way of creating problems in which the GA performs better than a simple hillclimber algorithm, again using implicit formae. Such problems have received much attention recently [6]. At the end of the section arguments are given supporting our opinion that these experiments illustrate the important role of the implicit formae

The following GA components are the same in all three examples: $C = \{0,1\}^{100}$, 1-point crossover, mutation with $P_m = 0.003$ and a population size of 100. $P_c = 0.6$ in the last example, otherwise $P_c = 1$. The selection used was elitist and proportional. To perform the experiments, GENESIS was used modified so that it could trace our non-traditional implicit formae. The algorithms were run until 10^4 function evaluations in every experiment in each case. All functions were maximized.

3.1 An Example for Illustration: the Equal Blocks Problem

The objective function f of this example was designed especially to illustrate the idea of implicit formae. However, it should be noted that it may very well happen that real problems have features like this one. Its domain is C and for an $x \in C$ $f(x)$ is counted as follows:

Let us fix an ideal block size $b = 5$. Let us divide x into blocks that contain only 1s or 0s (e.g. 111|0|11|000). For every block containing b' elements let us subtract a penalty $|b - b'|$ from the objective function value and let us fix the optimum value at 0. It is clear that the optimal individual will contain 20 blocks with 5 elements in each. For illustration, we give the two optimal solutions of the 30-bit equal blocks problem:

000001111100000111110000011111, 111110000011111000001111100000

This task meets our needs because formae (i.e. schemata) have little meaning and high fitness variance. It may be thought that schemata like

$$* \ldots * 0111110 * \ldots *$$

have high fitness. However, their fitness variance is considerable because the function is extremely epistatic and is quite insensitive to shifting due to its inherent properties.

Twenty independent experiments were performed with the GA and also with the uniform random search. The averages of the solutions found were −23.3 and −212.2, respectively. An explanation of this result can be given on the basis of the existence of implicit formae. Let us define a predicate over C.

Definition 9. $[y, z]$-blocknumber$\in \mathcal{P}(C)$, $x \in C$ $[y, z]$-blocknumber(x) iff the number of blocks contained in x is in the interval $[y, z] \subset \mathbb{N}$.

Figures 1b and 1a support the following hypotheses:

- $[20, 30]$-blocknumber *is a relevant implicit forma.* As shown in Fig. 1a, it gained a proportion of almost 100% so it must be relevant. It is also interesting to note that (as shown in Fig. 1b) the expected and observed growth fits well. This also indicates that $[20, 30]$-blocknumber is relevant.
- $[20, 30]$-blocknumber *has an important role in the search process.* The typical S-curve in Fig. 1a is familiar from the analysis of the above average and low order schemata of low fitness variance.

To summarize the first example, it have been shown that an implicit forma the existence of which is not trivial from the representation played an important role in the search.

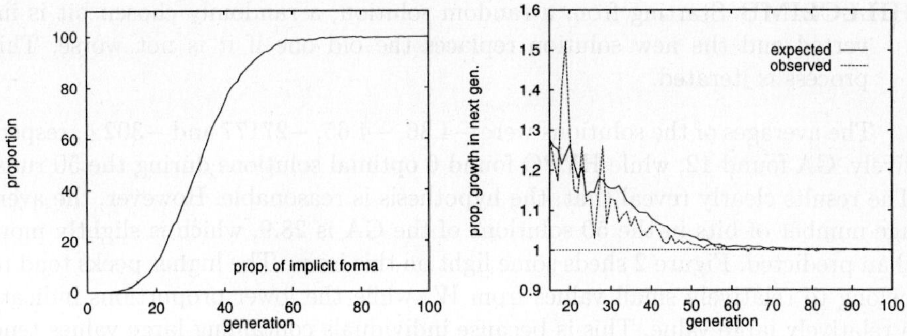

Fig. a
Fig. b

Fig. 1. (a) the proportion growth and (b) the expected and observed growth of the implicit forma [20, 30]-blocknumber. Average of 20 independent runs.

3.2 A Real Example: the Subset Sum Problem

We study the subset sum problem here. We are given a set $W = \{w_1, w_2, \ldots, w_n\}$ of n integers and a large integer M. We would like to find an $S \subseteq W$ such that the sum of the elements in S is closest to, without exceeding, M. This problem is NP-complete.

We used the same coding and objective function as suggested in [5]: If $x \in C$ ($x = (x_1, x_2, \ldots, x_{100})$), then let $P(x) = \sum_{i=1}^{100} x_i w_i$, and then

$$-f(x) = a(M - P(x)) + (1 - a)P(x)$$

where $a = 1$ when x is feasible (i.e. $M - P(e) \geq 0$) and $a = 0$ otherwise.

When creating a problem instance, elements of W were drawn randomly from the interval $[0, 10^4]$ instead of $[0, 10^3]$ (as was done in [5]) to obtain larger variance and thus a harder problem. The sum of all of the elements in W was 455784 and the sum to be created was 10^5. (It should be noted that optimal solutions do exist for the examined problem instance.)

After studying several experiments with the GA, a hypothesis seemed reasonable. The GA tends to sample individuals in which the number of 1s is close to $100 \cdot 10^5/455784 \approx 22$. That means that the numbers in W are treated as probability variables for which the expected value of the sum of any subset with 22 elements is 10^5. In other words, it is assumed by the hypothesis that the GA "figures out" how the problem instance was generated.

After forming the above hypothesis, four algorithms were run 50 times independently:

GA As described earlier.
HYPO A direct implementation of the hypothesis. Every bit is set to 1 with a probability of $22/100 = 0.22$ independently.
RAND Uniform random search.

HILLCLIMB Starting from a random solution, a randomly chosen bit is inverted and the new solution replaces the old one if it is not worse. This process is iterated.

The averages of the solutions were −4.36, −4.65, −27177 and −302.4, respectively. GA found 12, while HYPO found 6 optimal solutions during the 50 runs. The results clearly reveal that, the hypothesis is reasonable. However, the average number of bits in the 50 solutions of the GA is 28.9, which is slightly more than predicted. Figure 2 sheds some light on this issue. The higher peeks tend to belong to relatively small values from W, while the lower proportions indicate a relatively large value. This is because individuals containing large values tend to die off at the very beginning of the search.

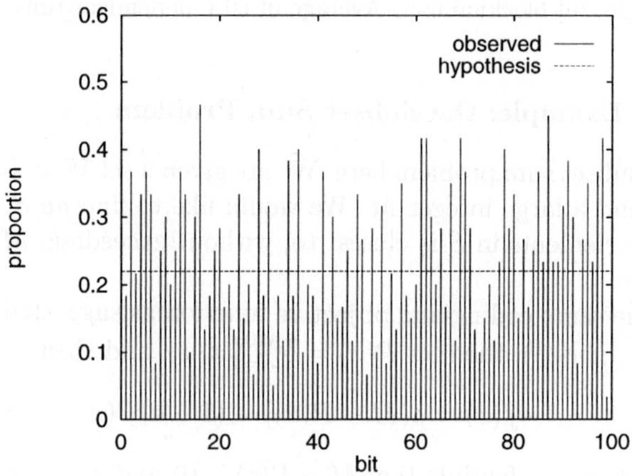

Fig. 2. Proportion of value 1 for a given bit over the solutions of the 50 independent runs of the GA. The proportion indicated by the hypothesis is also shown.

It is now time to explain exactly what the hypothesis means. Clearly, it says nothing about any particular element or subset of W. The only important feature is the number of 1s in an individual, according to the hypothesis. To express this in our terminology, there are implicit formae, based on the number of 1s in a chromosome, that play a mayor role in the optimization process. This motivates the following definition.

Definition 10. $[y, z]$-1s$\in \mathcal{P}(C)$, $x \in C$. $[y, z]$-1s(x) iff the number of 1s in x is in the interval $[y, z] \subset \mathbb{N}$.

$[24, 34]$-1s was traced by GENESIS and the statistics are shown in Figs 3b and 3a.

The graphs are very similar to those of the previous example, the equal blocks problem, so the conclusions are also very similar; in the case of the subset sum

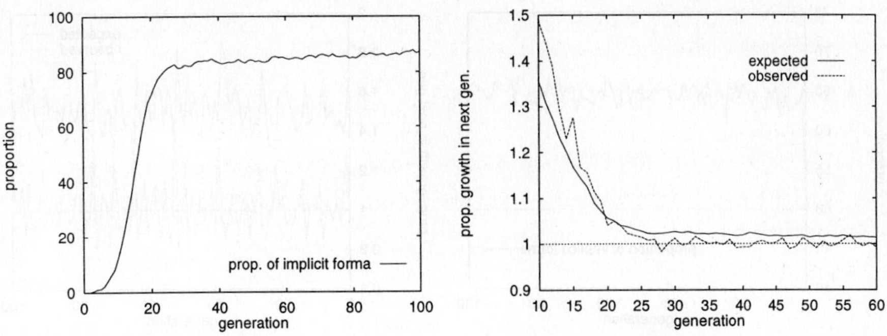

Fig. a **Fig. b**

Fig. 3. (**a**) the proportion growth and (**b**) the expected and observed growth of the implicit forma [24, 34]-1s. Average of 20 independent runs.

problem (with the GA components and the problem instance generation method used here), implicit formae play an important role.

3.3 When Will a GA Outperform Hillclimbing?

The title of this section is borrowed from [6]. Here, using implicit formae, we will try to point out some basic differences between the GA and hillclimbing through a simple example. We believe that this approach can be generalized, however. Moreover, using the definitions given in [9], more general representations could also be considered.

It is well known that functions that are easy for the GA (e.g. royal road functions) are easy (if not easier, see [6, 8]) for the bit-hillclimber, i.e. the algorithm HILLCLIMB in section 3.2. This is because HILLCLIMB can easily combine *explicit* formae (here schemata) in the case of such problems. But what about *implicit* formae? As we have seen, the GA can handle several implicit formae besides the explicit ones, and these implicit formae are not necessarily "relevant" for HILLCLIMB. The example of this section illustrates this effect. Let us consider the function

$$f(x) = \begin{cases} \|x\| \text{ if } \|x\| \text{ is even} \\ -\|x\| \text{ otherwise} \end{cases}$$

where $\|x\|$ is the number of 1s in x. This function is extremely hard for HILLCLIMB since every x with even $\|x\|$ is a local optimum from which HILLCLIMB cannot get out. On the other hand (as shown in section 2.2), EVEN is an implicit forma if $P_c < 1$ and $P_m = 0$. On the basis of this observation, P_c was set to 0.6.

20 independent experiments were performed with RAND, HILLCLIMB and the GA. The average best results were 67.7, 49.2 and 83.3, respectively. Observe that HILLCLIMB is considerably worse than RAND. Figure 4a indicates that EVEN is relevant with a relevance level of approximately 0.66.

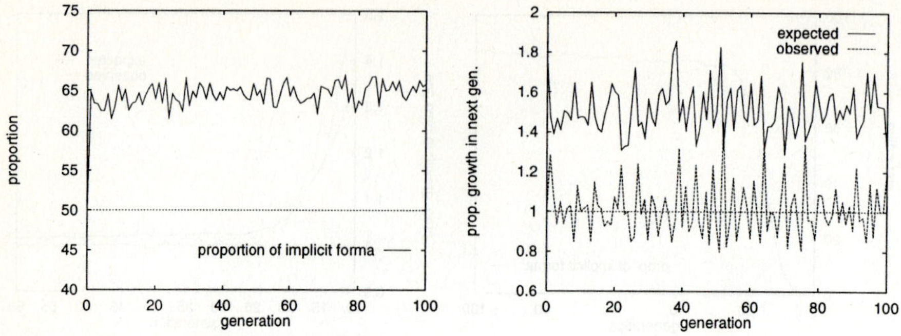

Fig. a **Fig. b**

Fig. 4. (**a**) the proportion growth and (**b**) the expected and observed growth of the implicit forma EVEN. Average of 20 independent runs and a typical single run, respectively.

As shown in Fig. 4b, in spite of the constantly strong pressure, EVEN cannot go further than 66% after a quick increase at the very beginning of the search. However, the relevance level of 0.66 is enough to outperform both RAND and HILLCLIMB.

Let us make a final remark. It may be thought that EVEN is a very artificial property which will not be encountered in the case of a real problem. However, for instance, it is a well-known fact in chemistry that atoms that have an *even* number of nucleons in their nuclei are always more stable than those with an odd number of nucleons.

3.4 Cause or Effect?

A natural question arises regarding the above results: is it the proportion growth of our implicit formae that causes the improvement of the solution or is this growth only a side effect of other factors that direct the search? To shed some light on this issue, imagine that only explicit formae (i.e. schemata in the examples of the paper) guide the search. In this case we could not have obtained results like Figs 1, 3 or 4 since the proportions of the implicit formae under consideration are practically independent of schemata (especially of short ones that receive many samples enough to guide the search). In other words, if expressed in the language of schemata, they define properties that need a high degree of *interaction* between the schemata. This of course does not mean that our implicit formae direct the search, however, it means that *there are* implicit formae that do this and are reasonably well approximated by or contained in the examined implicit formae.

This question would worth a more thorough examination but unfortunately it is out of the scope of this conference paper.

4 Happy or Sad Conclusions?

In this paper, we have seen implicit formae that can direct the genetic search as strongly and definitely as explicit formae. The only problem is that in the case of a particular problem we know only the explicit formae and this can make analysis of the behaviour of the GA quite difficult.

One solution could be to determine (enumerate) all of the implicit formae for a given task and examine all of them with the tools of the GA analysis. This may be a lot of work since it is not trivial at all what the important implicit formae of a given representation are, even if it is simple. In spite of this, for commonly used domains it may worth doing this analysis. However, for real applications, the representation (and thus the chromosome space C) and the operators tend to be different, difficult and problem-specific so the situation is not too hopeful.

On the other hand, this property of GAs of handling previously unknown implicit formae that have a high degree of relevance is very useful because it makes possible for the GA to be independent from the representation in the sense, that there is a probability of performing an effective search when only few information is available when designing the representation and so the schemata (or formae) does not seem to be too informative.

References

1. J.H. Holland (1975) *Adaptation in Natural and Artificial Systems.* University of Michigan Press (Ann Arbor).
2. N.J. Radcliff (1991) Equivalence Class Analysis of Genetic Algorithms. *Complex Systems*, 5(2):183-205
3. M.D. Vose (1991) Generalizing the Notion of Schemata in Genetic Algorithms. *Artificial Intelligence*
4. N.J. Radcliff (1992) Non-linear Genetic Representations. In R. Männer and B. Manderick editors, *Parallel Problem Solving from Nature 2.* pp259-268, Elsevier Science Publishers/North Holland (Amsterdam)
5. S. Khuri, T. Bäck, J. Heitkötter (1993) An Evolutionary Approach to Combinatorial Optimization Problems, in *The Proceedings of CSC'94.*
6. M. Mitchell, J.H. Holland (1993) When will a Genetic Algorithm Outperform Hillclimbing? (SFI working paper)
7. N.J. Radcliff, F.A.W. George (1993) A Study in Set Recombination. In *The Proceedings of ICGA'93.*
8. A. Juels, M. Wattenberg (1994) Stochastic Hillclimbing as a Baseline Method for Evaluating Genetic Algorithms. Technical Report, UC Berkeley
9. N.J. Radcliffe, P.D. Surry (1994) Fitness Variance of Formae and Performance Prediction. In L.D. Whitley and M.D. Vose editors, *Foundations of Genetic Algorithms III*, Morgan Kaufmann (San Mateo, CA) pp51-72
10. H. Kargupta (1995) Signal-to-noise, Croostalk and Long Range Difficulty in Genetic Algorithms. In *The Proceedings of ICGA'95.*
11. M.S White, S.J. Flockton (1995) Modeling the Behaviour of the Genetic Algorithm. In *The proceedings of GALESIA'95*

A Probabilistic Database Approach to the Analysis of Genetic Algorithms

Anil Menon[1], Kishan Mehrotra[1], Chilukuri K. Mohan[1], Sanjay Ranka[2]

[1] School of Computer & Information Science, 2–120 Center for Science and Technology, Syracuse University, Syracuse, NY 13244, *{armenon,kishan,mohan}@top.cis.syr.edu*

[2] 301 CSE Bldg, Department of CISE, University of Florida, Gainesville, FL 32611, *ranka@cis.ufl.edu*

Abstract. This paper takes a fresh look at some of the key ideas of genetic algorithms, using concepts drawn from the theory of majorization and probabilistic databases. We show the intimate relationships between GAs and the theory of probabilistic databases. We show how deception is well described using Saari's theorem, and its relationships with the Simpson and other paradoxes in decision theory. Reconstructability, a concept of fundamental importance in databases, is proposed as a useful substitute for deception. The database projection operator is connected with hyperplane partitions, and is used to show the nexus between point crossover operators and the join operator. Using results from probabilistic databases, we show that crossover may be considered as a majorization operator.

1 Introduction

A popular approach to explaining "how and why genetic algorithms work" is to use arguments based on the processing of schemas. While the *idea* of a schema has been undoubtedly useful in generating ideas, problems and solutions in GAs, the effectiveness of such arguments is in some doubt [6, 11]. We draw the attention of the community to alternative ways of looking at genetic algorithms, focusing on probabilistic databases and majorization theory. Space constraints preclude describing the many consequences in full detail[3].

2 GAs as Probabilistic Databases

Definition 2.1 (Probabilistic Database): A *probabilistic table* is a pair $D = (V, \boldsymbol{q})$ where, $V = \{v_1, \ldots, v_n\}$, referred to as the *scheme* of the probabilistic table, is a non-empty set of variables v_i, each taking values from a *finite* set S_i. Let $T(V) = \prod_i S_i$, denote the set of *tuples* of the table D. The *tuple occurrence function* is defined by $\boldsymbol{q} : T(V) \to [0, 1]$, such that $\sum_{\alpha \in T(V)} q(\alpha) = 1$. Thus, $\boldsymbol{q}$ assigns a value between 0 and 1 to every tuple in the table, such that the sum

[3] An expanded version of this paper is available [8].

Scheme V D = (V, p)

tuples

V_1	V_2	V_3	p
0	0	0	0.12
0	0	1	0.04
0	1	0	0.32
0	1	1	0.11
1	0	0	0.01
1	0	1	0.00
1	1	0	0.29
1	1	1	0.11

Figure 1: Probabilistic Table

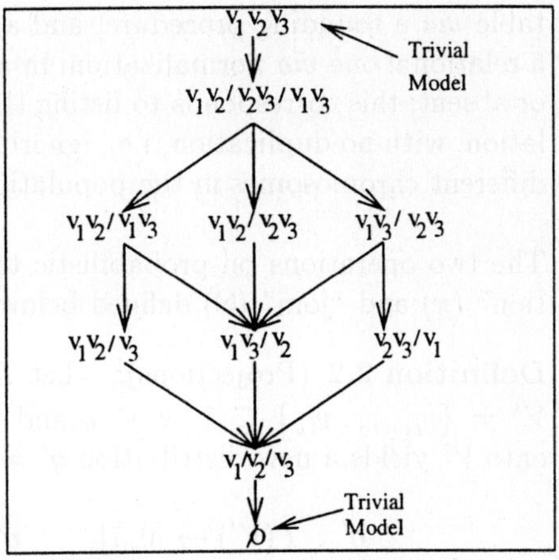

Figure 2: Lattice of All Models

of their values adds to one. A *model* of a scheme V is a set $X = \{V_1, \ldots, V_n\}$ such that $\cup_1^n V_j \subseteq V$ and $V_i \not\subseteq V_j, \forall i, j \in \{1, \ldots, n\}$. A model X, of a scheme V, is *non-trivial* iff $X \neq \{\emptyset\}$ and $X \neq \{V\}$. A collection of probabilistic tables $D_1, \ldots, D_k$ is a *probabilistic database* (see [1] for key theorems and references).

Figure 1 shows an example of a probabilistic table. The concept of a model is fundamental. Figure 2 shows the lattice of all the possible models over 3 variables. The lattice is induced *via* the partial order defined by set inclusion. We shall show that projection over models is intimately related to the analysis of hyperplane partitions.

The following conventions simplify definitions and notation. The tuples of a probabilistic table are denoted by small greek letters α, β, etc. We shall write q_α rather than $q(\alpha)$. The kth component of a tuple α, will be denoted by α_k. Given two schemes V and V' with $V' \subseteq V$, and tuple $\alpha \in T(V)$ then $\alpha[V']$ is the restriction of α to variables in V'.

In particular, schemes, variables, domain sets, tuples and the tuple occurrence function in a probabilistic database correspond to schemas, genes, allele sets, chromosomes and the net fitnesses of a population in a GA, respectively. One point needs special mention. In a probabilistic table, associated with every tuple α is a value $0 \leq q_\alpha \leq 1$. Correspondingly, associated with the ith chromosome α, is its *net* fitness $q_\alpha = p_\alpha f_\alpha / \bar{f}$. Thus the net fitnesses of a collection of n chromosomes with proportions p_i and fitnesses f_i adds to one. A special case is that of *relational tables*. A relational table is obtained from a probabilistic table *via* a rounding procedure, and a probabilistic table can be obtained from a relational one *via* normalization. In a relational table, a tuple is either present or absent; this corresponds to listing the fitnesses of the members of a GA population, with no duplication, i.e., ignoring the proportional representations of the different chromosomes in the population.

The two operations on probabilistic tables most relevant for GAs are "projection" (π) and "join" ($\bowtie$) defined below.

Definition 2.2 (Projections): Let $D = (V, \boldsymbol{q})$ be a probabilistic table. Let $V' = \{v_{i_1}, \ldots v_{i_k}\} \subseteq V$, $k \leq n$ and $T(V') = \prod_{j=1}^{k} S_{i_j}$. The *projection* of $\boldsymbol{q}$ onto V' yields a new distribution $\boldsymbol{q}' = \pi_{V'}(\boldsymbol{q})$, such that

$$\boldsymbol{q}' : T(V') \to [0,1]; \qquad \boldsymbol{q}'(\beta) = \sum_{\alpha \in T(V),\, \alpha[V]=\beta} \boldsymbol{q}(\alpha).$$

The projection of a distribution $\boldsymbol{q}$ onto a model, $X = \{V_1, \ldots, V_k\}$ is, $\pi_X(\boldsymbol{q}) = \{\pi_{V_1}(\boldsymbol{q}), \ldots, \pi_{V_k}(\boldsymbol{q})\}$. ∎

Example 2.1 Consider the probabilistic table $D = (V = \{v_1, v_2, v_3\}, \boldsymbol{q})$ shown in Figure 1. Let $X = \{V_1, V_2\} = \{\{v_1, v_2\}, \{v_2, v_3\}\}$. The projection of $\boldsymbol{q}$ over the model X yields two distributions, $\boldsymbol{q}'$ and $\boldsymbol{q}''$ where, $\boldsymbol{q}' = \pi_{V_1}(\boldsymbol{q})$ and $\boldsymbol{q}'' = \pi_{V_1}(\boldsymbol{q})$. For example, $q'_{\{v_1=0,v_2=1\}} = \sum_{v_3=0,1} q_{\{v_1=0,v_2=1,v_3\}}$. The projection over X yields a database with two tables given by,

v_1	v_2	$\boldsymbol{q}' = \pi_{\{v_1,v_2\}}$
0	0	0.16
0	1	0.43
1	0	0.01
1	1	0.40

v_2	v_3	$\boldsymbol{q}'' = \pi_{\{v_2,v_3\}}$
0	0	0.13
0	1	0.04
1	0	0.61
1	1	1.22

The relevance of projection operators is evident from a consideration of the *net* fitnesses of primary schemas. If S_i denotes any schema,

$$\text{net fitness of } S_i = \frac{f_{S_i} p_{S_i}}{\bar{f}} = \sum_{\alpha \in S_i} \frac{p_\alpha f_\alpha}{\bar{f}} \tag{1}$$

It follows that a tabulation of the net fitnesses of a primary schema partition is the projection of the original table of net fitnesses of the chromosomes over the appropriate subset of fixed positions. For example, consider a population consisting of 3-bit chromosomes, with the composition shown in Table 1. Table 2 shows the net fitness values of those primary schemas whose first two bits are fixed. An examination of the net fitnesses of the primary schemas shows that it is the projection of the net fitnesses of the chromosomes over the model $X = \{\{v_1, v_2\}\}$. Thus projections over models correspond in a natural manner to computing net fitnesses of primary schemas over different sets of fixed positions.

Table 1: Population composition

v_1 v_2 v_3	$p(\cdot)$	$f(\cdot)$	$p(\cdot)f(\cdot)/f$
0 0 0	0.12	1	0.0373
0 0 1	0.04	2	0.0249
0 1 0	0.32	6	0.5966
0 1 1	0.11	1	0.0342
1 0 0	0.01	0.8	0.0025
1 0 1	0.00	0.5	0.0
1 1 0	0.29	3	0.2704
1 1 1	0.11	1	0.0342

Table 2: Net fitness projections

v_1 v_2*	$p'(\cdot)$	$f'(\cdot)$	$p'(\cdot)f'(\cdot)/f$
00*	0.16	1.25	0.0622
01*	0.43	4.721	0.6308
10*	0.01	0.8	0.0025
11*	0.40	2.45	0.3046

Two tables $D = (V, \boldsymbol{q}')$, and $D = (V, \boldsymbol{q}'')$ may have the same projections with respect to a given model X. Projections are analogous to the marginals of a distribution. As is well known, more than one distribution many have the same marginals. In other words, a set of projections may be obtained from an infinite set of *reconstructions*. This leads to the notion of a "best" reconstruction w.r.t. some specific property. One very useful choice is to pick the reconstruction with the *maximum entropy*, referred to as the *join* reconstruction.

Definition 2.3 (Join): Let $\{D_i = (V_i, \boldsymbol{q}_i)\}$, $i = 1, \ldots, k$ be a probabilistic database, and $X = \{V_1, \ldots, V_n\}$ be a model for $V = \cup_i V_i$. Let $\mathcal{R}(X, \boldsymbol{q}_1, \ldots, \boldsymbol{q}_k)$ denote the set of all reconstructions of the database $\{D_i, i = 1, \ldots, k\}$, i.e., $\mathcal{R}(X, \boldsymbol{q}_1, \ldots, \boldsymbol{q}_k)$ is the set of all tables $D = (V, \boldsymbol{q})$ such that $\pi_X(\boldsymbol{q}) = \{\pi_{V_1}(\boldsymbol{q}), \ldots, \pi_{V_k}(\boldsymbol{q})\} = \{q_1, \ldots, q_k\}$. Assume the database $\{D_i, i = 1, \ldots, k\}$ is *consistent*, i.e., $\mathcal{R}(X, \boldsymbol{q}_1, \ldots, \boldsymbol{q}_k) \neq \emptyset$. The *join reconstruction* of the tables $\{D_i\}$ is defined to be the table $D_{\bowtie} = (V, \boldsymbol{q}^{\bowtie})$, such that $H(\boldsymbol{q}^{\bowtie})$, the Shannon entropy of $\boldsymbol{q}^{\bowtie}$, is maximum over all distributions in $\mathcal{R}(X, \boldsymbol{q}_1, \ldots, \boldsymbol{q}_k)$. ∎

$\boldsymbol{q}^{\bowtie}$ will be referred to as the *probabilistic join* of the distributions $\{\boldsymbol{q}_1, \ldots, \boldsymbol{q}_n\}$ and is denoted by $\boldsymbol{q}^{\bowtie} = \bowtie(\{\boldsymbol{q}_1, \ldots, \boldsymbol{q}_n\})$. Definition 2.3 is non-constructive, but there is a simple algorithm to compute the probabilistic join [1].

2.1 Point crossovers and Probabilistic Join

In one-point and two-point crossovers, the number of 0's and 1's is conserved at any position, e.g., if one starts out with a certain number of 0's and 1's at position no. 5 then repeated point crossovers do not change these numbers. In other words, the one dimensional marginals remain the same. The overall vector of proportions for the whole population, approaches the product of these marginals, i.e., the *join* of these marginal distributions[4].

We are interested in the behavior of a GA after a finite number of point crossovers. Consider a population of N binary chromosomes of length l, subjected to many

[4] For a population of N binary chromosomes each of length l, the number of one-point crossovers needed to randomize the population can be conjectured to be $O(Nl\ \ln(Nl))$, by analyzing random walks on permutation groups [8].

one-point crossover operations. Assume that the children produced do *not* replace their parents immediately. Instead they are stored in a separate list. After the crossover operations are complete, a sample of N chromosomes are drawn at random from it to replace the original population. In terms of databases, this process has an interesting interpretation. Collect all the children produced by crossover occurring at any given position between bits k and $k+1$ into a list L_k. This list of chromosomes is a subset of the set of chromosomes (tuples) that would have been produced had we taken the join of two projections of the original table; the first projection is over all variables to the left of the given position, and the other projection is over all variables to the right. In other words, L_k is a subset of the join of the projections of the original table with respect to the model of the form $X_k = \{\{v_1, \ldots, v_k\}, \{v_{k+1}, \ldots, v_l\}\}$ with $1 < k < n$. A similar statement holds for any other position. Overall, we see that one-point crossover samples the join distributions obtained by projecting the original table with respect to the models $X_2, \ldots, X_{n-1}$. Note that we ignore the fitnesses of the chromosomes in computing the projections and joins, and only deal with the table of chromosome proportions. The limitations of searching spaces by just considering these models out of the lattice of all possible models (which is exponential in the number of variables) is clear. Since any child obtained by two-point crossover can also be obtained by several applications of one-point crossover, the two are asymptotically equivalent. However, their finite behaviors are different. Two-point can explore a given set of models more efficiently than one-point in a given time interval. For either point crossover operator, the same set of a fixed number of models are explored, and as problem size increases, the chances of learning crucial data dependencies fall.

We do not claim that *all* crossover operators are variations of the join operator. But we emphasize the role played by model selection in designing new operators. One point and two point operators may perform poorly on problems where the relevant information-bearing models are not limited to the ones they explore.

On the other hand there is a similarity between the join operator and crossover operators in general, in that the latter usually result in an increase of entropy of the proportion vector. This holds for quadratic operators in general [12]. The following theorem shows that join results in the increase of not just entropy but that of any Schur convex function. The following definition is needed.

Definition 2.4 (Majorization) If $\boldsymbol{x}, \boldsymbol{y} \in \Re^n$, then $\boldsymbol{x}$ is said to *majorize* $\boldsymbol{y}$, denoted $\boldsymbol{y} \preceq \boldsymbol{x}$ (equivalently, $\boldsymbol{x} \succeq \boldsymbol{y}$) if the following conditions are satisfied [7, pp. 7,54]:

- $\sum_{i=1}^{k} x_{[i]} \geq \sum_{i=1}^{k} y_{[i]}, \quad \forall k = 1, \ldots, n-1$
- $\sum_{i=1}^{n} x_{[i]} = \sum_{i=1}^{n} y_{[i]}$

where $x_{[i]}$ denotes the ith largest element of the vector $\boldsymbol{x}$. A function $F : \Re^n \to \Re$ is said to be *Schur-convex*, if $\boldsymbol{x}, \boldsymbol{y} \in \Re^n$ and $\boldsymbol{y} \preceq \boldsymbol{x}$ implies that $F(\boldsymbol{y}) \leq F(\boldsymbol{x})$.

Schur's theorem states that if $\boldsymbol{y} \preceq \boldsymbol{x}$ then $\sum_i g(y_i) \leq \sum_i g(x_i)$ for any convex function $g : \Re \rightarrow \Re$.

Theorem 2.1 $D = (V, \boldsymbol{q})$ be a probabilistic table, and $X = \{V_1, \ldots V_k\}$ be a model for V. Project $\boldsymbol{q}$ over X to get the database $D_i = (V_i, \boldsymbol{q}^i)$, where $\boldsymbol{q}^i = \pi_{V_i}(\boldsymbol{q})$ for $i = 1, \ldots, k$. Let $D^{\bowtie} = (V, \boldsymbol{q}^{\bowtie})$ denote the probabilistic join of the tables D_i. Then, $\boldsymbol{q}^{\bowtie} \preceq \boldsymbol{q}$. In particular for any Schur-convex function $F : \Re^n \rightarrow \Re$, $F(\boldsymbol{q}^{\bowtie}) \leq F(\boldsymbol{q})$. ∎

The proof uses two facts: (1) by definition, the join distribution has the maximum entropy of all distributions with the same projections with respect to the underlying model, and (2) the entropy function is the sum of strictly concave functions. The theorem then follows from the Hardy, Littlewood, Polya theorem [7, pp. 108].

Proportional selection imposes a majorization in the reverse direction [9]. We have also shown that the popular quadratic differential models of crossover, used in mathematical genetics, also induce a majorization pre-ordering [10]. There, we argued that this constituted a strong case for treating any majorization operator as a form of crossover. Since point crossover and join operators are similar in the limit, Theorem 2.1 shows that point crossover operators implement majorization.

An important related concept is that of the *error distribution* $\boldsymbol{q}^{\epsilon}$, the difference between a distribution and its join obtained from a specified set of projections of the distribution, shifted and scaled so as to be in the unit simplex $S^n = \{(p_1, \ldots, p_n) : 0 \leq p_i \leq 1, \sum_i p_i = 1\}$. Given any two of the three distributions $(\boldsymbol{q}, \boldsymbol{q}^{\bowtie}, \boldsymbol{q}^{\epsilon})$, the third may be recovered. If $\boldsymbol{q} = \boldsymbol{q}^{\bowtie}$, then the probabilistic join of the marginals has produced no *new* tuples. The entropy of the error distribution is a convenient measure of how many new tuples have been produced, and is inversely related to the latter. It is important therefore, to know something about how the error distribution's entropy is related to those of the original distribution and the join. Theorem 2.2 is a majorization result similar to Theorem 2.1 for the error distribution. It also gives an upper bound on the entropy of the error distribution in terms of the difference of the entropies of constituent distributions. These results may be applied to bound the rate of convergence to the uniform distribution in repeated point crossover.

Theorem 2.2 Let $D, D_i, D^{\bowtie}, \boldsymbol{q}^i, \boldsymbol{q}^{\bowtie}$ and X have the meanings assigned to them in Theorem 2.1. Let $T(V)$ denote the number of tuples, and let $\boldsymbol{q}^{\epsilon} = \dfrac{\boldsymbol{e} + \boldsymbol{q} - \boldsymbol{q}^{\bowtie}}{T(V)}$ be the error distribution, where $\boldsymbol{e}$ is the vector of all ones. Then, $\boldsymbol{q}^{\epsilon} \preceq \boldsymbol{q}^{\bowtie}$. Consequently, for any Schur-convex function $F : \Re^n \rightarrow \Re$, $F(\boldsymbol{q}^{\epsilon}) \leq F(\boldsymbol{q}^{\bowtie})$. In particular, if ΔH denotes the difference in entropies of the distributions $\boldsymbol{q}^{\bowtie}$ and $\boldsymbol{q}$, then the entropy of the error distribution $H(\boldsymbol{q}^{\epsilon})$ is greater than or equal to $\lg \left\{ \frac{T(V)}{1 + \sqrt{\Delta H / 2}} \right\}$. ∎

In summary, we believe we have laid the groundwork for applying the theory of probabilistic databases to crossover. The convergence of results from dynamical models of crossover and from the database theoretic models is interesting, and support this approach. In the next section, we define the notion of reconstructability of a function with respect to a model. Such functions produce uniform error distributions and have a role in generalizing the notion of deception.

3 The Analysis of Deception

After Goldberg's introduction of the concept of deception [4], a considerable body of work has grown over this issue (see [5] for a list). Whitley's work emphasized the role of primary schema partitions in understanding deception [15], and Grefenstette forcefully argued that deception was based on a concept of relatively weak explanatory power, viz. the static building block hypothesis [5]. Central to his arguments were the facts that (1) GAs are essentially dynamic constructs, but (2) deception only deals with the problem of sums over *static* averages. We concur with this view. "Dynamic" deception would include the role of the varying chromosome proportions in determining whether a deceptive situation exists. Phenomena such as collateral convergence and large schema variance [5] then would not drop out of the analysis.

Probabilistic database theory offers a simple interpretation of static versus dynamic deception. Static deception is best understood as aggregation paradoxes over *relational* tables, while dynamic deception is about aggregation paradoxes over *probabilistic* tables. In relational tables as applied to GAs, we deal only with fitnesses (the "proportions" of the chromosomes are either 1 or 0), while in the probabilistic version, we deal with *net* fitnesses, which necessarily includes the chromosome proportions.

We first examine deception from the viewpoint of Saari's remarkable theorem, and relate it to Simpson's and other well known paradoxes in decision theory. We propose to replace deception by the notion of *reconstructability*.

3.1 Deception and Saari's Theorem

Deception addresses an aggregation paradox. A close examination of the examples in [15] or [4] shows that to exhibit deception in its simplest form, one requires to define 8 quantities. Abstractly, there are four units p, q, r, s (say), and four weights, w_1, w_2, w_3 and w_4. Define the first two units to be of type 'A', and the last two units to be of type 'B'. The weights are non-negative and normalized, i.e., $w_1 + w_2 = w_3 + w_4 = 1$. We aggregate over the A-type units (with respect to w_1, w_2), and correspondingly aggregate over the B-type units. It is given that,

$$p > r \quad \text{and} \quad q > s \tag{2}$$

$$\text{But,} \quad w_1 p + w_2 q < w_3 r + w_4 s \tag{3}$$

Thus, though each unit in a class is greater than a unit in the other class, the weighted aggregate fails to be so. In GAs, the associated semantics of the situation makes this "deceptive". Without loss of generality, let $p > q$. Then, a theorem due to Ijiri [14] states that there exist non-negative normalized weights which make (2) and (3) simultaneously true iff $r > q$. In the context of the minimal deceptive problem, Ijiri's conditions lead to Goldberg's conditions [4]. For the general case of several aggregates $A, B, C, \ldots$, with more than two units in an aggregate, similar necessary and sufficient conditions may be obtained via Saari's theorem [13] Three other important comments can be made:

1. Ijiri's theorem gives necessary and sufficient conditions for the occurrence of Simpson's paradox[14]. Structurally, deception is a close cousin of Simpson's paradox. In fact, similar connections with voting paradoxes, the ecological fallacy, and several "paradoxes" associated with statistical tests are all easily established *via* Saari's theorem.
2. Simpson's paradox is about a reversal of an ordering relation under aggregation. When there are several levels of aggregation, Saari's theorem can be used to construct examples where there is a reversal of ordering at each successive level of aggregation. This parallels Whitley's notion of fully deceptive functions [15].
3. Saari's necessary and sufficient conditions are weak and easily satisfied. This implies that deceptive situations are easily set up and should be expected to occur in practice, as supported by the considerable body of evidence available on the occurrence of Simpson's paradox[5].

On the one hand, when dealing with finite samples, it is advisable to make decisions based on as large a sample as possible (sampling error problem). In the context of GAs an extreme approach would be to use variables pertaining to the whole population, i.e., the schema "****...*". On the other hand, we know that information is lost under aggregation (as Simpson's paradox illustrates). From this perspective, an opposite approach would be to consider only individuals, and not use averages at all. This suggests that there is an optimal schema length, at which either horn of the dilemma can do the least harm. Estimates of this length can be obtained by using Cohen's statistical-test dependent uncertainty principle [2], or considerations based on the VC-dimension.

3.2 Deception and Reconstructability

If deception is to be studied in its original form, then Saari's theorem (and related body of work) offers fundamental insights. An alternative approach is to redefine the notion of deception, in terms of *reconstructability*, a concept fundamental in the study of probabilistic databases.

Definition 3.1 (Reconstructability): Let $D = (V, \boldsymbol{q})$ be a probabilistic table, and X be a model of V. Project $\boldsymbol{q}$ over X to obtain the marginal distributions

[5] See `http://www.cis.syr.edu/~mohan/html/simpson.html` for pointers to the vast literature on the subject.

$\pi_X(\boldsymbol{q})$. Let $\boldsymbol{q}^{\bowtie}$ denote the probabilistic join of the marginal distributions $\pi_X(\boldsymbol{q})$. If $\boldsymbol{q} = \bowtie(\pi_X(\boldsymbol{q})) = \boldsymbol{q}^{\bowtie}$, then D is said to be *reconstructable* with respect to the model X. ∎

The 3 variable table with tuple occurrence function $\boldsymbol{q} = (0.001, 0.054, 0.014, 0.126, 0.024, 0.216, 0.056, 0.504)$ is reconstructable w.r.t *all* of its models. Similarly, it is easy to construct examples of tables reconstructable w.r.t *none* of its models, or only some of its models.

If a distribution can be recovered from its marginal distributions by probabilistic join, then it is reconstructable with respect to those marginals. The following reasons support the use of reconstructability instead of deception.

- For relational tables and a given model, reconstructability coincides with what is usually referred to as static deception. Therefore, Definition 3.1 can be seen as a natural generalization to dynamic deception.
- It has the advantage of being theoretically tractable with key issues well understood. For example, theorems in [1, 3] give give necessary and sufficient conditions for a function to be reconstructable with respect to a model.
- Reconstructability can be studied in the algebraic framework of matroid theory; recall that greedy algorithms can be shown to optimal when a combinatorial optimization problem has the structure of a greedoid. A similar approach may be helpful to clarify the notions of *GA-easy*/*GA-hard* problems.
- Unlike deception, reconstructability is an intrinsically relative term. A function may be reconstructable with respect to one model and not so with respect to another. But, with respect to a given model, there are entropy ratio measures that can be used to estimate the degree of reconstructability [1]. For the class of *acyclic* models, there are simple entropy tests to determine if a function is reconstructable from its projections with respect to these models.
- Reconstructability is a concept with deep roots in contingency tables, functional dependencies and maximum entropy reconstruction techniques [1]. Its pedigree suggests that it will be of use in GAs as well.

4 Conclusion

We have applied the theory of probabilistic databases to genetic algorithms, showing that projection and join operators can play an important role in interpreting concepts in GAs. We establish the relationship between the join operator and point crossover, and elucidate the connection with majorization. We study deception in the context of Saari's theorem, and suggest that the concept of reconstructability is potentially more useful than deception.

References

1. R. Cavallo and M. Pittarelli. The theory of probabilistic databases. In P. M. Stocker, W. Kent, and P. Hammersley, editors, *Proceedings of the 13th International Conference on Very Large Data Bases*, pages 71–81. Morgan Kaufmann, 1987.
2. J. E. Cohen. An uncertainity principle in demography and the unisex issue. *The American Statistician*, 40(1):32–39, 1986.
3. R. Fagin. Degrees of acyclicity for hypergraphs and relational database schemes. *J. of the ACM*, 30(3):514–550, 1983.
4. D. E. Goldberg. Simple genetic algorithms and the minimal decptive problem. In L. Davis, editor, *Genetic algorithms and simulated annealing*, pages 74–78. Pitman, London, 1987.
5. J. Grefenstette. Deception considered harmful. In L. Whitley, Darrell, editor, *Foundation of Genetic Algorithms, Vol. 2*, pages 75–92. Morgan Kaufmann, 1993.
6. J. Grefenstette and J. Baker. How genetic algorithms work: a critical look at implicit parallelism. In G. J. E. Rawlins, editor, *Foundation of Genetic Algorithms*. Morgan Kaufmann, 1989.
7. A. W. Marshall and I. Olkin. *Inequalities: Theory of majorization and its Applications*. Academic Press, New York, 1979.
8. A. Menon. *Mathematical Models of Evolutionary Algorithms*. PhD thesis, School of Computer Science, Syracuse University, 1996 (forthcoming).
9. A. Menon, K. Mehrotra, C. Mohan, and S. Ranka. Selection, majorization and replicators. In *IEEE 3rd International Conference on Evolutionary Computation*, pages 606–610. IEEE Press, 1996.
10. A. Menon, K. Mehrotra, C. Mohan, and S. Ranka. Replicators, majorization and genetic algorithms: New models, connections and analytical tools. In *Foundations of Genetic Algorithms*. Morgan Kaufman, 1996 (to appear).
11. H. Mühlenbein. Evolution in time and space — the parallel genetic algorithm. In G. J. E. Rawlins, editor, *Foundation of Genetic Algorithms*, pages 316–338. Morgan Kaufmann, San Mateo, CA, 1991.
12. Y. Rabinovich, A. Sinclair, and A. Wigderson. Quadratic dynamical systems (preliminary version). In *Proc. 33rd Annual Symp. Foundations of Computer Science*, pages 304–313, Pittsburgh, 1992.
13. D. G. Saari. The source of some paradoxes from social choice and probability. *J. of Economic Theory*, 41:1–22, 1987.
14. S. Sunder. Simpson's reversal paradox and cost allocation. *J. of Accounting Research*, 21(1):223–233, 1983.
15. D. L. Whitley. Fundamental principles of deception in genetic search. In G. J. E. Rawlins, editor, *Foundation of Genetic Algorithms*. Morgan Kaufmann, San Mateo, CA, 1991.

Mean Field Analysis of Tournament Selection on a Random Manifold

Lutz Molgedey

Institut of Physics, Humboldt–University Berlin,
Invalidenstraße 110, 10115 Berlin, Germany
Email: molgedey@physik.hu-berlin.de

Abstract. A simple model of biological evolution based on q-tournament selection and uniform random mutations is presented and its time dependent behaviour analysed.

Life on Earth is too complex for quantitative modelling. Therefore we will focus here on a simple model of Darwinian evolution which is exactly solvable.

This model describes the competition of N species. The state of each species $i = 1, 2, \ldots, N$ is characterized by x_i, defined in a finite (discrete or continuous) space, and also by its assigned fitness value $E(x_i)$ which is to be maximized during the process of evolution.

The model is completely specified by the following rule: at each time step, q species are randomly chosen from the population (q-tournament [1]). The species with the lowest fitness value $E(x_i)$ is replaced by a randomly generated new one (mutation).

Normaly mutation is defined as variation of genetic material of the parent generation which will produce the new offspring generation. Here the creation of new species without varying genetic material should be called mutation too, since this can be treated as evolution in a totally rugged landscape [2, 3] where mutations can not benefit from correlations in the fitness landscape.

The dynamical mean field equation for this model, which becomes exact for infinitely large N, can be written as

$$P_{t+1}(x) = P_t(x) - \frac{1}{N} q P_t(x) Q_t(x)^{q-1} + \frac{1}{NV} \tag{1}$$

with

$$Q_t(x) = \mathbf{Tr}_{\{x'\}} \Theta(E(x') - E(x)) P_t(x') \tag{2}$$

where $P_t(x)$ is the probability density of finding a species at time t in state x and $Q_t(x)$ is the probability of finding a species with a better fitness than $E(x)$. The volume of the phase space is $V = \mathbf{Tr}_{\{x\}}\, 1$, where $\mathbf{Tr}$ is the trace defined as usual, i.e. the sum over all configurations. $\Theta(E)$ is the unit step function defined, by $\Theta(E) = 1$ if $E \geq 0$, and $\Theta(E) = 0$ if $E < 0$.

Instead of discussing (1), it is easier to analyse the corresponding equation for the integral quantity

$$Q_{t+1}(x) = Q_t(x) - \frac{1}{N} Q_t(x)^q + \frac{1}{N} \Xi(x) \tag{3}$$

with

$$\Xi(x) = \frac{1}{V}\mathbf{Tr}_{\{x'\}}\Theta(E(x') - E(x)) \tag{4}$$

$$= \int_{E(x)}^{\infty} \mathrm{d}E' \rho(E') \tag{5}$$

where the fitness value density

$$\rho(E) = \frac{1}{V}\underset{\{x\}}{\mathbf{Tr}}\,\delta(E - E(x)) \tag{6}$$

is, due to the simple nature of mutations in our model, the only characteristic function of the fitness landscape.

In fitness value representation equation (3) reads

$$Q_{t+1}(E) = Q_t(E) - \frac{1}{N}Q_t(E)^q + \frac{1}{N}\Xi(E) \tag{7}$$

with

$$Q_t(E) = \int_E^{\infty} \mathrm{d}E' P_t(E') \tag{8}$$

$$\Xi(E) = \int_E^{\infty} \mathrm{d}E' \rho(E') \tag{9}$$

$$P_t(E) = \frac{1}{V}\underset{\{x\}}{\mathbf{Tr}}\, P_t(x)\delta(E - E(x)). \tag{10}$$

The stationary solution of (7) simply is

$$Q_\infty(E) = \sqrt[q]{\Xi(E)} = \sqrt[q]{\int_E^{\infty} \mathrm{d}E' \rho(E')} \tag{11}$$

and, using (8), one obtains the stationary distribution of fitness values in the population

$$P_\infty(E) = -\frac{\mathrm{d}}{\mathrm{d}E}Q_\infty(E) = \frac{1}{q}\rho(E)\left(\int_E^{\infty} \mathrm{d}E' \rho(E')\right)^{\frac{1}{q}-1} \tag{12}$$

i.e., evolution tends to maximize the fitness. However, as expected, only for $q \to \infty$ the distribution is localized around the global optimum.

To study the nonstationary regime, we further discuss the corresponding differential equation (since N is large the long time behaviour is identical)

$$\frac{\mathrm{d}}{\mathrm{d}t}Q_t(E) = \frac{1}{N}\left(\Xi(E) - Q_t(E)^q\right), \tag{13}$$

which can be solved implicitly by partial fraction expansion. With

$$P_t(E) = -\frac{\mathrm{d}}{\mathrm{d}E}Q_t(E) \tag{14}$$

$$\rho(E) = -\frac{\mathrm{d}}{\mathrm{d}E}\Xi(E) \tag{15}$$

one obtains after some algebra the searched for fitness distribution of the population

$$P_t(E) = \frac{1}{q\Xi(E)}\rho(E)Q_t(E) + \frac{\Xi(E) - Q_t(E)^q}{\Xi(E)}\left(\frac{q-1}{qN}\rho(E)t + \frac{P_0(E)\Xi(E) - \frac{1}{q}Q_0(E)\rho(E)}{\Xi(E) - Q_0(E)^q}\right). \tag{16}$$

For a two–player tournament ($q = 2$), the explicit solution reads

$$Q_t(E) = \sqrt{\Xi(E)}\tanh\left(\frac{t\sqrt{\Xi(E)}}{N} + \operatorname{Arctanh}\frac{Q_0(E)}{\sqrt{\Xi(E)}}\right). \tag{17}$$

To be specific, let us now discuss a landscape where the state itself is the fitness value $E(x) = x$ in the intervall $[0, 1)$. The fitness value density is in this simple case constant $\rho(E) = 1$. The stationary solution of (3) as well as of (13) becomes now

$$Q_\infty(E) = \sqrt[q]{1-E} \tag{18}$$

and therefore

$$P_\infty(E) = \frac{1}{q}(1-E)^{\frac{1}{q}-1}. \tag{19}$$

The maximum of the distribution is located at the maximum fitness value $E_{max} = 1$, however, here too, the distribution converges to $P_\infty(E) = \delta(1-E)$ only for $q \to \infty$.

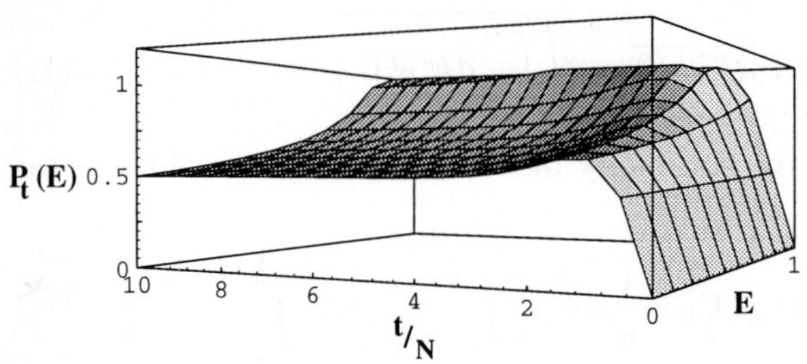

Fig. 1. *Time evolution of fitness distribution for two–player tournament.*

Fig. 1 shows the time evolution of the fitness distribution for two–player tournament. The initial distribution is $P_0(E) = \delta(E)$, i.e., all species have the worst fitness at time zero. For all fitness values $P_t(E)$ is first increasing monotonously with time and then decreasing to the stationary probability density $P_\infty(E)$. Only for the maximal fitness value, the probability density $P_t(E_{max} = 1)$ is increasing monotonously all the time.

The evolution for 2, 3, 4 and 5 player tournament is plotted in Fig. 2 for the fitness value 0.5. Since the maximal fitness value is $E_{max} = 1$ one would like to achieve as low a value of $P_\infty(E = 0.5)$ as possible, hence a large number of players in the tournament is needed.

The convergence velocities to the stationary solution are of the same order for all q. However, for each q-tournament one has to perform of order q^2 pairwise comparisons. If one is interested in computer–time, when tournaments are done sequentially, the natural time scale must be rescaled by q^2. To minimize the computer–time, it is better to start the algorithm with a small number of players in the tournament and to increase this number with time.

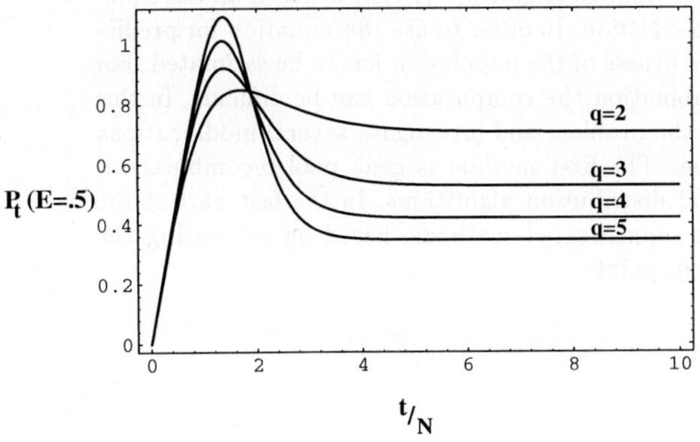

Fig. 2. *Time evolution of the probability density of finding a species with fitness* $E = 0.5$ *for* 2, 3, 4, 5 *player tournament.*

The model presented and analysed in this article was exactly solvable due to the simple nature of mutations. With the same method it should be easy to study other selection types, like ranking or proportional selection.

References

1. Goldberg, D. E. and Deb K.: A comparative analysis of selection schemes used in genetic algorithms, in Rawlins G. J. E. (editor): Foundations of Genetic Algorithms, Morgan Kauffmann Publishers, San Mateo, CA, 1991, 69–93
2. Derrida, B.: Random-Energy Model: Limit of a Family of Disordered Models. Phys. Rev. Lett. **45** (1980) 79–82
3. Kauffman, S. A., Weinberger, E. and Perelson, A. S.: Maturation of the immune response via adaptive walks on affinity landscapes. in Theoretical Immunology part 1, Santa Fe Institute Studies in the Sciences of Complexity, edited by Perelson, A. S., Addison-Wesley Reading, MA, 1988

From Recombination of Genes to the Estimation of Distributions I. Binary Parameters

H. Mühlenbein[1] and G. Paaß[1]

GMD – Forschungszentrum Informationstechnik, 53754 Sankt Augustin , Germany

Abstract. The Breeder Genetic Algorithm (BGA) is based on the equation for the response to selection. In order to use this equation for prediction, the variance of the fitness of the population has to be estimated. For the usual sexual recombination the computation can be difficult. In this paper we shortly state the problem and investigate several modifications of sexual recombination. The first method is gene pool recombination, which leads to marginal distribution algorithms. In the last part of the paper we discuss more sophisticated methods, based on estimating the distribution of promising points.

1 Introduction

The Breeder Genetic Algorithm (BGA) is based on the classical science of livestock breeding. The central part of the theory is the equation for the response to selection

$$R(t) = b(t) \cdot I \cdot \sigma(t) \tag{1}$$

Here R denotes the response, which is defined as the difference between the mean fitness of the population at generation $t+1$ and t, $b(t)$ is the *realized heritability*, I is the *selection intensity* and σ is the standard deviation of the fitness [12]. If $b(t)$ and $\sigma(t)$ can be estimated, the equation can be used for predicting the mean fitness of the population. In livestock breeding many methods have been developed to estimate the heritability [12], estimating the variance is still an open question [15].

But in evolutionary computation we have more freedom. We can design new recombination operators which have no counterpart in nature and use the above equation to evaluate the operators. In [13] we have made a further step away from the biological example and investigated *gene pool recombination* GPR. With GPR the genes of all selected parents are used to create offspring. The microscopic view of recombining two chromosomes in a Mendelian manner is abandoned.

In this paper we shortly show why the analysis of sexual recombination is so difficult, then we investigate two algorithms which use univariate marginal distribution of selected points to generate new points. In the last section the problem of estimating distributions is shortly discussed. The conditional distribution algorithm is outlined and applied to optimization problems known to be difficult for genetic algorithms.

2 Analysis of uniform crossover for two loci

The difficulty of analyzing Mendelian sexual recombination will be shown with a simple example, namely two loci and proportionate selection. In this case there are four possible genotypes: $(0,0),(0,1),(1,0)$, and $(1,1)$ which we index by $j=(0,1,2,3)$. We denote their fitness values f_0, f_1, f_2, and f_3 respectively. Let $q_j(t)$ be the frequency of genotype j at generation t. For simplicity we restrict the analysis to *uniform crossover* [18]. It is an example of *two parent recombination (TPR)*.

Theorem 1. *For proportionate selection and uniform crossover the gene frequencies obey the following difference equation*

$$q_j(t+1) = \frac{f_j}{\bar{f}(t)} q_j(t) + \frac{1}{2}\epsilon_j \frac{D_s(t)}{\bar{f}(t)^2} \quad j=0,1,2,3, \tag{2}$$

where $\epsilon = (-1,1,1,-1)$; $\bar{f}(t) = \sum_{j=0}^{3} f_j q_j(t)$ *is the average fitness of the population; and* $D_s(t)$ *is defined as*

$$D_s(t) = f_0 f_3 q_0(t) q_3(t) - f_1 f_2 q_1(t) q_2(t). \tag{3}$$

Proof: For proportionate selection the gene frequencies q_j^s after selection are given by

$$q_j^s(t) = \frac{f_j}{\bar{f}(t)} q_j(t)$$

Now we pair randomly between the selected parents and count how often genotype j arises after uniform crossover. We take $j=0$ as an example. We easily obtain

$$q_0(t+1) = q_0^s(t)\left(q_0^s(t) + q_1^s(t) + q_2^s(t) + 1/2 q_3^s(t)\right) + 1/2 q_1^s(t) q_2^s(t)$$

Using that $q_0^s(t) + q_1^s(t) + q_2^s(t) + q_3^s(t) = 1$ we obtain the conjecture for $j=0$. The remaining equations are obtained in the same manner. □

Equations (2) are identical to the ones known for diploid chromosomes in population genetics [6], despite the fact that the underlying genetic recombination is different. This shows that uniform crossover can be thought of as Mendelian recombination for haploid organisms. Note that $D_s(t) = 0$ if $q_0(t)q_3(t) = q_1(t)q_2(t)$ and $f_0 f_3 = f_1 f_2$. The first condition is called *linkage equilibrium* in population genetics.

This system of four nonlinear difference equations has not yet been solved analytically (see the discussion in [15]), but it is possible to derive an exact expression for the realized heritability.

Theorem 2. *The realized heritability* $b(t)$ *for uniform crossover is given by*

$$b(t) = 1 - \frac{1}{2}(f_0 - f_1 - f_2 + f_3)\frac{D(t)}{\bar{f}(t) V(t)}. \tag{4}$$

Proof: *By summation we obtain*

$$R(t) = \bar{f}(t+1) - \bar{f}(t) = \frac{V(t)}{\bar{f}(t)} - \frac{1}{2}(f_0 + f_3 - f_1 - f_2)\frac{D(t)}{\bar{f}(t)^2}, \tag{5}$$

where $V(t) = \sigma^2(t)$ *denotes the variance of the population. Using* $S(t) = V(t)/\bar{f}(t)$ *we obtain equation (4).* □

Uniform crossover in genetic algorithms, which models Mendelian recombination, leads to very difficult systems of difference equations. The genetic population moves away from linkage equilibrium. This makes an analysis of the algorithm almost impossible. But in genetic algorithms we may use recombination schemes which lead to simpler equations.

Simpler equation are obtained if the population is in linkage equilibrium. Without proof we note that linkage equilibrium is identical to the gene frequencies being in Robbins proportions [16]. Here the probability of a genotype $p(\mathbf{x})$ is given by

$$p(\boldsymbol{x}) = \prod_{i=1}^{n} p_i(x_i), \tag{6}$$

where $p_i(x_i)$ are the univariate marginal frequencies.

The assumption of linkage equilibrium is not as severe as one might think. We have numerically confirmed the conjecture that without selection, the gene frequencies of a population using uniform crossover will converge to linkage equilibrium. This means that linkage equilibrium can be considered to be the limiting distribution of any genetic recombination scheme applied without selection.

3 Univariate Marginal Distributions

There exist a simple recombination scheme that maintains the population in linkage equilibrium; we have called it *gene pool recombination (GPR)* [13]. In GPR, for each locus the two alleles to be recombined are chosen *independently* from the gene pool defined by the selected parent population. The biologically inspired idea of restricting the recombination to the alleles of two parents for each offspring is abandoned.

Definition: *In gene pool recombination the two "parent" alleles of an offspring are randomly chosen for each locus with replacement from the gene pool given by the parent population* **selected** *before. Then the offspring allele is computed using any of the standard recombination schemes for TPR.*

For a discussion of gene pool recombination and its analysis see [13]. Gene pool recombination leads to simple difference equations for the marginal frequencies $p_i(x_i)$ [13]. We generalize this idea and define a conceptual algorithm which uses univariate marginal frequencies directly.

Let $\mathbf{x} = (x_1, \ldots, x_n)$, $x_i \in \{0, 1\}$, $f(\mathbf{x})$ be its fitness and $q(\mathbf{x})$ its frequency. Then the univariate marginal frequencies can be computed from

$$p_i(x_i) = \sum_{\mathbf{x}|x_i} q(\mathbf{x}) \tag{7}$$

where the sum is taken over all $\mathbf{x}$ with x_i held fixed. The conceptual Univariate Marginal Distribution Algorithm (UMDA) is defined as follows.

UMDA

- **STEP0:** Set $t = 1$. Generate $N \gg 0$ points randomly.
- **STEP1:** Select $M \leq N$ points according to a selection schedule. Compute the marginal frequencies $r_{t;i}(x_i)$ of the selected set.
- **STEP2:** Generate N new points according to the distribution $q_{t+1}(\mathbf{x}) = \prod_{i=1}^{n} r_{t;i}(x_i)$. Set $t = t + 1$.
- **STEP3:** If not terminated, go to STEP1

Theorem 3. *For proportionate selection the marginal frequencies of UMDA obey the difference equation*

$$p_{t+1;i}(x_i) = p_{t;i}(x_i)\frac{\bar{f}_{t;i}(x_i)}{\bar{f}(t)} \tag{8}$$

where

$$\bar{f}_{t;i}(x_i) = \sum_{\mathbf{x}|x_i} f(\mathbf{x}) \prod_{\substack{j=1 \\ j \neq i}}^{n} p_{t;j}(x_j)$$

Proof: For proportionate selection the frequency of the selected points $\tilde{q}_t(\mathbf{x})$ is given by

$$\tilde{q}_t(\mathbf{x}) = \frac{f(\mathbf{x})}{\bar{f}^t} q_t(\mathbf{x})$$

From

$$r_{t;i}(x_i) = p_{t+1;i}(x_i) = \sum_{\mathbf{x}|x_i} \tilde{q}_t(\mathbf{x})$$

equation (8) follows. □

The difference equation (8) can also be written in the form

$$p_{t+1;i}(x_i) = p_{t;i}(x_i) + p_{t;i}(x_i)\frac{F_{t;i}(x_i)}{\bar{f}(t)} \tag{9}$$

where

$$F_{t;i}(x_i) = \bar{f}_{t;i}(x_i) - \bar{f}(t) \tag{10}$$

The term $F_{t;i}(x_i)$ was already introduced in [1] (there it is denoted $f_{(i)}(x_i)$). The terms $F_{t;i}(x_i)$ minimize the weighted quadratic error

$$\sum_{\mathbf{x}} q_t(\mathbf{x}) \left(f(\mathbf{x}) - \bar{f}(t) - \sum_{i=1}^{n} \alpha_i(x_i) \right)^2$$

The terms are used to define the *additive genetic variance* V_A, called V_1 in [1].

$$V_A(t) = \sum_{x_i} p_{t;i}(x_i)\left(F_{t;i}(x_i)\right)^2 \tag{11}$$

It is obvious that $p_{t+1;i}(x_i) = p_{t;i}(x_i)$ iff $F_{(i)}(x_i) = 0$ or $p_{t;i}(x_i) = 0$. Therefore we obtain:
Corollary: *For proportionate selection the UMDA stays in equilibrium iff $V_A = 0$.*

The response to selection is zero if the additive variance is zero. UMDA only exploits the additive genetic variance. It is interesting to note that this result is also used as a rule of thumb in livestock breeding. Up to now no rigorous mathematical proof is available.

The corollary also implies that UMDA is not a global optimization method for difficult fitness functions. This problem has already been discussed for gene pool recombination in [13].

The following theorem is a correct version of Fisher's Fundamental Theorem of Natural Selection [8], restricted to populations in linkage equilibrium.

Theorem 4. *For UMDA with proportionate selection the response to selection is given by*

$$R(t) = \frac{V_A(t)}{\bar{f}(t)} + \sum_{\boldsymbol{x}} \Delta q(\boldsymbol{x})\left(f(\boldsymbol{x}) - \bar{f}(t) - \sum_{i=1}^{n} F_{t;i}(x_i)\right) \tag{12}$$

where $\Delta q(\boldsymbol{x}) = q_{t+1}(\boldsymbol{x}) - q_t(\boldsymbol{x})$ is the difference of the frequencies of genotype $\boldsymbol{x}$.

Proof:

$$\begin{aligned}\sum_{\boldsymbol{x}} \Delta q(\boldsymbol{x}) \sum_{i=1}^{n} F_{t;i}(x_i) &= \sum_{i=1}^{n} F_{t;i}(x_i) \sum_{\boldsymbol{x}|x_i} \Delta q(\boldsymbol{x}) \\ &= \sum_{i=1}^{n} F_{t;i}(x_i) \Delta p_i(x_i) \\ &= \sum_{i=1}^{n} p_{t;i} F_{t;i}^2(x_i)/\bar{f}(t)\end{aligned}$$

Here $\Delta p_i(x_i) = p_{t+1;i}(x_i) - p_{t;i}(x_i)$. Equation (9) was used for the last step. By using $\sum_{\boldsymbol{x}} \Delta q(\boldsymbol{x}) f(\boldsymbol{x}) = R(t)$ and $\sum_{\boldsymbol{x}} \Delta q(\boldsymbol{x}) = 0$, the conjecture is obtained. □

Corollary: *The realized heritability of any algorithm based on univariate marginal distributions can be estimated by*

$$b(t) \approx \frac{V_A(t)}{V(t)}. \tag{13}$$

Proof: We have

$$R(t) \approx \frac{V_A(t)}{\bar{f}(t)} = \frac{V_A(t)}{V(t)} \frac{V(t)}{\bar{f}(t)} = \frac{V_A(t)}{V(t)} S(t). \quad \square$$

$V_A(t)/V(t)$ is called *heritability in the narrow sense* in livestock breeding [7], abbreviated by h_n^2. Estimating h_n is one of the most difficult parts in the science of livestock breeding.

4 A simple UMDA implementation

In order to implement UMDA, estimates for the marginal distributions are necessary. Especially the computation of $F_{t;i}(x_i)$ in Equation 9 is fairly computing intensive. Independently of the theory presented in this paper a simple algorithm has been already proposed in [2]. In this algorithm the univariate marginal frequencies are updated according to

$$p_{t+1;i}(x_i) = p_{t;i}(x_i) + \lambda(r_{t;i}(x_i) - p_{t;i}(x_i)) \tag{14}$$

where $r_{t;i}(x_i)$ are the marginal frequencies of the selected points and λ is a control parameter. The resulting algorithm we call the simple univariate marginal distribution algorithm (SUMDA).

SUMDA

- **STEP0:** Set $t = 1$. Set $p_{1,i}(x_i)$.
- **STEP1:** Generate N new points according to the distribution $q_{t+1}(\mathbf{x}) = \prod_i^n p_{t;i}(x_i)$.
- **STEP2:** Select $M \leq N$ points according to a selection schedule. Compute the marginal frequencies $r_{t;i}(x_i)$ of the selected set.
- **STEP3:** Update the marginal frequencies according to equation (14). Set $t = t + 1$.
- **STEP4:** If not terminated, go to STEP1

Note that λ influences the speed of convergence. The smaller λ, the less the convergence speed. Before we show some computational results, we qualitatively analyze the algorithm. We simplify the notation $p_{t;i}(x_i) \equiv p(t)$ and $r_{t;i}(x_i) \equiv r(t)$. We start with the simplest case.

Theorem 5. *Assume that* $r(t) \equiv c$ *with* $0 \leq c \leq 1$. *Then*

$$p(t+1) = p(1)(1-\lambda)^t - c(1-\lambda)^t + c \quad t = 0, 1, \ldots \tag{15}$$

The proof is straightforward and will be omitted. We obviously have

$$lim_{t \to \infty} p(t) = c$$

In a real algorithm $r(t)$ will oscillate. A qualitative analysis of the SUMDA algorithm has been first made in [11].

Theorem 6. *If the difference Equation (14) can be approximated by the differential equation*

$$\frac{dp(t)}{dt} = \lambda\left(r(t) - p(t)\right), \tag{16}$$

the solution is given by

$$p(t) = p(1)e^{-\lambda t} + \lambda e^{-\lambda t}\int_0^t r(\tau)e^{\lambda\tau}\,d\tau \tag{17}$$

If $r(t) \equiv c$ one obtains an approximation of equation (15). But in real simulations one observes that SUMDA often consists of two phases. In the first phase $(0 \leq t \leq t_1)$ $r(t)$ more or less randomly oscillates about a mean $< r(t) >_0^{t_1}$. If $p(t)$ gets more focused, then $r(t)$ changes accordingly.

In table 1 we give numerical results for the linear function $ONEMAX$. Note how λ influences the convergence speed. Because the size of the population, N, is very large, the speed of convergence is almost independent of the size of the problem n. For difficult multi modal fitness functions the success of SUMDA depends on the parameter λ and N. We have to omit this discussion here. But it should be obvious that SUMDA suffers from the problem, all algorithms using marginal distributions only have: they are not able to handle higher order gene interactions.

	$n = 30$		$n = 30$		$n = 60$		$n = 90$	
t	$\bar{p}$	$std(p)$	$\bar{p}$	$std(p)$	$\bar{p}$	$std(p)$	$\bar{p}$	$std(p)$
10	0.726	0.049	0.952	0.024	0.887	0.086	0.834	0.122
20	0.893	0.025	0.997	0.001	0.993	0.005	0.985	0.014
30	0.963	0.009	1.000	0.000	1.000	0.001	0.999	0.001

Table 1. SUMDA: $N = 1024; \lambda = 0.1, n = 30; \lambda = 0.25$ else

5 Conditional distributions

Gene pool recombination with two parent mating and uniform crossover as well as the two marginal distribution algorithms UMDA and SUMDA exploit the additive genetic variance mainly. The suitability of these algorithms for solving optimization problems with strongly interacting genes at different loci seems limited.

An extension of univariate marginal distribution algorithms are multivariate ones. Unfortunately it is difficult to generate the probabilty $p(\boldsymbol{x})$ of genotype $\boldsymbol{x}$ from multivariate marginal distributions. We demonstrate the problem with an example. For $n = 4$ loci for instance, we may use $p(\boldsymbol{x}) = p(x_1, x_2)\,p(x_3, x_4)$. But then four of the six bivariate distribution are left out. There are methods to solve this problem by using a system of equations as constraints, but the number of multivariate distributions scales exponentially. Therefore it seems easier to use *conditional distributions* $p(x_i|x_1,\ldots,x_{i-1},x_{i+1},\ldots,x_n)$ to reconstruct interactions between the variables. We use the notation

$$\boldsymbol{x}_{-i} := (x_1,\ldots,x_{i-1},x_{i+1},\ldots,x_n).$$

Then $p(x_i|\boldsymbol{x}_{-i})$ is the probability of x_i given $\boldsymbol{x}_{-i}$. Besag [3] has proven that the n different conditional distributions $p(x_i|\boldsymbol{x}_{-i})$, $i=1,\ldots,n$, completely determine the joint distribution $p(\boldsymbol{x})$. In our algorithm we will use conditional distributions $p(x_1,\ldots,x_m|x_{m+1},\ldots,x_n)$. In order to keep the description simple we will start with an algorithm using $p(x_i|\boldsymbol{x}_{-i})$ only.

There are a number of methods in statistics that estimate conditional distributions. We selected regression tree methods because they are reasonably accurate and computationally cheap. Algorithms for classification and regression trees date back to Sonquist and Morgan [17] and have been improved by Breiman et al.[4], see also [5] [14].

It turns out that the estimation of conditional distributions is very difficult. We are not able to describe our conditional distribution algorithm CDA here. It uses tree regression to estimate conditional distributions, and the Metropolis-Hastings algorithm to correct the estimates. In order to speed up the computation we use a cluster algorithm to compute the conditional distributions for correlated variables. Furthermore we scale the probability distribution $p(\boldsymbol{x})$ in order to concentrate its mass near the optima of $f(\boldsymbol{x})$.

In the next Section we give first numerical results.

6 Numerical results

Deceptive problems have been introduced by Goldberg [9] as a challenge to genetic algorithm. For these functions genetic algorithms will converge to suboptimal points. To overcome this problem, a radically different type of genetic algorithm called a *messy genetic algorithm* has been devised and tested by Goldberg and his coworkers. In a messy genetic algorithm the interaction of genes is tested with substrings in a primordial phase. Of crucial importance is the initialization. The interested reader should consult [10] for a recent update of the messy genetic algorithm applied to deceptive problems.

Our conditional distribution algorithm CDA tries to determine the important interactions more globally with well-known statistical techniques. The implementation of CDA is much more difficult than a genetic algorithm or an algorithm using univariate marginal distributions only.

For our numerical experiments we used the following deceptive functions.

$$f_3(d,\boldsymbol{x}) = \sum_{i=0}^{[n/3]-1} g_3(d,x_{3i+1},x_{3i+2},x_{3i+3}) \tag{18}$$

$$\tag{19}$$

where

$$g_3(d, x_1, x_2, x_3) = \begin{cases} 1-d, & \sum x_i = 0; \\ 1-2\,d, & \sum x_i = 1; \\ 0, & \sum x_i = 2; \\ 1, & \sum x_i = 3. \end{cases} \tag{20}$$

(21)

The function f_5 is defined similarly to f_3. The function $f_{(5,3)}$ has clusters of three and five interacting variables. By using an exponential transformation the marginal distributions of the clusters are independent from each other.

n	func	N	β	*eval*
50	$f_3,\ d = 0.1$	1000	$(4, 25)$	57000
50	$f_5, Goldberg$	1000	$(4, 45)$	121000
50	$f_5,\ d = 0.1$	2000	$(4, 45)$	710000
50	$f_{(5,3)},\ d = 0.1$	1000	$(4, 45)$	911000
100	$f_3,\ d = 0.1$	1000	$(5, 35)$	100000
100	$f_5,\ d = 0.1$	4000	$(5, 45)$	4960000
200	$f_3,\ d = 0.1$	1000	$(5, 45)$	500000

Table 2. Numerical results for CDA

Preliminary numerical results are presented in the Table 2. They clearly show that the algorithm is able to solve large deceptive problems. But the algorithm is at this stage more a conservative statistical estimation procedure than an optimization algorithm. It will take some time and lots of numerical experiments to end up with an efficient and reliable optimization algorithm.

Our results are not directly comparable to [10], because there a a deceptive function with a fitness value of 0.58 for the local optimum $x = (0, 0, 0, 0, 0)$ is used. We have used a fitness value of 0.9. Goldberg's deceptive function is substantially easier to solve, because the difference between the global and the local optimum is larger. Our algorithm needs for Goldberg's deceptive function of $n = 50$ about 1/6 function evaluations compared to our deceptive function.

Nevertheless, Goldberg's messy genetic algorithm seems to need substantially less function evaluations than our algorithm. But in our opinion, the messy genetic algorithm uses the cluster size as a priori information! Furthermore, the interacting variables are supposed to be contiguously located. Our algorithm detects all interactions without prior information. This is shown with the function $f_{(5,3)}$. Here clusters of size 3 and size 5 alternate, unknown to the algorithm.

From our statistical experience we believe that it is impossible to detect all important gene interactions by simply manipulating substrings like it is done in the messy genetic algorithm. Whether our conjecture is true the future will show, when experiments with a variety of deceptive functions are made.

References

1. H. Asoh and H. Mühlenbein. Estimating the heritability by decomposing the genetic variance. In Y. Davidor, H.-P. Schwefel, and R. Männer, editors, *Parallel Problem Solving from Nature*, Lecture Notes in Computer Science 866, pages 98–107. Springer-Verlag, 1994.
2. S. Baluja and R. Caruana. Removing the genetics from the standard genetic algorithm. In *Proc. of the 12th Intern. Conf. on Machine Learning*, Lake Tahoe, 1995.
3. J. Besag. Spatial interaction and the statistical analysis of lattice systems. *J. Royal Statistical Society, Series B*, pages 192–236, 1974.
4. L. Breiman, J.H. Friedman, R. Olshen, and C.J. Stone. *Classification and Regression Trees.* Wadsworth International Group, Belmont, California, 1984.
5. W. Buntine. Learning classification trees. *Statistics and Computing*, 2:63–73, 1992.
6. J. F. Crow and M. Kimura. *An Introduction to Population Genetics Theory.* Harper and Row, New York, 1970.
7. D. S. Falconer. *Introduction to Quantitative Genetics.* Longman, London, 1981.
8. R. A. Fisher. *The Genetical Theory of Natural Selection.* Dover, New York, 1958.
9. D.E. Goldberg. *Genetic Algorithms in Search, Optimization and Machine Learning.* Addison-Wesley, Reading, 1989.
10. D.E. Goldberg, K. Deb, H. Kargupta, and G. Harik. Rapid, accurate optimization of difficult problems using fast messy genetic algorithms. In S. Forrest, editor, *Proc. of the Fith Int. Conf. on Genetic Algorithms*, pages 56–64, San Mateo, 1993. Morgan-Kaufman.
11. V. Kvasnicka, M. Pelikan, and J. Pospichal. Hill-climbing with learning: An abstraction of genetic algorithm. Technical report, Slovak Technical University, Bratislava, 1995.
12. H. Mühlenbein and D. Schlierkamp-Voosen. The science of breeding and its application to the breeder genetic algorithm. *Evolutionary Computation*, 1:335–360, 1994.
13. H. Mühlenbein and H.-M. Voigt. Gene pool recombination in genetic algorithms. In J.P. Kelly and I.H Osman, editors, *Metaheuristics: Theory and Applications*, Norwell, 1996. Kluwer Academic Publisher.
14. K.V.S. Murthy. *On Growing Better Decision Trees from Data.* PhD thesis, The John Hopkins University, Baltimore, Maryland, 1995.
15. T. Naglyaki. *Introduction to Theoretical Population Genetics.* Springer, Berlin, 1992.
16. R.B. Robbins. Some applications of mathematics to breeding problems iii. *Genetics*, 3:375–389, 1918.
17. J.N. Sonquist and J.N. Morgan. *The Detection of Interaction Effects*, volume Monograph 35. Survey Research Center, Institute for Social Research, University of Michigan, 1964.
18. G. Syswerda. Uniform crossover in genetic algorithms. In H. Schaffer, editor, *3rd Int. Conf. on Genetic Algorithms*, pages 2–9, San Mateo, 1989. Morgan Kaufmann.

From Recombination of Genes to the Estimation of Distributions II. Continuous Parameters

H. Mühlenbein[1] and J. Bendisch[1] and H.–M. Voigt[2]*

[1] GMD – Forschungszentrum Informationstechnik, 53754 Sankt Augustin , Germany
[2] GFaI, Rudower Chaussee 5, 12484 Berlin, Germany

Abstract. The Breeder Genetic Algorithm (BGA) is based on the equation for the response to selection. In order to use this equation for prediction, the variance of the fitness of the population has to be estimated. For the usual sexual recombination this can be difficult. In this paper the new points (offspring) are generated from distributions, a uniform distribution and a distribution generated by univariate marginal distributions. For a class of unimodal fitness functions the performance of the BGA is analytically computed. The results are compared to gene recombination methods. The uniform distribution is approximately generated by line recombination; recombination methods acting independently on each gene approximate the second distribution.

1 Introduction

The Breeder Genetic Algorithm (BGA) is based on the classical science of livestock breeding. The central part of this theory is the equation for the response to selection

$$R(t) = b(t) \cdot I \cdot \sigma(t) \tag{1}$$

Here R denotes the response, which is defined as the difference between the mean fitness of the population at generation $t+1$ and t, $b(t)$ is the *realized heritability*, I is the *selection intensity* and σ is the standard deviation of the fitness [3]. If $b(t)$ and $\sigma(t)$ can be estimated, the equation can be used for predicting the mean fitness of the population after selection. In livestock breeding many methods have been developed to estimate the heritability [3], estimating the variance is still an open question [5].

Looking closer to the equation for the response to selection, we see that the equation does not use a microscopic genetic model at all. It needs the distribution of the fitness. In this paper we directly use distributions to generate new points (offspring). This facilitates the performance analysis for the algorithm. We compute the performance of the BGA for two different distributions. Comparisons are made with popular sexual recombination methods.

---

* HMV is also with the Technical University of Berlin

2 The uniform distribution BGA

We will use the following class of functions for a performance analysis

$$f_{n,k}(x) = \sum_{i=1}^{n} {x_i}^k \quad k = 1, 2, \ldots \tag{2}$$

These functions are to be minimized in

$$S_{n,k} = \{x | \sum_{i=1}^{n} x_i^k \leq 1, \quad 0 \leq x_i\}.$$

The unique minimization point is $x^* = 0$ with $f^*_{n,k} = 0$. The conceptual Uniform Distribution Breeder Genetic Algorithm (UDBGA) is defined as follows:

UDBGA

- **STEP0:** Set $t = 1$. Generate $N \gg 0$ points randomly in $S_{n,k}$.
- **STEP1:** Select the best $100 \cdot \rho\%$ points ($0 < \rho < 1$, truncation selection).
- **STEP2:** Generate N new points uniformly within the convex hull defined by the selected points. Set $t = t + 1$.
- **STEP3:** If not terminated, go to STEP1.

The above algorithm is conceptual, because the convex hull generated by the selected points maybe difficult to determine. For the above class of test functions, it is easy to see that truncation selection generates convex hulls $S_{n,k,\rho}(t)$, which are given by

$$S_{n,k,\rho}(t) = \{x | \sum_{i=1}^{n} x_i^k \leq d^k_{n,\rho}(t), \qquad 0 \leq x_i\} \tag{3}$$

For the analysis the value of $d_{n,\rho}(t)$ is needed. The following lemma gives the result.

Lemma 1: *The boundary value of the domain $S_{n,k,\rho}(t)$ is given by*

$$d_{n,\rho}(t) = \rho^{(t-1)/n} \tag{4}$$

Proof: We start with $d_{n,\rho}(1) = 1$. The next values are determined from the recursion $vol(S_{n,k,\rho}(t+1)) = \rho \cdot vol(S_{n,k,\rho}(t))$. Computing the volume of $S_{n,k,\rho}(t)$ in form of $vol(S_{n,k,\rho}(t)) = \gamma(n,k) \cdot d^n_{n,\rho}(t)$ gives the result. □

Note that $d_{n,\rho}(t)$ is independent of k. We are now able to formulate the main theorem.

Theorem 1. *The expected average fitness E_t of a population evolving according to UDBGA is given by*

$$E_t(f_{n,k}) = \frac{n}{n+k} d^k_{n,\rho}(t) \tag{5}$$

The variance V_t is given by

$$V_t(f_{n,k}) = \frac{n \cdot k^2}{(n+k)^2(n+2k)} d_{n,\rho}^{2k}(t) \tag{6}$$

Proof: For the proof $n-$dimensional integrals have to be computed. We used the following method, based on geometric arguments. Let $\varphi_k = f_{n,k}(x)$. With density

$$\theta_{n,\rho,t}(\varphi) = n \cdot d_{n,\rho}^{-n}(t) \cdot \varphi^{n-1}.$$

the expected fitness is obtained from

$$E_t(f_{n,k}) = \int_0^{d_{n,\rho}(t)} \varphi_k \theta_{n,\rho,t}(\varphi) d\varphi.$$

The variance is computed by the same method. □

In order to use the equation for the response to selection for prediction the selection intensity I and the coefficient of variation CV is needed. The selection intensity for an arbitrary fitness function f is defined as

$$I(f) = \frac{E_t(f) - E_t(f_\rho)}{V^{\frac{1}{2}}(f)},$$

where $E_t(f_\rho)$ denotes the expected mean of the fitness of the selected points at generation t. For our conceptual algorithm we obviously have a heritability of one, i.e. $E_t(f_\rho) = E_{t+1}(f)$. The coefficient of variation is defined for $f \geq 0$ as

$$CV(f) = \frac{V^{\frac{1}{2}}(f)}{E(f)}$$

From theorem 1 follows:

Theorem 2. *For UDBGA the selection intensity I is independent of t and given by*

$$I_{n,k,\rho} = \left(1 - \sqrt[n]{\rho^k}\right) \sqrt{\frac{n(n+2k)}{k^2}}. \tag{7}$$

The coefficient of variation CV is independent of ρ and given by

$$CV_{n,k} = \sqrt{\frac{k^2}{n(n+2k)}}. \tag{8}$$

Corollary: *In the limit we have*

$$\lim_{n\to\infty} I_{n,k,\rho} = \ln \frac{1}{\rho} \qquad 0 < \rho \leq 1 \tag{9}$$

Note that for *evolution strategies* exactly the same limit has been obtained for the progress coefficient $c_{1,\lambda}$ giving the maximum rate of progress ([1]).

Next we show how to use the above results in order to compute the computational complexity and the convergence rate of the algorithm.

3 Computational complexity and convergence

We recall the following definition from mathematical optimization theory.
Definition: *An optimization algorithm converges linearly if*

$$|f(x_{m+1}) - f^*| \leq c|f(x_m) - f^*| \quad 0 < c < 1 \tag{10}$$

For convenience we assume $f^* = 0$.

Theorem 3. *If the coefficient of variation $CV(f)$, the realized heritability b and the selection intensity I are independent of t, and $0 < b \cdot I \cdot CV(f) < 1$, the breeder genetic algorithm converges linearly*

$$E_{t+1}(f) = (1 - b \cdot I \cdot CV(f))\, E_t(f) \tag{11}$$

The proof follows directly from the equation for the response to selection.

Corollary: *For the previous class of test functions $f_{n,k}$ and truncation selection with parameter ρ UDBGA converges linearly in number of generations t*

$$E_{t+1}(f_{n,k}) = \sqrt[n]{\rho^k}\, E_t(f_{n,k}) \tag{12}$$

For unimodal functions it is obvious that the convergence speed increases with decreasing ρ, i.e severe selection is the best.

In order to evaluate the computational complexity, we introduce the notion of $\epsilon-$computational complexity.

Definition: *The $\epsilon-$computational complexity is defined as the number of steps t_ϵ needed to reduce the initial approximation error by a given fraction $\epsilon > 0$.*

Theorem 4. *For the class of test functions $f_{n,k}$ and truncation selection with parameter ρ UDBGA has a computational complexity of $O(n)$ in number of generations t_ϵ*

$$t_\epsilon(n, k, \rho) = \frac{n}{k} \frac{\ln \epsilon}{\ln \rho} \tag{13}$$

Proof: From Equations (4) and 5 we obtain

$$E_{t+1}(f_{n,k}) = \left(\sqrt[n]{\rho^k}\right) E_t(f_{n,k}) = \left(\sqrt[n]{\rho^k}\right)^t E_1(f_{n,k})$$

This gives

$$\frac{E_{t+1}(f_{n,k})}{E_1(f_{n,k})} = \left(\sqrt[n]{\rho^k}\right)^t = \epsilon$$

Taking the logarithm gives equation 13. □

The above results are given in number of generations t, not number of function evaluations. For the analysis it is assumed that the population is very large, so that the points are uniformly distributed in the statistical sense. In order to minimize the number of functions evaluations, the size of the population has to be as small as possible. This question leads to the difficult problem of the *minimal population size*. For binary genes this problem has been investigated in [4].

4 Line recombination

The conceptual UDBGA is based on the following principle. Generate initial points according to a uniform distribution. Do selection. Generate uniformly distributed new points in the domain implicitly defined by the selected points. The crucial questions for an implementation of this algorithm are: How to generate points uniformly in a given domain? How to identify the domain to be tested? It turns out that it is surprisingly easy to generate uniform distributed vectors in a convex polytope. This new recombination method will be investigated in a forthcoming paper. Here we will make a comparison to a more classical genetic algorithm with sexual recombination.

For convex domains, one of the easiest ways to create new points from two given points x and y is the linear combination

$$z = \alpha x + (1-\alpha)y \quad x, y \in R^n \tag{14}$$

These recombinations schemes are known as line recombination in genetic algorithms (see for instance [2]). For a certain number of generations, these recombination methods will generate points which are approximately uniformly distributed. Usually α is taken to be uniformly distributed in $[0,1]$, or even fixed at 0.5. Both methods have severe shortcomings because they reduce the variance. This will be shown with the following lemma.

Lemma 2 *Let x and y be independent random vectors from the same distribution with existing variance $V(x) = V(y)$. Let the stochastic real number α be independent from x and y and arbitrarily distributed with expectation $E(\alpha) = \bar{\alpha}$ and variance $V(\alpha) = v_\alpha$, then*

$$V(\alpha x + (1-\alpha)y) = (1 - 2\bar{\alpha} + 2\bar{\alpha}^2 + 2v_\alpha) \cdot V(x) \tag{15}$$

The proof has to be omitted. We use the above lemma to compute the variance of the fitness of line recombination methods. The lemma can be only applied for the linear function $f_{n,1}(x)$, for $k > 1$ higher moments have to be computed.

Theorem 5. *For $f_{n,1}(x) = \sum_{i=1}^n x_i$ and $z = \alpha x + (1-\alpha)y$ we have*

$$V(f_{n,1}(z)) = (1 - 2\bar{\alpha} + 2\bar{\alpha}^2 + 2v_\alpha) \cdot V(f_{n,1}(x)) \tag{16}$$

Example 1: For $\alpha \equiv 0.5$ we have $\bar{\alpha} = 0.5$ and $v_\alpha = 0$. Therefore the well known result $V(f_{n,1}(z)) = 0.5V(f_{n,1}(x))$ is obtained.

Example 2: For α uniformly distributed in $[0,1]$ we have $\bar{\alpha} = 0.5$ and $v_\alpha = 1/12$. Therefore $V(f_{n,1}(z)) = \frac{2}{3}V(f_{n,1}(x))$. The variance is severely reduced.

Example 3: Extended line recombination with α uniformly distributed in $[-d, 1+d]$ and $d \approx 3/8$ gives $V(f_{n,1}(z)) \approx V(f_{n,1}(x))$.

Example 4: For α derived from the bimodal fuzzy distribution defined in [7] we have $\bar{\alpha} = 0.5$ and $v_\alpha = 7/24$. Therefore $V(f_{n,1}(z)) = \frac{13}{12}V(f_{n,1}(x))$.

Example 5: For α uniformly distributed in $[-0.25, 0.25]$ and $[-0.75, 1.25]$ (two plateau distribution) we have $\bar{\alpha} = 0.5$ and $v_\alpha = 13/48$. This gives $V(f_{n,1}(z)) = \frac{25}{24}V(f_{n,1}(x))$.

Both in example 1 and example 2 we have a reduction of the variance. This can lead to premature convergence. The following table shows some numerical results. The initial points were uniformly placed in the cube $[0,1]^n$. For the initial population we have $E_0(f_{n,1}) = n/2$ and $V_0(f_{n,1}) = n/12$.

	D(1)			D(2)			D(3)		
t	$\bar{f}$	σ	CV	$\bar{f}$	σ	CV	$\bar{f}$	σ	CV
0	1.011	4.048	0.40	0.991	4.013	0.40	1.001	4.044	0.40
1	0.679	1.767	0.26	0.657	2.131	0.32	0.677	2.380	0.35
2	0.529	0.863	0.16	0.485	1.272	0.26	0.488	1.662	0.34
3	0.464	0.467	0.10	0.382	0.746	0.19	0.355	1.347	0.38
4	0.427	0.330	0.08	0.325	0.493	0.15	0.247	1.001	0.40
5	0.403	0.235	0.06	0.286	0.351	0.12	0.159	0.583	0.36
6	0.388	0.174	0.05	0.260	0.285	0.11	0.110	0.386	0.35
7	0.378	0.195	0.05	0.210	0.160	0.08	0.077	0.273	0.35

Table 1. Three line recombination methods ($k = 1, n = 2, \rho = 0.5$)

In Table 1 the results for three distributions of α are shown: (D1) $\alpha \equiv 0.5$, (D2) α uniform in $[0,1]$, and (D3) α uniform in $[-0.25, 0.25], [0.75, 1.25]$. The predicted CV from UDBGA is $CV_{2,1} = 0.35$. This value is fairly accurately reproduced by extended line recombination (D3). The other two line recombination methods ((D1),(D2)) reduce the variance too much, leading to premature convergence. For higher dimensions this problem gets also important for extended line recombination (D3).

	D(3)			D(3)		
t	$\bar{f}$	σ	CV	$\bar{f}$	σ	CV
0	2.00	0.5694	0.28	0.6710	0.4237	0.63
1	0.80	0.1744	0.21	0.3177	0.1909	0.60
2	0.36	0.0636	0.18	0.1538	0.0935	0.61
3	0.18	0.0352	0.19	0.0733	0.0465	0.63
4	0.11	0.0065	0.06	0.0338	0.0212	0.62
5	0.10	0.0042	0.04	0.0160	0.0086	0.53

Table 2. Two results for (D3) ($k = 1$, $n = 4, \rho = 1/24$; $k = 2, n = 2, \rho = 0.5$)

Table 2 gives some results for two other examples. In the first example the predicted CV from UDBGA is $CV = 0.20$. Here $CV \approx 0.20$ is achieved for only three generations, then it gets much smaller leading to premature convergence of the algorithm. The reason is the severe selection. A much larger population is needed to circumvent premature convergence. The second example shows that the UDBGA approximation can also be used for $k = 2$. The coefficient of variation for UDBGA is $CV = \sqrt{1/3} = 0.58$. This value is fairly accurately reproduced by extended line recombination.

We have done more simulations, all of which confirm our theoretical results. For large values of k the difference between UDBGA and line recombination based on (D3) gets larger. This shows that extended line recombination does not create uniformly distributed points in higher dimensions.

5 The univariate marginal distribution BGA

The uniform distribution does not take the fitness distribution into account. The search strategy of this algorithm is fairly conservative, i.e it does not exploit areas of good fitness values. In this section we will analyze a distribution which uses the fitness distribution. This distribution generates more points in areas where good fitness values are expected. The simplest way is to generate the new points according to the univariate marginal distributions of the selected points. The analysis of this algorithm is more difficult. We restrict the analysis to $k = 1$ and $k = 2$. The Univariate Marginal Distribution Breeder Genetic Algorithm (UMDBGA) is similar to the UDBGA, only the new points are generated from a different distribution.

UMDBGA

- **STEP0:** Set $t = 0$. Generate $N \gg 0$ points randomly within the unit cube $C_n(0)$.
- **STEP1:** Select the best $100 \cdot \rho\%$ points ($0 < \rho < 1$, truncation selection).
- **STEP2:** Generate N new points x according to $p(x) = \prod_{i=1}^{n} \theta(x_{i,\rho})$. Here $\theta(x_{i,\rho})$ denotes the univariate marginal distribution of variable $x_{i,\rho}$ in the domain of selected points.
- **STEP3:** If not terminated, go to STEP1

For the given fitness function, the domain defined by selection is $S_{n,k,\rho}(t)$ as before, but UMDBGA will generate new points non uniformly within a cube $C_{n,\rho}(t)$ with side length $d_{n,\rho}(t)$. Selection gives domain $S_{n,k,\rho}(t+1)$. Unfortunately, the determination of the marginal distributions within this domain turns out to be difficult, because the points are not uniformly distributed in the cube $C_{n,\rho}(t)$. We will use an approximation by assuming that we have a uniform distribution within the cube. For $k = 1$ we will use the density

$$\theta_{n,\rho,t}(x_{i,\rho}) = \frac{n}{d_{n,\rho}^n(t)} \left(d_{n,\rho}(t) - x_{i,\rho}\right)^{n-1}. \qquad (17)$$

Theorem 6. *The expected average fitness of a population evolving according to UMDBGA with the marginal distribution θ and fitness function $f_{n,1}$ is given by*

$$E_t(f_{n,1}) = \frac{n}{n+1} d_{n,\rho}(t). \tag{18}$$

The variance is given by

$$V_t(f_{n,1}) = \frac{n^2}{(n+1)^2(n+2)} d_{n,\rho}^2(t). \tag{19}$$

Proof: Let $d = d_{n,\rho}(t)$. We have

$$E_t(f_{n,1}) = n \cdot E_t(f_{1,1}) = n \int_0^d \frac{n}{d^n}(d-\xi)^{n-1}\xi d\xi = \frac{n^2 d^{n+1}}{n(n+1)d^n}$$

Similarly the variance is obtained from

$$V_t(f_{n,1}) = n \int_0^d \theta_{n,\rho,t}(\xi)\xi^2 d\xi - E_t^2(f_{n,1}). \quad \square$$

Corollary: For UMDBGA with marginal distribution (17) the coefficient of variation is

$$CV_{n,1} = \sqrt{\frac{1}{n+2}} \tag{20}$$

The computation of the side length $d_{n,\rho}$ seems to be difficult for the general case. We just give the solution for $n = 2$ and $\rho = 0.5$.

Lemma 3 *For dimension $n = 2$ and $\rho = 0.5$ the side length of the domain $C_{2,0.5}(t)$ is given by*

$$d_{2,0.5}(t+1) = 0.642 \cdot d_{2,0.5}(t) \quad d_{2,0.5}(1) = 1 \tag{21}$$

Proof: Let $d_{2,\rho}(t) = d(t)$. With truncation selection parameter ρ the side length $d(t+1)$ is obtained from

$$\int_0^{d(t+1)} \int_0^{d(t+1)} \frac{2}{d(t)^2}(d(t) - x_1)\frac{2}{d(t)^2}(d(t) - x_2) dx_1 dx_2 = \rho$$

This leads to the equation

$$\eta^4 - 8\eta^3 + 12\eta^2 - 6\rho = 0 \quad \eta = \frac{d(t+1)}{d(t)}$$

For $\rho = 0.5$ the result is obtained. □

Univariate marginal distributions are approximated by volume oriented sexual recombination schemes as used in genetic algorithms. In this case the recombination schemes discussed in the previous section are applied *independently* for each variable. We will show numerical results only for discrete recombination [2].

t	f	σ	CV	f Theory	σ Theory
0	1.000	0.406	0.40	1.000	0.401
1	0.662	0.278	0.41	0.666	0.333
2	0.430	0.196	0.45	0.428	0.214
3	0.274	0.128	0.46	0.275	0.138
4	0.166	0.078	0.47	0.176	0.088
5	0.101	0.047	0.46	0.113	0.057
6	0.063	0.024	0.38	0.073	0.037

Table 3. Discrete recombination ($n = 2, k = 1, \rho = 0.5$)

In table 3 simulation results are displayed for $n = 2$ and $\rho = 0.5$. In this case UMDBGA has $CV_{2,1} = 0.5$. Discrete recombination has a coefficient of variation, which is about 10% less. Note that the average fitness of the genetic recombination BGA and UMDBGA are very similar for the first generations. Then discrete recombination will of course lead to premature convergence.

UMDBGA can be also analyzed for other values of k. But the mathematical difficulties are tremendous. We just outline the case $k = 2$. The selected domain is now part of a hyper sphere. If the points would be uniformly distributed then the marginal distribution would be

$$\theta_{n,\rho,t}(x_{i,\rho}) = c\left(\sqrt{d^2_{n,\rho}(t) - x^2_{i,\rho}}\right)^{n-1} \tag{22}$$

c can be computed from the volume of the $(n-1)$-dimensional hyper-sphere. As for $k = 1$, we make the assumption that the marginal distribution is given by equation (22). The proof of the following theorem is based on sophisticated integration of n-dimensional integrals and has to be omitted.

Theorem 7. *The expected average fitness of a population evolving according to UMDBGA with marginal distribution (22) is given for odd $n \geq 3$ and $k = 2$ by*

$$E_t(f_{n,2}) = \frac{n}{n+2} d^2_n(t) \tag{23}$$

The variance is given by

$$V_t(f_{n,2}) = \frac{2n(n+1)}{(n+2)^2(n+4)} d^4_n(t) \tag{24}$$

Corollary: Under the assumptions of the above theorem the coefficient of variation of UMDBGA is given by

$$CV_{n,2} = \sqrt{\frac{2(n+1)}{n(n+4)}} \tag{25}$$

Note that for large n we have $CV_{n,2} = \sqrt{2/n}$. This value was already empirically determined for gene pool recombination with fuzzy recombination ([6]).

This shows that a UMDBGA accurately describes the behavior of a BGA with volume oriented genetic recombination.

6 Conclusion and outlook

We have shown that the performance of genetic algorithms is mainly governed by distributions. In this paper we have investigated algorithms based on two simple distributions. UDBGA using a uniform distribution is explorative, UMDBGA using marginal distributions is more exploitative. But using univariate marginal distributions is only the first step. For more complex fitness functions, like general quadratic forms, covariances and principal component analysis has to be used [6].

In order to predict the performance of classical genetic algorithms with sexual recombination, the distributions have to be estimated which are generated by recombination. We have shown that extended line recombination approximately generates uniformly distributed points; and volume oriented recombination methods approximate univariate marginal distributions. Now the questions arise: Why not directly using distributions instead of sexual recombination? Why not using multivariate distributions for fitness functions where the variables are correlated?

Acknowledgment: The authors thank Gerd Paaß, who proved lemma 2.

References

1. Hans-Georg Beyer. Toward a theory of evolution strategies: Some asymptotical results from the $(1, \lambda)$-theory. *Evolutionary Computation*, 1:165–188, 1994.
2. H. Mühlenbein and D. Schlierkamp-Voosen. Predictive Models for the Breeder Genetic Algorithm I. Continuous Parameter Optimization. *Evolutionary Computation*, 1:25–49, 1993.
3. H. Mühlenbein and D. Schlierkamp-Voosen. The science of breeding and its application to the breeder genetic algorithm. *Evolutionary Computation*, 1:335–360, 1994.
4. H. Mühlenbein and D. Schlierkamp-Voosen. The theory of breeding and the breeder genetic algorithm. In J. Stender, E. Hillebrand, and J. Kingdon, editors, *Genetic Algorithms in Optimisation, Simulation and Modelling*, Frontiers in Artificial Intelligence Applications, pages 27–64, Amsterdam, 1994. IOS Press.
5. T. Naglyaki. *Introduction to Theoretical Population Genetics.* Springer, Berlin, 1992.
6. H.-M. Voigt and H. Mühlenbein. Gene Pool Recombination and the Utilization of Covariances for the Breeder Genetic Algorithm. In Z. Michalewicz, editor, *Proc. of the 2nd IEEE International Conference on Evolutionary Computation*, pages 172–177, New York, 1995. IEEE Press.
7. H.-M. Voigt, H. Mühlenbein, and D. Cvetković. Fuzzy recombination for the continuous breeder genetic algorithm. In L. J. Eshelman, editor, *Proc. of the Sixth Int. Conf. on Genetic Algorithms*, pages 104–112, San Francisco, 1995. Morgan Kaufmann.

Searching in the Presence of Noise

Soraya Rana, L. Darrell Whitley, Ronald Cogswell

Computer Science Department, Colorado State University, Fort Collins, CO 80523
{rana, whitley, cogswell}@cs.colostate.edu

Abstract. In this paper, we examine the effects of noise on both local search and genetic search. Understanding the potential effects of noise on a search space may explain why some search techniques fail and why others succeed in the presence of noise. We discuss two effects that are the result of adding noise to a search space: the annealing of peaks in the search space and the introduction of false local optima.

1 Introduction

The two major components to any search problem are the algorithm we choose to use to traverse the search space and the function used to provide feedback to the algorithm (i.e. the objective function). When the objective function provides noisy feedback, the resulting behaviors and long term performance of search algorithms can be surprising.

By design, genetic algorithms should be effective search techniques in noisy environments. The genetic algorithm population preserves both highly fit points in the space and less fit points in a space which allows for a certain amount of variance for the fitness values of its members. Selection allocates trials to subpartitions of the search space based on the relative fitness values of sample strings the population: providing that the amount of noise is not overwhelming, this operation is still effective in the presence of noise. Thus, one advantage of using an evolutionary algorithm in a noisy environment is that it is not quick to discard valuable information.

Local search techniques, while often producing very good results in noiseless environments, are brittle in comparison to genetic algorithms in noisy environments. Local neighborhood search methods are often unable to accurately identify the best improving move or they may not be able to confidently identify a local optimum without strong a priori information about the amount of noise present relative to the expected change in the objective function for any given move. On the other hand, noise can sometimes have a soft annealing effect on the search space: even if one is currently in a local optimum, noisy evaluation can still potentially indicate that an improving move is possible. This can potentially make it possible for local search to actually perform well in the presence of noise. Levitan refers to this effect as "melting" [8].

It is difficult to predict how an arbitrary algorithm will behave in the presence of noise. This paper empirically examines the performance of various search algorithms in both noisy and noiseless conditions. We also include some old and new test functions, since the type of test function that is used also impacts the performance. We tested both the CHC as well as an elitist simple genetic algorithm along with Adaptive Simulated Annealing [7] and two local search techniques: random bit climbing and Line Search.

2 Background

Holland's *schema theorem* is based on the idea that selection acts not just on individual strings, but also on hyperplanes representing subpartitions of the search space. The *schema theorem*, in fact, is just a lower bound on the change in the sampling rate for a single hyperplane from generation t to generation $t+1$. Let P(H,t) be the representation of hyperplane H in the population at generation t; let P(H,t+s) be the proportional representation of hyperplane H in the population at a point intermediate between generation t and $t+1$ *after selection* but *before recombination.* Under fitness proportionate selection, using $\mathcal{E}$ to denote expectation:

$$\mathcal{E}P(H,t+s) = P(H,t)\frac{f(H,t)}{\bar{f}_t}$$

where f(H,t) is the average fitness of strings in the population that sample H at time t and $\bar{f}_t$ is the average population fitness. Now assume that random Gaussian noise is included as part of our fitness function. That is, for all strings i that are members of the current population,

$$f(H,t) = \sum_{i \epsilon H}(e(i) + G_i)$$

where $e(i)$ is the true evaluation of string i and G_i is noise added to string i. The noise is randomly drawn form a Gaussian distribution with $\mu = 0$. If we have a reasonably large sample for hyperplane H, then in expectation,

$$\mathcal{E}f(H,t) = \sum_{i \epsilon H} e(i) + \sum_{i \epsilon H} G_i = \sum_{i \epsilon H} e(i).$$

In other words, noise has no impact on the expected average fitness of a hyperplane subpartition if the number of samples from that partition is large. This suggests that selection on large hyperplane subpartitions is not seriously affected by noise if the population is also relatively large. This argument has been used to suggest that genetic algorithms are robust in the presence of noise, but there have been few empirical studies confirming this argument.

It should also be noted that this argument depends only on selection and that similar arguments might be applied to other evolutionary algorithms using other

$F101(x,y) = -x sin(\sqrt{\lvert x - \frac{(y+47)}{2}\rvert}) - (y+47) sin(\sqrt{\lvert y+47+\frac{x}{2}\rvert})$	$x,y \in [-512,511]$
$F102(x,y) = x sin(\sqrt{\lvert y+1-x\rvert}) cos(\sqrt{\lvert x+y+1\rvert}) + (y+1) cos(\sqrt{\lvert y+1-x\rvert}) sin(\sqrt{\lvert x+y+1\rvert})$	$x,y \in [-512,511]$

Table 1: Suite of test functions used in the experiments.

forms of selection. In the current study we look at CHC, which combines features of genetic algorithms and $(\mu + \lambda)$ evolution strategies. CHC also used small population sizes (i.e., 50) and truncation selection. This doesn't appear to fit the robust "hyperplane sampling" model very well, but nevertheless our results indicate that CHC is quite effective in the presence of noise.

Previous studies on the effects of noise on genetic algorithms performance have dealt mainly in analyzing specific components of specific genetic algorithms that may improve convergence properties, namely selection methods [10, 6]. Hammel and Back [6] also discuss the relationship between population size and sample size in terms of the potential benefit of one over the other. Greffenstette [4] provides both theoretical and empirical evidence that indicates that better performance can be achieved by choosing a large population over doing more work per evaluation to reduce the impact of noise on each string evaluation when using a traditional genetic algorithm. Mathias and Whitley [9] have done similar initial studies, but only looked at the random bit climbing, RBC, and also used a restricted set of test functions.

We test a suite of five test functions with and without the addition of noise. These include Rastrigin's function (F6), Schwefel's function (F7) and Griewangk's function (F8). We include these relatively simple functions in order to observe how noise impacts functions with very limited nonlinearity and whose optima can be found rather quickly using simple methods.

The remaining two functions were developed by Whitley et al. [11] (See Table 1). For all functions, every parameter is represented using a ten bit substring and Gray coded. All functions were scaled to 20 parameters. $F6$, $F7$ and $F8$ are scaled using a summation from 1 to 20 of each parameter evaluated using the basic subfunction that defines each function. For the functions in Table 1 Whitley et al. [11] describe methods for expanding functions of two variables into functions of N variables in a nonlinear manner. The method used here is the *wrap* method. A general formula illustrating the wrap method using a function of two variables F is as follows:

$$EF(x_1, x_2, x_3, .., x_n) = F(x_1, x_n) + \sum_{i=1}^{n-1} F(x_i, x_{i+1})$$

where EF is a function obtained by the *expansion* of F.

We examine the performance of five search algorithms: two evolutionary algorithms, two local search techniques and adaptive simulated annealing. We do not tune any of the algorithms to deal with the noise. The CHC adaptive search algorithm [3] (CHC) is run using a population of 50 with the HUX recombination operator while the elitist simple genetic algorithm uses tournament selection [5] (ESGAT) and a population size 200. For ESGAT, recombination is accomplished using a 2-point reduced-surrogate crossover operator [1] applied with probability 0.9 and mutation is applied to each individual bit with a probability of 1/L, where L is the length of the string. (We stress that testing the effect of increasing population size is one goal of our future work.)

The two local search techniques used here are Davis's Random Bit Climber and Line Search [11] (LINE). Davis' random bit climber (RBC) starts by changing 1 bit at a time beginning at a random position. Each improving move is accepted. The sequence in which the bits are tested is also randomly determined. After testing every bit in the string, a new random sequence for checking the bits is chosen and RBC again tests every bit for an improvement. If a local optima has been reached (i.e., there are no improving moves) RBC is restarted from a new random point in the space by generating a new random string.

Line Search works with any discretization of the space. Starting with a randomly chosen solution of n parameters, Line Search enumerates each parameter to find the best possible setting for that parameter. The order in which the parameters are enumerated is also randomly determined. If there are no nonlinear interactions between variables, then Line Search is an exact method guaranteed to find the global optimum *if the objective function is also exact.* Assuming each of the n parameters has k possible values, Line Search will have reached the global optimum after nk evaluations if there are no nonlinear interactions. $F6$ and $F7$ are exactly solved by Line Search since there are no nonlinear interactions between variables. On functions with nonlinear interactions, Line Search acts like a local search method searching a neighborhood of nk points.

The last algorithm that we use in our experiments is adaptive simulated annealing (ASA). The implementation used is ASA version 10.16 which was downloaded from the CalTech archive of Lester Ingber [7]. ASA is a simulated annealing algorithm first developed as Very Fast Simulated Reannealing (VFSR) in 1987. It differs from traditional simulated annealing algorithms by allowing for specialized annealing schedules for different parameters to address the issue of parameter sensitivity. For our application, tuning of the algorithm was minimal and limited to increasing performance on large parameter spaces. Reannealing is not utilized due to the high number of evaluation function calls required. Termination criteria was modified to prevent repeating evaluation values from ending the search.

FUNC	ALG	Mean Solution	σ	Mean Trials	σ Trials	Mean Rstrts	σ Rstrts	Nbr Slv
EF101	CHC	-939.880	0.000	93388	50333			30
	ESGAT	-809.875	73.102					0
	RBC	-668.569	23.400			243.69	6.39	0
	LINE	-752.234	30.299					0
	ASA	-740.462	43.479					0
EF102	CHC	-476.904	7.451					0
	ESGAT	-415.845	12.906					0
	RBC	-407.564	14.087			192.76	5.45	0
	LINE	-481.829	5.301					0
	ASA	-445.798	16.328					0
F6	CHC	0.000	0.000	158839	72048			30
	ESGAT	12.910	3.285					0
	RBC	23.198	1.879			422.89	2.53	0
	LINE	0.000	0.000	20500	0			30
	ASA	4.646	1.154					0
F7	CHC	-8379.655	0.000	30029	6397			30
	ESGAT	-8294.249	57.703					0
	RBC	-6994.345	188.166			468.20	2.36	0
	LINE	-8379.655	0.000	20500	0			30
	ASA	-8379.171	0.145					0
F8	CHC	0.000	0.000	50509	39451			30
	ESGAT	1.185	0.056					0
	RBC	0.000	0.000	82215	98985	56.90	69.45	30
	LINE	0.037	0.024	178789	113710			7
	ASA	0.869	0.113					0

Table 2: All four algorithms run on the suite of five test functions without the addition of noise.

3 Performance With and Without Noise

The first set of experiments were run using all four algorithms and all five test functions without the addition of any noise. The results are given in Table 2. ASA produces relatively good results; it is not the best performer but is also not the worst. As predicted, Line Search solves F6 and F7 on its first iteration. RBC produces surprisingly good results on $F8$ while Line Search performed significantly worse than RBC in terms of the number of times the global optimum is found. ESGAT performs better than RBC on four of the five functions tested and never outperforms Line Search. In fact, CHC usually outperforms all algorithms with the exception of Line Search. These experiments illustrate that Line Search and RBC can be competitive with the genetic algorithms without the presence of noise.

The next set of experiments involve the same functions with the addition of Gaussian noise (See Table 3). The Gaussian noise is drawn from a distribution with $\mu = 0$ and $\sigma = 6$. Assuming the global optimum is g and its evaluation is $e(g)$, search was terminated if a noisy evaluation is obtained that is less than or equal to $e(g) - 3$. The first two columns of Table 3 are the noisy mean and standard deviations for each algorithm based on 30 runs. The third and fourth

FUNC	ALG	Mean Solution	σ	Mean True Solution	σ	Mean Rstrts	σ Rstrts	Nbr Slv
EF101 +noise	CHC	-943.063	0.155	-939.294	0.220			30
	ESGAT	-840.927	82.007	-839.473	81.852			0
	RBC	-665.952	23.046	-663.263	22.935	370.33	6.65	0
	LINE	-737.868	50.032	-735.675	49.933			0
	ASA	-759.765	57.286	-756.886	57.346			0
EF102 +noise	CHC	-479.425	7.483	-478.582	7.466			0
	ESGAT	-411.256	14.053	-410.248	14.078			0
	RBC	-396.821	8.611	-394.252	8.727	399.46	7.57	0
	LINE	-482.405	6.861	-481.088	6.621			0
	ASA	-446.467	17.003	-444.356	17.088			0
F6 +noise	CHC	-2.270	1.779	0.660	0.186			23
	ESGAT	15.433	3.010	17.219	2.932			0
	RBC	27.161	3.550	29.772	3.660	434.36	5.98	0
	LINE	2.081	0.5265	4.048	0.754			0
	ASA	8.052	1.138	10.323	1.428			0
F7 +noise	CHC	-8382.810	0.157	-8379.099	0.220			30
	ESGAT	-8280.761	68.429	-8279.982	68.416			0
	RBC	-6977.993	168.510	-6975.396	168.516	393.16	5.06	0
	LINE	-8378.417	0.659	-8376.452	0.786			0
	ASA	-8379.029	0.826	-8376.451	0.991			0
F8 +noise	CHC	-0.380	1.296	2.231	0.544			0
	ESGAT	1.031	0.724	3.901	0.922			0
	RBC	1.561	0.649	4.523	0.711	427.79	6.52	0
	LINE	0.076	0.413	2.889	0.488			0
	ASA	-0.983	0.456	2.501	0.416			0

Table 3: All four algorithms evaluated on the suite of five test functions with noise added.

columns are the true mean and standard deviations for the same experiments. Typically, the performance of any algorithm on any function degrades when noise is added. However, the degree to which the performance changes varies not only from algorithm to algorithm but also from function to function. The performance of several of the algorithms is not significantly affected by the addition of noise on $EF101$, $EF102$ and $F7$ (verified using a two-tailed Student's T-test with $p = 0.05$). ESGAT's performance was particularly stable across $EF101$, $EF102$ and $F7$ and shows no significant change in performance when noise is added. RBC shows no significant change in performance on $EF101$ and $F7$ and Line Search and ASA show no significant change in performance on $EF101$ and $EF102$. The only function for which CHC does not show a significant change in performance is $F7$. When there are significant changes in performance (particularly for Line Search and CHC), it is usually because the functions were solved 30 out of 30 times when noise is not present. However, in those cases, the mean solutions found for the noisy function are often very close to mean solutions found for the corresponding non-noisy function.

The solutions for the noisy versions of $F6$ and $F8$ are categorically worse than the non-noisy results for all algorithms. In all cases, the mean of the best solutions found for each algorithms becomes significantly worse when noise is added.

3.1 Melting Optima Versus False Optima

There are at least two significant impacts of adding noise to an objective function: the soft annealing effect and the creation of false optima. Levitan [8], refers to the smoothing and soft annealing effect as "melting" of peaks. Noise can allow a local search algorithm to escape a local optimum by indicating an improving move is present when none in fact exists. Our results suggest that this effect can cause some algorithms to perform better on some functions with added noise–especially during the *initial* phases of search. However, the utility of the melting effect depends on the underlying function.

One primary difference between our experiments and those performed by Levitan are in the algorithms we tested. Levitan uses a single algorithm that is effectively the same as RBC without restarts. We attempted to use RBC without restarts but the resulting solutions were not competitive with those found using RBC with restarts simply because there is an advantage to sampling several points in the space as opposed to examining only one. An argument for removing the restarts is that their removal allows closer study of effects of noise on a given search space. However, it is also important to consider whether or not the algorithm will ultimately converge to a reasonably good solution even in the presence of noise. For this reason, we chose to report our results for RBC with restarts.

Like Levitan, we found evidence that supports the annealing effect. For $F7$, the number of restarts for RBC dropped significantly when noise was added to the function. This is evidence that the search space became "smoother" when noise was added; however, this was the only function in which this effect dominated and in the end RBC did not have an significant improvement in the quality of solutions it found. On functions $EF101$, $EF102$, $F6$ and $F8$, the number of restarts significantly increased when noise was added. This implies that the second effect, introduction of false optima, dominated in those functions.

We conjecture that if the objective function is relatively simple before the noise is added, the noise has little or no positive impact on search and only serves to make search more difficult. This effect is particularly evident in the performance on $F8$. Whitley et al. [11] show empirically and explain analytically that at higher dimensions $F8$ has smaller and more shallow local optima. Thus, scaling up $F8$ has a smoothing effect. At 20 variables the addition of noise to $F8$ caused a dramatic increase in the number of restarts for RBC. Given that the performance of RBC on $F8$ without noise was exceptionally good, its performance degraded dramatically when the noise was added.

4 Resampling Data During Search

Resampling data points is a common approach used to reduce the effects of noise. Other researchers [6, 4] point out that increasing the population size of a genetic algorithm can have similar effects as resampling data points. However, since

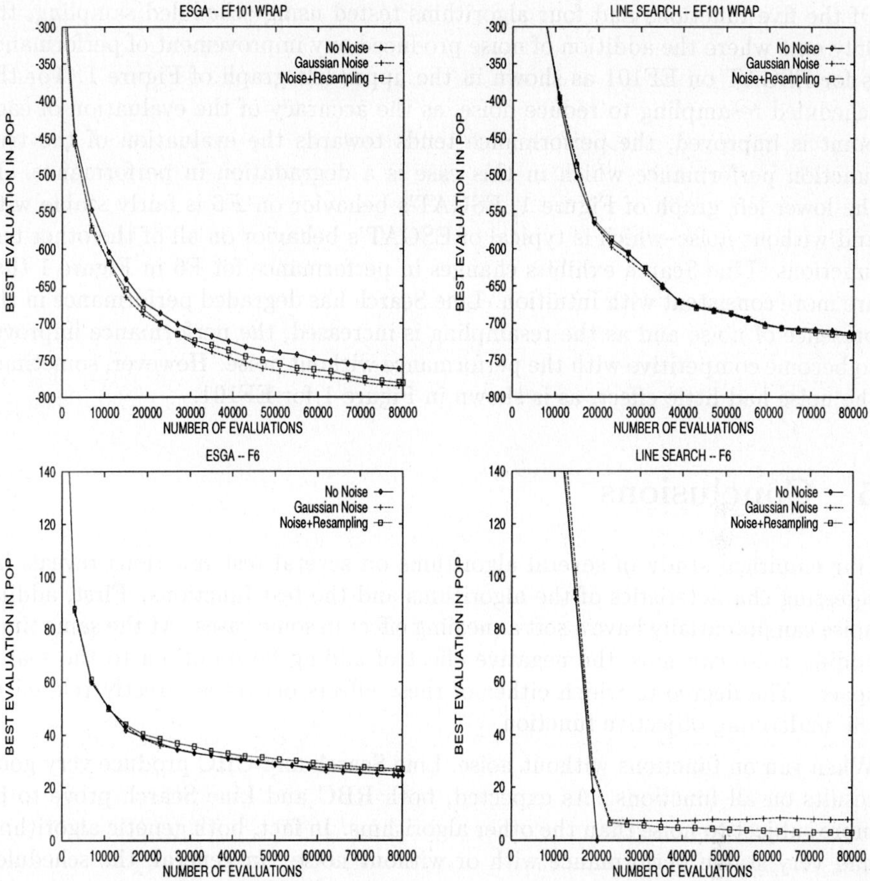

Figure 1: ESGAT (left) and Line Search (right) on EF101 (top), EF6 (bottom) without noise, with Gaussian noise added and with Gaussian noise with scheduled resampling.

two of our algorithms (ASA was not used in this set of experiments) are not population based, increasing the number of points sampled during execution by increasing population size was not used here. Instead, we wished to explore the benefits of sampling the evaluation function multiple times for a simple string in order to obtain more accurate evaluations as the execution progressed. A schedule is used so that we initially start out with 1 evaluation per string, then exponentially increase the number of evaluations per string every 20 thousand points sampled (20 thousand evaluations roughly corresponds to one iteration of Line Search.) This was done for both genetic algorithms and the local search techniques. The schedule is as follows:

```
 0-20K points: 1 evaluation     40K-60K points: 4 evaluations
20K-40K points: 2 evaluations   60K-80K points: 8 evaluations
```

Of the five functions and four algorithms tested using scheduled sampling, the only case where the addition of noise produced any improvement of performance is for ESGAT on EF101 as shown in the upper left graph of Figure 1. For the scheduled resampling to reduce noise, as the accuracy of the evaluation of each point is improved, the performance tends towards the evaluation of the true function performance which in this case is a degradation in performance. In the lower left graph of Figure 1, ESGAT's behavior on $F6$ is fairly stable with and without noise–which is typical of ESGAT's behavior on all of the other test functions. Line Search exhibits changes in performance for F6 in Figure 1 that are more consistent with intuition. Line Search has degraded performance in the presence of noise and as the resampling is increased, the performance improves to become competitive with the performance without noise. However, sometimes the noise had little effect, as is shown in Figure 1 for EF101.

5 Conclusions

Our empirical study of several algorithms on several test functions reveals interesting characteristics of the algorithms and the test functions. First, adding noise can potentially have a soft annealing effect in some cases. At the same time, adding noise can have the negative effect of adding false optima to the search space. The degree to which either of these effects occurs is directly related to the underlying objective function.

When run on functions without noise, Line Search and CHC produce very good results on all functions. As expected, both RBC and Line Search prove to be more subject to noise than the other algorithms. In fact, both genetic algorithms had very stable performance with or without noise. In general, the scheduled resampling did not improve the performance of the genetic algorithms. It is in the local search process where resampling of noisy data points has an opportunity to improve performance.

This work has been a preliminary study of the effects of noise on a variety of search techniques. Two future directions for this work is in the area of closer analysis of the behavior of local search methods in noisy environments and in additional experimentation with the population sizes of evolutionary algorithms. Levitan [8] introduced several mechanisms for closely analyzing the traversal of his *adaptive walk* (or our RBC with no restarts). Similar mechanisms can be integrated into our algorithms to more accurately determine whether or not the algorithms are benefiting or suffering from the addition of noise.

References

[1] Lashon Booker. Improving Search in Genetic Algorithms. In Lawrence Davis, editor, *Genetic Algorithms and Simulated Annealing*, chapter 5, pages 61–73. Morgan Kaufmann, 1987.

[2] Lawrence Davis. Bit-Climbing, Representational Bias, and Test Suite Design. In L. Booker and R. Belew, editors, *Proc. of the 4th Int'l. Conf. on GAs*, pages 18–23. Morgan Kauffman, 1991.

[3] Larry Eshelman. The CHC Adaptive Search Algorithm. How to Have Safe Search When Engaging in Nontraditional Genetic Recombination. In G. Rawlins, editor, *FOGA -1*, pages 265–283. Morgan Kaufmann, 1991.

[4] J. Michael Fitzpatrick and John Grefenstette. Genetic Algorithm in Noisy Environments. *Machine Learning*, 3:101–120, 1988.

[5] David Goldberg. A Note on Boltzmann Tournament Selection for Genetic Algorithms and Population-oriented Simulated Annealing. Technical Report Nb. 90003, Department of Engineering Mechanics, University of Alabama, 1990.

[6] Ulrich Hammel and Thomas Bäck. Evolution Strategies on Noisy Functions How to Improve Convergence Properties. In Y. Davidor, H.P. Schwefel, and R. Manner, editors, *Parallel Problem Solving from Nature, 3*, pages 159–168. Springer/Verlag, 1994.

[7] L. Ingber. Adaptive Simulated Annealing: Lessons Learned. *Control and Cybernetics*, 25(1):33–54, 1996.

[8] Bennett Levitan and Stuart Kauffman. Adaptive walks with noisy fitness measurements. *Molecular Diversity*, 1:53–68, 1995.

[9] Keith E. Mathias and L. Darrell Whitley. Noisy Function Evaluation and the Delta Coding Algorithm. In *Proceedings of the Conference on Neural and Stochastic Methods in Image and Signal Processing III*, 1994.

[10] Brad Miller and David Goldberg. Genetic Algorithms, Selection Schemes, and the Varying Effects of Noise. Technical Report IlliGAL Report No. 95009, Department of General Engineering, University of Illinois at Urbana-Champaign, 1995.

[11] Darrell Whitley, Keith Mathias, Soraya Rana, and John Dzubera. Evaluating Evolutionary Algorithms. *Artificial Intelligence Journal*, 85, August 1996.

The Density of States - A Measure of the Difficulty of Optimisation Problems

Helge Rosé, Werner Ebeling, Torsten Asselmeyer

Institut of Physics, Humboldt–University Berlin,
Invalidenstraße 110, 10115 Berlin, Germany
Email: rose@summa.physik.hu-berlin.de

Abstract. We introduce a classifying measure of fitness landscapes - the density of states - for continuous and discrete problems, especially optimisation of sequences and graphs. By means of the Boltzmann strategy we obtain a simple algorithm to calculate the density of states for a given problem. Knowing the density of states we are able to approximate the optimal fitness value of the problem which makes it feasible to assess the effectivity of practical optimisations.

1 Introduction

For discrete or high dimensional continuous search spaces it is very difficult to assess the structure of the fitness landscape. Any information about the structure is very fruitful to design a good representation and algorithm for practical optimisation. The general issue is the classification of fitness landscapes to understand the dynamics of optimisation leading to optimal search algorithms. To classify a given problem we need classification measures depending only on the structure of the fitness landscape. The *density of states* describes the number of solutions with a certain fitness value. Obviously this number is invariant with regard to the representation and depends only on the structure of the fitness landscape; thus it classifies the problem. Using a Boltzmann strategy we may easily determine the density of any optimisation problem. By means of the density it is possible to approximate the optimum of the problem and to assess the probability to find it by pure random search.

We shall investigate discrete optimisation problems for sequences and graphs. First we consider the frustrated game proposed by Engel (Ebeling et.al., 1990) and second the problem of low autocorrelation binary sequences (LAS), which plays an important role in communication theory (Golay, 1977,1982,1983) and in spin glass theory (Bernasconi, 1987,Bouchard and Mezard, 1994). We show that this problem is much more difficult than the Engel problem and its optimal fitness for sequences of length $L = 100$ is $f_{min} \approx 5.0$ approximately. Finally we determine the density of graphs for the problem of road network optimisation.

2 General Properties of a Fitness Landscape on Sequences

In the following we consider a set of N sequences of length L, forming a certain region in the sequence space. We assume that the elements of the sequence are taken from an alphabet consisting of λ different letters. The complete set of different sequences of length L consists of $N_L = \lambda^L$ elements. For $L \gtrsim 100$ this number is astronomical. In realistic systems the majority of possible sequences may be forbidden by hard constraints, leaving only a subset of N admitted solutions.

To measure the strength of a mutation we need a metric on the sequence space. A standard metric may be introduced by the Hamming distance defined by the number of non-coincidences of two sequences. The *neighbourhood structure* of the sequence space is given by means of the metric: Two sequences s, s' with a Hamming distance $h(s, s') = 1$ are neighbours. The neighbourhood structure is given by the adjacent matrix with $\mathcal{A}(s, s') = 1$ for neighbours and otherwise $\mathcal{A}(s, s') = 0$. A discussion of the neighbourhood structure can be found in (Asselmeyer et.al. 1996) for the case $L = 2$.

Without loss of generality we consider the sequences as the *genotypes* of the individuals. All possible sequences are elements of a metric space, the genotype space G. In the following we assume that each genotype s is associated with a real value $f(s)$, the fitness which we want to optimise $f : G \to \mathbb{R}_+$.

3 The Density of States

The notation *density of states* is borrowed from solid-state physics. We assume a bounded fitness $f_{min} < f(s) < f_{max}$ and define the total number of sequences having the value $f(s) < f$ by $N(f)$. Here $N(f)$ is a step function converging to the number N of admitted sequences.

The number of sequences in the interval $[f, f+df]$ forms the density of states $n(f)$. This density, which formally is the derivative of $N(f)$, consists of delta-peaks. To calculate $n(f)$ we consider the fitness function $f(s)$ in the interval $[f - \Delta f, f + \Delta f]$ then one obtains

$$n(f) = \lim_{\Delta f \to 0} \frac{vol(f^{-1}([f - \Delta f, f + \Delta f]))}{vol([f - \Delta f, f + \Delta f])} \quad . \tag{1}$$

As an example we consider the fitness function $f : \mathbb{R}^n \to \mathbb{R}$ over the n-dimensional space $\mathbb{R}^n$ with $f(x_1, \ldots, x_n) = x_1^2 + \ldots + x_n^2$. Thus one obtains

$$n(y) = \frac{d}{dy} vol(f^{-1}([0, y])) = \frac{n\pi^{n/2}}{\Gamma(\frac{n}{2}+1)} y^{n/2-1} \quad . \tag{2}$$

A key feature of the density of states is the fact that the zeros of the density approximate the highest (lowest) fitness values of the problem. In practice it is very important to know whether or not there is a fitness value better than the value found so far. To assess the effectivity of a further optimisation we can simply use the probability density $p(f)$ to approximate the probability of finding a better fitness value as the actual one. That means: the density of states gives an criterion to appreciate the benefit of further optimisation efforts and a termination rule for the search process.

To visualise the difference between the continuous and the discrete case we consider the following toy examples. The first example is given by the fitness function $f : \mathbb{Z}^n \to \mathbb{Z}$ with the same expression as above. Then the problem to determine all solutions of $f(m_1, \ldots, m_n) = k$ for $k, m_1, \ldots, m_n \in \mathbb{Z}$ is a well-known problem from number theory. Following a theorem of Siegel (see Husemoller and Milnor, 1973, Ch II, Th. 9.3) for large n the density of states reduces to the case (2) with k instead of y. In the second example we consider the adjacent matrix A of a directed graph given by a symmetric, positive definite matrix. We give every edge A_{ij} between i and j a value by a matrix $(A_{ij} i \cdot j) = f(1, \ldots, n) = G$ where n is the number of vertices. The weighted average of the density of states $n(G)$ (weighted with respect to equivalent graphs) scales with respect to the number of connections x as a formula of Siegel (Husemoller and Milnor, 1973, Ch. II, Th. 9.7)

$$n(G) \approx 0.705 (\frac{x}{2\pi e \sqrt{e}})^{x^2/4} (\frac{8\pi e}{x})^{x/4} / \sqrt[24]{x} \quad .$$

Later on we shall use these concepts for a structural characterisation of the landscape.

According to our work (Asselmeyer et al. 1996) there is another way to explain the meaning of the density of states: Genotypes with the same fitness value form an equivalence class which may be interpreted as the phenotype of the individual. The number of genotypes of a certain equivalence class forms the density of states (fig. 1). In this point of view it can be easily seen that the density of states is only related to the ordering of fitness values but there are no references to the geometry and topology of the search space. The density of states answers the question: How difficult is it to find a certain optimal value? The density and thus the probability to find a certain fitness level will be very low on high fitness levels. Problems with a very fast decay of $n(f)$ should be very hard to solve, because the probability to find a better solution decays also very fast. In this sense we may say: The density of states is a classifying measure of fitness landscapes. If we know $n(f)$ of two problems we are able to decide which problem is more difficult.

Our method of determining the density of states is based on a special model of evolutionary dynamics. We consider a genotype space of sequences $s \in G$ and choose a fixed numbering of the genotypes (Gödel number) $1, \ldots, i, \ldots, n$. The most simple model of an evolutionary dynamics is the Boltzmann strategy which is based on the assumption that competing objects $i = 1, \ldots, n$ have different transition rates. The evolutionary dynamics is given by the differential equations

$$\dot{x}_i = \sum_j [A_{ij} x_j - A_{ji} x_i] \tag{3}$$

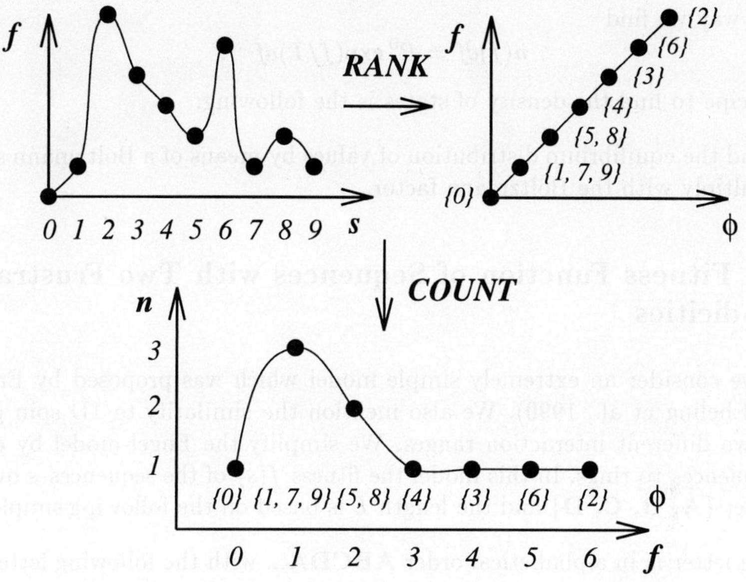

Fig. 1. *The RANK operator and the density of states n(f).*

with the transition rates A_{ij}:

$$A_{ij} = C_{ij} \begin{cases} 1 & \text{if} \quad f_i > f_j \\ \exp[(f_i - f_j)/T] & \text{else} \end{cases} \quad . \tag{4}$$

Here the real positive parameter T is the "temperature" of the Boltzmann search. The algorithm is also known as Metropolis algorithm and used in Simulated Annealing.

The Boltzmann distribution:

$$P_i^0 = Z^{-1} \exp(-f_i/T) \tag{5}$$

$$Z = \sum_j \exp(-f_j/T)$$

is a stationary solution of equation (3). On can easily prove that the functional

$$K(t) = -\sum_i P_i(t) \ln \frac{P_i(t)}{P_i^0}$$

is decreasing

$$\frac{d}{dt} K(t) \geq 0 \quad .$$

This guarantees that the solution converges to the Boltzmann distribution. From (3) we find that in the final state the probability to find a value in the interval df is given by

$$P^0(f)df = n(f) \exp(-f/T)df \quad .$$

In this way we find

$$n(f)df = P^0 \exp(f/T)df \quad . \tag{6}$$

The recipe to find the density of states is the following:

(i) Find the equilibrium distribution of values by means of a Boltzmann search.
(ii) Multiply with the Boltzmann factor.

4 A Fitness Function of Sequences with Two Frustrated Periodicities

Here we consider an extremely simple model which was proposed by Engel in 1989 (Ebeling et al., 1990). We also mention the similarity to 1D spin glasses with two different interaction ranges. We simplify the Engel-model by closing the sequences to rings. In this model the fitness $f(s)$ of the sequences s over the alphabet {**A, B, C, D**} and the length L is based on the following simple rules

(i) If a letter is in alphabetical order **ABCDA...** with the following letter then the fitness will increase by one, i.e., $f = f + 1$.
(ii) If letters on position i and $i + p$ are the same then $f = f + b$.

If the i-th element of a sequence s is denoted by S_i the fitness function is given by

$$f(s) = \sum_{i=1}^{L} [\alpha(S_i) + b\pi(S_i)] \tag{7}$$

where $\alpha(S_i) = 1$, if S_i, S_{i+1} in alphabetical order, and $\pi(S_i) = 1$, if $S_i = S_{i+p}$. Otherwise $\alpha(S_i) = \pi(S_i) = 0$. The first rule (1) favours alphabetical sequences **ABCDABCDABC...D** with period 4. The second rule (2) favours periodic repetitions with period p. If $p \neq 4$ then the tendencies to generate strings with period 4 or p are contradictory, i.e., the system is frustrated. We choose $p = 5$ and set $b = b_c = 1/L\,[L/p]$ (Ebeling et al., 1990). Then $b \ll b_c$ favours alphabetical sequences and $b \gg b_c$ p-periodic ones.

The fitness landscape f has a rugged structure, i.e., sequences which are quite close with respect to their Hamming distance may have very different values(fig. 2).

Figure 3 shows the density over the fitness levels $n(f)$, which is a very rugged function for short sequences $L = 7$.

Now we consider the density of states of long sequences and compare the results with an analytical calculation. To obtain the equilibrium density $P^0(f)$ we simulated an ensemble of $N = 10,000$ sequences of length $L = 100$ which carry out a Boltzmann strategy with the mutation rate (4) and the fitness (7). The density $P(f)$ is approximated by the frequency $N(f)/N$, where $N(f)$ is the number of individuals with $f \in [f, f + \Delta f)$. In the long time limit $P(f)$ tends towards the equilibrium density $P^0(f)$. After 10,000 time steps $P(f)$ relaxed into equilibrium. We double checked convergence up to 100,000 time steps. We

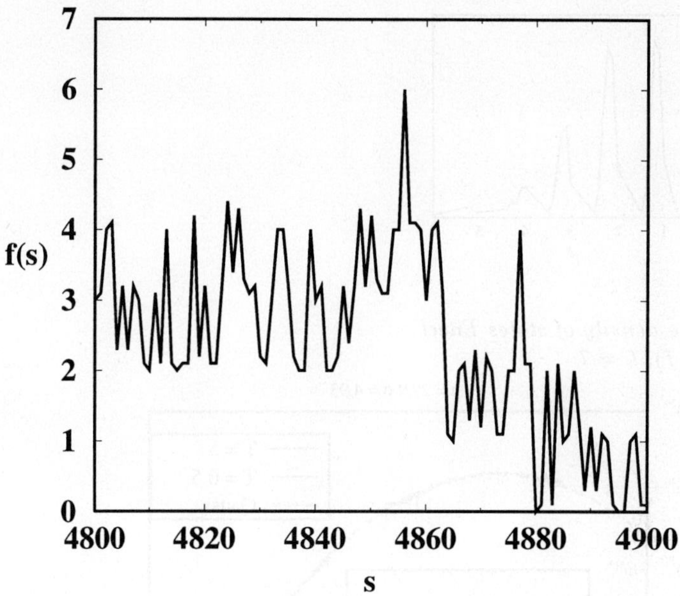

Fig. 2. *The fitness landscape on the genotype space, $L = 7$.*

did the simulation at two different temperatures to scan the whole range of f. The density of states of the problem (7) is a Gaussian distribution (see fig. 4).

We emphasize that the method also works for other fitness landscapes and is not restricted to sequences. The simulation of an ensemble of *Boltzmann searchers* is a general way to obtain the density of states and therefore a method to classify the fitness landscape of any optimisation problem.

In the special case of a fitness landscape like (7) we are able to calculate the structure of $n(f)$ by means of the simple structure of the mutation group $\mathcal{G}$ (Asselmeyer et al. 1996). To this end we introduce a map $n : \mathbb{R} \longrightarrow \mathbb{R}$ which gives for every fitness value the number of states occupying this value. We argue that for large sequence lengths L the number of combinatorial operations for every equivalence class is constant. Then with respect to the structure of the mutation group one obtains the Gaussian function in a qualitative way.

5 The LAS Problem

In this case one considers binary sequences of length L. Each position is valuated by a number $s_i = +1$ in the case of the letter **A** or $s_i = -1$ in the case of **B**. The fitness function is given by

$$f = \frac{1}{L} \sum_{k=1}^{L-1} R_k^2 \, , \quad R_k = \sum_{i=1}^{L-k} s_i s_{i+k} \quad . \tag{8}$$

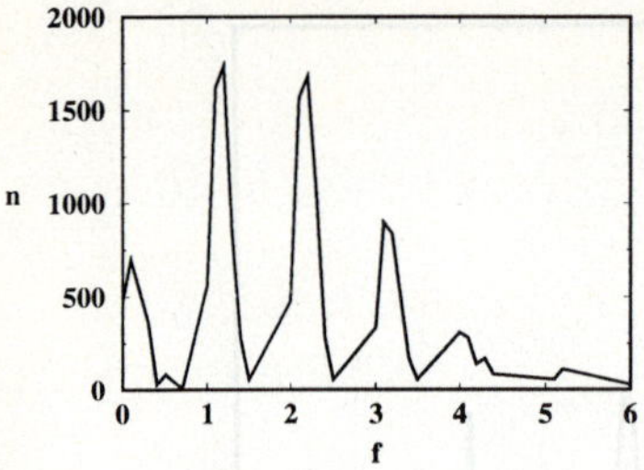

Fig. 3. *The density of states Engel problem $n(f)$, $L = 7$*

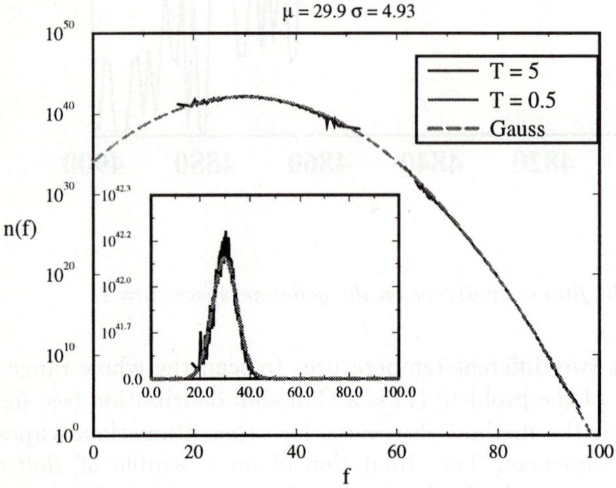

Fig. 4. *The density of states Engel problem $n(f)$, $L = 100$.*

That means the autocorrelations should be minimised. We considered $L = 100$ and applied the optimisation procedure described above. The best sequence we were able to find was

BAABBAABBBBAABBAAABBABAABBBBAAAABBABAABBB
BBABAAABAABBABBBABABAABBBABAAAABABBBBBABA
BABBABAAAAAAAAAAAAABAABBAABBBBAABBAAABBABA
ABBBBAAAABBABAABBBBBABAAABAABBABBBABABAAB
BBABAAAABABBBBBABABABBABAAAAAAAAAAAA

with $f = 7.82$. As we know this is one of the best values ever found for $L = 100$. Fig. 5 shows the density of states. We use the scaling formula (Golay, 1977, 1982; Bernasconi, 1987)

$$n(f) \sim f^{(L-3)/2} \exp(-f) \tag{9}$$

which is a Gaussian distribution with respect to R_k to approximate the numerical results. The criteria to determine the optimal fitness value is given by the condition $n(f_{min}) = 1$ which means that only one realisation for the value f_{min} exists. Together with the decreasing tendency we obtain a criteria to approximate the optimal fitness value. From the properties of the density of states above mentioned we are able to conclude:
The LAS problem is much more difficult than the Engel problem and has optimal fitness $f_{min} \approx 5.0$ approximately.

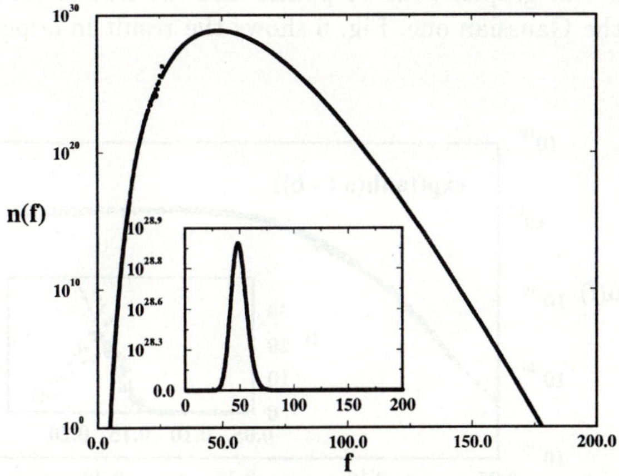

Fig. 5. *The density of states $n(f)$ of the LAS problem, $L = 100$. The optimal fitness value is $f_{min} \approx 5.0$.*

6 Road Networks

In our third application we simulated the optimisation of road networks. As a concrete example we apply evolutionary search to a street network of Martina Franca (Italy). A street network is a graph g connecting a given set of points $p_1, .., p_n$ in the plane. The edges of the graph g correspond to streets or highways, the nodes to houses or towns. There are two obvious factors to be minimised:
1.) The distance from each point to each other point shall be as small as possible.
2.) The network shall be as short as possible to minimise the cost of construction.
Thus the functional f we intend to optimise consists of two parts:

$$f(g) = (1 - \lambda)\, d(g) + \lambda\, l(g) \quad . \tag{10}$$

$$d(g) = \frac{1}{L} \sum_{i<j} l_{min}(i,j) - l_{ij} \qquad l(g) = \frac{1}{L} \sum_{i<j} a_{ij}\, l_{ij}$$

The first part d is the normalised detour, e.g. the difference between the shortest and direct path from point i to point j averaged over all pairs (i, j). l is the length of the network normalised by L, the length of the full connected network. The two contradicting aims are weighted by the price factor λ, which allows us to choose the importance of shortness or construction cost, respectively. If building routes is cheap we have a small λ resulting in a dense graph which approaches the fully coupled graph for $\lambda \to 0$. If on the other hand construction costs are very high the resulting graph is only sparsely coupled and approximates the minimum spanning tree in the limit $\lambda \to 1$.

With the help of the algorithm described above we obtain for the density of states for the set of graphs with 44 points and the fitness (10) a distribution different from the Gaussian one. Fig. 6 shows the result in a log-plot. We guess

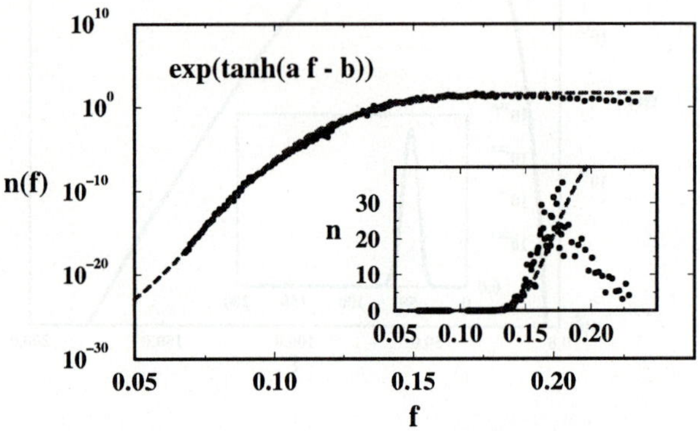

Fig. 6. *The density of states $n(f)$ of the network problem, log-scale*

that the curve decreases for large fitness values f because in general the set of best solutions is very sparse in the set of a possible networks or graphs.

7 Conclusions

The density of states and in particular its tail at optimal fitness values is a classifying measure of the difficulty of an optimisation problem. It is invariant to any choice of representation of the fitness landscape and characterises only the problem. The knowledge of this density allows to approximate the optimal fitness value of the given problem and to assess the benefit of the further optimisation process. This important fact makes it feasible to define a termination criterion which is relevant for practical optimisations. For any optimisation problem the density of states can be obtained by the *Boltzmann ensemble method* proposed in the paper. The method not only provides the density but also optimised solutions of the problem.

References

Andresen, B., 1989, Finite-Time Thermodynamics and Simulated Annealing, Proceedings of the Fourth International Conference on Irreversible Processes and Selforganization, Rostock.

Asselmeyer, T., Ebeling, W. and Rosé, H., 1996, Smoothing representation of fitness landscapes - the genotype-phenotype map of evolution, BioSystems 39, 63.

Bernasconi, J., 1987, Low autocorrelation binary sequences: statistical mechanics and configuration space analysis, J. Physique 48, 559.

Berry, R.S. and Kunz, R.E., 1993, Coexistence of Multiple Phases in Finite Systems, Phys. Rev. Lett. 71, 3987.

Boseniuk, T. and Ebeling, W., 1990, Boltzmann-, Darwin- and Haeckel-Strategies in Optimization Problems, (PPSN Dortmund).

Boseniuk, T., Ebeling, W. , Engel A., 1987, Boltzmann and Darwin Strategies in Complex Optimization, Phys. Lett. A 125, 307.

Bouchard, J.P. and Mezard, M., 1994, J. Phys. France 4, 1109.

Conrad, M. and Ebeling, W., 1992, M.V. Volkenstein, Evolutionary thinking and the structure of fitness landscapes, BioSystems 27, 125.

Ebeling, W., Engel, A., Feistel, R., 1990, Physik der Evolutionsprozesse. (Akademie-Verlag, Berlin).

Ebeling, W., Rosé, H., Schuchhardt, J., 1994, Evolutionary Strategies for Solving Frustrated Problems, Proceedings, IEEE-WCCI, Orlando, June 27-29 1994, 79-81.

Fogel, L.J., 1962, Autonomous automata. Ind. Research 4, 14.

Fogel, D.B., 1995, Evolutionary computation – toward a new philosophy of machine intelligence. IEEE Press, (Piscataway NJ).

Golay, M.J.E., IEEE Transactions on Information Theory, IT-23, 43 (1977); IT-28, 543 (1982); IT-29, 934 (1983).

Goldberg D.E., 1989, Genetic Algorithms in search, optimization and machine learning, (Readin, MA: Addison-Wesley).

Husemoller, D. and Milnor, J., 1973, Symmetric Bilinear Forms, (Springer Verlag, Berlin).

Koza, J.R., 1992, Genetic programming: On the programming of computers by means of natural selection, (Cambridge, MA. MIT Press).

Rechenberg, I., 1973, Evolutionsstrategien - Optimierung technischer Systeme nach Principien der biologischen Information, (Friedrich Frommann Verlag (Günther Holzboog K.G.) Stuttgart - Bad Cannstatt).

Sibiani, P., Pedersen, K.M. and Hoffmann, K.H. and Salamon, P., 1990, Monte Carlo dynamics of optimization: A scaling description, Phys. Rev. A 42, 7080.

On Interactive Evolutionary Algorithms and Stochastic Mealy Automata

Günter Rudolph

Informatik Centrum Dortmund, Joseph–von–Fraunhofer–Str. 20, 44227 Dortmund

Abstract. Interactive evolutionary algorithms (IEAs) are special cases of interactive optimization methods. Potential applications range from multicriteria optimization to the support of rapid prototyping in the field of design. In order to provide a theoretical framework to analyze such evolutionary methods, the IEAs are formalized as stochastic Mealy automata. The potential impacts of such a formalization are discussed.

1 Introduction

The idea of interactive optimization in the field of multicriteria optimization can be traced back at least to the early 1970s [1] and it was developed constantly ever since. The type of interaction between user and optimization algorithm may be very different and its actual realization touches many questions ranging from computer graphics [2] to psychological matters [3].

The typical situation leading to multicriteria optimization problems arises when the goals of the decision maker are conflicting. The plain approach to aggregate a vector–valued objective function $F : X^n \to \mathbb{R}^m$ $(m > 1)$ into a scalar–valued objective function $f : X^n \to \mathbb{R}$ via $f(x) = w' F(x)$ with some weight vector $w \in \mathbb{R}^m$ introduces a not negligible degree of uncertainty for the decision maker whether the chosen weights do reflect the importance of each original goal appropriately. In fact, as soon as a specific weight vector has been chosen, the original decision space is considerably and prematurely cut down *before* enough information could be gathered that might justify such a reduction. As a consequence, a huge number of potential good decisions are precluded *a priori*.

Interactive optimization may offer a remedy: The weights and other parameters are not fixed in advance and the decision maker interacts with the optimization algorithm in order to guide the optimization process in such a way as to keep the 'man–in–the–loop', using the decision maker to make judgments regarding the weights, certain complex constraints and tradeoffs. Evolutionary algorithms (EAs) enriched with visualizing and interactive components can be designed and used for this purpose [4].

Another field of application of interactive evolutionary algorithms (IEAs) is opened when the objectives are not explicitly identifiable and/or not quantifiable. For example, this situation arises when the evaluation of an admissible solution is made on basis of human taste [5]. It is clear that the presence of a graphical interface is inevitably here. This applies as well in situations in which formalized strategies with additional human judgments build a hybrid and synergistic optimization method. Applications of this type are of course not restricted to evolutionary methods [6, 7].

Further situations that make IEAs applicable are imaginable. The general theme that will be explored here, however, is less related to questions regarding additional fields of application — rather, the central questions will be of theoretical nature: Can IEAs be modeled in a probabilistic framework? If so, which theoretical properties could be investigated? And even more fundamental: Is there any utility of such models at all?

Note that EAs without interactions can be modeled and analyzed in a Markov chain framework [8, 9, 10, 11, 12]. Typical theoretical investigations are devoted to the finite time and the limit behavior of these evolutionary methods. The utility of this theory is obvious.

The situation changes in case of IEAs. As will be demonstrated in section 2, the Markov chain framework is too restricted to model IEAs. Thus, a more general theoretical framework is required to represent the interactions between machine and environment appropriately. Such a framework is offered by a specific class of stochastic automata whose theory is well-developed in several directions. But the question of whether or not IEAs can benefit from the existing theory will deserve careful scrutiny and it is addressed in section 3. Finally, some conclusions are drawn in section 4.

2 Stochastic Automata and Interactive Evolution

Stochastic automata were independently defined by several authors in the early 1960s. Since then the theory developed steadily in many directions. Here, only the very basic terminology and theory will be necessary [13, 14].

The tuple $< S, X, Y, P\{\, s', y \,|\, s, x\} >$ represents a *stochastic automaton* where S denotes the set of *states*, X the set of *input symbols*, Y the set of *output symbols* and $P : S \times X \times S \times Y \to [0,1]$ the *transition probabilities* that the stochastic automaton transitions from state $s \in S$ to state $s' \in S$ and outputs symbol $y \in Y$, provided that $x \in X$ was the input symbol. To keep the presentation simple it will be assumed that the sets S, X and Y are finite. Then it is clear that

$$\sum_{(s',y) \in S \times Y} P\{\, s', y \,|\, s, x\} = 1 \text{ for all } (s,x) \in S \times X$$

and that the conditional probabilities $P\{\, s', y \,|\, s, x\}$ can be gathered in a collection of *stochastic matrices* $A(y \,|\, x)$ with $a_{ss'}(y \,|\, x) = P\{\, s', y \,|\, s, x\}$. Some special cases of stochastic automata are presented below:

1. Markov chains:
   A stochastic automaton $< S, \emptyset, \emptyset, P\{\, s' \,|\, s\} >$ with empty input and output sets is a *Markov chain.*
2. Stochastic Mealy automaton:
   A stochastic automaton whose transition probabilities for a consecutive state

s' and a output symbol y are mutually independent for each input symbol x and each state s is a *stochastic Mealy automaton.* Thus, the relation $P\{s', y \mid s, x\} = P\{s' \mid s, x\} \cdot P\{y \mid s, x\}$ with

$$P\{s' \mid s, x\} = \sum_{y \in Y} P\{s', y \mid s, x\} \quad \text{and} \quad P\{y \mid s, x\} = \sum_{s' \in S} P\{s', y \mid s, x\}$$

is valid for all $(s', y, s, x) \in S \times Y \times S \times X$.

3. Stochastic automaton with deterministic output:
A stochastic automaton with $P\{y \mid s, x\} \in \{0, 1\}$ is a *stochastic automaton with deterministic output.* Thus, there exists a (deterministic) function $g : S \times X \to Y$ with

$$P\{y \mid s, x\} = \begin{cases} 1 & \text{, if } y = g(s, x) \\ 0 & \text{, otherwise} \end{cases} .$$

Evidently, every stochastic automaton with deterministic output is also a stochastic Mealy automaton.

Next, an abstract model of interactive evolutionary algorithms will be given in terms of the stochastic automata framework. It is obvious that the interactions between evolutionary algorithm and user can be represented by the input and output symbols. Since the input and output sets are empty for Markov chains it becomes clear that Markov chains cannot be used to model IEAs.

2.1 The abstract model

Evidently, it is sufficient to identify the state space, the input set, the output set and the transition matrices of an interactive evolutionary algorithm to specify an abstract stochastic automata model.

- The state space S:
Suppose there is a population $(i_1, \ldots, i_N)$ of N individuals $i_n \in \mathcal{S}$ where $\mathcal{S}$ is some finite space. Then the set $\mathcal{S}^N$ of all possible populations is of cardinality $|\mathcal{S}|^N < \infty$. Therefore, the state space of the stochastic automaton is just $S = \mathcal{S}^N$ and individual i_n may be referred to via $s(n) = i_n$ for $n = 1, \ldots, N$.
- The output set Y:
At some generation $t \geq 0$ the current population $s \in S$ is presented to the user in some manner. For example, each individual might be visualized by means of a graphical user interface. In any case the output is a deterministic function of the current state and may be omitted in the model. Thus, $Y = \emptyset$ and the transition matrix will not be parametrized by output symbols.
- The input set X:
After the current population has been presented to the user he selects some individuals that will serve as parents for the next generation. Since the number of all possible selections is finite, any of these actions can be symbolized by an element of X. For example, the user might select as follows: Choose

individual i_1 three times, individual i_2 twice, individual i_3 not at all, individual i_4 six times, and so forth until N selections have been made. Thus, there are $N\,(2\,N-1)!/(N!)^2$ different selection operations.

- The transition matrices $A(x)$:
  Let s be the current population. For every selection operation $x \in X$ of the user the parent population s'' is a deterministic function of the current population s and input x. Therefore, the entries of the matrices $U(x)$ describing the state transitions caused by the user are of the type $u_{ss''}(x) \in \{0,1\}$. Next, the parent population s'' might be modified by crossover and mutation resulting in a population s'. These probabilistic operations can be modeled by a transition matrix M as known from Markov models of EAs. Consequently, the transition matrices $A(x)$ of the stochastic automaton are determined by $A(x) = U(x) \cdot M$.

Summing up: Interactive evolutionary algorithms can be described as stochastic automata of the type IEA $= < \mathcal{S}^N, X, \emptyset, U(x) \cdot M >$. Since the output set Y is empty IEAs are stochastic Mealy automata.

The probabilistic behavior of the IEA for a given input sequence can be calculated as follows: Let $W = X \times X \times X \times \ldots$ be the set of words over alphabet X. The length of $w \in W$, denoted as $|w|$, is the number of symbols from X in w. The length of the *empty word* ϵ is $|\epsilon| = 0$. Let $A(\epsilon) = I$ be the unit matrix and $vw \in W$ be the concatenation of the words $v \in W$ and $w \in W$. Then the transition probabilities under input vw can be calculated via $A(vw) = A(v) \cdot A(w)$. This equation may be seen as an equivalent to the Chapman–Kolmogorov equation of discrete Markov chains. Similarly, the probability distribution of the state of the automata is given by $p(xvw) = p(x) \cdot A(v) \cdot A(w)$ where $p(\epsilon)$ is the initial distribution.

2.2 An explicit model

Suppose that the space of individuals is $\mathcal{S} = \mathbb{B}^\ell$ with $\mathbb{B} = \{0,1\}$ and that the individuals are modified by parametrized uniform crossover and mutation. The input of the crossover operator is a pair $(i,j) \in \mathbb{B}^\ell \times \mathbb{B}^\ell$ of individuals while the output is an preliminary individual $h' \in \mathbb{B}^\ell$ which is composed from the input pair by choosing each entry h'_k with probability $\chi \in (0,1)$ from individual i and with probability $1-\chi$ from individual j. Then individual h' is mutated to offspring h by inverting each entry independently with probability $\mu \in (0,1)$.

The first step to determine the transition matrix M is the derivation of the probability to generate the zero string from parents (i,j) by crossover and mutation. To this end note that crossover as well as mutation operate on each vector entry independently. Therefore, the probabilities to obtain an entry 0 at position k from (i_k, j_k) are given by

$$
\begin{aligned}
P\{\, h_k = 0 \,|\, (i_k, j_k) = (0,0)\} &= 1-\mu\,,\\
P\{\, h_k = 0 \,|\, (i_k, j_k) = (0,1)\} &= \chi\,(1-\mu) + (1-\chi)\,\mu\,,\\
P\{\, h_k = 0 \,|\, (i_k, j_k) = (1,0)\} &= \chi\,\mu + (1-\chi)\,(1-\mu) \text{ and}
\end{aligned}
$$

$$P\{\, h_k = 0 \,|\, (i_k, j_k) = (1,1)\} = \mu$$

for each $k = 1, \ldots, \ell$. Let $\oplus$ be the *exclusive-or* and $\otimes$ be the *logical and-operation* on bit strings while $|i|$ denotes the number of 1s in some bit string $i \in \mathbb{B}^\ell$. Then

$$\ell_{00} = \sum_{k=1}^{\ell} \bar{i}_k\, \bar{j}_k = |\bar{i} \otimes \bar{j}|,$$

$$\ell_{01} = \sum_{k=1}^{\ell} \bar{i}_k\, j_k = |\bar{i} \otimes j|,$$

$$\ell_{10} = \sum_{k=1}^{\ell} i_k\, \bar{j}_k = |i \otimes \bar{j}| \quad \text{and}$$

$$\ell_{11} = \sum_{k=1}^{\ell} i_k\, j_k = |i \otimes j|$$

denote the frequency of the positions (i_k, j_k) at which the parents have the values $(0,0)$, $(0,1)$, $(1,0)$ and $(1,1)$, respectively. The probability $m_{ij}(0)$ to generate the zero string from the input pair (i,j) is thusly

$$m_{ij}(0) = (1-\mu)^{\ell_{00}}\, [\chi\,(1-\mu) + (1-\chi)\,\mu]^{\ell_{01}}\, [\chi\,\mu + (1-\chi)\,(1-\mu)]^{\ell_{10}}\, \mu^{\ell_{11}}$$

which reduces to

$$m_{ij}(0) = 2^{-|i \oplus j|}\, \mu^{|i \otimes j|}\, (1-\mu)^{\ell - |i \otimes j| - |i \oplus j|}$$

for standard uniform crossover with $\chi = 1/2$. The probability to generate an arbitrary offspring $h \in \mathbb{B}^\ell$ from the pair of parents (i,j) can be obtained by using the relation [15, p. 33]

$$m_{ij}(h) = m_{i \oplus h, j \oplus h}(0).$$

Suppose that the pair (i,j) is drawn at random from population s by choosing two indices from $\{1, \ldots, N\}$ independently with uniform probability. Let

$$r_i(s) = \frac{1}{N} \sum_{n=1}^{N} 1_{\{i\}}(s(n))$$

denote the relative frequency of individual or pattern $i \in \mathbb{B}^\ell$ in population or state $s = (s(1), s(2), \ldots, s(N)) \in (\mathbb{B}^\ell)^N$. Then the probability that population s is modified by crossover and mutation to population s' is given by

$$m_{ss'} = \prod_{n=1}^{N} \sum_{i \in \mathbf{B}^\ell} \sum_{j \in \mathbf{B}^\ell} r_i(s)\, r_j(s)\, m_{ij}(s'(n))\,.$$

It remains to model the interaction with the user. Let the input symbol be of the type $x = (x_1, x_2, \ldots, x_N)$ where x_n denotes the number of times the user has selected individual $s(n)$ from population s. It is clear that the sum over the x_n must be N. Then the entries of the matrices $U(x)$ are as follows:

$$u_{ss'}(x) = 1 \quad \text{if} \quad s' = \underbrace{s(1) \cdots s(1)}_{x_1 \text{ times}} \underbrace{s(2) \cdots s(2)}_{x_2 \text{ times}} \cdots\cdots \underbrace{s(N) \cdots s(N)}_{x_N \text{ times}}$$

and zero otherwise. For example, with $\mathcal{S} = \mathbb{B}$ and a population size $N = 2$ the input set is $X = \{(2,0), (1,1), (0,2)\}$ leading to the three matrices

$U(2,0)$	00	01	10	11
00	1	0	0	0
01	1	0	0	0
10	0	0	0	1
11	0	0	0	1

$U(1,1)$	00	01	10	11
00	1	0	0	0
01	0	1	0	0
10	0	0	1	0
11	0	0	0	1

$U(0,2)$	00	01	10	11
00	0	0	0	1
01	0	0	0	1
10	1	0	0	0
11	1	0	0	0

where the input symbol is written in the upper left corner. When continuing this example with $\chi = 1/2$ matrix M becomes

M	00	01	10	11
00	$(1-\mu)^2$	$\mu(1-\mu)$	$\mu(1-\mu)$	μ^2
01	$1/4$	$1/4$	$1/4$	$1/4$
10	$1/4$	$1/4$	$1/4$	$1/4$
11	μ^2	$\mu(1-\mu)$	$\mu(1-\mu)$	$(1-\mu)^2$

yielding the transition matrices

$A(2,0)$	00	01	10	11
00	$(1-\mu)^2$	$\mu(1-\mu)$	$\mu(1-\mu)$	μ^2
01	$(1-\mu)^2$	$\mu(1-\mu)$	$\mu(1-\mu)$	μ^2
10	μ^2	$\mu(1-\mu)$	$\mu(1-\mu)$	$(1-\mu)^2$
11	μ^2	$\mu(1-\mu)$	$\mu(1-\mu)$	$(1-\mu)^2$

$A(0,2)$	00	01	10	11
00	μ^2	$\mu(1-\mu)$	$\mu(1-\mu)$	$(1-\mu)^2$
01	μ^2	$\mu(1-\mu)$	$\mu(1-\mu)$	$(1-\mu)^2$
10	$(1-\mu)^2$	$\mu(1-\mu)$	$\mu(1-\mu)$	μ^2
11	$(1-\mu)^2$	$\mu(1-\mu)$	$\mu(1-\mu)$	μ^2

and $A(1,1) = U(1,1) \cdot M = M$. Evidently, the interactive evolutionary algorithm of this example is completely formalized by the description of the stochastic automaton given above.

3 What might the formalization be good for?

Stochastic automata are a generalization of deterministic automata. Therefore it is not surprising that many theoretical questions regarding deterministic automata were also treated in the theory of stochastic automata. Typical topics are the equivalence of automata, the minimization of states, decompositions of automata and stochastic languages. Moreover, stochastic automata may be seen as a generalization of Markov chains. This leads to questions regarding the limit behavior of stochastic automata.

In the remainder two parts of stochastic automata theory associated with the above mentioned questions will be investigated in order to rate their applicability and usefulness with regard to interactive evolutionary algorithms. It should be kept in mind that this list is not complete and that some suggestions are of speculative nature yet.

3.1 Decompositions of stochastic automata

There exist techniques to decompose a stochastic automaton into a sequential combination of automata [13, 14]. Owing to this theory every IEA can be decomposed into a *controlled random source* and a deterministic automaton. In particular, a controlled random source is a single state stochastic automaton $< s, X, Y, P\{\, y \,|\, x\} >$ that returns an output symbol $y \in Y$ provided that $x \in X$ was fed in. It may be interpreted as follows: A realization of a random variable ξ and the input symbol $x \in X$ is passed to function R that returns $y = R(x, \xi)$. This symbol y is the input symbol of the deterministic automaton that calculates the new state.

At a first glance this result seems to be remarkable, but a closer look reveals that IEAs can be implemented in this manner easily. Consider the explicit model given in the previous section: In each generation two binomial random variables are drawn for mutation and additional two for crossover. Thus, there are 16 different potential realizations. Since the user may choose among three different selection operations, the size of the support of random variable ξ need not be larger than $3 \times 16 = 48$. These 48 potential realizations of ξ are the input to the deterministic automaton. It is clear that the new state/population can be calculated deterministically now. But when using the decomposition method described in [14, pp. 30–35] and choosing $(\chi, \mu) = (1/2, 1/8)$, it turns out that the size of the support of ξ need not exceed 11. Consequently, this IEA can be equivalently realized with less randomness in the operations than it was presented originally and one may speculate that this theory may give information about the extent of potential de–randomizations of the strategies.

3.2 Convergence of stochastic automata

Similar to the Markov theory of EAs one might inquire for the limit behavior of IEAs represented by stochastic Mealy automata. It is clear that the limit behavior must depend on the input sequences — besides the structure of the transition matrices. For example, let $f : S \to \mathbb{R}$ be some function with $\max\{|f(s)| \,:\, s \in S\} < \infty$ and let $(Z_t : t \in \mathbb{N})$ be the random sequence of states attained by the stochastic automaton. Then there exist conditions [16] that ensure convergence in expectation, i.e.,

$$E[f(Z_t) \,|\, Z_1 = s, w_1 w_2 \cdots w_t] = \sum_{s' \in S} f(s')\, a_{ss'}(w_1 w_2 \cdots w_t) \;\rightarrow\; E[f(Z_\infty)]$$

as $t \rightarrow \infty$ for a sequence of input words $(w_t : t \in \mathbb{N})$ and where $A(w) = (a_{ss'}(w))$. But it is likely that convergence issues will not play a major role with regard to IEAs since it is reasonable to assume that the user's interventions in the behavior of the optimization algorithm are intended to increase the flexibility of the entire man–machine system and that these interventions are not predictable with regard to the current state or time step. If they were predictable then the inputs $x \in X$ would be a function of the state/time and the stochastic automaton would reduce to an ordinary Markov chain.

4 Conclusions

It was shown that interactive evolutionary algorithms can be modeled as stochastic Mealy automata without output. At the current state of investigation, however, it is inconceivable yet to which extent a potential theory of IEAs can profit from stochastic automata theory, although some clues were given. Apparently, this work does not exhibit immediate utility with regard to practical applications — but this ought not to be surprising for the first steps towards a theory of IEAs.

Acknowledgment

Financial support by project EVOLALG, grant 01 IB 403 A, from the German Federal Ministry of Education, Science, Research and Technology (BMBF) is gratefully acknowledged.

References

1. A. Geoffrion, J. Dyer, and A. Feinberg. An interactive approach for multi–criterion optimization, with an application to the operation of an academic department. *Management Science*, 19:357–368, 1972.
2. P. Korhonen. Solving discrete multiple criteria problems by using visual interaction. In G. Fandel, M. Grauer, A. Kurzhanski, and A.P. Wierzbicki, editors, *Large–Scale Modelling and Interactive Decision Analysis*, pages 176–185. Springer, Berlin, 1986.
3. A. Lewandowski. User–machine interface and intelligent decision support. In G. Fandel, M. Grauer, A. Kurzhanski, and A.P. Wierzbicki, editors, *Large–Scale Modelling and Interactive Decision Analysis*, pages 161–175. Springer, Berlin, 1986.
4. C.M. Fonseca and P.J. Fleming. Genetic algorithms for multiobjective optimization: Formulation, discussion and generalization. In S. Forrest, editor, *Proceedings of the Fifth International Conference on Genetic Algorithms*, pages 416–423. Morgan Kaufmann, San Mateo (CA), 1993.

5. J. Graf. Interactive evolutionary algorithms in design. In D.W. Pearson, N.C. Steele, and R.F. Albrecht, editors, *Proceedings of the 2nd International Conference on Artificial Neural Networks and Genetic Algorithms*, pages 227–230. Springer, Vienna, 1995.
6. H. Adeli and K.V. Balasubramanyam. A synergetic man–machine approach to shape optimization of structures. *Computers and Structures*, 30(3):553–561, 1988.
7. W.B. Powell and Y. Sheffi. Design and implemetation of an interactive optimization system for network design in the motor carrier industry. *Operations Research*, 37(1):12–29, 1989.
8. A.E. Nix and M.D. Vose. Modeling genetic algorithms with Markov chains. *Annals of Mathematics and Artificial Intelligence*, 5:79–88, 1992.
9. T.E. Davis and J. Principe. A markov chain framework for the simple genetic algorithm. *Evolutionary Computation*, 1(3):269–288, 1993.
10. D.B. Fogel. Asymptotic convergence properties of genetic algorithms and evolutionary programming: Analysis and experiments. *Cybernetics and Systems*, 25(3):389–407, 1994.
11. G. Rudolph. Convergence properties of canonical genetic algorithms. *IEEE Transactions on Neural Networks*, 5(1):96–101, 1994.
12. J. Suzuki. A markov chain analysis on simple genetic algorithms. *IEEE Transactions on Systems, Man, and Cybernetics*, 25(4):655–659, 1995.
13. A. Paz. *Introduction to Probabilistic Automata*. Academic Press, New York and London, 1971.
14. R.G. Bukharaev. *Theorie der stochastischen Automaten*. Teubner, Stuttgart, 1995.
15. M.D. Vose and G.E. Liepins. Punctuated equilibria in genetic search. *Complex Systems*, 5(1):31–44, 1991.
16. E.-E. Doberkat. Convergence theorems for stochastic automata and learning systems. *Mathematical Systems Theory*, 12:347–359, 1979.

The Influence of Different Coding Schemes on the Computational Complexity of Genetic Algorithms in Function Optimization

Ralf Salomon

AI Lab, Computer Science Department, University of Zürich
Winterthurerstrasse 190, 8057 Zurich, Switzerland
FAX: +41-1-363 00 35; Email: salomon@ifi.unizh.ch

Abstract. Function optimization is a typical application domain for genetic algorithms (GAs). Traditionally, GAs work on bit strings of fixed total length l. Significant research has been done on designing and analyzing different coding schemes, of which Gray coding is one of the most used forms. Surprisingly little attention has been devoted to directly encoding the parameters by floating-point values provided by the programming language. This form of coding has been in favor in evolution strategy. This paper discusses several coding schemes and derives the resulting complexity when optimizing functions with n independent continuous parameters. It turns out that the direct use of real-valued parameters has certain advantages. First of all, it speeds up convergence by a factor of up to l^{q-1}, where q denotes the number of bits per parameter. Furthermore, the use of real-valued parameters allows for more flexibility in designing the mutation operator and eases many implementation issues. The theoretical analysis presented here strongly suggests that real-valued parameters (implemented by floating point values provided by the programming language) should be the best choice when applying a GA in the field of function optimization.

1 Introduction

Genetic algorithms (GAs) are a class of randomized optimization procedures that are based on natural selection and population genetics. For an introduction to GAs see, for example, [2, 5]. The basic scheme of a GA works on a population of individuals represented by fixed bit strings. In each iteration, also called generation, the GA produces new offspring by means of *mutation* and *recombination/crossover*. In the subsequent *selection* process, the GA selects the fittest individuals as parents for the next generation.

In the field of continuous parameter optimization, an algorithm has to find a set of n variables $\{x_1^o, \ldots, x_n^o\}$ such that the objective function $f(x_1^o, \ldots, x_n^o) =$ opt. The variables are denoted by x_i, $1 \leq i \leq n$, with n as the problem's dimensionality. Due to physical constraints and technical reasons, the search interval of each parameter is limited to a prespecified range $x_i \in [-\text{range}_i, \text{range}_i]$. It is sufficient to consider only symmetric search intervals; an asymmetrical interval $v_i \in [a_i, b_i]$ becomes symmetrical by using a simple translational transformation

$x_i = v_i - (a_i + b_i)/2$ and $\text{range}_i = (b_i - a_i)/2$. A randomized algorithm converges, if it finds at least one solution $\mathbf{x}_s$, $||\mathbf{x}_s - \mathbf{x}_o|| \leq \epsilon$ with a prespecified probability p and an arbitrary ϵ neighborhood of the optimum $\mathbf{x}_o$.

Many technical applications can be viewed as function optimization. Determining the weights of a neural network, optimizing the membership functions of a fuzzy controller, or optimizing the parameters of a classical controller are typical examples. The parameters, i.e., the weights, the membership coefficients, or the controller's parameters, can be either encoded by bit strings or represented by floating-point values provided by the programming language. This paper views the latter form as a higher-level representation, since the problem's structure (the parameters to be optimized) is reflected more naturally by the data structure of the programming language.

This paper presents a theoretical analysis of different coding schemes and their influence on the resulting convergence speed. The analysis presented here applies to most of the widely-used test functions, such as $f(\mathbf{x}) = \sum_i ix_i$ or Rastrigin's function $f_6(\mathbf{x}) = nA + \sum_i [x_i^2 - A\cos(2\,\pi\, x_i)]$, that have n independent parameters x_i. The parameters of the test functions considered in this paper are *separable*, since each test function can be reformulated as a sum of n independend sub-functions. An extensive discussion of test functions can be found in [2, 8, 9, 12, 14].

Section 2 describes the methods used, gives an overview of standard parameter settings, and compiles some important results obtained by previous research. Furthermore, Section 2 discusses the question whether a GA should use a constant or a dynamically-adapted mutation rate.

Traditionally, GAs work on bit strings of fixed length [4, 5]. Section 3 discusses two coding schemes that are often used and derives upper bounds of the complexity that are intrinsic to those coding schemes when using small mutation rates. It turns out that the upper bounds depend on both the coding scheme and the function type at hand.

Surprisingly little attention has been devoted to the direct use of real-valued parameters, which are usually used in evolution strategy [11, 13]. Section 4 discusses the direct use of real-valued parameters and describes several mutation operators, which can be implemented by adding small random numbers. The breeder genetic algorithm (BGA) [8, 9] is an example of a GA that represents all parameters by floating-point values. Theory and experiments [8, 9, 12] have shown that the BGA scales with $O(n \ln n)$ when applied to large variety of test functions. Some GA applications also use floating point values directly as is exemplified in [6].

Section 5 concludes with a discussion of the theoretical results. The main result is that using real-valued parameters allows for more flexibility in designing the mutation operator without suffering a performance loss. Furthermore, the direct use of real-valued parameters eases many implementation issues, which can further improve the runtime behavior of a GA. (see also [10]).

2 Methods and Standard Parameter Settings

Rather than deriving absolute values for the numbers function evaluations that a particular GA would need when applied to a chosen problem (fitness function), this paper aims at deriving general upper bounds for the computational complexity. The calculus of computational complexity considers only the most significant term and omits all constants. Thus, it is especially suited for describing the algorithm's behavior for a large number n of parameters to be optimized. This approach is very appropriate for GAs, since their goal is optimization in high dimensions as inspired by nature. A thorough discussion of computational complexity can be found in [3].

During the development of GAs, standard parameter settings have emerged [1, 2, 5, 8, 9, 10]. It is generally agreed that a GA should use a high recombination probability p_r and a small mutation probability p_m. Normally, the mutation probability is set to a value such that, on average, only one mutation per offspring occurs, i.e., $p_m = 1/l$ [10] for bit strings and $p_m = 1/n$ for real-valued parameters [8, 9] respectively. It should be noted that crossover can cause further changes in the genotype.

Another important consideration is (see, for example, [1, 7]) whether a GA should use a constant or a dynamically-adapted mutation rate. In [1, 7] it has been shown that a dynamic adaptation can significantly accelerate convergence. To this end, the algorithm has to know the distance of its the current bit string to the optimum. However, such an assumption is unrealistic. If an algorithm could measure its distance to the optimum, it would scale with $O(n)$. Thus, [1, 7] recommend constant mutation probabilities as already described. For (k, l)-deceptive functions, [7] recommends to increase the mutation probability by the factor k.

For a variety of algorithms and coding schemes, previous research [1, 7, 8] has derived a complexity of $O(n \ln n)$ or $O(l \ln l)$ respectively when applied to several fitness functions with n independent parameters. With $l = qn$, both complexities are identical, since they only differ in constants and lower order terms. The derivation of such complexities (cf. Appendix A) assumes that the complexity of optimizing a particular parameter x_i is constant and, thus, independent of n. This result can be generalized in the following way. In cases where the optimization of a particular parameter x_i depends on n, the resulting complexity is the product of both the term $O(n \ln n)$ and the complexity of optimizing the parameter x_i itself. For example, if the optimization of a parameter x_i was of complexity $O(n^2)$, optimization of n independent parameters would scale with $O(n^3 \ln n)$.

The complexity of a GA can be analyzed by looking at the processing of schematas and building blocks [5] or by looking at the response to selection [8] with respect to a complete GA. Normally, such analysis is done with respect to a full GA. However, for the sake of simplicity, this paper uses a simple bottom up approach as has been done by others [1, 7]. The analysis presented in this paper is based on the *success probability* of the mutation operator of a simple GA (see also [7]). The success probability is the probability p^+ that an applied mutation results in an improvement of the fitness function. This simple approach allows for a short derivation of the complexity and clear discussion of the results.

3 Bit Coding

Traditionally, a GA encodes each parameter by a certain number of q_x bits (cf. Fig. 1). Assuming that all n parameters are encoded by the same number of $q = q_x$ bits, the GA works on a bit string with total length $l = nq$. Then, the attached mapping function $f : [0,1]^q \rightarrow \mathbb{R}$ maps each bit encoding onto a real-valued number. The appropriate choice/design of the mapping function is an important issue, since the mapping function has a significant impact on the resulting convergence speed (see also [1]).

Standard binary coding is one of the simplest and easiest-to-implement methods. Using binary coding, the mapping function is defined as

$$f : [a_0, \ldots, a_{q-1}] \rightarrow \sum_{i=0}^{q-1} a_i 2^i \quad . \tag{1}$$

The major drawback of standard binary coding is that the Hamming distance between consecutive numbers is usually greater than 1. Due to this reason, the complexity of optimizing a particular parameter x_i is not constant, but may depend, in the general case, on n or $l = qn$ respectively. For an example, let us assume that the optimal value is 8 and that the GA has already obtained the value 7. In order to change the parameter from the value 7 to the value 8, the GA has to modify four bits simultaneously. The probability of changing four bits simultaneously is $p = (1/l)^4$. Even if the fitness function $f(\ldots, x_i, \ldots)$ is unimodal with respect to the parameter x_i, the attached mapping function makes the fitness function multimodal with respect to the underlaying coding scheme (see also [1]). The resulting complexity greatly depends on the location of the optimum. If, for example, the optimum was at $x_i^o = 0$, the complexity of optimizing parameter x_i would be constant. A further discussion of advantages and disadvantages of the so-called Haming cliffs associated with any bit coding scheme can be found in [14, pp. 153-155].

Further problems arise, if the fitness function $f(\ldots, x_i, \ldots)$ is multimodal with respect to the parameter x_i. Then, the fitness function is almost always multimodal with respect to the bit string too, since it is very unlikely that the multimodality of the mapping function cancels out the multimodality of the

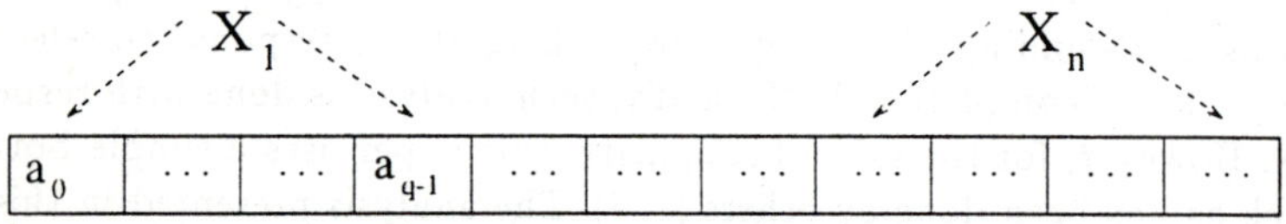

Fig. 1. Bit string coding. Superscripts for individual bits $a_i^{x_i}$ are omitted.

Table 1. Binary and Gray coding. Gray coding ensures that consecutive numbers have Hamming distance 1.

Gray Coding

Bits	Value	Bits	Value
000	0	110	4
001	1	111	5
011	2	101	6
010	3	100	7

Binary Coding

Bits	Value	Bits	Value
000	0	100	4
001	1	101	5
010	2	110	6
011	3	111	7

fitness function. Examples for multimodal functions are Rastigin's function, but also (k, l)-deceptive functions.

For simple binary coding, the upper bound of the resulting complexity can be expressed as follows. In the worst case, all q bits have to be changed simultaneously. The probability of this event is $p = (1/l)^q$, resulting in an overall complexity of $O(l^q \ln l)$. This result coincides with the estimates given in [1, 7]. Only when optimizing unimodal functions in which the optimum is located at very special points, e.g., $x_i^o = 0$, the complexity is reduced to $O(l \ln l)$.

The coding problems discussed above can be relieved by using Gray coding. As can be seen in Table 1, Gray coding ensures that consecutive numbers have always Hamming distance of 1. This makes the optimization of any unimodal function much easier for the GA. No matter where the optimum x_i^o is located, it can always be reached by a sequence of single bit flippings with monotonously increasing/decreasing fitness values. The length of this sequence is bounded by 2^q. Since the optimum can be found by a sequence of single bit flippings as opposed to flipping several bits simultaneously, the total complexity is bounded by $O(l \ln l)$.

However, optimizing multimodal fitness functions, a GA encounters the same problems already discussed. In the worst case, q bits have to be flipped simultaneously, which increases the overall complexity to $O(l^q \ln l)$. Again, a (k, l)-deceptive functions is an example of a multimodal fitness function, to which the derived complexity applies.

4 Real-Valued Parameters

Even though the direct use of real-valued parameters is straight forward for continuous parameter optimization, it is not very common in the GA community. The BGA [8, 9], however, does use real-valued parameters as its coding scheme. In order to apply mutation, on average, to only one parameter per offspring, the BGA uses a mutation probability $p_m = 1/n$, which is similar to using a $p_m = 1/l$ when considering bit strings.

When representing real-valued parameters by floating-point values, the mutation operator can be implemented as adding small random numbers. When

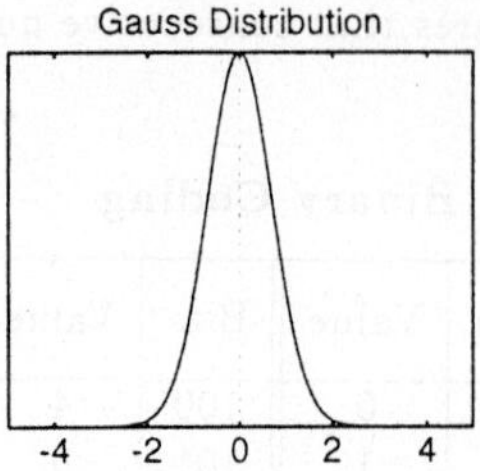

Fig. 2. $(0, \sigma)$-normal distributed random numbers.

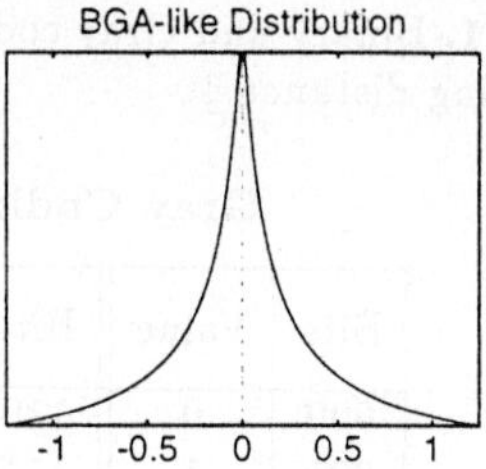

Fig. 3. BGA-like distribution of random numbers.

implementing the mutation operator, one can choose from many possible probability distributions. Two examples are given in Figs. 2 and 3. Figure 2 shows a $(0, \sigma)$-normal distribution, which is usually used in evolution strategy [11, 13]. In particular, the BGA uses the following random number generator

$$\delta = \sum_{i=0}^{15} \alpha_i \, 2^{-i} \tag{2}$$

where each α_i is set to the value 1 with a probability of 1/16 and set to the value 0 with a probability of 15/16 respectively. The probability distribution of the BGA's mutation operator is depicted in Fig. 3. By summing up 16 weighted α's, the BGA limits the obtainable precision to 16 bits. Before applying mutation, each random number is to be normalized such that the mutation operator generates random number in the whole search space of each parameter x_i (also called broad mutations in Appendix A).

The major advantage of directly using real valued parameters and implementing mutations by small random numbers is that the optimization of a particular independent variable x_i is always bounded by a constant. In the worst case, when optimizing a multimodal or deceptive function, the BGA's mutation operator has to set all α's to particular values 0 or 1 in order to yield any progress. Assuming a generalized version with m α's, the probability of this event is given by $p = (1/m)^m$ as opposed to $p = (1/l)^q$ when using bit strings. The probability $p = (1/m)^m$ might be small, but it is independent of the number n of parameters and still greater than the probability of flipping several bits simultaneously when using bit encodings.

The immediate consequence is that the BGA's complexity is $O(n \ln n)$ when optimizing independent parameters. Due to the fact that the complexity is independent of the particular probability density of the mutation operator, one gains much more flexibility in designing the mutation operator. The mutation operator can be tuned according to the problem's special requirements, such as fast convergence speed, high global convergence reliability, maintaining a large population diversity, or emphasizing on exploring search space.

Furthermore, the direct use of real-valued parameters speeds up convergence under epistatis between parameters, which can be seen as deception on a higher level. If, for example, epistatis between two parameters is present, the complexity increases to at most $O(n^2 \ln n)$.

5 Discussion

This paper has discussed different coding schemes and has derived several complexity estimates when optimizing functions with n independent parameters. When optimizing multimodal or deceptive functions, the encoding of parameters in bit strings yields a complexity that is bounded by $O(l^q \ln l)$ as opposed to real-valued parameters, where the complexity is only $O(n \ln n)$. Furthermore, it has been shown that the direct use of real-valued parameters allows for much more flexibility in designing the mutation operator.

The available literature provides many benchmark results on various test functions. When comparing these results, the BGA performs much better than most of the standard GAs. From this analysis it can be suspected that this performance advantage is due to the direct use of real-valued parameters.

In summary, the analysis of this paper strongly suggests that, in the field of function optimization, real-valued parameters should be the best choice. This paper has not considered recombination/crossover or different selection schemes. A comparison of different selection schemes can be found in [10]. If a GA uses one-point crossover, the analysis is likely to be still valid, since, as already pointed out in [1], one-point crossover corresponds to a crossover at segment boundary plus a mutation-like perturbation of the parameter in which crossover occurs. Furthermore, as long as the crossover rate is much smaller than n, the effect of crossover can be expected as small.

Acknowledgements

This work was supported in part by a Human Capital and Mobility fellowship of the European Union, grant number ERBCHBICT941266. Thanks to Rolf Pfeifer and Peter Eggenberger for helpful discussion.

References

1. Bäck, T., 1993, Optimal Mutation Rates in Genetic Search, in: *Proceedings of the Fifth International Conference on Genetic Algorithms*, S. Forrest (ed.) (Morgan Kaufmann, San Mateo, CA), pp. 2-8.
2. Bäck, T., Schwefel, H.-P.., 1993, An Overview of Evolutionary Algorithms for Parameter Optimization, *Evolutionary Computation* 1(1), pp. 1-23.
3. Cormen, T.H., Leiserson, C.E., and Rivest, R.L., 1990, *Introduction to Algorithms*, (The MIT Press, Cambridge, MA).
4. De Jong, K.A., 1975, An Analysis of the Behavior of a Class of Genetic Adaptive Systems, Ph.D. Thesis (University of Michigan).
5. Goldberg, D.E., 1989, *Genetic Algorithms in Search, Optimization and Machine Learning* (Addison-Wesley Publishing Company).

6. Nolfi, S., Parisi, D., 1995, Learning to Adapt to Changing Environments in Evolving Neural Networks, Technical Report 95-15, Institute of Psychology, National Research Council, Rome, Italy, WWW http://kant.irmkant.rm.cnr.it/public.html.
7. Mühlenbein, H., 1992, How genetic algorithms really work I: Mutation and hill climbing, in: *Proceedings of Parallel Problem Solving from Nature 2*, H.P. Schwefel and R. Männer (eds.) (Springer-Verlag), pp. 15-26.
8. Mühlenbein, H., Schlierkamp-Voosen, D., 1993a, Predictive Models for the Breeder Genetic Algorithm I, *Evolutionary Computation* 1(1):25-50.
9. Mühlenbein, H., Schlierkamp-Voosen, D., 1993b, The Science of Breeding and its Application to the Breeder Genetic Algorithm. *Evolutionary Computation*, 1(4):335-360.
10. Potter, M.A., De Jong, K.A., 1994, A Cooperative Coevolutionary Approach to Function Optimization, in: *Proceedings of Parallel Problem Solving from Nature 3*, Y. Davidor, H.P. Schwefel, and R. Männer (eds.) (Springer-Verlag), pp. 249-257.
11. Rechenberg, I., 1973, *Evolutionsstrategie* (Frommann-Holzboog, Stuttgart).
12. Salomon, R., 1996. Implicit Independence Assumptions; a Notorious Problem for Genetic Algorithms. To appear in *Soft Computing, SOCO'96*, Reading, England.
13. Schwefel, H.P., 1977, *Numerische Optimierung von Computer-Modellen mittels Evolutionsstrategie* (Birkhäuser Verlag, Basel and Stuttgart).
14. Schwefel, H.P., 1995, *Evolution and Optimum Seeking* (John Wiley and Sons, Inc, New York, Chicester, Brisbane, Toronto, Singapore).

Appendix A

This appendix gives a brief derivation of the convergence speed of GAs that use either real-valued parameters or bit strings. The performance analysis of the latter coding scheme is restricted to unimodal functions (see also [7]).

The notion of *broad mutations* is an important prerequisite for the derivation of the complexity. Let $pd(\mathbf{x}|\mathbf{x}_p)$ the probability density that mutation creates offspring $\mathbf{x}$ given parent $\mathbf{x}_p$. A mutation operator yields broad mutations, if for *all* possible parents $\mathbf{x}_p$ *and all* possible offspring $\mathbf{x}$ in search space the condition $pd(\mathbf{x}|\mathbf{x}_p) > 0$ holds. Thus, broad mutations generate mutations in whole search space with a probability strictly greater than zero. Flipping bits with a certain probability in certain bit encodings is an example for broad mutations. In addition, some implementations of the BGA's mutation operator are broad mutations as well, if the BGA's random numbers as defined in (2) are multiplied with a scaling factor $s \geq 0.5\,\text{range}_i$.

The following derivation of the convergence speed and its complexity makes the following four assumptions: (1) the objective function is decomposable, i.e., $f(\mathbf{x}) = \sum_{i=1}^{n} f_i(x_i)$, (2) a GA uses an elitist selection scheme (preserving the so far best solution), (3) the GA features an arbitrary broad mutation operator with probability $p_m = 1/n$, and (4) the GA does not feature any recombination.

First, consider the simple one-dimensional case. Since the probability density $pd(\mathbf{x}|\mathbf{x}_p)$ is strictly greater than zero, the probability p that an offspring $\mathbf{x}$ is in the ϵ-neighborhood of the optimum is greater than zero for arbitrary parents $\mathbf{x}_p$. Eventually, a GA converges to the optimum by applying mutation and using an elitist selection scheme. The number of generations and, thus, the convergence speed merely depend on the probability density associated with the mutation operator and the one-dimensional objective function. Hence, for any given combination, the number of required generations is bounded and, thus, the complexity is $O(1)$.

Now consider the n-dimensional case. For the sake of simplicity, it is assumed that one iteration is sufficient for a parameter x_i; further details for the case $k > 1$ can be found in [12]. A mutation probability of $p_m \leq 1/n$ implies that, on average, a GA modifies at most one parameter per offspring. By this means, such GAs decompose the optimization of a *decomposable* n-dimensional function into a sequence of n independent one-dimensional tasks. Since the complexity of the one-dimensional case is $O(1)$ (because k is independent of n), convergence in the n-dimensional case is given by the probability p that all parameters x_i, $1 \leq i \leq n$ have been chosen at least once. The probability q_i that a particular parameter x_i has *not* been chosen within g generations is given by $q_i = [(n-1)/n]^g$. Consequently, the probability p_i that it has been chosen at least once is $p_i = 1 - q_i = 1 - [(n-1)/n]^g$. Since the choice of each parameter x_i is independent of all other parameters, p can be expressed as follows

$$p = \prod_{i=1}^{n} p_i = \prod_{i=1}^{n} \left[1 - \left(\frac{n-1}{n}\right)^g\right] = \left[1 - \left(\frac{n-1}{n}\right)^g\right]^n \tag{3}$$

In order to guarantee that all n parameters have been chosen at least once within g generations, the number of generations $g > n$ has to be larger than n. Thus, the term $[1 - ([n-1]/n)^g]^n$ can be approximated by $1 - n\,[(n-1)/n]^g$

$$p \approx 1 - n\left(\frac{n-1}{n}\right)^g \Rightarrow g = \frac{\ln(1-p) - \ln n}{\ln(\frac{n-1}{n})} \quad . \tag{4}$$

For arbitrary n and a constant probability p the complexity is given by (all constant terms vanish)

$$g = O\left(\frac{-\ln n}{\ln(\frac{n-1}{n})}\right) \quad . \tag{5}$$

For large n, the value of $\ln(\frac{n-1}{n})$ approaches 0. A Taylor sequence of $\ln x$ at $x = 1$ leads to $\ln x \approx x - 1$. Substituting this approximation into (5) results in

$$g = O\left(\frac{-\ln n}{\frac{n-1}{n} - 1}\right) = O\left(\frac{-\ln n}{\frac{-1}{n}}\right) = O\left(n \ln n\right) \quad . \tag{6}$$

In summary, if a GA uses real-valued parameters, the derived convergence speed holds for all decomposable functions, whether multimodal, unimodal, or deceptive with respect to single parameters. If a GA encodes the parameters in bit strings, the result is limited to arbitrary unimodal functions.

An Analysis of the Effects of Neighborhood Size and Shape on Local Selection Algorithms

Jayshree Sarma and Kenneth De Jong

Computer Science Department
George Mason University
Fairfax, VA 22030
jsarma, kdejong@gmu.edu

Abstract. The increasing availability of finely-grained parallel architectures has resulted in a variety of evolutionary algorithms (EAs) in which the population is spatially distributed and local selection algorithms operate in parallel on small, overlapping neighborhoods. The effects of design choices regarding the particular type of local selection algorithm as well as the size and shape of the neighborhood are not particularly well understood and are generally tested empirically. In this paper we extend the techniques used to more formally analyze selection methods for sequential EAs and apply them to local neighborhood models, resulting in a much clearer understanding of the effects of neighborhood size and shape.

1 Introduction

Adapting evolutionary algorithms to exploit the power of finely-grained parallel architectures poses a number of interesting design issues. A standard approach is to use spatially structured populations in which local selection algorithms operate in parallel on small, overlapping neighborhoods [4, 7, 8, 9]. The effects of design choices regarding the particular type of local selection algorithm as well as the size and shape of the neighborhoods are not particularly well understood and generally tested empirically.

An EA, whether serial or parallel can be effective only when a proper balance between exploration (via well chosen operators) and exploitation (well chosen selection pressure) is maintained. Having some insights as to how the selection pressure can be varied in local neighborhood EAs will help in designing better parallel EAs.

In De Jong and Sarma 1995 [5] we studied the emergent global selection pressure induced on the entire population by standard local selection algorithms. Using standard small neighborhood sizes and shapes we presented results which indicated that the emergent global selection pressure of a particular local selection algorithm was qualitatively similar to its sequential counterpart, but quantitatively weaker.

In this paper we extend these results by looking more closely at the effects of local neighborhood size and shape. Our approach involves generalizing the techniques used to analyze selection methods for sequential EAs and apply them to local neighborhood models. In particular, we extend growth curve analysis to local neighborhood models resulting in a much clearer quantitative understanding of the effects that neighborhood size and shape have on the emergent global selection pressure.

2 Finely-grained Parallel EAs

There are a variety of finely-grained parallel EAs which have been proposed and studied (see, for example, [2, 4, 7, 10].) For this study we have adopted a fairly standard model to analyze. We assume a two-dimensional toroidal grid as the spatial population structure in which the neighborhood of a particular grid point is defined in terms of the number of steps taken (up, down, left, right) from that grid point. Every grid point has a neighborhood which overlaps with the neighborhoods of nearby grid points, and all neighborhoods are of identical size and shape.

Each grid point contains one individual of the population and, in addition, an evolutionary algorithm is assumed to be running simultaneously on each grid point, continuously selecting parents from the neighborhood of that grid point in order to produce offspring which replace the current individual assigned to that grid point. The overlapping neighborhoods provide an implicit mechanism for migration of genetic material throughout the grid. The amount of overlap is a function of the neighborhood size and shape.

Figure 1 illustrates four of the five neighborhood configurations used in this paper and these are neighborhoods that are typically used in the literature. The shape label L (linear) is assigned to neighborhoods defined as all points reachable in $\leq n$ steps taken in a fixed axial direction (north, south, east, or west) from the central grid point, while C (compact) neighborhoods contain the closest $n-1$ points to the central grid point.

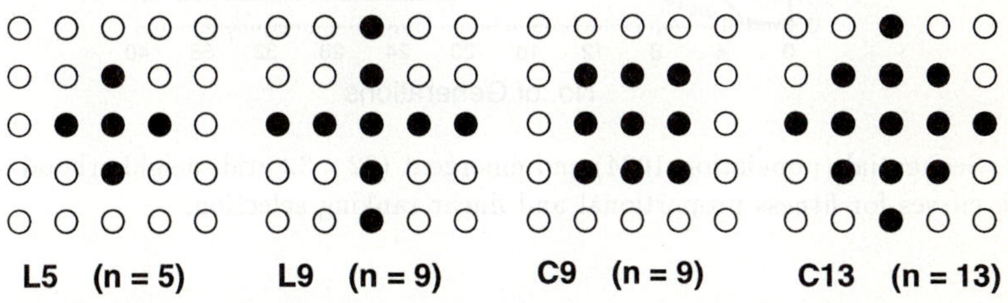

Fig. 1. Neighborhood Patterns

The selection algorithms used on the local neighborhoods are typically the same ones used for sequential EAs. In this paper we focus on just two: fitness proportional and linear ranking selection.

3 Growth Curve Analysis

A standard technique for studying and comparing selection algorithms for serial EAs is to characterize the selection pressure they induce on the individuals in a population in which only reproduction is active (i.e., no mutation, crossover, etc.). Of particular interest is the growth rate of the best individual in the initial population. For the standard selection algorithms, such as fitness proportional and linear ranking, these growth curves are logistic in nature but vary in their growth rates [1, 6]. Since the growth rate of fitness proportional selection is dependent on the fitness ratio, we kept the fitness ratio constant at 2.0 in all our studies in this paper.

Figure 2 illustrates how these growth rates change when we move to spatially structured populations with local neighborhood selection. In this particular case the growth curves exhibited by the best individual in a serial EA with a population size of 1024 using rank and fitness proportional selection are compared with the growth curves obtained from a parallel EA using a 2-dimensional 32×32 toroidal grid and a local neighborhood size of 9.

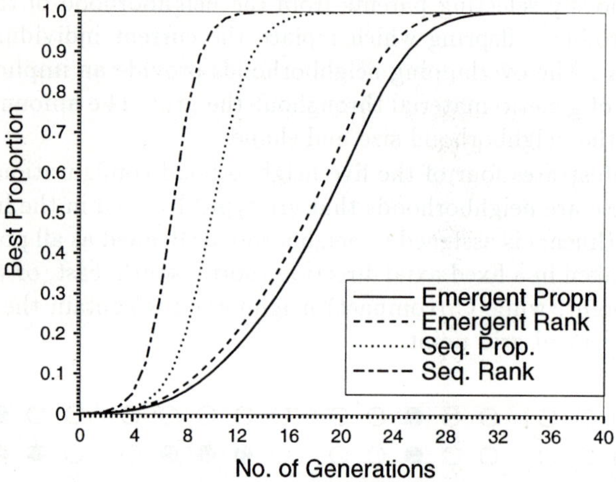

Fig. 2. Sequential (population 1024) and emergent (32×32 grid, neighborhood size 9) growth curves for fitness proportional and linear ranking selection.

Figure 2 is typical of what is consistently observed, namely the spatially structured EAs exhibit the familiar logistic growth curves but with lower growth rates. Note also that the rank order of the selection intensity is preserved: using weaker local selection pressure (in this case, proportional selection) induces a weaker emergent global selection pressure.

The intuitive explanation for this phenomenon is that it is the result of the combined effects of logistic growth occurring in each of the local neighborhoods and the propagation times necessary to spread the best individual globally throughout a spatially structured population. In De Jong and Sarma 1995 [5] we confirmed the first of these two hypotheses showing that the emergent global selection pressure of a local selection algorithm such as fitness proportional or linear ranking selection is qualitatively similar to that produced by fitness proportional or linear ranking in standard serial EAs with global mating pools. In this paper we focus on the second hypothesis involving the effects of propagation times on growth rates.

4 Effect of Neighborhood Size

Increasing the neighborhood size creates a larger overlap and decreases the propagation time. Thus one can see that propagation times are closely related to neighborhood size. Hence increasing local neighborhood sizes while keeping the grid size fixed should result in corresponding increases in selection intensity reflected by higher growth rates of the best individual.

Figures 3 and 4 illustrate typical results obtained on the same 32×32 toroidal grid used in the previous section. For both ranking and fitness proportional selection we analyzed the growth curves for five neighborhoods of different sizes (5, 9, and 13) and shapes (C and L).

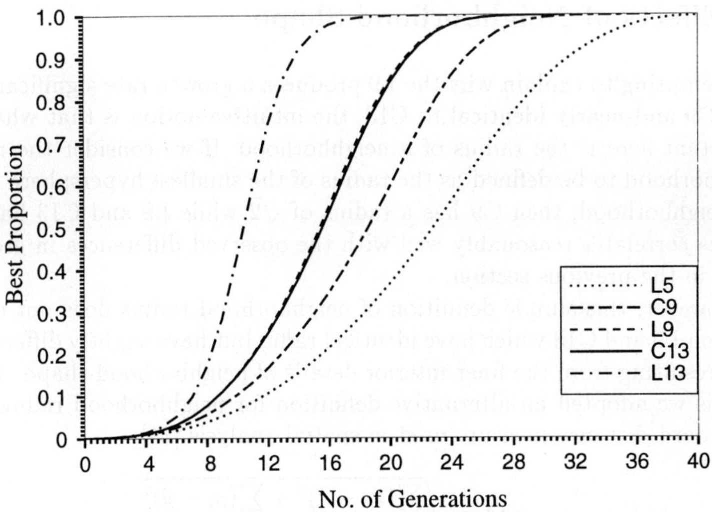

Fig. 3. Emergent growth curves for fitness proportional selection using different neighborhood sizes.

The results are fairly consistent with our expectation that selection intensity increases with increasing neighborhood size. However, there is an interesting "anomaly" in both Figure 3 and Figure 4. The L9 and C13 neighborhoods exhibit nearly identical growth curves even though C13 is almost 50% larger than L9. This suggests that neighborhood shape also plays an important role.

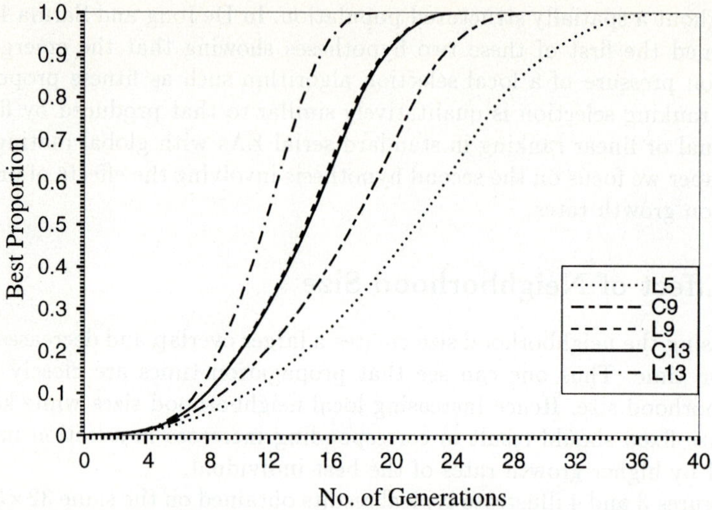

Fig. 4. Emergent growth curves for linear ranking selection using different neighborhood sizes.

5 Effects of Neighborhood Shape

In attempting to explain why the L9 produces a growth rate significantly higher than C9 and nearly identical to C13, the intuitive notion is that what is really important here is the radius of a neighborhood. If we consider the radius of a neighborhood to be defined as the radius of the smallest hypersphere containing the neighborhood, then C9 has a radius of $\sqrt{2}$ while L9 and C13 have radii of 2. This correlates reasonably well with the observed differences in growth rates noted in the previous section.

However, this simple definition of neighborhood radius does not distinguish between L9 and C13 which have identical radii, but have slightly different growth rates resulting from the finer interior details of neighborhood shape. To account for this we adopted an alternative definition for neighborhood radius based on a standard distance measure used in spatial analysis [11]:

$$rad = \sqrt{\frac{\sum(x_i - \bar{x})^2 + \sum(y_i - \bar{y})^2}{n}}$$

which measures the spatial dispersion of a point pattern and can be thought of as the radius of the circle centered on the mean center $(\bar{x}, \bar{y})$ of a neighborhood pattern of n points where

$$\bar{x} = \frac{\sum_{i=1}^{n} x_i}{n}, \qquad \bar{y} = \frac{\sum_{i=1}^{n} y_i}{n}$$

Using this definition, the radii of C9, L9, and C13 are 1.16, 1.49, and 1.47 respectively. A closer look at Figure 3 and Figure 4 indicates that this correlates well with the observed growth curves, with L9 actually exhibiting slightly higher growth rates than C13.

6 Effects of Neighborhood Radius

The results of the previous sections suggest a simple, intuitive model in which selection intensity varies as a function of radius of the local neighborhoods and can be driven arbitrarily close to the selection intensities of the corresponding serial EAs by choosing sufficiently large radii. Figure 5 illustrates this for three different radii on the same 32×32 grid as before using fitness proportional selection. Figure 6 shows the same results for linear ranking selection.

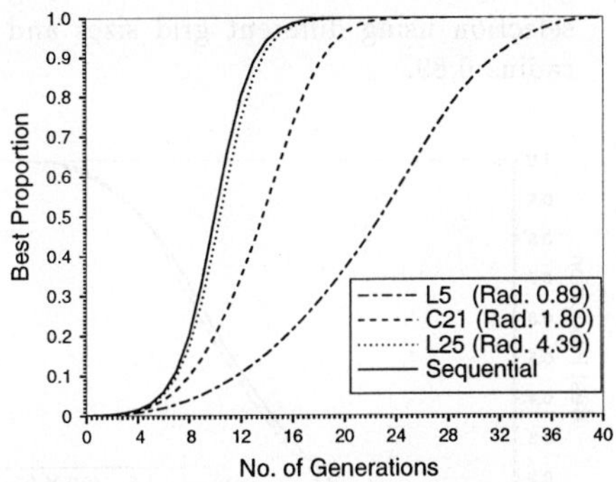

Fig. 5. Emergent growth curves for fitness proportional selection using different radius.

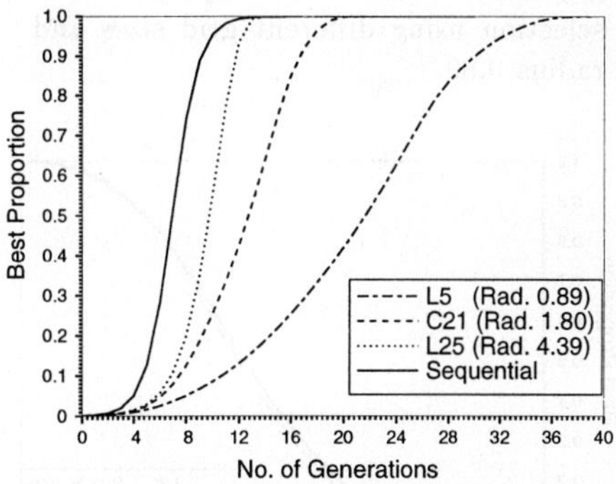

Fig. 6. Emergent growth curves for linear ranking selection using different radius.

If our hypothesis is correct, we should observe similar effects if we keep the neighborhood radius fixed and decrease the grid size. Figures 7 and 8 illustrate that this is precisely what happens when the radius is kept fixed at 0.89 and the grid sizes are changed.

This in turn suggests that the key factor in controlling selection intensity is the ratio of the neighborhood radius to the grid radius. Figures 9 and 10 illustrate that this is precisely the case. Here an L5 neighborhood on a 32×32 grid with a ratio of 0.06815 produces a growth curve nearly identical to a C21 neighborhood on a 64×64 grid with a ratio of 0.06891.

7 A Simple Quantitative Model for Selection Intensity

The observations of the previous section suggest how one might derive a simple quantitative model of selection intensity for these local neighborhood models. Like their sequential counterparts, all of the growth curves generated by the

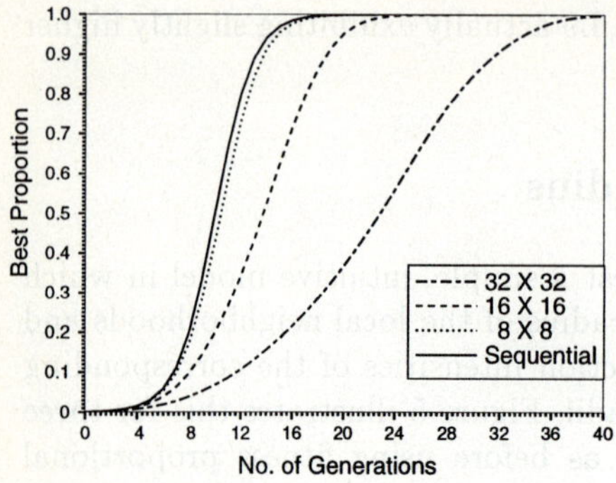

Fig. 7. Sequential and emergent growth curves for fitness proportional selection using different grid sizes and radius 0.89.

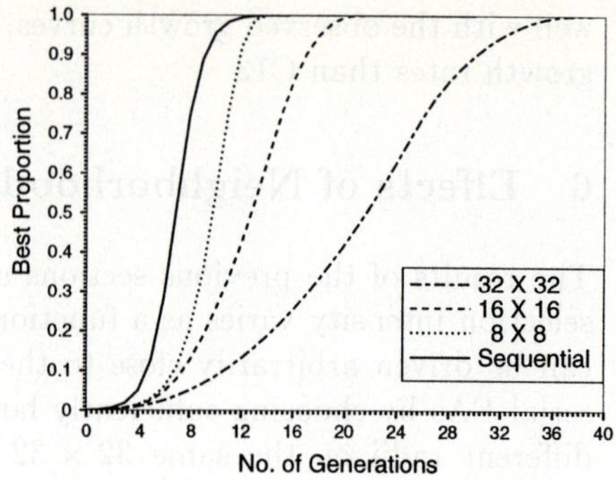

Fig. 8. Sequential and emergent growth curves for linear ranking selection using different grid sizes and radius 0.89.

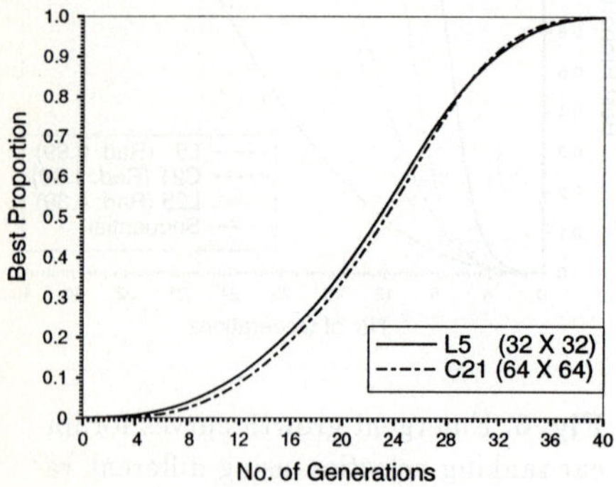

Fig. 9. Emergent growth curves for fitness proportional selection using constant radius ratios.

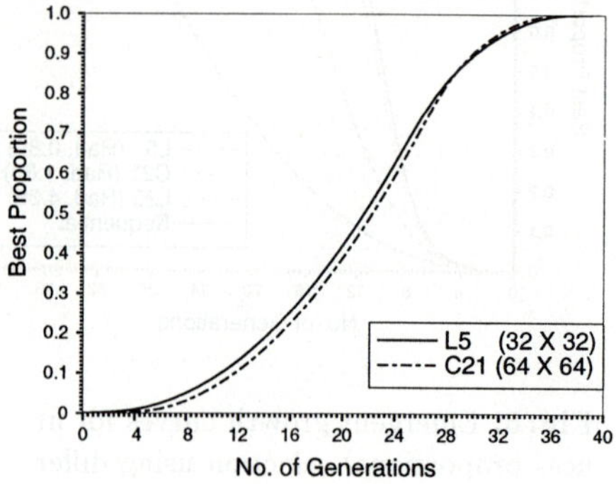

Fig. 10. Emergent growth curves for linear ranking selection using constant radius ratios.

local neighborhood models are well approximated by a logistic equation of the form:

$$N = \frac{N^*}{1 + (\frac{N^*}{N_0} - 1)e^{-at}}$$

where N^* is the asymptotic value of N for very large t and N_0 is the initial value of N [3]. Since in our case we know that N^* is 1.0 we can rewrite the equation as:

$$P_{b,t} = \frac{1}{1 + (\frac{1}{P_{b,0}} - 1)e^{-at}}$$

where a is the growth coefficient and $P_{b,t}$ is the proportion of the best in the population at time t. In this case the growth rate is controlled by a single parameter a, the coefficient in the exponent of the above equation.

In the case of sequential EAs the values of a is the natural logarithm of the fitness ratio for proportional selection and 1 for linear ranking [1, 6]. However, for spatially structured populations the growth coefficient a is dependent on the ratio of the neighborhood radius to the grid radius. It is fairly straight forward to plot the growth curves associated with various radius ratios in the interval $(0, 1)$ and estimate the associated value of a by using a least squares fit of the best logistic curve to the generated growth curves.

If we then plot the value of a as a function of increasing ratio r we obtain data of the sort illustrated in Figure 11. The perhaps not too surprising result is a very clear inverse exponential relationship between r and a with the case of $r = 1$ and the value of a corresponding to the sequential case.

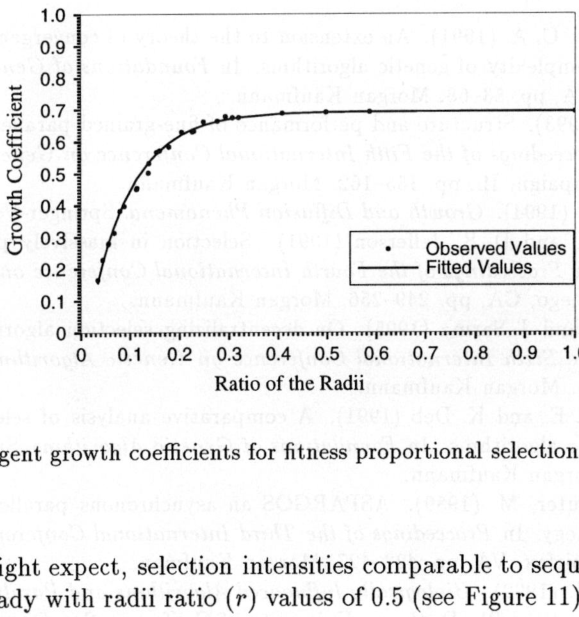

Fig. 11. Emergent growth coefficients for fitness proportional selection plotted against radii ratios.

As one might expect, selection intensities comparable to sequential EAs are achieved already with radii ratio (r) values of 0.5 (see Figure 11).

8 Discussion and Conclusions

Previous studies involving local neighborhood EAs selected the size and shape of local neighborhoods primarily on the basis of empirical tuning studies. The results presented in this paper provide a much clearer and more systematic way to make such decisions. It is shown that the critical parameter is the ratio of the radius of the neighborhood to the radius of the underlying grid. By varying this ratio the emergent selection intensity induced on the global population can be directly controlled. Moreover, a quantitative model of this relationship has been presented in which the coefficient of the growth rate of the best individual in the population is shown to be an inverse exponential function of this ratio.

A direct consequence of this analysis is the observation that typical neighborhood sizes and shapes used in the literature result in much lower selection pressures than their serial counterparts, but that comparable selection intensities can be obtained (if desired) by simply increasing this ratio to 0.5.

Effective EAs, whether serial or parallel, maintain a balance between exploration (via well chosen operators) and exploitation (well chosen selection pressure). Understanding how selection pressure can be directly controlled in local neighborhood EAs via a single parameter provides a simple means for adjusting that balance.

We believe that these observations will hold for other topologies and other local selection algorithms as well and are currently working on these issues.

References

1. Ankenbrandt, C. A. (1991). An extension to the theory of convergence and a proof of the time complexity of genetic algorithms. In *Foundations of Genetic Algorithm*, San Mateo, CA, pp. 53–68. Morgan Kaufmann.
2. Baluja, S. (1993). Structure and performance of fine-grained parallelism in genetic search. In *Proceedings of the Fifth International Conference on Genetic Algorithms*, Urbana–Champaign, IL, pp. 155–162. Morgan Kaufmann.
3. Banks, R. B. (1994). *Growth and Diffusion Phenomena*. Springer-Verlag.
4. Collins, R. J. and D. R. Jefferson (1991). Selection in massively parallel genetic algorithms. In *Proceedings of the Fourth International Conference on Genetic Algorithms*, San Diego, CA, pp. 249–256. Morgan Kaufmann.
5. De Jong, K. and J. Sarma (1995). On decentralizing selection algorithms. In *Proceedings of the Sixth International Conference on Genetic Algorithms*, Pittsburgh, PA, pp. 17–23. Morgan Kaufmann.
6. Goldberg, D. E. and K. Deb (1991). A comparative analysis of selection schemes used in genetic algorithms. In *Foundations of Genetic Algorithms*, San Mateo, CA, pp. 69–93. Morgan Kaufmann.
7. Gorges-Schleuter, M. (1989). ASPARGOS an asynchronous parallel genetic optimization strategy. In *Proceedings of the Third International Conference on Genetic Algorithms*, Fairfax, VA, pp. 422–427. Morgan Kaufman.
8. McInerney, J. (1992). *Biologically Influenced Algorithms and Parallelism in Nonlinear Optimization*. Ph. D. thesis, University of California, San Diego.
9. Mühlenbein, H. (1991). Evolution in time and space – the parallel genetic algorithm. In *Foundations of Genetic Algorithm*, San Mateo, CA, pp. 316–337. Morgan Kaufmann.
10. Spiessens, P. and B. Manderick (1991). A massively parallel genetic algorithm: Implementation and first analysis. In *Proceedings of the Fourth International Conference on Genetic Algorithms*, San Diego, CA, pp. 279–287. Morgan Kaufmann.
11. Unwin, D. (1981). *Introductory Spatial Analysis*. Methuen and Co. Ltd.

Evolutionary Computation at the Edge of Feasibility

Marc Schoenauer[1] and Zbigniew Michalewicz[2]

[1]CMAP – URA CNRS 756
Ecole Polytechnique
Palaiseau 91128, France
marc.schoenauer@polytechnique.fr.

[2]Department of Computer Science,
University of North Carolina,
Charlotte, NC 28223, USA
zbyszek@uncc.edu

Abstract. Numerical optimization problems enjoy a significant popularity in evolutionary computation community; all major evolutionary techniques use such problems for various tests and experiments. However, many of these techniques (as well as other, classical optimization methods) encounter difficulties in solving some real-world problems which include non-trivial constraints. This paper discusses a new development which is based on the observation that very often the global solution lies on the boundary of the feasible region. Thus, for many constrained numerical optimization problems it might be beneficial to limit the search to that boundary, using problem-specific operators. Two test cases illustrate this approach: specific operators are designed from the simple analytical expression of the constraints. Some possible generalizations to larger classes of constraints are discussed as well.

1 Introduction

For many years evolutionary techniques have been evaluated and compared with each other in the domain of function optimization. It seems also that the domain of function optimization will remain the primary test-bed for many new comparisons and new features of various algorithms. In particular, numerical optimization problems enjoy a significant popularity in evolutionary computation community; all major evolutionary techniques (genetic algorithms, evolution strategies, evolutionary programming) can be applied to these problems.

However, many of these techniques have difficulties in solving constrained numerical optimization problems. Several different search operators have been investigated; several different constraint handling techniques have been experimented with. For many test cases, the results of experiments were far from being satisfactory. It seems that one of the main reasons behind this failure was the inability of evolutionary systems to precisely search the boundary area between feasible and infeasible regions of the search space; in the case of optimization problems with active constraints, such ability is essential.

Some other heuristic methods recognized the need for searching areas close to the boundary of the feasible region. For example, one of the most recently developed approach for constrained optimization is strategic oscillation. Strategic oscillation was originally proposed in accompaniment with the strategy of scatter search [3], and more recently has been applied to a variety of problem settings in combinatorial and nonlinear optimization [4].

It seems that the evolutionary computation techniques have a huge potential in incorporating specialized operators which search the boundary of feasible and infeasible regions in an efficient way. In this paper we discuss some possible operators for such a search and illustrate this approach on a few test cases.

The paper is organized as follows. Section 2 briefly surveys constraint-handling techniques for numerical optimization problems, which have emerged in evolutionary computation over the years. Section 3 introduces a new approach for numerical constrained optimization, based on the idea of searching only the boundary of the feasible search space. This approach is illustrated in section 4 on two difficult problems on which it allows significant improvements over best known results. Section 5 proposes different methods to design operators searching a given surface of $\mathbb{R}^n$ in the general case. These methods are illustrated and discussed on both test cases of section 4.

2 Evolutionary Constraint-Handling Methods

Let us consider the following constrained numerical optimization problem:

$$\text{Find } x \in \mathcal{S} \subset \mathbb{R}^n \text{ such that } \begin{cases} f(x) = \min\{f(y);\ y \in \mathcal{S}\}, & (1) \\ g_i(x) \leq 0, for\ i = 1, \ldots, q, & (2) \\ g_i(x) = 0, for\ i = q+1, \ldots, m. & (3) \end{cases}$$

where f and g_i are real-valued functions on $\mathcal{S}$. The set of feasible points (i.e., points satisfying the constraints (2) and (3)) is denoted $\mathcal{F}$.

Restricting the search to the feasible region seems an elegant way to treat constrained problems: in [12], the algorithm maintains feasibility of all linear constraints using a set of closed operators, which convert a feasible solution (feasible in terms of linear constraints only) into another feasible solution.

However, for nonlinear constraints this ideal situation is generally out of reach, and during the last few years, several methods have been proposed for handling constraints by evolutionary algorithms. Most of them are based on the concept of penalty functions: Infeasible individuals are penalized by adding to their fitness $f(x)$ a penalty term $penalty(x)$, which is zero if no violation occurs, and is positive otherwise.

The most severe penalty method is death penalty ($penalty(x) = +\infty$) as in [1]. A usual form of penalty functions is $penalty(x) = \sum_0^q \alpha_i \max(0, g_i(x)) + \sum_{q+1}^m \alpha_i |g_i|$, where parameters α_i are either static parameters (see for instance [5] for a method to determine α_i), dynamically adjusted (as in [6]) or adaptive (two methods are proposed in [2, 19]). Many variations on the penalty approach have been implemented: in [16], an additional penalty term is added to ensure that any feasible point has worse fitness than any infeasible one; in [8], two populations are evolved with two different penalty coefficients. The idea of using two separate populations is also used in Genocop III [13]: a set of reference feasible points is maintained and used to repair infeasible points.

For an experimental comparison of some of these methods and some others on a few test cases, see [10, 15]. However, highly nonlinear constraints still present difficulties for evolutionary algorithms, as penalty parameters or strategies are then difficult to adjust.

3 Searching the boundary of the feasible region

It is a common situation for many constrained optimization problems that some constraints are active at the target global optimum. This optimum thus lies on the boundary of the feasible space. One the other hand, it is commonly acknowledged that restricting the size of the search space in evolutionary algorithms (as in most search algorithms) is generally beneficial. Hence, it seems natural in the context of constrained optimization to restrict the search of the solution to the boundary of the feasible part of the space.

We suppose in the rest of the paper that we are searching on a Riemanian surface S of dimension $n-1$ in the space $\mathbb{R}^n$. This surface is supposed to be regular, i.e., the gradient vector, orthogonal to the surface, is defined almost everywhere. The Euclidean measure of $\mathbb{R}^n$ thus classically induces a distance on that surface.

The basic components of an evolutionary search are the following.

An initialization procedure: This procedure must sample surface S as uniformly as possible according to the distance at hand. Though conceptually simple, this procedure can be quite hard to design: in many real-world engineering problems, the main difficulty can be to find just *one* feasible point.

Evolution operators on the surface: The first necessary conditions for the evolution operators is to be *closed*, i.e., transforming point(s) of the surface into point(s) of the surface. Moreover, these operators should (as much as possible) respect some empirically derived properties [17, 11]:

- recombination should be able to generate all points "between" the parents;
- mutation should be *ergodic*, having non-zero probability to reach any point within a finite number of application, and should respect the principle of *strong causality* [18], i.e., small mutations must result in small changes in the fitness function.

These ideas will be validated on two test cases in next section: specific evolutionary algorithms searching the boundary of the feasible regions will be designed.

4 Two test cases

4.1 Problem on an hyperboloid

An interesting constrained numerical optimization test case emerged recently; the problem [7] is to maximize $f(\mathbf{x}) = \left|\frac{\sum_{i=1}^{n} cos^4(x_i) - 2\prod_{i=1}^{n} cos^2(x_i)}{\sqrt{\sum_{i=1}^{n} i x_i^2}}\right|$, with constraints $\prod_{i=1}^{n} x_i \geq 0.75$, $\sum_{i=1}^{n} x_i \leq 7.5n$, and $0 \leq x_i \leq 10$ for $1 \leq i \leq n$.

Function f is nonlinear and its global maximum is unknown, lying somewhere near the origin. The problem has one nonlinear constraint and one linear constraint; the latter one is inactive around the origin and will be forgotten in the following

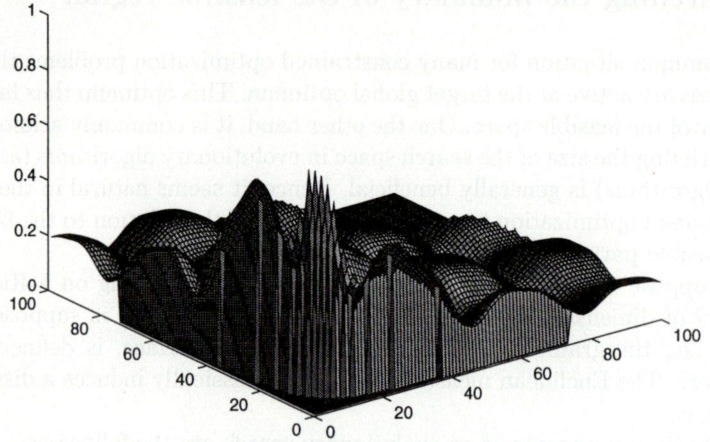

Fig. 1. The graph of function f for $n = 2$. Infeasible solutions were assigned value zero

Some potential difficulties of solving this test case are illustrated on Figure 1: infeasible points were assigned a value of zero. The F-surface is defined by the equation $\Pi x_i = 0.75$. It is a difficult problem, on which no standard method (be it deterministic or evolutionary) gave satisfactory results. In [7], a parallel GA with 12bit binary encoding using a modified Fiacco-McCormick constraint penalty function gets values like 0.76 after 20,000 evaluations (for $n = 20$).

This test case was the first one on which the idea of searching only the boundary was used [14]: due to the simple analytical formulation of the constraint, *ad hoc* specific initialization procedure and operators could be designed.

- **Initialization**: Randomly choose a positive variable for x_i, and use its inverse as a variable for x_{i+1}. The last variable is either 0.75 (when n is odd), or is multiplied by 0.75 (if n is even), so that the point lies on the F-surface.
- **Crossover**: The *geometrical crossover* is defined by

$$(x_i)(y_i) \rightarrow (x_i^{\alpha} y_i^{1-\alpha}), \text{ with } \alpha \text{ randomly chosen in } [0, 1]$$

  Figure 2 in section 5.2 illustrates the possible offspring from two parents on the F-surface for all values of α.
- **Mutation**: Pick two variables randomly, multiply one by a random factor q and the other by $\frac{1}{q}$ (restrict q to respect the bounds on the variables).

The simple evolutionary algorithm described above gave outstanding results in terms of quality of the solution. For the case $n = 20$ the system reached the value of 0.80 in less than 4,000 generations (with population size of 30, probability of crossover $p_c = 1.0$, and probability of mutation $p_m = 0.06$) in all runs. The best value found (namely 0.803553) was better than the best values of any method discussed earlier, whereas the worst value found was 0.802964. Similarly, for $n = 50$, all results (in 30,000 generations) were better than 0.83 (with the best of 0.8331937).

It was interesting to note the importance of geometrical crossover. With fixed population size (kept constant at 30), the higher values of probability of crossover p_c, the better results of the system were observed. Similarly, the best mutation rates were relatively low ($p_m \approx 0.06$).

4.2 Constrained problem on the sphere

The main interest of the sphere as a surface in $\mathbb{R}^n$ come from both its simple analytical expression and its nice symmetrical properties. Hence different methods to design evolution operators on the sphere can be used (see sections 5.3 and 5.2). However, we shall first present results of an *ad hoc* evolutionary algorithm that was designed in [14], based on the simple analytical formulation of the constraint.

The test problem for this case is to maximize $f(\mathbf{x}) = (\sqrt{n})^n \cdot \prod_{i=1}^n x_i$, with constraints $\sum_{i=1}^n x_i = 1$ and $0 \le x_i \le 1$ for $1 \le i \le n$.
The function has a global solution at $(x_1, \ldots, x_n) = (\frac{1}{\sqrt{n}}, \ldots, \frac{1}{\sqrt{n}})$ and the value of the function in this point is 1. The evolutionary algorithm uses the following components:

- **Initialization**: Randomly generate n variables y_i, calculate $s = \sum_{i=1}^n y_i^2$, and initialize an individual (x_i) by $x = y_i/s$ for $i \in [1, n]$.
- **Crossover**: The *sphere crossover* produces one offspring (z_i) from two parents (x_i) and (y_i) by:

$$z_i = \sqrt{\alpha x_i^2 + (1-\alpha) y_i^2} \ i \in [1, n], \text{ with } \alpha \text{ randomly chosen in } [0, 1]$$

- **Mutation**: Similarly, the problem-specific mutation transforms (x_i) by selecting two indices $i \neq j$ and a random number p in $\langle 0, 1 \rangle$, and setting:

$$x_i \to p \cdot x_i \text{ and } x_j \to q \cdot x_j, \text{where } q = \sqrt{(\frac{x_i}{x_j})^2 (1 - p^2) + 1}.$$

The simple evolutionary algorithm described above gave very good results. For the case $n = 20$ the system reached the value of 0.99 in less than 6,000 generations (with population size of 30, probability of crossover $p_c = 1.0$, and probability of mutation $p_m = 0.06$) in all runs. The best value found in 10,000 generations was 0.999866.

5 Surface-searching evolutionary operators

In this section, we propose possible approaches to the design of evolutionary operators on a general surface of dimension $n-1$ given in analytical form.

5.1 Curve-based operators

The first method to design suitable operators is based on *curves* drawn on the surface.

Crossover operators:
From curves joining two different points, one can derive a crossover operator by choosing as offspring one (two) point(s) on that curve. Minimal-length curves (termed *geodesical curves*) seem a priori a good choice: their existence is guaranteed, locally on any regular surface from standard Cauchy-Lipschitz theorem, and globally (i.e. joining any pair of points of the surface) if the surface is *geodesically complete*[1] (Hopf-Rinov theorem) [9]. Moreover, in the linear case, the geodesical curve between two points is the line segment between them, and the curve-based operator is nothing but the standard linear recombination operator [11]. But recent experiments suggest that other paths between both parents can be used successfully [14]: the minimal length requirement does not seem mandatory.

Mutation operators:
From a beam of curves starting from one point, one can derive a mutation operator by first choosing randomly one curve in the beam, then choosing a point on the chosen curve. A desirable property of the beam of curves related to the ergodicity of the resulting mutation operator is that a large enough neighborhood of the starting point is covered by such set of curves: the local geodesical curves defined from the parent point and one tangent direction are such sets, defined almost everywhere on regular surfaces [9]. On the sphere, for instance, the geodesical curves from a pole are the meridians, which in that case cover not only a whole neighborhood of the parent point, but the whole surface. Furthermore, a tight control of the distance between parents and offspring allows for a simple implementation of adaptive mutation respecting the strong causality principle.

Unfortunately, in the general case, even with analytical definitions of the constraints, the derivation of the geodesical curves (or the exponential curves beam) is not tractable: it involves heavy symbolic computations, plus the numerical solution of many local second-order systems of differential equations. Moreover, unavoidable numerical errors would probably move the solutions off the desired curves.

However, in some situations, the ideas presented above can be implemented, and evolutionary search on the boundary can be successfully performed without the need for exact geodesical curves. The geometrical and spherical crossovers

[1] A surface is geodesically complete if no geodesical curve encounters a dead-end.

presented in section 3 are particular examples of such curves. Next subsections will also present particular cases where such curves are available.

5.2 Parametric representation of the surface

From a parametric representation of a surface, it is easy to design a complete evolutionary algorithm on that surface. Suppose the surface S (of dimension $n-1$) is defined by $x_i = s_i(t_1, \ldots t_{n-1})$, $t_i \in [a_i, b_i]$, for $i = 1, \ldots, n$, where the functions s_i are regular functions from R^{n-1} into R. In the following, we denote this relation $(x_i) = S[(t_i)]$. The following elements can be designed:

- **Initialization**: A random choice of a point on S amounts to the choice of the $n-1$ values of the parameters $t_1, \ldots t_{n-1}$, uniformly on $\Pi[a_i, b_i]$.
- **Crossover**: The crossover can be defined by:
$$S[(t_i)], S[(u_i)] \rightarrow S[(\alpha t_i + (1-\alpha)u_i)]$$
for some α randomly chosen in $[0, 1]$.
- **Mutation**: Similarly, the mutation can be given by
$$S[(t_i)] \rightarrow S[(t_i + N(0, \sigma_i))]$$
where $N(0, \sigma)$ denotes the normal distribution with zero mean and σ variance. The parameters σ_i can be either user-supplied (eventually dynamically) or adaptive, i.e., encoded in the individual, as in evolution strategies.

In that context, the choice of a specific parametric representation fully determines the operators. Further subsection presents the common situation in which many different parameterization of surface S are available, for both cases of section 4.

Parametric operators on the hyperboloid. In the case of the hyperboloid (section 4.1), surface S is defined by the equation $\prod x_i = 0.75$. Any $n-1$ variables can be chosen as parameters, the last one is then defined by the equation of the surface itself. There are n different systems of such parametric representation, for the n different choices of $i_0 = 1, \ldots n$:
$$x_{i_0} = 0.75/\Pi_{i \neq i_0} x_i$$

Figure 2 presents three possible parametric crossovers (as defined above) in the case $n = 3$, termed C_i when variable i is taken as unknown, together with the geometrical crossover introduced in section 4.1 termed G. It is clear from that figure that the possible locations for the offspring depends on both the chosen parameterization and the position of the parents on the surface.

Parametric operators on the sphere. Similarly, an evolutionary algorithm can be defined as described earlier in this section from any standard spherical parametric representation (which are the straightforward extension of the usual spherical coordinates of $\mathbb{R}^3$). Here, there are $n!$ valid parametric representations for the sphere, corresponding to the permutations among coordinates. Figure 3-a gives an example of three curves defining these operators on the sphere in the case $n = 3$ (denoted P_1, P_2, and P_3), together with the geodesical curve (denoted G) and the curve corresponding to the spherical crossover presented in section 4.2 (denoted Sp).

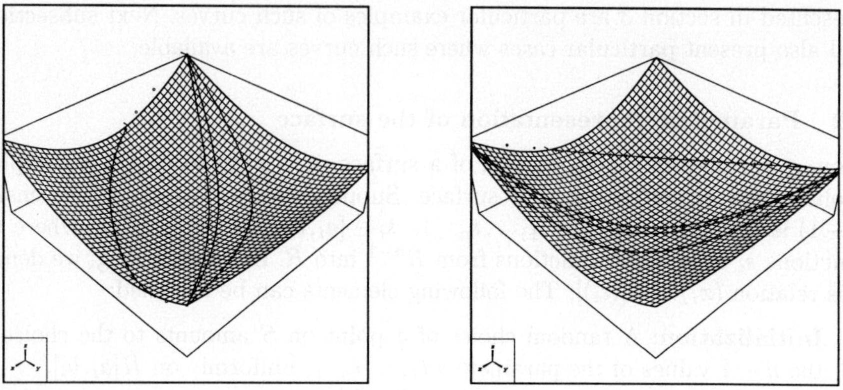

Fig. 2. Parametric crossovers for the hyperboloid problem, for different parametric representations and different parents. (a) From left to right, C_2, C_1, G, C_3 (b) From top to bottom, C_1, C_2, G, C_3

5.3 Plane-based operators

Another general method to design curves, and hence operators to evolve on a surface is to use the intersection of that surface with 2-dimensional planes.

Consider two points A and B belonging to S, and one vector $\mathbf{v}$ which are not collinear to $\mathbf{AB}$ and which is not orthogonal to the gradient vector at point A. Hence the plane defined by $(A, \mathbf{AB}, \mathbf{v})$ intersects the surface around A, defining a curve on S. If this curve is connected, a crossover operator can be designed as described in section 5.1. But this procedure can fail if the intersection is not connected (as for the "horse-shoe sausage" of R^3 with A and B at both end).

Similarly, the mutation operator can be designed by choosing the gradient at point A instead of vector $\mathbf{AB}$ above, with a prescribed distance off point A.

Examples of plane-based operators will now be given in the simple case where S is a sphere.

Plane-based operators on the sphere. In the case of the sphere, the derivation of curves joining two points by intersecting the sphere with a plane is straightforward calculation. Moreover, the geodesical curves are a particular case of such plane-based curves, corresponding to the case where the chosen plane goes through the center of the sphere.

Figure 3-b shows some plane-based curves for different values of the angle between the plane and the gradient of the surface. The angles were such that the resulting curves approximately match the curves of Figure 3-a, obtained by parametric operators (section 5.2) and by the *spherical* crossover of section 4.2. Obviously, in that particular case, plane-based operators are more general operators: particular plane-based crossovers can give almost the same resulting offspring than any other crossover presented here.

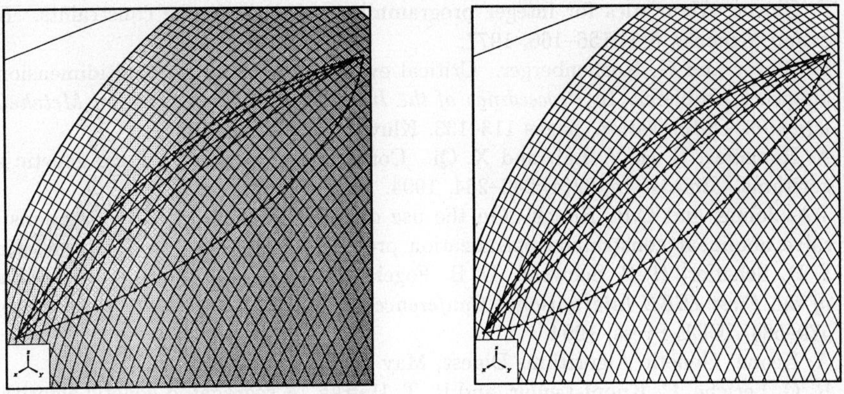

Fig. 3. Crossover operators on the sphere. (a) From top to bottom, P_1, P_2, G, Sp, P_3. (b) From top to bottom, angle between the plane and the gradient is $0, 15, 20, -15, -57$ (in degrees).

6 Conclusions

Using the geodesical curves constitute a theoretical method for constructing specific operators on a surface, but raises technical difficulties. The parametric operators represent an easy way when available with the inconvenience that these operators do depend a lot on the chosen parameterization (see Figure 2).

The plane operators provide another possibility, but they require more complex calculations, and possibly they may lead to pathological solutions (e.g., non-connected parts of curves). The case of the sphere illustrates all above-mentioned types of operators: plane-based operators end up in more general operators, sweeping a large region around the parents, thus avoiding the bias due to the choice of a single curve. Further comparative experiments are needed, on both test cases presented here as well as on other more complex surfaces.

Acknowledgments

This material is based upon work supported by the National Science Foundation under Grant IRI-9322400. Many thanks to C. Margerin (CMA-Ecole Polytechnique) for his helpful views on Riemanian geometry

References

1. T. Bäck, F. Hoffmeister, and H.-P. Schwefel. A survey of evolution strategies. In R. K. Belew and L. B. Booker, editors, *Proceedings of the* 4th *International Conference on Genetic Algorithms*, pages 2–9. Morgan Kaufmann, 1991.
2. J. C. Bean and A. B. Hadj-Alouane. A dual genetic algorithm for bounded integer programs. Technical Report TR 92-53, Department of Industrial and Operations Engineering, The University of Michigan, 1992.

3. F. Glover. Heuristics for integer programming using surrogate constraints. *Decision Sciences*, 8(1):156–166, 1977.
4. F. Glover and G. Kochenberger. Critical event tabu search for multidimensional knapsack problems. In *Proceedings of the International Conference on Metaheuristics for Optimization*, pages 113–133. Kluwer Publishing, 1995.
5. A. Homaifar, S. H.-Y. Lai, and X. Qi. Constrained optimization via genetic algorithms. *Simulation*, 62(4):242–254, 1994.
6. J.A. Joines and C.R. Houck. On the use of non-stationary penalty functions to solve nonlinear constrained optimization problems with GAs. In Z. Michalewicz, J. D. Schaffer, H.-P. Schwefel, D. B. Fogel, and H. Kitano, editors, *Proceedings of the First IEEE International Conference on Evolutionary Computation*, pages 579–584. IEEE Press, 1994.
7. A. Keane. Genetic Algorithms Digest, May 19 1994. V8n16.
8. R. G. Leriche, C. Knopf-Lenoir, and R. T. Haftka. A segragated genetic algorithm for constrained structural optimization. In L. J. Eshelman, editor, *Proceedings of the 6th International Conference on Genetic Algorithms*, pages 558–565, 1995.
9. C. Margerin. Une introduction à la géométrie. Course at ENSTA - Palaiseau - France, 1990.
10. Z. Michalewicz. Genetic algorithms, numerical optimization and constraints. In L. J. Eshelman, editor, *Proceedings of the 6th International Conference on Genetic Algorithms*, pages 151–158. Morgan Kaufmann, 1995.
11. Z. Michalewicz. *Genetic Algorithms+Data Structures=Evolution Programs.* Springer Verlag, New-York, 1996. 3rd edition.
12. Z. Michalewicz and N. Attia. Evolutionary optimization of constrained problems. In *Proceedings of the 3rd Annual Conference on Evolutionary Programming*, pages 98–108. World Scientific, 1994.
13. Z. Michalewicz and G. Nazhiyath. Genocop III: A co-evolutionary algorithm for numerical optimization problems with nonlinear constraints. In D. B. Fogel, editor, *Proceedings of the Second IEEE International Conference on Evolutionary Computation*, pages 647–651. IEEE Press, 1995.
14. Z. Michalewicz, G. Nazhiyath, and M. Michalewicz. A note on usefulness of geometrical crossover for numerical optimization problems. In L. J. Fogel, P. J. Angeline, and T. Bäck, editors, *Proceedings of the 5th Annual Conference on Evolutionary Programming*, 1996.
15. Z. Michalewicz and M. Schoenauer. Evolutionary Algorithms for Constrained Parameter Optimization Problems. *Evolutionary Computation*, 4(1), Spring 1996.
16. D. Powell and M. M. Skolnick. Using genetic algorithms in engineering design optimization with non-linear constraints. In S. Forrest, editor, *Proceedings of the 5th International Conference on Genetic Algorithms*, pages 424–430. Morgan Kaufmann, 1993.
17. N. J. Radcliffe. Equivalence class analysis of genetic algorithms. *Complex Systems*, 5:183–20, 1991.
18. I. Rechenberg. *Evolutionstrategie: Optimierung Technisher Systeme nach Prinzipien des Biologischen Evolution.* Fromman-Holzboog Verlag, 1973.
19. A. Smith and D. Tate. Genetic optimization using a penalty function. In S. Forrest, editor, *Proceedings of the 5th International Conference on Genetic Algorithms*, pages 499–503. Morgan Kaufmann, 1993.

Dimensional Analysis of Allele-Wise Mixing Revisited

Dirk Thierens

Department of Computer Science
Utrecht University, The Netherlands
dirk.thierens@cs.ruu.nl

Abstract. This paper revisits an important, yet poorly understood, phenomenon of genetic optimisation, namely the mixing or juxtapositioning capacity of recombination, and its relation to selection. Mixing is a key factor in order to determine when a genetic algorithm will converge to the global optimum, or when it will prematurely converge to a suboptimal solution. It is argued that from a dynamical point of view, selection and recombination are involved in a kind of race against time: the number of instances of good building blocks is quickly increased from generation to generation by the selection phase, but in order to create optimal solutions these building blocks have to be juxtaposed by the crossover operator and this also takes some time to occur. If the selection of building blocks goes too fast - relative to the rate at which crossover can juxtapose or mix them - then the population will prematurely converge to a suboptimal solution. Previous work (Goldberg, Deb & Thierens, 1993) made a first step toward a better understanding of mixing in genetic algorithms, and also introduced the use of dimensional analysis in GA modelling. In this paper we extend this work by integrating some of the insights gained from the modelling of the dynamic behaviour of GAs on infinite populations (Mühlenbein & Schlierkamp-Voosen, 1993; Thierens & Goldberg, 1994; Bäck, 1995; Miller & Goldberg, 1995). The resulting dimensional model quantifies the allele-wise mixing process: it specifies the boundary in the GA parameter space between the region of reliable convergence at one side, and the region of premature convergence at the other. Although the model is limited to simple bit-wise mixing, the lessons learned from it are quite general and are also valid for more difficult, building-block based problems.

1 Introduction

Genetic algorithms are complex adaptive systems and therefore it should come as no surprise that different modelling approaches are needed to highlight different aspects of their behaviour. Traditional analysis of genetic algorithms - as stated by the schema theorem - focuses on the selective growth of good building blocks and on the destructive effects of recombination on this growth (Holland, 1975; Goldberg, 1989). An alternative approach studies the GA convergence properties by modelling the dynamic change of the population fitness distribution (Vose & Liepins, 1991; Whitley, 1993; Mühlenbein & Schlierkamp-Voosen, 1993; Thierens

& Goldberg, 1994; Bäck, 1995; Miller & Goldberg, 1995). These analytical tools are all quite useful but unfortunately they do not answer all the questions one would like to get answered. For instance the analyses do not give an answer to the important question whether a finite sized population will prematurely converge or not, nor do they consider the effect of the different GA parameters on this phenomenon.

In this paper we study the dynamic interaction between the selection phase and the recombination phase. In contrast with the schema theorem analysis our attention is now focused on the constructive capacities of recombination. It is argued that selection and recombination are basically involved in a race against time. Selection makes copies of the best strings and since the population size is fixed a loss of diversity occurs. At the same time recombination has to mix or juxtapose the good genetic material, but due to the loss of diversity it has only limited time to achieve this. If selection goes too fast then recombination will have not enough time to bring all the optimal alleles together and the population will prematurely converge to a suboptimal solution.

A very useful methodology to quantify this selection-recombination race is the so called dimensional analysis methodology (Ipsen, 1960). Dimensional analysis tries to identify the basic dimensions or key features of a certain process and establishes the functional relationship between them. Important key features for genetic algorithms are the selection pressure, the recombination rate, the population size, the string length and the building block length. The dimensional analysis methodology was first applied to the study of GAs in (Goldberg, Deb & Thierens, 1993) where a first step at allele-wise modelling was performed. In (Thierens & Goldberg, 1993) the methodology was used to show the limitations of simple genetic algorithms when they have no linkage information about the building blocks. A general discussion of the methodological aspects and their use for GA analysis can be found in (Goldberg, 1994). This paper extends the work done in (Goldberg, Deb & Thierens, 1993) and builds a complete dimensional model for allele-wise mixing by integrating some of the insights gained from the modelling of the dynamic behaviour of GAs on infinite populations (Mühlenbein & Schlierkamp-Voosen, 1993; Thierens & Goldberg, 1994; Bäck, 1995; Miller & Goldberg, 1995). In addition we also perform an extensive set of experiments to check the validity of the dimensional model.

2 A Dimensional Model for Allele-Wise Mixing

The purpose of mixing analysis is to study the relationship between the key genetic algorithm parameters that determine whether or not the optimal solution will be found in a reliable way. When a given parameter choice violates this relationship the GA will prematurely converge to a suboptimal solution. In this paper we look at the mixing limitations on the level of alleles, and thus the modelling considers fitness functions with independent allele fitness contributions. Two extreme cases can be considered. In the first case all allele fitness values are equal - which gives us the well studied bit-counting function - and the proportion of the optimal alleles increases at the same rate in the entire string. In the second case the allele fitness values are exponentially scaled, which causes a domino-like convergence behaviour. The optimal alleles converge sequentially and at any time only a very limited number of genes is actually converging in the so called convergence window. Genes outside the convergence window are either already fully converged or they still have to start converging (Rudnick, 1992). From the mixing point of view, the domino convergence is an easy problem: only a few genes are actually converging at the same time and juxtaposing them is a simple matter. The mixing task becomes much harder with equal allele values because all genes are converging simultaneously and thus they all have to be juxtaposed simultaneously. It has also been shown that the time complexity of the convergence rate is of order $O(\sqrt{\ell})$ for equally scaled allele values, and of order $O(\ell)$ for the exponentially scaled allele values (Thierens, 1995). Since the convergence rate is faster for the uniform allele fitness distribution there is less time to mix all the alleles, and thus the most difficult situation for allele-wise mixing occurs when optimising the bit counting function. Therefore we will develop a dimensional mixing model for this case. The notation used throughout the text is summarised in table 1.

2.1 Recombination

n	population size	p_c	crossover probability
l	string length	p_x	allele swapping probability
s	tournament size	p_r	gene exchange probability
I	selection intensity	r	recombination rate ($= p_c p_r$)
t_x	mixing time	$p(t)$	proportion optimal alleles
t_s	selection time		

Table 1. *Notation.*

We start our dimensional modelling with the analysis of the recombinative capacity of crossover. Whether or not the GA will prematurely converge depends on the relative speed of selection and recombination. To quantify the recombination speed we express the recombinative capacity of crossover in terms of time or equivalently of number of generations.

First the probability that two arbitrary genes are exchanged is simply the probability of applying the crossover operator p_c times the probability p_r that an actual exchange between the two genes takes place. This exchange probability is dependent on the type of crossover operator used. For instance for 1-point crossover we have $p_r = \delta_{ij}/(l-1)$ (with δ_{ij} the distance between the two genes), while for parameterised uniform crossover the gene exchange probability is $p_r =$

$2p_x(1-p_x)$ (with p_x the allele swapping probability). We call the probability of gene exchange the recombination rate r:

$$r = p_c p_r$$

Under repeated use of crossover, the number of generations that are needed in expectation to exchange two arbitrary genes is thus given by $1/nr$. This gene exchange has to happen with all the l genes, so the number of generations that we have to apply recombination or the mixing time t_x is proportional to:

$$t_x \propto \frac{l}{nr} \qquad (1)$$

2.2 Selection

The speed at which selection makes the population converge is of course dependent on the selective pressure and on the particular selection algorithm used. A number of studies have derived an exact dynamical model of the convergence of different selection algorithms for normally distributed fitness functions such as the bit counting function (Mühlenbein & Schlierkamp-Voosen, 1993; Thierens & Goldberg, 1994; Bäck, 1995; Miller & Goldberg, 1995). For tournament selection and (μ/λ) or truncation selection this model is given by:

$$p(t) = 0.5(1 + sin(\frac{I}{\sqrt{l}}t + c_0))$$

where I is the selection intensity and $c_0 = arcsin(2p(0)+1)$ a constant dependent on the initial proportion of optimal alleles. For a randomly initialised population the number of generations needed to converge ($p(g_{conv}) = 1$) is thus given by:

$$g_{conv} = \frac{\pi}{2}.\frac{\sqrt{l}}{I}$$

The selection time t_s is therefore proportional to:

$$t_s \propto \frac{\sqrt{l}}{I} \qquad (2)$$

Note that for unscaled proportionate selection the time to convergence is given by $g_{conv} = l \log l$. Clearly this is unacceptably slow and in practice unscaled proportionate selection is never used so we will not consider it here.

2.3 Allele-wise mixing model

Now that we have a dimensional relation of both recombination and selection, we need to combine them. When selection acts more slowly than exchange - when $t_x \leq t_s$ - we expect the optimal alleles to have time to be juxtaposed and thus creating good strings which can then be given more copies by selection. This juxtapositioning of the target alleles can then subsequently proceed until all optimal alleles are put together. However when selection is too fast - when $t_s < t_x$ - too many copies are created of only a few good strings before recombination has had the time to exchange the optimal alleles. As a result some alleles will not be part of strings that receive extra copies and their proportion in the population will decline until they finally disappear. A lack of good mixing thus results in premature convergence.

To quantify this mixing failure we interrelate the previous dimensional relations (Equations 1 and 2) for the recombination and selection process. If we want to avoid a mixing failure we need $t_x \leq t_s$ or:

$$\frac{l}{nr} \leq c \, \frac{\sqrt{l}}{I}$$

where c is a constant factor since dimensional analysis gives us only the functional relationship between the parameters. Rearranging the selection and recombination parameters at one side and the size parameters at the other side we obtain the following mixing model:

$$\frac{\sqrt{\mathbf{l}}}{\mathbf{n}} \leq \mathbf{c} \, \frac{\mathbf{r}}{\mathbf{I}} \tag{3}$$

3 Experimental verification

The use of dimensional modelling allows us to build simple analytical models that expresses the functional relationship between the key parameters. For instance the model tells us that in order to maintain proper convergence the minimal population size needs to be increased by a factor $\sqrt{2}$ whenever the string length is doubled. Dimensional analysis forces us to take a birds eye view on the whole convergence process. It is therefore extremely important to validate the model with experimental results. Since we have four independent variables (population size n, string length l, selection pressure s and the recombination rate $r = p_c p_r$) we have $\binom{4}{2} = 6$ functional relations between two variables while keeping the other independent variables fixed. Exhaustively performing the 6 sets of experiments assures us of the correctness of the dimensional model. In the following experiments the results are obtained by doing 20 independent runs for all the parameter combinations shown. We call the experiments a success whenever in at least 19 of these 20 runs the population converged to the optimal string. At one side of the curve we have reliable convergence to the optimal solution, while at the other side premature convergence occurs. Although the 19-out-of-20 success criterion might seem rather arbitrary, the particular choice has no influence on the functional relationships. The value of the constant c in the dimensional model might change a little bit, but this is of no importance. All experiments are carried out with tournament selection with tournament size s. Since the selection intensity I is approximately proportional to the tournament size s ($\ln s \approx \sqrt{2}I$), we can quantify the selection pressure by the tournament size as was done in (Goldberg, Deb & Thierens, 1993).

1. **string length vs. selection pressure**
   First we look at the functional relation between the string length l and the selection pressure s. We fix the population size $n = 200$, the crossover probability $p_c = 1.0$ and the disruption probability $p_r = 0.3$. We use parameterised uniform crossover so the crossover swapping probability is $p_x = 0.18$ ($p_r = 2p_x(1 - p_x)$). Plugging these values into the mixing model (Equation 3) gives us a prediction of the boundary between successful and failing convergence:

$$\sqrt{l} = \frac{60\ c}{\ln s}$$

   Figure 1 shows the data and the corresponding fitted curve

$$l = \frac{320}{(\ln s)^2}$$

   The predicted functional relation and the data coincide quite well and the corresponding value of the constant factor in the dimensional model is approximately: $c = 0.298$.

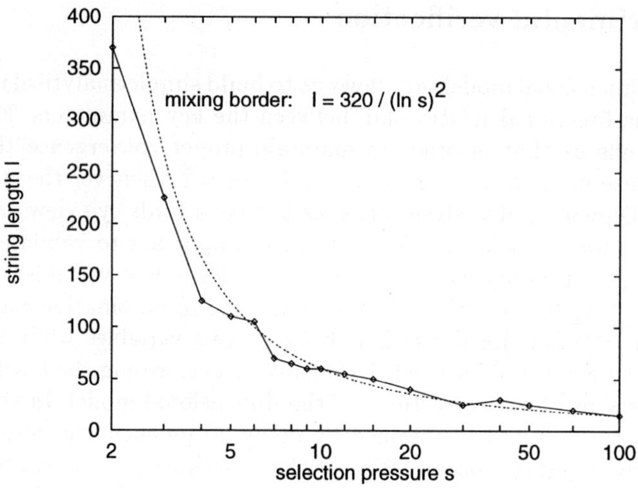

Fig. 1. *Dimensional relation between the selection pressure and the string length.*

2. **disruption probability vs. string length**
   The second experiment checks the relation between the disruption probability p_r and the string length l. The population size $n = 200$, the selection pressure $s = 10$ and the crossover probability $p_c = 1.0$. Note that the choice of the values of the fixed variables is such that the resulting mixing boundary falls within a reasonable range of the varying variables.

The predicted relation is now :

$$p_r = \frac{0.0115}{c} \sqrt{l}$$

Figure 2 shows a fitted curve equal to

$$p_r = 0.045\sqrt{l}$$

which gives us for the constant factor: $c = 0.256$.

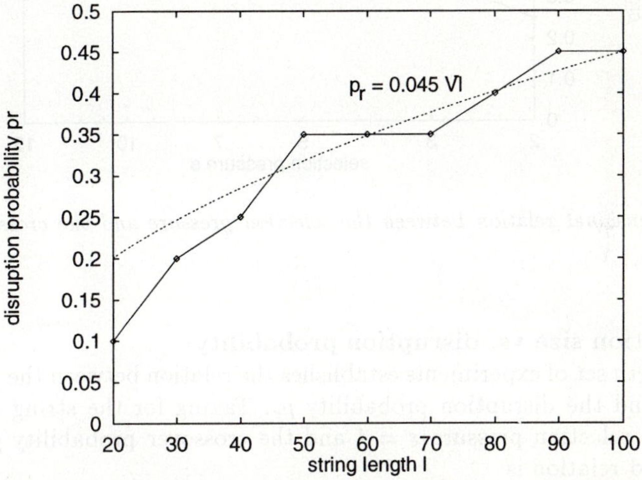

Fig. 2. *Dimensional relation between the string length and the disruption factor.*

The experimental data shows good agreement although for very low string lengths ($l < 30$) the necessary disruption probability is actually a little bit lower than predicted. This can be understood however if we realize that for such small string lengths the search problem becomes almost trivial.

3. **crossover probability vs. selection pressure**
For the relation between the selection pressure and the crossover probability we take the string length $l = 100$, the population size $n = 200$ and the disruption probability $p_r = 0.5$, the predicted functional relation now becomes:

$$p_c = \frac{\ln s}{10\ c}$$

Figure 3 shows the experimental results and the fitted curve:

$$p_c = 0.35 \ln s$$

which results in a constant factor : $c = 0.286$.
For large values of the selection pressure s the GA behaviour is no longer determined by the mixing but by the cross-competition between the genes (Goldberg, Deb & Thierens, 1993).

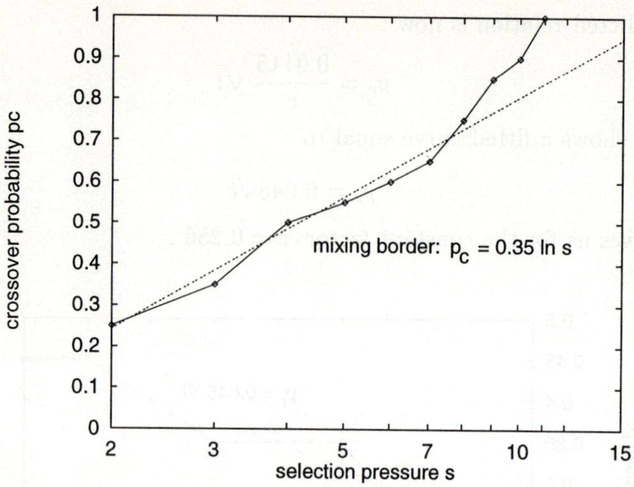

Fig. 3. *Dimensional relation between the selection pressure and the crossover probability.*

4. **population size vs. disruption probability**
   The fourth set of experiments establishes the relation between the population size n and the disruption probability p_r. Taking for the string length $l = 100$, the selection pressure $s = 4$ and the crossover probability $p_c = 1$ the predicted relation is:

$$n = \frac{13.86}{c\ p_r}$$

   Figure 4 shows the experimental results and the fitted curve:

$$n = \frac{50}{p_r}$$

   and a corresponding constant factor: $c = 0.277$.
5. **population size vs. selection pressure**
   For a string length $l = 100$, crossover probability $p_c = 0.75$ and disruption probability $p_r = 0.20$ ($\Rightarrow p_x = 0.11$) the relation between the population size n and the selection pressure s is:

$$n = \frac{66.67}{c} \ln s$$

   Experimental results (Figure 5) are

$$n = 236 \ln s$$

   or $c = 0.282$. Again we notice that for very large values of the selection pressure s cross-competition starts to influence the convergence results.

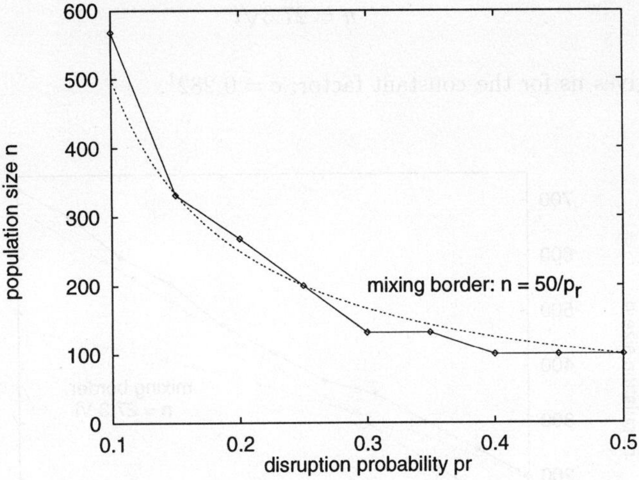

Fig. 4. *Dimensional relation between the disruption factor and the population size.*

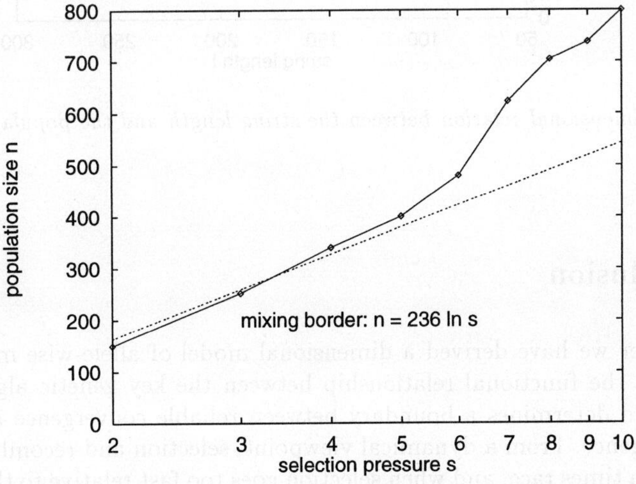

Fig. 5. *Dimensional relation between the selection pressure and the population size.*

6. **population size vs. string length**
   Finally the last set of experiments looks at the relation between the population size and the string length. Fixing the selection pressure $s = 2$, the crossover probability $p_c = 1.0$ and the disruption probability $p_x = 0.1 (\Rightarrow p_r = 0.18)$ the dimensional model predicts:

$$n = \frac{7.7}{c}\sqrt{l}$$

Experimental results are shown in Figure 6. The fitted curve is:

$$n = 27.3\sqrt{l}$$

which gives us for the constant factor: $c = 0.282$[1].

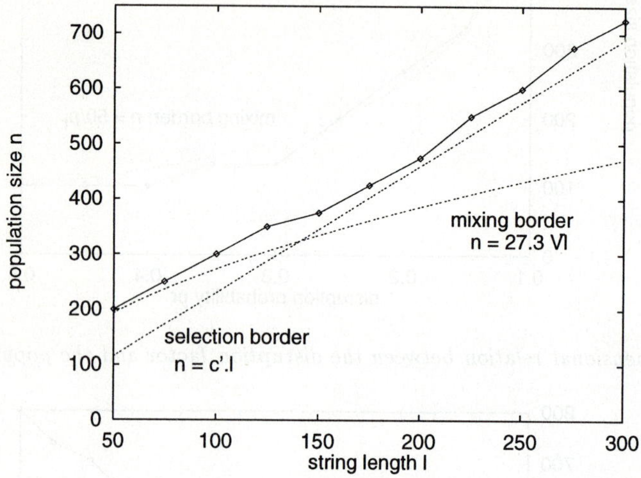

Fig. 6. *Dimensional relation between the string length and the population size.*

4 Conclusion

In this paper we have derived a dimensional model of allele-wise mixing. This model gives the functional relationship between the key genetic algorithm parameters and determines a boundary between reliable convergence and premature convergence. From a dynamical viewpoint, selection and recombination are involved in a times race, and when selection goes too fast relative to the recombination or mixing time, then the GA will fail to converge to the global optimum. The model quantifies the mixing boundary in terms of the selection pressure, the recombination rate, the population size, and the string length. Experimental results show good agreement with the predicted functional relations.

[1] The 6 fitted curves gave an approximate value to the constant factor of respectively $c = \{0.298,\ 0.256,\ 0.286,\ 0.277,\ 0.282,\ 0.282\}$. Considering the presence of the constant $\sqrt{\pi}$ in the normal distribution modelling of GA convergence it is interesting to note that: $1/2\sqrt{\pi} = 0.282$. However further analysis would be needed to test the sensitivity of the constant value on a number of factors, such as the choice of success criterion and the curve fitting method.

Acknowledgement

We would like to thank David E. Goldberg for the many useful discussions on the importance of dimensional modelling in complex systems analysis.

References

1. Bäck T. (1995). Generalised Convergence Models for Tournament- and (μ, λ)-Selection. Proceedings of the Sixth International Conference on Genetic Algorithms.
2. Goldberg D.E. (1989). *Genetic Algorithms in Search, Optimisation and Machine Learning.* Addison Wesley Publishing Company.
3. Goldberg D.E. (1994). *First Flights at Genetic-Algorithm Kitty Hawk.* IlliGAL Report No. 94008. University of Illinois at Urbana-Champaign, Illinois Genetic Algorithm Laboratory.
4. Goldberg D.E., & Deb K. (1991). A comparative analysis of selection schemes used in genetic algorithms. *Proceedings of Foundations of Genetic Algorithms FOGA-I.* ed. G. Rawlings. pp.69-93. Morgan Kaufmann.
5. Goldberg D.E., Deb K., & Thierens D. (1993). Toward a better understanding of mixing in genetic algorithms. *Journal of the Society for Instrumentation and Control Engineers, SICE Vol.32,* No.1 pp.10-16.
6. Holland J.H. (1975). *Adaptation in natural and artificial systems.* Ann Arbor: University of Michigan Press.
7. Ipsen D.C.(1960). *Units, dimensions, and dimensionless numbers.* McGraw-Hill.
8. Miller B. L., & Goldberg D. E. (1995). *Genetic algorithms, selection schemes, and the varying effects of noise* IlliGAL Report No. 95009. Illinois Genetic Algorithm Laboratory. University of Illinois at Urbana-Champaign,
9. Mühlenbein H. & Schlierkamp-Voosen D.(1993). Predictive Models for the Breeder Genetic Algorithm. I. Continuous Parameter Optimisation. *Evolutionary Computation 1(1):25-49,* MIT Press.
10. Rudnick M. (1992). *Genetic Algorithms and Fitness Variance with an Application to the Automated Design of Artificial Neural Networks.* Unpublished doctoral dissertation, Oregon Graduate Institute of Science and Technology, Beaverton.
11. Thierens D., & Goldberg D.E. (1993). Mixing in Genetic Algorithms. *Proceedings of the Fifth International Conference on Genetic Algorithms ICGA-93.* ed. S. Forrest. pp.38-45. Morgan Kaufmann.
12. Thierens D., & Goldberg D.E. (1994). Convergence Models of Genetic Algorithm Selection Schemes. *Lecture Notes in Computer Science, Vol. 866: Parallel Problem Solving from Nature PPSN-III.* Jerusalem (Il). eds. Y. Davidor, H.P. Schwefel, R. Männer. pp.119-129. Springer-Verlag.
13. Thierens D. (1995). *Analysis and Design of Genetic Algorithms.* PhD thesis, Dept. Electrical Engineering, Kath. Univ. Leuven, Belgium.
14. Vose M., & Liepins G. (1991). Punctuated Equilibria in Genetic Search. *Complex Systems 5:31-44*
15. Whitley D. (1993). An Executable Model of a Simple Genetic Algorithm. *Foundations of Genetic Algorithms II.* Morgan Kaufmann.

Gaussian Diffusion in a Simple Genetic Algorithm

Stefan Voget

Universität Hildesheim, Institut für Mathematik,
Samelsonplatz 1, D-31141 Hildesheim, Germany
e-mail: voget@informatik.uni-hildesheim.de

Abstract. We present a central limit theorem for the population process of a simple genetic algorithm. This theory approximates the discrete population process with finite population size by a continuous Gaussian - process. As a special application we consider a search space with only two elements. For this case we present a complete solution of the differential equation arising in the calculation of the Gaussian - process. This analysis gives first insight into the theory of the general case. Some applications of the theory and extensions to the general case are mentioned, too.

1 Introduction

Genetic algorithms (GA) adapt principles of natural evolution to combinatorial optimization problems. In 1975 Holland [6] introduced the concept. Since that time they have been applied to a lot of problems [2] [5]. A GA works by iterative application of operations like selection, crossover, and mutation. The aim is to propagate a population of possible solutions such that an optimal or at least very good solution can grow in an evolutionary process.
Though the algorithm is quite successful in applications, the mathematical theory of the operators selection, mutation, and crossover still seems to be incomplete. In this paper we shall study an approximation method from the theory of quantitative population genetics of biomathematics.
We present a complete mathematical model for the GA in section 2. Often such exact stochastic models are approximated by deterministic models with infinite population size (cp. [12], [16], and [17]). Other authors (for example Kargupta [7]) use a diffusion approximation originally introduced by Kimura [8] in biomathematics. We adapt another approximation approach which was originally introduced by Norman in [13] and applied in [14] and by Nagylaki in [11]. In section 3 we present a central limit theorem when population size tends to infinity. With the help of this theory the discrete population process of the GA with finite population size can be replaced by a continuous Gaussian - process. Such processes are widely examined. We introduced the limit theorem in our dissertation [16] and in another paper [18] before. In section 4 we consider the special case when the search space consists of two elements in detail. This situation helps to get more insight into the general case. Crossover is of no interest when there are only two individuals. Therefore we use a GA with selection and mutation. A complete theory incorporating crossover is contents of [18].

2 The Algorithm

Let $K \in \mathbb{N}$ and Ξ_k $(k = 1, ..., K)$ be finite sets. With a search space $\Xi = \prod_{k=1}^{K} \Xi_k$ and an optimization function $f : \Xi \to \mathbb{R}$ an optimization task is given with $\arg\max_{i \in \Xi} f(i)$. With N we denote the population size of the GA. A population of size N is defined by a vector $x^{(N)} = \left(x_i^{(N)}\right)_{i \in \Xi}$ with the properties

$$x_i^{(N)} \in \left\{0, \frac{1}{N}, ..., \frac{N-1}{N}, 1\right\}, \quad \sum_{i \in \Xi} x_i^{(N)} = 1.$$

The set of all populations of size N is denoted by $P^{(N)} := \{x^{(N)} | \, x^{(N)}$ population $\}$. Further we introduce populations of size infinity. A population with infinite population size is defined by a vector $x = (x_i)_{i \in \Xi}$ with the properties $x_i \in [0,1]$, $\sum_{i \in \Xi} x_i = 1$. The set of all populations of infinite size is denoted by $P := \{x | \; x$ population $\}$. Notice that $P^{(N)} \subset P$ for all $N \in \mathbb{N}$. Members of a population are called individuals. The coordinate of the population vector with the index i denotes the relative proportion of the individual i in the population x.

A genetic algorithm is given by iterative application of the following steps:

Step 1 (Selection) : Given a population $x(n)$ in a generation with number $n \in \mathbb{N}$ members of the population are selected independently. Individuals with higher fitness are preferred in the evolution process. But individuals with low fitness get a little chance for selection, too. The distribution of a randomly choosen individual $I^S(n)$ after selection is given by

$$\forall i \in \Xi : \; P(I^S(n) = i | \; X(n) = x(n) \,) := \frac{\sigma(f(i)) * x_i(n)}{\sum_{j \in \Xi} \sigma(f(j)) * x_j(n)},$$

with a selection function $\sigma : \mathbb{R} \to \mathbb{R}^+$. The selection function is of use for a scaling of the fitness function. This kind of selection is usually denoted by proportional selection. This one and other kinds of selection can be found for example in [1], [3], [4], [9], and [10].

Step 2 (Mutation) : The coordinates of an individual j are altered independently with a small probability μ. With i_k we denote the k'th coordinate of the individual i. If mutation occurs in the k'th coordinate the value of the coordinate is changed to one of the $|\Xi_k| - 1$ remaining values. Each one of the values is taken with equal probability. Further we make use of a scaling factor $\epsilon \in [0,1]$. The meaning of ϵ will be explained in the next section. The distribution of a randomly mutated individual $I^M(n)$ is given by

$$P(I^M(n) = i | \; I^S(n) = j) = \epsilon * \prod_{k=1}^{K} (1-\mu)^{\mathbf{1}_{\{i_k = j_k\}}} * \left(\frac{\mu}{|\Xi_k| - 1}\right)^{\mathbf{1}_{\{i_k \neq j_k\}}} =: \epsilon * \mu_{j \to i}$$

If i_k is not equal to j_k mutation has to occur in the k'th coordinate and has to produce the value i_k. Otherwise the coordiante must not be changed.

Step 3 (Production of the next generation) : The next generation is produced by reiteration of the first two steps. Produce N new individuals with selection and mutation. These individuals form the next generation. The new population is given by a polynomial distributed random vector, i.e. with the abbreviation $p_M(n,i) := P(I^M(n) = i|\ X(n) = x(n)\ )$ the distribution of the next population is given by

$$P\left(X(n+1) = x(n+1) \middle|\ X(n) = x(n)\right) = \frac{N!}{\prod_{i\in\Xi}(N*x_i(n+1))!} * \prod_{i\in\Xi} p_M^{N*x_i(n+1)}(n,i).$$

3 A Central Limit Theorem

The model of the last section gives an exact description of a simple GA with selection and mutation. In this section we present an approximation model in which population size converges to infinity. Simultaneously the parameters selection pressure and probability of mutation converge to zero. With this we are able to control the population process such that a central limit theorem can be given. Let $(\epsilon_N)_{N\in\mathbb{N}}$ be a sequence of real values fulfilling

$$\epsilon_N > 0,\ \epsilon_N \longrightarrow 0 \text{ and } N*\epsilon_N \longrightarrow \infty \tag{1}$$

for $N \to \infty$. In dependence of ϵ_N the selection function is restricted to $\sigma(f(i)) := 1 + \epsilon_N * f(i)$ for all $i \in \Xi$. This special choice of σ leads to another condition for the choice of ϵ_N. Because of the condition $\sigma \geq 0$ one has to choose ϵ_N such that

$$\forall i \in \Xi \text{ with } f(i) < 0\ :\ \epsilon_N \leq -\frac{1}{f(i)}. \tag{2}$$

The probability of mutation from an individual j to an individual i is restricted to $p_{j\to i} := P(I^M(n) = i|\ I^S(n) = j) := \begin{cases} \epsilon_N * \mu_{j\to i} & i \neq j \\ 1 - \epsilon_N * \sum_{k\in\Xi,k\neq i}\mu_{i\to k} & i = j \end{cases}$. The condition $P(I^M = i|\ I^S = j) \in [0,1]$ leads to another condition for the choice of ϵ_N. One has to choose ϵ_N such that

$$\forall i,j \in \Xi :\ \epsilon_N \leq \frac{1}{\mu_{j\to i}}, \tag{3}$$

where we set $\mu_{j\to j} := \sum_{k\in\Xi,k\neq i}\mu_{i\to k}$. For the presentation of the main result we need two further functions. They describe changes of the expectation and the covariance of a population after one step of the genetic algorithm in the limit $N \to \infty$ (cp. [16],[18].)

Definition 1. Define the function $m : \begin{cases} P \longrightarrow \mathbb{R}^{\Xi} \\ x \mapsto (m_i(x))_{i\in\Xi} \end{cases}$ by

$$m_i(x) := x_i * \left(f(i) - \sum_{j\in\Xi} f(j) * x_j \right) + \sum_{j\in\Xi} \mu_{j\to i} * x_j - x_i$$

Let the function

$v : \begin{cases} P \longrightarrow \mathbb{R}^{\Xi\times\Xi} \\ x \mapsto (v_{i,j}(x))_{i,j\in\Xi} \end{cases}$ be defined by $v_{i,j}(x) := x_i * (\delta_{ij} - x_j)$,

where δ_{ij} stands for the Kronecker - deltafunction, i.e. $\delta_{ij} = \begin{cases} 1 & i = j \\ 0 & \text{else} \end{cases}$.

Now we are able to formulate the main theorem.

Theorem 2. *Let $x(0) \in P$ a population and $z : \mathbb{R}^+ \to \mathrm{P}$ the unique solution of the differential equation system*

$$\frac{d\,z}{dt}(t) = m(z(t)\,) \tag{4}$$

with the condition $z(0) = x(0)$. Let a matrix $K(x)$ with $x \in P$ be given by $K_{i,j}(x) := \frac{\partial m_i}{\partial x_j}(x)$. Let $(\epsilon_N)_{N\in\mathbb{N}}$ be a sequence fulfilling (1), (2), and (3). With $n \in \mathbb{N}$ and $t := \epsilon_N * n$ the following probability vector

$$Z^{(N)}(n) := \sqrt{N * \epsilon_N} * \left[X^{(N)}(n) - z(t)\right].$$

is for $N \to \infty$ asymptotically equal distributed like a sequence of multivariate normal distributed random vectors with mean vector **0** *and covariance matrix*

$$\Sigma(t) := \int_0^t \left\{ \exp\left[\int_{t'}^t K(z(t''))dt''\right]\right\} * v(z(t')) * \left\{ \exp\left[\int_{t'}^t K(z(t''))dt''\right]\right\}^T dt'.$$

Proof. The proof is given in [16] and in [18]

Remark : In the applications of theorem 2 the stochastic process $(X^{(N)}(n)\,)_{n\in\mathbb{N}}$ of populations will be substituted by a continuous Gaussian - process with mean function $z(t)$ and covariance function $\frac{1}{t} * \Sigma(t)$. The main difficulty in the application of theorem 2 lies in the calculation of $z(t)$. The calculation needs a solution of a differential equation system. In the next section we present the complete solution of (4) in a search space with two individuals. Because of the condition $\sum_{i\in\Xi} x_i(0) = 1$ the differential equation system reduces in that case to an ordinary differential equation.

4 Search Space of Dimension $|\Xi| = 2$

Let $\Xi := \{i_1, i_2\}$ be a search space with two elements. The signification of this application for real size examples is given in the following two interpretations. First one may divide the search space into two classes of individuals. These are the 'good' ones and the 'bad' ones. The 'good' ones may be for example the ones with a fitness value above a border. This kind of classification is known from the theory of Simulated Annealing [15].
For a second interpretation one may sign one individual out of the population. This individual is compared with the 'rest of the world'. Will his heritage stay alife over several generations? Will the individual die because of a low fitness value? The 'rest of the world' may be represented by an expected fitness of the other individuals. If the fitness value of the signed individual is higher than the expected fitness, this individual will stay alife otherwise it will fall into the group which dies out after a few steps.
Because of the condition $x_{i_1}(0) + x_{i_2}(0) = 1$ it suffices to calculate an approximation for $X_{i_1}^{(N)}(n)$. For the model of this section we get with $x \in P$

$$m_{i_1}(x) = \mu_{i_2 \to i_1} - x_{i_1} * (\mu_{i_2 \to i_1} + \mu_{i_1 \to i_2}) + x_{i_1} * (1 - x_{i_1}) * (f(i_1) - f(i_2))$$

$$\text{and } v_{i_1 i_1}(x) = x_{i_1} * (1 - x_{i_1}). \qquad \text{Further} \quad \frac{d\, z_{i_1}(t)}{d\, t} = m_{i_1}(z(t)) \tag{5}$$

with the condition $z(0) = x(0)$. A differential equation of the form (5) is known under the name of Riccati - differential equation. If one has calculated z, the variance function is given by

$$\Sigma_{i_1 i_1}(t) = \int_0^t \exp\left(2 \int_u^t \frac{\partial m_{i_1}(z)}{\partial z}(\xi) d\xi\right) * v_{i_1 i_1}(z(u)) du.$$

The solution of (5) is separated into two cases. First we calculate the easy one.

4.1 The Case Without Selection - Pressure : $f(i_1) = f(i_2)$

If $f(i_1) = f(i_2)$ no individual is preferred in the selection step, i.e. no selection - pressure occurs. This is a case with mutation only.

$$\frac{d\, z_{i_1}}{dt}(t) = m_{i_1}(z(t)) = \mu_{i_2 \to i_1} - z_{i_1}(t) * (\mu_{i_2 \to i_1} + \mu_{i_1 \to i_2})$$

It is a linear differential equation with the solution (cp. [18])

$$z_{i_1}(t) = \left(x_{i_1}(0) - \frac{\mu_{i_2 \to i_1}}{\mu_{i_2 \to i_1} + \mu_{i_1 \to i_2}}\right) * \exp\left[-(\mu_{i_2 \to i_1} + \mu_{i_1 \to i_2}) * t\right] + \frac{\mu_{i_2 \to i_1}}{\mu_{i_2 \to i_1} + \mu_{i_1 \to i_2}}$$

Because of $t = \varepsilon_N * n$ we get the approximation

$$E\left(X_{i_1}^{(N)}(n)|\ X^{(N)}(0)=x(0)\right)\approx\left(x_{i_1}(0)-\frac{p_{i_2\to i_1}}{p_{i_2\to i_1}+p_{i_1\to i_2}}\right)$$
$$*\exp\left[-(p_{i_2\to i_1}+p_{i_1\to i_2})*n\right]+\frac{p_{i_2\to i_1}}{p_{i_2\to i_1}+p_{i_1\to i_2}}$$

for the population process. With the number of steps the influence of the start population $x(0)$ decreases exponentially. The ratio of production and destruction of the individual i_1 gets more and more important. The solution of the covariance function Σ is too long to present it here. It is given in detail in the dissertation [16].

4.2 The Case With Selection - Pressure : $f(i_1) \neq f(i_2)$

Define the abbreviations $a := \mu_{i_2\to i_1}$, $b := f(i_1) - f(i_2) - \mu_{i_2\to i_1} - \mu_{i_1\to i_2}$, and $c := f(i_2) - f(i_1)$. The differential equation (5) reduces to

$$\frac{d\,z_{i_1}}{d\,t}(t) = a + b * z_{i_1}(t) + c * z_{i_1}(t)^2. \qquad (6)$$

Lemma 3. *Special solutions of (6) are the constant solutions*

$$z_{i_1}(t) = -\frac{b}{2*c} \genfrac{}{}{0pt}{}{+}{-} \sqrt{\frac{b^2}{4*c^2}-\frac{a}{c}}$$

Proof. First we have to show the existence of the roots. But

$$\frac{b^2}{2*c^2}-\frac{a}{c}\geq 0 \Leftrightarrow (f(i_1)-f(i_2)+\mu_{i_2\to i_1}-\mu_{i_1\to i_2})^2+4*\mu_{i_2\to i_1}*\mu_{i_1\to i_2}\geq 0$$

Because all parameters are positiv the last inequality is true. It is easy to see, that the constant solutions fulfill $\frac{d\,z_{i_1}}{d\,t}(t) = 0$. Therefore both solutions remain unchanged for all $t \in \mathbb{R}$ and fulfill equation (6).

Consider the quadratic function $g(x) = a + b * x + c * x^2$. We are interested in a solution of (6) with $z_{i_1}(t) \in [0,1]$ for all $t \in \mathbb{R}^+$. With the conditions on the boundaries $g(0) = a = \mu_{i_2\to i_1} \geq 0$, $g(1) = a + b + c = -\mu_{i_1\to i_2}$ and the observation that the graph of g is an upwards (downwards) open parabola for $c > 0$ ($c < 0$) we get, if $f(i_1) > f(i_2)$ than the higher of the two solutions lies in $[0,1]$ else the lower one (cp. figure 1). The other solution lies out of the interval or on the boundary. For the common solution of (5) we try

$$z_{i_1}(t) = -\frac{b}{2*c}+\sqrt{\frac{b^2}{4*c^2}-\frac{a}{c}}+w(t).$$

Replacing this onset for z in (5) leads to the differential equation

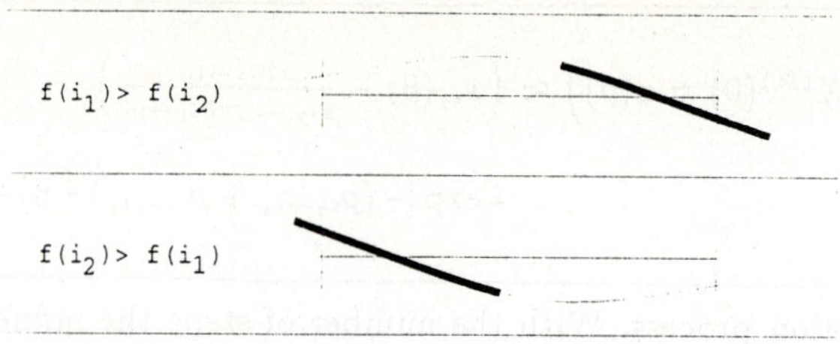

Fig. 1. Quality of solutions of (5) under different selection pressures

$$\frac{dw}{dt}(t) = h * w(t) + c * w^2(t) \tag{7}$$

with the abbreviation $h := 2*c*\sqrt{\frac{b^2}{4*c^2} - \frac{a}{c}}$. Here the further calculation ramifies into two subcases again.

The Case $h \neq 0$ **:** For $h \neq 0$ the differential equation (7) leads to the solution

$$\boxed{z_{i_1}(t) = -\frac{b}{2*c} + \sqrt{\frac{b^2}{4*c^2} - \frac{a}{c}} + \frac{1}{C_1 * e^{-h*t} - \frac{c}{h}}.}$$

Replacing t by $n * \epsilon_N$ one gets that z depends only on the parameters n, $\sigma(i_1)$, $\sigma(i_2)$, $p_{i_1 \to i_2}$, and $p_{i_2 \to i_1}$. The value of ϵ_N does not appear explicitly. For the calculation of the constant C_1 we use the condition $z(0) = x(0)$.

$$C_1 = \frac{1}{x_{i_1}(0) + \frac{b}{2*c} - \sqrt{\frac{b^2}{4*c^2} - \frac{a}{c}}} + \frac{c}{h} = \frac{1}{x_{i_1}(0) + \frac{b}{2*c} - \sqrt{\frac{b^2}{4*c^2} - \frac{a}{c}}} + \frac{1}{2 * \sqrt{\frac{b^2}{4*c^2} - \frac{a}{c}}}$$

Again the influence of the start population $x(0)$ decreases exponentially. For $t \to \infty$ we get the following limit

$$\lim_{t\to\infty} z_{i_1}(t) = \frac{1}{2} + \frac{\mu_{i_1\to i_2} + \mu_{i_2\to i_1}}{2 * (f(i_2) - f(i_1))} \pm \sqrt{\frac{(f(i_1) - f(i_2) + \mu_{i_2\to i_1} - \mu_{i_1\to i_2})^2 + 4 * \mu_{i_1\to i_2} * \mu_{i_2\to i_1}}{4 * (f(i_2) - f(i_1))^2}}$$

The "+" occurs if $f(i_1) > f(i_2)$ and the "-" occurs otherwise. The limit of $z_{i_1}(t)$ for $t \to \infty$ is the constant solution of lemma 3.

The Case $h = 0$ **:** Because we are in the case $c \neq 0$ the root has to be equal to zero $\sqrt{\frac{b^2}{4*c^2} - \frac{a}{c}} = 0$.

$$\Leftrightarrow \left(f(i_1) - f(i_2) - \mu_{i_1\to i_2} + \mu_{i_2\to i_1}\right)^2 + 4 * \mu_{i_1\to i_2} * \mu_{i_2\to i_1} = 0$$

$$\Leftrightarrow \begin{array}{c} (\ \mu_{i_1\to i_2} = 0 \wedge \mu_{i_2\to i_1} = f(i_2) - f(i_1)\ ) \\ \vee\ (\ \mu_{i_2\to i_1} = 0 \wedge \mu_{i_1\to i_2} = f(i_1) - f(i_2)\ ) \end{array}$$

In the first case we have no destruction of the individual i_1 by mutation ($\mu_{i_1 \to i_2} = 0$). The construction of i_1 by mutation is equal to his disadvantage in his fitness ($\mu_{i_2 \to i_1} = f(i_2) - f(i_1)$). In the second case the situation is reverse. We calculate

$$\boxed{z_{i_1}(t) = -\frac{b}{2*c} + \frac{1}{C_2 - c*t}}$$

with the constant $C_2 = \frac{1}{x_{i_1}(0) + \frac{b}{2*c}}$. For $t \to \infty$ we get the limit

$$\lim_{t \to \infty} z_{i_1}(t) = \frac{1}{2} + \frac{\mu_{i_1 \to i_2} + \mu_{i_2 \to i_1}}{2 * (f(i_2) - f(i_1))}$$

Again the limit of $z(t)$ for $t \to \infty$ is the constant solution of lemma 3.

4.3 Two Selected Applications of the Theory

In this subsection we present two applications of z given in subsection 4.2. If we take especially $\mu_{i_1 \to i_2} := \mu_{i_2 \to i_1} := 0$ and notice that $t = \epsilon_N * n$ and $\sigma(i_k) = 1 + \epsilon_N * f(i_k)$ for $k = 1, 2$ we get the approximation

$$E(X_{i_1}^{(N)}(n) |\, X^{(N)}(0) = x(0)\,)$$
$$\approx z_{i_1}(\epsilon_N * n) = \frac{1}{1 + \exp[-(\sigma(i_1) - \sigma(i_2)) * n] * \left(\frac{1}{x_{i_1}(0)} - 1\right)}.$$

For the experiments given in figure 2 we choose the constants $N = 1000$, $\sigma(i_1) = 1.1$, $\sigma(i_2) = 0.9$, and $x_{i_1}(0) = \frac{1}{2}$. The graphic shows the densities of $N * X_{i_1}^{(N)}(n)$ for $n = 2, 5, 7$ and 10 in constrast to simulated frequencies. The points of the simulated values are based on means of 10000 repetitions.

After two steps the frequency of the individual i_1 is grown up to 598 copies. In the following steps the expectation further increases. The variance increases first and decreases after a few further steps.

For another application consider the figure 3. It shows z_{i_1} in dependence of $mut := \mu_{i_1 \to i_2}$ and $fit := f(i_1)$. We choose especially $t = 10$, $x_{i_1}(0) := 0.1$, $f(i_2) := -f(i_1)$, and $\mu_{i_2 \to i_1} := \mu_{i_1 \to i_2}$. The value of z_{i_1} approximates the relative number of copies of the individual i_1. For small values of mut the individual i_1 dominates ($fit > 0$) the population or dies out ($fit < 0$) after a few steps. For higher values of mut destruction and production of i_1 are in balance. Disturbances of fit and mut are of no effect when mut takes a high value.

5 Summary

The central limit theorem introduced in section 3 denotes an approximation method for the population process of GA's. It approximates the process of finite population sizes by a continuous Gaussian - process. Such processes are well

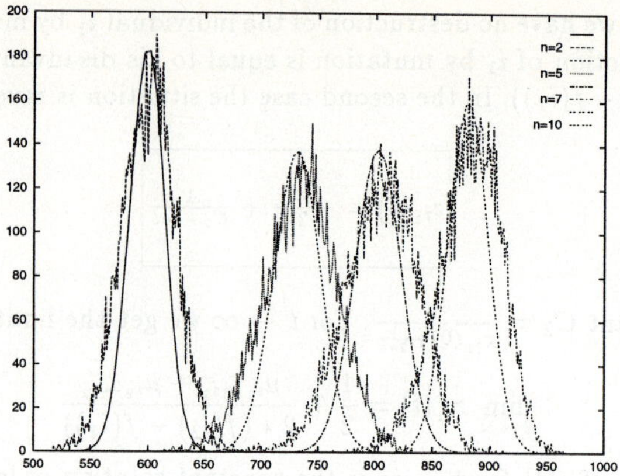

Fig. 2. Densities of $1000 * X^{(1000)}(n)$ for $n = 2, 5, 7$ and 10 (from left to right)

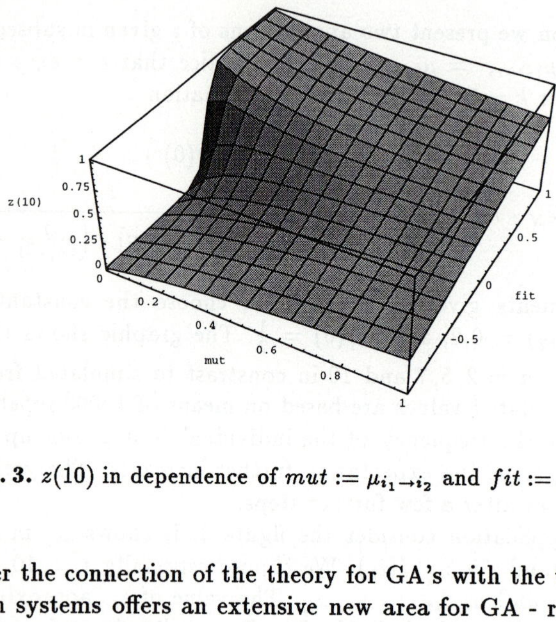

Fig. 3. $z(10)$ in dependence of $mut := \mu_{i_1 \to i_2}$ and $fit := f(i_1)$

known. Further the connection of the theory for GA's with the theory of differential equation systems offers an extensive new area for GA - researchers. The special case presented in section 4 can give only a first insight into the application of theorem 2. It shows in detail the convergence and the rate of convergence of the population process. Especially figure 2 shows how exactly the approximation models the real experiment. Because of limited space we refer to [16] and [18] for further applications including crossover.

6 Acknowledgement

The author would like to acknowledge the referees for their helpful comments.

References

1. Ankenbrandt. An extension to the theory of convergence and a proof of the time complexity of genetic algorithms. In Rawlins, editor, *Foundations of Genetic Algorithms*, pages 53–68. Morgan Kaufmann Publishers, 1991.
2. L. Davis. *Handbook of Genetic Algorithms*. Van Nostrand Rheinold, New York, 1990.
3. D.E. Goldberg. A note on boltzmann tournament selection for genetic algorithms and population-oriented simulated annealing. *Complex Systems*, 4:445–460, 1990.
4. D.E. Goldberg and K. Deb. A comparative analysis of selection schemes used in genetic algorithms. In G.J.E. Rawlins, editor, *Foundations of Genetic Algorithms*. Morgan Kaufmann Publishers, 1991.
5. D.E. Goldberg and P. Segrest. Finite markov chain analysis of genetic algorithms. *Proc. on Conf. Genetic Algorithms*, 2:1–8, 1987.
6. J.H. Holland. *Adaptation in Natural and Artificial Systems*. University of Michigan Press, 1975.
7. H. Kargupta. Drift, diffusion and boltzman distribution in simple genetic algorithm. preprint, 1994.
8. M. Kimura. Diffusion models in population genetics. *J. Appl. Prob*, 1:177–232, 1964.
9. S.W. Mahfoud. An analysis of boltzmann tournament selection. Report 91007, Illinois Genetic Algorithms Laboratory, March 1994.
10. M.de Maza and B. Tidor. An analysis of selection procedures with particular attention paid to proportional and boltzmann selection. In *International Conference on Genetic Algorithms*, pages 124–131, 1993.
11. T. Nagylaki. The gaussian approximation for random genetic drift. In S. Karlin and E. Nevo, editors, *Evolutionary Processes and Theory*, pages 629–644. Academic Press, 1986.
12. A.E. Nix and M.D. Vose. Modeling genetic algorithms with markov chains. *Annals of Mathematics and Artificial Intelligence*, 5:79–88, 1992.
13. M.F. Norman. A central limit theorem for markov processes that move by small steps. *The Annals of Prob.*, 2(6):1065–1074, 1974.
14. M.F. Norman. Approximation of stochastic processes by gaussian diffusions, and applications to wright - fisher genetic models. *SIAN J. Appl. Math.*, 29(2):225–242, 1975.
15. M.T. Tran. *Simulated-Annealing: Konstruktion und Analyse einer Auswahl stochastischer Optimierungsverfahren mithilfe inhomogener Markoff-Ketten*. PhD thesis, Universitaet Hildesheim, 1995. Cuvillier Verlag, Goettingen.
16. S. Voget. *Aspekte genetischer Optimierungsalgorithmen: mathematische Modellierung und Einsatz in der Fahrplanerstellung*. PhD thesis, Universitaet Hildesheim, 1995.
17. S. Voget. Theoretical analysis of genetic algorithms with infinite population size. *Hildesheimer Informatik Berichte*, 31/95:1–19, 1995.
18. S. Voget. A central limit theorem for the population process of genetic algorithms. *Complex Systems*, 1996. accepted for publication.

Erroneous Truncation Selection – A Breeder's Decision Making Perspective

Hans-Michael Voigt[1]* and Heinz Mühlenbein[2]

[1] GFaI, Rudower Chaussee 5, 12484 Berlin, Germany,
[2] GMD – Forschungszentrum Informationstechnik, 53754 Sankt Augustin, Germany

Abstract. Based on experiences from livestock breeding we introduce erroneous truncation selection for the Breeder Genetic Algorithm (BGA). The decision behavior of the breeder is given by a simple model. It is shown that there is no benefit to the BGA by using erroneous selection though the variance of the parent population is increased by increasing the decision error variance.

1 Introduction

Selection is one of the most fundamental operators in Evolutionary Algorithms, i.e. it is inherent to Genetic Algorithms, Evolution Strategies, Evolutionary Programming, and Genetic Programming. Generally, for all these algorithms a directed selection scheme is used which favors individuals having smaller – for minimization – or larger – for maximization – fitness values. With respect to Evolutionary Algorithms we will use the notion of fitness, trait, and character synonymously to characterize one measurable variable or function. Corresponding to the great variety of algorithms we also have a great variety of selection operators. This ranges from proportionate selection [5], tournament selection [6, 2], (μ, λ)–selection [12, 13, 1], Boltzmann selection [9], linear and exponential ranking selection [4, 17] to truncation selection [10, 3, 8].

Perhaps the most widespread used selection schemes in modern Evolutionary Algorithms are tournament selection and truncation or (μ, λ) selection.

With this paper we consider selection from a breeder's perspective. The ultimate selection scheme in livestock breeding is truncation selection. *The outward results of selection to a population* [8] is given by the *response to selection*

$$R(t) = \overline{f(t+1)} - \overline{f(t)}. \tag{1}$$

The amount of selection is measured by the selection differential

$$S(t) = \overline{f_s(t)} - \overline{f(t)}, \tag{2}$$

where $\overline{f_s(t)}$ is the average fitness of the selected parents. The equation for the response to selection relates R and S by

$$R(t) = b(t) \cdot S(t). \tag{3}$$

* HMV is also with the Technical University of Berlin

$b(t)$ is called the *realized heritability*. For many fitness functions and selection schemes the selection differential can be expressed as a function of the phenotypic standard deviation σ. For truncation selection (selecting the $T \cdot N$ best individuals) one obtains

$$S(t)/\sigma(t) = I. \tag{4}$$

I is called the *selection intensity*. With these notions the famous equation for the response to selection is obtained [3]:

$$R(t) = I \cdot b(t) \cdot \sigma(t). \tag{5}$$

Usually the response to selection equation is considered for a population having a normal fitness distribution. But it holds also for other unimodal fitness distributions [14, 16]. It should be noted that the response to selection equation does not explain *how selection changes the genetic composition of a population* [8].

Truncation selection in real breeding is hard to realize because of the precise truncation threshold which implies a perfect measurement of the trait under consideration. Therefore, breeders are well aware of possible errors in selection: *The kind of selection pictured in Fig. 1 (left) corresponds to that actually practiced for important traits in stock breeding where many different traits must be considered.* **Some animals which are mediocre or even inferior in the characteristic pictured are saved** *because they are unusually desirable in several other characteristics or* **because the breeder is careless or confused** [8].

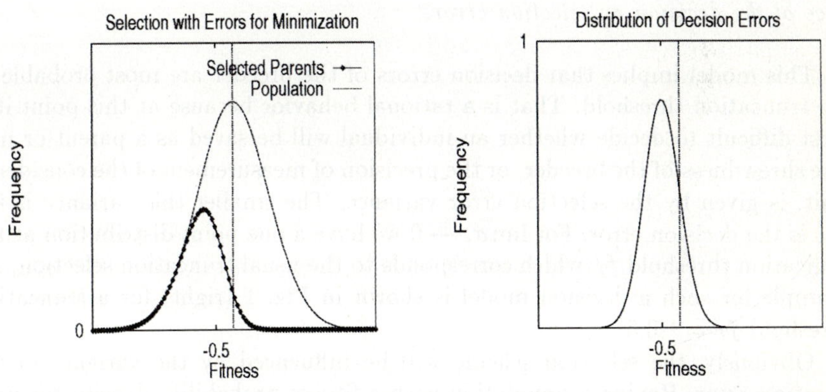

Fig. 1. Parent population selected from a population with erroneous truncation selection (left) and distribution of decision errors made by a breeder around the truncation threshold $f_T = -0.5$ (right)

In this paper we consider only one trait which is measured, and therefore selected with errors. The case of considering more then one trait is closely connected with multiobjective and/or subjective decision problems and will be analyzed in a forthcoming paper. A usual way breeders cope with such problems is the application of selection indices. Furthermore, we assume that selection is done without replacement.

The questions to be raised are: How does selection errors influence the behavior of an Evolutionary Algorithm? How can the decision behavior of a breeder be modeled? Is the response to selection equation sufficient for predicting the convergence of an Evolutionary Algorithm?

To give some first answers to these questions we proceed in the following way: Based on a very simple but comprehensive model for erroneous breeder decisions we present a general method for computing the selection intensity and the standard deviation of a parent population with respect to decision errors. This will be compared for selected fitness functions with empirical observations from simulation. Based on these results first conclusions concerning decision errors in truncation selection are presented.

2 Truncation Selection with Errors

The analysis of truncation selection with errors has to be based on a decision model for the breeder. As a first attempt we use the following model:

Definition 1 (Breeder decision model). *The decision behavior of a breeder is given by a probability density function (pdf) $p_e(f)$ with the expectation $E(f) = f_T$ and the variance $V(f) = \sigma_e^2$. f_T is the truncation threshold and σ_e^2 the variance of the decision or selection error.*

This model implies that decision errors of the breeder are most probable at the truncation threshold. That is a rational behavior because at this point it is most difficult to decide whether an individual will be saved as a parent or not. The shrewdness of the breeder, or the precision of measurement of the considered trait, is given by the selection error variance. The smaller this variance is the less is the decision error. For $\lim \sigma_e \to 0$ we have a one point distribution at the truncation threshold f_T which corresponds to the usual truncation selection. An example for such a decision model is shown in Fig. 1 (right) for a truncation threshold $f_T = -0.5$.

Obviously, the selection scheme will be influenced by the variance of the selection error. Having a population with a fitness probability density function $p(f)$ with expectation $E(f) = \overline{f}$ and variance $V(f) = \sigma^2$ we will analyze the dependency of the selection intensity $I = \overline{f}_p$ and the standard deviation of the selected parents σ_p on the decision error standard deviation σ_e.

We consider the standardized and normalized probability density function of the population fitness distribution which is given by $p(z)$ with

$$z = \frac{f - \overline{f}}{\sigma} \tag{6}$$

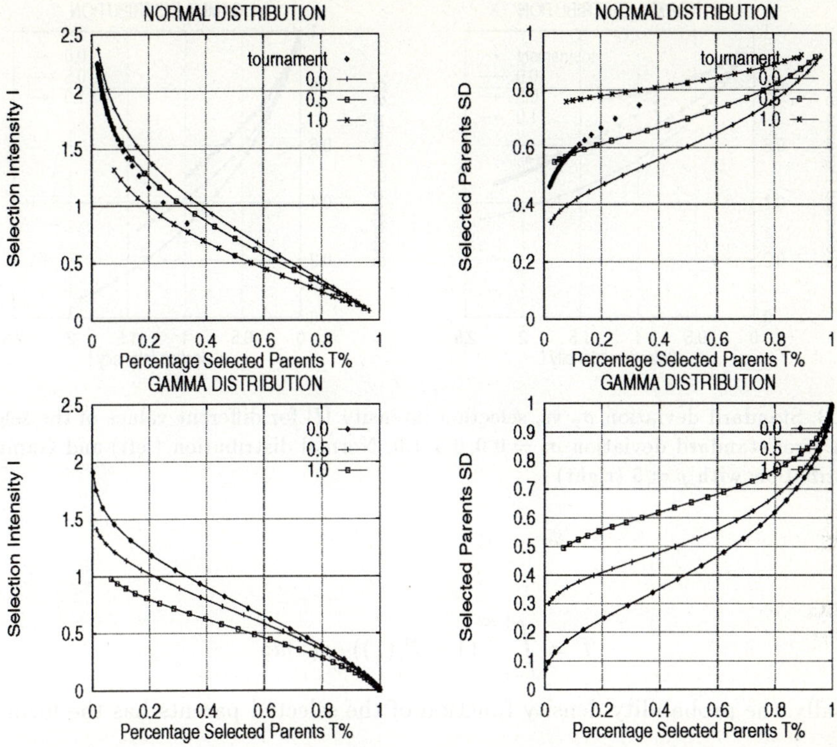

Fig. 2. Selection intensity $|I|$ (left) and standard deviation σ_p (right) of the selected parents for different values of the selection error standard deviation $\sigma_e = 0.0, 0.5, 1.0$ and different values of the proportion of selected parents T; Normal distribution (upper row) and Gamma distribution with $p = 5$ (lower row). For the normal fitness distribution there are also shown $|I|$ and σ_p for tournament selection with tournament sizes from 2 to 50 ($\diamond$) (upper row)

with $E(z) = \overline{z} = 0$ and $\sqrt{V(z)} = \sigma_z = 1$. This probability density function will be used subsequently. The decision error probability density function will be standardized in the same way, i.e. we have $p_e(z)$ with $E(z) = z_T = (f_T - \overline{f})/\sigma$ and $\sqrt{V(z)} = \sigma_e(f)/\sigma(f) = \sigma_e = k \cdot \sigma_z$. The cumulative density function (cdf) of the standardized decision error probability density function is given by

$$P_e(z) = \int_{-\infty}^{z} p_e(t)dt \tag{7}$$

such that the proportion of selected parents T with the smallest fitness values are given by

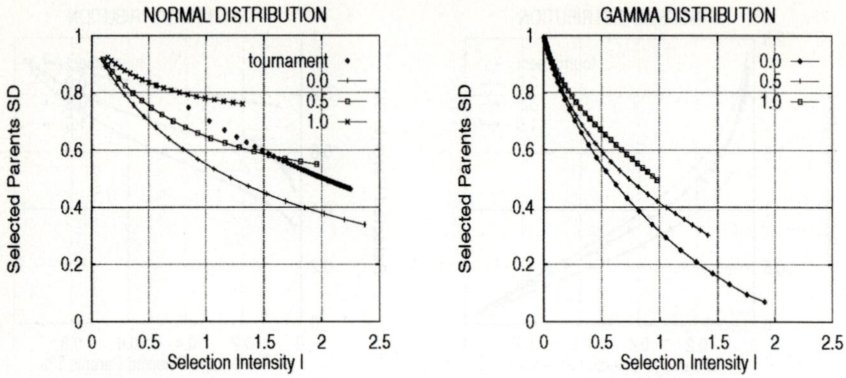

Fig. 3. Standard deviation σ_p vs. selection intensity $|I|$ for different values of the selection error standard deviation $\sigma_e = 0.0, 0.5, 1.0$, Normal distribution (left) and Gamma distribution with $p = 5$ (right)

$$T = \int_{-\infty}^{+\infty} (1 - P_e(z)) \cdot p(z) dz. \tag{8}$$

Finally, the probability density function of the selected parents has the form

$$p_p(z) = \frac{1}{T}(1 - P_e(z)) \cdot p(z). \tag{9}$$

Now we are able to compute the selection intensity I

$$E_p(z) = I = \int_{-\infty}^{+\infty} z \cdot p_p(z) dz \tag{10}$$

and the standardized fitness variance of the parents

$$V_p(z) = \sigma_p^2 = \int_{-\infty}^{+\infty} (z - I)^2 \cdot p_p(z) dz. \tag{11}$$

For a quantitative characterization of erroneous truncation selection we have to assume certain probability density functions for $p(z)$ and $p_e(z)$. A reasonable first assumption is a normal distribution for the breeder's decision errors, i.e.

$$p_e(z) = \frac{1}{\sqrt{2\pi}\sigma_e} \; \mathrm{e}^{-\frac{(z - z_T)^2}{2\sigma_e^2}}. \tag{12}$$

For the fitness distribution we assume a standardized and normalized normal distribution $p(z) = \frac{1}{\sqrt{2\pi}} \; \mathrm{e}^{-\frac{z^2}{2}}$ because up to now the quantitative analysis of selection schemes in quantitative genetics and Evolutionary algorithms is based on this assumption. Furthermore, we consider a standardized and normalized Gamma distribution $p(z) = \frac{\sqrt{p}}{\Gamma(p)}(z\sqrt{p}+p)^{p-1} \quad e^{-(z\sqrt{p}+p)}$ encountered already in the analysis of gene pool and fuzzy recombination schemes [14, 15].

For some values of the selection error standard deviation $\sigma_e = 0, 0, 0.5, 1.0$ the selection intensity I and the standard deviation σ_p of the selected parents dependent on the proportion of the selected parents T are shown in Fig. 2. The Figures in the upper row refers to a normal fitness distribution, the lower row to a Gamma distribution with $p = 5$. It it obvious that a smaller σ_e implies a larger selection intensity I and a smaller σ_p. In general, the selection intensity and the parents standard deviation for the Gamma distribution are lower then that for the normal distribution because the Gamma distribution is skewed to the right. It is interesting that I and σ_p for tournament selection can be generated by a suitable choice of σ_e. Fig. 3 depicts the dependence of σ_p on I for different values of σ_e.

The response to selection equation does not contain any information about the standard deviation σ_p of the fitness values of the selected parents. This gives rise to the question: What is the influence of σ_p on the response $R = \overline{f(t+1)} - \overline{f(t)}$? We will try to find first answers based on simulation experiments.

3 Empirical Observations

To study the effect of selection errors we consider the following optimization problem

$$\min_{x \in G} f(x) = f^* \quad \text{with} \quad G = R_+^n \tag{13}$$

with $R_+^N = \{x : x_i \geq 0, i = 1, ..., n\}$ for the following two functions

$$f_{\text{PLANE}}(x) = \sum_{i=1}^{n} x_i \quad \text{and} \quad f_{\text{SPHERE}}(x) = \sum_{i=1}^{n} x_i^2. \tag{14}$$

For both functions the optimal value is $f^* = 0$.

The simulations are done using discrete gene pool recombination (DGPR) [14, 11] with $\sigma_e = 0.0$, i.e. for pure truncation selection, and $\sigma_e = 1.0$, i.e. truncation selection with a rather high selection error. The proportion of selected parents $T = 0.2$ is chosen to be equal for all runs. DGPR was applied to avoid other stochastic influences which might be introduced using e.g. fuzzy gene pool recombination [15, 14].

Fig. 4 shows the results for the PLANE function. I and σ_p are dropping from high values at generation 1 to almost constant values after 3 ($\sigma_e = 0$) and 5 ($\sigma_e = 1$) generations, respectively. This is due to a non-stationary population fitness distribution which changes from an approximate symmetric distribution to a skewed to the right distribution. This change is shown for $\sigma_e = 1$ in Fig. 5. Therefore, in the beginning we have values for I and σ_p corresponding to that of the normal distribution from Fig. 2. These values are changing approximately to

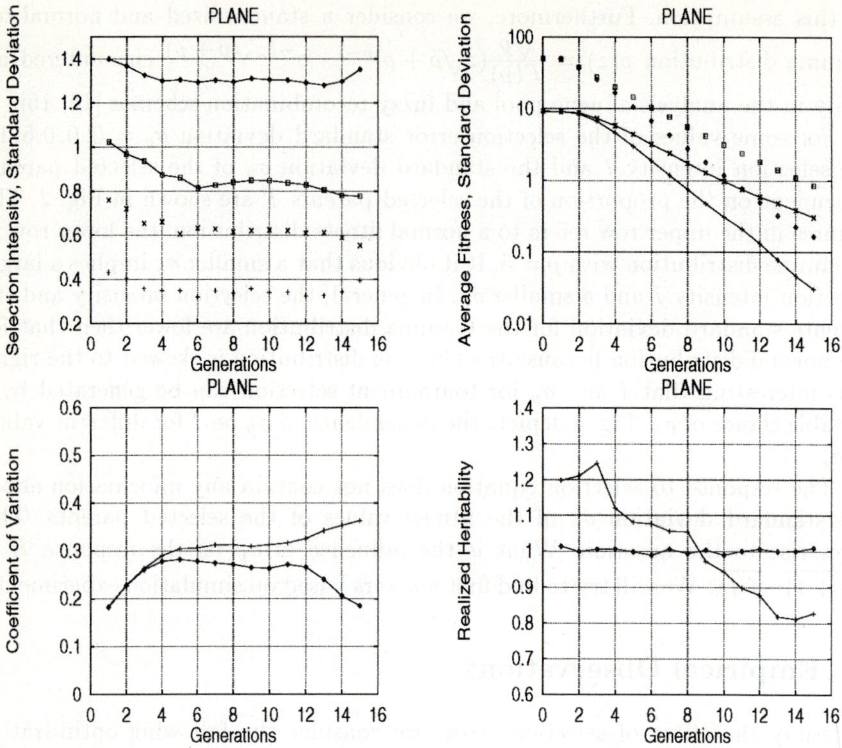

Fig. 4. **PLANE – Upper, left**: Selection intensity $|I|$ ($\sigma_e = 0$: –◇–), ($\sigma_e = 1$: –□–) and standard deviation σ_p of the selected parents ($\sigma_e = 0$: +), ($\sigma_e = 1$: ×), **upper, right**: average fitness $\overline{f}$ ($\sigma_e = 0$: ◇), ($\sigma_e = 1$: □) and standard deviation σ ($\sigma_e = 0$: –+–), ($\sigma_e = 1$: –×–) of the population, **lower, left**: coefficient of variation CV ($\sigma_e = 0$: –◇–), ($\sigma_e = 1$: –+–), **lower, right**; realized heritability b ($\sigma_e = 0$: –◇–), ($\sigma_e = 1$: –+–)

those of the Gamma distribution from Fig. 2. The deviation of the values of I and σ_p for $\sigma_e = 0$ is less then that for $\sigma_e = 1$ because the fitness distribution for the former case is less skewed then that for the latter case. This would support the idea that using a low selection error standard deviation leads to a low skewness of the fitness distribution of the population and vice versa.

To confirm this assumption we made a simulation with $T = 0.475$ and $\sigma_e = 0$. This gives approximately the same selection intensity as for the erroneous selection and a somewhat smaller $\sigma_p = 0.49$. The population fitness distribution is approximately symmetric for all considered generations. This leads to the same progress rate as for the erroneous selection though the standard deviation of the fitness of the selected parents σ_p is smaller.

The most striking property is the dramatic decline of the realized heritability

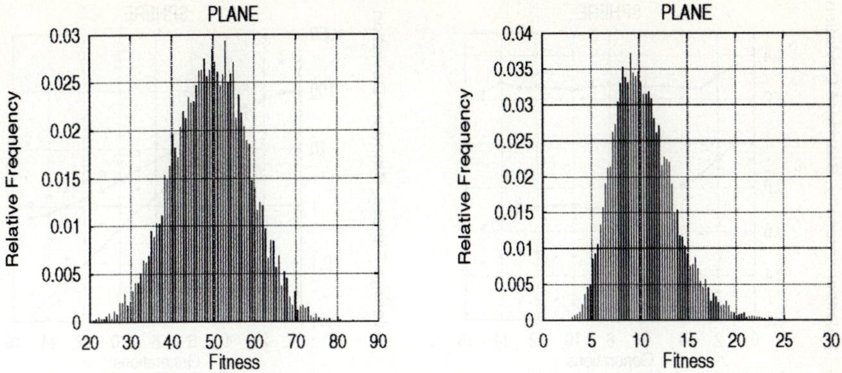

Fig. 5. **PLANE** Fitness distribution of the population at generations 1 and 6 for $\sigma_e = 1$

for erroneous selection over generations. Though we have a high fitness variability of the selected parents this will not ensure a high heritability. But this means that high fitness variability does not necessarily lead to high genetic variability.

We made much more simulations. In all cases of truncation selection with more or less severe selection errors we found a more or less rapid decline of the heritability. For pure truncation selection without errors we have an average $b = 1 =$ const. such that the lower fitness variability of the parents is compensated. Finally, the coefficient of variation $CV(t) = \sigma(t)/\overline{f(t)}$ is approximately constant and equal for both σ_e after some generations.

The results for the SPHERE function are similar to those of the PLANE function but the considered effects are stronger. They are shown in Fig. 6. The main difference is the definitely higher coefficient of variation for erroneous selection then that for pure truncation selection.

4 Conclusions

Summarizing the empirical observations leads to the conclusion that having pure and erroneous truncation selection with $I(\sigma_e = 0) = I(\sigma_e > 0)$, which means for an equal fitness distribution of the population that $\sigma_p(\sigma_e = 0) < \sigma_p(\sigma_e > 0)$, that pure truncation selection should be preferred because of its sustained higher heritability. Obviously, the selection error has a decisive influence on the skewness of the fitness distribution of the population which may contribute to the declining heritability. Since we are selecting without replacement erroneous truncation selection causes always the loss of individuals with good fitness values. The same may hold for tournament selection without replacement.

The advantage of pure truncation selection was already mentioned in [8]: Pure truncation selection *is the extreme kind of selection which might be practiced in a laboratory* (or computer) *experiment on selection for one trait alone, disregarding*

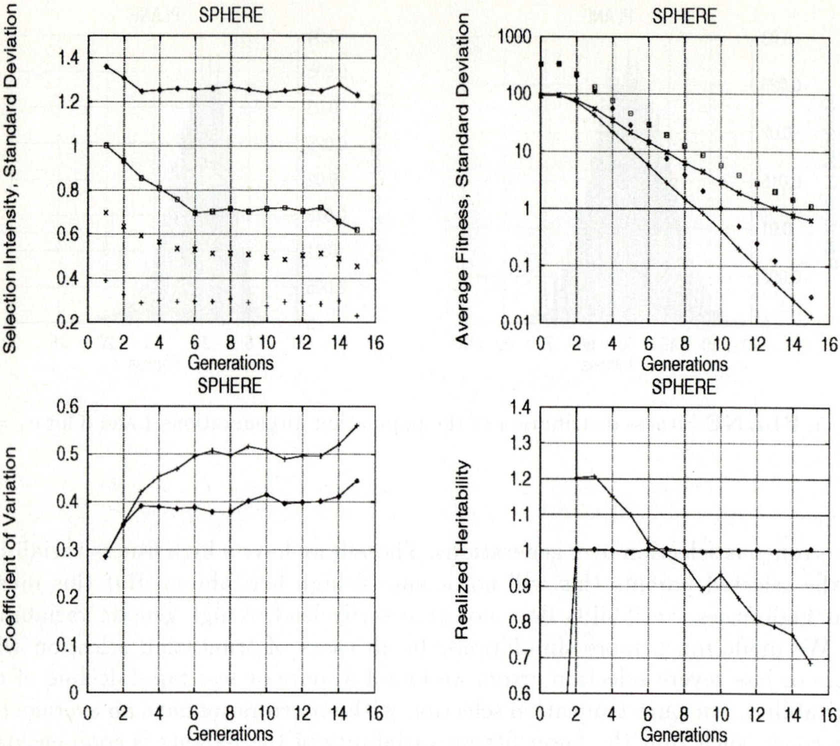

Fig. 6. **SPHERE** – **Upper, left**: Selection intensity $|I|$ ($\sigma_e = 0$: –◇–), ($\sigma_e = 1$: –□–) and standard deviation σ_p of the selected parents ($\sigma_e = 0 : +$), ($\sigma_e = 1 : \times$), **upper, right**: average fitness $\overline{f}$ ($\sigma_e = 0 : \diamond$), ($\sigma_e = 1$: □) and standard deviation σ ($\sigma_e = 0$: –+–), ($\sigma_e = 1$: –×–) of the population, **lower, left**: coefficient of variation CV ($\sigma_e = 0$: –◇–), ($\sigma_e = 1$: –+–), **lower, right**; realized heritability b ($\sigma_e = 0$: –◇–), ($\sigma_e = 1$: –+–)

all others. It *is, of course more effective if the percentage saved is the same as in* erroneous truncation selection.

From the experiments it can be seen that the best choice, at least for simple fitness functions as observed here, is the use of pure, error free truncation selection. With respect to the response to selection there is no benefit from a high parents standard deviation caused by erroneous selection as conjectured in [2]. A further analysis is necessary for erroneous truncation selection with replacement which is usually outside the scope of breeder decisions.

Finally, it should be noted that a further analysis is necessary to confirm these conclusions, e.g. for multi-modal fitness functions. But for these functions it is an open question whether the response to selection equation can be applied.

References

1. T. Bäck "Generalized Convergence Models for Tournament– and (μ, λ)–Selection". In: L. J. Eshelman (Ed.) "Proc. 6th Int. Conf. on Genetic Algorithms", 2–8, Morgan Kaufmann Publ. 1995
2. T. Blickle & L. Thiele "A Mathematical Analysis of Tournament Selection". In: L. J. Eshelman (Ed.) "Proc. 6th Int. Conf. on Genetic Algorithms", 9–16, Morgan Kaufmann Publ. 1995
3. D. S. Falconer "Introduction to Quantitative Genetics" Longman 1981
4. J. J. Grefenstette & J. E. Baker "How Genetic Algorithms work: A Critical Look at Implicit Parallelism. In: J. D. Schaffer (Ed.) "Proc. 3rd Int. Conf. on Genetic Algorithms", 20–27, Morgan Kaufmann Publ. 1989
5. D. E. Goldberg "Genetic Algorithms in Search, Optimization and Machine Learning" Addison–Wesley Publ. Comp. 1989
6. D. E. Goldberg, B. Korb & K. Deb "Messy Genetic Algorithms: Motivation, Analysis, and First Results" Complex Systems 3:493–530, 1990
7. D. E. Goldberg & K. Deb "A Comparative Analysis of Selection Schemes Used in Genetic Algorithms". In: G. J. E. Rawlins (Ed.) "Foundations of Genetic Algorithms", 69–93, Morgan Kaufmann Publ. 1991
8. J. L. Lush "Animal Breeding Plans" Iowa State University Press 1945
9. M. de la Maza & B. Tidor "An Analysis of Selection Procedures with Particular Attention Paid to Proportional and Boltzmann Selection". In: S. Forrest (Ed.) "Proc. 5th Int. Conf. on Genetic Algorithms", 124–131, Morgan Kaufmann Publ. 1993
10. H. Mühlenbein & D. Schlierkamp–Voosen "Predictive Models for the Breeder Genetic Algorithm I. Continuous Parameter Optimization". Evolutionary Computation 1:335–360, 1993
11. H. Mühlenbein & H.-M. Voigt "Gene Pool Recombination in Genetic Algorithms" In: J. P. Kelly & I. H. Osman (Eds.) "Proc. International Metaheuristic Conference", Kluwer Academic Publ. 1996
12. I. Rechenberg "Evolutionsstrategie '94" Frommann–Holzboog 1994
13. H.-P. Schwefel "Evolution and Optimum Seeking" Wiley 1995
14. H.-M. Voigt & H. Mühlenbein "Gene Pool Recombination and Utilization of Covariances for the Breeder Genetic Algorithm" In: "Proc. IEEE 2nd Int. Conf. on Evolutionary Computation", 172–177, IEEE Press 1995
15. H.-M. Voigt, H. Mühlenbein & D. Cvetcovic "Fuzzy Recombination for the Breeder Genetic Algorithm" In: L. J. Eshelman (Ed.) "Proc. 6th Int. Conf. on Genetic Algorithms",104–112, Morgan Kaufmann Publ. 1995
16. H.-M. Voigt & H. Mühlenbein "The Response to Selection Equation for Skew Fitness Distributions" To appear in: "Proc. IEEE 3rd Int. Conf. on Evolutionary Computation", IEEE Press 1996
17. L. D. Whitley "The GENITOR Algorithm and Selection Pressure: Why Rank–Based Allocation of Reproductive Trials is Best" In: D. E. Schaffer (Ed.) "Proc. 3rd Int. Conf. on Genetic Algorithms" 116–121, Morgan Kaufmann Publ. 1989

Modifications and Extensions of Evolutionary Algorithms

Genetic Operators and Problem Representation

Adaptation, Niching, and Isolation in Evolutionary Algorithms

Further Modifications and Extensions

Genetic Operators and Problem Representation

New Crossover Methods For Sequencing Problems

Tolga Aşveren and Paul Molitor

Institute of Computer Science
Department of Mathematics and Computer Science
Martin-Luther-Universität Halle-Wittenberg
06099 Halle(Saale), GERMANY

Abstract. In this paper we present two new crossover operators that make use of macro-order information and neighborhood information in sequencing problems. None of them needs local information, thus making them usable for a wide area of applications, e.g., optimal variable orders for binary decision diagrams, scheduling problems, seriation in archeology. The experimental results are promising. Especially they show that macro-order and neighborhood information is very important.

1 Introduction

Genetic Algorithms (GAs) are one of the stochastic search algorithms based on evolutionary and biological processes that enable organisms to adapt more to their environment over many generations. They are being successfully applied to problems in business, engineering and science [1]. GAs work on a set of possible solutions which is called the population. The most basic operations used by GAs are selection, crossover, and mutation. The selection operator identifies the individuals of the current population which will serve as parents for the next generation. Crossover randomly chooses pairs of individuals to combine properties of them by creating childs. Mutation is usually considered as a secondary operator, which makes small changes on single individuals to restore diversity of the population.

Hybrid Genetic Algorithms (HGA) uses local information during the process, i.e., information which is specific to the problem investigated in order to improve the solutions found by pure GAs. Of course, HGAs are not universal. Whenever the nature of the local information changes, a new algorithm has to be designed.

A very prominent and interesting class of combinatorial optimization problems is the class of sequencing problems. A sequencing problem is defined as follows: Given a finite set I of items and a cost function c which assigns costs to permutations of I, compute a minimum cost permutation of I. Problems as, e.g., the traveling salesman problem (TSP), the problem of computing good variable orders of Binary Decision Diagrams (BDD) which has to be solved for circuit verification and logic synthesis, scheduling problems, or seriation in archeology are representatives of this class.

In this paper, we discuss two new crossover operators for sequencing problems, namely the Neighborhood Relationship Crossover Operator (NRX) and the

Meta-Ordering Crossover Operator (MOX). Both do not use local information, i.e., they are applicable to any sequencing problem. The experimental results obtained for TSP (as representative of the class of sequencing problems) are promising. The new crossover operators outperform the operators known from literature by far in most cases. We have worked with parallel implementations of GAs using PVM 3.1 [11] in order to overcome long convergence times which are typical for GAs.

The paper is structured as follows. In Section 2 we outline the TSP problem and motivate 'blind' search methods, once again. In Section 3 the overall algorithm for sequencing problems is presented. In Section 4 the new crossover operators are introduced. We present experimental results in Section 5.

2 Traveling Salesman Problem

The most prominent member of the rich set of combinatorial optimization problems is undoubtly the traveling salesman problem (TSP). TSP is defined as follows: Given n cities, compute a minimal cost tour on which the salesman visits each city once. Obviously, TSP is a sequencing problem as defined above.

Many researchers have used TSP as test problem to measure the effectiveness of their GAs [2, 3, 4, 5, 6, 7]. The most famous technique used to improve the solutions found by GAs for TSP is an algorithm named 2-Opt. A 2-Opt move consists of eliminating two edges and reconnecting the two resulting paths in a different way to obtain a new tour. If the fitness of the modified tour is better than that of the original one, the change is kept, otherwise it is discarded. 2-Opt examines in this manner each of the $\frac{n(n-1)}{2}$ pairs of edges. If the edge lengths are known, this local information can be used by GA to compute the fitness of the new generated tour in constant time in order to determine whether the new fitness is better than the fitness of the original tour. However, this method will not be applicable to some other sequencing problems, as edge lengths (or something of this kind) are not available in any case (e.g., in optimal variable ordering in BDDs).

As we aim at efficient crossover operators applicable to any sequencing problem, we do not use local information in the following. We will only use the fact that the problem handled is a sequencing problem.

3 Algorithm

In the past few years, parallel genetic algorithms(PGAs) have been widely used. The basic motivation behind this was to reduce the processing time needed to reach an acceptable solution by hard problems. This was accomplished implementing PGAs on different parallel architectures [8, 9, 10]. In addition, it was noted that in some cases the PGAs found better solutions than comparably sized serial GAs.

We have implemented our algorithms by a network of workstations interconnected via Ethernet. We have used PVM 3.1, which is a software package that allows a heterogeneous network of parallel and serial computers to appear as a single concurrent computational resource [11]. We have used a coarse grained parallel method. In coarse grained PGA the population is divided into isolated subpopulations that exchange individuals by migration. Depending on the exchange model, the approach is called island model or stepping stone model. In the island model, migration can occur between any of the subpopulations. In the stepping stone model migration is restricted to neighboring subpopulations. The convergence time in the island model is less than in the stepping stone model. But in the stepping stone model the population diversity is higher. Thus the probability to hang up on a local optima is less than in the island model. We have used stepping stone model because we think that the effectiveness of crossover operators can be analyzed better in a model with longer convergence time.

Mutation plays an important role in our algorithm. In conventional GAs mutation is either not used or used with a small probability for every individual in the population. But with the time the idea has changed. Mühlenbein [12] has shown that mutation is a very important component of a GA and that it is a common mistake to believe that mutation is not important because the mutation rate is so small. Eshelman [13] has used a mutation operator to avoid decreasing diversity in the population. Whenever the population converges, the population is partially randomized for a restart by using the best individual so far as a template and creating new individuals by mutating this template. In our algorithm, when two subpopulations exchange their best individuals, the entire subpopulation is discarded and the new individuals are created by mutating the exchanged individuals and the best individual of this subpopulation. This method has the advantage that more new areas of the fitness landscape can be searched. Deletion of the old individuals of the subpopulation is reasonable because the "good" information of these individuals is already collected by the best individual of this subpopulation. We have used insertion, replacement, and 2-Opt as mutation operators. It should be noted that our 2-Opt is not a local improvement technique because all new individuals created by mutation are accepted for the new subpopulation, no matter what their fitness values are (i.e., the fitness has not to be computed during our 2-Opt).

As selection scheme, we have used a steady state, elitist selection. In each iteration a random pair is selected as parents and their offspring is created. Here each individual has equal chance to be selected. An offspring is accepted if it is not worse than the worst individual. In this case the offspring replaces the worst individual in the population.

Our method can be viewed as a parallel mixed Evolutionary / Genetic Algorithm method. In the subpopulations GA is used. The method used by the 'meta-population' can be stated as a evolutionary-like algorithm: only the best individuals are kept alive for the emigrant exchange and, after exchanging emigrants, the emigrants are mutated which is an operator like the neighborhood operator in Evolutionary Algorithms.

4 Crossover Operators

We will use terminology of TSP in the following. However, note that the ideas can be applied to any other sequencing problem, too.

The use of GAs on TSP presents specific difficulties: ommission or duplication of a city cause an illegal solution. Thus the traditional crossover and mutation operators cannot be used. For this reason many special crossover operators are implemented for TSP such as order crossover (OX) [3], cycle crossover (CX) [3], partially mapped crossover (PMX) [14], edge recombination (ER) [5].

We have designed two crossover operators for sequencing problems that make use of macro-order and neighborhood information. The experimental results at the end of the paper will show that they outperform the crossover operators mentioned above by far in most cases.

4.1 NRX Operator

Our first operator is called Neighborhood Relationship Crossover Operator (NRX) which is defined as follows: One city is chosen arbitrary (e.g., city A) and selected as a reference point. Then for each city x the number of cities through which the salesman has to run in order to travel from reference city A to city x is computed. The two distances of each city x which correspond to the two parents selected are added. In this operation the distances are multiplied with the fitness values of the parents. The child tour is computed according to the following algorithm.

```
for i = 0 to city number
   for j = i + 1 to city number
     if distance sum of city[j] < distance sum of city[i]
     then exchange city[i] and city[j];
```

Example

Let the tours A D G H C B F E and C G H A B D F E be the parents $parent_1$ and $parent_2$ selected. Assume the fitness of $parent_1$ to be 5 and that of $parent_2$ to be 2. Let city A be the reference city. The corresponding distance values of the cities are given in Table 1. The child, i.e., the new tour, is created by the process shown in Table 2.

Note that only the cities in the tour are exchanged, not their distance sum values. This allows the operator to make many replacements of the cities, thus it is very disruptive. However, replacements are only made for those cities whose distance sums are below a threshold value. This is the reason that the NRX operator works well if the cities that are to be replaced have high neighborhood relationship between each other. Neighborhood relationship of two cities is defined by the number of their common neighbors. A more accurate definition is given in the experimental part of this paper where the effect of neighborhood is analyzed in more detail. The crucial idea is that during the exchange phase the new generated solutions remain good if the neighborhood relationship is high,

city	$parent_1$	$parent_2$	distance sum
A	0	0	0
B	5	1	27
C	4	5	30
D	1	2	9
E	7	4	43
F	6	3	36
G	2	6	22
H	3	7	29

Table 1 Distance sums of the cities

step	$city[i]$	$city[j]$	$sum(city[i])$	$sum(city[j])$	new tour
1	B	C	27	30	ABCDEFGH
2	B	D	27	9	ADCBEFGH
3	B	E	27	43	ADCBEFGH
4	B	F	27	36	ADCBEFGH
5	B	G	27	22	AGCBEFDH
6	B	H	27	29	AGCBEFDH
7	C	D	30	9	AGBCEFDH
8	C	E	30	43	AGBCEFDH
9	C	F	30	36	AGBCEFDH
10	C	G	30	22	AGDCEFBH
11	C	H	30	29	AGHCEFBD
12	D	E	9	43	AGHCEFBD
13	D	F	9	36	AGHCEFBD
14	D	G	9	22	AGHCEFBD
15	D	H	9	29	AGHCEFBD
16	E	F	43	36	AGHCFEBD
17	E	G	43	22	AGHCBEFD
18	E	H	43	29	AGHCDEFB
19	F	G	36	22	AGHCDFEB
20	F	H	36	29	AGHCDBEF
21	G	H	22	29	AGHCDBEF

Table 2 The NRX approach

because the cities exchanged are in the neighborhood of their new adjacent cities in the tour with high probability.

4.2 MOX Operator

Our second crossover operator is named Meta-Ordering Crossover Operator (MOX) as it uses meta-order information. It can be defined by the following algorithm:

```
count₁ = 0; count₂ = 0;

BEGIN
    Select the first b cities from parent1 beginning by count1;
    Select only cities, which aren't already in the child tour;
    Order these cities according to their order in parent2;
    If the child tour is completed then exit;
    count1 = last selected city by parent1;

    Select the first b cities from parent2 beginning by count2;
    Select only cities, which aren't already in the child tour;
    Order these cities according to their order in parent1;
    If the child tour is completed then exit;
    count2 = last selected city by parent2;

    goto BEGIN;
```

If a parent encounters a city, which is already in the child tour, then he skips this city and goes to the next city. For the second child, the algorithm begins by $parent_2$ to select the first b cities.

Example

Let the tours D G I K B F H E C A J and G A D E K J I H F C B be the parents $parent_1$ and $parent_2$ selected. Let b be equal to 3. Then, the first child is created by the process shown in Table 3.

step	parent no	selected cities	new order	child tour
1	1	DGI	GDI	GDI
2	2	AEK	KEA	GDIKEA
3	1	BFH	HFB	GDIKEAHFB
4	2	CJ	JC	GDIKEAHFBJC

Table 3 The MOX approach

This operator has a parameter b. Obviously, the behavior of the MOX operator depends on b. However, it is very difficult to determine an optimal value of b for a given problem instance such that the MOX operator performs best. Therefore, we have coded b as a gene of each individual. b values which produce better results have greater chance to be selected as emigrants. Of course, b-genes are also mutated after changing emigrants.

5 Experimental Results

We have tested the NRX and MOX operator on the following TSP problems which we have taken from TSPLIB [15]: d198.tsp (city number: 198), kroA200.tsp (200), a280.tsp (280), lin318.tsp (318), and d1291.tsp (1291). We compared our operators to PMX, which is one of the best known and best performing operators as shown in [16]. We have implemented PMX in two different ways. In PMX1, we have used a look-up table for cities in order to find directly the position of a city in a tour. In PMX2, such a table is not available.

We made our experiments with 20 subpopulations each of 60 individuals and 50 subpopulation steps. A meta-generation is defined to be a process which starts by initialising 20 subpopulations at the parallel machine and stops after having obtained the best individuals from each of these sub-GAs which have run for 50 steps each.

Table 4 presents the average running times of one meta-generation for each of the crossover operators. By the experiments we have used a network of 10 workstations (SPARCclassic).

problem	PMX1	PMX2	NRX	MOX
d198.tsp	≈0.62s	≈0.68s	≈1.91s	≈0.64s
kroA200.tsp	≈0.60s	≈0.65s	≈1.86s	≈0.62s
a280.tsp	≈0.80s	≈0.91s	≈3.09s	≈0.81s
lin318.tsp	≈0.87s	≈1.00s	≈3.66s	≈0.88s
d1291.tsp	≈3.82s	≈5.08s	≈38.2s	≈3.74s

Table 4 Running times of a meta-generation

Figures 1 to 5 summarize the results for the TSP instances themselves. The horizontal axis denotes the running time in units of time needed by one meta-generation using PMX1. The vertical axis denotes the tour length. In Figure 4, e.g., the GA which uses NRX ($\triangle$) computes a tour of length about 100.000 in time in which the GA which uses PMX1 computes about 200 meta-generations. We have taken average of 10 runs.

Note that MOX performs always better than PMX, i.e., computes better tours in the same time. NRX is the winner by far, except for kroA200.tsp. The high performance of NRX still holds for a centralized GA which is demonstrated by Figures 2-5. The best individuals for benchmarks obtained by the end of the first meta-generation (before any exchange of emigrants) are superior to the results of the other operators (except for kroA200.tsp).

In order to better understand what happens when using NRX, we have computed the neighborhood relationships in the benchmarks. (Note that this is not done by our GAs!)

□=PMX1 △=NRX ◇=MOX

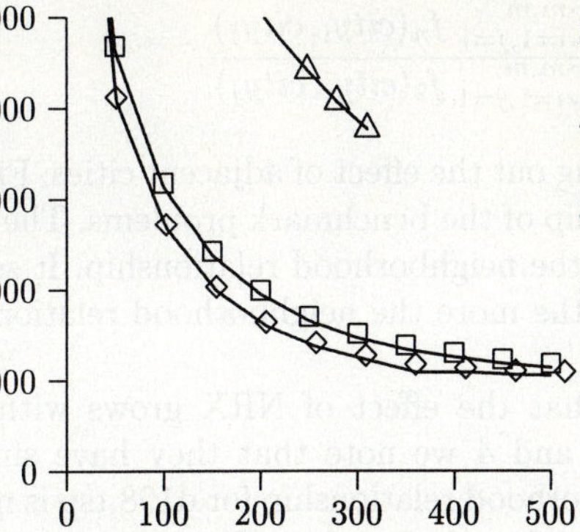

Figure 1 kroA200.tsp

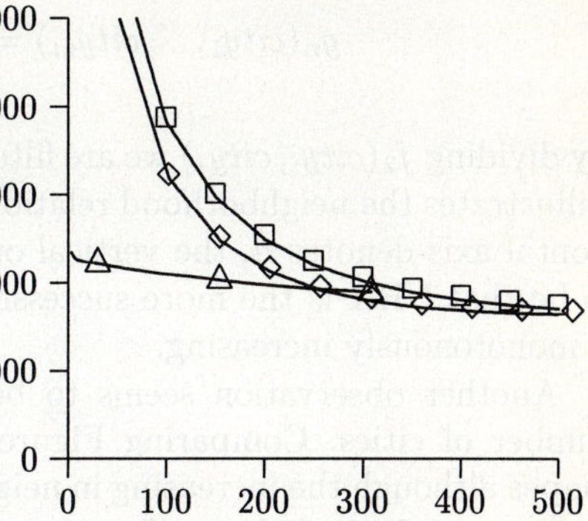

Figure 2 d198.tsp

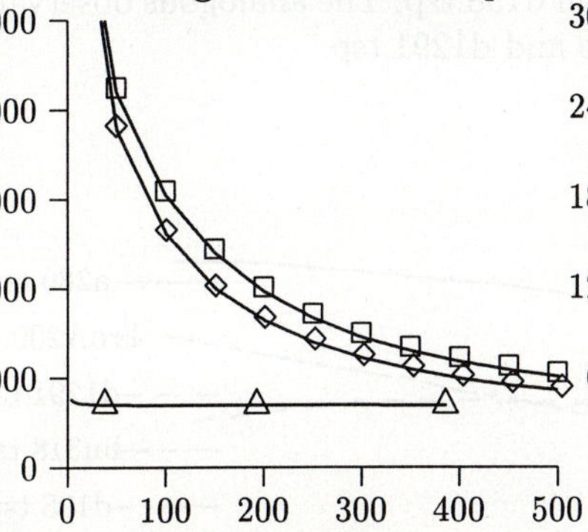

Figure 3 a280.tsp

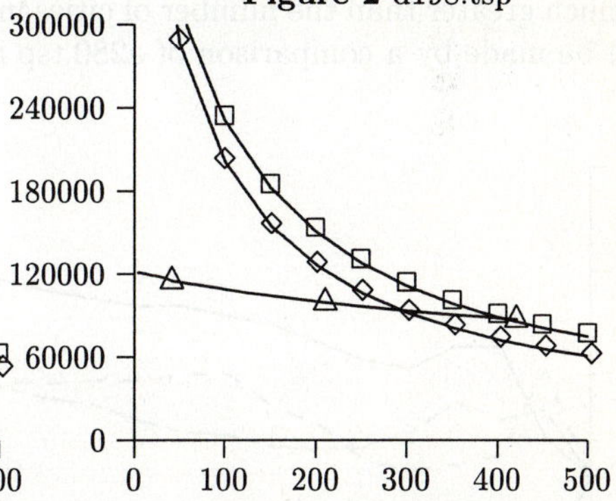

Figure 4 lin318.tsp

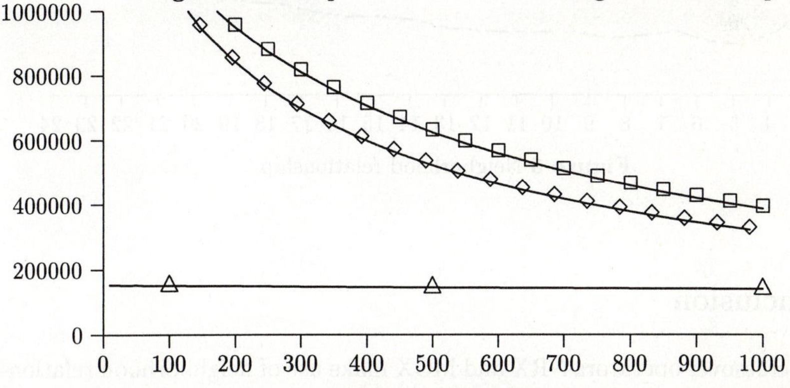

Figure 5 d1291.tsp

Let $f_n(city_1, city_2)$ be the number of cities which are among the n closest cities to city $city_1$ and among the n closest cities to city $city_2$ divided by the number of cities which are among the n closest cities to at least one of both. In the case that the set of the n closest cities is not well defined, we have chosen a permissible set at random. Now, the neighborhood relationship $g_n(city_1, ..., city_m)$

for a given problem instance is defined as

$$g_n(city_1, ..., city_m) = \frac{\sum_{i=1,j=1}^{m,m} f_n(city_i, city_j)}{\sum_{i=1,j=1}^{m,m} f_2(city_i, city_j)}.$$

By dividing $f_2(city_i, city_j)$ we are filtering out the effect of adjacent cities. Figure 6 illustrates the neighborhood relationship of the benchmark problems. The horizontal axis denotes n, the vertical one the neighborhood relationship. It seems to be that NRX is the more successful the more the neighborhood relationship is monotonously increasing.

Another observation seems to be that the effect of NRX grows with the number of cities. Comparing Figure 2 and 4 we note that they have similar shapes although the increasing in neighborhood relationship for d198.tsp is much higher than for lin318.tsp. However, note that the number of cities in lin318.tsp is much greater than the number of cities in d198.tsp. The analogous observation can be made by a comparison of a280.tsp and d1291.tsp.

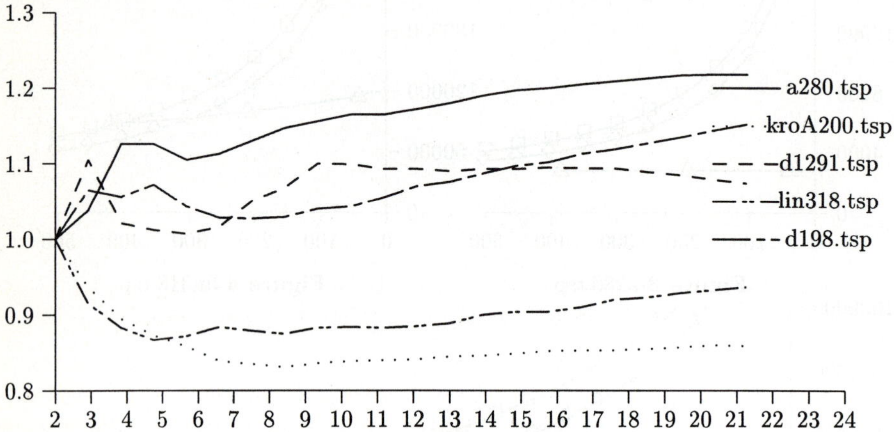

Figure 6 Neigborhood relationship

6 Conclusion

The new crossover operators NRX and MOX make use of neighborhood relationship and meta-order information, that have been neglected by the most of the known crossover operators. When the neighborhood relationship is high enough NRX outperforms PMX and MOX by far. MOX has outperformed PMX in all of the test problems. With growing city number, it needs less time for a meta-generation than PMX. The experimental results seem to imply that it may be a good idea to use NRX with another operator: first use NRX, then switch to the other operator, e.g., MOX.

A lot of sequencing problems can be attacked by the NRX approach just described. Note, however, that some sequencing problems will require modifications of the definition of the distance sum of a sequence.

References

1. Goldberg, D.E.: Genetic and Evolutionary Algorithms Come of Age. CACM, volume **37**(3), 1994.
2. Goldberg, D.E., Lingle J.R.: Alleles, Loci and the Traveling Salesman Problem. First Int'l Conf. on Genetic Algorithms and Their Applications, Erlbaum Associates, 1985.
3. Oliver, I.M., Smith, D.J., Holland, J.R.: A Study of Permutation Crossover Operators on the Traveling Salesman Problem. Second Int'l Conf. on Genetic Algorithms and Their Applications, 1987.
4. Prasanna, J., Jung, Y.S., Gucht, D.V.: The Effects of Population Size, Heuristic Crossover and Local Improvement on a Genetic Algorithm for the Traveling Salesman Problem. Third Int'l Conf. on Genetic Algorithms, 1989.
5. Whitley, D., Starkweather, T., Fuquay, D.: Scheduling Problems and Traveling Salesman: The Genetic Edge Recombination operator. Third Int'l Conf. on Genetic Algorithms, 1989.
6. Mathias, K., Whitley, D.: Genetic Operators, The Fitness Landscape and the Traveling Salesman Problem. Second Int'l Conf. on Parallel Problem Solving from Nature, pp.221-230, 1992.
7. Ulder, N., Aarts, E., Bandelt, H., van Laarhoven, P., Pesch, E.: Genetic Local Search Algorithms for the Traveling Salesman Problem. First Int'l Conf. on Parallel Problem Solving from Nature, pp.109-116, 1990.
8. Schleuter, M.G.: ASPARAGOS: An Asynchronous Parallel Genetic Optimization Strategy. Third Int'l Conf. on Genetic Algorithms, 1989.
9. Fogarty, T., Huang, R.: Implementing the Genetic Algorithm on Transputer Based Parallel Processing Systems. First Int'l Conf. on Parallel Problem Solving from Nature, pp.145-149, 1990.
10. Maruyma, T., Kanagaya, A., Konishi, I.: An Asynchronous Fine-Grained Parallel Genetic Algorithm. Second Int'l Conf. on Parallel Problem Solving from Nature, pp.561-570, 1992.
11. Geist, A., Beguelin, A., Dongorra, J., Jiang, W., Manchek, R., Sunderam, V.: PVM3 Users's Guide and Reference Manual. Technical Report, Oak Ridge National Lab, 1994.
12. Mühlenbein, H.: Evolution in Time and Space, the Parallel Genetic Algorithm. Foundations of Genetic Algorithms, Morgan Kaufmann, 1991.
13. Eshelman, L.J.: The CHC Adaptive Search Algorithm. Foundations of Genetic Algorithms, Morgan Kaufmann, 1991.
14. Goldberg, D.E.: Genetic Algorithms in Search, Optimization, and Machine Learning. Addison Wesley, 1989.
15. Bixby, B., Reinelt, G.: TSPLIB, A Traveling Salesman Problem Library. ORSA Journal on Computing **3**, pp.376-384, 1991. Access via http://ftp.zip-berlin.de/pub/mp-testdata/tsp/index.html.
16. Fox, B.R., McMahon, M.B.: Genetic Operators for Sequencing Problems. Foundations of Genetic Algorithms, Morgan Kaufmann, 1991.

The Effect of Extensive Use of the Mutation Operator on Generalization in Genetic Programming Using Sparse Data Sets

Wolfgang Banzhaf[1], Frank D. Francone[2] and Peter Nordin[1]

[1] Department of Computer Science, Dortmund University,
Joseph-vonFraunhofer-Str. 20, 44227 Dortmund, GERMANY
banzhaf,nordin@LS11.informatik.uni-dortmund.de
[2] Law Office of Frank D. Francone,
4806 Fountain Ave. #77, Los Angeles, California 90027, USA
ytns65a@prodigy.com

Abstract. Ordinarily, Genetic Programming uses little or no mutation. Crossover is the predominant operator. This study tests the effect of a very aggressive use of the mutation operator on the generalization performance of our Compiling Genetic Programming System ('CPGS'). We ran our tests on two benchmark classification problems on very sparse training sets. In all, we performed 240 complete runs of population 3000 for each of the problems, varying mutation rate between 5% and 80%. We found that increasing the mutation rate can significantly improve the generalization capabilities of GP. The mechanism by which mutation affects the generalization capability of GP is not entirely clear. What is clear is that changing the balance between mutation and crossover effects the course of GP training substantially — for example, increasing mutation greatly extends the number of generations for which the GP system can train before the population converges.

1 Introduction

Evolutionary Algorithms may be classified into two different groups based on their relative use of crossover and mutation. Genetic Algorithms ('GA') and Genetic Programming ('GP') tend to use little or no mutation. In these paradigms, crossover is by far the dominant operator [4, 3]. On the other hand, Evolutionary Strategies ('ES') and Evolutionary Programming ('EP') have their traditional focus on the mutation operator [11, 12, 2]. Recently, the crossover operator has been challenged by researchers as being relatively ineffective in both Genetic Algorithms [2] and in Genetic Programming [5]. This paper therefore undertakes the first systematic study of the effect of changing the relative balance of mutation and crossover in genetic programming.

We undertook this study with our Compiling Genetic Programming System ('CGPS'). Compiling Genetic Programming is the direct evolution of binary machine code. A CGPS program is a sequence of 32 bit binary machine instructions in memory. Genetic operators act directly on the 32 bit instructions. When executed, the instructions in a CGPS program cause the CPU to perform simple operations on the CPU's hardware registers.[1] By way of example, a CGPS program might, when executed, cause the CPU to add the value in register 1 to the value in register 2 and then place the result in register 3. Each such CGPS instruction corresponds to three nodes in a hierarchical (tree-based) GP-system. Functions of great complexity can be evolved with simple arithmetic functions in a register machine [9].

2 Specification of the experiments

Table 1 summarizes our experimental setup [4]. Some items merit separate discussion and for those items, the experimental setup is described in the text.

2.1 The CGPS mutation operator

The CGPS mutation operator flips bits inside the 32-bit instructions that comprise a CGPS program. The mutation operator ensures that only the instructions in the function set are generated and that the register and constant values are within the predefined ranges allowed in the experimental setup. To keep the number of individuals evolved even as between mutation and crossover, we either crossover or mutate two individuals each time a genetic operator is executed.

2.2 The data sets used in this study

The Gaussian 3D data set. Gaussian 3D is an artificially generated Classification problem. Both output classes are comprised of points with zero mean and normal distribution. The standard deviation of Class 0 is 1. The standard deviation of Class 1 is 2 [13] (p. 14). Using 5000 training samples, the ELENA [13] k-nearest neighbor (KNN) benchmark error rate is 22.2%. Therefore, a CGPS hit rate of 77.8% would match the benchmark. The Gaussian problem is by far the most difficult problem reported in this paper.

The phoneme recognition data set. The Phoneme recognition database requires a machine learning (ML-) system to classify two sets of spoken vowels into oral or nasal vowels. Using 5404 training samples, the KNN benchmark error rate is 14.2% [13] (p. 30-1).Therefore, a CGPS hit rate of 85.8% would be match the benchmark. This problem is the next most difficult problem reported in this paper.

[1] For a more detailed description of CGPS, please see [7, 8, 9, 10].

The IRIS data set. The IRIS database requires an ML system to classify measurements from photos of Irises into three different types of Irises. Using 150 training samples, the KNN benchmark error rate is between 0% and 7.3% (95% confidence interval)[13] (p. 35-6). Therefore, a CGPS hit rate of 92.7% would match the benchmark. The Iris data set is by far the easiest of the problems attacked here. It turned out to be almost trivial for CGPS to solve.

Sparse data sets. We made each of the above problems more difficult for CGPS by withholding between 50% and 98% of the data upon which the benchmarks were calculated. On Phoneme and Gaussian, we gave our system only 100 data points for training and another 100 for testing rather than the over 5000 data points used for the KNN Benchmarks[13]. For the Iris problem, we used 75 training examples as opposed to the 150 training samples for the benchmark.[13]

Table 1. Experimental specification. EDI's were enabled on half of the runs.

Description	*Value*
Objective :	Classification of data sets from ELENA Database
Terminal set :	Integer constants initialized from 0 - 255
Function set :	Addition, Multiplication, Subtraction, Division
Number of Hardware Registers :	One more than the number of classes in the data
Number of Fitness/Testing Cases :	100/100
Wrapper :	None
Population Size :	3000
Selection:	Tournament. 4/2
Maximum Individual Size:	256 instructions.
Total Number of Runs :	480 (Gauss), 240 (Phoneme), 240 (Iris)

2.3 Other important features of the system

Variable parameters/number of total runs. We varied three of the parameters from run to run. These parameters were: Parsimony Factor (0, 0.1, 1), Explicitly Defined Introns (enabled/not enabled), and Crossover/Mutation Mix (5%, 20%, 50%, 80% mutation). There are twenty-four different combinations of the above parameters (see Table 1). We ran each such combination on ten different random seeds. As a result, we conducted a total of 240 runs per problem set.

Measuring fitness. For our fitness function, we selected one hardware register as the output register. We also arbitrarily assigned a target output value to each class (the 'Class Target Value'). If a particular fitness case should have been classified as being a member of Class n, then the fitness of the individual for that fitness case is the absolute value of the difference between the value in the output register and the Class Target Value for class n. The sum of these absolute deviations over all fitness cases was the fitness of the individual.

Measuring hits. We counted a prediction as a 'Hit' if the absolute value of the difference between the output register and the Class Target Value was less than 50.

Measuring generalization. We assessed generalization by separating our data into training and testing sets. Each generation, the best individual on the training set is evaluated on the testing set and the results of that test are preserved. [2]

Terminating a run. We have previously reported that where destructive crossover falls to below 10% of all crossover events, all effective training is over [10]. Accordingly, we monitored the rate of destructive crossover during training. When destructive crossover fell to 10% of the total crossover events for any given generation, we terminated the run. This approach saves a substantial amount of CPU time. Otherwise, we terminated a run at 200 generations.

3 Results

We use two measures of how much mutation affected the performance of our GP system — the mean of all runs and the probability that a particular mutation rate would result in a particularly good run.

3.1 Results on the IRIS data set

We report the results on the Iris Data Set here because they are so straightforward. The Iris problem was very easy for CGPS. Almost all runs matched or exceeded the benchmark — most of the runs did so by the end of the first generation. On this data set, changes in the mutation operator had no measurable effect on generalization. The remainder of this Results section applies only to the more difficult Phoneme and Gaussian Data sets.

[2] While our method does provide much useful information about the generalization capabilities of our system[6] (pp. 335-376), the use of a third data set would improve it. The ability of the best generalizer from a run to generalize on this third data set would measure the performance of that run more accurately. We plan to implement this capability in the future.

3.2 Effect of varying mutation rates on the mean of the data set

Table 2 reports the effect of varying the mutation rate on the generalization capabilities of CGPS. The measure of generalization capabilities used is the performance in % hits on the testing set as a percentage of the ELENA KNN Benchmark.

Table 2. Effect of varying the mutation rate on CGPS generalization, including a statistical analysis: C.C.: Correlation Coefficient, S.S.: Statistical Significance.

Mutation Rate	*Gaussian 3D*	*Phoneme*
5%	72.3%	90.8%
20%	75.3%	90.6%
50%	75.7%	91.5%
80%	73.4%	91.4%
C.C.	0.199	0.111
S.S.	99%	92%

Thus, the effect of changing the mutation rate from 5% to 50% on the mean of 480 runs varies from a 1% to a 3.5% improvement on the testing set, depending on the problem. This effect is both important and statistically significant. Important, because in higher ranges small changes in generalization are disproportionally difficult to achieve and often make the difference between a successful prediction model and a failure. The result is also statistically significant. Table 2 shows the correlation coefficients and statistical significance level over all 480 runs for the correlation between the negative of the square of the mutation rate and the mean generalization capability over all 480 runs on both the Gaussian and Phoneme problem sets.

3.3 Effect of varying the mutation rate on the probability of evolving outstanding runs

In real world applications, the point is not to evolve a lot of runs with a somewhat higher mean. The point is to evolve one or a few runs where the best individual's generalization capability is outstanding. Our results strongly suggest that increasing the mutation rate dramatically increases the probability of generating such outstanding runs. Table 3 shows the proportion all runs that are in the top 5% of runs by mutation rate.

Table 3. Percentage of top 5% of runs comprised of various mutation rates. 480 runs. Phoneme and Gaussian data sets.

Mutation Rate	*Gaussian 3D*	*Phoneme*
5%	0%	0%
20%	33%	8%
50%	58%	58%
80%	8%	33%

This effect is statistically significant. Table 4 presents the correlation coefficients and the statistical significance levels of the coefficients for the top 5% , 10% and 20% of runs.

Table 4. Correlation coefficients and statistical significance levels for correlation between mutation rate and the probability that a run will be among the best runs. 480 runs. Gaussian and phoneme data sets.

	C.C.	*S.S.*
Top 5% of Runs	0.887	99%
Top 10% of Runs	0.760	95%
Top 20% of Runs	0.828	99%

Table 3 somewhat overstates the effect of higher mutation rates on the actual probability of a run being in the best 5% of runs. Simply put, it took longer for higher mutation runs to find a best generalizer than it took lower mutation runs. Table 5 shows the increases in the probability of a run being in the top 5% and the top 10% of runs adjusted for this difference in CPU Time.

Table 5. Effect in increasing mutation rate on probability of a run being one of the best runs. Adjusted for CPU time. Factors of increase in probability of run being in Top 5 and 10 %, respectively. 480 runs. Gaussian and phoneme data sets

Change in Mutation Rate	*Factor 5%*	*Factor 10%*
From 5% to 20%	1.8	1.7
From 5% to 50%	3.4	3.0
From 5% to 80%	1.6	2.3

A factor of 3.4 in Table 5 means that, adjusted for CPU time, a run with a 50% mutation rate is 3.4 times more likely to be in the top 5% of runs than a run with a 5% mutation rate. Put another way, one effect of higher mutation rates is to increase the size of the high generalization tail of the distribution of multiple runs.

3.4 Effect of varying the mutation rate on indicia of training

Introduction. Increasing the mutation rate profoundly changes the way a CGPS run trains. The purpose of this section is to describe some of those changes.

Table 6 sets forth the effect of various mutation rates on various training indicators. We discuss each of these items below.

Table 6. Various training indicators as a function of mutation rate. Mean of 480 runs: Introns as percent of total instructions; effective size of individual; number of generations to best generalizer / number of generations to termination of run.

Mutation Rate	*Introns*	*Effective Size*	*Best Generalizer*	*Run Termination*
5%	74%	7	12	151
20%	68%	12	22	167
50%	63%	12	24	176
80%	58%	9	26	175

Introns as a percentage of total instructions. First order introns are evolved single instructions that have no effect on the fitness calculation [8]. We have frequently observed first order introns in our previous work [10]. A typical first order intron is:

```
register1 = register1 + 0                                          (1);
```

During training we measured the percentage of all instructions in the population that were first order introns at the time the Best Generalizer was found. We found that increasing the mutation rate greatly reduces the proportion of the entire population that is comprised of introns, see Table 6. Our previous work suggests that changes of this magnitude shown in Table 6 are related to important changes in the training of a GP run [10].

Mean individual effective size. 'Effective Size' is the number of instructions in a GP individual that have an effect on the fitness of the individual [10]. We measured the effective size of all individuals in each GP run at the time the Best Generalizer was found and present the average for the population in Table 6. Here, raising the mutation rate significantly increases the average effective size of all the individuals in the population.

Mean generations to best generalizer. Increasing the mutation rate effectively doubles the number of generations before a run locates the best individual generalizer. Table 6.

Mean generations to run termination. Increasing the mutation rate increases the number of generations that it takes for a run to terminate. Table 6. In our system, this is mostly a measure of the time it takes for the number of introns to multiply so much that effective training is over [10]. This measure is, therefore, consistent with our observation above that there are more introns in low mutation rate runs. Table 6.

4 Discussion

Increasing mutation rates is a powerful way to improve the generalization capabilities of GP. Over a wide variety of parameters and over 480 runs, a 50/50 balance of mutation and crossover consistently performed better than the low mutation rates traditionally used in GP. However, higher mutation rates should only be expected to work on difficult data sets. As the data sets that we studied increased in difficulty, the effect of higher mutation rates also increased. The data sets we studied got more difficult in the following order: Iris, Phoneme and Gaussian. The effect of mutation on the mean of the generalization capabilities increases in the same order as follows: 0%, +1%, + 3.5%.

That said, the mechanism by which the mutation operator acts to improve generalization is not entirely clear. Several factors, however, point to increased diversity as a factor.

Diversity and introns. Increasing the mutation rate reduces the number of introns. Table 6. Consider the typical first order intron described in (1). Now, imagine the effect of the possible mutations that could be applied to (1). Changing the operator from "plus" to "times" or "minus" will convert the intron into working code. Changing the constant or changing the register of the argument or the result are also likely to convert the intron into working code. In short, mutation tends with high probability to destroy typical first order introns by converting them into code that effects the fitness calculation.[3]

[3] It is possible to imagine first order introns that would be resistent to mutation under the correct circumstances. An example of such an intron would be:

Diversity and effective length. Table 6 also shows that higher mutation rates are associated with longer effective length in the entire population. Effective length is a measure of the number of instructions in an individual that effect fitness. Longer effective length could easily be a reflection of a constant infusion of new effective code into the population. Such an infusion could easily be the result of the mutation operator converting typical introns, such as (1), into effective code. Of course, such an infusion of fresh genetic material would tend to maintain the diversity of the population longer.

But for this mechanism to supply a continual flow of new genetic material into the population, the supply of introns in the population must somehow replenish itself. Otherwise, the mutation opreator in high mutation rate runs should rapidly exhaust the population's supply of introns. But Table 6 shows that introns are merely reduced, not eliminated. Our previous research strongly suggests that introns are formed by a GP population in response to the crossover operator [10]. The mechanism that suggests itself then is that crossover creates introns and mutation changes them into fresh genetic material. That the mutation operator works best at a 50/50 balance of crossover and mutation suggests the balance between crossover and mutation is a key to maintaining the flow of new genetic material into the population.

Diversity and length of effective training. The effect of mutation on length of training is also consistent with our diversity explanation. Higher mutation runs continue to evolve better generalizing individuals for almost twice as many generations as do lower mutation runs, see Table 6. Of course, higher diversity in the population would be expected to cause such an effect. This observation hits at a central problem in GP — GP is plagued by premature convergence. That is, GP populations often lose their ability to evolve before the problem is solved. Increasing the mutation rate makes the runs continue to evolve for about twice as long (Table 6) - that is, a high mutation run maintans its ability to evolve for longer. This observation explains the better results in high mutation runs on difficult problems — with more time to explore the search space, such runs did better. This observation also explains why higher mutation rates did not effect the IRIS results. CGPS solved the IRIS problem almost immediately - most runs equalled or exceeded the benchmark by the end of the first generation. Simply put, CGPS did not need the extra evolvability lent by high mutation rates to solve the IRIS problem.

$register1 = register2 >> register3$ (2); "Shift-right" (>>) is effectively a division by powers of 2. In this example, mutations that change argument registers or the content of argument registers are less likely to have effects on fitness than the similar changes in the typical intron as shown in (1), provided values in the argument registers are in certain broad ranges. In short, a type (2) intron may be relatively more resistent to mutation than a type (1) intron. We have, indeed, observed these type (2) introns to proliferate heavily in individuals from runs with very high mutation rates. We have never observed such introns in our previous work in low mutation runs. This new type of intron is an area in which further research is suggested.

Conclusion. In conclusion, many factors point to the improved diversity of the population as a primary candidate for further research to explain how mutation improves the generalization in GP runs. One other area for future research would be to incorporate some of the ES and EP type mutation strategies into GP mutation operators.

Acknowledgments

We would like to thank the ELENA partners for assembling the ELENA database. Partial support from the Deutsche Forschungsgemeinschaft (DFG) under grant Ba 1042/5-1 is gratefully acknowledged.

References

1. T. Bäck: Optimal Mutation Rates in Genetic Search. In: S. Forrest (Ed.): Proc. 5th Int. Conference on Genetic Algorithms, ICGA-93. San Mateo: Morgan Kaufmann 1993
2. D. Fogel, L. Stayton: On the Effectiveness of Crossover in Simulated Evolutionary Optimization. Biosystems **32** 171 - 182 (1994)
3. D. Goldberg: Genetic Algorithms in Search Optimization & Learning, Reading: Addison-Wesley 1989
4. J.R. Koza: Genetic Programming. Cambridge (USA): MIT Press 1992
5. K. Lang: Hill Climbing Beats Genetic Search on a Boolean Circuit Synthesis Problem of Koza's. In: A. Prieditis, S. Russell (Eds.): Proc. 12th Int. Conference on Machine Learning. San Mateo: Morgan Kaufmann 1995
6. T. Masters: Advanced Algorithms for Neural Networks. New York: Wiley 1995
7. J.P. Nordin, J.P.: A Compiling Genetic Programming System that Directly Manipulates the Machine Code. In: K. Kinnear, Jr. (ed.). Advances in Genetic Programming. Cambridge MA: MIT Press 1994
8. J.P. Nordin, W. Banzhaf: Complexity Compression and Evolution. In: L. Eshelman (Ed.): Proc. 6th Int. Conference on Genetic Algorithms, ICGA-95. San Mateo: Morgan Kaufmann 1995
9. J.P. Nordin, W. Banzhaf: Evolving Turing Complete Programs for a Register Machine with Self Modifying Code. In: L. Eshelman (Ed.): Proc. 6th Int. Conference on Genetic Algorithms, ICGA-95. San Mateo: Morgan Kaufmann 1995
10. J.P. Nordin, F.D. Francone, W. Banzhaf: Explicitly Defined Introns and Destructive Crossover in Genetic Programming. In: K. Kinnear, Jr., P. Angeline (eds.): Advances in Genetic Programming 2. Cambridge MA: MIT Press 1996, in press
11. I. Rechenberg: Evolutionsstrategie 94. Stuttgart: Holzmann-Froboog 1994 (2nd. ed.)
12. H.P. Schwefel: Evolution and Optimum Seeking. New York: Wiley 1995 (2nd. ed.)
13. The ELENA Partners: C. Jutten, Project Coordinator: ESPRIT Basic Research Project Number 6891, Document Number R3-B1-P. Available via ftp at either ics.uci.edu or at satie.dice.ucl.ac.be, 1995

On Permutation Representations for Scheduling Problems

Christian Bierwirth, Dirk C. Mattfeld and Herbert Kopfer

University of Bremen, Dept. of Economics, D-28334 Bremen, Germany

Abstract. In this paper we concentrate on job shop scheduling as a representative of constrained combinatorial problems. We introduce a new permutation representation for this problem. Three crossover operators, different in tending to preserve the relative order, the absolute order, and the position in the permutation, are defined. By experiment we observe the strongest phenotypical correlation between parents and offspring when respecting the absolute order. It is shown that a genetic algorithm using an operator which preserves the absolute order also obtains a superior solution quality.

1 Introduction

The fundamental concept of permutations is widely used for the representational issue of combinatorial optimization problems. In the application of genetic algorithms to many of such problems, permutations can serve as chromosomes. It has been pointed out early that crossover has to respect the properties of the encoded problem, see e.g. Oliver et al. (1987).

The different properties of permutation crossover operators have been subject to various investigations, compare Kargupta et al. (1992). This area of research focused particularly on problems where a solution is represented in a natural way by reading a permutation either as a sequence or as a string of positions. Little attention has been paid to constrained permutation problems where a solution does not evolve until the permutation is decoded.

2 How to Read a Permutation

The solutions of assignment problems, sequencing problems, and mixtures thereof can be represented by permutation schemes. A model of these permutation problems is generally described in the following way.

A set of m resources is available to carry out n tasks. Assign all tasks to resources and sequence the assigned tasks for each resource such that an overall cost function is minimized. Here the solution is represented by the permutation

$$\{\underbrace{\pi_1,\ldots,\pi_{n_1}}_{\text{resource 1}},\underbrace{\pi_{n_1+1},\ldots,\pi_{n_2}}_{\text{resource 2}},\ldots,\underbrace{\pi_{n_{m-1}+1},\ldots,\pi_n}_{\text{resource } m}\}$$

of the task numbers $\{1,2,\ldots,n\}$, which is m-partitioned by the numbers $\{n_k\}$.

Several special cases of this model are well known. For $m = 1$ tasks may refer to jobs which have to be sequenced on a single machine. If job i precedes job j the machine setup may cost c_{ij} units. Thus the function $\sum_{i=1}^{n-1} c_{\pi_i \pi_{i+1}}$ has to be minimized. The Traveling Salesman Problem (TSP) is derived from the model in a similar way. Again $m = 1$ holds but tasks refer to cities here. The cost of a solution is determined by the distances between cities which are visited directly after each other. Solutions of both problems are represented by a permutation $\{\pi_i, \ldots, \pi_n\}$ of n tasks. Notice that this permutation is unpartitioned because assignment costs are neglected (just one resource is involved).

At the other extreme we face a case with $n = m$. Assume each resource has to carry out exactly one task. The Assignment Problem minimizes the function $\sum_{i=1}^{m} c_{i\pi_i}$. Here c_{ij} denotes the assignment costs for resource i to carry out task j. If resources refer to locations and tasks refer to certain objects we may wish to minimize the flow-intensity of objects between locations with respect to the distances of locations. This much more difficult to solve problem is known as the Quadratic Assignment Problem (QAP). Again solutions of both problems are represented by a permutation $\{\pi_i, \ldots, \pi_n\}$ of n tasks. But this time it is m-partitioned and the costs of sequencing are neglected (just one task is assigned to every resource).

The above considerations show that a permutation may express a pure sequence (TSP) as well as a pure assignment (QAP). In the former case the order of task numbers is of importance whereas their position in the permutation is meaningless. In the latter case things are completely reversed. Within the range of both extremes we find a variety of mixed assignment-sequencing problems, such as vehicle routing or multi-machine scheduling problems, compare Reeves (1993).

3 Representing the Job Shop Problem

For the purpose of this paper we concentrate on a representative of multi-machine scheduling. First we describe a representation of the Open Shop Problem in terms of the model introduced above. Then we derive a representation of the Job Shop Problem (JSP) capable of coping with the additional constraints of the problem.

A set of n operations (tasks) with known processing times has to be scheduled on m machines (resources). A group of m operations forms a complex called a job. Altogether N jobs are defined within the set of operations, i.e. the number of operations is the product of the number of jobs and machines ($n = N \times m$). Find a permutation

$$\{\underbrace{\pi_1, \ldots, \pi_N}_{\text{machine 1}}, \underbrace{\pi_{N+1}, \ldots, \pi_{2N}}_{\text{machine 2}}, \pi_{2N+1}, \ldots, \pi_n\}$$

of operation numbers $\{1, \ldots, n\}$ which is m-partitioned by the multiples of N such that the span of time to process all operations (makespan) is minimized. Notice, that each partition of the above permutation represents the solution of a single machine sequencing problem.

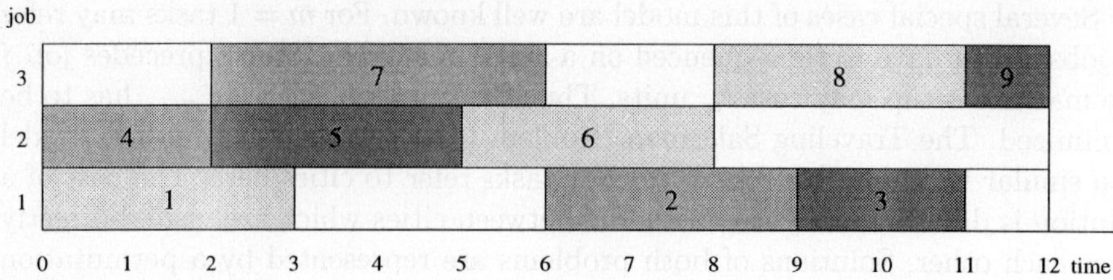

Fig. 1. The Gantt-chart representation of a JSP solution.

In an open shop environment, no prescribed technological processing order among the operations of a job exists, therefore the partitions can be sequenced independently of each other.

In a job shop environment the operations of each job have to pass the machines in a technological order. For an example we consider a JSP of three jobs and three machines. Figure 1 shows a JSP solution in the Gantt-chart representation which is referred to as phenotype. Each job consists of three operations (e.g. operation number 7, 8, and 9 for job 3) which occur in their prescribed technological order. Operations to be processed by the same machine appear in identical shading. The length of an operation corresponds to its processing time. The makespan of 12 time units can be taken directly from the abscissa.

The temporal order of machine assignments is restricted by dependencies among the operations. Consider a situation in which none of the operations 1, 4, and 7 in Fig. 1 are scheduled as the first operation of their dedicated machine. Other operations cannot be scheduled in the beginning because their technological predecessors have not been processed. This infeasible solution is represented by an m-partitioned permutation where none of the operations 1, 4, and 7 is placed in the first position of its partition.

The representation of infeasible solutions can be avoided for the JSP by a slightly modified permutation scheme, see Bierwirth (1995). Instead of using an m-partitioned permutation of operation numbers we change to an unpartitioned permutation with m-repetition of job numbers. Here, each job number occurs m times in the permutation, i.e. as often as there are operations belonging to this job. Scanning the permutation from left to right the k-th occurrence of a job number refers to the k-th operation in the technological order of this job. In this way we avoid scheduling operations whose technological predecessors have not been scheduled yet. Table 2 shows the permutation from which the Gantt-chart above is assembled.

permutation of jobs	1	2	2	3	1	2	3	1	3
index of occurrence	1	1	2	1	2	3	2	3	3
referred operation	1	4	5	7	2	6	8	3	9
partitioned permut.	4	7	2	1	6	8	5	3	9

Fig. 2. Pointer to technological constraint matrix.

The index line refers to the k-th occurrence of a job number. It is used to point to the corresponding operations while decoding. A permutation with repetition of job numbers merely expresses the order in which the operations of jobs are scheduled. The machine sequences are faded out in the representation and do not evolve until the permutation is decoded.

Nevertheless, the m-partitioned permutation can be easily established as shown in the last line of Fig. 2. The referred operations which belong to a single machine are assigned to the dedicated partition. Thereby the order among operations is kept.

4 Crossover for Permutations

It is well known that the crossover operator has to respect the semantical properties of the underlying problem representation, see Kargupta et al. (1992). We define three types of orderings for permutation chromosomes. Two genes may express meaningful information if they appear side by side (relative order). They may express information if one gene precedes the other gene in the chromosome (absolute order) regardless of how many genes lay in between. Finally information may be expressed by the position of a single gene in the chromosome.

As already mentioned, for the symmetric TSP the relative order of genes is meaningful whereas for the QAP the position of genes is of importance. Turning to the JSP, Syswerda (1991) conjectures that the order as well as the position of genes in the permutation are meaningful. To be more precise, we expect the absolute order to be of particular interest because it directly expresses precedence relations among operations in a schedule. Since we cannot valuate the ability of an operator to pass on meaningful information in advance, three different crossover operators are introduced in the following.

From the various permutation operators proposed we select two often used ones, Order Crossover and Partially Mapped Crossover. The techniques of both operators can be generalized to the demands of permutations with repetition.

Generalized Order Crossover (GOX) and its partially mapped counterpart (GPMX) assemble one offspring from two parental chromosomes (donator and receiver). In both techniques a substring is chosen from the donating chromosome. Then all genes of the substring are deleted with respect to their index of occurrence in the receiving chromosome. GOX implants the substring into the receiver at the position where the first gene of the substring has occured (before deletion) in the receiver. Different to GOX, GPMX implants the substring in the receiver at that position where it occurs in the donator. Examples of GOX and GPMX are given in Fig. 3.

parent 1	3	2	2	2	3	1	1	1	3
parent 2	~~1~~	1	3	2	~~2~~	1	~~2~~	~~3~~	3
GOX offspring	1	3	2	2	2	3	1	1	3
GPMX offspring	1	3	2	2	3	1	2	1	3

Fig. 3. Generalized position crossover (GPMX) in comparison to GOX.

In both operators the donator's substring is implanted without modifications whereas the receiving chromosome is disrupted. In order to pass on the same amount of characteristics from both parents, the length of the donating substring should be smaller than the receiving chromosome after deletion. The length of the donating substring varies within the range of 1/3 and 1/2 of the chromosome length.

Additionally we present the new Precedence Preservative Crossover (PPX) which perfectly respects the absolute order of genes in parental chromosomes. First the offspring chromosome is initialized empty. Then a vector of length n is randomly filled with elements of the set $\{1, 2\}$. This vector defines the order in which genes are drawn from parent 1 and parent 2 respectively. After a gene is drawn from one parent and deleted in the other one, it is appended to the offspring chromosome. This step is repeated until both parent chromosomes are empty and the offspring contains all genes involved.

parent 1	3	2	2	2	3	1	1	1	3
parent 2	1	1	3	2	2	1	2	3	3
gene of parent	1	1	2	2	2	2	1	1	1
PPX offspring	3	2	1	1	2	1	2	3	3

Fig. 4. Precedence Preservative Crossover (PPX).

In Fig. 4 PPX is applied in a two-point crossover fashion, i.e. the direction of choice between parental genes changes two times (third line). In order to apply PPX in a uniform crossover fashion the choices may alternatively change at random. However, the absolute order between any of two genes in the offspring has its origin in at least one of the parental chromosomes.

All operators proposed end up with a feasible offspring solution. In detail we expect GOX to pass on the relative order of genes. GPMX tends to pass on positions of genes by respecting the ordering to some extent. PPX respects the absolute order of genes resulting in a perfect preservation of precedence relations among genes.

5 Heredity of Schedule Characteristics

In order to explain the representational issue of absolute order for the JSP, precedence relations among operations itself are made to the subject of our consideration now. We map the permutation representation into a string of 0/1-decisions expressing the absolute order of any of two operations to be processed on the same machine. This mapping leads to the binary JSP representation proposed by Nakano and Yamada (1991). Each gene of the bit-string determines whether an operation v is sequenced prior to an operation w ($v \prec w = 1$) or not ($v \prec w = 0$). In case that a certain relation $v \prec w$ is specified, the inverse relation $w \prec v$ is redundant and therefore omitted. Since N jobs are processed by m machines we end up with a string of $m\frac{N^2-N}{2}$ bits.

For an example corresponding to the Gantt-chart in Fig. 1 all nine precedence relations are given below.

$2 \prec 4$	$2 \prec 7$	$4 \prec 7$	$1 \prec 6$	$1 \prec 8$	$6 \prec 8$	$3 \prec 5$	$3 \prec 9$	$5 \prec 9$
1	1	1	0	0	1	0	1	1

This binary mapping enables us to measure the differences and similarities of schedules on a phenotypical level by means of the Hamming-distance. The process is illustrated in Fig. 5. First two permutations are decoded into Gantt-charts. Next two bit-strings are derived from the two phenotypes. Finally the normalized Hamming-distance is calculated. In doing so the Hamming distance reflects the phenotypical characteristics of solutions instead of considering just genotypical information.

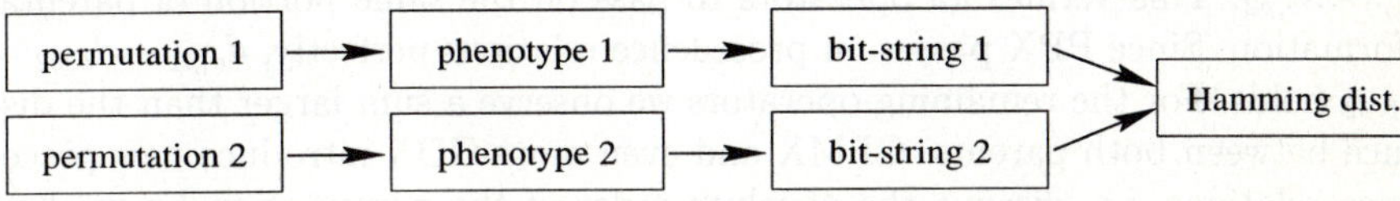

Fig. 5. Scheme for the calculation of the Hamming distance.

The normalized Hamming-distance between two bit-strings x and y is determined by $d_{x,y} = \frac{1}{l}\sum_{i=1}^{l} \mathtt{xor}(x_i, y_i)$, where l denotes the length of the bit-strings. For randomly generated permutations we might expect an average distance of $d = 0.5$. But actually this expectation fails. For the often treated challenging benchmark `mt10` (see e.g. Nakano and Yamada (1991)) we observe an average normalized distance of $d = 0.273$ only. The maximal observed distance in one million trials is $d = 0.4$. These values are explained by the fact that the majority of bit-strings do not represent feasible solutions. The technological constraints of a JSP strongly reduce the number of possible precedence constellations.

The described technique can be applied to valuate the outcome of the crossover operators outlined in the previous section. Crossover performed by GPMX, GOX or PPX results in one offspring. Ideally the offspring inherits one half of the characteristics from each parent. In the following experiment we determine the phenotypical distance $d_{p1,p2}$ between two randomly generated parents $p1$ and $p2$. Then crossover is performed and the distances of the offspring o to both parents $d_{o,p1}$ and $d_{o,p2}$ are calculated. Table 1 shows the results achieved for 1 000 calls to PPX, GPMX and GOX.

operator	$d_{p1,p2}$	$d_{o,p1}$	$d_{o,p2}$	$d_{o,p1}+d_{o,p2}$
PPX	0.273	0.137	0.136	0.273
GPMX	0.273	0.141	0.139	0.280
GOX	0.273	0.150	0.152	0.302

Tab. 1. Phenotypical preservation of crossover.

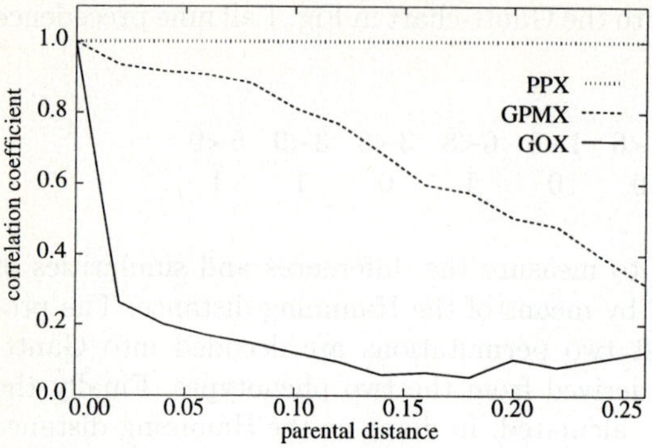

Fig. 6. Preservation of phenotypical properties by different crossover techniques.

As mentioned before, the average normalized Hamming distance between two arbitrary solutions is 0.273. For all three crossover operators we observe $d_{o,p1} \approx d_{o,p2}$. This verifies all operators to pass on the same portion of parental information. Since PPX passes on precedence relations perfectly, $d_{o,p1} + d_{o,p2} = d_{p1,p2}$ holds. For the remaining operators we observe a sum larger than the distance between both parents. GPMX and even more GOX introduce new precedence relations, i.e. disrupt the absolute order of the permutation by implicit mutations.

Thus far we have examined the crossover for arbitrary solutions. Next we examine crossover of parential solutions with varying similarity. Hereby we measure the correlation of the parental distance with the sum of the offspring distance to both parents. A related investigation on the correlation of fitness values has been done by Manderick et al. (1991).

In order to generate parents at different levels of phenotypical similarity, we generate parental pairs p_1, p_2 such that the normalized Hamming distance of a pair falls into one of the 11 intervals $[d_h, d_{h+1}]$ with $d_1 = 0.000, d_2 = 0.025, \ldots d_{11} = 0.275$. We generate p_1 randomly, then copy p_1 to p_2 and finally mutate p_2 iteratively until it falls into the desired cluster. In the experiment each cluster contains $T = 1\,000$ parental pairs. The normalized Hamming distances of parental pairs in each cluster are denoted as $x_t (1 \leq t \leq T)$. We produce offspring by applying crossover to each pair. The sum of the offspring distance to both parents results in $1\,000$ corresponding y_t values. The correlation coefficient $R_{x,y}$ is calculated for each cluster separately by

$$Cov_{x,y} = \frac{1}{T} \sum_{t=1}^{T} (x_t - \overline{x})(y_t - \overline{y})$$

$$\sigma_x = \frac{1}{T} \sum_{t=1}^{T} \sqrt{(x_t - \overline{x})^2}$$

$$R_{x,y} = \frac{Cov_{x,y}}{\sigma_x \sigma_y}.$$

This experiment is performed for each of the four crossover operators under consideration. The results obtained are shown in Fig. 6.

Concerning PPX the correlation coefficient is 1.0 for all clusters. This result is in accordance to the data of Tab. 1. Since PPX does not violate the absolute order among the operations, merely parental information is passed on to offspring regardless of the distance between both parents.

The correlation coefficient of GPMX declines continuously with an increasing parental distance. Nevertheless, GPMX performs well as long as the parents do not differ too much from each other. By respecting the position of the selected substring in the donator while implanting it in the receiver, the absolute order of genes is also kept in most cases, compare Fig. 3.

In contrast, GOX offspring do hardly correlate with their parents. Even for similar parents, the correlation coefficient is very low. Respecting the relative order of genes often forces a substring insertion in the receiver far away from its position in the donator. This change of the substring position causes a massively disturbance of the absolute order of genes.

6 Computational Validation

A purely phenotypical view on crossover operators cannot satisfy. In order to verify the expectations about phenotypical heredity we run the three operators considered on five benchmarks (`10x50e1`–`10x50e5`) taken from Storer et al. (1992). Although these JSP instances are relatively large ($m = 10$ and $N = 50$) they are known to be easy to solve. More difficult benchmarks would require the incorporation of a sophisticated base heuristic in order to gain near optimal solutions. But the use of a heuristic decoding procedure distorts the outcome of crossover.

The well known Simple-GA serves as a genetic algorithm template. In three versions SGA alternatively uses GOX, GPMX, and PPX crossover. The crossover rate is set to 0.6 while no explicit mutation takes place. The population size is set to 500 individuals and the algorithm terminates after 100 generations. Each of the three SGA versions is run for a total of 10 iterations on our benchmark suite. The relative error to the optimum and the standard deviation of the 10 runs are recorded and averaged over the five problem instances.

operator	rel. err.	std. dev.
GOX	12.63	1.28
GPMX	4.01	1.10
PPX	1.62	0.50

Tab. 2. Mean crossover performance.

Table 2 shows the results obtained. They match our expectations about the importance of the absolute order for the JSP. The better an operator preserves precedence relations among operations (compare Fig. 6) the better schedules are gained for easy problem instances. When solving more difficult instances, selection often misguides the search and eventually leads to a suboptimal convergence. In this situation a more disruptive crossover may help to escape from local entrapments. For this reason it is not surprising that even GOX leads to satisfying results in combination with a strong hill-climber, compare Mattfeld (1996).

7 Conclusions

Within this paper we have reflected the properties of permutation representations for combinatorial problems. The evident importance of relative order for the TSP and of position for the QAP is due to the fact that these problems are unconstrained in the permutation scheme. Turning to complex permutation problems the representation implicitly covers the constraints involved. Hereby other kinds of semantical dependencies become important. Unfortunately they are unknown in advance.

As an example we have described a representation for multi-machine scheduling problems in terms of m-partitioned permutations. This representation bears characteristics of both, relative order as well as position. It has been shown that another characteristic – denoted as absolute order – is of predominant importance for job shop scheduling problems. Therefore a new crossover has been presented which perfectly preserves the phenotypical properties of schedules. The comparison with standard crossover operators shows that the effort spent on reflecting a problem is worthwhile .

References

Bierwirth, C. (1995): A Generalized Permutation Approach to Job Shop Scheduling with Genetic Algorithms. OR Spektrum, vol. **17**, 87-92

Kargupta, H., Kalyanmoy, D., Goldberg, D. E. (1992): Ordering Genetic Algorithms and Deception. In: Männer, R., Manderick, B. (eds.): Parallel Problem Solving from Nature II, North Holland, Amsterdam, 47–56

Manderick, B., De Weger, M., Spiessens, P. (1991): The Genetic Algorithm and the Structure of the Fitness Landscape. In: Belew, R. K., Booker, L. B. (eds.): Proc. of the 4th Int. Conf. on Genetic Algorithms. Morgan Kauffman Publishers, San Mateo CA, 143–150

Mattfeld, D. C. (1996): Evolutionary Search and the Job Shop: Investigations on Genetic Algorithms for Production Scheduling, Physica Verlag, Heidelberg

Nakano, R., Yamada, T. (1991): Conventional Genetic Algorithm for Job Shop Problems. In: Belew, R. K., Booker, L. B. (eds.): Proc. of the 4th Int. Conf. on Genetic Algorithms. Morgan Kauffman Publishers, San Mateo CA, 474–479

Oliver, L. M., Smith, D. J., Holland, J. R. C. (1987): A Study of Permutation Crossover Operators on the Traveling Salesman Problem. In: Grefenstette, J. J. (ed.): Proc. of the 2nd Int. Conf. on Genetic Algorithms, Lawrence Erlbaum Associates, Hillsdale NJ, 224–230

Reeves, C. R. (1993): Modern Heuristic Techniques for Combinatorial Problems. Blackwell Scientific Publications, Oxford

Storer, R., Wu, D., Vaccari, R. (1992): New Search Spaces for Sequencing Problems with Application to Job Shop Scheduling. Management Science, vol. **38**, 1495-1509.

Syswerda, G. (1991): Schedule Optimization Using Genetic Algorithms. In: Davis, L. (ed.): Handbook of Genetic Algorithms. Van Nostrand Reinhold, NY, 332–349

Multi-Parent's Niche: n-ary Crossovers on NK-Landscapes

A.E. Eiben[1] and C.A. Schippers[2]

[1] Leiden University, The Netherlands, gusz@wi.leidenuniv.nl
[2] Vrije Universiteit Amsterdam, The Netherlands, adriaan@cs.vu.nl

Abstract. Using the multi-parent diagonal and scanning crossover in GAs reproduction operators obtain an adjustable arity. Hereby sexuality becomes a graded feature instead of a Boolean one. Our main objective is to relate the performance of GAs to the extent of sexuality used for reproduction on less arbitrary functions then those reported in the current literature. We investigate GA behaviour on Kauffman's NK-landscapes that allow for systematic characterization and user control of ruggedness of the fitness landscape. We test GAs with a varying extent of sexuality, ranging from asexual to 'very sexual'. Our tests were performed on two types of NK-landscapes: landscapes with random and landscapes with nearest neighbour epistasis. For both landscape types we selected landscapes from a range of ruggednesses. The results confirm the superiority of (very) sexual recombination on mildly epistatic problems.

1 Introduction

In previous papers the multi-parent scanning crossover and diagonal crossover were tested on numerical optimization problems, [3, 4, 5]. These tests were performed on a test suite of common EA test functions, still they were chosen somewhat arbitrarily, moreover the types of fitness landscapes they span are difficult to characterize. It was therefore not possible to look for 'multi-parent's niche', [6], in a systematic way. For a better analysis of the behaviour of GAs with multi-parent recombination a systematic way of defining different fitness landscapes was necessary. We found such a way in using NK-landscapes that allow characterization and user control of ruggedness of the fitness landscape, [10]. We define what NK-landscapes are in Section 2. We give a brief overview of multi-parent operators in EA in Section 3. Thereafter in Section 4 we describe the experimental setup, and in Section 5 we summarize the test results. Finally, we draw conclusions and sketch further research in Section 6.

2 NK-landscapes

The family of NK-landscapes was introduced by Kauffman as a class of problems where the fitness landscape can be gradually tuned from smooth to chaotic, [10]. The parameters N, respectively K specify the total number of bits (which will equal the chromosome length in the GA searching this landscape) and the number of bits that influence a particular bit. The same K is used for each bit $x_i (i = 1, \ldots, N)$, although the bits that influence x_i differ for every i. Actually, K determines the degree of epistatic interactions between bits. For a certain N, K can be gradually increased from 0 to $N-1$ leading to more and more epistasis, thereby decreasing the fitness correlation between neighboring points. Thus, for higher K's the landscape becomes more rugged.

Formally, using the NK-model each bit x_i of a bitstring $\bar{x}$ of length N is given a user defined fitness f_i and the fitness of $\bar{x}$ (to be maximized) is defined as the average of the fitness of its bits, i.e,

$$f(\bar{x}) = 1/N \cdot \sum_{i=1}^{N} f_i$$

The fitness f_i of x_i depends on K other bits $x_{i_1}, \ldots, x_{i_K}$, that is f_i is context dependent, where a context is a certain configuration of the values $x_{i_1}, \ldots, x_{i_K}$. Therefore, a lookup table of 2^{K+1} rows (2^K different contexts and 2 values for x_i) is needed to specify f_i. This lookup table is created by assigning each entry a random number between 0 and 1 drawn from a uniform distribution. If the bits that determine the fitness of x_i are chosen randomly, we have random neighbor interaction (RNI). If the interacting bits are the ones closest to x_i (assuming x_1 and x_N are neighbors) then we have nearest neighbor interaction (NNI).

NK-landscapes were used to investigate the relationship between characteristics of the fitness landscape and the performance of genetic operators, [11]. In [9] the usefulness of recombination is assessed comparing different (2 parent) crossovers and hill climbing on NK-landscapes with various ruggedness. Here we conduct an 'introspective' study, concentrating on crossover itself. In particular, we compare reproduction mechanisms where the extent of sexuality varies.

3 Multi-parent recombination

Genetic operators in EAs traditionally mimic natural reproduction mechanisms. Unary operators, such as mutation, correspond to asexual, while binary operators, such as crossover, correspond to sexual reproduction. Mutation is always used in an EA, recombination can be either used or not. In this sense sexuality is a Boolean feature: on or off. By the generalization of the binary n-point and uniform crossovers to diagonal, resp. scanning crossover (see below) recombination operators obtain an adjustable arity. Thus, sexuality looses its Boolean character and becomes a graded feature. So, the old question whether 'sexual reproduction is good or not' can be refined to 'how much sex is good'.

The first multi-parent mechanism was global recombination in ES, [1, 14] that produces one new individual that may inherit genes from more than two parents. Nevertheless, the number of parents is not determined, thus global recombination does not make sexuality a graded feature. The same holds for the recently introduced multi-parent Gene Pool Recombination [12, 17] and the Gene Linkage method [15] in GAs. A new extension of ES, the $(\mu/\rho, \lambda)$ multirecombinant strategy [2], does apply an adjustable operator arity ρ.

The first general multi-parent operators with adjustable arity in GAs are scanning crossover and diagonal crossover, introduced in [3] and further studied in [4, 5]. Scanning crossover generalizes uniform crossover, although creating only one child, by chosing one of the i-th genes of the n parents to be the i-th gene of the child. The choice can be random, based on a uniform distribution (uniform scanning), or biased by the fitness of the parents (fitnes based scanning). It can also be deterministic, based on the number of occurrences of the genes (occurrence based scanning). Diagonal crossover generalizes n-point crossover by selecting $(n-1)$ crossover points in the n parents and composing n children by taking the resulting n chromosome segments from the parents 'along the diagonals'. Figure 1 illustrates this idea.

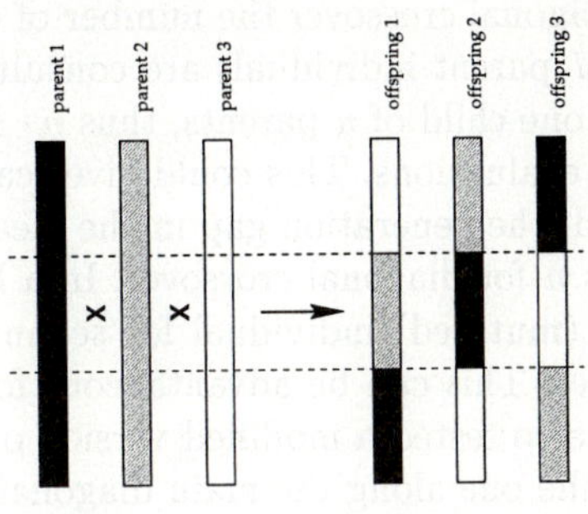

Fig. 1. Diagonal crossover with three parents

4 Experiment setup

In our experiments $N = 100$. We use two test suites, one with NNI and one with RNI. In both test suites we have landscapes for $K = 0, 1, 2, 3, 4, 5, 25$. For higher values, like $K = 50, 99$ it was shown in [9] that GAs cannot treat them well, therfore they are not tested here. Let the number of parents be denoted by P, the type of crossover operator by C and the type of epistatic interaction by I. For every combination of $\langle I, K\rangle$ 10 landscapes are generated and each test, i.e. each combination $\langle C, P\rangle$, is ran 10 times on each landscape. This results in 100 tests for each 4-tuple $\langle I, K, C, P\rangle$. We test 2, 4, 6, 8, 10, 12, 14 and 16 parents for both operators. (The NK-landscape generator can be ftp-ed from *ftp.santafe.edu*, */pub/terry/nk/nk$_l$andscapes.tar.gz*.)

The performance of the GA is measured by the mean distance percentage from the global optimum of the best individual at the end of the evolution. Since the global optimum of an NK-landscape is hard to find we assume the global optima to be the highest fitness found in all runs for a certain pair $\langle N, K\rangle$. When K increases, the validity of this assumption decreases. We performe maximization on the generated landscapes, hence the distance percentage is computed by

$$\Delta = \frac{f_{optimal} - f_{obtained}}{f_{optimal}} \times 100$$

chrom. length	100
GA type	steady state
crossover operator	diagonal crossover, uniform scanning
crossover rate	0.7
mutation rate	0.01 ($1/chrom.lenth$)
selection mechanism	linear rank biased (bias = 1.2)
pool size	200
stop condition	70.000 function evalutations

Table 1. GA setup

and for every combination $\langle I, K, C, P \rangle$ the Δ value presented in this article is the average over 100 tests.

Notice that using diagonal crossover the number of children equals the number of parents, hence M parent individuals are consulted for M fitness evaluations. Scanning creates one child of n parents, thus $n \cdot M$ parent individuals are consulted for M fitness evaluations. This could give scanning an 'unfair' advantage. On the other band, the generation gap in the steady state GA we use is 1 for scanning and equals n for diagonal crossover. In a homogeneous population this results in *one* new (mutated) individual for scanning and n new individuals for diagonal crossover. This can be advantageous for diagonal crossover. To eliminate this effect we also tested a modified version of diagonal crossover that creates only one child, the one along the main diagonal.

5 Experimental results

In figures 2 to 7 the performance results are given in a graphical form. The Δ values (vertical axis) are plotted against the number of parents used for crossover (horizontal axis). The results for $K = 0$ are not displayed, because every run terminated with the optimum. The figures show that the best performance was always achieved by a crossover using more than two parents.

We also tested asexual evolution, i.e. using only mutation. In Table 2 and Table 3 we present a comparison of asexual, (mutation only), sexual (2 parents) and 'very sexual' (16 parents) evolutions. For the sake of clarity, let's remark that in the latter two cases we used crossover **and** mutation and that we did not fine tune operator probabilities because of the extreme computational overhead.

To see regularities in the outcomes better we calculated the *gain in performance* when changing operator arities. $\Gamma^{\Delta}_{1vs.2} = ((\Delta^{mut} - \Delta_2)/\Delta^{mut}) \times 100$ is the gain in performance in terms of effectivity (Δ's) when shifting from asexual to 2-parent sexual reproduction. Similarily, $\Gamma^{\Delta}_{2vs.16} = ((\Delta_2 - \Delta_{16})/\Delta_2) \times 100$. We also observed that not only the mean distance percentage from the optimum is improving when using more parents, but also the standard deviation w.r.t. this mean. Tables 4 and 5 also show the gain of perfromance in terms of standard deviation results (σ's). As reference point we added the absolute σ values for mutation.

The results show that more parents do not only cause more effective search,

K	$\Delta^{mutation}$	$\Delta_2^{diagonal}$	$\Delta_{16}^{diagonal}$	$\Delta_2^{scanning}$	$\Delta_{16}^{scanning}$
1	0.407	0.126	0.004	0.119	0.110
2	1.765	0.843	0.344	1.020	0.837
3	2.824	1.547	0.710	2.193	1.872
4	4.069	2.630	1.340	3.478	3.260
5	5.098	3.377	2.317	4.624	4.681

Table 2. Mean distance percentage (Δ) from the global optimum of the best individual for asexual (mutation only), sexual (2 parents) and 'very sexual' (16 parents) reproduction on NNI

K	$\Delta^{mutation}$	$\Delta_2^{diagonal}$	$\Delta_{16}^{diagonal}$	$\Delta_2^{scanning}$	$\Delta_{16}^{scanning}$
1	0.310	0.277	0.171	0.167	0.153
2	1.817	1.173	0.852	0.857	0.907
3	3.208	3.059	2.083	2.395	2.144
4	4.328	4.328	3.139	3.742	3.375
5	4.808	4.856	4.837	4.400	4.271

Table 3. Mean distance percentage (Δ) from the global optimum of the best individual for asexual (mutation only), sexual (2 parents) and 'very sexual' (16 parents) reproduction on RNI

i.e. better approximation of the optimum (lower Δ's), but also a more robust search, i.e. lower σ's. However, there was a difference between the two test suites and the two crossovers. The highest gain in performance of using more parents is achieved on NNI (by diagonal crossover), the gains on RNI are smaller. Conform to our expectations diagonal crossover was better than scanning on NNI, while for RNI scanning proved to be better, at least for low K's (Fig. 5, 6).

Looking at the operators, we see that the performance of diagonal crossover is (quasi) monotonously increasing with the number of parents for NNI and, although less consistently, also for RNI with lower K's (Figures 2-7). We might get the impression that the curves of diagonal crossover are flattening as K grows. This is however caused by the different scales of the figures. Table 2-5 make clear that the absolute gain in performance increases while the relative gain decreases when K goes from 1 to 4. For uniform scanning the gains in performance are smaller and cannot be so simply related to the number of parents. This suggest that just a slight and inconsistent gain in effectivity can be expected from increasing the number of parents within the scanning scheme. Since uniform scanning is very similar to discrete global recombination in ES, this observation seems to confirm the experiences of Schwefel, [14] p. 146.

It is clear from the results that the GA performance becomes worse on more rugged landscapes. In this sense the multi-parent operators show similar behavior to the standard crossovers, [9].

	K	$\Gamma^{\Delta}_{1vs.2}$	$\Gamma^{\Delta}_{2vs.16}$	σ_{mut}	$\Gamma^{\sigma}_{1vs.2}$	$\Gamma^{\sigma}_{2vs.16}$
diag	1	69%	97%	0.381	39%	100%
	2	52%	59%	0.953	29%	41%
	3	45%	54%	1.147	35%	30%
	4	35%	49%	1.473	24%	32%
	5	34%	31%	1.536	14%	10%
scan	1	71%	8%	0.381	44%	13%
	2	42%	18%	0.953	26%	4%
	3	22%	15%	1.147	6%	19%
	4	14%	6%	1.473	6%	8%
	5	9%	-1%	1.536	-7%	7%

Table 4. NNI: gain in performance when switching from 1 to 2, resp. from 2 to 16 parents, w.r.t. the Δ values and the standard deviation of the Δ values (σ's)

	K	$\Gamma^{\Delta}_{1vs.2}$	$\Gamma^{\Delta}_{2vs.16}$	σ_{mut}	$\Gamma^{\sigma}_{1vs.2}$	$\Gamma^{\sigma}_{2vs.16}$
diag	1	11%	38%	0.308	-1%	29%
	2	35%	27%	1.188	24%	26%
	3	5%	32%	1.671	8%	30%
	4	0%	27%	1.567	-22%	17%
	5	-1%	0%	1.647	-16%	5%
scan	1	46%	8%	0.308	21%	26%
	2	53%	-6%	1.188	42%	2%
	3	25%	10%	1.671	27%	7%
	4	14%	10%	1.567	-9%	16%
	5	8%	3%	1.647	-19%	14%

Table 5. RNI: gain in performance when switching from 1 to 2, resp. from 2 to 16 parents, w.r.t. the Δ values and the standard deviation of the Δ values (σ's)

6 Conclusions and future work

Using diagonal and scanning crossover reproduction operators obtain an arity that can be set by the user, thus sexuality becomes a graded feature in EAs. Our main objective in this investigation was to relate the performance of EAs to the extent of sexuality used for reproduction on less arbitrary functions then those reported in the current literature. We performed experiments in a strict GA setting using 'pure' bit-problems with tunable ruggeddness. The results showed that sexual reproduction (in combination with mutation) is better than asexual reproduction (mutation only). Besides, we found that operators with a higher arity lead to better performance. Roughly speaking we observed that sex is good and more sex is even better.

Nevertheless, there are differences between the two operators we tested. Even though scanning achieves the best performance with more than two parents it shows no consistent improvement when the number of parents is increased. The lack of correlation between the number of parents and performance occured for both types of epistatic interactions and for every level of ruggedness. However, using other choice mechanisms within the scanning scheme (e.g. occurrence based or fitness based) may lead to different results. For diagonal crossover we could establish the advantages of more parents. Additionally, based on these experiments we can draw conclusions on the most promising area of application. On mildly epistatic problems it is worth to generalize the standard 2-parent crossover and to use diagonal crossover with higher n's instead. If moreover the interacting genes are close to one another, the gains of diagonal crossover are higher and come more consistently with increasing the number of parents then for a random spreading of interacting genes. The one-child version of diagonal crossover showed no significant difference in performance. This rejects the hypothesis that the source of diagonal crossover's success is the bigger generational gap.

So far, we have an explanation for some of our observations only. The advatage of more parents is most probably caused by the higher mixing of genes and the usage of a bigger sample (more parents) from the search space to base decisions upon. However, we cannot explain why using more parents consistently improves the performance of diagonal crossover and not the performance of uniform scanning. To answer this question we need additional tests. For instance looking at other performance measures, like speed or succes rate, can supply additional information.

The explanation for the performance differences between the two crossovers on NNI respectively RNI is rather straightforward. On NNI landscapes diagonal crossover outperforms uniform scanning, because it is better at preserving alleles that are near each other in the representation. Uniform scanning on the other hand, is better in preserving alleles that are spread all over the chromosome, and therefore outperforms diagonal crossover on RNI landscapes. In other words: both perform better on landscapes where they are better at preserving epistaticly interacting alleles.

Our results can also be related to those of Hordijk and Manderick [9], who concluded that sexual recombination is useful for low and medium epistasis (not very rugged landscapes). We found that on these very problems a generalization of 1-point 2-parent crossover (that they use) to n-parent diagonal crossover increases GA performance. Also the results of Schaffer and Eshelman, [13], come into mind looking at our observations. They conclude that crossover is useful on mildly epistatic non-deceptive problems. On such problems it is worth to use more parents (within the diagonal scheme), that is 'multi-parent's niche' is (at least) as big as usual crossover's niche, but comes with higher performance.

There is a growing number of studies on the usefulness of sexual recombination. Besides those within the GA paradigm [6, 13, 16], also comparisons of GAs and EP (where no recombination is used) have been performed. The results in [7, 8] indicate that EAs with mutation only can be better than EAs with crossover and mutation. Our observations on multi-parent crossovers and the comparisons between asexual and sexual reproduction can give new ammunition for the supporters of crossover. Further research is planned to compare asexual, sexual and 'very sexual' operators in EAs using floating point representations.

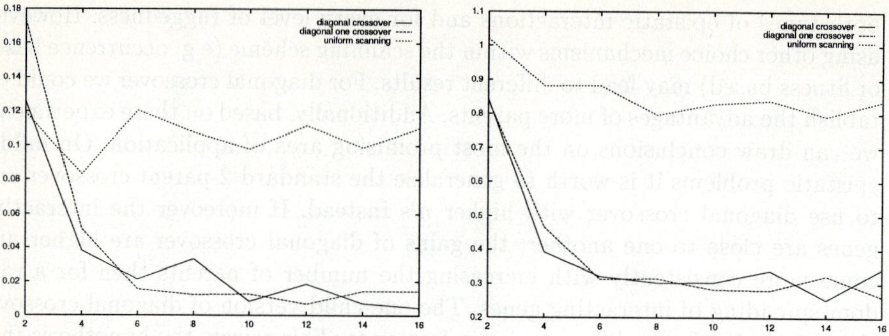

Fig. 2. NNI: mean distance percentage from global optimum (Δ_i) plotted against the number of parents (i) for $K = 1$ and $K = 2$.

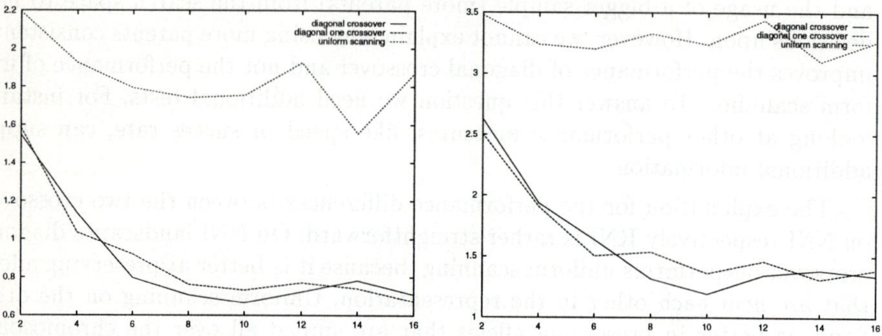

Fig. 3. NNI: mean distance percentage from global optimum (Δ_i) plotted against the number of parents (i) for $K = 3$ and $K = 4$.

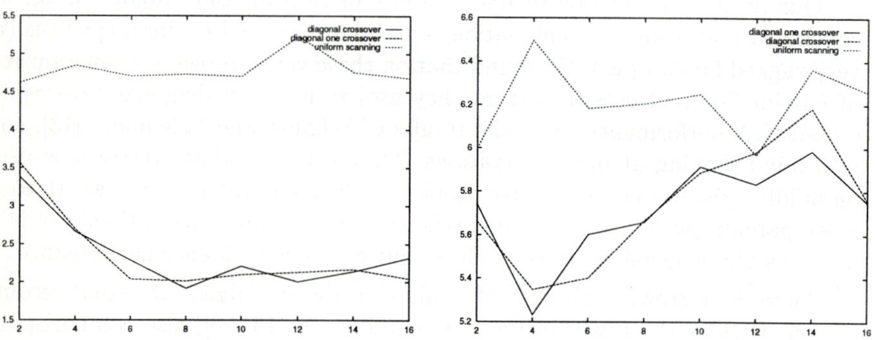

Fig. 4. NNI: mean distance percentage from global optimum (Δ_i) plotted against the number of parents (i) for $K = 5$ and $K = 25$.

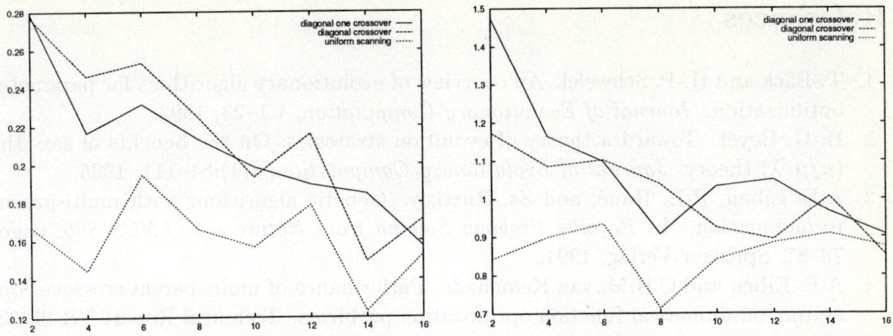

Fig. 5. RNI: mean distance percentage from global optimum (Δ_i) plotted against the number of parents (i) for $K = 1$ and $K = 2$.

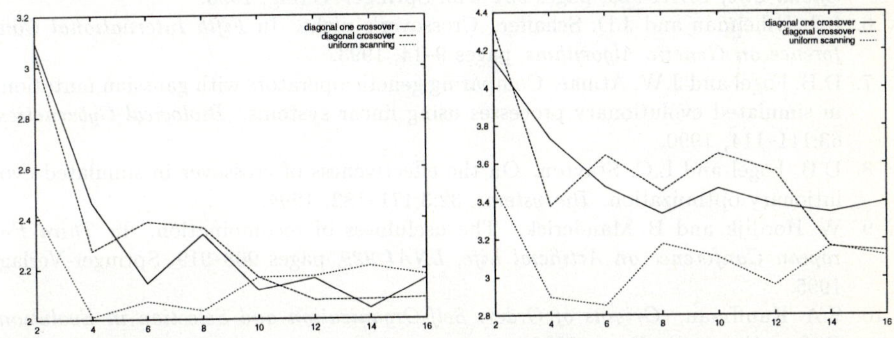

Fig. 6. RNI: mean distance percentage from global optimum (Δ_i) plotted against the number of parents (i) for $K = 3$ and $K = 4$.

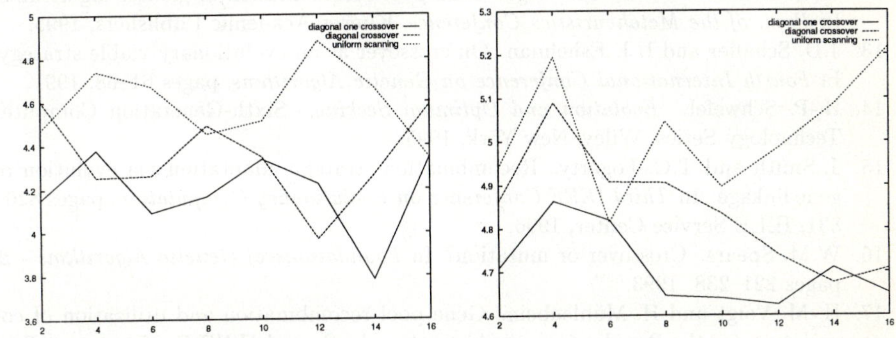

Fig. 7. RNI: mean distance percentage from global optimum (Δ_i) plotted against the number of parents (i) for $K = 5$ and $K = 25$.

References

1. T. Bäck and H.-P. Schwefel. An overview of evolutionary algorithms for parameter optimization. *Journal of Evolutionary Computation*, 1:1–23, 1993.
2. H.-G. Beyer. Toward a theory of evolution strategies: On the benefits of sex- the $(\mu/\mu, \lambda)$ theory. *Journal of Evolutionary Computation*, 3(1):81–111, 1995.
3. A.E. Eiben, P-E. Raué, and Zs. Ruttkay. Genetic algorithms with multi-parent recombination. In *Parallel Problem Solving from Nature - 3, LNCS 866*, pages 78–87. Springer-Verlag, 1994.
4. A.E. Eiben and C.H.M. van Kemenade. Performance of multi-parent crossover operators on numerical function optimization problems. Technical Report TR-95-33, also as ftp://ftp.wi.leidenuniv.nl/pub/CS/TechnicalReports/1995/tr95-33.ps.gz, Leiden University, 1995.
5. A.E. Eiben, C.H.M. van Kemenade, and J.N. Kok. Orgy in the computer: Multi-parent reproduction in genetic algorithms. In *Third European Conference on Artificial Life, LNAI 929*, pages 934–945. Springer-Verlag, 1995.
6. L.J. Eshelman and J.D. Schaffer. Crossover's niche. In *Fifth International Conference on Genetic Algorithms*, pages 9–14, 1993.
7. D.B. Fogel and J.W. Atmar. Comparing genetic operators with gaussian mutations in simulated evolutionary processes using linear systems. *Biological Cybernetics*, 63:111–114, 1990.
8. D.B. Fogel and L.C. Stayton. On the effectiveness of crossover in simulated evolutionary optimization. *Biosystems*, 32:3:171–182, 1994.
9. W. Hordijk and B. Manderick. The usefulness of recombination. In *Third European Conference on Artificial Life, LNAI 929*, pages 908–919. Springer-Verlag, 1995.
10. S.A. Kauffman. *Origins of Order: Self-Organization and Selection in Evolution.* Oxford University Press, 1993.
11. B. Manderick, M. de Weger, and P. Spiessens. The genetic algorithm and the structure of the fitness landscape. In *Fourth International Conference on Genetic Algorithms*, pages 143–150, 1991.
12. H. Mühlenbein and H.-M. Voigt. Gene pool recombination in genetic algorithms. In *Proc. of the Metaheuristics Conference.* Kluwer Academic Publishers, 1995.
13. J.D. Schaffer and L.J. Eshelman. On crossover as an evolutionary viable strategy. In *Fourth International Conference on Genetic Algorithms*, pages 61–68, 1991.
14. H.-P. Schwefel. *Evolution and Optimum Seeking.* Sixth-Generation Computer Technology Series. Wiley, New York, 1995.
15. J. Smith and T.C. Fogarty. Recombination strategy adaptation via evolution of gene linkage. In *Third IEEE Conference on Evolutionary Computation*, pages 826–831. IEEE Service Center, 1996.
16. W.M. Spears. Crossover or mutation? In *Foundations of Genetic Algorithms - 2*, pages 221–238, 1993.
17. H.-M. Voigt and H. Mühlenbein. Gene pool recombination and utilization of covariances for the Breeder Genetic Algorithm. In *Second IEEE Conference on Evolutionary Computation*, pages 172–177, 1995.

A Preliminary Investigation into Directed Mutations in Evolutionary Algorithms

Adam Ghozeil
David B. Fogel
Natural Selection, Inc.
3333 N. Torrey Pines Ct., Suite 200
La Jolla, CA 92037
dfogel@natural-selection.com

Abstract

The traditional mutation operator within evolution strategies and evolutionary programming relies on adding a multivariate zero mean Gaussian random vector to each parent solution. An alternative method is proposed that allows for optimizing the direction of such mutations. The notion of mutation in polar coordinates is adopted such that parents generate offspring in a selected direction with a random step size. Experiments on four functions suggest that the independent adjustment of direction of travel and step size can produce improvements in rate of convergence on some functions.

Introduction

There is a long history of applying evolutionary algorithms, including evolution strategies (Schwefel, 1995; Bäck, 1996) and evolutionary programming (Fogel, 1995), to real-valued continuous optimization problems (e.g., Rechenberg, 1973; Schwefel, 1981; Fogel and Atmar, 1990; Fogel et al., 1990; and many others). These procedures typically operate on a population of candidate solutions where each individual is represented as a vector in R^n. New solutions are created by adding a multivariate zero mean Gaussian random variable to each parent. The vector of associated standard deviations, and possibly also the rotations under conditions of correlated random variables, is determined using a form of self-adaptation (Schwefel, 1981; Fogel et al., 1992; Saravanan et al., 1995). As a result, the possible probability density functions for generating offspring are depicted in Figure 1. Although the use of independently adjustable step sizes and correlations aids in adapting the generating density function to the contours of the response surface being searched, the use of zero mean Gaussian mutations does not impart any true directionality to the search (e.g., in the one-dimensional case, it is just as likely to move toward an optimum as it is to move away from the optimum).

Although it is possible to impart directionality to the search by using non-zero mean Gaussian random variables (Ostermeier, 1992), or variations of fuzzy operators (Voigt and Anheyer, 1994), a more intuitive method would rely on a representational shift from

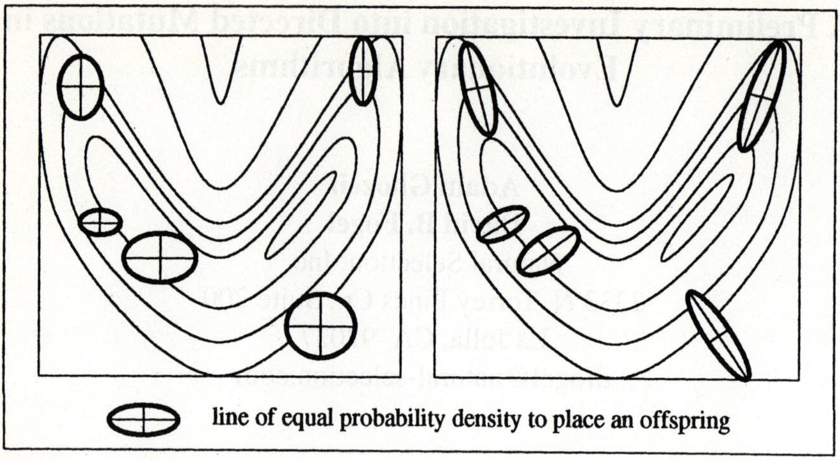

Figure 1. The use of correlated Gaussian mutations to parents allows for new trials to be generated in light of the contours of the response surface. Independent adjustment of the standard deviation in each dimension provides a mechanism for varying the width of the probability contour in alignment with each axis (left picture). Correlated standard deviations provide a mechanism for generating trials such that the probability contours are not aligned with the coordinate axes (right picture) (after Bäck et al., 1991).

"Cartesian" mutations to "polar" mutations. More specifically, rather than add Gaussian random variables to each Cartesian component of a parent, offspring can be generated by choosing a step size and direction vector (r,θ) to add to the parent. This is similar to a technique proposed by Bremermann and Rogson (1964), and Bremermann et al. (1965; 1968), in which offspring were generated by choosing a uniformly distributed direction from the parent such that the direction lay within a cone of a specified angle then stepping to a boundary of the cone (see also Schumer and Steiglitz, 1968). Bremermann's technique was developed for linear and convex programming problems, and the current method is offered as a more general instantiation of the fundamental concept.

Method & Analysis

Four mutation schemes were compared on the Quadratic, Bohachevsky, Ackley, and Rosenbrock functions:

$$f_1(\mathbf{x}) = \Sigma\, x_i^2,\ i \in [1, ..., n] \text{ (Quadratic)}$$
$$f_2(\mathbf{x}) = \Sigma(x_i^2 + 2x_{i+1}^2 - 0.3\cos(3\pi x_i) - 0.4\cos(4\pi x_{i+1}) + 0.7,\quad i \in [1, ..., n\text{-}1] \text{ (Bohachevsky)}$$
$$f_3(\mathbf{x}) = -20\exp[-0.2\sqrt{\Sigma x_i/n}] - \exp[1/n * \Sigma \cos(2\pi x_i)] + 20 + e,\quad i \in [1, ..., n] \text{ (Ackley)}$$
$$f_4(\mathbf{x}) = \Sigma(100(x_i^2 - x_{i+1})^2 + (1 - x_i)^2),\ i \in [1, ..., n] \text{ (Rosenbrock)}$$

in n = 5, 10, and 20 dimensions. Each trial was executed for 500 generations. Every generation, 30 parents generated one offspring each. Selection was conducted by using a standard evolutionary programming stochastic tournament based on $q = 3$ competitors (Fogel 1995). The initial populations were created with $x_i \in U(-5.12, 5.12)$, $i \in [1, \ldots, n]$, following De Jong (1975) and other literature. Thirty trials were executed to reduce the effects of noise on the mean results and allow statistical comparisons.

The first mutation scheme created offspring by adding to a parent vector x an n-dimensional Gaussian random variable with zero mean and a standard deviation:

$$\sigma = 1.224[\sqrt{f(\mathbf{x})}]/n$$

where $f(\mathbf{x})$ is the function to be minimized. This has been shown to be the optimal mutation rate for minimizing the quadratic bowl when using zero mean Gaussian perturbations in terms of maximizing the expected convergence rate (Rechenberg, 1973; Bäck et al., 1993).

The second method of mutation created offspring in a similar fashion, but with a self-adaptive value of σ, the procedure being a modified form of that offered in Schwefel (1981). For each offspring, the value of σ was mutated such that

$$\sigma' = \sigma * \exp[N(0,1)]$$

where N(0,1) is a Gaussian random variable with a mean of zero and a variance of 1. This mutated value σ' was used to produce the offspring's other parameters. The first generation was initialized with a value $\sigma_0 = 5$.

The third technique used polar coordinates for mutation, updating r and θ independently (Figure 2). In this case, r was equal to the magnitude (Euclidean norm) of an n-dimensional Gaussian variable with a mean of zero and a standard deviation σ_r which was subject to self-adaptation as above. This method produces step sizes identical to those generated using the previous method. The mutation on the direction was handled in the following fashion: the direction was defined as an n-dimensional unit vector in Cartesian coordinates. An n-dimensional Gaussian random variable with a mean of zero and a self-adaptive standard deviation σ_θ was added to this unit vector. The resulting vector was then normalized to produce the new direction vector (Figure 3). The first generation was initialized with $\sigma_r = \sigma_\theta = 5$ and a uniform direction vector.

The fourth technique employed the same mutation scheme for σ_r, σ_θ, and θ, but r was set equal to σ_r, so that the step size was deterministically linked to the mutation parameter (i.e., it was set equal to the parameter).

Results

Some representative results are given in Table 1. On the Quadratic, Ackley, and Bohachevsky functions, the optimal mutation rate for a bowl always produced a lower value after 500 generations than the others. On the Rosenbrock function, the directed, lognormal step was always statistically significantly superior to the others, and the self-adaptive variance produced lower scores than the optimum for a quadratic bowl. For each function, the directed, lognormal step produced lower final scores than the di-

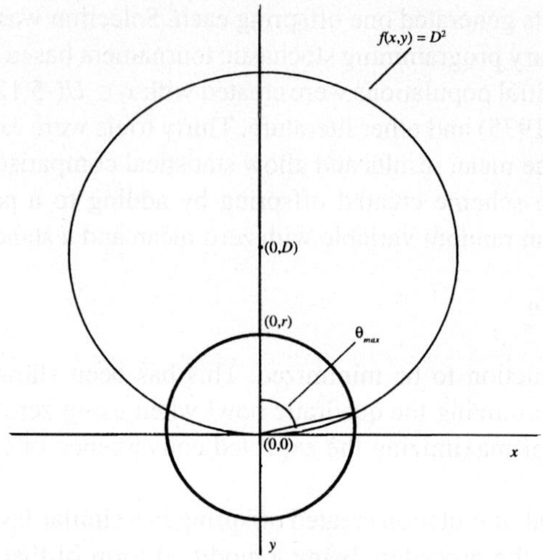

Figure 2. Depiction of contour line for the quadratic bowl at $f(x,y) = D^2$, the position of a parent (placed at the origin), and the circle of possible points that are one step away at a distance of r. Instead of distributing trials according to Gaussian perturbations, the figure suggests how polar coordinates can be used to define a direction and step size by which to mutate a parent solution.

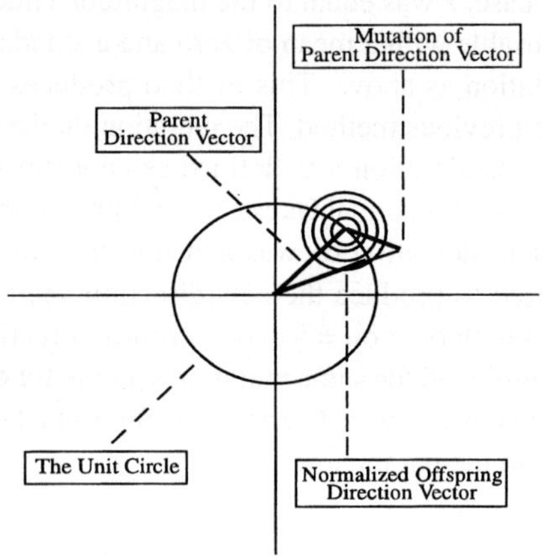

Figure 3. Creating a new direction vector under the third technique compared in the paper (see text). The parent direction vector is perturbed using a Gaussian density function (indicated by the concentric circles. The resulting vector is normalized to the unit circle to produce the new offspring direction vector.

rected, self-adaptive step, which produced scores comparable to those of the undirected, self-adaptive method.

Table 1. The mean best solution's objective value and associated sample standard deviation after 500 generations for 30 trials on the Quadratic, Bohachevsky, Ackley, and Rosenbrock functions. "Gauss-BO" refers to the classic method of generating offspring via zero mean multivariate Gaussian mutations with a standard deviation optimized for a quadratic bowl. "Gauss-SA" refers to a similar method, but with the standard deviation given by a self-adaptive parameter. "DSA" refers to a directed mutation with a step size equivalent to that produced by the self-adaptive Gaussian. "DLN" refers to a directed mutation with a lognormal distribution on the step size (see text). For the sake of space, only the 20-dimensional results are shown, but the same trends appear in 5 and 10 dimensions. Values that appear identical for different methods are simply the result of rounding to the second decimal place. The minimum value for all of the functions studied is zero.

Quadratic Bowl				
	Gauss-BO	Gauss-SA	DSA	DLN
Mean	2.07e-10	1.04e+2	1.05e+2	1.30e+1
Std. Dev	1.40e-10	1.40e+1	1.48e+1	2.20

Bohachevsky				
	Gauss-BO	Gauss-SA	DSA	DLN
Mean	1.01e+1	3.12e+2	3.09e+2	4.97e+1
Std. Dev	9.59e-1	4.47e+1	4.54e+1	5.56

Ackley				
	Gauss-BO	Gauss-SA	DSA	DLN
Mean	3.39e-1	8.98	8.98	4.66
Std. Dev	6.36e-1	4.46e-1	4.46e-1	2.20e-1

Rosenbrock				
	Gauss-BO	Gauss-SA	DSA	DLN
Mean	1.17e+5	1.16e+5	1.17e+5	3.03e+3
Std. Dev	2.58e+4	2.50e+4	2.58e+4	7.27e+2

Conclusions

The polar mutations employed provided convergence rates comparable to a common self-adaptive technique. There was little or no improvement using this method for preserving direction of travel when a step based on the magnitude of a multivariate Gaussian was used. However, an unexpected result of these experiments was the apparent superiority of taking a step with a size distributed as a lognormal over a step with a size given by the magnitude of a multivariate Gaussian random variable. More experiments would need to be conducted before general assessment can be made, but it suggests further research. Such adjustment of the distribution of the step size was only possible due to the polar nature of the mutations being employed. It is possible to exactly replicate a multivariate Gaussian mutation using the polar paradigm, and to produce numerous other distributions. Much thought has been given to the optimal step size under the assumption of Gaussian mutations (Schwefel, 1981; Fogel et al., 1992; Saravanan et al., 1995), but polar mutations allow research into the optimal probability distribution function of the step size, as well as its optimal mean. Even if polar mutations were used to only produce uniform angles, they would still provide more freedom than the traditional Cartesian, Gaussian approach. The fact that they also provide a mechanism for preserving direction of travel implies a wealth of possibilities for further development.

Acknowledgments

The authors thank the anonymous referees for the insightful and helpful criticisms. Thanks also are owed to V.W. Porto and M. Owen for providing comments on the final draft.

References

T. Bäck (1996) *Evolutionary Algorithms in Theory and Practice*, Oxford, NY.

T. Bäck, F. Hoffmeister, and H.-P. Schwefel (1991) "A Survey of Evolution Strategies," *Proc. of the Fourth Intern. Conf. on Genetic Algorithms*, R.K. Belew and L.B. Booker (eds.), Morgan Kaufmann, San Mateo, CA, pp. 2-9.

H.J. Bremermann and M. Rogson (1964) "An evolution-type search method for convex sets," ONR Tech. Report, Contracts 222(85) and 3656(58), Berkeley, CA.

H.J. Bremermann, M. Rogson, and S. Salaff (1965) "Search by evolution," *Biophysics and Cybernetic Systems*, M. Maxfield, A. Callahan, and L.J. Fogel (eds.), Spartan Books, Washington D.C., pp. 157-167.

H.J. Bremermann, M. Rogson, and S. Salaff (1968) "Global properties of evolution processes," *Natural Automata and Useful Simulations* (Proceedings of 1966 conference), H.H. Pattee, E.A. Edlsack, L. Fein, and A.B. Callahan, Spartan Books, Washington D.C., pp. 3-41.

I.O. Bohachevsky, M.E. Johnson, M.L. Smith (1986) "Generalized Simulated Annealing for Function Optimization," *Technometrics*, Vol. 28:3, pp. 209-217.

K.A. De Jong (1975) "The Analysis of the Behavior of a Class of Genetic Adaptive Systems," Ph.D. Dissertation, Univ. of Michigan, Ann Arbor.

D.B. Fogel and J.W. Atmar (1990) "Comparing Genetic Operators with Gaussian Mutations in Simulated Evolutionary Processes Using Linear Systems," *Biological Cybernetics*, Vol. 63, pp. 111-114.

D.B. Fogel, L.J. Fogel, and V.W. Porto (1990) "Evolving Neural Networks," *Biological Cybernetics*, Vol. 63:6, pp. 487-493.

D.B. Fogel, L.J. Fogel, W. Atmar, and G.B. Fogel (1992) "Hierarchic Methods of Evolutionary Programming," *Proc. of the First Annual Conference on Evolutionary Programming*, D.B. Fogel and W. Atmar (eds.), Evolutionary Programming Society, La Jolla, CA, pp. 175-182.

A. Ostermeier (1992) "An Evolution Strategy with Momentum Adaptation of the Random Number Distribution, " *Parallel Problem Solving from Nature, 2*, R. Männer and B. Manderick (eds.), North-Holland, Amsterdam, pp. 197-206.

I. Rechenberg (1973) *Evolutionsstrategie: Optimierung Technischer Systeme nach Prinzipien der Biologischen Evolution*. Stuttgart: Formman-Holzboog Verlag.

N. Saravanan, D.B. Fogel, and K.M. Nelson (1995) "A Comparison of Methods for Self-Adaptation in Evolutionary Algorithms," *BioSystems*, Vol. 36, pp. 157-166.

H.-P. Schwefel (1981) *Numerical Optimization of Computer Models*, John Wiley, Chichester, U.K.

M.A. Schumer and K. Steiglitz (1968) "Adaptive Step Size Random Search," *IEEE Trans. on Auto. Control,* Vol. 13, pp. 270--276.

H.-P. Schwefel (1995) *Evolution and Optimum Seeking*, John Wiley, NY.

H.-M. Voigt and T. Anheyer (1994) "Modal Mutations in Evolutionary Algorithms," *Proc. of the 1st IEEE Conference on Evolutionary Computation*, IEEE Press, pp. 88-92.

Heuristic Crossovers for Real-Coded Genetic Algorithms Based on Fuzzy Connectives*

Francisco Herrera and Manuel Lozano

Department of Computer Science and Artificial Intelligence
University of Granada
18071 - Granada, Spain

Abstract. A problem in the use of genetic algorithms is the premature convergence in a local optimum. Its main cause is the lack of diversity in the population due to a disproportionate relationship between exploitation and exploration. In this paper, we present heuristic crossover operators for real-coded genetic algorithms, which use the adaptation of the parents for generating the offspring. With these operators, diversity and convergence in the population may be modeled in order to avoid the premature convergence problem and to introduce good final behaviour.

1 Introduction

Different evolutionary algorithms based on real coding have been presented for tackling *parameter optimization problems*. They include *evolutionary strategies* ([1, 18]) and *real-coded GAs* (RCGAs) ([22, 21, 12, 3, 14, 8]). In this paper, we deal with RCGAs.

The GA's behaviour is strongly determined by the balance between exploiting what already works best and exploring possibilities that might eventually evolve into something even better. The loss of critical alleles due to the selection pressure, the selection noise, the schemata disruption caused by the crossover operators, and the poor parameter setting may mislead the exploitation/exploration balance and produce the lack of *diversity* in the population. Under these circumstances a preeminent problem appears: *the premature convergence*, i.e., the search becomes trapped in a local optimum before the global optimum is found.

The power of GAs arises from their crossover operator. It may be considered to be one of the algorithm's defining characteristics, and it is one of the components to be borne in mind to improve the GA's behaviour [10]. Crossover operator is a determinant element in the exploration and exploitation relationship kept by the GAs, so it may be taken into account for solving the premature convergence problem [2]. Therefore, new alternatives to this operator may be considered that allow suitable levels of exploration and exploitation to be established.

In [6, 9], the following were presented: the *fuzzy connectives-based crossovers* (FCB-crossovers), crossover operators for RCGAs based on the use of fuzzy connectives. Furthermore, a set of *offspring selection mechanisms* (OSM) was

* This research has been supported by DGICYT PB92-0933.

proposed, which choose the chromosomes (produced by the crossover) that form part of the new population. Different exploration and exploitation degrees are introduced by the FCB-crossover operators. The OSM establish a relationship between these degrees, so they induce different diversity levels in the population.

The results obtained in [6, 9] about the diversity levels, that are produced by different types of FCB-crossovers, motivated the presentation of *dynamic FCB-crossover operators* based on the use of parameterized fuzzy connectives [7]. These operators keep a suitable sequence between the exploration and the exploitation along the GA's run: "*to protect the exploration in the initial stages and the exploitation later*". This sequence is adequate for avoiding the premature convergence problem and for improving GA efficiency [12]. Other proposals for crossover operators based on fuzzy techniques may be found in [19, 16, 20].

In this paper, we present crossover operators for controlling the diversity and convergence of RCGAs: *heuristic FCB-crossover operators.* They use the fitness of the parents for leading the search process towards the most promising zones.

We shall present two types of crossover operators: one with *heuristic exploration properties*, called *dominated heuristic crossovers*, that attempt to introduce a useful diversity into the GA population; another with *heuristic exploitation properties*, called *biased heuristic crossovers*, that induce a biased convergence towards the best elements. Furthermore, we present the *dynamic heuristic FCB-crossover* operators, which put together the heuristic properties and the features of the dynamic FCB-crossover.

The paper is set up as follows: in Section 2, we present the heuristic crossover operators based on fuzzy connectives, in Section 3, we propose the dynamic heuristic crossover operators based on parameterized fuzzy connectives, in Section 4, we explain the experiments that were carried out in order to study the performance of the crossover operators presented along with others proposed in the literature, finally some conclusions are pointed out in Section 5.

2 Heuristic Crossover Operators

The heuristic crossover operators use the fitness of the parents for leading the search process towards the most promising zones. Subsection 2.1 presents a short analysis of the ways in which this is done. Subsection 2.2 reports two instances of the heuristic operators proposed in the literature. Subsection 2.3 reviews the gene combination functions proposed in [6, 9], which are used for presenting in Subsection 2.4 the heuristic fuzzy connectives-based crossover operators.

2.1 Use of the Fitness of the Parents by the Crossover Operator

The fitness of the parents may be useful for: 1) producing diversity and 2) inducing convergence:

1. Although the generation of diversity is a key issue for solving the premature convergence problem, it doesn't guarantee by itself the improvement of the GA's behaviour. Really, what it is needed is that diversity becomes useful i.e., it allows good elements to be reached ([11]). The generation of diversity

in zones close to the best parents allows the promising genetic material to be introduced into the population. It seems natural to consider that the neighbours of the good chromosomes have interesting properties. In this way useful diversity is included in the population.
2. The convergence may be produced by reducing the zones represented in the population towards the most promising ones. This may be achieved by sampling chromosomes near to the best known ones.

2.2 Antecedents

Two antecedents of heuristic crossover operators have appeared in the literature ([21, 17]); they are extensions of the averaging operators ([22, 4, 15]).

- *Wright's heuristic crossover* [21]
  Let's suppose two chromosomes $C_1 = (c_1^1 \dots c_n^1)$ and $C_2 = (c_1^2 \dots c_n^2)$ to be crossed, where C_1 is the one with the best fitness. Then, an offspring, $H = (h_1, ..., h_i, ..., h_n)$, is generated with $h_i = r \cdot (c_i^1 - c_i^2) + c_i^1$ where r is a random number belonging to $[0, 1]$.
- *Linear BGA crossover* [17]
  Under the considerations above, H is generated with $h_i = c_i^1 \pm rang_i \cdot \gamma \cdot \Lambda$, where $\Lambda = \frac{c_i^2 - c_i^1}{\|C_1 - C_2\|}$, the "−" sign is chosen with a probability of 0.9, $rang_i$ is usually $0.5 \cdot (b_i - a_i)$ and $\gamma = \sum_{k=0}^{15} \alpha_k 2^{-k}$ where $\alpha_i \in \{0, 1\}$ is randomly generated with $p(\alpha_i = 1) = \frac{1}{16}$.

2.3 Functions for the Combination of Genes

Let's consider $c_i^1, c_i^2 \in [a_i, b_i]$ $(c_i^1 \leq c_i^2)$ two genes to be combined. The action interval $[a_i, b_i]$ of these genes can be divided into three intervals $[a_i, c_i^1]$, $[c_i^1, c_i^2]$ and $[c_i^2, b_i]$ that bound three regions to which the resultant genes of some combination of c_i^1 and c_i^2 may belong. These intervals could be classified as exploration or exploitation zones. The interval with both genes being the extremes is an exploitation zone, the two remaining intervals are exploration zones.

With regards to these intervals, in [6] three monotone and non-decreasing functions are proposed: F, S and M, defined from $[a, b] \times [a, b]$ into $[a, b]$, $a, b \in \Re$, and which fulfill $\forall c, c' \in [a, b]$,

$$F(c, c') \leq \min\{c, c'\}, \; S(c, c') \geq \max\{c, c'\} \text{ and } \min\{c, c'\} \leq M(c, c') \leq \max\{c, c'\}.$$

Each one of these functions allows us to combine two genes giving results belonging to each one of the aforementioned intervals. Therefore, each function will have different exploration or exploitation properties depending on the range being covered by it.

T-norms, t-conorms and averaging operators used as fuzzy connectives may be considered to build these functions. A t-norm, T, a t-conorm, G and an averaging operator, P, are functions from $[0, 1] \times [0, 1]$ into $[0, 1]$, such that $\forall x, y \in [0, 1]$ they fulfill that $T(x, y) \leq \min\{x, y\}$, $G(x, y) \geq \max\{x, y\}$ and $0 \leq P(x, y) \leq 1$, respectively ([13]). We may associate to F a t-norm, to S a t-conorm and to M an averaging operator ([6, 9]). In order to do so, we need to transform the genes, that will be combined, from the interval $[a, b]$ into $[0, 1]$ and later, the results into $[a, b]$.

Different connective families may be considered for building sets of functions F, S and M. Table 1 shows those that will be used in this paper ([13]).

Table 1. Families of fuzzy connectives

Family	*t-norm*	*t-conorm*	*Averaging Fun.* $(0 \leq \lambda \leq 1)$
Logical	$T_1(x,y) = \min(x,y)$	$G_1(x,y) = \max(x,y)$	$P_1(x,y) = (1-\lambda)x + \lambda y$
Hamacher	$T_2(x,y) = \frac{xy}{x+y-xy}$	$G_2(x,y) = \frac{x+y-2xy}{1-xy}$	$P_2(x,y) = \frac{1}{\frac{y-y\lambda-xy+x\lambda}{xy}+1}$
Algebraic	$T_3(x,y) = xy$	$G_3(x,y) = x + y - xy$	$P_3(x,y) = x^{1-\lambda}y^{\lambda}$
Einstein	$T_4(x,y) = \frac{xy}{1+(1-x)(1-y)}$	$G_4(x,y) = \frac{x+y}{1+xy}$	$P_4(x,y) = \frac{2}{1+(\frac{2-x}{x})^{1-\lambda}(\frac{2-y}{y})^{\lambda}}$

Two types of heuristic crossover operators are defined using F, S and M functions: *dominated heuristic crossovers and biased heuristic crossovers.*

2.4 Dominated and Biased Heuristic Crossover Operators

Given two chromosomes, C_1 and C_2, to be crossed, with C_1 being the one with the best fitness (a minimization problem is assumed), we propose generating an offspring $H = (h_1, ...h_n)$, using the following crossover operators:

– *Dominated Heuristic Crossover*

$$h_i = \begin{cases} F(c_i^1, c_i^2) \text{ if } c_i^1 \leq c_i^2 \\ S(c_i^1, c_i^2) \text{ if } c_i^1 > c_i^2 \end{cases} \quad i = 1, ..., n.$$

This operator is based on functions with exploration properties, therefore it provides *heuristic exploration features.*

– *Biased Heuristic Crossover*

$h_i = M_i(c_i^1, c_i^2)$, $i = 1, ..., n$, where M_i should be appropriate for fulfilling that $|c_i^1 - h_i| \leq |c_i^2 - h_i|$. In order to keep this, we may build M_i using an averaging operator P_i (see Table 1) with

$$\lambda = 1 - \frac{\mathrm{f}(\mathrm{C}_1)}{\mathrm{f}(\mathrm{C}_1) + \mathrm{f}(\mathrm{C}_2)} \tag{1}$$

where $f(\cdot)$ is the fitness function. We need to point out that the gene of the best chromosome should be the second argument of M_i (see the definition of the M functions in Table 1). The tendency degree of the resultant M_i function towards c_i^1 depends on the relative importance of C_1 over C_2. Since biased crossover operators are based on an M function, they show *heuristic exploitation features.*

These heuristic FCB-crossover operators produce a child each whose components are closer to the corresponding component of its fitter parent, in terms of the fuzzy conectives used.

We use the Logical, Hammacher, Algebraic and Einstein F, S and M functions to build four dominated and biased crossover operators: the Logical, Hammacher, Algebraic and Einstein ones.

The application of these operators to the population will be carried out using the following strategy, that is denoted as ST: for each pair of chromosomes from a total of $p_c \cdot N$, two offspring are generated; one with a dominated heuristic crossover and the other with a biased heuristic crossover. Both offspring will be part of the new population. With this strategy, we are inducing the two heuristic properties in the population.

3 Dynamic Heuristic Crossover Operators

In [21], it was advised that the heuristic crossover operators should be applied in advanced stages of the GAs. Probably, the best chromosomes appearing in the initial stages are far away from the global optimum. If heuristic crossover operators are applied to them, the GA search direction is likely to be led towards a local optimum, and so, the risk of premature convergence increases. However, in the advanced generations, the best chromosomes may be considered near to the optimal regions and so, the heuristics may be useful.

According to this, we propose combining the two heuristic crossover operators presented and the dynamic FCB-crossover operators. This will favour diversity in the initial GA stages and the convergence in the final ones. We design *dynamic heuristic FCB-crossover operators* that allow the level of heuristic effects to be dependent on the current generation in which they are applied. At the beginning, this level is low and diversity high, later on, the heuristic level gradually increases.

Next, we present function families for the combination of genes that will be used for building dynamic heuristic FCB-crossovers.

3.1 Function Families for the Combination of Genes

For a GA with a maximum number of generations g_{max}, we propose an F function family $\mathcal{F} = (F^1, ..., F^{g_{max}})$, an S function family $\mathcal{S} = (S^1, ..., S^{g_{max}})$ and an M function family $\mathcal{M} = (M^1, ..., M^{g_{max}})$, which for $1 \leq t \leq g_{max} - 1$ fulfill:

$$F^t(c, c') \leq F^{t+1}(c, c') \text{ and } F^{g_{max}}(c, c') \cong min(c, c'),$$

$$S^t(c, c') \geq S^{t+1}(c, c') \text{ and } S^{g_{max}}(c, c') \cong max(c, c'),$$

$$M^t(c, c') \geq M^{t+1}(c, c') \text{ or } M^t(c, c') \leq M^{t+1}(c, c') \ \forall t \text{ and } M^{g_{max}}(c, c') \cong M_{lim}(c, c'),$$

where M_{lim} is an M function called M limit function. We shall denote $\mathcal{M}_+$ or $\mathcal{M}_-$ an $\mathcal{M}$ function family fulfilling the first and the second part of the last property, respectively.

$\mathcal{F}$ and $\mathcal{S}$ function families are built using a parameterized t-norm T^q converging on the logical t-norm and a parameterized t-conorms G^q converging on the logical t-conorm, respectively. In this paper, we use the following parameterized t-norms and t-conorms ([13]).

Table 2. Families of parameterized fuzzy connectives

Types	*Par. t-norms*	*Par t-conorms*
Frank $(q > 0), (q \neq 1)$	$T_1^q(x,y) = log_q[1 + \frac{(q^x-1)(q^y-1)}{q-1}]$	$G_1^q(x,y) = 1 - log_q[1 + \frac{(q^{1-x}-1)(q^{1-y}-1)}{q-1}]$
Dombi $(q > 0)$	$T_2^q(x,y) = \frac{1}{1+\sqrt[q]{(\frac{1-x}{x})^q+(\frac{1-y}{y})^q}}$	$G_2^q(x,y) = 1 - \frac{1}{1+\sqrt[q]{(\frac{x}{1-x})^q+(\frac{y}{1-y})^q}}$
Dubois $(0 \leq q \leq 1)$	$T_3^q(x,y) = \frac{xy}{x \vee y \vee q}$	$G_3^q(x,y) = 1 - \frac{(1-x)(1-y)}{(1-x)\vee(1-y)\vee q}$

We obtain $\mathcal{M}$ function families using parameterized averaging functions. An example of these functions is:

$$\forall x, y \in [0,1],\ 0 \leq q \leq 1,\ P^q(x,y) = qx + (1-q)y. \tag{2}$$

Now, we design two types of dynamic crossover operators using the $\mathcal{F}$, $\mathcal{S}$ and $\mathcal{M}$ function families defined earlier.

3.2 Dynamic Dominated and Biased Heuristic Crossover Operators

Let's suppose $C_1^t = (c_1^{1t}, ...c_n^{1t})$ and $C_2^t = (c_1^{2t}, ...c_n^{2t})$, two chromosomes which were selected to apply the crossover to them in a generation t. Let's also suppose that C_1^t is the one with the best fitness. Then, we may generate $H^t = (h_1^t, ..., h_n^t)$ using one of the following crossovers:

- *Dynamic dominated heuristic crossover*

  $$h_i^t = \begin{cases} F^t(c_i^{1t}, c_i^{2t}) \text{ if } c_i^{1t} \leq c_i^{2t} \\ S^t(c_i^{1t}, c_i^{2t}) \text{ if } c_i^{1t} > c_i^{2t} \end{cases} \quad i = 1, ..., n,$$

  where F^t and S^t belong to the function family $\mathcal{F}$ and $\mathcal{S}$, respectively.
  We use the $\mathcal{F}$ and $\mathcal{S}$ function families based on parameterized t-norms and t-conorms in Table 2 to specify three types of dynamic dominated heuristic crossover operators: the Frank, Dombi and Dubois ones.

- *Dynamic biased heuristic crossover*

  $h_i^t = M_i^t(c_i^1, c_i^2)$, $i = 1, ..., n$, where M_i^t belongs to a function family $\mathcal{M}_i^+$ if $c_i^{1t} \leq c_i^{2t}$ or to $\mathcal{M}_i^-$ otherwise. Both have the same M limit function, which fulfill $|c_i^{1t} - M_{lim}(c_i^{1t}, c_i^{2t})| \leq |c_i^{2t} - M_{lim}(c_i^{1t}, c_i^{2t})|$.
  We have used the parameterized averaging operator defined in (2) for building a dynamic biased heuristic crossover. To do that, we have also considered the following initial conditions: $M^1(c_i^{1t}, c_i^{2t}) = \frac{c_i^{1t}+c_i^{2t}}{2}$ and $M_{lim}(c_i^{1t}, c_i^{2t}) = (1-\lambda)c_i^{1t} + \lambda c_i^{2t}$ where λ is computed using (1).

The application of these operators is carried out according to the strategy denoted as DST: for each pair of parents, two offspring are generated, one with a dynamic dominated heuristic crossover and the other with a dynamic biased heuristic crossover.

4 Experiments

Minimization experiments on the following four well-known functions were carried out in order to study the efficiency of the crossover operators proposed. f_1 is the *sphere model*, f_2 the *generalized Rosenbrock function*, f_3 is the *generalized Rastringin function* and f_4 the *Ackley function*. f_1 and f_2 are unimodal functions whereas f_3 and f_4 are multimodal ones. We have considered $n = 25$.

Table 3. Test functions

Definition	Intervals	Optimum
$f_1(\mathbf{x}) = \sum_{i=1}^{n} x_i^2$	$-5.12 \le x_i \le 5.12$	$f_1^*(0,\ldots,0) = 0$
$f_2(\mathbf{x}) = \sum_{i=1}^{n-1} (100 \cdot (x_{i+1} - x_i^2)^2 + (x_i - 1)^2)$	$-5.12 \le x_i \le 5.12$	$f_2^*(1,\ldots,1) = 0$
$f_3(\mathbf{x}) = a \cdot n + \sum_{i=1}^{n} x_i^2 - a \cdot \cos(\omega \cdot x_i)$ $a = 10,\ \omega = 2\pi$	$-5.12 \le x_i \le 5.12$	$f_3^*(0,\ldots,0) = 0$
$f_4(\mathbf{x}) = -a \cdot \exp\left(-b\sqrt{\frac{1}{n} \cdot \sum_{i=1}^{n} x_i^2}\right) -$ $- \exp\left(\frac{1}{n} \cdot \sum_{i=1}^{n} \cos(\omega \cdot x_i)\right) + a + e$ $a = 20,\ b = 0.2,\ \omega = 2\pi$	$-32.768 \le x_i \le 32.768$	$f_4^*(0,\ldots,0) = 0$

For each type of crossover operator presented in this paper, we built an algorithm. The algorithms ga-H-Logical, ga-H-Hamacher, ga-H-Algebraic and ga-H-Einstein apply their respective dominated and biased heuristic crossover operators following the ST strategy. The algorithms ga-DH-Frank, ga-DH-Dombi and ga-DH-Dubois apply the DST strategy using their respective dynamic heuristic dominated crossover operators and the dynamic biased heuristic crossover operators proposed in Section 3. Furthermore, we implement some RCGAs based on crossover operators proposed in the literature, which were studied in [8] and showed good results: ga-Simple [12], ga-Linear [22], ga-BLX-α [3] with $\alpha = 0.3$, ga-Discrete [14]. We include an algorithm denoted as ga-ST2-Logical based on an FCB-crossover operator [6, 9] and another based on a dynamic FCB-crossover, which is denoted as ga-DRGA4 [7]. Finally two algorithms, ga-H-Wright and ga-Linear-BGA, based on Wright's heuristic and linear BGA crossover operators, respectively (see Subsection 2.2), are also implemented. The mutation operator used in ga-Discrete is Mühlenbein's mutation [14] and the non-uniform mutation is used for the remaining algorithms. A binary-coded GA (ga-bin) has also been included, which is based on a two-point crossover. For this purpose, we used the GENESIS program [5]. The number of binary genes assigned to each variable is 26 for f_4 and 11 for the remaining functions. Therefore, the precision is approximately 10^{-6}.

We carried out the experiments using the following parameters: the population size is 61, crossover probability $p_c = 0.6$, probability of chromosome update by mutation $p_u = 0.125$ ($p_m = 0.005$ per variable), the selection procedure was linear ranking and elitist selection and the sampling model used was stochastic universal sampling. We executed all the algorithms 15 times, each one with 5,000 generations. For each function, Table 4 shows the average values of the *best fitness* in 5,000 generations and the final *online* measure, which is considered here as a population diversity measure.

Table 4. Results

	f_1		f_2		f_3		f_4	
Algorithms	*Best*	*Online*	*Best*	*Online*	*Best*	*Online*	*Best*	*Online*
ga-bin	4.51e-09	3.01e+00	3.03e+01	2.49e+03	3.24e+01	4.17e+01	7.92e-05	2.72e+00
ga-Simple	6.68e-12	2.65e+00	3.16e+01	2.65e+03	1.24e-09	1.42e+01	1.09e-05	2.58e+00
ga-BLX-α	1.18e-13	1.24e+00	2.18e+01	1.11e+03	7.50e+00	4.43e+01	1.76e-06	2.50e+00
ga-Discrete	2.16e-09	1.54e+00	2.83e+01	1.55e+03	3.76e-07	8.94e+00	2.29e-04	1.48e+00
ga-Linear	9.70e-15	1.37e+00	2.10e+01	1.12e+03	1.70e+01	1.49e+02	4.13e-07	2.88e+00
ga-H-Wright	4.72e-04	6.01e+01	9.32e+01	1.11e+05	6.32e+01	4.55e+02	2.45e+00	1.26e+01
ga-Linear-BGA	1.08e-03	5.82e+00	4.13e+01	4.50e+03	3.23e+00	6.34e+01	2.17e-01	8.91e+00
ga-ST2-Logical	8.50e-17	4.84e-01	2.04e+01	5.18e+02	3.41e-14	6.11e+00	4.12e-08	9.17e-01
ga-DRGA4	4.74e-15	6.22e-01	1.99e+01	6.24e+02	1.10e-12	7.13e+00	2.93e-07	1.10e+00
ga-H-Logical	5.40e-14	4.65e-01	2.03e+01	5.04e+02	5.43e-12	5.52e+00	8.47e-10	8.36e-01
ga-H-Hamacher	1.09e-06	5.77e+01	1.73e+01	3.35e+04	1.01e+02	4.07e+02	9.61e+00	1.96e+01
ga-H-Algebraic	1.14e+00	1.35e+02	9.87e+01	1.36e+05	8.62e+01	5.07e+02	1.24e+01	2.13e+01
ga-H-Einstein	2.72e+00	1.85e+02	3.70e+01	2.14e+05	8.97e+01	5.44e+02	9.60e+00	2.14e+01
ga-DH-Frank	1.41e-02	1.02e+02	1.17e+02	1.21e+05	5.97e+01	3.86e+02	5.75e+00	1.85e+01
ga-DH-Frank	1.84e-04	5.89e+01	2.33e+01	7.27e+04	2.46e+01	2.90e+02	4.15e-02	1.35e+01
ga-DH-Frank	2.30e-23	5.12e-01	2.02e+01	5.61e+02	0.00e+00	5.92e+00	2.00e-11	9.20e-01

Next, we report some considerations about the algorithms based on the crossover proposed.

The increase in the *online* measure in the ga-H family from the logical algorithm to the Einstein one suggests that diversity is greater using functions distant from the logical one. The dominated heuristic crossovers based on other than the logical functions, generate an offspring which is far away from the best parent, that way, it produces a high diversity (compare the *online* measure with the remaining algorithms) and slows convergence. The case of ga-H-Logical is different, it returns results very similar to the best ones (the result for f_4 is the second best) and its *online* measure is good as well. Logical functions are adequate for building crossover operators for RCGAs with higher convergence.

ga-DH-Frank and ga-DH-Dombi return low results. The reason is that the function families of Frank and Dombi have a slow convergence towards the logical functions, and so, they induce higher diversity levels during the GA run (see the *online* measure for these algorithms). This causes the GA convergence to be slow and so no suitable refinements (local tuning) of the elements are produced at the end of the GA. On the other hand, ga-DH-Dubois is the best algorithm. It offers the best results for f_1, f_3 and f_4; for f_3 it was the only one that obtained the global optimum and its result for f_1 ($2.30e-23$) is much higher than the second best ($8.50e-17$). The convergence of the Dubois function families towards the logical functions is fast. So, at initial stages it offers diversity, and later on, a good local tuning is achieved (see the low online measure) since the functions used are similar to the logical ones, which are highly suitable.

The algorithms based on the crossover operators presented (in particular ga-H-Logical and ga-DH-Dubois) deal with the multimodal functions f_3 and f_4 in a suitable fashion. To explain this fact, we need to point out that these crossover operators may be included in the so-called *crowding methods*, which attempt to maintain stable subpopulations (niches) around the peaks of the function by replacing population elements with similar individuals. They are applied in order to: 1) locate and preserve multiple peaks in a multimodal function, or 2) preserve diversity for slowing down the premature convergence problem. One example of these methods is *deterministic crowding*, which works by randomly pairing all population elements in each generation. Each pair of parents undergoes crossover, possibly in combination with mutation or other genetic operators, to yield two offspring, which compete against the parents for inclusion in the population (see [11] for more information). Our heuristic crossovers generate offspring very similar to one of the parents (the best ones), this allows the diversity to be maintained (following the principle of the *crowding methods*) and so, some niches around the best elements are established. The heuristic diversity related to ga-DH-Dubois increased this effect, and so, more peaks could be held. For f_3, this diversity helped to include the *niche* to which the global optimum belongs. Later, an efficient heuristic convergence reached it.

5 Conclusions

In this paper, we have presented two crossover operator families for controlling the diversity and convergence of RCGAs: heuristic FCB-crossover and dynamic heuristic FCB-crossover operators. These operators are designed for leading the search process using the available information for each parent.

Results of experiments have highlighted the dynamic heuristic FCB-crossover operators based on Dubois' parameterized fuzzy connectives as *robust* crossover operators for RCGAs. An important feature of these operators is that they converge quickly towards the heuristic FCB-crossover operators based on Logical fuzzy connectives, which have returned very good results as well.

References

1. Bäck, T. & Schwefel, H.P.: An Overview of Evolutionary Algorithms for Parameter Optimization. Evolutionary Computation, **1**(1) (1993) 1-23.
2. Booker, L.: Improving Search in Genetic Algorithms. Genetic Algorithms and Simulated Annealing, L. Davis (Ed.), (Morgan Kaufmann Publishers, Los Altos, 1987), 61-73.
3. Eshelman L.J., Schaffer J.D.: Real-Coded Genetic Algorithms and Interval-Schemata. Foundations of Genetic Algorithms-2, L.Darrell Whitley (Ed.), (Morgan Kaufmann Publishers, San Mateo, 1993), 187-202.
4. Davis, L.: Handbook of Genetic Algorithms. New York: Van Nostrand Reinhold (1991).

5. Grefenstette J.J.: A User's Guide to GENESIS Version 5.0, (1990).
6. Herrera, F, Herrera-Viedma, E., Lozano, M., Verdegay, J.L.: Fuzzy Tools to Improve Genetic Algorithms. Second European Congress on Intelligent Techniques and Soft Computing (1994) 1532-1539.
7. Herrera, F., Lozano, M., Verdegay, J.L.: The Use of Fuzzy Connectives to Design Real-Coded Genetic Algorithms. Mathware & Soft Computing **1**(3) (1995) 239-251.
8. Herrera, F., Lozano, M., Verdegay, J.L.: Tackling Real-Coded Genetic Algorithms: Operators and Tools for Behavioural Analysis. To appear in Artificial Intelligence Review.
9. Herrera, F., Lozano, M., Verdegay, J.L.: Fuzzy Connective Based Crossover Operators to Model Genetic Algorithms Population Diversity. Technical Report #95110, Dept. of Computer Science and Artificial Intelligence. University of Granada (1995).
10. Liepins, G.E. & Vose, M.D: Characterizing Crossover in Genetic Algorithms. Annals of Mathematics and Artificial Intelligence **5**(1) (1992) 27-34.
11. Mahfoud, S.W.: Niching Methods for Genetic Algorithms. IlliGAL Report No. 95001 (1995).
12. Michalewicz, Z.: Genetic Algorithms + Data Structures = Evolution Programs. New York: Springer-Verlag (1992).
13. Mizumoto M.: Pictorial Representations of fuzzy connectives, Part I: Cases of t-norms, t-conorms and averaging operators. Fuzzy Sets and Systems **31** (1989) 217-242.
14. Mühlenbein H., Schlierkamp-Voosen D.: Predictive Models for the Breeder Genetic Algorithm I. Continuous Parameter Optimization. Evolutionary Computation **1** (1993) 25-49.
15. Radcliffe, N.J.: Equivalence Class Analysis of Genetic Algorithms. Complex Systems **5**(2) (1991) 183-205.
16. Sanchez, E.: Fuzzy Genetic Algorithms in Soft Computing Environment. Fifth IFSA World Congress, Seoul, (1993).
17. Schlierkamp-Voosen D.: Strategy Adaptation by Competition. Second European Congress on Intelligent Techniques and Soft Computing (1994) 1270-1274.
18. Schwefel, H.P.: Evolution and Optimum Seeking. Sixth-Generation Computer Technology Series. New York: Wiley (1995).
19. Voigt H. M.: Fuzzy Evolutionary Algorithms. Technical Report tr-92-038, International Computer Science Institute (ICSI) Berkeley, (1992).
20. Voigt, H.M., Mühlenbein, H. & Cvetković: Fuzzy Recombination for the Breeder Genetic Algorithm. Proc. of the Sixth Int. Conf. on Genetic Algorithms, L. Eshelman (Ed.), (Morgan Kaufmann Publishers, San Francisco, 1995), 104-111.
21. Wright A.: Genetic Algorithms for Real Parameter Optimization. Foundations of Genetic Algorithms, First Workshop on the Foundations of Genetic Algorithms and Classifier Systems, G.J.E. Rawlin(Ed.), (Morgan Kaufmann, Los Altos, CA, 1990), 205-218.
22. Wright A.: Genetic Algorithms for Real Parameter Optimization. Foundations of Genetic Algorithms-1, G.J.E Rawlin (Ed.), (Morgan Kaufmann, San Mateo, 1991), 205-218.

Are Evolutionary Algorithms Improved by Large Mutations?

C. Kappler

Institut für theoretische Physik, Humboldt Universität zu Berlin, Invalidenstr. 110, 10115 Berlin, Germany,

kappler@summa.physik.hu-berlin.de

Abstract. When optimizing with evolutionary algorithms in a continuous search space, mutations usually are distributed according to a Gaussian. A Gaussian distribution decays exponentially, i. e. very large mutations are highly unlikely. This bears the risk of the optimization getting caught in local extrema. A more slowly decaying distribution, e. g. a Cauchy distribution, may circumvent this problem. A Cauchy distribution allows for rare large mutations. In this paper the performance of Gaussian and Cauchy distributed mutations, in particular their robustness and rate of progress, are compared analytically and numerically in a number of examples. It turns out that, in one dimension, an algorithm working with Cauchy distributed mutations is both more robust and faster. This result cannot easily be generalized to higher dimensions, where the additional problem of finding the right direction for leaving a saddle point appears. The analysis of a simple two dimensional problem does not yet allow to draw final conclusions concerning which kind of mutations, if any, is preferable in higher dimensions.

1 Introduction

In this contribution the effect of different mutation distributions in an evolutionary algorithm is investigated. In a continuous search space, mutations usually are Gaussian distributed [1, 2, 3]. This distribution has a finite range: "large jumps", i. e. mutations to a very distant genotype are highly unlikely. This finite range bears the risk of the optimization getting caught in local extrema of the fitness function. It may thus make sense to work with a distribution instead that – very rarely – allows for large jumps also. The *Cauchy distribution* is such a long-tailed distribution.

We should specify what exactly we expect from such a distribution. The goal is that of a *robust* evolutionary algorithm, i. e. an algorithm that reliably works in a large variety of fitness landscapes, with as little a priori problem specific knowledge as possible. In the following we compare Gaussian and Cauchy distributed mutations in that respect. Next in importance, after robustness, is a high *rate of progress* of a strategy. This point will also be considered below.

The paper is organized as follow: First Cauchy distributions are introduced in detail (Sec. 2). Then evolutionary algorithms with Gaussian and Cauchy distributed mutations are compared in a number of simple examples: a one dimensional (1D) random fitness function of finite correlation length (Sec. 3), a nD inclined plane, bounded on top (Sec. 4), and finally a 2D inclined corridor, also bounded on top (Sec. 5). To close, conclusions and outlook are presented (Sec. 6). All problems are discussed with fixed step length.

Note added in proof: Michalewicz [10] introduces a non-gaussian mutation, the non-uniform or "triangle shape" mutation. However, it is defined only in finite spaces. Also its performance is not compared to that of gaussian mutations.

2 Cauchy and Gaussian distributions

In Fig. 1 Cauchy and Gaussian distributions are illustrated. They are described by

$$P^G(\mathbf{x}) = (2\pi\sigma)^{-\frac{n}{2}} \exp(-\frac{|\mathbf{x}|^2}{2\sigma^2}) \tag{1}$$

and

$$P^C(\mathbf{x}) = \mathcal{N}_n \frac{1}{(|\mathbf{x}|^2 + \sigma^2)^{\frac{n+1}{2}}} \tag{2}$$

for Gauss and Cauchy respectivly, where n is the number of dimensions. $\mathcal{N}_n$ is a normalization constant. Its analytic calculation for $n > 2$ is difficult, if not impossible. In one dimension, the Gaussian distribution decays exponentially, whereas the Cauchy distribution decays like $1/x^2$ for large x. The ratio of height to width of both distributions may in both cases be tuned by the parameter σ, the *step length*. Note, however, that Cauchy and Gaussian distributions with same σ are not directly comparable. For the Gaussian distribution, σ^2 also corresponds to the variance of the distribution. For the Cauchy distribution, the variance is infinite. Both Gaussian and Cauchy distributions are special cases of what

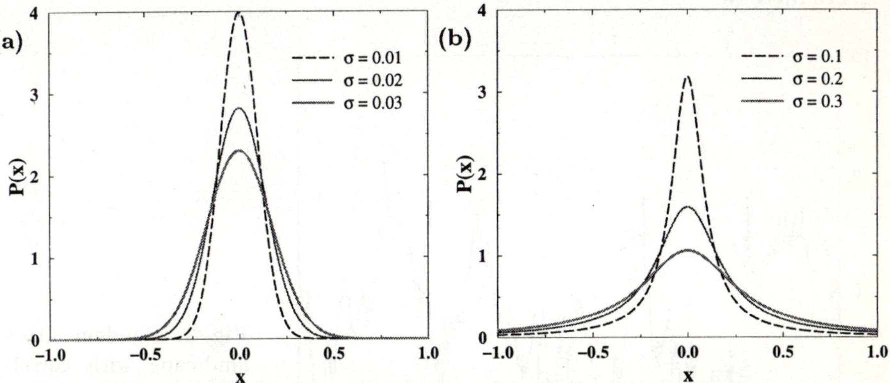

Fig. 1. (a) 1D Gaussian distribution, (b) 1D Cauchy distribution

is known as a *Levy distribution* [4]. Levy distributions are the family of *stable distributions* which are defined as follows: Let $x_1, \ldots, x_n$ be a set of independent stochastic variables, individually drawn according to a Levy distribution. Then their sum is also distributed according to a Levy distribution. Moreover, each

Levy distribution forms the basin of attraction for sums of numbers distributed according to other distributions: e. g., sums of numbers distributed according to any probability distribution decaying faster than $1/x^3$, for large x, in the limit $n \to \infty$ converge to a Gaussian distribution – this is the central limit theorem. However, sums of numbers distributed according to probability distributions decaying as $1/x^2$, for large x, all converge to a Cauchy distribution.

In Simulated Annealing a problem arises similar to that discussed here: An "offspring" must be produced in the vicinity of the last successful searcher. Usually vicinity is to mean Gaussian distributed. Recently, Fast Simulated Annealing [5] and Very Fast Simulated Annealing [6] were introduced, in which Cauchy distributions and a distribution decaying like $1/|\mathbf{x}|$, for $|\mathbf{x}|$ large, respectively, are successfully employed.

3 Gauss and Cauchy in a 1D random correlated fitness landscape

In this section the robustness and rate of progress of evolutionary algorithms with Gaussian and Cauchy distributed mutations are compared for a 1D random fitness landscape of finite correlation lengthi ξ. A (1+1) evolutionary algorithm [7] is employed, the result averaged over 400 runs. The fitness landscape in which optimization is to take place is depicted in Fig. 2. It was produced by an Ornstein-Uhlenbeck process [8]. This means the energy E at x_{n+1} was found as $E(x_n)$ plus a random number ϵ. The random number was drawn according to a gaussian with non-zero average. This average is related to the correlation length ξ of the fitness landscape. Periodic boundary conditions are used. The starting point for each simulation was picked uniformly distributed over the entire interval.

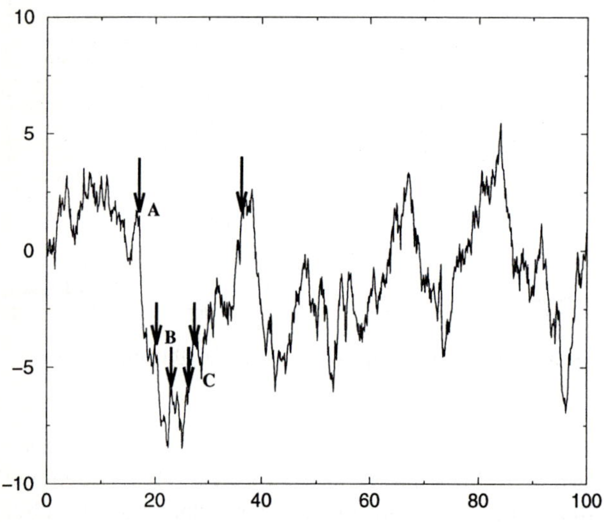

Fig. 2. Random fitness landscape with correlation length $\xi = 5$ and basins of attraction **A**, **B** and **C**. Basin **A** is located between the two outermost arrows etc.

In Fig. 2, three basins of attraction **A**, **B** and **C** are marked. Figure 3 shows how long the algorithm takes to enter each basin of attraction as a function of the step length σ, for Gaussian and Cauchy distributed mutations respectively.

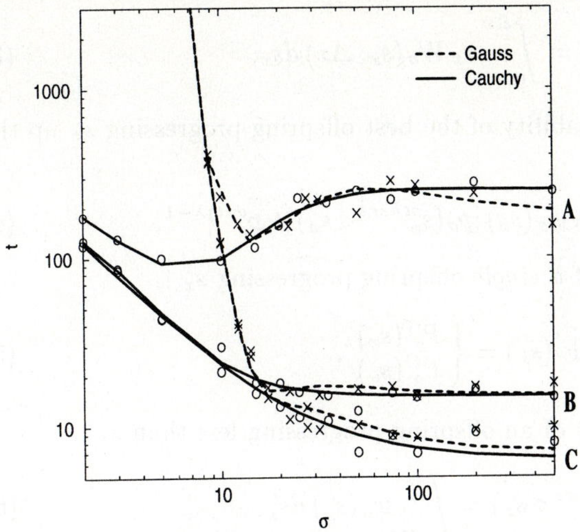

Fig. 3. Time t a (1+1) evolutionary algorithm takes to enter basins of attraction A, B and C from Fig. 2 as a function of step length σ for Gaussian and Cauchy distributed mutations. The lines are a guide to the eye.

The main result from Fig. 3 is that the algorithm with Cauchy distributed mutations is more robust: For Gauss, there is a certain cut-off value of the step length below which the algorithm does not converge (note the log-log scale). For Cauchy, however, the time of convergence is a slowly varying function of step length. Convergence is thus almost always guaranteed. Note that the point of this figure is **not** that of comparing data from Cauchy and Gaussian mutations for same value of σ, since σ has a different meaning in each distribution. The point is that of comparing the overall behaviour.

The minimal time of convergence that can be reached when tuning σ is somewhat better for Cauchy than for Gauss. Note that, because of the periodic boundary conditions, for $\sigma > 100$, both distributions become more and more equal to a uniform distribution, i. e. drawing locations at random or guessing. Therefore, for large σ, the time of convergence becomes constant and the same in both cases (differences are due to noisy data). We also see that for optimally tuned σ the time of convergence of an evolutionary algorithm is twice as high as that for guessing. Of course, for a less pathological fitness function, this difference would be greater.

4 Gauss and Cauchy on a bounded inclined plane

Next we compare the performance of the two distributions as the algorithm is trying to climb up a plane inclined in x-direction, until an upper bound is reached. The upper bound has a distance Δx from the current position. In this example robustness is not measured, since there are no local optima to get caught in. What is measured is the rate of progress only.

The rate of progress $\phi_\sigma(\Delta x)$ for (1+λ) strategies on a bounded inclined plane can be calculated analytically [1, 3]. It is the average progress s_x in x-direction, defined as follows:

$$\phi_\sigma(\Delta x) = \int_0^{\Delta x} s_x \, W_\sigma(s_x, \Delta x)\, ds_x, \tag{3}$$

where $W_\sigma(s_x, \Delta x)$ is the probability of the best offspring progressing s_x up the incline, given by

$$W_\sigma(s_x, \Delta x) = \lambda \, w_\sigma(s_x) \, [p_\sigma(s_x^{others} < s_x) + p_\sigma^{out}]^{\lambda - 1}, \tag{4}$$

with the probability $w_\sigma(s_x)$ of *a single* offspring progressing s_x

$$w_\sigma(s_x) = \begin{cases} P_\sigma^G(s_x) \\ P_\sigma^C(s_x) \end{cases}, \tag{5}$$

the probability $p_\sigma(s_x^{others} < s_x)$ of an offspring progressing less than s_x

$$p_\sigma(s_x^{others} < s_x) = \int_{-\infty}^{s_x} w_\sigma(s'_x)\, ds'_x, \tag{6}$$

and the probability p_σ^{out} of an offspring jumping beyond the bound

$$p_\sigma^{out} = \int_{\Delta x}^{\infty} w_\sigma(s_x)\, ds_x. \tag{7}$$

Note that Eqn. 4 means an offspring jumping beyond the upper bound is rejected, rather than drawn anew.

The rate of progress for this model is independend of the number of dimensions: it is the same for a 1D incline as for a nD inclined hyperplane. For the latter the algorithm will simply proceed in a random walk in $n-1$ dimensions.

A straight forward calculation gives the following results for the rate of progress:

$$\phi_\sigma^G(\Delta x) = \frac{\lambda\sigma}{\sqrt{2\pi}} \int_0^{\frac{\Delta x}{\sigma}} s_x \exp(-\frac{s_x^2}{2}) \, [1 + \frac{1}{2}\mathrm{erf}(\frac{s_x}{\sqrt{2}}) - \frac{1}{2}\mathrm{erf}(\frac{\Delta x}{\sqrt{2}\sigma})]^{\lambda-1} ds_x \tag{8}$$

for Gauss, and

$$\phi_\sigma^C(\Delta x) = \frac{\lambda\sigma}{\pi} \int_0^{\frac{\Delta x}{\sigma}} \frac{s_x}{1+s_x^2} \, [1 + \frac{1}{\pi}\arctan(s_x) - \frac{1}{\pi}\arctan(\frac{\Delta x}{\sigma})]^{\lambda-1} ds_x \tag{9}$$

for Cauchy. As is to be expected, the rate of progress increases linearly with the step length σ, when the distance Δx to be covered is scaled accordingly.

The above integrals must be evaluated numerically. The resulting curves are depicted in Fig. 4. We see that, generally, the rate of progress is higher for Cauchy distributed mutations than it is for Gaussian distributed mutations. Also, for Gauss, ϕ hardly depends on λ, whereas for Cauchy, the rate of progress strongly depends on it. This is not surprising: The largest step s_x taken is most

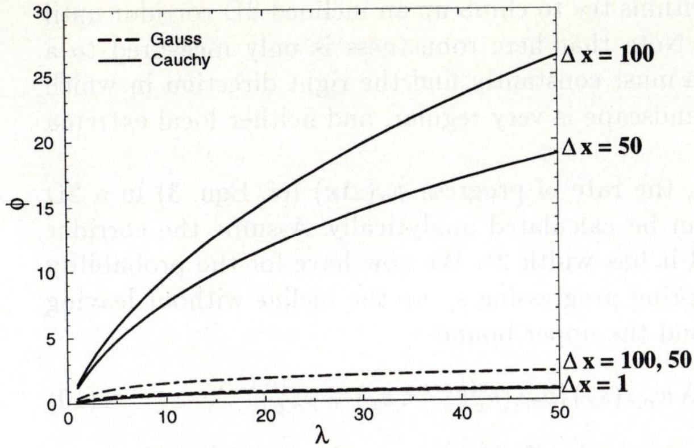

Fig. 4. Rate of progress ϕ for inclined plane as a function of the number of children λ ($\sigma = 1$ for both Cauchy and Gauss).

likely much higher for Cauchy than it is for Gauss, because of the slower decay of a Cauchy distribution – and the larger the number λ of children, the higher the probability a huge value of s_x occurs.

Furthermore it should be noted that for Cauchy distributed mutations ϕ strongly depends on the distance between parent and upper bound Δx. The bigger Δx, the higher the rate of progress. This is because the number of children jumping beyond the upper bound decreases with increasing Δx. In fact, ϕ diverges for $\Delta x \to \infty$. For Gaussian distributed mutations, the rate of progress hardly depends on Δx. Only when the distance to the upper bound becomes comparable to the standard deviation of the distribution, the rate of progress declines.

5 Gauss and Cauchy in a 2D bounded inclined corridor

As opposed to the nD inclined plane, the 2D inclined corridor truly has more than one dimension. The problems an optimization may run in into higher dimensions have a new quality: the landscape typically is dominated by saddle points [9].

Thus, in higher dimensions, the problem is less that of getting caught in local extrema, but rather that of finding the proper direction to progress, i. e. to leave a saddle point. Gaussian and Cauchy distributions both are rotationally symmetric, unless a direction sensitive step length control is employed, a possibility we disregard for now. Therefore it is not clear whether, in this case also, Cauchy distributed mutations outscore Gaussian distributed ones.

Note also that the Cauchy distribution (cf. Eqn. 2), while still decaying according to a power law, decays the faster, the higher the number n of dimensions. It may turn out that using a different probability distribution, the decay of which is independent of the number of dimensions, makes more sense. Of course, such a distribution would no longer be stable. A discussion of this point must be deferred to future research.

Also, a comprehensive comparison of Gauss and Cauchy distributions in high dimensions must be deferred to a later paper. For now we compare the respective rates of progress as the algorithms try to climb up an inclined 2D corridor until an upper bound is reached. Note that here robustness is only measured to a certain degree: the algorithm must constantly find the right direction in which to progress, but the fitness landscape is very regular, and neither local extrema nor saddle points exist.

As for the inclined plane, the rate of progress $\phi_\sigma(\Delta x)$ (cf. Eqn. 3) in a 2D bounded inclined corridor can be calculated analytically. Assume the corridor is inclined in x-direction and it has width $2b$. We now have for the probability $W_{\sigma,b}(s_x, \Delta x)$ of the best offspring progressing s_x up the incline without leaving the corridor or jumping beyond the upper bound

$$W_{\sigma,b}(s_x, \Delta x) = \lambda\, w_{\sigma,b}(s_x)\, [p_{\sigma,b}(s_x^{others} < s_x) + p_{\sigma,b}^{out}]^{\lambda-1}, \tag{10}$$

with the probability $w_{\sigma,b}(s_x)$ of a single offspring progressing s_x and not jumping beyond the walls of the corridor

$$w_{\sigma,b}(s_x) = \frac{1}{2b}\int_{-b}^{b}\int_{-b-y}^{b-y} \begin{cases} P_\sigma^G(s_x, s_y) \\ P_\sigma^C(s_x, s_y) \end{cases} ds_y\, dy. \tag{11}$$

Here we average over different initial postitions y, which are assumed to be uniformly distributed [1, 3]. Numerical experiments confirm this hypothesis.

The probability $p_{\sigma,b}(s_x^{others} < s_x)$ of an offspring progressing less than s_x, and not jumping beyond the walls of the corridor is as before (cf. Eqn. 6), with $w_{\sigma,b}(s_x)$ instead of $w_\sigma(s_x)$. Finally, the probability $p_{\sigma,b}^{out}$ of jumping into the forbidden region is

$$p_{\sigma,b}^{out} = 1 - \int_{-\infty}^{\Delta x} w_{\sigma,b}(s_x)\, ds_x. \tag{12}$$

Again, offspring jumping into the forbidden region is not considered further.

After some tedious integration one arrives at the following results:

$$\phi_{\sigma,b}^G(\Delta x) = \frac{\lambda\sigma}{\sqrt{2\pi}}\int_0^{\frac{\Delta x}{\sigma}} s_x \exp(-\frac{s_x^2}{2})\, p^{in\_b} \\ (1 + \frac{1}{2}\mathrm{erf}(\frac{s_x}{\sqrt{2}})\, p^{in\_b} - \frac{1}{2}\mathrm{erf}(\frac{\Delta x}{\sqrt{2}\sigma})\, p^{in\_b})^{\lambda-1} ds_x, \tag{13}$$

with the probability p^{in_b} of staying within the walls of the corridor

$$p^{in\_b} = \mathrm{erf}(\frac{\sqrt{2}b}{\sigma}) + \frac{\sigma}{\sqrt{2\pi}b}[\exp(-\frac{2b^2}{\sigma^2}) - 1]. \tag{14}$$

for Gauss. I. e. the result is just as that for the inclined plane (Eqn. 8) with all probabilities refering to progress along x multiplied by the probability p^{in_b} of not leaving the corridor in y-direction.

For Cauchy we have

$$\phi_{\sigma,b}^C(\Delta x) = \frac{\lambda\sigma^2}{2\pi b}\int_0^{\frac{\Delta x}{\sigma}} s_x\, [\frac{(s_x^2 + 1 + 4b^2/\sigma^2)^{\frac{1}{2}}}{s_x^2 + 2} - \frac{1}{(s_x^2+1)^{\frac{1}{2}}}]$$

$$\{1+\frac{1}{\pi}[\arctan(f_1(s_x))-\arctan(f_1(\frac{\Delta x}{\sigma}))]+\frac{\sigma}{4\pi b}[\ln(f_2(s_x))-\ln(f_2(\frac{\Delta x}{\sigma}))]\}^{\lambda-1}ds_x \tag{15}$$

where

$$f_1(t)=\frac{2b}{\sigma}\frac{t}{(t^2+1+4b^2/\sigma^2)^{\frac{1}{2}}}, \tag{16}$$

and

$$f_2(t)=\frac{[(1+\frac{1}{t^2})^{\frac{1}{2}}-1][(1+\frac{1}{t^2})^{\frac{1}{2}}+(1-\frac{4b^2/\sigma^2}{t^2+1+4b^2/\sigma^2})^{\frac{1}{2}}]}{[(1+\frac{1}{t^2})^{\frac{1}{2}}+1][(1+\frac{1}{t^2})^{\frac{1}{2}}-(1-\frac{4b^2/\sigma^2}{t^2+1+4b^2/\sigma^2})^{\frac{1}{2}}]}. \tag{17}$$

Note that for Cauchy the difference between the rate of progress on an inclined plane and that on a inclined corridor (Eqn. 9) is not just that of multiplying all probabilities with the same factor, as it was for Gauss. This is because for Gauss the probability distribution factorizes in contributions from each dimension, whereas for Cauchy it does not (cf. Eqns. 1 and 2). This is another reason why working with a different - slowly decaying - probability distribution might make sense (cf. beginning of this section)

The above integrals must again be evaluated numerically. The results are shown in Fig. 5.

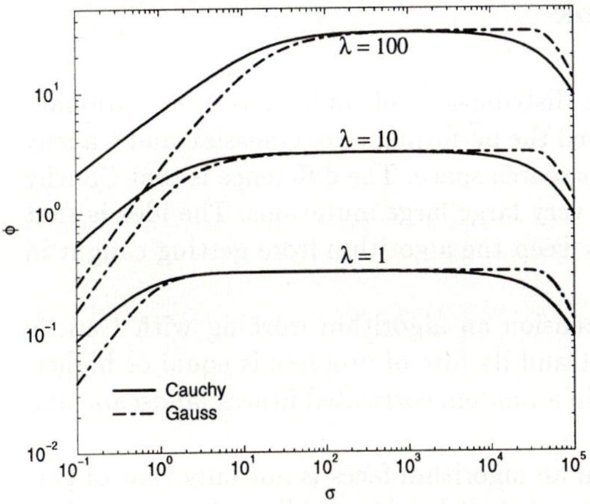

Fig. 5. Rate of progress ϕ versus step length σ for Gaussian and Cauchy distributed mutations in a 2D bounded inclined corridor. $(1+\lambda)$ strategy, width of corridor $2b = 2$, its length $\Delta x = 10^5$. Curves for different values of λ are presented.

The following may be read from Fig. 5. Note again that comparing the results for same values of σ for different distributions makes no sense. The shape and extrema of the curves are of interest here. For both Gauss and Cauchy, the rate of progress first increases with increasing step length, as it would on the inclined plane. In this regime at least one of the children remains within the walls of the corridor, while making increasing progress along its length. For $\lambda = 1$, the rate of progress saturates when the step length is of the order of the width of the corridor. As λ increases, saturation takes place at increasing values of σ, because the chances of producing suitable offspring increases. In this regime, the rate of progress is higher when Cauchy distributed mutations are used. This is because (cf. last section) for Cauchy the rate of progress along an incline is higher, while at the same time the effect of loosing offspring jumping beyond the walls is not yet felt strongly.

At some value of σ, which is the higher, the larger λ, longer steps along x are counterbalanced by more children jumping beyond the walls of the corridor, and the rate of progress becomes constant. The maximum value of ϕ_σ is the higher, the higher the number of children. Surprisingly, the value at which ϕ_σ saturates is the same for Gauss and Cauchy. This is although Cauchy's rate of progress starts off higher. From some value of σ on, Cauchy is more strongly affected by offspring jumping beyond the walls.

As the step length approaches the length Δx of the corridor, the rate of progress decreases. This effect is due to the increasing number of children leaving the corridor and also to offspring jumping beyond the upper bound, just as it was for the inclined plane. As in that case, the decline happens gradually for Cauchy, and more abruptly for Gauss. The number of children does not influence this behaviour.

To summarize, in a bounded inclined corridor, Gauss and Cauchy perform comparable for large values of step length. For small step lengths the rate of progress is higher for Cauchy. This effect is the more pronounced, the larger the number of children.

6 Conclusions and Outlook

We investigated the role of different distributions of mutations in evolutionary algorithms. In particular, we compared the performance of Gaussian and Cauchy distributed mutations in a continuous search space. The difference is that Cauchy distributed mutations allow for rare very large large mutations. The idea is that such occasional large mutations may keep the algorithm from getting caught in local extrema.

The results are that in one dimension an algorithm working with Cauchy distributed mutations is more robust and its rate of progress is equal or higher. This was demonstrated numerically in a random correlated fitness landscape and analytically on an inclined plane.

In higher dimensions the problem an algorithm faces is not only that of getting caught in local extrema but also that of leaving saddle points. As a first approach, the analytically found rates of progress in an inclined corridor were compared. For small step lengths and a large number of children, Cauchy distributed mutations again perform better. However, a final conclusion concerning which kind of mutations, if any, is better in high dimensions, cannot yet be drawn.

Acknowledgements

The author thanks the members of Project Evoalg for helpful discussions. Financial support by the German Federal Ministry of Education and Research (BMBF) (Grant 03040101, Project Evoalg) is gratefully acknowledged.

References

1. I. Rechenberg, "Evolutionsstrategie, Optimierung technischer Systeme nach Prinzipien der biologischen Evolution", Frommann-Holzboog, Stuttgart (1973)
2. I. Rechenberg, "Evolutionsstrategie '94", Vol. 1 of *Werkstatt Bionik und Evolutionstechnik*, Frommann-Holzboog, Stuttgart (1994)
3. H.-P. Schwefel, "Evolution and optimum seeking", John Wiley & Sons Inc. (1995)
4. J.-P. Bouchard and A. Georges, "Anomalous diffusion in disordered media: statistical mechanics, models and physical applications", Phys. Rep. **195**, 127 (1990)
5. H. Szu and R. Hartley, "Fast simulated annealing", Phys. Lett. A **122**, 157 (1987)
6. L. Ingber "Very fast simulated re-annealing", J. Math. Comp. Modelling **12**, 967 (1989)
7. An evolutionary algorithm without cross over is characterized by $(\mu \overset{+}{,} \lambda)$, where μ is the number of parents, and λ the number of children in each generation. In a (μ, λ) strategy, the μ parents of the next generation are the μ best of the λ children. In a $(\mu + \lambda)$ strategy, the parents of the next generation are the μ best of both parents and children of the last generation. See also Refs. [1, 2, 3].
8. C. W. Gardiner "Handbook of stochastic methods", 2nd ed., Springer (1994)
9. M. Conrad, W. Ebeling "M. V. Volkenstein, evolutionary thinking and the structure of fitness landscapes", BioSystems **27**, 125 (1992)
10. Z. Michalewicz "Genetic Algorithms + Data Structures = Evolution Programs", Springer (1992).

Mutation by Imitation in Boolean Evolution Strategies

Michèle Sebag[1] and Marc Schoenauer[2]

(1) LMS - URA CNRS 317 (2) CMAP - URA CNRS 756
Ecole Polytechnique, 91128 Palaiseau Cedex, France
Michele.Sebag@polytechnique.fr Marc.Schoenauer@polytechnique.fr

Abstract. Adaptive heuristics have been developed in the Evolution Strategy (ES) frame regarding the mutation of real-valued variables. But these heuristics poorly extend to discrete variables: when the rate or variance of mutation gets too small, mutation has no effect any more. To overcome this problem, we propose two mutation operators, that use the worst individuals of the current population as beacons indicating the limits of the current promising region:
Mutation by differentiation drives individuals away from the beacon-individuals. *Mutation by imitation* inversely assumes that beacon-individuals still contain relevant informations, and aims at moving the individual at hand nearer to the beacons. Mutation by imitation produces offspring that share the features of several "parents"; but in contrast with classical crossover, it allows one to control the distance between the offspring and the main parent, by fixing the number of bits to mutate. Mutation by imitation thus permits a tunable exchange of informations among individuals.
Both operators have been implemented in a boolean $(\mu + \lambda)$ ES framework, and experimented on four problems: the Royal Road problem, a GA-deceptive problem, the combinatorial multiple knapsack optimization problem and the Long Path problem. Comparative validation is presented and discussed.

1 Introduction

The three historical roots of evolutionary computation are known to be evolutionary programming (EP), evolution strategies (ES) and genetic algorithms (GA). Original ES were developed in the mid sixties [24, 23] to deal with real parameter optimization. EP was initially developed in the context of Finite State Machines [7], but was later modified and tuned to handle different representations, including real parameters. Last, early GAs heavily relied on the bitstring representation [10, 9], and were later extended to other representations [22].

No optimization method can accurately handle *all* optimization problems, according to the "No Free Lunch Theorem" [28]. The key question thus remains to choose the good evolutionary algorithm depending on the current problem. To address this issue, comparative validations have been conducted on many test-beds, most of them involving real-valued fitness functions (e.g. the DeJong test-suite [3]); see [2, 5, 6] among many others. Except in the GA literature, little attention has been paid to boolean problems, despite the fact that real-world problems often involve discrete features. The evolutionary landscape thus appears divided: GAs are to be preferred for discrete problems only [22, 12]; In the meanwhile, the efficient strategies developed in EP and ES to evolve real-valued features seem to transpose poorly to the discrete case [1].

This paper is concerned with the mutation of discrete features in the framework of evolution strategies. The idea is to use the current population as a reservoir of information. More precisely, the worst individuals in the current population are considered as beacons signaling the limits of the present promising region, which adaptively move as the population is driven toward regions of increasingly high fitness. These beacons give rise to two mutation operators: *mutation by imitation* moves the individual at hand toward the beacons, whereas *mutation by differentiation* rather moves the individual at hand away from the beacons. These mutation operators allow individuals to exchange information and directly influence each other. This was only possible so far through recombination. The advantage of the proposed mechanism is that it allows one to control the distance between offspring and parents by fixing the number of bits to mutate, whereas classical recombination offers no guarantee as to the distance between offspring and parents.

This paper is organized as follows. Section 2 briefly reviews the main trends regarding the mutation of real-valued and discrete features in EP and ES. Mutation by imitation and mutation by differentiation are described in section 3. These operators are experimented on four problems: the Royal Road [18, 19, 8], the Ugly (GA-deceptive) problem [27], the combinatorial multiple knapsack optimization problem [21, 14], and the Long Path problem [11]. Comparative results are discussed in section 4. We conclude with some avenues for further research.

2 State of the art

The general real-valued optimization problem is stated as: $\mathcal{F}$ being a real-valued function defined on $\mathbb{R}^n$, find $x \in \mathcal{E} \subseteq \mathbb{R}^n$, such that

$$\mathcal{F}(x) = Max\{\mathcal{F}(y), y \in \mathcal{E}\}$$

Real-valued evolutionary algorithms now exist in all three communities (see for instance [16] for an example of real-valued GA). Real-valued crossover is based on the linear combination of two or several parents [16, 2], or on classical n-point recombination. Real-valued mutation involves the addition of a Gaussian random variable:

$$x_i := x_i + N(0, \sigma_i)$$

where $N(0, \sigma)$ represents the Gaussian random variable of standard deviation σ. The main difficulty remains to adjust parameters σ_i.

Most real-valued GAs use fixed σ_i, or σ_i decreasing along generations according to a fixed schedule. Early ESs use the well-known 1/5 rule [23], where a global σ is modified according to the recent effects of mutation: if more than one-fifth of the mutations have been successful in the last generation (i.e. lead to an offspring more fit than the parent), increase σ, otherwise decrease σ. The schedule for increasing and decreasing σ is geometrical schedule (the factor suggested by Schwefel [24] is 1.1). Last, in early EP [4], the standard deviation of mutation was determined on the basis of the fitness of the individual at hand, in such way that most fit individuals undergo mutation with proportionally smaller standard deviations.

Both ES and EP finally turned to *adaptive mutation*: the standard deviations σ_i are encoded in the individuals, and themselves undergo evolution. The standard deviations are therefore adjusted "for free" along evolution [2].

This mechanism encounters several difficulties in the GA framework, which uses mutation very sparingly (mutation rate per bit is often around 10^{-3}): this gives little chance for the adaptive mutation of real-valued features to actually adapt. Further, Gaussian-like mutation seems to poorly evolve discrete features [1]: when the standard deviation gets very small, mutation comes to having no effect at all on discrete features. This violates the *strong causality* principle, stating that "a small change in the parameters should result in a small change in the fitness" [23]; as a matter of fact, no "small change" below the one-bit threshold is possible in the discrete case.

3 Evolution under Influence

This section presents three population-driven mechanisms to mutate discrete features in the ES framework.

3.1 Evolution and Induction

Our approach is loosely inspired from previous work devoted to the inductive control of evolution [26, 25]: evolution is considered a sequence of events (operators giving birth to new individuals), classified good or bad depending on whether the offspring are more or less fit than the parents. These events, gathered through either spying evolution or experimenting on the current population, are processed by Inductive Learning algorithms [17, 15]. Induction can thus construct online some "law of bad events", which may then be used in a variety of ways to guide the next generations (e.g. to control the disruptiveness of evolution operators, or prevent the loss of genetic diversity). The coupling of Evolution and Induction allows one to continually create, use and update knowledge about evolution.

The present paper is similarly based on the assumption that one can get valuable hints by observing evolution, and use them to guide the further steps of evolution. The difference is that what was previously observed was the evolution operators, whereas the present work directly considers individuals.

3.2 Imitation and Differentiation

Induction needs positive and negative examples; these are respectively set to the most fit and less fit offspring [1].

Indeed, the difference of fitness between a positive and a negative example is due to the difference of their gene values. From this fact, one may infer that mutation should preserve these differences, and preferably modify those bits which take same value for the good individual at hand, and the negative examples. Practically, for each individual Ex, the profile $(p_1, \ldots, p_N)$ of its differences with the negative examples is computed, where p_i is the fraction of negative examples differing from Ex on bit x_i. *Mutation by differentiation* then mutates bit x_i in individual Ex with a probability proportional to $1 - p_i$; the resulting offspring will be still farther from the negative examples, than the parent was. The number K of bits to mutate is set by the user, and it is presently constant along evolution and over the population. Mutation by differentiation expectedly leads to highly diversified populations: if most offspring share a given bit value, this bit will be mutated with high probability. This covers as a particular case strategies devised to restore genetic diversity (see [16] among others).

One could also consider that negative examples contain valuable, if not first-rate, information: after all, these individuals or their parents have survived up to now. This leads to *mutation by imitation*, where bit x_i in individual Ex is mutated with a probability proportional to p_i. Mutation by imitation tends to "repair" explorers whenever they have lost some information shared by the previous population; it favors uniformity.

Last, and since the two above operators have opposite virtues, a third possibility consists in alternating mutation by imitation and mutation by differentiation: this hopefully allies the conservative properties of mutation by imitation and the high rate of exploration of mutation by differentiation.

We finally propose three kinds of evolution "under influence": *evolution by imitation*, *evolution by differentiation* and *alternate evolution*. The two first schemes respectively use mutation by imitation and mutation by differentiation as single evolution operator. In the third scheme, even-numbered generations undergo mutation by imitation whereas odd-numbered generations undergo mutation by differentiation.

4 Experimental Validation

Evolution under influence has been implemented in a standard $(\mu + \lambda)$ ES frame, and compared to canonical GA, canonical ES (based on the 1/5 rule), and standard adaptive ES, on four problems.

[1] Care must be exercised in discarding individuals with intermediate fitnesses: otherwise hazardous conclusions can be drawn from making distinctions between almost equally fit individuals.

4.1 The problems

• The Royal Road problem was conceived by Holland, Mitchell and Forrest [18] to study into details the interaction of features most adapted to GA search. An analysis of the unexpected difficulties of this problem is found in [19, 8].

• The Ugly problem is a GA-deceptive problem [27], built by concatenation of 10 instances of the elementary problem, defined on $\Omega = \{0,1\}^3$, by F(x) = 3 if x = 111; F(x) = 2 for x in $0 \star\star$, and F(x) = 0 otherwise.

• The combinatorial multiple knapsack optimization problem [14] is defined as follows:

Given P knapsacks having respective capacities $c_1..c_P$,
Given N objects having respective costs $p_1..,p_N$,
Given the overall dimension $w_{i,j}$ of object i regarding knapsack j,
Determine a subset of objects noted $X = x_1,..x_N$, with x_i boolean, that is feasible, i.e. satisfies the constraints relative to the maximal capacities of all knapsacks, and maximizes the overall profit:

$$\text{Max}\,\{\sum_{i=1}^{N} p_i.x_i \;;\; \forall j = 1..P, \sum_{i=1}^{N} w_{i,j}x_i < c_j.\}$$

A usual heuristics in evolutionary constrained optimization [16] consists in reducing the fitness of non feasible individuals:

$$F(X) = \begin{cases} \sum_{i=1}^{N} p_i x_i & \text{if } X \text{ is feasible} \\ \frac{r}{2}\sum_{i=1}^{N} p_i x_i & \text{if } r \text{ is the percentage of satisfied constraints} \end{cases}$$

• The Long Path problem was conceived by Horn and Goldberg [11] as a unimodal problem hard for local searchers, that is, hill-climbers and the GAs mutation operator. The fitness landscape is composed of a large low-fitness plateau, within which a path of slowly increasing fitness leads to the unique optimum. This path is of length $2^{N/2}$ (N is the length of the bitstring). Two successive individuals on the path differ by one bit, while all other individuals on the path are at Hamming distance of at least 2.

4.2 Experimental settings

All results are averaged on 15 independent runs. The dynamics of evolution is visualized by plotting the (averaged) best fitness obtained for a number of fitness calculations. We compared six evolutionary schemes:

• A canonical GA (CGA) serves as reference [9]: the parents are selected based on their fitnesses with rank-based selection, 2-point crossover is applied at the rate of 0.6; the mutation is applied at the rate of $\frac{0.2}{N}$, where N denotes the length of the bitstring.

• A "traditional ES" (TES) is a boolean $(\mu + \lambda)$ evolution strategy involving a single mutation rate per bit σ ; σ is modified according to the 1/5 rule of Rechenberg [23]. The geometrical factor used to increase σ ranges from 1.1 to 2.

•An "adaptive ES" (AES) is a boolean $(\mu+\lambda)$ evolution strategy that transposes the adaptive mutation described in [1] with minor differences: Each individual is attached one mutation rate p (the probability of mutation of any single bit) which itself undergoes mutation according to Obalek's rule [20, 1]:

$$p := \left(1 + \frac{1-p}{p}.exp(\gamma \;.\; N(0,1))\right) \qquad \text{with } \gamma = \frac{0.5}{\sqrt{2\sqrt{N}}},$$

with a lower bound of $1/N$ on p to guarantee effective mutation.

• Mutations under influence have been implemented in the frame of a $(\mu + \lambda)$ ES. Positive and negative examples respectively are the μ most fit and μ less fit individuals among the λ offspring. Imitation- and differentiation-based evolutions respectively use mutation by imitation and mutation by differentiation as single evolution operators. Alternate evolution alternatively evolves populations through mutation by imitation and mutation by differentiation. Unless otherwise specified, the number K of bits to mutate is set to 1.

4.3 Comparative results

The Royal Road problem. The canonical GA evolves a population of 60 individuals; all other algorithms follow a $(30 + 60)$ ES scheme.

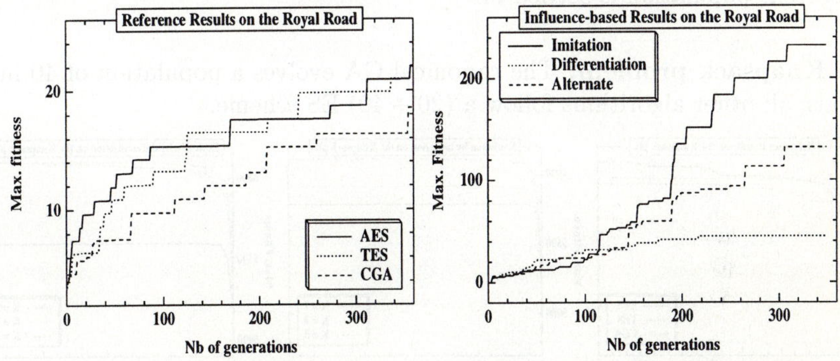

(a) Reference Results (b) Evolution under Influence

Figure 1 : The Royal Road, Dynamics of evolution (beware of the Y-scale).

The imitation scheme outstandingly outperforms all other schemes. This can be explained from the resemblance between mutation by imitation and crossover, and the fact that this problem explicitly relies on the building block hypothesis. In the meanwhile, the elitist $(\mu + \lambda)$ scheme prevents evolution from the fleeting discovery phenomenon [8], which was considered the main cause for the difficulties of standard GAs on this problem.

The Ugly problem. The canonical GA evolves a population of 40 individuals; all other algorithms follow a $(20 + 40)$ ES scheme.

The AES algorithm (ES with adaptive mutation) slightly supersedes the TES algorithm (ES following the 1/5 rule), and both significantly outperform the canonical GA algorithm on this GA-deceptive problem (Fig. 2(a)).

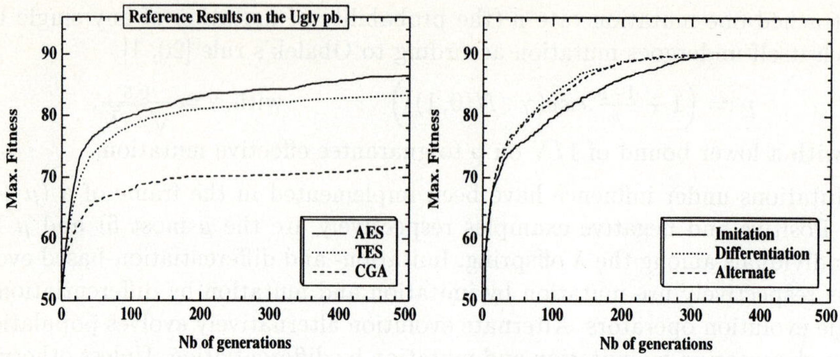

(a) Reference Results (b) Evolution under Influence

Figure 2 : The Ugly problem, Dynamics of evolution.

The differentiation scheme appears the best one on this problem, though the imitation scheme soon catches up; this can be interpreted as differentiation allows rejecting suboptimal solutions previously found (the deceptive schemata). Again, this is possible only because the $(\mu + \lambda)$ scheme counterbalances the disruptive effects of mutation by differentiation, which basically escapes any good schema the current population is settled in.

The Knapsack problem. The canonical GA evolves a population of 40 individuals; all other algorithms follow a $(20 + 40)$ ES scheme.

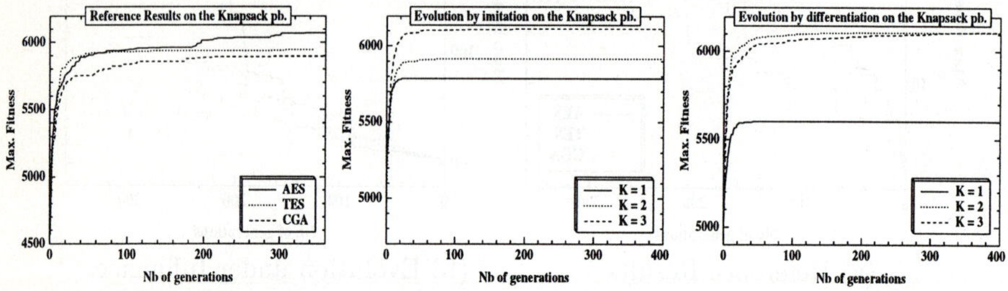

(a) Reference Results (b) Imitation Scheme (c) Diff. Scheme

Figure 3 : The Knapsack problem, Dynamics of evolution.

This problem includes a great many of local optima, and a strong mutation is needed to avoid premature convergence; mutating more than just one bit $(K = 2)$ demonstrates clearly beneficial in the Imitation and Differentiation schemes.

The Long Path problem. The canonical GA evolves a population of 21 individuals; all other algorithms follow a $(7+21)$ ES scheme. The size of the problem (number of bits of individuals) is 91. Parameter K is set to 2, the minimum jump for short-cuts on the path.

Figure 4 shows average results for 1000 generations. Note that the optimum will always be found by all methods in the (very) long run, by climbing up the path through mutations. What is measured here is the ability to find short-cuts in spite of the low-fitness plateau between different components of the path.

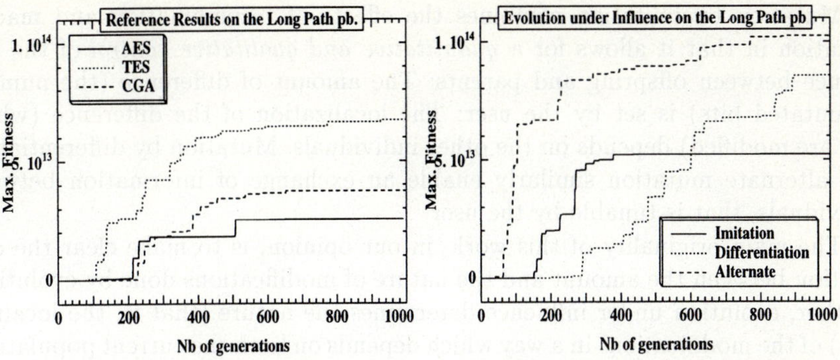

(a) Reference Results (b) Evolution under Influence

Figure 4 : The Long Path problem, Dynamics of evolution.

The long path problem presents intriguing particularities. First, the simple, traditional ES significantly supersedes CGA, whereas this problem was meant to be hard for mutation alone. Second, it demonstrates that alternate evolution can behave quite differently (and in fact, much better) than evolution by imitation or evolution by differentiation stand-alone. A tentative explanation is related to the accordion-like behavior of alternate evolution: mutation by imitation reduces the diversity and moves an individual toward the previous local optimum closest to this individual; then, mutation by differentiation re-increases the diversity and spreads individuals away. The combination of these two phases seemingly eases the discovery of shortcuts on the long and sneaky path toward the optimum.

5 Discussion and Perspectives

The central characteristics of evolution under influence is to allow individuals to exchange information along evolution. Such exchange is usually ensured by recombination, does it concern two parents or more [2]. And, according to the building blocks principle [10, 9], this exchange is the essential factor of biological and artificial evolution.

Another analysis [13] emphasizes that recombination can, in some contexts, be advantageously replaced by macro-mutation — equivalent to recombination with a random parent. It is noteworthy that macro-mutation and recombination offer different kinds of control on the difference between offspring and parents. Macro-mutation ensures that the offspring will be significantly different from the parent — but does not set any bias on the difference. In opposition, recombination is heavily biased: the localization, and hence the amount, of the difference between an offspring and a parent depends on the current population.

To sum up, macro-mutation controls *how much* offspring are different from parents, but does not care about *where*, that is, which bits are modified. Inversely, recombination tends to modify bits so as to copy other individuals in the population, which implies that it hardly has any effect when the population is on the verge of converging.

Mutation by imitation combines the effects of recombination and macro-mutation in that it allows for a *quantitative and qualitative control* of the difference between offspring and parents: The amount of difference (the number of mutated bits) is set by the user; The localization of the difference (which bits are modified) depends on the other individuals. Mutation by differentiation and alternate mutation similarly enable an exchange of information between individuals, that is tunable by the user.

The main originality of this work, in our opinion, is to make clear the distinction between the amount and the nature of modifications done by evolution. Further, evolution under influence determines the nature (that is, the localization) of the modifications in a way which depends on both the current population, and the individual at hand.

Many improvements can be brought to evolution under influence. Further research is concerned with adaptively adjusting the number of bits to mutate, and the kind of mutation (by imitation, differentiation, or alternate) to apply on a given individual. Mutation could also take into account, besides the difference between the current individual and the negative examples, its difference with other positive examples.

Last, this scheme will be extended to multi-modal fitness landscapes; the idea would be to evolve an individual depending on the negative examples nearest to this individual, in order to separately follow several tracks.

References

1. T. Bäck and M. Schütz. Evolution strategies for mixed-integer optimization of optical multi-layer systems. In J. R. McDonnell, R. G. Reynolds, and D. B. Fogel, editors, *Proceedings of the 4th Annual Conference on Evolutionary Programming.* MIT Press, March 1995.
2. T. Bäck and H.-P. Schwefel. An overview of evolutionary algorithms for parameter optimization. *Evolutionary Computation*, 1(1):1–23, 1993.
3. K.A. DeJong. *The Analysis of the Behavior of a Class of Genetic Adaptive Systems.* PhD thesis, University of Michigan, Ann Harbor, 1975. *Dissertation Abstract International*, 36(10), 5140B. (University Microfilms No 76-9381).
4. D. B. Fogel. An analysis of evolutionary programming. In D. B. Fogel and W. Atmar, editors, *Proceedings of the 1st Annual Conference on Evolutionary Programming*, pages 43–51. Evolutionary Programming Society, 1992.
5. D. B. Fogel. *Evolutionary Computation. Toward a New Philosophy of Machine Intelligence.* IEEE Press, Piscataway, NJ, 1995.
6. D.B. Fogel and L.C. Stayton. On the effectiveness of crossover in simulated evolutionary optimization. *BioSystems*, 32:171–182, 1994.
7. L. J. Fogel, A. J. Owens, and M. J. Walsh. *Artificial Intelligence through Simulated Evolution.* New York: John Wiley, 1966.
8. S. Forrest and M. Mitchell. What makes a problem hard for a genetic algorithms : Some anomalous results and their explanation. *Machine Learning*, pages 285–319, 1993.

9. D. E. Goldberg. *Genetic algorithms in search, optimization and machine learning.* Addison Wesley, 1989.
10. J. Holland. *Adaptation in natural and artificial systems.* University of Michigan Press, Ann Arbor, 1975.
11. J. Horn, D.E. Goldberg, and K. Deb. Long path problems. In Y. Davidor, H.-P. Schwefel, and R. Manner, editors, *Proceedings of the* 3rd *Conference on Parallel Problems Solving from Nature*, page 149:158. Springer Verlag, 1994.
12. C. Z. Janikow and Z. Michalewicz. An experimental comparison of binary and floating point representations in genetic algorithms. In R. K. Belew and L. B. Booker, editors, *Proceedings of ICGA'91*, pages 31–36. Morgan Kaufmann, 1991.
13. T. Jones. Crossover, macromutation and population-based search. In L. J. Eshelman, editor, *Proceedings of ICGA'95*, pages 73–80. Morgan Kaufmann, 1995.
14. S. Khuri, T. Bäck, and J. Heitkötter. The 0/1 multiple knapsack problem and genetic algorithms. In *Proceedings of the ACM Symposium of Applied Computation*, 1994. (http:\\www-cgi.cs.cmu.edu \afs\cs.cmu.edu\projet\ai-repository).
15. Y. Kodratoff. *Introduction to Machine Learning.* Pitman Publishing, London, 1988.
16. Z. Michalewicz. *Genetic Algorithms+Data Structures=Evolution Programs.* Springer Verlag, New-York, 1996. 3rd edition.
17. R.S. Michalski. A theory and methodology of inductive learning. In R.S Michalski, J.G. Carbonell, and T.M. Mitchell, editors, *Machine Learning : an artificial intelligence approach*, volume 1. Morgan Kaufmann, 1983.
18. M. Mitchell, S. Forrest, and J.H. Holland. The Royal Road for genetic algorithms : Fitness landscapes and GA performance. In F. J. Varela and P. Bourgine, editors, *Proceedings of ECAL-93*, pages 245–254. MIT Press, 1993.
19. M. Mitchell and J.H. Holland. When will a genetic algorithm outperform hill-climbing ? In S. Forrest, editor, *Proceedings of ICGA'93*, pages 647–654. Morgan Kaufmann, 1993.
20. J. Obalek. *Rekombinationsoperatoren für Evolutionsstrategieren.* PhD thesis, Universität Dortmund, Fachbereich Informatik, 1994.
21. C.C. Petersen. Computational experience with variants of the Balas algorithm applied to the selection of R & D projects. *Management Science*, 13:736–750, 1967.
22. N. J. Radcliffe. Equivalence class analysis of genetic algorithms. *Complex Systems*, 5:183–20, 1991.
23. I. Rechenberg. *Evolutionstrategie: Optimierung Technisher Systeme nach Prinzipien des Biologischen Evolution.* Fromman-Holzboog Verlag, Stuttgart, 1973.
24. H.-P. Schwefel. *Numerical Optimization of Computer Models.* John Wiley & Sons, New-York, 1981. 1995 – 2nd edition.
25. M. Sebag, C. Ravisé, and M. Schoenauer. Controlling evolution by means of machine learning. In L.J. Fogel, P. J. Angeline, and T. Bäck, editors, *Proceedings of the* 5th *Annual Conference on Evolutionary Programming.* MIT Press, 1996.
26. M. Sebag and M. Schoenauer. Controlling crossover through inductive learning. In Y. Davidor, H.-P. Schwefel, and R. Manner, editors, *Proceedings of the* 3rd *Conference on Parallel Problems Solving from Nature.* Springer-Verlag, LNCS 866, 1994.
27. D. Whitley. Fundamental principles of deception in genetic search. In G. J. E. Rawlins, editor, *Foundations of Genetic Algorithms.* Morgan Kaufmann, 1991.
28. D.H. Wolpert and W.G. Macready. No free lunch theorems for search. Technical report, Santa Fe Institute, 1995.

Formal Algorithms + Formal Representations = Search Strategies

Patrick D. Surry[a,b] & Nicholas J. Radcliffe[a,b]
{pds,njr}@quadstone.co.uk

[a]Quadstone Ltd, 16 Chester Street, Edinburgh, EH3 7RA, UK
[b]Department of Mathematics, University of Edinburgh, The Kings Buildings, EH9 3JZ, UK

Abstract. Most evolutionary algorithms use a fixed representation space. This complicates their application to many problem domains, especially when there are dependencies between problem variables (e.g. problems naturally defined over permutations). This paper presents a method for specifying algorithms with respect to *abstract* representations, making them completely independent of any *actual* representation or problem domain. It also defines a procedure for generating a concrete representation from an explicit *characterisation* of a problem domain which captures beliefs about its structure. This allows arbitrary algorithms to be applied to arbitrary problems yielding well-specified search strategies suitable for implementation. The process is illustrated by showing how *identical* algorithms can be applied to both the TSP and real parameter optimisation to yield familiar (but superficially very different) concrete search strategies.

1 Introduction

The traditional genetic algorithm (e.g. the Simple Genetic Algorithm of Goldberg, 1989) is defined over a fixed representation space, namely that of binary strings. A common perception is that to employ such an algorithm for a new problem, one need only define a fitness function. (Indeed, standard software packages exist which literally require only computer code for a fitness function, e.g. GENESIS; Grefenstette, 1984.) For problems defined explicitly over binary strings (one counting, royal road, etc.) this does not present any difficulty. For others, such as real-parameter optimisation, some encoding from the problem variables into binary strings must be formulated, in order that the fitness of binary chromosomes can then be calculated by decoding them. However, such "shoe-horning" may make much of the structure of the search problem unavailable to the algorithm in terms of heritable allele patterns (see for example the discussion of meaningful alphabets in Goldberg, 1990). For problems in which candidate solutions are more complicated objects (e.g. the travelling sales-rep problem) a direct binary encoding may be unnatural or even infeasible. A particular case is when the "natural variables" of the problem are not orthogonal, in that the valid settings of one variable depend on the value of another (e.g. permutations). Faced with such a situation, practitioners typically adopt an *ad hoc* approach, drawing on evolutionary "concepts" to define pragmatic new move operators perceived as appropriate in the new domain (e.g. operators such as subtour inversion, partially matched crossover and order crossover have been devised for the TSP; Oliver *et al.,* 1987).

Although the use of a fixed representation space is widespread, it is unsatisfactory for a number of reasons. Algorithms based on this idea fail to be truly independent of problem (particularly for problems with naturally non-orthogonal representations). As such, it is not possible to transfer a given algorithm to an arbitrary problem domain. Because such algorithms have only limited domains of applicability, it becomes difficult to make meaningful comparisons between different algorithms. (Attempting to compare, for instance, "genetic algorithms" and "simulated annealing" is futile until both a problem domain and set of move operators are specified, to define each algorithm precisely.) Finally, a fixed representation space makes it much more difficult to incorporate knowledge about the structure of the problem—one is forced to change either the growth function (the "genotype-phenotype" mapping) or the move operators, making the algorithm even less problem-independent.

In this paper we discuss a methodology by which these difficulties can be overcome. We show how (evolutionary) algorithms can be precisely specified independently of any particular representation or problem domain. We demonstrate that this allows us to instantiate such an algorithm for *any* appropriate representation of *any* particular problem class, and illustrate this with a compelling example.

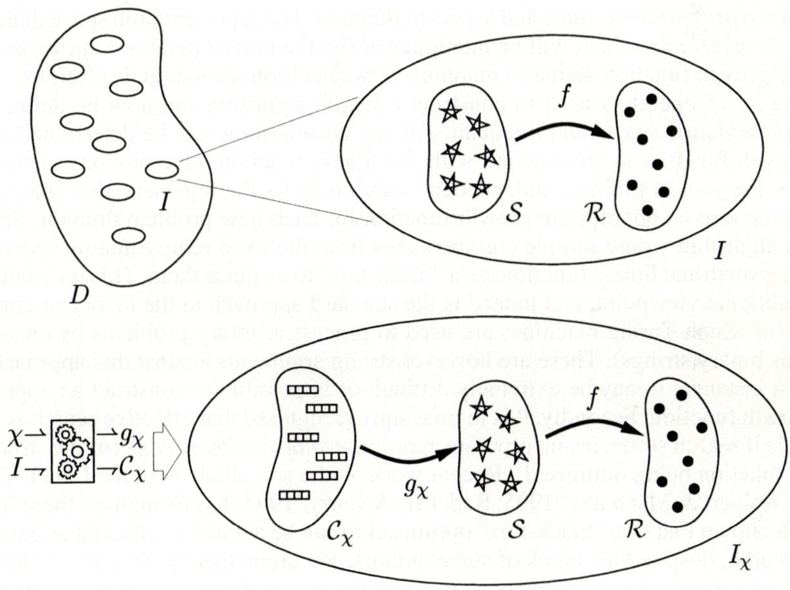

Fig. 1. A *problem domain* D consists of a set of *problem instances*. Each instance I defines a *search space* $\mathcal{S}$ of candidate solutions, a *fitness function* f and a set of objective values $\mathcal{R}$. A *characterisation* χ of the domain specifies a set of equivalences among the solutions for any instance I. These equivalences induce a *representation* made up of a *representation space* $\mathcal{C}_\chi$ (of *chromosomes*) and a *growth function* g_χ mapping chromosomes to the objects in $\mathcal{S}$. A chromosome x is a string of *alleles*, each of which indicates that x satisfies a particular equivalence on $\mathcal{S}$. Algorithms can be completely specified by their action on the alleles of these generalised chromosomes, making them totally independent of the problem domain itself.

In order to fix terminology, a *search problem* is taken to be the task of solving any problem instance from a well-specified problem domain, where by solve we mean finding some optimal or near-optimal solution from a set of candidate solutions. A *problem domain* is considered here to consist of a set of *problem instances,* each of which takes the form of a *search space* (of candidate solutions) together with some fitness function defined on that search space, as illustrated in the top part of figure 1. For instance, "symmetric travelling sales-rep problems" is a problem domain, with a particular set of $n(n-1)/2$ inter-city distances defining an instance (yielding a search space of $(n-1)!/2$ tours and an associated fitness function). A *search strategy* is then simply a prescription by which, for any problem instance, we successively sample candidate solutions from the search space, typically biasing the samples depending on the observed quality (fitness) of previously sampled points. Any such strategy can be viewed as utilising one or more *move operators* which produce new candidate solutions from those previously visited.

Because the objects in the search space can be arbitrary structures (e.g. real-valued vectors, TSP tours, neural-network topologies, etc.), it is often helpful to define search algorithms with respect to an abstract *representation* of the search space, allowing the transfer of search algorithms between problem domains. In general, a representation consists of a *representation space* and a *growth function*. The representation space defines a set of *chromosomes* which will be manipulated (by the move operators) during search, and the growth function defines a mapping between chromosomes and solutions.

The move operators used to construct a search algorithm can now be defined on the representation space, and the quality of any chromosome can be determined using the growth function in conjunction with the fitness function. One obvious method to achieve the goal of problem-independent search is to fix the representation space, and then to choose an appropriate growth function for each new problem domain. Such a search algorithm would sample chromosomes from the fixed representation space, using the growth and fitness functions as a "black-box" to evaluate them. This is essentially the traditional viewpoint, and indeed is the standard approach in the theory of computation (in which Turing machines are used to process arbitrary problems by encoding them as binary strings). There are however strong arguments against this approach. In the first instance, it may be extremely difficult or impossible to construct an appropriate growth function. Secondly, it is increasingly recognised that effective search is only possible if search strategies incorporate appropriate *domain knowledge* (of the structure of the function being optimised). Recent work on the so-called "No Free Lunch Theorem" (Wolpert & Macready, 1995; Radcliffe & Surry, 1995) has formalised these ideas, and has shown that true "black-box" optimisation can be at most as efficient as enumerative search, despite the claims of some authors. We argue that by abstracting the definition of a search algorithm away from a fixed representation-space (just as we strove for independence from a particular problem domain), we can realise the goal of a truly problem-independent algorithm while at the same time making the rôle played by domain knowledge much more explicit.

The formulation presented in section 2 postulates a problem-dependent characterisation χ which captures knowledge about a problem domain. This characterisation mechanically generates a *formal representation* (representation space and growth function) for any instance of the problem, by defining a number of equivalences over the search space, as shown in the bottom part of figure 1. These equivalences induce subsets of the search space thought to contain solutions with related performance; possibly as partitions[1] generated by equivalence relations, or simply as groups of solutions sharing some

[1] A partitioning of a set is a collection of disjoint subsets (partitions) covering the set.

characteristic. For a given solution, the pattern of its membership in the specified subsets is used to define its alleles (and possibly genes). Although in some problems the search space can be partitioned *orthogonally* (informally, meaning that all combinations of alleles represent legal solutions), this is not always the case. For example, in the travelling sales-rep problem, natural representations involve characterising tours by the edges (links) that they share, and it is clear that an arbitrary collection of edges does not always represent a valid tour.

In section 3 we show how *formal algorithms* can be precisely specified—completely independently of any particular representation—whose effectiveness is a direct function of the quality of the domain knowledge captured by the allele structure generated by the characterisation. All of the move operators used in such an algorithm are defined to manipulate solutions only in terms of their abstracted subset-membership properties (alleles). Because many problem domains are naturally characterised using non-orthogonal representations, the traditional operators are seen not to be fully general (e.g. consider one-point crossover between permutations). We provide examples of generalisations of N-point and uniform crossover, and of mutation and hill-climbing operators, and later show how they reduce to traditional forms in familiar problem domains.

We proceed in section 4 to show how *any* formal algorithm can be instantiated with *any* suitable representation of a problem domain of interest to produce a concrete *search strategy*. This is illustrated by defining a simple representation-independent evolutionary algorithm and instantiating it on the one hand to solve the TSP and on the other to solve a real-parameter optimisation problem. The resulting search strategies for the two problems look very different from each other but are both similar to evolutionary algorithms commonly applied in their respective domains. We thus prove the surprising result that two apparently quite different algorithms, in two completely different problem domains, are in fact *identical,* in a strong mathematical sense.

In section 5 we summarise the implications of this more formal approach. We see that by separating algorithm and representation, we achieve the goal of truly problem-independent algorithms. This separation also makes the rôle of domain knowledge in the search process much more explicit, allowing us to pose more carefully questions such as "What is a good algorithm given certain properties of the characterisation?" and "What is a good characterisation of a given problem domain?" Although this formalism might be argued to contain a certain degree of circularity, it is seen to yield practical benefits. For instance, we are able to transfer such algorithms between arbitrary problem domains and to compare different algorithms fairly, independent of a particular problem.

2 Formal Representations

In tackling a domain of search problems, we often prefer to search over a set of structures (chromosomes) representing the objects in the search space rather than directly over the objects themselves. Use of such a representation (made up of a representation space and associated growth function) makes the search algorithm much more generic. A general method for defining a representation is to classify subsets of solutions according to characteristics which they share.

In his seminal work, Holland (1975) proceeded using exactly this approach. He identified subsets of a search space of binary strings using *schemata*—sets of strings that share particular bit values. His Schema Theorem shows how the *observed* fitness of any schema in a population can be used to bound the *expected* instantiation of the same schema in the next generation, under the action of fitness-proportionate selection. Several authors then generalised the notion of a schema and have shown that the theorem applies to arbitrary subsets of the search space, provided that suitable disruption coefficients are chosen (Radcliffe, 1991a; Vose & Liepins, 1991).

In particular, Radcliffe (1991a, 1991b) has developed the idea of *forma analysis,* in which general subsets of the search space are termed *formae*. Typically, the formae are defined as the equivalence classes induced by a set of equivalence relations, although this need not be the case. Any solution can then be identified by specifying the equivalence class to which it belongs for each of the equivalence relations (provided the set of relations is sufficiently rich). Loosely speaking, we identify genes with a set of basic equivalence relations and alleles with the corresponding equivalence classes. For instance, in a search space of faces, "same hair colour" and "same eye colour" might be two basic equivalence relations, which would induce the formae "red hair", "brown hair", "blue eyes", etc. Higher order formae are then constructed by intersection, e.g. "brown hair and blue eyes". Chromosomes made up of strings of alleles can then be used to *represent* the original structures of the search space (faces in our example). These chromosomes make up the representation space and the objects they encode define the growth function.

In certain cases, the genes are orthogonal, meaning that any combination of allele values represents a valid solution, but in many cases this is not so (certain alleles are incompatible). It is also not always easy to define equivalence relations, so we simply identify particular subsets of the search space that share some characteristic. In such cases, genes are not defined and a chromosome consists simply of a set of "alleles". For instance, in the TSP, we could identify $n(n-1)/2$ subsets of the search space, each containing all tours in which city i is linked to city j. Then a particular tour would be represented by the set of (undirected) edges it contained. Although here each chromosome would have the same number of alleles, this need not be so, and the ideas generalise easily to variable-length chromosomes (Radcliffe, 1992).

A problem-dependent *characterisation* procedure is used to generate the required equivalences for any instance of a given problem (see figure 1), and captures all of the structure that will be exploited by a search algorithm. The selection of an appropriate characterisation for a particular problem domain is an open problem. However, several *design principles* have been previously proposed (Radcliffe, 1991a). The most important of these is that the generated formae should group together solutions of related fitness (Radcliffe & Surry, 1994a), in order to create structure which can be exploited by the move operators. (It must also be possible to find a member of any given formae in "reasonable" time without resorting to enumeration, but this is true of most "reasonable" characterisations.)

Examples of several representations designed for various problem domains are shown in table 1. These include the traditional binary representation for real parameters, the "Dedekind" representation[2] for real parameters introduced in Surry & Radcliffe (1996), two natural representations for the traveling sales-rep problem (for comparisons of these and others see Radcliffe & Surry, 1994a), and two representations for subset-selection problems (used in neural-network topology optimisation), one in which only set membership is considered to be important and one in which both membership and non-membership is used (Radcliffe, 1992).

[2] A Dedekind cut is a partitioning of the rational numbers into two non-empty sets, such that all the members of one are less than all those of the other. For example, the irrationals are defined as Dedekind cuts on the rationals (e.g. $\sqrt{2} \triangleq \langle \{x \mid x^2 > 2\}, \{x \mid x^2 < 2\} \rangle$).

Representation	Basic formae	Genes	Orthogonal	Degeneracy	Redundancy
Binary-coded reals	value has ith bit equal to j	yes	yes	none	none
Dedekind real parameters	value above/below cut at i	yes	no	none	huge
TSP: City positions	city i in position j	yes	no	$\times 2n$	low
TSP: Undirected edges	contains link ij	no	no	none	low
Subset-selection: inclusive	includes ith element	no	yes	none	none
Subset-selection: incl/excl	incl/excl ith element	yes	yes	none	none

Table 1. This table summarises the characteristics of several representations for different problem domains. Basic formae indicates the way in which basic subsets of the search space are identified, and the existence of genes is noted. Orthogonal representations are those in which any combination of alleles define a valid solution. Degeneracy occurs when multiple chromosomes represent the same solution, and redundancy is the amount of excess information in the chromosome.

3 Formal Algorithms

Traditional evolutionary algorithms are typically defined using a set of move operators which assume a particular form of the representation space. For example, many genetic algorithms assume chromosomes are binary strings, and most evolution strategies assume chromosomes are strings of real parameter values. Although some of the operators used by such algorithms can be generalised straightforwardly to related representation spaces (for example N-point crossover between binary strings is easily generalised to k-ary chromosomes), they typically are not general enough to handle arbitrary representations. In particular, variable-length genomes and non-orthogonal representations both present difficulties, and have generally led in the past to *ad hoc* construction of problem-specific move operators (for example in the traveling sales-rep problem).

We seek to define formal algorithms using move operators which manipulate the subset membership properties of chromosomes, as generated by *any* representation. Such algorithms are completely independent of representation, and can be applied to any problem domain by instantiating them with a representation appropriate to that domain.

A number of design principles have been proposed to facilitate the development of simple structure-preserving move operators. This has led to the definition of a number of *representation-independent* recombination and mutation operators, permitting the construction of truly representation-independent algorithms. These design principles (Radcliffe, 1991a; 1994) and associated operators include:

1. *Respect.* Respect requires that children produced by recombination are members of all formae to which both their parents belong. For example, if our representation included equivalence relations about hair colour and eye colour, then if both parents had red hair and green eyes, so should all of the children produced by a respectful crossover operator.

R^3: Random respectful recombination is defined as that operator which selects a child uniformly at random from the set of all solutions which share all characteristics possessed by both parents (their *similarity set*).

2. *Transmission.* A recombination operator is said to be *strictly transmitting* if every child it produces is equivalent to one of its parents under each of the basic equivalence relations (loosely, every gene is set to an allele which is taken from one or other parent). Thus, if one parent had red hair and the other had brown hair, then transmission would require that the child had either red or brown hair.
   RTR: The random transmitting recombination operator is defined as that operator which selects a child uniformly at random from the set of all solutions belonging only to basic formae present in either of the parents (their *dynastic potential*).
3. *Assortment.* Assortment requires that a recombination operator be capable of generating a child with any compatible characteristics taken from the two parents. In our example above, if one parent had green eyes and the other had red hair, and if those two characteristics are compatible, assortment would require that we could generate a child with green eyes and red hair.
   RAR: The random assorting recombination operator, a generalised form of uniform crossover, has been previously defined (Radcliffe, 1992). It proceeds by placing all alleles from both parents in a conceptual bag (possibly with different multiplicities), and then repeatedly draws out alleles for insertion into the child, discarding them if they are incompatible with those already there. If the bag empties before the child is complete, which can happen if not all combinations of alleles are legal (so that the representation is *non-orthogonal*) remaining genes are set to random values that are compatible with the alleles already present in the child.
   GNX: A generalised version of N-point crossover has also been defined (Radcliffe & Surry, 1994a). This proceeds in much the same way as standard N-point crossover, dividing the two parents with N cut-points, and then using genetic material from alternating segments. The alleles within each segment are tested in a random order for inclusion in the child, and any remaining gaps are patched by randomly selecting compatible alleles first from the unused alleles in the parents, and then from all possible alleles.
4. *Ergodicity.* This demands that we select operators such that it is possible to move from any location in the search space to any other by their repeated action. (Typically a standard mutation operator is sufficient.)
   BMM: Binomial minimal mutation, a generalisation of standard point-wise mutation, has been proposed in Radcliffe & Surry (1994a). Minimal mutations are defined to be those moves which change the fewest possible number of alleles in a solution (in non-orthogonal representations it may be necessary to change more than one allele at a time to maintain legality). BMM performs a binomially-distributed number (parameterised by the genome length and a gene-wise mutation probability) of minimal mutations, and does not forbid mutations which 'undo' previous ones.
   Hill-climbers: the definition of representation-independent "minimal mutation" allows us to define a number of representation-independent hill-climbing operators, and to define *memetic algorithms* based on the idea of searching over a sub-space of local-optima (Radcliffe & Surry, 1994b).

Using these operators, we can define algorithms which are independent from any particular representation or problem, such as the example shown below. Note that every step of the algorithm is precisely defined, and that given a representation of a problem domain, we can mathematically derive a concrete search strategy suitable for implementation on a digital computer (see section 4). This is different from traditional evolutionary algorithms, in which steps 4 and 5 would have to be modified for any problem domain which required a new representation space.

A representation-independent evolutionary algorithm

1. Generate an initial population by randomly sampling p times from the space of chromosomes.
2. Evaluate the p members of the initial population via the growth and fitness functions.
3. Select two parents using binary-tournament selection.
4. Recombine the parents using RAR.
5. Mutate the resulting child using BMM.
6. If the child does not exist in the population, evaluate it and replace the member with the worst fitness.
7. Repeat to step 3 until termination criterion.

4 Search Strategies

In order to construct a practical search strategy for a given problem domain, we simply combine a formal algorithm with an appropriate representation of the problem domain. There is no need to construct new move operators, as we simply instantiate those defined in the formal algorithm of choice. Since *exactly* the same formal algorithm (for example, that shown above) can be instantiated for two different representations (of either the same or different problem domains), one can make much more definite statements about the quality of the algorithm itself (as it is defined independently of any problem). It is also possible to fix the representation and vary the algorithm, allowing more meaningful comparisons between algorithms.

For several of the representations shown in table 1, the generalised operators defined in section 3 reduce to traditional forms. For example, for any orthogonal representation, R^3, RTR and RAR all reduce to uniform crossover (Syswerda, 1989), GNX reduces to N-pt crossover, and BMM becomes simple gene-wise point mutation. For the Dedekind real representation, R^3, RTR and RAR reduce to blend crossover with parameter $\alpha = 0$, as defined by Eshelman & Schaffer (1992) and widely used in evolution strategies (Baeck *et al.*, 1991), and BMM is equivalent to gaussian creep mutation (Surry & Radcliffe, 1996). If we consider the undirected edge representation for the traveling sales-rep problem, RAR becomes a variant of edge recombination (Whitley *et al.*, 1989) and R^3 reduces to a weaker version of the same operator. BMM here involves a binomially distributed number of sub-tour inversions, whereas for the city-position representation, BMM reduces to a binomially distributed number of city exchanges (Radcliffe & Surry, 1994a).

Such reductions imply that formal algorithms defined using these operators reduce to commonly used search strategies in the relevant problem domains. To illustrate, the algorithm shown above is instantiated below for both the traveling-sales rep problem using the undirected-edge representation, and for a real-parameter function optimisation problem using the Dedekind representation. This results on the one hand on a strategy based on edge-recombination and sub-tour inversions, and on the other in one based on blend-crossover and gaussian creep-mutation. Both of these strategies have been widely used in their respective domains, but it was not clear before now that they were exactly the same formal algorithm.

Search strategy as algorithm plus representation		
Problem domain:	**TSP**	**Real-parameter opt.**
Representation:	**Undirected-edges**	**Dedekind**
Choose initial population:	of random tours	of random vectors
Evaluate each solution:	by measuring tour length	using provided $f(\mathbf{x})$
Select two parents:	using binary-tournament selection	
Recombine parents using:	variant of edge-recomb.	BLX-0
Mutate the child with :	binomial number of sub-tour inversions	gaussian creep-mutation for each parameter
Evaluate, replace worst:	if the child does not exist in the population	
Repeat:	until termination criterion	

Note that both the representation and algorithm are mathematical constructions and need not be directly related to the actual way in which the data structures and computer code for the resulting search strategy is implemented on a digital computer[3]. Thus, rather than simply plugging together different bits of computer code, we plug together different bits of mathematics from which we can formally *derive* an actual implementation in a well-specified way. For example, the (formal) Dedekind representation for real numbers has (in the limit) an infinite number of genes, yet it is a simple matter to mathematically derive forms of the various operators suitable for (finite!) implementation.

5 Summary

This paper has presented a more formal approach to evolutionary search, by separating a search strategy into a representation and an algorithm. We have introduced a disciplined methodology for attacking new problem domains—instead of simply using evolutionary "ideas" to invent new operators, one need only provide a *characterisation* of the problem that explicitly captures beliefs about its structure, and then instantiate an existing algorithm with the derived representation. This applies equally to problems with non-orthogonal representations where traditional evolutionary algorithms are inapplicable. We have demonstrated, by way of example, that identical algorithms can be applied to both the TSP and real parameter optimisation, yielding familiar (but apparently quite different) concrete search strategies.

Because these formal algorithms are independent of any particular representation, it is possible to transfer them to arbitrary problem domains, and to make meaningful comparisons between them. By making the rôle of domain knowledge more explicit we are also directed to more reasoned investigation of what makes a good representation for a given problem. Further investigations will build on these ideas to construct a more complete taxonomy of representations, and to investigate issues of algorithmic performance and quality of representation.

[3] Thus the title of this paper has been inspired by but differentiated carefully from the prior works by Wirth (1976) and Michalewicz (1992).

References

T. Bäck, F. Hoffmeister, and H.-P. Schwefel, 1991. A survey of evolution strategies. In *Proceedings of the Fourth International Conference on Genetic Algorithms.* Morgan Kaufmann (San Mateo).

L. J. Eshelman and D. J. Schaffer, 1992. Real-coded genetic algorithms and interval schemata. In D. Whitley, editor, *Foundations of Genetic Algorithms 2.* Morgan Kaufmann (San Mateo, CA).

D. E. Goldberg, 1989. *Genetic Algorithms in Search, Optimization & Machine Learning.* Addison-Wesley (Reading, Mass).

D. E. Goldberg, 1990. Real-coded genetic algorithms, virtual alphabets, and blocking. Technical Report IlliGAL Report No. 90001, Department of General Engineering, University of Illinois at Urbana-Champaign.

J. J. Grefenstette, 1984. GENESIS: A system for using genetic search procedures. In *Proceedings of the 1984 Conference on Intelligent Systems and Machines*, pages 161–165.

J. H. Holland, 1975. *Adaptation in Natural and Artificial Systems.* University of Michigan Press (Ann Arbor).

Z. Michalewicz, 1992. *Genetic Algorithms + Data Structures = Evolution Programs.* Springer Verlag (Berlin).

I. M. Oliver, D. J. Smith, and J. R. C. Holland, 1987. A study of permutation crossover operators on the travelling salesman problem. In *Proceedings of the Third International Conference on Genetic Algorithms.* Morgan Kaufmann (San Mateo).

N. J. Radcliffe and P. D. Surry, 1994a. Fitness variance of formae and performance prediction. In L. D. Whitley and M. D. Vose, editors, *Foundations of Genetic Algorithms III*, pages 51–72. Morgan Kaufmann (San Mateo, CA).

N. J. Radcliffe and P. D. Surry, 1994b. Formal memetic algorithms. In T. C. Fogarty, editor, *Evolutionary Computing: AISB Workshop*, pages 1–16. Springer-Verlag, Lecture Notes in Computer Science 865.

N. J. Radcliffe and P. D. Surry, 1995. Fundamental limitations on search algorithms: Evolutionary computing in perspective. In J. van Leeuwen, editor, *Computer Science Today: Recent Trends and Developments, Lecture Notes in Computer Science, Volume 1000*, pages 275–291. Springer-Verlag (New York).

N. J. Radcliffe, 1991a. Equivalence class analysis of genetic algorithms. *Complex Systems*, 5(2):183–205.

N. J. Radcliffe, 1991b. Forma analysis and random respectful recombination. In *Proceedings of the Fourth International Conference on Genetic Algorithms*, pages 222–229. Morgan Kaufmann (San Mateo).

N. J. Radcliffe, 1992. Genetic set recombination. In D. Whitley, editor, *Foundations of Genetic Algorithms 2.* Morgan Kaufmann (San Mateo, CA).

N. J. Radcliffe, 1994. The algebra of genetic algorithms. *Annals of Maths and Artificial Intelligence*, 10:339–384.

P. D. Surry and N. J. Radcliffe, 1996. A formalism for real-parameter evolutionary algorithms and directed recombination. In *submitted to Foundations of Genetic Algorithms IV.* (San Diego).

G. Syswerda, 1989. Uniform crossover in genetic algorithms. In *Proceedings of the Third International Conference on Genetic Algorithms.* Morgan Kaufmann (San Mateo).

M. D. Vose and G. E. Liepins, 1991. Schema disruption. In *Proceedings of the Fourth International Conference on Genetic Algorithms*, pages 237–243. Morgan Kaufmann (San Mateo).

D. Whitley, T. Starkweather, and D. Fuquay, 1989. Scheduling problems and traveling salesmen: The genetic edge recombination operator. In *Proceedings of the Third International Conference on Genetic Algorithms.* Morgan Kaufmann (San Mateo).

N. Wirth, 1976. *Algorithms + Data Structures = Programs.* Prentice-Hall (Englewood Cliffs, NJ).

D. H. Wolpert and W. G. Macready, 1995. No free lunch theorems for search. Technical Report SFI-TR-95-02-010, Santa Fe Institute.

A Genetic Algorithm with Variable Range of Local Search for Tracking Changing Environments

F.Vavak - T.C.Fogarty - K.Jukes

Faculty of Computer Studies and Mathematics
University of the West of England
Bristol BS16 1QY, UK

{f_vavak, tcf}@btc.uwe.ac.uk & ka-jukes@csm.uwe.ac.uk

Abstract. In this paper we examine a modification to the genetic algorithm - a new adaptive operator was developed for two industrial applications using genetic algorithm based on-line control systems. The aim is to enable the control systems to track optima of a time-varying dynamic system whilst not being detrimental to its ability to provide sound results for the stationary environments. When compared with the hypermutation operator, the new operator matched the level of diversity introduced into the population with the "degree" of the environmental changes better because it increases population diversity only gradually. Although the new technique was developed for the control application domain where real variables are mostly used, a possible generalization of the method is also suggested. It is believed that the technique has the potential to be a further contribution in making genetic algorithm based techniques more readily usable in industrial control applications.

1 Introduction

The genetic algorithm is a proven search/optimisation technique [1] based on an adaptive mechanism of biological systems. The motivating context of Holland's initial work on genetic algorithms (GAs) was the design and implementation of robust adaptive systems in contrast to mere function optimisers [2]. Understanding GAs in this broader adaptive system context is a necessary prerequisite for understanding their potential application to any problem domain and for understanding their relevant strengths and limitations as argued in the previously quoted paper. One important limiting factor for the use of the GA in real time applications common to many real world applications, whose models are not stationary, is the need for the repeated initialization of the GA from a random starting point in the search space to enable tracking optima in such changing/dynamic environments. The use of a repetitive learning cycle has obvious implications in terms of the quality of the solutions available which presents limitations on the use of genetic techniques in dynamic environments such as on-line industrial control.

In this paper we present preliminary results of our research into techniques for genetic algorithm based robust systems which will continually evolve an optimal solution in changing environments while this feature will not be to the detriment of the GA's ability to provide sound results for stationary environments.

Studies carried out in the area discussed have looked into two modification strategies - increasing effective diversity in the population [3, 4] or expanding the memory of the GA [5, 6] to accommodate environmental changes. In the first two papers quoted, an adaptive hypermutation operator and random immigrants strategy are studied and discussed. The hypermutation operator temporarily increases the mutation rate to a high value (called the hypermutation rate) during periods when the time-averaged best performance of the GA worsens. Goldberg and Smith [5] examine the use of diploid representation and dominance operators to improve performance of the genetic algorithm in an oscillating environment, while Dasgupta and McGregor [6] present a modified genetic algorithm with a multi-layered structure of the chromosome which constitutes a "long term distributed memory".

2 Motivation

The method presented in this paper was designed for two industrial application projects concerned with load balancing problems in industry [7, 8] with the aim of enabling a GA based on-line control system to track the optima of a system in which dynamics vary with time (a fundamental problem in control). In both applications the parameters of the controlled system are not static and will drift as a result of variation of the working conditions of the system and external events that are difficult or impossible to predict or describe. Thus a traditional GA must be restarted periodically to accommodate such a changing environment which is a limiting factor in the use of the GA in these types of real time/world applications. Evaluation of all members in the GA population in the above mentioned applications is done by means of measurement of the controlled system output variables after a control action defined by a given chromosome has been performed. Because of the direct evaluation (through experimentation) of the weak individuals, an important consideration for the design of a tracking method was not only the off-line performance of the genetic algorithm but the on-line performance as well. Another important consideration was the quality of the worst members of the population, because direct evaluation of the weak individuals can have costly consequences in the real world applications.

3 Tracking

3.1 The Technique

The technique described in this section belongs to a class of strategies which employ various methods for increasing diversity in the population (e.g. the triggered hypermutation or the random immigrants method [4]) to compensate for changes encountered in the environment. Because of the requirement of sound performance in an environment which is not changing the tracking method is triggered only when the time averaged best performance of the population deteriorates, thus constituting an adaptive tracking mechanism as in the case of the triggered hypermutation [3].

The technique uses a mechanism of variable range local search around the locations in the search space which are represented by the chromosomes before a change of the environment has occurred. The tracking mechanism introduces diversity into the population of the GA gradually unlike, for example, the hypermutation operator discussed earlier. The gradual introduction of diversity into the population of chromosomes is in fact applicable to any problem encoding which use numerical variables as opposed to the categorical variables.

For simplicity, in the following text we will explain how the technique works in detail on the 1-dimensional problem with a binary coded integer variable although it can be easily extended to an n-dimensional problem, rational numbers and different encoding techniques.

3.2 Implementation

The tracking operator presented in this paper can be perceived as a "shift" operator with variable/switched range. When the time-averaged best performance of the population deteriorates, the tracking mechanism is triggered and the crossover and mutation operators are temporarily suspended. The tracking operator then sets randomly bits of the "shift" register whose length is initially R bits. The value represented by the shift register is with equal probability either added to, or subtracted from, the value expressed by the chromosome (a negative result or a value exceeding the maximum value which can be represented by the chromosome is not accepted) and the resulting value replaces the original value encoded in the chromosome. The shift operator effectively enables a local search around a current location in the search space expressed in the given chromosome. The boundary of the search is given by the biggest real value which can be represented by the shift register, i.e. the current range of the local search is determined as +/- $(2^{BITS}-1)$ where BITS is number of bits of the shift register. Figure 1a shows as an example a situation after the initial triggering of the shift operator - the chromosome consists of 10 bits and R=2. The shift size is limited to +/-3 relative to the current location in the search space. The shift operator is applied to all the members of the population and then the genetic algorithm will resume its typical iterations using crossover and the mutation operator on the population modified by the tracking operator.

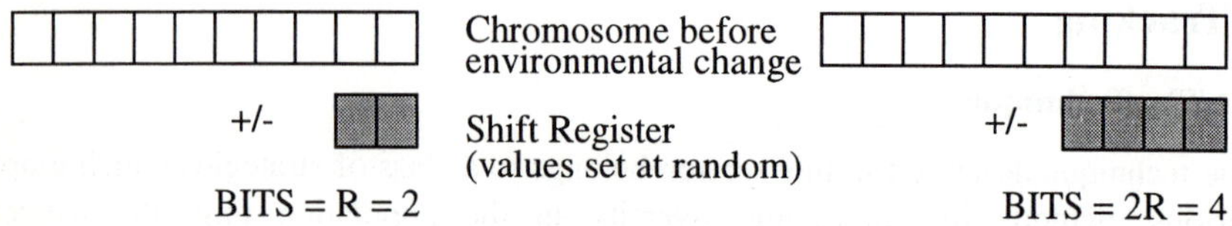

Fig. 1a. **Fig.** 1b.

If the running averaged performance of the best members of the population over a period of a selected number of populations does not improve (e.g. fitness does not reach its original value before the change of the environment) after a suitably defined period of time (e.g. after a given number of evaluations/generations), the range of the local search is modified, i.e. the search is extended to a wider neighbourhood of the current locations in the search space. Figure 1b shows the situation when the search was extended to the next higher range of the local search i.e. the size of the shift register is 2R bits. This search range switching can be initiated repeatedly (figure 2), gradually

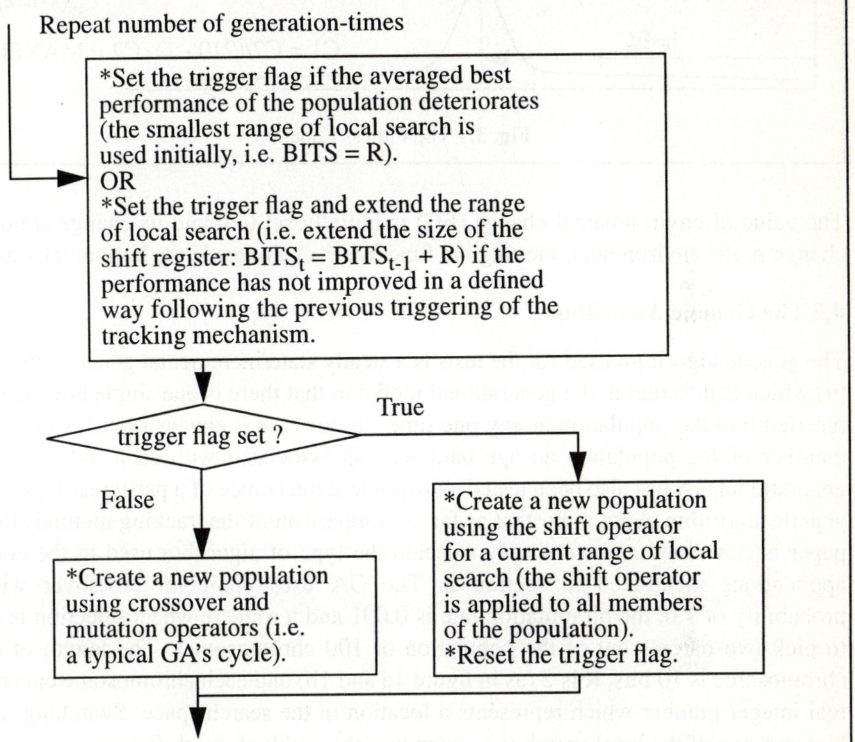

Fig. 2. - The GA Flowchart (simplified)

transforming the local search to a global search, provided a satisfactory optimum is not found on the way. If the time-averaged best performance of the population deteriorates after one is found, the shift operator will use the shift register R bits wide initially (i.e. the smallest range of the local search will again be used first). Thus it can be seen that the switching of the range of the local search can ultimately lead, in the last switching step, to an effective restart of the genetic algorithm and the random reinitialization of the population can be then used instead of the shift operator on this level.

4 Experiments

4.1 The Specific Problem

The problem used in this study for the preliminary tests of the new tracking technique was chosen so that analysis of results was easy and clear. The function F(x) to be optimised is a simple function of one independent variable (figure 3): it is a superposition of a normal distribution curve and an inverted absolute value of the independent variable x.

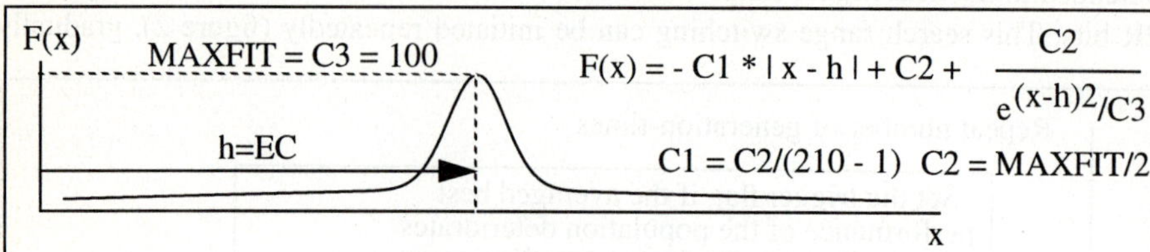

Fig. 3. - The Fitness Function

The value of environmental change (EC) is initially set to 0 and its change simulates change in the environment, moving the function F(x) alongside the horizontal x axes.

4.2 The Genetic Algorithm

The genetic algorithm used for the tests is a steady state/incremental genetic algorithm [9] which is different to the generational model in that there is one single new member inserted into the population at any one time. In our case it always replaces the oldest member of the population an age parameter is associated with each individual). A generational GA has also been tested showing that the choice of a particular type of the genetic algorithm is not important as far as comparison of the tracking methods in this paper is concerned and we simply selected the type of algorithm used in the control applications mentioned in section 2. The GA uses one-point crossover with a probability of 1.0, the bit mutation rate is 0.001 and a roulette wheel selection is used to pick two parents out of the population of 100 chromosomes. The length of each chromosome is 10 bits, R is 2 (as in figure 1a and 1b) and each chromosome encodes a real integer number which represents a location in the search space. Switching to the higher range of the local search (i.e. extending the width of the shift register) is carried out after three consecutive instances of deterioration or stagnation of the running average of the best performing members of the population.

The GA implementing the triggered hypermutation operator used for comparison is identical to the GA used in conjunction with our technique. The initial mechanism which triggers the tracking operator (initiated if the running average of the best performing members of the population over a given period of time drops below a predefined threshold level) is identical for both GAs as well. The best performing member of the population is selected after every 100 evaluations, i.e. after an equivalent of 1 generation of the generational GA.

4.3 Results

In our preliminary tests we compare the shift operator with the hypermutation operator which seems, due to its adaptive feature, to be an alternative mechanism for the kind of applications we are trying to approach. We compared both operators across the range of possible magnitudes of environment changes and for various settings of the mutation rate, the hypermutation rate and the parameters related to the triggering criterion and the criterion for switching the range of the shift operator. The following figures show the typical results. All values are averaged over 100 runs initiated with different random generator seeds. The same seeds were used for each set of experiments to eliminate effects of variables other than the tested parameters.

Figure 4a shows the results of the shift operator being applied to the optimisation problem when an environment change (EC) occurs every 2000 evaluations (i.e. equivalent of 20 generations of the generational GA) with EC=12 - the annotation of the curves for the figure 4a and 4b is identical. The first change of the environment takes place after 10000 evaluations from the start of the search of the GA from a random population. At that point the GA population is 74% converged to the optimum value (the maximum fitness is 100). The line denoted "cr" indicates the current range of the local search - e.g. cr = 0 means that the tracking mechanism will apply the smallest search range (i.e. the shift register will be R bits wide) when activated and cr=1 indicates that the shift register being used is 2R bits wide. To make the graphs clearer the cr value is multiplied by 5. The entropy line shows the values of the population entropy [10]. It is shown in [10] that each solution in the GA population can be viewed as a fixed-length array of symbols and therefore the population may be thought of as a matrix where each row is a solution. As all the symbols in the same column belong to the same alphabet, it is possible to evaluate the Shannon entropy for it and the population entropy is then evaluated as an average of all the columns. The population entropy is in our tests used as a measure of disorder/diversity in the population (i.e. entropy = 0 for a fully converged population) which is increased when the tracking of the changing environment is triggered. Figure 4b shows results obtained when the triggered hypermutation technique is applied to the same problem (the hypermutation rate is set to 0.1). The line denoted "h" indicates when the hypermutation operator is initiated (h=5 when the hypermutation operator is active, otherwise h=0).

It can be seen from the lines indicating population entropy that the triggered hypermutation technique introduces higher diversity into the population than the shift operator when the environmental change EC=12. Comparison of the on-line performance values in the figures 4a and 4b, which are 86.38 and 77.35 respectively, confirms that the triggered hypermutation technique introduced an extensive (i.e. higher than necessary) degree of diversity into the population. However, the rate of evolution to the optima (i.e. number of the evaluations needed to generate the first optimal solution) is 765 for the use of the shift operator and 483 for the hypermutation operator. (The number of evaluations needed to generate the first optimal solution after initial start of the GA is 633 for both cases.) Using Student's t-test for paired variates to compare on-line performance of the shift operator against the hypermutation operator shows that the result for EC=12 is highly significant (i.e. confidence level 99%) in favour of the shift operator.

It becomes apparent at this point that the overhead caused by the gradual extending the search range for the technique using the shift operator will become detrimental to the rate of convergence to the optima (and consequently to the on-line and off-line

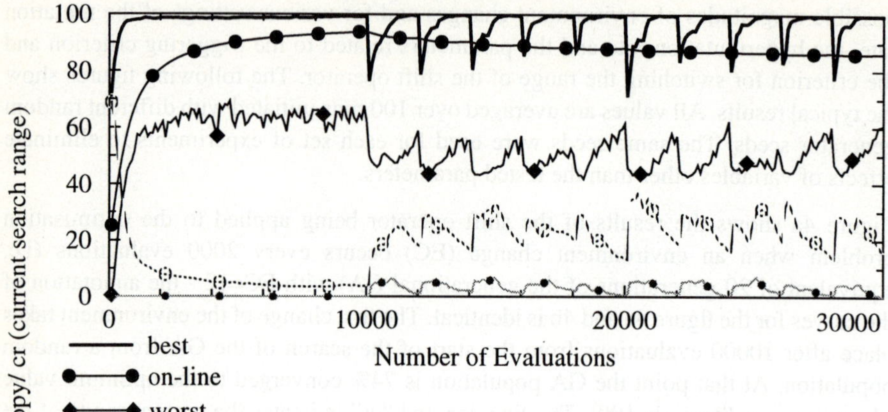

Fig. 4a. - Shift Operator Used

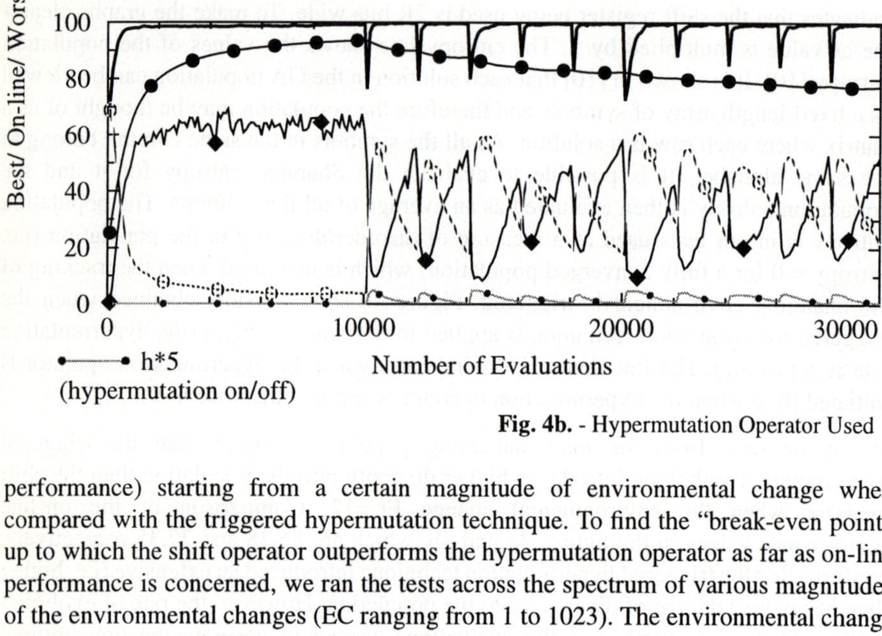

Fig. 4b. - Hypermutation Operator Used

performance) starting from a certain magnitude of environmental change when compared with the triggered hypermutation technique. To find the "break-even point" up to which the shift operator outperforms the hypermutation operator as far as on-line performance is concerned, we ran the tests across the spectrum of various magnitudes of the environmental changes (EC ranging from 1 to 1023). The environmental change always occurred 15000 evaluations after the start of the GA and the on-line measurements taken after 15000 more evaluations were compared. Figure 5 illustrates the results for the shift operator and EC=12 (the annotation of the curves and the x -axis is same as in the figure 4a). The results obtained for various degrees of the environmental change are summarized in the figure 6.

Figure 6 shows that, as was expected, the shift operator provides better results than the hypermutation operator for the smaller changes of the environment - the experimentally determined break-even point value is EC = 31. It is obvious that the experimentally

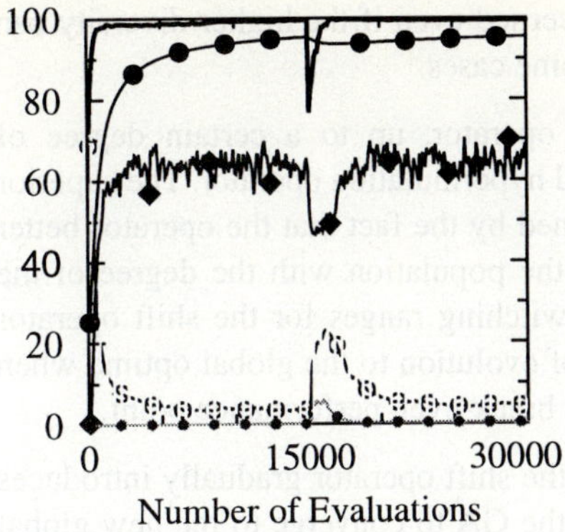

Fig. 5. - Shift Operator Used

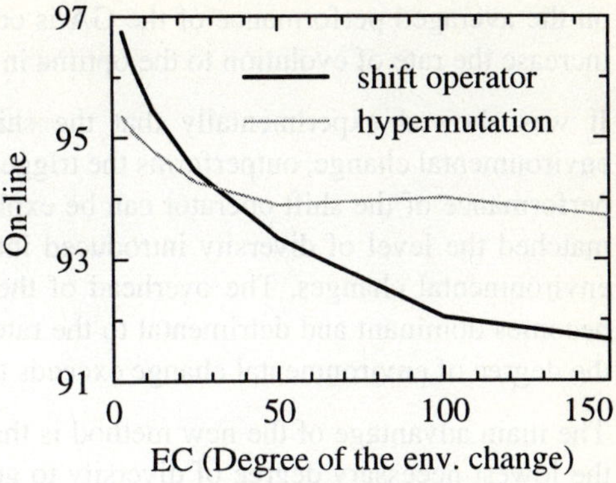

Fig. 6.

found value depends on the selection of the parameters controlling the search range switching as well as on the rate of the hypermutation used for the triggered hypermutation technique. The values of the parameters used for the tests were found to be optimal/near optimal for the particular problem. Statistical comparison of the results for various magnitudes of the environmental change suggest that there is a region of EC values, around the break-even point, where the on-line performance of either method is not significantly better.

5 Possible Generalization of the Technique

A potential criticism of the method is that it depends on having numerical variables. Despite the method being designed for control application where binary/Gray coded real variables are mostly used, a limited generalization of the technique is possible even for problems where categorical variables are used (e.g. bit matching task). The feature of the method which emphasizes gradual increase of the diversity of the population can be generalised when instead of using the shift operator the technique only gradually increases the mutation rate (e.g. in a few distinct bands). This is in fact only a modified triggered hypermutation technique and the penalty for gradual introduction of diversity is, similarly to the shift operator, decreased performance of the GA for the larger environmental changes as far as the Hamming distance of the genotype representation of the old and the new optimum locations is concerned.

6 Conclusions

As we have mentioned before, the tracking technique using the shift operator was developed for industrial control applications where on-line performance as well as the quality of the worst member of the population after the change of the environment was an important consideration for its design. These considerations are also taken into account when evaluating the results of the tests. In this context excessive diversity introduced into the population of the GA can be viewed as disturbance as far as its effect on the averaged performance of the GA is concerned even if the higher diversity can increase the rate of evolution to the optima in some cases.

It was showed experimentally that the shift operator, up to a certain degree of environmental change, outperforms the triggered hypermutation operator. The superior performance of the shift operator can be explained by the fact that the operator better matched the level of diversity introduced into the population with the degree of the environmental changes. The overhead of the switching ranges for the shift operator becomes dominant and detrimental to the rate of evolution to the global optima when the degree of environmental change exceeds the break-even performance point.

The main advantage of the new method is that the shift operator gradually introduces the lowest necessary degree of diversity to get the GA to converge to the new global optimum. This feature of the method corresponds with the requirement of the least possible adverse effect of the tracking method on the on-line performance and the performance of the worst members of the population of the GA during tracking of changing environments. This is an important feature for the use of the method for applications in on-line industrial control.

It can be concluded that the GA which implements the shift operator can continually evolve an optimal solution to the problem without the need for the inefficient periodical restarting of the GA. The method is particularly suitable for control applications where the environmental changes are relatively small or/and gradual. Nevertheless this limitation can be minimized by a suitable technique for self-adaptation of the search range as suggested in the following paragraph. It is believed that the technique will prove beneficial in the application of the GA based techniques to industrial control problems.

7 Further Work

In the application projects discussed in section 2 gradual and relatively small changes of the environment prevail. Nevertheless, a possible minimisation/elimination of the adverse effect of switching the search range on the GA average performance for the higher degrees of environmental changes was considered. It is possible to relate, for example, the degree of change to the width of the shift register, thus enabling self-adaptation of this important parameter to the different degrees of the environmental changes.

A more detailed investigation will be carried out in this area aiming to design a general self-adapting technique based on the shift operator for the control application domain. Another future research area is a study of a variety of the non-stationary environments in conjunction with suitability of the various triggering mechanisms for these environments.

Acknowledgements

The authors would like to thank Dr. Larry Bull for proof-reading of this paper.

References

1. Holland, J.H.: Adaptation in Natural and Artificial Systems. University of Michigan Press. (1975)

2. De Jong K.A.: Are Genetics Algorithms Function Optimizers? Parallel Problem Solving From Nature 2. Elsevier Science Publisher. (1992) 3-13

3. Cobb H.: An Investigation into the Use of Hypermutation as an adaptive Operator in Genetic Algorithm Having Continuous, Time-Dependent Nonstationary Environments. Naval Research Laboratory Memorandum Report 6760. (1990)

4. Cobb H., Grefenstette J.: Genetic Algorithms for Tracking Changing Environments. Proceedings of the 5th International Conference on Genetic Algorithms, Morgan Kaufmann Publishers, Inc. (1993) 523-530

5. Goldberg D., Smith R.E.: Nonstationary Function Optimization Using Genetic Dominance and Diploidy. Proceedings of the 2nd International Conference on Genetic Algorithms, Lawrence Erlbaum Associates, Inc. (1987) 59-68

6. Dasgupta D., McGregor D.: A Structured Genetic Algorithm. Technical report IKBS-8-92 University of Strathclyde. (1992)

7. Fogarty T.C., Vavak F., Cheng P.: Application of the Genetic Algorithm for Load Balancing of Sugar Beet Presses. Proceedings of the 6th International Conference on Genetic Algorithms, Morgan Kaufmann Publishers, Inc. (1995) 617-624

8. Vavak F., Fogarty T.C., Jukes K.: Use of the Genetic Algorithm for Load Balancing in the Process Industry. 1st International Mendelian Conference on Genetic Algorithms, PC-DIR Publishing, s.r.o. - Brno. (1995) 159-164

9. Whitley D., Kauth J.: GENITOR: A different Genetic Algorithm. Proceedings of the Rocky Mountain Conference on Artificial Intelligence, Denver. (1988) 118-130

10. Davidor Y., Ben-Kiki O.: The Interplay Among the Genetic Algorithm Operators: Information Theory Tools Used in a Holistic Way. Parallel Problem Solving From Nature 2. Elsevier Science Publisher. (1992) 75-84

Adaptation, Niching, and Isolation in Evolutionary Algorithms

An Evolution Strategy with Adaptation of the Step Sizes by a Variance Function

Joachim Born
Technische Universität Berlin, Bionik und Evolutionstechnik
Ackerstr. 71-76 (ACK1), D–13355 Berlin, Germany
born@fb10.tu-berlin.de

Abstract. In this paper we extend the classical Evolution Strategies by a new mechanism to adjust the step sizes. We propose an Evolution Strategy with Variance Function (ESV). The ESV can generate local and global random search procedures depending on the task.
The idea of the variance function approach is presented. A performance comparison of the ESV with other published Evolutionary Algorithms for global optimization problems is made. We report about some aspects of the analysis of the used multimodal test functions which concern the complexity of the fitness landscape.

1 Introduction

Evolution Strategies (ESs), founded by Rechenberg and Schwefel in the late 1960s (see [6], [8]), are numerical optimization methods inspired by principles of biological evolution. In this paper, we use a so-called (1 + 1)–ES schema corresponding to an iterative random search algorithm for solving continuous optimization problems.

In random search algorithms the step sizes must be adapted for an efficient search. The step sizes control is one of the most important parts of random search algorithms besides the iterative schema and, furthermore, it is closely linked with the convergence behaviour. This is also valid for the ESs . In ESs, the step sizes (i.e. the standard deviations of the normally distributed mutations) are not predetermined. They vary for a chosen variance. An adaptation is made by evaluating the success or failure of the random step for the generated step sizes.

Traditionally, the ES is mainly directed towards the optimization of unimodal functions (i.e. the minimum of a convex-quadratic function).

For the unimodal case, the ES is well advanced, see Rechenberg [7].

The use of the ESs for global optimization of multimodal functions is still in dispute among the ES protagonists. Rechenberg sceptically argues in [7] about global search variants. We believe the theoretical global convergence property of the ESs (see [1]) also has a practical relevance, e.g. in the simulation of natural and technical systems which lead to "complex" optimization problems. The unknown structure of optimization problems suggests the need to search for optimization procedures that have both global and local search abilities.

The proposed **E**volution **S**trategy with **V**ariance Function (**ESV**) is designed to generate local and global search procedures within a common framework. Our approach is motivated by the desire to tackle real–world problems in different manners. The ESV should be easy to handle within a common framework and the use of only a few strategy parameters.

The basic was first published by Born in [2]. In the present paper, we extend this approach and examine the performance in comparison with Evolutionary Algorithms (EAs) for global problems: The Breeder Genetic Algorithm (BGA) of H. Mühlenbein and D. Schlierkamp–Vosen (see [5]), and an extension of the BGA: the Evolutionary Algorithm with Soft Genetic Operators (EASY) of H. M. Voigt (see [11]).

2 Introducing the Variance Function

The main feature of the ESV approach is the use of a variance function.

Schwefel has proposed (see Schwefel [8] or [9]) the use of the log-normal distribution for a multiplicative generation of new step sizes.

Our proposal is to adjust the step sizes by a function, flexible enough to generate small and large steps over all iterations.

We construct the so called variance function as an inverse distribution function of a bounded random variable, depending on two parameters: *the mode* and *the dispersion*. The range for the step sizes is controlled by adaptation of the modes of the variance function:

- The step sizes are generated as exponentially distributed random variables, determined by the variance function.
- If the mutations were successful than the modes will be corrected by the step sizes used; else they will remain unchanged.

The dispersions are fixed over all iterations.

Let us illustrate the concept with the following Figure 1.

Three density functions of a variance function are depicted schematically. The functions are defined in the region $[v^l, v^u]$.

The *"mainly local search"* curve should illustrate: A small dispersion reduces the step sizes mainly to the order of the mode. In combination with the high selection pressure of the $(1+1)$ schema the mode would be quickly adapted to small values (near to v^l). This produces a mainly local search procedure.

The *"flexible local and global search"* curve shows the possibility to operate with small and large step sizes simultanously. The mode can be adapted to small values but the chance to generate "big jumps" will be large enough. As an extreme the *"blind search"* curve is shown. More precisely, this curve represents an equally distributed search within the bounds v^l, and v^u.

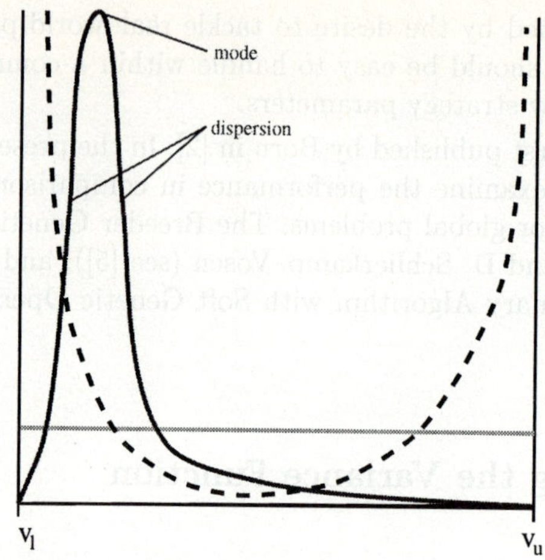

Fig. 1. Scheme of different density functions of a variance function

3 Algorithmic Description of the ESV

3.1 The Evolutionary Framework

We consider the following optimization problem:

$$\min \quad \{f(x) \mid x \in X\} \quad , \qquad X \subseteq R^n, f : R^n \longrightarrow R. \tag{1}$$

The step for the k–th generation is the well-known step of the $(1+1)$-ES[1]:

$$\overline{x}_i \quad = \quad x_i^k + N(0, \sigma_i), \quad i = 1, ..., n;$$

$$x_i^{k+1} \quad = \quad \begin{cases} \overline{x}_i & \text{if } f(\overline{x}) < f(x^k), \\ x_i^k & \text{else.} \end{cases}$$

The σ_i have been generated by using the variance function V (see next section).

---

[1] $N(e, s)$ denotes a normally distributed random variable with expected value e and dispersion s^2.

3.2 The Variance Function

Let z_i, $i = 1, ..., n$ be random variables, uniformly distributed within a given bounded spectrum $[v_i^l, v_i^u]$, $v_i^l < v_i^u$, $i = 1, ..., n$.

Let d_i be (fixed) dispersions and m_i^k, $i = 1, ..., n$ (free to adjust) modes of the variance function V.

Furthermore, let us make the following definitions :

$$v_i(z_i) = v_i^l + (v_i^u - v_i^l) \cdot V(z_i, m_i^k, d_i), \tag{2}$$

and

$$\sigma_i(v_i) = 10^{v_i}, \tag{3}$$

We define the variance function as (for seek of simplicity the indices i, and k are omitted):

$$V(z, m, d) = \begin{cases} 0 & \text{if } z \leq v^l, \\ \left(\frac{z-v^l}{m-v^l}\right)^d \cdot \frac{m-v^l}{v^u-v^l} & \text{if } v^l \leq z \leq m, \\ \frac{m-v^l}{v^u-v^l} + \left(\frac{z-m}{v^u-m}\right)^{\frac{1}{d}} \cdot \left(1 - \frac{m-v^l}{v^u-v^l}\right) & \text{if } m \leq z \leq v^u, \\ 1 & \text{if } z \geq v^u. \end{cases} \tag{4}$$

It is obvious that for $d > 0$ the variance function describes an inverse distribution function of the random variable v within the bounded spectrum $[v^l, v^u]$, with the mode m, and the dispersion d. For $d = 1$ the equal distribution follows.

3.3 Example of the Adaptation of the Modes

We wish to demonstrate the adaptation of the modes in the ESV. Let us apply the ESV to the test problem F7 (see section 4.1) with $n = 2$. The bounds for the variance function are set to $v_i^l = -2.0$, $v_i^u = 3.0$, $i = 1, 2$, and the dispersions are set to $d_i = 20.0$, $i = 1, 2$. These parameters realize a "flexible local and global search" within the constraints for F7.

Figure 2 shows the results of a simulation run and illustrates the choice of different modes by the ESV:
The chosen dispersions guarantee that the modes vary between the whole region $[-2.0, 3.0]$. The modes have been changed 11 times (corresponding to 11 successful iterations). "All four" combinations of the modes can be found, for example:

1^0 Both modes are small: after iteration 1, 31, 95, and 746.
2^0 Both modes are large: iteration no. 30, 92, 106 (, and 741).
3^0 m_1 is small, m_2 is large: after iteration 107, and 212.
4^0 m_1 is large, m_2 is small: after iteration 137.

The combinations 3^0 and 4^0 reflect that problem F7 is a separable one. Line search on the coordinate axis has been successful.

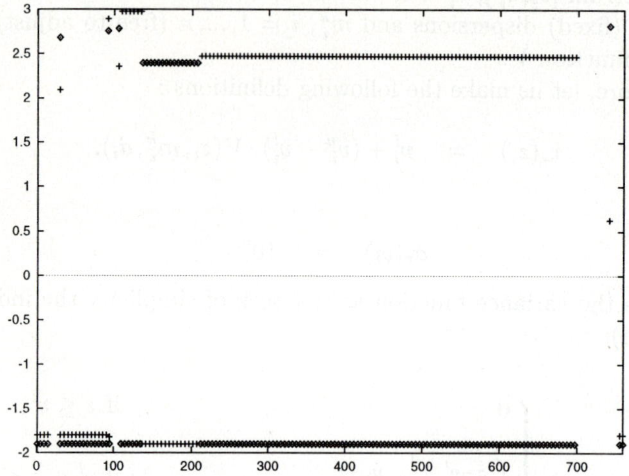

Fig. 2. Graph of the modes, produced in a run to solve problem F7 for $n = 2$ (x–axis – number of iterations, y–axis – values of the modes, $\diamond$ - m_1, $+$ - m_2).

3.4 The Complete Algorithm

Initial Step

Choose:

$v_i^l, v_i^u, \quad i = 1, ..., n$	- lower and upper bounds for the spectra of the variance function, $v_i^l < v_i^u$
$x_i^0, \quad i = 1, ..., n$	- a feasible point
$m_i^0, \quad i = 1, ..., n$	- a mode vector for the variance function, $v_i^l \leq m_i^0 \leq v_i^u$
$d_i, \quad i = 1, ..., n$	- dispersion vector for the variance function, $d_i > 0$
var_{mod_deter}	- a logical variable, determining the random adaptation of the modes
var_{step_stoch}	- a logical variable, determining the random adaptation of the step sizes
mut_{rate}	- a scalar, determining the probability to vary a component of the object vector $x_i^k, \quad i = 1, ..., n,$ $1/n \leq mut_{rate} \leq 1$

Iterative Scheme ($k \geq 0$)

1^0 **Control of the modes**

If $var_{mod\_deter} = .true.$ then
control the modes m_i^k, $i = 1, ..., n$ by the deterministic 1/5–success rule[2]
else
hold the modes.

2^0 **Variation**

Generate step sizes σ_i, $i = 1, ..., n$.
If $var_{step\_stoch} = .true.$ then
generate v_i by (2), and set σ_i by (3),
else
set $\sigma_i = m_i^k$.

Generate a new object vector $\overline{x}$ by

$$\overline{x}_i = x_i^k + N(0, \sigma_i), \quad i = 1, ..., n.$$

3^0 **Selection**

If $f(\overline{x}) < f(x^k)$ then
set $x_i^{k+1} = \overline{x}_i$, $i = 1, ..., n$;
and
set $m_i^{k+1} = v_i$, $i = 1, ..., n$;
only if $var_{mod\_deter} = .false.$
else
hold $x_i^{k+1} = x_i^k$, $i = 1, ..., n$;
and
hold $m_i^{k+1} = m_i^k$, $i = 1, ..., n$;

4^0 **Replace** k by $k+1$ and repeat the steps 1^0, 2^0, and 3^0 so termination criteria are not met.

In this scheme termination criteria are not included. ESV is implemented with the following termination criteria:

- Lower bounds for the improvements of the objective function (fitness function) and of variations in the object vector after a fixed number of generations both absolute and relative.
- A maximal number of evaluations of the objective function.

[2] An implementation is given in [9].

4 Numerical Tests

4.1 Test Problems

Performance evaluation of random search algorithms needs a representative suite of test functions. For this reason we choose the well known functions F1 and F6–8 (see Table 1) for minimization.

Problem/ or "Function"	Objective Function or Fitness Function	Constraints ($i = 1, ..., n$)	Const.
F1	$\sum_{i=1}^{n} x_i^2$	$-500 \leq x_i \leq 500$	
F6	$A \cdot n + \sum_{i=1}^{n} x_i^2 - A \cdot \cos(2\pi x_i)$	$-5.12 \leq x_i \leq 5.12$	$A = 10$
F7	$\sum_{i=1}^{n} -x_i \sin(\sqrt{\lvert x_i \rvert})$	$-500 \leq x_i \leq 500$	
F8	$\sum_{i=1}^{n} x_i^2/d - \prod_{i=1}^{n} \cos(x_i/\sqrt{i}) + 1$	$-600 \leq x_i \leq 600$	$d = 4000$

Table 1: Test suite for the ESV

These test problems have been used as a standard for measuring the performance of various Evolutionary Algorithms.

Function F1 is a unimodal function. Nevertheless, it is a standard problem. F6, F7, and F8 are multimodal.

4.2 Simulation Results

The strategy parameters and the inital values which have been used for the numerical tests are given in Table 2.

	F1	F6	F7	F8
$x_i^0, i = 1(1)n$	$\equiv$100.0	rnd(-5.12, 5.12)	rnd(-500.0, 500.0)	rnd(-600.0, 600.0)
$m_i^0, i = 1(1)n$	$\equiv$ 2.0	$\equiv$ 0.0	$\equiv$ 2.0	$\equiv$ 1.0
$v_i^l, i = 1(1)n$	$\equiv$ -15.0	$\equiv$ -2.0	$\equiv$ -2.0	$\equiv$ -3.0
$v_i^u, i = 1(1)n$	$\equiv$ 2.0	$\equiv$ 0.0	$\equiv$ 3.0	$\equiv$ 2.0
mut_{rate}	1.0	1/n	1/n	1/n
var_{step_stoch}	false	true	true	true
var_{mod_deter}	true	false	false	false
$d_i, i = 1(1)n$	$\equiv$ 0.0001	$\equiv$ 20.0	$\equiv$ 20.0	$\equiv$ 20.0

Table 2: Strategy parameters and initial values.[3]

For each problemwe made 20 runs. The results in the following tables are average numbers of function evaluations. The simulations were stopped if the following termination criteria (corresponding with [5] and [11]) were fulfilled:

[3] $rnd(a, b)$ denotes a of $[a, b]$ bounded, equally distributed random variable.
For the case $d <= 0.0001$ – the pure $(1+1)$–ES with 1/5 success rule is selected.

- F1: $f(x_k) <= \varepsilon$
- F6: $f(x_k) <= 9 \cdot 10^{-1}$
- F7: $f(x_k) <= f^{opt} + \cdot 5 \cdot 10^{-4}|f^{opt}|$; whereby $f^{opt} = -418,98288 \cdot n$.
- F8: $f(x_k) <= 10^{-3}$, or if no success happens in $5000 \cdot n$ generations (ESV).

The results of tests were compared with other EAs, in this case the BGA and the EASY.

First, we present results for F1 only for ESV. No data are available for the BGA and the EASY. Different values of the termination parameter ε are used to show the well-adapted step sizes control. The results for $\varepsilon = 9 \cdot 10^{-1}, 10^{-3}$ may be compared with the results for F6 and F8. F6 and F8 have F1 as "meta-function". Many more iterations are needed to find the (global) optimum, if the quadratic surface of the objective function is superposed by "waves".

F1	ε		
n	$9 \cdot 10^{-1}$	10^{-3}	10^{-15}
20	1800	2250	4950
100	7600	10450	22350
200	15000	22300	45950
400	35400	48750	100500
1000	85100	115400	230550

Table 3: Results for F1

F6	Algorithm		
n	ESV	EASY	BGA
20	7400	6098	3608
100	36600	45118	25040
200	83750	98047	52948
400	177150	243068	112634
1000	501250	574561	337570

Table 4: Results for F6

F7	Algorithm		
n	ESV	EASY	BGA
20	8700	10987	16100
100	42600	101458	92000
200	85300	241478	248000
400	170250	430084	699803
1000	422050	1067221	–

Table 5: Results for F7

F8	Algorithm		
n	ESV	EASY	BGA
20	43300	26700	66000
100	176500	77250	361722
200	339700	128875	748300
400	698583	229750	1630000
1000	1339750	563350	–

Table 6: Results for F8[4]

4.3 Remarks Concerning the Test Problems

The multimodal functions F6–8 have different levels of "difficulty" for a global optimization procedure. This set of problems was analyzed and evaluated for the first time in [4] and [10]. A recent examination of F6–8 which results in proposals of methodologies for "building better test functions" is presented in [12].

[4] The BGA and the EASY found the global optimum in all runs. ESV: The results have averaged on the successful runs. The global optimum was not found: for $n = 20$ in 17 runs, for $n = 100$ in 10 runs, for $n = 200$ in 6 runs, for $n = 400$ in 5 runs, and for $n = 1000$ in 2 runs.

Let us summarize the results of the examinations: All multimodal problems in our test suite are "semi-causal" ones (see [10]). Semi-causal means that the composition of the minima (and the maxima) fulfill an order relation. The extremes are not "chaotically" distributed. None of the test functions represents a "neadle in the haystack"– problem.

All functions – exept F8 – are separable and symmetric functions (see also [10]). The minima are located on rectangular grids. For details see [10].

Function F8 seems to be the most difficult problem in the test suite. The summation term induces a parabolic "meta–structure" disturbed by "waves". The waves are created by the cosine function in the product term. The product term induces the nonseparability of F8. The nonseparibility makes F8 resistant to coordinate oriented search. Some Evolutionary Algorithms prefer the line search on coordinate axis, if the mutation of a variable is depending on a probability distribution (such as in the case of BGA, EASY, and ESV). Convergence problems follow if small mutation rates are chosen.

In our numerical tests we found an apparently absurd behaviour of the ESV: The higher the dimensionality chosen, the better the rate of convergent runs! In the paper of Whitley et al. [12] the reason for this surprising effect is unmasked. The problem F8 becomes more simple and smoother, and thus easier to solve, as the dimensionality is increased.

The explored characteristica of the multimodal test functions explains the success of Evolutionary Algorithms, demonstrated in the previous presentation of test results.

5 Conclusions

In the unimodal case (F1), the superiority of ESV – in its parameter setting as the pure $(1+1)$–ES with deterministic step sizes control – is evident.

We have demonstrated that the ESV can be used as a tool for global search. It is possible to place the ESV within the spectrum of performance of such high sophisticated EAs for global optimization like BGA and EASY. As an secondary effect we were able to confirm the observations of Whitley et al. on the suitability of the chosen suite of test functions.

The easy handling of ESV is one of its benefits. We believe that the parameter setting (with default values for the variance function) approaches in our numerical tests a setting for tackling real–world problems. For instance, the parametric variant for F8 in Table 2 has also been used to adapt weights in an artificial neural network generator (see [3]).

In our opinion, the search for robust parameters, valid for the whole test suite, is a doubtful goal. We prefer to operate with basic variants having different search behaviour. Thus, we have presented the best parameter setting found for each problem. It was not the purpose to find a common best set of strategy parameters for the test suite.

Presenting the ESV we hope to contribute to the discussion on the use of Evolution Strategies as global optimization procedures. The ESV seems to be

a useful experimental tool to generate a spectrum of local and global search procedures based on the ES scheme.
Furthermore, an individual step sizes adaptation can be provided.

References

1. J. Born: Evolutionsstrategien zur numerischen Lösung von Adaptationsaufgaben. PhD thesis, Humboldt Universität zu Berlin, 1978.
2. J. Born: Adaptively Controlled Random Search - a Variance Function Approach. Systems Analysis, Modelling, Simulation, 2, pp.: 109–112, Akademie-Verlag, Berlin, 1985.
3. J. Born und I. Santibáñez-Koref: Untersuchungen und Erweiterungen zu Projection Pursuit Learning Networks. Internal Report, TU Berlin, Bionik und Evolutionstechnik, 1995.
4. H. Mühlenbein, M. Schomisch, and J. Born: The Parallel Genetic Algorithm as Function Optimizer. Parallel Computing 16, pp.: 619-632, 1991.
5. H. Mühlenbein, and D. Schlierkamp–Vosen: Predictive Models for the Breeder Genetic Algorithm, I. Continuous Parameter Optimization. Evolutionary Computation 1 (1):25– 49, 1993.
6. I. Rechenberg: Evolutionsstrategie: Optimierung technischer Systeme nach Prinzipien der biologischen Evolution. Frommann–Holzboog, Stuttgart. 1973.
7. I. Rechenberg: Evolutionsstrategie '94. Frommann–Holzboog, Stuttgart.1994.
8. H.P. Schwefel: Numerische Optimierung von Computermodellen mittels der Evolutionsstrategie. Interdisciplinary Systems Research; Birkhäuser, Basel and Stuttgart,vol. 26, 1977.
9. H.-P. Schwefel: Evolution and Optimum Seeking. Wiley. New York. 1994.
10. H.–M. Voigt, J. Born, and J. Treptow: The Evolution Machine – Manual. Institute for Informatics and Computing Techniques (iir), Inform., Inf., Rep. 7(1991) 7 - ISSN 0233-2582,1991.
11. H. M. Voigt: Soft Genetic Operators in Evolutionary Algorithms. In: W. Banzhaf and F.H. Eeckmann (Eds.): Evolution and Biocomputation. LN in Computer Science 899, pp. 123-141. Springer, Berlin. 1995.
12. D. Whitley, K. Mathias, S. Rana, and J. Dzubera: Building Better Test Functions. Proc. of the 6th Int'l. Conf. on Genetic Algorithms, pp.: 239–246, Morgan Kaufmann, San Francisco, 1995.

Every Niching Method has its Niche: Fitness Sharing and Implicit Sharing Compared

Paul Darwen and Xin Yao

School of Computer Science, University College UNSW
Australian Defence Force Academy
Canberra ACT 2600 AUSTRALIA

Abstract. Various extensions to the Genetic Algorithm (GA) attempt to find all or most optima in a search space containing several optima. Many of these emulate natural speciation. For co-evolutionary learning to succeed in a range of management and control problems, such as learning game strategies, such methods must find all or most optima. However, suitable comparison studies are rare. We compare two similar GA speciation methods, fitness sharing and implicit sharing. Using a realistic letter classification problem, we find they have advantages under different circumstances. Implicit sharing covers optima more comprehensively, when the population is large enough for a species to form at each optimum. With a population not large enough to do this, fitness sharing can find the optima with larger basins of attraction, and ignore the peaks with narrow bases, while implicit sharing is more easily distracted. This indicates that for a speciated GA trying to find as many near-global optima as possible, implicit sharing works well only if the population is large enough. This requires prior knowledge of how many peaks exist.

1 Motivation

1.1 Speciation in Co-evolutionary Learning

In a co-evolutionary GA, individuals are evaluated by how they perform against individuals in the same GA population, or perhaps another GA running in parallel. This is a promising way to learn game strategies [1] [3] [17] [21].

Without speciation, a GA will converge to only one high-fitness solution, due to genetic drift. So a co-evolutionary GA will converge and overspecialise to only one strategy for the game being learned. This generalises poorly, and is naïvely vulnerable to novel strategies not in the converged population [3].

To overcome this problem, speciation can greatly delay genetic drift [12], and prevent the convergence and overspecialisation that can otherwise happen in co-evolutionary learning [3]. Speciation with co-evolution can also find a repertoire of high-quality strategies for a game, giving improved generalisation [4]. However, this approach relies heavily on the speciated GA to find all (or most) good strategies — as speciation finds more high-quality strategies, generalisation ability improves [4, page 92]. So knowing what GA speciation method covers more peaks is important for co-evolutionary learning, not only for games but for other management and control tasks.

1.2 This paper

We compare two GA speciation methods, fitness sharing [5] and implicit sharing [20], in their ability to find as many peaks as possible. More comparative results are needed. Some studies evaluate GA speciation only on simple functions [18] [22], even though parallel hill-climbing is usually better on these [13, page 202]. Another comparison *forbids* fitness sharing from using a scaling function [13, pages 206-207]: this may be unfair, as it worked well with scaling [11], although scaling is not perfect [2]. So new GA speciation methods proliferate [15] [16] [18] without proper comparison of earlier methods. This paper helps fill that gap.

We find that implicit sharing works better when the population is large enough to form a species at each peak. With too many peaks, fitness sharing is less distracted by peaks with small basins of attraction. So implicit sharing is better *only if* the population is large enough to form a species at each peak of interest. A practical way to deal with this problem might be to do several runs, each with a larger population. When no more peaks are found, you have enough. With this caveat, it is feasible for a co-evolutionary GA with speciation to find most good strategies, and thus be suitable for strategy acquisition.

In Section 2, we describe two speciation methods, fitness sharing and implicit sharing. In Section 3, we describe the experimental setup, whose results are shown in Section 4, and discussed in Section 5. Section 6 concludes the paper.

2 Speciation Methods Based on Sharing

Many extensions to the GA let it locate multiple optima [13, pages 64-90]. Until recently, fitness sharing [5] was the only success [13, page 84], and is widely used. We study fitness sharing and its extension, implicit sharing [20].

2.1 Fitness Sharing

Fitness sharing modifies a search landscape by reducing payoff in densely-populated regions. This encourages search in unexplored regions, and causes subpopulations to form. Consider an individual i with fitness f_i. Its niche count m_i measures the number of other individuals with whom i shares fitness [10, page 191]. Shared fitness is $f_i^s = f_i/m_i$. Niche count m_i is calculated with a distance metric d_{ij} that measures the difference between individuals i and j:

$$m_i = \sum_{j=1}^{\text{population size}} \text{sh}(d_{ij}) \tag{1}$$

The *sharing function* $\text{sh}(d_{ij})$ makes distant individuals share less. Parameter α changes the sharing function's shape: $\alpha = 1$ gives a linear sharing function. More important is σ_s, the *sharing radius* or cutoff distance.

$$\text{sh}(d_{ij}) = \begin{cases} 1 - \left(\frac{d_{ij}}{\sigma_s}\right)^{\alpha} & \text{for } 0 \le d_{ij} < \sigma_s \\ 0 & \text{for } d_{ij} \ge \sigma_s \end{cases} \tag{2}$$

Fitness sharing has performed well in difficult search problems [11], but has flaws. Firstly, σ_s is fixed, so all optima in the search space must be equidistant or nearly so [20]. Secondly, to set σ_s, you need to know *a priori* how far apart optima are, and their (unshared) fitness. This important flaw is often overlooked by assuming there is perfect discrimination between peaks [13, pages 106, 158]. Also, scaling can cause problems [2]. To overcome these flaws, some fitness sharing extensions do not use a fixed sharing radius [20] [22].

2.2 Implicit Fitness Sharing

Implicit sharing [8] [20] modifies the fitness function according to Table 1. Individuals bid for the payoff of discrete objects. Originally, those were antigens in an immune system simulation [8] [20]. Another use is in learning a game: a strategy receives payoff when it has the best score against a test strategy [4] [17].

For each data point i to be matched, do the following C times:
1. From the GA population, select a sample of σ individuals. 2. Find the individual in that sample which achieves the highest match score against the single data point i. 3. The best in the sample receives payoff. In the case of a tie, payoff is shared equally among the tie-breakers.

Table 1. Payoff function for implicit sharing [20].

At first glance, Table 1 looks completely different to fitness sharing. Surprisingly, they share the same theoretical basis [20]. The sample size σ resembles the sharing radius σ_s: both control species size, and regulate the number of individuals who obtain payoff by specialising to the same part of the search space.

3 Experimental Setup

3.1 The Data

Frey and Slate's [9] letter recognition data has about 770 examples each of 26 capital letters. Each consists of a class (out of 26 letters), plus 16 integer values between 0 and 15 inclusive. What these measure is not important here. Accurate classification is not our main interest, it is to compare GA speciation methods.

We want the speciated GA to form a species at each cluster of same-letter data points. If the data contains a group of "A" points, close together with few non-A points intermingled, then want a species to "cover" this cluster, as in Figure 1. Such clusters exist, because nearest neighbour classification works well on this data [7]. The test phase classifies points by what species covers them.

Consider a subset of the data, by randomly taking only 2 letters out of 26. Table 2 shows how scattered this data is. Most data points (61.5% of S, 75.8% of V) are in a single cluster, i.e., there is a place in the 16-dimensional space, such

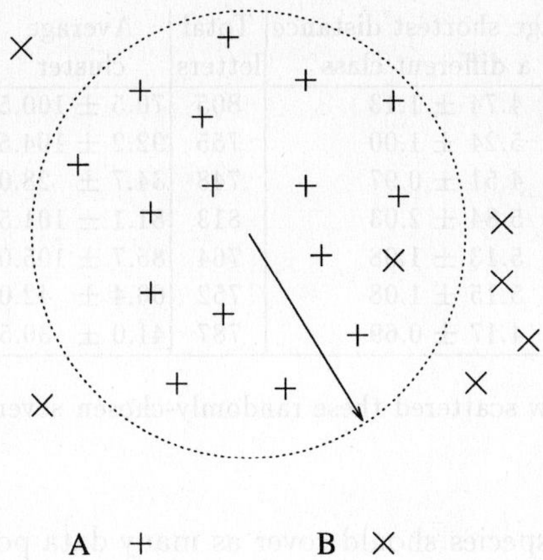

Fig. 1. A "cluster" of data points is when almost all the data near a certain point are of the same letter.

that 61.5% of the S data are closer to there than any V datum is. This place is where we want a species. Other clusters exist containing fewer S data.

Letter	Average shortest distance to a different class	Total letters	Average cluster	Largest cluster
S	7.93 ± 1.66	748	189.3 ± 225.3	460 61.5%
V	8.02 ± 1.45	764	278.7 ± 324.0	579 75.8%

Table 2. How scattered these two randomly-chosen classes are.

For more classes in Table 3, clusters of same-class data points get smaller because the letters are more intermingled. This requires more species (and thus a larger population) to successfully cover clusters. As the problem grows larger, the population needs to increase. Note that the number of *clusters* is different from the number of *classes* of data points.

Many methods can "cluster" data: a Holland-style classifier [9] gave worse accuracy (82.7%) than a simple nearest neighbour classifier (95.4%) [7] or several other non-GA classifiers [14, pages 140-142]. Again, we are less interested in classification accuracy as in comparing two GA speciation methods. For this reason, we will not follow the usual approach of separating learning and testing data. We will learn on the same data that we test with. However, generalisation has been considered in our definition of the payoff function.

3.2 Payoff Function

We represent GA individuals as points in the 16-dimensional integer space, with 4 bits to represent the 16 values of each of the 16 ranges, totaling 64 bits.

There are two desirable attributes we want reflected in the payoff function:

Letter	Average shortest distance to a different class	Total letters	Average cluster	Largest cluster
D	4.74 ± 1.13	805	70.5 ± 100.5	251 31.2%
I	5.24 ± 1.00	755	92.2 ± 104.5	204 27.0%
S	4.51 ± 0.97	748	34.7 ± 28.0	138 18.4%
U	5.84 ± 2.03	813	81.1 ± 101.5	226 27.8%
V	5.13 ± 1.08	764	85.7 ± 105.0	257 33.6%
W	5.15 ± 1.08	752	60.4 ± 42.0	213 28.3%
X	4.17 ± 0.69	787	41.0 ± 30.5	125 15.9%

Table 3. How scattered these randomly-chosen seven classes are.

1. **Quantity**: Each species should cover as many data points as possible. One species per data point needs a huge population.
2. **Quality**: Each species should classify data points as accurately as possible. We do not want a species to cover many data points with low accuracy.

Although we don't use a separate testing set, we do consider generalisation. Increasing the importance of the quality criterion allows a more complex solution, which is more specialised to the training data. Increasing the importance of the quantity criterion will allow a simpler solution which classifies less accurately. To balance these, the payoff function assigns equal fitness to an individual that covers many data points with reasonable accuracy, as to one that covers fewer points with higher accuracy. This is analogous to Occam's Razor.

Let c_i be the number of *correct* data points that are "covered" (in some sense) by individual i, and let n_i be the *total* number of points covered. Then let (unshared) fitness f_i be:

$$f_i = \left(\frac{c_i}{n_i}\right)^{\alpha} (c_i)^{\beta} \tag{3}$$

To set α and β, imagine one individual covers 100 data points of which 96 are of the same letter; and one that covers 200 data points, but only 180 are the same letter. We want these to have the same fitness:

$$\left(\frac{96}{100}\right)^{\alpha} (96)^{\beta} = \left(\frac{180}{200}\right)^{\alpha} (180)^{\beta} \Rightarrow \frac{\alpha}{\beta} = 9.740 \approx 10 \tag{4}$$

From Equation 4, we take $\alpha = 10$ and $\beta = 1$. The GA uses linear ranked selection, so only the relative values of α and β matter. Note that the payoff function means that smaller clusters of same-class data points do not necessarily form sub-optimal peaks in the search space: few data points with few errors pays the same as a large cluster with more errors.

What do we mean when an individual "covers" a data point? We tried giving every individual its own radius parameter, but this quickly evolved the maximum radius. So we use a nearest-individual approach: an individual "covers" a data point if it is closer to that data point than any other individual.

Population size was 50 for all runs. Other parameters were set as follows:

1. Sharing radius σ_s was 5, and the metric is Euclidean.
2. We used assortative crossover, so only similar individuals mate. This can improve a speciated GA [5, page 49]. Also, incest prevention [6] was used.
3. Mutation rate was 0.01, so a 64-bit genotype has a 53% chance of escaping unmutated. This is high, but assortative crossover reduces disruption.
4. The crossover rate was 1, and elitism was used.
5. Linear ranked selection was used. The highest scoring individual expects to receive 2 offspring, declining linearly to the worst expecting zero.

4 Results

At the fiftieth generation (by when each GA had stabilised), the test phase takes the best individuals of the final generation. We see which individual is closest to (i.e., covers) each data point. If the point is of a different letter to that individual, it is counted as an error. If they agree, it is a correct classification.

Classes	0% Cutoff	10% Cutoff	25% Cutoff	50% Cutoff	100% Cutoff
2	0.9368	0.9451	0.9452	0.9455*	0.9350
3	0.8404	0.8464*	0.8409	0.8338	0.8094
4	0.7445	0.7467*	0.7389	0.7254	0.6956
5	0.6528*	0.6339	0.6180	0.5964	0.5618
6	0.5756*	0.5401	0.5165	0.4982	0.4698
7	0.5391*	0.4975	0.4836	0.4669	0.4345

Table 4. Best scores are asterisked. Classification rates for 100 runs of fitness sharing, having rejected those who score less than the above fraction of the average payoff.

Table 4 shows the results for fitness sharing, and Table 5 for implicit sharing. "Cutoff" indicates how many low-performing individuals were excluded from the test phase: 10% cutoff rejects those who scored 10% or less of the final generation's average score. Individuals who score zero are always excluded, so 0% cutoff accepts all individuals with non-zero fitness.

Classes	0% Cutoff	10% Cutoff	25% Cutoff	50% Cutoff	100% Cutoff
2	0.9449	0.9505	0.9521	0.9528*	0.9513
3	0.8458	0.8648	0.8663*	0.8640	0.8514
4	0.7370	0.7529*	0.7454	0.7390	0.7163
5	0.6266	0.6541*	0.6450	0.6285	0.5909
6	0.5349	0.5468*	0.5292	0.5140	0.4757
7	0.4955*	0.4930	0.4776	0.4549	0.4117

Table 5. Best scores are asterisked. Classification rates for 100 runs of implicit sharing, having rejected those who score less than the above fraction of the average payoff.

Tables 4 and 5 show the classification rate for the test phase. One hundred times for each line, we randomly select letters from the alphabet, and run both

GA speciation methods on them. The best cutoff values are asterisked. Using their best cutoff values, Table 6 shows which method classified better.

Are the differences in Table 6 significant? We use a binomial test (as each set of letters are drawn randomly from the alphabet) [19], requiring the number of times one method is better, and ignoring ties. We try two different definitions of a tie in Table 6. The first: a method is better even if it classifies only one extra letter correctly. As this can be a narrow margin, we next take a tie as a difference in classification rate of less than 2% of the total number of letters.

Consider n non-ties, of which s were method A beating method B, so that method A seems to be better. When $p = q = 0.5$ in Equation 5, we find the probability that probability that both methods are equally good. These are shown in Table 6, and less than 0.05 (arrowed) indicates the difference is significant.

$$\text{Chance they're the same} = \frac{n!}{s!(n-s)!} p^s q^{n-s} \tag{5}$$

5 Discussion

An analytical explanation supports the empirical results. So although we only looked at one problem class, our results should be more widely relevant.

No. lets	Wins FS	IS	Ties	Tie margin	Prob same
2	43	57	0	0%	9.67e-02
3	40	60	0	0%	2.84e-02 ←
4	47	53	0	0%	3.09e-01
5	48	52	0	0%	3.82e-01
6	60	40	0	0%	2.84e-02 ←
7	72	28	0	0%	6.29e-06 ←
2	8	17	75	2%	5.39e-02
3	21	37	42	2%	2.40e-02 ←
4	41	44	15	2%	4.14e-01
5	38	46	16	2%	2.23e-01
6	52	33	15	2%	2.51e-02 ←
7	58	18	24	2%	2.36e-06 ←

Table 6. This shows how many runs (out of 100) in which one speciation method was better, out of fitness sharing (FS) and implicit sharing (IS). The right-hand column shows the probability that the two methods are in fact equal. When these probabilities are below 0.05 (arrowed), we can confidently say that it's not a fluke. Implicit sharing is better for few classes, fitness sharing is better for many classes.

In Tables 4 and 5, note that for few classes, ignoring poor performers brings better results. But as the problem grows too large for the population, we can no longer waste any non-zero scorers, and 0% cutoff gives the best results.

Also note the differences in ignoring poor performers. From Table 4, fitness sharing needs all individuals with non-zero payoff to best classify 5 classes; but in

Table 5, implicit sharing can ignore the worst performers at 5 classes. That is, it takes longer for the asterisks to move left in Table 5. This indicates that implicit sharing covers peaks more comprehensively when it has enough population.

Table 6 shows an interesting transition. With enough population for the problem, implicit sharing covers more comprehensively. With more classes (and more clusters to cover) and the same population, fitness sharing degrades less rapidly.

This is because implicit sharing is more discriminating. Consider the two similar individuals in Figure 2. Under fitness sharing, these will have a niche count of almost 2, halving the shared fitness. The only benefit for closer individual is a slightly higher payoff. There is little *relative* selection pressure.

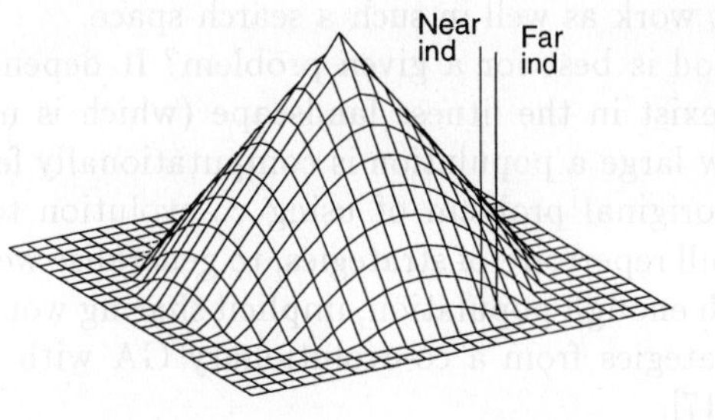

Fig. 2. Consider two similar individuals near a peak.

Recall Table 1: under implicit sharing, the probability that w individuals from this subset (of two individuals) are in a sample of size σ taken without replacement, from a population of size N, is given by [20]:

$$p(w, \sigma, N, 2) = \frac{C_w^2 C_{\sigma-w}^{N-2}}{C_\sigma^N} \qquad (6)$$

In these experiments, $N = 50$ and $\sigma = 38$. Equation 6 gives:

$$\begin{array}{ll} \text{Chance both in sample} & w = 2\; p = 0.574 \\ \text{Only near ind sampled} & w = 1\; p = 0.186 \\ \text{Only far ind sampled} & w = 1\; p = 0.186 \\ \text{Neither in sample} & w = 0\; p = 0.054 \end{array} \qquad (7)$$

Only the best in the sample receives payoff. For our two individuals in Figure 2, the closer individual will receive payoff when both are sampled ($w = 2$), and when it alone is sampled. The farther individual will only receive payoff when its neighbour (with its slightly higher unshared fitness) is not in the same sample. There are C samples for each data point, from Table 1. Equation 7 gives the expected fitness:

$$\begin{array}{l} f_{\text{near}} = (0.574 + 0.186)C \\ f_{\text{far}} \;= 0.186C \end{array} \Rightarrow \frac{f_{\text{near}}}{f_{\text{far}}} \approx 4$$

So there is greater *relative* selection pressure in implicit sharing. So implicit sharing covers peaks more comprehensively, given enough population. It also explains why the asterisks stayed to the right in Table 5 — implicit sharing could afford to ignore the poorest performers.

This is fine with a large enough population, or when the problem is simple enough for the population size. But with a small population (or a search space with more peaks) implicit sharing still exerts strong relative selection pressure, and tries to cover every peak when it can't.

Fitness sharing is not so easily sidetracked when there are too many peaks for the population size, and gives a higher classification rate for 6 and 7 letters in Table 6. In a previous study on a massively multimodal space with many sub-optimal peaks, fitness sharing worked well [11] (although it relied on scaling, which can cause problems for fitness sharing [2]). We conjecture that implicit sharing would not work as well in such a search space.

So what method is best for a given problem? It depends on how many interesting optima exist in the fitness landscape (which is usually not known in advance), and how large a population is computationally feasible.

Consider our original problem of using co-evolution to learn a game. We want to obtain a full repertoire of strategies, to generalise well against any expert opponent [4]. With enough population, implicit sharing would be best. Attempts to learn game strategies from a co-evolutionary GA with implicit sharing had some success [4] [17].

However, if the game has more strategies than we expected or our population is too small, then implicit sharing could get side-tracked and miss strategies it should have found, and we will generalise poorly. Normally, we don't know *a priori* how many near-global optima exist in a search space, so we don't know how large the population must be.

One possible way to deal with this problem might be to do several runs, each with a larger population. When a larger population does not find any more peaks of interest, it is big enough.

6 Conclusion

Both speciation methods are good in different ways. As shown in Table 6, implicit sharing performs better when the population is large enough for a species to cover each optima of interest. When the population is not large enough to do this, both methods degrade, but implicit sharing degrades considerably faster. This is because implicit sharing exerts a more discriminating evolutionary attraction between similar individuals, allowing it to covers peaks more comprehensively. This is fine with a large enough population, but with a small population it still tries to cover every single peak. In this situation, fitness sharing is not as easily distracted. By understanding their relative merits, we can create better GA speciation methods in future.

Acknowledgements

We thank UCI for making the database available, Robert I. McKay and Peter A. Whigham for comments, and the PPSN'96 reviewers for helpful feedback.

References

1. R. Axelrod. The evolution of strategies in the iterated prisoner's dilemma. In *Genetic Algorithms and Simulated Annealing*, pages 32–41. Morgan Kauffman, 1987.
2. P. Darwen and X. Yao. A dilemma for fitness sharing with a scaling function. In *1995 IEEE Conference on Evolutionary Computation*, pages 166–171, 1995.
3. P. Darwen and X. Yao. On evolving robust strategies for iterated prisoner's dilemma. In *Progress in Evolutionary Computation*, pages 276–292. Springer, 1995.
4. P. Darwen and X. Yao. Automatic modularization with speciation. In *1996 IEEE Conference on Evolutionary Computation*, pages 88–93, 1996.
5. K. Deb and D. E. Goldberg. An investigation of niche and species formation in genetic function optimization. In *ICGA-3*, pages 42–50, June 1989.
6. L. J. Eshelman and J. D. Schaffer. Preventing premature confergence in genetic algorithms by preventing incest. In *ICGA-4*, pages 115–122, 1991.
7. T. C. Fogarty. First nearest neighbor classification problem on Frey and Slate's letter recognition problem. *Machine Learning*, 9(4):387–388, Oct. 1992.
8. S. Forrest, B. Javornik, R. E. Smith, and A. S. Perelson. Using genetic algorithms to explore pattern recognition in the immune system. *Evolutionary Computation*, 1(3):191–211, 1993.
9. P. Frey and D. Slate. Letter recognition using Holland-style adaptive classifiers. *Machine Learning*, 6(2):161–182, Mar. 1991.
10. D. E. Goldberg. *Genetic Algorithms in Search, Optimization, and Machine Learning.* Addison-Wesley, 1989.
11. D. E. Goldberg, K. Deb, and J. Horn. Massive multimodality, deception, and genetic algorithms. In *PPSN2*, pages 37–46. North-Holland, 1992.
12. S. W. Mahfoud. Genetic drift in sharing methods. In *First IEEE Conference on Evolutionary Computation*, volume 1, pages 67–72, June 1994.
13. S. W. Mahfoud. *Niching Methods for Genetic Algorithms.* PhD thesis, University of Illinois at Urbana-Champaign, 1995.
14. D. Michie, D. J. Spiegelhalter, and C. C. Taylor. *Machine Learning, Neural and Statistical Classification.* Ellis Horwood, 1994.
15. A. Pétrowski. A clearing procedure as a niching method for genetic algorithms. In *1996 IEEE Conference on Evolutionary Computation*, pages 798–803, 1996.
16. S. Ronald. Finding multiple solutions with an evolutionary algorithm. In *1995 IEEE Conference on Evolutionary Computation*, pages 641–646, 1995.
17. C. D. Rosin and R. K. Belew. Methods for competitive co-evolution: Finding opponents worth beating. In *ICGA-6*, pages 373–380, 1995.
18. C. Ryan. Racial harmony and function optimization in genetic algorithms. In *1995 Evolutionary Programming Conference*, pages 296–307, 1995.
19. S. L. Salzberg. On comparing classifiers: A critique of current research and methods. Technical Report CS-1995-06, John Hopkins University, 1995.
20. R. E. Smith, S. Forrest, and A. S. Perelson. Searching for diverse, cooperative populations with genetic algorithms. *Evolutionary Computation*, 1:127–149, 1992.
21. R. E. Smith and B. Gray. Co-adaptive genetic algorithms: An example in Othello strategy. In *1994 Florida AI Research Symposium*, pages 259–264, 1994.
22. W. M. Spears. Simple subpopulation schemes. In *1994 Evolutionary Programming Conference*, pages 296–307. World Scientific, 1994.

Effects of Isolation in a Distributed Population Genetic Algorithm

Dr. Ian Robert East

Department of Computer Science, University of Buckingham,
Buckingham MK18 1EG, Great Britain
ian@buck.ac.uk

Dr. Jon Rowe

Artificial Intelligence Group,
Department of Computer Science, DeMontfort University,
Milton Keynes, Great Britain
jrowe@dmu.ac.uk

Abstract. An investigation is reported into the effects of isolation within a population upon its evolution under a genetic algorithm. The effects of varying population size were compared between a panmictic and a continuously distributed population, each offered an identical environment. Theoretical analysis predicted a logarithmic variation of performance with population size alone. Experiment confirmed such a variation in both populations. Although the distributed population always obtained superior peak fitness, no improvement in the ability to discover optima could be attributed to isolation. However, the distributed population was clearly observed to better maintain allelic diversity. Evidence was also found for the emergence of meta-stable geographical boundaries. Possible explanations are offered.

1 Introduction

1.1 Distributed Population Genetic Algorithms

The traditional genetic algorithm, established by Holland [17], was *panmictic* by nature. The deme (mating group) of every individual in the population comprised the population in its entirety. Perhaps the most obvious means of parallel execution of a genetic algorithm is simply to evaluate members of the population in parallel. However, the need for synchronisation once per generation would frequently render this inefficient. A perhaps equally obvious means is to partition the population. This has the appeal of natural precedent and leads to what is known as a "migration" algorithm and was first investigated by Grosso at The University of Michigan [16]. A number of other efforts were later reported at The Second International Conference on Genetic Algorithms (ICGA-2) [1, 18, 21]. These investigations were able to exploit both shared and distributed memory architecture. Much evidence accrued that such algorithms perform at least as well as the purely panmictic original across a variety of applications. It should be noted, though, that the original algorithm must be extended in order to periodically somehow select migrants who are swapped between sub-populations.

By the occasion of the Third International Conference on Genetic Algorithms (ICGA-3) the distribution of population across a "surface" had been followed to its logical conclusion by two groups, initially unbeknown to each other [7, 14]. One motive was that, according to the prevailing view in evolutionary biology, the existence of *isolation* within a population is crucial to evolution. Such isolation need only be the result of the population being spread out evenly over an extended surface.

It seemed attractive therefore to maximise isolation within any given population and exploit the rather simple mechanism of a neighbourhood mating system. Such an algorithm is known as a "diffusion" genetic algorithm because valuable genetic information diffuses via overlapping demes. They bear great similarity to other "cellular" means of computation, such as cellular automata and Markov random fields. The computing surface may have any number of dimensions. Each point process cyclically exchanges state with its neighbours then updates its own state. The deme comprises an individual, represented by the corresponding point process, and its neighbours. Cellular parallel algorithms have two great advantages. They are easy to render both deadlock-free and scalable [8].

The origin of the idea that creatures may profit from geographical isolation may be traced all the way back to a conjecture of Darwin [3]. Wright later developed the idea and expounded its importance [23]. He found only two plausible explanations of the evolution of any population, which he perceived as populating ever higher peaks upon an adaptive landscape. Inbreeding upon any individual peak would, he argued, lead inevitably to stagnation and extinction. First, a changing environment would force the mobility of utterly independent groups within a population. Some groups would become stuck and become extinct. Others would populate new and ever higher peaks. Second, groups with sufficient isolation (segregated by distance or other obstacle) would become genetically dynamic and thus retain diversity. The chances of populating the best niches, and of adapting to a changing environment are thus both increased. Success would require the right degree of isolation for the given environment. To quote, "In a small sufficiently isolated group all gene frequencies can drift irregularly back and forth about their mean values at a rapid rate...without reaching fixation...".

1.2 Aims

The "No Free Lunch" (NFL) theorem [22] states that for any optimisation problem where changed parameters improve the rate of convergence, there must exist another problem for which those same changes similarly degrade performance. It is no longer possible to define "improvements" to any algorithm for all applications. However, it *is* still possible to claim a performance advantage for a specific class of applications, or an improvement in the general ability for a population to adapt to a changing environment, or for it to be better able to populate multiple optima.

Early empirical investigations strongly suggested that a continuously distributed population discovered optima more rapidly than either a grouped migrating population or a panmictic one [7, 14]. The difference in performance was attributed to the presence of isolation. Yet there is to date no sound experimental evidence that isolation is truly responsible for any such improvement. Nor is there any empirical measure to quantify such an improvement or any sound theory to predict it. There has been only one systematic investigation, by Collins and Jefferson [2]. This employed a SIMD architecture and very large populations (2^{13} to 2^{19}). They found that a continuously distributed population did improve both quality and speed of convergence over panmixia, given the single problem of graph partitioning. They also reported very much improved maintenance of allelic diversity.

The purpose of the investigations reported here is to determine precisely what effect the scaling of isolation has upon a population. One concern was that the earlier results depend upon an extremely high degree of isolation. The largest deme size employed was of radius 30 in a huge population. We wished to verify that a more modest degree of isolation, in a small population, might still offer some advantage, and that it is indeed isolation that is responsible.

Genetic algorithms are perhaps too often regarded as mechanisms for locating a single stable optimum. Others have written concerning the relationship between such algorithms and optimisation tasks, e.g. [4]. A population may be regarded as a memory containing information which has been filtered according to its environment. It is possible, via direct replacement of parents with offspring, that allelic frequencies remain constant [5]. The information content of the population will still have been appropriately altered by the algorithm. Schema frequencies may still vary. However, it remains easier to quantify allelic, rather than schema, diversity, which will fall with time if the replacement strategy allows.

Diversity of the converged population offers an alternative quantifiable measure of algorithm performance to that of rate or quality of convergence. We thus set out to measure the variation of both quality and diversity of converged population with degree of isolation.

1.3 Varying Population Size

In the experiments described below, the degree of isolation within a population is varied along with population size. It is thus necessary to predict what effects result when population size is varied independently of the degree of isolation, as occurs with a traditional panmictic population.

One can begin an analysis by considering how the quantity of schemata varies with population size n. Overall, the number of schemata is bounded by 2^l and 3^l (l = genome length) since the genotype of a single individual displays 2^l and 3^l is the total number obtainable by varying the genotype. In a small population one might expect all members to possess very different genotypes and thus obtain roughly $n \times 2^l$ schemata. Note that this quantity varies linearly with population size but *exponentially* with genome length. However, as the population grows, it becomes more likely that schemata will recur, and thus any advantage due to increasing their quantity will diminish. At the same time, the computational task of population evaluation will grow linearly.

In an alternative approach, Goldberg and Rudnick [13] considered the variance of fitness among the instances of a given schema in a randomly initialised population. They estimated a lower bound for the size required of a population to allow the fittest schema to be distinguished from its nearest competitor, and thus for the Schema Theorem to remain a valid predictor of behaviour.

Goldberg [10] addressed the question of optimum population size by considering the trade-off between the total number of schemata occurring within a population of given size and the computation time required to evaluate every member. He chose as figure of merit the ratio of the quantity of schemata, in excess of the 2^l displayed by a single individual, to the size of the population. A simple power law was found to express the optimal population size n^*, given binary representation.

$$n^* \approx 1.65 \times 2^{0.21l}$$

In order to cater for parallel evaluation of a population, Goldberg [12] later suggested a slightly different figure of merit based upon an estimate of the average rate of schema processing. This, in turn, is based upon the expected total number of schemata displayed by the population and an estimate of the number of generations required for convergence. The time required for convergence is just the product of the number of generations and the number of computation steps, where one step computes an evaluation of one population member. To account for parallel evaluation, the number of computation steps is modelled by the following expression.

$$c = n^{1-\beta} \qquad 0 \le \beta \le 1$$

n = population size
c = #computation steps

Goldberg was able to show that the number of generations required for convergence (any required fraction of the population to become equated with the fittest genotype) is independent of population size. He was thus able to compute optimal population size versus genome length and degree of parallel evaluation. He predicted reasonable values for the size of panmictic populations but unreasonably large values for highly parallel evaluation. There is no evidence that very much larger population sizes are required for parallel genetic algorithms. The problem lies in the choice of convergence *rate*, rather than quality, as the figure of merit. It should also be noted that only parallel evaluation has been accounted for, not any change to the algorithm such as distributing the population to create overlapping or interacting demes.

Goldberg's analysis only accounts for the processing of schemata introduced by randomly initialising the population. A genetic algorithm must also explore the search domain by *sampling new schemata*. The rate at which it is able to do this depends upon the nature of the genetic operators employed and not upon population size. Some recombination operators sample new schemata at a significantly different rate than others. The size of a randomly initialised population is only important in providing complete allelic diversity [19] and in the diversity of schemata that it introduces. It defines the point from which the algorithm begins execution. If re-adaptation to a changed environment is called for then the population must remain large enough to maintain adequate diversity.

In some optimisation problems, the algorithm is extremely unlikely to discover certain schemata required to construct an optimum and gains great leverage from their presence in the initial population [20]. Suppose *m* schemata, each of order *o* are required for a certain optimum to be discovered. It can be shown that the minimum population size *n* that will exhibit all schemata with probability *p* is given by the following approximation.

$$n \approx 2^o \ln\left(\frac{m}{1-p}\right)$$

It is now clear that population size must increase exponentially with the order of the required schemata, but only logarithmically with their number. Similarly, it can be shown that the largest given schema that has a 50% chance of being found in the initial population has size $\lceil \log_2 n \rceil$.

Should the test function employed offer significant combinatoric difficulty, requiring a number of schemata that would not persist alone, then we might expect a performance that varies exponentially with the size of a panmictic population. The question remains, can a distributed population do better?

2 Experimental Method

2.1 Comparing Panmictic and Distributed Populations

In order to discover any change in behaviour that may be directly attributable to isolation alone, population size was allowed to vary in each of two distinct algorithms. The behaviour of a traditional panmictic genetic algorithm was compared with that of a distributed population diffusion algorithm. Each made use of the same evaluation function.

Clearly, no isolation exists within the panmictic population. Any advantageous schema may be expected to prosper simply according to the Schema Theorem [17]. The degree of isolation present within the distributed population will vary with population size. As yet, there is no theoretical confirmation that the Schema Theorem applies to a distributed population. Nor is there any other significant applicable predictive theory. Data recorded from the panmictic population offers an empirical way to decouple any direct effect of varying population size from that of varying degree of isolation. It should be possible to confirm or deny any observable effect of isolation upon population history.

The method of varying the degree of isolation by simply varying population size was chosen for its simplicity. The algorithms employed for panmictic and distributed populations are consistent. No extra operations are introduced as a result of distributing the population into overlapping demes. The only factors that vary in these experiments are degree of isolation and the initial diversity (allelic and schematic) available. Migration algorithms were deliberately avoided because they differ significantly with both panmixia and diffusion in that extra operations must be added. Emigrants must be selected somehow. Immigrants must replace members of the existing population somehow. No corresponding operations exist in either traditional or diffusion algorithm.

Collins and Jefferson [2] allowed an individual to conduct a random walk upon the mating surface in order to select a mate. Their method excludes the variation of population size with degree of isolation at the expense of introducing noise due to the random variation of length and orientation of the random walk. The walk was allowed to vary between 1 and 30 steps.

Two measures were made on population behaviour. First, the peak fitness attained after a fixed number of generations was recorded as a measure of performance. This was preferred over the time taken to converge because generally quality is valued over speed. Sometimes fitter individuals emerge after a protracted convergence. Second, allelic diversity was periodically recorded. Peak fitness data was obtained by repeatedly running the algorithm forty times for each of the following populations sizes: 9, 16, 25, 36, 49, 64, 81, 100, 121, 144. Diversity data was obtained similarly but with just twenty repetitions for each in a smaller set of populations sizes: 36, 49, 64, 81.

2.2 Algorithms

Mutation and recombination operators and parameters were identical in the algorithms applied to distributed and panmictic populations. Only the deme size and the selection and replacement strategies differed. Uniform crossover recombination was used, with an exchange probability of 0.8. The probability of recombination was 1.0. That of the mutation of each individual base was 0.02. Genetic representation was binary.

Introducing isolation includes the introduction of the concept of locus. Because of this, the random replacement employed in the traditional panmictic algorithm does not in itself constitute any extra algorithmic distinction with the distributed population where one parent is directly replaced according to an "elitist" strategy. This calls for the survival of the fittest individual, chosen from the set comprising both offspring and the current incumbent. Elitism seems to produce more rapid convergence across a range of applications [7, 14]. Since elitism offers a simple and sufficient means of introducing "selection pressure", selection of a second parent in the distributed population comprised the random choice of one immediate neighbour. Roulette wheel selection was used in the traditional algorithm for the panmictic population.

Any remaining purely algorithmic differences, that do not directly follow from distributing the population, should produce visible effects that are independent of population size and thus of degree of isolation.

2.3 Test Function

The test function employed was intended to offer a serious challenge to the genetic algorithms. A 50-bit problem was constructed by concatenation of ten 5-bit problems. The total score awarded was just the sum of the score for each 5-bit sub-string, which was equal to the number of bits set unless all bits are clear, whereupon a score of ten was given. The maximum fitness value (score) was thus 100 and the minimum 10.

While it is true that the algorithm has the opportunity to solve each subordinate problem independently, the subordinate problems themselves offer significant difficulty. The schemata corresponding to their solution become less likely to be constructed as the algorithm proceeds. No reasonable rate of mutation is likely to help.

There are only two ways in which the algorithm is likely to solve each sub-problem. First, occurrences of the desired schema, present in the initial population, may proliferate at a rate sufficient to avoid annihilation by unfortunate mutation or recombination. Second, occurrences, in the initial population, of components of the desired schema may be recombined successfully before their frequency decreases and the amount of construction necessary increases to the point where failure is inevitable. Once such schemata are constructed, they become "self-supporting". Selection will assist their survival.

The difficulties posed by such "trap functions", and related issues, are discussed in [20]. The notion of "deception" [11] is discredited as an indicator of difficulty for a genetic algorithm although it remains an interesting issue. It had earlier been criticised by others [9, 15]. To compose a *really* tough challenge to a genetic algorithm a fully combinatoric, non-decomposable, problem must be chosen. One such, referred to as the "scorpion", is proposed in [20]. However, there is little point in so doing here, where the purpose is to compare performance and behaviour between action upon distributed and panmictic populations.

3 Results

3.1 Comparing Performance

Table 1 (below) documents the variation of best fitness with population size after 100 generations.

Table 1 Best fitness after 100 generations versus population size.

Population Size	Best Fitness	
	Panmictic	Distributed
9	55.2 (±6.5)	65.3 (±7.1)
16	62.3 (±5.8)	69.0 (±6.7)
25	66.2 (±5.6)	73.1 (±4.9)
36	67.8 (±6.2)	75.8 (±4.9)
49	68.6 (±5.3)	77.1 (±5.4)
64	72.4 (±6.8)	78.8 (±5.2)
81	73.0 (±6.5)	78.0 (±4.8)
100	77.0 (±6.2)	80.3 (±4.2)
121	76.6 (±6.1)	82.1 (±4.2)
144	77.1 (±6.1)	81.9 (±3.5)

Figure 1 (overleaf) presents a graphical view of the data which clearly shows the benefit of increasing population size in improving convergence. In accordance with the theory presented earlier, the performance is plotted against the logarithm of population size. It can be seen that this produces linear variation for both panmictic and distributed populations. However, it fails to demonstrate any benefit that may be directly attributed to isolation, although it is clear that the distributed population consistently maintains better peak fitness performance.

It was hoped to reveal such a benefit via a greater gradient for the distributed population. No significant gradient differential is apparent. No data were recorded regarding the rate at which, or smoothness with which, convergence proceeded.

As pointed out above, the "No Free Lunch" (NFL) theorem limits the value of any conclusions regarding optimisation performance. It remains possible, however, to assert that increasing isolation offers a performance advantage for any specific class of problem. However, no such advantage was detected in the experiments conducted.

The scope of NFL is limited in certain other regards. It also remains possible to assert that a distributed population offers advantages for adaptive optimisation to a changing environment, or in the population of multiple optima. In such applications the maintenance of allelic diversity is important.

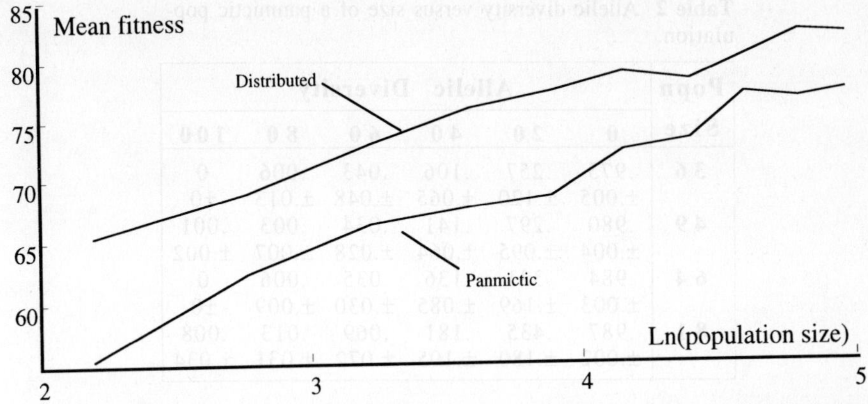

Fig. 1. Mean best fitness obtained versus size of both panmictic and distributed populations.

3.2 Maintenance of Diversity

It may be commonplace to *apply* a genetic algorithm to a problem of optimisation but the *function* of such an algorithm is rather to optimise an entire population to a given environment, without sacrifice of the ability to adapt to changes in that environment. The population may be perceived as a *memory* that stores information in the form of allelic frequencies and schema frequencies [6]. The ability to adapt depends crucially upon allelic diversity. A genetic algorithm balances the memories of adaptations, past and present, with an allelic diversity that will permit future adaptations.

Allelic diversity D may be expressed, given binary representation, via a mean over the entire genome as follows [2].

$$D = \frac{\sum_{i=0}^{l}\left(1-4(0.5-f_i)^2\right)}{l} \qquad f_i = \text{frequency of allele 0 (say) at locus } i$$

$$0 \le D \le 1$$

In the pursuit of evidence as to whether a distributed population offers any advantage regarding the maintenance of allelic diversity, that diversity was computed every twenty generations for both panmictic and distributed populations. The data is tabulated in Tables 1 and 2, and is plotted in Figure 2 (opposite).

The following may be clearly observed.

- The distributed population has maintained allelic diversity much more effectively than the panmictic one.
- Increasing population size benefits the distributed population far more than it does the panmictic one.

Table 2 Allelic diversity versus size of a panmictic population.

Popn Size	Allelic Diversity					
	0	**20**	**40**	**60**	**80**	**100**
36	.973 ±.005	.257 ±.120	.106 ±.065	.043 ±.048	.006 ±.013	0 ±0
49	.980 ±.004	.297 ±.095	.141 ±.064	.034 ±.028	.003 ±.007	.001 ±.002
64	.984 ±.003	.331 ±.169	.136 ±.085	.035 ±.030	.006 ±.009	0 ±0
81	.987 ±.002	.435 ±.180	.181 ±.105	.069 ±.072	.013 ±.031	.008 ±.034

Table 3 Allelic diversity versus size of a distributed population.

Popn Size	Allelic Diversity					
	0	**20**	**40**	**60**	**80**	**100**
36	.973 ±.005	.742 ±.042	.564 ±.173	.433 ±.207	.326 ±.213	.236 ±.231
49	.981 ±.004	.832 ±.047	.671 ±.118	.505 ±.189	.396 ±.227	.297 ±.240
64	.985 ±.003	.859 ±.043	.732 ±.096	.627 ±.158	.516 ±.209	.438 ±.241
81	.988 ±.002	.883 ±.037	.788 ±.084	.707 ±.128	.627 ±.191	.548 ±.213

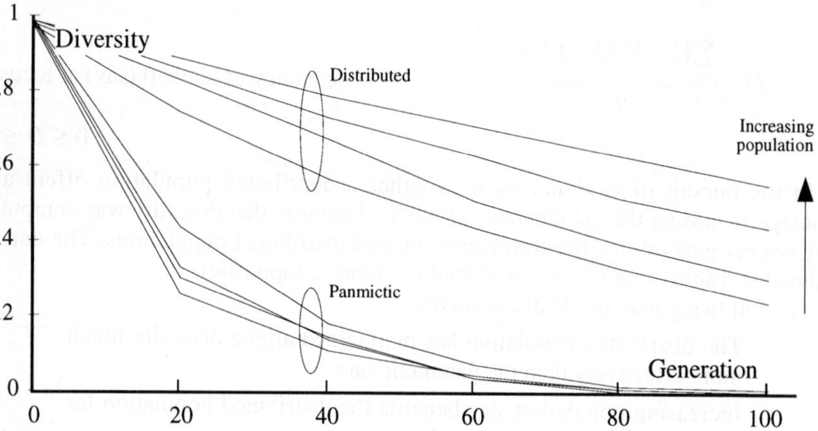

Fig. 2. Variation of allelic diversity with generation for panmictic and distributed populations and a range of population sizes.

3.3 Geographical Boundary Formation

A study of the standard deviation of allelic diversity reveals an interesting phenomenon. For both panmictic and distributed populations the initial value is small. As the traditional algorithm gets going on the panmictic population, the standard deviation increases quickly and then falls to zero as the population converges. However, with the diffusion algorithm, operating on the distributed population, it just keeps on increasing. The reason for this difference becomes clear when the distributed population is examined over an extended period.

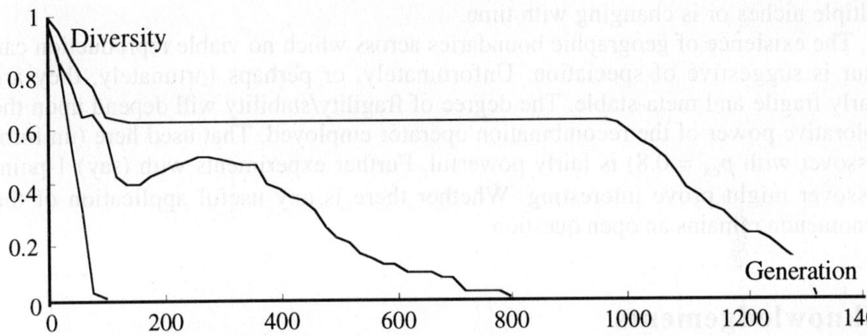

Fig. 3. Three different paths to convergence with a diffusion genetic algorithm.

Figure 3 depicts the variation of allelic diversity over time in three distinct distributed populations. One quickly converges, as would be expected given panmixia. In the intermediate case, diversity decreases at first but then increases for a while before reaching a peak from which it falls to zero as the population converges. What happened here was that, just as the population was beginning to converge, a new fit genotype is discovered. However, because of its distributed nature, it takes some time for the new beneficial genetic material to diffuse throughout the entire population. As it does so, diversity is observed to rise. Once it has spread everywhere, diversity again falls as convergence takes place.

In the third case, diversity is observed to remain static for an extended period before it eventually falls towards zero. This occurs whenever a number of genotypes of equal fitness are evolved in distinct regions. Borders form, across which procreation gives uncompetitive offspring. Such segmentation of the mating surface is only meta-stable. Either mutation comes to the rescue, or recombination eventually discovers a viable product.

Conclusion

Experiments have been conducted to investigate the effects upon performance and diversity of continuously distributing a population into overlapping demes. The size of a distributed population was scaled to vary the degree of isolation within it. Measures of peak fitness and diversity were recorded. In order to distinguish the effects of varying isolation alone, a reference panmictic population was studied with a corresponding variation of size.

The improvement detected in observed peak fitness over time could not be attributed to isolation. The observed trend could be explained theoretically as the effect of increasing population size, regardless of any isolation present.

Allelic diversity was observed to be better maintained over time when the population is distributed. Also, the distributed population was significantly better able to exploit increasing population size in this regard. This suggests that a distributed population might be more immune to premature convergence than a panmictic one. It would seem that continuously distributing a population into overlapping demes can do no harm, other than to perhaps slow down convergence. Yet, a distributed population should be better able to adapt to an environment that either contains multiple niches or is changing with time.

The existence of geographic boundaries across which no viable reproduction can occur is suggestive of speciation. Unfortunately, or perhaps fortunately, they are clearly fragile and meta-stable. The degree of fragility/stability will depend upon the explorative power of the recombination operator employed. That used here (uniform crossover with $p_{ex} = 0.8$) is fairly powerful. Further experiments with (say) 1-point crossover might prove interesting. Whether there is any useful application of the phenomenon remains an open question.

Acknowledgements

The work reported here was made possible by Grant GR/J 14301 from the Engineering and Physical Sciences Research Council (EPSRC) which provided necessary equipment and a post for one of the authors (Jon Rowe).

References

1. Cohoon, J. P., S. U. Hegde, et al.: Punctuated Equilibria: A Parallel Genetic Algorithm. Proceedings of the First International Conference on Genetic Algorithms. J. J. Grefenstette (ed.). Lawrence Erlbaum Associates. pp. 148-154. (1987)
2. Collins, R. J. and D. R. Jefferson: Selection in Massively Parallel Genetic Algorithms. Proceedings of the Fourth International Conference on Genetic Algorithms. R. K. Belew and L. B. Booker (eds). University of California, San Diego, Morgan Kaufmann. pp. 249-256. (1991)
3. Darwin, C.: On The Origin of Species by Means of Natural Selection. Penguin. (1859)
4. DeJong, K. A.: Genetic Algorithms Are NOT Function Optimizers. Foundations of Genetic Algorithms 2. L. D. Whitley (ed.). Morgan Kaufmann. pp. 5-17. (1992)
5. East, I. and J. Rowe: Direct Replacement: A Genetic Algorithm Without Mutation Which Avoids Deception. Workshop on Evolutionary Computation, 7th Australian Joint Conference on Artificial Intelligence. Armidale, NSW, Australia. (1994)
6. East, I. R.: Metaphors for Genetic Algorithm Operation: From Construction to Communication. PolyModel 16. University of Sunderland. (1995)
7. East, I. R. and D. MacFarlane: An Investigation of Several Parallel Genetic Algorithms. Proceedings of the Twelfth Technical Meeting of the Occam User Group. S. J. Turner (ed.). IOS Press. pp. 60-67. (1990)

8. East, I. R. and D. Macfarlane: Implementation in Occam of Parallel Genetic Algorithms on Transputer Networks. Parallel Genetic Algorithms: Theory and Applications Ed. J. Stender. IOS Press. pp. 43-63. (1992)

9. Forrest, S. and M. Mitchell: What Makes a Problem Hard for a Genetic Algorithm? Some Anomalous Results and Their Explanation. Machine Learning 13: pp. 285-319. (1993)

10. Goldberg, D. E.: Optimal Initial Population Size for Binary-Coded Genetic Algorithms. The Clearing House for Genetic Algorithms, Department of Engineering Mechanics, University of Alabama, Tuscaloosa, AL 35487-2908, USA. (1985)

11. Goldberg, D. E.: Simple genetic Algorithms and the Minimal, Deceptive Problem. Genetic Algorithms and Simulated Annealing. L. Davis (ed.). Pitman. pp. 74-88. (1987)

12. Goldberg, D. E.: Sizing Populations for Serial and Parallel Genetic Algorithms. Proceedings of the Third International Conference on Genetic Algorithms. J. D. Schaffer (ed.). George Mason University, Washington D. C., Morgan Kaufmann. pp. 70-79. (1989)

13. Goldberg, D. E. and M. Rudnick: Genetic Algorithms and the Variance of Fitness. Complex Systems **5**, 3, 265-278. (1988)

14. Gorges-Schleuter, M.: ASPARAGOS: An Asynchronous Parallel Genetic Optimization Strategy. Proceedings of the Third International Conference on Genetic Algorithms. J. D. Schaffer (ed.). George Mason University, USA, Morgan Kaufmann. pp. 422-427. (1989)

15. Grefenstette, J. J.: Deception Considered Harmful. Foundations of Genetic Algorithms 2. L. D. Whitley (ed.). Morgan Kaufmann. pp. 75-91. (1992)

16. Grosso, P.: Computer Simulations of Genetic Application: Parallel Subcomponent Interaction in a Multilocus Model. PhD Thesis. University of Michigan. (1985)

17. Holland, J. H.: Adaptation in Natural and Artificial Systems. University of Michigan Press. (1975)

18. Pettey, C. B., M. R. Leuze, et al.: A Parallel Genetic Algorithm. Proceedings of the Sec-ond International Conference on Genetic Algorithms. J. J. Grefenstette (ed.). Lawrence Erlbaum Associates. pp. 155-161. (1987)

19. Reeves, C. R.: Using Genetic Algorithms with Small Population Sizes. Proceedings of the Fifth International Conference on Genetic Algorithms. S. Forrest (ed.). Morgan Kaufmann. pp. 92-99. (1993)

20. Rowe, J. and I. East: Deception and GA Hardness. The First Nordic Workshop on Genetic Algorithms. Vaasa, Finland. (1995)

21. Tanese, R.: Parallel Genetic Algorithm for a Hypercube. Proceedings of the Second International Conference on Genetic Algorithms. J. J. Grefenstette (ed.). Lawrence Erlbaum Associates. pp. 177-183. (1987)

22. Wolpert, D. H. and W. G. Macready: No free lunch theorems for search. SFI-TR-95-02-010. Avaliable from , The Santa Fe Institute, 1399 Hyde Park Road, Santa Fe, NM 87501, U.S.A. (1995)

23. Wright, S.: The roles of Mutation, Inbreeding, Crossbreeding and Selection. Sixth International Congress on Genetics. pp. 356-366. (1932)

Self–Adaptive Genetic Algorithm for Numeric Functions

Robert Hinterding[1], Zbigniew Michalewicz[2] and T. C. Peachey[1]

[1] Department of Computer and Mathematical Sciences,
Victoria University of Technology,
PO Box 14428 MMC, Melbourne 3000, Australia
email: {rhh,tom}@matilda.vut.edu.au

[2] Department of Computer Science,
University of North Carolina,
Charlotte, NC 28223, USA
email:zbyszek@uncc.edu

Abstract. Self-adaption is one of the most promising areas of research in evolutionary computation as it adapts the algorithm to the problem while solving the problem. In this paper we extend self-adaption to operate on more than one aspect of evolutionary computation and at more than one level of adaption. We developed a genetic algorithm which self-adapts both mutation strength and population size; the results indicate that the approach works quite well.

1 Introduction

As evolutionary algorithms implement the idea of evolution, it is natural to expect self-adaption to be used in these techniques. Apart from evolution strategies and evolution programming, which incorporate some of its control parameters in the solution vectors, most other techniques use fixed representations, operators, and control parameters. Some promising research areas based on the inclusion of self adapting mechanisms are:

- representation of individuals (as proposed by Shaefer 1987; the Dynamic Parameter Encoding technique, Schraudolph & Belew 1992 and messy genetic algorithms, Goldberg et al 1991 also fall into this category).
- operators. It is clear that different operators play different roles at different stages of the evolutionary process. The operators should adapt (e.g., adaptive crossover Schaffer & Morishima 1987, Spears 1995). This is true especially for time-varying fitness landscapes.
- control parameters. There have been various experiments aimed at adaptive probabilities of operators (Davis 1989, Julstrom 1995, Srinivas & Patnaik 1994). However, much more remains to be done.

It seems that this is one of the most promising directions of research; after all, the power of evolutionary algorithms lies in their adaptiveness. The advantages of self-adaption are that for the parameters being self-adapted hand tuning is not required, they dynamically adapt to the changing requirements during the run and this is done while evolving a problem solution.

Angeline (1995) provides a classification of adaptive and self-adaptive evolutionary computation (EC) techniques:

> "Adaptive evolutionary computations can be separated largely by the level at which the adaptive parameters operate. *Population-level* techniques dynamically adjust parameters that are global to the entire population, such as global crossover frequency. *Individual-level* adaptive methods modify how a particular individual within the population is affected by the [...] operators. *Component-level* adaptive ECs dynamically alter how the individual components of each individual will be manipulated independently from each other."

Additionally, the EC systems can be classified as adaptive or self-adaptive on the basis of whether or not they evolve the values for the adaptive parameters.

In this paper we discuss a particular self-adaptive system (SAGA) for numerical optimisation problems, which combines population-level and individual-level techniques. The paper is organized as follows. The next section explains population-level and individual-level techniques incorporated in the proposed system; it also includes a discussion on adaptation of the population sizes. Section 3 reports the results of experiments and section 4 concludes the paper.

2 SAGA—A Self-Adaptive Genetic Algorithm

SAGA (Self-Adaptive Genetic Algorithm) uses population-level and individual-level adaptive parameters to self-adapt the population size and the mutation strength during the runs. While the self-adaptiveness for the mutation strength was explored in earlier work (Hoffmeister and Bäck 1992, Hinterding 1995), the addition of population-level techniques to control the size of the EC populations is discussed in this paper.

There have been empirical studies (De Jong 1975, Grefenstette 1986, Schaffer et al 1989) that address the question "how large should a GA population be for a given problem?"; there are also a number of heuristics on sizing GA populations. Some researchers studied the problem from a theoretical point of view, e.g., to maximize schemata processing ability (Goldberg 1989) or to maximize GA performance by insuring accurate sampling (Golberg et al 1992).

There are also two attempts reported at dynamically adjusting (self-adapting) the population size. One method (Smith 1993) is based on the absolute expected selection loss; the other (Arabas et al 1994) — on the concept of the age of individuals in the population. SAGA proposes a new approach which is based on the concepts of co-evolution: there is a community of three individual genetic algorithms (IGAs) with different population sizes. The population sizes are adapted by using a mutation function which is activated after a set number of function evaluations (an epoch) for each of the IGAs. This mutation function uses either the best fitness value or best fitness improvement found during an epoch to adjust the population size for each or the IGAs for the next epoch. We explain this process in detail in the next section of the paper.

Also, the IGA can self-adapt the mutation strength during the run. This requires addition of one value *ms* to each chromosome (which is allowed to vary from 0.000001 to 0.2); this value controls the standard deviation of the Gaussian mutation applied to the genes in the chromosome to be mutated. This value is allowed to participate in crossover and mutation, but does not contribute directly to the fitness of the solution. When the chromosome is to be mutated the following steps are followed:

1. decode the gene *ms* to a value,
2. apply Gaussian noise to the *ms* value using a standard deviation of 0.013 (meta-mutation).
3. use the *ms* value as the standard deviation for the Gaussian noise to mutate the other genes in the chromosome,
4. write the mutated genes (including *ms*) back to the chromosome.

During the initialization process, the value of *ms* for all chromosomes is set using a Gaussian distributed random variable with mean 0.1 and standard deviation 0.01. When fixed Gaussian mutation is used (for experiments described later in the paper), the standard deviation for the Gaussian noise is set to 0.1.

2.1 Adaptation of the population size

Three IGAs (with population sizes of P1, P2, and P3, respectively, and initial values of 50, 100 and 200) are used. The population sizes are adapted to maximize the performance of the IGA-P2 system; the best fitness found during an epoch of 1,000 evaluations for each IGA is used as the criteria to alter the population sizes.

Fitness refers to the fitness of the best individual or improvement of the best fitness value found, measured at the start and end of the epoch. IGA-P1, IGA-P2, and IGA-P3 are referred to as: P1, P2, and P3; P1 has always the smallest population, and P3 — the largest.

The population sizes are allowed to range from 10 to 1,000, and the differences between the population sizes are kept to at least 20. There are two categories of rules; those activated when the fitnesses of the IGAs converge and those activated when the fitness values are distinct.

The rules in the first category, when two or three fitnesses from the IGAs are the same ($< 1e{-}9$), are to move the populations further apart. That is, the smallest population size is decreased and the largest population size is increased. Given the assumption that population size affects performance, the justification for these rules is that if the fitnesses converge, the population sizes are too close together, or a (local) optimum has been found. In either case adjusting the population sizes so that they are further apart could help. Note that the case when P1, P2, and P3 have the same fitness is covered by the first rule as the fitness of P2 is not considered for this rule.

P1 & P3 have the same fitness: expand left and expand right
P1 & P2 have the same fitness: expand left
P2 & P3 have the same fitness: expand right

where the adjustment operator 'expand' is defined as:

expand left: size(P1) := size(P1)/2; rest unaltered
expand right: size(P3) := size(P3)*2; rest unaltered

The second category covers the situation where the best fitness values from P1, P2, and P3 are distinct. Here we try to adjust the population sizes so that the performance of P2 is maximized. The following set of rules gives a list of appropriate actions (in terms of adjustment operators being invoked) for each possible case (these cases are ordered by fitness, smallest fitness value on the left, largest on right):

P1 P2 P3: move right
P1 P3 P2 or P2 P1 P3: compress left
P2 P3 P1 or P3 P1 P2: compress right
P3 P2 P1: move left

where the adjustment operators 'move' and 'compress' are defined as:

move right: size(P1) := size(P2); size(P2) := size(P3); size(P3) := size(P3)*2
move left: size(P1) := size(P1)/2; size(P2) := size(P1); size(P3) := size(P2)
compress left: size(P1) := (size(P1) + size(P2))/2; rest unaltered
compress right: size(P3) := (size(P2) + size(P3))/2; rest unaltered

We justify these heuristic rules on the following grounds. As we used three IGAs (the minimum we thought would work), it seemed sensible to have rules that would maximize the performance of the "middle IGA" (i.e., the IGA with the middle population size). Then we could have rules that would adjust all the population sizes to be larger or smaller if the best population size could be outside the range of the current population sizes ('move' rules). We can also have rules to adjust the population size of the worse IGA so that it is closer in size to the others. The idea was to design rules that would explore different population sizes, try to maximize the performance of IGA-P2, and, if it was unclear how to adjust the population sizes then to take some action that could lead to future improvements.

As SAGA contains three IGAs we have the option of keeping the populations from the IGAs separate or we can allow them to mix at the end of each epoch. In the latter case, the three populations are collected into a single population pool at the end of an epoch, and after the sizes of the populations are adjusted, the three IGAs will draw their members from the population pool randomly. If the number of individuals in the population pool is insufficient to meet the needs of the IGAs, the number of individuals they get from the population pool is proportional to their desired population size. For example, if desired population sizes of the three IGAs are 10, 30 and 60, and the population pool contains only 50 individuals, then they will get 5, 15, and 30 individuals respectively.

When a population size is to decrease the worst individuals in the IGA or population pool are removed. When a population size is to be increased, we can either randomly generate new individuals and add them to the IGA or population pool or we can allow the population of an IGA to grow to the desired size by not deleting individuals for a number of generations.

2.2 The IGAs

The GA used for the IGAs is a steady-state GA (Davis 1991) using tournament selection with a tournament size of two. It uses bit-string representation, but the genes are considered to be the function variables rather than the binary bits. Crossover and mutation are used as independent reproduction operators; that is a new individual is produced by either crossover or mutation and never by both. The crossover/mutation rate determines the proportion of new individuals produced by crossover or mutation. Two point crossover is used and crossover points operate at the bit level. Mutation modifies genes and Gaussian mutation is used. Two parameters control mutation: Poisson mean—which is the mean number of genes that will be mutated in a chromosome; and mutation strength—which is the standard deviation of the Gaussian noise used in the mutation of a gene.

When a new individual is created, and it duplicates an individual already in the population, it is discarded and still counted as an evaluation. The other major parameter is the replacement rate, which is the percentage of the population to be replaced in one generation.

3 Experiments and Results

For the experiments, test functions have been taken from a number of sources, and more difficult functions have been included. F1 – F5 are from De Jong (1975, F6 – F8 are from Gordon & Whitley (1993), F1a and F9 are from Hoffmeister and Bäck (1992), and F10 is from Michalewicz (1994). The test functions include a range of function types and include nonlinear, non-separable and scalable functions. The functions are shown in Table 1. Gray coded binary representation was used for each function.

SAGA was allowed to run for up to 12 epochs on the test functions except for F10 where 20 epochs were allowed. All parameter settings for the IGAs, except for population size was taken from Hinterding (1995).

SAGA was run on these ten test functions in nine different configurations. The configurations can be divided into two major groups: where fixed strength Gaussian mutation was used (FM); and where self-adaption of the mutation strength was used (SAM). The sub-configurations common to both groups are:

- Control (CTRL) — Populations sizes remain fixed, populations are kept separate, extra individuals generated randomly.

Table 1. Test functions

Fn	Function	Domain
F1	$f(x_i)\mid_{i=1,3}) = \sum_{i=1}^{3} x_i^2$	$x_i \in [-5.12, 5.12]$
F1a	$f(x_i)\mid_{i=1,30}) = \sum_{i=1}^{30} x_i^2$	$x_i \in [-5.12, 5.12]$
F2	$f(x_i)\mid_{i=1,2}) = 100(x_1^2 - x_2)^2 + (1 - x_1)^2$	$x_i \in [-2.048, 2.048]$
F3	$f(x_i)\mid_{i=1,5}) = 30 + \sum_{i=1}^{5} \lfloor x_i \rfloor$	$x_i \in [-5.12, 5.12]$
F5	$f(x_i)\mid_{i=1,2}) = \frac{1}{K} + \sum_{j=1}^{25} \frac{1}{j + \sum_{i=1}^{2} (x_i - a_{ij})^6}$	$x_i \in [-65.536, 65.536]$ $K = 500$
F6	$f(x_i)\mid_{i=1,20}) = 20A + \sum_{i=1}^{20} x_i^2 - A\cos(2\pi x_i)$	$x_i \in [-5.12, 5.12]; A = 10$
F7	$f(x_i)\mid_{i=1,10}) = V + \sum_{i=1}^{10} -x_i \sin(\sqrt{\lvert x_i \rvert})$	$x_i \in [-512, 512]$ $V = 4189.827601614$
F8	$f(x_i)\mid_{i=1,10}) = \sum_{i=1}^{10} \frac{x_i^2}{4000} - \prod_{i=1}^{10} \cos(\frac{x_i}{\sqrt{i}}) + 1$	$x_i \in [-512, 512]$
F9	$f(x_i)\mid_{i=1,20}) = \sum_{i=1}^{20} (\sum_{j=1}^{i} x_j)^2$	$x_i \in [-65.536, 65.536]$
F10	$f(x_i)\mid_{i=1,45}) = \min(x_{45}^2 + \sum_{k=0}^{44} (x_k^2 + u_k^2))$ where $x_{k+1} = x_k + u_k$ and $x_0 = 100$	$x_i \in [-200.0, 200.0]$

- No Mix (NM) — Population size allowed to self-adapt, populations kept separate, extra individuals generated randomly.
- Mix (M) — Population size allowed to self-adapt, populations mix at epochs, extra individuals generated randomly.

The following three sub-configurations were only used with self-adaption of mutation strength.

- Mix, No Dups (MND) — population size allowed to self-adapt, populations mix at epochs, extra individuals generated randomly, duplicates removed from population pool.
- Mix, Grow (MG) - population size allowed to self-adapt, populations mix at epochs, populations grow to desired size.
- Mix, Grow, No Dups (MGND) — population size allowed to self-adapt, populations mix at epochs, populations grow to desired size, duplicates removed from population pool.

Results are produced by averaging the results from twenty (20) runs of SAGA on each of the functions. The results are summarised in Table 2. In this table, an entry consisting of a single number indicates the problem was always solved and gives the average number of epochs to solve the problem, while entries of the form x/y should be interpreted as follows: x gives the number of times the problem was solved and y gives the average best value found. Average number of epochs rather than average number of evaluations to solve are reported as SAGA can act as three independent GAs or as three interconnected GAs depending on whether or not the populations are allowed to mix.

The results from Table 2 show that for the set of runs where fixed Gaussian mutation is used, adaptation of the population size is not always beneficial, and (surprisingly) that allowing the populations to mix can also be detrimental. The situation is very different when we enable self-adaption of the mutation

Table 2. Results — average number of epochs or average best value

	FM — fixed mutation			SAM — self-adaptive mutation					
Fn.	CTRL	NM	M	CTRL	NM	M	MND	MG	MGND
F1	2.5	**2.3**	2.4	2.6	**2.2**	2.3	**2.2**	2.5	2.4
F1a	0/5.1e-2	0/2.8e-2	**0/9.2e-3**	0/2.6e-3	18/5e-4	19/1e-2	19/7e-4	**8.5**	19/3e-2
F2	**8/3e-6**	2/3.5e-5	8/3.6e-5	4.8	4.4	3.9	4.8	**3.3**	4.3
F3	**1.7**	1.8	1.8	1.7	1.7	1.8	1.8	2	1.9
F5	2.2	2.2	2.2	2.4	2.6	**2**	2.3	2.1	2.1
F6	0/4.2e0	0/2.4e0	**0/3.2e-1**	0/3.9e0	0/2.3e0	2/5.9e0	**4/2.3e0**	3/2.7e0	1/4e0
F7	**0/1.7e0**	1/1.5e1	8/6.1e0	8/1.3e1	6/2.2e1	14/3e1	**18/1e1**	14/3e1	**18/1e1**
F8	0/1.8e-1	**0/1.5e-1**	0/1.1e-1	0/7.7e-2	1/6.3e-2	1/7.3e-2	3/6.7e-2	1/8e-2	**0/8.2e-2**
F9	0/3.8e2	0/3.9e2	**0/1.9e2**	0/1.8e2	0/4.8e1	0/4.6e1	**0/3.5e1**	0/4.4e1	0/4.2e1
F10	0/5.2e4	0/3.7e4	**0/2.8e4**	0/4.6e4	0/3.2e4	**0/2e4**	0/2.1e4	**0/2e4**	0/2.2e4

strength. Now adaption of the population size and allowing the populations to mix both give improved results. In fact, except for the simple functions F1, F3, and F5, these configurations give the best results. The other point to notice is that the configurations where duplicates are removed give better results for the multimodal functions.

Table 3. Results — average total population size

Epochs	0	1	2	3	4	5	6	7	8	9	10	11	12
F1a	350	350	175	87	85.5	85.5	85	89.5	133				
F6	350	350	187.5	134	128.3	133	134.2	123.9	138.7	160.1	147.2	154.5	128.5
F8	350	350	212.5	154.9	112.2	101.2	130	104.9	131.7	203.2	347	340	415.4

Table 3 displays the trends in the total population sizes for a few of the functions in the following configurations: F1a – SAM, M; F6 & F8 – SAM, MND. For problem F1a (sphere in 30 dimensions) the trend is clearly to get the population sizes small and keep them small, as this is a simple function and exploitation (rather than exploration) gives better results. In a few of the runs, the population size increases at the end of the run as the values found by the three IGAs converge. With problems F6 (Rastrigin's function) and F8 (Griewank's function) the populations do not decrease to the same extent, and increase again to facilitate escaping local optima and to change the mode to exploration. In some runs (e.g., on F6), it can be seen that the population size fluctuates as the SAGA increases the population size to escape a local optimum and then decreases the population size again to find the next optimum (see Fig. 2).

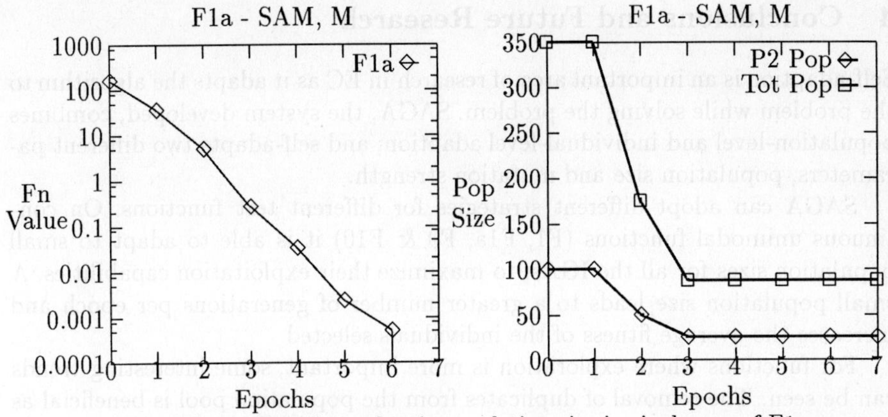

Fig. 1. Function value & population size in single run of F1a

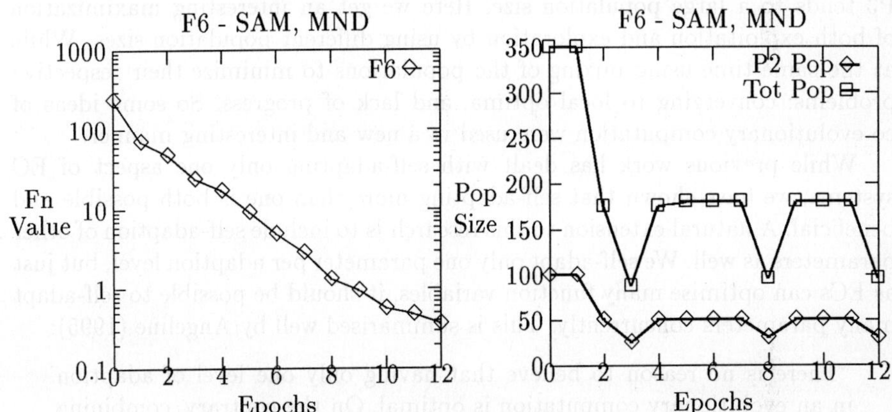

Fig. 2. Function value & population size in single run of F6

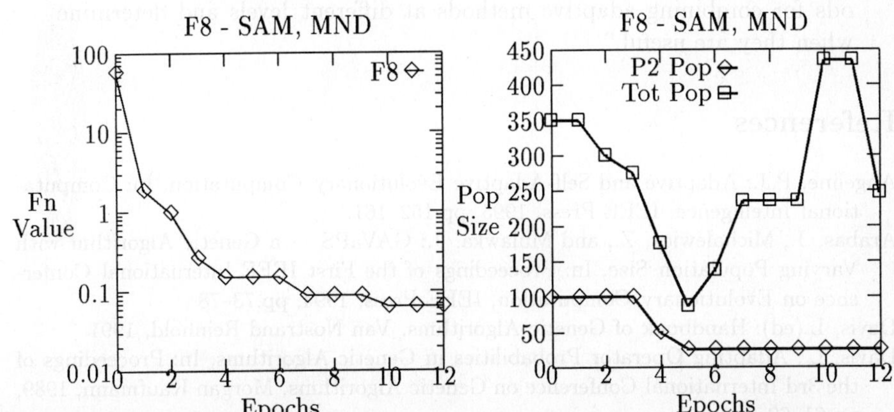

Fig. 3. Function value & population size in single run of F8

4 Conclusions and Future Research

Self-adaption is an important area of research in EC as it adapts the algorithm to the problem while solving the problem. SAGA, the system developed, combines population-level and individual-level adaption; and self-adapts two different parameters, population size and mutation strength.

SAGA can adopt different strategies for different test functions. On continuous unimodal functions (F1, F1a, F9 & F10) it is able to adapt to small population sizes for all the IGAs; to maximize their exploitation capabilities. A small population size leads to a greater number of generations per epoch and increases the average fitness of the individuals selected.

For functions where exploration is more important, some interesting trends can be seen. The removal of duplicates from the population pool is beneficial as this lowers the average fitness of individuals selected and increases the diversity of the population. IGA-P1 tends towards a small population size, and IGA-P3 tends to a large population size. Here we get an interesting maximization of both exploitation and exploration by using different population sizes. While at the same time using mixing of the populations to minimize their respective problems: converging to local optima, and lack of progress. So some ideas of co-evolutionary computation were used in a new and interesting manner.

While previous work has dealt with self-adapting only one aspect of EC systems, we have shown that self-adapting more than one is both possible and beneficial. A natural extension to this research is to include self-adaption of other parameters as well. We self-adapt only one parameter per adaption level, but just as ECs can optimise many function variables, it should be possible to self-adapt many parameters concurrently. This is summarised well by Angeline (1995):

> "There is no reason to believe that having only one level of adaption in an evolutionary computation is optimal. On the contrary, combining methods at different levels may actually provide significant advantages in some environments. Some effort is required to determine effective methods for combining adaptive methods at different levels and determine when they are useful."

References

Angeline, P.J.: Adaptive and Self-Adaptive Evolutionary Computation, In: Computational Intelligence, IEEE Press, 1995, pp.152–161.

Arabas, J., Michalewicz, Z., and Mulawka, J.: GAVaPS — a Genetic Algorithm with Varying Population Size, In: Proceedings of the First IEEE International Conference on Evolutionary Computation, IEEE Press, 1994, pp.73–78.

Davis, L.(ed): Handbook of Genetic Algorithms, Van Nostrand Reinhold, 1991.

Davis, L.: Adapting Operator Probabilities in Genetic Algorithms, In: Proceedings of the 3rd International Conference on Genetic Algorithms, Morgan Kaufmann, 1989, pp.61–69.

De Jong, K.A.: "An Analysis of the Behavior of a Class of Genetic Adaptive Systems", Doctoral dissertation, University of Michigan, 1975.

Goldberg, D.E.: Sizing Populations for Serial and Parallel Genetic Algorithms, In: Proceedings of the 3rd International Conference on Genetic Algorithms, Morgan Kaufmann, 1989, pp.51–60.

Goldberg, D.E., Deb, K., and Clark, J.H.: Accounting for Noise in the Sizing of Populations, In: D. Whitley (ed), *Foundations of genetic Algorithms 2*, pp. 127–140, Morgan Kaufmann, 1992.

Goldberg, D.E., Deb, K., and Korb, B.: Do not Worry, Be Messy, In: Proceedings of the 4th International Conference on Genetic Algorithms, Morgan Kaufmann, 1991, pp.24–30.

Gordon, V. S. & Whitley, D.: Serial and Parallel Genetic Algorithms as Function Optimizers, In: Proceedings of the 5th International Conference on Genetic Algorithms, pp 177-183, Morgan Kaufmann, 1993.

Grefenstette, J.J.: Optimization of Control Parameters for Genetic Algorithms, IEEE Transactions on Systems, Man, and Cybernetics, Vol. 16, No.1, pp.122–128, 1986.

Hoffmeister, F. and Bäck T.: Genetic Algorithms and Evolution Strategies: Similarities and Differences, Technical Report No. SYS-1/92 (Feb 1992), Systems Analysis Research Group, University of Dortmund, Germany.

Hinterding R.,: Gaussian Mutation and Self-adaption in Numeric Genetic Algorithms, In: Proc. of IEEE International Conference on Evolutionary Computation, IEEE Press, pp 384–389, 1995.

Julstrom, B.A.: What Have You Done for Me Lately? Adapting Operator Probabilities in a Steady-State Genetic Algorithm, In: Proceedings of the 6th International Conference on Genetic Algorithms, Morgan Kaufmann, 1995, pp.81–87

Michalewicz, Z.: Genetic Algorithms + Data Structures = Evolution Programs (2nd Ed), Springer - Verlag 1994.

Schaffer, J., Caruana, R., Eshelman, L., and Das, R.: A Study of Control Parameters Affecting Online Performance of Genetic Algorithms for Function Optimization, In: Proceedings of the 3rd International Conference on Genetic Algorithms, Morgan Kaufmann, 1989, pp.51–60.

Schaffer, J.D. and Morishima, A.: An Adaptive Crossover Distribution Mechanism for Genetic Algorithms, In: Proceedings of the 2nd International Conference on Genetic Algorithms, Lawrence Erlbaum Associates, 1987, pp.36–40.

Shaefer, C.G.: The ARGOT Strategy: Adaptive Representation Genetic Optimizer Technique, In: Proceedings of the 2nd International Conference on Genetic Algorithms, Lawrence Erlbaum Associates, 1987, pp.50–55.

Schraudolph, N. and Belew, R.: Dynamic Parameter Encoding for Genetic Algorithms, Machine Learning, Vol.9, No.1, pp.9–21, 1992.

Smith, R.: Adaptively Resizing Populations: An Algorithm and Analysis, In: Proceedings of the 5th International Conference on Genetic Algorithms, Morgan Kaufmann, 1993, p.653.

Smith, R., Population Size, section C6 of Handbook of Evolutionary Computation, Oxford University Press, New York, 1996.

Spears, W.M.: Adapting Crossover in Evolutionary Algorithms, in McDonnell, J.R., Reynolds, R.G., and Fogel, D.B. (Editors), In: Proceedings of the Fourth Annual Conference on Evolutionary Programming, The MIT Press, 1995, pp.367–384.

Srinivas, M. and Patnaik, L.M.: Adaptive Probabilities of Crossover and Mutation in Genetic Algorithms, In: IEEE Transactions on Systems, Man, and Cybernetics, Vol.24, No.4, 1994, pp.17–26.

Niche Search: An Evolutionary Algorithm for Global Optimisation

João Pedro Pedroso

Centre for Operations Research and Econometrics
34 Voie du Roman Pays,
B-1348 Louvain-la-Neuve, Belgium

Abstract. In this paper we describe niche search, a genetic-based optimisation approach which is characterised by an evolutionary search on two layers: the individual layer (which is comparable to search described in other genetic algorithms), and the niche layer.
Neither of these searches is directed: both individuals and niches evolve based on the selection of the fittest.
The numerical results obtained by niche search are quite promising, as our implementation has successfully handled all the tests carried out. The computational performance is considerably better than that of other algorithms of the same family analysed in the literature.

1 Overview

Niche search is a genetic algorithm version for whose conception special attention has been paid to the aspects that follow.

First, encode the reproduction operations that occur in nature, at the cellular and molecular level, more precisely and completely than the implementation proposed in the canonical genetic algorithm (CGA). In particular, it is proposed a simulation of the *meiosis* process in the reproduction of our artificial organisms. Meiosis is the main source of diversity in nature (for sexual reproduction), and is absent in the CGA.

Second, the overall population of individuals — the *ecosystem* — is assembled into different groups, each of them occupying a particular *niche*. This parallels what happens in nature: individuals of a given species are in general not found neither alone nor assembled in the same global pool. Furthermore, the parameters that control the reproduction (mutation probability, crossover probability, etc.) may vary from place to place, as may vary the way in which different species exploit different parameters. In the approach proposed, each niche is supplied its own set of these parameters by the ecosystem, in an arbitrary and endogenous way.

Finally, selection and reproduction act not only at the level of individuals, but also at the level of groups of individuals (niches). Individuals must compete in order to survive among their similars; niches must also compete between them for resources in the environment. Competition and selection between individuals of a particular niche is similar to what is proposed in the CGA; competition between niches is, to the best of our knowledge, proposed here the first time. *Niche selection* means that, at each generation, there are some poorly adapted niches which may disappear; niches whose adaptation is good remain.

Hence, niche search captures issues concerning evolution on both individual organisms and groups, or organisations of individuals. A diagram showing the general structure of the algorithm is presented in figure 1. The innovation, from the point of view of numerical optimisation, is that the adaptation of the main control parameters of the algorithm is made through an evolutionary approach — in contrast to what happens in evolutionary systems (ESs) and in evolutionary programming (EP), where auto adaption is directed by the program, based on the status of the system at each iteration. Our approach is also different from the one proposed by the *multilevel genetic algorithm* [8, 4].

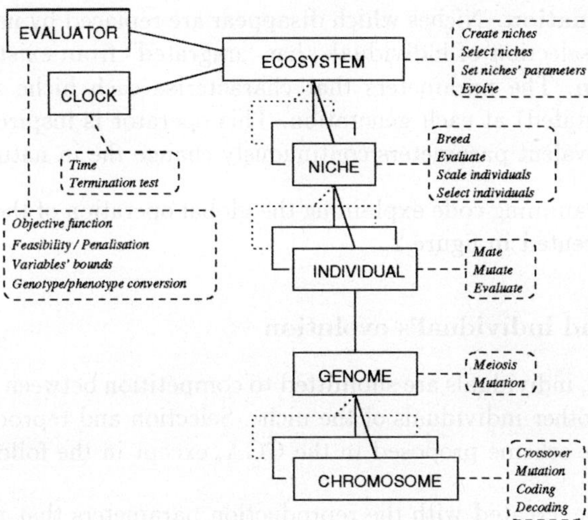

Fig. 1. Overview of the data structures and operators for niche search.

2 Niche search

2.1 The ecosystem and niches' evolution

What characterises a niche in an ecosystem is its set of individuals and the parameters of the environment where the niche is located (the reproduction factors). Parameters are imposed to the niches externally (and randomly) by the ecosystem; nothing directs niches to find the "best" reproduction parameters. Niches for which the parameters are good are likely to adapt faster to the pressures of the environment, and hence remain alive; those whose parameters are bad, are likely to adapt slower, and possibly extinguish.

Reproduction parameters imposed to the niches are: probability and intensity of mutation of the genes; probability and intensity of occurrence of crossover in the chromosome replication, and a selectivity factor (a factor that specifies how competitive an individual must be in relation to the average in order to have a favoured reproduction probability). Notice that the CGA corresponds to a single niche, where these parameters are set exogenously. The performance of that algorithm for difficult problems deeply depends on them; in niche search, they are endogenous, resulting from of an "evolutionary search".

Evolution at the niches level is based on the following operators (which parallel the operators found at the individual level):

Niche selection. Poorly adapted niches are likely to be extinguished, whilst better adapted ones remain.

Niche recombination. Niches which disappear are replaced by new ones; these emerge as a selection of individuals that "migrated" from existing niches.

Niche mutation. The parameters that characterise each niche are randomly changed (mutated) at each generation. This operator is inspired by the fact that the equivalent parameters continuously change the in natural life.

Pseudo programming code explaining the global operation of the niche search algorithm is presented in figure 2.

2.2 Niches and individual's evolution

Inside each niche, individuals are submitted to competition between their similars — i.e., with the other individuals of the niche. Selection and reproduction inside a niche follow the scheme proposed in the CGA, except in the following factors:

1. If a new niche, created with the reproduction parameters that the ecosystem supplies, is better than the progenitor niche, it can breed again (up to a maximum number of times) in the same "generation". The biological interpretation for this, is that when natural conditions are better, organisms tend to reproduce more and faster.
2. Not every new population generated is accepted. If both the average and the best individual are worse that their counterparts in the progenitor niche, then, with some probability, the offspring niche is rejected, and the old niche remains unchanged for the next generation[1].
3. We allow for the possibility of representing the chromosome of an individual by data structures other than bit strings. Our implementation supports both bit string and floating point genotypes.

[1] The natural interpretation for this in intuitive. Notice that this equivalent to what happens in Simulated Annealing: there, new solutions are accepted whenever there is an improvement, and may are rejected, with a given probability, when they are worse.

```
set t := 0                                              Start with an initial time.
set ecosystem(t) := InitEcosystem()                     Initialise the ecosystem:
    niches(t) = CreateNiches(t)            Create the desired number of niches for the run
    InitParameters(niches(t))   Randomly initialise the parameters that characterise each niche:
                                          crossover probability, mutation probability, etc.
    InitialisePopulation(niches(t))        Randomly initialise the population of each niche.
Evaluate(niches(t))    Evaluate the fitness of all the niches in the initial population. We propose an
    evaluation based on two parameters: the average fitness of the niches' population and the fitness of its
              best individual, and we use the sum of these factors as the niche's overall evaluation.
iterate                                                      Start the evolution process.
    strong(t) := SelectStrong(ecosystem(t))     Select the niches that will survive to the next
                                                                              generation.
    weak(t) := SelectWeak(ecosystem(t))                Select the niches that may extinguish.
    newniches(t) := Recombination(weak(t),strong(t))   With some probability, replace the
         populations of weak niches by a selection of individuals from the union of that niche with a
                                                                              strong one.
    InitParameters(newniches(t))           Randomly initialise the parameters of the created niches.
    Evaluate(newniches(t))                                             Evaluate the new niches.
    niches(t+1) := Selection(niches(t), new(t))        The new ecosystem is a selection of the
         best niches. In our implementation, we simply replace the the weak niches by the new ones.
    MutateParameters(niches(t+1))    With some probability, randomly perturb the parameters of
                                                                              each niche.
    Breed(niches(t+1))                     Create a new generation of individuals in each of the niches.
    t := t + 1                                                   Increase the time counter.
until Terminated()                                             Termination criteria: time.
display solution                                      Solution is the best individual found.
```

Fig. 2. Niche Search: pseudo code for the outer level

4. Niche search provides two parameters for mutation and two parameters for crossover, for controlling mating between individuals. One specifies the probability of occurrence of these operators, and the other determines its intensity.

The possibility of representing genotypes different from bit strings was suggested by several authors. In [5], the bit string representation receives considerable criticism: the precision of solutions represented by bit strings is considerably limited for a low number of bits, and the convergence for a large number of bits is rather slow. The success of the direct floating point representation of the phenotypes in ESs and EP also suggests the possibility of representing the chromosome as a floating point; in our implementation, floating point genotypes are values in the interval $[0, 1]$, whose phenotype can be assessed by scaling these values to the region defined by the lower and upper bound of the corresponding variable.

Mutation of individuals is based on two parameters: the mutation probability (which specifies the probability of a given chromosome being mutated) and the mutation intensity. This last, controls the magnitude of the mutation. In bit strings, this corresponds to the likelihood of any of the genes of the chromosome suffering a mutation. In floating point genomes this corresponds to a measure of the deviation that a mutation may produce, in relation to the original value.

On the same way, two parameters control the crossover: the crossover probability and the crossover intensity. On bit strings, higher intensity increases the number of potential mutation points (and hence the amount of "shuffling" between the two chromosomes). On floating point strings, crossover intensity specifies the likelihood of obtaining a solution which is intermediary between the two original values, instead of the value of either of them unchanged.

For pseudo programming code explaining the evolution process inside a niche, please refer to figure 3.

```
g := 0                                                   Initialise the "subgeneration" counter.
subpopulation(g) := population(t)     Select subpopulation for offspring production, i.e. the subset
    of the niche's elements that will be able to mate. (t is the global generation counter, in the ecosystem)
iterate                                                            Start the evolution process.
    parents(g) := Selection(subpopulation(g))      Select parents for offspring production, e.g.
                                                                 through roulette wheel selection.
    offspring(g) := Recombination(parents(g))       Recombine the genomes of two selected
                                                     parents, through the meiosis operator (figure 4).
    offspring(g) := Mutation(offspring(g))       With some probability, randomly perturb each of
                                                            the chromosomes of each individual.
    Evaluate(offspring(g))          Evaluate the objective of all the individuals in the niche's population.
                                                             Penalise and scale; obtain the fitnesses.
    subpopulation(g+1) := offspring(g)       New subpopulation: the offspring of the previous one.
    g := g + 1                                               Increase the subgeneration counter.
    population(t+1) := ChooseOne(population(t),subpopulation(g))                     Update the
                 niche's population. Always select the subpopulation is its performance is better; if the
                                           performance is worse, accept it with some probability.
until Terminated()     Termination criteria: maximum subgenerations achieved, or evaluation of current
                               subpopulation is worse than evaluation of last subgeneration's one.
```

Fig. 3. Niche search: pseudo code for the inner evolution (breeding) of a niche. This procedure is executed at each generation step of the ecosystem (the Breed() step, in figure 2).

2.3 Other differences between niche search and other GAs

Meiosis In niche search, the usual mutation and crossover operators on the genetic structure are complemented by a meiosis process, which is absent in other GAs. It performed as described in figure 4.

We view the meiosis operator as a considerable improvement over other GAs for the treatment of problems of larger dimension. The standard approach on GAs for multidimensional optimisation is to assemble all the components of a vector into a single chromosome string, loosing therefore the "independence" between the several chromosomes that our system provides, throught the association of each variable to a particular chromosome.

```
input(mother,father)   The originating (diploid) cell contains two copies of each of the chromosomes;
                       one coming from the father and the other coming from the mother.
for c = 1 to NumerOfChromosomes() do                          Start the meiosis process.
    origin := RandomChoose(FromMother(),FromFather())          Randomly select the
                       chromosome; either from the father's or from the mother's copy.
    if origin ?= FromMother()
        source(c) := mother(c)                This chromosome comes from the mother.
        genome(c) := Crossover(source(c), father(c))   With some probability, crossover
                                                   with the other chromosome occurs.
    else
        source(c) := father(c)                This chromosome comes from the father.
        genome(c) := Crossover(source(c), mother(c))   With some probability, crossover
                                                   with the other chromosome occurs.
    end if
done                                      Until all chromosomes in the genome are done.
return genome                                        Haploid cell (gamete) is created.
```

Fig. 4. Niche search: the meiosis process.

Time adaption The aim of niche search is to produce the best and most accurate achievable solution in a limited amount of generations. In order to get more precise solutions at the evolution goes on, we propose a way of gradually decreasing the intensity of the perturbations that the search operators produce. This allows a refinement of the solution obtained, as the number of performed generations gets closer the total number of generations. We named this feature *time adaption*.

Time adaption is optional: for any particular run, the user can select if it is performed or not. If not, the mutation and crossover intensities and the selectivity level are the same from the beginning until the end of a program run. This is what generally happens in other implementations of GAs. If there is time adaption, the intensity parameters are adapted at each generation, as follows:

- mutation intensity decreases proportionally to the time elapsed, starting with the value of the corresponding parameter set by the ecosystem and being close to zero at the end of the evolutionary run;
- crossover intensity and selectivity level start with values close to zero and increase proportionally to the time elapsed, being close to the values set by the ecosystem at the end.

This adaptation of the parameters allows for an increasing perfection of the individuals, leading to offspring that are closer and closer to their progenitors; at the end, the diversity in each of the niches is rather small. We expect to be, then, close to achieving species perfectly adapted to the environment. From another point of view, we expect to be close to the global optimum of the objective function.

The time adaption factor may take on different functions of the elapsed generations. Time adaption may be the most important factor for explaining the high precision of the solutions that niche search obtains.

Fitness: objective function and penalisation When the solution corresponding to a particular individual is outside the feasible region, the evaluation is composed of the objective function plus a penalty, which is supposed to be a value proportional to the severity of the infeasibility.

This value of the fitness for penalised individuals is the objective minus a value proportional to the penalty. It is computed as follows:

$$f'(x) = f(x) - (M - m) \cdot (1 + p(x) \cdot t) \quad (1)$$

where f' is the fitness, f is the objective function, M and m are respectively the maximum and minimum fitness for all the individuals in the population of the ecosystem at the current generation, $p(x)$ is the penalty, t is proportional to the number of generations elapsed.

Fitnesses determined this way guarantee that if there is any feasible solution, its fitness is higher than that of any infeasible one. As a consequence, if there is a feasible solution in the population, the "elite" will be feasible.

Computing the fitness this way allows infeasible individuals to survive at the beginning, while being progressively eliminated with the evolution process. This method proves to be quite interesting, specially when the optimum is found in a very narrow feasible region.

Generalised power law scaling Another difference between the niche search implementation and other GAs concerns the scaling operation.

The scaling method that we propose avoids the constraint, usual in other scaling procedures, that the objective functions must be positive in all the search domain. Another advantage is that it is independent of the absolute value of the fitness: adding a constant to all the fitnesses does not produce any change in the scaled value.

Scaled fitnesses are obtained as follow:

$$f''(x) = \left[\epsilon + \left(\frac{f'(x) - m}{M - m}\right) \cdot (1 - \epsilon)\right]^{\sigma} \quad (2)$$

where $f''(x)$ is the scaled fitness, $f'(x)$ is the (penalised) fitness, $\epsilon = 1/N$, m and M are minimum and maximum (also penalised) fitnesses in the niche, σ is the scaling power.

The first step consists on the normalisation of all the fitness values into the interval $[1/N, 1]$, where N is the number of elements in the niche. The second step consists on elevating this value to a power, greater or equal to zero, which is the *scaling power*. If there is time adaption, this value is itself the product of the selectivity parameter of the niche by the time adaption factor. Time adaption makes the niches more and more selective, as time goes on: at the beginning the selection is almost purely stochastic, whilst at the end a much increased weight is put on the best individuals.

The scaled fitness of the individual is used at the time of the selection.

Elitist niches In order for an evolutionary process to converge to the global optimum, it must assure that the best solution found always remains in the population. This is done through elitism.

In niche search, the ecosystem keeps the best solution found by all the niches. Further, we implement elitist modes in niches, which allow some of them to keep their best solution unchanged in their population.

By default, all the niches are *non-elitist* except two: the one which detains the best individual, and the one whose average is the best (which can be the previous one). The non-elitist niches can be performing their search in regions quite far away from the elitist ones; this proves to be a very powerful way of avoiding local optima. At the same time, the elitist niches perform a more localised search, in the neighbourhood of their best element.

3 Numerical tests

As our implementation provides the first results using the niche search approach, we found it necessary to proceed to an extensive set of tests. We relied on test functions that are commonly used by the evolutionary computation community, which are supposed to put in evidence the strengths and weaknesses of each implementation.

We have implemented the all test functions proposed by De Jong in his thesis dissertation [3], Schaffer's binary F6 function [7]. Each of the tests has been run at least 10 times. In none of the runs for each of the tests has the program failed to obtain the global optimum, in a considerably low number of function evaluations.

The sphere model, and Ackley's test function have also been implemented, the results being reported below. The solutions reported are the average of 10 runs performed, and the log of the evolution of the solution is that of an intermediate run. We have performed more than 100 runs for each of these tests; niche search has always found the global optimum.

3.1 Sphere model

This test consists of an extension of De Jong's first test function to 30 variables, with a wider search range:

$$\text{maximise } f(x) = -\sum_{i=1}^{n} x_i^2$$
$$x_i \in [-30, 30], \quad n = 30$$

Parameters used by niche search for this test: 750 generations, 3 niches with 3 individuals each. Average value of the solution found: $\bar{f}^* = -6.19 \cdot 10^{-04}$, $|\bar{x}_i^*| \leq 4.7 \cdot 10^{-3}$. Average number of function evaluations per run: 9089.

Experimental results for this test function have been provided, for ESs and EP, in [2]. There the model was for 40000 function evaluations, and the values obtained were $f^* \approx .4$ for and ES and $f^* \approx 200$ for EP. The niche search method reveals, therefore, a considerably improved performance. With 40000 evaluations, niche search obtains $f^* \approx 1.0 \cdot 10^{-13}$, $|\bar{x}_i^*| < 1. \cdot 10^{-07}, \forall i$.

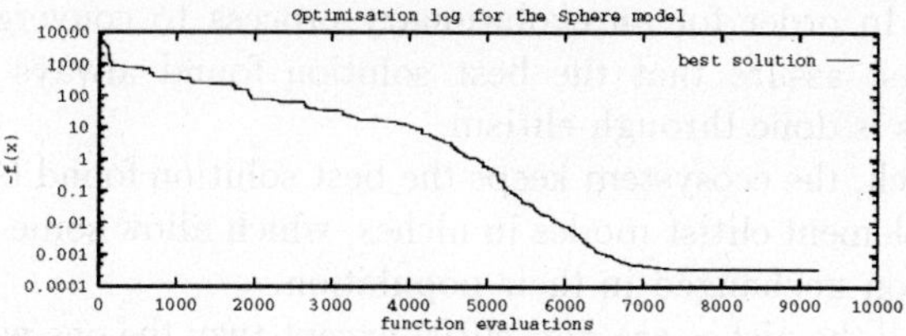

Fig. 5. Experimental run of niche search for the optimisation of the sphere model: best value obtained as a function of the number of objective evaluations.

3.2 Ackley function

Ackley test function is a strongly nonconcave and multimodal function, which has been proposed in [1].

$$\text{maximise } f(x) = 20 \cdot \exp\left(-0.2\sqrt{\frac{1}{n}\sum_{i=1}^{n} x_i^2}\right) + \exp\left(\frac{1}{n}\sum_{i=1}^{n}\cos(2\pi x_i)\right) - 20 - e$$

$$x_i \in [-30, 30], \quad n = 30$$

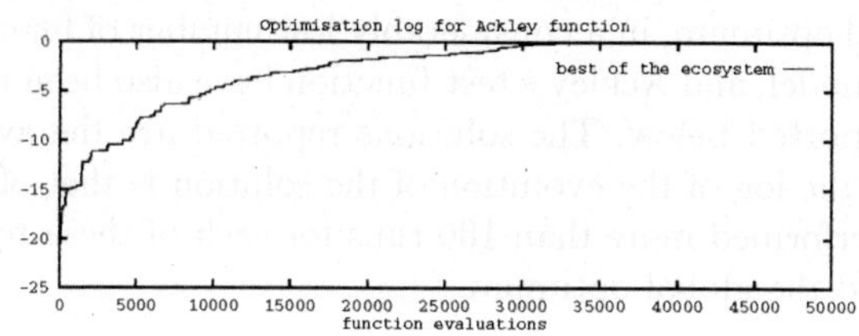

Fig. 6. Evolution log of an experimental run of niche search for the optimisation of Ackley's function: best value obtained as a function of the number of objective evaluations.

Parameters used by niche search for this test: 5600 generations, 3 niches with 3 individuals each. Average value of the solution found: $\bar{f}^* = -2.60 \cdot 10^{-9}$, $|\bar{x}_i^*| \leq 5.10 \cdot 10^{-10}$. Average number of function evaluations per run: 49539.

Experimental results for this test function have been provided, for ESs and EP, in [2]. They have run the model for 200000 function evaluations, and the values obtained are $f^* = 7.48 \cdot 10^{-08}$ for ES and $f^* = 1.39 \cdot 10^{-02}$ for EP. The niche search method has a considerably improved performance over both the systems, as approximately 25% of the evaluations were required to consistently obtain an equivalent solution. We also have run the model with close to 200000

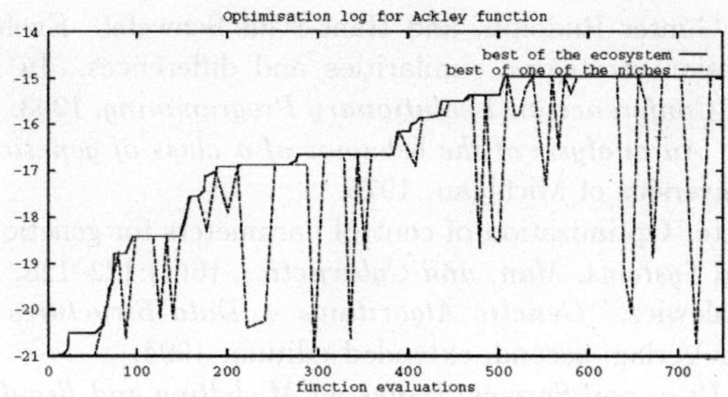

Fig. 7. Experimental run of niche search for the initial iterations of Ackley function's optimisation: best value obtained as a function of the number of objective evaluations, and best element of a particular niche. This shows how a particular niche can be far away form the best one during the search process.

function evaluations. The mean solution obtained was $\bar{f} = -3.5 \cdot 10^{-14}$, with $|x_i| < 1.4 \cdot 10^{-14}, \forall i$.

For a more complete set of benchmark tests, the reader is referred to [6].

4 Conclusion

Niche search is a genetic-based global optimisation solver that we have designed and implemented, trying to parallel closely the search operators on their biological equivalents. It is characterised by an evolutionary search on two layers: the individual layer and the niche layer. Neither of these searches is directed: both individuals and niches evolve based on the selection of the fittest.

The fact that different niches perform more localised searches in different regions of the search space strongly increases the probability of avoiding local optima. The possibility of using time adaption of the search parameters provides a way of improving the precision of the solution obtained, without drawbacks in terms of the global search. A penalisation method which allows for infeasible individuals to remain in the population was proposed. The aim of such a method is to increase the likeliness of finding the global optimum when it is located in narrow feasible regions; nevertheless, experimental support is not provided.

The numerical results obtained by niche search are quite promising, as our implementation has successfully handled all the tests carried out. The computational performance is considerably better than that of other algorithms of the same family analysed in the literature.

References

1. D. H. Ackley. *A Connectionist Machine for Genetic Hillclimbing.* Kluwer Academic Publishers, Boston, 1987.

2. Thomas Bäck, Gúnter Rudolph, and Hans-Paul Schwefel. Evolutionary programming and evolution strategies: similarities and differences. In *Proceedings of the Second Annual Conference on Evolutionary Programming*, 1993.
3. K. A. De Jong. *An analysis of the behavior of a class of genetic adaptive systems.* PhD thesis, University of Michigan, 1975.
4. J. J. Grefenstette. Optimization of control parameters for genetic algorithms. *IEEE Transactions od Systems, Man, and Cybernetics*, 16(1):122–128, 1986.
5. Zbigniew Michalewicz. *Genetic Algorithms + Data Structures = Evolution Programs.* Springer-Verlag, second, extended edition, 1994.
6. J. P. Pedroso. *Universal Service: Issues on Modelling and Regulation.* PhD thesis, Université Catholique de Louvain, 1996.
7. J. D. Schaffer, R. A. Caruana, L. J. Eshelman, and R. Das. A study of control parameters affecting online performance of genetic algorithms for function optimization. In J. D. Schaffer, editor, *Proceedings of the Third International Conference on Genetic Algorithms*, pages 51–59, San Mateo, CA, 1989.
8. R. Weinberg. *Computer simulation of a living cell.* PhD thesis, University of Michigan, 1970.

Adaptively Parameterised Evolutionary Systems: Self Adaptive Recombination and Mutation in a Genetic Algorithm

J.E.Smith & T.C.Fogarty
Evolutionary Computing Group
Faculty of Computer Studies & Mathematics
University of West of England
Bristol BS16 1 QY
{jim/tcf @ btc.uwe.ac.uk}

Abstract. It has long been recognised that the choice of recombination and mutation operators and the rates at which they are applied to a Genetic Algorithm will have a significant effect on the outcome of the evolutionary search, with sub-optimal values often leading to poor performance. In this paper an evolutionary algorithm (APES) is presented within which both the units of heredity and the probability that those units will subject to mutation are learnt via self adaptation of the genetic material. Using Kaufmann's NK model, this algorithm is compared to a number of combinations of frequently used crossover operators with "standard" mutation rates. The results demonstrate competitive times to find maxima on simple problems, and (on the most complex problems) results which are significantly better than the majority of other algorithms tested. This algorithm represents a robust adaptive search method which is not dependant on expert knowledge of genetic algorithm theory or practice in order to perform effectively.

1. Introduction

1.1 Background

In recent years the interaction between the Genetic Algorithm (GA) and Evolutionary Strategies communities has led to an increasing interest in the use of adaptive operators within genetic algorithms as it has been recognised that the optimal rate of application of a given operator will depend both on the nature of the landscape being searched and on the current state of the search.

Although self-adaptation of the search parameters presents an additional learning overhead compared to an algorithm tuned to a particular landscapes, different problems will require very different tuning. In general, particularly for "real world" problems, we do not know the structure of space being searched, and the priority is for a search strategy that will perform well on a wide variety of problem types, hence the interest in self-parameterising algorithms

Schaffer & Morishima [1] proposed an encoding whereby the GA learnt crossover points for two-parent recombination, and Spears [2] investigated the use of genetically encoded flags to determine the type of crossover used between two parents. Smith & Fogarty [3, 4] evaluated and analysed an algorithm (LEGO) within which the evolution of "blocks" of linked neighbouring genes within a genepool makes it possible for the recombination strategy to vary in both the amount of genetic material exchanged,

and in the number of parents contributing.
One result they observed when comparing its (competitive) performance with that of various "standard" recombination operators (one point, uniform [5] and Bit Simulated [6] crossover, and asexual reproduction) was that although these fixed recombination strategies all performed reasonably well given a suitable mutation rate, their performance was very sensitive to that rate, decreasing rapidly away from the optimal value.
Meanwhile Bäck [7] examined the application of the ideas from Evolutionary Strategies [8, 9] of genetically encoded mutation rates to generational genetic algorithms. Smith & Fogarty [10] combined Bäck's findings on the need for a very high selection pressure with results on the efficacy of adding local search to a GA and produced a steady state GA with self-adaptation of each individual's (single) mutation rate which outperformed a wide variety of fixed rates in empirical tests. Bäck experimented with both a single mutation rate applied to all elements of an individual, and with *n* mutation rates encoded (one for each of *n* sub-strings of an individual). He found that the optimal choice depended on the nature of the function, (since there is an overhead in learning many different mutation rates for a simple unimodal function). He also noted the importance of recombination to the process of "learning" mutation rates, concluding: "***Surely, new recombination techniques have to be used for n mutation rates...***".

1.2 Aims of this Work

This paper examines a representation which combines the ideas of adaptive mutation discussed above with the LEGO algorithm to produce an algorithm (APES) which optimises both recombination and mutation strategies via self adaptation of its genotype. This is done by learning useful "blocks" of linked genes and a suitable mutation rate for each block. The problem of decomposing the representation into a suitable number of sub-strings and mutation rates is solved since there are as many mutation rates in a given individual as there are discrete blocks of genes in it.
One effect of adding additional information about gene linkage and mutation rates to the genotype is to increase the size of the search space of the algorithm. A likely result is that on any given function it will be outperformed by the optimal combination of fixed operators and parameters for that function. However, this optimal combination is in general not known without recourse to solving the function itself a number of different times. The aim of this work is to produce a robust algorithm which will not exhibit the problems of sensitivity to parameter values that those using fixed operators suffer from.
In order to demonstrate this algorithm it is compared to a range of combinations of common recombination operators (one point crossover and uniform crossover) with a number of mutation rates suggested by empirical studies and commonly used as "default" values. To avoid any subjective bias, the class of landscapes chosen to investigate the behaviour of the algorithm is the well-studied NK family of landscapes which provide a tunable set of landscapes with increasing numbers of optima and decreasing fitness correlations as K is increased. The reader is referred to [11] for a full description.

2. Representation and Operators

2.1 Representation

The representation used for this work is as follows: an individual member *I* of the population of size *P* is considered to be a chromosome made up of *N* genes, where *N* is the length of the problem encoding. Each gene g_i ($0 \leq i < N$) is composed of four parts: $g_i = \{a_i, L_i, R_i, \mu_i\}$ the elements being defined as below.

$a_i \in \{0...A\text{-}1\}$ is the problem encoding, with cardinality *A*.

$L_i, R_i \in \{0, 1\}$ are Boolean flags denoting linkage (see below)

$\mu_i \in \{ r:\Re \mid 0.0 \leq r < 1.0 \}$ is the mutation rate encoding for that gene.

For the specific class of landscapes investigated in this work a binary encoding is used (i.e. $A = 2$) and for reasons of efficiency the mutation rates μ_i are encoded as integers in the range (0... 999) (which are divided by 1000 prior to use) thus we can denote the search space $S = (\{0,1\} \times \{0,1\} \times \{0,1\} \times \{0...999\})^N$.

2.2 Recombination

The recombination operator works by considering the population of solutions as a gene pool comprised of "blocks" of genes defined over certain loci, with these blocks potentially varying in size from a single gene to an entire chromosome. In order to achieve this each gene has associated with it two boolean flags determining whether it will link to the genes to its left and right, and two adjacent genes are said to be linked if the appropriate flags are both set to "*true*". Blocks are thus comprised of chains of linked genes. These blocks are maintained during recombination, i.e. they represent the "units of inheritance" of the algorithm.

This representation is similar to Schaffer and Morishima's use of "punctuation marks" to encode for crossover points [1], however in this case the recombination is not restricted to two parents. In this way the algorithm is able to benefit from the advantages of multi-parent recombination as discussed in [12,13] without the necessity of tuning the type of recombination to the nature of the problem.

This is shown schematically in Figure 1.

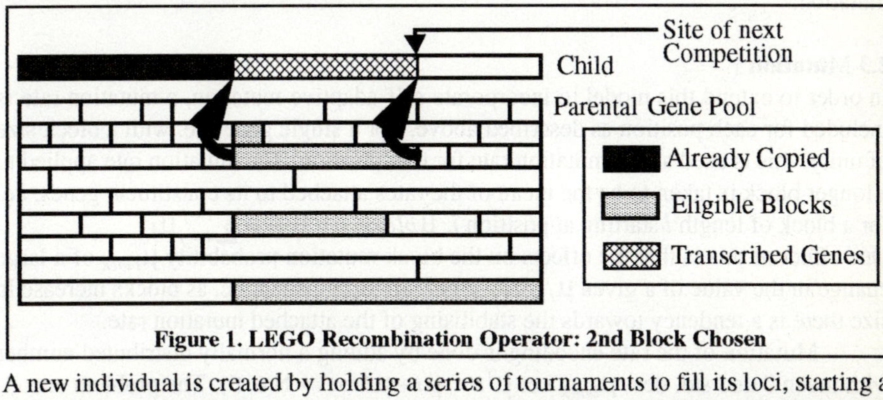

Figure 1. LEGO Recombination Operator: 2nd Block Chosen

A new individual is created by holding a series of tournaments to fill its loci, starting at the left hand edge.When a given position is being filled a number of eligible blocks (equivalent to the "tournament size" in selection algorithms for conventional crossover operators) are picked (with replacement) from the population according to the following method. Firstly, a random parent is selected from the population. If the block cov-

ering that position in the parent is not eligible (i.e. starts before that position) then a direction is picked at random and the population is stepped through in that direction until an eligible block is found. Since each block comes from a complete parent, it will always be possible to find at least one suitable candidate for each tournament, and at worst (P -1) tests for eligibility will be made for each.
Having selected a small number of blocks, the block coming from the fittest parent is chosen. That entire block (with its links) will be copied.A new tournament is then held to fill the next locus after the end of the block. The use of two bits to specify whether two adjacent genes are linked means that within a given individual there may be neighbouring blocks, one of which will have the appropriate end link bit set *"true"* - a *"free"* link. This phenomenon facilitates the building up of larger blocks during recombination via the juxtaposition of two blocks with the appropriate end links "free". The effect of this is to provide a counterbalance for the tendency of mutation to destroy larger blocks.
The algorithm is initialised with a variety of block sizes, and mutation is allowed to act on the linkage flags, providing the means for the evolution of recombination strategies. If all of the blocks are of unit length (no links) then this reduces to considering the problem as a set of separate populations of alleles (one for each locus) which is the basis of Bit Simulated Crossover. At the other extreme, if a chromosome is fully linked (one block extends over its whole length) then selection of this block for reproduction will result in an asexual strategy i.e. mutation only evolutionary search.
In practice the algorithm shows behaviour which varies between these extremes over the course of evolution, according to the nature of the landscape being searched and the degree of phenotypic convergence of the population. The recombination strategies which evolve are analysed in more depth in [4], to summarise briefly there is a tendency for the amount of linkage in the population to increase with the degree of epistasis of the problem. At the extremes, with zero interdependence (K = 0) the genepool evolves into separate populations of unlinked loci (cf. BSC) whereas for totally uncorrelated landscapes (K = 15) asexual strategies evolve and the search proceeds via mutation.

2.3 Mutation

In order to extend this model to incorporate self-adaptive mutation, a mutation rate is included for each position as described above. For a single gene (i.e. with a block size of unity) this is used as the mutation rate for that position. The mutation rate applied to a longer block is taken to be the mean of the rates attached to its constituent genes, i.e. for a block of length l starting at position j, $\mu block = (1/l) \times \sum_{i=j}^{l+j} \mu i$
One effect of this is that the effects on the block mutation probability μ_{block} of a large change in the value of a given μ_i ($j \leq i < j+l$) are diminished, i.e. as blocks increase in size there is a tendency towards the stabilising of the attached mutation rate.

Mutation of the rate encoding is done by adding a normally distributed number with mean 0 and std. dev. μ_{block} i.e. $\mu' i = \mu i + \mu block \times \mathrm{N}(0, 1)$ The problem encoding and boolean flags within each gene are subject to value-flipping with probability μ'_{block}
The steady state genetic algorithm used here is different to the generational models

used in [7] in that there is a single new member inserted to the population at any one time, which according to the standard nomenclature would correspond to a $(\lambda+1)$ strategy. However it has been shown empirically (and theoretically for certain simple problems [9]) that there is an optimal "acceptance" ratio of approximately 1:5. i.e. one individual should be incorporated into the population for every five created. The approach taken here is to create a single individual via recombination and then "clone" that individual a number of times. Each of these offspring then undergoes the mutation process and is evaluated before the fittest is chosen for potential insertion into the population.

Previously [10] we reported that using four "clones" (i.e. selecting one from a total of five offspring) provides a good compromise between exploration and exploitation over a range of problem types, an empirical confirmation of the 1:5 acceptance ratio noted above. It was also shown that the use of a single clone reduces the ability of the algorithm to escape from sub-optima on more complex landscapes.

This can be explained in terms of two effects. Firstly, the repeated mutation of a single individual's phenotype corresponds to a form of local search, which can be shown to enhance the performance of Genetic Algorithms on some functions e.g. [14]. Alternatively, it can be considered that having multiple copies of an individual, which are then subjected to mutation at differing rates prior to selection, allows the self-adaptive process to learn different mutation rates for different parts of the search space i.e. it facilitates the "decentralised" nature of the mutation operator.

In order to investigate whether the beneficial results obtained were due to the adaptive mutation operator or simply local search, the use of fixed mutation rates in an algorithm which used the same cloning strategy was also tested in [10]. It was shown that the addition of local search alone was not enough to enable algorithms using fixed mutation rates to escape from local optima as well as the adaptive mutation mechanism.

The APES reproduction algorithm can be summarised as follows:

```
Create a new individual via recombination (LEGO).
    Repeat 5 times
        {
            Copy new individual
            For each block in the copy
                {
                    Decode mutation rate of block μ_block
                    For each gene i in the block μ´_i = μ_i + N(0, μ_block)
                    Decode new mutation rate of block μ´_block
                    For each gene i in the block mutate (a_i, L_i, R_i) with prob. μ´_block
                }
            Evaluate this individual
        }
    Select best individual from the offspring.
    Replace oldest member of population if fitter.
```

Figure 2. Pseudo Code for APES Algorithm

3. Experimental Details

In order to test the effectiveness of the algorithm a series of experiments were run using the NK model with a length (N) of 16, and a set of values for K (0, 2, 4, 8, 15) which would represent a range of problem difficulty for the Genetic Algorithm from a simple unimodal hill climb (K = 0) to searching an entirely uncorrelated fitness landscape (K = 15).

For each value of K, 20 landscapes were created. Because the global maxima is not known for these landscapes, and the aim of this work is to provide a good reliable algorithm rather than necessarily the fastest, the approach taken was to compare the fittest member of the population after a fixed number of evaluations. The same initial populations and landscapes were used for all algorithms

All experiments were run for 20,000 evaluations, using a population of 100, with deletion of the oldest member of the population (if this was less fit than the candidate offspring), and parent (or block) selection via a tournament of size 2.

The APES algorithm was tested against a "standard" steady state algorithm (SGA) with the same population size and replacement strategies, but with reproduction creating a single offspring. The recombination operators chosen for comparison were one-point and uniform crossover (applied with 70% probability), and these were combined with each of four commonly used fixed mutation rates, described in the table below, creating eight versions of the SGA.

Symbol	Probability/bit	Source
D	0.001	DeJong [15]
G	0.01	Grefenstette [16]
S	$1.75/(\text{popsize}^* \sqrt{\text{length}})$	Schaffer et al. [17] reformulated in [7]
O	1/length	Mühlenbein [18] simplified in [7]

Table 1: Mutation Rates - Symbol, value and derivation

4. Comparison Results

In Table 2 the mean value (over the twenty landscapes) of the best member of the population after 20,000 evaluations is given for all nine algorithms. The results for K = 0 are not shown as all algorithms managed to reach the global optima on each of the 20 landscapes. Where this mean optima was reached before 20,000 evaluations, the time at which this happened (in 1000's of evaluations) is shown in braces.

In order to test the statistical significance of these results, the final best values of each of the twenty runs were noted and Student's t-test was applied to compare the performance of the adaptive algorithm with each of the others in turn. Shaded values in the table are those which are significantly worse than the adaptive algorithm at the 0.5% level. No algorithm is significantly better than APES at any value of K.

As can be seen, the performance of the APES algorithm progressively out-performs the SGA in it's various flavours as the complexity of the landscapes is increased. It is notable that the two fixed mutation rates which perform best in the SGA are those which take some account of the population and problem size.

Operators	*K = 2*	*K = 4*	*K = 8*	*K = 15*
Adaptive	723.1 (2.4)	752.7 (6.9)	778.45 (18.35)	774.75 (19.5)
1pt - D	722.65 (5.2)	744.5 (1.4)	746.5 (3.25)	715.4 (1.65)
1pt - G	722.9 (19.3)	750.3 (12.95)	758.95 (13.45)	730.8 (13.1)
1pt - O	723.1 (16.5)	753.6 (6.5)	775.4 (4.2)	750.55 (16.1)
1pt - S	723.1 (2.2)	754.55 (7.85)	775.6 (18.5)	767.55 (18.05)
Uni. - D	721.7 (1.5)	745.3 (3.25)	743.95 (48.5)	726.65 (19.5)
Uni. - G	722.75 (37.5)	751.85 (18.65)	753.5 (14.35)	730.8 (6.25)
Uni.- O	723.1 (1.35)	754.15 (14.75)	775.75 (5.25)	752.1 (11.1)
Uni. - S	723.1 (2.25)	755.95 (8.15)	778.40 (14.2)	768.35 (18.5)

Table 2: Mean Value of Best Individual after 20,000 evaluations

1pt refers to One Point, and Uni. is uniform crossover. The mutation rates are as denoted above.

The improved behaviour of APES on complex landscapes appears (from plots of performance vs. time) to be as a result of it's greater ability to escape from local optima. This is presumably as a result of the occasional creation of individuals with high (block) mutation rates and corresponding large "jumps" in search space from the parental gene pool.

At the outset it was suggested that the self-adaptive mechanism was designed to provide a robust algorithm which would perform reasonably well on a range of problem types rather than fine tuning it to do well on a particular sub-set of problems and suffering from poor performance on other subsets (as would be suggested by the "No Free Lunch" theorem [19]). The situation with K = 0 (a simple unimodal problem) might be expected to show up the deficiencies of the algorithm as a function optimiser (in terms of number of evaluations to reach the optimum) for the following reasons

1. Only one individual is incorporated into the population for every five evaluated, so on a simple problem there is a delay in taking advantage of good schema.

2 There is an additional overhead of learning suitable block sizes, and mutation rates for those blocks.

However this is not borne out by the results from the experiments, where the time at which the mean value (over all 20 landscapes) stopped increasing was noted. In this case all algorithms solved all 20 problems, so this is effectively the longest time taken to solve a 16 bit problem. The number of evaluations taken is shown in the Table below.

Unsurprisingly (given that this expression was formulated for the OneMax problem of which this is a generalisation) the SGA algorithms using a fixed rate of mutation O exhibited the least worst behaviour, and those using uniform crossover performed better than those using one-point crossover. More surprising is the result of the adaptive algorithm, which did not appear to suffer from the expected time-penalties of learning extra genes. The longest time taken by this algorithm to find the maxima on a 16 bit unimodal landscape was notably faster than that of the fixed mutation rate S, which was the only one which did not perform significantly worse on the more complex problems. It was also faster than rate D..

Adaptive		1200	
1pt - D	1750	Uni-D	1300
1pt - G	1200	Uni-G	1050
1pt - O	1100	Uni-O	1000
1pt - S	2100	Uni-S	1600

Table 3: Longest time to Solve 16 Bit Unimodal Problem

This can be explained by reference to the observed behaviour of the LEGO algorithm [4] on simple landscapes, where the linkages disappear, allowing all of the sub-problems (i.e. each locus) to be optimised independently. This behaviour was shown in [3] to be a much faster search strategy than traditional crossover operators. Thus it would appear that on landscapes of this type, the advantages of adapting to an optimal recombination strategy outweigh the disadvantages outlined above.

In order to test the validity of the performance metric, measurements of the on-line performance of the various algorithms were taken, again over 20,000 evaluations. Although these results are not shown for lack of space, they demonstrate exactly the same patterns as table 2, with the sole difference that for the lowest value of K = 0, the performance of the SGA with either crossover when used with a mutation rate S was significantly worse at the 5% level than that of the APES algorithm. This latter is a result of the longer time taken to reach the optimum by that algorithm as reflected in Table 3.

5. Conclusions

These results demonstrate the effectiveness of the algorithm as a function optimiser, and its ability to adapt to display different behaviours on different types of search space. Importantly it does not seem to suffer from a great "learning overhead" on simple problems as demonstrated by the competitive times to reach maxima on the unimodal problems, and on more complex functions it discovers significantly higher optima than the majority of other algorithms tested. This can attributed to the synergistic effects of simultaneously adapting both recombination strategy and mutation rates.

Whilst it might be reasonably argued that those other values are being used "out of context", they are frequently quoted as good "standard values" for general application, and will often be used by default. As has been shown the two most commonly quoted values (those of DeJong and Grefenstette) can yield poor performance on complex search spaces.

A second consideration is the use of the extended selection operator in the adaptive algorithm, This raises the possibility that the observed gains in performance on the more complex problems are due to this local search rather than the adaptive nature of the algorithm. The effect of adding local search to the SGA was investigated in [10], where it was shown that although it helped, the SGA-hybrid algorithm was outperformed by an algorithm similar to APES but using 1-point crossover. Noticably both the hybrid SGA algorithms and the "Adaptive Mutation-1-point Crossover" algorithm were slow to solve simple problems compared to a SGA, for the reasons noted above. Lack of space precludes the inclusions of the results of that algorithm or LEGO with fixed mutation rates, but as expected the former is much slower to solve simple problems and the latter is more easily trapped on sub-optima on complex landscapes.

At the outset it was stated that the original intention of this work was to find an algorithm which would perform "reasonably" well on all landscapes, and it was expected that on any given landscape one of the variants of the SGA used would outperform it. Surprisingly this has not proved to be the case, the performance being better than expected as a result of the synergy between the two types of self-adaptation. The next phase of work will require empirical testing on a wider variety of landscapes in attempt to identify problem types for which the algorithm is perhaps less suited. Current work is focused on analysis of the evolving behaviours, and means of representing these graphically.

6. References

1 Schaffer, J.D. & Morishima, A. (1987) *"An Adaptive Crossover Distribution Mechanism for Genetic Algorithms"* p36-40 in Grefenstette, J. (ed). "Proceedings of the Second International Conference on Genetic Algorithms". Lawrence Erlbaum.

2 Spears, W.M. (1995) *"Adapting Crossover in Evolutionary Algorithms"* in Proceedings of 4th Annual Conf. on Evolutionary Computing, ed Fogel, MIT Press.

3 Smith, J.E. & Fogarty, T.C. (1995) *"An Adaptive Poly-Parental Recombination Strategy"* in "Evolutionary Computing 2" ed. Fogarty,T.C. Springer Verlag.

4 Smith, J.E. & Fogarty, T.C. (1995) *"Recombination Strategy Adaptation via Evolution of Gene Linkage"*. pp 826-831 in "Proceedings of 1996 IEEE International Conference on Evolutionary Computing".

5 Syswerda G. (1989) *"Uniform Crossover in Genetic Algorithms"*. pp2-9 in "Proc. 3rd Int'n'l Conf. on Genetic Algorithms" ed. Schaffer, J.D. Morgan Kaufmann.

6 Syswerda, G. (1992) *"Simulated Crossover in Genetic Algorithms"* pp 239-255 in "Foundations of Genetic Algorithms" ed.Whitley 1992 Morgan Kaufmann

7 Bäck, T. (1991) *"Self Adaptation in Genetic Algorithms"*, pp 263-271 in Varela, F. & Bourgine, P. (eds.) "Towards a Practice of Autonomous Systems: Proceedings of the First European Conference on Artificial Life" MIT Press 1992.

8 Rechenberg, I. (1973) *"Evolutionsstrategie: Optimierung technischer Systeme nach Prinzipien der biologischen Evolution"* (Frommann-Holzboog Verlag, Stuttgart).

9 Schweffel, H-P. (1981) *"Numerical Optimization of Computer Models"* (Wiley, Chichester)

10 Smith, J.E. & Fogarty, T.C. (1995) *"Self Adaptation of Mutation Rates in a Steady State Genetic Algorithm"* pp 318 - 323 in "Proceedings of 1996 IEEE International Conference on Evolutionary Computing".

11 Kauffman, S.A. (1993) *"The Origins of Order"*, Oxford University Press.

12 Eiben, A.E., van Kemenade, C.H.M. & Kok, J.N. (1995) *"Orgy in the Computer: Multi Parent Recombination in Genetic Algorithms"* pp 934-945 in "Advances in Artificial Life: Proceedings of Third European Conference on Artificial Life", eds Moran, Moreno, Merelo & Chacon, Springer Verlag

13 Eiben, A.E., Raue, P.-E & Ruttkay, Zs *"Genetic Algorithms with Multi-parent Recombination"* pp78-87, "Parallel Problem Solving from Nature 3" eds. Davidor et al. Springer Verlag.

14 Bull L., & Fogarty T.C. 1994 *"An Evolutionary Strategy & Genetic Algorithm Hybrid: An Initial Implementation & First Results"* pp 95 - 102 in "Evolutionary Computing ed. T.C.Fogarty (Springer Verlag)

15 DeJong, K. (1975) *"An Analysis of the behaviour of a class of genetic adaptive systems"*. PhD. thesis, University of Michigan.

16 Grefenstette J.J. (1986). *"Optimisation of control parameters for genetic algorithms"*. pp 122-128, IEEE Transactions on Systems, Man & Cybernetics, SMC-16(1)

17 Schaffer J.D., Caruana R., Eshelman L.J., Das R. 1989 *"A Study of Control Parameters Affecting On-line Performance of Genetic Algorithms for Function Optimisation"*. in "Proceedings of 3rd International Conference on Genetic Algorithms", ed Schaffer (Morgan Kaufmann).

18 Mühlenbein, H. (1992) *"How Genetic Algorithms really work: 1 Mutation and hillclimbing"* pp 15-25. "Parallel Problem Solving from Nature 2" Männer & Manderick (eds) 1992, Elsevier, Amsterdam

19 Wolpert, D.H. & Macready, W.G. (1995) *"No Free Lunch Theorems for Search"* Tech. Report. SFI-TR-95-02-010, Santa Fe Institute, Santa Fe, NM. 1995

Obtaining Multiple Distinct Solutions with Genetic Algorithm Niching Methods

Alasdair Turner[1], David Corne[2], Graeme Ritchie[3] and Peter Ross[3]

[1] Department of Computer Science, University College London, Gower Street, London WC1E 6BT, UK. Email: A.Turner@cs.ucl.ac.uk
[2] Parallel, Emergent, and Distributed Architectures Laboratory, Department of Computer Science, University of Reading, Whiteknights, Reading RG6 2AY, UK. Email: D.W.Corne@reading.ac.uk
[3] Department of Artificial Intelligence, University of Edinburgh, 80 South Bridge, Edin. EH1 1HN, UK. Email:{peter,graeme}@aisb.ed.ac.uk

Abstract. This paper proposes a new technique for improving the number of usefully distinct solutions produced by a Genetic Algorithm (GA) when applied to multimodal problems. The *tribes* method builds on the spatial selection methods proposed by Collins and Jefferson [1]. We compare the technique with two well-known niching methods (crowding and sharing), spatial selection alone, and a simple control GA method, in the domain of simple timetabling problems. We demonstrate that the tribes technique can greatly improve the efficiency with which a GA can obtain multiple distinct solutions to a problem.

1 Introduction

Many methods have been developed to promote and prolong population diversity in Genetic Algorithms (GAs), many forming the basis of much continuing development, such as crowding [5], sharing [6], and local mating [1, 3]. Apart from an ability to improve solution quality, with in some cases little or no extra computational cost [3], such methods can also be viewed as advancing the ability of a GA to produce multiple distinct solutions in a single run. This is a useful but relatively-little studied property of a GA. In many application areas, such as scheduling or design, multiple different solutions to the same problem can form an important 'failsafe' resource. There is also evidence to suggest that the ability of an appropriately configured GA to naturally provide several different solutions in a single run can pull the GA back into favour in cases where simulated annealing and/or hillclimbing may otherwise seem better in terms of solution quality alone [9].

Here, we concentrate on a small collection of diversity-enhancement methods and examine them in the 'multiple distinct solutions' context, using simple timetabling problems as the test application area. The timetabling problem arena has the advantage of simplicity (we are able to construct artificial timetabling problems with known optima) and practicality.

The remainder of the paper is set out as follows. Section 2 reviews the small set of diversity-enhancement methods examined in the study, and describes the proposed 'tribes' method. Section 3 then describes the performance measures tailored towards examining relative quality in a 'multiple distinct solutions' context. Details of test problems and experimental setups are dealt with in section 4, and main results appear in section 5. We round off the paper with a summary in section 6.

2 Niching Methods

Paraphrasing Davidor [3], the chief motivation behind niching methods is to have a mechanism which controls and prevents an unbalanced proliferation of genotypes; such can be achieved via explicit testing of genotype diversity, but this would be computationally prohibitive. In the following we briefly review three well-known and one proposed method which differently aim to prevent this unbalanced proliferation of genotypes.

Crowding In crowding [5], a child chromosome replaces a member of the population with a similar genotype. This prevents undue domination of the population with similar genotypes, thus indirectly promoting sustained niche development. De Jong's scheme uses a crowding factor variable $CF(1 < CF < N$, where N is population size) which controls how keen the method is to ensure replacing highly similar current genotypes with new ones. A new child is compared to CF chromosomes chosen at random , and the most similar from this set to the new child is the one which the child replaces.

Sharing Sharing is intended to share the benefits of a particular facet of an individual (for example, a particular set of genes) among all the individuals in the population sharing that facet. This reduces the possibility that one set of individuals with a certain characteristic will dominate the whole population. Goldberg and Richardson [6] propose a sharing function to work out the degree to which individuals in the population must share their fitness. The shared fitness f' of an individual x_i is given by:

$$f'(x_i) = \frac{f(x_i)}{\sum_{j=1}^{N} Sh(x_i, x_j)} \tag{1}$$

Where N is population size, and the sharing function, which determines the amount of niche overlap between two individuals x_i and x_j, is given by:

$$Sh(x_i, x_j) = \begin{cases} 1 - \left(\frac{d_x(x_i,x_j)}{\sigma_{share}}\right)^{\alpha} & \text{if } d_x(x_i, x_j) < \sigma_{share} \\ 0 & \text{otherwise} \end{cases} \tag{2}$$

The function $d_x(x_i, x_j)$ is some measure of niche separation of the two individuals; this might be Hamming distance in the case of genotype sharing. The exponent α allows a non-linear sharing relationship.

Spatial Selection Following early work on deme-structures in genetic algorithms by Gorges-Schleuter [7], Collins and Jefferson [1] and Davidor [3] propose similar spatial selection methods which emulate some of the tenets of Wright's shifting balance theory of evolution [11]. The structure of Wright's model varies from *panmictic* islands (where parents in a subpopulation may be chosen from anywhere within the island), to islands joined by stepping stones (migration between subpopulations), to a state where the borders between subpopulations, or *demes*, have been eroded so far that they are only separated by a physical distance.

In Collins & Jefferson style 'local mating' method, chromosomes are placed on a notional n-dimensional grid. Parents are chosen by starting at a random location L on the grid and each taking a random walk of length R from L. The fittest chromosome found on a random walk is chosen as a parent. The child replaces the current occupant of L. We use a steady-state implementation of this method, in which it is useful to add the restriction that the child should be at least as fit as the chromosome it replaces.

Tribes Though better than panmictic GAs in this respect, spatial selection methods still suffer from successful genotypes rapidly dominating the whole spatial selection grid [10], destroying nascent demes as they advance. This prevents spatial selection from being as successful as it might be in finding multiple distinct solutions (see our results, in section 5).

In an attempt to allow multiple distinct solutions to be more effectively produced via spatially-oriented selection, without undue extra computational expense, we propose a simple strategy which we call 'tribes'. Like a variety of other methods, 'tribes' strives to maintain demes in the population. The difference with tribes (as is the difference among deme maintenance methods in general) is the way in which this is done. The 'tribes' method forms demes into rather racist 'tribes', who are collectively very choosy about who is allowed to join the tribe: the essential point is that a new chromosome which is a candidate for being inserted into the population must be similar to the chromosomes already present in the area — if not, the new chromosome is rejected without evaluation. The tribes hence protect themselves by rejecting children alien to themselves much as a mother rejects a mutant child, and are given time to converge to separate solutions. In other respects, the tribes method is identical to local mating [1].

A jarring feature of the tribes method as described is the rejection of 'alien' children *without evaluation*. This may of course lead to the disappearance of good, or even optimal solutions. On the other hand, this strategy has great benefits in terms of speed. We justify this approach partly with appeal to the speed issue, and also the notion that 'lost' improvements will often reappear and be accepted later. Indeed, since our interest is more in finding *many usefully distinct* solutions than in finding *a single best* solution, we can arguably be more relaxed about failing to evaluate some candidates. Most importantly though, the idea of *rejection without evaluation* is misleadingly emotive. It is actually a quick implementational treatment of the essentially equivalent idea of *operator direction*. That is, we could instead arrange that mutation was guaranteed to produce children acceptable in their surroundings. Later extensions to the method now under investigation will remove this idea entirely, however, by allowing new children to migrate to a maximally 'accepting' area of the population.

Some observations concerning the deme-interaction in spatially oriented local mating will help illustrate the extra 'protection' that the tribes method affords. Consider demes A and B, which share a border in a spatially-structured population, as illustrated in figure 1.

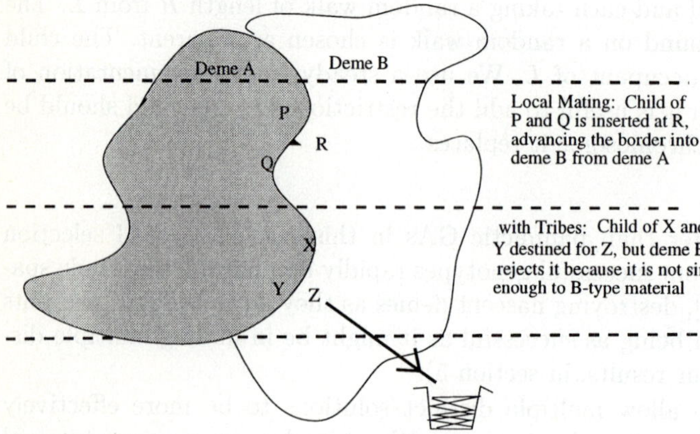

Fig. 1. Simple illustration of Tribes 'protection'

If A is a little ahead in terms of fitness, it may easily overcome B by virtue of grid cells near the border, but within B, such as R or Z in the figure, being replaced by children yielded from random walks which tended to end up in A. Eg: local mating may place a child of parents from P and Q (in deme A) into grid cell R in deme B. With tribes, however, such invaders from A's gene-pool will face a test of kinship with deme B's material before it is allowed in. Eg: parents from X and Y in deme A may yield a child which attempts to be inserted at Z in deme B, however the tribes method may reject this child, as illustrated in figure 1 if it is not similar enough to local genetic material. Hence B manages to stave off invasions more effectively than local mating alone.

We implemented a version of tribes using (genotypic) Hamming distance, measured between the current occupant on a spatial selection grid and the child to be inserted. If the distance is above a cut-off distance d_c, then the child is rejected without evaluation. A revised steady-state genetic algorithm can be written in pseudo code as follows:

```
BEGIN LOOP
    SELECT location; SELECT parents FROM NEAR location
    CROSSOVER parents TO FORM child
    IF d_H(child, chromosome at location) > d_c THEN
        REJECT child
    ELSE
        EVALUATE child TO GIVE fitness(child)
        IF fitness(child) > fitness(chromosome at location) THEN
            INSERT child IN PLACE OF chromosome at location
        END IF
    END IF
END LOOP
```

The cut-off distance d_c used in later experiments is indicated in the appropriate figures (ie: figures 2 and 3). The initial population is random; ie: there is no preprocessing or initialisation of demes.

3 Performance criteria

We use two performance criteria: a modified measure of the number of solutions found (the *effective trials*) and the effective trials per second of CPU time.

Effective Trials Imagine a method $M1$ which always tends to find one solution to a problem, and a method $M2$ which, in the same amount of time, tends to find two different solutions. Naively, we may suppose that $M2$ is 'twice as good' as $M1$ in some sense, since $M2$ seems equivalent to running $M1$ twice. The real difference is somewhat greater than that, however, since two independent runs of $M1$ are likely, half the time, to yield the same solution. The *effective trials* metric takes this into account, and is applicable when the number of solutions to the problem is known. It considers the difficulty of drawing a new solution from a bag of solutions with replacement. If a method were to find p distinct solutions on a single run, we call the number of runs it would take drawing one solution at a time to find p distinct solutions the effective number of trials. For a bag of q solutions, the expected number of draws (or trials) of solutions from the bag to find p distinct solutions one at a time with replacement is [10]:

$$\text{Expected number of trials} = q \sum_{i=q-p+1}^{q} \frac{1}{i} \tag{3}$$

We use a continuous approximation to this sum for our definition of effective trials [10]:

$$q \sum_{i=q-p+1}^{q} \frac{1}{i} \approx q \int_{q-p}^{q} \frac{1/x + 1/(x+1)}{2} dx = \left[q \ln \sqrt{x^2 + x} \right]_{q-p}^{q} \tag{4}$$

Hence we define effective trials, t_{eff}, for a method which finds on average p solutions on a single run as:

$$t_{eff} \equiv \left[q \ln \sqrt{x^2 + x}\right]_{q-p}^{q} \tag{5}$$

As with similar metrics, such as the chi-square-like diversity suggested by Deb and Goldberg [4], we assume that the number of solutions is known and that they are evenly distributed across the space. This is not, of course, directly applicable to real problems, in which we usually do not know the number of optima, and may not even have a good estimate. This measure suffices, however, in the context of comparative experiments on problems where q is known. The idea is that methods achieving high effective trials on such cases will do similarly well on real problems. In addition, again in common with chi-square-like diversity, we must cater for the no-solution case. We note that in our continuous definition, t_{eff} tends to zero in the limit as p tends to zero. This allows useful application of effective trials to a GA with a 'no solution' possible outcome by simply assigning those runs a t_{eff} of zero.

Efficiency Most studies do not consider the efficiency with which solutions are found using niching methods. Given the pragmatic nature of our work, relating niching methods to timetabling problems, we felt the overriding metric should be the speed with which solutions are produced.

We hence measure the *peak* efficiency with which the methods found solutions. We let the GA run until there is no longer an improvement in the average fitness of the population for an arbitrary number of generations (we typically chose values much higher than necessary to find the peak efficiency). We then measured the peak number of effective trials per second of CPU time during this period.

4 Experiments

We applied sharing, crowding, spatial selection and tribes to a test set of four fairly simple timetabling problems, using a 'direct' timetabling problem representation [2] where each gene represents an event and its allele represents the timeslot assigned to the event. Fitness depends on *edge constraints* which specify which events must not overlap in time, and also a few precedence constraints, specifying that certain events must occur before others. Four test problems were devised, consisting of 20 events to fit into 5 timeslots, with known different numbers of solutions. We refer to these later as: `tt10` (10 solutions), `tt30` (30 solutions), `tt60` (60 solutions), and `tt120` (120 solutions).

A good basic GA configuration was chosen as a template: steady-state reproduction with rank based selection (where applicable) and uniform crossover. In addition, a mutation rate of $1/\ell$ (chromosome length ℓ) was applied. The control GA used rank-based selection, steady-state reproduction, and new chromosomes replaced the current least-fit (if the new one was better or equal to it) in the population. The methods were tested over a range of population sizes. Starting with a population of 49 (to allow easy translation to spatial selection on a 7×7 grid), we experimented on population sizes increasing by a factor of roughly two, giving population sizes of 49, 100, 225 and 400.

For each niching method a single parameter was varied across a range of values. Crowding factors between 2 and 5 were used, according to the empirical observations of De Jong [5, in [3]]. We used genotype sharing, there being no way of assessing overlap of phenotypes; we extended Deb and Goldberg's analysis of theoretical values of σ_{share} [4] to the n-allele case [10] to give an appropriate range of σ_{share} (in normalised units, from 0.4 to 0.8). Spatial selection random walk paths were chosen as a ratio of population size, roughly according to the random walk lengths used by Collins and Jefferson [1]. Fairly arbitrary values of the cut-off distance d_c were used for tribes: again, from 0.4 to 0.8 in normalised Hamming distance units.

5 Results

Full results appear in [10]. We present here a summary of the main results, illustrated with an effective trials graph for problem `tt120`, and an efficiency graph (effective trials per second) for problem `tt10`

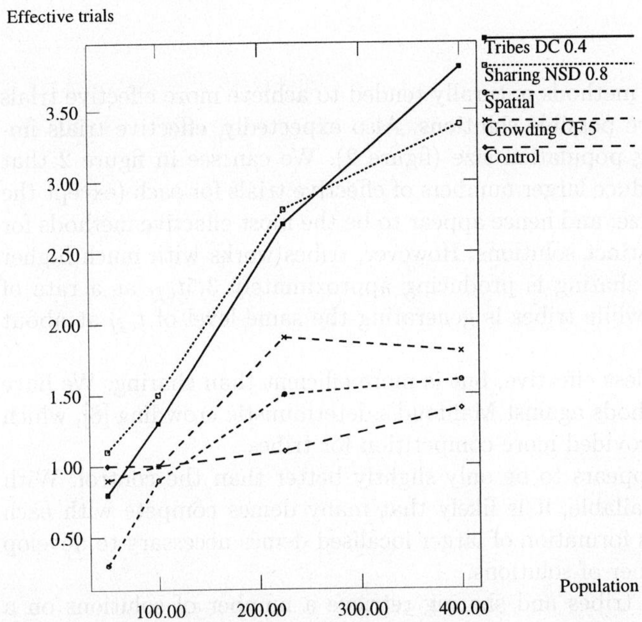

Fig. 2. Effective trials on the `tt120` problem

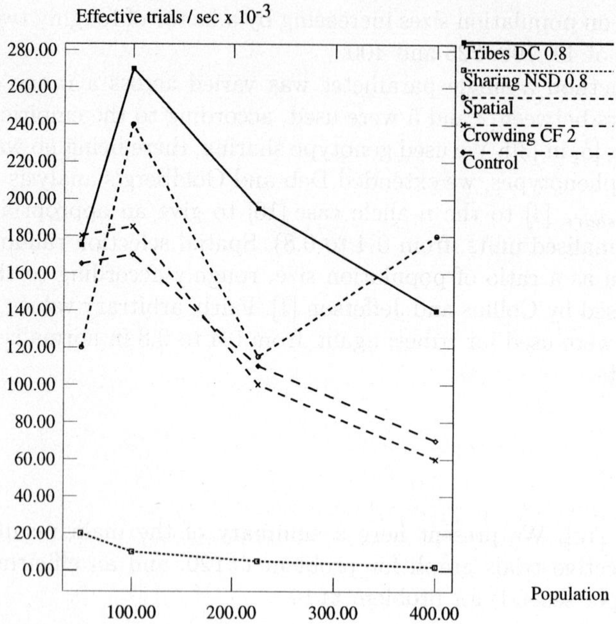

Fig. 3. Effective trials per second on the `tt10` problem

Many Solutions All methods naturally tended to achieve more effective trials on problems with more possible solutions. Also expectedly, effective trials improved with increasing population size (figure 2). We can see in figure 2 that sharing and tribes produce larger numbers of effective trials for each (except the smallest) population size; and hence appear to be the most effective methods for producing multiple distinct solutions. However, tribes works with much higher efficiency: in figure 2, sharing is producing approximately $3.5t_{eff}$ at a rate of less than $0.01t_{eff}s^{-1}$, while tribes is generating the same level of t_{eff} at about $0.14t_{eff}s^{-1}$.

Crowding appears less effective, but is more efficient than sharing. We have not yet tested the methods against Mahfoud's deterministic crowding [8], which perhaps would have provided more competition for tribes.

Spatial selection appears to be only slightly better than the control. With many solutions are available, it is likely that many demes compete with each other and this disrupts formation of larger localised demes necessary to develop into a reasonable number of solutions.

However, although tribes and sharing retrieve a number of solutions on a single run, neither are very *efficient* at finding solutions compared with the control on `tt120`. The control works at almost $0.30t_{eff}s^{-1}$ (double that of tribes)

with a population of 49. Ie: with many possible solutions, or perhaps on easier problems (not enough work has been done to distinguish between them), it seems better to iterate a simple GA than to employ a sophisticated niching method.

Few Solutions Figure 3 shows the efficiency of niching methods on the `tt10` problem. The methods are shown at their peak efficiency, rather than the peak t_{eff}, where they are producing an average of only 1 to 1.5 solutions per run. All work more efficiently, perhaps with the exception of sharing, when set to produce fewer solutions.

Both spatial selection and tribes perform well here, there being less conflict of interest between the smaller number of competing demes. Tribes works harder at allowing demes to converge independently, which seems consequently to reward it with the best efficiency result.

Crowding and the control method are very similar in efficiency. This is because we have chosen the peak efficiency for crowding, with a crowding factor of 2, which is quite close to a simple GA anyway. Higher crowding factors yield better effective-trials scores, but at expensive extra cost in convergence time, hence compromising efficiency.

Sharing suffers from a well-known high computational overhead as well as long converge time needs, and hence generally appears to be the least efficient method.

6 Summary

Our main findings are that all of the non-control methods are indeed better at producing many distinct solutions in a single run than the control GA. However, on the large number of solutions example, efficiency considerations suggest that many runs with a simple GA may be more effective in the long run at generating high effective trials. It remains true, of course, that solution quality considerations on particularly hard problems would mean that the 'better' non-control GAs are preferable. But if solutions are not very difficult to obtain, and there are very many, then an iterated simple GA (or perhaps a hillclimber) may be better than a more sophisticated GA. When there are fewer solutions to obtain, however, certain non-control methods are clearly more efficient at finding them. Sharing fares worst in this area, while crowding competes with the control GA only when the crowding factor is very small, but tribes seems the most effective method for most population sizes.

Overall, if generating multiple distinct solutions is the main measure of interest in a particular application, our results suggest that a simple GA is the best approach when the landscape is expected to contain very many solutions to find, since although 'enhanced-diversity' methods can obtain more effective trials in a single run, the extra convergence time needed means that they do so at lower overall efficiency. If there are only expected to be a handful of solutions, however, then certain enhanced-diversity methods, in particular the tribes method, become more effective than a simple GA.

Extrapolating these findings outwards from the simple test problems studied here is bound to be generally unsafe without much more study in connection with the interactions between many factors. Eg: in many cases a 'sharing' GA will be able to find much better solutions than a 'simple' GA, and hence efficiency considerations may be outweighed by solution quality.

The performance of the simple 'tribes' method is however encouraging, suggesting that methods based on the general idea will be useful in applications where multiple distinct solutions are required. In particular, several enhancements to the method can be imagined, such as the 'tribe-seeking' idea mentioned earlier, which may further improve its effectiveness.

References

1. Collins, R. J., Jefferson, D. R.: Selection in massively parallel genetic algorithms. Proc. 4th International Conference on Genetic Algorithms. Morgan Kaufmann (1991)
2. Corne, D., Fang, H.-L., Mellish, C.: Solving the modular exam scheduling problem with genetic algorithms. Proc. 6th Int'l. Conf. in Industrial & Engineering Applications of Artificial Intelligence & Expert Systems. Gordon & Breach Science Publishers (1993)
3. Davidor, Y.: A naturally occurring niche & species phenomenon: the model and first results. Proc. 4th International Conference on Genetic Algorithms. Morgan Kaufmann (1991)
4. Deb, K., Goldberg, D. E.: An investigation of niche and species formation in genetic function optimisation. Proc. 3rd International Conference on Genetic Algorithms. Morgan Kaufmann (1989)
5. De Jong, K. A.: An Analysis of the Behavior of a Class of Genetic Adaptive Systems. Dissertation Abstracts International 36(10), 5140B (University Microfilms No. 76-9381). PhD thesis, U. of Michigan, Ann Arbor (1975)
6. Goldberg, D. E., Richardson J. J., Genetic algorithms with sharing for multimodal function optimization. Proc. 2nd International Conference on Genetic Algorithms. Lawrence Erlbaum Publishers (1987)
7. Gorges-Schleuter, M., Explicit Parallelism of Genetic Algorithms through Population Structures. Parallel Problem Solving from Nature. Springer-Verlag, pp 150–159 (1990)
8. Mahfoud, S. W.: Crowding and preselection revisited. Männer R., Manderick B. (eds): Parallel Problem Solving from Nature 2. Elsevier (1992)
9. Ross, P., Corne D.: Comparing Genetic Algorithms, Simulated Annealing, and Stochastic Hillclimbing on Timetabling Problems. Evolutionary Computing: AISB Workshop, Sheffield 1995, Selected Papers, Springer-Verlag, T. Fogarty (ed), Springer Verlag (1995).
10. Turner, P. A.: Genetic Algorithms and Multiple Distinct Solutions. Unpublished MSc thesis, U. of Edinburgh (1994), Postscript version available via http://boom.cs.ucl.ac.uk/staff/A.Turner/pubs .
11. Wright, S., Evolution and the Genetics of Population, Volume 2: The Theory of Gene Frequencies. U. of Chicago Press (1969)

Cost Based Operator Rate Adaptation: An Investigation

Andrew Tuson and Peter Ross

Department of Artificial Intelligence, University of Edinburgh
80 South Bridge, Edinburgh EH1 1HN, U.K.
{andrewt,peter}@aisb.ed.ac.uk
Tel: +44 (0)131 650 2717

Abstract. In the vast majority of genetic algorithm implementations, the operator probabilities are fixed throughout a given run. However, it may be useful to adjust these probabilities during the run, according to the ability of the operators to produce children of increased fitness. Cost Based Operator Rate Adaptation (COBRA) periodically re-ranks operator probabilities according to a measure of operator performance. The effect upon genetic algorithm performance of COBRA upon both well-studied theoretical and practical problems is examined.

1 Introduction

It has long been acknowledged that the choice of operator probabilities have a significant impact upon GA performance. However, finding a good choice is somewhat of a black art. The appropriate choice depends upon the other GA components, such as the population model, the problem to be solved, its representation, and the operators used.

The above also ignores the case for varying operator probabilities during the course of a GA run. Davis [3] advocates the use of a time-varying schedule of operator probabilities.

The problem lies in knowing how to vary — this is harder that finding a good set of static operator probabilities. It may be advantageous, therefore, to employ a method that adjusts the operator probabilities according to a measure of the performance of each of the operators.

This paper investigates one such approach: COBRA (COst Based operator Rate Adaptation) [1], a method that was originally devised for adapting operator probabilities in timetabling problems.

2 What is COBRA?

First, some terminology will be described. Each operator available to the GA has a probability of being fired — an *operator probability.* This study makes a distinction between this and any parameters associated with a given operator (an *operator parameter*). For example, a GA could use uniform crossover 70% (operator probability) of the time, along with mutation 30% of the time, with the mutation operator possessing a bitwise mutation rate of 0.02 (operator parameter). This study concerns itself only with the adaptation of operator probabilities.

COBRA is a member of the group of 'learning-rule' adaptation methods, such as the techniques devised by Davis [2], and Julstrom [7]. This approach explicitly collects information on operator performance and uses this to adjust the operator probabilities. All of these methods are ad hoc in nature, and COBRA is no exception — the idea behind all of these techniques is to provide an operator adaptation mechanism that works in practice.

COBRA is implemented as follows. Given k operators $o_1, ..., o_k$, let $b_i(t)$ be the *benefit*, $c_i(t)$ the *cost* (the amount of computational effort to evaluate a child), and $p_i(t)$ the probability of a given operator, i at time t. We then apply the following algorithm:

1. The user decides on a set of initial probabilities p_i.
2. When a child is produced, $b_i(t)$ is updated.
3. After G (the gap between operator probability readjustments) evaluations, rank the operators according their values of b_i/c_i, and assign the operators their new probabilities according to their rank (i.e. the highest probability to the operator with the highest value of b_i/c_i).
4. Repeat step 2 every G evaluations.

This study used *operator productivity* as the measure of benefit. This is defined as the average increase in fitness when a child was produced that was fitter than its parents (i.e. if the child is worse than the parent, then the productivity is zero) over a set interval (in this case all operations since the last probability re-ranking).

The variables in the adaptation method come from two sources: firstly the gap between operator probability readjustments G, and secondly the initial operator probabilities provided by the user. The effect that these variables have upon the genetic algorithm will be investigated.

3 The Test Problems

In order to study the effectiveness (or otherwise) of adaptation using COBRA, a set of test problems need to be chosen. The first member of the test suite is a hard scheduling/operations research problem. The other members have been selected on account of their theoretical familiarity. Each will be briefly described in turn.

- **Flowshop Sequencing**. A Taillard [11] benchmark problem: 20 jobs and 20 machines with RNG seed 47934044.
- **Max Ones** of length 100.
- **Order-3 Deceptive** [5] of length 30.
- **Royal Road** (R1) [4] of length 64.
- **Long Path** [6] of length 29.

The representation used for the flowshop sequencing problem is a permutation of the jobs to be placed into the flowline, numbered 1 to n. The operators used were 'Modified PMX' crossover [8], and shift mutation [9].

The operators used for the binary-coded problems were: binary mutation with a bitwise mutation probability of $1/l$ (where l is the length of the string) and uniform crossover.

4 The Investigation

A full description how the genetic algorithm used was implemented is given in [12]. Two population models were used as part of this study, in order to see if this had any effect upon the success (or otherwise) of COBRA. The first population model used was ***steady-state*** reproduction with a ***kill-worst*** replacement policy; the second model was *generational* replacement with *elitism*, keeping the single best chromosome.

A large number of experiments were performed in this study. A summary of the results are given here, and the interested reader is directed to [12] for full results.

Two measures of performance were used: the quality of solution obtained after 10,000 evaluations, and the number of evaluations after which improvements in solution quality were no longer obtained (or 10,000 evaluations — whichever is smaller). This number of evaluations was chosen as preliminary investigations showed that the GA population had converged long before then.

Samples of 50 GA runs were taken, for each of the two population models, with a population size of 100 and a rank-based selection pressure of 1.5. Where differences in performance are reported to be significant, a t-test was applied in order to ascertain if this was the case.

4.1 The GA With Fixed Operator Settings

The effect of varying crossover probability on a genetic algorithm with fixed operator probabilities was investigated. An exhaustive search was made of the operator probabilities: a GA was run for crossover probabilities 0.05 to 0.95 with steps of 0.05 (mutation was applied otherwise). This will provide a benchmark against which the performance of a GA using COBRA will be compared, and measure how sensitive this operator setting is to GA performance. This will give some indication of how hard the GA is to tune, and will allow later comparison of tuning difficulty when co-evolution is used.

The operator probabilities found to be suitable for each problem/population model are given in Table 1. For each entry, the standard deviation is given in parentheses. Note that for the flowshop sequencing problem the aim is to *minimise* the makespan (fitness).

When the trends in performance against crossover probability are examined, some general patterns were observed (reflected somewhat in Table 1). The choice of operator probabilities appear to depend upon the problem to be solved, the

	Generational GA			Steady-State GA		
Problem	Xover	Fitness	Evaluations	Xover	Fitness	Evaluations
Flowshop	0.65	2444 (76)	8236 (1285)	0.35	2389 (69)	5064 (1616)
Max Ones	0.80	99.96 (0.20)	7714 (1025)	0.80	100.00 (0.00)	2172 (702)
Deceptive	0.05	289.68 (2.41)	5960 (1965)	0.20	289.12 (3.08)	3506 (2523)
Royal Road	0.35	35.52 (6.02)	7804 (1390)	0.95	40.64 (7.65)	3786 (1741)
Long Path	0.55	48686 (3441)	5370 (2138)	0.20	47312 (4765)	5129 (4088)

Table 1. The Mean Performance of the Standard GA Used To Compare COBRA

population model (interestingly, the steady-state GA gave consistently better performance), and the performance criterion being used. The final point is illustrated by the deceptive problem: a low crossover probability gives high quality results, a high crossover probability exchanges solution quality for a higher speed of search.

4.2 The Effect of Varying The Gap Between Probability Re-Rankings

The previous study [1] did not investigate the effect of varying G. This investigation examined a range of values of G (from 200 to 2000 evaluations in steps of 200). The mean performance (in terms of fitness and speed) for each of these problems is given in Tables 2 and 3.

	Re-Ranking Interval (G)									
Steady-State	200	400	600	800	1000	1200	1400	1600	1800	2000
Flowshop	2398	2397	2398	2401	2399	2397	2398	2392	2394	2395
Max Ones	100.00	100.00	100.00	100.00	100.00	100.00	100.00	100.00	100.00	100.00
Deceptive	287.72	287.52	287.44	288.04	287.96	287.92	288.08	288.32	288.40	288.44
Royal Road	40.00	39.36	40.80	40.48	40.32	40.48	40.80	40.64	40.96	40.64
Long Path	45675	43613	40568	41867	44704	44117	42998	43320	42055	42770
Generational	200	400	600	800	1000	1200	1400	1600	1800	2000
Flowshop	2445	2444	2444	2444	2444	2444	2444	2444	2444	2444
Max Ones	99.96	99.96	99.96	99.96	99.96	99.96	99.96	99.96	99.96	99.96
Deceptive	285.44	285.16	286.08	286.24	286.24	286.56	286.84	286.88	287.24	287.44
Royal Road	32.80	33.60	34.08	34.08	33.44	33.28	32.96	33.92	33.60	35.04
Long Path	47459	47843	48686	47887	47950	47696	48195	48687	48687	48687

Table 2. Mean Fitness Against Re-Ranking Interval (G)

	Re-Ranking Interval (*G*)									
Steady-State	200	400	600	800	1000	1200	1400	1600	1800	2000
Flowshop	5767	5979	5437	6081	5271	5862	5100	5993	5597	5470
Max Ones	2118	2139	2172	2172	2172	2172	2172	2172	2172	2172
Deceptive	2255	2463	2025	2334	2323	2119	2233	2220	2361	2349
Royal Road	3888	3741	3922	3910	4012	3845	3826	3800	3920	3830
Long Path	5120	6378	6326	6958	5575	5044	5305	5567	5555	5260
Generational	200	400	600	800	1000	1200	1400	1600	1800	2000
Flowshop	8098	8236	8236	8236	8236	8236	8236	8236	8236	8236
Max Ones	7714	7714	7714	7714	7714	7714	7714	7714	7714	7714
Deceptive	4322	4422	4194	4140	4244	4314	4160	4534	4204	4488
Royal Road	7664	7580	7728	7446	7616	7152	7026	7670	7410	7810
Long Path	5306	5344	5534	5418	5516	5536	5632	5434	5312	5280

Table 3. Mean Evaluations Reqd. With Re-Ranking Interval (G)

For three of the problems considered here, the choice of G had no significant effect upon GA performance. The exceptions were the deceptive and long path problems.

To interpret these results it is necessary for us to know what COBRA is doing during the course of a GA run. Therefore plots of the *operator productivities* were then obtained for a conventional GA with crossover probability 0.5, to see which operator was providing the most improvements at a given stage of a GA run. The plots shown in Figures 1 and 2 tend to be typical for the problems considered here — crossover is consistently the more productive operator.

In the case of the deceptive problem, a trade-off was observed — low values of G corresponding to an increased speed of search, although at the expense of solution quality: high values of G favouring a higher quality of solution. The reason for this behaviour is closely linked to the effect of the crossover probability for the static GA — high crossover probabilities lead the GA to the deceptive optimum more quickly, leading to a faster speed of search whilst sacrificing quality. As crossover was consistently the more productive operator the GA will assume a high crossover probability. For low G this will occur earlier in a GA run and favour speed over quality.

For the long path problem, behaviour varied according to the population model used. When a generational model was used, solution quality was affected, rising with increased G. Presumably the larger samples prevent spurious reranking due to noise in the operator productivity information.

The trends observed with a steady-state GA were quite the opposite: solution quality was degraded when compared to a conventional GA, declining further with increasing G. This is a result of crossover being the more productive operator, most of the time (Figure 2). Unfortunately the preferred crossover probability is low (0.2). Therefore COBRA will mostly adopt a high crossover probability with the effect of degrading solution quality. However, when G is

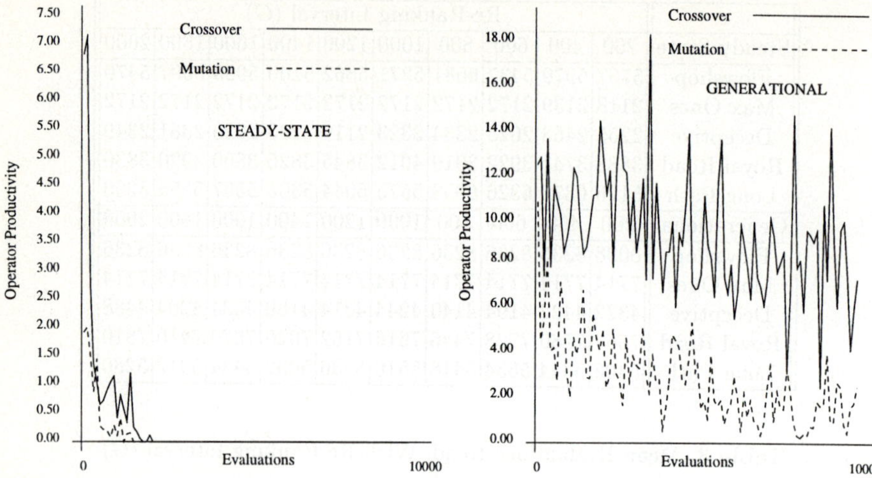

Fig. 1. Operator Productivities For The Deceptive Problem

small, there is a greater chance that 'spurious' re-rankings to a lower (i.e. better) crossover probability will occur which reduces the adverse effect of COBRA somewhat.

4.3 The Effect of Varying The Initial Operator Probabilities

The relationship between the performance of COBRA and the initial crossover probability was investigated. For all problems, the performance of crossover probabilities from 0.05 to 0.95 (in steps of 0.05 with the exception of 0.5) was examined. Table 4 displays the range of performance attained, for all problems and population models, with and without the use of COBRA. It was apparent, in most cases, that COBRA was less sensitive to the initial crossover probability, than a conventional GA. COBRA appears to mitigate the effect of bad choices somewhat.

But does this affect performance? The best performance attainable appears, in most cases, to be unaffected by COBRA. The exceptions are: the deceptive problem (for both population models), and the long path problem.

In the case of the deceptive problem, the best solution quality attained is reduced, but with a corresponding increase in speed. This trade off was found to be controllable by the initial crossover probability. The reason for this is similar to the reason for the trends for G — the higher productivity of crossover means that a high crossover probability is adopted, which favours speed of search at the expense of quality.

The results for the long path problem, however, are disappointing. When a steady-state model was used, solution quality was significantly degraded. The

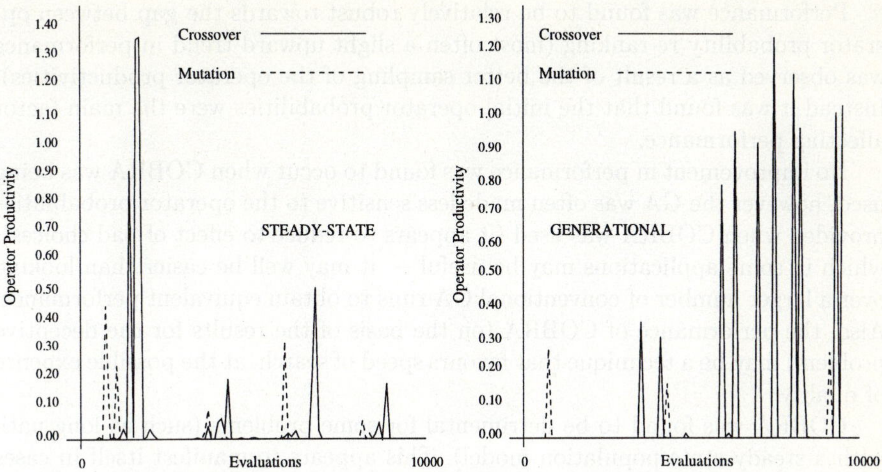

Fig. 2. Operator Productivities For The Long Path Problem

Problem	Generational GA: Static GA	Generational GA: GA w/COBRA	Steady-State GA: Static GA	Steady-State GA: GA w/COBRA
Flowshop: Fitness	2441-2453	2438-2454	2387-2420	2396-2411
Max Ones: Fitness	93.38-99.96	98.36-99.96	99.90-100.00	99.84-100.00
Deceptive: Fitness	284.20-289.68	284.92-288.04	286.28-289.28	286.28-288.48
Royal Road: Fitness	22.72-35.52	25.28-35.84	25.76-40.64	26.88-40.32
Long Path: Fitness	35824-48687	41407-49177	28287-48025	40955-44723
Flowshop: Evals	7714-8914	7824-8914	5064-7717	5045-6641
Max Ones: Evals	7714-9228	7714-8486	2172-5645	2172-6526
Deceptive: Evals	4484-6212	4244-6412	2192-4210	1979-3409
Royal Road: Evals	5626-7804	5596-7620	2876-3952	2607-4012
Long Path: Evals	3976-7848	4286-5702	5129-6736	5575-7437

Table 4. GA Performance With Crossover Probabilities In The Range 0.05-0.95

reason for this is, as for the trend in G, largely due to the predominantly higher crossover productivity (Figure 2). This results in COBRA adopting a high crossover probability, causing a reduction in solution quality.

5 Conclusions

First, it was established that, by examining the effect of the crossover probability on a conventional GA, that the choice of crossover probability depends upon the problem to be solved, the population model, and the performance measure used.

Performance was found to be relatively robust towards the gap between operator probability re-ranking (most often a slight upward trend in performance was observed as a result of the better sampling of the operator productivities). Instead it was found that the initial operator probabilities were the main factor affecting performance.

No improvement in performance was found to occur when COBRA was being used, however the GA was often made less sensitive to the operator probabilities provided when COBRA was used (it appears to reduce to effect of bad choices), which in some applications may be useful — it may well be easier than looking over a larger number of conventional GA runs to obtain equivalent performance. Also, the performance of COBRA (on the basis of the results for the deceptive problem) may be a technique that favours speed of search, at the possible expense of quality.

COBRA was found to be detrimental for some problems (such as long path with a steady-state population model). This appears to manifest itself in cases where the productivity of an operator is high (thus COBRA assigns it a high probability), but the preferred probability of the operator is low. In these cases COBRA should not be used.

This suggests that operator productivity is a poor basis with which to assign operator probabilities for a static GA, and possibly misleading for COBRA. Operator productivity is but one factor to consider; others include the maintenance of diversity lost by processes such as drift and premature convergence by the mutation operator.

Fortunately, one class of problems are known to exhibit improved performance when COBRA is used: timetabling problems. In addition, recent work [10] has shed some light upon what makes timetabling problems easy or hard for a genetic algorithm. Therefore it would be advantageous to use timetabling problems as a test-bed by taking examples for which COBRA was found to be effective and modifying them to see what effect it has.

To summarise, COBRA has promise as a means to remove some of the parameter tuning that can bedevil GA applications. But like many other such devices, there is the danger of being misled into a poor choice of operator probabilities by some problems.

6 Acknowledgements

Thanks to Dave Corne for his advice on COBRA. Thanks also to the Engineering and Physical Sciences Research Council for their support of Andrew Tuson via a research studentship with reference 95306458.

References

1. D. Corne, P. Ross, and H.-L. Fang. GA Research Note 7: Fast Practical Evolutionary Timetabling. Technical report, University of Edinburgh Department of Artificial Intelligence, 1994.

2. L. Davis. Adapting Operator Probabilites in Genetic Algorithms. In J. D. Schaffer, editor, *Proceedings of the Third International Conference on Genetic Algorithms and their Applications*, pages 61–69. San Mateo: Morgan Kaufmann, 1989.
3. L. Davis, editor. *Handbook of Genetic Algorithms.* New York: Van Nostrand Reinhold, 1991.
4. S. Forrest and M. Mitchell. Relative Building Block Fitness and the Building Block Hypothesis. In L. Darrell Whitely, editor, *Foundations of Genetic Algorithms 2.* San Mateo: Morgan Kaufmann, 1993.
5. D.E. Goldberg, B. Korb, and K. Deb. Messy genetic algorithms: Motivation, analysis, and first results. *Complex Systems*, 3:493–530, 1989.
6. J. Horn, D. E. Goldberg, and K. Deb. Long Path Problems. In Y. Davidor, H.-P. Schwefel, and R. Männer, editors, *Parallel Problem Solving from Nature, PPSN III*, pages 149–159. Springer Verlag, 1994.
7. Bryant A. Julstrom. What have you done for me lately? adapting operator probabilities in a steady-state genetic algorithm. In L. J. Eshelman, editor, *Proceedings of the Sixth International Conference on Genetic Algorithms*, pages 81–87, San Francisco, Ca., 1995. Morgan Kaufmann.
8. G. F. Mott. Optimising Flowshop Scheduling Through Adaptive Genetic Algorithms. Chemistry Part II Thesis, Oxford University, 1990.
9. C. R. Reeves. A genetic algorithm for flowshop sequencing. *Computers & Ops. Res.*, 22:5–13, 1995.
10. P. Ross and D. Corne. The phase transition niche for evolutionary algorithms in timetabling. In *Proceedings of the First International Conference on the Theory and Practice of Automated Timetabling*, Edinburgh, 1995. Napier University.
11. E. Taillard. Benchmarks for basic scheduling problems. *European Journal of operations research*, 64:278–285, 1993.
12. A. L. Tuson. Adapting Operator Probabilities In Genetic Algorithms. Master's thesis, Department of Artificial Intelligence, Univeristy of Edinburgh, 1995.

Further Modifications and Extensions

Genetic Algorithms and Relational Landscapes

Philippe Collard **Cathy Escazut** **Alessio Gaspar**

Laboratory I3S — CNRS-UNSA
250 Av. A. Einstein, Sophia Antipolis, 06560 Valbonne FRANCE
email: {pc,escazut,gaspar}@unice.fr

Abstract. A *DGA* is a genetic algorithm with novel features: *relational schemata.* These structures allow a more natural expression of relations existing between loci. Indeed, schemata in standard genetic algorithms can only specify values for each locus. Relational schemata are based on the notion of *duality*: a schema can be represented by two strings. The intent of this paper is to show the superiority of DGAs over conventional genetic algorithms in two general areas: efficiency and reliability. Thus, we show with theoretical and experimental results, that our algorithm is faster and perform consistently. The application chosen for test DGAs is the optimization of an extension of *Royal Road* functions we call *relational landscapes.*

1 Introduction

Standard genetic algorithms (SGAs) are adaptive methods used to solve search and optimization problems. They are based on the genetic processes of biological organisms. They encode a potential solution to a specific problem on a simple chromosome-like data structure to which operators of recombination are applied.

1.1 Basics of genetic algorithms

A GA works on a *population* of individuals, being a possible solution of a given problem. Members of this population are generally represented by a binary string of length λ which corresponds to the problem encoding. Each individual is assigned a *fitness score* according to how good solution it is. The highly fit individuals are given opportunities to "reproduce": they are first randomly *selected* following a scheme which favors the more fit members, and then recombined, typically using the mechanisms of *crossover* and *mutation.* Thus, this produces new "offsprings", which share features taken from each "parent". An new population is thus created, containing a higher proportion of the characteristics possessed by the good members of the previous generation. In this way, over many generations, good characteristics are spread throughout the population, being mixed and exchanged with other good characteristics as they go.

GAs manipulate individuals. However, most of the theoretical works focuses on the implicit processing of *schemata.*

1.2 Schemata and their properties

Schemata, also called *hyperplanes*, are implicit similarity templates: they identify subsets of individuals sharing certain characteristics. They are usually defined over the ternary alphabet {0,1,⋆} where '⋆' is a "don't care" symbol. The *schema theorem* proves that some schemata, called *building blocks* get an exponentially increasing number of representatives in the population [8, 6].

Radcliffe [10] defines four properties he thinks necessary to a useful representation for GAs. These are:

- the *closure*: the intersection of any pair of compatible schemata[1] should itself be a schema,
- the *respect*: crossing two instances of any schema should produce another instance of this same schema,
- the *proper assortment*: given instances of two compatible schemata, it should be possible to cross them to produce a child which is an instance of both schemata,
- the *ergodicity*: it should be possible, through a finite sequence of applications of genetic operators, to access any point in the search space given any population.

Unfortunately, schemata are not sufficient to represent all the hyperplanes of the space. Indeed, let us remember that hyperplanes of varying dimension in a λ-space describe schemata. For instance, in a two-dimensional space (λ=2), points of the space are schemata of order 2, lines are schemata of order 1, and the whole space is covered by the schema ⋆⋆ of order 0. One can notice that each schema is represented by only one hyperplane; but the converse is false. For instance the hyperplane {00,11} is not associated with any schema.

2 An implementation of relational schemata

Our objective is to increase the expressiveness of schemata in order to allow a more natural expression of solutions, while keeping the trueness of the properties. The approach we proposed is based on an implicit implementation of richer structures. The implicit character is due to the fact that the alphabet remains unchanged. The richness of the representation comes from taking into account the values on each loci, but also the relation between them. Indeed, in a standard schema, we can not enforce the equality or inequality of the values on different locus. Therefore we cannot adequately represent solutions which require to express links between different bits, as for the hyperplane {00,11}. This problem seems to disappear if we use variables [11], but this vastly increases the size of the search space. In order to express relations in schemata we have defined new structures, called *relational schema*.

[1] Two schemata, s_1 and s_2, are said *compatible* if there exists a chromosome being an instance of both s_1 and s_2.

2.1 Definition of relational schemata

A relational schema, or *R-schema* is defined as a string built over the alphabet {X,X',$\star$}. The symbol $\star$ is a "don't care" character, the two symbols X and X' represent complementary variables: if X is bound to 0 then X' stands for 1 and *vice versa.* Thus, a R-schema allows to express a relation between values on loci. In order to represent at least one relation, a R-schema must have at least two variables. As standard schemata, defined over the alphabet {0,1,$\star$}, only express values on loci, we call them *positional schemata* or *P-schemata.*

A R-schema can be identified with the set of its instances. For instance, the R-schema XX$\star$X' represent the set {0001,0011,1100,1110}, we call a *R-similarity set.* In order to guarantee for the uniqueness of the representation, we fix the first variable to X[2]. We can extend the notion of *order*, noted $\mathcal{O}$, to a R-schema: the order of a R-schema is the number of variables decremented by 1. For example, the order of X$\star$X' is 1. This definition is consistent with the one for P-schemata. Indeed, in both cases, the number of instances of an $\mathcal{O}$-order schema is $2^{\lambda-\mathcal{O}}$.

2.2 Implementation of R-schemata

Taking advantage of an *implicit* implementation of R-schemata, we expect a double benefit: on the one hand, we desire the alphabet to remain unchanged—we keep on using {0,1,$\star$}—on the other hand, we covet R-schemata to possess the four properties previously stated. We propose a quite simple implementation of this idea through a new encoding of the binary string. A *head-bit* is added to the string and manages the interpretation of the rest of the string. When the head-bit is set to '0', the rest of the string remains unchanged. If it is set to '1' the string is interpreted as its binary complement. For example, the string 0101 can be expressed as $\underline{0}\,0101$ or $\underline{1}\,1010$ (the head-bit is the underlined character). It is worth noticing that different chromosomes can be interpreted in the same way. Their *phenotypes* are identical (0101 in the example) while their *genotypes* are different ($\underline{0}\,0101$ and $\underline{1}\,1010$). We propose to call strings of such a pair, *dual chromosomes.*

Let us present the solution in a more formal way. Considering λ-bit strings, the search space is $\Omega = \{0,1\}^\lambda$. We define the *dual space* as $<\Omega> = \{0,1\} \times \Omega$. A GA only affects the dual space. We thus have to define a mapping T, so-called *transcription* function, from the dual space $<\Omega>$ to the basic space Ω as:

$$\forall \omega \in \Omega, \quad T(0\omega) = \omega \text{ and } T(1\omega) = \omega'$$

In other words, if the first bit is equal to '1', the rest of the chromosome is complemented. Thus, a string and its bitwise complement encode a single phenotype.

A fundamental point we wish to stress is that the GA is applied on the dual space $<\Omega>$ but via the transcription function, it is implicitly activated on the basic space Ω. Thus, the dual space is larger than the basic space. But, we can notice that the size of the phenotypical space remains unchanged.

---

[2] This restriction does not decrease the generality of the approach since the R-schemata X$\star$X' and X'$\star$X represent the same R-similarity set.

2.3 P-schemata versus R-schemata

We are going to establish a mapping between P-schemata of $<\Omega>$, i.e. strings of $\lambda+1$ characters over $\{0,1,\star\}$, and R-schemata of Ω, i.e., strings of λ characters over {X,X',$\star$}. This mapping founds our implicit implementation of R-schemata. According to the head-bit value of a P-schema of $<\Omega>$, we have two cases:

1. The head-bit is *specified* ('0' or '1'): the transcription is obvious. For instance, the P-schemata $\underline{0}\,1\star1$ and $\underline{1}\,0\star0$ of $<\Omega>$ are associated to 1$\star$1. More generally, each P-schema of Ω corresponds with two P-schemata of $<\Omega>$.
2. The head-bit is *undetermined* ('$\star$'): variables allow to describe a R-schema. For instance, the P-schema $\underline{\star}01\star0$ becomes the R-schema XX'$\star$X. Indeed, if the head-bit is for a '0' the transcription gives 01$\star$0; if the head-bit is for a '1', the result is 10$\star$1. These two schemata express that the first and last bits are identical, but different from the second one. More generally, the transcription of such a schema is a R-schema of Ω obtained as follows: (i) substitute the first specified value and its occurrences, for X, (ii) substitute all the complementary values for X', (iii) keep all the undetermined locus.

One can note that the transcription of a P-schemata of $<\Omega>$ for which the order is smaller than 2 is the P-schema $\star\ldots\star$ of Ω. More generally, R-schemata of Ω whose order is $\mathcal{O}$ are the transcriptions of P-schemata of $<\Omega>$ for which the order is equal to $\mathcal{O}+1$ and the head-bit is undetermined.

2.4 Properties of schemata in a DGA

Let us study R-schemata considering the properties previously stated. Our aim is not to show that R-schemata are better than P-schemata. The purpose is to show that they are two complementary models.

The closure : Before seeing if R-schemata own the closure property, let us extend the notion of compatibility: two R-schemata, r_1 and r_2 are compatible if there exists a chromosome being an instance of both r_1 and r_2. For instance, $\star$X$\star$X and XX'$\star\star$ are compatible. We refine the notion of compatibility, considering *corroborating* schemata: two compatible R-schemata are corroborating if they share at least one variable locus. For example, the two previous R-schemata are corroborating, while $\star$XX'$\star$ and X$\star\star$X' are not. The intersection of any pair of corroborating R-schemata is itself a R-schema. For instance, the intersection of $\star$X$\star$X and XX'$\star\star$ is the R-schema: XX'$\star$X'. We can note that two non-corroborating R-schemata are necessarily compatible. Nevertheless, their intersection cannot be expressed as a single R-schema; for instance, the intersection of $\star$XX'$\star$ and X$\star\star$X' can only be expressed by XYY'X' which is not a R-schema since there are two distinct variables. However, this expression can be represented by a disjunction of R-schemata: XYY'X' is equivalent to the disjunction (XXX'X' or XX'XX'). More generally, we can say that the intersection of any pair of non-corroborating R-schemata is a disjunction of R-schemata. In this sense, we say that R-schemata are *semi-closed* for intersection.

The respect : We have shown in [3] that explicit R-schemata do not own the respect property . Thus, we could think that they are not relevant for GAs. First, let us notice that the respect property is related to the crossover of schemata, which are strings explicitly handled by GAs. In our context, these strings are in the dual space. Moreover, for each R-schema, a choice between dual strings exists [2] and allows the crossover to respect R-schemata. Let ω be an instance of a R-schema of Ω, if the variable X corresponds to a '0' (respectively '1') in ω, we choose to represent ω in 0Ω (respectively 1Ω). We can show that this choice creates a R-similarity set in $<\Omega>$ closed by crossover. For example, let be the R-schema X⋆X', the R-similarity set in Ω, {001,011,100,110}, is not closed but the corresponding R-similarity set in $<\Omega>$, {$\underline{0}$ 001,$\underline{0}$011,$\underline{1}$011,$\underline{1}$ 001}, is the P-schema $\underline{\star}$0⋆1. We can conclude that a DGA through its choices between dual strings, allows to handle R-schemata of Ω which possess the respect property.

The proper assortment Traditional 1-point and 2-point crossover do not properly assort neither P-schemata nor R-schemata [3]. A uniform crossover properly assorts P-schemata but it does not assort R-schemata. We are going to show that our implicit implementation allows crossover operators to properly assort R-schemata. Let us consider the corroborating R-schemata ⋆X⋆X and XX'⋆⋆. Let 0000 and 0100 be two respective instances. A 1-point and a uniform crossover breed the children {0000,0100}. No offspring is an instance of the intersection XX'⋆X'. Let us choose to represent the string 0000 by the chromosome $\underline{1}$1111 and 0100 by $\underline{0}$0100. A uniform crossover allows to obtain $\underline{0}$0101 that can be transcripted by 0101 and which belongs to the intersection XX'⋆X'. More generally, let a and b be two instances of two corroborating R-schemata of Ω. Two equivalent strings a' and b' exist in the dual space and a uniform crossover between them generates an instance of the intersection. We can conclude that, through judicious choices between dual strings, a DGA allows uniform crossover to properly assort R-schemata.

The ergodicity The property of ergodicity makes possible to access any point in the search space, given any population, through a finite sequence of application of genetic operators. The mutation operator usually ensures this property. Obviously, by applying a sequence of mutations, it is possible to reach any point in the space. This property is qualitatively independent of the space (Ω or $<\Omega>$) on which we apply the mutation operator. The only improvement we can expect using the dual space is quantitative. In the basic space Ω, the minimum number of mutations between two strings is the Hamming distance. For two strings of $\Omega(\lambda)$, this number is smaller than the length λ. We can show that, in the dual space, $<\Omega>$, the minimum number of mutations between two points is smaller than $(\lambda/2)+1$. Let us consider a λ-dimensional space. Each point in this space can be considered as a vertex of the λ-dimensional unit hypercube. The greater Hamming distance between two points is equal to λ (this is the case when the two strings are complementary ones). So, with the standard approach, λ mutations are needed to go from one chromosome to the other. When we apply the mutation operator on the dual space, we are able to cross from a string in the basic space to its complement by only one mutation[3]. In this way, two complementary strings are at a Hamming distance of 1 from each other.

3 Royal Road functions

Now, we briefly introduce *royal road functions* and study the DGA's behavior in such an environment in comparison to a SGA. As DGAs are supposed to implicitly process R-schemata, these experiments are a study of the relevance of R-schemata versus standard P-schemata.

3.1 An historical overview

Royal Road functions (RRs) have been originally designed by M. Mitchell, S. Forrest and J. Holland [9, 5] as a set of easy problems for GAs. In practice, they reveal themselves difficult despite of the fact that they reward presence of user-specified building blocks in chromosomes. This should normally make easier their implicit processing by GAs. Their specification is supposed to offer a "royal road" for GAs' convergence but even with an increasing number of such blocks GAs encounter problems. Hence, as DGAs are particularly efficient to solve GA-hard problems [4] we confront them to RRs.

3.2 Structural definitions of Royal Road functions

There are two kinds of RRs. The *Royal Road Function 1* (R1) is composed by eight building blocks (each 8 bits long) rewarding presence of consecutive '1' within a 64 bits long chromosome. Thus, the global optima 111...111 features a fitness of 64 by combining all building blocks and associated rewards. The *Royal Road Function 2* (R2) introduces new building blocks rewarding presence of two consecutive R1's ones (Figure 1). Thus optimal fitness is increased up to 256.

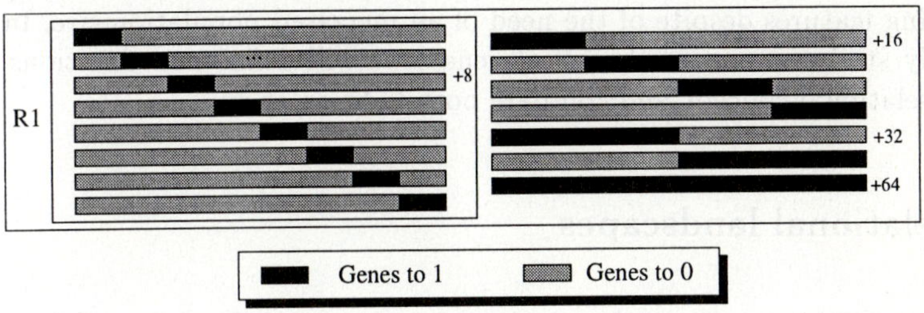

Fig. 1. Royal Road 1 and 2 Decomposition.

[3] A mutation on the head-bit.

3.3 Experiments

Experiments have been achieved with respect to specifications published in Mitchell and Al's papers. We used populations of 128 chromosomes, each 64 genes long, and measured at which generation an occurrence of the optima appeared. Each result has been averaged over 500 experiments.

A DGA doubles its search space by introducing a *head-bit*. But the populations manipulated by both GAs always contain 128 individuals. The difference of results obtained with the two systems remains constant, whether we faced them with R1 or R2. This advocates the fact that it only relies on the size of the population rather than on an hypothetic DGAs' weakness. Consequently, in order to obtain comparable results we have chosen to measure the number of evaluations computed before reaching the optima [4] rather than simply counting generations elapsed. DGAs have thus been allowed to work on a larger population (200) without altering the consistence of the measured criterion.

Results on Royal Road 1: The difference between both GAs remains constant, it takes 89472 for a SGA versus 95744 evaluations for a DGA to find the optimal string with populations of 128 chromosomes. If we adjust its size to 200, we get 78400 versus 84000 evaluations to reach a similar goal. According to the difference, their capabilities may be viewed as equivalent (with a little advantage to SGAs).

Results on Royal Road 2: When applying a SGA and a DGA to R2, we get more interesting results; it takes them respectively 202112 and 207872 evaluations to find the solution with population sized to 128 individuals. The difference has decreased and so they may really be considered as becoming equivalent as the function difficulty increases. When sized to 200 chromosomes, the population allows the DGA to find a solution within 248600 evaluations while it takes 251400 evaluations for the SGA.

At this stage, DGAs have proved to be as effective than SGAs when the environment get more complex. Thus, in our search for an universal, adaptive, and robust optimization method, we must advocate that a DGA offers multiple interesting features despite of the need of an increased population size. In order to deeply study reasons of this effectiveness we will define new functions based on the relational concept and compare both GAs on them.

4 Relational landscapes

This section is devoted to a description of our "extended royal road functions" featuring the use of R-schemata or a combination of R-schemata and P-schemata, instead of traditional P-schemata.

---

[4] This is simply accomplished by multiplying the average value of the halting generation by the population size.

4.1 Foundations

In a machine learning context, R-schemata have already featured interesting results [3]. This section introduces them in the field of optimization by adding to RRs the concept of *relational building-blocks.* While RRs only rely on P-schemata and thus only deal with positional informations about loci, we use R-schemata to build functions featuring more complex relations within binary chromosomes. Indeed, just as SGAs were supposed to implicitly process P-schemata, we now expect DGAs to naturally manage with R-schemata. The implicit handling of such schemata is sufficient to justify DGAs expected effectiveness on a landscape explicitly featuring such building blocks. So, we define *R-Landscapes* as such relational functions using R-schemata to describe their fitness landscapes. Similarly, using both P-schemata and R-schemata, we define *RP-Landscapes* that combines in a same structure relational and positional informations and thus features the maximal expressiveness for a binary chromosome. Furthermore, RP-Landscapes may become a generic definition of higher-level RR functions, allowing empirical studies and comparisons between different "enhanced GAs" able to handle more complex structures than P-Schemata.

4.2 Structural definitions of R-Landscapes

A *R-Landscape* is a set of R-schemata rewarded as detailed in figure 2. By rewarding alternation of 8-bits sequences of consecutive '1' and then '0' we introduce two global optima starting by '1' or '0' and both featuring a 64 points fitness. Similarly, a *RP-Landscape* is a set of R-schemata directly taken from the definition of R-Landscape and an additional P-schema that breaks its symmetry by rewarding the presence of a sequence of '1' at the beginning of the optimal string. This combination removes one of the prior optima and keeps only the one beginning with '1' for a fitness of 72.

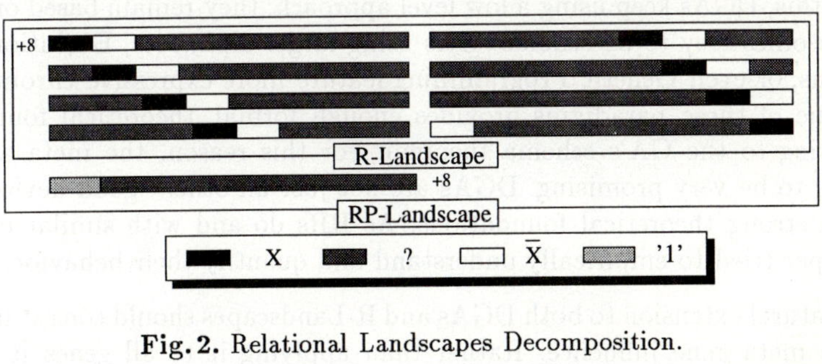

Fig. 2. Relational Landscapes Decomposition.

4.3 Experiments

In this second set of experiments we compare both GAs on functions taking into account loci's dependencies. Experimental conditions remain unchanged.

Results on R-Landscapes: The DGA finds more quickly the global optimum than the SGA (142848 generations against 210048 for the SGA). We can note that the difference is more significant than on classical RRs.

Results on RP-Landscapes: Results are more interesting with a RP-Landscapes since the DGA only needs only 125312 generations versus 212352 for the SGA.

As expected, DGAs revealed an unchallenged superiority on R-Landscapes which bring to us an example of P-schemata intrinsic limitations. The superiority is even more significant than the SGA's one on RRs. Furthermore, as we have not increased the population size during DGA's experiments, we should view those results as a lower bound. This advocates the hypothesis of the DGA's ability to deal with higher-level buildings blocks (*R-Building Blocks*). More generally R-Landscapes feature symmetry, they represent a new way to describe *multimodal deceptive functions* as the ones introduced by Goldberg in [7]. These dual functions represent a new perspective in optimization. After the deceptiveness, the multimodality and royal road structures, RP-Landscapes and more generally dual functions appear as a new promising gap.

5 Conclusion and future works

A DGA is an effective improved GA keeping close enough to the original one in order to be formally studied. We have introduced two new kinds of schemata, both expected to be implicitly processed by DGAs. The empirical study of DGAs over a positional and relational testbed leads to encouraging results: it has confirmed the DGA's superiority on the new testbed and its equivalent effectiveness on the classical one.

A brief overview of related work shows that many attempts to increase chromosome's expressiveness are based on an extension of their allelic alphabet. Unlike this, DGAs keep using a low level approach: they remain based on binary chromosomes easy to be studied. GAs using larger alphabets, Evolutionary Algorithms, or even Genetic Programming feature more expressive chromosomes, but none of these paradigms provides enough formal, theoretical foundations comparing to the GA's schema theorem. For this reason, the meta approach appears to be very promising. DGAs are not just an other "good device", they contain strong theoretical foundations. As RRs do and with similar methods, this paper tried to empirically understand and quantify their behavior.

A natural extension to both DGAs and R-Landscapes should consist in adapting the meta gene influence. Rather than applying it to all genes it may be relevant to restrict its effects to a few selected loci. This is a possible direct implementation of RP-schemata allowing the DGA to decide whenever it should use relational variables.

Next step will consist in defining a formal theory for meta-GAs inspired by traditional biology for example for which the *genome expression* remains an unresolved question, and by work concerning self adaptive GAs.

Among all these perspectives, on the one hand, DGAs appear as a privileged tool for applying R-schemata processing. On the other, RP-Landscapes provide a set of test functions for quantifying their effectiveness. Thus, studying these R-Landscapes as multimodal deceptive functions, should be an other relevant extension to this work continuing the one begun by Goldberg but providing a new easy method for defining such functions.

References

1. P. Collard and J.P. Aurand. DGA: An efficient genetic algorithm. In A.G. Cohn, editor, *ECAI'94: European Conference on Artificial Intelligence*, pages 487–491. John Wiley & Sons, 1994.
2. P. Collard and C. Escazut. Genetic operators in a dual genetic algorithm. In *ICTAI'95: Proceedings of the seventh IEEE International Conference on Tools with Artificial Intelligence*, pages 12–19. IEEE Computer Society Press, 1995.
3. P. Collard and C. Escazut. Relational schemata: A way to improve the expressiveness of classifiers. In L. Eshelman, editor, *ICGA'95: Genetic algorithms and their applications: Proceedings of the Sixth International Conference on Genetic Algorithms*, pages 397–404, San Francisco, CA, 1995. Morgan Kaufmann.
4. P. Collard and C. Escazut. Fitness Distance Correlation in a Dual Genetic Algorithm. In *ECAI 96: 12th European Conference on Artificial Intelligence*, 1996. To appear.
5. S. Forrest and M. Mitchell. Towards a stronger building-blocks hypothesis: Effects of relative building-blocks fitness on ga performance. In L. D Whitley, editor, *Foundations of Genetic Algorithms 2*, pages 109–126. Morgan Kaufmann, San Mateo, CA, 1993.
6. D. E. Goldberg. *Genetic algorithms in search, optimization, and machine learning.* Reading, MA: Addison-Wesley, 1989.
7. D. E. Goldberg, K. Deb, and J. Horn. Massive multimodality, deception and genetic algorithms. Technical Report 92005, Illinois Genetic Algorithms Laboratory, University of Illinois at Urbana-Champaign, Urbana, Il 61801, 1992.
8. J. H. Holland. *Adaptation in natural and artificial systems.* Ann Arbor: University of Michigan Press, 1975.
9. M. Mitchell, S. Forrest, and J. H. Holland. The royal road for genetic algorithms: Fitness landscape and GA performance. In F.J Varela and P. Bourgine, editors, *Proceedings of the First European Conference on Artificial Life*, pages 245–254, Cambridge, MA, 1992. MIT Press/Bradford Books.
10. N. J. Radcliffe. Forma analysis and random respectful recombination. In R. K. Belew and L. B. Booker, editors, *ICGA'91: Genetic algorithms and their applications: Proceedings of the Fourth International Conference on Genetic Algorithms*, pages 222–229, San Mateo, CA, 1991. Morgan Kaufmann.
11. L. Shu and J. Schaeffer. VCS: Variable classifier systems. In J. D. Schaffer, editor, *ICGA'89: Genetic algorithms and their applications: Proceedings of the Third International Conference on Genetic Algorithms*, pages 334–339, San Mateo, CA, 1989. Morgan Kaufmann.

IOGA:
An Instance-Oriented Genetic Algorithm

Richard S. Forsyth
Department of Mathematical Sciences
University of the West of England
Bristol BS16 1QY, UK.
email: rs-forsyth@csm.uwe.ac.uk

Abstract
Instance-based methods of classification are easy to implement, easy to explain and relatively robust. Furthermore, they have often been found in empirical studies to be competitive in accuracy with more sophisticated classification techniques (Aha et al., 1991; Weiss & Kulikowski, 1991; Fogarty, 1992; Michie et al., 1994). However, a twofold drawback of the simplest instance-based classification method (1-NNC) is that it requires the storage of all training instances and the use of all attributes or features on which those instances are measured -- thus failing to exhibit the *cognitive economy* which is the hallmark of successful learning (Wolff, 1991). Previous researchers have proposed ways of adapting the basic 1-NNC algorithm either to select only a subset of training cases ('prototypes') or to discard redundant and/or 'noisy' attributes, but not to do both at once. The present paper describes a program (IOGA) that uses an evolutionary algorithm to select prototypical cases and relevant attributes simultaneously, and evaluates it empirically by application to a set of test problems from a variety of fields. These trials show that very considerable economization of storage can be achieved, coupled with a modest gain in accuracy.
Keywords: Dimensionality Reduction, Evolutionary Computing, Feature Selection, Nearest-Neighbour Classification.

1. Introduction

A very simple form of learning is rote memory, that is, the storage of previously encountered examples. Rote memory is the basis for what is called case-based reasoning, in which previously solved problems are stored in a case library and novel problems are solved by first matching them to the most 'similar' stored problem in that library and then applying (sometimes adapting) the associated solution to the current situation. Currently, case-based reasoning is a growth area in Artificial Intelligence (Kolodner, 1993; Althoff et al., 1995).

Essentially the same idea lies at the heart of the well-tried method of nearest-neighbour classification (NNC) which was first proposed by Fix & Hodges (1951) and has been developed in several directions since then (Dasarathy, 1991). The basic form of this algorithm, single nearest-neighbour classification (1-NNC), works by holding the entire collection of training instances in memory: fresh cases are matched to each of these stored instances according to some similarity measure and assigned the class of the case they most closely resemble. It has been found on numerous past occasions (e.g. Forsyth, 1990; Aha et al., 1991; Fogarty, 1992; Michie et al., 1994; McKenzie & Forsyth, 1995) that, although conceptually very simple, this method frequently outperforms more sophisticated classification methods. Thus it was decided to use the 1-NNC algorithm as a basis for a novel evolutionary learning system.

2. Initial Benchmarking Trials

To begin with, a program was written in C, implementing essentially the 1-NNC algorithm as presented by James (1985). Some initial trials were conducted with this program on a collection of numeric data sets in order to: (1) establish a baseline performance level; (2) compare two different distance metrics (Euclidean versus City-block); (3) assess what level of decline in performance might typically be expected between training and test data when classifying with the nearest-neighbour technique.

No strong claims are made about this particular selection of data sets except that they have all been used by published authors in testing various statistical or machine-learning techniques. Table 1 gives information about the size of these data sets. For completeness, a name and brief description of each data set is given in Table 2. Further details may be found in the references cited.

Table 1 -- Details of Data Sets.

Name	No. of cases	No. of classes	No. of variables
BANKNOTE	206	2	7
CARDIAC	113	2	19
DIABETES	145	3	6
DIGIDAT	1001	10	12
DOGS	77	5	11
DRINKERS	345	3	5
FEDS	866	2	23
IRIS	150	3	4
QUIN	400	2	12
ZOOBASE	101	7	17

Table 2 -- List of Data Sets Used.

Data-Set Name & Source	Brief Description	Categories
BANKNOTE (Flury & Riedwyl, 1988)	measurements of images on genuine and counterfeit Swiss bank notes	0=forged; 1=genuine
CARDIAC (Afifi & Azen, 1979)	clinical data on patients admitted to a Los Angeles Hospital with heart failure	1=survived; 2=died
DIABETES (Andrews & Herzberg, 1985)	data on diabetic patients obtained by reaven & Miller (1979)	1=overt diabetes, 2=chemical diabetes, 3=healthy
DIGIDAT (Breiman et al., 1984)	quasi-random data simulating a faulty light-emitting diode display, plus four noise variables	numerals: 0 to 9
DOGS (Manly, 1994)	mandible measurements from jaws of five canine species, living and extinct	1=Thai dog; 2=golden jackal; 3=cuon; 4=Indian wolf; 5=prehistoric Thai dog
DRINKERS (Allaway et al., 1988)	blood enzyme measurements of healthy male volunteers obtained by BUPA, plus information about habitual alcohol consumption	0=light drinker or abstainer; 1=moderate drinker; 2=heavy drinker
FEDS (Mosteller & Wallace, 1984)	frequencies of 22 function words used in sections of essays by Alexander Hamilton and by James Madison	1=Hamilton; 2=Madison
IRIS (James, 1985)	data on petal and sepal sizes of three species of Iris, collected by Anderson (1935) and made famous by Fisher (1936)	1=Iris Setosa; 2=Iris Versicolor; 3=Iris Virginica
QUIN (Quinlan, 1987)	an artificial data set designed to model a task in which only probabilistic classification is possible and which requires a disjunctive concept description	0,1 (assigned by a stochastic rule)
ZOOBASE (Forsyth, 1990)	numeric (mostly binary) attributes describing 101 different animal species grouped into seven zoological classes	1=mammal; 2=bird; 3=reptile; 4=fish; 5=amphibian; 6=insect; 7=other

Essential to the concept of finding the nearest neighbour of a given instance is an operational definition of distance between points in multi-dimensional space. Many different distance measures have been proposed. Two of the the most popular are Euclidean distance (root summed squared deviation) and the 'city-block' metric (total absolute deviation). Both these were tried on the above data sets. In addition, performance levels on seen and unseen data sets were compared, to examine the susceptibility of 1-NNC to overfitting. This involved splitting each data set into two subsets of roughly equal size. Specifically, nine of these 10 data sets were divided randomly into two subsets, each case having a 0.5 probability of being allocated to either. After this approximate halving, the file which in fact contained more cases was designated the 'training' file and the other the test file. (The single exception was data-set FEDS, where whole essays were randomly assigned to test or training sets, then subdivided into segments of approximately equal length.)

The 1-NNC program was used to classify both training and test sets, producing the results given in Table 3. Note that a form of jack-knifing was employed (Mosteller & Tukey, 1977), here and subsequently; that is, when used on a single data set, the program finds the nearest neighbour by computing the distance of each case to all **other** instances, excluding the current case itself.

Table 3 -- Mean Percentage Correct Classifications with Split-Half Testing.

Distance Metric ↓	self-test (jack-knifed)	test on unseen data
Euclidean	72.15	71.54
City-block	73.66	72.57

A 2-way Analysis of Variance of deviations from the mean score on each problem (to eliminate the effect of problem difficulty, essentially a nuisance factor) was performed. There was no significant main effect of Distance Metric ($F_{1,37} = 1.06$, $p = 0.309$); nor was testing on useen data significantly different from self-test mode ($F_{1,37} = 0.48$, $p = 0.493$). These figures emphasize one of the most desirable properties of the 1-NNC technique, namely the fact that it normally gives what Breiman et al. (1984) call 'honest' error estimates. That is: a self-test on a random sample from a population (provided that jack-knifing is used) will tend to give an error-rate estimate that is not systematically biased towards either under- or over-estimation of the error rate to be expected on another random sample of comparable size from the same population. It was thought important to demonstrate these characteristics of the classic 1-NNC algorithm before turning to developments intended to improve it.

3. Some Disadvantages of 1-NNC

As shown above, 1-NNC is easy to implement and relatively robust. Nevertheless, it does suffer from some drawbacks:

(1) it requires all training cases to be stored, thus simulating memorization rather than learning, as that term is usually understood;

(2) in consequence, the classification phase is rather slow;
(3) it uses all features of each feature vector in assessing similarity to memorized cases, thus failing to compensate for, or exploit, the redundancy among variables found in most real data sets;
(4) since the 'knowledge base' is just the training data, it does not produce an intelligible **description** of what it has learned.

In an effort to alleviate the weaknesses listed above, a novel program was developed, based on the 1-NNC method but radically modified, as described in the next section.

4. An Instance-Oriented Genetic Algorithm

The need to store all training cases in nearest-neighbour classification has seemed wasteful of both storage space and computing time to previous researchers, and several ways of reducing this wastefulness have been devised. Many authors have proposed ways of selecting only a subset of the training cases (Hart, 1968; Swonger, 1972; Ullman, 1974; Ritter et al., 1974; Gabor, 1975; Tomek, 1976; Hand & Batchelor, 1978; Devijer & Kittler, 1982; Fukunaga & Mantock, 1984; Aha et al., 1991). Some also have proposed methods that involve the creation of 'archetypes', such as centroids, along with or instead of actual training instances (e.g. Batchelor, 1974; Chang, 1974; Batchelor, 1978; Geva & Sitte, 1991): this moves the nearest-neighbour technique away somewhat from pure rote memorization towards true learning in that it usually entails the storage of prototypical instances that were never actually encountered during training; thus it becomes rather like the Learning Vector Quantization, or LVQ, technique of Kohonen (1988). In addition, some authors have sought to avoid using spurious &/or redundant variables by methods of feature weighting &/or selection (e.g. Siedlecki & Sklansky, 1989; Kelly & Davis, 1991; Smith et al., 1994; Pei et al., 1995).

However, to the best knowledge of the present author, no previous reseacher has yet proposed a method of economizing on both cases stored and features used at the same time, the object of the program described in this section.

4.1 The IOGA Program

The selection of a suitable subset of variables and cases for nearest-neighbour classification can be seen as an optimization task. It could perhaps be performed in a sequential manner, as in a stepwise regression, but this approach is well known to be vulnerable to interaction effects among variables (McLachlan, 1992); and in the present case interactions among instances chosen and between variables and instances would also have to be considered. In theory, such an optimization could be performed by exhaustive search, but with a training set such as FEDS, containing 484 instances measured on 23 variables, that would entail looking at 2^{507} subsets -- clearly not a feasible option. Accordingly, since the genetic algorithm (GA), has been found to be a robust general-purpose optimization technique (Goldberg, 1989), this problem was tackled here using an evolutionary method.

IOGA (Instance-Oriented Genetic Algorithm) embodies principles common both to the evolution strategy of Rechenberg (1973) and the genetic algorithm of Holland (1975). These in turn are based on a biological model, namely the Darwinian idea of evolution by natural selection (Darwin & Wallace, 1858).

In any program of this kind there will be a population of structures representing potential solutions to the problem in hand which can be scored, or at least ranked, by some kind of fitness function. To emulate Darwinian "survival of the fittest", new candidate solutions are generated by a process analogous to reproduction. Ordinarily this involves a quasi-random selection, biased somehow in favour of higher-scoring members of the population, of two, or sometimes more, parents to which a crossover operation is applied (analogous to mating). A mutation operator is typically applied to the resultant offspring which is then inserted into the population, displacing a low-scoring individual. Within this general framework there are many variants, differing in details such as how crossover and mutation are implemented. In fact, the two most important attributes of any GA implementation are: (1) the representation scheme; (2) the fitness function used.

In IOGA the representation scheme is quite transparent: each item in the population is a string of R+V bits, where R is the number of records or instances and V is the number of variables in the training data. A 1 anywhere in the first R positions of this bitstring signifies that the corresponding case is to be included among the selected prototypes, a zero means that it is to be excluded. Similarly, 1 anywhere in the last V positions signifies that the corresponding variable in the feature vector is to be used in distance calculations, while a zero means that it is not. This representation is well suited to being chopped up and recombined by the GA operators.

The fitness of an individual bitstring is computed by running the jack-knifed 1-NNC procedure over the whole training set with only the selected instances used as prototypes and only the selected features employed in distance calculations. The number of correct classifications (K) is recorded during this evaluation. The fitness (F) of that gene-string is then given by

$$F = K - B/(R + V)$$

where B is the number of non-zero bits in the string and R+V, as before, is the total number of bits in the string. Essentially the subtraction of B/(R+V), the proportion of bits used, gives this fitness formula a bias towards brevity which acts as a tie-breaker: for bitstrings with equal error rate the one using less information is preferred. This may be seen as a crude operationalization of Occam's Razor. Note that K, the number of correct decisions, is summed over all cases in the training set, whether or not they are included by the bitstring in the prototype subset. Note also that, because jack-knifing is used, no case can be its own nearest neighbour.

The version of the GA used in IOGA is novel, though loosely based on a procedure called Iterative Genetic Search with Uniform Crossover (IGS-U) devised by Ackley (1987). An outline follows.

1. Create an initial population of random gene-strings, and compute their fitness scores.
2. Pick a parental gene-string at random from the population.
3. Pick a second parent by making P random probes in the population and retaining the gene-string with the highest fitness score (of the P strings sampled).
4. Make P random probes in the population and record the location of the gene-string with the lowest fitness score (out of P sampled).
5. Make a new offspring by applying the uniform crossover routine[1] to the two parental strings.
6. Randomly replace approximately 4% of the bits in the newly created string by random bits (0 or 1 with 0.5 probability). (This will make no difference half the time, by chance, so the effective mutation rate is in fact 2%.)
7. Replace the member of the population selected in step 4 by the newly created gene-string. Also, compute the new string's fitness and if it happens to have the best score seen so far, save a copy (outside the gene pool) for subsequent printout.
8. On a proportion of occasions (currently set at a third) apply the mutation routine to a randomly chosen member of the population (and keep a copy of it for later printout if it happens to be the best so far).
9. Increment counters and stop if enough work has been done; otherwise loop back to step 2.

   [In all experiments reported in this paper, P was equal to 4.]

The main point to notice about this particular GA is that it is <u>incremental</u> rather than <u>generational</u>. A generational GA consists of a main cycle in which most or all of the population is replaced, by their 'descendants', on each step. Generational GAs are more common than incremental ones (Forsyth, 1989; Goldberg, 1989). However, in performance there is generally little to choose between these two types of GA (Davis, 1991). The procedure used in IOGA sidesteps certain technical problems connected with fitness scaling (Whitley, 1989), and avoids the expense of sorting as well. To assess the amount of work done by a generational GA that it is necessary to multiply the number of generations by the population size to give the number of structures

---

[1] Uniform crossover makes an offspring by stepping through each string position in turn and at each position picking a binary digit from one or other parent with equal probability.

tested, while with an incremental GA it is only necessary to count the number of offspring made.

4.2 Results on Numeric Data Sets

A program, IOGA, implementing the method described above, was written in C, together with some supporting software including a program called NARC. NARC (Nearest Archetype Classifier) applies the 1-NNC procedure to a full datafile but uses only the instances and features selected by IOGA. These programs were applied to the 10 numeric data sets described in section 2, split into training and test sets. Results obtained are given in Table 4. These were obtained using NARC after IOGA had been run with a population size of 42 for 1200 trials (**not** 1200 generations, thus quite a short run as GA experiments go). To smooth out random fluctuations, the median value from three runs is quoted. Euclidean distance was used, as no significant advantage of City-Block distance had been found in section 2. The figures in the second and third columns are percentage success rates. The last two columns give the number of instances kept by IOGA and the number of variables, or features, selected.

Table 4 -- Results of Applying IOGA to Ten Data Sets.

Data Set	jack-knifed self-test (%)	test on unseen data (%)	Euclidean 1-NNC for comparison (%)	cases selected	variables used
BANKNOTE	100	98	99	4	2
CARDIAC	74.19	64.71	56.86	4	1
DIABETES	94.67	91.43	81.43	6	1
DIGIDAT	72.98	69.23	52.23	70	6
DOGS	89.74	84.21	76.32	9	3
DRINKERS	63.49	48.72	39.74	26	2
FEDS	76.03	64.66	61.26	80	8
IRIS	97.40	94.52	93.15	6	1
QUIN	74.15	67.18	67.69	7	2
ZOOBASE	88.46	79.59	87.76	10	4
Mean =	83.11	76.23	71.54	22.2	3.0

These results show firstly that the 'honesty' of jack-knifed self-testing has been lost: all 10 data sets show a decrease from self-test to test on unseen data.

Secondly there has been, as intended, a substantial reduction in size from the full data file to the archetype file, as shown by the number of cases and variables needed for nearest-archetype classification. These figures may be compared with Table 2. The best measure of storage required is the product of number of instances times number of features used. On this measure the mean size of the archetype files, as a percentage of the storage needed by the full training sets, was 3.34% -- a compression ratio of approximately 29 to 1. Thus there is indeed an economization of storage, but this would be of little value if it were accompanied by a loss of accuracy. However, the mean success rate of 76.23% obtained here on unseen data is actually higher than that of the basic 1-NNC using the full data set (71.54%). A paired (2-tailed) t-test shows that this difference is not significant ($t = 2.08$, $p = 0.067$). Nevertheless, it can be asserted that this genetic subset selection process has incurred no loss of accuracy.

In this connection it is interesting to note that Ritter et al. (1974) compared the performance of three different instance-selection algorithms (condensed, reduced and selective nearest-neighbour classification) on mass-spectrum data and found all three gave slightly worse performance than 1-NNC on the full training data. Likewise, Chang (1974) tested his prototype-based algorithm on some liver disease data and found it had a slightly higher error rate than 1-NNC on unseen data. In other words, it is somewhat unusual to find an instance-selecting version of the 1-NNC that gives better results than the standard algorithm.

5. Concluding Comments

IOGA exhibits to a high degree the compression that, as argued by Wolff (1991) among others, is a hallmark of learning. Indeed on this score it is very impressive, surprisingly so in view of the fact that the bias towards brevity in the fitness function was, in essence, only a tie-breaker. (Presumably the presence of spurious variables and rogue examples also creates selection pressure in favour of sparse subsets.) Nor was this thriftiness in storage bought at the cost of a decline in accuracy. Such compression also assists insight into the data (one of the aims of this selection process) by reducing the size of the problem. Details are given by Forsyth (1995).

The fact that IOGA/NARC gave respectable results in finding archetypal subsets in search spaces ranging from 2^{44} to 2^{519} points after testing a mere 1200 (less than 2^{11}) candidates is, in itself, a vindication of the Darwinian approach to optimization. Once again, evolutionary methods have been shown as robust and effective.

In summary, it may be said of this approach that:

(1) despite jack-knifing, there is a systematic difference between self-test mode and testing on unseen data;

(2) a huge reduction in storage requirement has been effected;

(3) there is no significant decrease in accuracy between the full 1-NNC and IOGA/NARC on unseen data (in fact, on seven out of 10 problems the latter does better);

(4) NARC runs faster than the full 1-NNC, at the cost of a slow training phase, especially with the larger data sets.

In essence, what IOGA does is exchange the fast training and slow classification normally found with 1-NNC algorithms for the reverse situation, though it should be noted that this is due primarily to the $O(N^2)$ nature of the underlying 1-NNC algorithm and not intrinsic to the GA itself. Thus strictly speaking, this is a problem of scalability rather than pure speed. The straightforward implementation described here is acceptably fast with data sets of modest size (roughly: where the product of variables times cases is less than 8,000) but hits a 'combinatorial explosion' quite soon after that. IOGA would need major modifications to deal with larger databases: however, the results outlined in this paper give evidence of sufficient promise to warrant further work on such modifications. Also more work needs to be done to assess the effect of preliminary standardization of feature values, e.g. by subtracting the mean then dividing by the standard deviation. Transformations of this sort are quite common in instance-based learning in order to equalize possibly arbitrary differences in scale among variables, but no such transformation was attempted here. Future studies will test whether this practice would lead to even better results than those reported above.

References

Ackley, D.H. (1987). An Empirical Study of Bit Vector Function Optimization. In: L. Davis, ed., *Genetic Algorithms & Simulated Annealing*. Pitman, London.

Afifi, A.A. & Azen, S.P. (1979). *Statistical Analysis: a Computer Oriented Approach*, 2nd. edition, Academic Press, New York.

Aha, D.W., Kibler, D. & Albert, M.K. (1991). Instance-Based Learning Algorithms. *Machine Learning*, 6, 37-66.

Allaway, S.L., Ritchie, C.D., Robinson, D. & Smolski, O.R. (1988). Detection of Alcohol-Induced Fatty Liver by Computerized Tomography. *J. Royal Soc. Medicine*, 81, 149-151.

Althoff, K-D., Auriol, E., Barletta, R. & Manago, M. (1995). *A Review of Industrial Case-Based Reasoning Tools*. AI Intelligence, Oxford.

Anderson, E. (1935). The Irises of the Gaspe Peninsula. *Bulletin of the American Iris Society*, 59, 2-5.

Andrews, D.F. & Herzberg, A.M. (1985). *Data: a Collection of Problems from Many Fields for the Student and Research Worker*. Springer-Verlag, New York.

Batchelor, B.G. (1974). *Practical Approaches to Pattern Classification*. Plenum Press, London.

Batchelor, B.G. (1978) ed. *Pattern Recognition: Ideas in Practice*. Plenum Press, N.Y.

Breiman, L., Friedman, J.H., Olshen, R.A. & Stone, C.J. (1984). *Classification and Regression Trees*. Wadsworth, Monterey, California.

Chang, C.L. (1974). Finding Prototypes for Nearest Neighbour Classifiers. *IEEE Trans. on Computers*, C-23(11), 1179-1184.

Darwin, C.R. & Wallace, A.R. (1858). On the Tendency of Species to Form Varieties; and on the Perpetuation of Varieties and Species by Natural Means of Selection. *Paper presented to the London Linnean Society, 1st July 1858*. In: D.C. Porter & P.W. Graham (1993). *The Portable Darwin*. Penguin, London, 86-104.

Dasarathy, B.V. (1991) ed. *Nearest Neighbour (NN) Norms: NN Pattern Classification Techniques*. IEEE Computer Society Press, Los Alamitos, California.

Davis, L. (1991) ed. *Handbook of Genetic Algorithms*. Van Nostrand Reinhold, New York.

Devijer, P.A. & Kittler, J. (1982). *Pattern Recognition: a Statistical Approach*. Prentice-Hall, New Jersey.

Fisher, R.A. (1936). The Use of Multiple Measurements in Taxonomic Problems. *Annals of Eugenics*, 7, 179-188.

Fix, E. & Hodges, J.L. (1951). Discriminatory Analysis -- Nonparametric Discrimination: Consistency Properties. *Project 21-49-004, Report No. 4*, USAF School of Aviation Medicine, Randolf Field, Texas, 261-279.

Flury, B. & Riedwyl, H. (1988). *Multivariate Statistics: a Practical Approach*. Chapman & Hall, London.

Fogarty, T.C. (1992). First Nearest Neighbor Classification on Frey & Slate's Letter Recognition Problem. *Machine Learning*, 9, 387-388.

Forsyth, R.S. (1989) ed. *Machine Learning: Principles & Techniques*. Chapman & Hall, London.

Forsyth, R.S. (1990). Neural Learning Algorithms: Some Empirical Trials. *Proc. 3rd International Conf. on Neural Networks & their Applications, Neuro-Nimes-90*. EC2, Nanterre.

Forsyth, R.S. (1995). *Stylistic Structures: a Computational Approach to Text Classification*. Doctoral Thesis, University of Nottingham.

Fukunaga, K. & Mantock, J.M. (1984). Nonparametric Data Reduction. *IEEE Trans. on Pattern Analysis & Machine Intelligence*, PAMI-6(1), 115-118.

Gabor, G. (1975). The eta-NN Method: a Sequential Feature Selection for Nearest Neighbour Decision Rule. In: I. Csiszar & P. Elias, eds., *Topics in Information Theory*. North-Holland, Amsterdam.

Geva, S. & Sitte, J. (1991). Adaptive Nearest Neighbor Pattern Classification. *IEEE Trans. on Neural Networks*, NN-2(2), 318-322.

Goldberg, D.E. (1989). *Genetic Algorithms in Search, Optimization & Machine Learning*. Addison-Wesley, Reading, Mass.

Hand, D.J. & Batchelor, B.G. (1978). An Edited Nearest Neighbour Rule. *Information Sciences*, 14, 171-180.

Hart, P.E. (1968). The Condensed Nearest Neighbour Rule. *IEEE Trans. on Info. Theory*, IT-14(3), 515-516.

Holland, J.H. (1975). *Adaptation in Natural & Artficial Systems*. Univ. Michigan Press, Ann Arbor.

James, M. (1985). *Classification Algorithms*. Collins, London.

Kelly, J.D. & Davis, L. (1991). Hybridizing the Genetic Algorithm and the K Nearest Neighbors Classification Algorithm. In: R.K. Belew & L.B. Booker, eds., *Proc. Fourth Internat. Conf. on Genetic Algorithms*. Morgan-Kaufmann, San Mateo, California, 377-383.

Kohonen, T. (1988). *Self-Organization & Associative Memory*, 2nd. edition. Springer-Verlag, Berlin.

Kolodner, J.L. (1993). *Case-Based Reasoning*. Morgan Kaufmann, California.

Manly, B.F.J. (1994). *Multivariate Statistical Methods: a Primer*. Chapman & Hall, London.

McKenzie, D.P. & Forsyth, R.S. (1995). Classification by Similarity: An Overview of Statistical Methods of Case-Based Reasoning. *Computers in Human Behavior*, 11(2), 273-288.

McLachlan, G. (1992). *Discriminant Analysis and Statistical Pattern Recognition*. Wiley, New York.

Michie, D., Spiegelhalter, D.J. & Taylor, C.C. (1994) eds. *Machine Learning, Neural and Statistical Classification*. Ellis Horwood, Chichester.

Mosteller, F. & Tukey, J.W. (1977). *Data Analysis and Regression*. Addison-Wesley, Reading, Mass.

Mosteller, F. & Wallace, D.L. (1984). *Applied Bayesian and Classical Inference: the Case of the Federalist Papers*. Springer-Verlag, New York.

Pei, M., Goodman, E.D., Punch, W.F. & Ding, Y. (1995). *Genetic Algorithms for Classification & Feature Extraction*. Technical Report: Michican State Univeristy, GA Research Group, Engineering Faculty.

Quinlan, J.R. (1987). Simplifying Decision Trees. *Int. J. Man-Machine Studies*, 27, 221-234.

Reaven, G.M. & Miller, R.G. (1979). An Attempt to Define the Nature of Chemical Diabetes using a Multidimensional Analysis. *Diabetologia*, 16, 17-24.

Rechenberg, I. (1973). *Evolutionsstrategie -- Optimierung technischer Systeme nach Prinzipien der biologischen Evolution*, Frommann-Halzboog, Stuttgart.

Ritter, G.L., Woodruff, H.B., Lowry, S.R. & Isenhour, T.L. (1974). An Algorithm for a Selective Nearest Neighbour Decision Rule. *IEEE Trans. on Info. Theory*, IT-21(6), 665-669.

Siedlecki, W. & Sklansky, J. (1989). A Note on Genetic Algorithms for Large-scale Feature Selection. *Pattern Recognition Letters*, 10, 335-347.

Smith, J.E., Fogarty, T.C. & Johnson, I.R. (1994). Genetic Selection of Features for Clustering and Classification. *IEE Colloquium on Genetic Algorithms in Image Processing & Vision*. London.

Swonger, C.W. (1972). Sample Set Condensation for a Condensed Nearest Neighbour Decision Rule for Pattern Recognition. In: S. Watanabe, ed., *Frontiers of Pattern Recognition*. Academic Press.

Tomek, I. (1976). An Experiment with the Edited Nearest-Neighbour Rule. *IEEE Trans. on Systems, Man & Cybernetics*, SMC-6(6), 448-452.

Ullman, J.R. (1974). Automatic Selection of Reference Data for Use in a Nearest Neighbour Method of Pattern Classification. *IEEE Trans. on Info. Theory*, IT-20(4), 541-543.

Weiss, S.M. & Kulikowski, C.A. (1991). *Computer Systems that Learn*. Morgan Kaufmann, San Mateo, CA.

Whitley, D. (1989). The GENITOR Algorithm and Selective Pressure: why Rank-Based Allocation of Reproductive Trials is Best. *Proc. Third Internat. Conf. on GAs*, 116-121, Morgan-Kaufmann, Palo Alto, CA.

Wolff, J.G. (1991). *Towards a Theory of Cognition and Computing*. Ellis Horwood, Chichester.

Explicit Filtering of Building Blocks for Genetic Algorithms

C.H.M. van Kemenade
kemenade@cwi.nl

CWI, Department of Software Technology,
P.O. Box 94079, 1090 GB Amsterdam, The Netherlands

Abstract. Genetic algorithms are often applied to building block problems. We have developed a simple filtering algorithm that can locate building blocks within a bit-string, and does not make assumptions regarding the linkage of the bits. A comparison between the filtering algorithm and genetic algorithms reveals some interesting insights, and we discus how the filtering algorithm can be used to build a powerful hybrid genetic algorithm.

1 Introduction

Genetic algorithms (GA's) with bit-based representation are usually regarded as general solvers for bit-coded problems. An interesting class of problems for a GA are the building block based problems. Solutions of such problems can be decomposed in a number of independent building blocks. These building blocks can be discovered separately, and then merged to create a good solution. The schema theorem [4, 7] describes how a canonical GA behaves on this class of problems. A schema is a string over the alphabet $\{\#, 0, 1\}$ of length n, where n is the length of an individual, which encodes a complete solution. A # is a so-called don't-care symbol, which can represent either 0 or 1. During a single generation of a GA 3^n schemata are processed simultaneously. Because each individual in the population is an instance of 2^n schemata, we get the so-called implicit parallelism [4], also called intrinsic parallelism [7]. Recently there has been discussion about the generality of the building block hypothesis, and therefore the schema theorem.

The ultimate goal of the AI-scientist is to create the general problem solver. Such efforts can be expected to fail, as the range of possible problems is too large: see for example the no free lunch theorem for optimization [10, 14]. Until now all efforts to find this general problem solver have failed. Each candidate has a limited class upon which it performs well. Hence for each new problem solver the (probably fuzzy) boundaries of the class upon which it performs well have to be determined. We think it can also be fruitful to take the opposite approach, and first define a broad class of problems. Next a solver is developed which uses knowledge search a solution rapidly. All information which is easily extractable and based on the class definition should be used. A standard GA deviates from this approach, as it only uses fitness of complete individuals to steer the search process. SEARCH, which is an acronym for Search Envisioned As Relation, and Class Hierarchizing, also touches this issue by emphasizing that one has to search for the set of bits that belong to the same building block [8].

In this paper we take the class of building block problems and develop a filtering algorithm using knowledge about this class. This filtering method is shown to perform well on (certain) problem instances. Then we outline how we can combine this method with genetic algorithms.

The rest of this paper is organized as follows. Section 2 discusses some of the reasons why GA's sometimes fail. Section 3 describes and briefly analyses the problems based on the fully deceptive trap functions, which are assumed to be an important representative for a large class of optimization problems. Based on these two sections a new filtering method is developed. This method is compared to GA's and messy GA's in section 5. Finally some conclusions are drawn in section 6.

2 Genetic Algorithms

In this section we discus some of the difficulties for genetic algorithms.

Before applying a GA we have to decide on a representation for solutions to problem we want to handle. An important issue is the linkage. Linkage is said to be tight if bits belonging to the same building block are next to each other on the chromosome, while loose linkage corresponds to a situation where bits belonging to the same building block are scattered over the chromosome. Loose linkage cause problems to GA's using operators that have a positional bias. A positional bias implies that the probability of two bits being taken from the same parent depends upon the (relative) position within the chromosome of these bits [2]. Problems due to linkage have already been studied by Holland [7], and the inversion operator is proposed as a remedy. It has been shown that the inversion operator acts too slow to be useful. Another approach to avoid linkage problems is taken in the (fast) Messy GA's [5, 6, 8], where a different representation without positional bias is introduced. On many (black-box) optimization problems the linkage between bits is not known in advance, so handling loose linkage is of crucial importance for a general optimizer.

Another issue is the number of defined bit-positions of a building block. Even when tight linkage can be assured most genetic operators will introduce a bias. Smaller building blocks are less likely to be disturbed during crossover, and therefore are more likely to be propagated than larger building blocks giving a similar fitness contribution.

Other troubling factors for a GA are genetic hitch-hiking, genetic drift [1], mixing problems [11, 12] and sampling errors due to low order schemata of relative high fitness that are not contained in any of the building blocks. This is for example the case in the fully deceptive trap functions discussed in section 3. Several of these problems are rooted in the iterated character of a GA. A GA continuously applies selection and production to a population which only contains a very small sample of the search-space. A small decision error might easily initiate an avalanche of effects during subsequent iterations.

3 Building Block problems

Many problems involve a search-space which is too large to search it completely. In order to find solutions to large problem instances we have to make some assumptions regarding structures in the search-space, and use these structures to develop a faster optimizer.

An interesting assumption is to assume that a solution is made up of a number of building blocks. If these building blocks can be discovered independently and combined afterwards, we get a tractable problem. A difficult instance of this class can be created by using the parameterized set of fully deceptive trap functions [3]. A fully deceptive trap (sub)function of order k has value [8]

$$f(x) = \begin{cases} k & \text{if } u(x) = k \\ k - u(x) - 1 & \text{otherwise} \end{cases}$$

where $u(x)$ is a function that counts the number of 1-bits in x. The global optimum of this function is the string consisting of k 1-bits resulting in the maximal fitness contribution k. The second best solution is a string consisting of k 0-bits having value $k-1$. As decreasing the number of one bits usually increases fitness, except for the optimal string, hill-climbing algorithms will be strongly attracted by the second best optimum.

By concatenating m of these order k subfunctions we create a building block problem, that has a solution which can be represented by a bit-string of length $l = m \times k$. When the bits belonging to the some subfunction are always next to one another we have a building block function with tight linkage. When the bits of a single subfunction are spread over the total bit-string we talk about loose linkage.

Given a random bit-string of length l, the probability that at least one building block is present within this string is

$$\mathbb{P}[\textit{at least one BB}] = 1 - (1 - \frac{1}{2^k})^m \leq \frac{m}{2^k}$$

Figure 1 shows this probability for $l = 30, 100, 300$ as a function of the order of the building blocks k. We see that the probability a building block is present decreases rapidly as k increases. This Figure also shows a number of additional problems for a genetic algorithm. In order to be certain that all building blocks are present in the initial population, a large population is required. Application of mutation will not help us much in this case. A mutation rate of $1/l$, which is commonly used, will concentrate on bit-strings at Hamming distance 1. The only solution seems to be a highly disruptive crossover, such as uniform crossover, which can discover new schemata easily combined with a reasonably high selective pressure in order to prevent the loss of already observed building blocks.

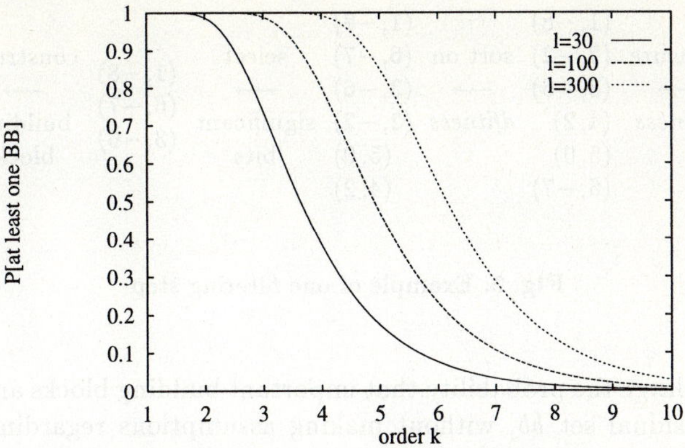

Fig. 1. The probability $\mathbb{P}[\textit{at least one BB}]$ for random bit-string coding a solution to a concatenation of fully deceptive trap functions of order k

4 Filtering of building blocks

In this section we introduce the filtering algorithm for building block problems.

Informally, the filtering method tries to locate building blocks in a bit-string s. In order to do so it measures the change in fitness when individual bits of s are flipped. Using this information a set of most influential bits is selected which is likely to contain the building blocks present within s.

The actual algorithm is as follows

function filter(*string*, *partial_sol*)
  $bb \leftarrow \emptyset$
  for all i where $\neg$defined(i, *partial_sol*)
    $bb \leftarrow bb \cup (i, string_i, dfitness(string, i))$
  sort bb on field *dfitness*
  truncate(bb)
  return bb

The parameter *partial_sol* is used to carry information regarding the bits have been determined already. The set bb is filled with tuples $(i, b_i, dfitness(b, i))$, where i is the index of a bit, b_i is a bit-value, and $dfitness(b, i)$ is the change in fitness when the value of bit b_i is flipped within string string b. The set bb is ordered on field *dfitness* after which the set is truncated on the position where the largest change in field *dfitness* between subsequent tuples appears. The rationale for this truncation rule is that the set of bits that makes the largest fitness contribution is selected. By truncating on the largest gradient in

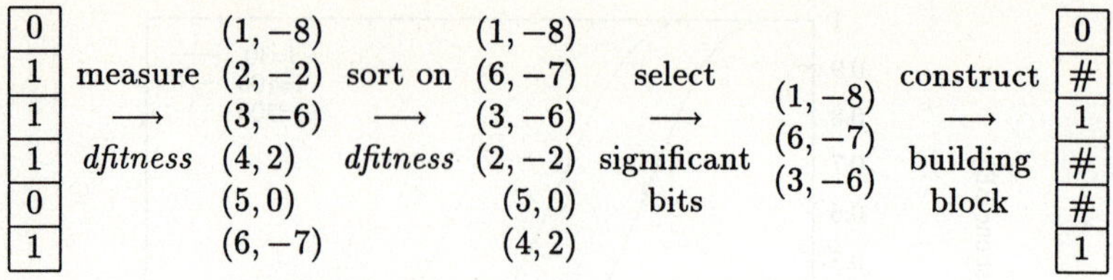

Fig. 2. Example of one filtering step

dfitness we enlarge the probability that important building blocks are completely within the residual set *bb*, without making assumptions regarding the actual fitness contribution of a building block. This truncation rule does not give any guarantees, but if a bit is removed from set *bb*, then the current value of this bit is not likely to be necessary to maintain a building block present within set *bb*.

An example of the application of this filtering procedure is shown in Figure 2. On the left we see a bit-string of length 6. Let us assume that the main fitness contribution within this string is coming from a building block containing bits 1, 3 and 6, resulting in a fitness contribution of +6 when the schema 0#1##1 is present. During the first step the individual fitness contribution, *dfitness* of each bit is measured by flipping this bit and observing the change in fitness, and a set of tuples of type (position, *dfitness*) is created. Flipping bit 1, 3 or 6 will break schema 0#1##1 and therefore result in a relatively large value of *dfitness*. During the second step, these tuples are sorted on *dfitness*. Next the significant tuples are selected by truncating the ordered set of tuples on the position of the largest jump in *dfitness*. In our example the largest jump is between the third and the fourth tuple, where *dfitness* increased from -6 to -2. Based on the remaining tuples a candidate building block can be reconstructed.

The filtering procedure does only a detection of building blocks which are present, so in order to operate, this procedure has to be provided bit-strings which are likely to contain building blocks. In order to test the performance of the algorithm the main loop shown in Figure 3 is used. The loop is entered with an empty partial solution. During each iteration it creates a baseline population of size N_{base}, consisting of bit-strings that have random bit-values for those bits which are not defined by the partial solution. The fitness of each such bit-string is calculated, and the best N_{sel} strings from this baseline population are selected. For each selected bit-string a filtering process is applied, which tries to locate a building block contained within this string that is responsible for the relative high fitness of this string. These building blocks are added to the set *BB*. At the end of each iteration a partial solution is created by combining all obtained building blocks. If two building blocks define opposite values for a bit, the value of the bit is taken from the first discovered building block. The main loop is terminated if the obtained partial solution is complete, i.e. specifies a value for each bit, or if no progress is achieved for more than 5 iterations.

Based on the size of the baseline population N_{base} the expected maximal

```
BB ← ∅
partial_sol ← ∅
repeat
   Base ← ∅
   /* create a baseline population */
   for i ← 1 to N_base do
      bstring ← random_string(partial_sol)
      Base ← Base ∪ (bstring, fitness(bstring))

   /* select high quality subset and do filtering */
   Sbase ← best_tuples(N_sel, Base)
   for a ∈ Sbase do
      bb ← filter(a, partial_sol)
      BB ← BB ∪ bb

   /* merge building blocks to partial solution */
   partial_sol ← merge_bb(BB)
until complete(partial_sol) ∨ no_progress()
```

Fig. 3. Pseudo-code of main loop of filtering algorithm

order of discovered building blocks can be estimated as $\lfloor {}^2\log(N_{base}) \rfloor$. If the filter process produces a large block, then this block mainly consists of noise, or it contains a large number of low order building blocks. Currently we use $\lfloor {}^2\log(N_{base}) \rfloor$ as an upper limit on the size of filtered block. Larger blocks are ignored. Note that this will deteriorate the performance of the method in case the order k of the building blocks is small.

As the solutions of many binary problems are assumed to be decomposable in a set of independent building blocks, the filtering algorithm is a valuable method. It is not necessary to know the linkage between bits in advance. As each sample represents 2^n schemata simultaneously we also have a kind of implicit parallelism. A further advantage of the method is that it yields the actual parts that compose a solution instead of just a complete solution. Such a decomposed solution allows for analysis, which helps in getting a better understanding of the specific problem at hand, and of the behavior of the filtering method on this problem. This is an important advantage over the genetic algorithm, where one usually only gets the (well performing) bit-string, without any knowledge about internal structure of the search-space, or an indication of the confidence one can have in this particular solution.

5 Experiments

A comparison is made between the following algorithms:

GGA1 a generational genetic algorithm with population size 1000, $P_{cross} = 0.7$, $P_{mut} = 1/l$, and tournament selection with tournament size 2,

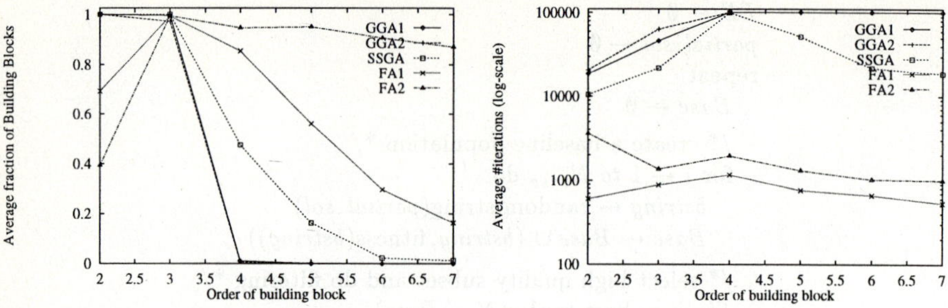

Fig. 4. Average fraction of all building blocks found (left) and average number of function evaluations (right) as a function of the order k of the building block ($l \approx 30$).

GGA2 same as GGA1 except for 2-point crossover being used,

SSGA a steady-state genetic algorithm with population size 1000, $P_{cross} = 1.0$, $P_{mut} = 1/l$, uniform selection, and worst fitness deletion [13],

messy GA the messy genetic algorithm [8],

FA1 the destructive building block filtering method with $N_{base} = 200$, and $N_{sel} = 10$, and

FA2 same as FA1 except for having an upper bound of $\lfloor {}^2\log(Nbase) \rfloor$ on the number of bits that can be discovered simultaneously.

The settings of the GGA1 and GGA2 are the standard ones. SSGA is shown to perform well on a set of numerical optimization problems [13]. For the messy GA we only make a comparison to results from recent literature [8].

During all experiments the building block problems are based on the deceptive trap function. As we are interested in solving problems without any knowledge of the linkage between bits, it seems appropriate to assume a worst-case scenario: loosely coupled building block problems. All the results are averaged over 100 independent runs. The GA's are terminated when the optimum is found, the fitness variance over the population has decreased to zero, or the maximal number of function evaluations is reached.

The first set of experiments investigates scaling of different methods with respect to k. All the problem instances require a bit-string of approximately 30 bits. The exact sizes for m, k, and l are:

k	2	3	4	5	6	7
m	15	10	8	6	5	4
l	30	30	32	30	30	28

Figure 4 shows the average fraction of building blocks in the best solution detected (left) and the average number of function evaluations until termination (right) as a function of the order k of the building blocks. The FA methods outperform the GA's for all problem instances having building blocks of order $k \geq 3$. Amongst the GA's the SSGA method seems to perform best. It finds the

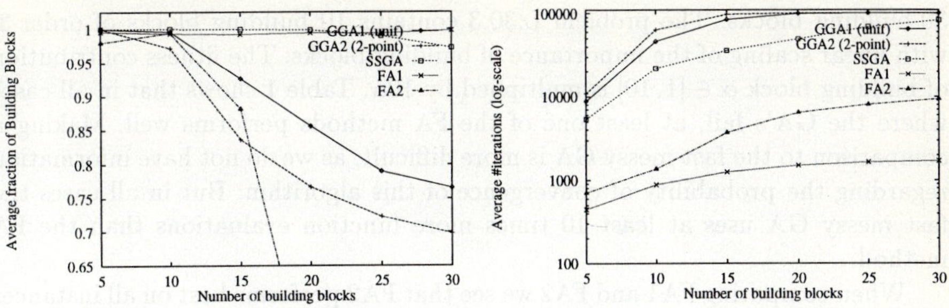

Fig. 5. Average fraction of all building blocks found (left) and average number of function evaluations (right) as a function of the number of building blocks m ($k = 3$).

Problem		fast mGA	GGA1	GGA2	SSGA	FA1	FA2
P.90.3	P_{succ}	—	0.0	0.0	0.51	0.94	0.0
	Av. #iter	256,500	100,000	100,000	83,290	1,703	9,398
P.100.5	P_{succ}	—	—	—	0.0	0.06	0.76
	Av. #iter	1,000,500	—	—	30,870	1,825	4,902
P.150.5	P_{succ}	—	—	—	—	0.03	0.63
	Av. #iter	425,000	—	—	—	2,845	11,284
L.30.3	P_{succ}	—	0.84	0.86	0.99	0.01	0.71
	Av. #iter	>120,000	67,270	63,550	24,316	687	2,342

Table 1. Comparison between methods

optimum more often than the GGA's. An additional advantage of the SSGA is that it is able to terminate if the optimum is not found, which limits the amount of computation (see Figure 4, right). The value $k = 3$ seems to mark a region where the GA's start to get in trouble. A second set of experiments is performed during which k is set to a fixed value 3, while m takes the successive values 5, 10, 15, 20, 25, and 30. Figure 5 shows the results. The SSGA and FA1 method show comparable performance. The FA2 methods breaks down, as too many order-3 building blocks will be discovered simultaneously, resulting in a violation of the length constraint.

When looking at the graphs to the right in Figures 4 and 5 we see that both FA methods use only a moderate number of function evaluations. During all experiment the FA method uses approximately 10 times less function evaluations than the GA's.

Making a comparison to fast messy GA's is more difficult as our only source of information [8] just contains the outcomes of a single run. Our results are again averaged over 100 independent runs. The results are shown in table 1. Problem P.90.3 consists of a 90 bit problem containing 30 deceptive trap functions of order 3, P.100.5 consist of 20 building blocks of order 5, and P.150.5 contains

30 building blocks. The problem L.30.3 contains 10 building blocks of order 3, with linear scaling of the importance of building blocks. The fitness contribution of building block $\alpha \in [1, 10]$ is multiplied by 10α. Table 1 shows that in all cases where the GA's fail, at least one of the FA methods performs well. Making a comparison to the fast messy GA is more difficult, as we do not have information regarding the probability of convergence of this algorithm. But in all cases the fast messy GA uses at least 10 times more function evaluations than the FA method.

When comparing FA1 and FA2 we see that FA2 performs best on all instances having building blocks of order larger than 3. This result is to be expected as the only difference between these two methods is the additional constraint on the order of the obtained block of bits in FA2. As building blocks of low order are easy to find, the bit-strings selected from the baseline population will contain many building blocks having a combined length that violates this additional constraint. FA2 performs well in all those cases where the GA seemed to fail during our experiments.

It is not known yet how the filtering methods will behave on more complex problems containing overlapping building blocks or having building blocks which are not completely independent. On such problems the simple merging rule we used in this paper might be far from optimal. But we are convinced that discovering linkage stays important and therefore that the filtering method is usefull. Powerful solvers can be obtained by combining genetic algorithms with the filtering algorithm. For example, we can use the filtering algorithm as a pre-processing stage to identify the linkage between bits. Based on such linkage-information a specialized set of crossover masks can be constructed, or the genetic algorithm can be used to find the best combination of the actual building blocks discovered by the filtering algorithm. Another approach would be to incorporate the filtering in the GA. This approach is taken in GEMGA, where the a weight is computed for each bit of a chromosome. These weights are used during recombination operations to determine which sets of bits should be determined by the same parent [9].

6 Conclusions

Genetic algorithms were developed to be general problem solvers for arbitrary bit-coded problems based on the evolution principle. Most practical applications incorporate problem-specific knowledge in order to get a competitive algorithm. This deviates from the original idea of the GA as a general problem solver. We propose to incorporate general knowledge instead. One way to do so is to restrict the class of problems, and use the additional knowledge to enhance the genetic algorithm.

In this paper we have restricted ourselves to the class of building block problems. We have defined a filtering algorithm to locate building blocks without making assumptions about the linkage between bits. The results look promising. In this paper we have suggested several ways to combine the filtering algorithm with genetic algorithm in order to construct a fast hybrid genetic algorithm that requires less strong assumptions about the linkage of bits and the defining length of building blocks.

Remarks: Measuring the fitness contribution of individual bits and usage of this information has been developed independently by Hilol Kargupta [9]. Furthermore I would like to thank Joost N. Kok for his useful comments.

References

1. H. Asoh and H. Mühlenbein. On the mean convergence time of evolutionary algorithms without selection and mutation. In *Parallel Problem Solving from Nature - 3*, pages 88–97, 1994.
2. L.J. Eshelman, R.A. Caruana, and J.D. Schaffer. Biases in the crossover landscape. In *Third International Conference on Genetic Algorithms*, pages 10–19, 1989.
3. D.E. Goldberg. Genetic algorithms and walsh functions: Part II, deception and its analysis. *Complex Systems*, 3:153–171, 1989.
4. D.E. Goldberg. *Genetic Algorithms in Search, Optimization, and Machine Learning.* Addison-Wesley, 1989.
5. D.E. Goldberg, K. Deb, H. Kargupta, and G. Harik. Rapid, accurate optimization of difficult problems using the fast messy genetic algorithms. In *Fifth International Conference on Genetic Algorithms*, pages 56–64, 1993.
6. D.E. Goldberg, B. Korb, and K. Deb. Messy genetic algorithms: Motivation, analysis, and first results. *Complex Systems*, 3:493–530, 1989.
7. J.H. Holland. *Adaptation in natural and artificial systems: an introductory analysis with applications to biology, control, and artificial intelligence.* The university of Michigan Press/Longman Canada, 1975.
8. H. Kargupta. SEARCH, polynomial complexity, and the fast messy genetic algorithm. Technical Report IlliGAL-95008, University of Illinois, October 1995.
9. H. Kargupta. Search, evolution, and the gene expression messy genetic algorithm. Technical Report 96-60, Los Alamos National Laboratory, February 1996.
10. N.J. Radcliffe and P.D. Surry. Fundamental limitations on search algorithms: Evolutionary computing in perspective. In J. van Leeuwen, editor, *Computer Science Today — Recent Trends and Developments*, volume 1000 of *Lecture Notes in Computer Science*, pages 275–291. Springer–Verlag, 1995.
11. D. Thierens. *Analysis and Design of Genetic Algorithms.* Doctoral dissertation, University of Leuven, Belgium, 1995.
12. D. Thierens and D.E. Goldberg. Mixing in genetic algorithms. In S. Forrest, editor, *Fifth International Conference on Genetic Algorithms*, pages 38–45. Morgan Kaufmann, 1993.
13. C.H.M. van Kemenade, J.N. Kok, and A.E. Eiben. Controlling the convergence of genetic algorithms by tuning the disruptiveness of recombination operators. In *Second IEEE conference on Evolutionary Computation*, pages 345–351. IEEE Service Center, 1995.
14. D.H. Wolpert and W.G. Macready. No free lunch theorems for search. Technical Report SFI-TR-95-02-010, The Santa Fe Institute, July 1995.

Multi-Objective Optimization by Means of the Thermodynamical Genetic Algorithm

Hajime KITA, Yasuyuki Yabumoto, Naoki Mori and Yoshikazu NISHIKAWA

Department of Electrical Engineering, Graduate School of Engineering,
Kyoto University
Yoshidahonmachi, Sakyo, Kyoto 606-01, JAPAN

Abstract. Recently, multi-objective optimization by use of the genetic algorithms (GAs) is getting a growing interest as a novel approach to this problem. Population based search of GA is expected to find the Pareto optimal solutions of the multi-objective optimization problems in parallel. To achieve this goal, it is an intrinsic requirement that the evolution process of GA maintains well the diversity of the population in the Pareto optimality set. In this paper, the authors propose to utilize the Thermodynamical Genetic Algorithm (TDGA), a genetic algorithm that uses the concepts of the entropy and the temperature in the selection operation, for multi-objective optimization. Combined with the Pareto-based ranking technique, the computer simulation shows that TDGA can find a variety of Pareto optimal solutions.

1 Introduction

The Genetic Algorithm (GA) is a search and optimization technique based on the mechanism of natural evolution[1, 2]. Recently, as an application of GA, studies on multi-objective optimization (MO) have been receiving a growing interest. Populations based search of GA is expected to find the Pareto optimal solutions, a set of rational solutions to the multi-objective optimization problem, in parallel.

1.1 Multi-objective Optimization and Pareto Optimal Solutions

The multi-objective optimization problem(MOP) is formulated as follows:

$$\min_{x \in F} \quad f_1(x), f_2(x), \cdots, f_M(x) \tag{1}$$

where $f_1(x), f_2(x), \cdots, f_M(x)$ are the objective functions to be minimized simultaneously, x is the decision variable and F is the feasible region.

If there exist a feasible solution x^* such that $\forall x \in F$, $\forall m = 1, \cdots, M$, $f_m(x^*) \leq f_m(x)$, the solution x^* is an optimal solution of the problem. However, there usually exist trade-off relations among the objective functions, and in such a case, the problem has no optimal solution. Hence another concept of solution called the Pareto optimal solution is used in MOP.

Let's suppose two feasible solutions x_A and x_B. If $\forall m = 1, \cdots, M, f_m(x_A) \leq f_m(x_B)$ and $\exists m, f_m(x_A) < f_m(x_B)$, we say that x_A *dominates* x_B. If a feasible solution x_P is not dominated by $\forall x \in F$, we call x_P a *Pareto optimal solution.* Further, if there exists no $x \in F$ which satisfies $f_m(x) < f_m(x_P), \forall m = 1, \cdots, M$, we call x_P a *weakly Pareto optimal solution.*

We also call the set consisting of all the Pareto optimal solutions *the Pareto optimality set.* Since a Pareto optimal solution is a rational solution of MOP, the first goal of solving MOP is to obtain the Pareto optimality set (or, to sample solutions from it uniformly).

Since the study of VEGA by Schaffer[8], there has been proposed several methods for solving MO by GA[2, 8, 9, 10, 11]. So far, the most successful approach to MO by GA seems to be a combination of *the Pareto-based ranking* and *the fitness sharing*[12].

The Pareto-based ranking is a method of evaluating the individual by its degree of Pareto optimality in the current population. Goldberg has suggested an algorithm of assigning the fitness values to the individual based on their Pareto optimality[2]. Fonseca and Fleming have also proposed a similar technique[9]. Horn et al. have used a tournament selection based on domination[10].

While the Pareto-based ranking makes it possible to find Pareto optimal solutions by GA, a good (basically uniform) sampling of the solutions from the Pareto optimal set is not guaranteed only by this technique. That is, the population converges to small number of solutions due to the random genetic drift. To avoid this phenomenon, some devices to maintain the diversity of the population are also required.

For maintenance of the diversity, techniques of fitness sharing have been used[2, 9, 10, 11]. In this method, the fitness value of each individuals is reduced if there exist other individuals in its neighborhood, and therefore the individuals located in more crowded area leaves less offsprings. Thus the distribution of the population gets uniform over the Pareto optimality set. However, to make the fitness sharing work well, several factors such as a similarity measure between individuals, sharing function and sharing parameters should be decided carefully.

In this paper, the authors propose another approach of maintaining the diversity of the population required in MO by GA. An algorithm called the *Thermodynamical Genetic Algorithm* (TDGA)[4], which utilizes the concepts of temperature and entropy as in the simulated annealing (SA)[3], is used in GA being combined with the Pareto-based ranking technique. In the followings, after a brief description of TDGA, it is applied to MOP. Computer simulation is carried out by taking a simple two-objective problem as an example.

2 Thermodynamical Genetic Algorithm (TDGA)

2.1 The Principle of the Minimal Free Energy

In the stochastic process used in SA, the stationary distribution of the state is given by the Gibbs distribution[7]. Further, it is also known that this distribution minimizes the free energy F defined by:

$$F = \langle E \rangle - HT, \tag{2}$$

where $\langle E \rangle$ is the mean energy of the system, H is the entropy and T is the temperature. It is called 'the principle of the minimal free energy.'

From the viewpoint of GA, by regarding $-\langle E \rangle$ as the fitness value in GA, minimization of the free energy can be interpreted as taking a balance between minimization of the energy function (the first term in the RHS of Eq.(2), or equivalently maximization of the fitness function in GA) and maintenance of the diversity (the second term in the RHS of Eq.(2)), where the diversity can be controlled explicitly by adjusting the temperature parameter T.

2.2 Algorithm of TDGA

The algorithm of TDGA is as follows:

[TDGA]

1. Select appropriate values for
   N_{p}: the population size,
   N_{g}: the number of generations, and
   $\mathcal{T}(t)$: the annealing schedule of the temperature.
2. Let $t = 0$, and construct the initial population $\mathcal{P}(0)$ randomly.
3. Let $T = \mathcal{T}(t)$.
4. Pair all the individuals in $\mathcal{P}(t)$ randomly. Apply the crossover operator to all the pairs, and obtain N_{p} offsprings. Then, apply the mutation operator to all the N_{p} parents and N_{p} offsprings. Let $\mathcal{P}'(t)$ be the population consisting of the above $2N_{\mathrm{p}}$ individuals.
5. Let $i = 1$, and make the population $\mathcal{P}(t+1)$ at the next generation empty.
6. We refer to an individual in $\mathcal{P}'(t)$ by its number $h = 1, \cdots, 2N_{\mathrm{p}}$. Let $\mathcal{P}(t+1, i, h)$ be the population which consists of already selected $i-1$ individuals for $\mathcal{P}(t+1)$ and the h-th individual of $\mathcal{P}'(t)$, and calculate the free energy of $\mathcal{P}(t+1, i, h)$ for all $h = 1, \cdots, 2N_{\mathrm{p}}$.

$$F = \langle E \rangle - T \sum_k H_k$$
$$= \frac{\sum_{l=1}^{i-1} E_l + E'_h}{i} - T \sum_{k=1}^{M} H_k(i,h), \tag{3}$$

where

$$H_k(i,h) = -\sum_{j \in \{0,1\}} P_j^k(i,h) \log P_j^k(i,h), \tag{4}$$

E_l is the energy of the l-th individual of $\mathcal{P}(t+1)$, E'_h is the energy of the h-th individual of $\mathcal{P}'(t)$, $H_k(i,h)$ is the entropy of the k-th locus of $\mathcal{P}(t+1, i, h)$,

and $P_j^k(i,h)$ is the ratio of gene j on the locus k of $\mathcal{P}(t+1,i,h)$[1]. Find the individual h that minimizes the free energy given by Eq.(3) from $\mathcal{P}'(t)$. Add the individual h to $\mathcal{P}(t+1)$ as the i-th individual. Repeated selection of the same individual in $\mathcal{P}'(t)$ is allowed.
7. Let $i = i+1$. If $i \leq N_{\rm p}$, go to Step 6.
8. Let $t = t+1$. If $t < N_{\rm g}$, go to Step 3, otherwise terminate the algorithm.

TDGA has been successfully applied to single-objective optimization problems such as the knapsack problem[4] and the traveling salesman problem[5]. Further, the authors are also studying adaptation ability of TDGA to a changing environment[6].

3 Multi-objective Optimization by Means of TDGA

We use TDGA for the multi-objective optimization combined with the Pareto-based ranking suggested by Goldberg[2]. The algorithm of the Pareto-based ranking is as follows:

[Pareto-based Ranking]
1. Let the rank counter $k = 1$.
2. Find all the non-dominated solutions (individuals) in the population, and give them the rank k.
3. Remove all the non-dominated solutions.
4. If the population is empty, terminate the algorithm.
5. Let $k = k+1$
6. Go to Step 2.

We have simply used the above procedure to evaluate the energy value in TDGA. That is, the energy value E used in Step 6. of TDGA is the rank calculated by the above procedure.

Since the energy function decided by the Pareto-based ranking is normalized, and TDGA adjusts the diversity via the free energy, it is expected that the suitable temperature does not vary largely depending on the domain of the applied problem.

4 Initial Results

We use the following two-variable and two-objective problem as a test problem:

$$\max_{x_1,x_2} \; f_1 = -x_1^2 + x_2 \tag{5}$$

$$\max_{x_1,x_2} \; f_2 = \frac{1}{2}x_1 + x_2 + 1 \tag{6}$$

[1] The entropy of the population is evaluated in a locus-wise manner to cope with the problem that the population size is much smaller than the number of the possible species[4].

subject to

$$\frac{1}{6}x_1 + x_2 - \frac{13}{2} \leq 0 \tag{7}$$

$$\frac{1}{2}x_1 + x_2 - \frac{15}{2} \leq 0 \tag{8}$$

$$5x_1 + x_2 - 30 \leq 0 \tag{9}$$

$$x_1 \geq 0 \tag{10}$$

$$x_2 \geq 0 \tag{11}$$

Figure 1 (a) shows the feasible region of the problem. In Fig. 1 (a), the line segment AB is the Pareto optimality set, and the line segment BC is also included in the weakly Pareto optimal set. They correspond to the curved segment XY and the line segment YZ, respectively, in the objective function space shown in Fig. 1 (b).

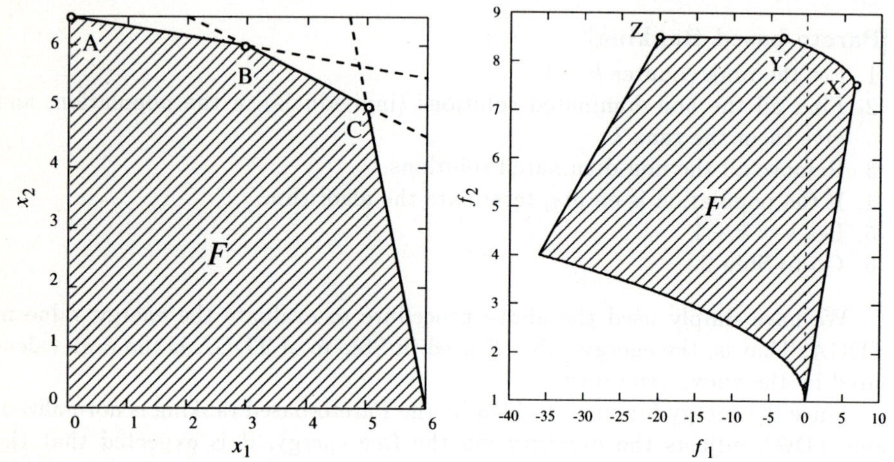

(a) Feasible Region in the Decision Variable Space

(b) Feasible Region in the Objective Function Space

Fig. 1. Test problem.

We have carried out a computer simulation with the following setup:

- Population size: $N_p = 100$.
- Maximal generation: $N_g = 100$.
- Each variable is encoded in the 10-bit binary code with a linear scaling to adjust the range of the variable. Hence the total length of the chromosome is 20 bits.

- The energy values of the infeasible solutions are set to infinity.
- The uniform crossover is used.
- One-bit flip is used as a mutation operation with probability 0.02 per locus.
- Temperature is set constant at 0.005.

Simulation results are shown in Figs. 2 and 3. These figures show the evolution of the population with the proposed method.

Since the temperature is set low in order not to select individuals of greater ranks, only few solutions (and their duplicates) having rank 1 in the initial population survive after selection in the first generation (Fig.2 (a) and (b)). However, the population spreads toward the Pareto optimality set gradually(Fig.2 (c) through (f)). Within the 20th generation, the population is able to cover the range of the Pareto optimality set (Fig.3 (a), and (b)). In the later generations, the distribution of the population gets more uniform and accurate (Fig.3 (c) through (f)).

In this simulation, we have fixed the temperature to examine the ability of the proposed method in maintaining the diversity. The result shows that a satisfactory distribution of the population near the Pareto optimality set is obtained while the diversity loss occurred in the first stage of evolution. The diversity loss in the first generation may not be favorable in more complicated tasks. In such a case, it will be avoided by introducing an annealing schedule of the temperature.

The authors have also carried out simulation runs with various values of the temperature, and the results show that satisfactory distributions of the population near the Pareto optimality set have been obtained at the temperature around 0.01. It is also shown that even if we lengthen the maximal generation, the proposed method keeps a good distribution of the solution avoiding convergence to small number of solutions.

5 Conclusion

In this paper, we apply the thermodynamical genetic algorithm (TDGA) to a multi-objective optimization problem(MOP). Combining TDGA with Pareto-based ranking, a good sampling from the Pareto optimality set is achieved. While the computer simulation is carried out using only a simple example, the obtained results are quite encouraging.

The followings are the subjects of further study:

- To examine the behavior of the proposed algorithm more in detail. Especially its dependency on the system parameters such as the population size should be made clear.
- To design an effective annealing schedule of the temperature.
- To carry out a comparative study with other genetic algorithms for multi-objective optimization(GAs for MO). Especially comparison of the proposed method with GAs for MO using fitness sharing will make the difference of maintaining diversity in the both approaches clear.

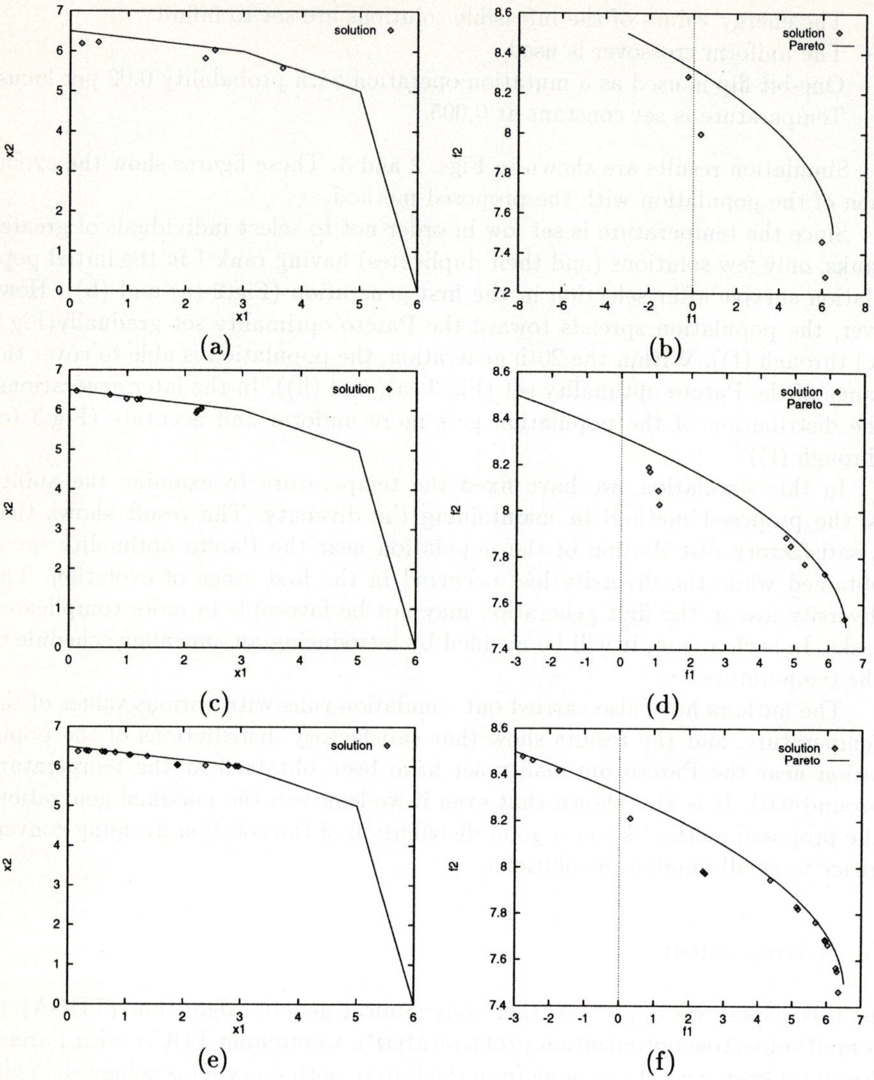

Fig. 2. Solutions obtained by TDGA. Left panels are populations plotted in the decision variable space, and the right panels in the objective function space. The rows of panels are, from the top, the snapshots of the population at the generations 1, 5 and 10.

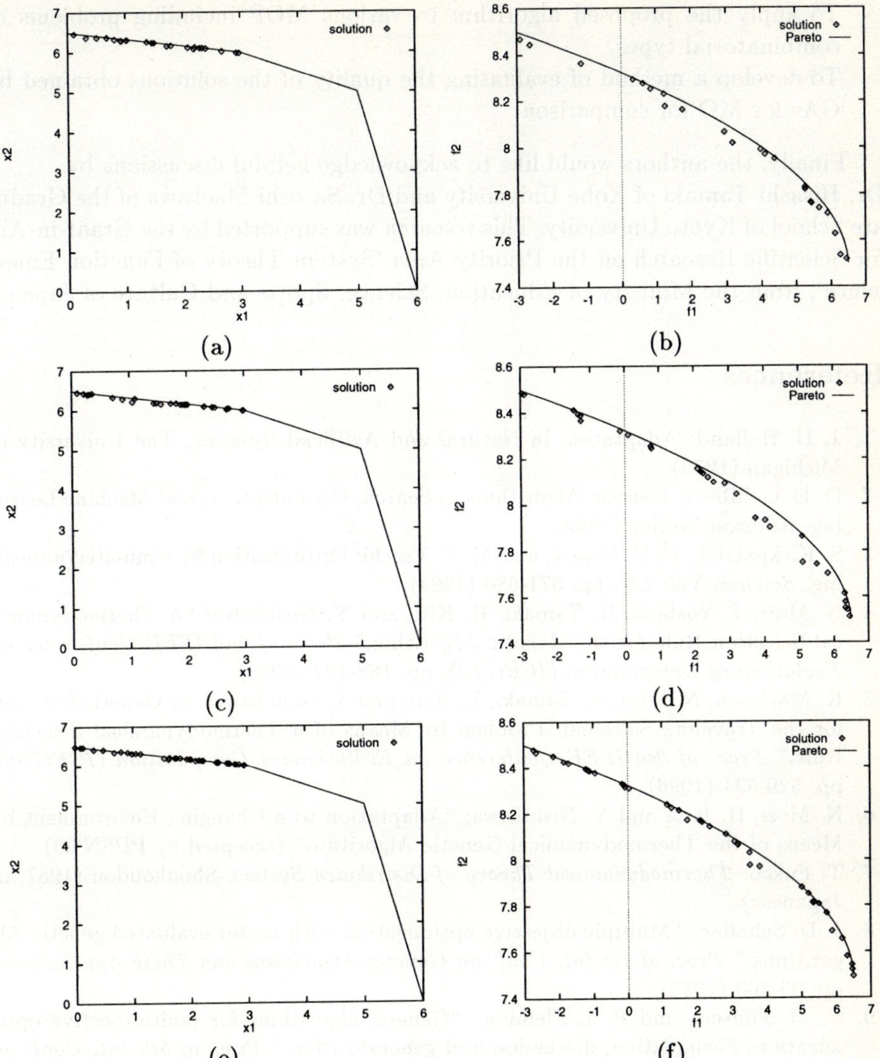

Fig. 3. Solutions obtained by TDGA (Continued). The rows of panels are, from the top, the snapshots of the population at the generations 20, 60 and 100, respectively.

- To apply the proposed algorithm to various MOP including problems of combinatorial types.
- To develop a method of evaluating the quality of the solutions obtained by GAs for MO for comparison.

Finally, the authors would like to acknowledge helpful discussions by Dr. Hisashi Tamaki of Kobe University and Dr. Satoshi Maekawa of the Graduate School of Kyoto University. This research was supported by the Grant-in-Aid for Scientific Research on the Priority Area 'System Theory of Function Emergence', from the Ministry of Education, Science, Sports and Culture of Japan.

References

1. J. H. Holland: Adaptation in Natural and Artificial Systems, The University of Michigan (1975).
2. D. E. Goldberg: Genetic Algorithms in Search, Optimization, and Machine Learning, Addison-Wesley (1989).
3. S. Kirkpatrick, C. D. Gelatt, and M. P. Vecchi: Optimization by simulated annealing, *Science*, Vol. 220, pp. 671-680 (1983).
4. N. Mori, J. Yoshida, H. Tamaki, H. Kita and Y. Nishikawa: "A Thermodynamical Selection Rule for the Genetic Algorithm," *Proc. of 2nd IEEE Conference on Evolutionary Computation* (*ICEC'95*), pp. 188-192 (1995).
5. K. Maekawa, N. Mori, H. Tamaki, H. Kita and Y. Nishikawa: "A Genetic Solution for the Traveling Salesman Problem by Means of a Thermodynamical Selection Rule," *Proc. of 3rd IEEE Conference on Evolutionary Computation* (*ICEC'96*), pp. 529-534 (1996).
6. N. Mori, H. Kita and Y. Nishikawa: "Adaptation to a Changing Environment by Means of the Thermodynamical Genetic Algorithm" (accepted by PPSN'96).
7. T. Fukao: *Thermodynamical Theory of Distributed System*, Shoukoudou (1987, in Japanese).
8. J. D. Schaffer: "Multiple objective optimization with vector evaluated genetic Algorithms," *Proc. of 1st Int. Conf. on Genetic Algorithms and Their Applications*, pp. 93-100 (1985).
9. C. M. Fonseca and P. J. Fleming: "Genetic algorithms for multiobjective optimization: Formulation, discussion and generalization," *Proc. of 5th Int. Conf. on Genetic Algorithms*, pp. 416-423 (1993).
10. J. Horn, N. Nafpliotis and D. E. Goldberg: "A niched Pareto genetic algorithm for multiobjective optimization," *Proc. of 1st IEEE Conf. on Evolutionary Computation*, pp. 82-87, (1994).
11. N. Srinivas and K. Deb: "Multiobjective optimization using nondominated sorting in genetic algorithms," *Evolutionary Computation*, Vol. 2, No. 3, pp. 221-248 (1994).
12. C. M. Fonseca and P. J. Fleming: "An Overview of Evolutionary Algorithms in Multiobjective Optimization," *Evolutionary Computation*, Vol. 3, No. 1, pp. 1-16 (1995).

Adaptation to a Changing Environment by Means of the Thermodynamical Genetic Algorithm

Naoki MORI, Hajime KITA and Yoshikazu NISHIKAWA

Department of Electrical Engineering, Graduate School of Engineering, Kyoto University
Yoshidahonmachi, Sakyo, Kyoto 606-01, JAPAN

Abstract. In the genetic algorithm (GA), maintenance of the diversity of the population is an important issue to enhance its optimization and adaptation ability. The authors have proposed the thermodynamical genetic algorithm (TDGA), which can maintain the diversity explicitly and systematically by evaluating the entropy and the free energy of the population. In adaptation to changing environment, the maintenance of the diversity is quite essential because it is a key factor of generating novel search points. This paper discusses adaptation to changing environment by means of TDGA by taking a time-varying knapsack problem as an example.

1 Introduction

The Genetic Algorithm (GA) is a search and optimization technique based on the mechanism of natural evolution[1, 2]. GA consists of the selection, the crossover, and usually the mutation operators. In the selection operation, an individual having larger fitness value is allowed to yield more offsprings in the next generation. While it is a basic mechanism to find the optimal solution, it also brings about loss of the diversity of the population.

In solving optimization problems with GA, there is a problem called 'premature convergence.' It is a phenomenon that the system often loses diversity of the population at an early stage of searching. Recently, a variety of studies have been reported on avoiding the premature convergence[2, 6, 7]. While these methods are effective to some extent, they are not sufficiently systematic in maintaining diversity of the population.

The authors have proposed the algorithm called the *Thermodynamical Genetic Algorithm* (TDGA)[9], which utilizes the concepts of temperature and entropy as in the simulated annealing (SA)[5], and maintains diversity of the population explicitly and systematically.

In consideration of adaptation to changing environment, since loss of the diversity reduces the ability of adaptation, maintenance of the diversity is essential. Several studies have been reported on GAs for solving non-stationary optimization problems. There have been proposed methods of controlling the mutation rate[3, 4], of using the diploid model[2], and of using directed evolution theory[8].

This paper discusses adaptation to changing environment by means of TDGA which can maintain the diversity explicitly. The performance and the ability of TDGA in maintaining the diversity are compared with those of the Simple GA (SGA)[2] by taking a time-varying knapsack problem[11] as an example.

2 Thermodynamical Genetic Algorithm (TDGA)

In this section, we describe the outline of TDGA.

2.1 The Principle of the Minimal Free Energy

Let's consider the stochastic process used in SA. With a fixed temperature, the stationary distribution of the state obtained by the Metropolis method, a typical transition rule of SA, is given by the Gibbs distribution[10]. Further, it is also known that this distribution minimizes the free energy F defined by:

$$F = \langle E \rangle - HT, \tag{1}$$

where $\langle E \rangle$ is the mean energy of the system, H is the entropy and T is the temperature. It is called 'the principle of the minimal free energy.'

From the viewpoint of GA, by regarding $-\langle E \rangle$ as the fitness value in GA, minimization of the free energy can be interpreted as taking a balance between minimization of the energy function (the first term in the RHS of Eq.(1), or equivalently maximization of the fitness function in GA) and maintenance of the diversity (the second term in the RHS of Eq.(1)), where the diversity can be controlled by using the temperature parameter T explicitly.

2.2 Algorithm of TDGA

The algorithm of TDGA is as follows:

1. Select appropriate values for
   N_{p}: the population size,
   N_{g}: the number of generations, and
   $\mathcal{T}(t)$: the annealing schedule of the temperature.
2. Let $t = 0$, and construct the initial population $\mathcal{P}(0)$ randomly.
3. Let $T = \mathcal{T}(t)$.
4. Preserve the individual having the minimum energy function as an elite.
5. Pair all the individuals in $\mathcal{P}(t)$ randomly. Apply the crossover operator to all the pairs, and obtain N_{p} offsprings. Then, apply the mutation operator to all the N_{p} parents and N_{p} offsprings. Let $\mathcal{P}'(t)$ be the population consisting of the above $2N_{\mathrm{p}}$ individuals and the elite preserved in Step 4.
6. Let $i = 1$, and make the population $\mathcal{P}(t+1)$ at the next generation empty.

7. We refer to an individual in $\mathcal{P}'(t)$ by its number $h = 1, \cdots, 2N_\mathrm{p}+1$. Let $\mathcal{P}(t+1, i, h)$ be the population which consists of already selected $i-1$ individuals for $\mathcal{P}(t+1)$ and the h-th individual of $\mathcal{P}'(t)$, and calculate the free energy of $\mathcal{P}(t+1, i, h)$ for all $h = 1, \cdots, 2N_\mathrm{p}+1$.

$$
\begin{aligned}
F &= \langle E \rangle - T \sum_k H_k \\
&= \frac{\sum_{l=1}^{i-1} E_l + E'_h}{i} - T \sum_{k=1}^{M} H_k(i,h),
\end{aligned}
\tag{2}
$$

where

$$
H_k(i,h) = - \sum_{j \in \{0,1\}} P_j^k(i,h) \log P_j^k(i,h),
\tag{3}
$$

E_l is the energy of the l-th individual of $\mathcal{P}(t+1)$, E'_h is the energy of the h-th individual of $\mathcal{P}'(t)$, $H_k(i,h)$ is the entropy of the k-th locus of $\mathcal{P}(t+1,i,h)$, and $P_j^k(i,h)$ is the ratio of gene j on the locus k of $\mathcal{P}(t+1,i,h)$[1] . Find the individual h that minimizes the free energy given by Eq.(2) from $\mathcal{P}'(t)$. Add the individual h to $\mathcal{P}(t+1)$ as the i-th individual. Repeated selection of the same individual in $\mathcal{P}'(t)$ is allowed.
8. Let $i = i + 1$. If $i \leq N_\mathrm{p}$, go to Step 7.
9. Let $t = t + 1$. If $t < N_\mathrm{g}$, go to Step 3, otherwise terminate the algorithm.

3 Adaptation to a Changing Environment

Before applying TDGA to the problem of adaptation to a changing environment, we make the framework of the problem clear.

3.1 Online Adaptation and Offline Adaptation

To adapt to the changing environment, there are two approaches. One is a direct approach, i.e., the adaptation is achieved by a trial-and-error method directly committing the real world. We call this approach 'the online adaptation'.

Another approach is an indirect one, where first, the changed environment is identified. Then, adaptation scheme is computed based on the identified problem by, e.g., the computer simulation. We call this approach 'the offline adaptation'.

Although the real lives achieve the adaptation in an online way, use of this is not adequate in engineering applications of GA because it requires large amount of fitness evaluation. Hence, here we consider the offline adaptation.

---

[1] The entropy of the population is evaluated in a locus-wise manner to cope with the problem that the population size is much smaller than the number of the possible species[9].

3.2 Periodicity of Environmental Change

If a certain situation of the past environment appears repeatedly, to memorize the result of the past adaptation scheme and to retrieve it will be a powerful strategy of adaptation. We call such a situation the 'periodic change of the environment'. On the other hand, if the environment changes to an unexperienced situation, search by a trial-and-error way becomes indispensable. We call such a situation the 'non-periodic change of the environment'. In this study, we treat the latter situation.

4 Changing Environment Problem

We use the following time-varying knapsack problem as an example of the changing environment problem.

Time-varying Knapsack Problem

$$\max_{x_i(t)\in\{0,1\}} \quad z = \sum_{i=1}^{N} c_i(t)x_i(t)$$

$$\text{sub. to} \quad \sum_{i=1}^{N} a_i(t)x_i(t) \le b(t)$$

$$t = 1, 2, \cdots,$$

where N is the number of items, a_i and c_i are the weight and the value of item i, respectively, b is the weight limit and t is discrete time. In this paper, we use the following two time-varying knapsack problems to examine the adaptation performance of TDGA.

4.1 Irregularly Varying Knapsack Problem (IVKP)

The number of items in the knapsack problem N is 100. The weight a_i and the value c_i are set randomly in the range $1 \sim 100$. These parameters are kept constant. The weight limit $b(t)$ is changed according to an autoregressive process of one-degree (AR(1)).

Let the mean and the variance of $b(t)$ be μ and σ, respectively. With a white noise u_i of unity variance, $b(t)$ is given by

$$b(t) = \mu(1-\phi) + \phi b(t-1) + (1-\phi^2)\sigma^2 u_i, \tag{4}$$

where ϕ is a parameter which represents the magnitude of change. We have fixed as $\phi = 0.5$, $\sigma = 500$, and $\mu = b(0) = 0.5\sum_{i=1}^{N} a_i$. This problem is called the 'irregularly varying knapsack problem (IVKP)'. Figure 1 shows the variation of weight limit and the optimal value of this problem in each time.

4.2 Staircase Knapsack Problem(SKP)

The number of items in the knapsack problem N is 100. All the weight a_i and the value c_i are fixed at 10. The weight limit $b(t)$ is reduced by 100 every 10 generations from 1000 to 100. This problem is called the 'staircase knapsack problem (SKP)'. Figure 2 shows the variation of weight limit and the optimal solution of this problem.

Since the parameters a_i and c_i of all the items are identical, the optimal solution is obviously to select arbitrary $b(t)/10$ items. However, as the weight limit $b(t)$ is reduced, the optimal solution at a time will become infeasible. The aim of the using this problem is to observe the behaviors of the algorithms in such a situation.

4.3 Setup of GA

The genetic representation for problems IVKP and SKP is a 100 bit binary code. The fitness of individual which satisfies the constraint is the value of the objective function itself. The fitness of an infeasible individual is given by

$$f = (b_{\text{sum}} - (\sum_{i=1}^{N} a_i(t)x_i(t) - b(t))) \times 0.01. \tag{5}$$

We use the following parameter I as the index of adaptation performance:

$$I = \frac{1}{T_{\max}} \sum_{t=1}^{T_{\max}} \frac{f_{\text{best}}(t)}{f_{\text{opt}}(t)}, \tag{6}$$

where $T_{\max}$ is the time horizon of the simulation, $f_{\text{best}}(t)$ is the best objective function value in the population in the generation t, and $f_{\text{opt}}(t)$ is the optimal solution in generation t.

5 Computer Simulation

First, IVKP is solved by TDGA and SGA. In this simulation, the temperature in TDGA is fixed. In SGA, the following liner scaling of the fitness function is used:

$$f_{\text{new}} = \frac{A - B}{f_{\max} - f_{\min}} f_{\text{old}} + \frac{B \cdot f_{\max} - A \cdot f_{\min}}{f_{\max} - f_{\min}} \tag{7}$$

where f_{old} and f_{new} are the fitness values before and after scaling, respectively, $f_{\max}$ and $f_{\min}$ are the maximum and the minimum fitness values, respectively, and A and B are constant parameters. In the following simulation, The uniform crossover is used both in TDGA and SGA with unity crossover rate.

In SGA, we set the population size to 200, i.e., twice as large as that in TDGA (100) in order to make the number of fitness evaluation equal.

We have applied the elitism to both TDGA and SGA. The parameters, mutation rate in each locus, fixed temperature (TDGA only) and scaling parameter (SGA only), of the algorithms have been set to the best values after a preliminary parameter tuning. These parameters are shown in Table 1.

Table 1. Parameter list

	Mutation Rate	Temperature	Scaling Parameter
TDGA	0.05	1	–
SGA	0.01	–	$A = 10$, $B = 1$

We set generation size of GA to 100. Change of the environment according to Eq.(4) occurs every p generations.

Figure 3 shows the simulation results for IVKP. The abscissa indicates the fluctuation interval p, and the ordinate indicates the performance index I.

In the simulation shown in Fig.3, the performance of TDGA is quickly improved as fluctuation interval p becomes longer, while the performance of SGA is not improved so much. This result shows that the adaptation ability of TDGA is superior to that of SGA when the environmental change occurs slowly. In contrast, when the environmental change occurs at high rate, the performance of TDGA is rather inferior to that of SGA. In this case, we have observed frequently that all the individuals become infeasible because weight limit $b(t)$ gets down suddenly. In such a situation, the entropy term HT becomes dominant in the free energy F of Eq.(1) in TDGA. Therefore TDGA only works to maintain diversity and can hardly find feasible solutions. This is the reason why the performance of TDGA declines. On the other hand, since SGA uses the linear scaling, SGA can find feasible solutions much better than TDGA. Figures 4, 5 and 6 show the search process of SGA and TDGA for IVKP with $p = 5$.

Second, we solve SKP in order to observe maintenance of the diversity. In this simulation, we have fixed the temperature of TDGA and used the linear scaling in SGA. The crossover operation, the elitism and the population size are identical with those in the above simulation. We have set the mutation rate in each locus to 0.02 and have fixed the temperature of TDGA as $T = 0.1$ and $T = 20$. Figures 7(a), (c) and (e) show the search process of SGA and TDGA, and Figs.7(b), (d) and (f) show the ratios of gene '1 ' in the population.

It is shown in Fig.7(a) that the search by SGA follows the environment change well. Fig.7(b) shows that the ratio of gene 1 in the population decreases with change of the problem in SGA. It is shown in Fig.7(c) that, at a low temperature ($T = 0.1$), TDGA puts more emphasis on searching than maintaining diversity. Fig.7(d) shows that the ratio of gene 1 in the population is almost equal to that of the optimal solution. Once the optimal solution is found, the population becomes occupied by this solution very quickly.

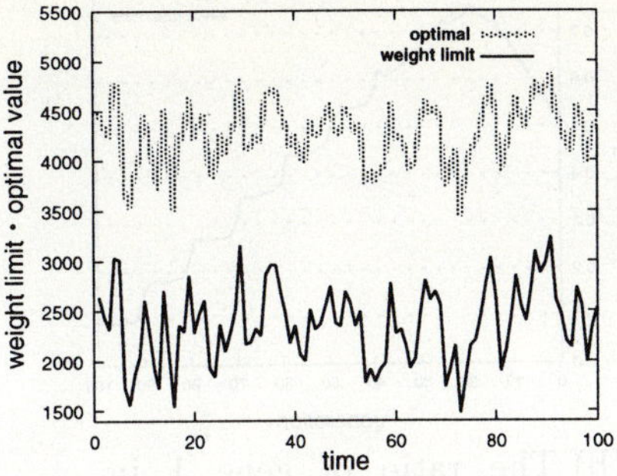

Fig. 1 Irregularly varying knapsack problem.

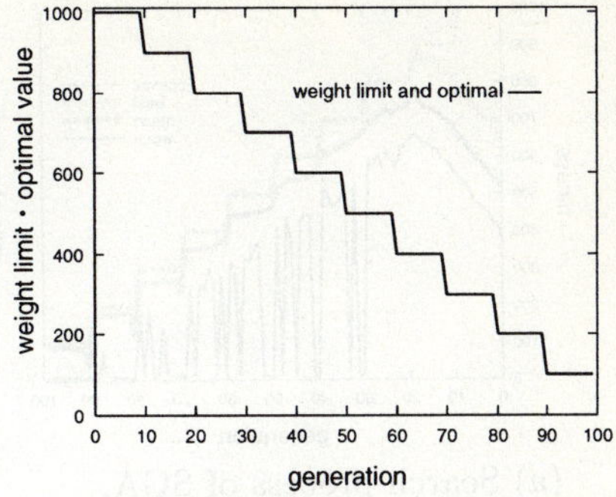

Fig. 2 Staircase time-varying knapsack problem.

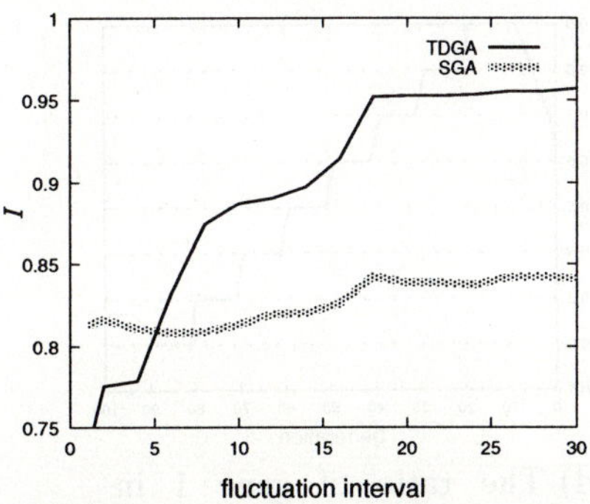

Fig. 3 Comparison of TDGA and SGA in IVKP.

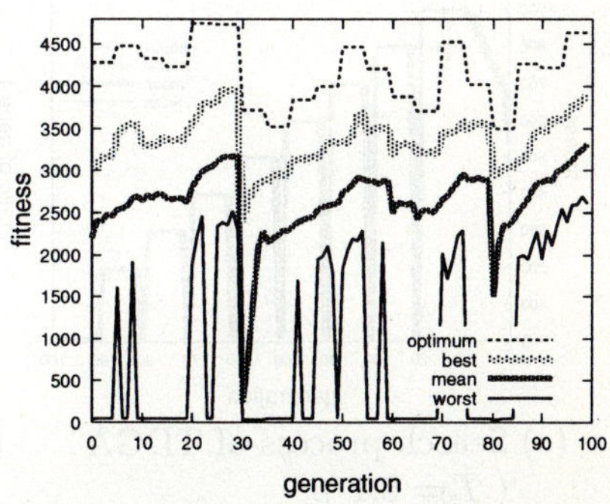

Fig. 4 Search process of SGA in IVKP.

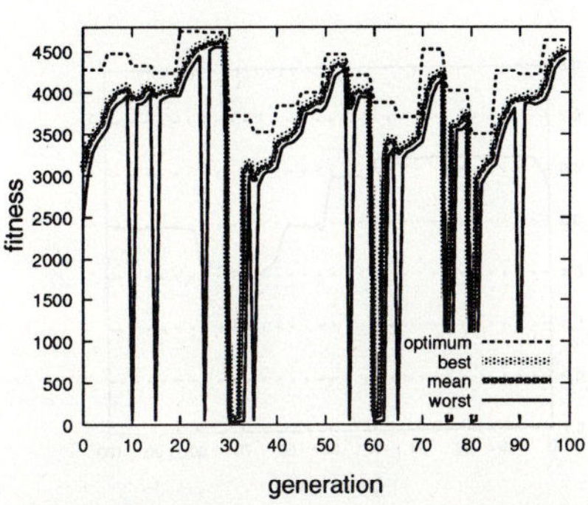

Fig. 5 Search process of TDGA ($T = 1$) in IVKP. The lines for the best and the mean solutions are almost overlapped.

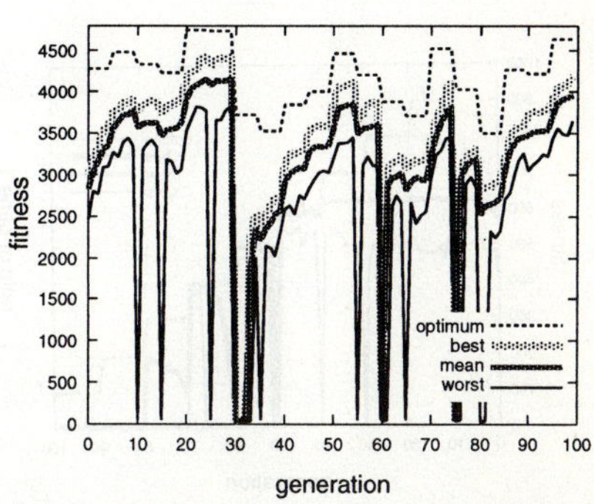

Fig. 6 Search process of TDGA ($T = 20$) in IVKP.

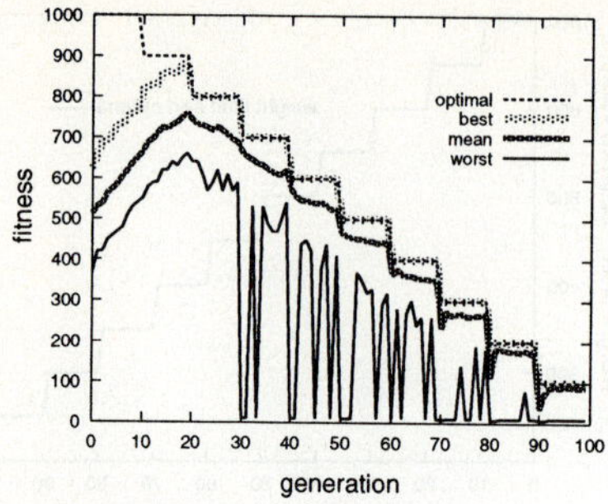

(a) Search process of SGA. The lines for the optimal and the best solutions are almost overlapped.

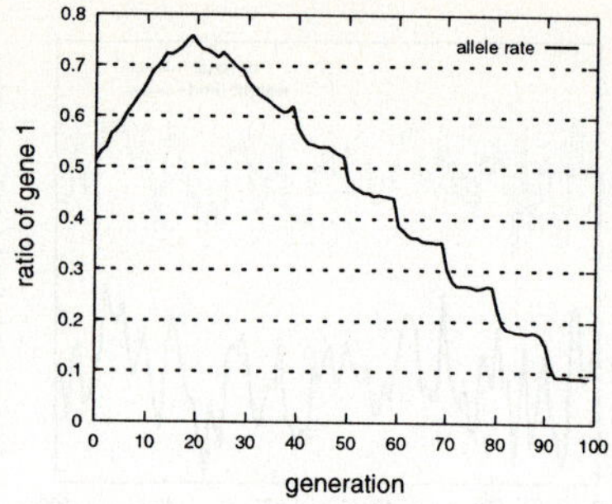

(b) The ratio of gene 1 in SGA.

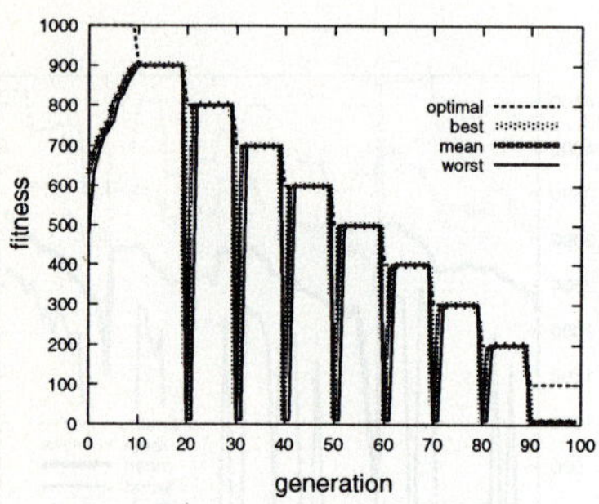

(c) Search process of TDGA ($T = 0.1$). The lines for the optimal, the best and the mean solutions are almost overlapped.

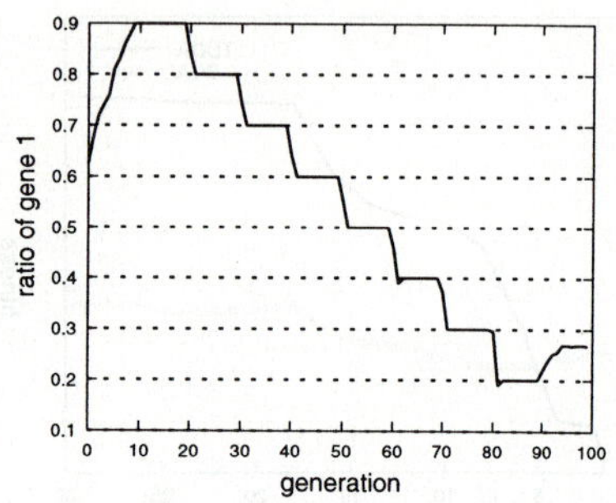

(d) The ratio of gene 1 in TDGA ($T = 0.1$).

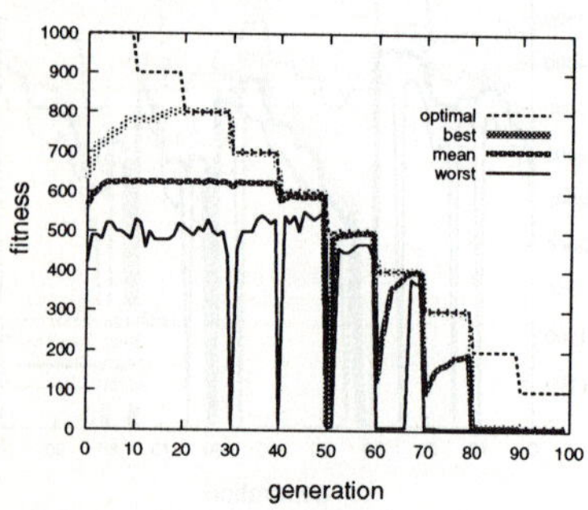

(e) Search process of TDGA ($T = 20$).

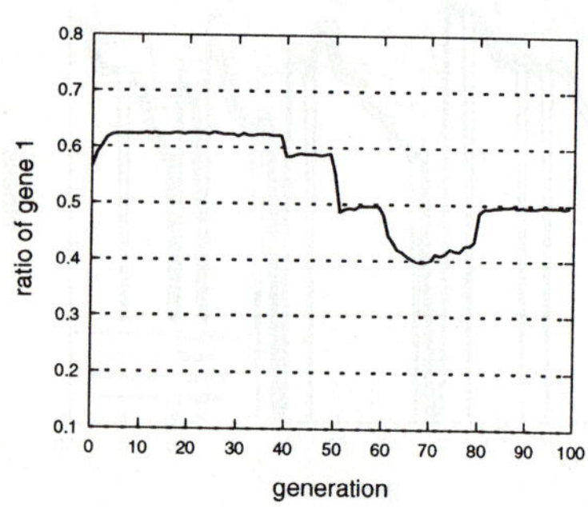

(f) The ratio of gene 1 in TDGA ($T = 20$).

Fig. 7. Comparison of TDGA and SGA in SKP.

On the other hand, at a high temperature ($T = 20$), TDGA puts emphasis on maintaining diversity (Fig.7(e)), and then the searching performance gets poorer. When the weight limit b is quite large or quite small, the performance of TDGA is poor. Especially, the case of $b = 100$ and 200, the feasible solution can not be found. Fig.7(f) shows that the ratio of gene 1 stays around 0.5. It is observed remarkably when the weight limit is small. As mentioned before, in these cases, all the individuals are infeasible, therefore the entropy term HT becomes dominate in the free energy F. This phenomenon is an essential problem in maintaining diversity explicitly. To avoid this shortcoming, the following methods should be considered.

1. Adjust temperature T to give a desirable balance between the variance of energy E and the entropy H.
2. In TDGA, minimization of the free energy is quite rapid. Find a method of controlling its speed.

6 Conclusion

In this paper, we apply the thermodynamical genetic algorithm (TDGA) to a changing environment problem and examine its behavior through the comparison of TDGA with SGA. Under the changing environment, maintenance of the diversity is essential, and TDGA shows a satisfactory performance if the environmental change is slow. However, it is also shown that achieving a desirable balance between minimization of the fitness and maintenance of the diversity is difficult in some cases. It occurs when the environmental change is so rapid and all the individual become infeasible. To overcome this difficulty by, e.g., adjusting temperature automatically is a subject of further study.

Finally, the authors would like to acknowledge helpful discussions by Dr. Hisashi Tamaki of Kobe University and Dr. Satoshi Maekawa of the Graduate School of Kyoto University. This research was supported by the Grant-in-Aid for Scientific Research on the Priority Area 'System Theory of Function Emergence', from the Ministry of Education, Science, Sports and Culture of Japan.

References

1. J. H. Holland: Adaptation in Natural and Artificial Systems, The University of Michigan (1975).
2. D. E. Goldberg: Genetic Algorithms in Search, Optimization, and Machine Learning, Addison-Wesley (1989).
3. J. J. Grefenstette : Genetic algorithms for changing environments, *Problem Solving from Nature 2*, Vol. 2, pp.137-144 (1992).
4. H. G. Gobb and J. J. Grefenstette : Genetic Algorithms for Tracking Changing Environments, *Proc. of 5th ICGA*, Vol. 5, pp. 523-529 (1993).
5. S. Kirkpatrick, C. D. Gelatt, and M. P. Vecchi: Optimization by simulated annealing, *Science*, Vol. 220, pp. 671-680 (1983).

6. H. Tamaki and Y. Nishikawa: A Paralleled Genetic Algorithm based on a Neighborhood Model and Its Application to the Jobshop Scheduling, *Parallel Problem Solving from Nature 2* (*PPSN'92*), North-Holland, pp. 573-582 (1992).
7. Y. Ichikawa and Y. Ishii: Retaining Diversity of Genetic Algorithms Based on Allele Distribution, *Trans. SICE*, Vol. 30, No. 10, pp. 1242-1250 (1994, in Japanese).
8. K. Ohkura and K. Ueda: A Genetic Algorithm for Nonstationary Function Optimization Problems, *Trans. SICE*, Vol. 8, No. 6, pp. 269-276, (1995).
9. N. Mori, J. Yoshida, H. Tamaki, H. Kita and Y. Nishikawa: "A Thermodynamical Selection Rule for the Genetic Algorithm," *Proc. of 2nd IEEE Conference on Evolutionary Computation* (*ICEC'95*), pp. 188-192 (1995).
10. T. Fukao: *Thermodynamical Theory of Distributed System*, Shoukoudou (1987, in Japanese).
11. S. Martello and P. Toth: Knapsack Problems, Wiley (1990).

The Development of a Dual-Agent Strategy for Efficient Search Across Whole System Engineering Design Hierarchies

I C PARMEE, Director

Plymouth Engineering Design Centre, University of Plymouth

email: iparmee@plymouth.ac.uk

Abstract. Evolutionary and adaptive search (AS) strategies for diverse multi-level search across a preliminary, whole-system design hierarchy defined by both discrete and continuous variable parameters is described. Such strategies provide high-level decision support when integrated with preliminary design software describing the major elements of an engineering system. Initial work has involved a Structured Genetic Algorithm (stGA) with appropriate mutation regimes to encourage search diversity. The shortcomings of the stGA approach are identified and a dual agent strategy is introduced (GAANT). Results are compared to those of the stGA. Appropriate communication between search agents concurrently manipulating the discrete and continuous variable parameter sets results in a more efficient search across the hierarchy than that achieved by the stGA whilst also simplifying the chromosomal representation. This simplification allows the further development of the preliminary design hierarchy in terms of complexity. The technique therefore represents a significant contribution to preliminary design where multi-level, mixed discrete/continuous parameter problems can be prevalent.

1. Introduction

The research is primarily concerned with the feasibility/bid stages of the design process. These early stages are characterised by a high degree of uncertainty related to limited available data and lack of definition in the initial design brief. A degree of necessary assumption is therefore required and a breadth-first approach is evident. The detail of any system modelling must be commensurate with the degree of confidence in the available data and it therefore follows that caution must be exercised when interpreting the results from such preliminary design tools. Engineering judgement based upon case-based reasoning, problem-specific knowledge and an understanding of the shortfalls of the software plays a significant role.

The hypothesis underlying the research described is that during these early stages of design the engineer requires a flexible tool that will provide an efficient search of a high-dimensional design space rather than a stiff optimiser. The search will result in the identification of high-performance solutions from diverse regions of a design hierarchy described by both discrete design decisions and continuous variables. The genetic algorithm (GA) generation of a number of high-performance solutions based upon quantitative criteria provides sufficient information for the engineer to form a qualitative judgement. This benefits the significant requirement for caution related to problem uncertainties and allows conflicting criteria to be taken into consideration [1]. The selection of the most appropriate solutions results in a significant reduction in the size of the design space and subsequent concentration of further search in the most appropriate areas. The objective is not to locate the global optimum of the space described by the mathematical model but to select some local optima that best satisfies all qualitative criteria relating to the current design requirements. This will represent the optimal design direction at that stage in terms of least risk and best performance.

The research concerns the utilisation of the GA to achieve an efficient concurrent, multi-level search through the hierarchical structure described by both discrete and continuous variable parameters. The objective is the development of a high-level, decision support tool which will reduce lead times during feasibility and tendering stages of design whilst allowing a more extensive search of the available design alternatives within budget and time constraints. This results in the identification of regions containing competitive solutions that may have been overlooked during the problem decomposition processes of traditional heuristic design. The research is generic in the sense that the developed techniques can be applied to any mixed discrete/continuous variable parameter problem. The dual-agent aspect refers to the final concurrent utilisation of two differing adaptive search regimes. Appropriate high and low level communication between these search 'agents' results in the required breadth of search across the hierarchy whilst allowing a very significant reduction in the complexity of chromosomal representation.

2. The Engineering System

The design domain comprises of a hierarchy describing the major design elements of a large-scale hydropower system (figure 1). At the current state of development the model of the hydropower system must be regarded as representative as opposed to definitive. To date work has been concentrated upon the recognition of those characteristics that enable the search process to concurrently investigate diverse regions of the design hierarchy. However, although not definitive, the model represents practical design aspects of most of the relevant major subsets of hydropower system design. The following variable parameters are considered:

- Five *Sites* are considered each with differing valley cross-section and longitudinal valley sections.
- Two *Dam Types* are considered - Concrete Gravity and Embankment.
- Three *Material Types* are available at varying cost (dependant upon location) for the embankment dams. *Dam Height* represents another variable parameter related to valley depth.

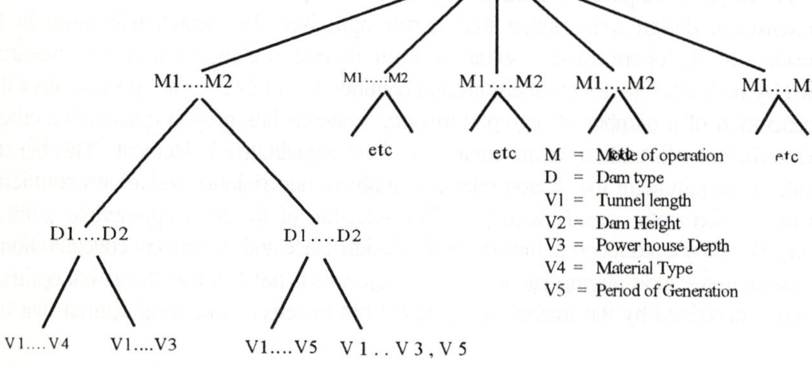

Figure 1: Basic Design Hierarchy

- The length of *The Pressure Tunnels* is represented as a single continuous variable at each site within the limits of the longitudinal valley section.
- It is assumed that tunnel length is related to *Powerhouse Depth* ie the deeper the powerhouse the less circuitous the tunnel route to satisfy minimum overburden requirements.
- Two distinct *Modes of Operation* are considered: Baseload supply where all of the available flow is constantly utilised for power generation and peak power supply where generation is restricted to those periods providing an increased unit price.
- The *Period of Generation* sets the number of hours of energy production per day where peaking output is concerned.

Diversion tunnel length; spillway cost and a factor applied to the concrete gravity dam option related to ground stabilisation requirements are also taken into consideration. The overall objective is to minimise the unit cost of power out calculated from net present worth of both the capital cost and power-out over a twenty-five year period.

The incorporation of a Structured Genetic Algorithm (stGA) (2) provided an appropriate starting point for the development of a suitable global search paradigm [3]. The preliminary design model was therefore initially integrated with the stGA. The stGA allows parameters defining the characteristics of each site to be encoded in the same chromosome string. Controlling discrete parameters, relating to site, mode of operation and dam type then 'switch on' the relevant parameters within the chromosome string which relate to the appropriate configuration. The 'live' parameters are subsequently passed to the design model (see figure 2). Other values remain dormant within the string unless activated in a later population as a result of crossover or random mutation. This process eliminates the possibility of non-feasible parameter combinations being passed to the mathematical model. The stGA therefore defines the hierarchical structure consisting of both discrete variables (ie site, mode of operation and dam and material types) and continuous variables (dam height, tunnel length, powerhouse depth, flow-rate etc) as shown in figure 1.

3 Initial Results

Initial runs of a real-number stGA showed a rapid convergence upon relatively high-performance solutions. Figure 3 however, illustrates the degree of search diversity across the hierarchy where a uniform mutation probability of 0.02 has been applied throughout the 100 chromosome population over fifty generations In this case, an elitist strategy was implemented.

SITE (1 to 5) || MD_1 MD_2 MD_3 MD_4 MD_5 || DT_{11} DT_{12} DT_{21} DT_{22} DT_{31} DT_{32} DT_{41} DT_{42} DT_{51} DT_{52} etc || MT_{111} MT_{112} MT_{121} MT_{122} MT_{211} MT_{212} MT_{221} MT_{222} MT_{311} etc || PD_{111} PD_{112} PD_{121} PD_{122} PD_{211} etc || TL_{111} TL_{112} TL_{121} etc || DH_{111} DH_{112} DH_{121} etc || GP_{111} GP_{112} GP_{121} etc

where:

MD = Mode of operation; DT = Dam type; MT = Material type; PD = Powerhouse depth; TL = Tunnel length; DH= Dam height; GP = Generation period

therefore site 4, peaking generation and embankment dam (rockfill) is represented by:

SITE MD_4 DT_{42} MT_{421} PD_{421} TL_{421} DH_{421} TL_{421} GP_{421}

Figure 2: Chromosome Representation of stGA

Each line represents one of the twenty discrete branches of the hierarchy as described by the three high-level parameters (site, mode of operation and dam type). The 'number of calls' represents the number of times the stGA has visited each of the branches. It is apparent that an optimal solution has been achieved at the expense of search effort along the majority of the branches ie very little search across the system has taken place. The results represent averages from 100 runs each commencing from randomly selected starting points. The fitness of the solutions are shown as a percentage of the best fitness from the initial results of the dual-agent approach (section 6). The lines merely illustrate the diversity of search across the hierarchy.

The overall objective is to develop a search methodology that allows concurrent processing of far more complex hierarchies than the one under investigation here. Such systems will likely involve discrete branching below levels described by continuous variables. There must therefore be a high probability that the search algorithm is sampling each region of the hierarchy to the extent that high performance regions can be identified. The development of suitable mutation regimes that ensure that the discrete elements of the hierarchy have a significantly higher probability of mutation was considered necessary to allow an acceptable degree of investigation of the hierarchy and of the relevant lower-level continuous variables. The greater diversity was therefore initially achieved by assigning independent mutation probabilities to the high-level discrete parameter set (set A) and the continuous variable parameter set (set B). Independent mutation probabilities of 0.2 for discrete set A and 0.02 for continuous set B were combined with a non-elitist strategy. This produced the required diverse search with a much higher proportion of the design hierarchy being visited and a number of high-performance solutions located [3]. A hybrid approach was then developed in which the dual mutation regime with no elitism is implemented for the first fifty generations at which point single mutation plus elitism takes over for a further fifty generations. In this case a population of 100 chromosomes was implemented with a single-point crossover probability of 0.6. The results from this hybrid approach (figure 6) indicated the possibility of both improving upon the optimal solutions found by either of the independent mutation regimes whilst still

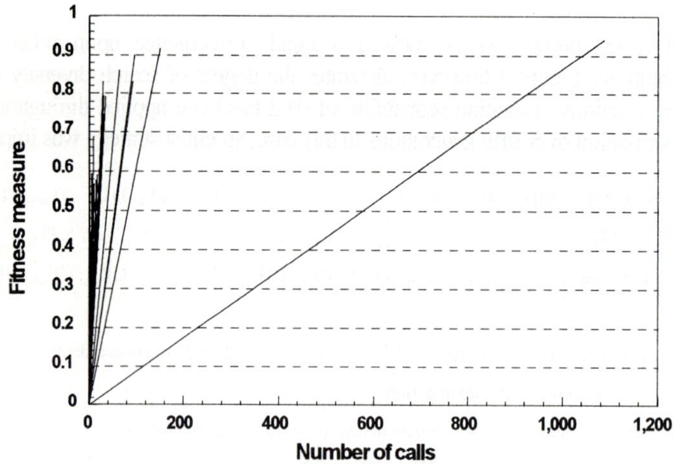

Figure 3: Results from a simple stGA manipulation of the design hierarchy

maintaining a diverse search across the structure. Typically around sixty percent of the solutions are better than those found by the individual techniques.

4. Deficiencies of the stGA and Mutation Regime Strategy

For the strategies so far discussed crossover can be potentially disruptive to the desired formation of high performance parameter sets particularly in the earlier generations. A high diversity of system configuration described by the three main discrete parameters (set A) in early generations leads to a high level of crossover of the continuous variables (set B) between differing configurations. This leaves little opportunity for the evolution of better continuous variable sets for any particular discrete configuration. Crossover merely perturbs either A or B depending upon the location of the crossover site creating a simple 'hill climber' with little relevant improvement in the continuous variables when related to a particular site, mode of operation or dam type. The situation improves as a degree of convergence becomes apparent. The probability of crossover between 'like' configurations then increases and there is therefore an increased opportunity for an overall relevant improvement in parameter set B. This represents a serious problem in that the opportunities for premature convergence are prevalent. The initial hydropower hierarchy is simple and a significant increase in complexity will result from further development. This is bound to involve additional sets of discrete parameters at lower levels of the hierarchy which will likely exacerbate the problem and increase the probability of premature convergence.

Another area for concern is the inherent parameter redundancy within each of the stGA's parameter strings. In order to prevent the generation of non-feasible (lethal) parameter combinations it is necessary to include parameter representations for each of the discrete design options. This requires a string containing ninety-six parameters of which only eight (ie those relevant to the discrete configuration) will be passed to the design model as shown in figure 2. A high proportion of crossover and mutation could therefore be ineffective unless restricted to those areas of the string currently active. Added to this are the problems associated with the excessive number of parameters required in an stGA representation as the hierarchy is developed and problem complexity increases.

5. Simplifying the Parameter Representation

The ideal representation would be a strategy that ensures the avoidance of lethal parameter sets whilst allowing the information exchange evident during traditional crossover. Crossover could be restricted to parameter strings that are identical in terms of the discrete parameter set (ie set A). This would allow an exchange of information relevant to a particular design configuration and the subsequent evolution of that configuration in terms of the continuous variables (set B) whilst also allowing a straightforward eight parameter chromosome representation.

However this crossing of 'like' configurations in terms of the discrete parameters does not allow their perturbation and their subsequent improvement. This problem could be addressed by introducing the variable mutation probability approach described earlier ie introduce a high mutation probability in set A and a lower probability to set B. The overall strategy would therefore involve two individual search agents that are operating autonomously ie a simple hill climber manipulating the discrete set A and a genetic algorithm manipulating the continuous set B. Communication is inherent and exists at a lower level between the individual chromosomes of the continuous set B via information exchange during crossover and at a higher level between the two search agents via the evaluation of each string and subsequent selection using roulette wheel [4]. An improvement upon this approach can be achieved by introducing lower-level information exchange between the discrete sets, A, of each generation. Elements of the Ant Colony metaphor [5,6] have therefore been integrated for the manipulation of the discrete set to form the GAANT algorithm. Two particular Ant Colony 'operators' are of interest:

- *fitness proportionate distribution:* similar to fitness proportionate reproduction - in this case the number of software 'ants' distributed down each 'trail' is proportionate to the relative strength (ie fitness) of that trail. Each discrete path of the hierarchy represents a possible 'trail'.
- *evaporation:* if the strength of a particular 'trail' does not improve over a preset number of iterations then that 'trail' is evaporated and the released 'ant' resource is redistributed around the better 'trails'.

The concepts supporting these two operations have been adapted slightly and integrated with the manipulation of the discrete parameter set. The pseudo-code of figure 4a illustrates this integration. To further explain the process, the values of set A, are randomly selected in generation 1 and combined with a randomly selected population of set B. The initial population of discrete parameters survives for a preset number of generations (*n*) while the associated continuous parameters are manipulated by a simple GA (figure 4b). A combination of like parameter sets during crossover and reproduction is controlled by means of a classification of the discrete parameters into like configurations. Crossover then only occurs between members of the same class. Evolution of set B continues over each generation whereas improvements in set A are achieved as follows: The average fitness of each chromosome is calculated over *n* generations then compared to the average fitness of the *nth* generation. Evaporation, duplication and perturbation of the discrete parameter sets are then established in accordance with their relative fitness (*rfit*) in terms of their average fitness (*fitn*) and *nth* generation average fitness (*fitall*) ie *rfit=fitn/fitall*. This allows the following communication:

- low-level communication between the chromosomes of set B resulting in the evolution of the continuous parameters within the bounds imposed by their discrete system configuration
- low-level communication every *nth* generation between the discrete parameter sets which results in their gradual improvement
- high-level communication between the two agents in the form of the relative fitness of an entire string over *n* generations

Evaporation, duplication and perturbation are controlled at the *n*th generations by introducing two thresholds Rf_1 and Rf_2 (figure 5). If *rfit* is less than Rf_1 then the trail is evaporated ie the chromosome is not reproduced. If *rfit* is greater than Rf_2 then the trail is maintained (ie the chromosome is reproduced) and further resource is allocated from the evaporated trails (ie the population deficit created by trail evaporation is made good by randomly selecting chromosomes from those with a fitness higher than Rf_2). Finally, if *rfit* lies between Rf_1 and Rf_2 the trail is maintained and the direction changed (ie a random perturbation is applied to the discrete parameter set).

```
DISCRETE PARAMETER SET (A)
do I=1,25
      if generation =1
        randomly select initial
        population of A
      endif
      if generation>1 and mod(generation,n) > 0
        reproduce population
        of A
      endif
    elseif mod(generation,n) = 0
        rfit=fitn/fitall
        if rfit<Rf1
          evaporate trail
          elseif Rf1< rfit <Rf2
               maintain trail and
               perturb discrete parameters
             elseif rfit > Rf2
                 maintain trail with no
                 perturbation
                 allocate further
                 resource
      endif
enddo
```

(a)

```
CONTINUOUS PARAMETER SET (B)
do I=1,150
      if generation =1
        randomly select initial
          population of B
          classify population in terms of
          discrete parameters
          assess fitness of complete
        chromosome (sets A & B) and
          implement roulette wheel
      apply crossover between 'like' classes
        apply mutation to set B only
        endif
      if generation>1 and mod(generation,n) > 0
          reproduce selected sets into
           'like' classes
           assess fitness of complete
        reproduced chromosomes
        apply crossover between 'like'
        classes
          apply mutation to set B only
  etc
```

(b)

Figure 4: Pseudo-code describing the search agent algorithms of GAANT

6. Results and Discussion

Initial results displayed in the same format as figure 3 are shown in figure 7 and should be compared to the hybrid stGA results of figure 6. All results are based upon a population size of 100 chromosomes with $n = 5$ generations; $Rf_1 = -0.75$ and $Rf_2 = 0.75$ (in terms of standard deviations from the mean). Table 1 shows a more detailed comparison between the dual mutation regime approach and GAANT. Initial results show the change in performance related to the overall number of calls to the fitness function and the setting of n. Fitness is shown relative to that of the initial GAANT implementation with $n = 5$ and number of calls = 2500. The results are based upon 100 runs of the various algorithms. Standard deviation (SD) of the number of calls along the best path and of the fitness along that path over the 100 runs is shown. The table also shows the number of times individual runs have failed to visit paths and the worst case showing the max number of 'misses' related to a particular path over the 100 runs.

It is apparent from figures 6 & 7 and from the number of solutions greater than 0.8 in table 1 that the GAANT approach can provide improved performance in terms of maximum fitness across a larger number of paths than the dual mutation regime. The standard deviation (SD) of the calls and of the fitness along the best path has been calculated to give an indication of the robustness of the two approaches. The very high SD of the hybrid stGA approach prompted further investigation of the results which showed a far from normal distribution and indicates a lack of robustness. This is further supported by the number of paths that are not visited over the 100 generations of the test runs. The GAANT approach however shows far

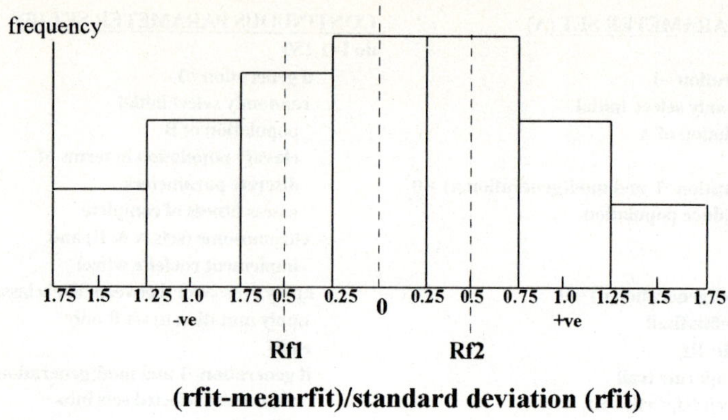

Figure 5: Scaling of *rfit* and introduction of *Rf* thresholds

greater stability both from the standard deviations and the complete cover of the twenty discrete paths. Although both of the techniques finally converge upon the same configuration (ie best discrete path) the GAANT solution from that path is significantly better than that found by the stGA.

Other aspects currently under investigation include the values of Rf_1 and Rf_2 and the redistribution and evaporation strategies of the ant colony manipulation of the discrete parameters. Extensive experimentation is planned based upon a number of test hierarchies of varying complexity.

	HYBRID stGA APPROACH		GAANT IMPLEMENTATION			
	n = 5		n = 5		n = 10	
	2500 CALLS	5000 CALLS	2500 CALLS	5000 CALLS	5000 CALLS	7500 CALLS
Max Solution	0.95	0.97	1	1.01	1	1.01
No of solutions > 0.9	3	3	3	3	3	3
No of solutions > 0.8	5	5	7	9	9	10
No of calls along best path	611	1727	711	1277	1287	2545
SD of No of Calls (Best Path)	580	1706	207	460	413	738
SD of Ftness (Best Path)	0.21	0.17	0.05	0.05	0.05	0.04
No of Missed Paths	93	78	0	0	0	0
Max No of misses of any path	20	26	0	0	0	0

Table 1: Initial Results

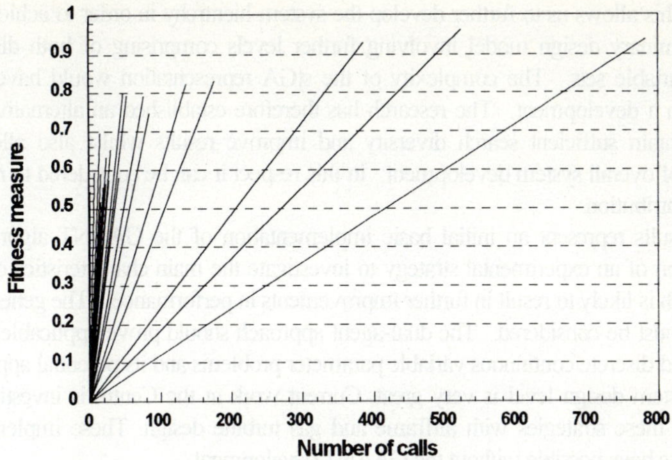

Figure 6: Hybrid stGA approach

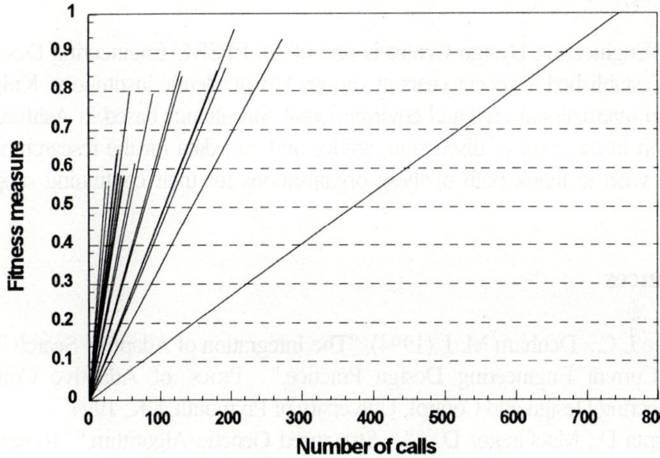

Figure 7: GANT implementation

7. Conclusions

A comparison of the GAANT approach with the previous work involving the stGA shows that the strategy can find better solutions for a greater number of discrete configurations. Diversity of search is thus maintained and with fewer calls to the model in some cases (figure 7). The GAANT technique is also exhibiting a much greater degree of robustness than the stGA approach. Of equal if not more significance during these early stages of development is that this improvement has been achieved using a basic chromosomal representation of the eight variable parameters that describe the system. The extensive chromosomes of the stGA are no longer required thus problems concerning redundancy and complexity of implementation can be avoided. This allows us to further develop the system hierarchy in order to achieve a more realistic preliminary design model involving further levels comprising of both discrete and continuous variable sets. The complexity of the stGA representation would have seriously restricted such a development. The research has therefore established an alternative strategy that can maintain sufficient search diversity and improve results whilst also allowing the continuation of overall system development. In this respect it can be considered to represent a significant contribution.

The results represent an initial basic implementation of the GAANT algorithm. The implementation of an experimental strategy to investigate the main characteristics of the dual agent approach is likely to result in further improvements in performance. The generic aspects of the work must be considered. The dual-agent approach should prove applicable to a wide range of mixed discrete/continuous variable parameter problems and its potential application at the whole system design level is very great. Current work at the Centre is investigating the integration of these strategies with airframe and gas turbine design. These implementations would not have been possible without the GAANT development.

8. Acknowledgements

The Plymouth Engineering Design Centre is one of six EPSRC Engineering Design Centres that have been established in recent years at various UK academic institutions. Knight Piesold and Partners, an international civil and environmental consultancy based in Ashford, Kent has provided support in the form of discussion, advice and cost data for the research described in the paper. We wish to thank both of these organisations for their continuing support of our activities.

9. References

1. Parmee I. C., Denham M. J. (1994), "The Integration of Adaptive Search Techniques with Current Engineering Design Practice." Procs. of Adaptive Computing in Engineering Design and Control; University of Plymouth, UK; 1994.
2. Dasgupta D., MacGregor D., "A Structured Genetic Algorithm." Research Report IKBS-2-91, University of Strathclyde, UK.
3. Parmee I. C., 'Diverse Evolutionary Search for Preliminary Whole System Design.' Procs. 4th International Conference on AI in Civil and Structural Engineering , Cambridge University, Civil-Comp Press, August 1995
4. Goldberg D. E., "Genetic Algorithms in Search, Optimisation & Machine Learning". Addison - Wesley Publishing Co., Reading, Massachusetts, 1989
5. Coloni A., Dorigo M., Maniezzo V. An Investigation of Some Properties of the Ant Algorithm. Procs. PPSN '92, Elsevier Publishing pp 509-520.
6. Bilchev G., Parmee I. C., "The Ant Colony Metaphor for Searching Continuous Design Spaces." Procs. AISB Workshop on Evolutionary Computing; Lecture Notes in Computer Science 993, Springer-Verlag, ISBN 3 540 60469 3, 1995.

A Parallel Cellular Genetic Algorithm Used in Finite Element Simulation

A. Schoneveld, J.F. de Ronde, P.M.A. Sloot and J.A. Kaandorp

Parallel Scientific Computing and Simulation Group
Faculty of Mathematics, Computer Science, Physics and Astronomy
University of Amsterdam
Kruislaan 403, 1098 SJ Amsterdam
The Netherlands, http://www.wins.uva.nl/research/pscs/
e-mail:{arjen,janr,peterslo,jaapk}@wins.uva.nl

Abstract. In this paper we will formulate a framework for a parallel population based search process: an Abstract Cellular Genetic Algorithm (ACGA). Using the ACGA as a template, various parallel search algorithms can be formulated, e.g. parallel Genetic Algorithms and parallel Simulated Annealing. As a case study we will investigate the influence of locality on the behaviour of a Cellular Genetic Algorithm (CGA), that is constructed according to this framework. A neighbourhood structure is imposed upon the population, which results in overlapping local cell-populations. Using varying neighbourhood sizes, we will discuss experiments with CGAs ranging from maximally local to effectively global. The CGA has been applied to a load balancing problem: the NP-hard problem of mapping a process graph onto a processor topology in parallel finite element simulations.

Introduction

Many problems from the natural sciences can be considered as optimisation problems. One approach to solve these problems is to use numerical methods. Another attractive approach is to use stochastic or natural solvers (NS) (for an introduction to the concept of NS see e.g. [15]). Two typical natural solvers are Simulated Annealing (SA)[10] and Genetic Algorithms (GA)[8]. A fundamental problem is that both methods are difficult to parallelise to a level of high scalability. Classical GAs use global knowledge for their selection process. There does not exist a spatial relation between the different chromosomes. An essential problem in SA is that the method is inherently sequential. Our approach to parallelise both methods is to introduce adjustable ranges of locality by using an explicit mapping onto Cellular Automata. Examples in which a GA is mapped onto Cellular Automata can be found in e.g. [11], [7], and [17].

In the general case it is not possible to map SA on Cellular Automata. However, locality can be imposed to SA by applying a population based algorithm [6]. Another approach is to use simultaneous independent searches, which is basically the same method without interactions[2].

In [1] a generic algorithm, the so-called Abstract Genetic Algorithm (AGA), for both SA and GA was introduced. However, the AGA was not designed to facilitate parallelisation. The purpose of this paper is to describe an Abstract

Cellular Genetic Algorithm suitable for parallelisation. In this ACGA the locality is introduced by mapping both GA and population based SA on Cellular Automata.

In this paper we will address the consequences of the imposed locality on a CGA applied to a specific optimisation problem: the *Load Balancing Problem*. This optimisation problem occurs in the mapping of parallel processes onto a specific parallel processor topology. This is one of the fundamental problems in applied scientific computing. The objective is to balance the load equally over all processors and at the same time minimise the communication overhead. Both process and processor topologies can be modelled as graphs. Load balancing has been identified as a major problem present in for instance parallel finite element simulations (see e.g.[16]). Finding the optimal mapping is an NP-hard problem (see section 1.3).

In section 1.1 we will introduce the ACGA and instances of search strategies that can be formulated within this framework. Also some formal convergence proofs will be given. In section 1.3 we will introduce the methodology of redundant decomposition to solve the Load Balancing Problem. In section 1.4 we will discuss the modelling of the process and processor topologies as chromosomes. Furthermore an objective function to control the selection process is formulated. Section 1.5 is dedicated to time complexity and implementation aspects of the parallel algorithm, such that it can be used for verifying speedup results. In section 2 we will discuss the experiments of mapping a specific finite element mesh onto a canonical processor architecture (a grid topology). Emphasis is on the relation between the ranges of locality and the quality and speed of a Cellular Genetic Algorithm instance of the ACGA. Furthermore parallel speedup results will be compared to the formal time complexity derived in 1.5. Finally, in section 3, we will discuss the results and suggest some approaches for future work.

1 Theoretical background and methods

1.1 An Abstract Cellular Genetic Algorithm

To avoid the use of global information which is necessary in the Abstract Genetic Algorithm of Aarts et al. [1], we introduce a local spatial neighbourhood structure. In [1] a neighbourhood is assigned to the value of a chromosome, not its location. The main idea behind the proposed ACGA in this paper is to make an analogy between the chromosome (or solution vector) and a cell in Cellular Automata. Each chromosome is assigned to a cell, which explicitly defines its neighbourhood structure. All communication is local and cells can only interact with direct neighbours. Consequently we can formulate the ACGA:

```
Initialise
DO
    FOR EACH cell in the population
        DO
            Choose a parent list (choice)
            Recombine parent list (production)
            Mutate the offspring
```

```
        Evaluate offspring
      IF offspring meets some criterion (selection)
      THEN
        accept offspring
      ELSE
        leave the current chromosome in its place
      ENDIF
    ENDFOR
  UNTIL maximum number of generations (iterations)
```

From the ACGA pseudo-code above a parallel CGA with local selection can be derived straightforwardly. We only have to select the various genetic operators. First the selection operator. A conventional GA uses a global method to select the parents.

One example is roulette wheel selection. With a CGA the parents are selected from a neighbourhood of size $(2r+1)^2$, where r is the radius, using a fitness function F. A cell is chosen as a parent by picking a uniformly distributed random number $\xi \in [0, 1)$ which satisfies the following rule:

$$\xi < \frac{F(x_m)}{\sum_{x_j \in A_{k(r)}} F(x_j)}. \tag{1}$$

where $A_{k(r)}$ is the neighbourhood with radius r of cell x_k, including x_k, and $x_m \in A_{k(r)}$.
We call this selection mechanism Local Roulette Wheel (LRW).

Another possibility is tournament selection, which we identify by Local Tournament Selection (LTS) in the case of CGA. There is an advantage in using LTS over LRW in small neighbourhoods, because LRW suffers from sampling errors when used on small populations.

As a recombination operator we can take the unchanged GA-crossover operator. Also the GA-mutation operator can be used. Crossover between two cells is done by taking a uniformly distributed random number $\psi \in$ [0, *length (chromosome)*] as the splitting location. Mutation is realized e.g. by "bit-flipping" every bit of a chromosome with a probability p_m. Where a bit is an n-ary number ($n \geq 2$). Evaluation means calculating the fitness of the new chromosome. Because only one child out of the two created can be accepted, a child selection criterion must be applied. In the experiments we only accepted the fittest child. Note that a maximum radius for the CGA is identical with a GA with child selection. We will use this observation to investigate the gradual change from a local to a global CGA.

Another instance of the ACGA is a special variant of Simulated Annealing: Cellular Simulated Annealing (CSA). To introduce locality in the SA algorithm we use an alternative approach whereby several configurations exist together on a 2-dimensional (2D) grid. These configurations only know of the existence of other configurations in their direct neighbourhood. This neighbourhood is defined as a localised spatial structure on the grid. If a new configuration has to be evaluated for acceptance, not only the previous configuration is taken into account, but also its neighbourhood set. Rejection of a new configuration can cause any of the configurations in a neighbourhood set to take over the current spatial grid location. Experiments with CSA for the Travelling Salesperson Problem were reported elsewhere [15].

1.2 Selective behaviour in local neighbourhoods

We already mentioned that LTS is used as the selection mechanism for our experiments. Before discussing the experimental results, the influence of the neighbourhood size on the selection behaviour is analysed. It is shown that the neighbourhood size has no significant influence on the selection process (using LTS). This implies that significant differences in the convergence behaviour are caused by recombination operators acting on localised parts of the population.

Let's consider the expected number of current best chromosomes in the next population, using the LTS mechanism. Let $P_r(best)$ be the probability of choosing the best chromosome in one selection round (choose two chromosomes) given a certain neighbourhood size. Assuming that there is only one best chromosome present in the current population, we can derive the following formula:

$$P_r(best) = \frac{2(2r+1)^2 - 1}{(2r+1)^4}. \tag{2}$$

Furthermore the expected number of best chromosomes is given by:

$$E_r[best] = (2r+1)^2 \times P_r(best) = \frac{2(2r+1)^2-1}{(2r+1)^2} = 2 - \frac{1}{(2r+1)^2}. \tag{3}$$

Note that $\lim_{r\to\infty} E_r[best] = 2$. If $r = \frac{n-1}{2}$ we have global tournament selection. The convergence of the above limit is fast. This indicates that only for small r a deviation of the normal GA tournament selection should be expected. Comparable arguments are valid for other chromosomes in the population. Therefore it is to be expected that the composition of next generations is not influenced significantly by the radius size.

1.3 Preprocessing: redundant decomposition

The problem of finding an efficient mapping of a set of parallel tasks is generally referred to as the load balancing problem (LBP). In [4] it is posed that a practical approach to the LBP is to split the problem into two distinct phases: domain decomposition followed by mapping.

Many applications (like finite element) work on data domains of considerable size. In general the intrinsic parallelism (often denoted by "problem size" N) is much higher than the available number of processors (p) in a parallel system. Finding the optimal mapping is an NP-hard problem, which requires, in the worst case, $O(p^N)$ different mappings to be evaluated. It is obvious that the size of solution-space is too large to find the best mapping in a reasonable time.

It is therefore essential to reduce this solution space. This can be done by clustering N parallel tasks into M clusters where M is of $O(p)$ (decomposition). The decomposition determines the connectivity between the clusters as well as their relative computational weight. In this way the LBP is reduced to the mapping of M parallel tasks instead of the N atomic parallel tasks.

The M clusters can then be grouped into (a maximum) of p "super-clusters", by means of some optimisation method.

In summary we can motivate the two-phase approach as follows: decomposition is necessary to separate the domain of an application in an acceptable number of segments (parallel tasks). Mapping is necessary for optimisation of the parallel execution time. It is important that a near optimal solution is still present in the reduced solution space. The chances of this are significantly increased by decomposing into M clusters where $M > p$ (redundant decomposition). For experimental results on redundant decomposition we refer to [4] and [3].

1.4 Process/processor modelling and the objective function

A good candidate for a generic formalism to describe the performance of static parallel processes is the static execution graph description. The vertices of the graph correspond to work load while the edges model communication load in the parallel process graph.

A parallel machine can be modelled analogously. Now a vertex corresponds to a processor and the attribute is processing power, while an edge corresponds to the physical network connection between processors and the attribute there is link speed or bandwidth. The processor graph should be fully connected. This means that every processor can communicate with every other processor in the topology, although they may be not linked to each other directly in the physical topology.

Using the graph formulation a solution is encoded as a chromosome as follows: each gene corresponds to a process number and is assigned a processor number. The length of the chromosome is determined by the total number of processes.

Having modelled the mapping problem in terms of a compact parameter set we have to define a function that expresses the quality of a mapping. The function (4) e.g. has the property that it has a minimal value in case of optimal load balancing, see e.g. [12], [9] and [3] for other examples of such cost functions.

$$C = \max_{q \in \mathcal{Q}} \left(\sum_{u_i \in \mathcal{U}^q} W_{u_i} P_q + \max_{u_i \in \mathcal{U}^q, u_j \in \mathcal{A}(u_i)} P_{pq} W_{u_i u_j} \right), \tag{4}$$

where

- u_i is a task in the execution graph, called a unit
- $\mathcal{Q}$: the set of processors
- $\mathcal{A}(u_i)$: the set of neighbouring units for unit u_i
- $\mathcal{U}^q$: set of units u_i residing on processor q
- W_{u_i}: Work associated with unit u_i (e.g. in terms of Flops)
- P_q: $\frac{1}{processorspeed}$ for processor q (e.g. in s/Flops)
- $W_{u_i u_j}$: Number of bytes to be sent between host processor of unit u_i and unit u_j (the logical connectivity).
- P_{pq}: $\frac{1}{bandwidth}$ of route between processor p and q (in $(bytes/s)^{-1}$).

It is a property of this specific function that it assumes that the execution time is determined by the "slowest" processor in the parallel machine.

1.5 Time complexity and implementation

In order to compare with scalability experiments we consider the time complexity for executing one iteration of a parallel 2D CGA, implemented on a distributed memory parallel architecture. The total parallel time $T^r(N,p)$ (p processors, radius r and population size N) is given by:

$$T^r(N,p) = T^r_{calc}(N,p)\tau_{calc} + T^r_{comm}(N,p)\tau_{comm}. \tag{5}$$

Where $T^r_{calc}(N,p)$ corresponds to the basic steps performed in the calculation process and $T^r_{comm}(N,p)$ corresponds to the number of basic units communicated every iteration step. The machine specific parameters are τ_{calc} and τ_{comm}. $T^r_{calc}(N,p)$ can be written as:

$$T^r_{calc}(N,p) = (T^r_{select}(N,p) + T^r_{cross}(N,p) + T^r_{eval}(N,p))\frac{N}{p} + \frac{N}{p}. \tag{6}$$

Where N is the size of the population. Both T^r_{select} and T^r_{cross} are $O(1)$ in p and r. T^r_{select} is $O(1)$ for LTS selection. Finally, $T^r_{comm}(N,p)$ can be written as:

$$T^r_{comm}(N,p) = 4r(\sqrt{\frac{N}{p}} + 2r). \tag{7}$$

Combining Eq. 6 and Eq. 7 gives us:

$$T^r(N,p) = (\frac{2N}{p})\tau_{calc} + (4r\sqrt{\frac{N}{p}} + 8r^2)\tau_{comm}. \tag{8}$$

In the Eqs. above $\sqrt{\frac{N}{p}}$ is integer, otherwise appropriate floor and ceiling functions must be introduced. We will use Eq. 8 to verify experimentally obtained parallel timings. It is important to note that due to the absence of any global communication step, the system is optimally scalable. We have implemented a CGA parallel kernel using the MPI message passing library[5]. The CGA is implemented as a back-end program to a front-end mapping tool. The back-end currently runs on a 32-node Parsytec PowerXplorer, which consists of PowerPC 601 processors physically ordered on a grid.

2 Results

Initial work has been done with the CGA on the "de Jong's test functions"[15]. The results were very promising from the perspective of solution quality and convergence speed. Here we apply the CGA to a real world problem occurring in many industrial applications: load balancing of a decomposed mesh for parallel finite element simulations. As a test case we have used a car mesh (see Fig. 1). First domain decomposition was applied, using recursive spectral bisection (RSB , see e.g. [14]), to partition the mesh in 32 clusters. As a target architecture we

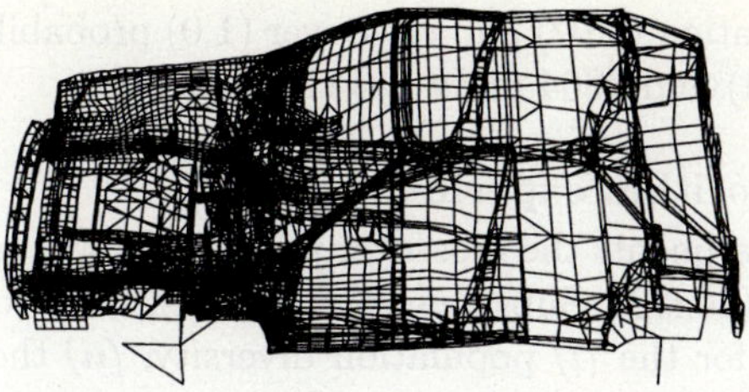

Fig. 1. A finite element mesh of a car. Courtesy provided by ESI-SA (Paris) in the framework of the ESPRIT-III project CAMAS (nr. 6756).

employed a 16 processor grid topology, which is a model of a 16 processor partition of the 32-node PowerXplorer mentioned in section 1.5. With the resulting parallel execution- and processor topology graph, a series of experiments has been performed. Although only 1 specific instance of the LBP experiments is shown, the results are of general nature with respect to the LBP for finite element applications. The experiments only discuss the relative solution quality for different mutation rates and neighbourhood sizes. Actual solution quality is discussed elsewhere [3].

First, the theoretical time complexity of section 1.5 is compared with scalability measurements, in order to validate that the CGA is highly scalable. Secondly, results are presented for the genetic behaviour when two important parameters are varied: radius size (r) and mutation probability (μ). In all experiments, averages and deviations are taken over 25 runs.

2.1 Scalability measurements

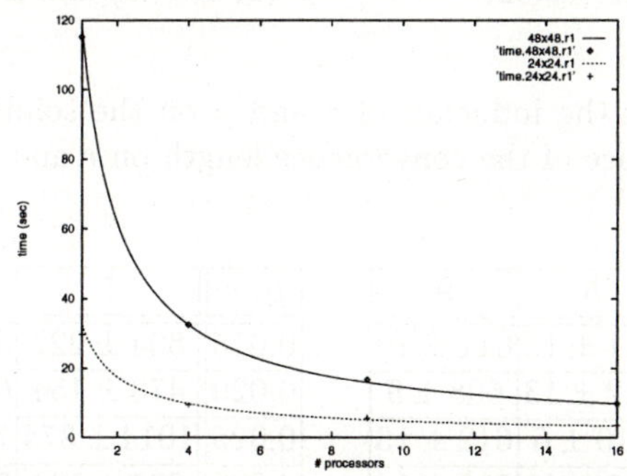

Fig. 2. Running time for 100 iterations for an 24x24 and 48x48 population with $r = 1$. The curves are given by Eq. 8.

In Fig. 2 timing results as well as theoretical predictions are displayed for running 100 iterations of the CGA on 1, 4, 9 and 16 processors. For these experiments we have used fixed mutation (0.02) and crossover (1.0) probabilities and population sizes of 576 (24 × 24) and 2304 (48 × 48) chromosomes.

2.2 Genetic Algorithm experiments

In the following experiments the crossover probability was set to 1, and the population size to 400 (20x20). Subsequently the sensitivity to parameter changes has been measured for the *(i)* population diversity, *(ii)* the convergence of the fittest chromosome and *(iii)* the number of convergence steps. The algorithm is assumed to have converged when the best chromosome has not changed for 300 iterations.

Population diversity is defined as a mean hamming distance over the population. The hamming distance between two chromosomes is defined as the number of different genes. Figs. 3 and 4 show the evolution of the diversity for varying radii with fixed μ.

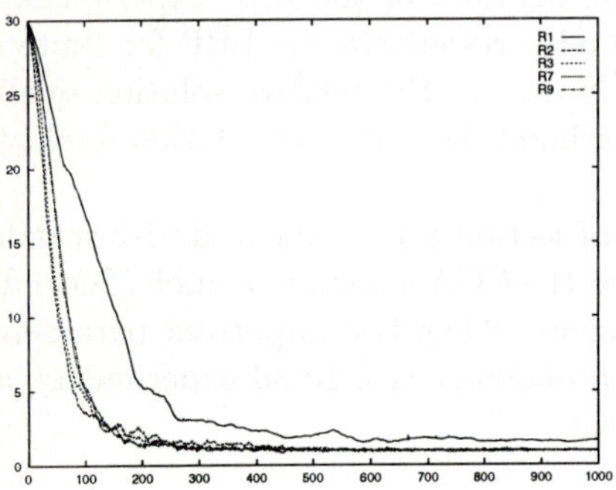

Fig. 3. Diversity evolution for different r (1, 2, 3, 7, 9) and $\mu = 0.02$.

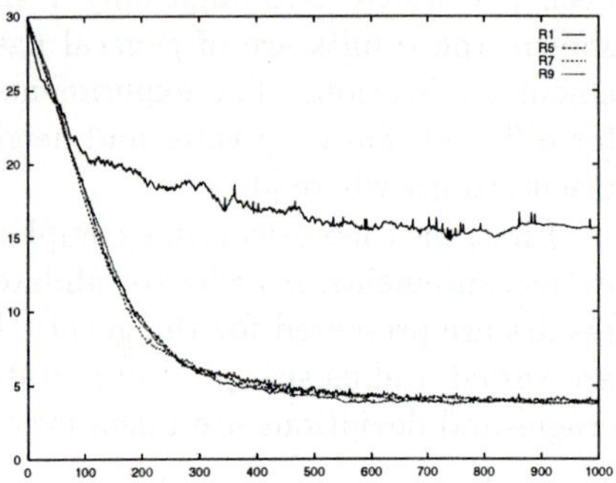

Fig. 4. Diversity evolution for different r (1, 5, 7, 9) and $\mu = 0.03$.

Next, Table 1 shows the influence of r and μ on the solution quality. Table 2 depicts the dependence of the convergence length on r and μ.

μ, r	1	5	9
0.015	606 ± 12	611 ± 12	611 ± 10
0.020	618 ± 18	612 ± 13	608 ± 9
0.025	618 ± 17	610 ± 6	612 ± 13
0.030	646 ± 19	619 ± 13	612 ± 14
0.040	683 ± 24	786 ± 86	770 ± 84

Table 1. Cost of final solution for varying μ and r.

μ, r	1	5	9
0.015	804 ± 222	657 ± 155	650 ± 165
0.020	473 ± 154	692 ± 181	681 ± 165
0.025	1014 ± 374	756 ± 214	848 ± 172
0.030	684 ± 194	772 ± 262	752 ± 256
0.040	624 ± 261	619 ± 250	651 ± 221

Table 2. Convergence length for varying μ and r.

3 Discussion and future work

3.1 Discussion of the results

Fig. 2 shows that the measured values behave conform the theoretical predictions of Eq. 8. Similar experiments were performed for larger radii, resulting in comparable behaviour. Again correspondence with the theoretical predictions was obtained.

Fig. 3 shows that the evolution of the population diversity is not significantly dependent of r. Except for $r = 1$, the behaviour differs from the global selection mechanism. This is in correspondence with our theoretical predictions from section 1.2. This difference is even more manifest for larger μ (see Fig. 4).

According to the formal derivation in section 1.2 the behaviour of the selection process cannot be notably influenced by radius size. Therefore, observable differences must be due to local recombination operations. This is the motivation for studying the dependence on r and μ of the solution quality (Table 1) as well as the convergence length (Table 2).

The diversity is inherently higher for $r = 1$ (see Fig. 3 and Fig. 4), therefore it is expected that, for $r = 1$, a mutation probability must be chosen which is lower than the optimal values for $r > 1$ in order to reach comparable convergence behaviour.

The final solution quality in Table 1 appears to have a lower best μ in the case of $r = 1$ than for larger, near global r, which supports our previous assumption. The convergence lengths shown in Table 2 tend to be highly sensitive to variations in μ for $r = 1$. We intend to investigate this phenomenon in more detail in the near future.

A preliminary conclusion is that the behaviour of the CGA is identical to GA. Except for r near 1 a small difference exists. It should be noted that this has only been validated for GAs based on tournament selection. Furthermore the results show that both solution quality as well as convergence length of CGA (for $r > 1$) are comparable to GA.

Since CGA allows for (theoretically) highly scalable implementations, and shows good convergence behaviour, it appears to be a very fruitful approach for large optimisation problems.

3.2 Future work

Extensive research on the subject of dynamic load balancing in our group has resulted in a prototype dynamic load balancing system for cluster computing[13]. Part of the future work includes embedding a (parallel) mapping algorithm, based on the techniques presented above, into the task scheduler of this cluster computing environment. Furthermore, application of the CGA to various other optimisation problems is scheduled.

Further investigation of the behaviour of CGA in particular and localised parallel search methods in general will be pursued in the near future. This work is part of a long term research initiative in our group on the applicability of parallelism in complex system simulations (see also [15]).

References

1. E.H.L. Aarts, A.E. Eiben, and K.H. van Hee. Global convergence of genetic algorithms: a Markov chain analysis. In H.P. Schwefel, editor, *Parallel problem solving from Nature I*, pages 4–12, Berlin, 1990. Springer-Verlag.
2. R. Azencott. *Simulated annealing: parallelization techniques.* Wiley & sons, New York, 1992.
3. J.F. de Ronde, A. Schoneveld, and P.M.A. Sloot. A genetic algorithm based tool for the mapping problem. accepted for Advanced School for Computing and Imaging Conference'96.
4. J.F. de Ronde, A. Schoneveld, P.M.A. Sloot, N. Floros, and J. Reeve. Load balancing by redundant decomposition and mapping. In H. Liddell, A. Colbrook, B. Hertzberger, and P. Sloot, editors, *High Performance Computing and Networking*, volume 1067 of *Lecture Notes in Computer Science*, pages 555–561, 1996.
5. Message Passing Interface Forum. MPI: A message-passing interface standard. *International Journal of Supercomputer Applications*, 8(3/4), 1994.
6. D. Goldberg. A note on Boltzmann tournament selection for genetic algorithms and population oriented simulated annealing. Technical report, University of Alabama, 1990. TCGA Report 90003.
7. M. Gorges-Schleuter. A asynchronous parallel genetic optimization strategy. In J.D. Schaffer, editor, *3rd International Conference on Genetic Algorithms*, pages 422–427, San Mateo, 1989. Kaufmann.
8. J.H. Holland. *Adaptation in natural and artificial systems.* University of Michigan Press, Ann Arbor, 1975.
9. J. De Keyser and D. Roose. Load balancing data parallel programs on distributed memory computers. *Parallel Computing*, 19:1199–1219, 1993.
10. S. Kirckpatrick, C.D. Gelatt, and M.P. Vecchi. Optimization by simulated annealing. Technical report, IBM, 1982. Research Report RC 9355.
11. B. Manderick and P. Spiessens. Fine grained parallel genetic algorithms. In J.D. Schaffer, editor, *3rd International Conference on Genetic Algorithms*, pages 428–433, San Mateo, 1989. Kaufmann.
12. N. Mansour and G. Fox. Allocating data to multicomputer nodes by physical optimization algorithms for loosely synchronous computations. *Concurrency: practice and experience*, 4(7):557–574, 1992.
13. B.J. Overeinder, P.M.A. Sloot, R.N. Heederik, and L.O. Hertzberger. A dynamic load balancing system for parallel cluster computing. In P.M.A. Sloot, editor, *FGCS*, 1996. Accepted for publication in FGCS special issue on resource management in parallel and distributed systems.
14. H. D. Simon. Partitioning of unstructured problems for parallel processing. *Computing Systems in Engineering*, 2(2/3):135–148, 1991.
15. P.M.A. Sloot, J.A. Kaandorp, and A. Schoneveld. Dynamic complex systems (dcs): A new approach to parallel computing in computational physics. Technical Report TR-CS-95-08, University of Amsterdam, 1995.
16. P.M.A. Sloot and J. Reeve. Executive report on the camas workbench. ESPRIT III-CEC CAMAS-TR-2.3.7, University of Amsterdam, Amsterdam, 1995.
17. M. Tomassini. The parallel genetic cellular automata: application to global function optimization. In R.F. Albrecht, C.R. Reeves, and N.C. Steele, editors, *Artificial neural nets and genetic algorithms*, pages 385–391, Wien, 1993. Springer-Verlag.

A Robust Solution Searching Scheme in Genetic Search

Shigeyoshi Tsutsui[1], Ashish Ghosh[2] and Yoshiji Fujimoto[3]

[1] Department of Management and Information Science, Hannan University
5-4-33 Amamihigashi, Matsubara, Osaka 580 Japan
tsutsui@hannan-u.ac.jp

[2] Department of Industrial Engineering, College of Engineering
Osaka Prefecture University
1-1 Gakuen-cho, Sakai, Osaka 593 Japan

[3] Department of Applied Mathematics and Informatics
Faculty of Science and Technology, Ryukoku University
1-5 Yokoya, Seta Ooe, Ohtsu, Shiga 520-21 Japan

Abstract. Many of the studies on GAs give emphasis on finding the global optimal solution. In this paper, we propose a new method which extend the application of GAs to domains that require detection of *robust solutions*. If a global optimal solution found is on a sharp-pointed location, there may be cases where it is not good to use this solution. In nature, the phenotypic feature of an organism is determined from the genotypic code of genes in the chromosome. During this process, there may be some perturbations. Let X be the phenotypic parameter vector, $f(X)$ a fitness function and Δ a noise vector. As can be easily understood from the analogy of nature, actual fitness function should be of the form $f(X+\Delta)$. We use this analogy for the present work. Simulation results confirm the utility of this approach in finding robust solutions.

Keywords: Genetic Search, Robust Solutions, Adding noise

1 Introduction

Over the years, genetic algorithms (GAs) have proved useful in a variety of search and optimization problems [6]. There are many theoretical and empirical studies to improve the performance of GAs to solve difficult problems such as the multimodal and deceptive problems [5, 7, 10, 12, 13]. As a matter of fact, these researches put emphasis on finding the global optimal solution.

There are a number of investigations which emphasizes on finding multiple solutions (peaks) including local optima. These include the crowding method of De Jong [3], the sharing method of Goldberg et al. [8], the deterministic crowding method of Mahold [11], and the sequential niche method of Beasley et al. [2]. These approaches extend the application of GAs to domains that require the location of multiple solutions.

In this paper, we propose a new method which extend the application of GAs to domains that require the location of *robust solutions*. If the global optimal solution detected is a very sharp point, then there may be cases where it is not good to adopt this solution. This is especially true in areas such as setting the control parameters of aerospace control system, nuclear power control system, where a kind of robustness against the perturbation of the environmental features are important.

In nature, the phenotypic feature of an organism is determined from the genotypic code of genes in the chromosome. In this transformation, there may be some perturbations, for example, caused by an abnormal temperature, a nutritionally imbalance condition, existence of injurious matter etc. If in an organism these perturbed phenotypic features have low fitness, then the organism can not survive or produce offspring. Thus a species having a good genotypic material, if its phenotypic features become sensitive to perturbations, it would die out. On the other hand, the species which is robust against this perturbations would survive and evolve.

To emulate this sort of genetic feature, we can develop a genetic search scheme which can produce *robust solutions*. The proposed approach uses the effect of noise in the calculation of fitness values. Approaches on evolutionary computation which give consideration to existence of noise in calculating the fitness function are discussed in [3, 9]. Let $\boldsymbol{X} = (x_1, x_2, ..., x_m)$ be a phenotypic parameter vector, $f(\boldsymbol{X})$ the fitness function and $\Delta = (\delta_1, \delta_2, ...,\delta_m)$ a noise vector. They used the form $f(\boldsymbol{X}) + \delta$, i.e. add noise δ with fitness value. As can be understood from the analogy of nature that noise is added during transformation from genotype to phenotype. Thus we can use an evaluation function of the form $f(\boldsymbol{X}+\Delta)$. By this approach, we can search for robust solutions. We call this approach *Robust Solution Searching Scheme* (RS^3) in genetic search.

In the following sections, first a model of the RS^3 in genetic search is outlined. Next, a mathematical model of RS^3 is described. Finally, empirical results are shown which confirm the effectiveness of the approach.

2 Description of the Robust Solution Searching Scheme (RS^3)

In this paper, we are primarily concerned with finding the robust solutions (against perturbations of $\boldsymbol{X}$) which maximize the function $f(\boldsymbol{X})$. Then the problem becomes as follows:

Find $\boldsymbol{X}$ which maximizes $f(\boldsymbol{X}+\Delta)$.

Let $\boldsymbol{G}$ be a genotype string (or *chromosome*) which generates parameter $\boldsymbol{X}$. The model of the GA with RS^3 becomes as shown in Fig. 1. Here, it should be noted that adding noise in the form of $f(\boldsymbol{X}+\Delta)$ may look like a mutation operation on real valued coding, but it is completely different from mutation, since it does not affect the individual. The perturbations are used only for selection operation purpose.

```
gen = 0;
Pop(gen) = randomly initialized population (G^1, G^2, ..., G^N)
Transform each G^i to X^i;
Y^i = X^i + Δ;
Evaluate fitness of each Y^i in Pop(gen);
while( termination condition == false ){
        gen += 1;
        Select Pop(gen) from Pop(gen - 1) based on the fitness value f(Y^i);
        Apply genetic operators to G^1, G^2, ..., G^N in Pop(gen)
        Transform each G^i to X^i;
        Y^i = X^i + Δ;
        Evaluate fitness of each Y^i in Pop(gen);
}
Evaluate fitness of each X^i in Pop(gen)
```

Fig. 1 Model of the GA with RS^3

3 Mathematical Model

In this section we describe a simple mathematical model of RS^3. Although there are major differences between high- and low-dimensional problems, we consider $\boldsymbol{X}$ to be one dimensional to demonstrate the effect of adding noise more clearly and denote $\boldsymbol{X}$ by x. Extension of it to multi-dimension can be performed in a similar manner.

3.1 Effective Fitness Function in GA with RS^3

Let us consider the Schema Theorem of a GA using a proportional selection scheme and single-point crossover [6]:

$$M(H,t+1) \geq M(H,t) \cdot \frac{f(H,t)}{\overline{f(t)}} \left[1 - p_c \frac{d(H)}{L-1} - o(H) p_m \right], \tag{1}$$

where H represents a schema in population $P(t)$, $f(H,t)$ is the average fitness of representatives of H in $P(t)$, $\overline{f(t)}$ denotes the average fitness of the individuals in $P(t)$, p_c is the crossover rate, p_m is the mutation rate, $d(H)$ is the defining length of H, $o(H)$ is the order of H, L is the string length and $M(H,t)$ is the expected number of representatives of schema H at generation t. $\overline{f(t)}$, the average of the individuals in $P(t)$, is taken as

$$\overline{f(t)} = \sum_{i=1}^{N} f(x^i) / N, \tag{2}$$

where N is size of the population. If noise is added to the fitness function $f(x)$, it becomes $f(x+\delta)$; then

$$\overline{f(t)} = \sum_{i=1}^{N} f(x^i + \delta) / N . \tag{3}$$

The same logic holds true for calculating $f(H,t)$. If we assume the noise δ to be independent of time, the effective average fitness $\overline{F(t)}$, i. e., the average fitness $\overline{f(t)}$ over the distribution of δ, can be obtained as follows:

$$\begin{aligned}\overline{F(t)} &= \int_{-\infty}^{\infty} \sum_{i=1}^{N} f(x^i + \delta) \cdot q(\delta) d\delta / N \\ &= \sum_{i=1}^{N} \left[\int_{-\infty}^{\infty} f(x^i + \delta) \cdot q(\delta) d\delta \right] / N ,\end{aligned} \tag{4}$$

where $q(\delta)$ is the density function of noise δ.

From Eqs. 2 and 4, we can conclude that the *effective fitness function* $F(x)$ can be formulated as

$$\begin{aligned}F(x) &= \int_{-\infty}^{\infty} f(x + \delta) \cdot q(\delta) d\delta \\ &= \int_{-\infty}^{\infty} f(y) \cdot q(y - x) dy .\end{aligned} \tag{5}$$

Thus, we can calculate the effective fitness function $F(x)$ from fitness function $f(x)$ and noise density function $q(\delta)$.

If we assume $q(\delta)$ to be symmetric, i. e., $q(\delta) = q(-\delta)$, then $F(x)$ can be written as

$$F(x) = \int_{-\infty}^{\infty} q(x - y) \cdot f(y) dy . \tag{6}$$

Eq. 6 has the form of convolution integral. Let $\hat{F}(\omega)$, $\hat{f}(\omega)$ & $\hat{q}(\omega)$ be Fourier transform of functions $F(x)$, $f(x)$ & $q(x)$, respectively. Then, we can get $\hat{F}(\omega)$ as

$$\hat{F}(\omega) = \hat{q}(\omega) \cdot \hat{f}(\omega) \tag{7}$$

It is very natural to assume the noise to be a Gaussian noise N(0, σ) as it is the sum of various perturbations. Then, $\hat{q}(\omega)$ is obtained as

$$\hat{q}(\omega) = \frac{1}{\sqrt{2\pi}} e^{\frac{-\sigma^2 \omega^2}{2}} . \tag{8}$$

Function $\hat{q}(\omega)$ decreases as ω increases. Thus, we can understand that adding Gaussian noise to phenotypic parameters acts as a low-pass filter as in a signal processing system. Also we can see that the effect of low-pass filtering is strengthened as the value of σ increases.

3.2 Calculation of the Effective Fitness Functions

For mathematical manipulation let us chose (for the sake of simplicity) a *peak* of fitness function by a rectangular function with height h and width $2w$ as follows:

$$f(x) = \begin{cases} h: & -w \le x \le w \\ 0: & \text{otherwise}. \end{cases} \tag{9}$$

Then, from Eq. 6 we can calculate effective fitness function of Eq. 9 as follows:

$$\begin{aligned} F(x) &= h\int_{-w}^{w} q(x-y)dy \\ &= h\left[\Phi\left(\frac{x+w}{\sigma}\right) - \Phi\left(\frac{x-w}{\sigma}\right)\right], \end{aligned} \tag{10}$$

where a Gaussian noise N(0, σ) is assumed and $\Phi(y)$ is the distribution function of the standard Gaussian noise defined by

$$\Phi(y) = \int_{-\infty}^{y} \frac{1}{\sqrt{2\pi}} e^{\frac{-y^2}{2}} dy. \tag{11}$$

By setting the derivative of the function $F(x)$ to zero, the peak point is obtained at $x = 0$ and the peak value $\max F(x)$ is obtained as

$$\begin{aligned} \max F(x) &= F(0) \\ &= h\left[2\Phi\left(\frac{w}{\sigma}\right) - 1\right]. \end{aligned} \tag{12}$$

Fig. 2 plots the $\max F(x)$ values vs. w/σ. Fig. 3 shows the relationship between the fitness function $f(x)$ and the effective fitness function $F(x)$ for w/σ = 4.0, 2.0, 1.0, 0.5 & 0.25.

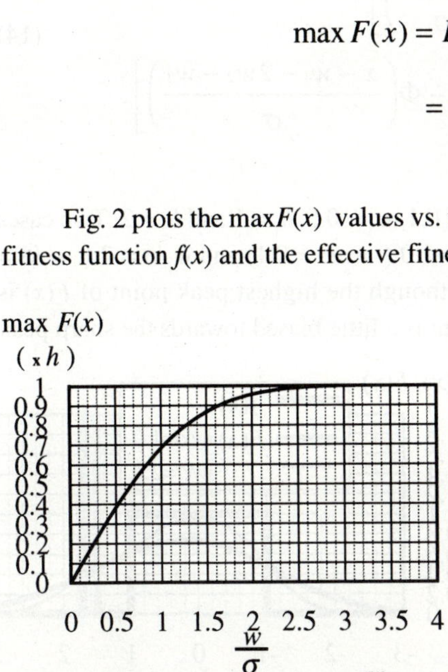

Fig. 2. max $F(x)$ vs. $\frac{w}{\sigma}$

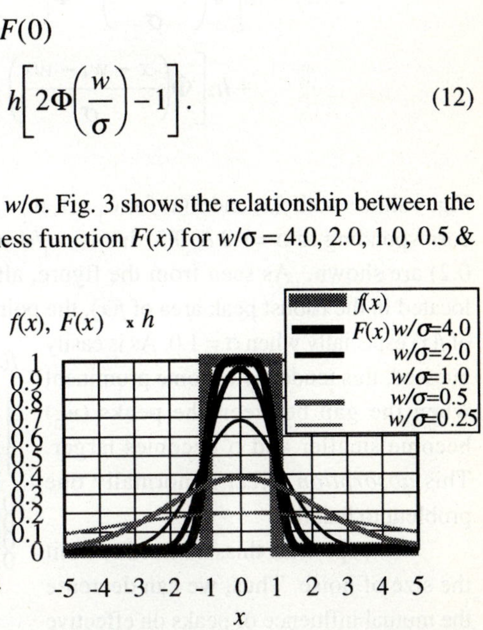

Fig. 3. Relationship between $f(x)$ and $F(x)$

0.25. From Figs. 2 and 3, we can confirm that adding Gaussian noise to phenotypic parameters acts as a low pass filter as discussed in Section 3.1. We can estimate σ value as follows. Let $2w_0$ be the width of a sharp peak with height h. If we take σ in the range $2w_0$ - $4w_0$, then w/σ has values in the range 0.5 - 0.25 and the effective peak value would lie between $0.197h$ and $0.383h$. Thus, we can roughly estimate σ value.

3.3 An Absorption Effect

Let us consider a fitness function $f(x)$ with one robust peak with width $2w_1$ and height h_1, one sharp peak with width $2w_2$ and height h_2 and a gap w_3 between them as follows:

$$f(x) = \begin{cases} h_1: & -w_1 \le x \le w_1 \\ h_2: & w_1 + w_3 \le x \le w_1 + 2w_2 + w_3 \\ 0: & \text{otherwise}. \end{cases} \tag{13}$$

Here, we assume $w_1 >> w_2$ and $h_1 < h_2$. The effective fitness function $F(x)$ of $f(x)$ can be obtained as follows:

$$\begin{aligned} F(x) = h_1&\left[\Phi\left(\frac{x+w_1}{\sigma}\right) - \Phi\left(\frac{x-w_1}{\sigma}\right)\right] \\ +h_2&\left[\Phi\left(\frac{x-w_1-w_3}{\sigma}\right) - \Phi\left(\frac{x-w_1-2w_2-w_3}{\sigma}\right)\right]. \end{aligned} \tag{14}$$

Fig. 4 shows both $f(x)$ and $F(x)$ for $w_1 = 1$, $w_2 = 0.1$, $w_3 = 0.5$, $h_1 = 1$ and $h_2 = 2$. Two cases corresponding to σ =1.0 & 0.5, that is, $w_1/\sigma = 1.0$ (: $w_2/\sigma = 0.1$) and $w_1/\sigma = 2$ (: $w_2/\sigma = 0.2$) are shown. As seen from the figure, although the highest peak point of $F(x)$ is located in the robust peak area of $f(x)$, the point is a little biased towards the sharp peak of $f(x)$ especially when σ = 1.0. As is easily guessed, this tendency become prominent when the gap between the peaks (w_3) become smaller and σ becomes larger. This *absorption effect* is normally one problem to handle.

To cope with this, we need to limit the size of noise. Thus, we can decrease the mutual influence of peaks on effective fitness function. In this paper, we propose

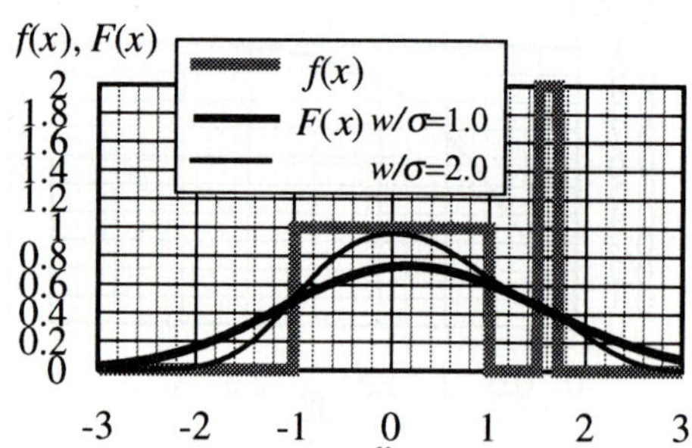

Fig. 4. The Absorption Effect

to use the following *modified Gaussian noise* N'(0, σ):

$$q(y) = \begin{cases} \dfrac{1}{C\sqrt{2\pi\sigma}} e^{\frac{-y^2}{2\sigma^2}} & : \quad -k\sigma \le y \le k\sigma \\ 0 & : \quad \text{otherwise}, \end{cases} \tag{15}$$

where k is a control parameter and C is a normalizing constant calculated as

$$C = 2\Phi(k) - 1. \tag{16}$$

In our experiment, we used $k = 1$.

Although the form N'(0, σ) is useful, there still remains a point to be considered. Let us consider a fitness function where the gap between a robust peak and a sharp peak (w_3 in this section) is very small. In this case, it may so occur that the peak of the effective fitness function is located in the gape. This problem can also be tackled if we are careful in using the RS^3. Due to the presence of noise, individuals in the converged population are distributed according to the effective fitness function (see Figs. 6 & 7). Thus, each individual is a candidate to be adopted. We should choose a solution from these candidates.

4 Empirical Study

To show the utility of RS^3, we studied two functions. We use a simple GA with stochastic universal sampling [1]. GA parameters were kept constant for all the simulations as $p_m = 0.006$, $p_c = 0.6$, population size $N = 50$, maximum number of trials = 3,000, and string length = 30 (Gray coded).

(1) Function f_a

f_a is a function (shown in Fig. 4) with two peaks in the range $-3 \le x \le 3$. We assume $\sigma = 0.4$ ($w_2/\sigma = 0.25$). Fig. 5 shows the mean value of parameter x in the population with trials. Simple GA converged to the highest sharp peak with mean value 1.6 (the center of the highest peak). GA with RS^3 converged to the lower robust peak. Fig. 6 shows a typical distribution of the individuals in the population after 3,000 trials for both simple GA and the proposed model.

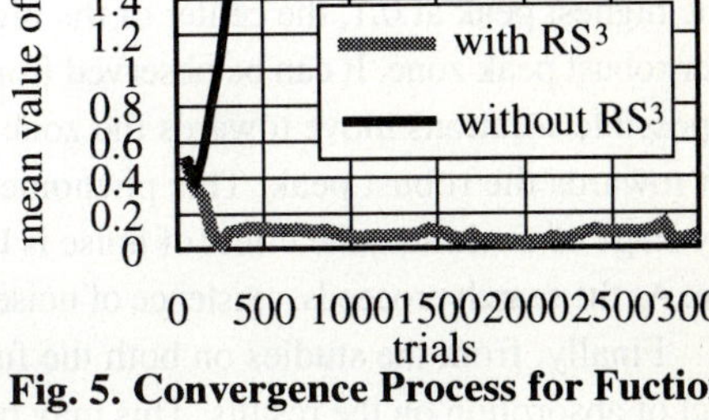

Fig. 5. Convergence Process for Fuction f_a

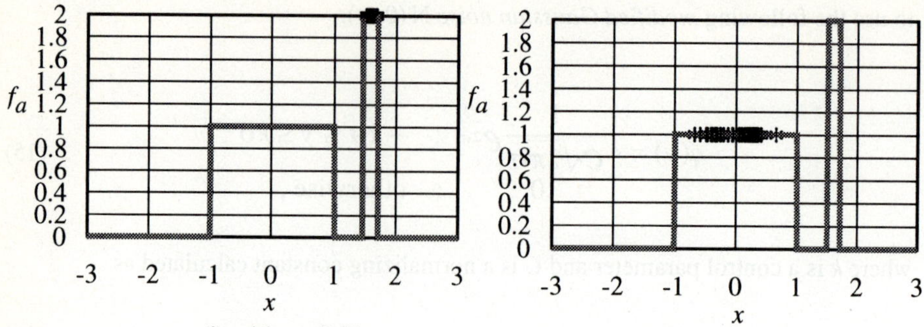

(i) without RS³ (ii) with RS³

Fig. 6. State of the Population on Function f_a

(2) Function f_b

Function f_b has five unequal peaks in the range $0 \le x \le 1$ and is a variant of the function used in [4] defined as follows:

$$f_b = \begin{cases} e^{-2\ln 2\left(\frac{x-0.1}{0.8}\right)^2} |\sin(5\pi x)|^{0.5} & : 0.4 < x \le 0.6 \\ e^{-2\ln 2\left(\frac{x-0.1}{0.8}\right)^2} \sin^6(5\pi x) & : \text{otherwise}. \end{cases} \tag{17}$$

As shown in Fig. 7, global optimum is located at $x = 0.1$ with value 1.0. All peaks except the third one are sharp. The third peak is robust compared to the other four peaks and is located at $x = 0.486$ with peak value 0.715. The effective width $2w$ of the sharp peaks can be estimated as follows:

$$1 \times 2w \approx 1 \times \int_0^{0.2} \sin^6(5\pi x)\,dx = 1/16 \quad \Rightarrow \quad w \approx 1/32\,. \tag{18}$$

Referring to Fig. 2, w/σ can be chosen in (0.25, 0.5] so as to reduce the effective fitness value by 50%. We choose $w/\sigma = 0.5$. Thus, $\sigma = 1/16$ ($\because \sigma = w/0.5 = 2 \times 1/32$) is used.

Fig. 7 shows a typical distribution of the individuals in the population after 3,000 trials for both simple GA and the proposed model. From the figures, we can say that in the GA with RS³ the population converges to the robust peak. Fig. 8 shows a convergence process of the mean values of parameter x in the population. GA without RS³ converges to the highest peak at 0.1, the center of the highest peak. GA with RS³ converges to the lower robust peak zone. It can be observed from Fig. 8 that at the first stage of searching, the possible solutions move towards the zone where the highest peak exists. Then they shift towards the robust peak. This phenomenon may be explained as follows. In the early stage of evolution, the effect of noise is low since the diversity of the population is large. As the search proceeds, existence of noise gradually affects and moves the solutions.

Finally, from the studies on both the function f_a and f_b we notice that there is no effect of absorption on the results. This may be due to the fact that we added noise with

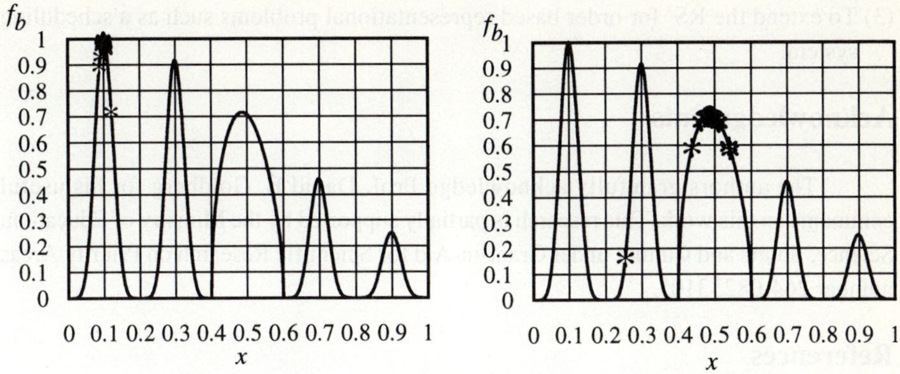

(i) without RS[3] (ii) with RS[3]

Fig. 7. State of the Population on Function f_b

modified Gaussian distribution and appropriate value of σ.

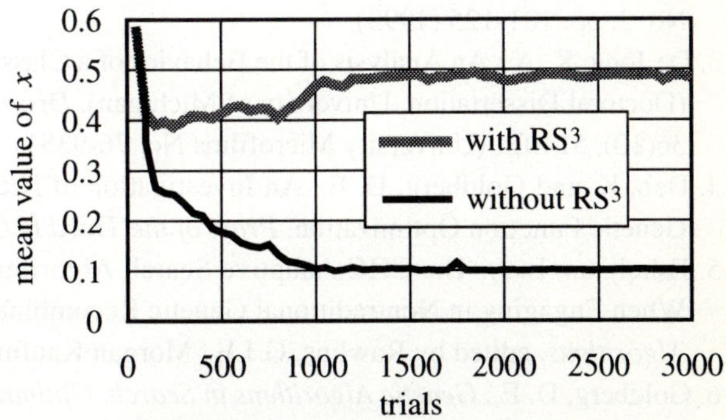

Fig. 8. Convergence Process on Fuction f_b

5 Conclusions

The *robust solution searching scheme* (RS^3), a new method which extends the application of GAs to domains that require detection of *robust solutions*, is proposed in the present article. In nature, the phenotypic feature of an organism is determined from the genotypic code of genes in the chromosome. In this process, there may be some perturbations. Even with these perturbation, strong organisms can survive. To emulate this sort of genetic feature, we added noise while evaluating the fitness of a function.

We developed a mathematical model of RS^3 and analyzed using simple functions. This analysis provides a guideline to determine the amount of noise to be added. The effectiveness of the RS^3 is demonstrated by maximizing functions having robust and sharp peaks.

Future work will focus on the following items:

(1) Combining the RS^3 with niche-formation methods, such as a sharing method, remains to be an interesting topic to be studied for more fruitful search.

(2) To analyze the influence of RS^3 on the convergence properties of high-dimensional and more complex problems.

(3) To extend the RS^3 for order based representational problems such as a scheduling system.

Acknowledgments

The authors gratefully acknowledge Prof. David E. Goldberg for his useful comments on this work. This research is partially supported by the Ministry of Education, Science, Sports and Culture under Grant-in-Aid for Scientific Research on Priority Areas number 264-08233105.

References

1. Baker, J. E.: Reducing Bias and Inefficiency in the Selection Algorithm, *Proc. of the Fifth ICGA*, pp. 14-21 (1987).
2. Beasley, D., Bull, D. R. and Martin, R. R.: A Sequential Niche Technique for Multimodal Function Optimization, *Evolutionary Computation*, MIT Press, Vol. 1, No. 2, pp. 101-125 (1993).
3. De Jong, K. A.: An Analysis of the Behavior of a Class of Genetic Adaptive Systems (Doctoral Dissertation, University of Michigan). *Dissertation Abstract International* 36(10), 5140B. (University Microfilms No. 76-9381)
4. Deb, K. and Goldberg, D. E.: An Investigation of Niche and Species Formation in Genetic Function Optimization, *Proc. of the Third ICGA*, pp. 42-50 (1989).
5. Eshelman, L. J.: The CHC Adaptive Search Algorithm: How to Have Safe Search When Engaging in Nontraditional Genetic Recombination, *Foundations of Genetic Algorithms*, edited by Rawlins, G.J.E., Morgan Kaufmann, pp.265-283 (1991).
6. Goldberg, D. E.: *Genetic Algorithms in Search, Optimization and Machine Learning*, Addison-Wesley Publishing Company, Inc. (1989).
7. Goldberg, D. E., Deb, K. and Korb, B.: Messy Genetic Algorithms Revisited: Studies in Mixed Size and Scale, *Complex Systems*, vol. 4, pp. 415-444 (1990).
8. Goldberg, D. E. and Richardson, J.: Genetic Algorithms with Sharing for Multimodal Function Optimization, *Proc. of the Second ICGA*, pp. 41-49 (1987).
9. Hammel, U. and Back, T.: Evolution Strategies on Noisy Function How to Improve Convergence Properties, *Proc. of Third Conf. on Parallel Problem Solving from Nature*, North-Holland, pp. 159-168 (1994).
10. Mathias, K and Whitley, L. D.: Changing Representations During Search: A Comparative Study of Delta Coding, *Evolutionary Computation*, MIT Press, Vol. 2, No. 3, pp. 249-278 (1994).
11. Mahfoud, S. W.: Crowding and preselection revisited, *Proc. of Second Conf. on Parallel Problem Solving from Nature*, North-Holland, pp. 27-34 (1992).
12. Tsutsui, S. and Fujimoto, Y.: Forking Genetic Algorithm with Blocking and Shrinking Modes, *Proc. of the Fifth ICGA*, pp. 206-213 (1993).
13. Tsutsui, S. and Fujimoto, Y.: Phenotypic Forking Genetic Algorithms (p-fGA), *Proc. of the 1995 IEEE ICEC*, pp. 566-572 (1995).

Comparison of Methods

Solving *MasterMind* Using GAs and Simulated Annealing: A Case of Dynamic Constraint Optimization

J. L. Bernier, C. Ilia Herráiz, J. J. Merelo, S. Olmeda, A. Prieto

Department of Electronics and Computer Technology; University of Granada (Spain)
e-mail: `jmerelo@kal-el.ugr.es`, `http://kal-el.ugr.es/jj/jj.html`

Abstract. MasterMind is a game in which the player must find out, by making guesses, a hidden combination of colors set by the opponent. The player lays a combination of colors, and the opponent points out the number of positions the player has found out (black tokens) and the number of colors that are in a different place from the hidden combination (white tokens). This problem can be formulated in the following way: the target of the game is to find a string composed of l symbols, drawn from an alphabet of cardinality c, using as constraints hints that restrict the search space. The partial objective of the search is to find a string that meets all the constraints made so far the final objective being to find the hidden string.This problem can also be located within the class of *constrained optimization*, although in this case not all the constraints are known in advance; hence its dynamic nature.Three algorithms playing MasterMind have been evaluated with respect to the number of guesses made by each one and the number of combinations examined before finding the solution: a random-search-with-constraints algorithm, simulated annealing, and a genetic algorithm. The random search and genetic algorithm at each step plays the optimal solution i.e., the one that is consistent with the constraints made so far, while simulated annealing plays the best found within certain time constraints. This paper proves that the algorithms that follow the optimal strategy behave similarly, getting the correct combination in more or less the same number of guesses; between them, GA is better with respect to the number of combinations examined, and this difference increases with the size of the search space, while SA is much faster (around 2 orders of magnitude) and gives a good enough answer.

1 Introduction

MasterMind is a game in which the player must find out a hidden combination of colors set by the opponent. The player lays a combination of color pegs, and the opponent points out the number of pegs which appear in the same position in the guess and the hidden combination, (black tokens, or *bulls*) and the number of color pegs that appear in the hidden combination, but in a different place (white tokens, or *cows*). No hint is given about which of the pegs laid by the player are the correct ones. These hints placed by the opponent will be called *constraints* or *rules*, since they restrict the search space. The problem of finding the secret combination can be formulated in the following way: the target is to find a string composed of l symbols, each one drawn from an alphabet of cardinality c, using as constraints hints that restrict the search space. During each step, the partial objective of the search is to find a string, which will not necessarily be the correct one, that meets all the constraints made so far, the final objective being to find the hidden string. The best player is the one that finds a solution in a minimal number of guesses, on average.

The optimal strategy to play *MasterMind* is then to play at each step a combination that is consistent with the constraints made so far; i. e., such that, if it was the secret combination, the *bulls* and *cows* (black and white tokens) set so far would be the same. An algorithm following this optimal strategy will try to find such a combination and play it at each step; suboptimal algorithms will try to find one that meets as many constraints as possible. Not all optimal strategies will behave in the same way, because at each step (except the last one) there are many combinations in the subset that meet all constraints, and some of them will restrict the remaining space more than others. For instance, it has been suggested that the best ones try to diversify as much as possible the number of colors [1]. However, if no attempt is made to further select the played combination, all optimal strategies, on average, should behave in the same way.

There are many possible ways of following this optimal strategy. They are all search algorithms that seek one of the optimal combinations at each step. The first obvious approach is *exhaustive search.* The space of all possible combinations is generated; each combination is examined in turn and played or ruled out. This approach is possible when the search space is small, compared with the typical computer memory available, but impossible when the search space is too big for the memory space in the computer. A *random search algorithm* can also be used; new combinations are generated randomly and played if they meet all current constraints; a variant of this algorithm would cache the number of constraints met by already examined combinations, so that the evaluation would be faster. Finally, a *heuristic approach* would try to play in the same way a human would do. A common strategy is to play at the beginning combinations with only one color, "to get the colors right" [2], until all the colors in the combination are found out; then different combinations with the colors already known are tried. This approach, while usually good for the standard *MasterMind* (4 pegs, 6 colors) fails in the generalized case, for instance, if there are many colors; there would be as many initial guesses as colors.

Different algorithms will consist, then, in different ways of searching the combination space for both the partial and the final solution. Solutions will be better if they are found in a minimal amount of guesses, and, if possible, examining a minimal subset of the search space, but for the generalized game, this might take too much time, and a suboptimal solution will often be good enough, if the time it takes is orders of magnitude smaller.

This problem has been approached from the AI, combinatorics and game theory fields.Several algorithms have been described in the literature that try to follow an optimal strategy. Two of them have been published in the Journal of Recreational Mathematics [3, 4]. The first one manages to solve the standard game in, at most, 5 moves; the latter, using exhaustive search, proves that the optimal average number of moves is 4.340, if a maximum of 6 guesses are allowed, or 4.341, if only 5 guesses are allowed. This result has been slightly improved by Neuwirth [5], using several strategies taken from game theory. Viaud [6, 7] also presents a general framework to play *MasterMind*. A *Prolog* language program is also described in [8], which takes "an average of 4 to 6 guesses, with a maximum of 8"; other programs that play *MasterMind* using Prolog can be found in AI software repositories. V. Chvatal [9] (mentioned in [10]), proved that the strategy of selecting vectors at random is close to optimal in the general case.

A contest, with 5 positions and 7 numbers, is played in the Web site *Web-Meninges*. The best player so far is called `pc_test1`, and achieves an average of 5.08 moves. The algorithm is not known, although an educated guess would be that it uses exhaustive search (in a space of $7^5 = 16807$ combinations).

The paper is organized as follows: section 2 describes the genetic algorithm used for playing *MasterMind*, pointing out the problems it faces and the solutions proposed; section 3 presents the simulated annealing algorithm proposed to solve the same problem suboptimally. Section 4 is devoted to a comparison the previous two algorithms and a random search algorithm, and finally, these results are discussed in section 5, along with future lines of research.

2 A Genetic Algorithm playing Master Mind

As has been said, playing *MasterMind* is a restricted search problem, but it can also be approached as a constrained optimization problem; i. e., looking for the best solution within some constraints; in this case, the *fitness* of the solution is computed directly from the number of constraints it meets. Several genetic algorithms have been proposed to solve such problems. A popular approach involves a *penalty function*, substracted from the fitness, whose value increases with the badness of the constraint break [11]. Another solution proposed by Schoenauer et al. [12] is to change the fitness function each time a constraint is met, and then restart the population with a new fitness function to optimize another constraint.

On the other hand, a new constraint is added every time a combination is played, so that the genetic search itself develops in a changing environment. The main problem in this kind of environment, as pointed out by Cobb et al. [13], is to maintain diversity so that the changing fitness landscape can be explored efficiently. Grefenstette et al. [14] have proposed several strategies, mainly based on a randomization of the population: an operator called *hypermutation*, which mutates a part of the population with a high rate , *random replacement*, and simply a high mutation rate; a similar "restart" operator is presented by Maresky et al. in [15]. This sort of "frontal assault" approach to GAs is explicitly discarded by Goldberg in [16], but more natural approaches like de Jong's *crowding factor* [11] or Ryan's *pygmy algorithm* [17] keep diversity in a more natural way, while yielding more or less the same results. In any case, a mechanism to maintain diversity must be used to properly solve *MasterMind*. Schoenauer et al.'s [12] approach skillfully reduces the problem mentioned in the first paragraph to this one; the solution proposed includes a *hypermutation* phase, each time a constraint is met; it also emphasizes the need to maintain diversity.

The two previous problems (which could be reduced to one, following Schoenauer et al. [12]), along with the fact that only one combination in the whole search space is correct, and the need to restrict the search space at each game step, call for an adaptation of one of the usual GAs, instead of a standard approach. Thus, a GA will be presented that tries to fiend a hidden combination following an optimal strategy; i.e., it plays a combination as soon as one suitable is found.

Nevertheless, the standard binary **representation** is used. The genetic algorithm acts on a population of binary strings representing combinations. The maximum number of colors allowed is 8, so that each color is represented in the chromosome string by 3 bits. Thus, the chromosome is 3*(length of the combination) long. If the number of colors is less than 8, the color of the combination played (phenotype) will be the remainder of dividing the gene value by the number of colors; this means it is a "redundant" coding, since two different bit strings can result in the same combination. Although this reprsetentation introduces a bias for a number of colors not a power of two, it has been chosen because it is more compact than others (integer or floating point), while being able to support the same kind of operations.

The **fitness function** must be obviously related to the optimal strategy mentioned in the introduction; i.e., to the number of rules a combination meets. However, instead of simply using that amount, as in previous approaches [18], more weight is given to black pegs (10) than to white pegs (1); thus, each time a rule is met, the fitness increases by 10*(number of black pegs) + (number of white pegs). This means that a rule with 0 blacks/0 whites adds 0 to fitness, but this is not usually a problem for the range of colors and length of combinations used (it could be, however, for longer combinations or more colors). This approach has the advantage over the previous one [18] of making some combinations better than others, if they meet "better" rules, even if the number of rules met is the same. Thus, solutions are built from the "best" rules, those with the most black pegs.

This election of fitness function increases the efficiency of the selection procedures over previous choices [18], but, nevertheless, it is not very efficient, since fitness increases by leaps, not gradually. This once again calls for an increase of "exploration", or diversity-creation, operators, instead of "exploitation" operators, since groups in the population will have exactly the same fitness.

The importance of maintaining a high diversity becomes apparent in the operator and parameter choices related to population. The theory with respect to **population size** usually indicates that it must grow with the chromosome size. In this case, the population size P is quite high compared with usual approaches: for a chromosome size of 18 bits (6 colors, 6 pegs), for instance, 500-chromosome populations are used; and, besides, experiments show that P must grow faster than lineally to accomodate variations in the search space size, to the point that a 10000-chromosome population is used for length 10 combinations.

The **selection procedure** used is *steady state*; a proportion of the population is kept in each generation. New individuals are generated in 3 different ways:

- From two parents, using 2-point crossover, which does not consider gene (color) boundaries. This operator allows the mixture of combinations that meet two different rules to give a new one that meets both. Just as gene breaking has the effect of random mutation, this factor once again increases diversity. A low proportion X of the population P is created using this operator, $X = 0.15..0.30$; one of the parents is chosen from the $X \cdot P$ ranked best among the population.
- From only one parent, using mutation. This procedure is called *cloning with mutation*. The mutation operator performs bitflipping, and the rate is adjusted in such a way that at least a bit will be changed in each chromosome that undergoes cloning with mutation. Such a proportion C changes each time a new combination is played, and is proportional to the length of the combination less the number of black and white pegs for the *last* combination played. In this way, it goes down to 0 when all the colors in the combination are known, and only the correct position must be found out. An adaptive operator rate has already been used by Julstrom [19] to improve performance; however, in this case, it has been used to change the space that is being searched and the rate at which the search space is explored.

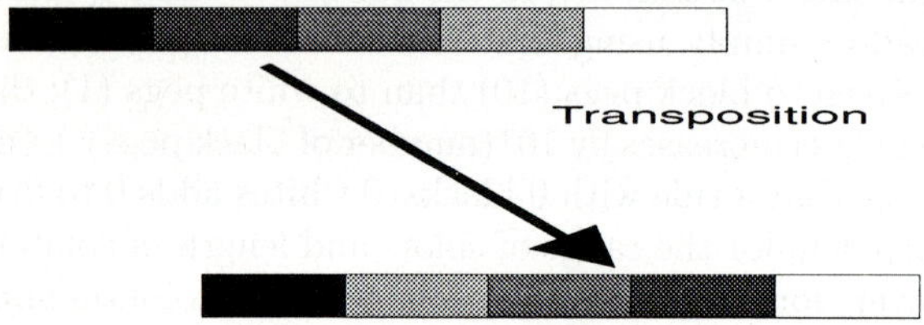

Fig. 1. Transposition operator used in this paper, in this case acting on 5-gene chromosomes. Genes 2 and 4 are interchanged.

- From only one parent, using *inversion* or *transposition* (*cloning with transposition*). This operator, which interchanges the values of whole genes in a chromosome (see Figure 1) is rather unusual in GAs, although mentioned by Holland [20] and Fogel [21]; however, it is specially suitable for this problem, since it can turn a combination with white pegs into another with color pegs in the correct position. That is the reason why the proportion of chromosomes cloned with inversion is proportional to the number of white pegs in the last combination played.

These last two operators are only applied to chromosomes whose fitness is not among the X best, ie, those ranked in the $P - 2X$ central positions. Among these, $0.4(l - n_b - n_w)$ undergo cloning with mutation, and $0.4 \cdot n_w$ undergo cloning with transposition. These parameters have been found by tuning. The total population P and the percentage of population undergoing crossover X vary with the length of the combination; the other parameters stay the same through all tests made.

3 Simulated annealing

Simulated annealing (SA) has also been used for solving combinatorial problems [22, 23]. In a classical SA problem, a cost function to be minimized is defined and then, from an initial solution, different solutions are derived and compared with the retained solution; the solution with the least cost is kept, but retaining a solution with a greater cost is allowed with a certain probability. The probability of keeping a worse solution decreases with a parameter called temperature.

In the case of *MasterMind*, the objective is to find a combination that meets all the rules to make a new guess. Thus, SA is applied to discover a combination that meets the maximum number of rules within a limited time; if the stopping condition is to find a combination that meets all rules the procedure will become very similar to a random algorithm.

Each combination is compared with the previously played guesses, the number of different white and black pegs are computed and added to the cost, that is defined as $C = \sum_{i=1}^{n} abs(\Delta n_w^i) + abs(\Delta n_w^i + \Delta n_b^i)$ where n is the number of guesses played and Δn_w^i and Δn_b^i are the white and black peg differences between the target combination and the guess i. In this way, the cost increases with the number of unsatisfied rules, exactly the opposite of the fitness defined in section 2.

The SA algorithm is the usual, except that two operations are used to generate a combination from the previous one: permutation and mutation. While a permutation changes the order of two pegs, the mutation changes the color of a peg; in both cases the pegs are randomly chosen. The values of the parameters were fixed to the following ones: $T_f = 1e - 30$, $\alpha = 0.98$. In this way, the combination payed meets a suboptimal number of rules in the worst case, but the time to find it is short. The number of guesses needed to obtain the final solution is usually acceptable. This algorithm finds the solution very quickly as the number of combinations to check is small.

4 Results

These two algorithms, along with a random search algorithm that plays the optimal strategy, have been tested in games with 6 colors, and 4 to 10 pegs. Using different randomly generated combinations to be guessed, 20 games were played for each color/peg combination for random and GA, and 100 for SA. Different parameter values were tested for the GA; results are presented for the best combination of parameters. The number of guesses made and the number of combinations evaluated were recorded.

A program using the previous algorithm [18] is also running on our Web server, using 6 colors and 6 pegs, and has so far obtained an average of 5.62 for 693 games played (GA) and 5.98 for 232 games played (SA). The current version has been evaluated with the *WebMeninges* setup, scoring an average of 5.45±0.67 guesses, and evaluating an average of 7755 ± 4286 combinations, placing it among the best 30. The other results are represented in figure 2, with averages and standard deviation. Times have not been measured accurately,

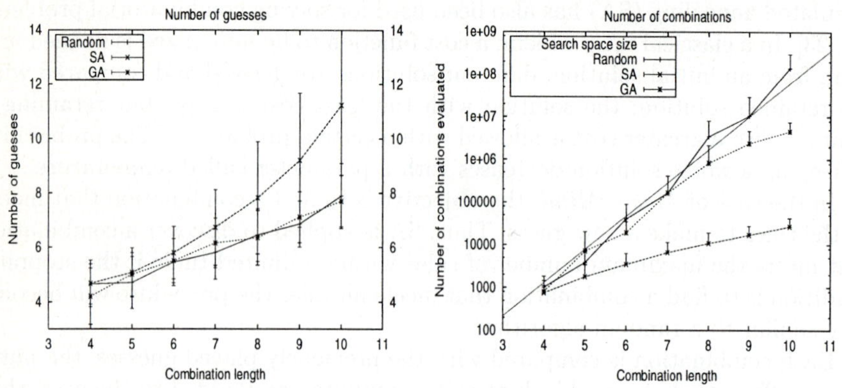

Fig. 2. Graph comparing the average number of guesses made and number of combinations evaluated, with standard deviation, by the three algorithms.

except for SA, only order of magnitude measures: SA takes from tens of milliseconds to 10 seconds, GA from seconds to hours, and the random algorithm from milliseconds to tens of hours (in fact, not all measures could be taken for length = 10). The algorithms following optimal strategy, GA and random, beat the SA in number of guesses, and are thus better players, but SA is much faster than either of them: at worst, only 25 seconds elapse before reaching a solution. It can be clearly seen that the GA and random algorithm are almost equal in average number of guesses made, and SA slightly worse, with the difference increasing with the combination length. This is due to the fact that SA does not follow the optimal strategy. However, the number of combinations examined by SA is orders of magnitude smaller than any of the other algorithms; the number of combinations evaluated by the random algorithm increases exponentially, almost at the same rate as the size of the search space, while it grows slower than exponentially for SA and GA. For the longest combination tested, l= 10, the number of combinations evaluated is two orders of magnitude bigger for SA than for GA, and 1 order of magnitude bigger for random than for GA, which explains the time taken by each one of them. In any case, the GA does not need to search the whole space to find the solution; for $l = 10$, only 4% of the search space is examined on average. Two other things must be taken into account: first, the number of actual combinations examined by the GA is, on average, 2/3 of the one shown, since the chromosome-combination mapping is not one to one (see section 2. Relatively better results would be obtained for a representation in which genotype and phenotype were the same. Second, the worst result in combinations would be the number of guesses (the search space size) times 0.5, since, in any algorithm, the combinations already examined are not retained. This would be reduced to (the search space size) times 0.5 in the case of exhaustive search, but this possibility has not been examined.

How then, would a GA-endowed automated player fare against a SA-engine and a random challenger? To find this out, it must first be pointed out that it is not the same when a player always gets the hidden combination in 5 guesses, as when part of the time it is achieved in 4, and the rest in 6; while having similar averages, the latter would beat the former if it manages to score 4 once more than 6. Thus, the number of guesses each algorithm makes have been compared by plotting the proportion of times one algorithm would beat the other, and the number of draws. As can be seen in figure 3, the GA would beat SA more times than the other way round, even for small-length combinations; but for greater length combinations, these results improve to the point where it is almost impossible for the SA to win even one match. To enphasize the extent

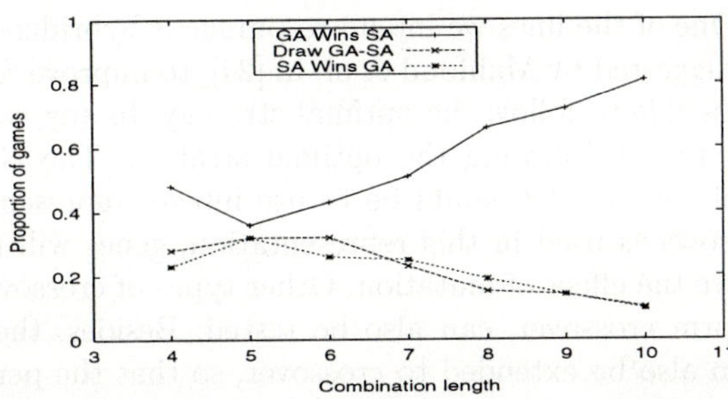

Fig. 3. The proportion of times each of GA and SA would beat the other, and the number of draws, is plotted for different combination length.

to which a GA is better than a random search algorithm, while averaging more or less the same number of guesses, figure 4 presents a *time-to-solution* graph for the extreme case: length 9. This graph represents the number of combinations evaluated in the x axis, and the accumulated proportion of runs that reach the solution in that number of guesses. On this extreme case, the GA always find the solutions in less than 10% of the time the random search algorithm needs.

5 Discussion

Examining the behavior of three algorithms on a combinatorial search problem, playing the game of Mastermind, we have found out that GA is a robust search algorithm, performing well through a wide range of problem sizes, and it is efficient, since it finds the solution with enough speed, while examining a small portion of the search space. Simulated annealing is very fast, but cannot play

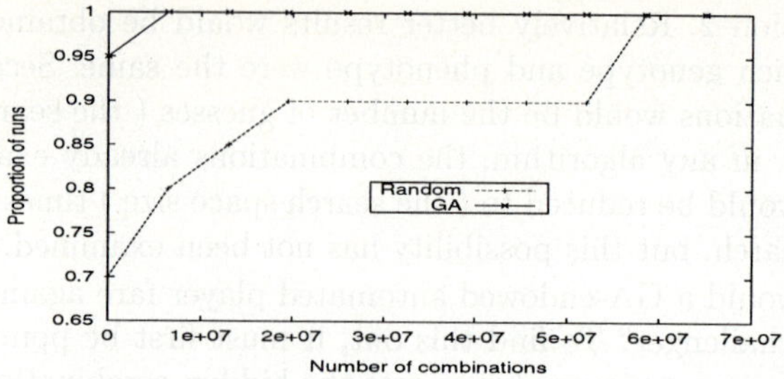

Fig. 4. Graph comparing the number of combinations a GA and a random search algorithm need to reach a solution for $l = 9$. The proportion of runs (over 20) is plotted on the y axis, and the number of combinations needed on the x axis.

optimally since it would reduce itself to a random search algorith; and the random search algorithm performs as expected, but is the slowest; it is good enough, nevertheless, for small search spaces. SA has the advantage that its optimality can be fixed in advance.

Several improvements can be made to the basic GA and SA algorithms to improve results. One of the lines we intend to pursue is hybridization of SA and GA, in the style suggested by Mahfoud et al. in [24], to improve SA performance and to make it possible to follow the optimal strategy. In any case, the current SA setup will be tested following the optimal strategy. The GA can also be improved. One interesting test would be to use integer representation, instead of binary; if crossover is used in this representation, genes will not be broken, and it will not have the effect of mutation. Other types of crossover, like 1-point crossover or uniform crossover, can also be tested. Besides, the adaptivity of operator rates can also be extended to crossover, so that the percentage of the population generated by crossover also changes through time. These modifications attempt to decrease the amount of invalid combinations generated. With respect to diversity, some other strategies can also be tested, like, for instance, the *pygmy* algorithm [17], or niching strategies like the one proposed originally by de Jong.

This procedure can also be used in other restricted combinatorial search problems. It could probably be used too in other games, like "Battleships" or "Scrabble"; in these cases, the search space is much bigger, but the techniques described in this paper could be adapted.

Acknowledgements I would like to acknowledge the help of Marc Schoenauer.

References

1. Melle Koning. Mastermind. newsgroup `comp.ai.games`, archived at `http://www.krl.caltech.edu/~brown/alife/news/ai-games-html/0370.html`.
2. Tim Cooper. Mastermind. newsgroup `comp.ai.games`, archived at `http://www.krl.caltech.edu/~brown/alife/news/ai-games-html/0313.html`.
3. Donald E. Knuth. The computer as Master Mind. *J. Recreational Mathematics*, (9):1–6, 1976-77.

4. Kenji Koyama; T. W. Lai. An optimal Mastermind strategy. *J. Recreational Mathematics*, 1994.
5. E. Neuwirth. Some strategies for mastermind. *Zeitschrift fur Operations Research. Serie B*, 26(8):B257–B278, 1982.
6. D. Viaud. Une strategie generale pour jouer au Mastermind. *RAIRO-Recherche Operationelle*, 21(1):87–100, 1987.
7. D. Viaud. Une formalisation du jeu de Mastermind. *RAIRO-Recherche Operationelle*, 13(3):307–321, 1979.
8. Leon Sterling; Ehud Shapiro. *The Art of Prolog: Advanced Programming Techniques.* MIT press, 1986.
9. V. Chvatal. Mastermind. *Combinatorica*, 3(3-4):325–329, 1983.
10. Risto Widenius. Mastermind. newsgroup `comp.ai.games`, archived at `http://www.krl.caltech.edu/~brown/alife/news/ai-games-html/1311.html`.
11. Zbigniew Michalewicz. *Genetic Algorithms + Data Structures = Evolution programs.* Springer-Verlag, 2nd edition edition, 1994.
12. Marc Schoenauer; Spyros Xanthakis. Constrained GA optimization. In Forrest [25], pages 573–580.
13. John J. Grefenstette. Genetic algorithms for changing environments. In R. Maenner; B. Manderick, editor, *Parallel Problem Solving from Nature, 2*, pages 137–144. Elsevier Science Publishers B. V., 1992.
14. Helen G. Cobb; John J. Grefenstette. Genetic algorithms for tracking changing environments. In Forrest [25], pages 523–530.
15. A. Barak J. Maresky; Y. Davidor; D. Gitler; G. Aharoni. Selective destructive re-start. In Eshelman [26], pages 144–150.
16. David E. Goldberg. Zen and the art of genetic algorithms. In J. David Schaffer, editor, *Procs. of the 3rd Int. Conf. on Genetic Algorithms, ICGA89*, pages 80–85. Morgan Kauffmann, 1989.
17. Conor Ryan. *Advances in Genetic Programming*, chapter Pygmies and Civil Servants. MIT press, 1992.
18. J. J. Merelo. Genetic Mastermind, a case of dynamic constraint optimization. GeNeura Technical Report G-96-1, Universidad de Granada, 1996.
19. Bryant A. Julstrom. What have you done for me lately? Adapting operator probabilities in a steady-state Genetic Algorithm. In Eshelman [26], pages 81–87.
20. John J. Holland. *Adaptation in Natural and Artificial Systems.* University of Michigan Press, 1975.
21. D. B. Fogel. *Evolutionary Computation: Towards a New Philosophy of Machine Intelligence.* IEEE press, 1995.
22. J. Aarts, E.; Korst. *Simulated Annealing and Boltzmann Machines.* John Wiley & Sons, 1989.
23. C. H. Papadimitriou; K. Steiglitz. *Combinatorial Optimization: Algorithms and Complexity.* Prentice-Hall, New York,, 1982.
24. S. W. Mahfoud; D. E. Goldberg. Parallel recombinative simulated annealing: A genetic algorithm. Technical report, IlliGAL Report no. 92002, Dept. Of General Engineering, UIUC., 1992.
25. Stephanie Forrest, editor. *Proceedings of the 5th International Conference on Genetic Algorithms.* Morgan Kaufmann, 1993.
26. Larry J. Eshelman, editor. *Proceedings of the 6th International Conference on Genetic Algorithms.* Morgan Kaufmann, 1995.

Evolving Compact Solutions in Genetic Programming: A Case Study

Tobias Blickle

Computer Engineering and Communication Networks Lab (TIK)
Swiss Federal Institute of Technology (ETH)
Gloriastrasse 35, 8092 Zurich
Switzerland
blickle@tik.ee.ethz.ch

Abstract. Genetic programming (GP) is a variant of genetic algorithms where the data structures handled are trees. This makes GP especially useful for evolving functional relationships or computer programs, as both can be represented as trees. Symbolic regression is the determination of a function dependence $y = g(\mathbf{x})$ that approximates a set of data points $(\mathbf{x}_i, y_i)$. In this paper the feasibility of symbolic regression with GP is demonstrated on two examples taken from different domains. Furthermore several suggested methods from literature are compared that are intended to improve GP performance and the readability of solutions by taking into account introns or redundancy that occurs in the trees and keeping the size of the trees small. The experiments show that GP is an elegant and useful tool to derive complex functional dependencies on numerical data.

1 Introduction

Genetic Algorithms (GA) are probabilistic search algorithms characterized by the fact that a number N of potential solutions (called *individuals*) of the optimization problem simultaneously sample the search space. This *population* is modified according to the natural evolutionary process: after initialization, selection and recombination are executed in a loop until some termination criterion is reached. Genetic Programming (GP) uses the same principle as GA and the representation of the individuals is done by trees. Especially in control systems the ability of GP to generate symbolic solutions makes it an interesting optimization tool for many problems, e.g., symbolic regression is such a problem where functional dependencies are searched. Symbolic regression can be described as the following task: Determine a functional dependency $y = g(\mathbf{x})$ such that the error $E(g)$ of approximating a set of n data points $\{(\mathbf{x}_1, y_1), (\mathbf{x}_2, y_2), \ldots, (\mathbf{x}_n, y_n)\}$ is minimized. A common goal is, for example, to minimize the average squared differences over the data set.

This task is similar to the system identification problem, where the behavior of an unknown system is to be learned and predicted based on examples given as input-output data. Time-series prediction, pattern recognition and the classification problem also belong to this problem class (see, e.g. [3]). Often the generalization capability of the approximation function $g(\mathbf{x})$ is crucial, i.e. the accuracy of the approximation on unseen data.

The approximation function $g(\mathbf{x})$ may be of predefined shape, for example a polynomial of a certain degree. In this case the regression simply consists of adjusting coefficients. Hence one is faced with a numerical optimization problem and all methods for numerical optimization may be applied, e.g., gradient methods, hill climbing methods, tabu search, genetic algorithms, evolution strategies.

If the appearance of the function $g(\mathbf{x})$ is unknown in advance these methods are not applicable. In this case GP is a perfect candidate for solving the problem. One specifies basic functions and terminals from which the approximation formula g can be composed and GP automatically evolves the shape and size of the formula.

The intention of this paper is twofold. First, to show the feasibility of symbolic regression on complex data. We outline this general approach in Sect. 2. One example is the approximation of a complex integral equation that represents a continuous optimization problem. On the other hand, the determination of a Boolean multiplexer function is a typical example for a discrete optimization task. Second, to empirically analyze the size problem in GP. This problem is related to "introns" or "redundancy" in the trees and has been addressed by several investigations [8, 1, 7, 9, 5]. A comparison of several configurations that make use of methods to reduce the "garbage" in the trees is carried out for the two examples. The size problem is of special interest for symbolic regression as one usually looks for short, compact, and "readable" solutions. The different explanations will be introduced in Sect. 3. The subsequent section compares the results and Sect. 5 gives some conclusions.

2 Symbolic Regression Using GP

The basic approach of using GP for symbolic regression has already been outlined by Koza [4]. The advantages of using GP for symbolic regression can be summarized as follows:

- Size and shape of the approximation function need not be known in advance.
- A small risk of over-fitting the data.
- Arbitrary complex functions can be supported in the function set. Thereby allowing application specific knowledge to be included in the search process.

In addition to the problem of tree size explosion, addressed in the next section, there are several items that have to be considered in order to use GP successfully for symbolic regression. In particular, these are

- *The handling of mathematical exceptions during fitness evaluation:* As we are looking for mathematically valid expressions we do not accept any illegal mathematical operation and add a penalty term for each violation.
- *The handling of floating point or integer constants:* All individuals with a fitness value better than a certain threshold f_{th} are selected for constant optimization. The optimization consists of sequentially changing all constants

in the tree by a fixed amount $\delta = 0.1$ and accepting the new value as long as the fitness is improved or a maximum number of optimization steps s_{max} have been performed.

- *The choice of the fitness function:* The fitness function consists of three terms: The first term measures the error $E(g)$ of an individual g. This depends on the specific task and is introduced in the context of the experiments (Sect. 4). Furthermore, a penalty term is added for mathematical exceptions together with the parsimony pressure that depends on the complexity $C(g)$ of the function and is scaled by a factor α. This topic will be discussed in detail in the next section. In summary, the fitness (to be minimized) of an approximation function g is given by:

$$f(g) = E(g) + \alpha\, C(g) + j\text{PENALTY} \tag{1}$$

where $j \in \{0, \ldots, n\}$ gives the number of occurrences of mathematical exceptions during evaluation of the fitness function.

3 Controlling the Tree Size

In this section we will consider a crucial point of GP, the tree size explosion or bloating phenomenon. It is well known from several investigations that the tree size in GP tends to grow even (or especially) when no improvement in the population is made [8, 1, 5, 6]. However for symbolic regression a small tree size is desirable in order to be able to interpret the evolved results. Furthermore, several investigations indicate that short solutions generalize the training data better [5, 9].

There are several approaches dealing with the problem of tree size explosion. Most commonly, some kind of parsimony pressure is introduced, i.e., adding a factor to the fitness value of an approximation related to its size, i.e., $f(g) = E(g) + \alpha C(g)$, as stated above.

Also in [5, 6] it is argued that Evolutionary Algorithms have a built in property of favoring short solutions and that a large fraction of the code of a GP solution are "introns" and hence the effective size of the code is much smaller. Nordin *et al* introduce the term of Explicitly Defined Intron (EDI). For our purposes it is sufficient to know that EDIs can be considered as an edge weight in the tree. The probability of crossover at a particular edge is proportional to the weight of that edge. The authors conclude that EDIs may replace and interact with implicit introns and under the presence of some parsimony pressure lead to more compact solutions. Another effect of the "weighted crossover" is the potential emergence and encapsulation of useful building blocks possibly leading to the faster discovery of high fit individuals.

In a different approach dealing with the bloating phenomenon is the suggestion of a special crossover operator, the *deleting crossover*, based on the *marking crossover* citeBT94. The basic idea is to mark all edges in a tree that were traversed during evaluation of the fitness function. All remaining edges were never used to calculate the fitness and hence the subtrees at these edges are redundant.

These subtrees are deleted and replaced with a single randomly chosen terminal. In particular, this approach should be suited for discrete problems.

A straightforward idea to address the size problem is to restrict the maximum tree size during the run of the GP, e.g., to set the maximum tree size to 10. However, one problem with this approach is the diversity of the population. In order to have sufficient genetic material in the population, one has to use large population sizes. More important is the fact that the tree size needed to solve a particular problem is often not known in advance.

The difficulty in all the approaches mentioned above stems from balancing the parsimony pressure. Especially if the fitness function is real valued, one has to face the problem that if the parsimony pressure is too high, the GP may favor a short solution to a better one.

Zhang and Mühlenbein solve this problem by a method called "adaptive balancing of accuracy and parsimony" [9]. The parsimony pressure α (also called *Occam factor*) is automatically adapted to the current quality of the best solution. The proposed heuristic is derived from a detailed statistical analysis. The principle is a low parsimony in the beginning of the optimization, as long as the error $E(g)$ is above a user-specified accuracy limit ϵ. When this limit is reached, the parsimony pressure is increased in order to reduce the size of the solution.

In this paper, we will compare four basic setups:

- **Simple** setup: Standard GP with a constant parsimony pressure α.
- **EDI** setup: The usage of standard GP with EDIs and a constant parsimony pressure α. The initialization range of the EDIs is [10, ..., 1010], as recommended in [6].
- **Deleting** setup: The use of standard GP with deleting crossover as described above and a constant parsimony pressure α.
- **Adaptive** setup: The usage of standard GP with adaptive parsimony pressure as suggested in [9], with the accuracy limit $\epsilon = 0.02$.

4 Experiments

In the following we will test the four setups on two problems taken from different domains: the symbolic regression of a unknown complex integral equation as one-dimensional continuous regression problem and the determination of a Boolean 6-multiplexer function as an example of a 6-dimensional discrete regression problem.

The parameter settings of the GP are summarized in Table 1.

4.1 Regression for a Continuous Problem

During the theoretical investigation of selection selection schemes [2], several difficult integral equations were obtained. In the following, we will consider one of these equations, namely:

$$V_T(t) = \int_{-\infty}^{\infty} t\, x^2\, \frac{1}{\sqrt{2\pi}} e^{-\frac{x^2}{2}} \left(\int_{-\infty}^{x} \frac{1}{\sqrt{2\pi}} e^{-\frac{y^2}{2}} dy \right)^{t-1} dx - I_T(t)^2 \qquad (2)$$

Table 1. The global parameters of the genetic program.

Selection method	Tournament Selection 10
Crossover method	crossover limiting tree size
Crossover probability	$p_c = 0.9$
Constant-optimization threshold	$f_{th} = 1.0$
Maximum number of constant-optimization steps	$s_{max} = 10$
Complexity measure ($v(g)$= # of nodes)	$C(g) = \frac{v(g)}{v_{max}}$
Penalty value	$PENALTY = 100.000$

where $I_T(t)$ is given by

$$I_T(t) = \int_{-\infty}^{\infty} t\, x \frac{1}{\sqrt{2\pi}} e^{-\frac{x^2}{2}} \left(\int_{-\infty}^{x} \frac{1}{\sqrt{2\pi}} e^{-\frac{y^2}{2}} dy \right)^{t-1} dx$$

For this equation an analytic expression may not exist but the equation can be easily solved numerically. However, an analytic expression is desirable, since it allows further investigation of the relationships expressed by the initial integral equation. Even an approximation formula is of great interest, if it is good enough. The maximum relative error over all data points assures that for each data point the error is below a certain value:

$$E_c(g) = \max_{i=1,\ldots,n} \left| \frac{g(\mathbf{x}_i) - y_i}{y_i} \right| \tag{3}$$

Equation 2 describes the selection variance of tournament selection as a relationship with the tournament size t (see [2] for details). As the tournament size is a discrete parameter (only integer tournament sizes are possible) the data points for approximating this equation consist of the tournament sizes and the corresponding selection variances, i.e., $\{(1, V_T(1)), (2, V_T(2)), \ldots, (30, V_T(30))\}$. The values V_T have been computed by numerical integration. Values of larger tournament sizes ($t > 30$) are of no practical relevance. Hence we only consider the interval $t = \{1, \ldots, 30\}$ and need not verify the approximation formula on unseen data, i.e., the generalization capabilities of the approximation formula are not taken into account.

For this experiment the function set was $\mathcal{F}$={Plus, Subtract, Times, Divide, Log, Sqrt, Exp} and the terminal set was $\mathcal{T}$ = {t, π, RFPC}, where RFPC symbolizes a random floating point constant. Twenty runs were carried out for each setup and each experiment.

Results The results of the experiments are shown in Table 2. The first column describes the setup used and the next four columns give the the corresponding parameter settings. The entry E_{best} gives the maximum relative error (in percent) of the best approximation formula found in the final generation. E_{av} gives the average error (in percent) of the best approximations found in the 20 runs. Similar v_{best} describes the complexity (in number of nodes) of the best solution found and v_{av} is the average complexity of all 20 best solutions.

Experiment 1: In the first experiment the four setups **Simple** , **EDI** , **Deleting** , and **Adaptive** have been compared with a small maximum tree size (number of nodes per tree) $v_{max} = 15$, a high population size of $N = 10000$, and an maximum of 30 generations ($k_{max} = 30$). This parameter setting is designed for the **Simple** setup. The first observation to make is that GP is well suited to this problem as short solutions with high accuracy have been found even with the **Simple** setup. This indicates that the choice of a maximum tree size of 15 was sufficient to solve this problem. The approximation accuracy was at least 4%. The best result found had an maximum relative error of 0.56% and can be simplified to:

$$V_T(t) \approx \frac{0.918}{\ln(1.186 + 1.328t)} \quad ; t \in \{1, \ldots, 30\} \tag{4}$$

The results for the **EDI** and **Deleting** setup are of the same quality and there seems to be no advantage in using one of these more complicated setups. In the **Adaptive** setup the error is slightly increased and the complexity slightly decreased. The small differences in the results seem reasonable as the restricted tree size and the small number of generations probably do not allow enough time and space for the more sophisticated approaches to evolve.

Table 2. Results of the experiments with four different setups (**Simple, EDI, Deleting, Adaptive**) to evolve an approximation formula for the integral equation 2. For the values marked with (*) refer to the text.

Exp	Setup	N	v_{max}	k_{max}	α	E_{best}[%]	E_{av}[%]	v_{best}	v_{av}
1	**Simple**	10000	15	30	0.01	0.56	1.8	12	12.75
	EDI	10000	15	30	0.01	0.30	1.6	12	12.38
	Deleting	10000	15	30	0.01	0.34	2.0	13	12.17
	Adaptive	10000	15	30	*var*	0.98	1.8	11	11.85
2	**Simple**	3000	45	100	0.01	0.08	0.56	29	26.92
	EDI	3000	45	100	0.01	0.08	152* /0.62*	21	26.23
	Deleting	3000	45	100	0.01	0.10	0.76	25	26.38
	Adaptive	3000	45	100	*var*	0.84	1.6	8	13.5
3	**Adaptive + EDI**	3000	45	100	*var*	0.37	1.86	17	16
	Adaptive + Deleting	3000	45	100	*var*	0.43	1.5	14	12.73

Experiment 2: A second experiment was set up with a higher maximum number of generations ($k_{max} = 100$) and a larger maximum tree size ($v_{max} = 45$) but a smaller population size ($N = 3000$). This setup should give sufficient time (generations) for the **EDI** and **Adaptive** setup to work.

The quality of the best and average best solution for **Simple**, **EDI**, and **Deleting** setup has improved dramatically. But in all cases this is countered by a more than doubled solution complexity compared with the first experiment. This means that the optimization worked towards smaller approximation errors but not towards smaller complexity values. This is remarkable because of the relatively high parsimony pressure at the end of the optimization. If we take a look, for example, at the best approximation found for the **Simple** setup we see that $C_{best} = \frac{29}{45} \approx 0.64$ and $E_{best} = 0.0008$. As $\alpha = 0.01$ this means that the contribution of the complexity to the fitness (according to equation 1) is about 8 times the contribution of the accuracy.

The **EDI** setup does not seem to have any advantages over the **Simple** setup. In contrary, the average error of the best solutions is very high (152%) (marked with (*) in the table). This occurs because in two runs the GP found very bad solutions. This phenomenon has also been reported in [6] where, on the other hand, the good solutions were found very quickly. This could not be observed in our experiments. If the two "runaways" are neglected the average error is 0.62%.

The **Deleting** approach seems to have no advantages. All results are similar to those of the **Simple** setup.

The **Adaptive** setup seems to be very well suited to reduce the complexity of the solutions. Although the maximum tree size could grow up to 45 nodes, the average complexity of the solutions was only 13.5 nodes. The fact that the accuracy of approximation is one magnitude worse than those of the **Simple** , **EDI** , and **Deleting** setup is plausible as the accuracy limit was set to $\epsilon = 2\%$.

Experiment 3: In the last experiment the **Adaptive** setup was combined with the **EDI** and **Deleting** setup. In both cases this results in a slightly more accurate best approximation formula (E_{best}=0.37% for **Adaptive + EDI** , E_{best}=0.43% for **Adaptive + Deleting** , but E_{best}=0.84% for **Adaptive** alone). However the averaged error and the average complexity remain more or less constant.

4.2 Regression of a Discrete Problem

The task of the 6-multiplexer-problem consists in the determination of a Boolean function that performs the 6-multiplexer function. The data points are the n = 64 possible combinations for the six input variables that form the terminal set $\mathcal{T} = \{d_0, d_1, d_2, d_3, d_4, d_5\}$. No numerical constants are used. The function set is $\mathcal{F}$ ={IF, AND, OR, NOT}. For this discrete optimization problem the accuracy is measured by the number of incorrect classified data samples, i.e.,

$$E_d(g) = \sum_{i=1}^{64} \begin{cases} 0 & : \quad g(\mathbf{x_i}) = y_i \\ 1 & : \quad else \end{cases} \tag{5}$$

Hence, an optimal individual fulfills $E_d(g_{opt}) = 0$. We performed 100 runs for each setup and each run was continued to the 50 generation maximum even if a perfect individual had been found.

A peculiarity of the **Adaptive** setup must be mentioned: the best accuracy that can be achieved is $E_d(g) = 0$. But the method assumes that a perfect accuracy is never reached; an assumption that makes sense as long as one works with continuous data. In order to be able to use this method on the discrete problem, a constant factor of 0.01 was added to the error measure.

Results The results are summarized in Table 3. The first four columns show the parameter settings. Note that the constant parsimony pressure is $\alpha = 1$, as the smallest possible increase in accuracy is 1. E_{best} gives the accuracy of the best solution found and p_{succ} the probability of success, i.e., the percentage of runs that found a perfect solution. Finally, v_{av} reports the average complexity (in number of nodes) over all individuals of the last generation and runs.

The first thing to notice is that every setup found some perfect individuals ($E_{best} = 0$). This is to be expected as the task is not especially difficult. More interesting are the success rates. The **EDI** approach performs worse than the **Simple** approach. The **Adaptive** setup is clearly better than **Simple** . The best performer is the **Deleting** setup obviously due to the IF-function in the function set allowing redundancy to be exploited.

Perhaps of more interest is the fact that there is no need to use the **Adaptive** setup to reduce the complexity of the trees. All setups end up with almost the same average complexity, because a relatively high constant parsimony pressure can be exceeded without having a negative effect on the accuracy (due to the discrete character of the error function in this problem).

Table 3. Results of the experiments with four different setups (**Simple**, **EDI**, **Deleting**, **Adaptive**) to determine a Boolean 6-multiplexer function.

Exp	Setup	N	v_{max}	k_{max}	α	E_{best}	p_{succ} [%]	v_{av}
4	**Simple**	250	100	50	1.0	0	52	12.75
	EDI	250	100	50	1.0	0	44	12.03
	Deleting	250	100	50	1.0	0	66	12.32
	Adaptive	250	100	50	var	0	59	13.64

4.3 Discussion

In summary, there seems to be no advantage in using the **EDI** or **Deleting** approach for the particular continuous problem in order to reduce the complexity of the solutions. They both work as well as the **Simple** setup. Probably, in a continuous problem, no subtrees are "completely" redundant or "complete" introns but may contribute only "very little" to the quality of an approximation. Introns are not recognized by these methods and consequently they do not have the intended effect. This conjecture is supported by the good performance of the **Deleting** setup on the (discrete) 6-multiplexer problem. However it remains open as to why the **EDI** approach fails to work for this example.

The **Adaptive** setup seems to reduce the complexity of the solutions for both examples. This can also be observed in Fig. 1 which shows the average number of nodes in trees of a population, averaged over all runs with respect to time (generations) for the example of continuous regression. At the early stages, all methods behave indistinguishably: the number of nodes grows quickly in the first 18 generations up to an average tree size of 27-30 nodes. After that, two different behaviors can be observed. In all methods with constant parsimony pressure, the tree size remains more or less the same (around 27 nodes), whereas methods using the adaptive parsimony pressure show a significant decrease in tree size before the size stabilizes at 15 nodes.

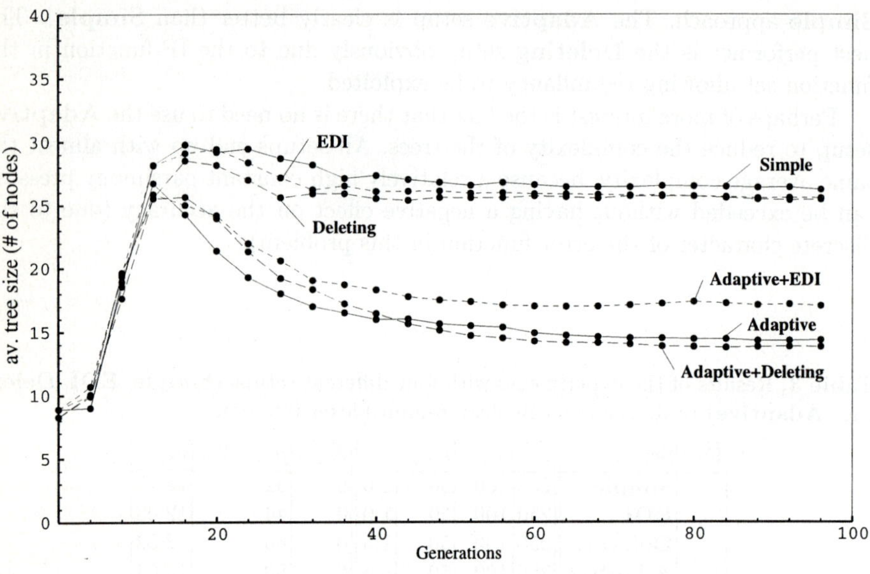

Fig. 1. Comparison of the average tree size in the population (averaged over 20 runs each) for the different setups and experiment 2 and 3. The tree size is given in number per generation.

5 Conclusion

In this paper the feasibility of symbolic regression with GP on complex data has been demonstrated. Several suggested methods from literature to control the tree size complexity have been compared, in particular, the use of Explicitly Defined Introns (EDI) [6], the deleting crossover [1] and the use of an adaptive parsimony pressure [9]. The results for the two specific problems investigated in this paper seem to indicate that the use of EDIs or deleting crossover give no advantages for continuous problems and that deleting crossover can be successful on discrete problems. The superior method to obtain compact and accurate solutions is the method of adaptive parsimony pressure that worked well on both problems. The evolved solutions were compact and accurate within the user-specified limits. For discrete problems there may be no need for this method as a constant parsimony pressure is sufficient to evolve compact solutions.

References

1. Tobias Blickle and Lothar Thiele. Genetic programming and redundancy. In J. Hopf, editor, *Genetic Algorithms within the Framework of Evolutionary Computation (Workshop at KI-94, Saarbrücken)*, pages 33–38. Max-Planck-Institut für Informatik (MPI-I-94-241), 1994.
2. Tobias Blickle and Lothar Thiele. A comparison of selection schemes used in genetic algorithms (2. edition). Technical Report 11, Computer Engineering and Communication Networks Lab (TIK), Swiss Federal Institute of Technology (ETH) Zurich, Gloriastrasse 35, CH-8092 Zurich, Dec 1995.
3. Hitoshi Iba, Takio Kurita, Hugo de Garis, and Taisuke Sato. System identification using structured genetic algorithms. In Stefanie Forrest, editor, *Proceedings of the Fifth International Conference on Genetic Algorithms*, pages 279–286, San Mateo, CA, 1993. Morgan Kaufmann Publishers.
4. John R. Koza. *Genetic programming: on the programming of computers by means of natural selection.* The MIT Press, Cambridge, Massachusetts, 1992.
5. Peter Nordin and Wolfgang Banzhaf. Complexity compression and evolution. In L. Eshelman, editor, *Proceedings of the Sixth International Conference on Genetic Algorithms (ICGA95)*, pages 310–317, San Francisco, CA, 1995. Morgan Kaufmann Publishers.
6. Peter Nordin, Frank Francone, and Wolfgang Banzhaf. Explicitly defined introns and destructive crossover in genetic programming. In Justinian P. Rosca, editor, *Proceedings of the Workshop on Genetic Programming (at Twelfth Int. Conf. on Machine Learning)*, pages 6–22. Technical Report 95.2, University of Rochester, 1995.
7. Justinian P. Rosca and Dana H. Ballard. Genetic programming with adaptive representations. Technical Report 489, The University of Rochester, Computer Science Department, Rochester, New York 14267, 1994.
8. Walter Alden Tackett. *Recombination, Selection, and the Genetic Construction of Computer Programs.* PhD thesis, Faculty of the Graduate School, University of Southern California, 1994.
9. Byoung-Tak Zhang and Heinz Mühlenbein. Balancing accuracy and parsimony in genetic programming. *Evolutionary Computation*, 3(1):17–38, 1995.

Climbing Up NP-Hard Hills

D. Duvivier* and Ph. Preux** and E-G. Talbi***

Abstract. Evolutionary algorithms are sophisticated hill-climbers. In this paper, we discuss the ability of this class of local search algorithms to provide useful and efficient heuristics to solve NP-hard problems. Our discussion is illustrated on experiments aiming at solving the job-shop-scheduling problem. We focus on the components of the EA, pointing out the importance of the objective function as well as the manner the operators are applied. Experiments clearly show the efficiency of local search methods in this context, the trade-off between "pure" and hybrid algorithms, as well as the very good performance obtained by simple hill-climbing algorithms. This work has to be regarded as a step towards a better understanding of the way search algorithms wander in a fitness landscape.

1 Introduction

Our work aims at assessing what evolutionary algorithms (EAs) are good for in the context of combinatorial optimization with regards to other search methods (both exact and non exact). We think that stochastic local search algorithms can bring something to this field. Exact methods are limited in the size of the problems they can handle because of their time/space requirements. Local searches suffer from the lack of demonstrated bounds with regards to the solutions they are able to find [PS97]. However, hybrid algorithms might provide some useful methods, able to handle large instances, and able to relax in some measure these theoretical limitations. To achieve our goal, we put a strong emphasis on a better understanding of the structure of seach spaces related to how search algorithms wander in them. In particular, we want to understand whether, given an instance of a problem, we can predict what kind of algorithm is more likely to perform the best. This paper is grounded on experiments. Theoretical work is under work.

To achieve our goal, we concentrate ourselves on the resolution of the job-shop-scheduling problem (JSP), the traveling salesman problem (TSP), and the quadratic assignment problem (QAP), and we investigate how the evolutionary paradigm may be used (see [BPT96] for the QAP). Though sophisticated ones, EAs are hill-climbers: given a collection of points of the search space, the EA forms a new collection and keeps, deterministically or not, the best points among these two collections. The discriminating feature of EAs from a "standard" hill-climber is the use of recombination operators. Hence, comparing an EA with a standard hill-climber using

* Laboratoire d'Informatique du Littoral, BP 719, 62228 Calais Cedex, France, `duvivier@lil.univ-littoral.fr`

** Laboratoire d'Informatique du Littoral, `preux@lil.univ-littoral.fr`

*** Laboratoire d'Informatique Fondamentale de Lille, URA CNRS 369, Cité scientifique, 59655 Villeneuve d'Ascq Cedex, France, `talbi@lifl.fr` only mutation-like (asexual) operators may shed some lights on the importance of recombination as well as its efficiency. However, care has to be taken when drawing conclusions on the efficiency of recombination because of the mixed effect of mutation and recombination.

In this paper, we will restrict ourselves to one problem, namely the job-shop-scheduling on which we have obtained some significant results. There are several variants of the JSP (see [P94]). We consider here the simple JSP where J jobs, each composed of M operations are to be realized. There are also M machines. Each operation may be realized on a single machine. Each job has an operation which has to be performed on each machine. Then, the aim of the search is to find a planning of occupation of the machines that minimizes the total makespan, that is the total time of realization of the J jobs. This planning indicates, for each time slot, the operation it is processing. A planning is said to be active iff none of its operation may be started earlier resulting in a reduction of the overall makespan. It is known that the optimal planning is active [GT69]. A critical operation is one that, if started earlier, would reduce the makespan. Hence, critical operations are good target for local optimization of a planning.

In section 2, we discuss the encoding of solutions. In section 3, we detail the algorithms we have used so far. Section 4 gives our current results using the OR-LIB benchmarks [Bea90], that is a set of about 150 instances of size ranging from simple instances to very difficult ones. Finally, we discuss these results and give our perspectives.

2 Encoding schemes

In this section, we discuss the encodings of solutions that we have used in our algorithms. Basically, two classes of encodings may be considered for the JSP. They are qualified either as direct, or indirect.

2.1 Indirect encoding

When using an indirect encoding, the data structure is not a planning. Rather, given a data structure, a decoder is required to express the planning. According to the information that is present in the data structure, the decoder has more or less work to do to be able to derive a planning. Constraints are handled by the decoder and guarantee the validity of the planning that is derived. We use a table of $J \times M$ entries. Each job is assigned a class of markers. All the markers associated to one job have the same tag. The markers are then shuffled in the array. The decoder considers this array from the "left to the right". For each entry, it schedules as soon as possible the next not-yet scheduled operation of the job associated to the marker that has been found.

2.2 Direct encoding

In the case of a direct encoding, the data structure actually represents a planning. Hence, no decoder is required. We use a two-dimensional encoding, one dimension ranging among jobs, the other one among machines. For each machine, we have the list of operations that are performed with their time slot. For each job, we have the list of operations tagged with their time slot. This encoding makes it easier to detect available time slots.

3 Algorithms

We have mainly worked with three classes of primitive algorithms: "standard" hill-climber, tabu search and evolutionary algorithms. We have also investigated hybrid algorithms tinkered with these three algorithms as building-blocks. Let us now turn to a detailed presentation of these algorithms.

3.1 Multi-start Hill-climber

The hill-climber is considered as a very simple heuristic that does not require heavy computational resources. A hill-climber is very easy to design. However, it may easily be trapped in a local optimum. We also use a variant of the basic hill-climber, namely a multi-start hill-climber. Starting at a random point, the hill-climber tries to move uphill. When, after a certain amount of attempts, it always fails to climb, the current best point is recorded and the climbing is restarted from another point in the space, chosen at random. To be more precise, it performs the algorithm displayed in figure 1.

The delicate part in using a hill-climber lies in the choice of the move operator. Using an indirect encoding, the basic move turns out to be a swap of markers. Accordingly, using a direct encoding, the basic move is an exchange of two operations. Using one encoding or the other, the solutions that are obtained are equivalent.

3.2 TABU search

The TABU search is a hill-climber which is able to escape from local optima [Glo89a, Glo89b]. The TABU search has only been used with the direct encoding. The basic move swaps two operations of two different jobs. We use an aspiration criterion which accepts a movement even though it is taboo if it leads to the best ever found planning. The size of the taboo list varies dynamically during the run according to [HW95].

3.3 Evolutionary algorithm

As the TABU, the EA only works with the direct encoding. The operators, the objective function, the basic scheme of the algorithm have been tailored for the resolution of the JSP and are described below.

Encoding The encoding of solutions should fit with the problem, as well as the operators that act on them. In this regard, an encoding providing as much information as possible, or at least as much as useful, is worthy. An indirect encoding clearly lacks a lot of information. Thus, we use the direct encoding in the EA. Using this encoding, we can detect the critical operations of a planning.

```
current_schedule := random_schedule
best_ever_found_schedule := current_schedule
best_schedule := current_schedule
for i := 1 to number_of_periods do
  for j := 1 to threshold do
    candidate_schedule := perform move from current_schedule
    if candidate_schedule is better than current_schedule then
      current_schedule := candidate_schedule
    fi
  done
  if current_schedule is better or equal to the best_schedule then
    best_schedule := current_schedule
    if current_schedule is better than the best_ever_found_schedule then
      best_ever_found_schedule := current_schedule
    fi
  else /* Trigger a new experiment */
    best_schedule := current_schedule := random_schedule
  fi
done
output ("I have found " best_ever_found_schedule)
```

Fig. 1. The multi-start hill-climber algorithm that we use.

Recombination operator We use a recombination operator largely inspired by the GA/GT crossover introduced in [NY92]. This operator relies on Giffler and Thompson's algorithm [GT69] to produce an offspring given two parents. The principle of the GT algorithm is:

- $C \leftarrow$ first operation (which is not yet scheduled) of each job
- compute ECT of operations $\in C$
- repeat
  1. select $O^* \in C$ which has minimum ECT
  2. $G \leftarrow$ operations $\in C$ sharing the same machine with O^* and conflicting with O^* (processing overlaps)
  3. choose an operation $O^{**} \in G$ at random
  4. schedule O^{**} as soon as possible according to ECTs
  5. update C and ECTs
- until all operations are scheduled

where C is a "cut", G is a set of operations conflicting with O^*, and ECT means Earliest Completion Time.

A property of this GA/GT operator is that it always produces active plannings.

The mutation operator The mutation performs a swap of two operations. To lead to a valid planning, the swap should only consider operations on one machine chosen at random and re-schedule all the operations that are not yet scheduled. This mutation operator always produces semi-active plannings which, in general, are not active.

The objective function For the simple JSP, aiming at optimizing the makespan, the usual idea is to design the objective function as returning the makespan of a planning/solution. However, close observations of the behavior of the EA in this case (it is still more salient in the case of the hybrids described below) led us to work further the objective function. Initially, our criterion to stop the EA was a null standard deviation of the performance of the members of the population, that is all individuals have the same makespan. However, this does not involve that all individuals are the same planning. As long as there is (genotypic) diversity in the population, the population can evolve. Thus the halting criterion is not the good one. However, it is not easy to assess the equivalence of two plannings. Thus, it is difficult to assess the diversity of the population when all individuals have the same makespan. The number of critical operations may be used as a clue of the goodness of an individual: the less critical operations it has, the better it is. Hence, to distinguish two individuals, we used the sufficient (but not necessary) condition: if two plannings have a different number of critical operations, they are different. Hence, we use an objective function which combines the makespan and the number of critical operations. Using this new objective function, the quality of found solutions has been improved substantially.

Basic scheme of the EA We have observed that, because we are typically using a high rate of mutation and a sophisticated recombination operator, the benefit of the application of the crossover is often destroyed by the mutation applied afterwards. Hence, we use a different scheme of application of the operators. More precisely, the EA performs as follows:

- initialize the population of plannings at random and make them all active
- while completion criterion is not fulfilled do
  - reproduce
  - apply operators on offsprings
  - operated offsprings form the next population

The operators are applied as follows:

1. pick up two individuals χ_1 and χ_2 in the population
2. perform cross-over on them and keep one of the two resulting individuals: χ_1'. The best of the two is more likely to be kept than the worst.
3. perform mutation on one individual among χ_1 and χ_2 choosing one or the other at random. This results in χ_2'
4. put χ_1' and χ_2' in the population of offsprings

This non-conventional scheme of application of operators has proven to perform better.

3.4 Hybrid algorithms

Various hybridization schemes are possible (see [PT95]). We have currently experimented one scheme on the JSP, namely the synchronous hybridization which uses a search algorithm as the mutation operator. Only direct encodings have been used in the case of hybrid algorithms (all algorithms are then working on the same representation). We have used a simple hill-climber (HC) as the search algorithm in the hybrid denoted EA+HC below. It iterates a certain amount of moves, starting from a planning which is the individual it is applied on. The amount of moves that are allowed while there is no improvement is set to 200. When this threshold is reached, the algorithm continues to move as long as it climbs up. We use populations of 300 individuals, stochastic universal sampling reproduction strategy, generational elitist selection. GA/GT is applied with probability 0.6, swap mutation is applied to all the individuals, and the hill-climber to 5 % of the population.

4 Results

We now turn to the results we have obtained with previously reviewed algorithms (*cf.* table 1). In our benchmark suite, we use the Muth and Thompson's instances, the 8 Carlier's instances, as well as 6 Lawrence's instances, and 5 Taillard's instances of big size. The size of the instances ranges from 6×6 to 100×20.

4.1 Performance of our algorithms

Generally speaking, the hybrid EA+HC always performs better than the EA alone. The hybrid has found the optimal planning for some instances (MT6 $\times$ 6, MT10 $\times$ 10, car1, car2, car3, car4, car6, car7, la01, la02, la03, la04, and la05) while the EA did only find the optima of the MT6 $\times$ 6, la01, and la05 which are found by all the algorithms.

For their parts, the hybrid EA, MSHC, and TABU all achieve the same kind of results, lying within a few percents from the optimal planning. When considering the distribution of points found in a series of experiments with a given algorithm, it clearly appears that the standard deviation of optimal plannings is very different from one algorithm to another, and from one series of instances to another. The MSHC generally has a low to moderate standard deviation, the EA and the hybrid EA+HC a moderate one, the TABU heuristic quite a high one. Furthermore, for all heuristics, the standard deviation obtained on the Carlier's instances is much higher than the standard deviation obtained for Muth and Thompson's and Lawrence's instances. Hence, on the test-suite, the MSHC always finds the same quality of makespans, while the TABU finds various quality of plannings.

Concerning the mean time of execution of the various algorithms, the very short time of execution of the MSHC is noteworthy. The EAs (both pure and hybrid) have moderate times of execution. For the TABU, no such conclusion might be easily drawn with regards to the size of the instance for the MT's. It should be pointed out that the EA+HC was run during 2000 generations. However, the best planning that the EA+HC is able to find in a run is usually synthesized during the first hundreds generation. Hence, that means that the EA+HC can be stopped after a few hundreds

Instance	Size	optimum	EA	EA+HC	MSHC	Tabu
mt6x6	6x6	55	55 (0)	55 (0)	55 (0)	55 (0)
mt10x10	10x10	930	953 (2)	930 (0)	947 (2)	930 (0)
mt20x5	20x5	1165	1180 (1)	1178 (1)	1175 (<1)	1165 (0)
car1	11x5	7038	7101 (<1)	7038 (0)	7038 (0)	7038 (0)
car2	13x4	7166	7576 (6)	7166 (0)	7166 (0)	7166 (0)
car3	12x5	7312	7594 (4)	7312 (0)	7312 (0)	7399 (1)
car4	14x4	8003	8423 (5)	8003 (0)	8003 (0)	8003 (0)
car5	10x6	7702	8047 (4)	7720 (≈0)	7738 (≈0)	7720 (≈0)
car6	8x9	8313	8699 (5)	8313 (0)	8313 (0)	8313 (0)
car7	7x7	6558	6680	6558 (0)	6558 (0)	6558 (0)
car8	8x8	8264	8407 (2)	8264 (0)	8294 (≈0)	8294 (≈0)
la01	10x5	666	666 (0)	666 (0)	666 (0)	666 (0)
la02	10x5	655	711	655 (0)	655 (0)	655 (0)
la03	10x5	597	624	597 (0)	597 (0)	597 (0)
la04	10x5	590	620	590 (0)	590 (0)	590 (0)
la05	10x5	593	593 (0)	593 (0)	593 (0)	593 (0)
abz7	20x15	(655, 665)	757	685	682	682
la36	15x15	1268	1408 (11)	1292 (<2)	1281 (1)	1291 (<2)
ta21	20x20	(1539, 1658)	1968	1721	1725	1712
ta31	30x15	(1764, 1766)	2098	1907	1807	1774
ta41	30x20	(1859, 2026)	2551	2262	2143	2117
ta51	50x15	2760	3225 (15)	2909 (5)	2760 (0)	2776 (<1)
ta71	100x20	5464	6065 (10)	5723 (<5)	5744 (5)	5609 (<3)

Table 1. This table sums up our results. The instances are identified with their name in the Orlib. The second column gives the size of the instance. The third one gives the value of the optimum if it is known, a range of it when it is unknown. The fourth column gives the best result obtained using the evolutionary algorithm. The fifth column gives the result obtained with the hybrid EA+hill-climber (EA+HC), the sixth with the multi-start hill-climber (MSHC), the seventh with the Tabu. In columns 4, 5, 6, and 7, we have indicated in () the percent from the optimum the best found planning lies in. All algorithms have been run from 10 to 20 times.

of generations without losing, most of the times, the best solution that it would have been able to find in the run. It also means that we can perform 10, or 20 runs in the time of 1, and have much more odds to obtain better solutions while using the same amount of computational resources. However, the remark should be tempered by the fact that, as noted earlier, our objective function has changed, resulting in a change in the halting criterion. Thus, the genotypic diversity of the population is now better taken into account to stop the algorithm when the "natural" evolution of the population is actually ended.

It is noteworthy that for big instances, the research space is huge and only a very minute fraction of it is visited by the algorithms.

It is also noteworthy that using EAs with a population 2, or 4 times bigger does not improve the quality of best found plannings. The rapid loss of diversity probably accounts for this fact.

We would like to put the emphasis on the performance achieved by the (multi-start) hill-climber. The best found plannings are either the optimal planning or very close to it. This prompts us with two remarks. First, the design of the hill-climber is very simple while the design of the EA is not so easy (notably because of the recombination operator). Second, the basic movement of the MSHC is similar to the mutation that was used in the EA. Hence, this questions the efficiency of the GA/GT operator.

4.2 Comparison with other works

In table 2, we have summarized the results obtained by several authors on the Muth and Thompson's instances. We have only taken into consideration works with pure EAs with random initial population. (However, in some of these works, the initial plannings are generated at random, and made active before going any further.)

Reference	Algo-rithm	MT 6 × 6	MT 10 × 10	MT 20 × 5
Carlier and Pinson [CP89]	B&B	55	930	1165
Nakano and Yamada [NY91]	EA	**55**	965	1215
Nakano and Yamada [NY92]	EA	55	**930**	1184
Dorndorf and Pesh [DP92]	–	55	938	1178
Fang, Ross and Corne [FRC93]	EA	–	949	1189
Juels and Wattenberg [JW94]	EA	–	937	1174
Soares [Soa94]	EA	58	997	–
Kobayashi *et al* [KOY95]	EA	–	930	–
Our results (best obtained results)	EA	55	937	1178
Optimum		**55**	**930**	**1165**

Table 2. This table displays the results obtained by different authors on the Muth and Thompson instances. The first column gives the references to the work. The second column indicates the kind of algorithm that have been used. The three subsequent columns give the results that are reported (best found makespan) for the 3 instances. [NY91] uses an indirect encoding. [NY92] uses a direct encoding with the GA/GT operator. [JW94] uses the indirect encoding. They use an other recombination operator.

The Branch-and-Bound (B&B) is an exact method. Carlier and Pinson [CP89] have obtained the optimal solutions using this method.

Using an EA with an indirect representation, Nakano et Yamada [NY91] have obtained the optimal solution to the MT6×6. Nakano et Yamada [NY92] have obtained the optimal solution to MT10×10. They had turned to a direct representation and the GA/GT as the recombination operator. The optimal planning of the MT20×5 has not been found using the same algorithm. It should be noted that the optimal planning of the MT10×10 has only been found in 4 experiments out of 600. [KOY95], using a new operator (a crossover coupled with a hill-climber), have obtained the optimum of the MT10×10 51 times out of 100 experiments, that is much more often than Nakano and Yamada. It should also be emphasized that among the reported results, only Kobayashi *et al* [KOY95] work solely with active plannings.

Using an EA, only Nakano and Yamada [NY92] and [KOY95] have obtained the optimum of the MT10 × 10. No one has obtained the optimum of the MT20 × 5.

5 Discussion and perspectives

In this paper, we have compared different stochastic meta-heuristics on a test-suite composed of job-shop-scheduling instances, ranging from small size to big size. The meta-heuristics are hill-climbers, TABU search and evolutionary algorithms. Best plannings that were found, standard deviation, times to obtain this planning are discussed for 4 algorithms. The hybrid algorithm achieves better results than the pure EA. Furthermore, a simple multi-start hill-climber often obtains very good solutions. For this kind of algorithms, the trade-off between its design and its efficiency is then very good.

Given the results obtained with the pure EA and the hill-climber, we are prompted to question the efficiency of the recombination operator as long as this is the real difference between these two algorithms. This observation is radically different from the one we obtained on the set partitioning problem where the EA worked much better (both with regards to the solution that was obtained and the time to obtain it) than several kinds of hill-climbers (see [Tal93]). Hence, further studies on the role of the recombination are required.

As it was observed in our experiments, different classes of problem hardness seem to exist. Very pragmatically, we would like to say that an instance is easy if it can be solved optimally with a simple algorithm. This way, we optimize the trade-off between the time of design of the algorithm and the quality of solutions it is able to find. Furthermore, the multi-start hill-climber has also proved to be very fast to find optimal solutions on a series of instances.

We are currently working towards a deeper understanding of the structure of search spaces in cunjunction with how algorithms search the space. We are on our way to characterize some features of instances that involve a certain structure of search spaces as well as the ability of a certain kind of algorithm to search a given space. In [BPT96], we have begun to apply these ideas to the quadratic assignment problem. Along this line, encouraging results have also been obtained for the traveling salesman problem. These features are now being sought for the JSP which is a more complex problem than the TSP, and the QAP in its definition. They should explain why, on one or an other instance, one or an other search algorithm performs the best.

References

[BPT96] Vincent Bachelet, Philippe Preux and El-Ghazali Talbi. Parallel Hybrid Meta-Heuristics: Application to the Quadratic Assignment Problem. *Proc. of the Parallel Optimization Colloquium*, Versailles, France, March 1996.

[Bea90] J.E. Beasley. OR-Library: distributing test problems by electronic mail. *Journal of the Operational Research Society*, **41**(11):1069–1072, 1990. acces to the library via anonymous ftp on `mscmga.ms.ic.ac.uk:/pub`.

[CP89] J. Carlier and E. Pinson. An algorithm for solving the job-shop problem. *Management Science*, **35**(2):164–176, 1989.

[DP92] U. Dorndorf and E. Pesh. Evolution-based learning in a job shop scheduling environment. Technical Report RM 92-019, Rijksuniversiteit Limburg, The Netherlands, 1992.

[FRC93] Hsiao-Lan Fang, Peter Ross, and Dave Corne. A promising genetic algorithm approach to job-shop scheduling, rescheduling, and open-shop scheduling problems. In Stephanie Forrest, editor. *Proc. of the Fifth International Conference on Genetic Algorithms*, Urbana-Champaign, IL, USA, July 1993. Morgan Kaufmann, San Mateo, CA, USA, pages 488-493.

[Glo89a] F. Glover. Tabu search — part I. *ORSA Journal of Computing*, **1**(3):190–206, 1989.

[Glo89b] F. Glover. Tabu search — part II. *ORSA Journal of Computing*, **2**(1):4–31, 1989.

[GT69] B. Giffler and G. L. Thompson. Algorithms for solving production scheduling problems. *Operations Research*, 8:487–503, 1969.

[JW94] Ari Juels and Martin Wattenberg. Stochastic hillclimbing as a baseline method for evaluating genetic algorithms. Technical Report csd-94-834, University of California, 1994.

[HW95] Alain Hertz and Marino Widmer. *La méthode TABOU appliquée aux problèmes d'ordonnancement.* Automatique, Productique, Informatique Industrielle, **29**(4-5), pages 353–378, 1995.

[KOY95] Shigenobu Kobayashi, Isao Ono, and Masayuki Yamamura. An efficient genetic algorithm for job shop scheduling problems. In Larry J. Eshelman, editor. *Proc. of the Sixth International Conference on Genetic Algorithms*, Pittsburgh, PA, USA, July 1995. Morgan Kaufmann, San Mateo, CA, USA, pages 506–511.

[NY91] Ryohei Nakano and Takeshi Yamada. Conventional genetic algorithm for job shop problems. In Richard K. Belew and Lashon B. Booker, editors. *Proc. of the Fourth International Conference on Genetic Algorithms*, La Jolla, CA, USA, July 1991. Morgan Kaufmann, San Mateo, CA, USA, pages 474–479.

[NY92] Ryohei Nakano and Takeshi Yamada. A genetic algorithm applicable to large-scale job-shop problems. In R. Männer and B. Manderick, editors. *Proc. of the Second Conf. on Parallel Problem Solving in Nature.* Elsevier Science Publishers, Amsterdam, 1992, pages 281–290.

[PS97] Christos Papadimitriou and Kenneth Steiglitz. On the complexity of local search for the traveling salesman problem. *SIAM Journal Computing*, **6**(1):76–83, 1977.

[P94] Bernard Penz. *Constructions agrégatives d'ordonnancements pour des job-shops statiques, dynamiques et réactifs.* PhD dissertation, Université de Grenoble I, 1994.

[PT95] Ph. Preux and E-G. Talbi. Assessing the evolutionary algorithm paradigm to solve hard problems. In *Constraint Processing, workshop on really hard problem solving*, September 1995. An extended version is available as report LIL-95-4 from the Laboratoire d'Informatique du Littoral (`ftp://ftp-lil/pub/preux/papers/lil-95-4.ps.gz`)

[Soa94] C. Soares. Evolutionary computation for the job-shop scheduling problem. Technical Report UU-CS-1994-52, Utrecht University, The Netherlands, December 1994.

[Tal93] E. G. Talbi. *Allocation de processus sur les architectures parallèles à mémoire distribuée.* PhD thesis, Institut National Polytechnique de Grenoble, Mai 1993.

On the Performance Assessment and Comparison of Stochastic Multiobjective Optimizers

Carlos M. Fonseca and Peter J. Fleming

Department of Automatic Control and Systems Engineering
The University of Sheffield
Mappin Street, Sheffield S1 3JD, U.K.
C.Fonseca@shef.ac.uk, P.Fleming@shef.ac.uk

Abstract. This work proposes a quantitative, non-parametric interpretation of *statistical* performance of stochastic multiobjective optimizers, including, but not limited to, genetic algorithms. It is shown that, according to this interpretation, typical performance can be defined in terms analogous to the notion of median for ordinal data, as can other measures analogous to other quantiles.
Non-parametric statistical test procedures are then shown to be useful in deciding the relative performance of different multiobjective optimizers on a given problem. Illustrative experimental results are provided to support the discussion.

1 Introduction

The growing interest devoted to evolutionary algorithms for multiobjective optimization is well reflected by the increasing number of different approaches being proposed in the literature (see [1] for a review). Unfortunately, and although the power and usefulness of such techniques is recognized, a well-established approach for the quantitative characterization of the performance of multiobjective evolutionary algorithms, which could, in turn, enable their comparison also in quantitative terms, is still lacking. Arguments for and against the methods currently available have thus remained largely based on qualitative aspects of the evolutionary process, e.g. on whether or not the population tends to cover "well" the, often unknown, trade-off surface of a particular problem.

This work proposes a quantitative, non-parametric interpretation of *statistical* performance of stochastic multiobjective optimizers based on the notion of goal attainment. It then discusses how, and to what extent, the performance of different multiobjective approaches *on a given problem* can be compared based on the proposed interpretation.

2 Performance of a Stochastic Optimizer

The notion of performance of an optimizer inevitably involves the quality of the solutions it is able to produce and the amount of computation effort it requires to arrive at those solutions. In some cases, it is possible to actually guarantee that the optimum will be found, or at least approached at a certain rate, as long as the problem itself satisfies certain conditions. More generally, if there is ultimately no such guarantee, then the performance of the algorithm may still be evaluated experimentally on selected problems. Depending on the algorithm, it then may or may not be possible to correctly extrapolate the results obtained to other problems in the same class as that considered.

In the case of stochastic optimizers, such as evolutionary algorithms and simulated annealing, and generally, in that of any optimizer for which no performance guarantee exists under the given experimental conditions (e.g. limited computation time, multiple local optima), performance characterization is often attempted by repeated, independent experimentation.

In the remainder of this work "performance" will simply refer to the quality of the *final* solutions produced by the optimizer under study on a given problem, regardless of the termination criterion chosen. Evolutionary algorithms, for example, are often applied under the condition of limited computation time (typically measured in terms of elapsed time, CPU time, or number of function evaluations).

2.1 The Single-Objective Case

In the single-objective case, where results from multiple runs of an optimizer can at least be ordered according to their quality (as measured by the objective function which defines the problem), the distribution of the quality of such results can usually be represented easily by means of histograms and/or empirical distribution functions, and summarized by measures such as the median in combination with other statistics of the same type (e.g. upper and lower quartiles, best and worst result, other quantiles).

Moreover, a whole range of (non-parametric) statistical test procedures exist [2] which enable a comparison of the results produced by different optimization methods on a given problem, provided that each method can be independently applied to that problem a number of times. Typically, such procedures make only very weak assumptions about the (unknown) distributions the properties of which they attempt to compare.

If, additionally, the quality of a solution can be represented in terms of a numeric figure, then other measures of location and dispersion can also be used, namely the mean and the standard deviation. Both of these measures are, however, tied to the particular scale in which the objective function is expressed. In contrast, a simple genetic algorithm with rank-based fitness assignment, for example, or an evolution strategy, are insensitive to that scale. Even if the optimizer does depend on the scaling of the objective function, as does simulated annealing and GAs with proportional selection, mean and standard deviation alone would seem insufficient to summarize the performance of such algorithms. Note that the distribution of the results of many runs has unknown shape and cannot generally be expected to approximate a normal distribution (e.g. it is bounded below, assuming minimization, and thus asymmetric).

2.2 The Multiobjective Case

In the multiobjective case, the outcome of an optimization run will generally consist of a varying number of non-dominated solutions. Informally, one would like to obtain a "diverse" sampling of the trade-off surface which was, simultaneously, as close to the real trade-off surface as possible. A possible sampling of a given trade-off surface is illustrated in Fig. 1, for the simultaneous minimization of two objectives.

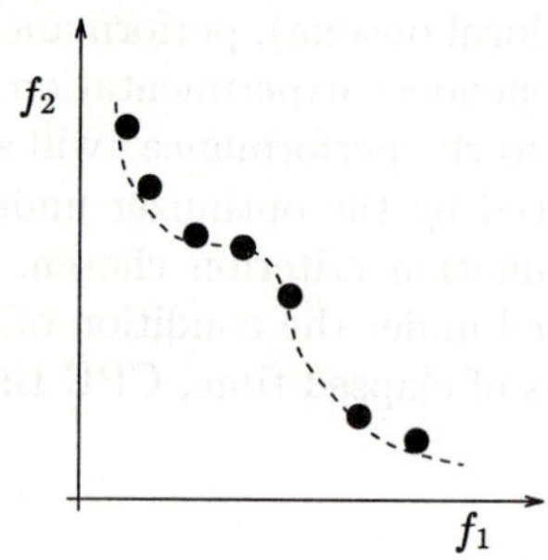

Fig. 1. Visualisation of non-dominated data in two dimensions. From [3].

Interpolating between the data to obtain a smooth representation of the trade-off surface is, however, not generally correct, firstly because there may be no guarantee that it will actually be smooth, and secondly because actual solutions corresponding to those intermediate objective vectors, even if they exist, are not known. At most, one could draw a boundary in objective space separating those points which are dominated by or equal to at least one of the data points, from those which no data point dominates or equals. Such a boundary (see Fig. 2) can also be seen as the locus of the family of tightest *goal vectors* which, given the data, are known to be attainable. It will be called an *attainment surface.*

An attainment surface actually combines information about the quality and the distribution of the corresponding individual non-dominated points across the trade-off surface. On the one hand, the closer to actually non-dominated the approximate solutions are, the closer to the real trade-off surface the attainment surface will be. On the other hand, any "holes" in the distribution of these solutions will have the opposite effect, i.e., will result in the corresponding region of the attainment surface being drawn away from the real trade-off surface, as Fig. 2 also illustrates. Thus, both types of information are expressed in terms of the *location* of the points which constitute the boundary, relative to the real trade-off surface. However, note that the way in which information is combined is independent of the scale in which objectives are expressed, as it relies solely on an ordinal relation, in this case, $\leq$.

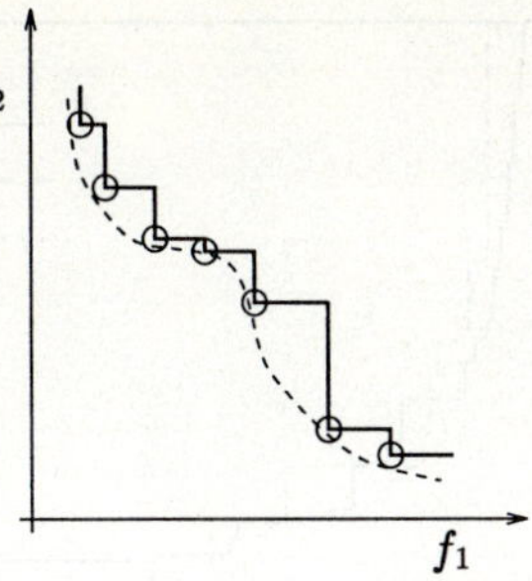

Fig. 2. The family of tightest goals known to be attainable as a result. From [3].

2.3 Multiple Runs

In order to gain some insight into how a certain multiobjective optimizer may typically perform on a given problem, multiple runs can of course be performed. Simply super-imposing non-dominated points obtained from various runs of a multiobjective optimizer does give an idea of how good individual points found in each run tend to be, but, unfortunately, information on how they tend to be distributed along the trade-off surface is largely lost, as Fig. 3 illustrates.

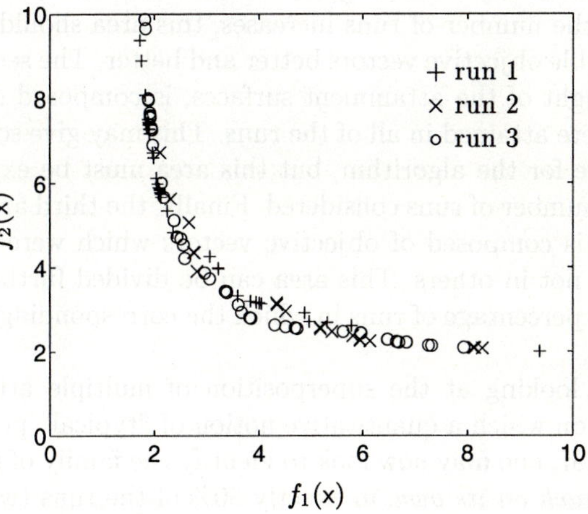

Fig. 3. The superposition of 3 sets of non-dominated points. From [3].

On the other hand, the superposition of the corresponding attainment surfaces preserves both kinds of information better. In Fig. 4, the uneven distribution of some of the sets of non-dominated solutions along the trade-off surface is more apparent. Nevertheless, for a large number of runs, even these plots rapidly become too dense and, therefore, difficult to interpret.

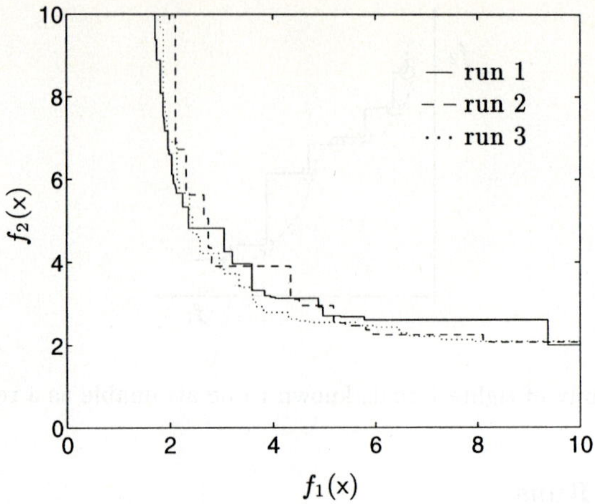

Fig. 4. The superposition of the 3 corresponding boundaries. From [3].

2.4 Statistical Interpretation

Plots such as that in Fig. 4 clearly divide the objective space into three main areas. The first area, located down and to the left of the attainment surfaces, is composed of all those objective (or goal) vectors which were never attained in any of the runs. As the number of runs increases, this area should approximate the real set of infeasible objective vectors better and better. The second area, located up and to the right of the attainment surfaces, is composed of those objective vectors which were attained in all of the runs. This may give some idea of worst-case performance for the algorithm, but this area must be expected to depend strongly on the number of runs considered. Finally, the third area, located within the boundaries, is composed of objective vectors which were attained in some of the runs, but not in others. This area can be divided further into sub-areas, according to the percentage of runs in which the corresponding objective vectors were attained.

This way of looking at the superposition of multiple attainment surfaces provides a basis on which a quantitative notion of "typical" performance can be built. In particular, one may now look to identify the family of goal vectors likely to be attained, *each on its own*, in exactly 50% of the runs (what will be called the 50%-attainment surface of the optimizer). In order to estimate this, consider the points of intersection of a set of attainment surfaces obtained experimentally with an *arbitrary* auxiliary straight line, diagonal to the axes and running in the direction of improvement in all objectives, as illustrated in Fig. 5.

These points can be seen to define a sample distribution which is essentially uni-dimensional and, thus, can be strictly ordered. The desired result can be obtained through the successive estimation of the median of all possible samples defined in this way. Note that this result is independent of the slope of the auxiliary lines used to produce it, as long as they remain diagonal to the axes

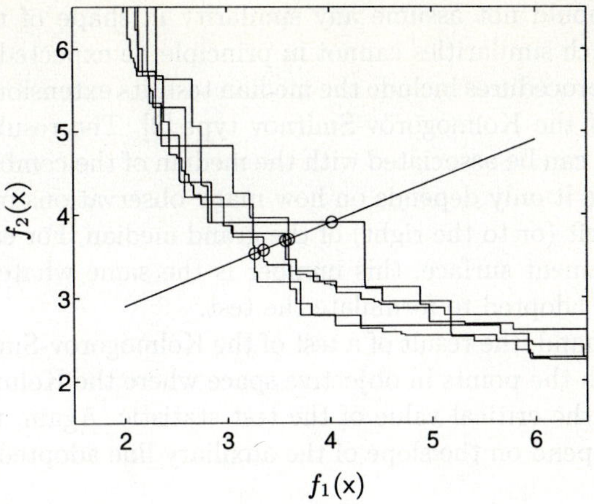

Fig. 5. The points of intersection with a line diagonal to the axes. From [3].

and running in the direction of improvement in all objectives.

Estimates for the 25% and 75% attainment surfaces could be produced exactly in the same way by estimating the lower and upper quartiles instead of the median. In Sect. 4, 25%, 50% and 75%-attainment surfaces estimated in this way from 21 independent runs of each of two different algorithms on a sample problem will be given, as well as the corresponding experimental lower and upper bounds.

3 Performance Comparison

The above considerations on how the performance of a multiobjective optimization approach may be described apply equally well when the performance of two or more different approaches is to be compared. In that case, the intersection of an auxiliary line with the experimental attainment surfaces will define not one, but two (or more) univariate-like samples, each sample corresponding to one approach. The properties of their underlying distributions can then be compared, one set of samples at a time, by means of standard non-parametric statistical test procedures. Provided that

1. the result of testing on a pair (or set) of samples can be associated with a point (or a region) in objective space, and that
2. the result associated with a point (or a region) in objective space is the same independently of the auxiliary line used to arrive at it,

it should be possible to identify those regions in objective space where a statistically significant difference between (the relevant aspects of) the localized performance of the methods under study can be found. As in the single-objective case, the tests should not assume any similarity in shape of the distributions involved, since such similarities cannot in principle be expected.

Suitable test procedures include the median test, its extensions to other quantiles, and tests of the Kolmogorov-Smirnov type [2]. The result of the median test, for example, can be associated with the median of the combined samples (or grand median), as it only depends on how many observations from each sample there are to the left (or to the right) of the grand median. For each point on the grand 50%-attainment surface, this number is the same whatever the slope of the auxiliary line adopted to formulate the test.

On the other hand, the result of a test of the Kolmogorov-Smirnov type could be associated with the points in objective space where the Kolmogorov-Smirnov distance exceeds the critical value of the test statistic. Again, the result of the test would not depend on the slope of the auxiliary line adopted to formulate it.

4 Experimental Results

Two different multiobjective genetic algorithms were run for 100 generations, 21 times each, on the optimal regulator design problem described in [4]. Algorithm A did not include sharing or mating restriction, whereas Algorithm B included sharing and mating restriction in the phenotypic domain. In this case, the niche sizes were computed at each generation depending on the distribution of the population, as proposed in [5]. The results for each algorithm are presented in Figs. 6 and 7.

In both plots, the lower grey line indicates the best trade-off approximation known as a consequence of all the runs, while the upper grey line delimits the set of goal vectors attained in all the runs. The thick black line provides an estimate of the real 50%-attainment surface of each algorithm, and the thin black lines provide analogous estimates, but for 25% and 75%.

These plots can be seen to convey information about the location, dispersion, and even skewness of the distributions of the results in each region (considered in isolation) of the trade-off surface, much like the box plot used in statistics.

By looking at the 50%-attainment surface in each plot, Algorithm B would appear to produce better results more often than Algorithm A in the upper-left region of the trade-off surface. Differences in other regions of the trade-off surface are not clearly apparent. To assess in which regions of the trade-off surface the two methods may have significantly different 50%-attainment performance, the grand 50%-attainment surface may be computed, and a sufficiently large number of median tests performed along this surface, as suggested above. In practice, since the samples are finite, so is the number of *different* tests that may be performed.

Figure 8 presents test results, plotted on the grand 50%-attainment surface, for a 95% confidence level. The regions where no significant difference between the points of the 50%-attainment surfaces of the two algorithms could be found are indicated in light grey, whereas those regions where the points of the two surfaces were found to differ with the given confidence level are plotted in black.

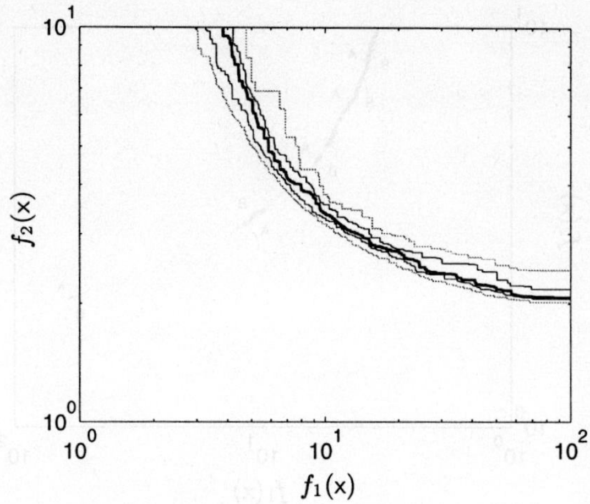

Fig. 6. Representation of the statistical performance of Algorithm A (21 runs).

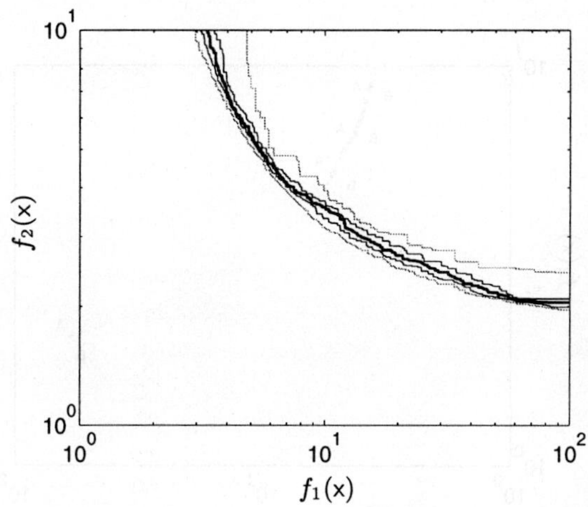

Fig. 7. Representation of the statistical performance of Algorithm B (21 runs).

The labels A and B indicate on which side of the grand 50%-attainment surface each algorithm has its own 50% attainment surface.

It is interesting to note that, although the addition of niche induction techniques in Algorithm B may be said to have improved performance in the extreme regions of the trade-off surface, this was at the expense of degradation in the middle region. This could be explained by the fact that forcing the population to spread more actually weakens its exploitative ability in those regions of the trade-off surface where it would otherwise be more concentrated. However, choosing a higher confidence level (99%) for the individual tests, this degradation is no longer statistically significant. The corresponding plot is shown in Fig. 9.

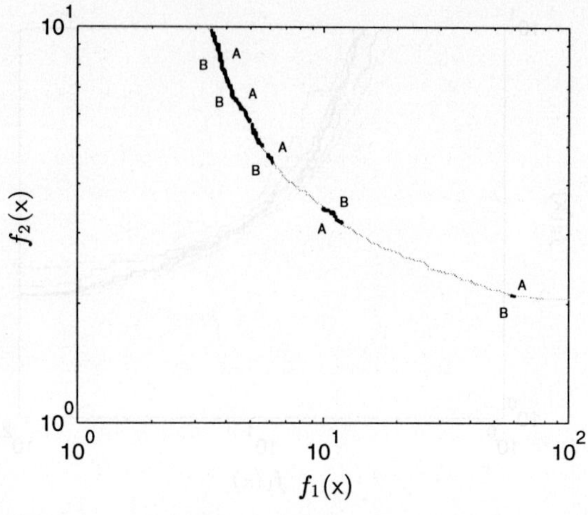

Fig. 8. Comparison of the 50%-attainment surfaces of algorithms A and B (95% confidence).

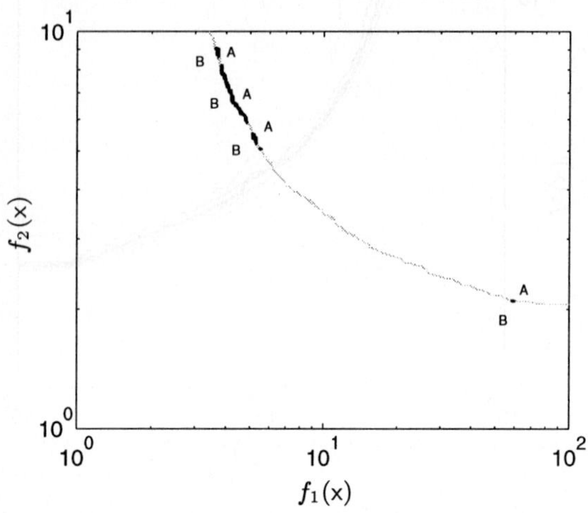

Fig. 9. Comparison of the 50%-attainment surfaces of algorithms A and B (99% confidence).

5 Concluding Remarks

The proposed interpretation of the statistical performance of a multiobjective optimizer in terms of the probability of the optimizer attaining arbitrary goals provides the grounds on which a much needed assessment and comparison of the performance of current and future multiobjective evolutionary approaches can be based. Rather than attempting such a comparison here, a simple example was given in order to illustrate the proposed methodology.

From the initial results presented, such a comparative study would most likely fail to elect an overall "best" algorithm, even for the same optimization problem. Instead, it might find a number of "non-dominated" approaches, in the same spirit of multiobjective optimization itself. On what basis a single, overall "best" approach could be selected, and with what significance level, are questions which are still difficult to answer, especially due to the multiple testing involved and to the likely dependence between tests performed close to each other in objective space.

Perhaps the main limitation of the present results is that the notion of probability of attainment applies only to individual points, separately. How to estimate similar surfaces for given probabilities of attaining the whole surface *simultaneously*, if at all possible, remains unclear.

Finally, although all examples given here involve two objectives only, the considerations made are clearly valid for any number of objectives. The development of software and visualisation tools to support more than two objectives is the subject of further work.

Acknowledgement The authors wish to acknowledge the support of the UK Engineering and Physical Sciences Research Council under Grant GR/J70857.

References

1. C. M. Fonseca and P. J. Fleming, "An overview of evolutionary algorithms in multiobjective optimization," *Evolutionary Computation*, vol. 3, pp. 1–16, Spring 1995.
2. W. J. Conover, ed., *Practical Nonparametric Statistics*. New York: Wiley, 1971.
3. C. M. Fonseca, *Multiobjective Genetic Algorithms with Application to Control Engineering Problems*. PhD thesis, University of Sheffield, 1995.
4. C. M. Fonseca and P. J. Fleming, "Multiobjective optimal controller design with genetic algorithms," in *Proc. IEE Control'94 International Conference*, vol. 1, (Warwick, U.K.), pp. 745–749, 1994.
5. C. M. Fonseca and P. J. Fleming, "Multiobjective genetic algorithms made easy: Selection, sharing and mating restriction," in *First IEE/IEEE International Conference on Genetic Algorithms in Engineering Systems: Innovations and Applications*, (Sheffield, UK), pp. 45–52, The Institution of Electrical Engineers, 1995.

Paginating the Generalized Newspapers - A Comparison of Simulated Annealing and a Heuristic Method

Krista Lagus[1,2], Ilkka Karanta[1] and Juha Ylä-Jääski[1]

[1] VTT Information Technology, FIN-02044 VTT, Finland
(e-mail ilkka.karanta@vtt.fi)
[2] Currently on leave at Helsinki University of Technology,
Neural Networks Research Unit, FIN-02150 Espoo, Finland

Abstract. We consider the problem of placing ready-made boxes (containing e.g. articles) on the pages of a generalized newspaper. Three methods – one utilizing heuristic search, and two utilizing simulated annealing – are presented and compared. The second simulated annealing implementation emerged as the best method. It uses only one simple but powerful state transformation. In our view its success is due to clever use of domain knowledge in the design of the model.

1 Introduction

One important phase of the newspaper production process that has hitherto rather persistently resisted automatization is pagination, or the placement of articles and other material on the pages. There are several reasons for this, the main one beyond aesthetic considerations being that the problem is a two-dimensional bin-packing problem, and as such, np-hard.

There are several ways to characterize a pagination task. A central consideration is whether we can choose a selection from a large corpus of material or must all the material be paginated, and whether we can choose the scope (e.g. pages) of pagination or is the scope given beforehand.

The size of the problem naturally contributes to the complexity of the task. In the general case, the output of the pagination process normally consists of the chosen material together with page number and x and y coordinates for each item. There are several pages and several columns on each page, and the y coordinate may be a real number. A limitation in the range of any of these will reduce the complexity.

In this paper, we consider only pagination to a single page from a large corpus of editorial material. This is a fixed-space, varying contents problem. Such a problem emerges e.g. in the pagination of so-called fax newspapers. These are typically single page publications filled with actual articles from a newspaper, and faxed abroad to tourist centers, embassies etc. The problem emerges also when some section of the newspaper spanning only one page is being paginated. Furthermore, pagination to a single page can be considered as a step in paginating a whole newspaper.

A third potential application may emerge when markup languages start supporting multiple-column page layouts; this kind of enhancement is likely to appear in distributed hypertext systems of the future, such as the World Wide Web (WWW). If one then wants to create a WWW page with varying contents that fits on the screen of the user, these techniques will be readily applicable.

We describe and compare three approaches to the problem. One is based on a heuristic algorithm, whereas the other two utilize simulated annealing.

2 Background

Pagination with fixed size and varying contents involves two interrelated decisions: selection of *article forms* to be paginated to the page, and the actual placement of the article forms to create a page layout. An article form is a box with fixed size, shape and contents; one article may have many alternative article forms.

Not much literature exists on pagination problems. Our research group has a relatively long tradition in solving various pagination problems for yellow pages [2], newspaper advertisements [9], and generalized newspapers [8]. [7] describes the system that formed the basis for this paper. The search for optimal page layout was handled there in the heuristic way described in section 3. This system was then modified to allow for a simulated annealing search method, among other enhancements, and two simulated annealing approaches were implemented [6].

Pagination of article material can be handled as a generalization of two-dimensional multiple-knapsack problem (fixed space, varying contents) or as a two-dimensional bin-packing problem (fixed contents, varying space). Some literature for handling the latter kind of problems exists [5], but we have not been able to find any literature concerning the fixed space, varying contents problem outside the publications of our own research group.

The varying size, fixed contents problem can be treated as a *layout problem* [3], for which a number of optimal algorithms has been developed. However, due to the np-completeness of the quadratic assignment problem, these cannot be used to solve large-scale problems such as problems with fifteen or more items [4].

Several types of suboptimal algorithms have been designed to solve the layout problem. Some are based on heuristic search [7], some on simulated annealing (cf. [4]) and some on genetic algorithms [5]. The first two approaches will be discussed in the following sections. For the third approach the main difficulty has been encountered in developing a representation of the bin-packing problem that is suitable for a GA and is not limited to cuttings representable by slicing trees. However, according to [5], solutions found by heuristic algorithms can be improved by the application of GA's.

The three methods described in this paper were implemented to take care of the automatic pagination task of V·I·P^E, a system for automatic pagination of fax papers[3]. The input for V·I·P^{E}consists of a database of available material

[3] The heuristic method and the second of the simulated annealing methods were ac-

categorized into topics and sub-topics, a set of page frame descriptions (size, the number of columns etc.), a topic category for each page (or sub-page), and for each pagination task, an order from the customer, which directs both the selection of material and the search for best visual layouts. Based on this information V·I·P^{E}paginates selections of the available material to each page, also taking care of database management. The paginated pages may then be modified further via a graphical user interface, if deemed necessary. V·I·P^{E}also produces PostScript descriptions of the pages.

3 A heuristic method for pagination

The main problem in paginating articles with arbitrary size and (rectangular) shape is the combinatorial explosion. This led to the idea of reducing the problem size by discretizing the layout space not only vertically (which is done for newspaper articles anyway as they are presented in columns) but also horizontally. Typically, the page is divided into 4-6 horizontal sections, which together with the vertical division to columns constitute a sparse grid. The contents of each article are first paginated into several different modularized article forms by a rough layout. These forms are then passed to pagination, which selects at most one of them to a page.

The actual search algorithm is a mixture of best-first and branch and bound techniques. The status of the page at any state is represented as a graph that describes the places of the material inserted so far. This description forms the state of the search at each instant. In each state, the algorithm proceeds by searching through the empty spaces on the layout. Each maximal rectangular area of empty space is treated as a *region*, one possible position where to place an article form. Figure 1 illustrates the concept of a region.

At each state, the transition from a father to a child in the state diagram takes the following steps:

1. select N most suitable regions for pagination, and
2. for each such region, find out all the possible combinations of article boxes from the available article shapes in such a way that their combined width does not exceed the width of the region. Select M "best" combinations out of these.

Next, a number of selected region-box-combinations will be expanded to create new nodes of the search graph by inserting the box combinations to the regions. Each node is expanded further until no more articles can be added to the page. Finally, the best page according to given criteria is selected from all the states.

The heuristics of the approach reside in the ordering of empty regions (phase 1) and article combinations (phase 2) into a best-first order. It is difficult to formulate good rules for these ordering tasks.

---

tually implemented in place, whereas the first simulated annealing method was implemented only experimentally.

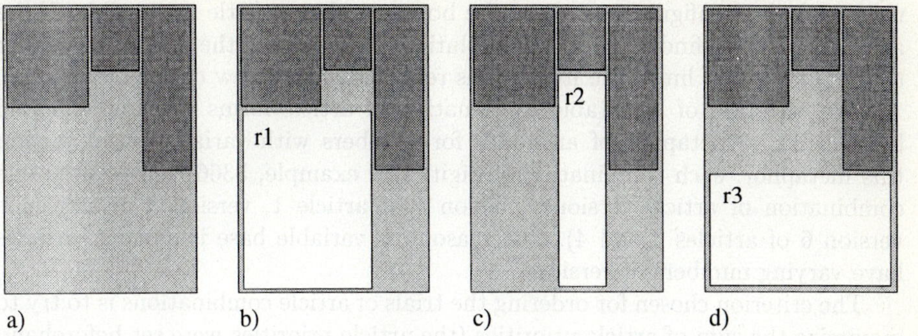

Fig. 1. a) A sample layout in the middle of pagination, with three articles placed. b), c) and d) The three maximal empty regions r1, r2 and r3 that can be found from the layout.

This approach has the merit that the resulting pages look tranquil. A major drawback is that the approach occasionally results in quite a lot of empty space on the page. This is due to two factors. First, because of the modularization, the article forms often contain empty space. Second, the actual search cannot be guaranteed to find a solution with minimal space usage given the article forms, because many alternative paths have been cut during the search based on the heuristic rules just described.

4 Application of simulated annealing

Simulated annealing is a stochastic method for selecting a state change, and within this context may be used to decide which change out of the possible ones to introduce to the layout at any time. First, a state is randomly selected from among the possible ones. If the state results in a lower cost, it is selected for expansion. If it results in a higher cost, it is with a certain probability chosen for expansion anyhow. This probability depends on a parameter called *temperature*, so that as the temperature is decreased the probability of selecting a worse solution becomes smaller. Finally, only changes improving the layout are allowed. The rate at which the temperature is decreased is called *cooling schedule.* For an excellent description of the method the reader is referred to [1].

In the following two subsections, we describe two methods for fixed-space, variable contents pagination that utilize simulated annealing.

4.1 Method SA1

In this approach, the two tasks of pagination – selection of material and creation of the layout – are separated, and the requirement that two distinct boxes do not overlap on the page is relaxed. First, an attempt is made to select material consisting of boxes with fixed size, shape and contents, and then annealing is used to find a configuration where the boxes overlap as little as possible. If the algorithm fails to find an acceptable solution, or one where the overlap is smaller than a predefined limit, the iteration is repeated with a new choice of material.

The selection of a suitable combination of article forms was implemented by utilizing a metaphor of an adder for numbers with variable base. Within this metaphor, each combination of digits (for example, 5366) represented one combination of article versions (version 5 of article 1, version 3 of article 2, version 6 of articles 3 and 4). The reason for variable base is evident: articles have varying numbers of versions.

The criterion chosen for ordering the trials of article combinations is to try to maximize the sum of article priorities (the article priorities were set beforehand manually for each article, and reflect its judged relative importance). This is accomplished by assigning the articles to digit positions in the order of their priority, and arranging the different versions of each article in the order of size from large to small. This ordering tends to maximize the amount of higher priority material on the page before descending to material of lower priorities, and produces an order roughly from best to worst in terms of total priority of the material on the page. Here we define total priority as

$$\sum_i \text{area}(i) \times \text{priority}(i), \tag{1}$$

where i runs through the prospective article forms.

Four criteria are used to prune out useless article form combinations before actually trying to place them on the page. The first criterion is that all the articles should, at least in principle, fit to the page judged by their area:

$$\sum_i \text{area}(i) \leq \text{area}(page), \tag{2}$$

where i runs again through article forms. Another criterion states that if the combined width of two article forms is greater than the width of the page, their combined height should be less than the height of the page. The other criteria are heuristic, and concern the minimum allowed area that is occupied by the material on page, and the minimum acceptable priority value for the whole page, respectively.

These criteria and the specific order of trial selections of material make it possible to prune whole branches of the search tree whenever the root of the branch is found unsuitable. For example, when constraint 2 is violated in some node of the search tree, it is not necessary to search through article form combinations whose combined area is even higher.

The actual search of article combinations that fit to the page involves the relaxation that the article forms may overlap on the page in the intermediate stages of optimization. The final requirement of no overlappings is coded into the cost function to be minimized,

$$\min E = \sum_{i,j,i \neq j} \text{area}(\text{box}(i) \cap \text{box}(j)). \tag{3}$$

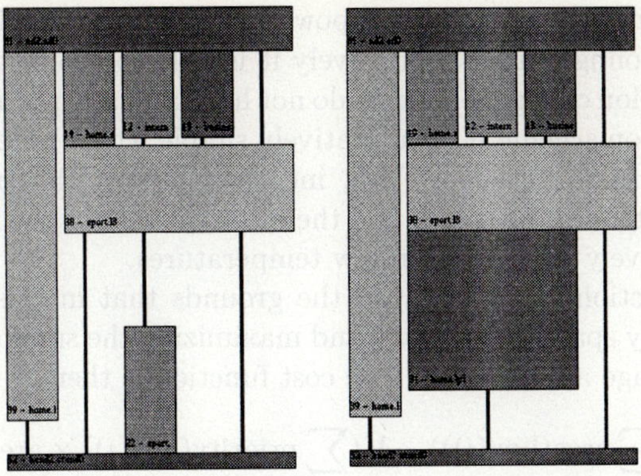

Fig. 2. An insert article transition during the annealing for a 5-column page. The shaded boxes are articles, darker boxes representing articles with higher priority value. The thick black lines stand for individual gaps, i.e. empty space.

State transitions were defined so that an article might at one transition move 1-30 rows within the same column, or alternatively move one column to either direction on the same row, with equal probabilities.

Annealing schedule for the search of article combinations was chosen so that in the initial temperature almost all attempts (over 90 %) were accepted. The end temperature was chosen so that less than 10 % were still accepted.

4.2 Method SA2

In this approach, the tasks of selection of material and finding the layout are integrated into a single optimization task. The approach utilizes a single transition insert article and replace if overlap occurs (called insert article in the following) that randomly chooses an article to be placed on the page, and also randomly finds a corner of empty space for it. Then articles that would overlap with this one are removed from the page, and the article is placed in the chosen empty spot.

In practice, empty spaces on the page are represented by regions described in section 3. An advantage of this representation is that regions give both form and size information that can be used in deciding where to put the chosen article. In addition, finding the regions in a given state is a relatively simple task, and it does not contribute much to the computational burden.

The operation of insert article are illustrated in figure 2. Here the insertion of article 31 results in an overlap with article 22, which is therefore removed.

The transition insert article has several important advantages. First of all, empty space cost is now a perfectly valid measure of the goodness of a state change. With this transition the neighbouring states will extremely rarely have exactly the same amount of empty space on the layout. Second, as no pure deletions are made, the process shows a quicker tendency to proceed towards full layouts. Third, the transition is powerful enough to produce a very great variety of page configurations (intuitively it is able to produce any conceivable article configuration on a page, but we do not have a formal proof of this). Fourth, the state transition scheme is comparatively simple which potentially renders it analyzable by formal methods. Fifth, increases in cost that result from state transformations tend to be small, and therefore chances of getting stuck at local optima are relatively small even in low temperatures.

The cost function was chosen on the grounds that in this approach, both minimizing empty space on the page and maximizing the sum of priorities of the articles on the page are essential. The cost function is then

$$E = U(A - \sum_i \text{area}(\text{box}(i))) - V(\sum_i \text{priority}(\text{box}(i)) \times \text{area}(\text{box}(i))), \quad (4)$$

where A is the total available space on the page, and $U, V \geq 0$ are weights that tell how much we stress each single criterion.

In the average about 1500 rounds (i.e., suggested transitions) were used in annealing, with a final period of 30 rounds at zero temperature to further ensure being in at least a local minimum.

5 Comparison of the approaches

The heuristic method presented in section 3 is based on going systematically through a number of relevant configurations. Combinatorial explosion is avoided by restricting the form of relevant page configurations rather dramatically. This results in the relative efficiency of the implementation, but wastes layout space.

In our experience, a common pitfall of heuristic methods in pagination is that it is not easy to formulate heuristics that at the same time are sufficiently general, valid, and result in moderate run times. This stresses the criticality of available human resources since it is necessary to rethink the heuristics for each class of pagination tasks (for example, in extending our fax system to multi-page newspapers).

The simulated annealing method SA1 (section 4.1) resulted in awkwardly long annealing times for a fax newspaper. This is due to the vastness of the state space. The problem is underlined by the fact that when the articles to be put on the page are not known in advance, the tedious simulated annealing round must be repeated for every combination of articles that are to be tried. Another serious drawback of the method is that the resulting page layouts are not in many cases good or even acceptable (see figure 3).

Method SA2 (section 4.2) resulted in both acceptable run times and good quality page layouts. For example, paginating a set of 130-150 article forms 10 of which actually ended up on the page took less than half a minute on a Sun Sparcstation 20/m71 workstation. Run times were generally an order of magnitude shorter than with SA1. The actual difference in run times might be even larger since SA1 was implemented in C and SA2 in Common Lisp, which is usually considered to produce slower code than C.

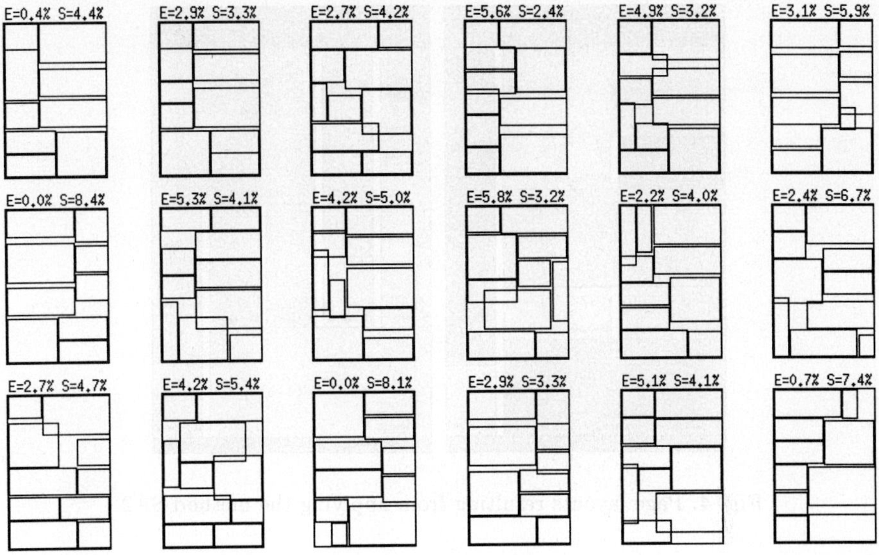

Fig. 3. Page layouts resulting from applying the method SA1. Notice the partial overlap of the articles.

The resulting page layouts were usually aesthetically pleasing. However, in some cases, the resulting pages were cluttered. The situation can be improved by post-pagination operations such as equalizing the spacings on the page automatically, but the fact remains that in some cases, manual reordering of the articles on the page or even repagination is necessary if aesthetics is a major concern.

A typical page layout produced by SA2 is presented in figure 4.

The good performance of SA2 is largely due to the design of state space and state transitions. Especially the transition insert article turned out to reduce the local discontinuity of the search space with respect to the cost function, which enabled considerable improvements even in the frozen annealing state.

Although SA2 is the most promising of the three approaches, it still is not quick enough for pagination that is a part of an interactive user interface. However, it can be used in the task it was designed for: pagination of a fax newspaper page that is delivered to the customers at most a few times a day.

6 Conclusions

We have presented and compared three methods, one based on heuristic search and two based on simulated annealing, in the application of automatic pagination of newspaper editorial material. The heuristic method is based on placing the boxes into a prechosen grid. The first simulated annealing method (SA1) is based on placing the boxes randomly and then applying simulated annealing to state

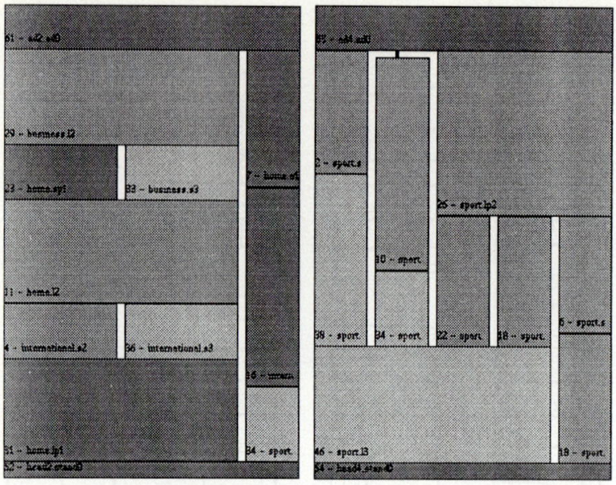

Fig. 4. Page layouts resulting from applying the method SA2.

transformations while trying to minimize overlap between articles. The second method (SA2) is based on applying simulated annealing with only one kind of state transformation: select a box to be placed on the page, find a suitable space for it, and remove any boxes that it would overlap on the page.

It is difficult to say whether better results in terms of speed and memory use could be obtained by using heuristic methods than when using simulated annealing. The main reason is that one can never say whether a better heuristic algorithm for the problem at hand could be designed if no currently known algorithm reaches optimal performance (and if one can define what the optimal performance is). Based on our long experience in development of heuristic methods for automatic pagination it seems evident, however, that using simulated annealing – or other search methods based on controlled randomization – will shorten development times of solution procedures considerably. This seems to be so since when using SA it is not necessary to investigate the problem area as thoroughly as when trying to end up with a good heuristic. Thus, SA provides an effective and well-analyzed vehicle of highly controllable randomization; the control is exercized when designing the state space and the cost function.

On the other hand, SA2 emerged as the winner of the two simulated annealing approaches. It seems to be no coincidence that SA2 is also the one that is based on a more thorough understanding and utilization of the special properties of the problem area. Therefore simulated annealing – or any other method – cannot be held as a substitute of genuine understanding of the problem. Rather, the degree of randomness brought by SA should be used in situations where it is difficult to set computationally simple and reliable rules to guide the search.

A future research direction is to combine the two approaches so that simulated annealing controls the global search, and heuristic methods guide local search in the neighborhood of an initial solution given by simulated annealing.

A demanding future research task is to find a means of analyzing the effects of state transitions. The analysis should both shed light on the performance and complexity of the methods and models in different pagination tasks, and on whether a particular search scheme is in principle capable of finding all possible page layouts from a given material.

Finally, two important research tasks concern the realm of subjective judgments. The first is to find an appropriate measure of the aesthetic appeal of page layouts. This could then be used in the cost function (or even in selecting which state expansion to take into consideration at each situation). The other is to find good ways to calculate the priority of an article, especially for a single user (or a group). This would allow to automatically customize the contents of the page for different customers. This topic is currently under research in our group.

References

1. E. Aarts and J. Korst. *Simulated annealing and Bolzmann machines.* John Wiley & Sons, 1989.
2. Hannu Ahonen and Petri Viertiö. Knowledge-based pagination. In Hannu Jaakkola and Seppo Linnainmaa, editors, *Proceedings of the second Scandinavian Conference on Artificial Intelligence*, pages 607–611, Amsterdam, Springfield Va., Tokyo, 1989. IOS Press.
3. S.S. Heragu. Recent models and techniques for solving the layout problem. *European Journal of Operations Research*, 57:136–144, 1992.
4. S.S. Heragu and A.S. Alfa. Experimental analysis of simulated annealing based algorithms for the layout problem. *European Journal of Operations Research*, 57:190–202, 1992.
5. S.-M. Hwang, C.Y. Kao, and J.-T. Horng. On solving rectangle bin packing problems using genetic algorithms. In *Proceedings of the 1994 IEEE International Conference on Systems, Man and Cybernetics*, volume 2, pages 1583–1590, Piscataway, NJ, USA, 1994. IEEE Press.
6. Krista Lagus. Automated pagination of the generalized newspaper using simulated annealing. Master's thesis, Helsinki University of Technology, 1995.
7. T. Veijonen, H. Ahonen, V. Leikola, J. Niku-Paavola, and J. Ylä-Jääski. Automatic page layout for electronic news distribution. In B. Furht, editor, *Proc. IASTED/ISMM International Conf. Distributed Multimedia systems and Applications*, Anaheim-Calgary-Zurich, 1994. IASTED/ISMM - Acta Press.
8. T. Veijonen, H. Ahonen, J. Niku-Paavola, and J. Ylä-Jääski. Knowledge-based system for the design of newspaper structure. In J. Liebowitz, editor, *Proceedings of the World Congress on Expert Systems*, pages 2172–2179. Pergamon Press, 1991.
9. J. Ylä-Jääski and H. Ahonen. Knowledge-based newspaper pagination. In *Applications of artificial intelligence VIII*, volume 1293, pages 767–774. SPIE, 1990.

A Comparison of Optimization Techniques for Integrated Manufacturing Planning and Scheduling

M. McIlhagga[1], P. Husbands, R. Ives

COGS, University of Sussex, Brighton, BN1 9QH, UK.

Abstract. We describe a comparison between Simulated Annealing (SA), Dispatch Rules (DR), and a Coevolutionary Distributed Genetic Algorithm (DGA) solving a random sample of integrated planning and scheduling (IPS) problems. We found that for a wide range of optimization criteria the DGA consistently outperformed SA and DR. The DGA finds 8-9 unique high quality solutions per run, whereas the other techniques find only one. On average, each DGA solution is 10-15% better than SA solutions and 30-35% better than DR solutions.

1. Introduction

This paper describes a comparison of SA, DR, and a Coevolutionary DGA applied to a highly generalized class of job-shop scheduling problems. These problems involve the simultaneous optimization of a number of flexible manufacturing plans. The application of Coevolutionary GAs to this class of problems has been investigated in [Husbands P and Mill F, 1991, Husbands P, 1993]. Prior to that Khoshnevis and Chen used DR to solve problems from a restricted subset of the class [Khoshnevis B and Chen Q, 1990]. Recently Palmer applied SA to a range of industrial problems of this sort [Palmer G, 1994]. To date the relative performance of all three approaches has not been measured. In his Ph.D. thesis Palmer [Palmer G, 1994] detailed algorithms for generating random IPS problems. He used these to compare his SA method with Khoshnevis and Chen's approach on sets of 100 industrially realistic problems.

A comparison of the results obtained with a coevolutionary DGA with those in Palmer's thesis is reported here. His problem generation algorithms have been reimplemented, as have his evaluation criteria: makespan, mean flow time, total tardiness and proportion of tardy jobs. The coevolutionary approach was found to significantly outperform the two other techniques on all these measures. This work involved adapting an earlier 'ecosystems' model of integrated production for use with a new set of problems and cost functions. This turned out to be relatively straightforward, supporting the claim that the coevolutionary model is very general [Husbands P, 1993].

Section 2 explains IPS more fully. This is followed by an overview of each technique used in this study. The problem, cost function and implementation details are then given before the results of the comparison are presented.

1. malcolm@cogs.susx.ac.uk, http://www.cogs.susx.ac.uk/users/malcolm

2. Integrated Manufacturing Planning and Scheduling

The traditional academic view of job-shop scheduling (JSS) is shown in Figure 1 [French S, 1982; Zweben M and Fox M, 1994]. A number of *fixed* plans, one for each component to be manufactured, are interleaved by a scheduler so as to minimize some criteria such as total schedule length.

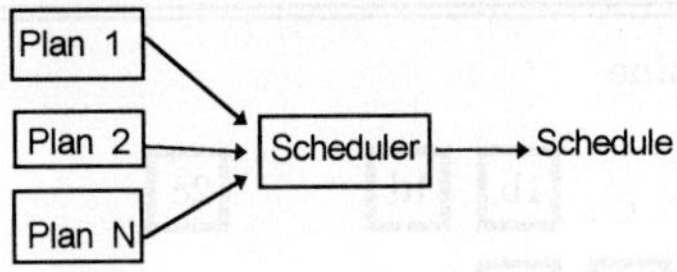

Figure 1: Traditional Scheduling

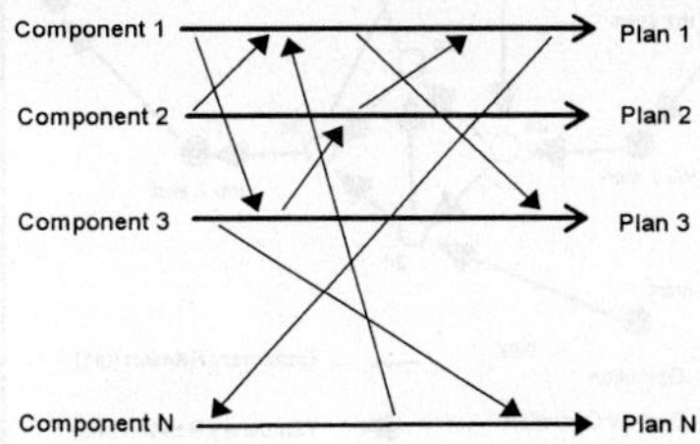

Figure 2 Emergent Scheduling

A problem that would often be more useful to solve is that illustrated in Figure 2. Here the intention is to optimize the individual manufacturing plans *in parallel*, taking account of the numerous interactions between them resulting from the shared use of resources. This is a harder and more general problem than traditional JSS.

In many manufacturing environments there are a vast number of legal component plans. These vary in the number of manufacturing operations, the ordering of the operations, the machines used, the tool used for an operation and orientation of the work-piece (setup) given the machine and tool choices. All these choices are subject to constraints on the ordering of operations, and technological dependencies between operations. Optimizing a single process plan is an NP-hard problem [Husbands P and Mill F, 1991]. Optimizing several in parallel requires a powerful search technique. It is this class IPS with which we are concerned.

3. Approaches to Integrated Planning and Scheduling

Section 3 reviews the three approaches to IPS investigated in this study.

3.1 Simulated Annealing

SA is a stochastic search technique fully described in the literature [Aarts E and Korst J, 1989; Kirkpatrick S, Gelatt C D, Vecchi M P, 1983]. By sometimes allowing temporary jumps to worse solutions using the Boltzman distribution the technique tends to avoid local minima. In order to apply SA to a problem it is necessary to have a solution representation and a set of operators to move from the current solution to new candidate solutions. Palmer chose to represent solutions to the IPS problem as digraphs [Palmer G, 1994]. Such a graph is shown in Figure 3 and the schedule it represents is shown in Figure 4. The solid arrows represent ordering constraints between operations and the shaded arrows represent particular linearisations of the process plans which are combined in parallel to form the overall schedule.

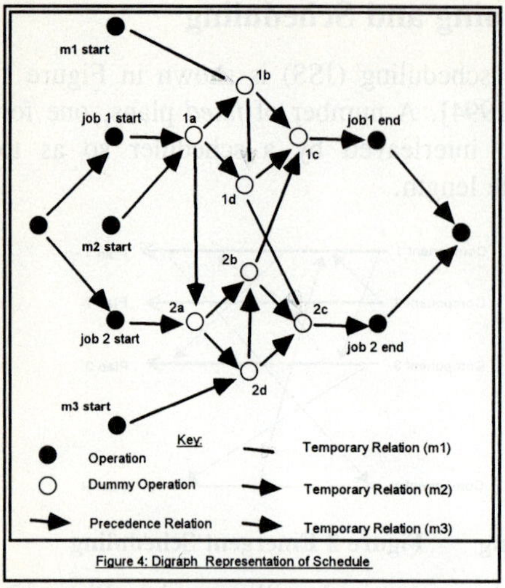

Figure 3: Digraph Representation

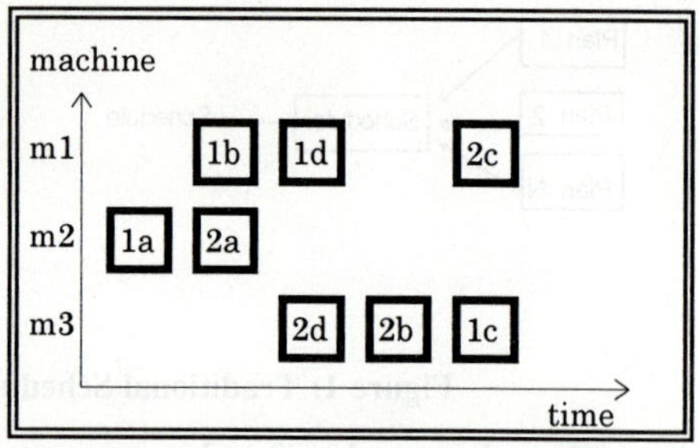

Figure 4: Gantt Chart of Schedule

He implemented three plan change operations which respect problem ordering and operation/machine constraints: reverse two sequential machine operations; reverse the order of two sequential operations within a job; change the machine performing an operation. Each move was generated by one randomly chosen operator from the set above. Where N is the number of problem variables. The annealing schedule reduced the temperature by 10% every 10N moves, or after N moves without any improvement since the last drop in temperature, whichever came first.

3.2 Khoshnevis and Chen's Dispatching Rules Approach

Dispatching (priority) rules are a popular heuristic used to solve classical JSS problems [French S, 1982]. Often used with simple constructive search algorithms to choose the next operation to process, the most common are: **SPT,** Shortest Processing Time; **FCFS,** First Come First Served; **MWKR,** Most Work Remaining; **LWKR,** Least Work Remaining; **MOPNR,** Most Operations Remaining; **RDM,** Random. [Khoshnevis B and Chen Q, 1990] use a dispatching rule based on slack time (the difference between time remaining to due date and anticipated total process time). Whenever a machine becomes available, the job chosen to be processed next is the one with least slack time (LST). Their approach allows process plan flexibility in the order of operations within a job and the machine chosen for each operation. To decide between candidate operation/machine combinations in the next job to be processed, they use the SI (Shortest Imminent Processing Time) rule. Thus IPS is tackled using a LST rule to choose between jobs, and the SI rule to choose an operation-machine combination within a job.

3.3 Distributed GAs & the Coevolutionary Ecosystem Model

The DGA model is fully described in [Husbands P, 1992; McIlhagga M, Husbands P, Ives R, 1996]. In the basic DGA [Collins R and Jefferson D, 1991] a population of chromosomes is kept in a non-ordinal data structure similar to that of a traditional GA [Goldberg D E, 1989]. However a landscape grid (a 2D torus) is maintained, allowing geographically local selection and replacement strategies (Figure 5). That is, members of the population mate with other members nearby on the 2D grid and their offspring are placed in the same 'neighbourhood'. The advantages of a DGA are: low variance in best solutions found over multiple runs; high variance in good solutions represented in the population at the end of a run; better quality and quantity of solutions found and faster decent to very good solutions [McIlhagga M, Husbands P, Ives R, 1996; Collins R and Jefferson D, 1991].

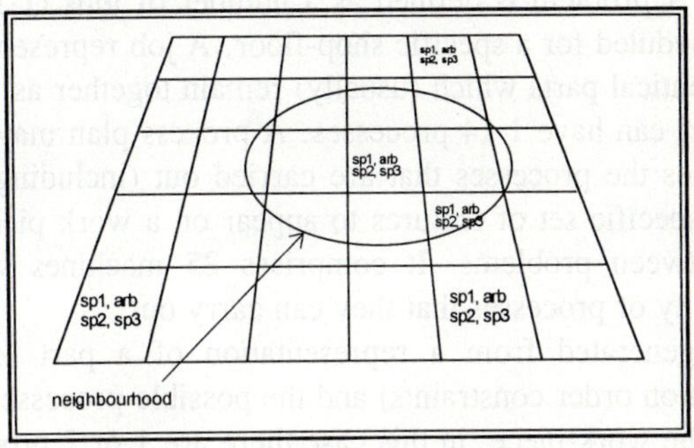

Figure 5: Distributed Set of Species

In the ecosystems model for handling the IPS problem, a number of different species coevolve on the 2D grid. Each cell on the grid contains one member of each species. This is illustrated in Fig 5. The genotype of each species represents a plan for a component to be manufactured in the machine shop. Separate populations evolve under the pressure of selection to find near-optimal plans for each component. However, their costs account for shared resources in their common world (a machine shop model). This means that without the need for an explicit scheduling stage, a low cost schedule will emerge as the plans are being optimized. Manufacturing data is used to randomly construct populations of plan structures, one for each component. Arbitrator chromosomes, who resolve conflicts between members of the other populations, are an important part of this model—their fitness depends on how well they achieve this. Each population, including Arbitrators, evolve under the influence of selection, crossover and mutation [Husbands P, 1993].

Selection works by using a ranking scheme within a 12 chromosome neighbourhood: the fittest individual is twice as likely to be selected as the median. Offspring replace individuals from their parents' neighbourhood. Replacement is probabilistic using the inverse scheme to selection. Genetic material remains spatially local and a robust and coherent coevolution (particularly between Arbitrators and process plans) is allowed to unfold.

The cost, hence selection, functions for plan organisms involve two stages: first, population specific criteria (machining costs) and the second takes into account interactions between populations. Arbitrators are only evaluated at the second stage, their fitness depending on how well they reduce conflicts between plans. The second stage of the plan cost function involves simulating the simultaneous execution of several plans, one for each component manufactured. These plans (plus an Arbitrator) are taken from the same cell on the grid—an important factor in allowing coherent coevolution. Any waiting time due to interactions between plans (resource conflicts) are added to manufacturing costs to give the total plan cost.

4. Description of the Problems

The test problems were generated from data collected from David Brown Vehicles Ltd. [Palmer G, 1994]. The statistics shown later are mean figures taken from 100 sample problems. A problem is defined as a number of jobs (1-14), each of which requires a plan scheduled for a specific shop-floor. A job represents the manufacture of one or more identical parts which (usually) remain together as they move through the shop. Each part can have 1-14 processes. A process plan may be either fixed or flexible, it describes the processes that are carried out (including possible ordering constraints) for a specific set of features to appear on a work piece. The shop-floor does not alter between problems. It comprises 25 machines which vary in the number and diversity of processes that they can carry out.

Each plan is generated from a representation of a part (descriptions of its features and operation order constraints) and the possible processes that can generate those features on the work-piece; in this case there are 1 or 2 processes per feature. Most processes can be carried out on a large selection of machines, greatly increasing the search space for this IPS problem.

4.1 Problem Generation

The problems used were generated according to plan templates as detailed in [Palmer G, 1994]. A template forms the basis of a job, giving possible operations, machine options and ordering constraints. The number of operations for a particular job is chosen at random within the limits defined in the template. The ordering constraints and machine options in the generated (flexible) plans form the basis for the IPS search space. The major problem parameters were as follows:

- 1-14 operations per job (generated at random from a plan template)
- 5-10 jobs per problem (generated at random)
- 1-2 applicable methods per operation (generated from a plan template)

There were 24 available operation methods. The earliest availability date for each machine was randomly generated. Release and due dates, set-up and machine times, were generated using lookup tables and random functions [Palmer G, 1994]. Operation times were calculated using the company's estimation program.

4.2 The Cost Function

All of Palmer's results reproduced here were found using the compound cost function *mean flowtime plus twice the total tardiness* (MFTT2). The more distributed coevolutionary GA approach uses slightly different cost functions. These were adapted from Palmer's to fit the coevolutionary architecture. It should be pointed out that results from the two methods were compared over exactly the same set of statistical evaluation criteria.

Each job j has the following data associated with it:

- release date r_j
- due date d_j
- completion time C_j
- flowtime $F_j = C_j - r_j$
- lateness $L_j = C_j - d_j$
- tardiness $T_j = \max(0, L_j)$
- processing time of job j on machine i, P_{ij}

The following cost functions can then be calculated:

- makespan: $C_{\max}$
- mean flowtime: $\bar{F} = \frac{1}{N}.\sum_{j=1}^{N} F_j$
- total tardiness: $\sum_{j=1}^{N} T_j$
- proportion of tardy jobs.

In addition, machine utilization, U, for each machine can be calculated:

$$U_i = \frac{1}{c_{\max} - a_i}.\sum_{j=1}^{N} P_{ij}$$

Where a_i is the initial available date of machine i.

Below we show the results for two cost functions used with the coevolutionary DGA: **Grp**. and **Cont**. The difference between these two costing criteria is as follows. **Cont**. stands for *contribution*. Here the plan chromosomes have a cost that is in part proportional to it's own efficiency and in part proportional to the efficiency of the group that is belongs to. Each cell on the DGA grid contains a single group comprising one unique plan for each part being planned plus an arbitrator. The evaluation of an individual may be tardiness or plan cost (includes machine set-up and machining costs). **Grp**. stands for *group*, here each chromosome in the group is given the same cost: a weighted sum of the efficiency of *all* of the chromosomes in a cell. Below, P_G and P_C are the Grp. and Cont. process plan chromosomes cost functions respectively. A_G and A_C are the Grp. and Cont. arbitrator cost functions respectively.

PG = MFTT2, PC = (flowtime + 2*tardiness)*N (N is No of plans),
AG = MFTT2, AC = total wait time + 2*total tardiness.

5. The Coevolutionary DGA Implementation

Section 5 describes problem specific details of the DGA implementation.

5.1 Plan Encoding

Each job is encoded in a separate fixed length chromosome (this varies between jobs). Chromosomes have two sections, the first deals with method (machine) choices and the second with sequence (ordering) choices. Currently, all methods that have a choice have two options and are represented in binary. Lookup tables translate these values into a machine choice. Method choices are held on the genome in an order which maps to a set of known operations (1-N). For each job, the cost function maintains a tree containing the space of legal sequences of operations. Sequence choices on the chromosome are interpreted as routes down the tree for that job (see figure 6). The default sequence is always legal, so in cases where the problem description constrains the genome to only one legal sequence, the sequencing information is implicit. The evaluation function is a set of routines that traverse a given tree, following a given route, returning a valid operation sequence.

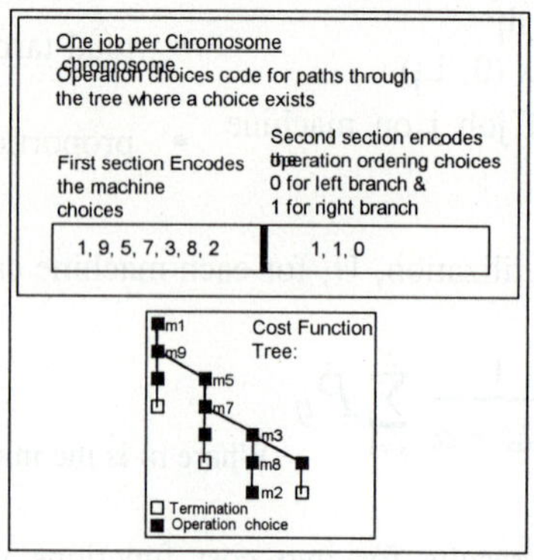

Figure 6: Chromosome Encoding

The sequence choices may be much larger than the method choices, depending simply on the branch rate of the tree. Thus, a separate data structure is maintained to hold the maximum possible value of each gene. Legal crossover is made trivial with this representation, provided it only occurs at gene boundaries. Translocation is not possible with this scheme.

5.2 Arbitrator Encoding

An arbitrator is a series of lookup tables, flattened into a bit string, used to resolves resource (machine) conflicts between different plans. The Nth table encodes preference relationships for the Nth manufacturing operations. Relationships for every possible component pairing are represented. See [Husbands P, 1994] for details. The event-processing in the cost function responds to a request for the use of a machine as follows:

1. If machine is unoccupied, provisionally put the operation on that machine.
2. If the machine is already provisionally occupied by another operation, an arbitrator will decide whether the new operation is placed on the machine instead, and the first operation placed in a waiting state, or whether the second operation should wait until the machine is released.

The provisional status of an operation placement is lost when the **time** in the event-processing routines reaches the operation completion time. As operations cannot be performed **in part**, an operation taken off a machine is said to have been waiting all along. No consideration is made for the time an operation has provisionally occupied a machine when conflict arises. The binary table encodes which of the two plans wins machine-use.

6. Results

The results for the SA and dispatch rule algorithms presented here are reprinted from [Palmer G, 1994]. Due to time constraints, we chose not to re-implement these algorithms. The results in [Palmer G, 1994] show the mean results over a set of 100 problems. Here we present our results along side those shown in his thesis. Statistics were derived from 100 problems. The number of objective function calls per run was 525,000.

Algorithm	Make span	Proportion Tardy	Total Tardiness	Total Time Machining	Machine Utilization	Mean Flowtime
GPDGA cont	81.22	0.14	5.84	171.75	0.18	34.86
GPDGA grp	80.40	0.15	5.47	172.23	0.18	34.63
SA	89.09	0.18	8.87	191.22	0.18	36.10
DR	95.96	0.31	30.28	218.13	0.19	41.37

Table 1: Problem Set Comparison Over Assorted Cost Functions

Objective function:	Contribution, Group
popsize:	1500.
Evaluations per problem:	525,000

Table 2: Parameters

The DGA outperforms SA and DR for all optimisation criteria (Table 1). Mean improvements over SA, averaged over all optimization criteria (not machine utilization), were **16.58%** and **15.75%** for GPDGA cont. and grp. respectively. The mean improvements over DR, averaged over the optimization criteria, were **37.60%** and **39.00%** for GPDGA cont. and grp. respectively. See section 4.2 for an explanation of the two GPDGA cost functions. The DGA performs ≈1% better when the cost function reflect the efficiency of an individual and not just the group that it came from.

One advantage of using the coevolutionary DGA over SA is that in one run it is capable of generating more than one solution to the problem at hand. Table 3 shows the mean number of chromosomes within 5% of the best found. The figures are averages over 100 problems. The data is taken from the same set of experiments used to generate Table 1. This emphasizes the fact that the DGA is not only finding good solutions to an NP-Hard problem, but is finding multiple different near optimal solutions. It is impossible to make a detailed comparison of the solutions found by different techniques (other than mean costs over 100 problems) because Palmer does not include problem solutions in his thesis [Palmer G, 1994].

Algorithm	MFTT2	Mean No. Competing Solutions
GPDGA Cont.	46.54	8.76
GPDGA Grp.	45.56	9.74
SA	53.84	N/A
DR	101.93	N/A

Table 3: MFTT2 Comparison

Further analysis indicated the presence of a few aspects which significantly swung the results for the Total Tardiness criterion. These occur in cases where a problem includes a number of plans generated from the same templates-section. In such cases, the due-dates turn out to be similar for a number of jobs which largely demand the same machines (i.e. the method flexibility required to avoid waiting-times turns out to be particularly limited). Because there are 14 job-types, and 5-10 different jobs per problem, the probability of getting three or more jobs from the same job-type class is ≈0.071 (given 105 jobs, an average of ≈7.5 jobs would be the same as at least two others). This aspect adds to the difficulty of the problem by making the total tardiness hard to minimize. Table 4 shows the results for two identical DGA runs using two different sets of 100 problems.

Algorithm	Makespan	Proportion Tardy	Total Tardiness	Total time Machining	Machine Utilization	Mean Flowtime
GPDGA 1st	62.75	0.18	16.67	112.86	0.16	23.93
GPDGA 2nd	63.50	0.16	12.89	117.22	0.16	23.99
SA	89.09	0.18	8.87	191.22	0.18	36.10
K&C	95.96	0.31	30.28	218.13	0.19	41.37

Table 4: Comparison of Two sets of 100 Problems (GPDGA Cont. cost function)

The results stay reasonably constant except for tardiness factors. Thus the effect of the MFTT2 in Table 5. This suggests that, although 100 problems would provide statistical significance for most of the optimization criteria, the sample may not be large enough to give a fair comparison of tardiness.

Algorithm	MFTT2
GPDGA 1st	57.27
GPDGA 2nd	49.77
SA	53.84
K&C	101.93

Table 5: MFTT2

7. Conclusions

We found that for all the optimization criteria described in [Palmer G, 1994] the coevolutionary DGA consistently outperformed SA and the DR. Results suggest that variance in costs due to sample size should be calculated in this sort of comparative study. It is clear that some optimisation criteria are more sensitive to this effect than others. A larger sample than that provided by Palmer would have been desirable. Both DGA cost function configurations investigated improved on the performance of the SA by a factor of over 15%, and on the dispatching rule by more than 35%. The results suggest that a cost function that includes factors that are related to both its individual performance as well as it's group performance will outperform, by about 1%, one which only accounts for the group performance. Unlike the other techniques, the DGA produced a number of unique, high quality solutions, to the problem on each run (typically 8 or 9).

8. References

Aarts E and Korst J, 1989. Simulated Annealing and Boltzmann Machines. Wiley.

Collins R and Jefferson D, 1991. Selection in massively parallel genetic algorithms. In Belew R and Booker L B (Eds.), Proceeding on the fourth International Conference on Generic Algorithms, ICGA-91, pp. 249-256. Morgan Kaufmann, 1991.

French S, 1982. Sequencing and Scheduling. Ellis Horwood.

Garey M and Johnson D, 1979. Computers and Intractability. W H Freeman.

Goldberg D E, 1989. GAs in Search, Optimization and Machine Learning, Reading, Massachusetts: Addison Wesley.

Husbands P and Mill F, 1991. Simulated Co-evolution as the mechanism for Emergent Planning and Scheduling. In: R. K. Belew and L. B. Booker Eds. Proceedings of the Fourth International Conference on GAs, ICGA-91. Morgan Kaufmann Publishers.

Husbands P, 1992. GAs in Optimization and Adaptation. In L. Kronsjö and D. Shumsheruddin, Eds. 1992. Advances in Parallel Algorithms, pp. 227-276. Blackwell Scientific Publications.

Husbands P, 1993. An Ecosystems Model for Integrated Production Planning. International Journal of Computer Integrated Manufacturing, Vol. 6, nos. 1 & 2, pp. 74-86.

Husbands P, 1994. Distributed coevolutionary Genetic Algorithms for muti-criteria and multi-constraint optimisation. In: Fogarty T, Ed., *Evolutionary Computing, AISB Workshop selected papers,* pp. 150-165. Springer-Verlag, Lecture Notes in Computer Science Vol. 865, 1994.

Khoshnevis B and Chen Q, 1990. Integration of Process Planning and Scheduling Functions. Journal of Intelligent Manufacturing. pp. 165-176.

Kirkpatrick S, Gelatt C D, Vecchi M P, 1983. Optimisation by Simulated Annealing, Science 220, 671-680.

McIlhagga M, Husbands P, Ives R, 1996. A Comparison of Various Search Techniques on a Wing-Box Optimization Problem. In Parallel Problem Solving From Nature IV (this volume).

Palmer G, 1994. An Integrated approach to Manufacturing Planning (Ph.D. thesis, University of Huddersfield).

Rinnooy Kan A, 1976. Machine Scheduling Problems. Martinus Nijhoff, the Hauge.

Zweben M and Fox M, 1994. Intelligent Scheduling. Morgan Kaufmann.

A Comparison of Search Techniques on a Wing-Box Optimisation Problem

Malcolm McIlhagga, Phil Husbands and Robert Ives

School of Cognitive and Computing Sciences,
University of Sussex, Brighton, BN1 9QH, UK

Abstract. This paper describes a thorough comparison of ten different search techniques applied to a wing-box design optimisation problem. The techniques used vary from deterministic gradient descent to stochastic Simulated Annealing (SA) and Genetic Algorithms (GAs). The stochastic techniques produced as good solutions as the best found by the deterministic techniques. However, only the stochastic techniques consistently produced very good solutions every run. Significantly, only a distributed genetic algorithm (DGA) and hybrid methods (SA with gradient descent, DGA with gradient descent) had a reliable fast decent to good regions of solution space. Of these the hybrid DGA was significantly better than anything else. The issue of generating solutions stable to perturbations of the problem variables, without greatly increasing the runtime of the objective function, is also discussed. We describe a method for producing highly stable solutions with the DGA while increasing the run time of the objective function by a factor of only 4. No explicit term dealing with stability was added to the objective function.

1 Introduction

Many engineering design optimisation problems involve search spaces with a highly complex structure. Stochastic techniques such as simulated annealing and genetic algorithms have been successfully applied to a number of these [4, 10], and folklore states that these are among the sorts of problems to which these techniques are best suited, having advantages over other methods [6, 4]. However, with a few notable exceptions [7], there has been a tendency to neglect large-scale comparative studies of many optimisation techniques applied to problems of this nature. We believe that studies of this kind are necessary in order to gain greater insight into the relative merits and weaknesses of different techniques, and to form an understanding of what kinds of problems they are most appropriate for. This is particularly important for genetic algorithms, where the body of empirical and theoretical work is still relatively small.

As a contribution to knowledge in this area, we made a thorough (at least 5×10^7 objective function calls per technique) comparative study of ten optimisation techniques applied to an industrially-based structural design optimisation problem. The search techniques used were: random search; brute force search; local gradient descent; gradient descent; Powell's method; simulated annealing; a distributed genetic algorithm (DGA); the Alopex method; hybridized simulated annealing and gradient descent; and hybridized DGA and local gradient descent.

The next section describes the structural design problem. Section 3 explains the solution representation used in this study. Section 4 outlines the implementation of each of the techniques used. This is followed by a presentation of the results. The paper continues with a discussion of the issue of stability of solutions, and a simple DGA-based technique that produces highly stable solutions is described. Finally, conclusions are drawn.

2 Description of the Wing Box Problem

Research in the design of aircraft structures, such as airframes and their components, often considers problems in which it is necessary to develop structures of minimum weight that can withstand a given load. For this study a simplified wing-box design optimisation task, based on industrially-realistic data, was formulated with the help of British Aerospace. The problem was simplified in such a way as to greatly reduce the computational cost of the evaluation function, but at the same time preserve many of the most salient features of the real problem. Hence a solution to the simplified problem gives a good 'ball park' indication of areas of the design space of the full problem to investigate in detail.

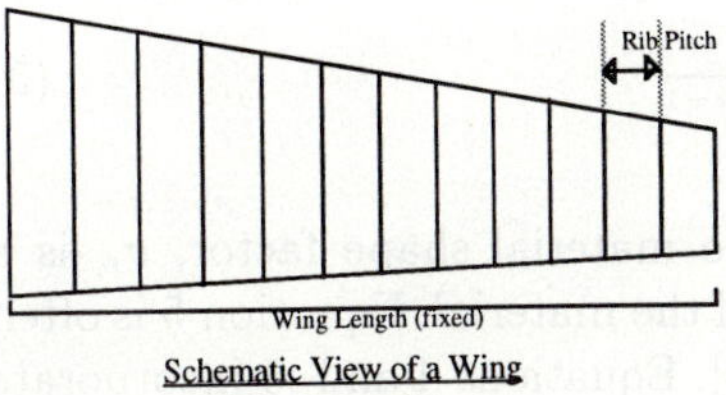

Fig. 1. Schematic view of wing

The wing box problem can be simply described as the task of finding the number of panels needed in an aircraft wing topskin and the thickness of each of those panels while minimising the mass of the wing and ensuring that none of the panels buckle under maximum operational stresses. Figure 1 shows a schematic plan view of the wing discussed in this document.

It was assumed that the topskin panels can be modelled as flat plates, and that a panel undergoes uniform compressive stresses. It was also assumed that the spacing between ribs (rib pitch) is uniform and that the thickness of all ribs is the same. Hence the aim is to find the rib pitch, dictated by the number of panels, and the thickness of the top panels, such that the structure has minimum weight and will not buckle under the compressive stresses produced by the bending moments of a 2g manoeuvre.

2.1 The Objective Function

The objective function (to be minimised) used throughout is given in Equation 1:

$$C = \sum_{i=1}^{i=n} M_i(P_i + 1) \; + \; RM \tag{1}$$

Where n is the number of panels, M_i is the mass of the ith panel, P_i is the penalty term described in Equation 2 and RM estimates total rib mass.

$$P_i = \begin{cases} \frac{\sigma_i}{\sigma_t^i} \text{ if } \sigma_i > \sigma_t^i, \\ 0 \text{ otherwise.} \end{cases} \tag{2}$$

Where σ_i is the compressive stress in the ith panel and σ_t^i is a threshold stress that must not be exceeded in that panel; σ_i is calculated using Equation 3.

$$\sigma_i = \frac{\left(\frac{BM_i}{EH_i}\right) \times Rs}{CS_i} \tag{3}$$

Where BM_i is the mean bending moment on the ith section, found by interpolating from tables of empirical data [1]; EH_i is the height of the ith section, found by interpolating from tables; Rs is a safety factor and CS_i is the cross sectional area of the ith section. Referring back to Equation 2, σ_t^i is calculated using Equation 4.

$$\sigma_t^i = K \times \sqrt{E_t \times LI_i} \tag{4}$$

Where K, the material structural efficiency, is a constant; E_t is the tangent modulus of elasticity which is calculated from Equation 5; and LI_i is the loading index on the ith section calculated using Equation 6.

$$\frac{E_t}{E} = \frac{1}{1 + \left(\frac{\sigma_i}{\sigma_n}\right)^{m-1}} \tag{5}$$

Where m is an index corresponding to the material shape factor, σ_n is a reference stress and E is the Young's modulus of the material. Equation 5 is often referred to as the Ramberg-Osgood equation [9]. Equations 4 and 5 incorporate the assumption that the top skin can be treated as a flat plate in which the thickness is small compared to the other dimensions. In these circumstances the tangent modulus of elasticity has been shown to give conservative values for buckling stress corresponding closely to test results [9].

$$LI_i = \frac{\left(\frac{BM_i}{EH_i}\right) \times Rs}{w_i \times l_i} \tag{6}$$

Where w_i is the width of the middle of the ith section and l_i is the length of the section (distance between ribs).

The mass of a panel is calculated using Equation 7.

$$M_i = t_i \times \alpha \times A_i \times \rho \tag{7}$$

Where t_i is the thickness of the ith panel, α is a correcting factor for the stiffening action of stringers which effectively increases the skin thickness. This is based on the procedure described in [5]. A_i is the planform area of the ith panel, taking into account wing tapering, and ρ is the density of the skin material.

Finally, RM, the total rib mass estimate, is calculated using Equation 8.

$$RM = (a \times Rp - b) \times Rp + c \qquad (8)$$

Where Rp is the rib pitch and a, b and c are constants. This Equation was derived by fitting a quadratic to empirical data [1]. The rib mass is scaled from a datum aircraft based on rib pitch and equivalent top skin thickness. As the rib pitch increases, the total rib weight decreases.

The values used in this study for the various constants mentioned above were: $Rs = 1.5$; $K = 0.7746$; $E = 71000N/mm^2$; $\sigma_n = 511N/mm^2$; $m = 45.6$; $\alpha = 1.116$; $\rho = 2800Kg/m^3$; $a = 0.021$; $b = 37.56$; $c = 23385.92$.

3 Solution representation - the delta encoding

A solution to the problem is represented by defining for each section, apart from the one nearest to the fuselage, a term by which the thickness of that section should be increased/decreased from the previous one.

Figure 2 illustrates the encoding. $\delta_{n-th\ panel}$ is the amount by which the thickness of the n-th panel is bigger or smaller than that of the (n-1)th panel.

Number of Ribs	Thickness of 1st Panel	$\pm\partial$ 2nd Panel	...	$\pm\partial$ Nth Panel

Fig. 2. Delta Encoding used by all Search Techniques

Most of the search techniques used in this study could not handle variable dimensionality search spaces, so they were run on separate problems defined for each possible number of panels in the range 45–65. However, the GA easily handled variable numbers of panels in a single run by having a fixed length encoding allowing a maximum of 65 panels, but specifying how many panels to consider as one of the variables. The thickness of the initial panel was defined to be in the range 5-15 mm (discretized into multiples of 0.125 mm), and $\delta_n \in \{-0.25, -0.125, 0.0, 0.125, 0.25\}$. This gives a search space of size $\sum_{n=45}^{n=65} \frac{10}{0.125} \times 5^{n-1}$, where n is the number of panels.

4 Overview of Search Techniques

Random Search simply consisted of generating a random solution and checking if it was better than the current best. This process was continued until the stop condition of 5×10^7 evaluations was met.

Brute Force Search consisted of a systematic search through every possible combination of panel thicknesses until 5×10^7 evaluations were reached.

A simple implementation of the standard **Gradient Descent** technique was used. A move from the current solution to the next solution is defined by taking the set of solutions that are one increment and decrement of each dimension of the space away from the current solution, and moving to the solution with the best evaluation. The stop condition of one run of the search is to find no better solution within that set of immediate neighbours to the current solution.

Local Gradient Descent is a simple variant on gradient descent. When evaluating all immediate perturbations of the current solution, instead of taking the best solution of that set, the algorithm moves to the first solution found that is better than the current solution.

Powell's Direction Set Algorithm is detailed in [11]. It can be briefly described as follows: given a set of conjugate directions (initially the basis vector directions), and a current position, record the fitness gain of movement in each dimension. From the directional fitness gain information gleaned, extrapolate a new vector direction that should lead to movements of greatest value. Minimise along this direction, using a single variable technique. If there is a significant gain, then add it to the direction set, replacing the direction of greatest descent from the last move.

Simulated Annealing is a well know stochastic technique fully described in the literature [8]. In the implementation used in this study, a new solution was generated from the current solution as follows: with a probability of 0.6 a simple mutation was applied, with a probability of 0.4 a heuristic mutation was applied. The heuristic mutation favoured changes being made to the thickest part of the topskin. After a thorough empirical investigation of possible annealing schedules, an accept:reject ratio[1] of 1.6N:16N was adopted for the main study, where N is the number of dimensions of the problem. The stopping condition for a run was 7,500 drops in temperature or 200 drops in temperature without any improvement, whichever came sooner. The initial temperature was set at 2.8×10^{12}.

Distributed Genetic Algorithms differ from standard generational GAs [6] in their use of an underlying conceptual model of a population spread out over a 2D grid with local asynchronous mating. There is mounting evidence that this sort of GA, whether implemented in parallel or sequentially (essentially simulating parallelism) gives very good reliable results over a range of problems [3]. The algorithm used was as follows:

1. Create random genotypes and place in cells on a 2D toroidal grid
2. Pick cell on grid, **C**, this holds genotype C_g
3. Create a set of cells, **S**, in neighbourhood of **C**
4. Select (proportional to fitness) a genotype, **m**, from one of the cells in **S**
5. Create offspring, **O**, from **m** and C_g
6. Select a genotype, **d**, at a cell in **S**
7. Replace **d** with **O**
8. Goto 2.

The set creation at step 3 simply used the nearest 12 neighbours to cell **C**. Selection at step 4 used fixed linear selection probabilities determined by the rank of elements of set **S**. The least fit element of **S** was replaced at step 7. This sort of algorithm allows very fierce local selection, but because neighbourhoods overlap, there is rapid diffusion around the grid of better than average genotypes. In this

[1] For an accept:reject ratio of A:R, the temperature is lowered after A accepted moves or R rejected moves, whichever comes sooner.

study a population of 1500 on a 50x50 grid was employed. Two point cross-over and mutation were the genetic operators used. Each run was terminated after 1×10^6 evaluations.

The Alopex Method is relatively unknown (see [12]), so it will be briefly described here. It is a stochastic algorithm that causes the simultaneous convergence of a number of parameters, using a biased random walk. On a given iteration, movement is made in every dimension of the search space by a small increment. Whether the move is positive or negative in the dimension considered will depend on: the previous move made in that dimension, correlated with the overall fitness gain of the previous move. Formally, $x_i^n = x_i^{n-1} + \delta_i^n$, where $\delta_i^n = \begin{cases} \delta & \text{with probability } p_i^n, \\ -\delta & \text{with probability } 1 - p_i^n. \end{cases}$, $p_i^n = \frac{1}{1+e^{\frac{\pm\Delta_i^n}{T}}}$, and $\Delta_i^n = (x_i^{n-1} - x_i^{n-2})(F^{n-1} - F^{n-2})$. Here x_i^n is the value on the nth iteration of the ith member of the vector of values making up a solution to the problem; δ_i^n is the amount to alter x_i^{n-1} by in producing the next solution; T is the 'temperature'; and F^n is the cost of the solution on the nth iteration. As the fitness changes on each iteration decrease towards a converged solution, the temperature drops, thus causing automatic annealing: $T = \langle|\Delta_i|\rangle$. In the implementation used here, the initial temerature was set at 1000 and the step size in all dimensions was fixed at 0.0625. The maximum number of iterations performed on any run was 1×10^6.

Hybrid Simulated Annealing with Gradient Descent involved gradient descent to a local optima after every SA move.

In order to cut down the potential number of evaluation function calls, it was decided to **Hybridise the DGA with Local Gradient Descent** rather than ordinary gradient descent. Local gradient descent was run for N_e evaluations, or to the nearest minima – whichever came sooner, on each new offspring before placing it in the population. Their genetic material *was altered* during the local search, and their cost was taken to be the value returned by the gradient descent phase. Each run terminated after 2×10^6 evaluations, and N_e decreased linearly from 200 to 0 during the course of a run.

A Re-evaluating DGA was developed to deal with stability issues and is dealt with in Section 6.

5 Results

This section presents the data generated by the various search techniques. Each technique was run for 5×10^7 evaluations to allow water-tight statistics. Note that a test with this number of evaluations for a single technique comprised many runs of the method; each run was started from a new random position in the search space. Table 1 summarises the results of the comparative study.

All of the deterministic methods (with the exception of Brute Force search) found comparatively good solutions within the liberal time-constraints allowed. However, the very large standard deviations for most of these techniques indicates that although they can find good solutions, this is very unlikely and in

Search Technique	Legal Solution ?	Best Solution (Kg)	Mean Solution (Kg)	SD Solutions (Kg)
Random search	YES	13345.8	13663.8	336
Brute Force Search	NO	9.6×10^{8}	2×10^{11}	6.6×10^{11}
Local Gradient Descent	YES	12761.9	1.9×10^{9}	7.1×10^{10}
Gradient Descent	YES	12761.6	3×10^{9}	9.8×10^{10}
Powell	YES	13015.8	13456	145.7
SA	YES	12763.2	12770	9.1
DGA	YES	12859.5	12921	26.6
Alopex	YES	13077.3	5313578.3	36588508
Hybrid SA and Gradient Descent	YES	12759.5	12764.4	5.3
Hybrid DGA and Local Grad. Desc.	YES	12815	12856	40.6

Table 1. Comparison of all techniques

general these techniques have to be run many many times for very large numbers of evaluations before a high quality solution is found. It should be noted that the random search results are for one single run of 5×10^{7} evaluations. The mean and standard deviation refer to the set of best-solution-so-far found during the course of the run, which necessarily monotonically decreases. Hence these figures should not be compared with those given for the other techniques. Results from the gradient descent methods give empirical credence to the belief that the search space is highly convoluted with many local minima.

The GA and SA methods proved much better at avoiding the many local optima around the 13000–14000 Kg region of the search space. Both the DGA and SA consistently found very good solutions, i.e. had very low standard deviations of best solution. The DGA and SA methods were also able to handle variable numbers of panels rather than assuming a fixed number as was the case with the other techniques.

The Alopex method did not fare well. This appears to have been because there are complex interactions between the large number of variables in the problem. Always changing all variables at once is unlikely to retain the valuable parts of previous solutions.

The DGA descended into the region of very good solutions much faster than SA; it typically reached solutions within 5% of the best found after only 100,000 evaluations, whereas SA needed several million calls to the objective function to proceed that far. Hybridized SA and Gradient Descent was as reliable as SA and found comparably good solutions. However, it produced them much faster. The performance of the hybridized DGA and Local Gradient Descent was very similar to that of the hybrid SA method in terms of reliability and quality of solution found. However, it was significantly faster again at descending into very low cost regions of the search space.

Clearly the GA and SA based methods were head and shoulders above the other techniques tried, with the hybrids providing quality, reliability and speed.

6 Calculating the Stability of a Solution

All the results reported so far have assumed a simplified *and idealised* evaluation function. Idealised in the sense that exact floating point values are given for panel thicknesses. This does not take into account real-world contingencies, such as manufacturing tolerances, which mean that exact values cannot be assumed. This section reports on an investigation into the stability of solutions found under random perturbations of the panel thicknesses. In many cases it is found that the best solutions obtained are highly unstable, i.e. very slight changes in just one panel thickness renders the solution untenable due to constraint violation. A promising DGA method for overcoming this problem is introduced.

In order to simulate tolerances in the manufacturing of wing-boxes, the thickness of each panel was probabilistically perturbed. Each solution was perturbed 100 times and some summary statistics calculated.

For each search algorithm employed, we took the best design (from the fifty million evaluation runs) and subjected it to a number of 'manufacture and test' phases. To gain some measure of stability, we then calculated the mean difference between the mass of the original design specification and the mass of the 'manufactured' wing. Additionally, the standard deviation of these differences is assessed. The following formulas should sum this up. If manufacturing stability is S and the number of panels in a wing is L, then

$$S = \frac{\sum_{i=1}^{i=100L} M_i}{100L} \tag{9}$$

Where M_i is the mass returned from the objective function (Equation 1) when passed a solution formed by perturbing the original solution whose stability it is desired to measure. Each perturbated solution is formed by producing new panel thicknesses according to:

$$t_n = t_o + \delta \tag{10}$$

Where δ is a random variable with normal distribution about zero and standard deviation equal to half the minimum manufacturing tolerance (0.0625mm).

Should a modified wing buckle the evaluation function adds a penalty 'mass' to its cost. This component is somewhat misleading as far as a calculation of mass stability is concerned. Therefore, in cases where a design leads to manufactured wings which buckle during evaluation, their cost will not be included in the statistics, *but rather the percentage of wings that buckle will be given.* Table 2 gives stability results for the best solutions found with each of the ten search techniques used in this study.

Surprisingly, we found that even very small tolerances lead to the manufacture of wings which regularly break buckling constraints. This can be explained, at least in terms of the problem at hand, as the result of fully optimising the wing-box up to the edge of the buckling constraint (i.e. the search algorithms are discovering points at the bottom of narrow fitness precipices).

Search Technique	Mean Deviation	SD from Solution	% buckling
Random search	3.52	2.67	13.1
Brute Force Search	NA	NA	100
Local Gradient Descent	6.00	3.24	98.9
Gradient Descent	4.54	3.18	96.4
Powell	4.80	3.35	95.1
SA	5.67	3.41	99.0
DGA	4.29	3.07	93.0
Alopex	3.63	2.73	59.8
Hybrid SA and Gradient Descent	4.69	3.18	97.14

Table 2. Stability of Best Solutions Results

As a general solution to this, our recent work centres on extending the distributed GA in such a way as to avoid potentially unstable solutions. The method employed here is novel, and exceptionally simple (compared with techniques such as cluster analysis etc), and as such is worth considering for a range of other manufacturing stability problems. On evaluating a given solution during the running of the GA, we employ the following technique:

- Generate n 'manufactured' versions of the design, complete with small tolerances as outlined above.
- Cost each of these separately, and of these evaluations consider the worst to be the cost of the solution being tested.

The DGA employing this strategy is referred to as a **Reevaluating DGA**. The re-evaluating idea is based on techniques used in evolutionary robotics [2].

We find that small values of n are sufficient to dramatically reduce the instability of solution space, typically in a run we take the worst of 4 trials. Because of the asynchronous geographic nature of the DGA, good solutions tend to remain on the grid for substantial time periods undergoing repeated evaluations. Hence an implicit pressure for stable solutions is maintained. The re-evaluating DGA operates with no explicit criterion of stability, but it will nevertheless efficiently avoid unstable solution space.

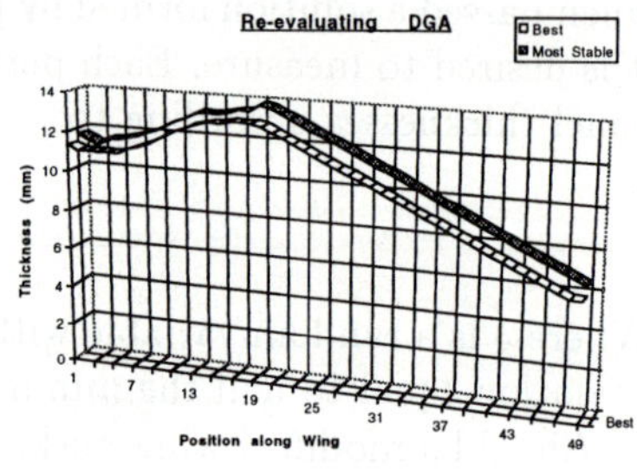

Fig. 3. Re-evaluating DGA, wing profiles

The profiles shown in figure 3 depict the lowest mass solution found by the re-evaluating GA and the most stable solution. As would be expected, the lowest mass solution achieved is far more stable than those found by other methods. Importantly, the most stable solution has *0% buckling* under the criteria explained at the beginning of this section *while at the same time having only fractionally more mass than the lowest mass solution.* On each run many very stable low cpst (and different) solutions were present in the final population.

7 Conclusions

As far as we are aware, this is one of the most extensive comparative studies of different optimisation methods applied to a problem of this nature. However, because there are so many parameters associated with the various techniques that could be altered, it is inevitably far from exhaustive. Nevertheless, it does suggest strongly that hybridized stochastic search is the correct route for problems such as the simplified wingbox design task. One obvious direction for future work, then, is a more thorough investigation of hybrid algorithms.

We have also described a DGA model where stability can be a factor driving selection, but which does not need an index of stability explicitly.

This research was supported by EPSRC grant GR/J40812. Many thanks to Phil Green and colleagues from BAe Airbus, and to A. Wright of BAe Sowerby Research Centre for help with the work discussed in this paper.

References

1. L Aston and G Lucas. Vla aircraft 14 wingbox structural layout. Technical Report B57N/VLA/LA/GFL/hjs/3129, Future Projects Office, BAe Airbus Ltd., 1992.
2. D. Cliff, I. Harvey, and P. Husbands. Explorations in evolutionary robotics. *Adaptive Behavior*, 2(1):73–110, 1993.
3. R. Collins and D. Jefferson. Selection in massively parallel genetic algorithms. In R. K. Belew and L. B. Booker, editors, *Proceedings of the Fourth Intl. Conf. on Genetic Algorithms, ICGA-91*, pages 249–256. Morgan Kaufmann, 1991.
4. L. Davis. *The Handbook of Genetic Algorithms.* Van Nostrand Reinhold, 1990.
5. Emero. Optimisation of multirib and multiweb wing-box structures under shear and moment loads. 1965.
6. David E. Goldberg. *Genetic Algorithms in Search, Optimization and Machine Learning.* Addison-Wesley, Reading, Massachusetts, USA, 1989.
7. A. J. Keane. Structural design for enhanced noise performance using genetic algorithms and other optimisation techniques. In R. Albrecht, C. Reeves, and N. Steele, editors, *Proceedings of ANNGA93, the Intl. Conf. on Neural Networks and Genetic Algorithms*, pages 536–543. Springer-Verlag, 1993.
8. S. Kirkpatrich, C. Gelatt, and M. Vecchi. Optimisation by simulated annealing. *Science*, 220:671–680, 1983.
9. D. Peery and J. Azar. *Aircraft Structures.* McGraw-Hill, 1982.
10. D. Powell and M. Skolnick. Using genetic algorithms in engineering design optimization with non-linear constraints. In S. Forrest, editor, *Proc. 5th Int. Conf. on GAs*, pages 424–431. Morgan Kaufmann, 1993.
11. W. Press, W. Vetterling, S. Teukolsky, and B. Flannery. *Numerical recipes in C (2/e).* CUP, 1992.
12. K. Unnikrishnan and K. Venugopal. Learning in connectionist networks using the alopex algorithm. In *Proceedings IJCNN 1992*, pages I–926 – I–931. IEEE Press, 1992.

A Comparative Study of Evolutionary Algorithms for On-Line Parameter Tracking

André Neubauer

Duisburg Gerhard-Mercator-University, Department of Communication Engineering, Bismarckstr. 81, 47048 Duisburg, Germany

Abstract. Adaptive filters are systems in digital signal processing designed to work in environments with unknown or time-varying statistical characteristics — according to non-stationary stochastic signals. In order to achieve this capability the adaptive filter's adaptation algorithm has to be able to adapt the filter to a time-dependent error criterion. I.e., given a filter topology, the filter parameters have to be estimated on-line. In this paper, a comparative study of several *evolutionary algorithms* — *evolution strategies* (ES), *genetic algorithms* (GA) and *micro-genetic algorithms* (μGA) — is presented for the on-line adaptation of adaptive filters. The adaptive filter's task is to predict a time-discrete and non-stationary stochastic signal. This important problem arises in a variety of applications, e.g. stochastic signal estimation, system identification and echo cancellation. The evolutionary algorithms optimize the adaptive filter's parameters on-line, with one generation corresponding to one time step of the stochastic signal. Hence, the evolutionary algorithms' ability to adapt to rapidly changing and noisy environments and to track time-varying parameters is of special interest in this study.

1 Introduction

Evolutionary algorithms are optimization and adaptation procedures based on an abstract formulation of natural evolution. Two important representatives of evolutionary algorithms are *evolution strategies* and *genetic algorithms.* Developed in the sixties at the Technical University of Berlin by Rechenberg and Schwefel [10] and at the University of Michigan by Holland [4], respectively, they both share the underlying assumption that the mimicking of natural evolution as an optimization or adaptation process is promising for many applications. Nevertheless, important differences exist between these algorithms — as outlined e.g. by Rechenberg [10]. This requires the comparison of these algorithms for a given problem.

The application that is considered in this paper is part of adaptive filter theory and digital signal processing. Especially, the on-line adaptation of adaptive filters for the prediction of non-stationary stochastic signals using evolutionary algorithms is studied. Given the filter topology, the adaptive filter's parameter vector embodies the statistical properties of the stochastic signal. In order to track temporal changes in the signal statistics for non-stationary stochastic signals, the adapted parameter vector has to be time-varying. Thus, this study treats the on-line adaptation capability of evolutionary algorithms.

Section 2 gives an introduction to the application of adaptive filters to stochastic signal prediction and estimation. Evolutionary algorithms are described in Sec. 3. Special emphasis is given to the structure of *evolution strategies*, *genetic algorithms* and *micro-genetic algorithms* for on-line adaptation. In Sec. 4, experimental results are presented and discussed for the prediction of two classes of non-stationary stochastic signals. A conclusion is given, summarizing the essential results of this study.

2 Adaptive Filters for Stochastic Signal Estimation

Modern techniques for the estimation of stochastic signals are based on parameterized stochastic signal models [3]. A time-discrete, i.e. $t \in \mathbf{Z}$, stochastic signal process $\{x(t)\}$ is assumed to be generated by a stationary white GAUSSian noise process $\{e(t)\}$. One unobservable realization $e(t)$ of the noise process $\{e(t)\}$ provides the input signal of a system — the *stochastic signal model.* This hypothetical system is defined by a corresponding difference equation. A commonly used linear system is given by the difference equation

$$x(t) + \sum_{i=1}^{p} a_i(t) x(t-i) = e(t) \tag{1}$$

leading to the *autoregressive* or AR(p) stochastic signal model. For time-varying AR-parameters $a_i(t)$ non-stationary stochastic signal processes are obtained.

A suitable approach to stochastic signal estimation is to use an adaptive filter $\mathcal{F}$. Given one realization $x(t)$ of the stochastic process $\{x(t)\}$ with a priori unknown or time-varying statistical characteristics, the adaptive filter extracts the desired information about the signal statistics from the realization $x(t)$. This is achieved by using the adaptive filter as a *predictor* that predicts the present sample $x(t)$ according to an error criterion $E(t)$ with the help of past samples $x(t-i)$, $i = 1(1)p$. The adaptive filter — its topology and estimated filter parameter vector $\widehat{\boldsymbol{\theta}}(t) = (\widehat{\theta}_1(t), \ldots, \widehat{\theta}_N(t)) \in \mathbf{R}^N$ — then yields the estimated signal model for the stochastic signal process $\{x(t)\}$ that incorporates the corresponding statistical information. By using a suitable adaptation procedure the adaptive filter is able to track temporal changes in the signal statistics.

The task of estimating the statistical characteristics of the stochastic autoregressive signal process $\{x(t)\}$ of order p thus becomes a task of estimating the AR-parameters $\theta_i(t) = a_i(t)$, $i = 1(1)p$, with the help of an adaptive predictor filter $\mathcal{F}$. The adaptive filter's difference equation for the prediction of $x(t)$ is given by [6]

$$\widehat{x}(t) = -\sum_{i=1}^{p} \widehat{a}_i(t) x(t-i) \ . \tag{2}$$

The estimated AR-parameters $\widehat{\theta}_i(t) = \widehat{a}_i(t)$, $i = 1(1)p$, are obtained via an adaptation procedure that optimizes the time-varying *least squares* criterion

$$E(t) = \sum_{\tau=0}^{L-1} \widehat{e}^2(t-\tau) \overset{\widehat{\theta}(t)}{\longrightarrow} \text{minimum} \tag{3}$$

with residual $\widehat{e}(t) = x(t) - \widehat{x}(t)$ and window length L.

An extension of (1) leads to the *autoregressive moving average* or ARMA(p, q) stochastic signal model that is defined by the difference equation

$$x(t) + \sum_{i=1}^{p} a_i(t)x(t-i) = e(t) + \sum_{j=1}^{q} b_j(t)e(t-j) \ . \tag{4}$$

Again, the ARMA-parameters $\theta_i(t) = a_i(t)$, $i = 1(1)p$, and $\theta_{p+j}(t) = b_j(t)$, $j = 1(1)q$, have to be estimated from one realization $x(t)$ of the stochastic signal process $\{x(t)\}$. According to the above-mentioned estimation procedure an adaptive predictor filter $\mathcal{F}$ is defined by the difference equation [6]

$$\widehat{x}(t) = -\sum_{i=1}^{p} \widehat{a}_i(t)x(t-i) + \sum_{j=1}^{q} \widehat{b}_j(t)\widehat{e}(t-j) \ . \tag{5}$$

The $N = p + q$ estimated ARMA-parameters $\widehat{\theta}_i(t) = \widehat{a}_i(t)$, $i = 1(1)p$, and $\widehat{\theta}_{p+j}(t) = \widehat{b}_j(t)$, $j = 1(1)q$, are adapted according to criterion (3).

3 Evolutionary Algorithms

Evolutionary algorithms are optimization and adaptation procedures taking pattern from natural evolution. Their success in a variety of engineering domains motivates their application to the adaptation of adaptive filters in digital signal processing. In this section, the evolutionary algorithms under study — *evolution strategies* (ES), *genetic algorithms* (GA) and *micro-genetic algorithms* (μGA) — are formulated for the task of on-line parameter adaptation, taking into account the problem of stochastic signal prediction and estimation as outlined in Sec. 2.

3.1 Evolution Strategies

The $(\mu/\mu, \lambda)$-ES with self-adaptation of strategy parameters is used [10]. This algorithm works on a population $P(t) = (\,(\widehat{\boldsymbol{\theta}}_1(t), \sigma_1(t)), \ldots, (\widehat{\boldsymbol{\theta}}_\mu(t), \sigma_\mu(t))\,)$ of μ parental tuples $(\,\widehat{\boldsymbol{\theta}}_m(t), \sigma_m(t)\,)$, $m = 1(1)\mu$. Each parental tuple consists of an estimated adaptive filter's parameter vector $\widehat{\boldsymbol{\theta}}_m(t)$ and the strategy parameter $\sigma_m(t)$. In order to create one of the λ offspring tuples $(\,\overset{\circ}{\widehat{\boldsymbol{\theta}}}_l(t), \sigma_l^\circ(t)\,)$, $l = 1(1)\lambda$, the operators *multi recombination* and *mutation* are used. The multi recombination operator is applied by selecting each component of vector $\overset{\bullet}{\widehat{\boldsymbol{\theta}}}_l(t)$ uniformly at random from the set of the corresponding components of all parental parameter vectors $\widehat{\boldsymbol{\theta}}_m(t)$, $m = 1(1)\mu$. This corresponds to *discrete* multi recombination of problem parameters. According to *intermediary* multi recombination, the strategy parameters are calculated

$$\sigma_l^{\bullet}(t) = \frac{1}{\mu}\sum_{m=1}^{\mu} \sigma_m(t) \ . \tag{6}$$

The mutation operator is then applied to the strategy parameters

$$\sigma_l^{\circ}(t) = \begin{cases} \sigma_l^{\bullet}(t)\cdot\alpha & \text{with probability } \frac{1}{2} \\ \sigma_l^{\bullet}(t)/\alpha & \text{with probability } \frac{1}{2} \end{cases} \tag{7}$$

with $\alpha > 0$. The offspring parameter vector is mutated yielding

$$\overset{\circ}{\widehat{\boldsymbol{\theta}}}_l(t) = \overset{\bullet}{\widehat{\boldsymbol{\theta}}}_l(t) + \frac{1}{\sqrt{N}}\cdot\sigma_l^{\circ}(t)\cdot\mathbf{z} \tag{8}$$

using a random vector $\mathbf{z}$ with independent $N(0,1)$-distributed components.

With the help of the parameter vector $\overset{\circ}{\widehat{\boldsymbol{\theta}}}_l(t)$ the sequence $\widehat{e}_l(t-L+1), \ldots, \widehat{e}_l(t)$ is produced by the corresponding adaptive filter $\mathcal{F}_l$ and the error criterion $E_l(t)$ is calculated. The λ offspring tuples are ranked according to $E_l(t)$ and the μ best individuals are selected as parents for the next time step $t+1$ (see Fig. 1). The

Set $t = 0$ and initialize population $P(0)$ at random.
- FOR ($l = 1$; $l \leq \lambda$; l++)
  - Apply multi recombination to all μ parents in $P(t)$ yielding $(\overset{\bullet}{\widehat{\boldsymbol{\theta}}}_l(t), \sigma_l^{\bullet}(t))$.
  - Mutate $(\overset{\bullet}{\widehat{\boldsymbol{\theta}}}_l(t), \sigma_l^{\bullet}(t))$ leading to $(\overset{\circ}{\widehat{\boldsymbol{\theta}}}_l(t), \sigma_l^{\circ}(t))$.
  - Calculate $E_l(t)$ for $\overset{\circ}{\widehat{\boldsymbol{\theta}}}_l(t)$ at time t.
- Select the μ best offspring individuals and store them in $P^{\circ}(t)$.
- Set $P(t+1) = P^{\circ}(t)$ and increment t by 1.

UNTIL end of adaptation

Fig. 1. Evolution Strategy $(\mu/\mu, \lambda)$-ES.

parameters that have to be specified are μ, λ and α. In order to produce a single estimate $\widehat{\boldsymbol{\theta}}(t)$ for the adaptive filter's parameter vector at time t, the parameter vector of the best offspring individual with index $l^{\star}$ is chosen, i.e.

$$\widehat{\boldsymbol{\theta}}(t) = \widehat{\boldsymbol{\theta}}_{l^{\star}}(t) \quad \text{with} \quad E_{l^{\star}}(t) \leq E_l(t) \quad \forall l = 1(1)\lambda \ . \tag{9}$$

3.2 Genetic Algorithms

Genetic algorithms are based on a population $P(t)$ of M individuals $\Theta_h(t)$, $h = 1(1)M$ [4]. Each individual $\Theta_h(t) = (\vartheta_{h,1}(t), \dots, \vartheta_{h,\ell}(t))$ is given by an ℓ-tuple of binary alleles $\vartheta_{h,k}(t) \in \{0,1\}$, $k = 1(1)\ell$. This ℓ-tuple represents one parameter vector $\widehat{\boldsymbol{\theta}}_h(t)$ of the adaptive filter $\mathcal{F}$ by coding each parameter using a K-bit binary code. Again, in order to calculate the fitness of $\Theta_h(t)$ the corresponding adaptive filter $\mathcal{F}_h$ produces the sequence $\widehat{e}_h(t-L+1), \dots, \widehat{e}_h(t)$ leading to the error criterion $E_h(t)$. Each individual $\Theta_h(t)$ is ranked according to $E_h(t)$ with rank $r_h(t) \in \{1, \dots, M\}$ and $r_h(t) < r_{h'}(t) \Rightarrow E_h(t) \le E_{h'}(t)$. Using BAKER's *linear ranking* procedure [1] with maximal expected number of offspring η, individuals are selected to produce offspring $\Theta_h^\circ(t)$, $\Theta_{h+1}^\circ(t)$ with the help of genetic operators *crossover*, *mutation* and *partial hypermutation* [2, 4]. The crossover operator is applied with probability p_C by selecting two individuals from the population $P(t)$ and crossing the two ℓ-tuples. Each allele of the two offspring tuples is then mutated with probability p_M by the mutation operator. The partial hypermutation operator generates genetic variability by introducing the average of Mp_H 'random immigrants' [2] in one generation.

The GA's structure for on-line adaptation is given in Fig. 2 [7, 8, 9]. The parameters that have to be specified are K, M, p_C, p_M, p_H and η. The parameter vector of the best individual $\Theta_{h^\star}(t)$ is chosen as the estimated adaptive filter's parameter vector $\widehat{\boldsymbol{\theta}}(t)$ at time t.

Set $t = 0$ and initialize population $P(0)$ at random.

- Calculate $E_h(t)$ for each individual $\Theta_h(t)$ in $P(t)$ at time t.
- FOR $(h = 1;\ h < M;\ h += 2)$
  - Select individuals $\Theta_i(t)$ and $\Theta_j(t)$ from $P(t)$.
  - Apply crossover, mutation and partial hypermutation to $\Theta_i(t)$, $\Theta_j(t)$ to create $\Theta_h^\circ(t)$, $\Theta_{h+1}^\circ(t)$ and store $\Theta_h^\circ(t)$, $\Theta_{h+1}^\circ(t)$ in $P^\circ(t)$.
- Set $P(t+1) = P^\circ(t)$ and increment t by 1.

UNTIL end of adaptation

Fig. 2. Genetic algorithm GA.

3.3 Micro-Genetic Algorithms

Micro-genetic algorithms are variants of the GA discussed above with a small population size M. They were designed by KRISHNAKUMAR for non-stationary environments where the calculation of $E_h(t)$ underlies time-constraints [5]. Using merely crossover genetic variability is generated by a restart procedure. After having detected convergence in population $P(t)$ — e.g. by measuring the mean relative HAMMING distance of all ℓ-tuples $\Theta_h(t)$ in $P(t)$ — the best individual is maintained while randomly generating all other $M-1$ individual ℓ-tuples. A further difference lies in the selection procedure; *tournament selection* is used.

The coding of individual ℓ-tuples $\Theta_h(t)$, the calculation of $E_h(t)$ and the choice of the best individual's parameter vector as the single estimate for the adaptive filter's parameter vector $\widehat{\boldsymbol{\theta}}(t)$ is as discussed above with the GA. The μGA's structure for on-line adaptation is given in Fig. 3. The parameters that have to be specified are K, M, p_C and ε.

Set $t = 0$ and initialize population $P^\circ(0)$ at random.
- Increment t by 1 and set $P(t) = P^\circ(t-1)$.
  - Calculate $E_h(t)$ for each individual $\Theta_h(t)$ in $P(t)$ at time t.
  - Determine the best individual $\Theta^\circ_M(t)$ in $P(t)$ and store it in $P^\circ(t)$.
  - FOR $(h = 1;\ h < M-1;\ h+=2)$
    - Select individuals $\Theta_i(t)$ and $\Theta_j(t)$ from $P(t)$.
    - Apply crossover to $\Theta_i(t)$, $\Theta_j(t)$ to create $\Theta^\circ_h(t)$, $\Theta^\circ_{h+1}(t)$ and store $\Theta^\circ_h(t)$, $\Theta^\circ_{h+1}(t)$ in $P^\circ(t)$.
  - UNTIL convergence (e.g. mean relative HAMMING distance $\le \varepsilon$)
  - Randomly generate $M-1$ new ℓ-tuples $\Theta_h(t)$, $h = 1(1)M-1$, in $P^\circ(t)$.

UNTIL end of adaptation

Fig. 3. Micro-genetic algorithm μGA.

4 Experimental Results

The evolutionary algorithms are applied to the estimation of AR and ARMA stochastic signal models in order to study their adaptation properties. In Tab. 1, the strategy parameters are given. For the GA and the μGA each parameter of the adaptive predictor filter is coded in the interval $[-2, 2]$ with a $K = 32$-bit binary code. Additionally, $p_H \in \{0, 0.1\}$ in case of the GA. A window length $L = 100$ for the least squares error criterion (3) and a white GAUSSian $N(0,1)$ stochastic process $\{e(t)\}$ are used throughout the experiments. In order to obtain statistically significant results 50 simulations are carried out for each experiment. In the first example an AR(2) stochastic signal model with parameters

$$a_1(t) = \begin{cases} 0.5, & 0 \le t < 500 \\ -0.5, & 500 \le t \le 1000 \end{cases} \quad \text{and} \quad a_2(t) = 0.95$$

is considered. In Fig. 4, the mean $\overline{\widehat{a}_i}(t)$ of the estimated parameters $\widehat{a}_i(t)$ (solid lines) and the standard deviation $s_{\widehat{a}_1}(t)$ obtained with the ES are shown. The

Table 1. The strategy parameters for the ES, GA and μGA.

ES		GA		μGA	
μ	10	M	30	M	5
λ	30	p_C	0.95	p_C	1.0
α	1.3	p_M	0.01	ε	0.05
		η	2.0		

true parameter values $a_i(t)$ (dotted lines) are quickly approximated with high reproducibility — according to small standard deviations $s_{\widehat{a}_i}(t)$. Further, the ES is able to track the time-varying parameter $a_1(t)$.

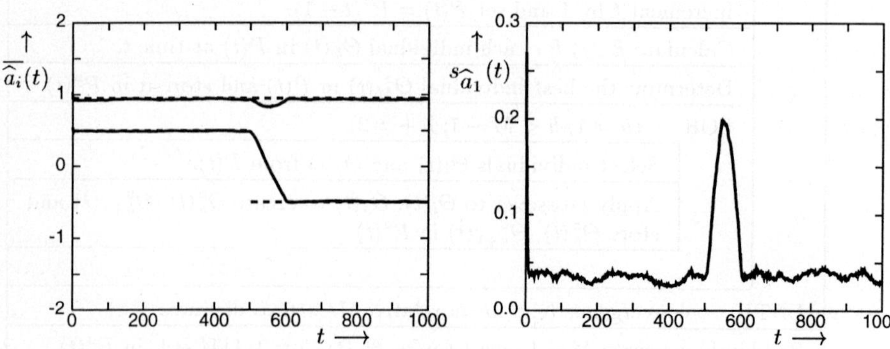

Fig. 4. Mean $\overline{\widehat{a}_i}(t)$ and standard deviation $s_{\widehat{a}_1}(t)$ for AR(2) model using ES.

The results obtained with the GA using $p_H = 0$ are given in Fig. 5. It is evident that the GA without partial hypermutation ($p_H = 0$) is not capable of steadily adapting filters in non-stationary environments. As shown in Fig. 6, the GA with partial hypermutation ($p_H = 0.1$) is able to track the time-varying parameter $a_1(t)$. The incorporation of partial hypermutation leads to a diversification of the population $P(t)$ and the ability to work in rapidly changing environments [2].

Figure 7 shows the mean $\overline{\widehat{a}_i}(t)$ of the estimated parameters $\widehat{a}_i(t)$ obtained with the μGA. Though its small population size M the μGA is able to approximate the true parameters. The standard deviations as indicated by $s_{\widehat{a}_1}(t)$ in Fig. 7 are, however, slightly higher.
The second example is an ARMA(2,1) stochastic signal model with parameters

$$a_1(t) = \begin{cases} -0.6, & 0 \le t < 500 \\ 0.6, & 500 \le t \le 1000 \end{cases}, \quad a_2(t) = 0.9 \quad \text{and} \quad b_1(t) = -0.8 \ .$$

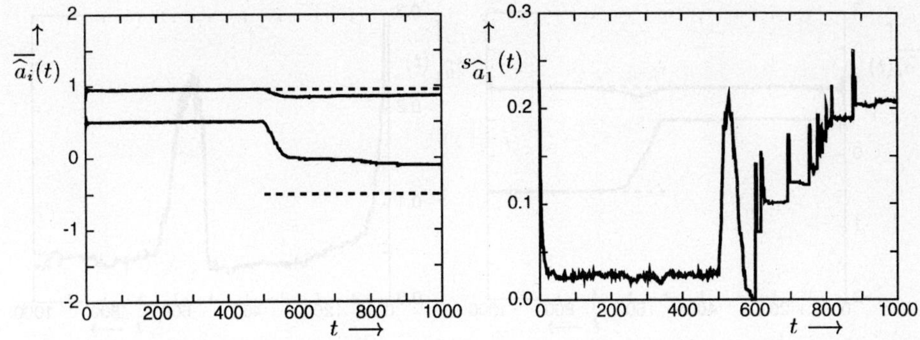

Fig. 5. Mean $\overline{\widehat{a}_i}(t)$ and standard deviation $s_{\widehat{a}_1}(t)$ for AR(2) model using GA ($p_H = 0$).

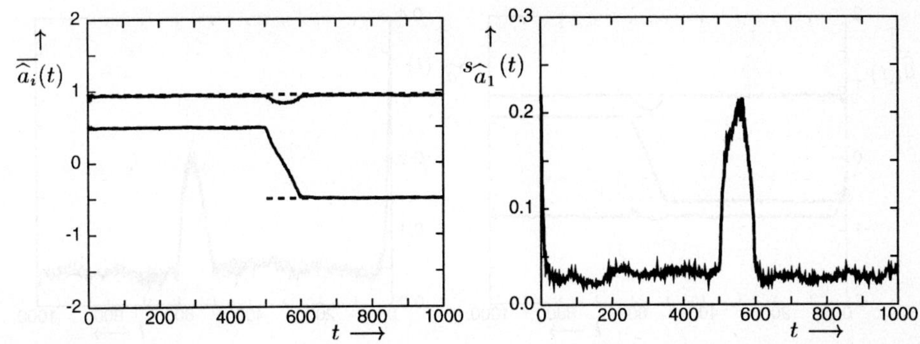

Fig. 6. Mean $\overline{\widehat{a}_i}(t)$ and standard deviation $s_{\widehat{a}_1}(t)$ for AR(2) model using GA ($p_H = 0.1$).

In Fig. 8, 9 and 10, the mean $\overline{\widehat{\theta}_i}(t)$ of the estimated parameters $\widehat{\theta}_i(t)$ obtained with ES, GA ($p_H = 0.1$) and μGA are shown. All evolutionary algorithms are able to approximate the true parameters quickly and to track the time-varying parameter $a_1(t)$. Whereas ES and GA produce similar results, the μGA is slightly worse with regard to adaptation speed and accuracy.

5 Conclusions

A study of several evolutionary algorithms — *evolution strategies*, *genetic algorithms* and *micro-genetic algorithms* — as on-line adaptation procedures for adaptive filters in stochastic signal prediction and estimation was presented. The $(\mu/\mu, \lambda)$-ES with self-adaptation of strategy parameters was able to adapt to the time-varying parameters of the true stochastic signal model with high reproducibility. The standard GA was not suitable for the on-line adaptation of adaptive filters. The incorporation of partial hypermutation in the GA led to an

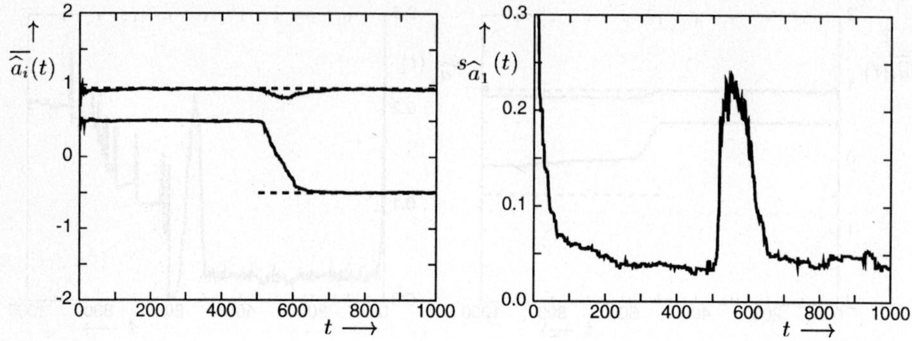

Fig. 7. Mean $\overline{\widehat{a}_i}(t)$ and standard deviation $s_{\widehat{a_1}}(t)$ for AR(2) model using μGA.

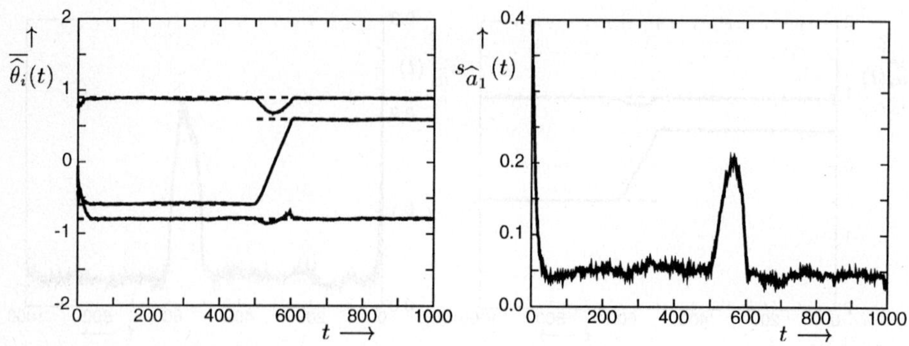

Fig. 8. Mean $\overline{\widehat{\theta}_i}(t)$ and standard deviation $s_{\widehat{a_1}}(t)$ for ARMA(2,1) model using ES.

adaptation algorithm that produced results similar to those obtained with the ES. The lower computational complexity of the μGA due to the small population size came with slightly worse results with regard to adaptation speed, accuracy and reproducibility.

References

1. BAKER, J.E.: *An Analysis of the Effects of Selection in Genetic Algorithms.* Ph.D., Vanderbilt University, 1989
2. GREFENSTETTE, J.J.: *Genetic Algorithms for Changing Environments.* In: MÄNNER, R.; MANDERICK, B. (Eds.): *Parallel Problem Solving from Nature II.* Amsterdam: Elsevier Science Publishers, pp. 137-144, 1992
3. HAYKIN, S.: *Adaptive Filter Theory.* Englewood Cliffs: Prentice Hall, 1986
4. HOLLAND, J.H.: *Adaptation in Natural and Artificial Systems.* Cambridge: MIT Press, 1992
5. KRISHNAKUMAR, K.: *Micro-Genetic Algorithms for Stationary and Non-Stationary Function Optimization.* In: *Intelligent Control and Adaptive Systems.* Proc. of the SPIE, Vol. 1196, pp. 289-296, 1989

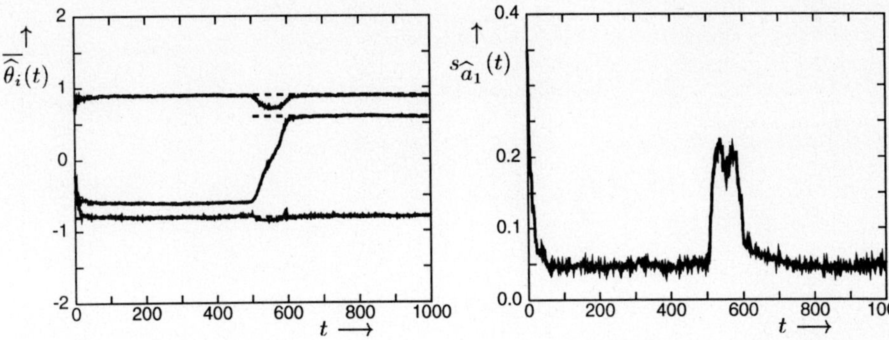

Fig. 9. Mean $\overline{\widehat{\theta}_i}(t)$ and standard deviation $s_{\widehat{a}_1}(t)$ for ARMA(2,1) model using GA ($p_H = 0.1$).

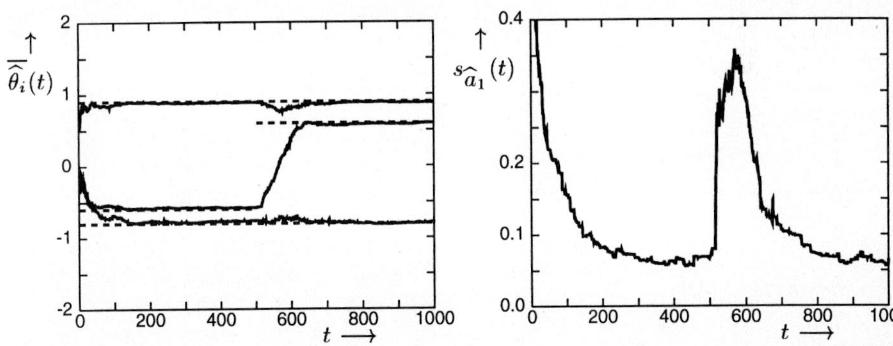

Fig. 10. Mean $\overline{\widehat{\theta}_i}(t)$ and standard deviation $s_{\widehat{a}_1}(t)$ for ARMA(2,1) model using μGA.

6. NEUBAUER, A.: *Linear Signal Estimation Using Genetic Algorithms.* In: *Systems Analysis Modelling Simulation.* Vol. 18/19, Switzerland: pp. 349-352, 1995
7. NEUBAUER, A.: *Real-Coded Genetic Algorithms for Bilinear Signal Estimation.* In: SCHIPANSKI, D. (Hrsg.): *Tagungsband des 40. Internationalen Wissenschaftlichen Kolloquiums.* Ilmenau: Band 1, pp. 347-352, 1995
8. NEUBAUER, A.: *Non-Linear Adaptive Filters Based on Genetic Algorithms with Applications to Digital Signal Processing.* In: *Proc. of the 1995 IEEE International Conference on Evolutionary Computation.* Perth: Vol. 2, pp. 527-532, 1995
9. NEUBAUER, A.: *Genetic Algorithms for Non-Linear Adaptive Filters in Digital Signal Processing* (Invited paper). In: *Proc. of the 1996 ACM Symposium on Applied Computing.* Philadelphia: pp. 519-522, 1996
10. RECHENBERG, I.: *Evolutionsstrategie '94.* Werkstatt Bionik und Evolutionstechnik, Band 1, Stuttgart: frommann-holzboog, 1994

Other Metaphors

Modeling Urban Growth by Cellular Automata

Thomas Bäck[1], Holger Dörnemann[2], Ulrich Hammel[2] and Pierre Frankhauser[3]

[1] Informatik Centrum Dortmund, Center for Applied Systems Analysis (CASA), Joseph-von-Fraunhofer-Str. 20, D–44227 Dortmund
[2] Universität Dortmund, Fachbereich Informatik, LS XI, D–44221 Dortmund
[3] Institut de Recherche et d'Analyse des Dynamiques Economiques et Spatiales, 32 rue Mégevand, F–25030 Besancọn cedex

Abstract. The structural development of human settlements can be characterized as a complex highly feedbacketed process. The assumption that this process is governed by rather few fundamental laws stimulated a considerable research in the field of urban growth during the last decade. Aiming at the comprehension of the basic underlying dynamics different approaches from the field of self-organizing systems have been proposed. In this paper we present a "cellular model" of urban growth dynamics based on the work of White, Engelen and Uljee. As a starting point this model throws some light on the mechanism of urban growth. But even more important, it raises a lot of questions concerning the requirements for a sound modeling technique. One of these questions is how to assess the complex patterns produced by single simulation runs. Here we make especially use of fractal measures reducing the contained information to a manageable size. No doubt, this field of research is still in its infant state, and we are far from being able to hand a reliable tool to the decision maker. But promising results will stimulate future investigations which we hope will lead to a deeper insight into the nature of cities to improve the living conditions of their inhabitants.

1 Introduction

One main task of town planers is the foresighted and careful design of cities, which are "worth living" for their inhabitants, and therefore succesful [5, 17].

As most development intentions are (expensive) long term concerns, town planners would like to have decision support tools at their disposal, giving prospective insights in the consequences of the realization of particular plans. The simulation of urban development processes may serve as one part of such a decision support tool, demonstrating future urban evolution as a basis for interpretation by the planner. Against the background of the socio-economical crisis and the introduction of assessments of environmental impact, the simulation of urban development becomes important to both public institutions and industry.

In this paper we demonstrate the feasibility of "cellular geography"-models [16], which make use of a fascinating, nature-analogous and massively parallel modeling technique based on the concept of "cellular automata" [11], in contrast to traditional modeling techniques based on system dynamics approaches [2, 8], which suffer from their insufficient degree of spatial resolution, detail and design complexity. As one example, we focus on the so-called "White-model" for the forecast of changes in land-use patterns [18, 19]. Changes in land-use are only one but important aspect of urban development. Instead of giving a complete list of reasons for this, we would like to stress on the following (translated) quotation: "Changes in settlement structures are the most perceptible expression of social changes within a society. Nearly all social structures, processes and problems find their expression in spatial structures, changing land-use and more or less clearly seperated territories." [15, p. 233].

Cellular automata are inherently spatial models by their regular arrangement of cells in space. Hence it is easy to regard a cell of a cellular automaton as part of a regular intersected map. In this sense, every cell covers an attribute, which may be identified in the corresponding grid square in the city map (e.g. land-use, population size, etc.).

Apart from this profane – but obviously important – feature of cellular automata, one might find more scientific reasons for the use of this modeling technique as well. Consider the parallel processing of information for example, which is typical of natural and socio-economic processes. As a consequence of the parallel update of cell states, cellular automata show self-organizing behavior as all cells work individually without the necessity of a global control instance. Again, this is a typical feature of socio-economic processes.

Cities show a really complex structure, which is often interpreted as a necessary feature [19] and it is fascinating to regard the city's complex morphology as the consequence of simple morphogenetic principles. This is in fact one main aspect of cellular automata dynamics, where simple rules serve to generate a complex (self-organized) overall behavior.

The morphology of cities may be regarded as a balance between ordered and disordered structuring elements, a phenomenon, which has already been identified for some cellular automata by Wolfram [20] and Langton [12]. Again, this feature of cellular automata (important within the field of "artificial life") seems to be ideal for the application in question. Regarding both, complex morphology of cities and of cellular automata configurations it is evident that there exists some common (inherent) order principle in the spatial organization of cells, which may be identified by fractal investigations.

We tried to find out whether the concept of cellular automata combined with "artificial life"-paradigms is a feasible solution for an adequate modeling of the development of urban land-use [7]. The starting point was a variety of existing cellular geography models (i.a. [3, 6, 14]) with an emphasis on White's model [19], because of ongoing work, promising published results and references to "artificial life" work. The reader should keep in mind that most of the cellular automata models used in geography differ from the original concept, so that it is often more appropriate to speak of "cellular models". But it is common knowledge in geography that "cellular models" are the most promising approach for the adequate spatially detailed modeling of complex urban socio-economic processes.

The main stream of White's model is a correlation of neighboring land-use patterns, covering some simple development rules (see section 3). This concept shows an amazing, somehow realistic evolution of urban areas. Nevertheless, we identified some inconsistencies and problems of the model, which will lead us stepwise to more realistic cellular models.

In section 2, we introduce morphological measures for cities which are necessary for analyzing city maps and which are used in section 4 to evaluate the outcome of a simulation run. The White-model is described in section 3. As our main goal is to improve cellular urban models, we conclude our paper by summarizing the main observations and critical questions regarding the model.

2 Morphological Measures

As we are dealing with a spatial development process of change in land-use, we need a method which allows us to compare simulated city maps to really observed ones, in order to assess the quality of any simulation run. This task, however, is not very easy to deal with because the complex nature of urban development is modeled by a probabilistic component of the simulation model. Consequently, we never might expect two simulations to be identically and simulation runs will differ from the observed situation at least quantatively, but not necessarily qualitatively. Therefore the easiest method – comparing maps cell by cell [19] – is expected to produce less valuable results [7], and this is why we need more abstract measures, identifying *qualitatively equal structures*, which will be found in simulated as well as in observed maps.

The presently most promising approach is based on "fractal geometry" [13], which serves as an appropriate tool for describing natural structures in a quite abstract way (using extended definitions of Euclidean dimension). It would go beyond the scope of this paper to give detailed reasons for the adequacy of different fractal analysis techniques for characterizing urban structures (see [4, 7, 9, 10] for details). However, the analysis of fractal scaling behavior gives a qualitative evidence about the spatial distribution of the build-up area of urban agglomerations in form of characteristic "scaling laws". The so-called "radial dimension" and "cluster-size frequency" have shown to be particularly well suited morphological measures for cities [4, 9, 19].

The radial analysis takes advantage of a typical urban peculiarity: the dilution of the build-up area from the center to the border (suburbs). In order to understand the meaning of the radial dimension, think of a filled circle, intersected in equal parts (regular lattice). In an iterative procedure we count all occupied points $N(r)$ within a radius of r from the circle's center, which is actually the area covered by the circle in distance r. This occupied area is – of course – proportional to the square of r (a well-known scaling law, stating that a filled circle is a *2*-dimensional object): $N_{circle}(r) \propto r^2$. Now we have a look at city maps. As the center is more dense than the border region we might expect a scaling law $N(r) \propto r^{D_{rad}}$, where D_{rad} is the radial dimension. In other words, with increasing radius r we will find less and less occupied points $N(r)$ than needed to cover a (filled) circle with the same radius:

$$\rho(r) = \frac{N(r)}{N_{circle}(r)} \quad \propto \quad \frac{r^{D_{rad}}}{r^2} = r^{D_{rad}-2} \tag{1}$$

In equation (1) $\rho(r)$ may be interpreted as a relative density.

Reformulating the scaling law in the form $\log N(r) \propto D_{rad}\ \log r$, it is obvious that the radial dimension can be estimated by the slope of the curve which results from plotting the data points $(r, N(r))$ in a double-logarithmic diagram. But as natural structures are not regular fractals, we should not expect the existence of exactly one matching linear regression but different ones (multi-fractality) [10]. We finally decided to consider the course of the resulting curve rather than estimated slope values for this reason [7].

A reformulation of equation (1) as $D_{rad} \propto 2+\frac{\log \rho(r)}{\log r}$ yields a second method of visualizing the measured data points, the so-called "fractal signature", which gives evidence about the stability of the radial dimension [4]. In this case the (approximated) radial dimension is plotted against the distance from the fractals centre $(r, 2+\frac{\log \rho(r)}{\log r})$.

A less common method for analyzing urban structures is called "cluster-size frequency" (csf) analysis. It is based on the assumption that cities show a hierarchial construction: places, streets, commercial areas etc. of different (hierarchial) sizes. In fact, one should expect to find a few number of large places (for instance public ones) but a large number of small places (e.g. backyards) [7, 9]. In analogy to equation $N(r) \propto r^{D_{rad}}$ this leads to the assumption $H(c) \propto c^{D_{cluster}}$, where $H(c)$ is the frequency of cluster-size c and $D_{cluster}$ is the characteristic "csf dimension". As written above, we might estimate $D_{cluster}$ from the slope of the curve spanned by the data-points $(c, H(c))$.

The described analyzing techniques are built-in features of our simulator URBSIM. As we found out, meaningful results for the csf-method may only be observed for large sample sizes (number of different cluster sizes), which is only achieved by a high resolution of the underlying map (i.e. a large number of cells). For the simulation run presented in this paper – based on an 80×80 grid – no csf-analysis is provided because the typical sample sizes are too small (often less than 5 different cluster sizes); no fractal signatures are shown due to a lack of space.

3 Urban Growth Modeling Based on White's Approach

This section gives a brief introduction to the basic cellular automata model implemented in our simulator URBSIM and presents some of the features of this simulator. Essentially, the implementation follows the model description given by White, Engelen, and Uljee [18, 19].

3.1 The Model

The simulated city grows on a regular quadratic $(m \times n)$-grid with identical cell automata located at each grid position (i, j). In our case, a grid dimension of $m = n = 80$ is chosen for reasons of the computational costs that scale with $m \cdot n$.

Each cell automata may take on a certain state from a state set $\mathcal{S} = \{s_{\text{vacant}}\} \cup \mathcal{S}_{\text{active}} \cup \mathcal{S}_{\text{fixed}}$ which contains three different sorts of states: A special state s_{vacant} which characterizes "free" space on the map, a set $\mathcal{S}_{\text{active}} = \{s_{a1}, \ldots, s_{a\eta}\}$ of different land uses (here $\mathcal{S}_{\text{active}} = \{\text{housing, industry, commerce}\}$), and a set

$\mathcal{S}_{\text{fixed}} = \{s_{f1}, \ldots, s_{f\kappa}\}$ of fixed states ($\mathcal{S}_{\text{fixed}} = \{\text{road}, \text{rail}, \text{river}\}$). State transitions are only possible from a vacant into an active state and from an active state into another active state.

The cell automata, however, are not equally well suited for all states which are possible in principle, i.e., depending on the coordinates (i, j) of a cell some states are more likely than others (this feature of the model is incorporated to reflect some explicit knowledge about the geographical, political, or socio-economical situation of the particular city). To achieve this, a vector $\mathbf{q}_{(i,j)} = (q_1, \ldots, q_\eta) \in [0,1]^\eta$ is given for each cell, and an entry q_k of $\mathbf{q}_{(i,j)}$ specifies the *suitability* of this cell for an active state s_{ak}. The η $(n \times n)$-matrices $\mathbf{Q}_k = ((\mathbf{q}_{(i,j)})_k)$ are called *suitability maps* and are fixed in advance for a particular city simulation.

The neighborhood of a cell automaton is defined as all cells that fall within a radius $r \in N$ around the actual cell. Using the idea of a *neighborhood template* $N_s(r) = \{(i_1, i_2) \mid \text{dist}((i_1, i_2)) \leq r\} =: \{\mathbf{n}_1, \ldots, \mathbf{n}_{|N_s(r)|}\}$, where $\text{dist}((i_1, i_2)) = \sqrt{i_1^2 + i_2^2}$, the relative index tupels of all neighbors of a particular cell are collected in the set $N_s(r)$ [12]. In contrast to more traditional cellular automata, the neighborhood radius r is typicall chosen quite large ($r = 6$, resulting in 113 neighboring cells), because medium and far reaching interactions are also important in urban dynamics. Neighborhood members are classified according to equal values of $\text{dist}(\cdot)$ into $m(r)$ distance classes (in our application, $m(r) = m(6) = 19$).

The state transition function $\delta : (\{s_{\text{vacant}}\} \cup \mathcal{S}_{\text{active}})^{|N_s(r)|} \to \mathcal{S}_{\text{active}}$ depends on *state transition potentials* $\mathbf{p}_{(i,j)} = (p_1, \ldots, p_\eta)$ characterizing the potential of a cell to change into each of the active states:

$$p_k = \nu \cdot q_k \cdot \left(1 + \sum_{i=1}^{|N_s(r)|} w_k(s_{\mathbf{n}_i}, \text{dist}(\mathbf{n}_i)) \right) + H_k \quad . \tag{2}$$

The potential p_k depends on the suitability q_k for state k, the weighted impact of all neighboring cells $\mathbf{n}_1, \ldots, \mathbf{n}_{|N_s(r)|}$ on the actual cell, an inertia term H_k that favors retention in the actual state of a cell ($H_k > 0$, if the actual cell is already in state k; otherwise, $H_k = 0$), and a noise term $\nu = 1 + (-\ln u)^\alpha$ where $u \sim U(0,1)$ is a uniformly distributed random number and α allows to tune the noise variance (a setting of $1.5 \leq \alpha \leq 2.5$ is claimed to yield a realistic degree of complexity for the simulated city).

The impact $w_k(s_{\mathbf{n}_i}, \text{dist}(\mathbf{n}_i))$ of a neighboring cell i on the potential of the actual cell to change into state k depends on i's state $s_{\mathbf{n}_i}$ and on its distance $\text{dist}(\mathbf{n}_i)$ to the actual state. The corresponding $(|\mathcal{S}| \times m(r))$-*influence matrices* $\mathbf{W}_k$ reflect the complete influence of all possible states in all relevant distances on a particular active state. These matrices numerically reflect the rules of the dynamics of the cellular automata model by encoding information such as "housing districts nearby commercial centers promote further growth of commerce." Of course, however, the exact numerical quantification of such rules overestimates their precision and causes a major problem of calibrating the $\mathbf{W}_k$ matrices to a certain application.

After calculating the transition potentials for all active cells, state transitions are executed by taking a global, exogenous growth control vector $N_t =$

$(N_1, \ldots, N_\eta)$ into account. The N_k cells having largest values p_k are changed to state s_{ak} in time step t of the simulation.

Notice that, although the approach of modeling urban growth by cellular automata is very promising and most terms of equation (2) have a reasonable interpretation, the model also raises a number of questions and difficulties, including the following:

1. The noise parameter α has no clear semantic background, and the nonlinear transformation from u to ν also lacks any reasonable interpretation. It is certainly necessary to include probabilistic state transitions into the model, but after a suitable scaling the transition potentials could be used directly as transition *probabilities*.
2. The model has a large number of free parameters that need to be set in order to calibrate the model for a particular city simulation: η suitability maps of n^2 entries each, η influence matrices of $|\mathcal{S}| \cdot m(r)$ entries, each, inertia values and the α parameter. So far, these parameters require a laborious calibration by hand.
3. Due to the stochastic perturbation term ν and the stochastic nature of the whole process, a comparison of simulation runs and the resulting land use patterns is difficult, both concerning the definition of a quantifyable metrics and the automatic assessment whether a land use pattern corresponds to a "typical" city or not.
4. The time scale relation between a single iteration of the model and real time is completely unknown. So far, only the growth control vector N_t combined with the total number of steps to simulated attempts to relate both by prescribing the number of cells that may change their state at each time step — introducing an additional number of parameters for calibration. Especially there is no way to make a distinction beetween sub-processes taking place on different time scales (see [3]).
5. So far, only few rules are encoded in the influence matrices $\mathbf{W}_k$, and the numerical representation is unreadable and too precise. A more flexible way to formulate the rules of urban growth is desirable, e. g. in form of "colloquial rules" including fuzziness instead of exactness.
6. The assumption of fixed states for rail and road corresponds to fixed infrastructural elements and is unrealistic. Similarly, the assumption of fixed suitability maps corresponds to fixed development plans, which is also unrealistic. In fact, the model lacks to simulate directed development of streets or railways and only supports spreading of (undirected) areas.

Consequently, one of the rationales behind the implementation of a simulator was to develop a tool for investigating some of these topics.

3.2 The Simulator

The simulator URBSIM [7] combines an implementation of the model presented in the previous section with an on-line analysis of the morphological measures according to section 2. A graphical user-interface (figure 3.2) allows for the direct observation of a complete simulation run, including the visualization of the cellular map and morphological measures (radial dimension and cluster size frequency), state information, and control panels for simulation parameters. The specific data for parameterizing the simulator (suitability maps, influence matrices, initial configuration, parameter values) are collected in a number of input files. For practical purposes, URBSIM also provides an editor for land use patterns and suitability maps.

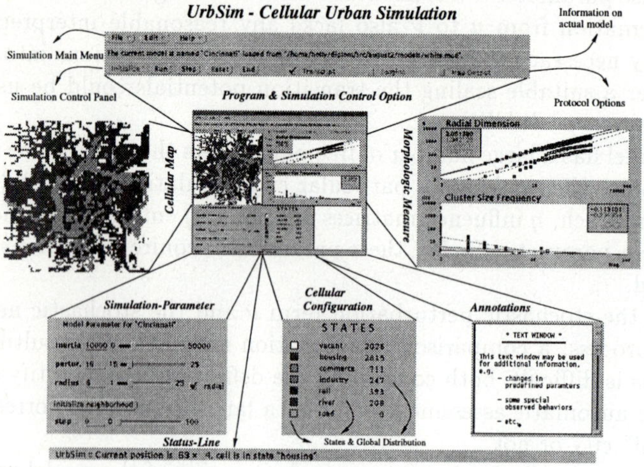

Fig. 1.: Overview of the user interface of the simulator

4 Observations and Assessments

Presently, it is still difficult to get appropriate land use data maps and development plans for applying the simulator to a particular real city — most of the data is simply not available or not recorded electronically. Geographical information systems (GIS), however, are promising tools for feeding simulators such as URBSIM in the near future, when the data is electronically recorded (which is a very time-consuming task).

To solve the input data problem, the simulator discussed here uses the original maps provided by White et al. [19], scanned from the publications. The initial configuration shows the city Cincinnati in the year 1850, and the goal is to simulate the period until 1960. The influence matrices are also taken from [19]. The noise parameter is typically set to a value $\alpha = 2.0$, and inertia terms $H_k = 10,000$ are set to a heuristic value determined by experiments (White et al. do not give the exact value of H_k they used in their experiments). The growth control values N_k are determined from the initial number of active cells by fixed growth rates of 7% (for housing and commerce) and 8% (for industry) per iteration. A simulation run is terminated after 50 generations, corresponding to the total growth (in terms of occupied land cells) of Cincinatti between 1850 and 1960. An example run of the simulator is presented in figure 4, which shows each fifth land use pattern from the complete simulation between initial and final configuration.

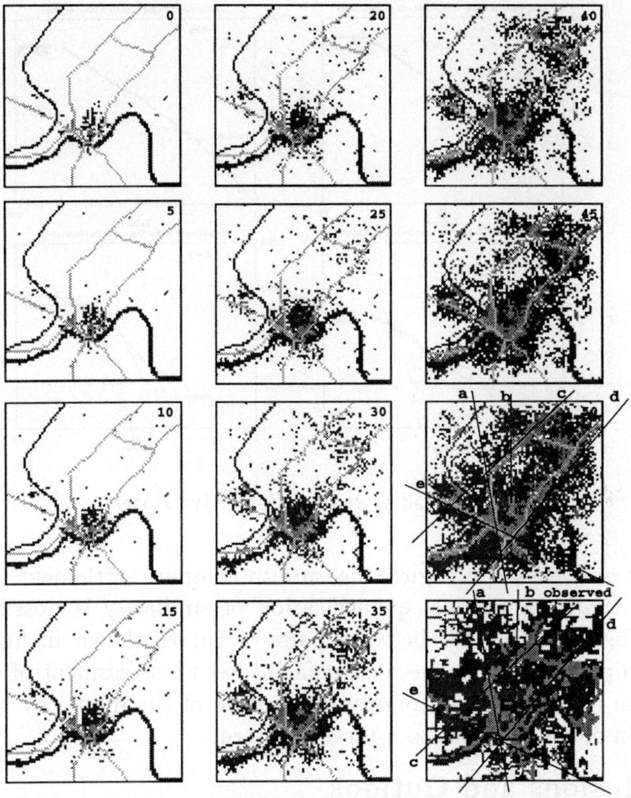

Fig. 2.: Sample run of the simulator.

The maps show a city development that looks quite realistic and proceeds to some degree along the infrastructure elements. In the final configuration and in the target configuration, the main axes are clarified by the lines a-e to facilitate a better comparison of simulation result and target map. Of course, both are not exactly identical, but the strong similarity is obvious. A human observer certainly feels that the simulation yields a realistic result.

To facilitate a better analysis of the results, however, a quantifyable similarity measure for land use patterns is strongly desirable, but presently only available in form of fractal measures introduced in section 2.

We demonstrate the feasibility of this method by applying the radial dimension analysis to compare the final configuration and the target configuration. For the analysis, log-log plots of the number of cells $N(r)$ occupied by a certain active state depending on the measurement radius r are generated. These plots are shown for the states housing, commerce and industry and the union of these in the four plots of figure 4, comparing the curve of the simulation result and the target configuration in each of these plots.

The similarity between the actual and the desired curve is striking for all of these plots. This result confirms the expectation that the fractal dimension

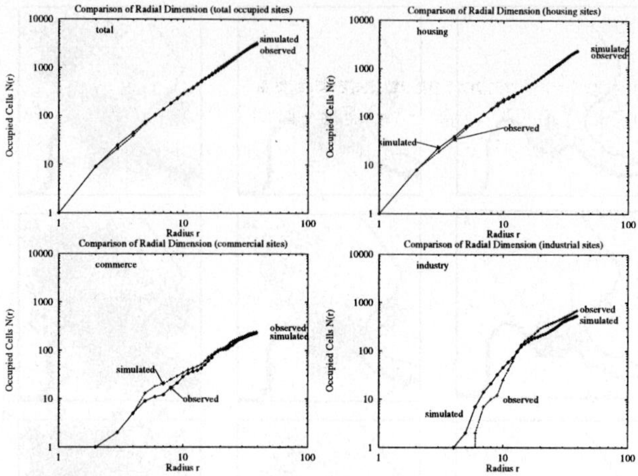

Fig. 3.: Radial analysis for active states.

is a suitable global morphological measure to compare settlement patterns and it indicates that a numerical quantification of similarity is possible (e.g., by defining a distance measure between pairs of curves shown in figure 4). This result is of high importance, because it facilitates an assessment of the outcome of simulation runs and an automatic calibration of the model by performing a minimization of the distance to a target pattern.

5 Conclusions and Outlook

So far we presented a "cellular model" of urban growth producing some promising results. But obviously the model suffers from several shortcomings presented in chapter 3.1. Future work will concentrate on simplifications (neighborhood relationship, suitability map, etc.) and validations (noise versus probabilistic state transitions, time scale, etc.). In order to do so we need reliable tools to classify and discriminate different patterns of land use, growth dynamics and so on. Consequentially, we have to enhance our analysis techniques based on fractal dimensions and probably add additional ones to our tool set, e.g., neural networks.

It is our belief that to understand the underlying fundamental rules of pattern formation the model is still much to complex. Consequently, case studies based on strongly simplified models will be investigated.

However, even the simplest model will have a certain degree of freedom which requires identification. This calibration has to be based on the minimization of the deviation between simulations and real world observations. Sophisticated optimization algorithms like evolutionary algorithms might be a good choice.

Finally, it is intended to incorporate expert knowledge into the rules of state transitions during a later stage of the project. For this knowledge naturally being "crisp" the application of fuzzy CAs [1] will be investigated.

Acknowledgements The authors gratefully acknowledge support by the German DAAD and the French A.P.A.P.E. within the PROCOPE program. The first author also acknowledges support by the German BMBF within the project EVOALG, grant 01 IB 403 A.

References

1. A. J. Adamatzky. *Identification of Cellular Automata.* Taylor & Francis, London & Bristol, 1994.
2. P. Allen and M. Sanglier. A Dynamic Model of Growth in a Central Place System. *Geographical Analysis*, pages 256–272, 1979.
3. M. Batty and Y. Xie. From Cells to Cities. *Environment and Planing B*, 21:31–48, 1994.
4. M. Batty. Cities as Fractals: Simulating Growth and Form. In A. Crilly, R. Earnshaw, and H. Jones, editors, *Fractals and Chaos*, pages 43–69. Springer Verlag, New York, 1991.
5. U. L. Businario. Technology and the Future of Cities. Technical report, Commission of the European Communities, Directorate-General Science, Research and Development, 1994. Report FOP 380 (FAST Programme).
6. H. Coucelis. Cellular Worlds: a Framework for Modeling Micro-Macro Dynamics. *Environment and Planing A*, 17:585–596, 1985.
7. H. Dörnemann. Zelluläre Automaten zur Simulation von Stadtentwicklungsprozessen am Beispiel des WHITE-Modells. Diplomarbeit, Universität Dortmund, Fachbereich Informatik, Lehrstuhl für Systemanalyse, Oktober 1995.
8. J. W. Forrester. *Urban Dynamics.* The M.I.T. Press, Massachusetts Institute of Technology, Cambridge, 1969.
9. P. Frankhauser. Fractal Properties of Settlement Structures. In *Proceedings of the 1st International Seminar of Structural Morphology*, pages 357–368, Montpellier-La Grande Motte, September 1992.
10. P. Frankhauser. *La Fractalité des Structures urbaines.* Collection Villes. Anthropos, Paris, 1994.
11. M. Garzon. *Models of Massive Parallelism.* Springer Verlag, New York, 1995.
12. C. G. Langton. Computation at the Edge of Chaos: Phase Transitions and Emergent Computation. *Physica D, North Holland*, 42:12–37, 1990.
13. B. B. Mandelbrot. *Die fraktale Geometrie der Natur.* Birkhäuser, Basel, 1987. Deutsche Ausgabe.
14. M. Phipps. Dynamical Behavior of Cellular Automata under the Constraint of Neighborhood Coherence. *Geographical Analysis*, 21(3):187–215, July 1989.
15. B. Schäfers. *Gesellschaftlicher Wandel in Deutschland: Ein Studienbuch zur Sozialstruktur und Sozialgeschichte der Bundesrepublik.* Enke Verlag, Stuttgart, 1990.
16. W. Tobler. Cellular Geography. In G. O. S. Gale, editor, *Philosophy in Geography*, pages 279–386. D Reidel. Dodrecht, 1979.
17. M. Wegener and K. Spiekermann. Efficient, Equitable and Ecological Urban Structures. In *WCTR 1995 – 7th World Conference on Transport Research, Sydney, Australia*, 1995.
18. R. W. White and G. Engelen. Cellular Automata and Fractal Urban Form: A Cellular Modelling Approach to the Evolution of Urban Land Use Patterns. *Environment and Planing A*, 25:1175–1193, 1993.
19. R. W. White, G. Engelen, and I. Uljee. Cellular Automata Modelling of Fractal Urban Land Use Patterns: Forcasting Change for Planning Applications. *Eighth European Colloquium on Theoretical and Quantitative Geography, Stockholm*, 1993.
20. S. Wolfram, editor. *Theory and Applications of Cellular Automata.* Advanced Series on Complex Systems. World Scientific Publishing, Singapore, 1986.

Democratic Optimization for Discrete and Continuous Systems

Frank-Michael Dittes

Research Center Rossendorf, Institute for Nuclear and Hadronic Physics, D-01314 Dresden, Germany

Abstract. A novel strategy for finding optimal solutions to complex problems with many competing requirements is proposed. It consists in a simultaneous optimization of the energy, cost or fitness function of the system itself, and of sub-systems of all sizes with an appropriate weight function. For various travelling salesman problems and spin glasses as well as for an example of a continuous-valued system (the optical multilayer problem) the corresponding Monte Carlo algorithm is shown to yield results superior to those obtained by previous optimization techniques.

1 Introduction

The description of complex systems with many competing requirements generically leads to multi-peaked or "rugged" functions: the energy, cost or fitness landscape (over the space of all possible configurations of the system) is characterized by a complicated structure with many local optima. In a physical context typical examples are the energy functions of many-body systems with a high amount of frustration: glasses, antiferromagnetics and many random systems. In a broader setting rugged landscapes describe, e. g., the fitness of biological species (as a function of the pheno- or genotype), the "payoff" of economical or social actions (as a function of the sequence of possible decisions) or the cost or time required to achieve a certain aim. Finding the global optimum of such systems is a highly non-trivial problem since fulfilling one requirement often leads to an increase in the mismatch of others. In the notion of energy or fitness landscapes such situations correspond to *local* optima, i. e., to situations from which no way out by undertaking a single step is possible.

Various strategies have been proposed to tackle this problem, adopting ideas from different areas of science. Most prominent examples are simulated annealing (SA) and its recent developments [1, 2, 3, 4] (based on the thermodynamically motivated Metropolis algorithm [5]), evolutionary and genetic algorithms imitating adaptive processes in biological systems [6, 7] and neural network techniques [8]. All these strategies orient themselves exclusively on the energy or cost E of the *total* system by specifying the acceptance rule for configuration changes purely on behalf of E.

It is the aim of the present contribution to formulate an alternative approach based on the assumption that an optimal (or near-optimal) solution to complex problems can be found by an interplay of *individual* interests, synchronized to a certain extent by group and system regulations. This assumption allows to formulate an efficient and robust Monte Carlo optimization algorithm, often performing better than previously used techniques. Apparently, a motivation for this approach stems from one of the most complex systems — human society – relying, at least partially, on similar principles. Vice versa, the mathematical formulation presented below might allow a more detailed insight into why *democratic* structures allowing individuals and groups of them to follow their own interests — taking into account those of other individuals as well as of the system as a whole — are most capable of solving complex problems.

2 The Algorithm

In order to be specific I use a physical terminology and try to find a global minimum ("ground state") of the energy E of a system with N degrees of freedom (called spins or sites). Every configuration of the system can be specified by a vector $\mathbf{s} = \{s_1, \ldots, s_N\}$, and the energy landscape is given by a map from the set of all possible configurations into the real numbers: $\mathbf{s} \to E(\mathbf{s})$. The aim of a Monte Carlo algorithm is to evolve a random initial configuration into the ground state (or close to it) by randomly generating configuration changes. The optimization *strategy* is determined by the criterion according to which a configuration change is accepted or discarded.

The starting point of the approach is the representation of the total energy function $E(\mathbf{s})$ as a sum of k-spin interaction terms, $E(\mathbf{s}) = \sum_{k=0}^{N} E_k(\mathbf{s})$, where the general form of E_k reads $E_k(\mathbf{s}) = \sum_{i_1=1}^{N} \cdots \sum_{i_k=1}^{N} e_k(s_{i_1}, \ldots, s_{i_k})$. The basic objects of the algorithm are the *single-spin energies* $E^{[1]}_{\{n\}}$ defined as the sum over all interaction terms in which the spin with label n occurs:

$$E^{[1]}_{\{n\}}(\mathbf{s}) = \frac{1}{N} E_0 + \sum_{k=1}^{N} \sum_{i_1,\ldots,i_k=1}^{N} e_k(s_{i_1}, \ldots, s_{i_k}) \, \frac{1}{k} \sum_{j=1}^{k} \delta_{n i_j} \,. \qquad (1)$$

From expression (1), the set of multiple-spin energies is constructed by defining $E^{[2]}_{\{n_1,n_2\}}(\mathbf{s}) = E^{[1]}_{\{n_1\}}(\mathbf{s}) + E^{[1]}_{\{n_2\}}(\mathbf{s})$, etc. Note that, in particular, $E^{[N]}_{\{n_1,\ldots,n_N\}}(\mathbf{s}) \equiv \sum_{1 \le i \le N} E^{[1]}_{\{i\}}(\mathbf{s}) = E(\mathbf{s})$, i. e., the $E^{[1]}_{\{n\}}$ defined by eq. (1) realize a complete decomposition of the total energy function into single-spin energies each of which depends, however, on the total configuration.

The key idea of the proposed optimization strategy is to search for minima not on the single landscape E, but on the *ensemble* of landscapes defined above — looking at each moment of time for steps diminishing the value of a randomly chosen member of this landscape ensemble. There are two properties of the ensemble that make this approach work:

1. Different landscapes are not independent of each other but synchronized in the sense that, for all K, the average value of K-energies is proportional to the system's energy: $\sum_{1 \le i_1 < \ldots < i_K \le N} E^{[K]}_{\{i_1,\ldots,i_K\}}(\mathbf{s}) \sim E(\mathbf{s})$. Therefore, *on average*,

an optimization of group energies brings the system closer to its global energy minimum.
2. The structure of *local* minima is, at least for sufficiently random systems, different for different landscapes. As a consequence, switching from the optimization of E to that of an $E^{[K]}$, and vice versa, avoids the danger of getting trapped into local minima.

The general scheme realizing this approach in form of a Monte Carlo algorithm looks as follows:
1. Specify the class of elementary configuration changes ("steps", ECS).
2. For each ECS select a set of energy landscapes (EL) affected by it.
3. Define a probability distribution, p, over the set of ECS, and another one, P, over the set of EL. (If the latter has $K_{\max}$ elements then P is given by the $K_{\max}$ numbers $P(K)$, $K = 1, \ldots, K_{\max}$.)
4. Randomly choose pairs of ECS and EL (according to $p \times P$). Accept an ECS if and only if it lowers the value of the corresponding EL.

Obviously, the performance of such an algorithm depends on the choice of the weight functions p and P. Whereas p can be taken to be flat (i. e., all ECS occur with equal probability), a non-trivial structure of P is indispensable. Based on the assumption that an optimal search strategy for sufficiently complicated problems should include configuration changes on all scales, a power-law ansatz known to adequately represent the fluctuation properties of many complex systems [9] seems to be appropriate. Specifically, $P(K)$ has been constructed in the following way: generate a random number x uniformly distributed between 0 and 1 and determine K according to $K = K_{\max} + 1 - [(1 - x + x/(K_{\max} + 1)^{\alpha})^{-\frac{1}{\alpha}}]$, where α is a small non-negative number being roughly proportional to $1/K_{\max}$; $[\ldots]$ denotes the integer part.

Note that the parameter α characterizes, loosely speaking, the "amount of democracy" in the algorithm. Large positive α almost completely exclude spin flips preferable for individuals only, corresponding to a "totalitarian", "centralized" evolution, whereas for large negative α the amount of purely "egoistic" moves prevails — leading to an "anarchic" behavior; in both cases the performance of the optimization algorithm is poor. The best choice turns out to be in between: $P(K)$ should have its maximum at large K (since we are aiming to minimize the *system's* energy) while being not too small at $K \approx 1$ (in order to provide enough flexibility for leaving local minima). This is what could be called a "democratic" balance: a high amount of individual freedom preserving, nevertheless, the dominance of global interests.

The scheme outlined above has been successfully applied to a number of specific problems described in the following sections.

3 Travelling Salesman Problems

One of the most intensively investigated hard combinatorial problems is that of the Travelling Salesman (TSP). The aim is to find the shortest cyclic tour connecting a given number of points ("cities"). Characterizing a tour by the order the cities are visited, for a problem with N cities each tour may be represented as a permutation of $\{1, \ldots, N\}$. Given any configuration, another one can be obtained by cutting the tour at two segments (connecting, say, sites i and j, and sites k and l) and inverting one of the parts, i. e., by replacing the configuration $\ldots, i-1, i, j, j+1, \ldots, k-1, k, l, l+1, \ldots$ by $\ldots, i-1, i, k, k-1, \ldots, j+1, j, l, l+1, \ldots$ [10]. The "energy" to be minimized is the length of the tour defined as the sum of distances d_{ij} between the cities: $E = \sum_{n=1}^{N} d_{nn+1} = \frac{1}{2}\sum_{n=1}^{N}(d_{nn-1} + d_{nn+1})$, where the numbering is assumed to go along the tour, and all indices are to be taken modulo N. In line with the algorithm, single-site energies $E^{[1]}_{\{n\}}$ are defined by $E^{[1]}_{\{n\}} = \frac{1}{2}(d_{nn-1} + d_{nn+1})$, since the index n appears exclusively in this combination. The requirement $E(\mathbf{s}) = \sum_{1\leq i\leq N} E^{[1]}_{\{i\}}(\mathbf{s})$ is fulfilled in an obvious way.

The number of elementary configuration changes (within the class described above) is given by $(N-1)(N-2)/2$, and any such ECS affects only four sites (in the above representation, those with indices i, j, k, and l). As a consequence, any given flip influences exactly $2^4-1=15$ energy landscapes ($E_1 = E^{[1]}_{\{i\}}, E_2 = E^{[1]}_{\{j\}}, E_3 = E^{[1]}_{\{k\}}, E_4 = E^{[1]}_{\{l\}}, E_5 = E^{[2]}_{\{i,j\}}, E_6 = E^{[2]}_{\{i,k\}}, E_7 = E^{[2]}_{\{i,l\}}, E_8 = E^{[2]}_{\{j,k\}}, E_9 = E^{[2]}_{\{j,l\}}, E_{10} = E^{[2]}_{\{k,l\}}, E_{11} = E^{[3]}_{\{i,j,k\}}, E_{12} = E^{[3]}_{\{i,j,l\}}, E_{13} = E^{[3]}_{\{i,k,l\}}, E_{14} = E^{[3]}_{\{j,k,l\}}, E_{15} = E^{[4]}_{\{i,j,k,l\}}$). The value $K_{\max}$ equals, therefore, 15. Using these values, the scheme outlined in sect. 2 takes the following form: For each moment of (discrete) time, randomly choose an ECS (with uniform probability $2/((N-1)(N-2))$. Randomly select one of the 15 EL E_K affected by that ECS by applying the procedure described in sect. 2: generate a random number x uniformly distributed between 0 and 1 and determine K according to $K = K_{\max} + 1 - [(1 - x + x/(K_{\max}+1)^{\alpha})^{-\frac{1}{\alpha}}]$, with $K_{\max} = 15$. Accept the chosen ECS if and only if it lowers the value of the selected E_K.

This algorithm has been tested on three problems for which the optimal configuration is known [11]; a good value for the single parameter α turned out to be 2.5 (in all presented examples, α has not been varied with time):
1. The 100 city tour kroA100. In a series of 25 runs the algorithm found the true optimum within 4×10^5 to 3×10^7 trial flips. These numbers can be improved by adopting the heuristic rule [12] that configuration changes are promising only if the affected cities are close to each other in the plane. Allowing only such trial flips for which the site with index k is one of the nb cities located closest to site i good results can be obtained already for nb=7: The algorithm finds quickly configurations close to the optimal one at the 1 % level and needs between 1×10^5 and 12×10^6 trial flips (with a mean value of about 3×10^6) in order to find the global minimum. This is illustrated in Fig. 1 where the resulting curves are compared to that of another recently proposed Monte Carlo technique [4].
2. Grötschel's 442-problem (pcb442). With the same parameters as above, the best tour found by the algorithm within a series of 10 runs, each continuing over 2×10^7 trial flips was of length 50,936, 0.3% above the global optimum and slightly improving the results reported in Ref. [12].

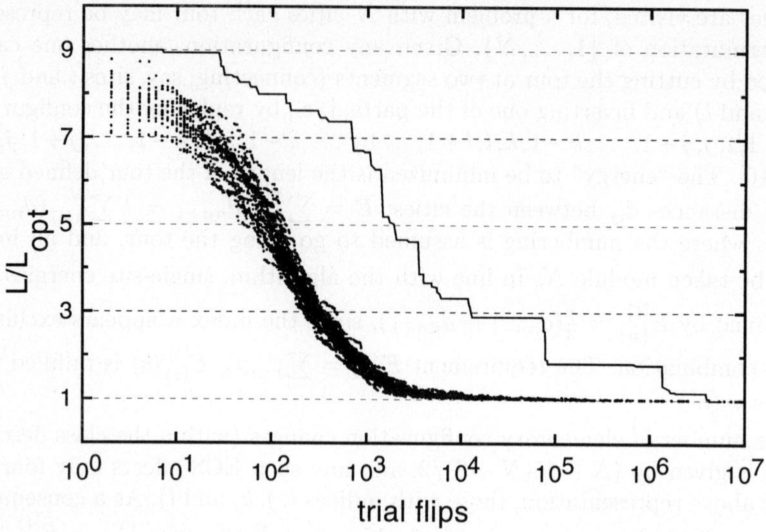

Fig. 1. Length of the best-so-far tour as a function of time for the TSP problem kroA100. A total of 25 runs is displayed and compared to the curve published in Ref. [4]

3. The 532-city problem of Padberg and Rinaldi [13] (att532) where the optimal solution is of length 27,686. The algorithm found 27,802, less than 0.4% above the true minimum.

4 Spin Glasses

Spin glasses (SG) are many-body systems for which the number of possible states for each element is restricted to be a finite number, usually two. The elements ("spins") are subject to a (possibly long-range) interaction.

For SG a natural choice for ECS are single-spin flips. Since for long-range interactions the number of EL affected by a given EL is huge ($\sim K_{\max}!$, where $K_{\max}$ is the "interaction radius", i. e. the number of sites interacting with the flipping site), only a restricted number of EL can be included into the algorithm. In particular, one can consider the chain of "K-neighborhoods", $K = 1, \ldots, K_{\max}$, given by the flipping site, and the $K-1$ sites most adjacent to it. Accordingly, the weight function $P{=}P(K)$ defines the probability of choosing a specific neighborhood size K. For the time evolution I used the "fitter updating" [14, 15] known to be effective for SG when the acceptance rate of ECS is smaller than the inverse number of spins: For each moment of discrete time examine *all* possible single-spin flips and accept a randomly chosen one which leads to lower energy of *its* K-neighborhood.

The algorithm has been tested on the following SG:

4.1 The $N-k$ model

Kauffman's $N-k$ model [16] describes a system of N spins, each interacting with k others. The system's energy is given by

$$E(\mathbf{s}) = \frac{1}{N}\sum_{i=1}^{N} E_i(s_i; s_{i_1}, \ldots, s_{i_k}) . \tag{2}$$

The k sites $i_1, \ldots, i_k$ are assumed to be adjacent to i on a twodimensional lattice and the E_i are random numbers uniformly distributed between 0 and 1. The number of local optima of (2) changes from 1, for k=0, to $\mathcal{O}(2^N/N)$ for k=$N-1$, and their energies are known to be normally distributed for large k [17]. A numerical test on 200 randomly chosen local minima for N=24^2 and k=12 yielded a mean energy per spin m of 0.314, with a standard deviation σ of about 0.007.

The $N-k$ model served as a testing ground for a first attempt to use the minimization of sub-system energies for the optimization of the total E. The approach followed by Kauffman et al. [14] assumed a static division of the system into "patches" of equal size selfishly trying to minimize their energy. It has been found that an optimal choice of the patch size allows the system to reach energies better than m by 2σ [see the dashed line in Fig. 2]. In the same Figure, the results of 25 runs of the algorithm formulated above are shown for α=1. After 5000 time steps, i. e., less than 10 executed flips per spin, an average energy per spin of $\approx$0.266 has been reached, corresponding to almost 7σ below m (solid line). One clearly sees the advantage of the algorithm proposed — demonstrating the importance of using sub-systems of *all* sizes and trying to find a permanent balance between individual, group and system energies.

4.2 The low autocorrelation binary sequence model

The low autocorrelation binary sequence (LABS) problem [18] originates from communication engineering and consists in finding the low lying states of an ordered onedimensional spin glass with long-range 4-spin interaction given by the energy function [19, 15]

$$E(\mathbf{s}) = \frac{1}{N}\sum_{k=1}^{N-1}(\sum_{i=1}^{N-k} s_i s_{i+k})^2 \; ; \; s_i = \pm 1 . \tag{3}$$

The problem is very hard, the deep minima of $E(\mathbf{s})$ being presumably of "golf-hole like" character [19]. The exact ground states are known only for $N \leq 32$, within a restricted class of configurations up to $N = 71$ [20]. For larger system sizes the best results obtained by algorithms based on SA differ by a factor of almost 2 from the ground state energies expected on the basis of ergodicity arguments [18, 19] as well as from an extrapolation of the small-N energies. With

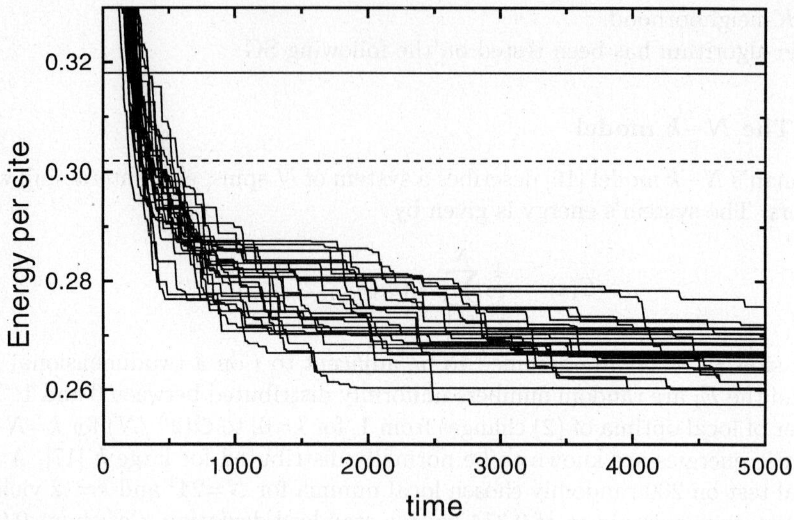

Fig. 2. Best-so-far energies of 25 runs for the N–k model (2) with N=24^2 and k=12. The full straight line indicates the value of the mean local minimum, the dashed line – the best result of Ref. [14]

$\alpha = 0$ (corresponding to the long-range character of the problem, $K_{\max} = N$) the algorithm presented above easily recovers the exact results for small N and makes a considerable step beyond the results of other techniques for larger N: In a series of 25 runs each over 100000 time steps, it found for $N = 101$ an *average* minimum energy per spin of 0.079, reaching quickly the best known configuration at energy $E_{\min}/N = 0.059798...$ [21, 20] – corresponding to 6 σ below the mean local energy minimum ($m = 0.137, \sigma \approx 0.013$). Note that the number of Monte Carlo steps necessary to reach the above mentioned energies within SA can be estimated to be 10^{19} for $E/N = 0.08$ and 10^{200} for $E/N = 0.06$ [19]! For still larger N the algorithm systematically encounters new minima, e. g., $E_{\min}/N = 0.0727...$, for $N = 141$, and $E_{\min}/N = 0.0799...$, for $N = 181$ – as compared to the previously known best values of 0.0772 and 0.0861, correspondingly [20].

4.3 Coulomb glasses

Coulomb glasses are frustrated many-body systems formed by a number of interacting electric charges [22]. I considered a specific example of N=500 static charges randomly distributed within the unit cube:

$$E(\mathbf{s}) = \sum_{i=1, i\neq j}^{N} \sum_{j=1}^{N} \frac{s_i s_j}{|\mathbf{r}_i - \mathbf{r}_j|} \tag{4}$$

with fixed $\mathbf{r}_i$ and $s_i = \pm 1$. The positions of 25 randomly chosen local minima for each value of the neighborhood size K are plotted in Fig. 3. One can see the existence of an optimal patch size in Kauffman's sense of the order of 3, followed by a counterreaction between sizes of 20 – 40, and a slow relaxation towards the local minima of $E(\mathbf{s})$ itself. The latter have a mean value of m=−8490, with a σ of about 80. Fig. 3 also shows a typical time evolution generated by the optimization algorithm (with α=0), reaching energies below −9000 after $\approx 3\times 10^4$ fitter steps. The best value found by the algorithm was −9094 — again more than 7 σ below m.

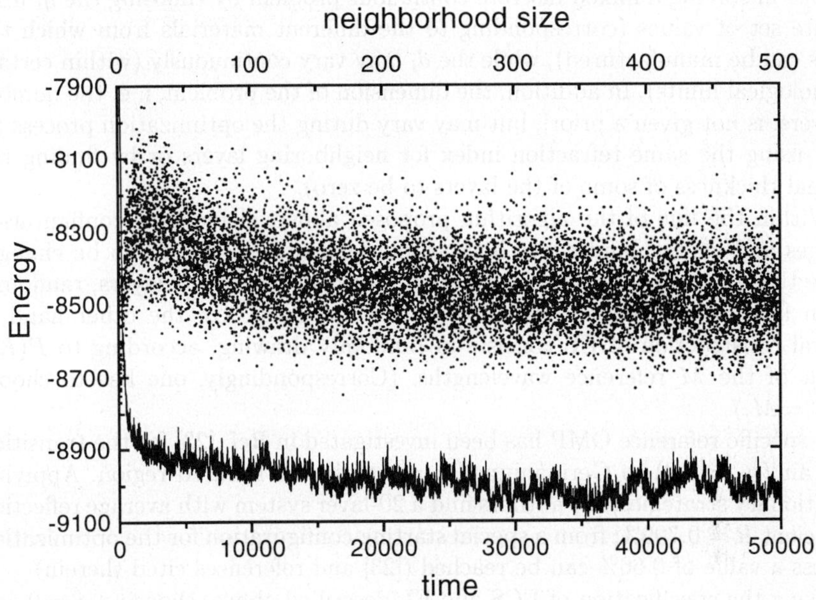

Fig. 3. Points: Values of 25 local minima of the Coulomb glass (4) as a function of the neighborhood size K. Curve: Time evolution of a single run of the algorithm for this energy function. Note the typical "Manhattan" panorama

I conclude that for spin glasses with < 500 sites the algorithm is capable of finding, after a few 10^4 time steps, energies which are about 7 standard deviations below the mean local energy minimum.

5 The Optical Multilayer Problem

In the previous sections the formulated algorithm has been tested on different discrete systems. In the following, results for a simple optimization problem including the necessity of performing an optimal choice of *continuous-valued* variables will be presented.

The aim of an optical multilayer system is to minimize the reflection coefficient R at a surface separating two homogeneous media with refraction indices η_0 and η_s by covering it with a sequence of thin optical layers with thicknesses d_i and refraction indices η_i. The reflection and transmission coefficients of any of the layers depend periodically on the wavelength of the incoming light so that the problem becomes highly frustrated if one is interested in a small *average* R, over a set of, say, M different wavelengths. (The reflection coefficient of the total multilayer depends in a non-linear way on the thicknesses and refraction indices of all layers.)

From the optimization point of view the optical multilayer problem (OMP) consists in solving a mixed discrete-continuous problem by choosing the η_i from a finite set of values (corresponding to the different materials from which the layers can be manufactured), while the d_i may vary continuously (within certain technological limits). In addition, the dimension of the problem, i. e. the number of layers, is not given a priori, but may vary during the optimization process (e. g. by using the same refraction index for neighboring layers or by finding the optimal thickness of some of the layers to be zero).

Within the line of the algorithm proposed above, elementary configuration changes and energy landscapes have to be defined. I used ECS to be changes of the thickness (and/or of the refraction index) of one of the layers, randomly drawn from a Gaussian around the present thickness. On the other hand, a natural construction of EL consists in randomly drawing, according to $P(K)$, K out of the M reference wavelengths. (Correspondingly, one has to choose $K_{\max} = M$.)

A specific reference OMP has been investigated in Ref. [23] for the transition from air ($\eta_0 = 1.0$) to Germanium ($\eta_s = 4.0$) in the infrared region. Applying evolutionary strategies, the authors find a 20-layer system with average reflection coefficient $R = 0.709\%$; from a special starting configuration for the optimization process a value of 0.66% can be reached ([23] and references cited therein).

Using the specification of ECS and EL described above, choosing $\alpha = 0$ and taking starting values for the number of layers between 20 and 50 the presented algorithm finds a variety of solutions improving the above cited values. E. g., the 17-layer system $\{d_i\} = \{0.2079, 0.2407, 2.2481, 1.0573, 1.8382, 1.0158, 1.5171, 0.1261, 0.3374, 0.7549, 0.2080, 1.3427, 1.2282, 0.1096, 0.5263, 0.6027, 1.0846\}$, $\{\eta_i\} = \{2.2, 2.4, 2.2, \ldots\}$ reaches $R = 0.62\%$, whereas with the help of 23 layers R can be lowered to 0.55%, with 25 layers to 0.49%, with 35 - to 0.45%.

Note that the specification of EL chosen above opens the possibility of highly parallelizing the algorithm since the calculation of any of the "energies" $R_k, k = 1, \ldots, M$ can be performed completely independent of the others.

6 Summary and Conclusions

In summary, a new optimization strategy for finding optimal or near-optimal solutions to problems with many competing requirements has been proposed. It is based on the *simultaneous* optimization of the fitness, cost or energy landscape of the system, and of the individuals forming it — with a weight function realizing an optimal, "democratic" balance between interests of different scales. On its basis, a Monte Carlo algorithm has been formulated and tested for a number of TSP and of SG as well as for an example of a continuous-valued problem. The proposed algorithm turns out to be superior to other general purpose Monte Carlo techniques in quality and speed, reaching its most significant advantage for very hard problems.

Acknowledgment: I am indebted to Stuart Kauffman for the stimulating discussion of Ref. [14]. Fruitful discussions with W. Ebeling and H.-P. Schwefel are gratefully acknowledged.

References

[1] S. Kirkpatrick, D. C. Gellat, and M. P. Vecchi, Science **220** (1983) 671
[2] H. Szu and R. Hartley, Phys. Lett. A **122** (1987) 157
[3] T. J. P. Penna, Phys. Rev. E **51** (1995) R1
[4] B. Hesselbo and R. B. Stinchcombe, Phys. Rev. Lett. **74** (1995) 2151
[5] N. Metropolis, A. W. Rosenbluth, M. N. Rosenbluth, A. H. Teller, and E. Teller, J. Chem. Phys. **21** (1953) 1087
[6] I. Rechenberg, *Evolutionsstrategie* (Friedrich Frommann Verlag, Stuttgart, 1973)
[7] J. Holland, *Adaption in natural and artificial systems* (MIT Press, Cambridge, Mass., 1992)
[8] J. J. Hopfield and D. W. Tank, Biol. Cybern. **5** (1985) 141
[9] P. Bak, C. Tang and K. Wiesenfeld, Phys. Rev. Lett. **59** (1987) 381
[10] S. Lin and B. W. Kernighan, Oper. Res. **21** (1973) 498
[11] ftp://titan.cs.rice.edu/public/tsplib.tar
[12] G. Dueck and T. Scheuer, J. Comput. Phys. **90** (1990) 161
[13] M. Padberg and G. Rinaldi, Oper. Res. Lett. **6** (1987) 1
[14] S. Kauffman, W. G. Macready, and E. Dickinson, Preprint SFI-94-06-031, Santa Fe, 1994; S. Kauffman, *At Home in the Universe* (Oxford University Press, Oxford, England, 1995)
[15] W. Krauth and M. Mézard, Z. Phys. B **97** (1995) 127
[16] S. Kauffman, *The Origins of Order* (Oxford University Press, Oxford, England, 1993)
[17] E. D. Weinberger, Phys. Rev. A **44** (1991) 6399
[18] M. J. E. Golay, IEEE Trans. Inform. Theory **IT-23** (1977) 43
[19] J. Bernasconi, J. Physique **48** (1987) 559
[20] C. de Groot, D. Würtz and K. H. Hoffmann, Optimization **23** (1992) 369
[21] M. J. E. Golay and D. A. Harris, Preprint, 1989
[22] M. Pollak, Discuss. Faraday Soc. **50** (1970) 13; A. L. Efros and B. I. Shklovskii, J. Phys. C8 (1975) L49
[23] Th. Bäck and M. Schütz, Proceedings of the Fourth Annual Conference on Evolutionary Computation (Evolutionary Programming IV), The MIT Press, Cambridge MA, 1995, p. 33

A Study of Some Properties of Ant-Q

Marco Dorigo and Luca Maria Gambardella

IDSIA, Corso Elvezia 36, CH-6900 Lugano, Switzerland

dorigo@idsia.ch, luca@idsia.ch

Abstract. Ant-Q is an algorithm belonging to the class of ant colony based methods, that is, of combinatorial optimization methods in which a set of simple agents, called ants, cooperate to find good solutions to combinatorial optimization problems. The main focus of this article is on the experimental study of the sensitivity of the Ant-Q algorithm to its parameters and on the investigation of synergistic effects when using more than a single ant. We conclude comparing Ant-Q with its ancestor Ant System, and with other heuristic algorithms.

1 Introduction

In this paper we study some properties of Ant-Q, a novel distributed approach to combinatorial optimization based on reinforcement learning. Ant-Q (Gambardella and Dorigo, 1995) finds its ground in one of the authors previous work on the so-called Ant System (Colorni, Dorigo and Maniezzo, 1991; 1992; Dorigo, 1992; Dorigo, Maniezzo and Colorni, 1996), and in the Q-learning algorithm (Watkins, 1989). Ant System (AS), which will not be discussed here, is a distributed algorithm loosely based on the observation of ant colonies behavior, hence its name. It has been applied to various combinatorial optimization problems like the symmetric and asymmetric traveling salesman problems (TSP and ATSP respectively), and the quadratic assignment problem (Maniezzo, Colorni and Dorigo, 1994). Ant-Q is an extension of AS, which is reinterpreted in the light of reinforcement learning and in particular of Q-learning recent literature. This paper is devoted to a study of some of Ant-Q characteristics, and to a comparison of Ant-Q with AS and other heuristics, in which we show Ant-Q superiority. Ant-Q is different from Q-learning in that while typical applications of Q-learning see one single agent exploring the state space, Ant-Q uses a set of cooperating agents. These agents cooperate exchanging information in the form of AQ-values (the analogous of Q-values in Q-learning). Last, Ant-Q agents have some memory: this is necessary, as explained in Section 2, due to the different nature of our application problems (combinatorial optimization) with respect to typical Q-learning applications.

The article is organized as follows. In Section 2, we briefly describe the Ant-Q approach by means of its application to the traveling salesman problem. In Section 3 we discuss a few characteristics of the Ant-Q family of algorithms. In Section 4 we investigate Ant-Q by experimentation on TSP and ATSP problems. A brief conclusion is given in Section 5.

2 The Ant-Q Approach to Combinatorial Optimization

The easiest way to introduce the Ant-Q algorithm is by its application to the traveling salesman problem (TSP) or to the more general asymmetric traveling salesman problem (ATSP). They are defined as follows.

TSP

Let $V = \{v_1, \dots, v_n\}$ be a set of cities, $A = \{(i,j) : i,j \in V\}$ be the edge set, and $d_{ij} = d_{ji}$ be a cost measure associated with edge $(i,j) \in A$.
The TSP is the problem of finding a minimal length closed tour that visits each city. In the case cities $v_i \in V$ are given by their coordinates (x_i, y_i) and d_{ij} is the Euclidean distance between i and j, then we have an Euclidean TSP.

ATSP

If $d_{ij} \neq d_{ji}$ for at least some *(i,j)* then the TSP becomes an ATSP.

In the following of this section we will talk generically of ATSP problems, which include TSP as a special case.

Let k be an ant whose task is to make a tour: visit all the cities and return to the starting one. Associated to k there is the list $J_k(r)$ of cities still to be visited, where r is the current city (this is equivalent to say that ant k remembers already visited cities). An ant k situated in city r moves to city s using the following rule, called *pseudo-random-proportional* action choice rule (or state transition rule) :

$$s = \begin{cases} arg \max\limits_{u \in J_k(r)} \left\{ [AQ(r,u)]^\delta \cdot [HE(r,u)]^\beta \right\} & \text{if } q \le q_0 \\ S & \text{otherwise} \end{cases} \tag{1}$$

where:

- *AQ(r,s)*, read Ant-Q-value, is a positive real value associated to arc *(r,s)* and is the Ant-Q algorithm counterpart of Q-learning Q-values. *AQ(r,s)*'s are changed at run time and are intended to indicate how useful it is to make move s (i.e., to go to city s) when in state r.
- *HE(r,s)*, is a heuristic function which evaluates the goodness of move s when in city r. For example, in the ATSP *HE(r,s)* is the inverse of the distance between cities r and s.
- Parameters δ and β weigh the relative importance of the learned *AQ*-values and the heuristic values.
- q is a value chosen randomly with uniform probability in [0, 1], and q_0 ($0 \le q_0 \le 1$) is a parameter: the smaller q_0 the higher the probability to make a random choice.
- S is a random variable selected according to the distribution given by formula (2) which gives the probability with which an ant in city r chooses the city s to move to.

$$p_k(r,s) = \begin{cases} \dfrac{[AQ(r,s)]^\delta \cdot [HE(r,s)]^\beta}{\sum\limits_{z \in J_k(r)} [AQ(r,z)]^\delta \cdot [HE(r,z)]^\beta} & \text{if } s \in J_k(r) \\ 0 & \text{otherwise} \end{cases} \tag{2}$$

As we said, the goal of Ant-Q is to learn AQ-values such that they can favor, in probability, the discovery of good ATSP solutions. AQ-values are learned by the following rule[1]:

$$AQ(r,s) \leftarrow (1-\alpha)\cdot AQ(r,s) + \alpha \cdot \left(\Delta AQ(r,s) + \gamma \cdot \underset{z \in J(s)}{Max}\; AQ(s,z) \right) \tag{3}$$

The update term is composed of a reinforcement term and of the discounted evaluation of the next state. In general, the reinforcement ΔAQ can be local (immediate) or global (delayed). In the current version of Ant-Q local reinforcement is always zero, while global reinforcement, which is given after all the ants have finished their tour, is computed by the following formula:

$$\Delta AQ(r,s) = \begin{cases} \dfrac{W}{L_{Best}} & \text{if } (r,s) \in \text{ tour done by the best agent} \\ 0 & \text{otherwise} \end{cases} \tag{4}$$

where L_{Best} is the length of the tour done by the best ant, that is the ant which did the shortest tour in the current iteration, and W is a parameter. The Ant-Q algorithm used in this paper is shown in Fig. 1 (the detailed algorithm can be found in (Gambardella and Dorigo, 1995)).

```
Ant-Q algorithm
/* Initialization phase */
    Set an initial value for AQ-values
/* Main algorithm */
Loop   /* This loop is an iteration of the algorithm */
  1.   /* Initialization of ants data structures */
       Choose a starting city for ants
  2.   /* In this step ants build tours and locally update AQ-values */
       Each ant applies the state transition rule (1) to choose the city
       to go to, updates the set Jk and applies formula (3) to locally
       update AQ-values (in formula (3) ΔAQ(r,s)=0)
  3.   /* In this step ants globally update AQ-values */
       The edges belonging to the tour done by the best ant are updated
       using formula (3) where ΔAQ(r,s) is given by formula (4)
Until (End_condition = True)
```

Fig. 1. The Ant-Q algorithm

In words it can be described as follows. First, there is an initialization phase in which an initial value AQ_0 is given to AQ-values. Then comes the main algorithm loop which comprises three steps. In the first step each ant k is placed on a city $r_{k\text{-}initial}$ chosen according to some policy, and the set $J_k(r_{k\text{-}initial})$ of the still to be visited cities is initialized. Then, at Step 2, a cycle, in which each of the m ants makes a move and the $AQ(r,s)$'s are updated using only the discounted next state evaluation, is repeated until each ant has finished its tour and is back in the starting city. Last, in Step 3 the edges belonging to the shortest tour are updated using formulas (3) and (4). The loop

---

1 The form of this updating rule, which is very similar to the updating rule used by Q-learning, is the most relevant difference between Ant System and Ant-Q. In Ant System formula (3) reduces to $AQ(r,s) \leftarrow (1-\alpha)\cdot AQ(r,s) + \Delta AQ(r,s)$.

is repeated until a termination condition is met. Usually the termination condition is verified after a fixed number of iterations, or when no improvement is obtained for a fixed number of iterations.

3 The Family of Ant-Q Algorithms

To apply the Ant-Q algorithm of Fig. 1 a set of somewhat arbitrary choices have to be done. These are: the value of parameters δ, β, and q_0 in formula (1), α and γ in formula (3), the constant W in formula (4), the initial AQ-values AQ_0, and the number m of ants and the choice of their starting city $r_{k\text{-initial}}$. Moreover, some structural characteristics like the state transition rule (1), the chosen heuristic function, and the kind of global reinforcement used, are worth investigating. In this section we discuss some of the most interesting alternative choices.

3.1 Parameters

In the experiments reported in this paper the value of parameters was determined as follows. Each of the parameters was optimized using Ant-Q applied to a set of benchmark problems: grid problems[2], Oliver30 (see for example Whitley, Starkweather and Fuquay, 1989), ry48p (see TSPLIB, in Reinelt, 1994). The experimentally determined best values are δ=1, β=2, q_0=0.9, α=0.1, γ=0.2÷0.6, W=10, AQ_0=1/(average_length_of_edges·n). Regarding the number m of ants and their initial positioning we decided to use m=n ants and to put one ant in each city. Results on the parameters α, γ, q_0, and m are discussed in Section 4.

3.2 Structural Choices

The Ant-Q approach to combinatorial optimization provides a family of algorithms. Members of the family are characterized by: (*i*) the action choice rule, (*ii*) the heuristic used to bias the choice of the next city, and (*iii*) the kind of global reinforcement provided to the system.

(*i*) The action choice rule we use in our experiments, called *pseudo-random-proportional*, is a compromise between the *pseudo-random* action choice rule typically used in Q-learning (with the pseudo-random rule the chosen action is the best one with probability q_0, and a random one with probability 1-q_0), and the *random-proportional* action choice rule typically used in Ant System[3] (with the random-proportional rule the action is chosen randomly with a probability distribution given by the AQ-values). Experiments reported in (Gambardella and Dorigo, 1995) have shown that the pseudo-random-proportional action choice is by far the best choice for Ant-Q algorithms.

(*ii*) A result of our experiments is that the heuristic function *HE* is fundamental in making the algorithm find good solutions in a reasonable time. In fact, if we set β=0 the algorithm does not find any good solution at all. The use of *HE* requires to define its form, which in this paper has been chosen to be the inverse of the distance, and the way in which it is used to direct the search. We chose to multiply *HE* by the corresponding AQ-value, as shown in formulas (1) and (2). This choice was suggested by

---

2 A grid problem is a problem in which cities are evenly distributed on a squared grid.

3 A random-proportional rule is also often used in genetic algorithms to select individuals to reproduce.

the desire of favoring AQ-values belonging to shorter edges; also, it maintained a continuity with our previous work on Ant System; other ways of composing *HE* and *AQ*-values may be worth investigating.

(*iii*) In the experiments presented in this paper only the best performing ant in the current iteration contributes to the global reinforcement. In previous work on Ant System all the ants contributed to the global reinforcement: the contribution of each ant was proportional to how short was its tour. This and other ways to provide reinforcement are discussed in (Gambardella and Dorigo, 1995).

4 Ant-Q: Experimental Study

In this section we experimentally study the functioning of the Ant-Q algorithm. Tests were run on the following problems: 6x6 grid and Oliver30, two TSP problems, and ry48p, an ATSP problem. Each trial was divided into two phases: a learning phase and a test session. The learning phase follows the algorithm reported in Fig. 1, while in the test session the updating of *AQ*-values is switched off and each ant deterministically chooses the arc with the highest *AQ*-value among those leading to a not yet visited city. The result of the trial is given by the performance of the best ant. Each experiment consisted of at least 30 trials, so to have some statistical information. In all experiments of this section the parameters, except when differently indicated, were set to the values reported in Section 3.1.

This section is divided into three parts. First, we study the synergistic effect generated by the use of more than one ant; here we used Oliver30 as a test-bed. Second, we study the behavior of Ant-Q with respect to α, γ, and q_0 again using Oliver30. Last, we repeat a similar study on the ry48p problem. It is important to note that while the 6x6 grid and Oliver30 are relatively simple problems that are easily solved to optimality by many general purpose (like genetic algorithms) and specialized algorithms, ry48p is much more difficult (Fischetti and Toth, 1992; 1994) and the fact that Ant-Q was able to find the optimal value is remarkable and encouraging.

4.1 Multiple Ants: Synergistic Effects

Cooperation between ants is one of the key characteristics of Ant-Q. In this section we show that ants cooperation is essential, and that this cooperation bears a synergistic effect. We show the importance of cooperation by setting δ=0 in formulas (1) and (2): This corresponds to a complete inhibition of communication between ants, which are no longer guided by *AQ*-values. The result is a very low performance level.

To further investigate the existence of synergistic effects, we ran the following experiments: (i) we evaluate the performance of Ant-Q varying the number *m* of ants from 1 to *n*, given a fixed number of iterations (200 iterations per trial); (ii) we evaluate the performance of Ant-Q varying the number of ants from 1 to *n*, given a fixed number of ants tours (6,000 tours per trial). In both experiments in the initialization phase in each city was placed at most one ant. In the first experiment, by fixing the number of iterations we fix the number of times global reinforcement is given, which therefore is independent of the number *m* of ants; on the contrary, the computational effort changes with *m* given that each ant causes the application of formula (3) at each state transition. In the second experiment, we fix the total number of ants tours

(6,000), and therefore the computational effort is independent of the number m of ants; on the contrary, in experiments with fewer ants (that is, with a small m) the trials last a greater number of iterations (the number of iterations is given by $6{,}000/m$) and therefore the number of times that global reinforcement is provided is greater. Results of the first experiment clearly show that, given the same total amount of global reinforcement, the performance of the algorithm increases with the number of ants. In fact, the number of times Ant-Q finds the optimal solution increases with m, as shown in Fig. 2. Moreover, Fig. 3 shows that for all experiments with $m \geq 20$ (with the only exception of m=28) the result of the test session is as good as the best result of the learning phase. This result suggests that for $m \geq 20$ the learnt AQ-values are effectively used by the ants to find short tours.

The second experiment, see Figures 4 and 5, shows that, given the same number of ant tours per trial, which implies a higher number of global reinforcements for trials with lower values of m, the number m of ants used is less important. In fact, the number of optimal values found by the ants is largely independent of m. Nevertheless, Fig. 5 shows that good test session performances where achieved only for high values of m. In particular, the test session solution was much worse than the best solution of the learning phase for most values of $m \leq 20$. These results were confirmed by further experiments run on the ry48p problem.

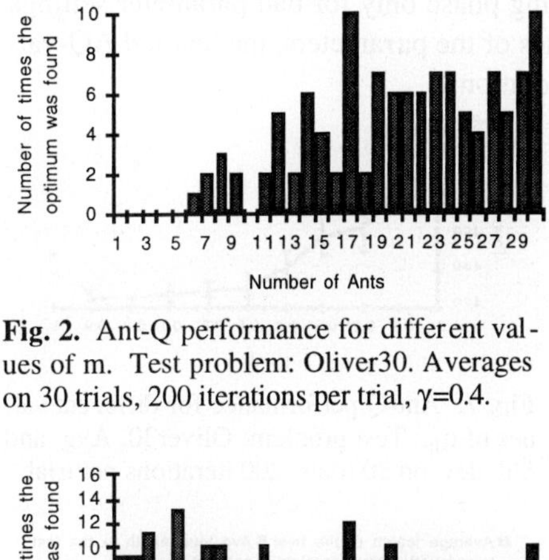

Fig. 2. Ant-Q performance for different values of m. Test problem: Oliver30. Averages on 30 trials, 200 iterations per trial, γ=0.4.

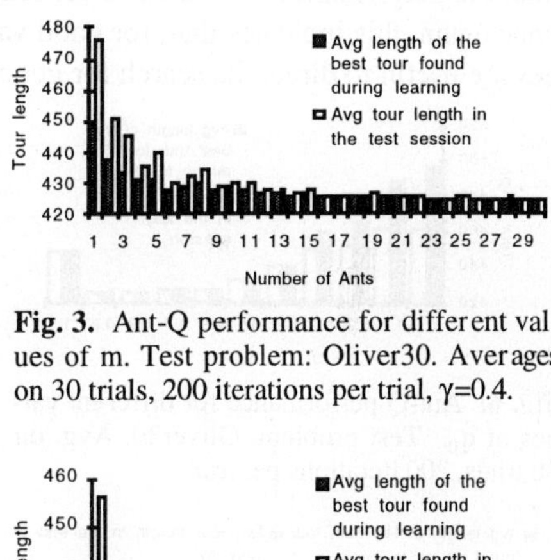

Fig. 3. Ant-Q performance for different values of m. Test problem: Oliver30. Averages on 30 trials, 200 iterations per trial, γ=0.4.

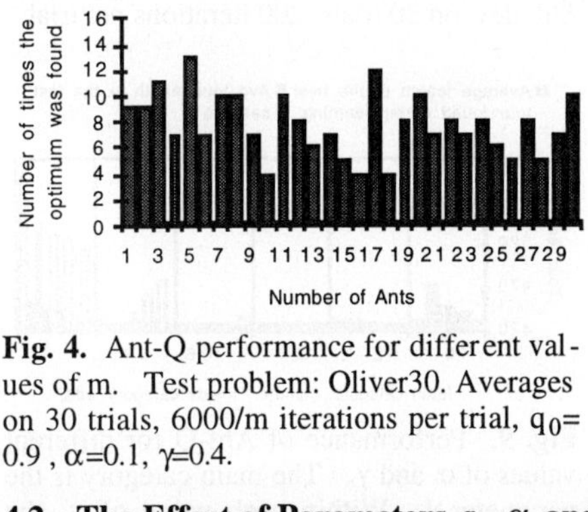

Fig. 4. Ant-Q performance for different values of m. Test problem: Oliver30. Averages on 30 trials, 6000/m iterations per trial, q_0= 0.9 , α=0.1, γ=0.4.

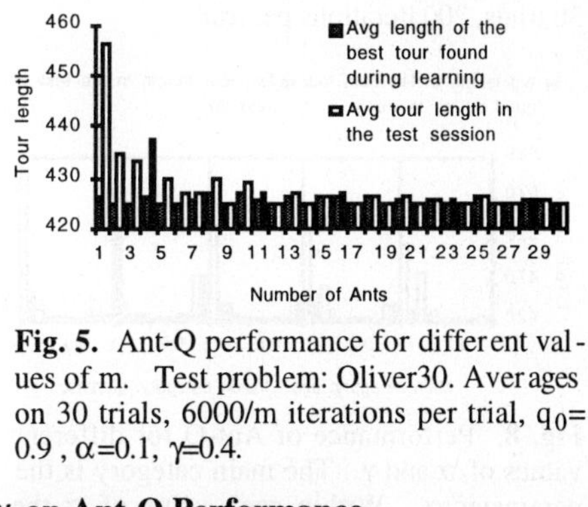

Fig. 5. Ant-Q performance for different values of m. Test problem: Oliver30. Averages on 30 trials, 6000/m iterations per trial, q_0= 0.9 , α=0.1, γ=0.4.

4.2 The Effect of Parameters q_0, α, and γ on Ant-Q Performance

In this section we report the results of some experiments run to evaluate the best value for the following parameters: q_0, α, and γ. Each experiment consists of 30 trials, and each trial was stopped after 200 iterations of the algorithm. In the experiment to evaluate q_0 we set γ=0.4.

In Fig. 6 we show the average length of the best tours found by Ant-Q during the learning phase and in the test session. It is interesting to note that the result of the test session is always equal to or better than the best found solution during learning. This result suggests that the learnt AQ-values are effectively used by the ants to find short tours. Another interesting observation is that the algorithm performance suddenly decreases when q_0 changes from 0.9 to 1. This indicates that exploration is necessary to find good solutions. Ant-Q was able to find the best known solution (423.741) only for $0.6 \le q_0 \le 0.9$, and the best result was obtained with q_0=0.9: in this case Ant-Q found the optimal value 10 times out of 30 trials, with an average number of iterations of 96.6. In Fig. 7 we show the average length of the best tour found by Ant-Q and its standard deviation.

In Figures 8 and 9 we show the behavior of Ant-Q when changing α and γ. These bar graphs show that γ is much more important than α. In particular, good values of γ are found in the range 0.2÷0.6, while the value of α seems to be irrelevant. Further analysis of the results, and in particular of the number of times the algorithm was able to find the optimum, suggested that α=0.1 was the best value for this parameter. An interesting observation is that the performance of Ant-Q in the test session is worse than the performance measured in the learning phase only for bad parameter settings: once again, this indicates that, for good values of the parameters, the learned AQ-values are useful to direct the search for good solutions.

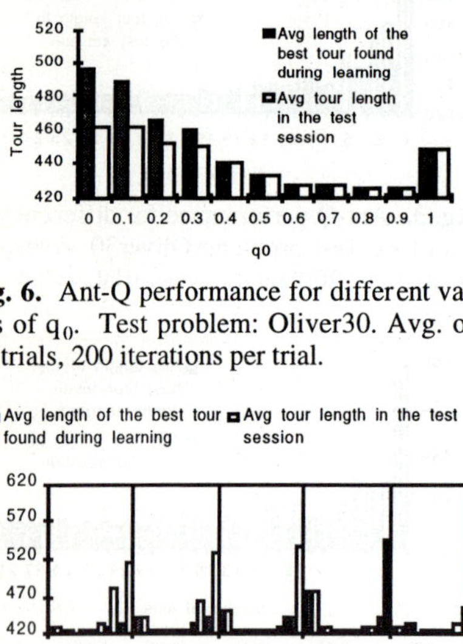

Fig. 6. Ant-Q performance for different values of q_0. Test problem: Oliver30. Avg. on 30 trials, 200 iterations per trial.

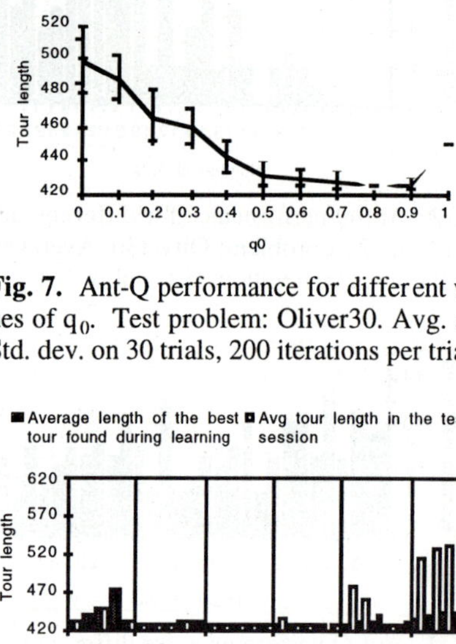

Fig. 7. Ant-Q performance for different values of q_0. Test problem: Oliver30. Avg. and Std. dev. on 30 trials, 200 iterations per trial.

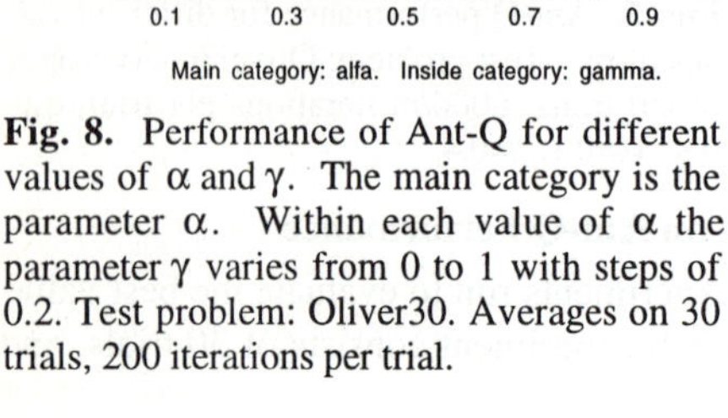

Fig. 8. Performance of Ant-Q for different values of α and γ. The main category is the parameter α. Within each value of α the parameter γ varies from 0 to 1 with steps of 0.2. Test problem: Oliver30. Averages on 30 trials, 200 iterations per trial.

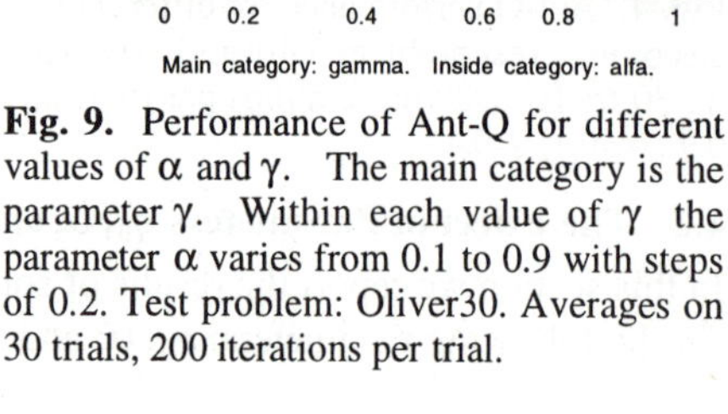

Fig. 9. Performance of Ant-Q for different values of α and γ. The main category is the parameter γ. Within each value of γ the parameter α varies from 0.1 to 0.9 with steps of 0.2. Test problem: Oliver30. Averages on 30 trials, 200 iterations per trial.

4.3 Ant-Q Applied to ry48p

In this last experiment we apply Ant-Q to a rather difficult asymmetric TSP, ry48p. Beside the fact that Ant-Q was able to find the optimal result for this problem, it is interesting to note that the (experimentally obtained) optimal value of most parameters remained the same as for the Oliver30 experiments (this property was found to hold also for a set of experiments run on grid problems whose results are not reported here because of space constraints). In Figures 10 and 11 we report the results of two experiments in which we show the influence that γ and α have on Ant-Q performance. Here the influence of α is higher than in the previous experiment on Oliver30.

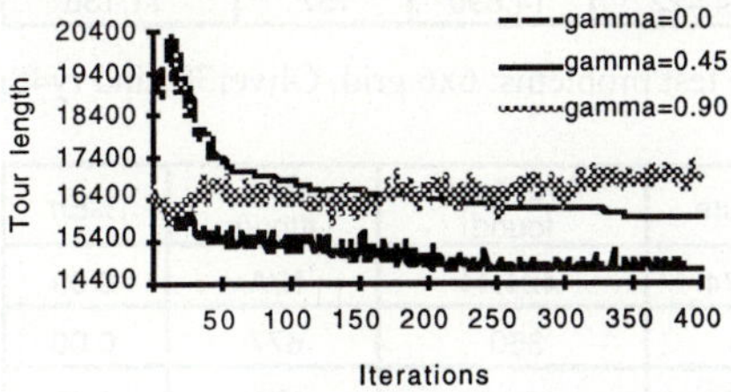

Fig. 10. Performance of Ant-Q for different values of γ. Test problem: ry48p. Averages on 5 trials, 400 iterations per trial.

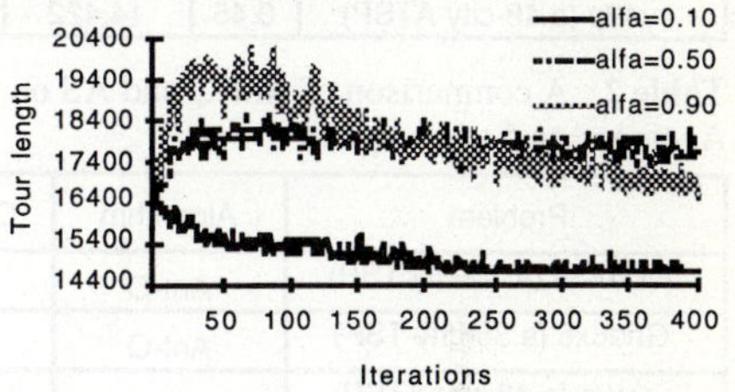

Fig. 11. Performance of Ant-Q for different values of α; γ was set to 0.45. Test problem: ry48p. Avg on 5 trials, 400 iterations per trial.

5 Ant-Q: A Summary of Results

In this section we present a summary of results obtained on some test problems. (Most of the test problems we used can be found in TSPLIB: http://www.iwr.uni-heidelberg.de/iwr/comopt/soft/TSPLIB95/TSPLIB.html.) First, we report detailed results obtained with Ant-Q. For each of three test problems (Oliver30, 6x6 grid, and ry48p), in Table 1 we report the value of parameter γ used by Ant-Q (as always in this section, not tested parameters have the values reported in Section 3.1), the optimal solution, the best solution found by Ant-Q, and the number of tours (that is, the number of iterations of the algorithm multiplied by the number m of ants) it took to find it.

Second, in Table 2 the same three test problems are used to compare Ant System and Ant-Q. We report the optimum, and the average over five trials of the best-found solution, of the number of tours which were necessary to find it (only in case the algorithm always found the optimal solution), and of the error percentage (computed as 100·((Ant-Q_best_result - Optimum)/Optimum)). The main observations are that Ant-Q always outperformed AS, and that Ant-Q was in the average always very close to the optimal solution.

Third, we compare Ant-Q with other approaches using as test problems Eil50, Eil75, and KroA100. We compared ACS with the genetic algorithm (GA), evolutionary programming (EP), and simulated annealing (SA). In Table 3 we report the best integer tour length, the best real tour length (in parentheses) and the number of tours required to find the best integer tour length (in square brackets). Results using EP are from (Fogel, 1993) and those using GA are from (Bersini, Oury and Dorigo, 1995) for KroA100, and from (Whitley, Starkweather and Fuquay, 1989) for Eil50, and Eil75. Results using SA are from (Lin, Kao and Hsu, 1993). Eil50 and Eil75 are from (Eilon, Watson-Gandy and Christofides, 1969), and are included in TSPLIB with an additional city as Eil51.tsp and Eil76.tsp. KroA100 is also in TSPLIB. Results show that the ACS performance is always better than that of the other algorithms: the only case in which EP found a slightly better solution it took a much higher number of tours.

Table 1. Best results obtained by Ant-Q on three test problems: 6x6 grid, Oliver30, and ry48p.

Problem	γ	Optimum	Best-found	Mean	Std.dev.	#tours best-found
Oliver30 (a 30-city TSP)	0.46	423.74	423.74	424.44	0.46	180
6x6 grid (a 36-city TSP)	0.40	360	360	360	0	72
ry48p (a 48-city ATSP)	0.45	14,422	14,422	14,690	157	11,136

Table 2. A comparison of Ant-Q and AS on three test problems: 6x6 grid, Oliver30, and ry48p. Averages on 5 trials, γ=0.4.

Problem	Algorithm	Optimum	Avg. best-found	Avg. #tours	%Err
Oliver30 (a 30-city TSP)	Ant-Q	423.74	424.44	N/A	0.09
Grid6x6 (a 36-city TSP)	Ant-Q	360	360	677	0.00
ry48p (a 48-city ATSP)	Ant-Q	14,422	14,690	N/A	1.47
Oliver30 (a 30-city TSP)	AS	423.74	425.46	N/A	0.41
Grid6x6 (a 36-city TSP)	AS	360	360	2160	0.00
ry48p (a 48-city ATSP)	AS	14,422	14,889	N/A	3.30

Table 3. Comparison of Ant-Q with some others "nature inspired" algorithms. We report the best integer tour length, the best real tour length (in parentheses) and the number of tours required to find the best integer tour length (in square brackets). The best result for each problem is in boldface.

Problem name	Ant-Q	GA	EP	SA
Eil50 (50-city problem)	**426** (428.83) **[10,640]**	428 (N/A) [25,000]	**426** **(427.86)** [100,000]	443 (N/A) [68,512]
Eil75 (75-city problem)	**535** **(542.31)** **[8,970]**	545 (N/A) [80,000]	542 (549.18) [325,000]	580 (N/A) [173,250]
KroA100 (100-city problem)	**21282** **(21,285.44)** **[59,150]**	21761 (N/A) [103,000]	N/A (N/A) [N/A]	N/A (N/A) [N/A]

6 Conclusions

In this paper we studied some aspects of the functioning of Ant-Q, an algorithm belonging to the class of ant colony based search methods, and we presented some interesting computational results (e.g., Ant-Q was able to find the optimal solution of a difficult 48-city ATSP). Current research directions include the study of the meaning of AQ-values, and the identification of the set of problems that can be efficiently solved by Ant-Q.

Acknowledgments

This research has been funded by the Swiss National Science Fund, contract 21–45653.95 titled "Cooperation and learning for combinatorial optimization". Helpful comments were made by Hugues Bersini.

References

Bersini H., C. Oury and M. Dorigo, 1995. Hybridization of genetic algorithms. *Tech. Rep. No. IRIDIA/95-22*, IRIDIA, Université Libre de Bruxelles, Belgium.

Colorni A., M. Dorigo and V. Maniezzo, 1991. Distributed Optimization by Ant Colonies. *Proceedings of ECAL91 - European Conference on Artificial Life*, Paris, France, F.Varela and P.Bourgine (Eds.), Elsevier Publishing, 134–142.

Colorni A., M. Dorigo and V. Maniezzo, 1992. An Investigation of some Properties of an Ant Algorithm. *Proceedings of the Parallel Problem Solving from Nature Conference (PPSN 92)*, Brussels, Belgium, R.Männer and B.Manderick (Eds.), Elsevier Publishing, 509–520.

Dorigo M., 1992. *Optimization, Learning and Natural Algorithms*. Ph.D.Thesis, Politecnico di Milano, Italy. (In Italian.)

Dorigo M., V.Maniezzo and A.Colorni, 1996. The Ant System: Optimization by a colony of cooperating agents. *IEEE Transactions on Systems, Man, and Cybernetics–Part B*, 26, 2, 29–41.

Eilon S., C.D.T. Watson-Gandy and N. Christofides, 1969. Distribution management: mathematical modeling and practical analysis. *Operational Research Quarterly*, 20, 37–53.

Fischetti M. and P.Toth, 1992. An Additive Bounding Procedure for the Asymmetric Travelling Salesman Problem. *Mathematical Programming*, 53, 173–197.

Fischetti M. and P.Toth, 1994. A polyhedral approach for the exact solution of hard ATSP instances. *Tech. Rep. OR-94*, DEIS, Università di Bologna, Italy, April 1994.

Fogel D., 1993. Applying evolutionary programming to selected traveling salesman problems. *Cybernetics and Systems: An International Journal,* 24, 27–36.

Gambardella L. and M. Dorigo, 1995. Ant-Q: A Reinforcement Learning approach to the traveling salesman problem. *Proceedings of ML-95, Twelfth International Conference on Machine Learning,* Tahoe City, CA, A. Prieditis and S. Russell (Eds.), Morgan Kaufmann, 252–260.

Lin F.–T., C.–Y. Kao and C.–C. Hsu, 1993. Applying the genetic approach to simulated annealing in solving some NP-hard problems. *IEEE Transactions on Systems, Man, and Cybernetics,* 23, 1752–1767.

Watkins C.J.C.H., 1989. Learning with delayed rewards. *Ph. D. dissertation*, Psychology Department, University of Cambridge, England.

Whitley D., T. Starkweather and D. Fuquay, 1989. Scheduling Problems and Traveling Salesman: the Genetic Edge Recombination Operator. *Proc. of the Third International Conference on Genetic Algorithms*, Morgan Kaufmann, 133–140.

Immunoid: An Immunological Approach to Decentralized Behavior Arbitration of Autonomous Mobile Robots

Akio ISHIGURO, Toshiyuki KONDO,
Yuji WATANABE and Yoshiki UCHIKAWA

Dept. of Information Electronics, Graduate School of Eng., Nagoya University,
Furo-cho, Chikusa-ku, Nagoya, 464-01, Japan

Abstract. Conventional artificial intelligent (AI) system have been criticized for its brittleness under hostile/dynamic changing environments. Therefore, recently much attention has been focused on the reactive planning systems such as behavior-based AI. However, in the behavior-based AI approaches, how to construct a mechanism that realizes adequate arbitration among competence modules is still an open question. In this paper, we propose a new decentralized consensus-making system inspired from the biological immune system. And we apply our proposed method to behavior arbitration of an autonomous mobile robot as a practical example. To verify the feasibility of our method, we carry out some experiments. In addition, we propose an adaptation mechanism, and try to construct a suitable immune network for adequate action selection.

1 Introduction

In recent years much attention has been focused on *behavior-based artificial intelligence(AI)*, which have already been demonstrated its robustness and flexibility against dynamically changing world[1, 2, 3, 4]. However, in this approach, how to construct a mechanism that adequately arbitrates multiple competence modules (i.e. simple behavior/action) is still an open question.

On the other hand, the immune system has various interesting features such as immunological memory, immunological tolerance, pattern recognition and so on, viewed from the engineering standpoint. Recent studies on immunology have clarified that the immune system plays important roles to maintain its own system against dynamically changing environments (i.e. *anitigens*) through the interaction among *lymphocytes/antibodies*. Therefore, the immune system would be expected to provide a new methodology suitable for dynamic problems dealing with unknown/hostile environments rather than static problems.

Based on the above facts, in this paper, we propose a new decentralized consensus-making system inspired from the biological immune system. We then apply to behavior arbitration of an autonomous mobile robots as a practical example. In order to verify the validity of our proposed method, we perform some experiments. In addition, we try to evolve the proposed artificial immune network using reinforcement signals. Finally, we show an another evolutionary mechanism from the selectionist standpoint.

2 Overview of the biological immune system

For the sake of convenience in the following explanation, we introduce several terminology in immunology. The portion on an antigen recognized by an antibody is called *epitope* (antigen determinant), and the one on the antibody that recognizes the corresponding antigen determinant is called *paratope*. Recent studies on immunology have clarified that each type of antibody also has its specific antigen determinant called *idiotope* (see Fig.1(a)).

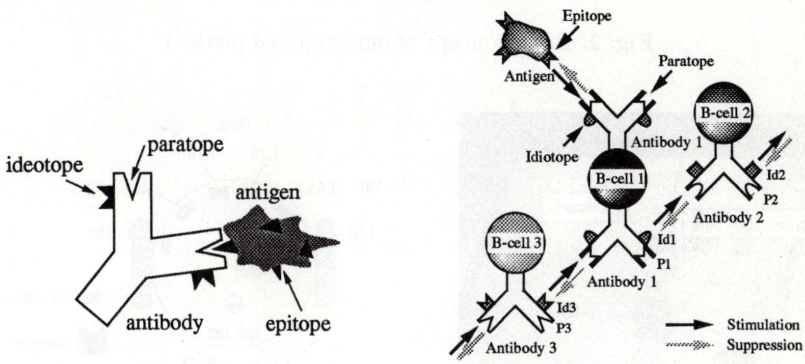

(a) Antigen and antibody. (b) Idiotypic network hypothesis.

Fig. 1. Biological immune system.

Based on this fact, *Jerne* proposed a remarkable hypothesis which he has called the *"idiotypic network hypothesis"*, sometimes called "immune network hypothesis" [8, 9, 10, 11, 12]. This network hypothesis is the concept that antibodies/lymphocytes are not just isolated, namely they are communicating to each other among different species of antibodies/lymphocytes. This idea of *Jerne's* is schematically shown in Fig.1(b).

3 Proposed consensus-making network based on the biological immune system

3.1 Action selection and Immune system

Fig.2 schematically illustrates the action selection system for an autonomous mobile robot in the behavior-based approach and the immune network architecture. As shown in this figure, current situations, for example, distance and direction to the obstacle detected by the installed sensors work as antigens, and a prepared competence module (simple behavior) can be regarded as an antibody (or B-lymphocyte), while the interaction between modules is represented by stimulation and suppression between antibodies. The basic concept of our method is that the immune system equipped with the autonomous mobile robot selects a competence module (antibody) suitable for the detected current situation (antigen) in a bottom-up manner.

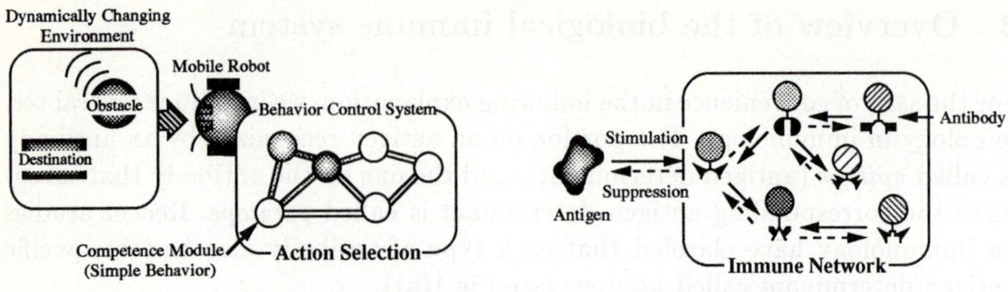

(a) Action selection mechanism. (b) Immune network.

Fig. 2. Basic concept of our proposed method.

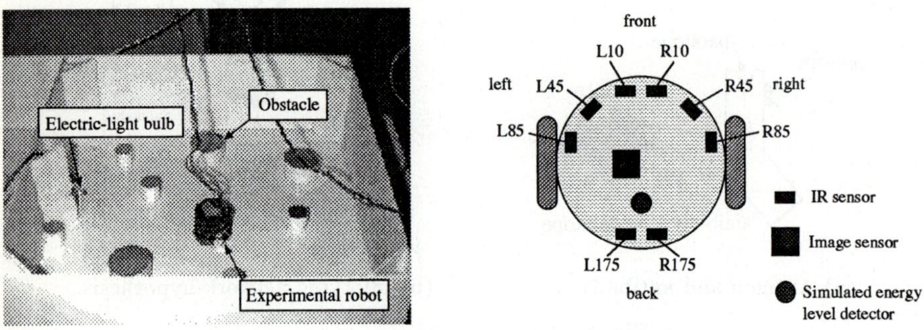

(a) (b)

Fig. 3. Experimental setup.

3.2 Problem

For the ease of the following explanation, we firstly describe the experimental setup used to confirm the ability of an autonomous mobile robot with our proposed immune network-based action selection mechanism (for convenience, dubbed *"immunoid"*). Fig.3(a) shows the experimental setup. The arena is surrounded by white polystyrene walls (approximately 50cm x 50cm), and contains the following two kinds of objects: 1) *multiple obstacles*(movable) and 2) *one charging station*. As seen in the figure, the charging station is represented by an electric-light bulb. And we assume that prespecified quantity of initial energy is given to the immunoid at the beginning of each trial, and the current energy level can be detected by the simulated internal sensor installed in the immunoid.

For quantitative evaluation, we use the following assumptions:

1. if the immunoid moves, it consumes energy due to the *metabolism*.
2. if the immunoid collides with an obstacle, it loses some energy.
3. if the immunoid reaches the charging station, it instantaneously obtains full energy. However, if the energy level of the immunoid is high, `go_to_charging_station` behavior might not emerge to avoid over-charging.

Fig.3(b) indicates the structure of the immunoid used in the experiments. As illustrated in the figure, the immunoid has eight infrared(IR) proximity sensors, one image sensor and one simulated energy level detector. Each IR sensor can detect the existence of obstacles within approximately 3cm. On the other hand, the image sensor can recognize the direction of the charging station within 36 degrees in the front.

3.3 Definition of the antigens and antibodies

In this study, each antigen informs the existence of obstacle, charging station and current energy level. Based on this, we describe the detected antigen in the following manner: *object* (i.e. obstacle or charging station)—*direction* (i.e. front, right, left, back (only obstacle), none), or *current energy level*—*state* (high, low). Note that the concentration of the antigen concerned with the current energy level is varied according to the remaining energy quantity, while those of another antigens are constant.

Next, we explain how we describe an antibody in detail. To make the immunoid select an antibody suitable for the current antigen, we must look carefully into the definition of the antibodies. Moreover, we should notice that our immune-network-based arbitration mechanism selects an antibody in a bottom-up manner by interacting among antibodies. To realize the above requirements, we defined the description of antibodies as follows. As mentioned in the previous section, the identity of each antibody is generally determined by the structure (e.g. molecular shape) of its paratope and idiotope. Fig.4 depicts our proposed definition of antibodies. As depicted in the figure, we assign a pair of desirable condition and the corresponding action to the paratope, and the ID–number of the disallowed antibodies and their degrees of disallowance to the idiotope, respectively. The structure of the desirable condition is the same as the antigen described above.

In addition, for the adequate selection of antibodies, we assign one state variable called *concentration* to each antibody.

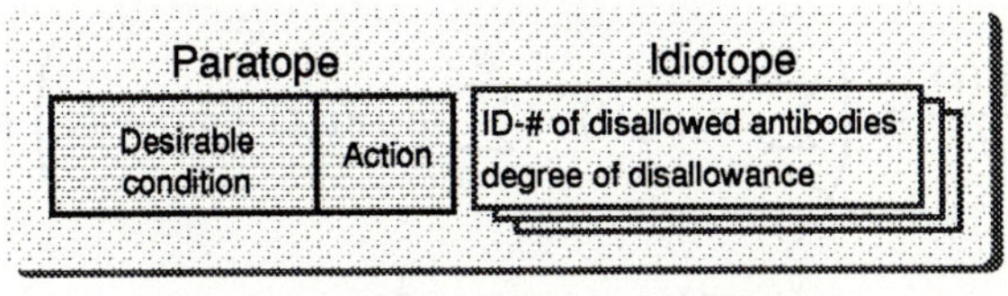

Fig. 4. Definition of the antibody.

3.4 Interaction between antibodies

Next, we explain the basic principle of our immunological consensus-making networks in detail.

For the ease of understanding, we assume that the immunoid is placed in the situation shown in Fig.5 as an example. Suppose that the listed four antibodies are prepared in advance. For example, antibody 1 means that if the immunoid detects the charging station in the right direction, this antibody can be activated and would cause `turn_right` action. However, if the current energy level is high, this antibody would give way to other antibodies represented by its idiotope (in this case, antibody 4) to prevent over-charging.

Now assume that the immunoid has enough energy, antibodies 1, 2 and 4 are stimulated by the antigens. As a result, the concentration of these antibodies increases. However, there are interactions indicated by arrows among the antibodies through their paratopes and idiotopes. Consequently, the concentration of each antibody varies. Finally, antibody 2 will have the highest concentration, and then permitted to be activated.

In the case the immunoid has not enough energy, antibody 1 tends to be selected in the same way.

As observed in this example, the interactions among the antibodies work as a priority adjustment mechanism.

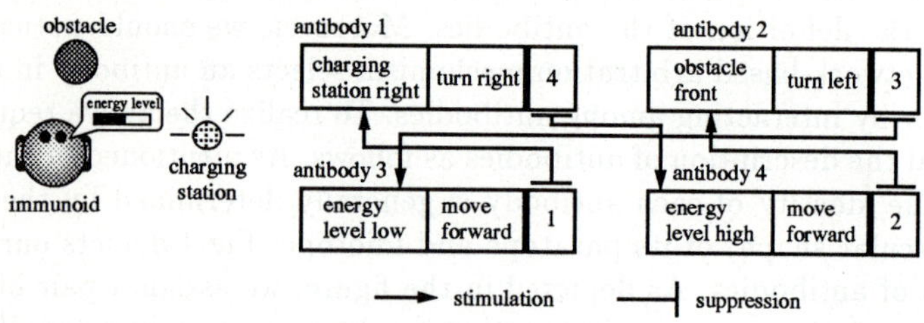

Fig. 5. An example of consensus-making network by interacting among antibodies.

3.5 Dynamics

The concentration of i-th antibody, which is denoted by a_i, is calculated as follows:

$$\frac{dA_i(t)}{dt} = \left(\sum_{j=1}^{N} m_{ji} a_j(t) - \sum_{k=1}^{N} m_{ik} a_k(t) + m_i - k_i \right) a_i(t) \tag{1}$$

$$a_i(t+1) = \frac{1}{1 + \exp(0.5 - A_i(t))} \quad , \tag{2}$$

where, in equation (1), N is the number of antibodies. m_{ji} and m_i denote affinities between antibody j and antibody i (i.e. the degree of disallowance), and antibody i and the detected antigen, respectively. Equation (2) is a squashing function used to ensure the stability of the concentration. In this study, selection of antibodies is simply carried out by a *roulette-wheel selection* based on the concentrations of the antibodies.

3.6 Results

To verify the feasibility of our proposed method, we carried out some experiments. As a rudimentary stage of investigation, we prepared 18 antibodies of which paratope and idiotope are described a priori (Fig.6). In the figure, note that the degrees of disallowances are omitted in each idiotope for lack of space. At the beginning of the experiments, we equipped the immunoid with the maximum energy level (i.e. 200). Obtained results are as follows: while the energy level is enough, the immunoid moves around the arena avoiding obstacles. As the remaining energy runs out, the immunoid tends to select an antibodies concerned with `go_to_charging_station` and/or `search_for_charging_station` behaviors. After successful reaching the station, the immunoid starts to move around again. Such a regular behavior could be frequently observed in the experiments.

In order to evaluate the arbitration ability of our proposed mechanism, we furthermore carried out simple experiments by varying the remaining energy level. Fig.7(a) depicts the initial position of the immunoid. As shown in the figure, in this situation, both the obstacles and the charging station exist in the front of the immunoid. Fig.7(b), (c) and (d) are the resultant trajectories of the immunoid in the case where the initial energy level is set to 200 (maximum), 80 and 60, respectively. Fig.8(a), (b) and (c) shows the transition of the concentrations ofthe prepared antibodies under the same conditions of Fig.7, respectively. In case 1, it can been seen that the immunoid mainly pays attention to avoiding obstacles since the concentration of the antigen concerned with energy level high is higher than that of energy level low. In case 2, the immunoid firstly tries to avoid obstacles and then shifts to `go_to_charging_station` behavior. In case 3, due to the critical energy level, the immunoid thrusts its way through the obstacles and goes straight to the charging station. From these results, in spite of the simple experiments, it is understood that the immunoid selects an action (antibody) according to the current situation (antigen) by flexibly changing the priorities of the prepared competence modules.

4 Adaptation mechanisms

For more usefulness, as some researchers have been pointed out, the introduction of some adaptation mechanisms is highly indispensable. Adaptation mechanism is generally classified into two types: *adjustment* and *innovation* [13, 14, 15]. In the followings, we propose an adjustment mechanism suitable for the proposed system, and show a possible/promising innovation mechanism.

4.1 Adjustment mechanism

For an adequate consensus-making, it is necessary to appropriately determine the disallowed antibody and its degree of disallowance m_{ij}, i.e. priorities among antibodies. To realize this aim, we propose an on-line adaptation mechanism using the advantages of the prementioned description of antibodies. Additionally,

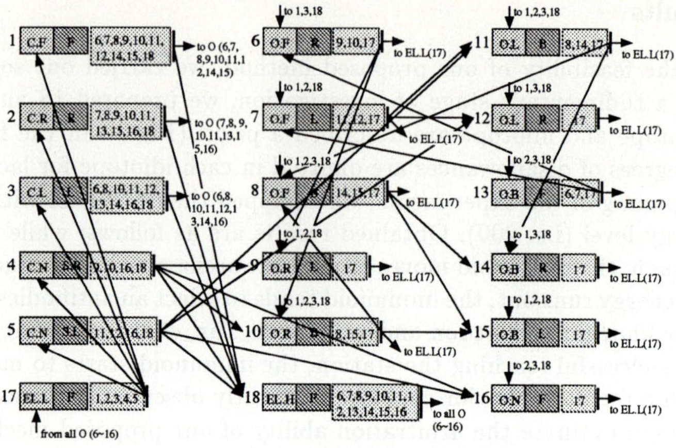

Fig. 6. Prepared immune network.

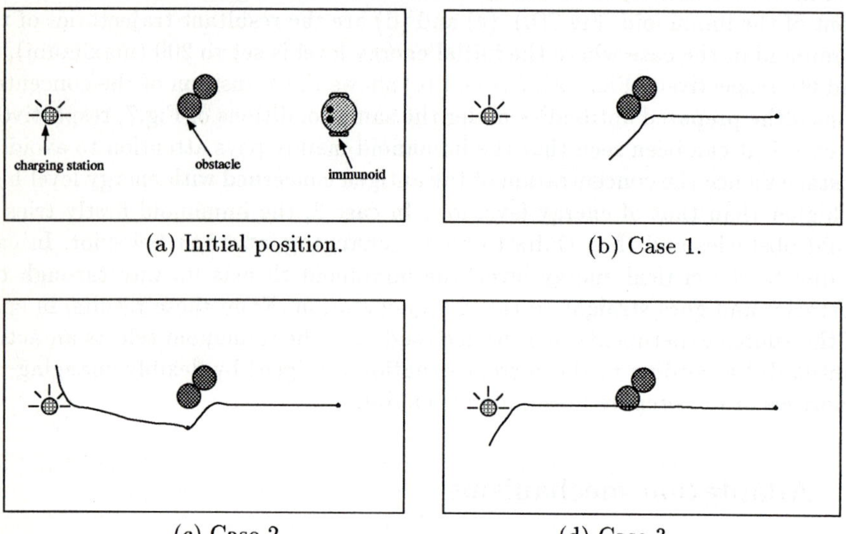

(a) Initial position.

(b) Case 1.

(c) Case 2.

(d) Case 3.

Fig. 7. Experimental results.

it is desired that this mechanism can even work under the situation where the idiotopes of the prepared antibodies are initially *tabula rasa* through the obtained reinforcement signals.

For the ease of the following explanation, we assume that antigen 1 and 2 invade into the immunoid's interior (see Fig.9(a)). In this example, antibody 1 (Ab_1) and 2 (Ab_2) are simultaneously stimulated by each antigen. Consequently, the concentration of each antibody increases. However, since the priority between Ab_1 and 2 is unknown (because idiotopes are initially *tabula rasa*, there are

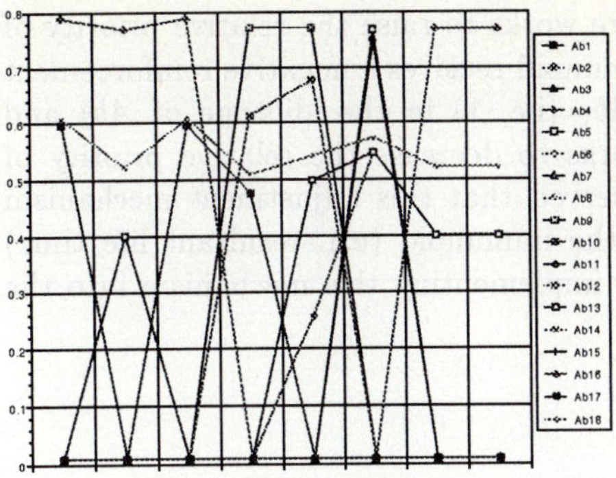

(a) Case 1.

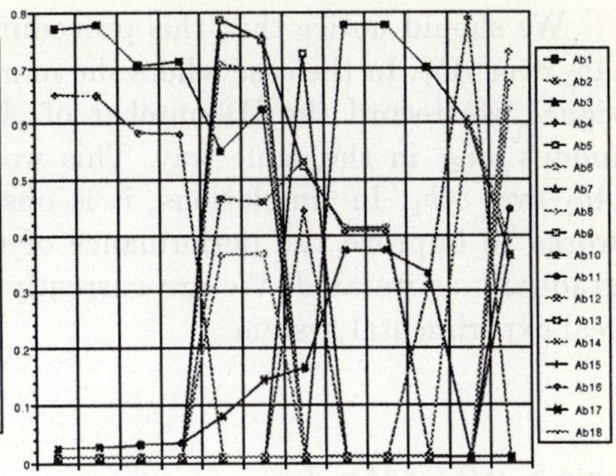

(b) Case 2.

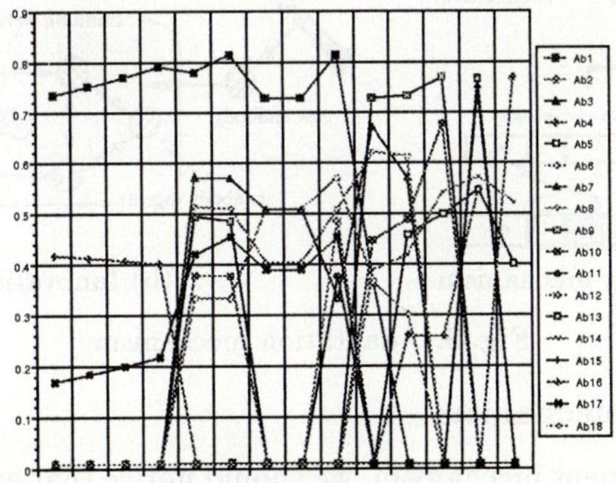

(c) Case 3.

Fig. 8. Transition of the concentrations of the antibodies.

no stimulation/suppression chain), in this case, either of them can be selected randomly.

Now, assuming that the immunoid randomly selects Ab_2 and then receives a positive reinforcement signals as a reward. To make the immunoid tend to select Ab_2 under the same or similar antigens(situation), we record the ID-number of Ab_2 (i.e. 2) in the idiotope of Ab_1 and increase a degree of disallowance m_{12}. In this study, we simply modify the degree of disallowance as:

$$m_{12} = \frac{T_p^{Ab_1} + T_r^{Ab_2}}{T_{Ab_2}^{Ab_1}} \tag{3}$$

$$m_{21} = \frac{T_r^{Ab_1} + T_p^{Ab_2}}{T_{Ab_2}^{Ab_1}}, \tag{4}$$

where $T_p^{Ab_1}$ and $T_r^{Ab_1}$ represents the number of times of receiving penalty and reward signal when Ab_1 is selected. $T_{Ab_2}^{Ab_1}$ denotes the number of times when both Ab_1 and Ab_2 are reacting to their specific antigens.

We should notice that this procedure works to raise the relative priority of Ab_2 over Ab_1. In the case where the immunoid receives a negative reinforcement signal, we record the ID–number of Ab_1 (i.e. 1) in the idiotope of Ab_2 and modify m_{21} in the same way. This works to decrease the relative priority of Ab_2 over Ab_1. In simulations, it is observed that this adjustment mechanism works to improve the performance of the immunoid (e.g. resultant life time) gradually as iterated. We are currently implementing this mechanism into the real experimental system.

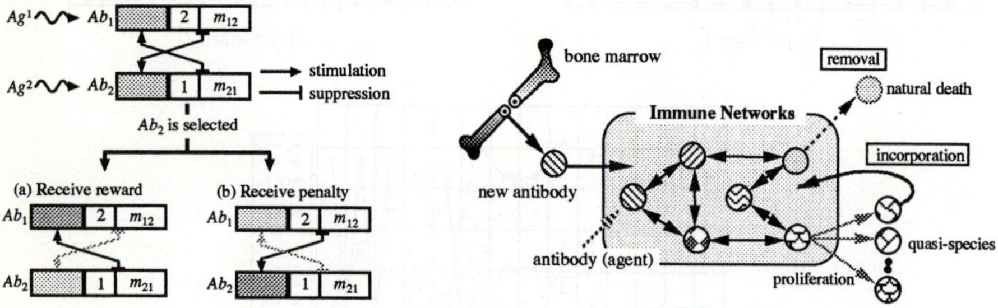

(a) Adjustment mechanism. (b) Innovation mechanism.

Fig. 9. Adaptation mechanism.

4.2 Innovation mechanism

In the above adjustment mechanism, we should notice that we must still describe the paratope of each antibody in a top-down manner. One obvious and promising candidate to avoid such difficulties is to combine an innovation mechanism with the proposed adjustment mechanism. In the biological immune system, the *metadynamics function* can be instantiated as an innovation mechanism. The metadynamics function works to maintain adequate repertoire of antibodies by incorporating new types (these are generally generated as *quasi-species* through the proliferation process of the activated antibodies) and removing useless ones. Fig.9(b) schematically shows the concept of the metadynamics function. Incorporating this mechanism is currently under investigation.

5 Conclusions and Further work

In this paper, we proposed a new decentralized consensus-making mechanism based on the biological immune system and confirmed the validity of our proposed system by applying to an action arbitration for an autonomous mobile robot as a practical example. And we showed an adaptation mechanism for an adequate arbitration using reinforcement signals.

Since this study is still in a rudimentary stage of investigation, we designed antibodies a priori in a top-down manner. For more usefulness, we must clarify how to combine the proposed adjustment and innovation mechanisms. This is currently undertaking.

Acknowledgments

This research was supported in part by Grant-Aid for Scientific Research on Priority Areas from the Japanese Ministry of Education, Science, Sports and Culture (No. 07243208).

References

1. R.Brooks: *"A Robust Layered Control System for a Mobile Robot"*, IEEE Journal of R&A, Vol.2, No.1 (1986) 14–23
2. R.Brooks: *"Intelligence without reason"*, Proc. of IJCAI–91 (1991) 569–595
3. P.Maes: *"The dynamic action selection"*, Proc. of IJCAI–89 (1989) 991–997
4. P.Maes: *"Situated agent can have goals"*, Designing Autonomous Agents, MIT Press (1991) 49–70
5. A. Ishiguro, S. Ichikawa and Y. Uchikawa: *"A Gait Acquisition of 6-Legged Walking Robot Using Immune Networks"*, Journal of Robotics Society of Japan, Vol.13, No.3 (1995) 125–128 (in Japanese), also in Proc. of IROS '94, Vol.2 (1994) 1034–1041
6. A. Ishiguro, Y. Watanabe and Y. Uchikawa: *"An Immunological Approach to Dynamic Behavior Control for Autonomous Mobile Robots"*, in Proc. of IROS '95, Vol.1 (1995) 495–500
7. A. Ishiguro, T.Kondo, Y. Watanabe and Y. Uchikawa: *"Dynamic Behavior Arbitration of Autonomous Mobile Robots Using Immune Networks"*, in Proc. of ICEC'95, Vol.2 (1995) 722–727
8. H.Fujita and K.Aihara: *"A distributed surveillance and protection system in living organisms"*, Trans. on IEE Japan, Vol. 107–C, No.11 (1987) 1042–1048 (in Japanese)
9. J.D.Farmer, N.H.Packard and A.S.Perelson: *"The immune system, adaptation, and machine learning"*, Physica **22D** (1986) 187–204
10. N.K.Jerne: *"The immune system"*, ScientificAmerican, Vol.229, No.1 (1973) 52–60
11. N.K.Jerne: *"The generative grammar of the immune system"*, EMBO Journal, Vol.4, No.4 (1985)
12. N.K.Jerne: *"Idiotypic networks and other preconceived ideas"*, Immunological Rev., Vol.79 (1984) 5–24
13. H.Bersini and F.Varela: *"The Immune Learning Mechanisms: Reinforcement, Recruitment and their Applications"*, Technical Report, IRIDIA (1993)
14. B.Manderick: *"The importance of selectionist systems for cognition"*, in R.Paton(ed.) Computing with Biological Metaphors, Chapman & Hall (1994)
15. J.D.Farmer, S.A.Kauffman, N.H.Packard and A.S.Perelson: *"Adaptive Dynamic Networks as Models for the Immune System and Autocatalytic Sets"*, Technical Report LA–UR–86–3287, Los Alamos National Laboratory, Los Alamos, NM (1986)

Parallelizable Evolutionary Dynamics Principles for Solving the Maximum Clique Problem

Marcello Pelillo [1] and Immanuel M. Bomze [2]

[1] *Dipartimento di Matematica Applicata e Informatica*
Università "Ca' Foscari" di Venezia
Via Torino 155, 30173 Venezia Mestre, Italy

[2] *Institut für Statistik, Operations Research und Computerverfahren*
Universität Wien
Universitätsstraße 5, A-1010 Wien, Austria

Abstract

An algorithm for approximately solving the maximum clique is presented which uses relaxation labeling neural network techniques, focusing on the continuous problem formulation: maximize a quadratic form over the standard simplex. We employ somewhat surprising connections of the latter problem with dynamic principles of evolutionary game theory, and give a detailed report on our numerical experiences with the method proposed.

1 Introduction

During the last 30 years, many algorithms have been created by analogies to natural processes. The practical interest of these has increased considerably by the emergence of massively parallel computers. The most commonly known procedures in this class include evolutionary programming, genetic algorithms, evolution strategies, simulated annealing, classifier systems, and neural networks. In this paper, we show how simple dynamical equations developed to model evolutionary processes on a (population) genetic level, and surprisingly related to certain relaxation labeling techniques widely employed in machine vision, are capable of approximately solving the maximum clique problem (MCP), a well-known *NP*-hard optimization problem [11] which is computationally intractable even to approximate well [24]. The problem is frequently encountered in such diverse domains as cluster analysis, information retrieval, computer vision, and experimental design, to name just a few, and turns out to be intimately related to a number of other difficult graph problems. Although the proposed method is different, the articles within the abundant literature which seem to be most closely related are [7, 22]. The reverse research direction, namely optimization approaches to biological modeling is covered, e.g., by [2, 13].

A wide variety of algorithms have been proposed to solve the MCP, and the literature on this subject has now grown considerably. An up-to-date review (with 260 references) has recently been offered by Pardalos and Xue [24]. The approach described in this paper is based on a result due to Motzkin and Straus [21] which allows us to formulate the MCP as a continuous optimization problem with linear constraints, a problem that is then naturally mapped onto a relaxation labeling neural network. We present results over graphs with as many as 2000 vertices and about one million edges. The computational time required to complete a single run of our algorithm over one such graph was approximately 30 minutes on a SparcStation 10. Moreover, because of its inherent massive parallelism, the overall computational time can be dramatically reduced, if the algorithm is implemented on a parallel machine (see [18] and references therein for practical parallel implementations of this kind of algorithms). One distinctive feature of our algorithm is that, unlike most neural-style clique finding models, it is completely devoid of operational parameters which typically require a lengthy, problem-dependent tuning phase, and this makes the model extremely simple to implement and use.

2 Evolutionary approach to quadratic programming on the standard simplex

Consider the following quadratic optimization problem

$$\begin{array}{ll} \text{maximize} & x'Ax \\ \text{subject to} & x \in S^n \end{array} \tag{1}$$

where a $'$ denotes transposition, A is an arbitrary symmetric $n \times n$ matrix, and S^n is the standard simplex in n-dimensional Euclidean space $\mathbb{R}^n$:

$$S^n = \{x \in \mathbb{R}^n : x_i \geq 0 \text{ for all } i = 1 \ldots n, \text{ and } e'x = 1\} \ .$$

Here and in the sequel, the letter e is reserved for a vector of appropriate length, consisting of unit entries exclusively. Note that the maximizers of (1) remain the same if A is replaced with $A + \gamma ee'$ where γ is an arbitrary constant. So without loss of generality we assume henceforth that all entries of A are positive.

Quadratic optimization problems like (1) are *NP*-hard, so the challenging task remains to devise algorithms for solving them. The procedure proposed in this paper will generate a local solution of (1) quite quickly; in a second step one then has to escape from an inefficient local maximizer in a way such that improvement in the objective is guaranteed [3].

Most of the following results seem to be folklore in theoretical biology [20] and evolutionary game theory [29], but appear to be somehow scattered in the literature. Proofs with an optimization theory flavor can be found in [3] with the exception of the convergence result in Theorem 1 below which goes back to [19].

To formulate the results, we need some notions and notations. First, consider the *generalized Lagrangian* $L(x;\lambda,\mu) = \frac{1}{2}x'Ax + \lambda'x + \mu(e'x-1)$ of problem (1) where the multipliers λ_i and μ may have arbitrary sign. Call a critical point x of the generalized Lagrangian a *generalized* Karush-Kuhn-Tucker point if $L(x;\lambda,\mu) = \frac{1}{2}x'Ax$ irrespective of the sign of λ_i.

Next recall that a point $x \in S^n$ is said to be a *(symmetric) Nash (equilibrium) strategy* if and only if $y'Ax \le x'Ax$ for all $y \in S^n$. Furthermore, a Nash strategy x is said to be a *neutrally stable strategy* (NSS) if and only if

$$y'Ax = x'Ax \quad \text{implies} \quad x'Ay \ge y'Ay \,, \tag{2}$$

and an *evolutionarily stable strategy* (ESS) if and only if the inequality in (2) is strict for $y \ne x$.

Finally, consider the following dynamical systems which operate on S^n:

$$\dot{x}_i(t) = x_i(t)[(Ax(t))_i - x(t)'Ax(t)]\,, \quad i = 1\ldots n \tag{3}$$

where a dot signifies derivative w.r.t. time t, and a discrete time version

$$x_i(t+1) = x_i(t)\frac{(Ax(t))_i}{x(t)'Ax(t)}\,, \quad i = 1\ldots n\,. \tag{4}$$

The *stationary points* under these dynamics, i.e. the points satisfying $\dot{x}_i(t) = 0$ for (3) or $x_i(t+1) = x_i(t)$ for (4), are the solutions of the equations

$$x_i[(Ax)_i - x'Ax] = 0\,, \quad i = 1\ldots n\,. \tag{5}$$

Hence the stationary points for both dynamics coincide, and it will turn out below that all local solutions of (1) are among these. Of course, there are quite many stationary points, e.g., all vertices. However, only those which can be approximated by all nearby starting trajectories are serious candidates for strict local solutions: a stationary point x is said to be *asymptotically stable* if every solution to (3) or (4) which starts close enough to x, will converge to x as $t \to \infty$.

We note that the preceding equations can easily be implemented in a parallel relaxation network of n locally-interacting computational units, the strength of the connection from unit i to unit j being simply the (i,j) entry of the matrix A, i.e., a_{ij}. Let $x_i(t)$ represent the state of unit i at time t, and define the state of the network as a whole at time t to be the n-vector $x(t) = (x_1(t),\cdots,x_n(t))'$. The system starts out with an initial state vector $x(0)$ and iteratively and synchronously updates its own state according to the replicator dynamical equations (3) or (4), until convergence to a stationary point. In practical computer implementations it is customary to prefer the discrete time version (4).

Both (3) and (4) are called *replicator dynamics* in theoretical biology, since they are used to model evolution over time of relative frequencies $x_i(t)$ of interacting, self-replicating entities. Equation (3) has been introduced in [28] to model evolution of behavior in intraspecific conflicts under random pairwise mating in a large, ideally infinite population. It formalizes the idea that the growth rates $\dot{x}_i/x_i$ of relative frequency x_i of the i-th behavior pattern $(i = 1 \ldots n)$ is equal to the (dis)advantage $(Ax)_i - x'Ax = \sum_j a_{ij}x_j - \sum_{j,k} x_k a_{kj} x_j$, measured by incremental fitness relative to the average performance within the population in state $x = (x_1, \cdots, x_n)'$. Here a_{ij} denotes incremental individual fitness attributed to an i–individual when encountering a j-individual, and $A = [a_{ij}]$ is the resulting fitness matrix. The behavior patterns $i \in \{1, \cdots, n\}$ are often called "pure strategies" in evolutionary game theory, in which context the interaction matrix A is also termed "payoff matrix."

Similar arguments provide a rationale for the discrete time version (4). This dynamics corresponds also to a particular instance of a general parallel relaxation algorithm widely popular in computer vision. The model was introduced heuristically by Rosenfeld *et al.* [27] to solve certain labeling problems arising in the 3-D interpretation of ambiguous line drawings, and have since found applications in a variety of practical tasks. The theory of these *relaxation labeling* processes has later been developed by Hummel and Zucker [15], and the heuristic original model has recently been the subject of a thorough theoretical analysis [25]. These discrete dynamical equations can also be regarded as a very special case of a general class of dynamical systems studied in [1].

The same dynamics (3, 4) arise in population genetics under the name *selection equations* in a model assuming separate (non-overlapping) generations, large population size, random union of gametes, and a selection acting only upon one chromosomal locus through different viabilities (i.e., survival probabilities), given by the the fitness matrix A of the genotypes, i.e., pairs of genes drawn from a set $\{1, \cdots, n\}$ of alleles for a single chromosomal locus. Here x_i is the gene frequency of the i-th allele. Obviously the matrix A is in this context always symmetric, since permuted gene pairs belong to the same genotype. The models (4) and (3) as selection equations go way back to Fisher [10] and Kimura [17].

From an optimization point of view, the difference between symmetric and non-symmetric matrices A is also crucial. Indeed, in the symmetric case the quadratic form $x(t)'Ax(t)$ is increasing along trajectories of the replicator dynamics; this is the Fundamental Theorem of Selection, see, e.g. [9, 14].

Theorem 1 *If $A = A'$ then the function $x(t)'Ax(t)$ is strictly increasing with increasing t along any non-stationary trajectory $x(t)$ under both continuous time (3) and discrete time (4) replicator dynamics. Furthermore, any such trajectory converges to a stationary point.*

Under replicator dynamics in continuous time, the trajectory approaches its limit most efficiently in the sense that (3) is a gradient system if one uses the (non-Euclidean) Shahshahani metric [14], which for any point $p \in S^n$ is defined by

$$d_p(x, y) = \sum_{i:p_i>0} x_i y_i / p_i \,, \quad x, y \in S^n \,.$$

This efficiency result is called Kimura's maximum principle.

Now we provide the characterization results which links three different fields: optimization theory, evolutionary game theory, and qualitative theory of dynamical systems.

Theorem 2 *Let $A = A'$ be an arbitrary symmetric $n \times n$ matrix and $x \in S^n$. Consider the following properties:*

(a1) x is an evolutionarily stable strategy;
(a2) x is a strict local solution of (1);
(a3) x is an asymptotically stable stationary point of (3) and (4);
(b1) x is a neutrally stable strategy;
(b2) x is a local solution of (1);
(c1) x is a Nash strategy;
(c2) x is a Karush-Kuhn-Tucker point for (1);
(d1) x is a stationary point under (3) or (4), i.e., satisfies (5);
(d2) x is a generalized Karush-Kuhn-Tucker point for (1).
Then (a1) $\Leftrightarrow$ (a2) $\Leftrightarrow$ (a3) $\Rightarrow$ (b1) $\Leftrightarrow$ (b2) $\Rightarrow$ (c1) $\Leftrightarrow$ (c2) $\Rightarrow$ (d1) $\Leftrightarrow$ (d2).

From Theorem 1 we know that the replicator dynamical system, starting from an arbitrary initial state $x(0)$, will iteratively maximize the function $x'Ax$ over the simplex S^n. Due to Theorem 2, the iterates $x(t)$ will eventually approach a stationary point x^* which is a strict local maximizer of problem (1) with probability one. Note that strictness will play an important role in the representation theorem (Theorem 3) below. To escape from an inefficient local maximizer one could use the method proposed in [3], but this is beyond the scope of this article.

3 Evolution towards the maximum clique

Let $G = (V, E)$ be an undirected graph, where $V = \{1, \cdots, n\}$ is the set of vertices, and $E \subseteq V \times V$ is the set of edges. We will assume that the graph has no loops, i.e., $(i, i) \notin E$ for all $i \in V$. A *clique* of G is a subset of V in which every pair of vertices is connected by an edge. A clique is called *maximal* if no strict superset of C is a clique; i.e., no vertex external to C can be connected with more than $|C| - 1$ vertices of C. A clique C is called *strictly maximal* if every vertex external to C is connected with even less than $|C| - 1$ vertices of C. A *maximum* clique is a clique having largest cardinality (note that a maximal clique is not necessarily a maximum one). Hence, the MCP consists of finding a clique of maximum size of a graph G. In the following, given a set S of vertices in G, we will denote by x^s its characteristic vector, defined as $x_i^s = 1/|S|$ if $i \in S$ and $x_i^s = 0$ otherwise, where $|S|$ denotes the cardinality of S.

Given a graph G, consider the following quadratic program

$$\begin{array}{ll} \text{maximize} & f(x) = x' A_g x \\ \text{subject to} & x \in S^n \end{array} \tag{6}$$

where $A_g = (a_{ij})$ is the adjacency matrix of G (i.e., $a_{ij} = 1$ if $(i, j) \in E$, and $a_{ij} = 0$ if $(i, j) \notin E$).

The following theorem expands on a remarkable result due to Motzkin and Straus [21] (see [26, 12] for proof). It relates local and global maxima of (6) to maximal and maximum cliques of G in the following way:

Theorem 3 *Let C be a subset of vertices of a graph G, and let x^c be its characteristic vector.*

(a) C is a maximum clique of G if and only if x^c is a global solution of (6). Its size is then given by $k = 1/(1-\alpha)$ where $\alpha = f(x^c)$.

(b) If C is a maximal clique of G, then its characteristic vector x^c is a local solution of (6).

(c) If x^c is a strict local solution of (6), then C is a strictly maximal clique of G.

Note that the Motzkin-Straus result provides us with a method to solve the "evaluation" version of the MCP, i.e., given a graph determine the *size* of its maximum clique (not the clique itself): this can be accomplished by maximizing in S^n the polynomial f, and then applying Theorem 3. We note that this problem formulation is essentially equivalent to its original "optimization" counterpart. Straightforward recursive or iterative procedures are in fact available to determine the vertices comprising the maximum clique once we have a means to compute its size [23].

The computational significance of the previous result is that if the (strictly local or global) maximum of f over S^n is attained at a point x^* of the form $x_i^* = 1/k$ if $i \in C$ and $x_i^* = 0$ if $i \notin C$, for some subset C of vertices, then we can say that C is a maximal or maximum clique of G. In this case, we need not resort to such iterative procedures to derive the vertices of the maximum clique, since they are directly encoded into x^* itself. Note that, in general, maximizer of (6) do not necessarily correspond to maximal cliques, i.e., they may well be non-characteristic vectors. This was earlier observed by Pardalos and Phillips [23], and has recently been formalized by Pelillo and Jagota [26], who showed that problem (6) can have in fact infinitely many such "spurious" solutions. One possible approach to avoid spurious solutions is to regularize the objective function by adding some penalty terms, e.g. to use $A_g + \frac{1}{2}I$ instead of A_g in (6). This regularization goes back to Comtet [8] and is used in [3, 4] to obtain the maximal cliques directly.

Once that the MCP is formulated in terms of maximizing a quadratic polynomial over S^n, the use of the previously defined replicator model immediately suggests itself. In this case, the model will have as many behavior patterns as there are vertices in G, and the (symmetric and nonnegative) fitness matrix given by

$$A = A_g \tag{7}$$

where A_g is the adjacency matrix of G.

The solution obtained using the replicator process can then be employed to get an estimate of the *size* of the maximum, as seen in Theorem 3. Note that, since the algorithm essentially performs a gradient ascent search in S^n, we are not in principle guaranteed that it will eventually converge to a global maximum of (6). In the light of the preceding results, therefore, what we can say is that the process can find only maximal cliques of G, hoping they have a large size. This is a common feature of most heuristic clique finding procedures [24]. Using an escape procedure like in [3] one can then try to improve the cliques obtained.

4 Experimental results

In order to assess the effectiveness of the proposed clique finding model, extensive simulations were carried out over randomly generated graphs of various sizes and densities.[1] The experiments were conducted using the discrete time version (4) of the replicator equations. In the first part of this study, we considered graphs with a relatively small number of vertices, i.e., with up to 500 vertices and over 60,000 edges. This allowed us to compare our results with those obtained using well-known exact clique finding algorithms. In particular, the Bron-Kerbosch (BK) backtracking-based procedure [5], and the partially enumerative algorithm developed by Carraghan and Pardalos (CP) [6] were employed for comparison. We found the BK algorithm attractive because it is able to generate *all* cliques of a graph, and this allowed us to better understand certain phenomena associated with our replicator model. When the computational time of BK became prohibitively long, we resorted to the CP algorithm, which is considerably faster than BK, but finds just *one* maximum clique.

The sizes considered in this series of experiments were $n = 10, 25, 50, 75, 100, 250, 500$ and the densities were $\delta = 0.10, 0.25, 0.50, 0.75, 0.90$. Indeed, for 250- and 500-vertex graphs the densities 0.75 and 0.90 were excluded, because even the CP algorithm became excessively slow in these cases. For each pair (n, δ), 100 different graphs with n vertices and approximate density δ were obtained so that, overall, 3100 graphs were employed. For each of them, the corresponding replicator network was constructed as described in the previous section and then run by starting the process from the vector $x(0) = (1/n, \cdots, 1/n)'$, which corresponds to the center of the domain S^n. To get a high-precision final solution, the process was allowed to iterate until the (squared) distance between two successive states became smaller than 10^{-10}. Each of the 3100 graphs were also given as input to the BK/CP algorithms in order to determine its actual maximum clique size k. Specifically, the BK algorithm was run over all graphs whose size n was less than or equal to 100; the exception was the 100-vertex 0.90-density case where, for reasons of computational expediency, we resorted to the CP algorithm. The CP algorithm was also employed for all 250- and 500-vertex graphs.

The results of the simulations are summarized in Table 1 which contains, for each n and δ, the average clique sizes found by both the replicator and the BK/CP algorithms. The entries are of the form k_{repl}/k_{opt}, where k_{repl} and k_{opt} denote the average maximum clique size found by the replicator process and the BK/CP algorithms, respectively. As can be seen, the replicator model, despite its inability to escape from local optima, did a good job of approximating the

[1] The density δ of a graph G with n vertices is defined to be the ratio between the number of edges in G and $\binom{n}{2}$.

Table 1: Average clique sizes found by replicator (left) and BK/CP algorithms (right)

δ / n	0.10	0.25	0.50	0.75	0.90
10	2.10/2.10	2.70/2.70	3.57/3.57	4.93/4.93	6.07/6.07
25	2.85/2.85	3.79/3.79	5.56/5.56	8.82/8.82	12.49/12.49
50	3.08/3.08	4.50/4.51	7.19/7.21	12.31/12.36	20.21/20.22
75	3.32/3.50	5.06/5.08	8.11/8.35	14.47/15.14	24.17/24.96
100	3.36/3.93	5.16/5.51	8.48/9.10	16.31/16.87	27.71/29.22
250	3.82/4.51	5.50/6.84	9.41/11.41	—	—
500	4.09/5.01	6.02/7.70	10.28/13.14	—	—

size of the maximum cliques, even for high values of n and δ. This suggests that global maxima of the objective function f have large basins of attraction.

In order to evaluate the scaling properties of the proposed algorithm, in the second part of our study we concentrated on larger problem dimensions. The number of vertices considered in this case were $n = 1000$, 1500, and 2000, whereas the only density considered was $\delta = 0.50$. For each size n, ten graphs were generated randomly and then given as input to the replicator network. In this case, the process was terminated when the squared distance between two successive states became smaller than 10^{-7}. Unlike the previous series of experiments, where conventional exact algorithms were capable of solving the problem within reasonable computational time, in this case no such procedure is known to exist. Hence, to gauge the quality of the solutions found we resorted to a well-known result due to Matula, which accurately predicts the size of the maximum clique in a random graph, when the number of vertices is sufficiently large [16]. Let

$$M(n,\delta) = 2\log_{1/\delta} n - 2\log_{1/\delta}\log_{1/\delta} n + 2\log_{1/\delta}\frac{e}{2} + 1 \,. \qquad (8)$$

Matula proved that, as $n \to \infty$, the size of the maximum clique in an n-vertex δ-density random graph is either $\lfloor M(n,\delta)\rfloor$ or $\lceil M(n,\delta)\rceil$ with probability tending to 1, where $\lfloor x\rfloor$ denotes the largest integer less than or equal to x, and $\lceil x\rceil$ denotes the smallest integer greater than or equal to x. Interestingly, it was also shown that the size of the smallest maximal clique is expected to be $M(n,\delta)/2$ [16]. The results of our simulations are reported in Table 2, where the average clique size found by our algorithm (denoted by k_{repl}), the expected maximum clique size $M(n, 0.5)$, and the expected size of the smallest maximal clique $M(n, 0.5)/2$ are shown, together with the median number of iterations performed by the replicator process. The results are encouraging. The clique sizes found by the replicator network are in fact significantly larger than the estimated minimum, thereby contradicting what is known as the Jerrum conjecture [16], which states that in a large 0.5-density random graph it may be hard to find a clique whose size is even a bit larger than that of the smallest maximal clique. A conclusion similar to ours has also been drawn by Jagota

Table 2: Results over large 0.5-density graphs

n	k_{repl}	$M(n, 0.5)$	$M(n, 0.5)/2$	Iterations
1000	11.10	15.18	7.59	196
1500	11.70	16.19	8.09	193.5
2000	12.00	16.91	8.45	197

in [16]. It is interesting to note how the number of iterations of the replicator process was approximately constant, that is independent on the number of vertices in the graph. We report that the algorithm took about 30 minutes on a SparcStation 10 to converge, when run on a 2000-vertex graph.

5 Conclusions

We have shown how the classical problem of finding the maximum clique of an undirected graph can be approximately solved using simple yet powerful evolutionary dynamical equations related to certain relaxation neural networks models. Based on a result due to Motzkin and Straus, we have seen how the MCP can naturally be mapped onto a relaxation labeling network which is capable of maximizing quadratic polynomials over a certain linearly constrained domain. The model is especially suited for parallel implementation, and is attractive for its operational simplicity, since no operational parameters need to be determined. Extensive simulations over randomly generated graphs with up to 2000 vertices and about one million edges have demonstrated the effectiveness of the proposed approach both in terms of quality of solutions and speed.

One problem associated with the proposed relaxation model relates to the existence of spurious solutions in the Motzkin-Straus program which have been found both theoretically and experimentally. Spurious solutions should be avoided because they do not allow us to determine the nodes comprising the clique directly from the structure of the final solution. In [4] we report on the numerical behavior of the Comtet regularization of the Motzkin-Straus program which avoids spurious solutions.

References

[1] L. E. Baum and G. R. Sell (1968). Growth transformations for functions on manifolds. *Pacif. J. Math.* **27**(2), 211–227.

[2] I. M. Bomze (1991). Cross entropy minimization in uninvadable states of complex populations. *J. Math. Biol.* **30**, 73–87.

[3] I. M. Bomze (1995). Evolution towards the maximum clique. *J. Global. Optim.*, in press.

[4] I. M. Bomze, M. Pelillo, and R. Giacomini (1996). Evolutionary approach to the maximum clique problem: Empirical evidence on a larger scale. In I. M. Bomze, T. Csendes, R. Horst, and P. Pardalos (Eds.), *Developments in Global Optimization*. Kluwer Academic Publishers, Dordrecht, The Netherlands.

[5] C. Bron and J. Kerbosch (1973). Finding all cliques of an undirected graph. *Comm. ACM* **16**(9), 575–577.

[6] R. Carraghan and P. M. Pardalos (1990). An exact algorithm for the maximum clique problem. *Oper. Res. Lett.* **9**, 375–382.

[7] B. Carter and K. Park (1993). How good are genetic algorithms at finding large cliques: An experimental study. *Technical Report BU-CS-93-015*, Computer Science Department., Boston University.

[8] L. Comtet (1974). *Advanced Combinatorics.* Reidel, Dordrecht.

[9] J. F. Crow and M. Kimura (1970), *An Introduction to Population Genetics Theory.* Harper & Row, New York.

[10] R. A. Fisher (1930). *The Genetical Theory of Natural Selection.* Clarendon Press, Oxford.

[11] M. R. Garey and D. S. Johnson (1979). *Computers and Intractability: A Guide to the Theory of NP-Completeness.* W. H. Freeman, New York.

[12] L. E. Gibbons *et al.* (1996). Continuous characterization of the maximum clique problem. *Math. Oper. Res.*, to appear.

[13] A. Hastings and G. A. Fox (1995). Optimization as a technique for studying population genetics equations. In W. Banzhaf and F. H. Eeckman (Eds.), *Evolution and Biocomputation* (pp. 18–26). Springer-Verlag, Berlin.

[14] J. Hofbauer and K. Sigmund (1988). *The Theory of Evolution and Dynamical Systems.* Cambridge University Press.

[15] R. A. Hummel and S. W. Zucker (1983). On the foundations of relaxation labeling processes. *IEEE Trans. Pattern Anal. Machine Intell.* **5**(3), 267–287.

[16] A. Jagota (1995). Approximating maximum clique with a Hopfield network. *IEEE Trans. Neural Networks* **6**(3), 724–735.

[17] M. Kimura (1958). On the change of population fitness by natural selection. *Heredity* **12**, 145–167.

[18] S. Y. Lin and Z. Chen (1992). A flexible parallel architecture for relaxation labeling algorithms. *IEEE Trans. Signal Process.* **40**(5), 1231–1240.

[19] Yu. Lyubich, G.D. Maistrowskii, and Yu.G. Ol'khovskii (1980), Selection-induced convergence to equilibrium in a single-locus autosomal population. *Problems of Information Transmission* **16**, 66–75.

[20] J. Maynard-Smith (1982). *Evolution and the Theory of Games.* Cambridge University Press.

[21] T. S. Motzkin and E. G. Straus (1965). Maxima for graphs and a new proof of a theorem of Turán. *Canad. J. Math.* **17**, 533–540.

[22] H. Mühlenbein, M. Gorges-Schleuter, and O. Krämer (1988). Evolution algorithms in combinatorial optimization. *Parallel Computing* **7**, 65–85.

[23] P. M. Pardalos and A. T. Phillips (1990). A global optimization approach for solving the maximum clique problem. *Int. J. Computer Math.* **33**, 209–216.

[24] P. Pardalos and J. Xue (1994). The maximum clique problem. *J. Global Optim.* **4**, 301–328.

[25] M. Pelillo (1994). On the dynamics of relaxation labeling processes. *Proc. IEEE Int. Conf. Neural Networks*, Orlando, FL, 1006–1011.

[26] M. Pelillo and A. Jagota (1995). Feasible and infeasible maxima in a quadratic program for maximum clique. *J. Artif. Neural Networks* **2**(4), 411–419.

[27] A. Rosenfeld, R. A. Hummel, and S. W. Zucker (1976). Scene labeling by relaxation operations. *IEEE Trans. Syst. Man Cybern.* **6**(6), 420–433.

[28] P. Taylor and L. Jonker (1978). Evolutionarily stable strategies and game dynamics. *Math. Biosci.* **40**, 145–156.

[29] J. W. Weibull (1995). *Evolutionary Game Theory.* MIT Press, Cambridge, MA.

Significance of Locality and Selection Pressure in the Grand Deluge Evolutionary Algorithm

Günter Rudolph[1] and Joachim Sprave[2]

[1] Informatik Centrum Dortmund, Joseph-von-Fraunhofer-Str. 20, 44227 Dortmund
[2] Universität Dortmund, Fachbereich Informatik XI, 44221 Dortmund

Abstract. This paper presents the results of a parameter study of the Grand Deluge Evolutionary Algorithm, whose special features consist of local interactions between individuals within a spatially structured population and a self-adjusting control mechanism of the selection pressure. Since both ingredients are parametrizable this study aims at the identification of the significance and sensitivity of the parameter settings with regard to the performance of the algorithm, especially under the transition from one- to two-dimensional neighborhood patterns.

1 Introduction

In [11] we presented the Grand Deluge Evolutionary Algorithm (GDEA), which combines the traditional proportionate selection operator with a self-organizing acceptance threshold schedule. The population of the GDEA possesses a spatial structure to allow scalable parallel implementations, which means that the individuals are distributed over the vertices of a connected graph and that the genetic operators are applied locally in some neighborhood of each individual. This algorithm was embedded in the framework of *probabilistic automata networks* and could be proven to be globally convergent with probability one under the assumption that the genotypes of the individuals are binary strings. The parameter study made in [11] employed a multiple knapsack problem as objective function and investigated the significance of the parameters with regard to performance by varying the delay of adjusting the threshold values (selection pressure) and the neighborhood size (locality) in a ring topology, i.e., with one-dimensional neighborhood structures. While the overall performance of the GDEA was great compared to a traditional genetic algorithm (GA), the results were disappointing with respect to parallelism, where small neighborhood sizes are preferred to obtain low communication requirements. But instead the parameter study resulted in a relatively large optimal neighborhood size of about 40 individuals. Since the ring topology is only one possible implementation of the GDEA, the next step was to run the same experiments with a different topology. We chose a toroid grid for two reasons: it seems to be the most natural extension of a topology just to increase the dimension, and the torus is the most popular structure for parallel implementations.

A description of the GDEA is given in section 2, with emphasis on the design of local reproduction operators for individuals distributed over the vertices of a connected graph and the realization of a self-adjusting threshold control. Section 3 first presents our selection of neighborhood structures and test problems, before the results of the parameter study are discussed. Finally, we draw some conclusions in section 4.

2 Description of the Algorithm

It is assumed that the reader is familiar with the basics of evolutionary algorithms (EA). For a recent comprehensive overview see the monograph by Bäck [1]. The genetic operators of the GDEA for individuals with binary genotype are based on those of the traditional GA as described by Goldberg [4]. Since mutation and crossover remain unchanged they are not explicitly defined here. The changes only affect reproduction and offspring acceptance.

2.1 Local Reproduction

Since all individuals in a population compete with each other for the chance to produce offspring, a traditional EA requires information about the fitnesses of all individuals during the reproduction phase. This kind of global knowledge makes an algorithm unsuitable for an efficient parallel implementation. Therefore, most parallel implementations of EAs base on local reproduction rules [7, 5, 13, 8, 12, 9, 14] which can be applied simultaneously to smaller subsets of the population.

In order to be comparable to a standard GA, in [11] a localized proportionate selection was defined for a ring topology. In the following a more general definition is given which does not even depend on homogeneous neighborhood structures.

Let be n the population size, ℓ the dimension of the search space, $P^t = \{x_i^t \in \mathbb{B}^\ell : 0 \leq i < n\}$ the population at generation t, and $\mathcal{N}_\nu \in \mathcal{P}\{0, \ldots, n-1\}$ a set of indices defining the neighborhood $\mathcal{N}_\nu$ of the individual x_ν^t. $\mathcal{N}_\nu$ is a family (not a set) consisting of all x_k^t with $k \in \mathcal{N}_\nu$. The fitness function $F : \mathbb{B}^\ell \mapsto \mathbb{R}^+$ is normally the result of windowing and scaling techniques applied to the objective function. If the search space of the objective function is $D \neq \mathbb{B}^\ell$, e.g. $D \subseteq \mathbb{R}^N$, a mapping function $m : \mathbb{B}^\ell \mapsto D$ must be applied additionally.

The *ν-local relative fitness* of an index μ can now be defined as

$$p_\nu^t(\mu) := \frac{F(x_\mu^t)}{\sum\limits_{k \in \mathcal{N}_\nu} F(x_k^t)}$$

and the *ν-local cumulative relative fitness* of an index μ as

$$\mathrm{CRF}_\nu^t(\mu) := \sum_{k \in \mathcal{N}_\nu : k \leq \mu} p_\nu^t(k).$$

Proportionate selection can now be applied in a canonical way. For each parent to select, a random number ξ is drawn uniformly from $[0, 1)$ and the individual with index k is chosen with

$$\mathrm{CRF}_\nu^t(k) = \min\{i \in \mathcal{N}_\nu : \mathrm{CRF}_\nu^t(i) \geq \xi\}.$$

As an example, figure 1 shows a small torus and the population indices of the individuals. In case of a von–Neumann neighborhood structure, the individuals inside of the dashed line belong to the neighborhood of the individual with index 7, so $\mathcal{N}_7$ would be $\{2, 6, 7, 8, 12\}$.

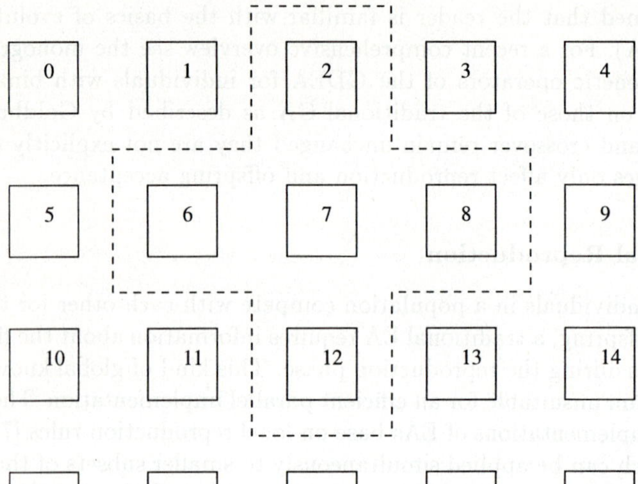

Fig. 1: Example of a neighborhood structure on a torus.

The following table lists the (fictional) fitness values and the resulting local relative fitnesses:

μ	2	6	7	8	12
$F(x_\mu^t)$	16	8	12	20	4
$p_7^t(\mu)$	4/15	2/15	3/15	5/15	1/15
$\mathrm{CRF}_7^t(\mu)$	4/15	6/15	9/15	14/15	15/15

The generation of offspring can be performed in parallel. For each position in the population, two parents are chosen from the neighborhood by local proportionate selection, and one child is generated by recombination and mutation. The individual at the current position is replaced by the new child if the latter is accepted, otherwise it remains unchanged.

2.2 Threshold Adjustment

As shown in [10], a standard GA with proportionate selection is not globally convergent to the optimum. Motivated by the *Grand Deluge Algorithm* of Dueck [3], an adaptive threshold acceptance schedule was added in [11]. For the convergence proof, the reader is referred to the original work. In the GDEA, the local threshold τ_k^t at index k and generation t is defined as

$$\tau_k^t := \begin{cases} F(x_k^0) & \text{, if } t < \delta \\ \max\{\tau_k^{t-1}, F(x_k^{t-\delta})\} & \text{, otherwise.} \end{cases} \tag{1}$$

The *threshold delay* $\delta \in \mathbb{N}$ specifies the lag of generations that a current fitness value will enter the threshold update rule (1). A new offspring at a given position in the population is only accepted if its fitness value exceeds the local threshold τ_k^t. This "tidal value" is the maximum of the fitness of the predecessor at this position δ generations in the past, and the tidal value of the last generation. Evidently, the local tides are monotonic rising by definition.

Since the value of δ determines how many generations without improvement are tolerated at most, it is a control parameter of the selection pressure. For $\delta = 1$, only improvements are accepted, whereas values beyond the maximum number of generations turn off the threshold acceptance. In conjunction with large neighborhoods, the latter case is very close to a traditional GA.

2.3 Outline of the Algorithm

The following pseudo code gives a sketch of the algorithm:

```
initialize population
REPEAT
   FOR EACH node
      select two neighbors
      recombine them
      mutate resulting offspring
      evaluate offspring
      IF F(offspring) > threshold
      THEN
         accept offspring
      ENDIF
      update local threshold
   ENDFOR
UNTIL maximum number of generations
```

3 Computational Experiments

3.1 Choice of Neighborhoods

In [11] we assumed that the population's directed graph $G = (V, E)$ with edges $E = \{(\nu, \mu) : \nu \in V, \mu \in \mathcal{N}_\nu\}$ was embedded into a processor network with bidirectional ring topology. To keep the (virtual) communication load low we decided to use neighborhoods of the following type: Let $R \in \mathbb{N}$ denote the *neighborhood radius* and $\mathcal{O} = \{a \in \mathbb{Z} : |a| \le R\}$ a set of offsets. The neighborhood set of the individual with label ν is $\mathcal{N}_\nu = \{(\nu + n + a) \bmod n : a \in \mathcal{O}\}$ where n is the population size. We shall say (with some lack of precision) that the population is living on a ring or that the optimization problem is treated on a ring whenever a neighborhood of the above type is used.

Since the ring topology is not the only admissible choice for a neighborhood structure there arises the obvious question whether two–dimensional neighborhood patterns would result in a qualitative change of performance or a change of significance of the parameters controlling locality and selection pressure. Therefore the individuals were placed on a toroidal processor network where each individual possesses the same two–dimensional neighborhood pattern. These patterns can be defined by a mask or matrix $M = (m_{ij})$ with an odd number of columns and rows whose central element refers to the current individual with label $\nu \in V$. An entry of M with $m_{ij} = 1$ indicates that the corresponding individual on the torus belongs to the neighborhood set of individual ν, otherwise the entry is zero. This is enough to calculate the neighborhood sets:

The matrix $M = (m_{ij})$ with r rows, c columns (r, c odd), $m_{ij} \in \{0, 1\}$ for all $i \in I = \{0, 1, \ldots, r-1\}$, $j \in J = \{0, 1, \ldots, c-1\}$ and $m_{r/2,c/2} = 1$ is called the *neighborhood mask*. The set

$$\mathcal{O}_M = \left\{ \left(i - \frac{r}{2},\, j - \frac{c}{2}\right) \in \mathbb{Z}^2 : m_{ij} = 1,\ (i, j) \in I \times J \right\}$$

is termed the *offset set* of neighborhood mask M. For example, the neighborhood mask

$$M = \begin{pmatrix} 0 & 0 & 1 & 0 & 0 \\ 0 & 1 & 1 & 1 & 0 \\ 1 & 1 & 1 & 1 & 1 \\ 0 & 1 & 1 & 1 & 0 \\ 0 & 0 & 1 & 0 & 0 \end{pmatrix}$$

defines a neighborhood pattern that is related to the maximum norm in $\mathbb{Z}^2$, i.e., the offset set is $\mathcal{O}_M = \{w \in \mathbb{Z}^2 : \|w\|_\infty \le 2\}$ or explicitly

$$\mathcal{O}_M = \{(0,0), (0,\pm 1), (0,\pm 2), (\pm 1, 0), (\pm 2, 0), (\pm 1, \pm 1), (\pm 1, \mp 1)\}.$$

Let the pair $(n, k) \in \mathbb{N}^2$ such that $n = k \cdot q$ with $q \in \mathbb{N}$ and where n is the population size. The function $\delta_k(\nu) = (\nu \operatorname{div} k\,,\ \nu \bmod k)$ with its inverse $\delta_k^{-1}(a, b) = a \cdot k + b$ will serve to map the population into a grid and vice versa. Now the neighborhood set can be defined easily:

$$\mathcal{N}_\nu = \{\delta_k^{-1}((\delta_k(\nu) + (i, j) + (q, k)) \bmod (q, k)) : (i, j) \in \mathcal{O}_M\}.$$

In this formalism the experiments made on the ring [11] can be described by setting $k = n$ and $\mathcal{O} = \{w \in \mathbb{Z}^2 : w_1 = 0, \|w\|_\infty \le R\}$.

While the neighborhood size in a ring can be increased gradually the neighborhood size defined by regular two–dimensional patterns increases in larger steps when usual distance measures (norms in $\mathbb{Z}^2$) are used. Therefore, the comparability of the effects of locality between one– and two–dimensional patterns would be hardly possible. As a consequence, we defined neighborhood masks whose patterns were inspired by chamfer–distances [2] in order to "smooth" the transitions to larger neighborhood sizes. For example, the matrix C below characterizes 9 different neighborhood masks with neighborhood sizes ranging between 5 and 49:

$$C = \begin{pmatrix} 9&8&7&5&7&8&9 \\ 8&6&4&3&4&6&8 \\ 7&4&2&1&2&4&7 \\ 5&3&1&0&1&3&5 \\ 7&4&2&1&2&4&7 \\ 8&6&4&3&4&6&8 \\ 9&8&7&5&7&8&9 \end{pmatrix}$$

The mask M_d is defined via $m_{ij} = 1$ if $c_{ij} \le d$ for $d = 1, \ldots, 9$ and zero otherwise. Our experiments were made with patterns of the above type resulting in the neighborhood sizes $\{5, 9, 13, 21, 25, 29, 37, 45, 49, 81, 121, 169, 225\}$ where the steps between the last five sizes were enlarged intentionally to reduce the computation time required for our study.

3.2 Objective Functions

Our experiments were made on two problems: a pseudo–boolean and a pseudo–continuous one. The first one was a NP–hard multiple knapsack problem already investigated for populations on a ring in [11]. The problem can be formalized as follows:

$$f_1(x) = c^T x \quad \to \max! \\ \text{s.t. } Ax \le b$$

with $x \in \mathbb{B}^\ell$, $c \in \mathbb{R}_+^\ell$, $b \in \mathbb{R}_+^m$ and $A \in \mathbb{R}_+^{m,\ell}$. The constraints were included into the objective function by a penalty technique in the same manner as in [6]:

$$f_1(x) = c^T x - \beta \cdot c_{max} \quad \to \max!\ ,$$

where β denotes the number of violated constraints and c_{max} the largest entry in the cost vector c. Here, the problem had dimension $\ell = 50$ and $m = 5$ constraints.

The objective function of the second test problem was a version of the well–known Rastrigin function:

$$f_2(x) = 5000 - \sum_{i=1}^{20} \{x_i^2 + 10\,[1 - \cos(2\,\pi\,x_i)]\} \quad \to \max!$$

where each x_i was represented by a Gray–coded binary string of length 20 such that $|x_i| \le 5.24288$ for each $i = 1, \ldots, 20$. Thus, the string length of an individual is $\ell = 400$.

3.3 Computational Results

The population size was set to 500 for both the ring and torus topology. While the labels of the individuals in the ring were arranged in linear order, a grid of 20×25 was the basis of the labeling in the torus.

For the multiple knapsack problem, the neighborhood size $|\mathcal{N}_\nu|$ was varied from 3 to 200 for the ring topology (results taken from [11]), and from 5 to 225 for the torus. In both cases, the threshold delay δ ranged from 1, which can be seen as a local elitist selection, to 500 which was the maximum number of generations. For each combination of δ and $|\mathcal{N}_\nu|$ the success frequency, which is the ratio of the number of runs that found the global optimum to total number of runs, was calculated from 200 independent experiments.

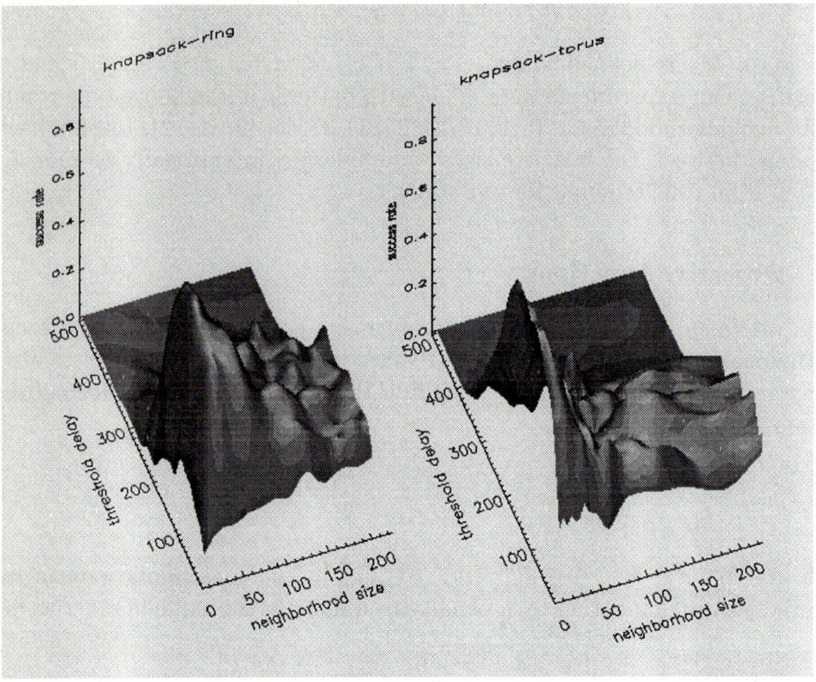

Fig. 2: Success frequency for the multiple knapsack problem with varying parameters.

Figure 2 summarizes the success frequencies depending on δ and $|\mathcal{N}_\nu|$ in both ring and torus topology, i.e., for one– and two–dimensional neighborhood patterns. In contrast to the results of the same experiment in the ring topology, the highest success rates in the torus were obtained by the smallest neighborhood sizes. In fact, the optimal settings were approximately $(|\mathcal{N}_\nu|, \delta) = (40, 100)$ for the ring and $(|\mathcal{N}_\nu|, \delta) = (5, 140)$ for the torus. These settings achieved a success frequency of about 85 % and 95 %, respectively. An interesting observation is the fact that the torus neighborhood yields better results when properly tuned, whereas the ring topology behaves slightly more robust against missetting of the neighborhood sizes. But in both cases, it is obvious that a retarded initiation of selection pressure is the key to success: Missing selection pressure (too large δ) as well as too strong selection pressure (small δ) decays the success frequency to almost zero.

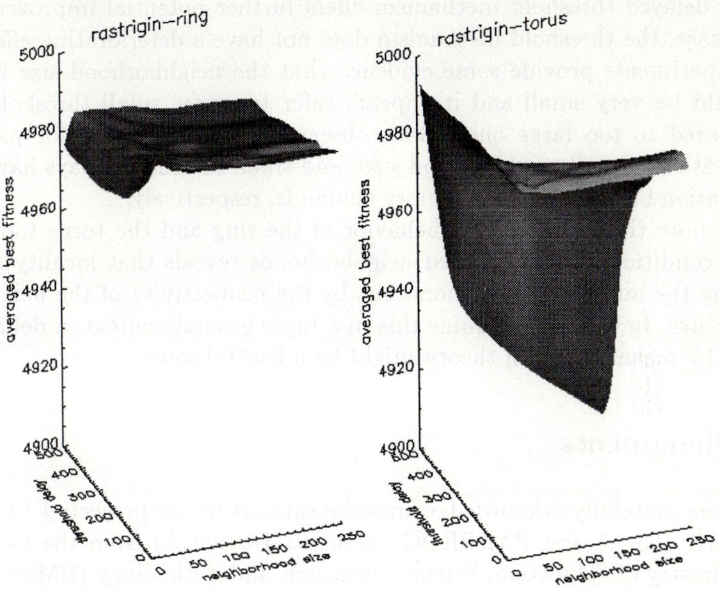

Fig. 3: Averaged best fitness for the Rastrigin test problem with varying parameters.

In contrast to the first test problem, success frequencies are not an appropriate quality measure for a continuous function such as the Rastrigin problem. Instead, the best results after 500 generations were averaged out of 100 runs. Figure 3 shows the response of the GDEA to the variation of δ and $|\mathcal{N}_\nu|$ for the Rastrigin function using ring and torus topology. Again, the best performance of the torus can be observed with the smallest neighborhood sizes while the ring requires a neighborhood size similar to the first experiment. It is quite evident that the ring is much more robust against parameter missettings than the torus: The influence of both the threshold delay value and the neighborhood size in the ring is remarkably small. In contrast, the torus is insensitive with respect to the delay value only if the neighborhood size is small, and it is insensitive with respect to neighborhood size only if the threshold delay is minimal (implying strong selection pressure).

4 Conclusions

Speaking in terms of biology, the parameters examined in this paper are selection pressure (threshold delay) and locality (neighborhood size). Obviously, a moderately retarded initiation of selection pressure causes a speed–up of the GDEA on its way to the global optimum. With respect to parallelism (and on base of our two test problems), we can state that locality does not harm the performance of the EA. Rather, the performance of the spatial structured EA was better equal than the traditional panmictic (not spatially structured) EA. The additional usage of the delayed threshold mechanism offers further potential improvements — in any case, the threshold mechanism does not have a deteriorating effect.

Our experiments provide some evidence that the neighborhood size in the torus should be very small and it appears safer to prefer small threshold delays compared to too large ones. Both observations are pleasant for parallel implementations: Small neighborhood sizes and small threshold delays have low communication bandwidth and memory demands, respectively.

Finally note that the different behavior of the ring and the torus topology under the condition of equally sized neighborhoods reveals that locality is not provided by the number of neighbors, but by the connectivity of the neighborhood structure. In order to examine this in a more general context, a definition of locality by means of graph theory might be a fruitful route.

Acknowledgments

Both authors gratefully acknowledge financial support by the projects EVOALG (grant 01 IB 403 A) and PARPROG (grant 01 IR 509 A) from the German Federal Ministry of Education, Science, Research and Technology (BMBF).

References

1. T. Bäck. *Evolutionary Algorithms in Theory and Practice.* Oxford University Press, New York, 1996.
2. G. Borgefors. Distance transformations in arbitrary dimensions. *Computer Vision, Graphics, and Image Processing*, 27:321–345, 1984.
3. G. Dueck. New optimization heuristics: the great deluge algorithm and the record–to–record travel. *Journal of Computional Physics*, 104:86–92, 1993.
4. D.E. Goldberg. *Genetic Algorithms in Search, Optimization, and Machine Learning.* Addison Wesley, Reading (MA), 1989.
5. M. Gorges-Schleuter. ASPARAGOS: an asynchronous parallel genetic optimization strategy. In J.D. Schaffer, editor, *Genetic Algorithms, Proceedings of the 3rd International Conference on Genetic Algorithms*, pages 422–427. Morgan Kaufman, San Mateo, 1989.
6. S. Khuri, Th. Bäck, and J. Heitkötter. The zero/one multiple knapsack problem and genetic algorithms. In E. Deaton, D. Oppenheim, J. Urban, and H. Berghel, editors, *Proceedings of the 1994 ACM Symposium on Applied Computing*, pages 188–193. ACM Press, New York, 1994.
7. H. Mühlenbein, M. Gorges-Schleuter, and O. Krämer. Evolution algorithms in combinatorial optimization. *Parallel Computing*, 7:65–88, 1988.
8. M.E. Palmer and S.J. Smith. Improved evolutionary optimization of difficult landscapes: Control of premature convergence through scheduled sharing. *Complex Systems*, 5:443–458, 1991.

9. G. Rudolph. Parallel approaches to stochastic global optimization. In W. Joosen and E. Milgrom, editors, *Parallel Computing: From Theory to Sound Practice, Proceedings of the European Workshop on Parallel Computing (EWPC 92)*, pages 256–267. IOS Press, Amsterdam, 1992.
10. G. Rudolph. Convergence properties of canonical genetic algorithms. *IEEE Transactions on Neural Networks*, 5(1):96–101, 1994.
11. G. Rudolph and J. Sprave. A cellular genetic algorithm with self–adjusting acceptance threshold. In *Proceedings of the First IEE/IEEE International Conference on Genetic Algorithms in Engineering Systems: Innovations and Applications*, pages 365–372. IEE, London, 1995.
12. P. Spiessens and B. Manderick. A massively parallel genetic algorithm: Implementation and first analysis. In R.K. Belew and L.B. Booker, editors, *Proceedings of the Fourth Conference on Genetic Algorithms*, pages 279–286. Morgan Kaufmann, San Mateo, 1991.
13. J. Sprave. Parallelisierung Genetischer Algorithmen zur Suche und Optimierung. Diplomarbeit, University of Dortmund, Department of Computer Science, 1990.
14. J. Sprave. Linear neighborhood evolution strategies. In A.V. Sebald and L.J. Fogel, editors, *Proceedings of the 3rd Annual Conference on Evolutionary Programming*, pages 42–51. World Scientific, River Edge (NJ), 1994.

Parallel Computing with DNA: Toward the Anti-Universal Machine

Klaus-Peter Zauner and Michael Conrad

Wayne State University, Dept. of Computer Science,
Detroit MI 48202, USA, e-mail: biocomputing@cs.wayne.edu,
www: http://www.cs.wayne.edu/biolab/

Abstract. A DNA-based biomolecular string processing scheme demonstrated by Adleman has attracted wide attention. While it is not known to what degree the scheme can scale up, it nevertheless introduces a new and interesting concept which seems so far to have been overlooked. The key point is that the Adleman scheme involves building specific hardware for a single problem instance. This opens a design degree of freedom that is not limited to biomolecular architectures.

1 Introduction

DNA computing, first developed by L. Adleman [1], raises novel questions about the relationship between the structure and function of computational systems. The scheme has primarily been discussed from the point of view of its programmability [13]. The implication is that it shares the main property of a conventional digital computer, namely the property of being general purpose and in the limit being computation universal.

The universality property has in fact been demonstrated for the scheme as a whole [11]. However, caution is necessary, since this is a class property, not a property of the actual systems that can be constructed. This sharp deviation from the usual concept of universality is due to the fact that the structure of any given realization is specific for a particular problem instance. Nevertheless such extreme special purposiveness can in principle afford computational advantages for certain problem domains. We will illustrate the reasons for this by developing a close analysis of the manner in which the Adleman system works. Though the scheme does not have practical value at the present time [10], it serves as a good springboard for identifying features that should apply to other possible machines and to biological organisms.

2 Universality versus Specificity

In the absence of space and time bounds general purpose machines would be universal [7]. The universal Turing machine is the simplest and best known example. Such a machine (or formalism) can emulate any other machine. Actual machines are, of course, never universal in this arbitrary sense, since they are always subject to memory and time limitations. We call such finite machines quasi-universal and adopt the convention that the state includes the memory. The program can then be regarded as encoded in the state.

Universality is not always an advantage. In general higher performance can be achieved with specialized hardware. A typical example is an analog computer used to solve a differential equation. The equation is fixed in the physical structure, but the parameter values and initial conditions can be varied. The hardware in this case is clearly problem specific, since the physical structure has to be changed to deal with different differential equations.

The difference between quasi-universal and problem specific machines is that the problem is represented in the state in the former case and in the physical structure in the latter. The physical structure might be viewed as a material state, but the two cases differ widely in the amount of energy required to change the state. Thus when a digital computer is reprogrammed we ordinarily view it as the same machine, whereas an analog computer (or a specially cut digital circuit) would more naturally be viewed as a different machine. As noted above, both machine types can process different instances of a problem, and in both cases this is achieved by starting from different initial states. For present purposes we will therefore distinguish the structure of a system from the state of this structure, using the latter to refer to changes in a given machine structure.

The opposite extreme of universality would be a machine that encodes a single problem instance in its structure. We will call such a machine an *instance machine*. The distinguishing feature of an instance machine is that it is not possible to process different instances of a problem by starting from different initial states. More generally, any computing device with the following two properties qualifies as an instance machine:

1. The physical structure of the machine is specific for a single problem instance (but we exclude the trivial case of a system that can only be used to answer questions about its own behavior).
2. The time evolution of the machine leads to a state or structure that can be interpreted as a solution to the problem (i.e., representation of the problem in the system structure should lead to the development of a solution).

3 Key features of DNA computing

The Adleman scheme may be the first which employs actual instance machines. In fact all realizations of it are instance machines.

Each realization is a probabilistic parallel machine with a high degree of fine-grained parallelism. The new feature is that the self-assembly properties of DNA are used to achieve this high degree of parallelism. Problems are represented with DNA sequences. The solution of the problem proceeds through the free energy minimization associated with the self-assembly (or annealing) of these DNA molecules. That the physical structure of the machine is specific for a single problem is due to the fact that special DNA sequences are necessary for each problem instance.

The actual computation proceeds in three phases (Fig. 1). First, in a synthesis phase, a structural representation of the input (i.e., the problem instance) is created. In the second phase the structures formed during the synthesis stage undergo a state to state development driven by free energy minimization. In the third stage the result of the computation is extracted from an analysis of the final structure.

Let us concretize this picture by tracing an example through the three stages. Given a directed graph and a choice of a start and an end vertex in the graph,

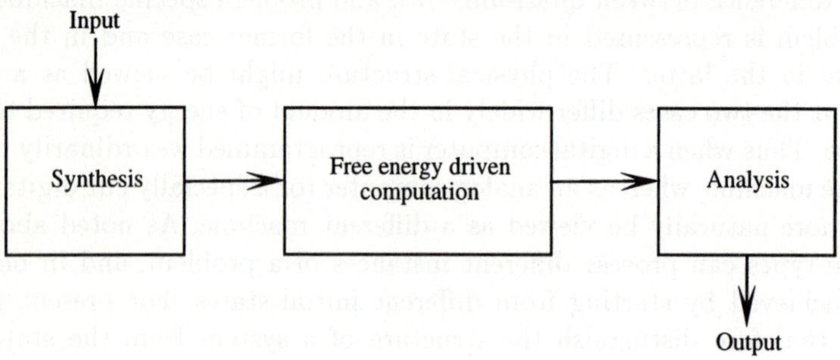

Fig. 1. The three phases of the DNA based computation.

the question can be asked: does there exist a path from the start vertex to the end vertex that visits every vertex in the graph exactly once? Such a path, called a (directed) Hamiltonian path, is frequently of interest in optimization problems. For the graph in Fig. 2 and the choice of A and D as the start and end vertices a Hamiltonian path exists and is indicated in the figure by solid arrow heads.

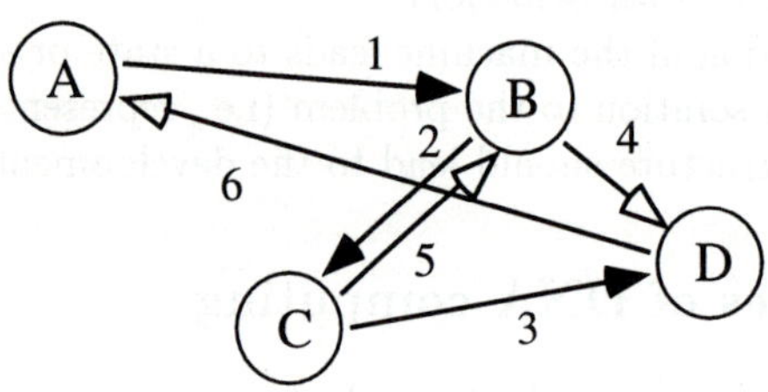

Fig. 2. Hamiltonian path problem.

The first phase of the computation is the encoding of the graph in DNA base sequences. To this end a short oligonucleotide of fixed size with an arbitrary, but unique base sequence is formally assigned to each vertex in the graph. The oligonucleotides are illustrated in Fig. 3 as dashed boxes. The first half of the sequence is indicated by the lower case letter of the vertex and the second half by the primed lower case letter.

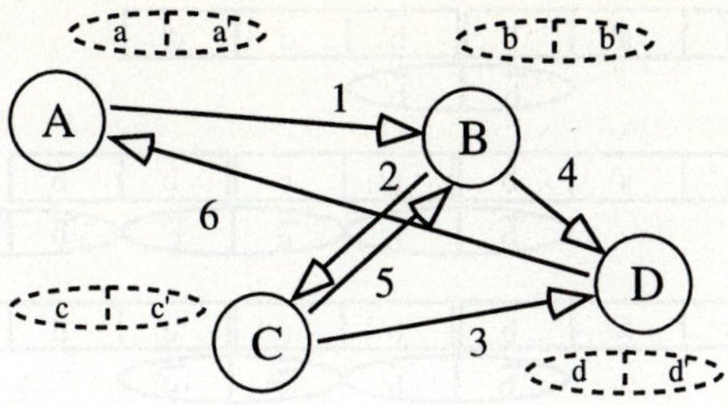

Fig. 3. Encoding of the vertices through base sequences.

From this formal assignment a molecular representation of the graph is derived as follows. For each edge in the graph a nucleotide sequence is synthesized with the property that its first half is identical with the second half of the sequence formally assigned to the vertex from which it originates. The second half of the sequence that represents the edge is identical to the first half of the sequence assigned to the vertex that the edge enters. (See edge 2 in Figs. 3 and 4 and note that the start A and the end D are exceptions.)

Then for each intermediate vertex, such as B and C in the example graph, the oligonucleotide corresponding to the complement of the sequence formally assigned to the vertex is synthesized. The set of molecules which represents the graph displayed in Fig. 2 is shown in Fig. 4, with complements indicated by bars over the lower case letters. The structure of the eight molecules completely specifies the graph.

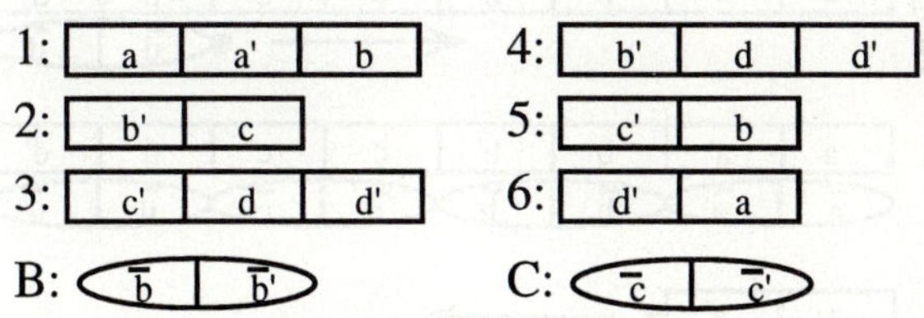

Fig. 4. Molecular representation of the directed graph shown in Fig. 2 and 3.

At this point phase 2 of the computation begins. The molecules that represent the graph interact with each other to form self-assembled supermolecular complexes through the association of complementary base sequences. Each of the complexes is a structural representation of a path in the graph. Three examples from the set of possible complexes are shown in Fig. 5. If a Hamiltonian path exists in the graph encoded in the reactant molecules then with high probability a self-assembled complex will be formed that represents this path.

Phase 3 involves extracting the solution. The self-assembled (or hybridized) complexes are held together by hydrogen bonds. Sequences that are lined up next to each other in these complexes are first enzymatically linked to form

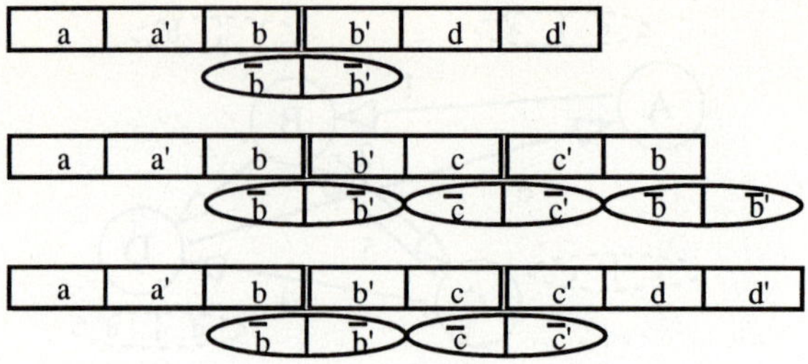

Fig. 5. Examples of complexes produced in the self-assembly phase.

continuous strands. The strands are then analyzed to extract the molecules that encode the Hamiltonian path, if such molecules exist. (More than one molecule may be possible, first because the problem may have more than one solution and second because a given solution is typically encoded by more than one strand.)

Molecules corresponding to a Hamiltonian path must satisfy three conditions. The first is that the molecule must start with the sequence encoding the start vertex and end with the sequence encoding the end vertex. If in a polymerase chain reaction (PCR) the primers are chosen according to the sequences that encode for the start and the end vertex, only DNA segments that encode for a path with the correct start and end vertices will undergo exponential amplification (Fig. 6). Such specific amplification is the key feature of the PCR technique.

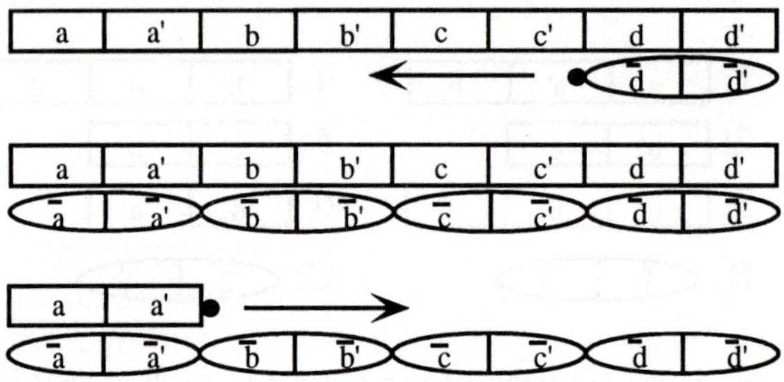

Fig. 6. Selective amplification by polymerase chain reaction (PCR).

The second necessary condition is that the molecules corresponding to problem solutions have exactly the length of the sequences assigned to the vertices multiplied by the number of vertices in the graph. Gel electrophoresis provides a method of ensuring this by separating DNA strands migrating through a polymer gel according to their length (Fig. 7).

The molecules that are known to encode the correct start and end vertices and to have the correct length are checked for whether they encode all intermediate vertices. Hybridization probes of the sequences complementary to the

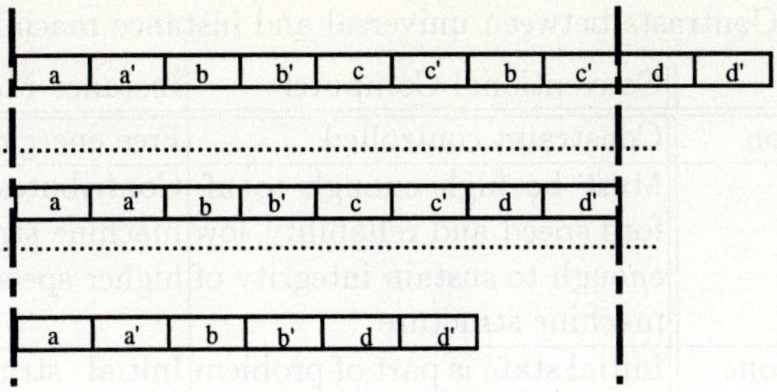

Fig. 7. Separation through gel electrophoresis.

ones formally assigned to the vertices are used to ensure this third necessary condition. Each vertex is checked separately. The probe is attached to a solid support and DNA molecules that encode the vertex in question will bind to this probe; other DNA molecules can be washed out. The process is illustrated in Fig. 8 for vertex C.

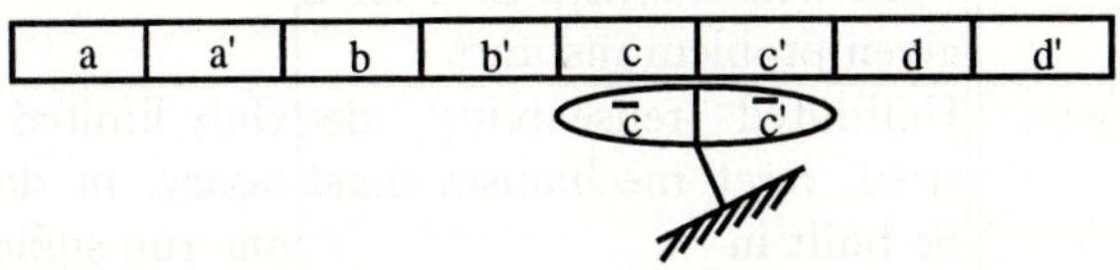

Fig. 8. Identification with hybridization probes.

Finally, the molecules that remain can be sequenced to yield the Hamiltonian path.

4 General Instance Machine Characteristics

At first sight it might seem that instance machines, such as used in the Adleman scheme, would always be less desirable than quasi-universal machines or than machines that are designed for a specific class of problems. This is not necessarily the case. Under some circumstances instance machines may be able to solve larger problems or be able to deal with an important case in a shorter amount of time.

The DNA example considered in the previous section provides a useful paradigm. We can use this example to elicit the main characteristics of instance machines, and to consider how these bear on issues of size and speed.

Table 1 summarizes the main characteristics and compares them to those of conventional (digital) computers. Recall that self-assembly (or annealing) is the key to DNA computing. This means that the state transitions are primarily

Table 1. Contrasts between universal and instance machine computing

	Conventional Computer	Instance Machine
State transition	Constraint controlled	Free energy dominated
Dissipation	Must be high enough to afford speed and reliability, low enough to sustain integrity of machine structure	Contributes to integrity of machine structure, allows for higher speed and reliability
Initial conditions	Initial state is part of problem representation, course of computation narrowly prescribed	Initial structure (or family of states) specifies problem, course of computation not sensitive to initial state
Potential size of state set	Programming requires precise control of system state, potential barriers limit number of states	Programming through control of system structure allows for closely similar states, expanded state set possible
Minimum size of state set	State set must be large enough to accommodate all classes of tasks, typically only a fraction of states used for a given problem instance	Only states relevant to problem instance need to be supported
Machine life cycle	Unlimited reuseability desired, reset mechanism must be built in	Only limited reuseability necessary, in deterministic case one run sufficient

driven by either energy minimization or entropy maximization. In a digital computer, by contrast, energy is irrelevant to the course of the computation. The designer takes great care to ensure that the different states of the machine are as similar as possible from the energy point of view and that any differences that do occur are precluded from affecting the state transitions. This feature is key to conventional programmability. The programmer therefore has the freedom to prescribe the course of the computation by setting constraints that restrict the dynamic degrees of freedom without considering energy/entropy aspects [12]. Constraints play a role in all computational systems, including DNA instance machines, but in the latter the energy differences between different states are the main controlling factor. Consequently the dynamics are self-organizing.

Of course digital computers must be plugged into a source of energy and must export heat to the environment. The energy serves to push the system over the potential barriers that separate the different possible states. For this reason dissipation is closely connected to both speed and reliability. It is possible on paper to construct universal computing models that are practically reversible [2], but these systems are nearly as likely to run backwards as forwards. Also, to ensure that the system undergoes correct state transitions it is important for states to be separated by significant potential barriers. The constraints that encode the program followed by a digital machine limit the amount of dissipation that is possible, however. Clearly the rate of heat export must be high enough so that these constraints do not melt. This limitation is much less severe for systems with self-organizing dynamics, since the course of the computation as a whole, including structural changes, is driven by dissipation. The speed and reliability attainable is therefore potentially greater than for conventional machines.

The high parallelism of DNA computing actually has its origin in this speed and reliability property, since it depends on the high speed and reliability of DNA hybridization. The scheme also illustrates the distinction between programming by structure preparation as opposed to state preparation. The outcome of a conventional computation is highly sensitive to the initial state, since this encodes the program. The DNA computer, by contrast, encodes the problem it solves in its initial structure, and therefore in a large family of states. The course of the computation is accordingly highly stable to perturbations, since it follows a basin of attraction. Unlike a conventional constraint controlled machine, it is not necessary to support the existence of possible states that are never relevant to the problem at hand. Furthermore, the number of possible states that a conventional machine can assume is limited by the requirement for significant potential barriers.

Since an instance machine by definition deals with only one instance of a problem it is in principle unnecessary to reset it to its initial structure and run it again. Some rerunning would be useful for randomized computations and for testing the machine. The potential advantage is that it is unnecessary to restrict the design to materials with high reversibility (i.e., reuseability) and unnecessary to support reset mechanisms. The latter could be costly with free energy driven devices. In the case of the Adleman system the effort and energy required to use the same DNA bases for a different computation would be much greater than that required to start with a new batch of material. The machine is not only an instance machine, but a throw away instance machine.

5 Is there a Niche for Anti-Universality?

For an instance machine to be worthwhile the problem instance would have to be very important. The number of instances could be combinatorially explosive, but in practice it is often a particular instance that is of interest. Economic decision makers, for example, often are presented with particular instances of large graph problems. Another example would be the need to rapidly recognize a particular pattern in a complex background. In some domains it may be sufficient to have solutions for a small number of arbitrary instances. This is the case when it is required to judge the quality of a particular heuristic, approximate, or suboptimal solution procedure. The availability of a small number of optimal solutions provides a useful benchmark. Developing test sets against which to assess genetic algorithms would be an example [14].

DNA computing is far from being competitive with conventional machines in any of these domains, and may never become so. The Hamiltonian path problem originally used to illustrate its operation is NP complete. Thus it is almost certainly the case (though not yet proved) that the number of resources required to solve the problem increases exponentially with problem size. The Adleman system cannot overcome this combinatorial explosion, just as conventional systems cannot. The advantage that it could conceivably have would be its enormous parallelism that converts the exponential time burden that conventional machines face into an exponential materials burden in terms of the amount of DNA required. Currently, however, it is not possible to exploit this tradeoff due to numerous practical limitations connected with the biochemical techniques available.

But the instance machine approach illustrated by DNA computing carries over to other technologies, where aspects of it may find more immediate application. This would be the case for conventional electronic and optical computers, where limits are set by the effect of state changes on machine structure. For example, the lifetime of a transistor is limited by electromigration (i.e., the effect of switching operations on the distribution of atoms). This puts a limit not only on transistor size, but on the materials and geometries that can be used. These limitations would be irrelevant to an instance machine since the number of switching operations could be extremely small. Similarly, many materials with highly desirable optical computing properties have been discovered but cannot be used for conventional purposes because of low reversibility. The course of the computation in these designs would not be driven by free energy minimization, but admitting changes in the machine structure opens up a new design degree of freedom.

Device proposals that utilize protein self-assembly for pattern recognition go a step further [5, 6]. Input signals are coded as molecular shapes, which then self-assemble to form higher level structures whose shape features represent different classes of input patterns. Enzymes specific for these shape features control the output of the device. The pattern recognition problem is thus converted to a free energy minimization process. Unlike Adleman DNA computing, which is also based on self-assembly, the protein self-assembly device is not programmable in a conventional sense, since a fixed set of formal (physics independent) rules is not available for ascertaining the effect of protein modifications. This is actually an advantage from the standpoint of potential computing power, since the number of interactions that can contribute to the computation is much less restricted. Such systems must be bred to perform desired functions through an evolutionary procedure [4, 3].

Biological evolutionary systems also make use of structure creating and destroying processes to maintain the potentiality of solving new problems without having to pay the price of maintaining the capacity to solve all problems. This is possible because their problem solving capabilities are represented in their structure as determined by strong chemical bonds [15, 8], as it is in DNA computing or in the protein self-assembly design. The structure-based computing principle illustrated by the instance machine concept is arguably better suited to the analysis of natural biological systems than is the state-based computing concept utilized in conventional computing models.

Acknowledgment This work was supported by the U.S. National Science Foundation under Grant No. ECS-9409780.

References

1. Adleman, L.M.: Molecular computation of solutions to combinatorial problems. Science **266** (1994) 1021–1024
2. Bennett, C.H.: Logical reversibility of computation. IBM J. Res. Dev. **17** (1973) 525–532
3. Conrad, M.: Information processing in molecular systems. Currents in Modern Biology (now BioSystems) **5** (1972) 1–14
4. Conrad, M.: The price of programmability. In: The Universal Turing Machine: A Fifty Year Survey (Herken, R. ed.) pp. 285–307. Oxford: Oxford Univ. Press (1988)
5. Conrad, M.: Molecular computing. In: Advances in Computers (Yovits, M.C., ed.), vol. 31, pp. 235–324. Boston: Academic Press (1990)
6. Conrad, M.: Molecular computing: the lock-key paradigm. Computer IEEE **25** (1992) 11-20
7. Hopcroft J.E., Ullman, I.: Introduction to Automata Theory, Languages, and Computation, pp. 146–170. Reading: Addison-Wesley (1979)
8. Kondo, H.,Yamamoto, M., Watanabe, M.: Reversible intracellular displacement of the cytoskeletal protein and organelles by ultracentrifugation of the sympathetic ganglion. J. Submicrosc. Cytol. Pathol. **24** (1992) 241–250
9. Landauer, R.: Uncertainty principle and minimal energy dissipation in the computer. Int. J. Theoret. Phys. **21** (1982) 283–297
10. Linial, M., Linial, N.: On the potential of molecular computing. Science **268** (1995) 481
11. Lipton, R.J.: DNA solution of hard computational problems. Science **268** (1995) 542–545
12. Pattee, H.H.: Physical problems of decision-making constraints. In: The Physical Principles of Neuronal and Organismic Behavior (Conrad, M., Magar, M., eds.), pp. 217–225. New York: Gordon and Breach, Science Publishers (1973)
13. Reif, J.H.: Parallel molecular computation: models and simulations. Seventh Annual ACM Symposium on Parallel Algorithms and Architectures (SPAA95), Santa Barbara, June 1995 (to appear)
14. Schwefel, H.-P.: Evolution and Optimum Seeking, pp.105–164. New York: Wiley (1995)
15. Skoultchi, A.I., Morowitz, H.J.: Information storage and survival of biological systems at temperatures near absolute zero. Yale J. Biol. Med. **37** (1964) 158–163

Applications of Evolutionary Computation

Evolutionary Computation in Machine Learning, Neural Networks, and Fuzzy Systems

Evolutionary Computation in Electrical, Electronics, and Communications Engineering

Evolutionary Computation in Computer Science and Operations Research

Evolutionary Computation in Mechanical, Chemical, Biological, and Optical Engineering

Evolutionary Computation in Machine Learning, Neural Networks, and Fuzzy Systems

Tackling the "Curse of Dimensionality" of Radial Basis Functional Neural Networks Using a Genetic Algorithm

Brian Carse[1] and Terence C. Fogarty[2]

1. Faculty of Engineering
University of the West of England, Bristol
Frenchay Campus, Coldharbour Lane
Bristol BS16 1QY, UK
b-carse@uwe.ac.uk

2. Department of Computer Studies
Napier University
Craiglockhart Campus, 219 Collinton Road
Edinburgh EH14 1DG, UK
T.Fogarty@dcs.napier.ac.uk

Abstract. Radial Basis Function (RBF) neural networks offer the possibility of faster gradient-based learning of neuron weights compared with Multi-Layer Perceptron (MLP) networks. This apparent advantage of RBF networks is bought at the expense of requiring a large number of hidden layer nodes, particularly in high dimensional spaces (the "curse of dimensionality"). This paper proposes a representation and associated genetic operators which are capable of evolving RBF networks with relatively small numbers of hidden layer nodes and good generalisation properties. The genetic operators employed also overcome the "competing conventions" problem, for RBF networks at least, which has been a reported stumbling block in the application of crossover operators in evolutionary learning of directly encoded neural network architectures.

1 Introduction

Radial Basis Function (RBF) neural networks [1,2] originate from the use of radial basis functions in the solution of the real multivariate interpolation problem. Such networks have been applied successfully to applications including image processing, speech recognition, time series analysis and adaptive equalisation. In its basic form (Figure 1) an RBF neural network involves three functionally distinct layers. The input layer is simply a set of sensory units. The second layer is a hidden layer of sufficient dimension which applies a non-linear transformation of the input space to a higher-dimensional hidden-unit space. The third and final layer performs a linear transformation from the hidden-unit space to the output space. Compared to multi-layer perceptron (MLP) networks, RBF networks differ in a number of respects [3]. An RBF network employs a single hidden layer whereas an MLP network may have one or more hidden layers. Nodes in an MLP network share a common neural model whereas hidden and output nodes of an RBF network are functionally distinct. Another difference is that MLP networks construct "global" function approximations whereas RBF networks construct "local" function approximations using exponentially decaying localised non-linearities. The significance of this is that MLP networks have better generalisation in regions of the input space where no training data are available, but RBF networks are capable of faster learning and display reduced sensitivity to the order of presentation of training data.

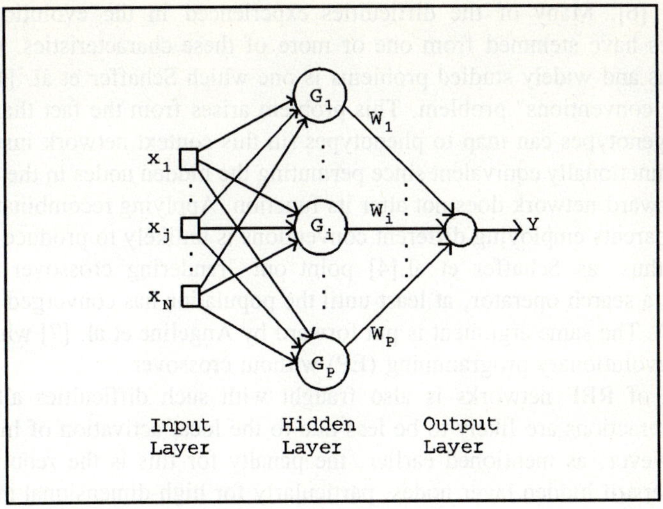

Fig. 1 RBF Network

The latter advantages of RBF networks are bought at the expense of a potentially large number of radial basis functions required to span the input space adequately. Both MLP and RBF networks have been proved to be universal approximators and therefore there exists an RBF network which is functionally equivalent to any MLP network and vice-versa. However, while theoretically extremely important results, these existence proofs offer little insight into how networks may be designed or learned efficiently.

An enormous amount of research effort has recently been applied to evolutionary learning of MLP networks in both straight feedforward and recurrent forms. Since the extensive literature on this work has already been thoroughly reviewed by a number of authors [4,5], we do not attempt an exhaustive review here, but rather intend to summarise the essence of the primary approaches proposed and problems encountered, and to relate these to our discussion of evolution of RBF neural networks. The taxonomies suggested in the different GA/MLP reviews are broadly similar and include the following three combinations: (1) Evolution of connection weights for fixed MLP architectures. (2) Evolution of MLP architectures often combined with gradient-based learning for weight determination. This includes direct representations, where network topology is directly coded onto the genome, and also indirect codings of grammar structure which generate architectures by development ("neurogenesis"). (3) Evolution of selected training data, learning rules and associated parameters. In this paper, we are primarily concerned with the second of these categories, and in particular, direct representations where the genome encodes network topology directly. The problem of evolving MLP neural network topologies (nodes and connections) is a difficult one, since the search surface (fitness landscape) is effectively infinitely large, complex, strongly epistatic, deceptive and highly multimodal [6]. Many of the difficulties experienced in the evolution of MLP architectures have stemmed from one or more of these characteristics. One of the most serious and widely studied problems is one which Schaffer et al. [11] call the "competing conventions" problem. This problem arises from the fact that a number of distinct genotypes can map to phenotypes (in this context network instantiations) which are functionally equivalent since permuting the hidden nodes in the same layer of a feedforward network does not alter its function. Applying recombination to two successful parents employing different conventions is unlikely to produce successful offspring, thus, as Schaffer et al.[4] point out "rendering crossover essentially impotent as a search operator, at least until the population has converged to a single convention". The same argument is put forward by Angeline et al. [7] who advocate the use of evolutionary programming (EP) without crossover.

Evolution of RBF networks is also fraught with such difficulties although the epistatic interactions are likely to be less due to the local activation of hidden layer nodes. However, as mentioned earlier, the penalty for this is the requirement for large numbers of hidden layer nodes, particularly for high-dimensional input/output spaces (the "curse of dimensionality"). In this paper we describe a representation and associated genetic operators for the evolution of "economical" RBF network parameterisations in an attempt to learn accurate functional mappings with relatively small numbers of hidden layer nodes. The approach is based on the premise that many functional mappings of interest vary highly in their local complexity over the input/output space and therefore the density of RBF hidden layer nodes and their basis function widths should reflect the underlying functional complexity. The paper is organised as follows. The next section provides a summary of recent work conducted in evolutionary learning of RBF networks. Section 3 gives details of our proposed representation and operators. Section 4 describes experimental results employing the proposed approach and finally, in section 5, we conclude and suggest areas for further investigation.

2 Evolution of Radial Basis Function Networks using the Genetic Algorithm - Related Work

Much less attention has been paid to the artificial evolution of RBF networks compared to that directed towards their MLP counterparts, although both direct and indirect encodings have been investigated, along with evolution of learning parameters, and hybrid GA and gradient-based learning combinations. In this section we offer a summary of recent work.

In [8], Whitehead and Choate present an elegant approach which evolves "space filling curves" to determine basis function centres in conjunction with gradient-based learning to learn weights. Rather than encoding individual basis function centres and widths directly on the genome, this approach applies the GA to binary coded strings representing parameters for an algorithm which generates basis function centres. The learning rate employed in gradient-based learning for evaluation of individual fitness during evolution is encoded on the genotype and is evolved along with the space-filling curve parameters. Networks with large numbers of hidden nodes are indirectly penalised by setting the number of passes through the training data during the gradient-based learning phase to be inversely proportional to the number of hidden nodes. The method is applied to learning of a chaotic time-series and RBF networks are evolved that outperform networks determined using the k-means clustering algorithm in conjunction with gradient-based learning, using fewer hidden nodes, although the reported GA/RBF learning approach takes about 35-40 times as much CPU time as the k-means based algorithm.

In [9] Chen et al. describe a two level learning approach for RBF networks using a regularised orthogonal least squares (ROLS) algorithm at the lower level to learn connection weights. The ROLS learning algorithm employs a regulation parameter λ and basis function width ρ. The GA operates at a higher level by evolving values for λ and ρ to be applied during ROLS learning. Hence the GA is essentially being used to evolve both an architecture related parameter (basis function width) and a learning parameter. Regularisation is a technique used to improve the generalisation properties of trained networks by minimising a cost functional $\mathscr{E}(F) = \mathscr{E}_s(F) + \lambda\mathscr{E}_c(F)$, where F is the learned functional mapping, $\mathscr{E}_s$ is the standard error term (e.g. sum squared error) and $\mathscr{E}_c$ is the regularising term. The effect of regularisation in learning is to engender smoother input-output function mappings from a finite set of training examples, possibly containing noise. The regularisation parameter λ determines the relative contributions of the standard error term and the regularising term to the cost functional to be minimised during training. In the approach of Chen et al. networks are trained using the ROLS algorithm on a training set for particular values of λ and ρ. The trained networks are then tested on a separate test set and the inverse of the generalisation performance is the fitness for that particular (λ,ρ) pair used by the GA. This hybrid approach is successfuly applied to learning of a simple scalar function with added noise; to learning prediction of Mackey-Glass time series; and to learning prediction of sunspot time series. In reported experiments, the GA operating on λ and ρ together gave significantly better results compared with the GA operating on ρ only.

In [10] Neruda addresses the matter of functionally equivalent network parameterisations [11] in relation to the evolution of directly encoded RBF networks using the GA. This again raises the issue of the "competing conventions" problem described by Schaffer et al.[4] in relation to MLP networks. As with MLP networks, exchanging two hidden layer nodes in an RBF network together with their weights produces a network with identical input/output characteristics to the original. Neruda proposes a solution to the problem by selecting a single parameterisation for each class ("convention") called a canonical parameterisation. and restricting the search space of the GA accordingly. Crossover and mutation operators are defined which ensure that the offspring generated by the GA are consistent with the canonical parameterisation. Although no experimental results are presented in Neruda's paper, the arguments presented are compelling and next in section 3 we describe an RBF genome representation and associated genetic operators, independently arrived at and derived from studies in evolution of fuzzy controllers, which effectively implement a "canonical parameterisation".

3 A Representation and Genetic Operators for Evolving Radial Basis Function Neural Networks

In this section we introduce a genome representation for evolving RBF networks and describe associated genetic operators. The representation and operators are adapted from those described in [13,14] applying the GA to evolution of fuzzy rule-based systems. The similarity between RBF networks and specific types of fuzzy rule-based systems has been established by Jang and Sun [12], and their work suggests that an interchange of learning mechanisms between the two fields is of possible benefit. In [13] a Pittsburgh-style fuzzy classifier system is proposed which is evaluated in [14]. This system employs a variable length genome directly encoding fuzzy relations and membership functions, and uses a crossover operator based on crosspoints in the input variable space (and therefore the space of possible fuzzy rule membership function centres) instead of position on the genome string. This operator was devised to preserve building blocks of fuzzy rules whose input membership functions overlap and experiments reported in [14] demonstrate that the new crossover operator significantly outperforms simple one-point and two-point crossover operators in a function identification task and a control task using reinforcement learning.

In our own (admittedly simplistic) translation between fuzzy rule base language and RBF parlance, membership functions in fuzzy logic become RBF basis function centres and widths, and fuzzy relations (rules) become RBF hidden nodes. Bearing in mind the demonstrated similarities between RBF networks and fuzzy inference systems, it seems reasonable to extend the aforementioned GA/Fuzzy approach to the evolution of RBF network architectures, supplementing it with gradient-based learning.

The genome employed comprises a variable length concatenated string of composite "genes", where each gene encodes the parameters (basis function centre and widths) of a single hidden layer node together with the node's output connection weights. Using a variable length genome allows the number of hidden RBF network nodes encoded on the genome to evolve. Each composite gene, G_i, which encodes parameters for a hidden layer node is represented by the 2N-tuple

$$(C_{i1}, R_{i1}, \dots C_{ij}, R_{ij}, \dots, C_{iN}, R_{iN})$$

where N is the number of inputs, (C_{ij}, R_{ij}) is the centre and width of the Gaussian radial basis function of the hidden node for the jth input variable. All parameters are encoded as real numbers. We employ a modified version of the 2-point crossover operator described in [14] which operates as follows. Two vector crosspoints X_{1j} and X_{2j}, where each crosspoint vector contains an element for each input variable (N inputs), are chosen as follows:

$$X_{1j} = MIN_j + (MAX_j\text{-}MIN_j).Rd_1$$
$$X_{2j} = X_{1j} + (MAX_j\text{-}MIN_j).(Rd_2)^{1/N}$$

Rd_1 and Rd_2 are selected randomly in the range [0,1] with uniform probability density. $[MIN_j, MAX_j]$ is the allowed range of the jth input variable. After crossover, Child 1 contains those "genes" (i.e. encoded hidden layer nodes) which satisfy:

$$\forall j, ((C_{ij}>X_{1j}) \text{ AND } (C_{ij}<X_{2j})) \text{ OR } ((C_{ij} + MAX_j - MIN_j)<X_{2j})$$

together with "genes" from Parent 2 which do not satisfy this condition. Child 2 contains the remaining "genes" from both parents. The effect of this crossover operator is to exchange encoded hidden layer nodes whose radial basis function centres fall within the "hypervolume" (in the N-dimensional space of input variables) defined by X_{1j} and X_{2j}. A property of this crossover operator when applied to encodings of RBF networks is that it sidesteps the aforementioned "competing conventions" problem. Since crossover is carried out with reference to the space of the input variables rather than distance along the genome string, two strings which are different but interchange equivalent (i.e. represent different permutations of the same set of hidden layer nodes and therefore belong to different "conventions") are treated as identical for the purposes of crossover. Put another way, building blocks are viewed as existing in the input space as opposed to the space of positions in the genome string. Mutation operators are relatively straightforward. Real number creep is applied to basis function centres and widths, and is intended to perform the role of local search. Hidden layer node creation and deletion operators are employed. The node creation operator introduces a new hidden layer node with random centre and width and zero output weight. The node deletion operator simply deletes a hidden layer node selected at random.

Fitness evaluation employs network training to modify hidden layer output connection weights using the Least-Mean-Square(LMS) algorithm (please see [3] for a full description of the LMS algorithm). The number of training epochs is varied as evolution proceeds. In early stages of evolution, when encoded network architectures may be highly suboptimal, fewer training cycles are applied. As higher quality network architectures evolve, a larger number of training cycles are applied to more fully evaluate the merit of encoded networks.

4 Experimental Results and Discussion

The first set of experiments described pertain to a relatively simple single-input, single-output (SISO) function identification task, that of learning the SINESQUARE function $y = \sin(20x^2)$ in the input range [0,1]. This function is chosen since the input-output mapping varies in complexity over the input space and the discovery of "economical" (i.e. low order) assemblies of RBF network hidden layer nodes is important for scaling to higher dimensions. In a second set of experiments we apply the proposed learning method to a benchmark problem of prediction of a chaotic time series. This problem involves a 4-input 1-output RBF network.

4.1 SineSquare Function Experiments

To evaluate the performance of the proposed representation and crossover operator, experiments were carried out to compare it against straightforward one-point and two-point crossover. Fixed length genomes were employed in experiments using one/two-point crossover. These experiments were performed with 8, 10, 12, 15 and 20 encoded hidden layer nodes. In experiments using the proposed variable length genotype, the maximum allowed number of encoded hidden layer nodes were restricted to these values. The GA was run for 50 generations, replacing the weakest 40 individuals at each generation, using rank-based selection with s = 1.8. The chromosome mutation rate was 0.2 and the crossover rate 0.8. The LMS learning algorithm was run for 10 training epochs over a set of 40 equally spaced input points in the range [0,1] with the learning rate parameter, η , set to 0.3. Hidden layer node weights were set to zero before LMS learning was applied and weights were not inherited. The evaluation function is the inverse of the sum squared error over the training set after training. In each case, node creation and node deletion operators were applied to new offspring with probability 0.1. For fixed length genomes, these two operators were applied together. Encoded hidden layer node centres and widths were assigned randomly in the range [0,1] and [0,1/NumberOfNodes] respectively. Figure 2 shows the sum square error of the best evolved networks for different network sizes and different crossover operators. These results are the average of 20 runs in each case using a different random seed for each run. The new crossover operator outperforms the straightforward one-point and two-point operators, particularly so in the evolution of networks with small numbers of hidden nodes. For larger networks (e.g. 15, 20 hidden nodes) the performance improvement is not so significant, presumably because the learning problem becomes easier as the number of hidden layer nodes is increased.

The best evolved networks were fully trained and their perfomance compared with fully trained networks with fixed, equally spaced basis function centres and equal widths. The results are shown in Figure 3. When the number of hidden nodes is small (e.g. 8,10) evolved networks significantly outperform the fixed networks. At larger network sizes, the fixed networks' performance improves dramatically. There is a simple explanation for this - networks with a small number of equally spaced basis functions are incapable of accurately learning in regions of the input space where the input/output mapping complexity is high. For the SINESQUARE function this complexity, in terms of the frequency of oscillation of the function, increases with increasing x. With large numbers of nodes, the fixed networks have a sufficient density of basis functions in this region to accurately learn the function. However this is at the expense of having an equal density of basis functions in regions where the input/output mapping is less complex, which is hardly economical. When the centres and widths of basis functions of evolved networks were inspected, these were observed to yield a much more economical spread. Figure 4 depicts an evolved 7-node network. Each horizontal line represents a hidden layer node basis function centre and width, with the vertical displacement showing the trained output weight of the node. An interesting feature of this evolved solution is in the input region [0.5,1.0]. A single large width basis function (N2) is "pulling" the output high over the entire region. Two other, smaller width, basis functions pull the output low near the troughs in the function. This might be viewed as a form of basis function "default hierarchy", which clearly provides a mechanism for the learning of economical networks with small numbers of hidden nodes.

4.2 Scaling Up - Mackey Glass Time Series Prediction

In this section experiments are described in learning the chaotic time series generated by the Mackey-Glass differential equation [15]:

$$\frac{dx(t)}{dt} = -bx(t) + a.\frac{x(t-T)}{1+x(t-T)^{10}}$$

A sample of the Mackey-Glass time series is shown in Figure 5. Following previous research [8], the time series was generated with the parameter values a = 0.2, b = 0.1 and T = 17, and the training data consisted of 500 randomly selected points in the time series. Test data consisted of 500 points in sequence following the training data. As in previous work, the task for the neural network is to predict the value of the time series at point x[t+I] from the earlier points x[t], x[t-D], x[t-2D] and x[t-3D] where D = 6 timesteps, and I = 85 timesteps into the future. Encoded RBF networks therefore have four inputs and one output. For this more difficult problem, the GA is supplemented with a cover operator which generates a new hidden layer node if an input vector is encountered which does not activate any of the encoded basis functions. The fitness of each individual is based on the normalised error over the training set after training is completed. This normalised error is calculated in the same way as in [8] and is the root-mean-squared error over the training set divided by the standard deviation of the set of correct outputs. Rank based selection is employed with s = 1.8. After evolution, the best evolved RBF networks were fully trained using the LMS algorithm over the training set, then finally evaluated using the test data set.

Experiments were carried out which restricted the maximum of the variable hidden layer size to 20, 40, 60, 80 and 100 nodes. Figure 6 shows the results of applying different operators using 200 generations and averaged over five independent runs. Results using the new crossover operator compare well with those obtained by Whitehead and Choate[8] using k-means clustering and using evolved space filling curves. For example, we obtained normalised errors of 0.25, 0.18 and 0.15 respectively for RBF networks with a maximum of 40, 60 and 100 hidden layer nodes. Results presented in [8] report normalised errors of approximately 0.34, 0.28 and 0.19 (using k-means clustering) and approximately 0.32, 0.20 and 0.13 (using evolved space-filling curves) respectively for networks containing 40, 70 and 110 hidden layer nodes. The results we have obtained compare well since the maximum number of single weight changes (which represents the innermost loop of the hybrid learning algorithm) was 220 million compared with 1 billion employed in [8].

5 Conclusions and Further Work

We have described a representation and associated genetic operators for evolving economical radial basis function neural networks. A crossover operator, initially devised for fuzzy classifier systems, and which overcomes the competing conventions problem for evolution of RBF networks, has been described and evaluated. Initial

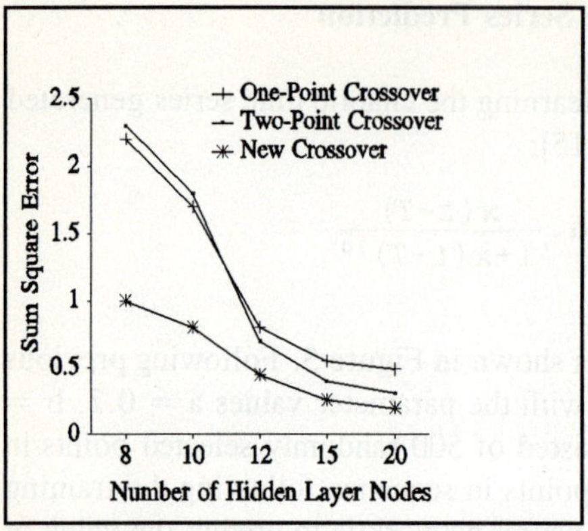

Fig. 2 Error vs. Network Size for Different Crossover Operators

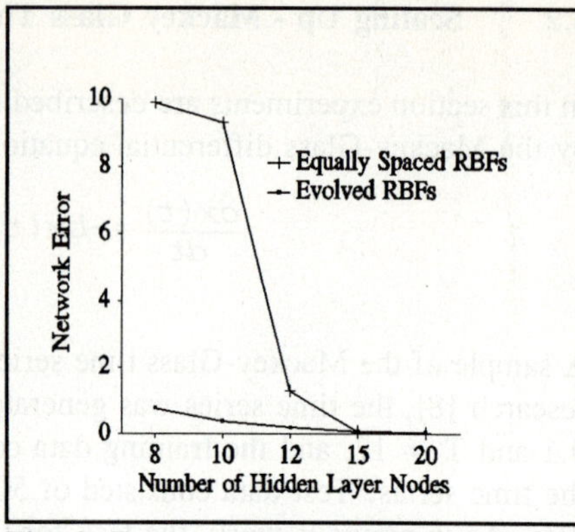

Fig. 3 Error vs. Network Size for Evolved and "Fixed" RBF Networks

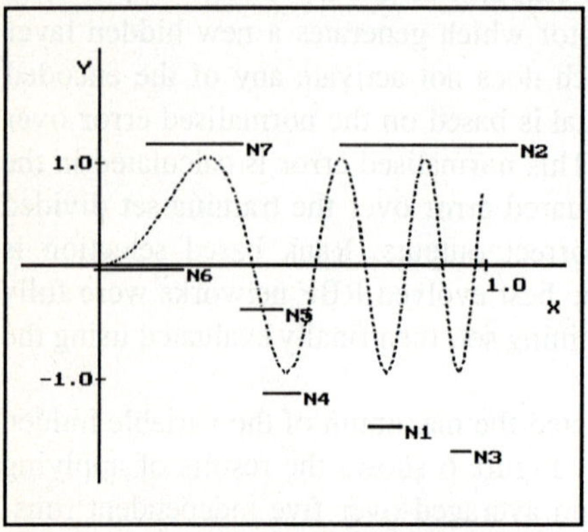

Fig. 4 Evolved Network Basis Functions

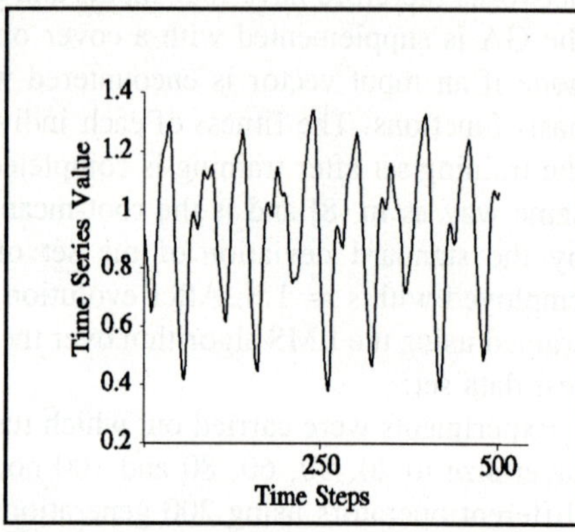

Fig. 5 Sample of Mackey-Glass Time Series

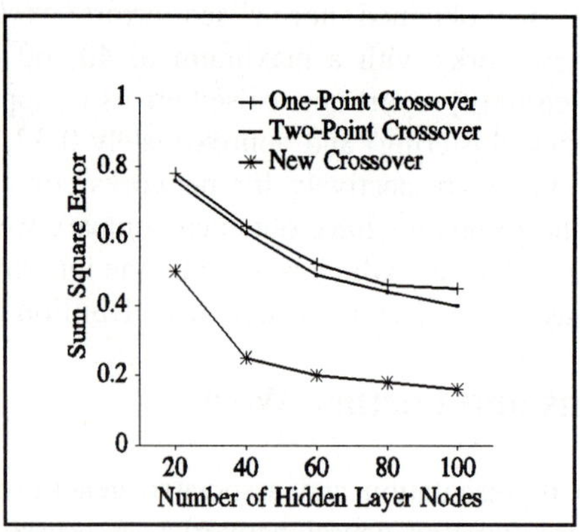

Fig. 6 Error using Different Crossover Operators on the Mackey-Glass Problem

experimental results indicate that the proposed hybrid learning system is able to produce high performance RBF networks with relatively few hidden nodes and using relatively few weight changes during the evolutionary process. Interactions between the gradient-based learning process and evolution of RBF networks requires further attention, empirically and theoretically.

References

[1] Broomhead D.S. and Lowe D., Multivariable functional interpolation and adaptive networks. Complex Systems 2, 321-355, 1988.

[2] Poggio T. and Girosi F., Networks for approximation and learning. Proceedings of the IEEE 78, 1481-1497, 1990.

[3] Haykin S. Neural Networks. Macmillan College Publishing Company, New York, NY, 1994.

[4] Schaffer J.D., Whitley D. and Eschelman L.J., Combinations of genetic algorithms and neural networks: a survey of the state of the art. In Proceedings of the International Workshop on Combinations of Genetic Algorithms and Neural Networks (COGANN-92), IEEE, pp1-37, 1992.

[5] Yao X., A review of evolutionary artificial neural networks. International Journal of Intelligent Systems, 8, pp539-567, 1993

[6] Miller G.F., Todd P.M., Hegde S.U., Designing neural networks using genetic algorithms. Complex Systems 4, pp461-476, 1990.

[7] Angeline P.J., Saunders G.M. and Pollack J.B., An evolutionary algorithm that constructs recurrent neural networks. IEEE Transactions on Neural Networks, 5, 1, pp54-65, January 1994.

[8] Whitehead B.A. and Choate T.D., Evolving space-filling curves to distribute radial basis functions over an input space. IEEE Transactions on Neural Networks, 5, 1, pp 15-23, January 1994.

[9] Chen S., Wu Y. and Alkadhimi K., A two-layer learning method for radial basis function networks using combined genetic and regularised OLS algorithms. In Proceedings of the 1st IEE/IEEE International Conference on Genetic Algorithms in Engineering Systems: Innovations and Applications, pp245-249, 1995.

[10] Neruda R., Functional equivalence and genetic learning of RBF networks. In Pearson D.W., Steele N.C. and Albrecht R.F. (eds) Artificial Neural Nets and Genetic Algorithms, pp53-56, Springer-Verlag, 1995.

[11] Hecht-Nielson R., On the algebraic structure of feed-forward network weight spaces. In Advanced Neural Computers, pp129-135, Elsevier, 1990

[12] Jang J.R. and Sun C.T. (1993). Functional equivalence between radial basis function networks and fuzzy inference systems. IEEE Transactions on Neural Networks,4,1. pp156-159.

[13] Carse B. and Fogarty T.C. (1994). A fuzzy classifier system using the Pittsburgh approach. In Davidor Y., Schwefel H.P. and Maenner (eds) PPSN III- Proceedings of the International Conference on Evolutionary Computation, pp260-269. Springer-Verlag Berlin Heidelberg.

[14] Carse B., Fogarty T.C. and Munro A., Evolving fuzzy rule based controllers using genetic algorithms. To appear in Fuzzy Sets and Systems, 1996.

[15] Mackey M.C. and Glass L., Oscillation and chaos in phsiological control systems, Science vol. 197, pp287-289, 1977.

A Three-Stage Method for Designing Genetic Fuzzy Systems by Learning from Examples *

Oscar Cordón, Francisco Herrera and Manuel Lozano

Dept. of Computer Science and Artificial Intelligence.
E.T.S. de Ingeniería Informática.
University of Granada, 18071 - Granada, Spain.
e-mail: ocordon, herrera, lozano@robinson.ugr.es

Abstract. In this paper, we present a three step method for designing Genetic Fuzzy Systems combining an iterative and increasing rule derivation stage and two genetic-based simplification and tuning processes. The performance of the method proposed is shown by measuring the accuracy of the Fuzzy Logic Controllers designed in the fuzzy modeling of two three-dimensional control surfaces and comparing them with others generated by using Wang and Mendel's method, one of the most widely known iterative rule derivation processes.

1 Introduction

Fuzzy Logic Controllers (FLCs) are now considered as one of the most important applications of Fuzzy Set Theory proposed by Zadeh in [10]. FLCs are knowledge-based controllers that make use of the known knowledge of the process, expressed in the form of fuzzy linguistic control rules collected in a knowledge base (KB), to control it. The advantage of this approach with respect to the classical *Control Theory* is that it has no need for expressing the relationships existing in the system by means of a mathematical model, which constitutes a very difficult task in many real situations presenting non linear characteristics or complex dynamics.

Nowadays, FLCs [4] have been succesfully applied to a wide range of engineering control processes. Several tasks have to be performed in order to design an intelligent control system of this kind for a concrete application. One of the most important and difficult ones is the extraction of the expert known knowledge from the controlled system. The difficulty presented by the human process operators to express their knowledge in the form of control rules has made researchers develop automatic techniques for performing this task. Over the last few years, many different approaches have been presented taking the Genetic Algorithms (GAs) as a base, obtaining the so-called Genetic Fuzzy Systems (GFSs).

In this paper, we present a three-stage process for designing GFSs combining an iterative and increasing rule derivation method and two genetic-based simplification and tuning processes, and compare its behaviour with the iterative method proposed by Wang and Mendel in the fuzzy modeling of two three-dimensional control surfaces.

In order to put this into effect, this paper is set up as follows. The next section presents some guidelines on the GFSs design. In Sect. 3, the proposed method is introduced by describing in detail each one of the three stages composing

* This research has been partially supported by DGICYT PB92-0933

it. Section 4 presents the two control surfaces selected for studying the process accuracy while Sect. 5 shows the experiments developed and the different results obtained. Finally, in Sect. 6 some concluding remarks are pointed out.

2 Designing Genetic Fuzzy Systems

Recently, numerous papers and applications combining fuzzy concepts and GAs have been published and there is increasing interest about the integration of these two topics. In particular, there are a great number of publications exploring the use of GAs for designing FLCs by deriving their KBs. These kinds of systems are generically called GFSs.

GAs [5] have demostrated to be a powerful tool for automating the KB definition since adaptive control, learning and self-organization can be considered in a lot of cases as optimization or search processes.

The KB is the FLC component containing the expert knowledge known about the controlled system. It is comprised of two components, a *Data Base* (DB), containing the definitions of the fuzzy control rule linguistic labels, and a *Rule Base* (RB), constituted by the collection of fuzzy control rules representing the expert knowledge.

In view of the GFS approaches for designing FLCs developed in the last few years, it is possible to distinguish among three different groups according to the KB components involved in the design process. These ones are the following (a more complete description of each family and several methods belonging to each one of them is to be found in [2], and for a complete bibliography refer to [3], section 3.13):

1. *Genetic definition of the* FLC DB: One of the FLC DB definition modes is based on the genetic tuning of this FLC component. Taking as a base a previously primary DB definition, the different DB parameters are set up in order to obtain high-performance FLCs.
2. *Genetic derivation of the* FLC RB: The purpose of the methods belonging to this family is to derive an FLC RB by assuming the existence of a previously defined DB. A common characteristic for most of them is that they consider the RB represented in the form of a decision table. In this kind of structure, each table cell represents a fuzzy control rule that may belong to the RB.
3. *Genetic learning of the* FLC KB: This last group is based on learning complete FLC KBs, that is, developing a DB genetic definition and an RB genetic derivation in the same process. This is the one for which more the most contributions have been made in the last few years.

3 Description of the Three-stage Genetic Fuzzy System Design Method

In this section, we present a GFS design method belonging to the third family mentioned above. In this way, making use of our process it will be possible to automatically generate a complete FLC KB when a training set formed by numerical input-output (state-control) problem variable pairs recorded experimentally is available.

The method proposed consists of the following three steps, whilst maintaining the generic structure used in [8]:

1. An iterative and increasing RB generation process of desirable fuzzy control rules able to include the complete knowledge of the set of examples,
2. A genetic rule simplification process, which finds the final RB able to approximate the input-output behaviour of the real system. It is based on eliminating some unnecessary rules from the rule set obtained in the previous stage, avoiding thus the possible overlearning.
3. A genetic tuning process of the DB used in order to improve as far as possible the accuracy of the final KB.

3.1 The Rule Base Generation Process

The first stage consists of an increasing RB generation process based on an iterative exploration of the problem search space. Apart from the training data set E_p, a previously defined DB, constituted by uniform fuzzy partitions with triangular membership functions crossing at height 0.5, is considered. The number of linguistic terms forming each one of them can be specified by the GFS designer in order to obtain the desired granularity level. Figure 1 shows the generic structure of a fuzzy partition with seven linguistic labels:

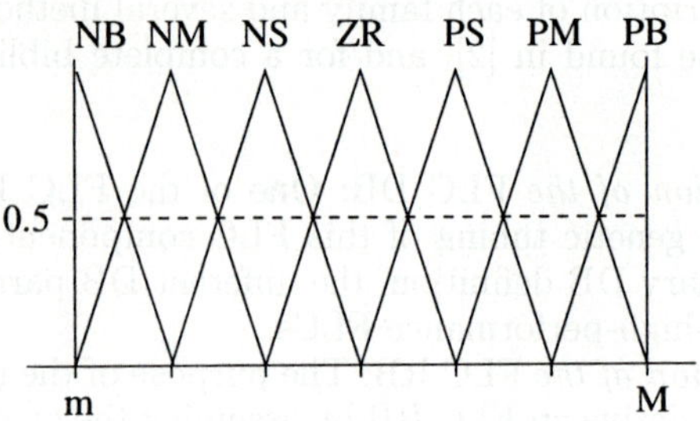

Fig. 1. Graphical representation of a possible fuzzy partition

This component allows us to obtain a set of Mamdani-type fuzzy control rules B^g describing the system behaviour. In order to do that, it is necessary to establish a condition for it. This is the requirement of covering all possible situation-action pairs, $e_l \in E_p$, the *completeness property* [6, 8]. This may be formalized for a constant $\tau \in [0,1]$, it requires the non-zero union of fuzzy sets $A_i(\cdot), B_i(\cdot), i = 1, ..., T, T = |B^g|$, and is formulated by the following expressions:

$$C_R(e_l) = \bigcup_{i=1..T} R_i(e_l) \geq \tau \quad , \quad l = 1, ..., p \qquad (1)$$

$$R_i : \text{If } x_1 \text{ is } A_{i1} \text{ and ... and } x_n \text{ is } A_{in} \text{ then } y \text{ is } B \qquad (2)$$

$$e_l = (ex_1^l, \ldots, ex_n^l, ey^l) \qquad (3)$$

$$R_i(e_l) = *(A_i(ex^l), B_i(ey^l)) \tag{4}$$

$$A_i(ex^l) = *(A_{i1}(ex_1^l), ..., A_{in}(ex_n^l)) \tag{5}$$

where $*$ is a t-norm, and $R_i(e_l)$ is the *compatibility degree* between the rule R_i and the example e_l.

Given a set of rules R, the *covering value* of an example e_l is defined as

$$CV_R(e_l) = \sum_{i=1}^{T} R_i(e_l) \tag{6}$$

and we require the following condition

$$CV_R(e_l) \geq \epsilon \quad l = 1, ..., p. \tag{7}$$

A good set of rules must satisfy both the conditions presented above, to verify the completeness property and to have an adequate final covering value.

The RB is derived rule by rule, selecting the most accurated one at each step in the algorithm. Once this rule is obtained, its covering over the training set examples is taken into acccount. Those examples covered in a degree higher than a value ϵ specified by the GFS designer are removed from the training set. Hence, the increasing example covering guides the search to other promising space zones at each step.

Each time the best rule have to be selected in the generation process, the accuracy of the candidates is measured by using a multicriteria fitness function. This function is designed taking into account the following three criteria allowing to ensure the completeness and consistency of the final KB generated:

a) *High frequency value* [8]
The frequency of a fuzzy control rule, R_i, through the set of examples, E_p, is defined as:

$$\Psi_{E_p}(R_i) = \frac{\sum_{l=1}^{p} R_i(e_l)}{p} . \tag{8}$$

b) *High average covering degree over positive examples* [8]
The set of positive examples to R_i with compatibility degree greater than or equal to ω is defined as:

$$E_\omega^+(R_i) = \{e_l \in E_p / R_i(e_l) \geq \omega\} . \tag{9}$$

When $n_\omega^+(R_i) = |E_\omega^+(R_i)|$, the *average covering degree* on $E_\omega^+(R_i)$ can be defined as:

$$G_\omega(R_i) = \sum_{e_l \in E_\omega^+(R_i)} R_i(e_l) / n_\omega^+(R_i) . \tag{10}$$

c) *Small negative examples set* [6]
The set of the negative examples to R_i is defined as:

$$E^-(R_i) = \{e_l \in E_p / R_i(e_l) = 0 \text{ and } A_i(ex^l) > 0\} \ . \qquad (11)$$

An example is considered negative for a rule when it better matches some other rule that has the same antecedent but a different consequent. The negative examples are always considered over the complete training set.
With $n^-_{R_i} = |E^-(R_i)|$ being the number of negative examples, the *penalty function on the negative examples set* will be:

$$g_n(R_i{}^-) = \begin{cases} 1 & \text{if } n^-_{R_i} \leq k \cdot n^+_\omega(R_i) \\ \frac{1}{n^-_{R_i} - kn^+_\omega(R_i) + exp(1)} & \text{otherwise} \end{cases} \ . \qquad (12)$$

where we permit up to a percentage of the number of positive examples, $k \cdot n^+_\omega(R_i)$, of negative examples per rule without any penalty. This percentage is determined by the parameter $k \in [0, 1]$.

Therefore these three criteria are combined into a fitness function using any aggregation function increasing in the three variables. In this paper, we work with the product in the following way:

$$F(R_i) = \Psi_{E_p}(R_i) \cdot G_\omega(R_i) \cdot g_n(R_i{}^-) \ . \qquad (13)$$

Rules getting a higher value in this function will be more accurate.

Taking the previous comments into account, the generation method is developed in the following steps:

1. Initialization:
   (a) To introduce the k, ω, and ϵ parameter values.
   (b) To set the example covering degree $CV[l] \leftarrow 0$, $l = 1, ..., p$.
   (c) To initialize the final Rule Base B^g to empty.
2. To initialize the candidate fuzzy rule set B^c to empty.
3. For every $e_l \in E_p$, generate the fuzzy rule R_c best covering it by taking the linguistic label matching best with the e_l component value for each variable. If $R_c \notin B^c$, add it to B^c.
4. To evaluate all the fuzzy rules contained in B^c and to select the one getting a higher value in the fitness function, R_r.
5. To introduce R_r into the set of rules B^g.
6. For every $e_l \in E_p$ do
   (a) $CV[l] \leftarrow CV[l] + R_r(e_l)$.
   (b) If $CV[l] \geq \epsilon$ then remove e_l from E_p.
7. If $E_p = \emptyset$ then Stop else return to Step 2.

3.2 The Genetic Rule Base Simplification Process

Due to the iterative nature of the generation process, an overlearning phenomenon may appear. This occurs when some examples are covered at a higher degree than the desired one and it makes the RB obtained perform worse. In order to solve this problem and improve its accuracy, it is necessary to simplify the rule set obtained from the previous process, removing the redundant rules for deriving the final RB allowing the system to be controllled.

The simplification process used was proposed in [8]. It is based on a binary coded GA, in which the selection of the individuals is developed using the stochastic universal sampling procedure proposed by Baker in [1] together with an elitist selection scheme, and the recombination is put into effect by using the classical binary multipoint crossover (performed at two points) and uniform mutation operators.

The coding scheme generates fixed-length chromosomes. Considering the rules contained in the rule set derived from the previous step counted from 1 to m, an m-bit string $C = (c_1, ..., c_m)$ represents a subset of candidate rules to form the RB finally obtained as this stage output, B^s, such that,

$$If\ c_i = 1\ then\ R_i \in B^s\ else\ R_i \notin B^s \ . \tag{14}$$

The initial population is generated by introducing a chromosome representing the complete previouslly obtained rule set B^g, that is, with every $c_i = 1$. The remaining chromosomes are selected at random.

As regards to the fitness funtion, $E(\cdot)$ it is based on an application specific measure usually employed in the design of GFSs, the medium square error (SE) over a training data set, E_{TDS}, which is represented by the following expression:

$$E(C_j) = \frac{1}{2|E_{TDS}|} \sum_{e_l \in E_{TDS}} (ey^l - S(ex^l))^2 \ , \tag{15}$$

where $S(ex^l)$ is the output value obtained from the FLC using the RB coded in C_j, $R(C_j)$ when the state variable values are ex^l, and ey^l is the known desired value.

Anyway, there is a need to keep the *control rule completeness* property considered in the previous stage. An FLC must always be able to infer a proper control action for every process state. We shall ensure this condition by forcing every example contained in the training set to be covered by the encoded RB in a degree greater than or equal to τ,

$$C_{R(C_j)}(e_l) = \bigcup_{j=1..T} R_j(e_l) \geq \tau, \quad \forall e_l \in E_{TDS} \text{ and } R_j \in R(C_j) \ , \tag{16}$$

where τ is the minimal training set completeness degree acepted in the simplification process. Usually, τ is less than or equal to ω, the compatibility degree used in the generation process.

Therefore, we define a *training set completeness degree* of $R(C_j)$ over the set of examples E_{TDS} as

$$TSCD(R(C_j), E_{TDS}) = \bigcap_{e_l \in E_{TDS}} C_{R(C_j)}(e_l) \ . \tag{17}$$

and the final fitness function penalizing the lack of the completeness property is:

$$F(C_j) = \begin{cases} E(C_j) & \text{if } TSCD(R(C_j), E_{TDS}) \geq \tau \\ \frac{1}{2}\sum_{e_l \in E_{TDS}} (ey^l)^2 & \text{otherwise.} \end{cases} \tag{18}$$

3.3 The Genetic Data Base Tuning Process

Finally, a modified version of the genetic tuning method presented in [7] is applied. The process is based on the existence of a previous complete KB, that is, an initial DB definition and an RB constituted by m fuzzy control rules.

Each chromosome forming the genetic population will encode a complete DB definition that will be combined with the simplified RB obtained in the previous stage in order to evaluate the individual adaption.

The GA designed for the tuning process presents real coding issue, uses the stochastic universal sampling [1] as a selection procedure and Michaelewicz's non-uniform mutation operator. As regards to the crossover operator, the Max-Min-Arithmetical [7], which makes use of fuzzy tools in order to improve the GA behaviour, is employed.

As we have commented before, the primary fuzzy sets considered in the initial linguistic variables fuzzy partitions are triangular-shaped (see Fig. 1). Thus, each one of the membership functions has an associated parametric representation based on a 3-tuple of real values and a primary fuzzy partition can be represented by an array composed by $3 \cdot N$ real values, with N being the number of terms forming the linguistic variable term set. The complete FLC DB for a problem in which m linguistic variables are involved is encoded into a fixed length real coded chromosome C_r built by joining the partial representations of each one of the variable fuzzy partitions as is shown in the following:

$$\begin{aligned} C_{ri} &= (a_{i1}, b_{i1}, c_{i1}, \ldots, a_{iN_i}, b_{iN_i}, c_{iN_i}) \ , \\ C_r &= C_{r1}\ C_{r2}\ \ldots\ C_{rm} \ . \end{aligned} \tag{19}$$

The initial gene pool is created making use of the initial DB definition. This is encoded directly in a chromosome, denoted as C_1. The remaining individuals are generated by associating an interval of performance, $[c_h^l, c_h^r]$ to every gene c_h in C_1, $h = 1 \ldots \sum_{i=1}^{m} N_i \cdot 3$. Each interval of performance will be the interval of adjustment for the corresponding gene, $c_h \in [c_h^l, c_h^r]$.

If (t mod 3) = 1 then c_t is the left value of the support of a fuzzy number. The fuzzy number is defined by the three parameters (c_t, c_{t+1}, c_{t+2}), and the intervals of performance are the following.

$$\begin{aligned} c_t &\in [c_t^l, c_t^r] = [c_t - \tfrac{c_{t+1}-c_t}{2}, c_t + \tfrac{c_{t+1}-c_t}{2}] \ , \\ c_{t+1} &\in [c_{t+1}^l, c_{t+1}^r] = [c_{t+1} - \tfrac{c_{t+1}-c_t}{2}, c_{t+1} + \tfrac{c_{t+2}-c_{t+1}}{2}] \ , \\ c_{t+2} &\in [c_{t+2}^l, c_{t+2}^r] = [c_{t+2} - \tfrac{c_{t+2}-c_{t+1}}{2}, c_{t+2} + \tfrac{c_{t+2}-c_{t+1}}{2}] \ . \end{aligned} \tag{20}$$

Therefore we create a population of chromosomes containing C_1 as its first individual and the remaining ones initiated randomly, with each gene being in its respective interval of performance.

The fitness function $E(\cdot)$ defined in the previous stage is used for evaluating the adaptation of each individual of the population in the genetic tuning process as well.

4 Examples Selected: Fuzzy Modeling of Some Complex Control Surfaces

In order to analyze the accuracy of the method proposed, we have selected two n-dimensional mathematical functions for using them to derive theoretical three-dimensional control surfaces. Three different ways of fuzzy modeling these surfaces are going to be compared by using the following design methods:

1. the widely employed Wang and Mendel's (WM) method [9],
2. a two-stage method based on obtaining a complete KB by deriving the RB by means of the WM method and defining the DB by means of the genetic tuning method constituting the third stage of the method proposed, and
3. the GFS design method proposed in this paper.

The mathematical functions and the variable universes of discourse considered are shown below. The *spherical model*, F_1, is an unimodal function while the *generalized Rastrigin function*, F_2, is a strongly multimodal one, as may be observed in their graphical representations shown in Fig. 2:

$$\begin{array}{c} F_1(x_1, x_2) = x_1^2 + x_2^2, \\ x_1, x_2 \in [-5, 5], F_1(x_1, x_2) \in [0, 50] \ . \end{array} \tag{21}$$

$$\begin{array}{c} F_2(x_1, x_2) = x_1^2 + x_2^2 - cos(18x_1) - cos(18x_2), \\ x_1, x_2 \in [-1, 1], F_2(x_1, x_2) \in [2, 3.5231] \ . \end{array} \tag{22}$$

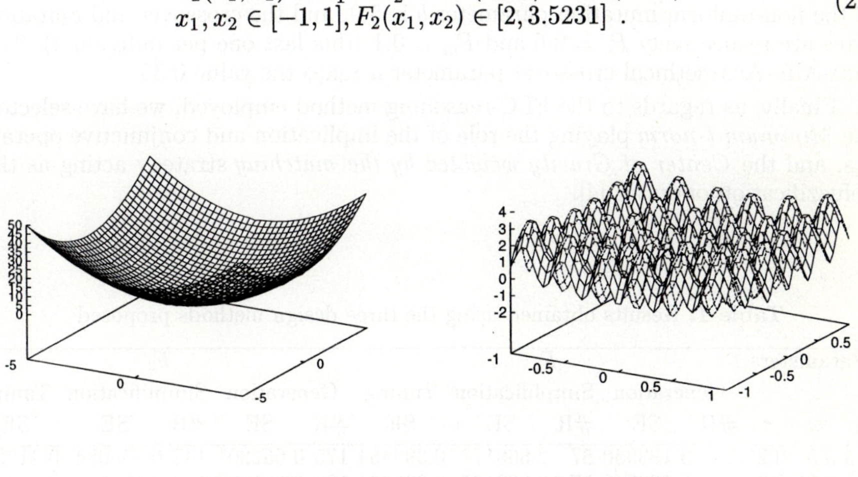

Fig. 2. Graphical representation of F_1 and F_2

5 Experiments Developed and Results Obtained

For each one of the functions presented in the previous section, a training data set uniformly distributed in the three-dimensional definition space has been obtained experimentally. In this way, two sets with 1681 values have been generated by taking 41 values for each one of the two state variables considered to be uniformly distributed in their respective intervals.

Two data sets have been generated for their use as test sets for evaluating the performance of the learning method, avoiding any possible bias related to the data in the training set. The size of these data sets is a percentage of the corresponding training set one, which is ten percent to be precise. The data are obtained by generating, at random, the state variable values in the concrete universes of discourse for each one of them, and computing the associated output variable value. Hence two test sets formed by 168 data are used to measure the accuracy of the FLCs designed by computing the Square Error for them.

The initial DB used in the three aforementioned methods is constituted by three primary fuzzy partitions (two corresponding to the state variables and one associated to the control one) formed by *seven linguistic terms* with triangular-shaped fuzzy sets giving meaning to them (as shown in Fig. 1), and the adequate scaling factors to translate the generic universe of discourse into the one associated with each problem variable.

The following parameter values, corresponding to the first two stages, are combined to determine the different runs of the method to be carried out: $\omega = 0.05, 0.5$, $\epsilon = 0.5, 1.0, 1.5$, and $\tau = 0.25, 0.5$. It leads to an overall number of 12 runs for each function. With respect to the remaining parameters, in all the runs performed in the generation process, the parameter k takes the fixed value 0.1 and the t-norm $*$ used in the rule generation process is the Minimum. The genetic simplification and tuning processes run over 500 and 1000 generations respectively. In both cases, the population is formed by 61 individuals, the value of the non-uniform mutation parameter b is 5.0, and the crossover and mutation rates are respectively $P_c = 0.6$ and $P_m = 0.1$ (this last one per individual). The Max-Min-Aritmethical crossover parameter a takes the value 0.35.

Finally, as regards to the FLC reasoning method employed, we have selected the *Minimum t-norm* playing the role of the implication and conjunctive operators, and the *Center of Gravity weighted by the matching* strategy acting as the defuzzification operator [4].

Table 1. Results obtained using the three design methods proposed

Parameters			F_1					F_2				
			Generation		Simplification		Tuning	Generation		Simplification		Tuning
ϵ	ω	τ	#R	SE	#R	SE	SE	#R	SE	#R	SE	SE
0.5	0.5	0.25	73	5.183930	57	2.660177	0.399484	175	0.652201	147	0.585084	0.412264
0.5	0.05	0.25	73	5.183930	57	2.660177	0.399484	182	0.635634	156	0.571281	0.410232
1.0	0.5	0.25	122	4.582979	63	2.121200	0.359204	272	0.665791	191	0.540436	0.420476
1.0	0.05	0.25	118	4.710966	65	2.066748	0.323362	281	0.639040	198	0.541107	0.423427
1.5	0.5	0.25	167	3.498697	91	1.622512	0.317471	367	0.672863	242	0.505367	0.385740
1.5	0.05	0.25	167	3.498697	91	1.622512	0.317471	373	0.672165	243	0.518951	0.393275
0.5	0.5	0.5	73	5.183930	63	4.723776	0.336022	175	0.652201	171	0.644315	0.419001
0.5	0.05	0.5	73	5.183930	63	4.723776	0.336022	182	0.635634	177	0.619592	0.413059
1.0	0.5	0.5	122	4.582979	76	2.434697	0.377507	272	0.665791	216	0.563345	0.416299
1.0	0.05	0.5	118	4.710966	74	2.402340	0.397477	281	0.639040	214	0.553970	0.415261
1.5	0.5	0.5	167	3.498697	97	1.735540	0.313888	367	0.672863	251	0.532816	0.405507
1.5	0.05	0.5	167	3.498697	97	1.735540	0.313888	373	0.672165	263	0.518454	0.382833
W	*M*		49	4.651811			0.463816	49	2.094091			0.970021

The results obtained in the different experiments are collected in table 1 where $\#R$ stands for the number of rules of the corresponding KB. The last table row shows the results corresponding to both design processes based on the WM RB generation method (the Generation columns are related to the single WM method and the Tuning column to the two-stage design process). In view of these results, the good behaviour presented by the proposed method may be clearly observed. The KBs obtained using it are always more accurate than those obtained from the other two processes. It has to be noted that the ones obtained from both WM design processes present less rules. Although this fact may be considered as an advantage in real-time control applications, in our case the purpose is to obtain the best possible fuzzy identification of the control surfaces so that this factor does not present a significative influence. Another important conclusion that can be drawn is the good performance of the genetic tuning process, even working regardless of the complete three step method. This may be viewed studying the high accuracy improvement obtained over the WM RBs.

6 Concluding Remarks

A three-stage method for designing GFSs combining an iterative and two genetic processes has been presented. The proposed method has been compared with two other design processes based on the WM method in the fuzzy modeling of two three-dimensional control surfaces. It has clearly shown the best performance.

References

1. Baker, J.E.: Reducing Bias and Inefficiency in the Selection Algorithm. Proceedings of the Second International Conference on Genetic Algorithms, Lawrence Erlbaum, Hillsdale, NJ (1987) 14–21.
2. Cordón, O., Herrera, F.: A General Study on Genetic Fuzzy Systems. J. Periaux, G. Winter, M. Galán, and P. Cuesta (Eds.), Genetic Algorithms in Engineering and Computer Science. John Wiley and Sons (1995) 33–57.
3. Cordón, O., Herrera, F., Lozano, M.: A Classified Review on the Combination Fuzzy Logic-Genetic Algorithms Bibliography. Technical Report DECSAI–95129, Dept. of Computer Science and A.I., University of Granada, Spain (November 1995) (last version May 1996). Available at `http://decsai.ugr.es/~herrera/fl-ga.html`
4. Driankov, D., Hellendoorn, H., Reinfrank, M.: An Introduction to Fuzzy Control. Springer-Verlag (1993).
5. Goldberg, D.E.: Genetic Algorithms in Search, Optimization, and Machine Learning. Addison-Wesley, New York (1989).
6. González, A., Pérez, R. Completeness and Consistency Conditions for Learning Fuzzy Rules. Technical Report DECSAI-95103, Dept. of Computer Science and Artificial Intelligence, University of Granada, 18071 Granada, Spain (November 1995).
7. Herrera, F., Lozano, M., Verdegay, J.L.: Tuning Fuzzy Controllers by Genetic Algorithms. International Journal of Approximate Reasoning **12** (1995) 299–315.
8. Herrera, F., Lozano, M., Verdegay, J.L.: A Learning Process for Fuzzy Control Rules Using Genetic Algorithms. Technical Report DECSAI–95108, Dept. of Computer Science and A.I., University of Granada, Spain (February 1995).
9. Wang, L.X., Mendel, J.M.: Generating Fuzzy Rules by Learning from Examples. IEEE Transactions on Systems, Man, and Cybernetics **22** (1992) 1414–1427.
10. Zadeh, L.A.: Fuzzy Sets. Information and Control **8** (1965) 338–353.

Learning Heuristics for OBDD Minimization by Evolutionary Algorithms

Rolf Drechsler, Nicole Göckel, Bernd Becker

Institute of Computer Science
Albert-Ludwigs-University
79110 Freiburg im Breisgau,Germany
email: <name>@informatik.uni-freiburg.de

Abstract. *Ordered Binary Decision Diagrams (OBDDs) are the state-of-the-art data structure in CAD for ICs. OBDDs are very sensitive to the chosen variable ordering, i.e. the size may vary from linear to exponential.*

In this paper we present an Evolutionary Algorithm (EA) that learns good heuristics for OBDD minimization starting from a given set of basic operations. The difference to other previous approaches to OBDD minimization is that the EA does not solve the problem directly. Rather, it developes strategies for solving the problem.

To demonstrate the efficiency of our approach experimental results are given. The newly developed heuristics are more efficient than other previously presented methods.

1 Introduction

Decision Diagrams (DDs) are often used in CAD systems for efficient representation and manipulation of Boolean functions (see e.g. [7]). The most popular data structure is the *Ordered Binary Decision Diagram* (OBDD) [6]. Recently, several approaches in logic synthesis have been presented that make use of OBDDs. Especially the good testability properties of circuits derived from OBDDs make them an interesting candidate for circuit design for testability [1, 2]. In [21] an OBDD-based method for low-power design has been proposed. Better results than using conventional synthesis tools could be obtained. Using OBDDs becomes also more and more popular in the area of *Field Programmable Gate Arrays* (FPGAs) [26]. There OBDDs have also been integrated in commercial FPGA tools [22]. It should be mentioned that in these applications a small gain (counted in the number of nodes) can tremendously simplify the problem to be solved by OBDDs.

One drawback of this data structure is that it is very sensitive to the variable ordering, i.e. the size may vary from linear to exponential. Finding the optimal variable ordering is an NP-complete problem [5] and the best known algorithm has runtime $O(n^2 \cdot 3^n)$ [13, 19], where n denotes the number of variables.

This is the reason why in the last few years many authors presented heuristics for finding good variable orderings [24, 15, 25, 14, 16]. The most promising methods are based on *dynamic variable ordering* [17, 29, 27]: OBDDs for some Boolean functions could be constructed for which all other topology oriented methods failed.

Recently, new methods based on non deterministic algorithms have been proposed for OBDD minimization, e.g. GAs [11] and *Simulated Annealing* (SA)

[28, 4]. The major drawback of these approaches is that in general they obtain good results with respect to quality of the solution, but the running times are often much larger than that of classical heuristics[1]. Due to the high complexity of the design process of CAD of ICs often "fast" heuristics are used. These heuristics are developed by the designer himself. But they also often fail for specific classes of circuits. Thus it would help a lot, if the heuristics could learn from previous examples, e.g. from benchmark examples.

Recently, a theoretical model for learning heuristics by *Genetic Algorithms* (GAs) has been presented [20, 9]. The new aspect of this model is that the GA is not directly applied to the problem. Instead the GA developes a good heuristic for the problem to be solved. First applications to multi-level synthesis and to 2-level AND/EXOR minimization have been presented. There the model has not fully been used, i.e. only a part of the features has been implemented.

In this paper we present an *Evolutionary Algorithm* (EA)[2] based approach to learn heuristics for OBDD minimization. Several heuristics have been proposed in the past few years (as described above). Our EA learns heuristics starting from some simple basic operations that are based on dynamic reordering. The learning environment is a set of benchmark examples, that is called the *training set*. We show by experiments that our EA finds out a heuristic that improves the results obtained by iterated sifting [29] by up to 60%. Furthermore the runtimes of the developed heuristics are low, since the costs of the heuristic are minimized during the learning process.

2 The Learning Model

In [9] a learning model has formally been introduced. In this section we briefly review the main notations and definitions to make the paper self-contained.

It is assumed that the problem to be solved has the following property: There is defined a non empty set of optimization procedures that can be applied to a given (non-optimal) solution in order to further improve its quality. (These procedures are called *Basic Optimization Modules* (BOMs).) These BOMs are the basic modules that will be used. Each heuristic is a sequence of BOMs. The goal of the approach is to determine a good (or even optimal) sequence of BOMs such that the overall results obtained by the heuristic are improved.

In the following we assume that the reader is familiar with the basic concepts and notations of evolutionary approaches. For simplicity of the description we use multi-valued strings, i.e. strings that may assume various values from a fixed finite range. (For more details see [18, 8, 3].)

The set of BOMs defines the set H of all possible heuristics that are applicable to the problem to be solved in the given environment. H may include problem specific heuristics but can also include some random operators.

To each BOM $h \in H$ we associate a *cost function*

$$cost : H \rightarrow \mathbf{R},$$

[1] This observation also holds for many other applications of CAD of ICs (see e.g. [23, 12, 20, 10].)

[2] In our application we make use of a modified GA, i.e. the GA works on multi-valued strings. Thus we call our implemented algorithm an EA.

where **R** denotes the real valued numbers. *cost* estimates the resources that are needed for a heuristic. We measure the fitness *fit* of a string $s = (h_1, h_2, \ldots, h_l)$ of length l (representing a heuristic composed from l BOMs) by

$$fit(s) = c_c / fit_c(s) + c_q \cdot fit_q(s),$$

where

$$fit_c(s) = \sum_{i=0}^{l-1} cost(h_i)$$

is the cost fitness of string s and

$$fit_q(s) = \sum_{i=0}^{\#\ of\ examples} quality(example_i)$$

is the quality fitness of string s. c_c and c_q are problem specific constants.

The cost fitness measures the cost for the application of the string. If this cost is relatively high the resulting heuristic will take long time. If the heuristic has a low cost fitness it will terminate quickly.

The quality fitness measures the quality of the heuristic that is represented by the string s by summing up the results for a given *training set*.

The constants c_c and c_q are used to influence the primary goal of the heuristic: If c_c is set to 0 the GA will only optimize the heuristic with respect to the quality of the result, i.e. it will not care about the expenditure of the BOMs. If c_q is set to a small value the GA will determine a very fast heuristic, but the quality of the result will not be very good. Using these parameters the designer can influence the trade-off between runtime and quality and he can determine the primary goal of the GA: Should the heuristic focus on fast runtime or on good results?

For more details about the learning model see also [9].

3 Problem Domain

The essential definitions and properties of OBDDs [6] are briefly reviewed. Then the exchange of neighbouring variables that is the basic operation of our BOMs are given.

3.1 Binary Decision Diagrams

As well-known each Boolean function $f : \mathbf{B}^n \rightarrow \mathbf{B}$ can be represented by a *Binary Decision Diagram* (BDD) [6], i.e. a directed acyclic graph where a Shannon decomposition is carried out in each node.

A BDD is called *ordered* if each variable is encountered at most once on each path from the root to a terminal and if the variables are encountered in the same order on all such paths. A BDD is called *reduced* if it does not contain vertices either with isomorphic sub-graphs or with both edges pointing to the same node.

Reduced, ordered BDDs are a canonical data structure for Boolean functions and allow efficient manipulations [6]. In the following only reduced, ordered BDDs are considered and for briefness these graphs are called OBDDs.

The example from [6] shows the importance of the variable ordering for OBDDs:

Example 1. Let $f = x_1x_2 + \ldots + x_{2n-1}x_{2n}$. If the variable ordering is given by $(x_1, x_2, \ldots, x_{2n})$ the size of the resulting OBDD is $2n$. On the other hand if the variable ordering is chosen as $(x_1, x_{n+1}, x_2, x_{n+2}, \ldots, x_{2n})$ the size of the OBDD is $\Theta(2^{n-1})$. Thus the number of nodes in the graph varies from linear to exponential depending on the variable ordering. In Figure 1 the OBDDs of the function $f = x_1x_2 + x_3x_4 + x_5x_6$ with variable orderings $x_1x_2x_3x_4x_5x_6$ and $x_1x_3x_5x_2x_4x_6$ are illustrated. The left (right) outgoing edge of each node x_i denotes $f_{x_i=1}$ ($f_{x_i=0}$). As can be seen the choice of the variable ordering largely influences the size of the OBDDs.

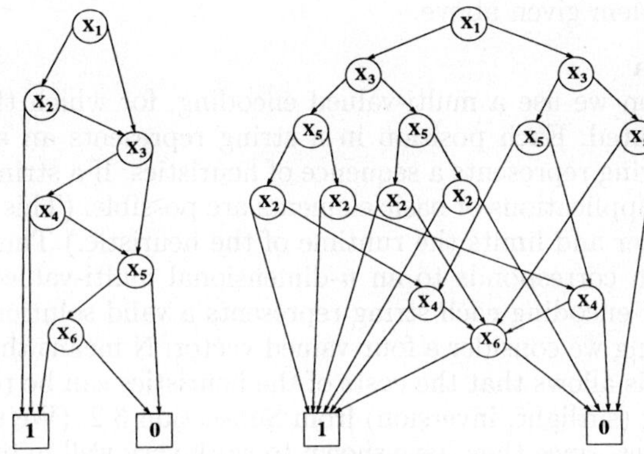

Fig. 1. OBDDs of the function $f = x_1x_2 + x_3x_4 + x_5x_6$

We now consider the following problem that will be solved using EAs:

> *How can we develop a good heuristic to determine variable orderings for an OBDD representing a given Boolean function f such that the number of nodes in the OBDD is minimized?*

Notice once more that we do *not* optimize OBDDs by GAs. Instead we optimize the heuristic that is applied to OBDD-minimization.

3.2 Dynamic Variable Ordering

It is well-known that in the case of OBDDs, the size of the decision diagram can be minimized by exchange of adjacent variables [17]. The exchange is performed very quickly since only edges must be redirected. This exchange is the basic operation for different algorithms for dynamic variable ordering, e.g the sifting algorithm, window permutation, and exact minimization algorithms [29, 19].

In the following we briefly describe the algorithms that are used as BOMs in the EA in the next section:

Sifting (S) [29]: By the sifting algorithm, the variables are sorted into decreasing order based on the number of nodes at each level and then each variable is traversed through the OBDD in order to locate its locally optimum position while all other variables remain fixed.

Siftlight (L): Siftlight is a restricted form of sifting that does not allow the algorithm to do any hill climbing, i.e. the variables are directly located in the next minimum. (The algorithm is much faster than "normal" sifting, but in general the results are worse.)

Inversion (I): The variable ordering of the OBDD is inverted.

4 Evolutionary Algorithm

In this section we briefly describe the *Evolutionary Algorithm* (EA) that is applied to the problem given above.

Representation

In our application we use a multi-valued encoding, for which the problem can easily be formulated. Each position in a string represents an application of a BOM. Thus a string represents a sequence of heuristics. If a string has n components at most n applications of basic elements are possible. (This upper bound is set by the designer and limits the runtime of the heuristic.) Thus, each element of the population corresponds to an n-dimensional multi-valued vector. Using this multi-valued encoding each string represents a valid solution.

In the following we consider a four-valued vector: N means that no operation is performed. This allows that the costs of the heuristics can be reduced. S (L, I) represents sifting (siftlight, inversion) from Subsection 3.2. (We restrict to these simple alternatives, since they have shown to work very well in our application.)

Objective Function and Selection

As an *objective function* that measures the *fitness* of each element we apply the heuristics to several benchmark *training sets.* Obviously the choice of the benchmarks largely influences the (quality of the) results. On the other hand the designer can create several different heuristics for different types of circuits, e.g. a fast but simple heuristic for very large problem instances or a very "time consuming" heuristic for small examples. The function *quality* was calculated by constructing the OBDD and counting the number of nodes for each example. The function *cost* is given by a measure that represents the execution time that is used for the application of the newly generated heuristic. In our approach the setting is given by

$$cost(\text{S}) = 4 \quad cost(\text{L}) = 2 \quad cost(\text{I}) = 1.$$

The constant values approximate the (relative) average execution time of the BOMs for some examples of Boolean functions.

The selection is performed by *roulette wheel selection*, i.e. each string is chosen with a probability proportional to its fitness. Additionally, we also make use of *steady-state-reproduction* [8]. A part of the best elements of the old population is included in the new one anyway. This strategy guarantees that the best element never gets lost and that a faster convergency is obtained.

Initialization
At the beginning of each EA run an initial population is randomly generated. The fitness is assigned to each element.

Operators
As operators we used *reproduction*, *crossover* and *mutation*. All operators are directly applied to the four-valued strings of length n that represent elements in the population. The parent(s) for each operation is (are) determined by the mechanisms described above. All operators only generate valid solutions, if they are applied to the four-valued strings.

Algorithm
Using the genetic operators our algorithm works as follows:

1. The initial population of size 10 is generated randomly and the length of the strings is set to 20.
2. Then $\frac{pop}{2}$ elements are generated by the genetic operators *reproduction* and *crossover*. The parent elements are selected by the method described above. The newly created elements are then mutated with a probability of 15%. After each iteration the size of the population is constant.
3. If no improvement is obtained for 200 generations the algorithm stops.

A sketch of the algorithm is given in Figure 2.

```
evolutionary_algorithm (training set) {
  generate_random_population () ;
  calculate_fitness () ;
  {
    apply_operators_with_corresponding_probabilities () ;
    calculate_fitness () ;
    update_population () ;
  } while (improvement obtained) ;
  return ;
}
```

Fig. 2. Sketch of basic algorithm

5 Experimental Results

In this section we present results of experiments that were carried out on a *SUN Sparc 20* workstation. All runtimes *time* are given in CPU seconds. We performed our experiments using examples of Boolean functions that are taken from LGSynth91 [30].

In a first series of experiments we developed a heuristic for OBDD minimization on *training set 1* that is composed of small functions up to 15 variables. The results are given in Table 1. *in* (*out*) denotes the number of inputs (outputs) and *optimal* denotes the exact algorithm from [13]. *size* gives the number of nodes that is needed for the representation of the benchmark. $sift_{iter}$ denotes the size of the OBDD after sifting has iteratively applied until no further improvement could be obtained. The newly developed heuristic that is learned on *training set 1* by our EA is given in column EA_{L1}. Each OBDD minimization algorithm starts with an initial variable ordering. EA_{L1} **always** obtained the optimal OBDD sizes and the execution times are much better than the runtimes of the exact algorithm. In contrast, $sift_{iter}$ fails to determine the exact solution for 3 out of the 5 benchmarks in *training set 1*. The order of the BOMs of heuristic EA_{L1} is: ILSLL. The learning time for EA_{L1} given in the last row is about 20 minutes. Notice that our EA implicitly makes use of the cost function, i.e. redundant BOM sequences like "II" are filtered out.

name	*in*	*out*	*optimal*		$sift_{iter}$		EA_{L1}	
			size	*time*	*size*	*time*	*size*	*time*
add6	12	7	28	19.4	54	0.1	28	0.1
addm4	9	8	163	5.4	163	0.2	163	0.1
cm85a	11	3	27	4.1	35	0.1	27	0.1
m181	15	9	54	332.0	56	0.2	54	0.2
risc	8	31	65	0.5	65	0.1	65	0.1
Learning time								1152.2

Table 1. Training set 1

Next, we applied the newly developed heuristic EA_{L1} to new small benchmarks that were not in *learning set 1*, i.e. that were not known during the learning process. As can be seen in Table 2 EA_{L1} fails for some examples by more than 10%. Hence, we extend *training set 1* by the examples that are in the bottom part of Table 2, i.e. the examples where EA_{L1} does not obtain satisfying results. Now the EA learns a heuristic on the extented set of benchmarks. The learning results are given in Table 3 in column $\mathrm{EA}_{L1_{ex}}$. Notice, that the OBDD sizes of the newly inserted functions are reduced. The application of $\mathrm{EA}_{L1_{ex}}$ to new benchmarks is also given in Table 2 in column $\mathrm{EA}_{L1_{ex}}$. The order of the BOMs for $\mathrm{EA}_{L1_{ex}}$ is given by: ISILSILLS. Now, the newly developed heuristic generates smaller OBDDs than $sift_{iter}$ and EA_{L1} and furthermore the runtimes are competitive.

In the next experiments we consider *training set 2* that includes larger examples for which the optimal solution can not be determined (within reasonable time bounds) due to the exponential worst case runtime of the exact algorithm. Table 4 shows the results obtained by the resulting heuristic that is called EA_{L2}. The results obtained by the new heuristic are never worse than those obtained by $sift_{iter}$. In contrast, for 50% of the considered benchmarks EA_{L2} creates OBDDs that need less nodes for the representation than sift_{iter}.

Additionally, EA_{L2} is applied to some new benchmarks that were not included in *training set 2*. The results are given in Table 5. As can easily be seen the newly developed heuristic never obtained much worse results than $sift_{iter}$ (3 nodes in the worst case), but in some cases is much better (see e.g. vg2).

name	*in*	*out*	*optimal*		*sift*$_{iter}$		EA_{L1}		$EA_{L1_{ex}}$	
			size	*time*	*size*	*time*	*size*	*time*	*size*	*time*
Z5xp1	7	10	41	0.6	41	0.1	50	0.1	41	0.1
alu4	14	8	349	1460.0	449	2.5	354	1.4	353	2.8
cm151a	12	2	16	24.8	16	0.1	16	0.1	16	0.3
cm162a	14	5	29	37.1	29	0.1	37	0.1	35	0.1
cm163a	16	5	25	110.0	25	0.1	26	0.1	25	0.1
cmb	16	4	27	176.6	27	0.1	27	0.1	27	0.1
cu	14	11	31	45.8	31	0.1	31	0.1	34	0.1
sqn	7	3	48	0.3	55	0.1	56	0.1	54	0.1
gary	15	11	289	955.0	293	0.3	306	0.2	289	0.5
s1494	14	25	368	615.0	372	1.0	383	0.4	373	0.9
tial	14	8	563	958.0	600	2.0	611	1.0	565	2.1

Table 2. Application to new benchmarks

name	*in*	*out*	$EA_{L1_{ex}}$	
			size	*time*
add6	12	7	28	0.1
addm4	9	8	163	0.4
cm85a	11	3	27	0.1
m181	15	9	54	0.3
risc	8	31	65	0.1
gary	15	11	289	0.5
s1494	14	25	373	0.9
tial	14	8	565	2.2
Learning time				1505.3

Table 3. Extended training set 1

name	*in*	*out*	*sift*$_{iter}$		EA_{L2}	
			size	*time*	*size*	*time*
bc0	26	11	522	1.0	522	2.3
ex7	16	5	77	0.3	77	0.6
frg1	28	3	89	13.0	75	19.8
ibm	48	17	209	2.5	206	1.8
in2	19	10	252	2.9	230	4.0
s1196	32	32	597	3.7	597	4.3
ts10	22	16	145	2.0	145	2.7
x6dn	39	5	243	12.3	239	6.1
Learning time						22783.0

Table 4. Training set 2

name	*in*	*out*	$sift_{iter}$ *size*	$sift_{iter}$ *time*	EA_{L2} *size*	EA_{L2} *time*
apex2	39	2	473	58.6	353	61.6
apex7	49	37	292	1.4	291	1.7
bcd	26	38	589	1.5	567	2.1
chkn	29	7	261	4.5	305	4.8
cps	24	109	699	2.2	699	3.1
in7	26	10	76	0.5	76	0.6
pdc	16	40	601	1.6	601	2.2
s1494	14	25	372	1.0	368	0.9
t1	21	23	116	0.1	114	0.2
vg2	25	8	184	0.3	79	0.4

Table 5. Application to new benchmarks

6 Conclusions

We presented an *Evolutionary Algorithm* that learns heuristics for OBDD minimization. The EA optimizes the heuristics with respect to size and time. It has been shown by experiments that the heuristics learned by our EA on a training set obtain *very good* results for these elements. The newly developed heuristic also works well on *new* functions that were unknown during the learning process.

The learning algorithm only takes a few CPU hours on a workstation and the resulting heuristics that obtain better results than the best previously known are very fast, i.e. they take less than 10 CPU seconds for most examples.

We also studied the extension of the learning set during the run of the EA. In this case the EA adapts the heuristic in a way that the newly integrated functions are optimized, too, and thus the quality of the heuristic is improved.

References

1. P. Ashar, S. Devadas, and K. Keutzer. Gate-delay-fault testability properties of multiplexor-based networks. In *Int'l Test Conf.*, pages 887–896, 1991.
2. P. Ashar, S. Devadas, and K. Keutzer. Path-delay-fault testability properties of multiplexor-based networks. *Integration the VLSI Jour.*, 15(1):1–23, 1993.
3. T. Bäck and H. Schwefel. An overview of evolutionary algorithms for parameter optimization. *Evolutionary Computation*, 1(1):1–23, 1993.
4. B. Bollig, M. Löbbing, and I. Wegener. Simulated annealing to improve variable orderings for OBDDs. In *Int'l Workshop on Logic Synth.*, pages 5b:5.1–5.10, 1995.
5. B. Bollig, P. Savicky, and I. Wegener. On the improvement of variable orderings for OBDDs. *IFIP Workshop on Logic and Architecture Synthesis, Grenoble*, pages 71–80, 1994.
6. R.E. Bryant. Graph - based algorithms for Boolean function manipulation. *IEEE Trans. on Comp.*, 8:677–691, 1986.
7. R.E. Bryant. Symbolic boolean manipulation with ordered binary decision diagrams. *ACM, Comp. Surveys*, 24:293–318, 1992.
8. L. Davis. *Handbook of Genetic Algorithms.* van Nostrand Reinhold, New York, 1991.

9. R. Drechsler and B. Becker. Learning heuristics by genetic algorithms. In *ASP Design Automation Conf.*, pages 349–352, 1995.
10. R. Drechsler, B. Becker, and N. Göckel. A genetic algorithm for minimization of Fixed Polarity Reed-Muller expressions. In *Int'l Conf. on Artificial Neural Networks and Genetic Algorithms*, pages 392–395, 1995.
11. R. Drechsler, B. Becker, and N. Göckel. A genetic algorithm for variable ordering of OBDDs. In *Int'l Workshop on Logic Synth.*, pages P5c:5.55–5.64, 1995.
12. H. Esbensen. A macro-cell global router based on two genetic algorithms. In *European Design Automation Conf.*, pages 428–433, 1994.
13. S.J. Friedman and K.J. Supowit. Finding the optimal variable ordering for binary decision diagrams. In *Design Automation Conf.*, pages 348–356, 1987.
14. H. Fujii, G. Ootomo, and C. Hori. Interleaving based variable ordering methods for ordered binary decision diagrams. In *Int'l Conf. on CAD*, pages 38–41, 1993.
15. M. Fujita, H. Fujisawa, and N. Kawato. Evaluation and improvements of boolean comparison method based on binary decision diagrams. In *Int'l Conf. on CAD*, pages 2–5, 1988.
16. M. Fujita, H. Fujisawa, and Y. Matsunaga. Variable ordering algorithms for binary decision diagrams and their evolution. *IEEE Trans. on CAD*, 12:6–12, 1993.
17. M. Fujita, Y. Matsunga, and T. Kakuda. On variable ordering of binary decision diagrams for the application of multi-level synthesis. In *European Conf. on Design Automation*, pages 50–54, 1991.
18. D.E. Goldberg. *Genetic Algortithms in Search, Optimization & Machine Learning.* Addision-Wesley Publisher Company, Inc., 1989.
19. N. Ishiura, H. Sawada, and S. Yajima. Minimization of binary decision diagrams based on exchange of variables. In *Int'l Conf. on CAD*, pages 472–475, 1991.
20. A. Kuehlmann and L.P.P.P. van Ginneken. Grammar-based optimization of synthesis scenarios. In *Int'l Conf. on Comp. Design*, pages 20–25, 1994.
21. L. Lavagno, P. McGeer, A. Saldanha, and A.L. Sangiovanni-Vincentelli. Timed shannon circuits: A power-efficient design style and synthesis tool. In *Design Automation Conf.*, pages 254–260, 1995.
22. V.V. Le, T. Besson, A. Abbara, D. Brasen, H. Bogushevitsh, G. Saucier, and M. Crastes. ASIC prototyping with area oriented mapping for ALTERA/FLEX devices. In *SASIMI*, pages 176–183, 1995.
23. J. Lienig and K. Thulasiraman. A genetic algorithm for channel routing in VLSI circuits. *Evolutionary Computation*, 1(4):293–311, 1993.
24. S. Malik, A.R. Wang, R.K. Brayton, and A.L. Sangiovanni-Vincentelli. Logic verification using binary decision diagrams in a logic synthesis environment. In *Int'l Conf. on CAD*, pages 6–9, 1988.
25. S. Minato, N. Ishiura, and S. Yajima. Shared binary decision diagrams with attributed edges for efficient boolean function manipulation. In *Design Automation Conf.*, pages 52–57, 1990.
26. R. Murgai, Y. Nishizaki, N. Shenoy, R.K. Brayton, and A. Sangiovanni-Vincentelli. Logic synthesis for programmable gate arrays. In *Design Automation Conf.*, pages 620–625, 1990.
27. S. Panda and F. Somenzi. Who are the variables in your neighborhood. In *Int'l Conf. on CAD*, pages 74–77, 1995.
28. D.E. Ross, K.M. Butler, R. Kapur, and M.R. Mercer. Functional approaches to generating orderings for efficient symbolic representations. In *Design Automation Conf.*, pages 624–627, 1992.
29. R. Rudell. Dynamic variable ordering for ordered binary decision diagrams. In *Int'l Conf. on CAD*, pages 42–47, 1993.
30. S. Yang. Logic synthesis and and optimization benchmarks user guide. Technical Report 1/95, Microelectronic Center of North Carolina, Jan. 1991.

Improving the Generalization Performance of Multi–Layer–Perceptrons with Population–Based Incremental Learning

Elvis Galić[1] and Markus Höhfeld *[2]

[1] Department of Theoretical Physics, Würzburg, Germany
Corporate Research Siemens AG, München, Germany
[2] Corporate Research Siemens AG, München, Germany

Abstract. Based on Population–Based Incremental Learning (PBIL) we present a new approach for the evolution of neural network architectures and their corresponding weights. The main idea is to use a probability vector rather than bit strings to represent a population of networks in each generation. We show that crucial issues of neural network training can effectively be integrated into the PBIL framework. First, a Quasi–Newton method for local weight optimization is integrated and the moving average update rule of the PBIL is extended to continuous parameters in order to transmit the best network to the next generation. Second, and more important, we incorporate cross–validation to focus the evolution towards networks with optimal generalization performance. A comparison with standard pruning and stopped–training algorithms shows that our approach effectively finds small networks with increased generalization ability.

1 Introduction

We consider the problem of designing Multi–Layer–Perceptrons (MLP) using evolutionary algorithms. Given a fixed architecture powerful and fast procedures exist for optimization of the network's real valued weights. Unfortunately, there exists no systematic approach to the design of neural architectures for a given task. To optimize the architecture one has to search a discrete space of high dimensionality. It has been shown that evolutionary algorithms are powerful in this domain [10] [11]. We present a combination of methods based on Population–Based Incremental Learning (PBIL) [1] and a Quasi–Newton (QN) method [3]. This approach enables us to simultanously optimize the discrete architecture and the corresponding real valued weights.

We focus our work on the improvement of the network's generalization ability as this is the major obstacle in network training. The question is: How complex can the network be allowed to be, given a fixed set of noisy data. While a small

* This author gratefully acknowledges support by the German BMBF (project EVOALG, a cooperation of Informatik Centrum Dortmund, Siemens AG München, and Humboldt–Universität zu Berlin), grant 01 IB 403 A.

network will fail to represent the structure of the data, a large network tends to model the noise contained in the data. The later behaviour is termed overlearning and causes a decrease in the generalization performance of the network.

A variety of authors have examined this problem and suggested several strategies for complexity adaptation. Most of the work was done in complexity reduction by pruning weights from the network [5] [7]. Other methods, also used in combination with pruning, are adding a penalty term to the cost function used to steer learning towards low complexity networks [9] and stopping training as soon as the error on some validation data begins to increase [5]. Especially the experience with pruning shows that the generalization performance of a MLP can be increased by optimizing the network's architecture.

Applying evolutionary algorithms to architecture optimization, the main problem lies in the discrete nature of the neural architecture. The variation of architectural features from one generation to the next is a discontinuous process and it is difficult to transmit the relevant features to the offspring. It will be shown that the PBIL algorithm together with appropriate extensions is an elegant solution to this problem.

Similar work to ours was done by [4] and [2], who evolve MLPs for real world tasks with genetic algorithms [10]. While [4] have to use special codings tailored for specialized cross–over operators, we can use a direct coding shema. [2] omit cross–over and use specialized mutation operators to use direct coding. Similarly to our work they incorporate cross–validation but evolve networks for classification tasks.

2 Generalization Performance of Neural Networks

A MLP [12] specifies a functional relationship between an input vector $\mathbf{x} \in \Re^M$ and an output $y \in \Re$. It is common practice to use this for approximating a target function y_0 from $\Re^M$ to $\Re$. A fully connected network with one linear output unit, L hidden hyperbolic tangent units, and M input units represents the function:

$$y = \sum_{i=1}^{L} w_i \tanh\Big(\sum_{j=1}^{M} w_{ij} x_j + w_{i0}\Big) + w_0 \tag{1}$$

where $\mathbf{w}$ is a vector containing all weights of the network including the hidden layer biases w_{i0} and the output bias w_0. Usually a MLP operates in two ways, separated in a learning and a generalization phase. In the first one the weights $\mathbf{w}$ of the network are learned using a data set D consisting of n examples of input vectors $\mathbf{x}$ and targets t.

$$D := \{(\mathbf{x}_1, t_1), ..., (\mathbf{x}_n, t_n)\} \tag{2}$$

The aim of learning is to map each pair of examples correctly by equation (1). The learning task is designed to minimize the mean squared error (MSE).

$$\mathbf{w} = \arg\min_{\mathbf{w}} \frac{1}{n} \sum_{i=1}^{n} (y_i - t_i)^2 \tag{3}$$

After adaptation of the weights, the network represents a nonlinear approximator $y = f(\mathbf{x}, \mathbf{w})$ for the target function $y_0 = f(\mathbf{x}_0)$.

After training, the knowledge about the structure of the data is stored in the weights of the network. For this reason the network can make predictions v on new input vectors which were not trained before. An easy way to measure the generalization performance of the trained network is to hold back some of the examples during training and use these for validating the generalization performance. [6] shows in detail why such cross–validation techniques can be used for model selection. The splitting of the dataset D leads to a training set D_t and a validation set D_v. The validation error E_v on the set D_v is used to obtain knowledge of the expected performance on m novel examples.

$$E_v = \frac{1}{m}\sum_{j=1}^{m}(v_j - t_j)^2 \tag{4}$$

In the following we use the training error E_t to optimize the network's weights and the validation error E_v to select the network's architecture. Therefore, to evaluate the evolved networks, we need a third data set, the generalization or test set D_g. The error E_g on the data set D_g is used to measure the generalization performance of the evolved networks.

We consider small and noisy data sets. For this it will be assumed that we can only obtain noisy samples of the function y_0. In the case of noisy data it is however difficult to decide what constitutes the structure and what should be regarded merely as noise. To avoid overlearning one has to find a procedure which eliminates those input nodes and thus those components of the patterns which mainly represent noise. Since the remaining input nodes feed further noise into the network it is additionally necessary to optimize the total number of weights and their values.

3 Population–Based Incremental Learning

In this section we review the basics of the PBIL algorithm. PBIL was introduced as an optimization technique for binary coded optimization problems in 1995 [1]. The main idea addresses the representation of the current generation. While genetic algorithms keep a whole population of binary solution vectors $\mathbf{x}$, PBIL only keeps a vector of probabilities $\mathbf{p}$, specifying the probabilities for each bit position of an individual containing a 1. In each generation a new population is resampled according to this vector.

The algorithm is initialized with a probability of 0.5 in each component of $\mathbf{p}$. Sampling from this vector yields equal probability for generating 1 or 0. During the search, the values in the probability vector gradually move towards 1 or 0. The best individual $\mathbf{x}_{best}$ is used to update $\mathbf{p}$. Using a moving average update with exponential forgetting in time t, $\mathbf{p}$ is shifted with learning rate α towards solutions with best fitness according to:

$$\mathbf{p}_{t+1} = (1-\alpha)\mathbf{p}_t + \alpha\mathbf{x}_{best,t} \tag{5}$$

Mutation is introduced in the way that a component p_i of the probability vector is occassionally disturbed with mutation shift β according to

$$p_{i,t+1} = (1-\beta)p_{i,t} + \beta b \tag{6}$$

where b is randomly chosen as either 0 or 1. After the probability vector is updated, a new population is produced and the cycle is continued. The entire algorithm together with extensions concerning network optimization is summarized in section 4.2.

[1] contains in depth discussions about the relation between PBIL and genetic algorithms and about PBIL results on real world tasks. We would like to add that the PBIL update rule embodies different ideas known from the evolution strategies [11]. From the (μ,λ)–strategy it borrows rank based selection and the idea that evolutionary search should accept individuals which are worse than their parents. Furthermore, sampling each component individually when generating a new population is closely related to uniform binary cross–over, where individuals inherit each component from one of the parents randomly. For our work on network optimization it is important, that PBIL learns in small steps. This approach helps to overcome local minima in the beginning of the search without the need for prohibitively large populations.

4 Evolutionary Design of Neural Architectures

4.1 Network Representation

The PBIL algorithm does not use a cross–over like reproduction operator. Unlike [4], we can therefore use a direct coding scheme where each connection is specified by a bit. If the connection exists, the bit is 1, else the bit is 0. The network is thus represented by a binary vector $\mathbf{x}$ and the corresponding sparse weight vector $\mathbf{w}_{sp}$, the element–by–element product of $\mathbf{x}$ and $\mathbf{w}$. The vector $\mathbf{w}_{sp}$, together with the inputs, determines the network mapping according to equation (1).

4.2 The PBIL Framework

The basic elements of our algorithm are one probability vector $\mathbf{p}$ and one weight vector $\mathbf{w}$. In the beginning, each component of $\mathbf{p}$ is initialized with the value 0.5. The weights $\mathbf{w}$ are initialized uniformly distributed from the interval $[-0.03, 0.03]$. It is important to note that we initialize our networks with many small weights and thus start with large and linear models. In the beginning, when search is mainly driven by chance, this approach reduces the risk of badly disturbing the network function when adding or deleting weights.

Depending on $\mathbf{p}$, each generation, a binary vector $\mathbf{x}_j$ is generated for each individual j. Next a sparse vector of weights $\mathbf{w}_{sp,j}$ is generated for each individual. The totally available data are split into two random disjoint subsets in each generation. Training the weights of the networks on one set and optimizing their architectures on the other one yields networks with improved generalization performance. Dividing the data again in each generation allows training of the weights on the whole set of available data points. Of course, one has to avoid the specialization of weights on a particular data distribution. For this reason the weights are trained only a small number of epochs in each generation. After training each individual with QN, yielding the optimized weight vectors $\mathbf{w}^*_{sp,j}$, their fitnesses are evaluated according to the objective function F_j:

$$F_j = E_{v,j} + \delta \sum_i x_{i,j} \tag{7}$$

Since oversized networks tend to overlearn the data, the second term counts the number of connections. With the parameter δ the influence of this complexity term and thus the selection pressure towards small networks can be controlled. This will be shown to be sufficient to evolve small networks with good generalization abilities. The vector $\mathbf{x}_j$ of the best individual is used to update $\mathbf{p}$ according to (5).

Extending the PBIL update rule to continuous parameters we use the weights of the best individual to create initial weights for the next generation:

$$\mathbf{w}_{t+1} = (1-\gamma)\mathbf{w}_t + \gamma \mathbf{w}^*_{best,t} \tag{8}$$

Unlike [2], we chose this way to transmit weight information into the next generation rather than to transmit the weights directly. Choosing the learning rates α and γ small will guarantee that architecture and weights of the current generation are on average close to that of the parent generation. This strategy lowers the risk that architectures and weights produced by the update rules do not match. In the following we summarize the algorithm:

$t := 0$
Initialization: $p_i = 0.5, \mathbf{w} \in [-0.03, 0.03]$
while(... $\neq$ **true**)**do**:
Generate population: $\mathbf{x}_j, \mathbf{w}_{sp,j}$
Split data: D_t, D_v
Optimize weights: $\mathbf{w}^*_{sparse,j} \longleftarrow QN(\mathbf{w}_{sp,j}, D_t)$
Fitness evaluation: $Fitness_j \longleftarrow F(\mathbf{w}^*_{sp,j}, D_v)$
Ranking: $F(best) \leq F(j)$
Update $\mathbf{p}$: $\mathbf{p} = (1-\alpha)\mathbf{p} + \alpha \mathbf{x}_{best}$
Mutate p_i: $p_i = (1-\beta)p_i + \beta b$
Update $\mathbf{w}$: $\mathbf{w} = (1-\eta)\mathbf{w} + \eta \mathbf{w}^*_{best}$
$t := t+1$
od

5 Simulation Results

5.1 The Learning Tasks

We tested our procedure with two different kinds of data: First, we used artificial data as introduced in [5]. The advantage here is, that the structure of the data remains equal for all patterns. Furthermore one is able to test the algorithms ability to prune those input nodes which input noisy components of the patterns to the network, simply by adding components of patterns which contain noise instead of structure. We chose two data sets for presentation. These are a sum of sinus functions with a medium noise level (sin–6–n; signal to noise ratio 0.6) and a sum of linear functions with a high noise level (id–8–n; signal to noise ratio 0.8). The data generation process was the following: The targets $y_i \in \Re$ were calculated from the inputs $x_i = (x_i^1, ..., x_i^{10}) \in [-1, 1]^{10}$, where

$$y_i = \sum_{k=1}^{5} \sin(\alpha^k x_i^k) + u_i; \; \alpha^k \in \Re \tag{9}$$

for sin–6–n, and

$$y_i = \sum_{k=1}^{5} \alpha^k x_i^k + u_i; \; \alpha^k \in \Re \tag{10}$$

for id–8–n. The index i corresponds to the patterns. The nodes $x^1, ..., x^5$ are the relevant inputs, the nodes $x^6, ..., x^{10}$ the irrelevant inputs. The variable u_i represents the stochastic disturbance. The input data and the disturbance variables were generated by independent drawings from a uniform distribution from the interval $[-1, 1]$. The total data was then split into two random disjoint subsets D_t and D_v with 200 patterns respectively in each generation. The third data set D_g with 1000 patterns was created the same way, but without additive noise. The initial networks had a size of 10 input nodes, 10 hidden nodes and one output node.

Secondly, we used the sunspot series, a common benchmark for time series prediction algorithms. The series is a record of the annual average sunspot activity for the period 1700–1979. It is believed to be generated by a noisy, chaotic, dynamic system. Its spectrum has a 12 year period. The tapped delay architecture used 12 data points from the past, corresponding to 12 input nodes, to forecast one data point in the future, corresponding to 1 output node. The data set was split into one set for 1700–1920 and two generalization sets, namely $D_{g,1}$ for 1921–1955 and $D_{g,2}$ for 1956–1979. The set for 1700-1920 was then split into new training and validation sets of equal size in each generation. The initial networks had a size of 12 input nodes, 12 hidden nodes and 1 output node.

5.2 Experiments

A number of experiments were performed. The parameters for the presented test runs were:

Learning rate: $\alpha = 0.1$; Mutation probability: $p_{mut} = 0.02$; Mutation shift: $\beta = 0.05$; Learning rate: $\gamma = 0.03$; Populationsize: 40 individuals; Parameter for complexity reduction term: $\delta = 0.001$; Learning steps for QN: 20 epochs

The following figures show typical behaviour on the sunspot data. At the end of the section we summarize the results for all data sets together with benchmark results. For evaluation we monitored the mean squared error E^0 for the fittest

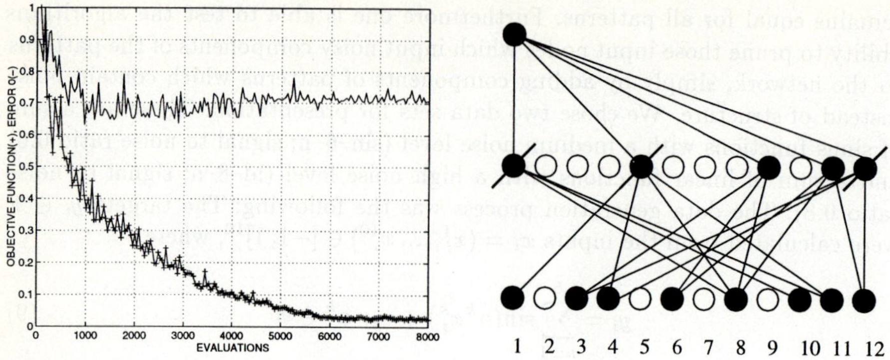

Fig. 1. Left: Objective function F (+) and error E^0 (-) (both normalized to unity) versus the number of fitness evaluations. **Right**: Network architecture of the best network evolved at evaluation 2900. A bar through a unit indicates an active threshold. The network only uses the latest three points of the sunspot series (nodes 10–12) and a reduced number of the other ones

network per generation, calculated for the whole available training and validation data. In fig. (1) the error E^0 and the objective function F of the best network per generation versus the number of fitness evaluations is shown. While F is decreasing the error E^0 starts to increase slightly after 4000 evaluations. We interpret this as an effect of overpruning the network. Therefore we chose the best network to be the one with lowest E^0 evolved within 4000 evaluations. On the right hand side of fig. (1) we show a typical network, in this case, evolved at evaluation 2900. The errors on the generalization data sets, normalized by the variance of the specific data set were then used to evaluate the evolved networks after retraining them with QN on the whole available training and validation data for 400 epochs.

5.3 Overlearning

The left hand side of fig. (2) shows the performance of a fully connected network with 12 input nodes, 8 hidden nodes and 1 output node. Overlearning was observed. The training error is a decreasing function but the generalization errors start increasing after some learning steps. The right side of fig. (2) shows the performance of the evolved network from fig. (1). Retraining the evolved network shows no overlearning. The training, as well as, the generalization errors are decreasing. The evolutionary algorithm has successfully reduced the complexity of the network. This reduced network is sufficient to represent the structure of the limited dataset. The generalization errors $E_{g,1}$ for the years 1921–1955 and $E_{g,2}$ for 1956–1979 show lower values compared to those from the fully connected network.

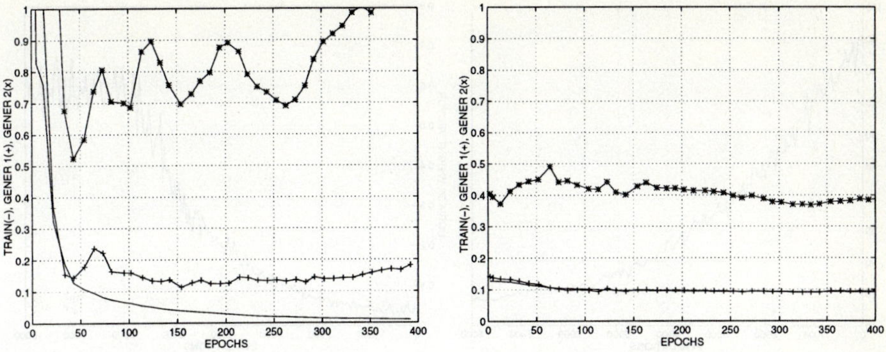

Fig. 2. Left: Training error E_t (-) and generalization errors $E_{g,1}$ (+) and $E_{g,2}$ ($\star$) of a fully connected network with 12 input nodes, 8 hidden nodes and one output node is shown after training for 400 epochs on the sunspot data. Overlearning was observed. **Right**: Training error E_t (-) and generalization errors $E_{g,1}$ (+) and $E_{g,2}$ ($\star$) of the evolved network with 8 input nodes, 5 hidden nodes and 1 ouput node is shown after retraining for 400 epochs on the sunspot data. The evolved network shows no overlearning.

5.4 Evolution of Connections and Weights

The left hand side of fig. (3) shows the number of weights of the best network per generation versus the number of fitness evaluations. One can see that the number of weights is reduced. Shown in the figure are also redundant weights, e.g. weights to a hidden node which has no connection to the output node. After removing these weights the best evolved networks had about 20–25 weights. Within the pruning process a number of input nodes were eliminated. Most evolved networks selected the same inputs. All used the three most recent inputs and several among the older ones. Similar behaviour was observed in [7] while pruning with a method called Optimal Brain Damage (OBD). We like to note that OBD as other pruning techniques rely on a set of sophisticated test criteria to identify and eliminate irrelevant weights. In contrast, our method eliminates weights and nodes solely depending on the validation error.

Considering the artificial data the algorithm was able to prune all weights from all irrelevant input nodes.

The right hand side of fig. (3) shows the evolution of the norm of the weight vector divided by the number of weights of the best network per generation. The values of the weights are increased in smaller networks. This is important, because only large arguments to the hyperbolic tangent units yield nonlinear mapping. This shows that our algorithm effectively shifts small networks into regions of nonlinearity, thus exploiting the full representational power of MLPs for nonlinear function approximation.

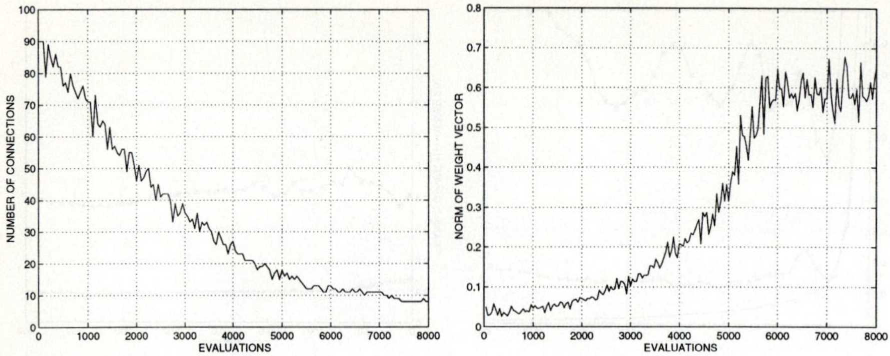

Fig. 3. Left: Number of connections of the best network per generation versus the number of fitness evaluations. It can be seen that the overall number of connections and thus the number of weights is reduced. **Right**: Norm of the weight vector divided by the number of weights of the best network per generation versus the number of fitness evaluations. The curve shows the increase of the average weight value.

5.5 Comparison to other Methods

In the following we compare the generalization errors of the evolved networks (PBIL–NN) with results from other techniques. The individual runs differ due to random effects in initialization and search. Therefore we present averaged results over 10 runs. As benchmarks for the results we used fully connected stopped training networks (STOP) with 10 input nodes, 10 hidden nodes and 1 output node for the artificial data, stopped training networks with 12 input nodes, 8 hidden nodes and 1 output node for the sunspot data, threshold autoregression (TA) [8], MLP pruning (PRUNE) [7] and weight decay (DECAY) [9] algorithms, linear models (LINEAR) [7] and pruning by an expert with the commercial tool SENN (EXPERT), which is successfully used by Siemens AG in the domain of finance and process data prediction and modelling.

From table (1) it is clear, that the generalization performance of the evolved networks is comparable to the best of other techniques and that it outperforms the linear as well as the stopped training network. On the artificial data, PBIL–NN evolved networks with a similar number of parameters compared to the expert's pruning procedure. The number of parameters of the evolved networks on the sunspot data lies in between the number of parameters from the other MLP techniques (DECAY and PRUNE).

6 Conclusion

We presented an evolutionary algorithm based on PBIL but specifically tailored to evolve neural networks with improved generalization performance. It was

Data	Model	$E_{g,1}$	$E_{g,2}$	Parameters
Sunspot	TA	0.097	0.28	16
	DECAY	0.086	0.35	43
	LINEAR	0.130	0.37	13
	STOP	0.107 ± 0.005	0.50 ± 0.05	113
	PRUNE	0.082 ± 0.007	0.35 ± 0.05	12–16
	PBIL–NN	0.085 ± 0.008	0.35 ± 0.07	20–25

Data	Model	E_g	Parameters
sin–6–n	EXPERT	0.0003	8
	STOP	0.0008 ± 0.0002	121
	PBIL–NN	0.0004 ± 0.0002	7–9
id–8–n	EXPERT	0.0012	9
	STOP	0.03 ± 0.01	121
	PBIL–NN	0.0020 ± 0.0005	7–10

Table 1. Comparison to other models

shown that PBIL–NN with the appropriate extensions consistently converges to small networks and that it removes irrelevant inputs from the networks. The evolved networks outperform the stopped training method and achieve a generalization performance comparable to the currently available model selection techniques.

Those techniques however rely on a set of sophisticated test criteria and require an experienced network designer to interactively choose parameters and threshold values. We are confident that the inclusion of these test criteria will lead to further improvement of our method.

An open research issue is the convergence analysis of PBIL, which will provide further insight into different design choices and parameter settings. It is expected that results can be achieved much easier than for standard genetic algorithms, because the representation is very convenient from a theoretical point of view. We expect that the analysis will give rise to minor changes in the PBIL update rule in order to provide even easier–to–handle control knobs to adjust the trade–off between exploration and exploitation.

References

1. Baluja, C., Caruana R.: Removing the genetics from the standard genetic algorithm, Proc. of the Twelfth Int. Conference on Machine Learning (1995)
2. Braun, H., Zagorski, P.: ENZO–M, A Hybrid Approach for Optimizing Neural Networks by Evolution and Learning, Parallel Problem Solving from Nature, Springer (1994)
3. Fletcher, R. Practical methods for optimization, John Wiley and Sons, Chichester (1995)

4. Harp, S., Samad, T., Guha, A.: Designing application–specific neural networks using the genetic algorithm, Advances in Neural Information Processing Systems 2, Morgan Kaufmann, San Mateo, CA (1990)
5. Hergert, F.,Finnoff, W. and Zimmermann H.: A comparison of weight elimination methods for reducing complexity in neural networks, Int. Joint Conf. on Neural Networks, Baltimore (1992)
6. Liu, Y.: Neural Network Model Selection using Asymptotic Jackknife Estimator and Cross–Validation, Advances in Neural Information Processing Systems 4, Morgan Kaufmann, San Mateo, CA (1992)
7. Svarer, C., Hansen, L., Larsen, J.: On design and evaluation of tapped–delay neural network architectures, IEEE International Conference on Neural Networks, San Francisco (1993)
8. Tong, H., Lim, K,: Threshold autoregression, limit cycles and cyclical data, Journ. Roy. Stat. Soc. B, 42 (1980) 245
9. Weigend, A., Rummelhart, D., Huberman, B.: Predicting the future: A connectionist approach, Int. Jour. of Neural Systems (1990)
10. Goldberg, D.: Gentic Algorithms in Search, Optimization and Machine Learning, Addison–Wesley, Redwood City (1989)
11. Schwefel, H.–P.: Evolution and Optimium Seeking, John Wiley and Suns, Chichester (1995)
12. Hertz, J., Krogh, A. and Palmer, R. Introduction to the theory of neural computation, Addison-Wesley, Redwood City (1991)

Robust GP in Robot Learning

Naohiro HONDO[1] Hitoshi IBA[2] Yukinori KAKAZU[1]

[1] Complex Systems Engineering,
Division of Systems and Information Engineering,
Hokkaido University. N-13 W-8, Sapporo, Hokkaido 060, Japan
{hondo, kakazu}@complex.hokudai.ac.jp
+81-11-706-6445

[2] Machine Inference Section, Electrotechnical Lab.
1-1-4 Umezono, Tukuba Science City, Ibaraki, 305, Japan.
iba@etl.go.jp
+81- 298-58-5195

Abstract. This paper presents a new approach to Genetic Programming (i.e. GP). Our goal is to realize robustness by means of the automatic discovery of functions. In traditional GP, techniques have been proposed which attempt to discover certain subroutines for the sake of improved efficiency. So far, however, the robustness of GP has not yet been discussed in terms of knowledge acquisition. We propose an approach for robustness named COAST, which has a library for storing certain subroutines for reuse. We make use of the Wall Following Problem to illustrate the efficiency of this method.

1. Introduction

This paper presents a new approach to robust Genetic Programming using the automatic discovery of functions. The ultimate goal of this paper is to construct a GP that is robust toward a changeable environment.

As an additional facility to GP, the automatic discovery of functions is proposed. The purpose of this automatic discovery of functions is to reduce the size of individuals and decompose problems into subproblems thereby reducing computational effort [Koza 92b]. A number of methods for the automatic discovery of functions have been proposed. For example, Automatically Defined Functions (i.e., ADF) has been proposed by Koza [Koza 94], Module Acquisition by Angeline [Kinnear 92], and Adaptive Representation by Rosca [Rosca 94]. These methods are effectual for the above purposes. In particular, ADF gives a high performance in constructing subroutines as solutions for the subproblems mentioned above.

However, so far the robustness of GP using automatic discovery of functions has not yet been discussed. The robustness of the GP is a critical element in any automatic programming system. In order to realize this facility, we introduce a new method based on ADF, called COAST (i.e. COllecting Adf for Subroutine acquisiTion). COAST extends ADF so as to establish a library for acquiring effective subroutines with each generation. As the generations proceed, the subroutines acquired by COAST are shared among the population, whereby any individual in COAST can use this generalized knowledge by referring to the library.

As a result, through these shared subroutines, COAST gives robustness to the system.

The rest of this paper is structured as follows: Section 2 describes our approach to a robust GP and our method, COAST is proposed. Section 3 describes some experimental results, by which the effectiveness of COAST is demonstrated. Section 4 discusses these results and the feasibility of our approach, followed by some conclusions in Section 5.

2. Robust GP: COAST

2.1 An Approach to Robust GP

In this paper, robustness means flexibility with regard to changeable objects or stability within a changeable environment. In general, standard GP tends to be delicate in a changeable environment. This is because programs generated by standard GP are not structured to certain subroutines. That is, programs generated by standard GP are described from the starting point to the end of the process. Even if there are similar routines within a process, the program must describe each solution without omission. On the other hand, programs generated by humans are constructed of a main part and some subroutines. All subsolutions included in this process are represented as subroutines. This difference between GP and humans results in the lack of robustness found in standard GP. When an environment changes, standard GP must remake its program to match the new environment from the beginning. On the other hand, a program structured from subroutines can be remade merely by rearranging those subroutines in the environment. As a result, the program can adapt to the environment more quickly.

There is also another reason for the lack of robustness in standard GP. Let us use the example of robot learning known as the Wall Following Problem: The goal of this problem is to generate a program which can navigate a robot to follow the wall. In this problem, changeable environment means change in the location of obstacles. As mentioned above, any program generated by standard GP is described from the starting point to the end of the process. In such a case, the program is described as the trajectory of the robot. Thus, the program describes only map information. Therefore, if a map changes, any program consisting of only previous map information is useless for the new map. In short, the second reason for the lack of robustness in standard GP is that such programs describe only map information. In other words, standard GP doesn't learn the movement of the robot but the map. The most important thing for robustness, therefore, is to acquire the general movements of the robot.

Moreover, even if standard GP can acquire the general movements of a robot, it can't store those movements. Thus, when a GP converges to a certain environment, it must discard previously effective subroutines when that environment changes. It must then acquire similar subroutines all over.

To overcome those first and second problems, methods for the automatic discovery of functions have been proposed by some researchers. Their objective is to reduce the size of individuals and to construct subroutines. Koza has proposed the

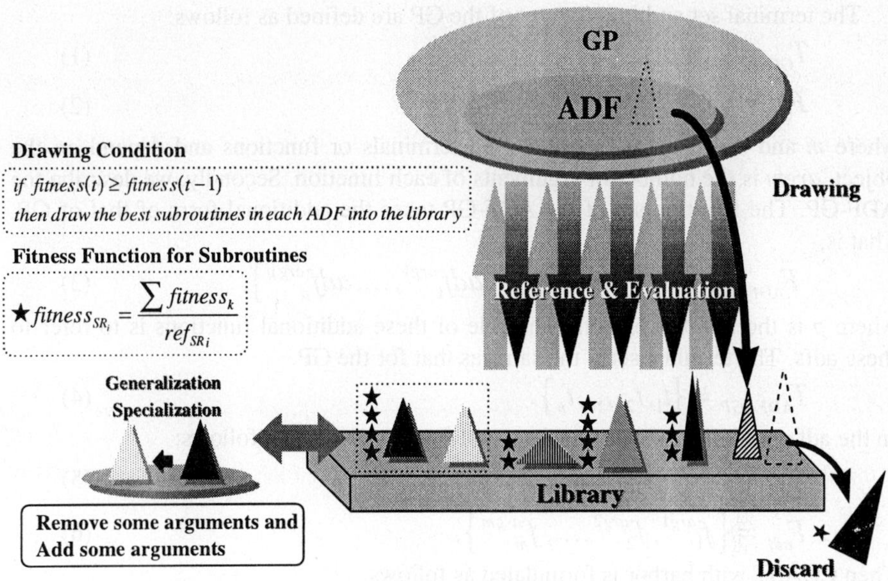

Figure 1. COAST.

Automatically Defined Functions (i.e., ADF), which is capable of realizing the above objectives. That is, ADF generates subroutines automatically in its evolutionary process. Each subroutine is expected to work as a subsolution of subproblems included in the original problem.

ADF can solve the first and second problems mentioned above, but can't overcome the third problem. In this paper, we propose a new method based on ADF with the addition of a library aimed at giving robust GP. This proposal is called COAST (COllecting Adf for Subroutine acquisiTion). In COAST, the part which generates those effective subroutines (as general movement in the above example) is realized as ADF, and the part which stores those acquired subroutines is realized as a library in order to reuse them. Moreover, we introduce two additional operations for the subroutines in the library to give a bias. These operations constitute a generalization and specialization to the subroutines. The objective of these operations is to give diversity for the subroutines. The following sections describe the structure of COAST and of the operations.

2.2 Description of COAST

COAST is structured into two main parts: The former part generates the main solutions and subroutines and is based on ADF-GP. The latter part stores the effective subroutines acquired by this ADF. These subroutines acquired by ADF are drawn into a library according to a rule. Any subroutine in the library (called *SR* here) may be referred to by any individual in the main GP. That subroutine is the given fitness by the individual which referred to it. The subroutine which has the lowest fitness is discarded and a new subroutine, generated by the ADF, is added to the library.

The terminal set and function set of the GP are defined as follows:

$$T_{GP} = \{t_1, t_2, \ldots, t_n\}, \quad (1)$$

$$F_{GP} = \{f_1^{arg1}, f_2^{arg2}, \ldots, f_m^{argm}\}. \quad (2)$$

where *m* and *n* are the number of used terminals or functions and depend on the object. *argm* is the number of arguments of each function. Secondly, we describe the ADF-GP. The function set of the ADF-GP takes the additional form of that of GP. That is,

$$F_{ADF-GP} = \{f_1^{arg1}, \ldots, f_m^{argm}, adf_1^{arg1}, \ldots, adf_p^{arg\,p}\}, \quad (3)$$

where *p* is the number of adfs. The role of these additional functions is to refer to these adfs. The terminal set is the same as that for the GP.

$$T_{ADF-GP} = \{t_1, t_2, \ldots, t_n\}. \quad (4)$$

In the adf population, the terminal set and function set are as follows:

$$T_{adf} = \{t_1, \ldots, t_n, arg_1, \ldots, arg_q\}, \quad (5)$$

$$F_{adf} = \{f_1^{arg1}, f_2^{arg2}, \ldots, f_m^{argm}\}. \quad (6)$$

Then COAST with harbor is formulated as follows:

$$COAST := \left\{ \begin{array}{c|ccc|c} body_1 & adf_{11}^{arg1} & \cdots & adf_{p1}^{arg\,p} & SR_1 \\ \vdots & \vdots & \vdots & \vdots & \vdots \\ body_M & adf_{1M}^{arg1} & \cdots & adf_{pM}^{arg\,p} & SR_w \end{array} \right\} \quad (7)$$

Moreover, the function set of COAST is given additional functions to refer SR_i in the library.

$$F_{COAST} = \left\{ \begin{array}{l} f_1^{arg1}, \ldots, f_m^{argm}, \\ adf_1^{arg1}, \ldots, adf_p^{arg\,p}, \\ SR_1^{arg1}, \ldots, SR_w^{argw} \end{array} \right\}. \quad (8)$$

The terminal set of COAST is as follows.

$$T_{COAST} = \{t_1, \ldots, t_n\}. \quad (9)$$

The subroutine for the drawing operation into the library would be executed under the following condition:

$$if\ f_{\max}^{t} \geq f_{\max}^{t-1}\quad then\, draw\, into\, the\, library, \quad (10)$$

where f_{max}^{t} is the maximum fitness value in generation *t*. Then, the SR_i already in the library is discarded based on each SR_i fitness. The SR_i fitness is defined in the following equation.

$$fitness_{SR_i} = \frac{\sum fitness_k}{ref_{SR_i}}, \quad (11)$$

where $fitness_k$ is the fitness value of individual k which refers to SR_i, and ref_{SR_i} is the total number of referred SR_i. The SR_i with the lowest fitness is discarded and replaced with a new subroutine acquired by the ADF-GP.

2.3 Generalization and Specialization

In library, to obtain the SR_i with the salient number of ref_{SR_i}, a *generalization* operation may be implemented. The aim of generalization here is to own a wholly stable mean for each subroutine so as to exclude any argument. Therefore, for some subroutines, the argument *argi* may be changed to other terminals stochastically. The conditions governing whether or not the operation is executed are as follows:

$$if\ ref_{SR_i} = 0\ then\ operate\ to\ Generalization. \tag{12}$$

The *specialization* operation means to limit the function to fix its argument. For example, suppose that a function has three arguments, arg0, arg1, and arg2. If the specialization operation is implemented to this function (Indeed, it is not a function but a subtree. However, as I discussed in the previous chapter, it may be regarded as a function), one of the arguments is removed and converted to a fixed value, such as 1, so the function has only two arguments to use. The criterion employed in implementing this operation is the same that for generalization operation.

3. Experiments

We tested COAST using the Wall Following Problem [Koza 91]. The aim of this problem is to acquire a program which can navigate a robot to follow a closed wall within a map. A problem space is represented by a field which is divided into grids and surrounded by a wall along which some tiles have been set. The robot can obtain a reward if it passes a tile. However, there are some obstacles near the wall and the tiles are set alongside those obstacles.

The robot can move within the space with no effect on the grid. The robot can select from the following actions: *MoveForward*, *MoveBack*, and rotating left or right at 45° (*LeftTurn*, *RightTurn*). Moreover the robot has eight sensors(from 12 o'clock by counter clock, $s0, s1, \ldots, s7$) and can measure its distance from the wall. The robot consumes its energy (E) through its movement and sensing. Its energy decreases E-1 units if it moves over a tile, E-2 units if it moves in the field and E-1 units if it senses. If E=0, the robot stops. The evaluation of the program which navigates the robot is given as the number of passed tiles (i.e. rewards). Table 1 gives a more detailed description of the problem.

The experiments make use of 2 different types of conditions:

I. **ex. 1**: this makes use of the map shown in Figure 2. Notice here is that the robot starts from a random starting point within the map.

II. **ex. 2**: this makes use of the 2 maps shown in Figure s 2 and 3. Those maps are used in turn every 5 generations.

The objective of this experiment in using this particular problem is to examine the robustness of COAST towards a changeable and/or unstable environment. Therefore, in this experiment, the environment, i.e., the field of the robot, is changeable. To realize this effect, we use a random starting point and two maps to

Table 1. Tableau for the wall following problem.

Objective:	Find a program to control a robot so that it moves to follow to the wall.
Terminal set:	TurnLeft, TurnRight, MoveForward, MoveBack, s0,s1,...,s7. May include arg0, arg1, and arg2 when using ADF and COAST.
Function set:	IFLTE (4), Prog (2), [{adf0 (2), adf1 (3)}, SR (2,3)] where, the number in parentheses is its argument.
Fitness cases:	One fitness case consisting of a field surrounded by wall.
Raw fitness:	Raw fitness is the amount of the tiles passed within maximum allowed number of its energy.
Standardized fitness:	Standardized fitness is a total number of the passed tile until the robot stops.
Hits:	Not used.
Wrapper:	Not used.
Parameters:	Population size (M) = 70. Maximum generation (G) = 61
Success predicate:	When one individual has a raw fitness = 0.

learn the trajectory of the robot. In ex. 1, the program must include its general movement in following the wall. In ex. 2, the robot learns two maps (i.e., two environments) in turn. Under those conditions, in general, a robot which learns the maps using standard GP learns only a map. So after the robot learns one map (called map A), it doesn't learn the other (called map B). The behavior of the robot in the second map is same as that in map A. Therefore, if there are some obstacles in the second map which didn't exist in map A, the robot can't move as it collides with them.

To show the efficiency of COAST, we apply standard GP and ADFGP to the same environment. Also, all the results in this paper are averaged over 10 trials, and the default library size of COAST is set to 7.

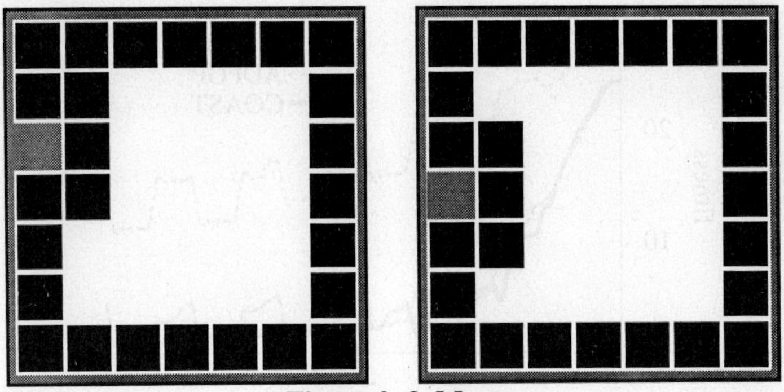

Figure 2, 3. Map.

3.1. Result of ex. 1

Figure 4 shows the transition of the best fitness of standard GP, ADFGP, and COAST in each generation.

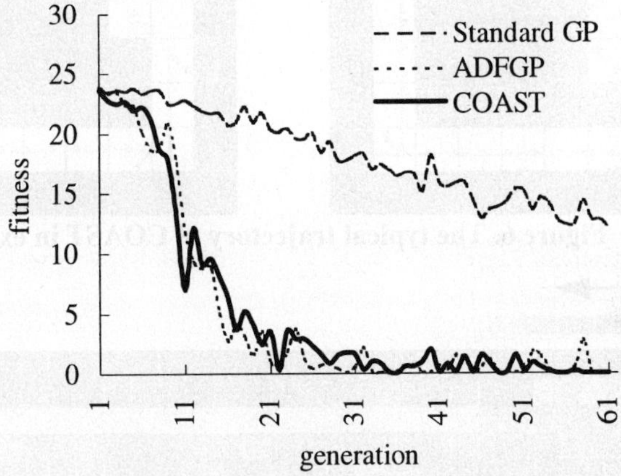

Figure 4. The best fitness in ex. 1.

3.2 Result of ex. 2

This experiment is of central interest in this paper. The objective is , of course, to examine the robustness of COAST. Figures 6 and 7 show the best trajectory and the transition of the SR functions.

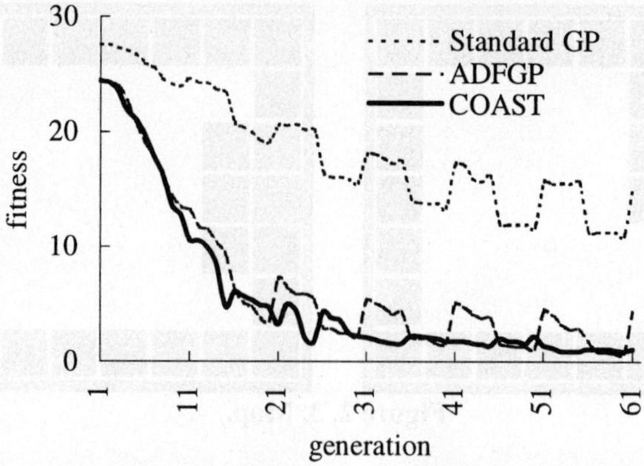

Figure 5. The best fitness in ex. 2.

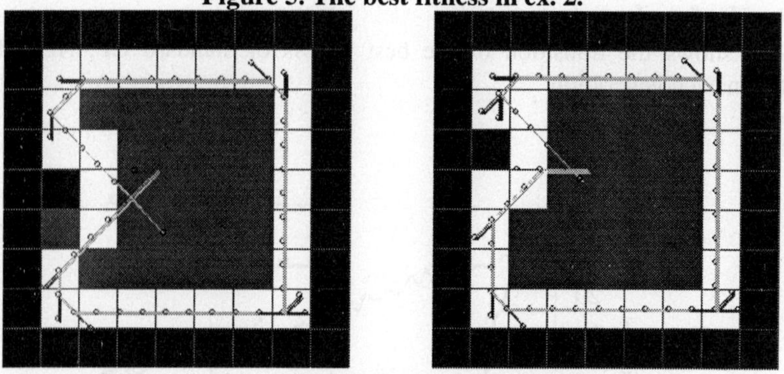

Figure 6. The typical trajectory of COAST in ex. 2.

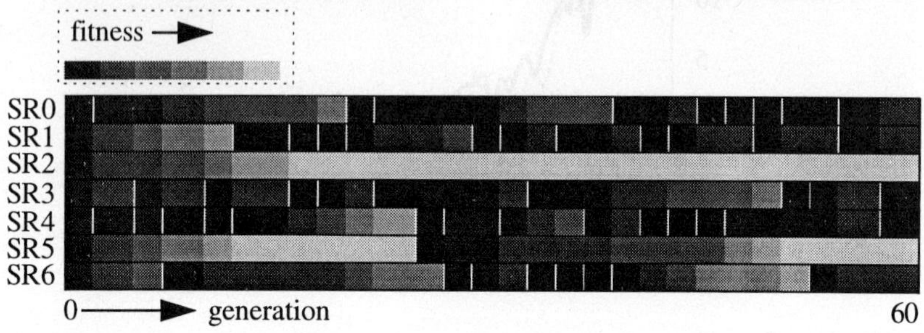

Figure 7. Transition of SR function.

4. Discussion

4.1. ex. 1

The robot has to learn the trajectory at each generation. That is, because the starting point altered, the last program in the last generation was not used. The robot has to remake its program on all such occasions.

The limitations of standard GP are already visible here. Standard GP generated a poor program towards random environments. In contrast to this result, COAST and ADFGP ended in a good performance. These results, of course, were produced by effective subroutines. As each subroutine was generated and used, the robot could adapt to the random environment. Indeed, the graph was continually oscillated at random. However, in almost all the generations, the robot could follow the wall accurately.

4.2. ex. 2

The result of this experiment is presented in Figure 5. This graph represents well the typical characteristics of COAST. First of all, standard GP was scarcely able to adapt to the two maps. This can be seen from the line of the standard GP in Figure 5. The fitness failed completely at every map change, giving a rectangular wave. The knowledge acquired from one map wasn't used in the next. This is because that standard GP can't store effective knowledge when an environment changes. Moreover, programs generated by standard GP have an inclination to learn only map form. Therefore, when the map changes, the program can't follow the transition.

In previous experiments, ADFGP gave the same result as COAST. However, in this experiment, a clear difference appears. ADFGP could generate a program which could completely adapt to one map. However, it couldn't adapt to another. In the second map, the robot failed to follow the wall completely. This phenomenon can be explained from another view point. That is, as the ADFGP converged quickly, it was deprived of its flexibility. As a result, it could adapt to only one map.

On the contrary, COAST showed no drop with the change of maps. In other words, COAST could imbibe the alternation of maps using subroutines obtained from the library. That is, by storing the effective subroutines, the robot could behave robustly after the map has changed. Therefore, reusability emerged effectively in this experiment.

Figure 6 indicates the typical trajectory of COAST. This trajectory is included in specific strategy. In Figure 6, (1) the robot approached the wall, (2) the sensor sensed the distance to the wall. (3) The robot moved back and turned left. (4) it moved forward. (5) The robot sensed the distance to the wall again. (6) The robot moved back and turned left again. This series of movements could be applied to every corner so the robot was able to move smoothly regardless of any change in map.

5. Conclusion

This paper proposed COAST for the scaling up of GP from the point of view of its robustness. The effectiveness of our proposal was shown experimentally through the Wall Following Problem. COAST showed a stable performance, even under a fluctuating environment.

Reference

[Kinnear 92] Kinnear, K.: Alternatives in Automatic Function Definition: A Comparison of Performance in Advances in Genetic Programming, K. E. Kinnear, Jr., Ed. Cambridge, MA: MIT Press.

[Koza 91] Koza, J.: Evolution of subsumption using genetic programming, Proc. of the First European Conference on Artificial Life (ECAL 91), MIT Press, 1991.

[Koza 92a] Koza, J.: Genetic Programming, On the Programming of Computers by Means of Natural Selection, MIT Press, 1992.

[Koza 92b] Koza, J.: Scaleable Learning in Genetic Programming using Automatic Function Definition: in Genetic Programming, K. E. Kinnear, Jr., Ed. Cambridge, MA: MIT Press.

[Koza 94] Koza, J.: Genetic Programming II : Automatic Discovery of Reusable Subprograms, MIT Press, 1994.

[Rosca 94] Justinian P. Rosca. and Dana H. Ballard.: Hierarchical Self-Organization in Genetic Programming, Machine Learning, Proc. 11th International Conference, p251-258, 1994.

A Pattern Recognition System Using Evolvable Hardware

Masaya Iwata[1] Isamu Kajitani[2] Hitoshi Yamada[2]
Hitoshi Iba[1] Tetsuya Higuchi[1]

[1] 1-1-4,Umezono,Tsukuba,Ibaraki,305,Japan
Electrotechnical Laboratory
[2] 1-1-1,Tennoudai,Tsukuba,Ibaraki,305,Japan
University of Tsukuba

Abstract. We describe a high-speed pattern recognition system using Evolvable Hardware (EHW), which can change its own hardware structure by genetic learning in order to adapt best to the environment. The purpose of the system is to show that EHW can work as a recognition device with such robustness for the noise as seen in the recognition systems based on neural networks. The advantage of EHW compared with a neural network is the high processing speed and the readability of the learned result. The readability means that the result is understandable in terms of Boolean functions. In this paper, we describe the architecture, the learning algorithm and the experiment on the pattern recognition system using EHW.

1 Introduction

The interests on evolvable hardware (EHW) are growing rapidly since the idea of EHW was proposed independently in Japan and in Switzerland around 1992 [Higuchi94],[Marchal94]. And in 1995, the first international workshop on evolvable hardware was held in Lausanne. EHW is a hardware which can adapt to the new environment which the designer doesn't anticipate. This contrasts with the conventional hardware where the adaptive changes are not allowed. EHW, built on programmable logic devices (PLDs), is an adaptive hardware whose architecture can be reconfigured by using genetic algorithms to adapt to the new environment.

EHW is best suitable for applications where hardware specifications can not be given in advance. Applications solved by artificial neural network (ANN) are such examples because pattern classifier functions can be obtained only after learning is complete.

The purpose of this paper is to show that EHW may have the possibility to take the place of ANN when used for a pattern recognition system. EHW is expected to work as ANN-like robust pattern recognizer which realizes noise-insensitive recognition. Advantages of EHW over ANN are as follows. First the processing speed is at least two orders of magnitude faster than ANN systems whose executions are mostly software-based. Second the the learned results of

EHW are readable. That means that the learned result is easily expressed in terms of readable Boolean functions. In ANN, on the contrary, it is difficult to read the learned result because it is represented just by the enumeration of real values for thresholds and weights.

This paper consists of the following sections. Section 2 describes the EHW concept. Section 3 describes the pattern recognition using EHW. It introduces MDL (Minimum description length) and VGA (Variable length chromosome genetic algorithm) for increasing the capability of noise-insensitive recognition. Section 4 describes an architecture of the pattern recognition system using EHW and the experiment on the recognition of numerical characters. Section 5 discusses about the recognition system and Section 6 concludes this paper.

2 Evolvable Hardware (EHW)

2.1 Basic Idea

Evolvable Hardware (EHW) is a hardware which modifies its own hardware structure according to the environmental changes. EHW is implemented on a programmable logic device (PLD), whose architecture can be altered by downloading a binary bit string, i.e. *architecture bits.* The architecture bits are adaptively acquired by genetic algorithms (GA).

The basic idea of EHW is to regard the architecture bits of a PLD as a chromosome for GA (see Fig. 1). The hardware structure is adaptively searched by GA. These architecture bits, i.e. the GA chromosome, are downloaded onto a PLD, on and after the genetic learning. Therefore, EHW can be considered as an on-line adaptive hardware.

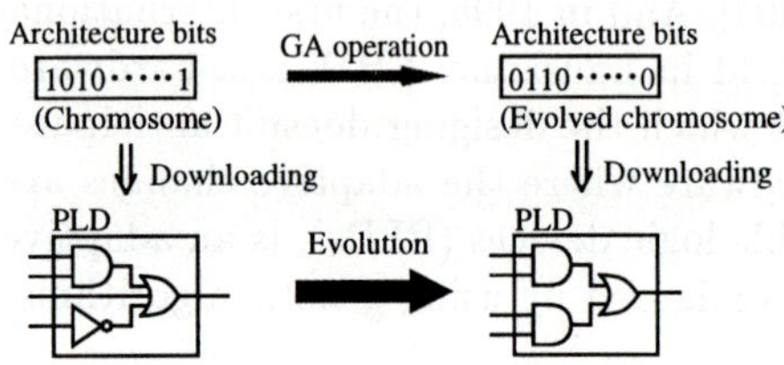

Fig. 1. Evolvable Hardware (EHW)

2.2 Programmable Logic Device (PLD)

We explain in more detail about PLD using the simplified model as shown in Fig. 2.

A PLD consists of *logic cells* and a *fuse array.* In addition, architecture bits determine the architecture of the PLD. These bits are assumed to be stored in an architecture bit register (ABR). Each link of the fuse array corresponds to a bit in the ABR.

The fuse array determines the interconnection between the device inputs and the logic cell. It also specifies the logic cell's AND-term inputs. If a link on a particular row of the fuse array is switched on, which is indicated by a black dot in Fig. 2, then the corresponding input signal is connected to the row. In the architecture bits, these black and white dots are represented by 1 and 0 respectively.

Consider the example PLD shown in Fig. 2. The first row indicates that I_0 and $\overline{I_2}$ are connected by an AND-term, which generates $I_0\overline{I_2}$. Similarly, the second row generates I_1. These AND-terms are connected by an OR gate. Thus, the resultant output is $O_0 = I_0\overline{I_2} + I_1$.

As mentioned above, both of the fuse array and the functionality of the logic cell are represented in a binary string. The key idea of EHW is to regard this binary bit string as a chromosome for the sake of GA-based adaptive search.

The hardware structure we actually use is a FPLA device, which is a commercial PLD (Fig. 3). This architecture mainly consists of an AND and OR arrays. A vertical line of the OR array corresponds to a logic cell in Fig. 2.

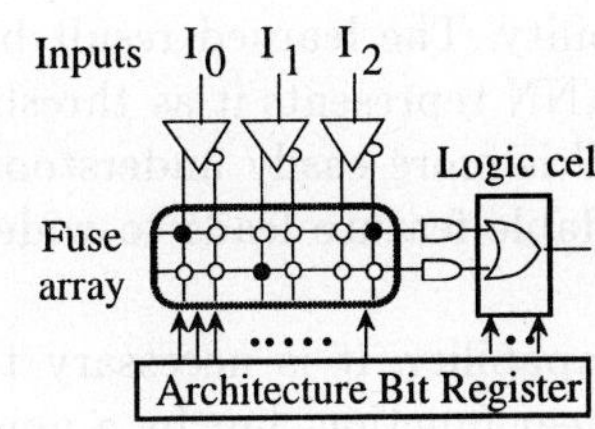

Fig. 2. A Simplified PLD (Programmable Logic Device) Structure

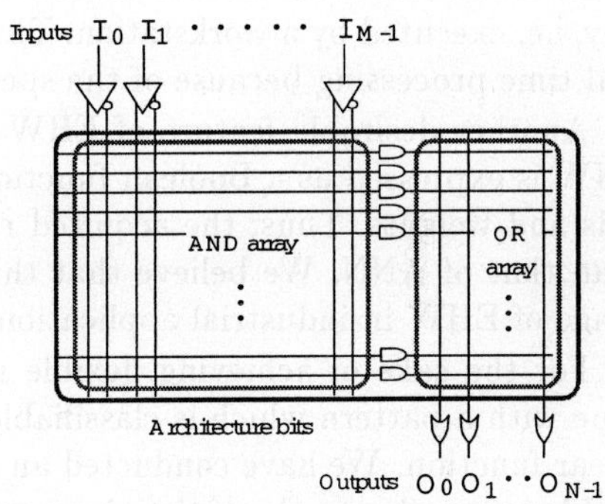

Fig. 3. A FPLA Architecture for EHW

2.3 Genetic learning

We describe the genotype representation of EHW and the genetic learning method.

In our earlier works, the architecture bits were regarded as the GA chromosome and the chromosome length was fixed. In spite of this simple representation, the hardware evolution was successful for combinatorial logic circuits (e.g. 6-multiplexer [Higuchi93]) and sequential logic circuits (e.g. 4-state machine, 3-bit counter [Higuchi94]).

However, this straightforward representation had a serious limitation in the hardware evolution. All the fuse array bits should have been included in the genotype, even when effective bits in the fuse array were only a few. This made the chromosome too long to be effectively searched by evolution.

Therefore, we have introduced a new GA based on variable length chromosome called *VGA* [Kajitani95]. VGA is expected to evolve a large circuit more quickly. The chromosome length of VGA is smaller than the previous GA, especially when evolving a circuit with large inputs. VGA is described in more detail in section 3.

The fitness evaluation of GA is basically determined by the correctness of the EHW's output for the training data set. In the pattern recognition system we introduce MDL (Minimum Description Length) [Rissanen89] for the fitness evaluation. Using MDL, the ability of robustness in recognizing noisy pattern is expected to increase. (For more details, see section 3.3)

3 Pattern Recognition

3.1 Motivation

EHW has been applied to high-speed pattern recognition in order to establish a robust system in noisy environments [Iwata96]. This ability, i.e. robustness, seems to be the main feature of ANN. ANN is mostly run in a software-based way, i.e. executed by a workstation. Thus, current ANN may have difficulty with real-time processing because of the speed limit of the software-based execution.

Another desirable feature of EHW is its readability. The learned result by EHW is expressed as a Boolean function, whereas ANN represents it as thresholds and weights. Thus, the acquired result of EHW is more easily understood than that of ANN. We believe that this understandable feature leads to wider usage of EHW in industrial applications.

For the sake of achieving flexible recognition capability, it is necessary to cope with a pattern which is classifiable not by a linear function, but by a non-linear function. We have conducted an experiment in learning the exclusive-OR problem in order to check the above capability. From the simulation result, we confirmed that EHW can learn non-linear functions successfully [Higuchi95]. In other words, EHW is supposed to fulfill the minimum requirement towards the robust pattern recognition.

3.2 Procedure of pattern recognition

The pattern recognition procedure consists of two phases as shown in Fig. 4. The first is the learning phase of training patterns. The training patterns are genetically learned by EHW. We use VGA and MDL-based fitness described in section 3.3 and 3.4. The second phase is the recognition of test patterns. Our aim is the noise-insensitive pattern recognition.

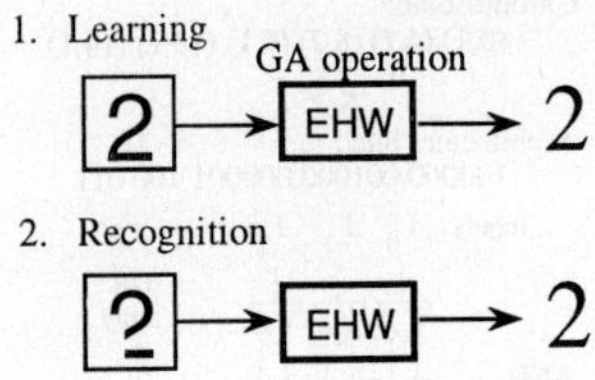

Fig. 4. The Procedure of Pattern Recognition using EHW

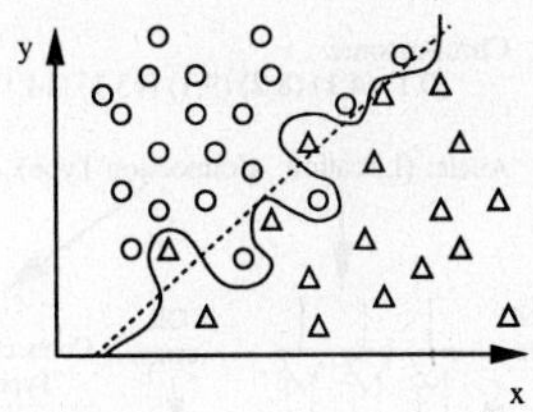

Fig. 5. An Example of Pattern Classification using MDL

3.3 Fitness evaluation by MDL (Minimum Description Length)

MDL (Minimum Description Length) is an information criteria in machine learning in order to predict the rest of the data set with the given data set [Rissanen89]. Using MDL for pattern recognition, a noise-insensitive classifier function is obtained effectively.

A classifier function which is noise-insensitive is more desirable than a classifier which is noise-sensitive, since the latter is susceptible to noise and overfitting occurs. For example, in Fig. 5, the function denoted with solid line classifies two patterns in very strict way, but the function denoted with dotted line is better as the classifier function because it is noise-insensitive [Itoh92]. Thus, MDL is defined so as to choose more simple and more general classifier functions.

We have introduced the above MDL criterion into the GA fitness evaluation. The purpose is to establish a robust learning method for EHW. In general, the greater the number of "don't care" [1] inputs, the more robust (i.e. noise-insensitive) the evolved hardware. Thus, we regard the number of "don't care" inputs as an index of MDL.

More formally, the MDL value for our EHW is written as follows:

$$\mathrm{MDL} = A_c \log(C+1) + (1 - A_c)\log(E+1), \qquad (1)$$

where C denotes the complexity of the EHW. E is the error rate of the EHW's output.

The C value (i.e. the complexity of the EHW) determines the performance of the MDL. We introduce three types of C definitions as described in Appendix.

To use MDL as the fitness function of GA, it must be normalized so that it has the range of $0 \leq \mathrm{MDL} \leq 1$. Thus the fitness is expressed as follows.

$$\mathrm{Fitness} = 1 - \mathrm{MDL} \qquad (2)$$

[1] We call an input "don't care" if it is not included in the output expression. For instance, if $O = I_1 + I_2$ in case of a PLD shown in Fig. 2, then I_0 is a "don't care" input.

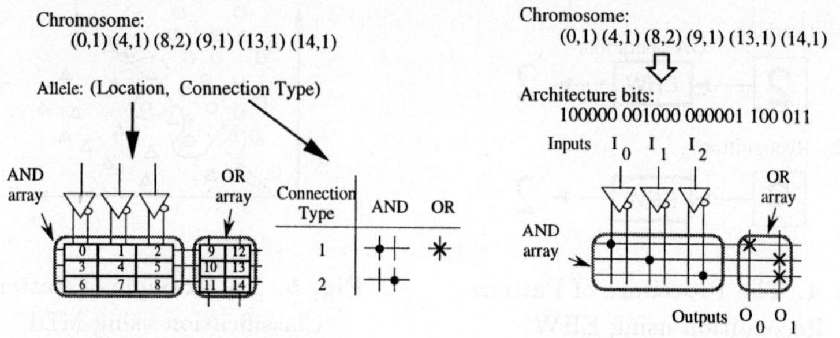

(a) Representation of an Allele (b) An Example of a Chromosome

Fig. 6. Chromosome Representation of Variable Length Chromosome GA

3.4 Variable length chromosome GA (VGA)

We introduce a new GA based on variable length chromosome called VGA to increase the performance of GA. In conventional EHW, the whole architecture bits of PLDs were regarded as a chromosome of GA. We call this method simple GA (called SGA). However, in pattern recognition problem of 2D image here, many inputs are needed. This causes the increase of chromosome length, leading to the increase of GA learning time, and the restriction to evolved circuit size.

Comparing with SGA, the chromosome length of VGA is smaller especially when evolving a circuit with large inputs. This is because VGA can deal with a part of architecture bits, which effectively determine the hardware structure. Because of this short chromosome, VGA can increase the maximum circuit size and establish an efficient adaptive search.

The coding method of VGA is described in Fig. 6. An example of a chromosome and representation of an allele is shown in Fig. 6 (a). An allele in a chromosome consists of a location and a connection type. The location is the position of the allele in the fuse array. There are two kinds of connection type. The AND connection type defines the input of the AND array to be either positive or negative. The OR connection type defines the output of the AND array to be connected or not to the input of the OR array. For example, an allele (0,1) means that the connection type at location 0 is 1. By converting each allele into the connection pattern of the PLD, the chromosome is converted into the the architecture bits defining the PLD as shown in Fig. 6 (b).

We use the roulette wheel selection strategy. Recombination operators are *cut* and *splice*, which are used in the messy GA [Goldberg93]. The splice operator is slightly different in the sense that a gene with the same locations (for instance, (0,1) and (0,2)) are not allowed in one chromosome. A mutation operator is applied so as to change the values of the location and the connection type randomly. Splice operator concatenates two chromosomes.

For more details of VGA, refer to [Kajitani95].

4 Pattern recognition system

4.1 The pattern recognition system

We have developed the pattern recognition system (Fig. 7). The organization of the system is shown in Fig. 8. It consists of an EHW board including 4 FPGA chips (Xilinx 4025), a DOS/V machine, and an input tablet for drawing patterns. The DOS/V machine handles GA operations, the control of EHW board and the display of patterns. The PLD on FPGA is reconfigurable, which means that the system can be used as a universal EHW system.

The overview of the EHW board is shown in Fig. 9. and the block diagram is shown in Fig. 10. In the EHW board, there are four FPGA (hatched area in the figure), board control registers, and SRAM which stores the configuration data of FPGA. In the EHW, a circuit represented by a chromosome is realized by an ABR (architecture bit register) and a PLD. The ABR stores architecture bits of the PLD. The PLD has the architecture of FPLA device (Fig. 3). In this figure, there are K individuals, i.e. K pairs of an ABR and a PLD in a FPGA chip. In the first version of this system, we designed a genetically reconfigurable hardware device with four FPGAs. The processing time of the EHW board is 720 ns.

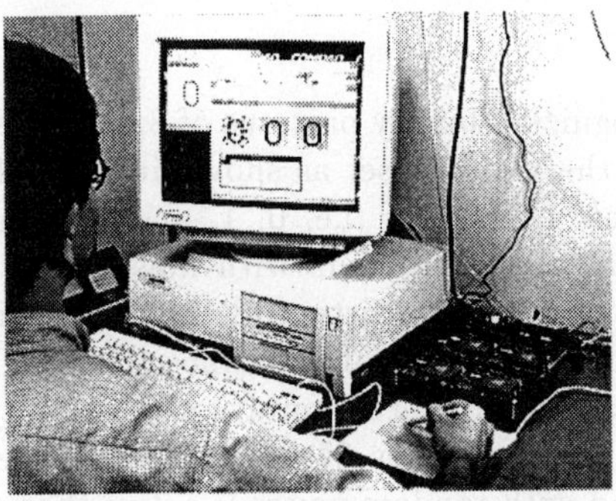

Fig. 7. Pattern Recognition System using EHW

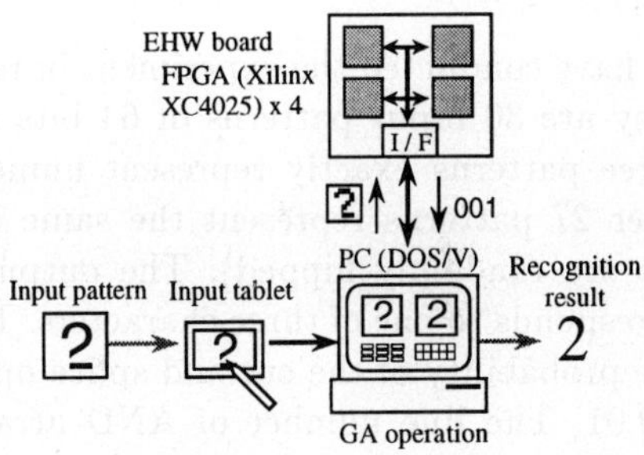

Fig. 8. Block Diagram of Pattern Recognition System

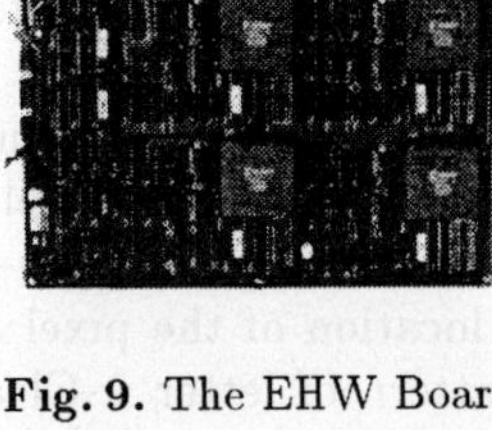

Fig. 9. The EHW Board

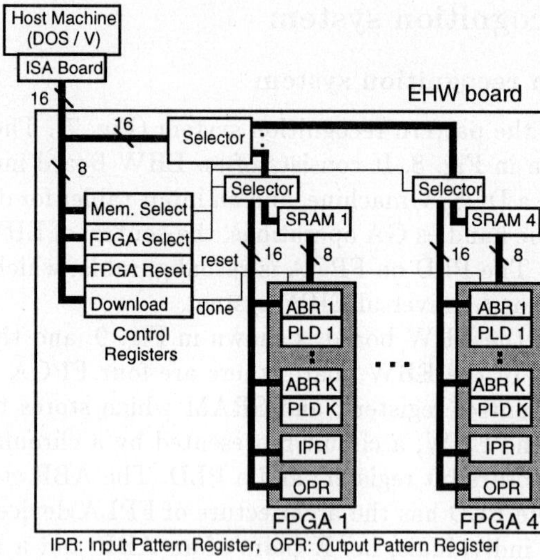

Fig. 10. Block Diagram of EHW Board

4.2 Experiment

We have conducted the experiment in recognizing binary patterns of 8×8 pixels. They are 30 input patterns of 64 bits in the training set as shown in Fig. 11. Three patterns exactly represent numerical characters (i.e. 0, 1, and 2). The other 27 patterns represent the same numerical characters with noises (i.e. 5 bits are randomly flipped). The outputs of EHW consists of 3 bits; each bit corresponds to one of three characters. The initial length of a chromosome is 100. The probability of the cut and splice operators is 0.1. The mutation probability is 0.01. The line number of AND array in the PLD is 24. The test data set consists of 30 patterns, which are generated with random noises (i.e. less than 5 bits are flipped randomly).

For different learning methods were examined, i.e. MDL-based EHW with three types of MDL definitions (MDL1, MDL2 and MDL3 which correspond to equations (3), (4), and (5) in Appendix, respectively) and non-MDL EHW. The recognition result of the test set is plotted in Fig. 12. From the figure, it is clear that MDL-based EHWs give better performance for noisy patterns than EHW without MDL.

An important feature of EHW is that the resultant expression can be represented by a simple Boolean function. For example, in one run, learned results in case of MDL3 are $O_0 = \overline{I_{34} I_{38}}, O_1 = \overline{I_{22} I_{38}} + \overline{I_{13}}$, and $O_2 = I_{37}$, where $I_i (0 \leq i \leq 63)$ indicates the location of the pixel in the pattern and O_i is the recognition output for the pattern of letter i. Clearly, the results obtained by EHW are easier to understand, compared with ANN.

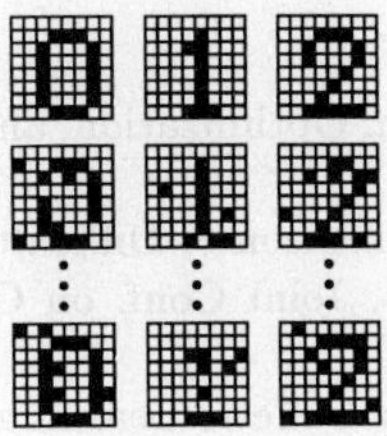

Fig. 11. Training Patterns

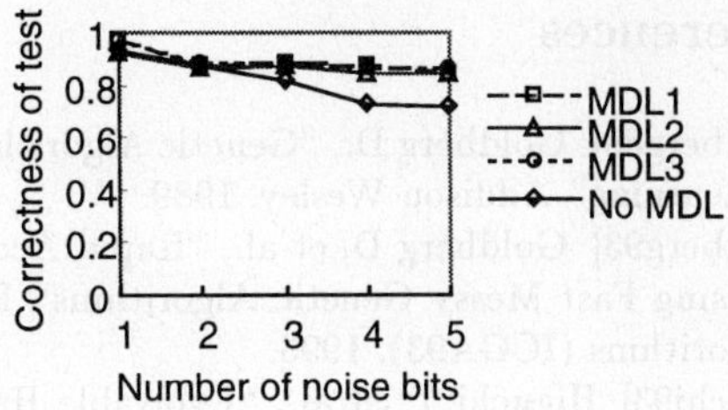

Fig. 12. Recognition Result of Test Set

5 Discussion

In this section we discuss about 1) the Boolean function which has high recognition ability for noisy patterns, 2) the advantage of VGA over SGA.

First we discuss the Boolean function which has high recognition ability for noisy patterns. Roughly speaking, the Boolean function with better recognition ability is the function which has less inputs, that is, the function with more "don't care" inputs. We confirmed that we can get such a function using MDL. However, we can get more robust functions by adding more terms in the equation. The method to obtain such functions is the subject of the future research.

In the pattern recognition system, we used VGA instead of SGA. The main advantage of VGA in pattern recognition is that we can handle larger inputs than using SGA. For example, EHW could learn three patterns of 16 inputs by SGA with the chromosome length of 840. On the other hand, by VGA, EHW can learn three patterns of 64 inputs with the chromosome length of 187.6 in average. In addition, the learning by VGA is much faster than SGA; 416.7 generation by VGA, 4053 by SGA. The reason why VGA can handle larger inputs than SGA is that VGA encodes into the chromosome only the inputs which actually generate AND terms. So, the chromosome length can be kept small. If SGA is used for problems of this nature, we suffer the increase of the chromosome length because of many inputs, leading to the increase of GA execution time. In addition, VGA has a very good matching with MDL because MDL directs the GA search to find smaller circuits. Thus, we can say that VGA is suitable for pattern recognition problems because it handles many inputs and learns small circuits.

6 Conclusion

In this paper, we described the pattern recognition system using EHW. The system aims to recognize noisy patterns as neural networks do. We described the learning algorithm using MDL (Minimum Description Length) and VGA (Variable length chromosome GA). The noise-insensitive function was obtained effectively by using MDL as a fitness function of GA. By using VGA, EHW could handle larger inputs with faster learning speed than using simple GA. We developed the pattern recognition system to show the feasibility of EHW for noise-insensitive recognition. We conducted experiments of recognizing noisy patterns and we confirmed that EHW has the ability to recognize noisy patterns.

References

[Goldberg89] Goldberg D., "Genetic Algorithms in Search, Optimization, and Machine Learning" Addison Wesley, 1989.

[Goldberg93] Goldberg D. et al., "Rapid Accurate Optimization of Difficult Problems using Fast Messy Genetic Algorithms" Proc. 5th Int. Joint Conf. on Genetic Algorithms (ICGA93), 1993.

[Higuchi93] Higuchi T. et al., "Evolvable Hardware with Genetic Learning" in Proc. Simulation of Adaptive Behavior, MIT Press, 1993.

[Higuchi94] Higuchi T. et al., "Evolvable Hardware with Genetic Learning" in Massively Parallel Artificial Intelligence (eds. H. Kitano), MIT Press, 1994.

[Higuchi95] Higuchi T. et al., "Evolvable Hardware and its Application to Pattern Recognition and Fault-tolerant Systems" in 1st Int. Workshop Towards Evolvable Hardware, Springer Verlag, 1996.

[Itoh92] Itoh, S., "Application of MDL principle to pattern classification problems" (in Japanese), J. of Japanese Society for Artificial Intelligence, Vol. 7, No. 4, 1992.

[Kajitani95] Kajitani I. et al., "Variable Length Chromosome GA for Evolvable Hardware" in Proc. 3rd Int. Conf. on Evolutionary Computation (ICEC96), 1996

[Marchal94] P. Marchal et al., "Embryological Development on Silicon" Artificial Life IV, 1994.

[Rissanen89] Rissanen, J., Stochastic Complexity in Statistical Inquiry, World Scientific Series in Computer Science, Vol. 15, 1989.

Appendix Definition of Complexity value for MDL

We describe the C value which is the complexity value for MDL. The C value (i.e. the complexity of the EHW) determines the performance of the MDL. We introduce three types of C definitions as follows:-

$$C_1 = \sum_i \mid AND_{Oi} \mid, \tag{3}$$

$$C_2 = \mid AND \mid \times \mid OR \mid, \tag{4}$$

$$C_3 = \sum_i \mid AND_{Oi} \mid \times \mid OR_{Oi} \mid . \tag{5}$$

Where $\mid AND_O \mid$ and $\mid OR_O \mid$ are the numbers of ANDs and ORs connected to the output O. $\mid AND \mid$ ($\mid OR \mid$) is the number of ANDs (ORs) on the AND (OR) array. Consider Fig. 6(b) for instance. ANDs and ORs are represented as black dots and $\times$ marks in the figure. The values of C_1, C_2 and C_3 are 3 ($= 1 + 2$), 9 ($= 3 \times 3$) and 5 ($= 1 \times 1 + 2 \times 2$) respectively, because $\mid AND_{O0} \mid$, $\mid OR_{O0} \mid$, $\mid AND_{O1} \mid$, $\mid OR_{O1} \mid$, $\mid AND \mid$, and $\mid OR \mid$ are 1, 1, 2, 2, 3 and 3.

The definition of C_1 is not very precise because it does not include the information of OR gates. On the other hand, C_2 and C_3 are expected to give more exact MDL values. We tested several other definitions of the complexity. In this paper we tested best three definitions.

Topology Design of Feedforward Neural Networks by Genetic Algorithms

Slawomir W. Stepniewski[1] and Andy J. Keane[2]

1 Department of Electrical Engineering, Warsaw University of Technology, ul. Koszykowa 75, 00-662 Warszawa, Poland, E-mail: step@bsdi.iem.pw.edu.pl.

2 Department of Mechanical Engineering, University of Southampton, Highfield, Southampton, SO17 1BJ, U.K, E-mail: andy.keane@soton.ac.uk

Abstract. For many applications feedforward neural networks have proved to be a valuable tool. Although the basic principles of employing such networks are quite straightforward, the problem of tuning their architectures to achieve near optimal performance still remains a very challenging task. Genetic algorithms may be used to solve this problem, since they have a number of distinct features that are useful in this context. First, the approach is quite universal and can be applied to many different types of neural networks or training criteria. It also allows network topologies to be optimized at various level of detail and can be used with many types of energy function, even those that are discontinuous or non-differentiable. Finally, a genetic algorithm need not be limited to simply adjusting patterns of connections, but, for example, can be utilized to select node transfer functions, weight values or to find architectures that perform best under certain simulated working conditions. In this paper we have investigated an application of genetic algorithms to feedforward neural network architecture design. These neural networks are used to model a nonlinear, discrete SISO system when only noisy training data are available. Additionally, some incidental but nonetheless important aspects of neural network optimization, such as complexity penalties or automatic topology simplification are discussed.

1. Introduction

When designing feedforward neural networks for the purpose of nonlinear approximation, typically architectures with one or two hidden layers are used. Because there is no precise guidance on how to choose the number of nodes in each layer or the size of the whole network, designing such a structure is usually a trial and error procedure. For a given problem many different network architectures may be able to reconstruct a desired input-output mapping with similar error levels. Moreover, using cross-validation techniques, it is possible to train even oversized architectures, since this kind of approach is designed to avoid overfitting [6]. For this reason, the application of neural networks may seem to be quite simple and straightforward. If no serious mistakes are made and the problem is suitable for modelling by a feedforward neural network (the function being approximated is for example smooth, continuous and has bounded values), many configurations should work fairly well despite wide variations in their sizes, types and interconnection patterns. On the other hand, however, a designer usually wants to be assured that the proposed network is optimal or close to optimal in some sense. Also, in some cases, maximal performance may be very desirable. This type of problem arises for example in control schemes that utilize basic or inverse plant models. The controlling capabilities of such schemes improve as the synthesized model better matches the object. Automated design methods start to become attractive in such situations. Here, we present several new results concerning the application of genetic algorithms to the automated design of network topologies.

2. Initial Network Architecture

Before applying a genetic algorithm to neural network topology optimization, information about the network architecture must be converted into an appropriate format that can be processed by the method. Binary strings are used most often with genetic algorithms, although it is also possible to utilize custom designed encodings together with relevant recombination and mutation operators [9]. Here, we have adopted binary chromosomes that are built from the elements corresponding to network synapses only. A value of one indicates that a link exists, zero means that the connection is removed. All hidden and output nodes are always biased. Because it is not desirable to delete biases, bits indicating their presence are not included in the encoding.

Figure 1 illustrates the type of network considered in this paper. All hidden units have sigmoid ($f(x)=\tanh(x)$) transfer functions. The output node has a linear ($f(x)=x$) transfer function. The initial topology to be pruned is a two layer architecture with additional direct connections from each hidden and input node to the network output. This kind of topology was chosen for the following main reasons:

1. Additional links that skip adjacent layers allow the genetic algorithm to remove a whole layer of nodes while still keeping the network functional.
2. Some additional shortcut connections, e.g., those between the network input and output [12], may ease training and therefore the whole genetic topology optimization may become faster.
3. The architecture adopted has a better capability to realize mappings with linear trends, due to the direct links between the input and output layer (for training we have used raw data without any preprocessing to remove DC components or linear trends).
4. Because all the networks pruned here have only one output, the length of the chromosome string does not increase significantly; it rises by the total number of hidden and input units in comparison to a layered architecture with only adjacent units connected.

Other choices for the initial neural network topology are discussed in [11].

The choice of bit locations in the chromosome is not addressed in detail here. It is worth noting, however, that the bits associated with one node are initially bound together but the genetic algorithm applied uses inversion to alter gene ordering and attempts to discover arrangements that help to preserve valuable building blocks.

It should be noted that the binary encoding used here may be difficult to apply to large scale networks (e.g. >1,000 links) but for modelling applications encountered in control

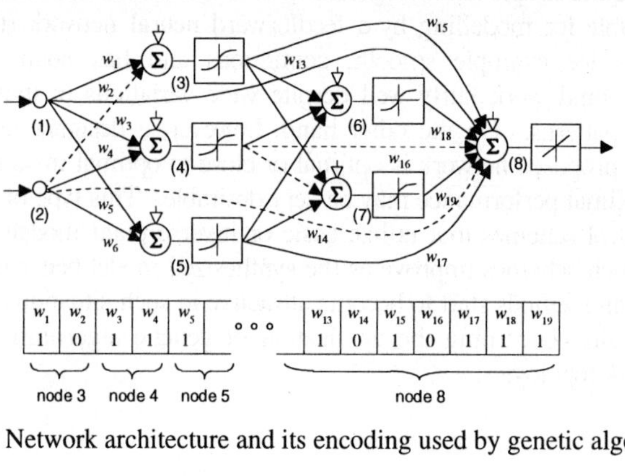

Figure 1: Network architecture and its encoding used by genetic algorithm.

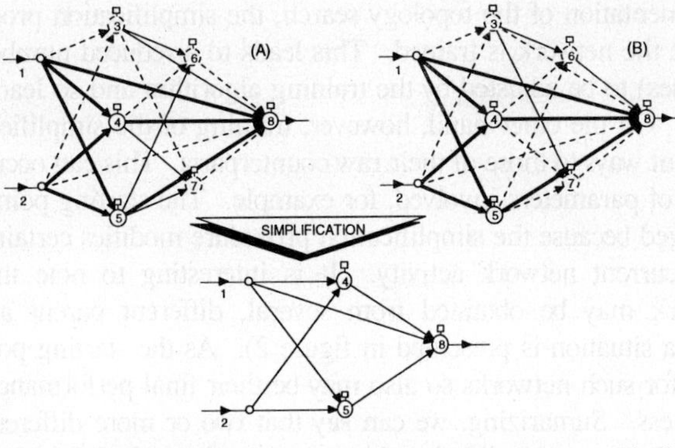

Figure 2: An example of the topology simplification procedure. The bold lines of networks (A) and (B) represent active connections, hairlines correspond to the passive links and dotted lines show deleted synapses.

engineering it is rather unusual to construct neural networks with more than 200 or 300 free parameters (weights and biases). Besides, this kind of encoding allows a search space to be sampled quite precisely and can be used with almost any genetic software package. Any kind of genetic operation always produces a valid neural network (we assume that the architecture is valid if it does not violate the principle of the feedforward transmissions of signals, i.e., there are no explicit closed loops inside the network, althought it is permitted for some input signals not to reach the network outputs). Of course, with this kind of encoding, it is easy to create architectures that obviously will not work correctly, e.g., networks that do not process any input signals. We have never found this possibility to be a real problem; when such configurations occur, this should rather be treated as an indication that some parameters of the topology optimization are adjusted incorrectly (e.g., an excessive penalty on network complexity may give rise to this kind of behaviour) or the task to be implemented by the network is trivial so very few nodes are sufficient to perform the desired function approximation. A genetic algorithm is then likely to sample extremely small networks including those with no active synapses.

3. Topology Simplification

It is clear that topologies generated by a genetic algorithm may contain many superfluous components such as single nodes or even whole clusters of nodes isolated from the network input. Such units (we call them passive nodes) do not process the signals applied to the network sensors and produce only constant responses that are caused by the relevant biases. These passive nodes, if finally connected to active nodes (those transmitting network input signals), function simply as extra biases (e.g., the connection between node 3 and 8 of network A, figure 2). A simplification procedure (a similar idea was used for example in [7]) can therefore be used to remove passive nodes and links and modify true biases so that the input/output mapping of the network remains unchanged. In addition, the simplification procedure deletes all totally isolated links and nodes that have no influence on the network output (e.g., the connection between nodes 5 and 7 of network A, figure 2). A genetic algorithm has no chance to perform this type of simplification efficently by itself as the existance of spare connections has little or no influence on the value of the fitness function. A detail diagram of the simplification algorithm used here is presented in figure 3.

In our implementation of the topology search, the simplification procedure is always carried out before the network is trained. This leads to a reduced number of parameters (weights and biases) to be adjusted by the training algorithm and so learning is typically performed faster. On the other hand, however, training of the simplified networks may proceed in different ways to those of their raw counterparts. This can occur because of the different number of parameters involved, for example. The starting point of the training can also be changed because the simplification procedure modifies certain biases in order to preserve the current network activity. It is interesting to note that a particular, simplified network may be obtained from several, different parent architectures (an example of such a situation is presented in figure 2). As the starting points for training may be different for such networks so also may be their final performance and thus their estimated usefulness. Sumarizing, we can say that two or more different chromosomes corresponding to the same simplified architecture may be assigned various fitness values due to different network performance achieved.

The topologies obtained after simplification are used to asses the real (effective) complexity of the encoded network. Obviously, this task cannot be accomplished by simply calculating the number of '1's in the chromosome because some bits may refer to passive links. Figure 2 is based on such an example of two different size, raw architectures that are functionally equivalent; for network A, five existing links are redundant while network B has only three such connections.

4. Objective Function

Using a genetic algorithm for network topology optimization requires an objective function to be constructed which allows comparison of the usefulness of the network architectures examined (in fact, this approach could be treated as hierarchical optimization with one stage involving network training and the second one being connection pruning). The objective function may combine several factors that reflect the overall quality of a particular network architecture, e.g., number of nodes, number of synaptic connections, learning accuracy, generalization ability and so on. Some components of the objective function, such as generalization ability cannot be evaluated precisely. They depend heavily on many hidden factors that are difficult to quantify by a simple formula, e.g., the choice of training algorithm, its internal parameters and starting point, the effectiveness of training data, termination condition, etc. Other parameters associated with network complexity (number of weights, biases, nodes or inputs) can be calculated directly but converting this information into a useful coefficient that robustly describes network topology is also not trivial (to help in this process we have used the results provided by the topology simplification process discussed ealier).

The fundamental parameter that reflects the usefulness of a feedforward network with analog output remains, however, its generalization ability. Although this factor cannot be evaluated easily it should form a major part of the objective function. Despite the relatively high cost of estimating generalization (it of course involves training each network) some of its properties still make assessing and comparing network quality difficult.

- First, generalization is evaluated with finite accuracy and therefore some differences between networks remain unrevealed. The maximum level of generalization is constrained, for example, by the target learning error (assuming this error level is reachable for a given training algorithm or the maximum number of training

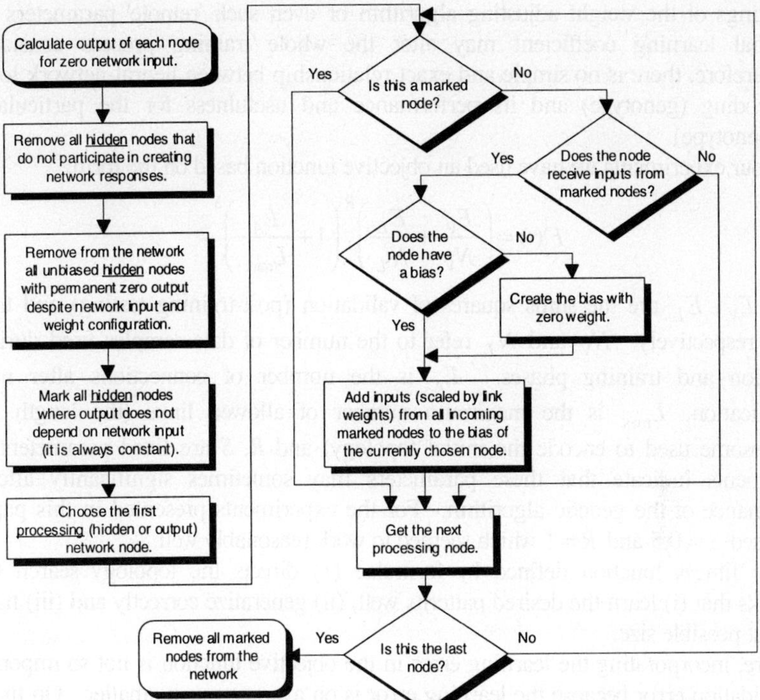

Figure 3: A general flowchart of the simplification routine that can be applied to networks built using both biased and unbiased nodes.

iterations). Since training is always stopped when the network error achieves some required accuracy, typically the generalization error per one data sample should not be lower than the preset, target training error.

- Second, the generalization ability of a given network is estimated after training. The intermediate step of training allows different networks to be adjusted to perform a requested function approximation with similar degrees of performance. The longer and more efficient the training algorithm is, the greater the portion of the networks examined that achieve a given accuracy level. This phenomenon means that when more precise training is used, a genetic algorithm may face difficulties distinguishing between various design options and extracting features that help to build superior networks (it is easier to recognize badly functioning outliers rather than to identify exceptionally valuable individuals). On the other hand, using crude network evaluation may also be inappropriate since no useful information may be provided to the topology optimizer except parameters that are obvious, i.e., network size. Although the genetic algorithm is known as a robust optimization method that can function in noisy environments, allowing inaccurate training may mean that the final 'winners' of the network topology optimization will not achieve the expected performance when subsequently trained more precisely.
- Finally, generalization assessment is affected by many types of disturbances that cannot be totally compensated for. Any fluctuation of the training starting point, or the number of data points may influence the training algorithm. Also, the internal

settings of the weight adjusting algorithm or even such 'remote' parameters as the initial learning coefficient may alter the whole training process considerably. Therefore, there is no simple and exact relationship between neural network topology encoding (genotype) and its performance and usefulness for the particular task (phenotype).

In our experiments we have used an objective function based on the form:

$$F(\cdot)=\left(\frac{E_V}{N_V}+\frac{E_L}{N_L}\right)^R\left(1+\frac{L_A}{L_{\max}}\right)^S \tag{1}$$

where E_V, E_L are the sums squares of validation (post-training testing) and training errors, respectively. N_V and N_L refer to the number of data samples used during the validation and training phases. L_A is the number of connections after network simplification, $L_{\max}$ is the maximum number of allowed links (the length of the chromosome used to encode the initial topology) and R, S are fixed parameters. Our experiments indicate that these parameters may sometimes significantly affect the performance of the genetic algorithm. For the experiments presented in this paper we have used $S = 0.5$ and $R = 1$ which seemed to work reasonably well.

The fitness function defined by formulae (1) directs the topology search toward networks that (i) learn the desired patterns well, (ii) generalize correctly and (iii) have the smallest possible size.

Here, incorporating the learning error in the objective function is not so important as the validation error because the learning error is on average much smaller. On the other hand, however, the value of E_L also carries some information about network performance and we treat it as a 'second order' correction factor. The difference between these two components depends on many aspects of the training process, e.g., the stopping criteria. Employing the cross-validation technique usually prohibits the learning error from having very small values while allowing the validation error to be rather higher. In our test, when the cross-validation method was used, E_V was usually about 4 to 5 times higher than the learning error E_L. Nonetheless, we decided to keep the learning error in the objective function (1) to assure that the networks that fail to train correctly or those which produce rare results when $E_V < E_L$ have a high objective function and are then likely to be rejected by the genetic algorithm[1].

The term $(1+L_A/L_{\max})$ in the objective function (1) can be interpreted as a complexity penalty factor. In some cases, especially when the initial, unpruned network is small, this penalty factor may be difficult to adjust precisely using the parameter S. The penalty function may still overly reward small networks and remove too many links. In such cases, a modified complexity penalty factor Θ can be applied:

$$F(\cdot)=\left(\frac{E_V}{N_V}+\frac{E_L}{N_L}\right)^R\left[1+(\gamma-1)\left(\frac{L_A}{L_{\max}}\right)^S\right]=\left(\frac{E_V}{N_V}+\frac{E_L}{N_L}\right)^R\Theta\left(L_A/L_{\max}\right) \tag{2}$$

---

[1] Our version of the genetic algorithm utilizes an extinctive selection scheme so that the worst chromosomes are always removed from consideration in the process of creating a new population.

The parameter γ $(\gamma \geq 1)$ affects the maximum value of the complexity penalty while the exponent S controls the shape of the function Θ: for S approaching unity the penalty is close to linear but as S increases a stronger penalty is applied to the biggest networks leaving smaller and medium size architectures relatively unpenalized.

5. Genetic Algorithm

The genetic algorithm tested here uses all four standard operators: crossover (crossover probability, $P_C = 0.8$), mutation ($P_M = 0.01$), inversion ($P_I = 0.2$) and selection. The selection[2] scheme is generational, linear ranking and extinctive, allowing the best 80% of the current population to breed and discarding the remaining 20% of chromosomes (this allows those chromosomes that correspond to the networks that were not trained successfully to be rejected). The selection operator is also 1-elitist so that the best performing individual of each generation is assured of being included in the next population unchanged. To prevent the genetic algorithm from being dominated by a few moderately good designs that may block further exploration of the search space a fitness sharing scheme is employed as described in [5, 8]. This method performs a cluster analysis of the current population and modifies the raw objective function so that the chances of creating individuals in overcrowded regions are reduced. A somewhat opposite operation, inbreeding, is launched if, despite the niche penalty, a particular cluster remains numerous.

For all the experiments presented in this paper the population size was chosen to be 50 and the genetic algorithm was run for 10 generations. Because the genetic algorithm reuses some top performing designs when a new population is created, the actual number of different network evaluation is slightly less than 500; typically it was 5 to 8% lower.

6. Experimental Results

We have applied the the pruning technique as described above to the problem of designing a neural network that is employed to model a discrete time, noisy, non-linear system. The neural network is treated as a one step predictor. The system to be identified has one input and one output (SISO class). Its behavior at discrete points may be described by a non-linear equation of the form:

$$y(k) = G\big(y(k-1),\ldots,y(k-n_a),u(k-1),\ldots,u(k-n_b),e(k),\ldots,e(k-n_c)\big) \qquad (3)$$

where $y(k-1),\ldots,y(k-n_a)$ are past system outputs, $u(k-1),\ldots,u(k-n_b)$ are relevant system inputs and $e(k),\ldots,e(k-n_c)$ is a disturbance sequence. Because feedforward neural networks propagate signals with no delays, to emulate the dynamics of a non-linear system the MLP is fed with several, time shifted signals that come both from the system input and/or output. Here, we consider an idealized situation when the number of network inputs is chosen to match the mathematical description of the modelled plant. The plant behaviour is described by the following discrete equation:

$$y(k) = \frac{y(k-1)+0.5u(k-1)+3.6y(k-1)u(k-1)+y(k-1)e(k)}{1+y^2(k-1)+u(k-1)e(k)} - 1.5 \qquad (4)$$

[2] The terminology used to describe selection follows the definitions presented by Bäck and Hoffmeister in [2].

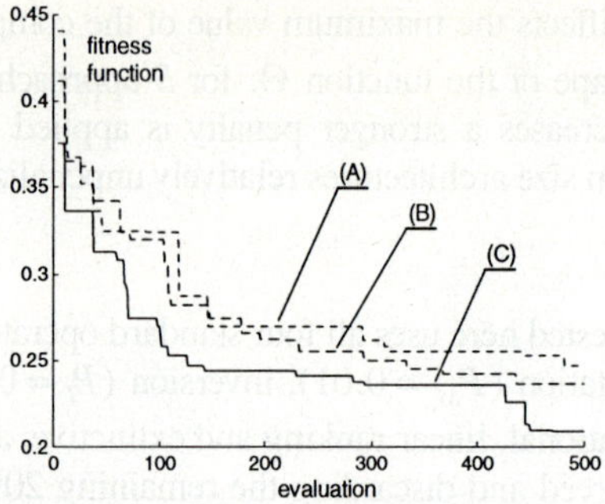

Figure 4: Average performance of a genetic search for increasing sizes of validation data pools: A - 100 samples, B - 400 samples, C - 800 samples.

where $e(k)$ is non-additive, normally distributed white noise of variance 0.05. This is a modified version of the problem that was investigated in [3]. The plant was excited with a uniform, zero mean signal $u(k)$ ranging between -2.0 and 2.0. All networks were trained using the RPROP [10] algorithm. The number of training data was 100 (30% of which were used for cross-validation); three sets of post-training, verification data were used with 100, 400 and 800 samples. The initial network topology to be trimmed was 2-6-6-1 with 62 connections and 13 biases.

When a plant is affected by significant noise that cannot be filtered out, some kind of noise estimator may be established to make prediction more accurate and this is identified along with the main object model (see [1] for a tutorial treatment of this subject). Also, the influence of noise can be reduced by modification of the identification algorithm and utilization of model outputs $\hat{y}(k)$ as regressors instead of the real plant values, but this kind of identification approach (instrumental variable method or output-error model) requires a more complicated iteration process for finding model parameters and larger amounts of training data to obtain valid results However, our task here is not to create a good predictor *per se* but to investigate the performance of the genetic algorithm for network topology design when neural networks are trained using data corrupted by noise. Therefore, the approach used in constructing the neural models does not utilize noise estimation or modified network training.

Optimizing neural network topology when noisy training and validation data are used creates a new situation for the genetic algorithm. Seemingly, there is no longer a lack of diversity in the problem because of the stronger fluctuations in network training and performance. However, this will not help a genetic search, since values of the fitness function are likely to be erroneously evaluated. Indeed, when neural networks were trained and verified on small numbers of data points, the genetic algorithm did not converge: after creating the initial population, usually, no improvements were encountered or successful steps were isolated and rare. We may suspect that the final results produced were flukes rather than the effect of the choosen search strategy. This situation starts to improve as we increase the quantity of training and validation data. Obviously, the training pool cannot be expanded without limit since it slows down the whole topology optimization. It is, however, possible to test inexpensively a network, even on a very large data sets, after completing training. We have found that utilizing larger post-taining validation tests steadily improves the performance of a genetic algorithm in finding good designs (figure 4).

Method/Ratio	Objective function	Generalization	Number of links
GA - search	2.067095e-01	2.013831e-02	20
enumeration	3.893958e-01	5.939192e-02	35
GA/enumeration ratio	0.53	0.34	0.57
GA - search	2.009306e-01	1.430509e-02	30
enumeration	3.319947e-01	5.892727e-02	19
GA/enumeration ratio	0.61	0.24	1.58
GA - search	2.212368e-01	2.730137e-02	14
enumeration	2.710268e-01	1.717330e-02	53
GA/enumeration ratio	0.81	1.59	0.26
GA - search	2.048909e-01	1.781993e-02	24
enumeration	4.095443e-01	6.307428e-02	35
GA/enumeration ratio	0.50	0.28	0.69
GA - search	2.117007e-01	1.978875e-02	22
enumeration	2.662749e-01	2.509494e-02	35
GA/enumeration ratio	0.80	0.79	0.63

Table 1: Comparison of the best networks for problem (4) found by a genetic algorithm and by sequential evaluation.

So far we have focused on the performance of the genetic algorithm alone. However, an important question is whether it is worth applying this method as an alternative to a simple trial and error approach that can also lead to successful solutions. For this reason, we have finally compared the performance of genetically optimized neural networks with manually crafted designs. The latter approach was emulated by a sequential evaluation of fully connected architectures obtained after removing increasing numbers of hidden nodes from the initial topology used to start the genetic algorithm. For the initial architecture 2-6-6-1 this led to training 36 different networks (topologies: 2-6-6-1, 2-6-5-1,...,2-6-1-1, 2-5-6-1, 2-5-5-1, and so on) in 5 series (each one started from different random seeds) and a comparison, according to the fitness function, of the best result found by both methods. Tables 1 summarizes these results.

For the problems studied here the genetic algorithm was *always* able to find a better neural network topology with respect to the chosen fitness function. In most cases both smaller size and better generalization ability could be achieved, although in some instances only one of these parameters has superior fitness. The results of creating neural models of the noisy plant are promising as they suggest that genetic algorithms may be a useful tool for solving these difficult problems. The results obtained also reveal that architectures with problem specific patterns of connections may indeed perform better than more restrictive, fully connected topologies arranged into geometrically regular layers. Besides, their size as measured by the number of connections may be expected to be smaller as well.

7. Conclusions

In this paper we have presented a network topology optimization method that is based on using a genetic algorithm. Various aspects of this technique, such as topology simplification, complexity assessment and the impact of network training on a genetic search have been discussed. Although, the simplification procedure was integrated quite closely with a topology optimizer, the same method of removing inactive or redundant connections may also be useful when other pruning techniques like OBS or OBD [6] are used and the initial feedforward architecture has connections that skip adjacent layers.

The method presented is CPU expensive due to the exceptionally laborious process of neural network training. This time consuming procedure requires a designer to choose carefully the number of training data sets and the initial, unpruned topology to avoid unnecessary computations. We have stressed that precise training may not guarantee ultimate success in finding superior architectures. A proper construction of the fitness function is an equally important (if not crucial) factor. Also, post-training validation is an essential part of network evaluation, as it detects not only the precision of weight adjustment but also the adequacy of the model structure. It is also worth noting that, although in the present study we have treated neural networks as one step predictors, the results presented in [4] suggest that utilizing them as multiple-step ahead predictors (autoregressive models only) may reveal topological deficiencies more clearly.

The genetic algorithm investigated here has proven to be a robust optimization technique, capable of operating in noisy environments while still producing superior results than could be obtained by manual, trial and error approaches. The genetic algorithm cannot be applied blindly, however. Although the method is well behaved and the wide range of investigations conducted elsewhere confirm that it does not need very precise tuning of its parameters, a good knowledge of the underlying problem modelling is definitely required.

References

[1] Åstrom K. J., Wittenmark B., Computer Controlled Systems - Theory and Design, Prentice-Hall, 1984.

[2] Bäck T., Hoffmeister F., Extended Selection Mechanisms in Genetic Algorithms, Proc. 4th Int. Conf. on Genetic Algorithms, Morgan Kaufmann, 1991.

[3] Billings S.A., Zhu Q.M., Nonlinear model validation using correlation tests, Int. J. Control, 1994, vol. 60, no. 6, pp. 1107-1120.

[4] Billings S.A., Jamaluddin H.B., Chen S., Properties of neural networks with applications to modeling non-linear dynamical systems, Int. J. Control, 1992, vol. 55, no. 1, pp. 193-224.

[5] Goldberg D. E., Genetic Algorithms in Search, Optimization and Machine Learning, Addison-Wesley, 1989.

[6] Haykin S., Neural Networks - A Comprehensive Foundation, Macmillan College Publishing, 1994.

[7] Kitano, H., Neurogenetic learning: an integrated method of designing and training neural networks using genetic algorithms, Physica D 75, 1994, pp. 225-238.

[8] Keane A.J., The Options Design Exploration System, Reference Manual and User Guide, 1994, available at http://www.eng.ox.ac.uk/people/Andy.Keane/.

[9] Kuscu I., Thornton C., Design of Artificial Neural Networks Using Genetic Algorithms: review and prospect, Cognitive and Computing Sciences, University of Sussex, 1994.

[10] Schiffmann W., Joost M., Werner R., Optimization of the Backpropagation Algorithm for Training Multilayer Perceptrons, Technical Report, University of Koblenz, 1992.

[11] Stepniewski S.W., Keane A.J., Pruning backpropagation neural networks using modern stochastic optimization techniques, (accepted for publishing by Neural Computing & Applications).

[12] Whitley D., Starkweather T., Bogart C., Genetic Algorithms and Neural Networks: optimizing connections and connectivity, Parallel Computing 14, 1990, pp. 347-361.

An Evolution Strategy for On-line Optimisation of Dynamic Objective Functions

J.C.W. Sullivan and A.G.Pipe

Intelligent Autonomous Systems Group
Faculty of Engineering, University of the West of England
Coldharbour Lane, Frenchay, Bristol BS16 1QY
United Kingdom
email : jcw-sull@uwe.ac.uk, ag-pipe@uwe.ac.uk
www http://gate.uwe.ac.uk:8000/cgi-bin/count/eng/ias/ias-lab.html

Abstract. We review recent research in Evolution Strategy (ES) operators with particular emphasis on improving convergence within small populations. We then report on the results of applying some of these operators in a problem domain where performance is critically dependent on population size and where the objective function is dynamic, i.e. changing shape as optimization proceeds. The ES must operate quickly and efficiently, acting as the exploration component of a larger on-line learning architecture. We found that the use of a derandomised mutation operator and intermediate recombination resulted in a considerable performance improvement.

1 Introduction

We have recently been experimenting with a Reinforcement Learning Adaptive Heuristic Critic (AHC) [9] architecture for maze-solving in mobile robotics which employs an Evolution Strategy (ES) as the exploration element. This architecture has been described elsewhere [6],[5], and here we restrict ourselves to reporting on the use of more advanced operators in order to improve ES efficiency in terms of convergence rate with small populations in dynamic environments.

The ES attempts to establish the best straight line move of a mobile robot from its current position in a maze. Each population member has two parts, direction relative to the current heading and distance to move. The objective function is provided by a form of environmental model stored in the "critic" part of the AHC architecture, of which we hope the following brief description will suffice. A radial basis function neural network comes to approximate a measure of the "real" (as opposed to Euclidean) distance, and therefore fitness, of maze locations from a goal position. Two factors modify the shape of this function. Firstly, each time an ES member is evaluated in the environment, if it would cause a collision then the function is modified to a fixed low value at the collision point and the ES member is modified to this position. Secondly, a Temporal Difference learning algorithm (which is executed after each move i.e. at the end of an ES run) passes back a portion of any change in fitness to moves which led to the current position, once a "punishment for zero reward" has been subtracted. These factors place interesting constraints on the ES.

- The population size and number of generations are severely limited compared with typical off-line optimization problems.
- Due to the effects of the learning algorithm, the shape of the objective function changes as a result of individual member evaluations,
- The region of the search may be multi-modal and it is important that the ES avoids local maxima, however climbing to the very top of the global maximum in a region is not normally necessary.
- In some scenarios the ES fitness function is initially flat across the whole region to be optimized. Under these circumstances, until the goal is reached, it is only the effects described above which create a fitness "landscape" to be optimized at all.

In the work described below we review some recent research into new operators for Evolution Strategies and then apply these to our maze-learning architecture in order to maximise efficiency of our ES in this application.

2 Evolution Strategy Operators

2.1 Notation and Representation

In the following discussion we adopt the notation of Bäck and Schwefel[1] :

μ	size of parent population
λ	size of offspring population
ρ	number of parents involved in the production of a single offspring
$N(0,1)$	standard normal deviate
$\mathbf{N}(\mathbf{0}, \boldsymbol{\sigma}', \boldsymbol{\alpha}')$	generalised $n-$dimensional normal distribution
c_{ij}	covariance matrix of generalised$n$ – dimensional normal distribution

Search points in ESs are n-dimensional vectors $\mathbf{x}$, in this implementation $n = 2$ and $\mathbf{x} = (r, \theta)$ represents the coordinates of the current search point in a local (polar) coordinate frame whose origin is located at the last point on the selected path. Additionally, each individual may include a vector of *strategy* variables $\boldsymbol{\sigma}$ which evolve together with the *object* variables in a process which has been termed *self-adaptation* by Schwefel [8]. The third element of an ES individual is its *fitness* which is identical to the objective function (in this case supplied by the Radial Basis Function neural network).

2.2 Selection

Selection is completely deterministic in ESs, in contrast to GAs where it is usually a probabilistic process. There are two main classifications :-

1. *Extinctive* – (μ, λ) strategies – parents live for a single generation only.
2. *Preservative* – $(\mu + \lambda)$ strategies – selection operates on the joined set of parents and offspring, very fit individuals may survive indefinitely.

Schwefel stated that (μ, λ) strategies outperform $(\mu+\lambda)$ strategies, even in static environments [8]. The explanation given was that, if by chance a large step-size should result in a very fit individual, that individual would have a large step-size variance parameter and would consequently be lost from the population in the next generation of a (μ, λ) strategy, resulting in a short-term regression but ultimately improved convergence. However the $(\mu+\lambda)$ strategy would 'stagnate' at this sub-optimal point.

The ratio μ/λ is known as selection pressure. Hoffmeister and Bäck [3] have stated that (μ, λ)-ESs with $\mu/\lambda \approx 1/6$ are tuned for a maximum rate of convergence, and as a result tend to reduce their genetic variability, i.e. the number of different alleles (specific parameter settings) in a population, as soon as they are attracted by some local optimum. With increasing ratio μ/λ the bias towards local search is shifted towards global search, which in the limit ($\mu/\lambda = 1$) is nothing but a parallel random walk.

2.3 Mutation

Mutation consists of the addition of a normally distributed random number to each component of the object variable vector, corresponding to a step in the search space. The variance of the step-size distribution may itself be subject to mutation as a strategy variable. In the general case of an n-dimensional search space there may be n independent step-size distributions, or, the step-sizes may be sampled from a generalised n-dimensional normal distribution, in which case the $n(n-1)/2$ covariances c_{ij} would become additional strategy variables.

Correlated Mutations. The maximum rate of convergence in an ES has been shown to be inversely proportional to the number of object variables [7]. As a consequence ESs have the tendency to reduce the search space by adjusting some step sizes towards zero in order to achieve a higher rate of convergence. This might result in a restricted search along some coordinate axes only, eventually yielding a poor rate of overall convergence. In order to counteract this tendency, Schwefel [7] proposed the concept of *correlated mutations*, introducing additional strategy parameters

$$\alpha_{ij} \;\; (i \in \{1, \ldots, n-1\}, j \in \{i+1, \ldots, n\})$$

which represent the angles of the principal axes of the generalised n-dimensional normal distribution ($\tan 2\alpha_{ij} = 2c_{ij}/(\sigma_i^2 - \sigma_j^2)$) [1]. In the two-dimensional case (n=2), this reduces to a single rotation parameter α. After being itself subject to mutation, this parameter is used together with the mutated step sizes $\boldsymbol{\sigma}'$ to define the sampling distribution for mutations of the object variable. Formally :-

$$\sigma_i' = \sigma_i e^{(\tau' \mathrm{N}(0,1) + \tau \mathrm{N}_i(0,1))}$$

$$\alpha'_j = \alpha_j + \beta \cdot \mathrm{N}_j(0,1)$$
$$\mathbf{x}' = \mathbf{x} + \mathbf{N}(\mathbf{0}, \boldsymbol{\sigma}', \boldsymbol{\alpha}')$$

This can be visualised by considering surfaces of equal probability density for the next step from a given population member. If there is only one step-size parameter, the surface will be a hyper-sphere and all components of the step vector are equally distributed, whereas in the general case it will be a hyper-ellipse. Correlated mutation introduces a rotational degree of freedom which enables the ellipse to align itself (adaptively) to the topology of the fitness landscape and hence take advantage of larger step sizes. The benefit, in terms of increased progress rate, would be most marked in a landscape which featured long narrow, non-axis-parallel valleys or ridges.

Schwefel's claim is that there is an implicit link between an appropriate *internal model* and good fitness values and so good values of the strategy parameters will emerge from the population and accelerate the rate of convergence. He likens this linear correlation process to the *epigenetic apparatus* or transmission mechanism between genotype and phenotype, whereby a single gene can influence several phenotypic characteristics (pleiotropy) and vice versa (polygeny).

The problem of *self-adaption of step-sizes* has been approached in two ways :-

1/5 success rule – Rechenberg postulated that the ratio of successful mutations to all mutations should be 1/5: if greater than this fraction, the variance should be increased. However this method can only be used with a single step-size parameter, and as Schwefel pointed out [7], it may lead to premature convergence even in the case of unimodal functions if there are discontinuities.

mutative step-size control – the strategy parameters are treated similarly to the object variables. They are incorporated in the genome of the individual and thus are affected by recombination, mutation and selection.

Schwefel [8] has reported a surprising result when attempting to use mutative step-size control with more than one step-size parameter : the adaptation process only works when the parent population consists of more than one individual (i.e. $\mu > 1$) and a recombination operator is used.

Derandomised Mutative Step-size Control. Ostermeier et al [4] have claimed that mutative control is not effective in small populations, and pointed to two deficiencies in the standard algorithm :-

1. Step-size variations are only stochastically dependent on parameter variations, since each is produced by a separate random number instantiation.
2. Step-size variations between individuals in one generation are identical with those between one generation and the next, whereas ideally the latter would be smaller to reduce random fluctuations.

In order to overcome these problems, Ostermeier et al proposed *derandomised mutative step-size control* The main elements of this algorithm are :-

1. Local step size factor
$$\xi_i = exp\{|z_i| - \sqrt{2/\pi}\}$$
where z_i denotes a separate random normal deviate for each component.
2. General step size factor
$$\xi = \alpha; 1/\alpha \text{ with equal probability}$$
3. Object variable mutation
$$x'_i = x_i + \xi \cdot \sigma_i \cdot z_i$$
where z_i is the same random number instantiation as above.
4. Step size increment in next generation
$$\sigma'_i = (\xi)^{\beta} (\xi_i)^{\beta scal} \sigma_i$$
where $\beta << 1$, thus ensuring that the random fluctuation of step-size change from one generation to the next is less than that within the population at any instant in time.

Ostermeier et al. compared the performance of this algorithm using a simple (1,10)-ES with that of a conventional (15,100)-ES over a range of test problems. They found that the derandomised ES exhibited faster progress than the (15,100)-ES in most cases (measured in terms of function evaluations to compensate for the different population sizes) and concluded that it allows reliable adaptation of individual step-sizes even in small populations. Additionally the $\beta scal$ parameter provides control of speed and precision of the adaptation process – small values of $\beta scal$ result in slow adaptation but the final approximation to the "correct" step-size distribution is very precise, whereas larger values result in faster adaptation but more stochastic fluctuation of the individual step-sizes.

2.4 Recombination

The two main classes of recombination operators are :-

1. *Intermediate* – the genotype / phenotype vector of each offspring is obtained by taking the mean vector of its parents' vectors. This is similar to the "blending" theory of genetics widely accepted before the rediscovery of Mendel's work.
2. *Discrete* – also referred to as "dominant" in the literature, but actually more equivalent to the "particulate" theory of genetics – can be regarded as a dynamic n-point crossover : each component of the genome of the offspring is produced by choosing either the vector component of the first or the second parent with equal probability

Each of these has *global* and *local* variants : in global recombination the parent population is sampled anew for each component of the vector and consequently results in greater mixing than local recombination where the same parents supply all the genetic material for a given offspring.

An additional complication is introduced if more than two parents are allowed to participate in the production of a single offspring, resulting in a $(\mu/\rho, \lambda)$-ES where ρ indicates the number of parents involved in mating. It has been claimed [2] that such *multi-recombinant* strategies exhibit remarkably high progress rates, particularly in the case where $\rho = \mu$.

2.5 ES based search : convergence, reliability and robustness

Theoretical results concerning the convergence of ESs have been slow to develop and most of the results published have been based on empirical testing using a set of model test functions. However, recently Beyer has given some interesting results for the convergence velocity of $(\mu/\mu, \lambda)$-ESs [2].

Beyer attributes the high progress rates of such strategies to *genetic repair* rather than the combination of "good properties" of the parents which would be more consistent with Holland's building block hypothesis. The implication of this hypothesis is that there is a probability that the offspring of two parents will have properties that are superior to those of either parent. However, using intermediate recombination, the offspring will only have the average properties of its parents. In Beyer's analysis he decomposed the mutations into components in the optimum direction and perpendicular to it. The latter components constitute the "harmful part" of the mutation, and Beyer showed that μ/μ intermediate recombination reduced these by approximately $1/\sqrt{\mu}$ – a process which he named genetic repair. It might appear that such an approach will lead to rapid 'homogenisation' of the population and a strong tendency to premature convergence. Such problems are not indicated in Beyer's analysis which assumes optimal mutation strength. Our empirical tests do not seem to indicate such a trend.

Hoffmeister and Bäck [3] compared the convergence velocity and reliability of several variants of ESs and GAs using two "standard" model functions. Firstly Schwefel's problem, a unimodal function which presents two difficulties : the gradient is not oriented along any axis, and there is a narrow "valley", the best GA variants suffered from premature convergence, whereas the (μ, λ)-ES strategy with correlated mutations was able to exploit the surface information presented by the offspring and converge successfully. On Rastrigin's problem the multi-modality presented a substantial difficulty to the best (8,50)-ES which was trapped by a local optimum due to its setup for a high rate of convergence but a (40,50)-ES with suitable initial step-sizes clearly outperformed the GAs with respect to rate of convergence and quality of solution. They concluded that, if the selection pressure of an ES is chosen to give rapid convergence, then global convergence may be less reliable. However, with the appropriate parameter settings they can outperform GAs in terms of global search reliability and convergence.

3 Empirical Testing

The following operators were implemented and tested :-

1. **Mutation**
   (a) *Uncorrelated* – a simple mutation operator incorporating two step-size variance parameters, each of which is mutated by either multiplication with, or division by, a constant with equal probability.
   (b) *Correlated* – a version of Schwefel's [7] correlated mutation algorithm, involving sampling from a bi-variate normal distribution. We have used Schwefel's recommended values for exogeneous parameters.
   (c) *Derandomised* mutation. This operator has been adapted for use in a (μ, λ)-ES from the version given by Ostermeier [4] who used it in the context of a $(1, \lambda)$-ES. Again the standard values have been used for exogenous strategy parameters, following Ostermeier's recommendations.
2. **Recombination**
   (a) *Intermediate* μ/μ Following Beyer's theoretical work on recombination [2], this operator effectively takes the 'center of mass individual' as the basis for further mutations. The justification for this is the assertion that recombination assists progress by a process of 'genetic repair'.
   (b) *Intermediate object, discrete strategy variable* This operator was intended to retain the advantages of intermediate recombination of the object variables, but, using discrete recombination to promote greater exploration in the space of strategy parameters.

Our focus here is on the relative performance of different ES operators, and consequently the initial tests were carried out with a simple two-object maze as shown in Fig. 1. We have previously reported on learning more complicated environments with this architecture [5].

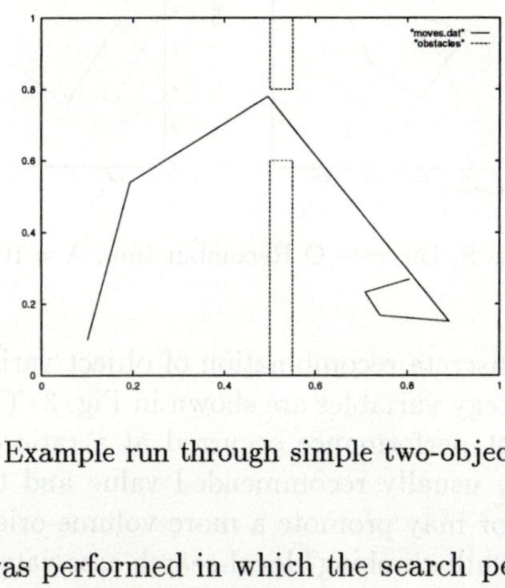

Fig. 1. Example run through simple two-object maze

A series of tests was performed in which the search performance was measured at a range of values of selection pressure and with different recombination and mutation operators. Figure 2 shows the amount of exploration (search effort as measured by the total distance travelled) and the average path-length of the route chosen by each of the variants using intermediate recombination of both strategy and object variables. It can be seen that the optimal search strategy here uses derandomised mutation and selection pressure of 0.2. With a population size of ten this the closest possible value to the 1/7 recommended as being optimal for convergence rate by Schwefel [8]. Also the good performance of the derandomised mutation operator with this small population is encouraging and appears to confirm, or at least add weight to, Ostermeier's claims [4]. Results

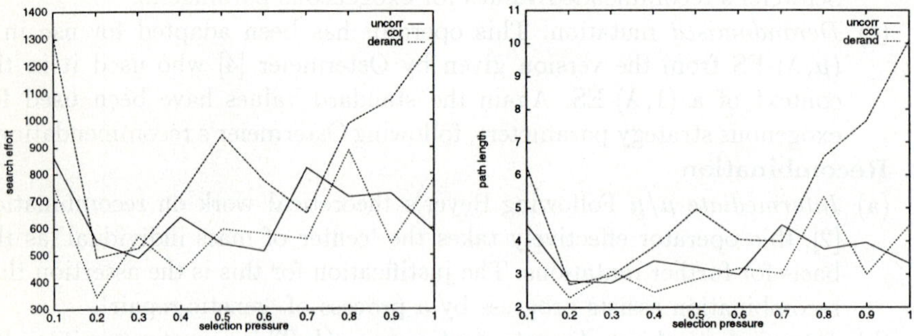

Fig. 2. Intermediate Recombination, $\lambda = 10$, average of 10 runs

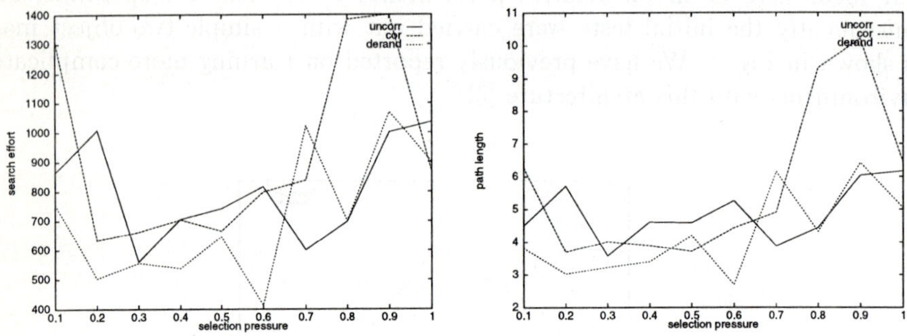

Fig. 3. Intermediate S, Discrete O Recombination, $\lambda = 10$, average of 10 runs

for the variant with discrete recombination of object variables but intermediate recombination of strategy variables are shown in Fig. 3. The most striking result here was that the best performance occurred at a ratio of $\mu/\lambda = 0.6$ which is much higher than the usually recommended value and this indicates that this recombination operator may promote a more volume-oriented search behaviour rather than the more "hill-climbing" local-search associated with higher selection pressure. In all of the tests carried out the derandomised mutation operator gave better performance than the others: indeed the correlated mutation performed rather badly in comparison with the other two variants.

The initial testing showed that the choice of selection pressure, mutation and recombination operators could have quite a large effect on the performance of the robot in a simple maze. A more complicated maze was designed which, as well as reducing the probability that a random walk would reach the goal introduced a "blind-alley" feature close to the goal. An example run through this maze is shown in Fig. 4. A series of tests was carried out with this maze, using the most

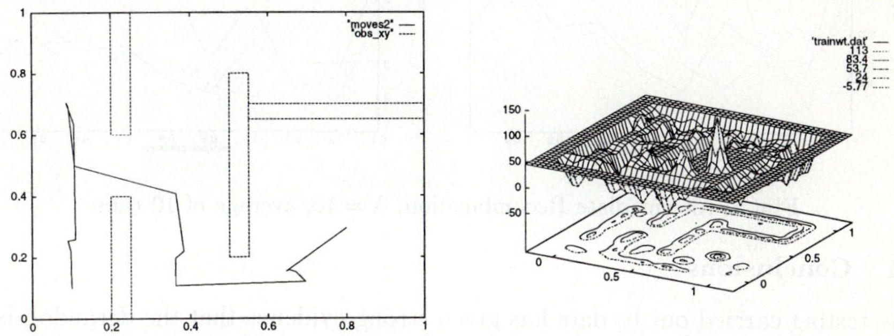

Fig. 4. Example run through more complicated maze and resulting fitness function

promising parameter settings from the earlier tests, but this time measuring not just the average distances traveled in the run, but also an estimate of the standard deviation of these variables. Again, these results were based on a sample of ten runs. Tests were run using a range of population sizes, keeping the selection pressure constant where possible. The aim here was to determine the smallest feasible population size whilst still retaining the genetic search principle. Note that there seems to be little advantage in terms of the solution quality to be gained from increasing the population size, and search effort is inevitably increased.

Table 1. Derandomised ES Performance on Maze 2

	Search Effort		Path Length	
λ	Average	Std. Dev.	Average	Std. Dev.
5	322.1	161.1	4.18	1.72
10	621.1	294.8	4.54	2.03
20	1191.6	359.0	4.31	1.08

A further series of tests was carried out in order to examine the ability of the system to cope with re-learning the maze using initial neural-network weights inherited from a previous run (see Fig. 4). This gives the ES a more complicated initial function to optimise, but should provide more feedback from the environment to guide the search. Results from these tests (Fig. 5) show the same trends as those with the simple two-object maze, but with small improvements in search efficiency. It appears that the ability to learn from previous exploration outweighs the added difficulty of starting with a more complicated objective function.

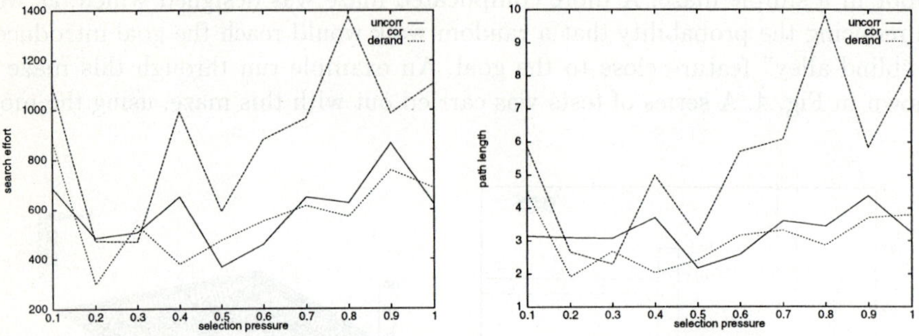

Fig. 5. Intermediate Recombination, $\lambda = 10$, average of 10 runs

3.1 Conclusions

The testing carried out to date has given strong evidence that the derandomised mutation operator can enhance convergence velocity in this application without adversely affecting reliability, particularly in small populations. By comparison the correlated mutation operator did not perform well and this seems to support Ostermeier's claims [4] that self-adaptation of strategy parameters is less effective in small populations.

References

1. T. Bäck and H-P. Schwefel. An overview of evolutionary algorithms for parameter optimization. *Evolutionary Computation*, 1(1):1—23, 1993.
2. H-G. Beyer. Towards a theory of evolution strategies : On the benefits of sex – the $(\mu/\mu, \lambda)$ theory. *Evolutionary Computation*, 3(1):81—111, 1995.
3. F. Hoffmeister and T. Bäck. Genetic algorithms and evolutionary strategies: Similarities and differences. In *PPSN1*, pages 455–469, 1990.
4. A. Ostermeier, A. Gawelczyk, and N. Hansen. A derandomized approach to self-adaptation of evolution strategies. *Evolutionary Computation*, 2(4):369—380, 1995.
5. A.G. Pipe, T.C. Fogarty, and A. Winfield. Hybrid adaptive heuristic critic architectures for learning in mazes with continuous search spaces. In *PPSN3*, pages 482–490, 1994.
6. A.G. Pipe, Y. Jin, and A. Winfield. A hybrid adaptive heuristic critic architecture for learning in large static search spaces. In *Proc. 9th Int. Symp. Int. Control*, 1994.
7. H-P. Schwefel. *Numerical Optimization of Computer Models.* Wiley, 1981.
8. H-P. Schwefel. Collective phenomena in evolutionary systems. In *Preprints of the 31st Meeting of the Int. Soc. for Gen. Systems Research*, pages 1025–1032, 1987.
9. R.S. Sutton. *Temporal Credit Assignment in Reinforcement Learning.* PhD thesis, University of Massachusetts, 1984.

Evolutionary Computation in Electrical, Electronics, and Communications Engineering

Exploiting Competing Subpopulations for Automatic Generation of Test Sequences for Digital Circuits [1]

Fulvio Corno, Paolo Prinetto, Maurizio Rebaudengo, Matteo Sonza Reorda
Politecnico di Torino, Dip. di Automatica e Informatica, Torino, Italy

Abstract. The paper describes the application of a Parallel Genetic Algorithm to Automatic Test Pattern Generation (ATPG) for digital circuits. Genetic Algorithms have been already proposed to solve this industrially critical problem, both on mono- and multi-processor architectures. Although preliminary results are very encouraging, there are some obstacles which limit their use: in particular, GAs are often unable to detect some hard to test faults, and require a careful tuning of the algorithm parameters. In this paper, we describe a new parallel version of an existing GA-based ATPG, which exploits competing sub-populations to overcome these problems. The new approach has been implemented in the PVM environment and has been evaluated on a workstation network using standard benchmark circuits. Preliminary results show that it is able to improve the results quality (by testing additional critical faults) at the expense of increased CPU time requirements.

1. Introduction

Testing of integrated circuits is an increasingly important problem which nowadays accounts for a significant percent of the total design and production costs of ASIC. For this reason, a large amount of research efforts have been devoted in the last years to the development of more efficient algorithms for the Automatic Test Pattern Generation (ATPG) for digital circuits [1]. In particular, due to their wide use in industrial design, synchronous sequential circuits have been a major subject for researchers.

One of the most promising approaches in this area is based on Genetic Algorithms (GAs) [9], and several prototypical tools [11] [12] [14] now exist, which implement this idea. The main advantages of GA-based ATPGs when compared with other approaches, like the topological [10] or the symbolic ones [4], are their lower CPU time requirements, the higher fault coverage they can reach, and the capability of dealing with larger circuits (more than 30,000 gates). On the other side, their main drawback consists in the lack of completeness (they can not identify untestable

[1]This work is partially supported by European Union through the PCI project #9452 94 204 70 (PETREL).

Contact Person: Matteo SONZA REORDA, Politecnico di Torino, Dip. di Automatica e Informatica, Corso Duca degli Abruzzi 24, I-10129 Torino, Italy, tel. +39 11 564 7055, fax +39 11 564 7099, E-mail sonza@polito.it faults) and, more in general, in their difficulty in finding a test sequence for the hard-to-test faults. Moreover, using a GA-based ATPG often requires a careful setting of many parameters which strongly affect its performance, and no method yet has been found, able to fully automate the parameter tuning phase.

Several GA-based tools (see Fig. 1) have been developed at our institution to experimentally evaluate the effectiveness of Evolutionary Computation techniques when applied to the ATPG problem. GATTO [6] is the ancestor of all of them: a brief description of the GATTO algorithm is provided in Section 2. An improved version, named GATTO+, is described in [7]. In the GATTO approach, one genetic experiment is activated for every fault to be covered: this represents a major advantage with respect to other GA-based ATPGs which activate a single genetic experiment for the whole ATPG process. In fact, the GATTO solution allows us to use a fitness function which is much more focused to the goal. Based on the GATTO code, a parallel version of the same tool has been developed, whose name is GATTO*: in GATTO*, whose characteristics are outlined in Section 3, the computational power of a parallel or distributed system can be exploited either to reduce the time required to reach a given Fault Coverage with respect to the mono-processor version, or to improve the Fault Coverage without increasing the time. Although very successful, GATTO* proved to have difficulties in generating test sequences for some very-hard-to-test faults. CGATTO is an attempt to overcome this limit by providing an alternative technique which can possibly be followed at the end of a GATTO* experiment, when it possibly left untested a too high number of faults.

The CGATTO approach is based on competing sub-populations [13] and exploits the power of a parallel or distributed system in order to improve the result quality, rather than to decrease the CPU time requirements. As it uses the PVM library [8], the code is highly portable and can be easily migrated to a large number of parallel and distributed platforms.

In Section 2 and 3 we briefly overview the main characteristics of the GATTO and GATTO* tools; Section 4 introduces CGATTO, the new ATPG algorithm based on competing sub-populations; Section 5 reports some preliminary results assessing the method effectiveness, and Section 6 draws some conclusions.

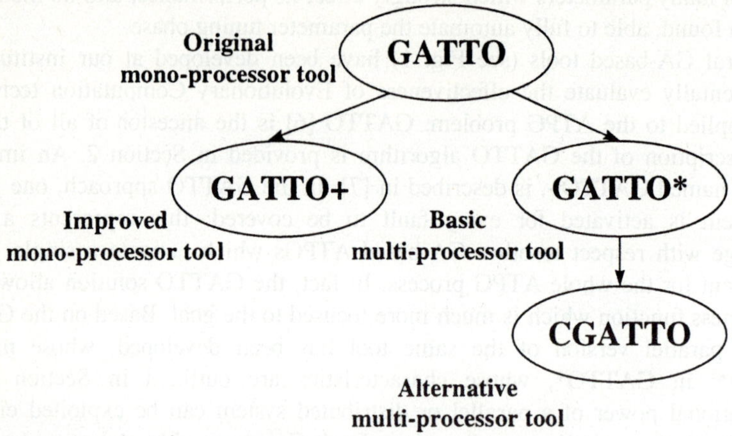

Fig. 1: The GATTO family.

2. GATTO

The GATTO algorithm, first presented in [11], is organized in three phases:

- the first phase aims at selecting one fault (denoted as *target* fault); this phase consists of randomly generating test sequences and fault simulating them with respect to the untested faults. As soon as one sequence is able to excite at least one fault, the fault is chosen as target fault;
- the second phase aims at generating a test sequence for the target fault with a Genetic Algorithm: each individual is a test sequence to be applied starting from the reset state; cross-over and mutation operators are defined to modify the population and generate new individuals; a fitness function evaluates how close each individual is to the final goal (i.e., detecting the target fault); this function is a weighted sum of the numbers of gates and Flip-Flops having a different value in the good and faulty circuit. After a maximum number of unsuccessful generations the target fault is aborted and the second phase is exited;
- the third phase is a fault simulation experiment which determines whether the test sequence possibly generated in phase 2 detects other faults (*fault dropping*).

The three phases are repeated until either all the faults have been tested or aborted, or a maximum number of iterations has been reached.

3. GATTO*

The GATTO algorithm spends most of its time in fault simulation, because:

- in phase 1, it is necessary to determine whether each untested fault has been detected and, if not, to compute the evaluation function for each sequence and for each fault;
- in phase 2, only one target fault is considered, and both the detection check and the fitness function computation are performed;
- in phase 3, all the untested faults are considered, and their possible detection is investigated.

By distributing the fault simulation task among the machines of a parallel system, on the other hand, we can exploit its great computational power. In GATTO* [5], a master-slave approach is adopted: a *master* process executes the kernel of the overall algorithm on one processor, while the *slave* processes are distributed among all the other processors and handle the fault simulation activity.

In phases 1 and 2, the sequences to be simulated are partitioned among the slaves; in phase 3, the list of undetected faults is partitioned, and the tasks distributed to the slaves amounts to simulating a sequence on different subsets of faults. Several fault simulation processes thus work in parallel in the three phases. Synchronization points are placed at the end of phase 1, at the end of each generation in phase 2, and at the end of phase 3. When the master reaches these points, it waits until all the slave processes finish their work, thus guaranteeing the global correctness of the whole algorithm.

The master process:

- does all the I/O operations, towards both the user and the file system, to read the netlist and the fault list and to store the generated test sequences;
- spawns the slave processes on the available machines;
- initially distributes a copy of the internal format of the netlist and fault list to each slave process;
- starts executing the algorithm through the three phases: as soon as a sequence has to be fault-simulated, a slave process is activated by an appropriate message; when the slave finishes its work, the master updates the global data structures (such as the global fault list and the fitness of each individual).

Please note that all the data structures required by the Genetic Algorithm (e.g, the population) are stored and updated by the master, which is also in charge of performing the crossover and mutation operators. The only task which is distributed is the evaluation of the fitness function, as it requires executing the fault simulation of the corresponding sequence.

4. CGATTO

In order to obtain the best results in the generation of test sequences with GATTO, optimal values of various parameters have to be found. Unfortunately, optimal values often change from one circuit to another, and even from one fault to another in the same circuit. In order to overcome this obstacle, a mechanism to dynamically set up the parameter values should be found. CGATTO exploits the availability of several processors for this purpose.

In CGATTO, phases 1 and 3 are implemented in a similar way to GATTO*: in phase 1, a test sequence partitioning is adopted, so that every processor fault simulates a different sequence, while the fault list remains the same for all the processors; in phase 3, a fault partitioning technique is used, according to which all the processors simulate the same sequence on a sub-set of the whole fault list.

In phase 2, as many genetic experiments are performed in parallel, as the number of available processors. The experiments differ in the value assigned to the parameters. In particular, every processor executes an independent GA experiment, aiming at finding a test sequence for the same target fault starting from the same population of sequences. However, processors are organized in *groups*, and the parameter values used by the processors in different groups are different, so that the evaluation function orients the search towards different areas of the search space. Each processor autonomously runs its own genetic experiment: periodically, the best results obtained in every group are analyzed and compared, and processors are moved from the most unsuccessful group towards the most successful one (Fig. 2). In this way, the algorithm dynamically evaluates the most suitable parameter values and increases the computational resources allocated to the most successful ones, thus implementing a mechanism very similar to the one described in [13]. Please note that no migration is performed of any individual from one population to another.

The effectiveness of our algorithm, which is proved by the experimental results provided below, mainly stems from the fact that several populations evolve independently; as they use different parameter values, they explore different sub-spaces of the total search space. The periodical comparison among the results attained by the populations and the possible movement of processors from one group to another aims at favoring the parameter values appearing as most successful and handicapping the others. However, the existence of each group is guaranteed up to the end of each experiment (at least one processor is left to each group no matter how bad the results it produces are), thus avoiding any concentration of all resources in a local minimum.

To preliminarily evaluate the effectiveness of the approach, we identified a critical parameter and used it to differentiate the experiments performed by the groups. GATTO adopts an evaluation function which is based on the number of Flip Flops having a different value in the good and faulty circuits. It is a common practice to weight the Flip Flops according to some Controllability (i.e., difficulty in forcing to a value) and/or Observability (i.e., difficulty in observing the value) measure; we observed that for many faults the adoption of special values for the Flip Flop weights is crucial for the capability of the algorithm to test the fault. Unfortunately, these values are neither known, nor are the same for all the faults. We thus adopted the set of Flip Flop weights as the parameter characterizing each group. A different set of values is assigned to the experiments performed by the processors in each group, and the best set is identified by evaluating the best results obtained by each of them: processors are moved from one group to another according to the relative effectiveness of the achieved results.

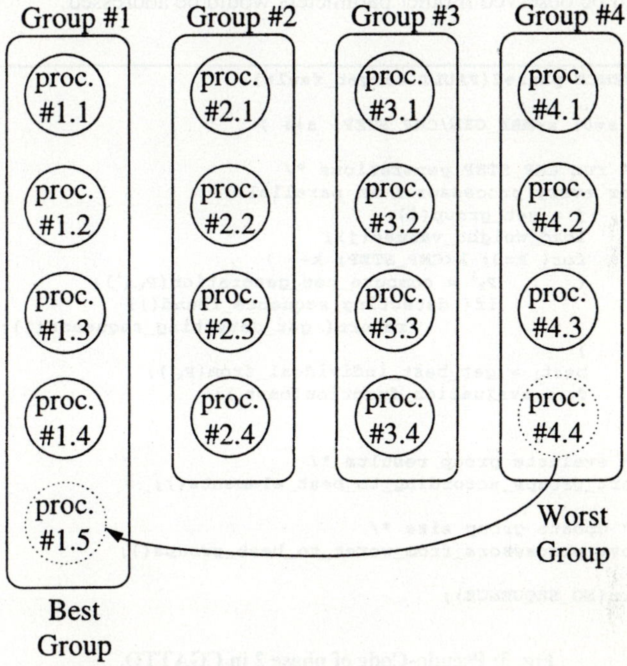

Fig. 2: Moving one processor from the worst group to the best one.

A pseudo-code of the algorithm adopted in phase 2 is reported in Fig. 3.

5. Experimental Results

CGATTO has been implemented in C using the PVM library and its performance has been evaluated on a workstation network composed of 16 DEC Alpha AXP 3000/500 workstations interconnected through a GIGAswitch.

Tab. 1 reports some preliminary results (in terms of Fault Coverage and elapsed time) for a selected subset of the standard ISCAS'89 benchmark circuits [3]. It is important to emphasize the fact that the attainable Fault Coverage is not always 100%, as untestable faults exist in some circuit (i.e., faults for which there is no test sequence at all). Circuits s420 and s838 are well-known examples, where this phenomenon is particularly evident.

In Tab. 2 we report a comparison between the results gathered with CGATTO, and the ones published in [5] for GATTO* for some of the largest benchmark circuits. It is evident that CGATTO is able to improve the Fault Coverage at the expense of larger time requirements. However, the latter ones still remain very limited. The additional faults detected by CGATTO are due to the algorithm capability of identifying the best parameter values. We expect that the same capability could be observed if other parameters would be addressed.

```
TEST_SEQUENCE phase2(FAULT target_fault)
{
      for( s=0; s<MAX_GEN/CMP_STEP; s++ )
      {
          /* run CMP_STEP generations */
          for every processor i in parallel
          {     j = get_group(i);
                load_weight_values(j);
                for( k=0; k<CMP_STEP; k++ )
                {        Pk^i = compute_new_generation(Pk-1^i);
                         if( detecting_sequence_found())
                                   return( get_detecting_sequence());
                }
                best_i = get_best_individual_from(Pk^i);
                f_i = evaluation_function(best_i);
          }

          /* evaluate group results */
          sort_groups_according_to_best_elements();

          /* update group size */
          move_processors_from_worst_to_best_groups();
      }
      return(NO_SEQUENCE);
}
```

Fig. 3: Pseudo-Code of phase 2 in CGATTO.

6. Conclusions

GAs have been recognized as a valuable approach in the Automatic Generation of Test Sequences for synchronous sequential circuits. However, they are often not able to deal with the hardest to test faults, and require a careful tuning of several algorithm parameters.

To overcome these limits, we devised a new algorithm, named CGATTO, which is based on Competing Subpopulations: several groups of processors run the same experiment in parallel, each exploiting a different set of values for some crucial parameter. Periodically, the best results produced by each group are compared, and processors are moved from the most unsuccessful group to the most successful one. Experimental results show the effectiveness of the approach. In particular, better results can be obtained (in terms of covered critical faults), and parameters are automatically tuned.

Work is currently being done to extend the use of this approach to the selection of the optimal values of other parameters.

Circuit	# Faults			FC	Time
	Total	*Detected*	*Aborted*	%	*[s]*
S208	215	150	65	69.77	45
S298	308	273	35	88.64	47
S382	399	366	33	91.73	51
S400	424	380	44	89.62	58
S420	430	204	226	47.44	71
S444	474	422	52	89.03	89
S526	555	436	119	78.56	62
S641	465	406	59	87.31	61
S713	581	480	101	82.62	61
S820	850	781	69	91.88	76
S838	857	303	554	35.36	92
S1196	1242	1236	16	99.52	54
S1238	1355	1282	74	94.61	72
S1423	1515	1459	114	96.30	68
S1488	1486	1446	3	97.31	61
S1494	1506	1277	3	84.79	63

Tab. 1: Experimental results on 16 workstations.

Circuit	FC		Time	
	CGATTO	GATTO*	CGATTO	GATTO*
	%	%	[s]	[s]
S1196	99.52	98.71	54	34
S1238	94.61	94.02	72	40
S1423	96.30	83.5	68	65
S1488	97.31	90.44	61	9

Tab. 2: CGATTO vs. GATTO*.

7. Acknowledgments

The authors wish to thank USTL *(Université de Science et Technologies de Lille)*, Lille (France) for access to its workstation network. The contributions of Patrick Degremont and Flavio Bianchi in the implementation of CGATTO are also acknowledged.

8. References

[1] M. Abramovici, M.A. Breuer, A.D. Friedman: "Digital Systems Testing and Testable Design," Computer Science Press, 1990

[2] V.D. Agrawal, K.-T. Cheng, P. Agrawal, "CONTEST: A Concurrent Test Generator for Sequential Circuits," *Proc. 25th Design Automation Conference*, 1988, pp. 84-89

[3] F. Brglez, D. Bryant, K. Kozminski, "Combinational profiles of sequential benchmark circuits," *Proc. Int. Symp. on Circuits And Systems*, 1989, pp. 1929-1934

[4] H. Cho, G.D. Hatchel, F. Somenzi, "Redundancy Identification/Removal and Test Generation for Sequential Circuits Using Implicit State Enumeration," *IEEE Trans. on CAD/ICAS*, Vol. CAD-12, No. 7, pp. 935-945, 1993

[5] F. Corno, P. Prinetto, M. Rebaudengo, M. Sonza Reorda, E. Veiluva, "A Portable ATPG Tool for Parallel and Distributed Systems," *Proc. IEEE VLSI Test Symposium*, 1995, pp. 29-34

[6] F. Corno, P. Prinetto, M. Rebaudengo, M. Sonza Reorda, "A Genetic Algorithm for Automatic Test Pattern Generation for Large Synchronous Sequential Circuits," to appear on the *IEEE Transactions on Computer Aided Design*

[7] F. Corno, P. Prinetto, M. Rebaudengo, M. Sonza Reorda, R. Mosca, "*Advanced Techniques for GA-based sequential ATPGs,*" *IEEE Design & Test Conf.*, Paris (France), March 1996, pp. 75-379

[8] A. Geist, A. Beguelin, J. Dongarra, W. Jiang, R. Manchek, V. Sunderam, "PVM 3 User's Guide and Reference Manual," Oak Ridge Nat. Lab., Internal Report ORNL/TM-12187, 1993

[9] D.E. Goldberg, "Genetic Algorithms in Search, Optimization, and Machine Learning," Addison-Wesley, 1989

[10] T. Niermann, J.H. Patel, "HITEC: A Test Generator Package for Sequential Circuits," *Proc. European Design Automation Conf.*, 1991, pp. 214-218

[11] P. Prinetto, M. Rebaudengo, M. Sonza Reorda, "An Automatic Test Pattern Generator for Large Sequential Circuits based on Genetic Algorithms," *Proc. Int. Test Conf.*, 1994, pp. 240-249

[12] E.M. Rudnick, J.H. Patel, G.S. Greenstein, T.M. Niermann, "Sequential Circuit Test Generation in a Genetic Algorithm Framework," *Proc. Design Automation Conf.*, 1994, pp. 698-704

[13] D. Schlierkamp-Voosen, H. Mühlenbein, "Strategy Adaptation by Competing Subpopulations," *Proc. Int. Conf. on Parallel Problem Solving from Nature*, 1994, pp. 199-208

[14] D.G. Saab, Y.G. Saab, J. Abraham, "CRIS: A Test Cultivation Program for Sequential VLSI Circuits," *Proc. Int. Conf. on Computer Aided Design*, 1992, pp. 216-219

Constraint Handling in Evolutionary Search: A Case Study of the Frequency Assignment*

Raphaël Dorne and Jin-Kao Hao

LGI2P
EMA-EERIE
Parc Scientifique Georges Besse
F-30000 Nîmes
France
email: {dorne,hao}@eerie.fr

Abstract. In this paper, we present the constraint handling techniques developed to tackle a real world optimization application: the frequency assignment problem (FAP) in cellular radio networks. The main goal of this application consists in finding assignments which minimize electromagnetic interference due to frequency reuse and minimize the number of frequencies used. An acceptable assignment of the FAP must satisfy a set of multiple constraints such as traffic constraints and interference constraints. We present how each type of constraint can play a different role in EAs. In particular, we show how co-station constraints can be used to reduce the search space efficiently. The effectiveness of the constraint handling techniques combined with a regeneration technique is tested on big and hard FAP instances. Results show that limiting the degree of unfeasible solutions is beneficial for this application.

1 Introduction

Constraint handling is an important issue in evolutionary algorithms (EAs) for tackling complex applications such as optimization and constraint problems. There are essentially three approaches for handling constraints [8]. The first totally forbids unfeasible solutions (which violate constraints) during the search and uses constraints to limit the search space by eliminating unfeasible solutions. This is often done via specialized genetic operators tailored to the application at hand. The second approach consists in using some repair mechanisms to produce feasible solutions from unfeasible solutions [2]. The third approach tolerates unfeasible solutions and uses constraint violation as a means of defining penalty functions [7, 6]. Each approach has relative advantages and disadvantages with respect to particular applications although the third is the most general approach. Finally, it will also be interesting to relate the above constraint handling techniques and recent work on the multi-objective approach to constraint optimization [8, 4].

* Supported by the CNET (French National Research Center for Telecommunications) under the grant No.940B006-01.

In this paper, we present the constraint handling techniques we developed to tackle a real world optimization application: the frequency assignment problem (FAP) in cellular radio networks in the field of telecommunications. The main goal of this application consists in finding assignments which minimize electro-magnetic interference due to frequency reuse and minimize the number of frequencies used. The difficulty of this application comes from the fact that an acceptable assignment of the FAP must satisfy a set of multiple constraints: traffic constraints which specify the minimum number of frequencies required by each station and interference constraints which specify the minimal distances between frequencies assigned to a station or to adjacent stations. We present how these constraints can play different roles in EAs. In particular, we show how co-station constraints can be used to reduce the search space efficiently. The effectiveness of the constraint handling techniques is tested on large and hard instances having up to 350 stations, 60 available frequencies and 35,000 interference constraints. Results show that our EAs integrating these constraint processing techniques and a population regeneration technique are very efficient for this application.

The paper is organized as follows. In Section 2, we introduce the various constraints in the FAP. In Section 3, we present the techniques for efficiently handling these constraints. We define also our EAs combined with these handling techniques. In Section 4, we give the results of our EAs on a set for real-size problems.

2 Frequency Assignment Problem

2.1 Constraints

The general objective of the frequency assignment problem is to provide the maximal number of communications over the network with a sufficient quality of transmission. More concretely, this involves assigning to each radio station one or more frequency values taken from a limited radio spectrum in such a way that a set of constraints is satisfied. These constraints can be classified into three categories which are defined as follows.

1. The *frequency constraint* specifies the number of available frequencies (channels) in the radio spectrum. This constraint is imposed by national and international regulations.
2. The *traffic constraints* specify the minimum number of frequencies required by each station to serve the communications within its geographic area. These constraints are empirically determined by the telecommunications operators.
3. The *interference constraints* are further classified into two families:

   adjacent-station constraints: the frequencies assigned to two adjacent stations must be sufficiently separated in the frequency domain. Two stations are adjacent if they emit within a common area even if they are not geographically adjacent.

   co-station constraints: any pair of frequencies assigned to a station must have a certain distance between them.

Constraints in the frequency assignment problem are therefore multiple and some of them are conflicting. The most severe constraint concerns the very limited number of available frequencies. This constraint imposes a high degree of frequency reuse by the stations and consequently increases the difficulty of satisfying the interference constraints.

Different optimization versions of the FAP could be developed such as maximizing all the traffic, minimizing the number of frequencies used and minimizing the interference over the network. In this paper, we minimize the frequency interference while using a minimum number of frequencies.

2.2 Modeling

Let *NS* be the number of stations in the network, *NF* the number of available frequencies in the radio-spectrum, *NA* the number of adjacency constraints, and *NC* the number of co-station constraints. The FAP can be modeled with a quadruple <X,D,C,F> representing a constraint optimization problem (COP) with:

X = $\{S_i |\ S_i$ is a station in the network, i $\in$ [1..NS]$\}$.
D = $\{F_i \mid F_i$ is an available frequency in the spectrum, i $\in$ [1..NF]$\}$.
C = TC $\cup$ AC $\cup$ CC
 TC = $\{T_i \mid T_i$ minimal number of frequencies necessary for Si, i $\in$ [1..NS]$\}$.
 AC = $\{A_i \mid A_i$ adjacent-station constraints for any pair of frequencies assigned to two adjacent stations, i $\in$ [1..NA]$\}$.
 CC = $\{C_i \mid C_i$ co-station constraints for any pair of frequencies assigned to the same station, i $\in$ [1..NC]$\}$.
F = the number of frequencies used to cover all the traffic in the network.
To solve the FAP problem, assignments satisfying all the constraints in C must be found and F must be minimized.

3 Constraint Handling

In this section, we show how the different types of constraints can be efficiently handled in evolutionary algorithms. Some constraints may be solved easily and others may be used to guide the search process. Note that this study have been done with EAs without a crossover operator. A study concerning crossover for the FAP has been already carried out in [5] and showed a marginal efficiency of this operator for this problem.

3.1 Frequency Constraint

This constraint requires the minimization of the frequencies used by all the stations. To do this, we proceed as follows: beginning with a certain number K of frequencies, we look for an interference-free assignment. If such an assignment is found, we start again with K-1 frequencies and so on. Details are given in Section 3.4.

3.2 Traffic Constraints

These constraints are static, that is, they will not change during the optimization process. Therefore these constraints could be directly included in the chromosome encoding as follows:

A frequency assignment is associated with a chromosome and one frequency value of a station is associated with one gene. The length of a chromosome is thus equal to the total traffic of all the stations in the network. Fig.1 gives an example where three stations require respectively two, one and four frequencies and $f_{i,j}$ represents the jth frequency value of the ith station S_i.

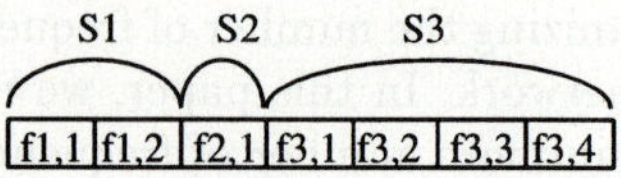

Fig. 1. Chromosome Encoding

3.3 Interference Constraints

Each interference constraint describes the minimal distance between any pair of frequencies assigned to two adjacent stations or to the same station. This set of constraints is represented by a symmetrical matrix M of NS*NS :

- M[i,j] with i $\neq$ j represents the minimal number of channel separations required to satisfy the adjacency constraints between the stations S_i and S_j. $\forall n \in [1..T_i], \forall m \in [1..T_j], |f_{i,n} - f_{j,m}| \geq M[i,j]$
- M[i,i] represents the channel separations necessary to satisfy the co-station constraints: $\forall n, m \in [1..T_i], n \neq m, |f_{i,n} - f_{i,m}| \geq M[i,i]$
- M[i,j]=0 means there is no interference constraint between the stations S_i and S_j.

In general, both co-station and adjacent-station constraints can be used to define the fitness function. This is perhaps the easiest technique to deal with them. However, as explained below, there are much more efficient techniques for co-station constraints. In what follows, we show first how co-station constraints can be used by EAs to reduce the search space and then how adjacent-station constraints are used to guide the search process.

Co-station Constraints

With the chromosome encoding presented above, different ways of handling co-station constraints will lead to a search space of different sizes. In fact, given S_i a station requiring T_i frequencies, and NF the available frequency values, the search space SP can be defined by:

$$SP = \prod_{i=1}^{NS} NP(i)$$

with $NP(i)$ being the number of possible combinations of frequencies for S_i.

Using this definition for the search space, we now investigate three ways of dealing with co-station constraints, in increasing order of their capacity to reduce the search space.

case 1: *Co-station constraints are not taken into account at all by the chromosome.* In this case, each gene may independently take any of the NF possible values. Therefore, for each station S_i, we have $NP(i) = NF^{T_i}$ possible combinations of frequencies. This implies a total search space of size

$$SP = \prod_{i=1}^{NS} NP(i) = NF^{\sum_{j=1}^{NS} T_j}$$

case 2: *Co-station constraints are taken into account by the chromosome, but an order is introduced among the frequencies of the same station.* That is, for a station S_i having a traffic of T_i, if a *list* of frequencies $(f_{i,1}, f_{i,2} \ldots f_{i,T_i})$ satisfying the co-station constraints is assigned to S_i, there are still other $T_i! - 1$ valid frequency assignments (lists) for S_i using the same frequencies. In this case, for each station S_i, the possible combinations of frequencies are reduced to

$$NP(i) = nbposs(T_i, NF, i) * T_i! \text{ with}$$

$$nbposs(T_k, N, k) = \begin{cases} N \text{ if } T_k = 1 \\ \sum_{j=1}^{N-(M[k,k]*(T_k-1))} nbposs(T_k - 1, N - (j + M[k,k] - 1, k) \text{ otherwise} \end{cases}$$

case 3: *Co-station constraints are taken into account by the chromosome and no order is imposed among the frequencies of the same station.* That is, for a station S_i having a traffic of T_i, if a *set* of frequencies $\{f_{i,1}, f_{i,2} \ldots f_{i,T_i}\}$ satisfying the co-station constraints is assigned to S_i, other $T_i! - 1$ possible frequency assignments for S_i using the same frequencies will be considered to be *equivalent* to this assignment. In this case, for each station S_i, the possible combinations of frequencies are reduced to

$$NP(i) = nbposs(T_i, NF, i)$$

For example, given a FAP instance of 75 stations with 8 available frequencies ($NF = 8$), a uniform traffic of 3 ($T_i = 3, \forall i \in [1..75]$) and a minimal separation distance of 3 for frequencies assigned to the same station ($M[i,i] = 3, \forall i \in [1..75]$), we obtain for each case above these results for the search space:

- **case 1**: $NP(i) = 8^3 = 512 => SP = 512^{75}$
- **case 2**: $NP(i) = 4 * (3!) => SP = 24^{75}$
- **case 3**: $NP(i) = 4$, which are: {1,4,7},{1,4,8},{1,5,8},{2,5,8} $=> SP = 4^{75}$

It is clear that, for this example, the application of co-station handling in cases 2 and 3 allows us to greatly reduce the initial search space by a factor of about 21^{75} and 128^{75} respectively. In general, the larger the initial search space, the bigger the reduction which may be obtained. It is also clear that the difficulty of implementation increases when we go from case 1 to case 3. In what follows, we outline how cases 1, 2 and 3 may be implemented in EAs.

For case 1, there is no special treatment for co-station constraints, and they are used together with adjacent constraints to build the fitness function. Since each gene may take any value from [1..NF], there is no need to adapt our genetic operators.

For case 2, the implementation consists in modifying the mutation operator[2] and the way in which the initial population is generated. For the initial population, we ensure that all of the co-station constraints are satisfied by each chromosome, i.e. any two frequencies assigned to the same station have the required minimal distance. It should be remembered that the mutation operator is based on a three-step choice strategy [3]:

- *choice of a station* S_i: randomly take one from among conflicting stations. A station is conflicting if some of its frequencies violate interference constraints;
- *choice of one frequency for* S_i: randomly take one from 1 to T_i;
- *choice of a frequency value* $f_{i,k}$: take the best one from 1 to NF, which is different from the current value.

In order to carry out co-station constraint processing of case 2, we enhance the third choice for selecting the frequency value; we now refuse to assign a value which violates co-station constraints. More precisely, this choice becomes:

- *choice of a frequency value* $f_{i,k}$: take the best one from 1 to NF which is different from the current value *and* which does not violate co-station constraints.

For case 3, the implementation consists once again in modifying the mutation operator and the way in which the initial population is generated. Here, an initial chromosome will be the concatenation of a list of NS sublists $(L_1, L_2, ..., L_{NS})$ where each L_i is one of S_i's $NP(i)$ valid combinations of frequencies. When mutation is applied, a sublist L_i of the chromosome will be replaced by another sublist L_i', which is always taken from S_i's $NP(i)$ valid combinations of frequencies. For the moment, case 3 is not implemented yet.

Adjacent-station Constraints

Having presented the techniques for handling the frequency constraint, traffic constraints and co-station constraints, we now study how adjacent constraints can be used. These constraints can neither be integrated into the chromosome encoding like traffic constraints nor be satisfied like the co-station constraints. However, they are useful to guide the search process. To do this, we use them to define the fitness function *Eval* which associates with each chromosome, an integer value corresponding to the number of interference constraints violated by the chromosome. The fitness will thus be a value in the interval [0...NA+NC] if the co-station constraint handling is not applied; otherwise, this interval becomes [0...NA].

Therefore, a chromosome I is a solution (a frequency assignment without interference) if and only if $Eval(I) = 0$. Evidently, different assignments could have this evaluation value and thus be solutions to the problem.

---

[2] If crossover is used, it should also be adapted.

3.4 Algorithm

The general algorithm we used to process the tests is described below:

```
begin
  NF ← MAXfreq ; success ← false ; failed ← 0 ; gen ← 0 ;
  generate(P_0) ;evaluate(P_0) ;P_best ← P_0;
  while (failed < MAXfailed) do
    success ← false ; gen ← 0 ;
    while (gen < MAXgen and success = false) do
      P_sel ← selection(P_gen) ;
      P_gen+1 ← mutation(P_sel) ;
      gen ← gen + 1 ;
      evaluateP_gen ;
      if (Bestof(P_gen)) is a solution(without interference) then
        P_best ← P_gen ; success ← true ;
    if (success = true) then
      NF ← NF-1 ; failed ← 0;
      P_0 ← regenerate(P_gen, NF) ;
    else
      failed ← failed + 1;
      P_0 ← regenerate(P_best, NF) ;
  return NF + 1 ;
end;
```

P_{best} is the last population containing at least one individual having an evaluation equal to 0, i.e. an interference-free assignment with a certain number K of fixed frequencies. P_i represents the population of the ith generation.

An initial population is randomly generated with the maximum number of available frequencies $MAXfreq$ (if co-station constraint processing is applied, the initial population will be forced to satisfy all the co-station constraints). This population evolves until one of its individuals becomes a solution to the problem or the maximum number of generation cycles $MAXgen$ is reached.

In the first case, the number of available frequencies NF is decremented and the population is regenerated using the following process: for each gene having a frequency value greater than the decremented NF, it is given a new value which is randomly determined in the interval $[1..NF]$ (if co-station handling is applied, this new value will satisfy all the co-station constraints); other genes remain unchanged. We call this process the *population regeneration* technique.

In the second case, we consider this attempt as a failure. The population is regenerated using the best population P_{best} and then the evolution starts again for $MAXgen$ generations. If we get the maximal number of failed attempts $MAXfailed$ for the same number of available frequencies, the current run is finished and the last minimal number of frequencies used for an assignment which does not contain unsatisfied constraints is returned.

4 Results

Different EAs have been developed and tested on 10 FAP instances: four instances with a uniform traffic of two frequencies per station, and six instances with non-uniform traffic from 2 to 4 frequencies per station.

The name of each instance consists of three numbers *ns.nf.nc* which are respectively the number of stations, the sum of the traffic (frequencies) required by all the stations, and the number of interference constraints. For example, 150.300.12634 defines a problem composed of 150 stations, a total traffic of 300 frequencies and 12,634 constraints.

We compare below four algorithms with/without Co-station Constraint Handling (CCH) (an implementation of Case 2 described in Section 3.3.) and/or Population Regeneration (PR) described in Section 3.4.

EA: EA with no special techniques.
EA+PR: EA with only population regeneration.
EA+CCH: EA with only co-station constraint handling.
EA+CCH+PR: EA with co-station constraint handling and population regeneration.

These algorithms have the following common characteristics. We used a population of 20 individuals with SUS selection [1], no crossover, and the three-steps choice mutation described in Section 3.3. The maximum number of generation was set at 10,000.

To compare these algorithms, the following criteria are used:

- **NF**: the minimum number of frequencies used to find a frequency assignment without any constraint violation (average over 5 runs).
- **Eval**: the number of evaluations (in thousands) necessary to solve the FAP instance.
- **Time**: the average time per run in seconds excluding failed attempts. Our tests have been carried out on a Silicon Graphic Power Station with a R8000 processor.
- **Fail**: the average of failed attempts per run (see Section 3.4) over 5 runs to find the best solution.

Table 1 shows the performance of the four algorithms according to the chosen criteria. Given that the computing time for some instances is very high (>10 hours), the results are the mean of only 5 independent runs for 10 tests.

In this table, the instances are classified from the easiest to the hardest for the two families (uniform and non-uniform traffic). All the algorithms are compared in terms of solution quality (NF), efficiency (Time and Eval) and robustness (Fail). Several remarks concerning the data in the table may be made.

First, EA and EA+PR perform in a similar way except for two relatively easy instances (119.140.5918, and 168.372.4099) for which the PR option becomes more efficient (up to ten times faster). In general, at the beginning of an evolutionary optimization process, only a small number of generations is needed to satisfy most of the constraints, followed by a long series of generations to satisfy the remaining constraints. Therefore, starting a search process with the

problems	EA				EA+PR				EA+CCH				EA+CCH+PR			
	NF	Eval.	T[sec]	Fail.	NF	Eval.	T[sec]	Fail.	NF	Eval.	T[sec]	Fail.	NF	Eval.	T[sec]	Fail.
75.150.2231	15	1260	600	6.2	15.40	1300	680	5.8	14.20	1200	620	5.0	13.20	1440	740	7.8
75.150.3247	14.60	1400	760	6.8	13.60	1600	1060	6.2	13.20	1280	780	5.4	13.20	600	400	4.8
75.150.3203	18.20	2200	1380	6.4	18.20	1840	1200	6.6	17.20	2980	1880	5.8	17	1300	820	5.2
150.300.12634	25.60	2000	2400	5.8	23.40	2560	3200	9.0	20	11840	12860	6.0	18	3200	3700	5.6
119.140.5918	45	1452	889	0.0	45	190	120	0.0	45	1300	836	0.0	45	168	106	0.0
168.372.4099	45	1301	458	0.0	45	149	53	0.0	45	1186	918	0.0	45	145	54	0.0
343.966.35104	54	11926	10969	0.0	54	1461	1203	0.0	54	10375	15866	0.0	54	1326	1110	0.0
168.538.8197	45.40	3539	1530	0.0	45	585	292	0.0	45	2749	2436	0.0	45	380	176	0.0
119.335.11058	46.50	43362	45923	7.0	45.20	38428	43487	4.4	45	8800	8820	2.0	45	1280	1240	1.6
59.158.6043	56	30868	29267	4.0	56	22036	20766	3.0	56	25451	44348	4.0	55.60	6820	7040	4.6

Table 1. Comparative results

PR option is interesting if the instance is easy or if the last solution obtained is close to a final solution. Note that the PR option is designed to carry out efficient exploitation rather than exploration. Consequently, PR may put the search process in a local optimum. Many generations may be required to release the search process from this local optimum.

Second, EA+CCH gives solutions of better quality than EA and EA+PR on all the instances especially on the hardest ones. This point confirms the theoretical expectation about the search space reduction provided by CCH (c.f. Section 3.3). In terms of efficiency, EA+CCH is faster because co-station constraints are no longer a part of the fitness function and solved implicitly. Consequently, for the same number of mutation applications, the number of required evaluations is reduced. EA+CCH is also more robust than EA and EA+PR because even for a solution of better quality this algorithm has comparable failure values. Note, however, that EA+PR is more efficient for solving some easy instances of the second family.

Third, EA+CCH+PR gives far better results than other algorithms for all the instances. This is certainly due to the CCH and PR options. An important example concerns 150.300.12634 which is the hardest instance of the first family. In fact, EA+CCH+PR uses 7.6 fewer frequencies than EA and 2.0 fewer frequencies than EA+CCH. For the same instance, this algorithm divides the number of evaluations and computing time by four compared with EA+CCH. EA+CCH+PR is also robust since it gives much better results with comparable failures. In conclusion, the combination of CCH and PR is definitely very efficient. This may be explained as follows. When co-station handling is used, the co-station constraints which are harder to solve are already satisfied by all the individuals of the population. This will facilitate the search since only adjacency constraints remain. Applied to such individuals, the PR option becomes more efficient for exploitation. Moreover, the fact that CCH is applied means that the co-station constraints are removed from the fitness function. Thus, this function becomes simpler and more refined, which in turn favors a better exploration of the search space.

5 Conclusions

In this paper, we have presented a set of techniques for handling various constraints in the frequency assignment problem. Traffic constraints are solved by a direct integration into the chromosome structure. Interference constraints related to adjacent stations are used to build the evaluation function and guide the search process. Co-station constraints are used to greatly reduce the search space. We have also presented a technique for population regeneration. We have shown that this technique is powerful for exploitation. Results of experiments show that all these techniques integrated into the evolutionary framework give efficient EAs which allow us to solve hard FAP instances. Our results also show that for this application, it is beneficial to limit unfeasible solutions.

We are currently working on the last technique described in Section 3.3 in order to improve co-station constraint handling. As shown in that section, this processing will allow us to further reduce the search space. Finally, we are testing the techniques and ideas presented in this paper on other optimization and constraint problems. We hope to be able to report new results in the near future.

Acknowledgments

We would like to thank the CNET which supported this work. Special thanks go to A. Caminada and R. Mignone from the CNET for their assistance.

References

1. J.E. Baker. Reducing bias and inefficiency in the selection algorithm. In *Proc. of Intl. Conf. on Genetic Algorithms (ICGA'87)*, pages 14–21, 1987.
2. L. Davis and D. Orvosh. Shall we repair? genetic algorithms, combinatorial optimization and feasibility constraints. In *Proc. of Intl. Conf. on Genetic Algorithms (ICGA'93)*, page 650, 1993.
3. R. Dorne and J.K Hao. An evolutionary approach for frequency assignment in cellular radio networks. In *IEEE International Conference on Evolutionary Computation (ICEC'95)*, pages 539–544, Perth, Australia, 1995.
4. C. M. Fonseca and P. J. Fleming. Multi-objective optimisation and multiple constraint handling with evolutionary algorithms 1: a unified formulation. Technical Report 564, University of Sheffield, UK, 1995.
5. J.K Hao and R. Dorne. Study of genetic search for the frequency assignment problem. In *Lecture Notes in Computer Science vol. 1063, Artificial Evolution (AE'95)*, pages 333–344, Brest, France, 1995.
6. Z. Michalewicz. *Genetic Algorithms + Data Structures = Evolution Programs.* Springer Verlag, Berlin, 1992.
7. J. T. Richardson and M. R. Palmer. Some guidelines for genetic algorithms with penalty functions. In *Proc. of Intl. Conf. on Genetic Algorithms (ICGA'89)*, pages 191–197, 1989.
8. P. D. Surry, N. J. Radcliffe, and I. D. Boyd. A multi-objective approach to constrained optimisation of gas supplay networks: the comoga method. *Lecture Notes in Computer Science vol. 9,AISB Workshop on Evolutionary Computing*, 1994.

An Application of Genetic Algorithms and Neural Networks to Scheduling Power Generating Systems

Claus Hillermeier[1] and Joachim Keppler[2]

[1] Siemens AG, Corporate Research (ZFE), 81730 München, Germany
[2] Siemens AG, Power Generation (KWU), 91050 Erlangen, Germany

Abstract. This paper presents an effective strategy to schedule fossil-fuel power plant systems with so-called power-heat coupling. Due to the simultaneous production of electricity, heat and steam such systems reach a higher efficiency than pure electric power plants. The goal is to minimize the total costs for the production of the predicted load demand of the next day. We employ a genetic algorithm to determine the unit commitment, while the economically optimal load distribution among the operating units is performed by a conventional constraint optimization method. Our approach is based on exact thermodynamic simulations of the unit efficiency, taking into account the current plant state and environmental conditions. In order to make this high modeling precision available within short computation times we employ neural networks for the storage and interpolation of simulation data.

1 Introduction

The optimal production policy of a fossil-fuel power generating system has to take into account two cost factors: fuel costs and costs for starting up generating units. To that end, power generating systems are usually scheduled over a certain time horizon (e.g. 24 hours) on the basis of a forecast of future demand. The scheduling task involves two decisions: 'unit commitment' and 'economic dispatch'. Unit commitment (UC) establishes which generating units to place in operation in each period of the scheduling horizon. Economic dispatch is the minimum cost allocation of load among the generating units committed for operation during a period.

Scheduling power generating systems is a complex mathematical optimization problem with both integer and continuous variables which are subject to a variety of constraints. For the partial task of UC an exact solution can be obtained by complete enumeration of all possible schedules. This approach, however, cannot be applied to larger power systems due to its excessive computation time requirements. In view of the drawbacks of conventional UC methods, a Genetic Algorithm (GA) was recently proposed as an efficient suboptimal UC algorithm [1].

The economic load dispatch requires knowledge about the degree of efficiency of the individual generating units. Modern power plants simultaneously produce electricity, heat and steam and, by this so-called power-heat coupling, reach a higher efficiency than pure electric units. The efficiency of such units depends in a complex, nonlinear way on the three types of provided load. Approximating the unit efficiency by a simple (e.g. linear or quadratic) mathematical function, as is done in all UC algorithms known to us, cannot take into account these nonlinear effects adequately. We therefore evaluate the unit efficiency by a detailed simulation of the water-steam cycle. For most types of power plants, computer programs performing such simulations have been developped in order to facilitate plant design. Schedule optimization, however, requires too many evaluations of the unit efficiency to have time for simulation in each case. As a solution to that dilemma we produce simulation data off-line and store them by means of neural networks.

Summarizing, this paper gives a solution to the described scheduling task by a combination of GA and Neural Networks. Like [1], we apply a GA for the solution of the UC problem. Apart from that, we make the modeling precision of simulations available for the optimization by storing and interpolating simulation data by means of neural networks. Thereby, the optimization capability of GA is combined with the modeling capability of neural networks. Neural networks accelerate the evaluation of the fitness of GA-generated schedules.

2 Problem Formulation

Starting point of the scheduling task is a forecasted load demand which lists for each of the k time slices of the time horizon the respective demands for electric power P_{el}, thermal heat P_h and steam m_s. An economical distribution of these loads to the n units of the power generating system has to take into account that each unit can either be completely switched off or must be operated above some minimum power. Scheduling the power plant system, therefore, implies the following decisions:

- A schedule for UC has to be fixed. Such a schedule can be described by an $n \times k$-matrix which for each time slice and each unit contains a binary on/off-signal.
- On the basis of a UC schedule, for each time slice the load demand has to be economically shared between those units which are switched on. The result can be written as a series of n unit-specific $3 \times k$-matrices which for each type of load and each time slice state the load assigned to that unit.

The total costs due to the chosen schedule are given by

$$\text{costs}_{\text{tot}} = \sum_i \sum_j \left[\text{costs}^{\,i}_{\text{fuel}}(t_j) + \text{costs}^{\,i}_{\text{start}}(t_j)\right] \qquad (1)$$

where i runs over all units and j over all time slices.

A correct schedule has to satisfy a variety of constraints. The necessity of power balance couples the whole plant system:

$$\sum_{\text{units } i} P^i(t_j) = P_{\text{demand}}(t_j) \qquad (2)$$

for all time slices j and all types of load. The feasible power range of units is given in two ways. First, by explicit minimum and maximum values for each type of load. In addition to these linear boundaries between possible and impossible loads there are complex nonlinear boundaries due to power-heat coupling. A further type of constraints, namely minimum-up and minimum-down times, couples the time slices.

Summarizing, we are confronted with a complex optimization problem involving nk binary and $3nk$ continuous parameters as well as $3k$ balance equations and nk power range checks as constraints. For larger power systems ($n > 2$), finding the global optimum will not be possible within a realistic computation time. The most prominent conventional methods to find suboptimal solutions are Priority List methods, Dynamic Programming and Lagrange Relaxation. A discussion of the drawbacks of these methods can be found in [1].

3 Hierarchical Problem Solution

In this paper we propose a scheduling algorithm which decomposes the task into three stages (see Figure 1):

- At the topmost level a GA generates possible UC schedules. The GA exclusively operates on the binary $n \times k$-matrices recording the on/off-status. Each generated UC schedule is tested whether it complies with the minimum-up and minimum-down times and is rated by means of the total costs it implies over the whole scheduling period.
- In order to evaluate the fuel costs resulting from a UC schedule, for each time slice the demanded load has to be economically dispatched. This dispatch can be performed for each time slice independently. The efficiency of power units with power-heat coupling depends on the load in a most complicated way, making the dispatch problem and the constraints nonlinear. To solve that task, we employ the most effective nonlinear programming method at present, the Sequential Quadratic Programming (SQP) algorithm [2]. Since these economic dispatch calculations consume the largest share of the total computation time, the results are stored in a $(2^n \times k)$-matrix.
- Economic dispatch tries to minimize the total fuel costs spent by the operating units. This requires knowledge about the nonlinear efficiency of each unit. Thus, at the lowest stage of our algorithm the efficiency has to be calculated in dependency of the assigned power release. Details of this unit modeling are discussed in section 5.

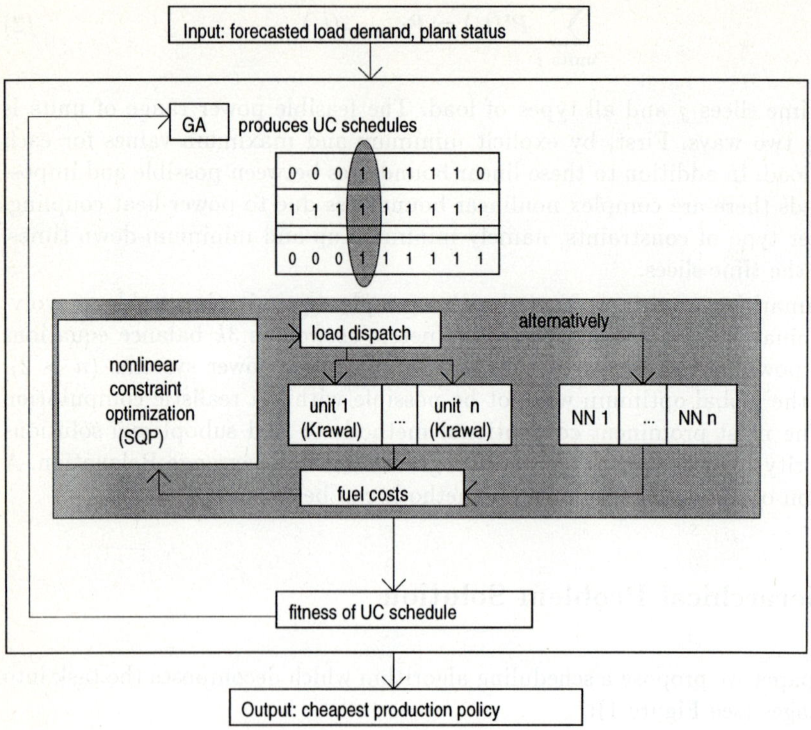

Fig. 1. Hierarchical solution scheme for scheduling power generating systems (see text). NNi denotes the system of neural networks modeling unit i (see secion 5).

4 Genetic Algorithm for the Unit Commitment

Every single UC schedule generated by the GA is interpreted as an individual. As the optimization proceedes, we always keep a constant number of typically 30 schedules (individuals) simultaneously. In applying the genetic operators *selection*, *recombination* and *mutation* the population of schedules moves into a domain of the search space which contains the global optimum or at least a quasi optimum. The most economic UC schedule of such a converging population is finally interpreted as the solution of the UC problem.

Each UC schedule is described by a binary $n \times k$-matrix (row index = unit index, column index = time slice index). This description directly serves as genetic encoding of the individual. It should be emphasized that this representation is a major advantage of the GA-method, since the UC problem is not decomposed either by time or by unit (cf. the criticism of conventional UC methods in [1]). Rather, each individual contains the full information about the on/off-status of all units at all time slices and therefore enables an easy treatment of time dependent and time coupling constraints. Since there are 2^n possible on/off-combinations per time slice, each column of the binary matrix is interpreted as an integer between 0 and $2^n - 1$. Initialization of a population is done by generating these integers at random.

As a robust selection procedure for parents of new individuals we choose the so-called *2 of 3 scheme*[3]. Here 3 individuals of a population are randomly selected and rated on the basis of their fitness, i.e. their total costs given by eq. (1). The worst is replaced by an offspring of the two best, in the following called *father* and *mother*. In addition to its transparency and robustness this procedure has the advantage that in any case the best individual remains in the population.

The combination of two parent individuals to form an offspring is achieved by means of the multi-point-crossover operator. An application of this operator leads to randomly selected cross-over points $t_1 < t_2 < \ldots$ between 1 and k. Up to t_1 the resulting schedule inherits the information (i.e. the columns of the binary matrix) from the father, between t_1 and t_2 from the mother, and so on. Passing on intact columns of the parent UC schedules to the offspring, pure recombination does not require new load dispatch calculations.

In order to introduce new information into a population, i.e. to create new on/off-combinations in the columns of the binary matrix, we subject the offspring to a sequence of mutation operators. First we apply the standard mutation operator which sequentially acts on all time slices by flipping a randomly selected bit with a small probability. Apart from this, we employ five more mutation operators that act on building blocks rather than single bits (cp. [1]). Building blocks are low-order, highly fit parts of the genotype which are to be recombined to form higher-order and even more highly fit genetic schemes and to finally form the complete solution string [4]. Once a good building block has been found, it is preserved with high probability through the evolution process. Building-block operator one exchanges the bits of two randomly chosen units during a time period of several hours. Operator two randomly selects a unit and a time period. Then it mutates all on/off-bits of the unit in the time period, turning all of them to 1s or all of them to 0s. Once a new *best* individual of the population has emerged, building block operators three through five are applied for further improvement. These are stochastic hill climbing operators, whose actions are only accepted if they produce better solutions. Operators three and four sequentially act on all time slices of the scheduling period. For each time slice, operator three exchanges the on/off-bits of two randomly selected units, whereas operator four flips the on/off-bit of a randomly chosen unit. Each single mutation is only accepted if it improves the fitness. Building block operator five randomly selects two units. A time window of random length is aligned with the beginning of the scheduling period, and the two selected units exchange their bits in that window. If this mutation gives a better solution, it is kept, otherwise the original state is restored. Then the window is shifted one time slice up, and the above procedure is repeated, until finally the time window reaches the last hour of the scheduling period.

If for a given number of generations the fitness of the best individual has not improved any more or if a maximum number of generations has been exceeded, the GA is stopped. The most economical operation schedule of the final population represents the output of the GA.

5 Modeling of the Unit Efficiency by Neural Networks

As already mentioned in section 1, the fuel costs of units with power-heat coupling depend in a complicated and nonlinear way on the released quantities of P_{el}, P_h and m_s. The boundaries separating feasible values of (P_{el}, P_h, m_s) from non-feasible ones are complex and nonlinear, too. On top of that, fuel costs as well as feasibility-boundaries depend on the actual plant configuration (e.g. shutdown of feedwater heaters or condenser tube bundles) and on ambient conditions (e.g. temperature of cooling water). In order to achieve the most economic dispatch of the load demand, we model these functional dependencies very precisely by simulating the water-steam cycle of the power generating unit, taking into account details like the geometry of the turbine. The computer program performing the simulation, called KRAWAL, was developped by the manufacturer of power plants, Siemens KWU, for the purpose of plant design [5].

Since a single run of KRAWAL takes about 5s on a SUN Sparc 20 workstation, KRAWAL cannot be employed in a straightforward way during the whole optimization procedure. To make nevertheless use of the modeling precision of KRAWAL, we store offline-produced simulation data and, during optimization, look up the values of the unit efficiency in that storage. As type of storage we choose neural networks since they require small storage space, enable a fast look-up and are capable of interpolating.

Each run of KRAWAL gives two important informations. First, it checks whether the particular combination of P_{el}, P_h and m_s, which is assigned to the respective unit, can be fulfilled given the actual plant status and ambient conditions. Second, if this check returns the signal 'feasible', the precise consumption of primary energy required for this load combination is calculated. In the framework of our concept both functionalities of KRAWAL have to be mimiced by neural networks. Task 1, the classification of feasibility, is done by a 3-layer perceptron with one tanh-activated output neuron. Task 2, the modeling of the I/O-relation of fuel consumption versus power releases (and plant parameters), is made more difficult by discontinuities for the cases $P_h \to 0$, $m_h \to 0$ and $P_h \to 0 \wedge m_s \to 0$ due to technical, plant-internal reasons. To solve task 2, we employ a 'mixture of local experts' (see, e.g., [6]), i.e. a system of several different 'expert' networks each of which has been trained for a specific I/O-regime. When the mixture-of-experts network is asked for an I/O-approximation, a smooth gating function decides which of the experts should be used. The single expert networks are 3-layer perceptrons with one linearly activated output neuron. Training is done by means of the BFGS-version of the Quasi-Newton method (see [2]). The trained mixture-of-experts network is a very precise neural approximation of KRAWAL with an average deviation of less than 0.2 %.

6 Results

The efficiency of a GA for the UC problem as compared to conventional UC methods has already been proven in [1]. Here, we want to verify that the precise modeling of power plants with power-heat coupling allows to find load dispatch solutions whose fuel costs are reduced by an economically relevant amount. For that demonstration we choose the case which gives the least hope for cost reductions by sophisticated load dispatch, namely a power generating system consisting of 2 identical (800 MW) units in an identical plant state. Table 1 shows for three load examples the load dispatches resulting from SQP on the basis of unit-modeling by neural networks (including a subsequent fine tuning on the basis of KRAWAL-simulations). In case 1, a feasible solution can only be found by means of precise unit modeling. The symmetric assignment of load is not a feasible solution for that demand. Cases 2 and 3 give examples of reductions of fuel costs (as compared to the symmetrical load dispatch) by making use of nonlinear effects of the power-heat coupling. The achieved cost reductions (1.3% and 2.9%, respectively) have to be rated against the background that for the modelled power generating system an average cost reduction of 0.5% in the course of one year would amount to a cost reduction in the order of magnitude of 1 million DM. In order to test the performance of the presented scheduling

	load demand (MW)	load dispatch (MW) unit 1	unit 2	$Q_{opt}(MW)$	$Q_{symm}(MW)$	cost reduction
case 1	P_{el} : 1400	659	741	3187	–	
	P_h : 300	201	99			
	m_s : 100	0	100			
case 2	P_{el} : 800	114	686	1919	1944	1.3%
	P_h : 100	11	89			
	m_s : 100	0	100			
case 3	P_{el} : 800	91	709	1879	1935	2.9%
	P_h : 80	0	80			
	m_s : 100	0	100			

Table 1. Reduction of fuel consumption by an economic load dispatch which takes into account nonlinear effects of power-heat coupling (3 examples). Q_{opt} indicates the fuel consumption for the optimal load dispatch, Q_{symm} for the symmetrical load dispatch.

algorithm as a whole, we chose an example of a 5-unit power system (real world data) and performed for 10 realistic sample forecasts each time 5 optimization runs. In all cases our algorithm achieved very good solutions.

7 Conclusions

We have presented a new algorithm for scheduling fossil-fuel plant systems with power-heat coupling. A GA solves the UC problem and is assisted by neural networks which accelerate the evaluation of the fitness of generated UC schedules. The employment of neural networks enables a precise modeling of nonlinear effects of the power-heat coupling within justifiable computation times and, thus, makes possible economically relevant cost reductions.

The proposed method to integrate neural networks in the framework of a GA to accelerate the fitness evaluation is not restricted to scheduling power plant systems. Rather, the method seems promising in all *real-world* optimization problems where

- many time consuming simulations are necessary in order to evaluate the fitness in a precise and situation-adapted way
- many of the simulation runs have similar input parameters, and
- the output of a simulation depends on the input parameters in a sufficiently continuous way.

Given these conditions, it seems promising to store simulation results by neural networks and to make use of their ability of interpolation and, possibly, of their gradient information.

References

1. Kazarlis, S., Bakirtzis, A., Petridis, V.: A Genetic Algorithm Solution to the Unit Commitment Problem. Presented at the Winter Meeting of the IEEE Power Engineering Society, NY (1995)
2. Bazaraa, M., Sherali, H., Shetty, C.: Nonlinear Programming, Theory and Algorithms. John Wiley, NY (1993)
3. Nagel, K.: Private Communications, Siemens AG, Corporate Research, München (1994)
4. Goldberg, D.: Genetic Algorithms in Search, Optimization and Machine Learning. Addison Wesley, Reading, Mass. (1989)
5. Description of the simulation program KRAWAL. Internal report, Siemens/KWU, Erlangen, (1983)
6. Jacobs, R., Jordan, M., Nowlan, S., Hinton, G.: Adaptive Mixtures of Local Experts. Neural Computation **3** (1991), 79-87

Evolutionary Algorithms for the Calculation of Electron Distributions in Si-MOSFETs

J. Jakumeit

II. Physikalisches Institut, Universität zu Köln, Zülpicher Str. 77, D-50937 Köln, Germany

Abstract. The prediction of electron distributions in semiconductor devices is compulsory for the design of modern computer chips. In spite of increasing computation facilities the calculation of electron distributions at high energies is difficult resulting in significant deviations between theoretical predictions and measurement results. With evolutionary algorithms, however, it is possible to search for electron distributions which fit to experimental results and in this way backward calculate the distribution from measurements. Hereby the possibility to support the optimization of the evolutionary algorithm by a physical mutation operator which modifies individuals due to physical rules is important. This new approach was applied to the calculation of electron distributions and gate currents in Si-MOSFETS. The results demonstrate that the combination of physical model and evolutionary optimization is an interesting tool to compare theoretical models with experimental results.

1 Introduction

Computer simulation is an important tool to design semiconductor devices. [1] The Monte-Carlo method [2], which simulates directly the motion of carriers in semiconductor devices due to external forces and scattering, is the most flexible and common used technique. Many effects can be nicely simulated by this technique, but there are still a number of problems like the calculation of electron distributions at high energies, where measurement results are difficult to predict. The usefulness of evolutionary algorithms (EA) [3] for the determination of energy distributions of electrons in semiconductors was already demonstrated in [4]. In this work a significantly improved EA was used to minimize the gap between theoretical predictions and measurements of physical quantities related to electron distributions in Si-MOSFETs. Compared to other mathematical or combinatory optimization techniques EAs are favourable mainly for the following three reasons.
First, for an efficient use of standard optimization methods it is necessary to describe the electron distribution by a rather small set of parameters. This parametrization often limits significantly the possible forms of distributions. As shown below the optimization with an EA is possible with a simple discretization of the distribution function which does not limit the form of the distribution.
Second, due to the inevitable experimental errors as well as approximations and

not well defined parameters in the model neither the experimental nor the theoretical results are precise . Thus not the optimum solution of the mimimum problem is of interest but near optimum solutions, which lead to a fit between theory and experiment within their error limits. This fits well to the characteristic of EAs, which often find near optimum solutions rather quick but may not reach the global minimum within a reasonable time.
Third, the natural optimization technique of EAs makes it possible to influence the optimization by physical information. New individuals can be created from old ones using a physical mutation operator which modifies individuals not arbitrary but due to physical rules. The physical mutation operator pushes the search for near optimum solutions into a physical reasonable direction and improves the convergence speed.
Especially the last point can only be incoporated into natural optimization techniques and is essential for the calculation of hot electron effects in Si-MOSFETs.

2 Gate current in Si-MOSFETs

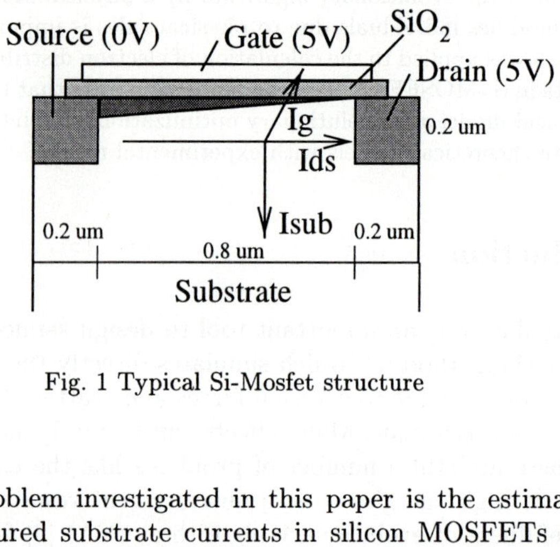

Fig. 1 Typical Si-Mosfet structure

The physical problem investigated in this paper is the estimation of gate currents from measured substrate currents in silicon MOSFETs (Metal Oxid Semiconductor Field Effect Transistors). Fig. 1 shows the principle structure of a Si-MOSFET. The current from source to drain I_{ds} is controlled by the voltage applied to the gate V_g. A positive voltage at the gate accumulates electrons at the interface between Si and SiO_2 and yields a conducting channel between source and drain. To improve the speed of Si-MOSFETS, the channel length $L_{channel}$ is drastically reduced into the submicron region in modern devices. This leads to very high electric fields F in the channel, because the drain voltage V_d remains at 5 V or 3.3 V ($F = U_d/l_{channel}$). High fields heat the electrons in the channel to energies of several electron volts. Electrons with a kinetic energy higher than 1.1 eV can ionize an electron from the valence band and thus create an electron-hole pair. The positive hole is pushed towards the substrate by the applied gate voltage and leads to the substrate current I_{sub}. Electrons above an energy of about 3.2 eV can cross the barrier of the SiO_2 and result in a gate current I_g (see fig. 1). A fraction of these hot electrons get trapped inside the SiO_2-layer before reaching the gate. These trapped electrons shield the field of the gate and lead to a reduced device performance. After several months or years of operation a hugh number of electrons may be accumulated in the SiO_2-layer and may cause a failure of the device. In modern computer chips, millions of Si-MOSFETs are integrated and the failure of one transistor often ruins the complete chip. Thus an estimation of the gate current and of the number of trapped electrons is crucial for the silicon technology.

Substrate and gate currents can be calculated if the energy distribution of electrons along the channel $f(E,x)$, i.e. the electron density at a certain point x and energy E in the channel, is known. The substrate current is limited by the hole creation rate and thus given by:

$$I_{sub}^{calc} = K \cdot e \cdot \int_{channel} \int_0^{\infty} f(E,x) W_{ii}(E) dE dx \quad , \tag{1}$$

where $W_{ii}(E)$ is the impact ionization rate [5] which is equal to the hole creation rate in this case. $K = 1$ holds if all created holes contribute to the substrate current.

The gate current can be calculated in the same way if the probability to cross the SiO_2-layer $P_{trans}(E,x)$ for an electron at location x and energy E is known:

$$I_{gate}^{calc} = e \cdot \int_{channel} \int_0^{\infty} f(E,x) P_{trans}(E,x) dE dx \quad . \tag{2}$$

The theory for the calculation of $P_{trans}(E,x)$ is not yet as well established as the calculation of the impact ionization rate. The results shown below are calculated by the formulas given by Huang et al. in [6].

The Monte-Carlo simulation, mentioned above, yields $f(E,x)$ at low energies and source-drain currents can be calculated which are in agreement with measurements. Even the substrate current can often be correctly estimated from the electron distribution obtained by a MC simulation, when high electric fields heat many eletrons to energies above 1.1 eV. But the electron density at 3 eV or higher energies, which is important for the gate current, is several orders of magnitude smaller than the density at low energies even in high electric fields. Thus the simulated electrons in a MC only seldom reach such energies and the MC must run for a very long time in order to resolve the distribution without a large statistical noise.

This study demonstrates that an EA is a helpful tool to calculate the electron distribution above 3 eV. The EA was used to search for electron distributions up to 5 eV, which fit a given substrate current, obtained by measurements or from Monte-Carlo results.

3 Calculation of electron distribution with EAs

The EA used in this work can be seen as a real-coded genetic algorithm [3, 7, 8] using special mutation and recombination operators which fit to the physical problem. Electron distributions $f(E,x)$ discretized over E and x were used as individuals, represented by a real-coded array. The enery interval between 0 eV and 5 eV was discretized by 250 equally distributed points while up to 50 points represent the x-direction. Thus a subarray of 250 real numbers can be seen as a gene, giving the energy distribution at a certain poisition and each individual consists of up to 50 genes. $f(E,x)$ was normalized to 1 or the x-dependent carrier density $n(x)$. The negative relative mistake between the goal substrate current I_{sub}^{goal} und the substrate current calculated from $f(E,x)$ was used as objective function:

$$F(f(E,x)) = -\frac{|I_{sub}^{goal} - I_{sub}^{calc}(f(E,x))|}{I_{sub}^{goal}} \tag{3}$$

Parent-selection was performed by the roulette wheel method. [7] The new generation was selected from the old and the newly created individuals by a Threshold Acceptance process [9] which selects new individuals for the new population if their fitness is not smaller than the maximum fitness of the old population reduced by a threshold. If not enough new individuals fullfill this requirement, the new population is filled with the best individuals from the old population. Two random mutation operators were used, one increases or decreases the high energy part of the distribution (fig. 2(a)) and the other varies a randomly chosen local part of the distribution (fig. 2(b)) Again the magnitude of these changes was chosen randomly but never exceeds 10 %. Two individuals were recombined

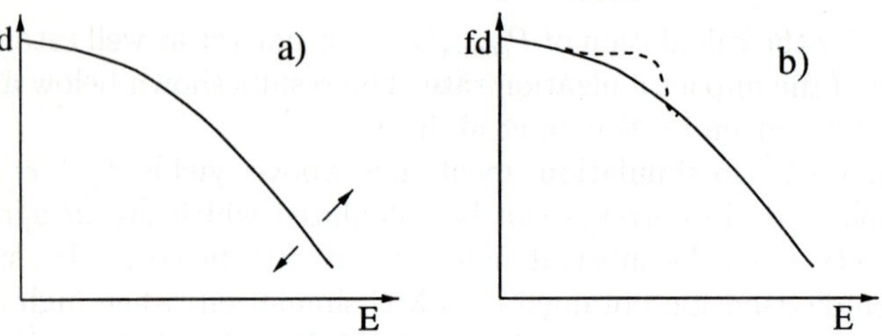

Fig. 2 Random mutation operators

by exchanging randomly chosen parts between electron distributions. Both the rekombination and the mutation operators may change more than one gene if the individual consists of more than one gene. With these mutation, recombination and selection operators it is possible to run the EA and the algorithm will find distributions with a very small deviation between I_{sub}^{goal} and I_{sub}^{calc} within a reasonable amount of CPU-time. But in general these distributions will not be physically meaningful but just arbitrary, because from many electron distributions a substrate current can be calculated using equation 2 which is equal to I_{sub}^{goal}. But these distributions are not necessarily close to a physical meaningfull distribution. It is not practical to limit the searchspace to the region of physical meaningful distributions by restrictions. Instead the search for the electron distribution was pushed towards a physical meaningful solution by the help of a physical mutation operator. This mutation operator is based on the Monte-Carlo method described above. A randomly chosen part of the distribution is transfered into a simulation electron and the drift and scattering of this electron inside the devices is simulated based on the knowledge of the electric fields, bandstructure and scattering rates in the device. When the simulation electron has suffered a certain number of scattering events, the electron density represented by the electron is given back to the distribution at the final energy- and x-value of the electron (see fig.3). Because the EA uses not only the physical mutation

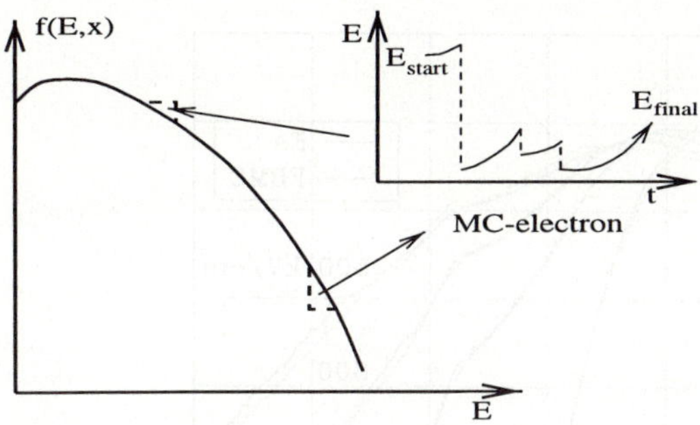

Fig. 3 Principle of the physical mutation operator

operator but aims at measurement results the physical model inside the physical mutation operator can be rather simple without leading to wrong solutions. Here a simple effective mass approach is used for the bandstructure with the effective mass m_{eff} of the electron as calibration parameter. The scattering rates for electron phonon scattering and impact ionization were calculated using a full band approach [2, 10]. The scattering rates for both effects were multiplied by an additional factor, f_{phonon} and f_{impact} respectively, which artificially increase or decrease the scattering rates. These factors are necessary to calibrate the simple physical model. The EA was stopped when the relative difference between I_{sub}^{goal} and I_{sub}^{calc} was less than 0.001 or the number of created individuals exceeds 10000.

4 Results for silicon and Si-MOSFETs

The new approach was first tested by calculating the electron distributions in n-doped bulk silicon, i.e. the material of the channel of Si-MOSFETs without any device structures like gate or contacts. In this case no measurement results like gate or substrate current exist and the EA was tested assuming that the results of the well established full-band Monte-Carlo (FBMC) simulation method describe the physics in bulk silicon correctly. Substrate currents calculated from the electron distribution given by the FBMC (equation 2) were used as goal value

I_{sub}^{goal} for the EA. The best convergence of the algorithms was found when a two step optimization scheme was used. First the physical mutation operator was applied several thousand times to a randomly chosen initial distribution without any optimization, until a steady state was reached. This can easily be done by choosing a population size of one and a very high threshold for the selection of the new population, using only the physical mutation operator to create a new individual from the old one. In the second step the electron distributions obtained in this way by the physical mutation operator were taken as initial populations for the full EA with selection, random mutation, physical mutation and recombination.

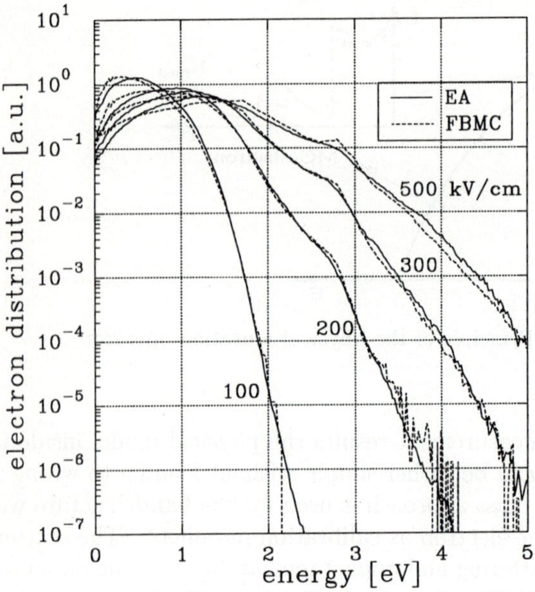

Fig. 4 Electron energy distributions in bulk silicon for different electric fields typically found in modern Si-MOSFETs

With the parameter set $m_{eff} = 1.0$, $f_{phonon} = 1.0$ and $f_{impact} = 1.6$ in the physical mutation operator, the EA found distributions with a relative difference smaller than 0.001 between the substrate current calculated from the FBMC and the EA result within 5 generations. In order to reduce the statistical noise in the solution found in one EA run an average over 100 results of single runs were taken. Fig. 4 compares these averaged curves (full lines) with results of the FBMC (dotted lines) for different electric fields typically found in the channel of a Si-MOSFET. The electron distributions obtained by the EA agree well with the results of the FBMC over almost the whole energy range. The high energy tail of the distribution, which is the aim of this work, is nicely reproduced with a smaller statistical noise.

The rather quick convergence of the EA is mainly due to the good initial population created using the physical mutation operator. For more complex

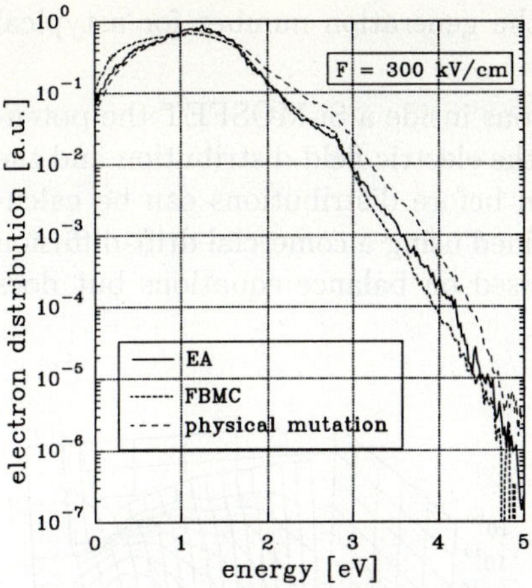

Fig. 5 Electron distributions obtained by the physical mutation operator and the EA for $f_{phonon} = 0.8$.

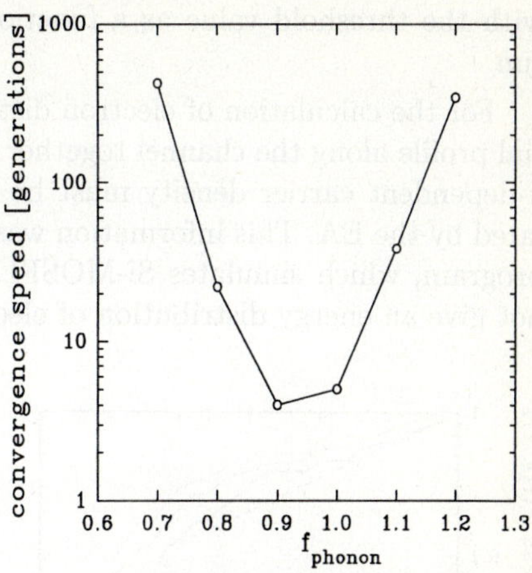

Fig. 6 Convergence speed of the EA as a function of f_{phonon}.

problems like Si-MOSFETs one can not expect that a simple physical mutation operator yields solutions close to the optimum. In this case the optimization facilities of the EA should be more important. To demonstrate this, the factor f_{phonon}, which adjusts the strength of the phonon scattering rate, was changed to a value below or above the optimum of 1.0, leading to an artificially wrong physical model. Fig. 5 compares the initial distribution obtained by the physical mutation operator and the final solution of the EA with the FBMC result for $f_{phonon} = 0.8$. As to expect the physical mutation operator with reduced phonon scattering yields a too high tail of the distribution. But the EA still finds a solution very close to the FBMC result by aiming at the substrate current, calculated from the FBMC result. Fig. 6 shows the influence of f_{phonon} on the convergence speed of the EA, measured by the generations needed to find a satisfactory solution. Obviously the convergence speed is linked to the quality of the physical model. A slow or no convergence indicates a wrong or oversimplified physical model inside the physical mutation operator.

Testing different parameter sets of the EA revealed that recombination by exchanging parts between distributions does not influence the convergence speed. But a population size of 10 individuals increased the convergence speed compared to population size 1, due to the possible parent selection and the smaller probability to loose a good individual in the selection of the new generation. The influence of the random mutation operators and the physical mutation operator has to be carefully balanced in order to obtain satisfactory results. The roulette wheel selection of the parents was linearly scaled giving the best individual a probability of 2 to become parent. The threshold of the Threshold Acceptance selection was reduced by a constant factor in each generation. The slope of this exponential decrease should be linked to the convergence speed. Fig. 7 shows the maximum, average and minimum fitness found in the actual population together with the threshold value as a function of the generation number for a typical run.

For the calculation of electron distributions inside a Si-MOSFET the potential profile along the channel together with the electric field distribution and the x-dependent carrier density must be known before distributions can be calculated by the EA. This information was obtained using a comercial drift-diffusion program, which simulates Si-MOSFETS based on balance equations but does not give an energy distribution of electrons.

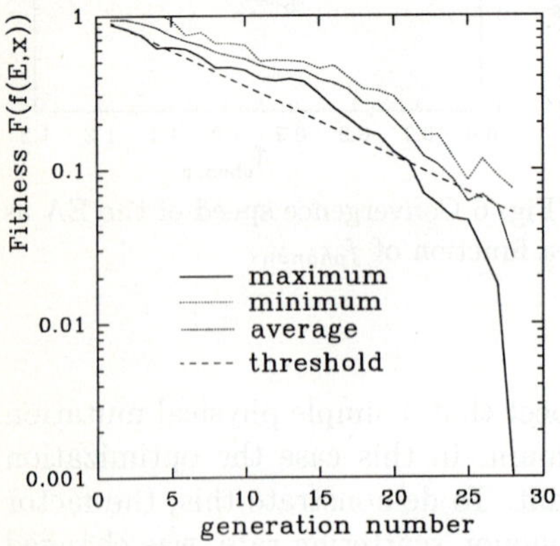

Fig. 7 Typical convergence of the EA with population size 10.

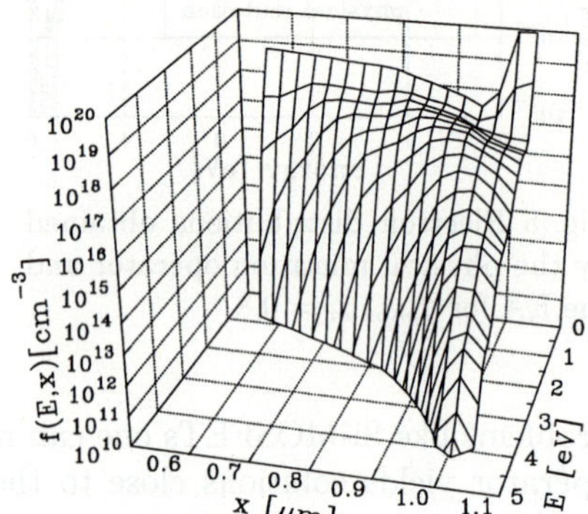

Fig. 8 Electron distribution for a 0.8 μm Si-MOSFET with V_d = 6V and V_g = 7V.

Fig. 8 shows the electron distribution calculated for Si-MOSFET with a channel length of 0.8μm calculated by the EA for a gate voltage of 7 V and a drain voltage of 6 V. The channel reaches from 0.2μm to 1.0μm and only the region close to the drain contact is shown. The heating of the electron gas in the high field region before the drain is clearly visible. The electron distribution obtained by the EA is in qualitatively agreement with calculations within the FBMC method. From such distributions substrate and gate currents can be calculated using equations 1 and 2 , respectively. In Fig. 9 results of the EA for $V_d = 6, 7$ V and $V_g = 5, 6, 7, 8$ V are compared with measurements by Ng et al. [11]. The EA aimes at the substrate current and the calculated I_{sub} therefore agree with the measurement results. For V_d = 6 V gate currents calcualted from the electron distribution given by the EA are in good agreement with the measurements but the results for V_d = 7 V reveal a deviation of almost one order of magnitude for V_g = 7 V and 8 V. This deviation shows that further improvements of this new method, especially a better calibration of the physical mutation operator and the calculation of the gate current, are necessary. But the agreement with the experimental results is good compared to results of Monte-Carlo algorithms. In addition the EA needs less computation time than a FBMC-program and yields a higher resolution of the electron distribution above 3 eV.

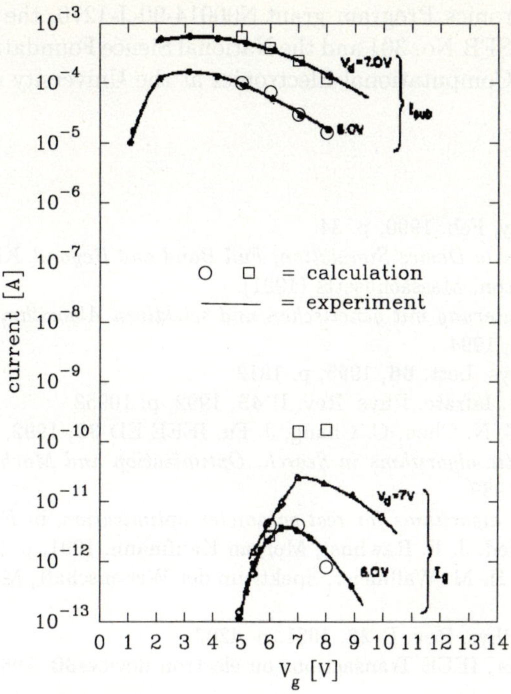

Fig. 9. Comparison between experimental results (taken from [11]) and substrate and gate currents calculated by the EA.

5 Conclusion

In conclusion an EA was used to minimize the gap between the theoretical predictions of electron distributions and correlated experimental results. The main advantage of the EA compared to other optimization techniques is the possiblity to influence the search for an optimal solution by physical information using a physical mutation operator, which modifies individuals due to physical rules. This new approach was applied to the calculation of electron energy distributions in Si-MOSFETs. First results indicate that this new method might be an interesting alternative to standard simulation methods like the Monte-Carlo method. Electron distributions in bulk silicon, which agree with the results of a full-band Monte-Carlo program, could be calculated by the EA. Estimations for gate currents in a 0.8 μm long Si-MOSFET are close to measurement results. A further investigation of this method including a transfer to other physical problems is promising.

6 Acknowledgement

The work was mainly influenced by the colaboration with K. Hess, U. Ravaioli, A. Pacelli and A. Duncan at the University of Illinois. It was supported by the Joint Services Electronics Program grant N00014-90-J-1270, the Deutsche Forschungsgemeinschaft SFB No. 301 and the National Sience Foundation through the National Center for Computational Electronics at the University of Illinois.

References

1. K. Hess, Physics Today, Feb. 1990, p. 34
2. K. Hess, ed., *Monte Carlo Device Simulation: Full Band and Beyond*, Kluwer Academic Publishers, Boston, Massachusetts (1991).
3. W. Kinnebrock, *Optimierung mit genetischen und selektiven Algorithmen*, Oldenburg Verlag, München, 1994
4. J. Jakumeit, Appl. Phys. Lett. **66**, 1995, p. 1812
5. J. Bude, K. Hess, G. J. Iafrate, Phys. Rev. B **45**, 1992, p. 10958
6. C. Huang, T. Wang, C. N. Chen, C. Chang, J. Fu, IEEE ED **39**, 1992, p. 2562
7. D. E. Goldberg, *Genetic algorithms in Search, Optimization and Machine Learning*, Addison-Wesley, 1989
8. A. H. Wright, *Genetic algorithms for real parameter optimization*, in *Foundations of genetic algorithms* (ed. J. E. Rawlins), Morgan Kaufmann, 1991, p. 205
9. D. Dueck, T. Scheuer, H. M. Wallmeier, Spektrum der Wissenschaft, March 93, p. 42
10. H. Shichijo, K. Hess, Phys. Rev. B **23**, 1981, p. 4207
11. K. K. Ng, G. W. Taylor, IEEE Transactions on electron devices**30**, 1983, p. 871

Refueling of a Nuclear Power Plant: Comparison of a Naive and a Specialized Mutation Operator

C. Kappler[1], T. Bäck[2], J. Heistermann[3], A. Van de Velde[4], M. Zamparelli[1]

[1] Institut für theoretische Physik, Humboldt Universität zu Berlin, Invalidenstr. 110, 10115 Berlin, Germany, {kappler, michele}@summa.physik.hu-berlin.de

[2] Informatik Centrum Dortmund, Center for Applied Systems Analysis (CASA), Joseph-von-Fraunhofer-Str. 20, 44227 Dortmund, Germany, baeck@home.informatik.uni-dortmund.de

[3] Siemens AG, ZFE T SN 4, Otto-Hahn-Ring 6, 81730 München, Germany, Jochen.Heistermann@zfe.siemens.de

[4] Siemens AG / KWU - BTMC, Bunsenstr. 43, 91058 Erlangen, Germany, Antoine.VandeVelde@bte.kwu.siemens.de

Abstract. An evolutionary algorithm is applied to the refueling of a nuclear power plant. Refueling plans so far are designed by experts on the basis of the experience and intuition. An automatization of this process is desirable because of its high commercial and scientific interest. We develop an appropriate fitness function and parallelize the optimization process. The focal point of this paper is the comparison of two mutation operators: a naive operator, and one in which more problem specific knowledge, in particular knowledge about the symmetry of the problem, is incorporated. The latter operator reduces the search space considerably. This specialization involves the risk of excluding the best solutions from consideration. We expound a method by which to acquire some certainty that this is not the case. The method also shows how the specialized mutation operator smoothes the search space. Finally, it allows a rough estimate of the best fitness value. At this time, refueling plans found by the algorithm compare favorably with those developed by experts, but they do not yet reach the estimated optimal fitness.

1 Introduction

We present an evolutionary algorithm for optimizing the performance of a nuclear power plant. In particular we show how the algorithm itself becomes more efficient by the use of a well-designed mutation operator. This is demonstrated by a method which allows to compare the performance of different mutation operators. The algorithm has been developed in a collaboration of university and industry and is now in active testing phase in view of its effective implementation.

The problem is the following. The core of a reactor consists of an array of fuel assemblies. The burn-up of the reactor is not homogeneous: because of finite size effects, the fuel assemblies at the boundary of the core burn up more slowly than those in the center. Usually, a reactor is stocked such that after about a year the output drops below a certain threshold and new fuel has to be added. Refueling consists of replacing fuel assemblies with the greatest burn-up by new ones, and then, because of the inhomogeneous burn-up, shuffling all assemblies such that fuel is used optimally. The time between two subsequent refueling operations is called a cycle. More details will be given in Sec. 2.1.

Optimal refueling is a difficult task which so far is tackled by experts. Our evolutionary algorithm allows to automate the process. In Sec. 2.2 we describe how experts develop a refueling plan and how the problem was made tractable for an evolutionary algorithm. In Sec. 2.3, the fitness function is introduced.

Because of the long CPU time each evaluation of the goal function requires, it makes sense to parallelize the optimization procedure (Sec. 2.4).

An important ingredient to any evolutionary algorithm is the mutation operator. We compare the performance of two different mutation operators: one "naive" operator, and one in which problem specific expertise, in particular knowledge about the symmetry of the problem, is built-in (Sec. 3.1). However, such a specialized mutation operator must be treated with caution: the optimization process is accelerated by excluding a large fraction of possible solutions from consideration. While one can never be sure the optimal solution is not among those excluded, we present a method by which to acquire some certainty. The method also shows how the search space is smoother when the specialized symmetric mutation operator is used (Sec. 3.2).

To our knowledge, reactor refueling is one of the economically most ambitious problems tackled by evolutionary algorithms so far. The costs of refueling a single nuclear power plant amount to about US$ 100 million per year, with potential savings predicted to be of several percent.

2 Problem Description

2.1 The design of the reactor core

The fuel assemblies in the core of a typical pressurized water reactor are arranged circularly on a square lattice. A cross section is shown in Fig. 1.

From the beginning, the fuel assemblies are not identical, but contain different quantities of reactive material. An unequal distribution of fuel (which thus exists even in the first cycle) promotes in positive feedback the development of greater inhomogeneity: An individual assembly of high reactivity constitutes a "hot spot" which accelerates its own burn-up and those of the surroundings. Thus, at the end of a cycle, there is a large number of fuel assemblies of different reactivity. Additionally, because of the finite size of the assemblies, most assemblies have an internal burn-up gradient.

2.2 Development of a refueling plan

As pointed out above, composing a refueling plan is a complex problem, which so far is solved by experts, for each cycle of each individual nuclear power plant.

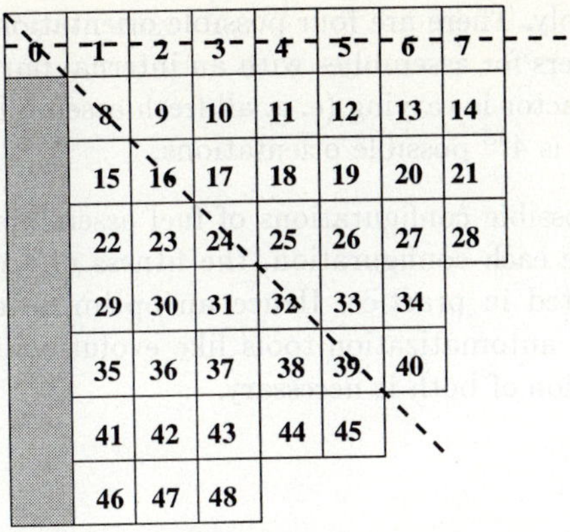

Fig. 1. Simplified cross section of the core of a nuclear reactor. Shown is only a quarter, the remainder is to be completed symmetrically. Each square corresponds to one fuel assembly. Note the mirror symmetries along the dashed lines.

Manual design of a refueling plan To design the next refueling plan, an expert first analyses data describing the fuel assemblies at the end of the last cycle. A simplification arises by only working with a quarter core (cf. Fig. 1). The remainder of the reactor is stocked symmetrically and thus burned up symmetrically also. A typical data set contains the ID and position of all fuel assemblies in the quarter core, the ID of the three assemblies in equivalent position, the reactivities and internal gradients. Based on this data the designer develops a prototype plan of which assemblies to discard, by which assemblies to replace them, and how to shuffle the assemblies. This proposal will then be translated into a set of input cards fed into a computer for a simulation of the next cycle. The simulation of one cycle needs about 90s CPU time on modern workstations and produces up to 5 MB output data. The expert interprets the, according to current design criteria, relevant parts of the output, and appropriately adapts the original plan. The process is repeated until a satisfactory solution is reached.

In the process described above, the interpretation of the 5MB output from the simulation is done without a mathematically defined fitness function. The knowledge and experience of the expert allow to decide on the quality of a specific refueling plan.

Automated design of a refueling plan Automated design of the refueling plan requires two steps: The automated proposal of a new configuration of assemblies in the reactor, and an automated interpretation of the results of the simulation, i. e. a fitness function. For previous work on the subject see Ref. [1]

Let us see why it is impossible to exhaustively evaluate all possible configurations. The quarter core of our example reactor contains 48 fuel assemblies (the center assembly always remains in place). Also 21 fresh assemblies are available.

Composing a new configuration consists of three steps:

1. Choice of which fuel assemblies to use in the next cycle. There are $\binom{69}{48}$ possible configurations.
2. Choice of position for each of the 48 assemblies in the reactor. The number of permutations is 48!.

3. Choice of orientation of each assembly. There are four possible orientations. Of course the orientation only matters for assemblies with an internal burn-up gradient. Their number in the reactor is varying (e. g. all fresh assemblies have no gradient). An upper bound is 4^{48} possible orientations.

Thus, in total there are about 10^{107} possible configurations of fuel assemblies. With 90s CPU time needed to evaluate each configuration, the fitness of only a tiny fraction of these can be computed in practice. Hence an optimization procedure based on human experience, automatization tools like evolutionary algorithms, or an appropriate combination of both is necessary.

2.3 The fitness function

An evolutionary algorithm needs a simple way to evaluate a given refueling plan. It is so far impossible to mathematically express all qualities figuring in their design. We therefore restrict ourselves to the most important ones. We introduce a fitness function f which presently is a sum of 4 terms:

$$f(\mathbf{x}) = \frac{a_1}{x_1} + \frac{x_2}{a_2} + \frac{x_3 + x_4}{a_3} + \frac{1}{a_4} max(x_3, x_4) \tag{1}$$

where the x_i characterise a given configuration and the weights a_i are chosen such that each term would optimally become one. Thus the theoretically optimal value of the fitness function is $f_{min} = 4.0$. "Fitness" is to be minimized in this case.

The meaning of the individual terms is as follows

- Maximization of cycle length (x_1).
- Minimization of the number of fresh fuel assemblies (x_2).
- Minimization of the maximal local power peaking factor after 6 days (x_3).
- Minimization of the maximal local power peaking factor for the rest of the cycle (x_4).

The last two conditions assure a flat power distribution and avoid local power peaks during the entire cycle length.

Besides optimizing the fitness function, a refueling plan must meet hard constraints, such as a cycle length within a certain given intervall and safety conditions. We incorporate these conditions by quadratic penalty terms.

Refueling plans with a fitness function value of less than 4.2 usually preserve the cycle length with few fresh fuel assemblies and with a flat power distribution.

2.4 A parallel evolutionary algorithm

The problem presented here is a typical representative of problems based on simulation models where evolutionary algorithms are identified as promising methods (see e.g. [2]): The simulator is given as a "black box" (in fact, only a binary executable is provided by the industrial partner), which was extended by special input- and output-interfaces. The input-interface accepts a configuration of fuel assemblies and passes it on to the simulator in the appropriate format. The output interface accepts the large output generated by the simulator and returns the scalar fitness function according to Eqn. (1).

Besides algorithmic difficulties, the optimization of simulation models is typically hampered by technical difficulties such as licensing problems or resource consumption of the simulation runs. As mentioned above, a single simulation run takes about 90 sec. CPU-time on a workstation (this time will soon increase to four minutes, when the present simulator is coupled to a second one that performs an enhanced post-processing of the data), and needs at least 28MB of RAM, and 50MB disk space for temporary data. These are strong reasons for evaluating refueling plans in parallel within a local area network of workstations. The appropriate parallelization paradigm uses a simple *master-slave* algorithm consisting of the master process (which runs the evolutionary algorithm) and a number Γ of identical slave processes which evaluate individuals asynchronously parallel on different computers. The structure of the master-slave algorithm is shown in Fig. 2.

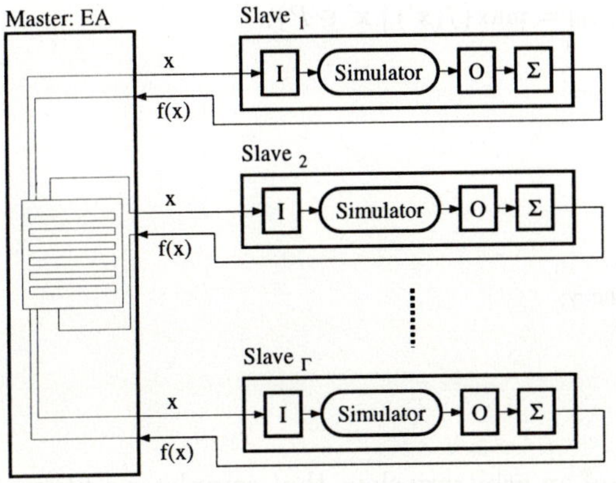

Fig. 2. Structure of the master-slave evolutionary algorithm. The master maintains a population of refueling plans, which are evaluated by the slaves. Each slave consists of an input interface "I," the simulator, an output interface "O," and the fitness function.

The master process runs the evolutionary algorithm with a population of refueling plans and the typical loop of recombination, mutation, evaluation and selection (see e.g. [3]). For evaluation, a core reload pattern $\mathbf{x}$ is send to a free slave, where $\mathbf{x}$ is evaluated. Finally, the result $f(\mathbf{x})$ is send back to the master.

The present implementation of the algorithm does not use a generational synchronization of the evaluation of individuals but relies on an asynchronous update of the population when an objective function value is received: The worst individual of the population is replaced by a newly created and evaluated individual, if the new individual performs better (*steady-state* [4] or $(\mu+1)$-selection

[5]). After performing this selection step, the algorithm creates a new individual and sends it to the free slave for evaluation. The asynchronous update of the population guarantees an optimal use of the available CPU resources. The implementation of the algorithm using PVM [6] follows the following pseudocode description:

```
Master: μ, Γ, i_max, p

initialize P := (x_1, ..., x_μ);
for i = 1 to Γ do
   send x_i to slave i;
for i = Γ+1 to μ do
   receive (x, f(x)) from slave γ;
   send x_i to slave γ;
od
while (i < i_max) do
   receive (x, f(x)) from slave γ;
   select:    if       f(x) ≤ f(x_worst)
              then     x_worst := x;
              where    f(x_worst) = max{f(x') | x' ∈ P};
   recombine: x' := r(P);
   mutate: x'' := m_{p}(x');
   apply heuristics to x'';
   send x'' to slave γ;
   i := i + 1;
od
for i = 1 to Γ do
   receive (x, f(x)) from slave γ;
   select;          {as above}
od
return x_best;
```

```
Slave:

while not terminate do
   receive x from master;
   call simulator with input x;
   calculate f(x) from simulator output;
   send (x, f(x)) to master;
od
```

Here, γ denotes the index of an arbitrary slave that completes a fitness function evaluation, returns its result, and receives a new individual created by recombination and mutation. The main loop of the master constantly receives results from slaves, inserts the new individual into the population, and creates a new offspring by means of recombination and mutation for sending it to the free slave. The slave processes on the other hand receive an individual $\mathbf{x}$ for evaluation from the master, call the simulator with the input configuration corresponding to $\mathbf{x}$, calculate $f(\mathbf{x})$ from the simulator output, and send the result $(\mathbf{x}, f(\mathbf{x}))$ back to the master. The slave processes are started and terminated by the master process.

The input parameters of the algorithm include the population size μ, the number of slave processes Γ, the maximum number $i_{\max}$ of evaluations permitted, and the mutation probability p for the mutation operator.

The recombination operator used is the order cross over operator (see [7], pp. 170–174 for further information). The mutation operator will be described in detail now.

3 Performance of the symmetric mutation operator

The most obvious mutation operator is the following. Randomly pick one fuel assembly in the quarter core. Randomly pick a second one, either from the quarter core or among the fresh assemblies. Exchange the two. With a certain probability rotate one or both assemblies by one of the possible rotation angles. This operator we call the *asymmetric* mutation operator.

Much can be gained by considering the symmetries of the problem consistently. In addition to the fourfold symmetry, there is a reflection axis along the diagonal (dashed line in Fig. 1). Intuitivly it is clear that, after each cycle, assemblies should be exchanged such that all symmetries are conserved. Thus the mutation operator should respect these symmetries. We now present details of the *symmetric* mutation operator, and subsequently compare the performance of the symmetric and the asymmetric mutation operator in depth.

3.1 Description of the symmetric mutation operator

We must distinguish two kinds of symmetric configurations: Those that are symmetric only concerning the reactivity of the fuel assemblies, and those that also are symmetric concerning the reactivity gradients. The symmetric mutation operator presented here only respects symmetry concerning bulk-reactivity.

The implementation of the symmetric mutation operator is straight forward. Instead of picking *any* element among those in the quarter core, only pick among those between main axis and diagonal, and fresh assemblies. Each mutation is completed symmetrically below the diagonal also. Assemblies on the diagonal and main axis are "single" and treated as before. Rotate assemblies as before.

For both the symmetric and the asymmetric mutation operator, *heuristics* are included. These are empirical rules known to lead to good configurations. We distinguish between deterministic rules (e. g. no new elements in the border) which are always obeyed, and stochastic rules (e. g. no neighboring new elements) which with a certain probability may be violated. These rules make certain parts of the configuration space unaccessible or less accessible.

3.2 Symmetric or asymmetric configurations - which are best?

A sophisticated mutation operator such as the symmetric one bears a risk: a huge number of possible configurations is excluded from inspection. In our case the number of possible configurations drops from about 10^{107} to about 10^{59}. We should therefore make sure the searched for best configurations are not among those left out.

A first insight can be gained by counting the number of configurations per fitness value in a small (10^4) sample of symmetric and asymmetric configurations (see Ref. [8]). This procedure shows, that *on average* symmetric configurations have a better fitness. However, because of the small size of the sample, little can be said about the searched-for very good configurations, because here the statictics become unreliable.

We developed a method which circumvents this problem. To explain it properly, we first need to review some statistical physics.

Picture a gas of particles at a certain temperature T. For each temperature there is a different probability distribution of the energy of the individual particles. The average energy of the particles is the lower, the lower the temperature. This energy distribution can be found by a *Metropolis Algorithm* [9], which in practical terms corresponds to Simulated Annealing at constant temperature: A new particle is generated and accepted with probability one if its energy is lower, and it is accepted with probability $\exp(-\Delta E/kT)$, if its energy is higher than that of the preceeding particle. In the limit of infinitely many steps, the energy distribution of the set of particles thus produced is the equilibrium energy distribution of a gas at that temperature. In practice the number of steps is not infinite but we require the average energy of the last n particles generated to be constant. The number n of course must be chosen with care.

In our case, we have a gas the particles of which are *nuclear power plants* with different fuel-assembly configurations. The energy of the nuclear power plant – particle is given by the fitness of its fuel assembly configuration. The average energy, or fitness, $\overline{F(T)}$ at different temperatures is found according to the method described above. The lower the temperature, the better (i. e. lower) the average fitness, and $\lim_{T\to 0}\overline{F(T)} = F_{optimal}$. We now investigate how the weighted average fitness of symmetric configurations compares with that of asymmetric configurations. Two scenarios are possible. Either we have

$$\lim_{T\to 0}\overline{F^{asym}(T)} < \lim_{T\to 0}\overline{F^{sym}(T)}. \qquad (2)$$

In this case the best configuration is asymmetric. Or else we have

$$\lim_{T\to 0}\overline{F^{asym}(T)} = \lim_{T\to 0}\overline{F^{sym}(T)}. \qquad (3)$$

This is because the set of symmetric configurations is included in the set of asymmetric configurations. In this case the best configuration is symmetric.

We investigate the behaviour of both $\overline{F^{asym}(T)}$ and $\overline{F^{sym}(T)}$ by running a Metropolis Algorithm with an asymmetric and with a symmetric mutation operator. The average fitness was computed from samples of 2500 and 5000 configurations for the symmetric and asymmetric mutation operator respectivly.

Fig. 3 shows that at all temperatures $\overline{F^{asym}} > \overline{F^{sym}}$. It seems unlikely the two curves will cross at lower temperatures. Rather (from the argument given above) we expect the two curves converge slowly.

We conclude that, with great probability, the best configuration is symmetric. It is therefore safe to use the symmetric mutation operator, thereby excluding a large fraction of configuration space from consideration and speeding up the optimization.

Still more may be read from Fig. 3. The data concerning asymmetric configurations is considerably more noisy than that for symmetric ones — although for asymmetric data about twice as many configurations were sampled. This means, when a asymmetric mutation operator is used, an optimization procedure is

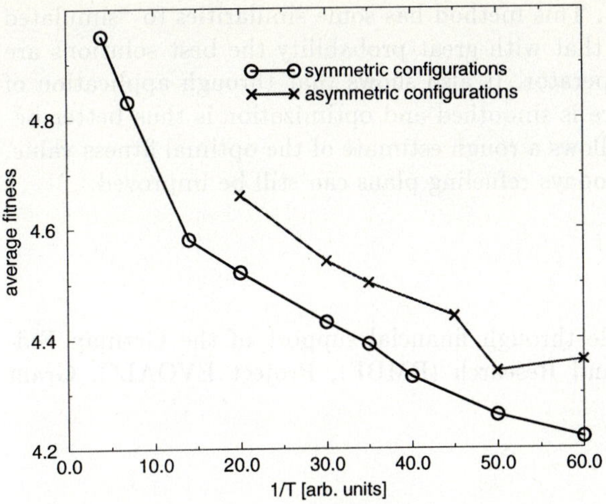

Fig. 3. Weighted average fitness of symmetric and asymmetric configurations as a function of inverse temperature

caught in saddlepoints more easily. Assuming symmetric configurations are generally better, this is not surprising: With the asymmetric mutation operator at least two mutations are necessary to move from one symmetric configuration to another one. Symmetric configurations are thus separated by ridges of asymmetric configurations.

To summarize, the symmetric operator not only diminishes the number of configurations that need to be searched but also *smoothes* the fitness landscape, making optimization better behaved.

It is also possible to make predictions concerning the best fitness value from Fig. 3. The best fitness value is that to which both curves converge in the limit of zero temperature. A rough estimate is an optimal fitness between 4.0 and 4.1. At that point, the best refueling plans reach fitness values of about 4.12. Thereby, plans found by the evolutionary algorithm compare favorably with those developed by experts. However, as pointed out in Sec. 2.3, comparisons of automatically generated refueling plans with those developed manually must be handled with care.

4 Conclusion

In this paper we presented an evolutionary algorithm which automatizes the refueling of a nuclear power plant. We derived a fitness function and parallelized the algorithm. This last step considerably accelerates the optimization because each evaluation of the fitness function consumes vast resources and time on the individual computer. We then discussed in detail two different mutation operators: one naive operator, the asymmetric operator, and one operator, in which more problem specific knowledge has been incorporated, the symmetric mutation operator. The advantage of a specialized operator is the reduction of search space. Its drawback is that the best solutions may be excluded from consideration. We developed a method which allows to compare the performance of these two operators in detail. This method has some similarities to "simulated annealing". It demonstrates that with great probability the best solutions are reached by the symmetric operator. It also shows that through application of this operator the search space is smoothed and optimization is thus better behaved. Finally, the method allows a rough estimate of the optimal fitness value. According to this estimate, todays refueling plans can still be improved.

Acknowledgements

This work was made possible through financial support of the German Federal Minstry of Education and Research (BMBF), Project EVOALG, Grant 03040101.

References

1. P. W. Poon, G. T. Parks, Optimizing Pressurized Water Reactor Reload Core Designs, *Proceedings of PPSN 2*. Bruxelles, 1992.
2. Th. Bäck, U. Hammel, and H.-P. Schwefel, Modelloptimierung mit evolutionären Algorithmen, in A. Sydow ed., *Simulationstechnik: 8. Symposium in Berlin*, Fortschritte in der Simulationstechnik, p. 49–57. Vieweg, Wiesbaden, 1993.
3. Th. Bäck and H.-P. Schwefel, An overview of evolutionary algorithms for parameter optimization, *Evolutionary Computation*, 1(1):1–23, 1993.
4. D. Whitley. The GENITOR algorithm and selection pressure: Why rank–based allocation of reproductive trials is best, in J. D. Schaffer, ed., *Proceedings of the 3rd International Conference on Genetic Algorithms*, p. 116–121, Morgan Kaufmann Publishers, San Mateo, CA, 1989.
5. Th. Bäck, F. Hoffmeister, and H.-P. Schwefel, A survey of evolution strategies, in R. K. Belew and L. B. Booker, eds., *Proceedings of the Fourth International Conference on Genetic Algorithms*, p. 2–9. Morgan Kaufmann, San Mateo, CA, 1991.
6. A. Geist, A. Beguelin, J. Dongarra, W. Jiang, R. Manchek, and V. Sunderam, *PVM: Parallel Virtual Machine — A User's Guide and Tutorial for Networked Parallel Computing*, The MIT Press, Cambridge, MA, 1994.
7. D. E. Goldberg, *Genetic algorithms in search, optimization and machine learning*, Addison Wesley, Reading, MA, 1989.
8. Th. Bäck, J. Heistermann, C. Kappler, and M. Zamparelli, Evolutionary algorithms support refueling of pressurized water reactors, in *Proceedings of the Third IEEE Conference on Evolutionary Computation*, IEEE Press, 1996, in press.
9. K. Binder in *Monte Carlo Methods in Statistical Physics*, K. Binder Ed., Springer, Berlin 1979.

Genetic Algorithms Applied to the Physical Design of VLSI Circuits: A Survey

Jens Lienig and James P. Cohoon

Department of Computer Science
University of Virginia
Charlottesville, VA 22903, U.S.A.
E-mail: jens/cohoon@virginia.edu

Abstract. Electronic design automation is concerned with the design and production of VLSI systems. One of the important steps in creating a VLSI circuit is its physical design. The input to the physical design step is a logical representation of the system under design. The output of this step is the layout of a physical package that optimally or near-optimally realizes the logical representation. Physical design problems are generally combinatorial in nature and have very large problem sizes. In this paper we review genetic algorithms for physical design and observe and analyze the common traits of the superior contributions. For example, many of these investigations use genetic operators that incorporate expert knowledge. We believe this review can stimulate and steer further applications.

1 Introduction

A major computer science application area is the field of electronic design automation. The goal of this field is to facilitate the creation of VLSI (Very Large Scale Integration) systems. There are five major steps in the process of creating a VLSI system.

- *Specification*: produce a functional specification of the system under design.
- *Logic design*: transform the functional specification into a logical representation. The logical representation is typically given as a collection of *logic cells* or *gates* and a *netlist* collection of sets of logic cells that must be interconnected for the system to be realized. The logic cells, themselves, are predesigned circuit elements taken from a technology-specific library.
- *Physical design*: convert the logical representation into a physical package representation. The physical package representation is specified through a set of mask descriptions which specify how the individual layers of the integrated circuit are to be produced.
- *Fabrication*: use the physical package representation to fabricate an actual integrated circuit.
- *Testing*: determine whether there are manufacturing errors that prevent the integrated circuit from implementing the functional specification.

Traditionally computer science researchers and developers have concentrated on the first three steps. The physical design step has received particular attention. A good overview of electronic design automation in general and physical design in particular is [22].

In developing a VLSI system, the designer is typically seeking not just a feasible system, but a system with optimal or near-optimal performance characteristics. A inferior solution is rejected by the system designer since it will almost assuredly be rejected in the marketplace. The standard figure of merit is some combination of the speed in which the system can compute its result, the size of the physical package, and the amount of power necessary for circuit operation. Because of the desire for optimality, the problems arising in carrying out the five design steps are generally combinatorial in nature.

What makes electronic design automation problems particularly difficult compared to traditional combinatorial optimization problems is that the instance sizes that must be handled can be quite large–a circuit can be easily composed of over one-million gates. As such, design automation practitioners have a strong tradition of quickly considering and adapting new and alternative solution techniques. For example, simulated annealing is an optimization technique that emulates the annealing of crystals. This combinatorial optimization method was first proposed in the literature in 1983 and by the following year, the major design automation conferences had multiple sessions on simulated annealing for design automation [24]. Early adoption was again repeated on neural networks [25] which simulate the organizing principles of nervous systems.

Although design automation did not immediately add genetic algorithms to its basic tool chest, genetic algorithms have been consistently used in the field for the last ten years.

In the remainder of this paper we first briefly give a more in-depth description of the VLSI physical design process. We then present a systematic review of genetic algorithm investigations for the physical design process. These contributions are generally different than standard genetic algorithm investigations. One difference is that the crossover and mutation operators for physical design genetic algorithms are typically very problem-specific. This specificity occurs because of the extreme importance of determining very high quality solutions–therefore expert information on the likely form of solutions is included as much as possible. Another difference is the concern for robustness. There exists a rich collection of design automation benchmarks (e.g., [23]) and for a solution method to be accepted, it must be demonstrated to work consistently well on those benchmarks.

2 Overview of VLSI Physical Design

The major steps in a typical VLSI design process are shown in Figure 1. In particular, the substeps of physical design are given.

The physical design phase is an important part of this process. Its input is generally a logical description of the circuit, often in the form of a netlist. The task of the physical design step is to produce a layout, an assignment of geometric

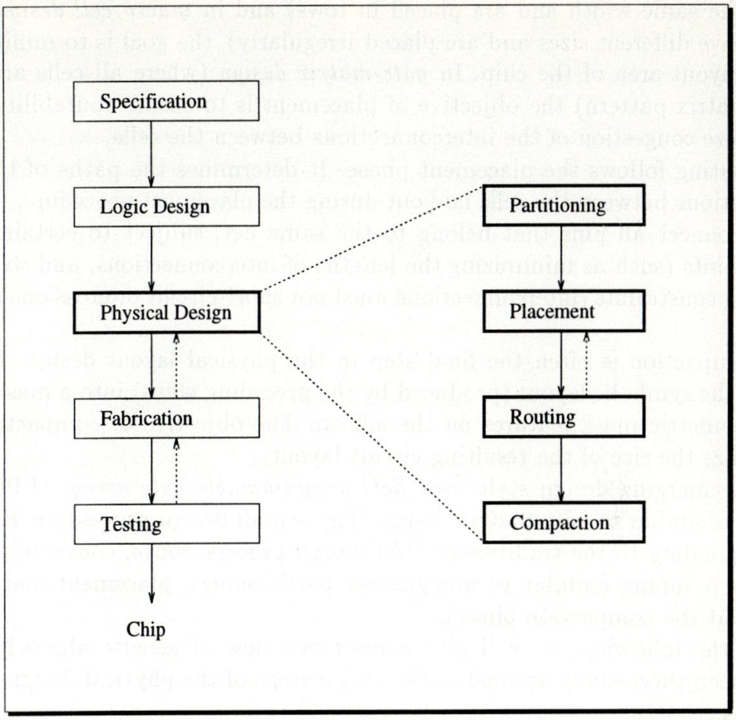

Fig. 1. The design process of VLSI chips.

coordinates to the circuit components, either in the plane or in a specified number of planar layers. The layout must satisfy the requirements of the fabrication technology (sufficient spacing between components of the circuit, and so on) and should minimize certain cost criteria (the lengths of the interconnections, etc.).

Due to its complexity, the physical layout problem is generally divided into subproblems which can be solved sequentially. These subproblems are still NP-hard, but they reduce the practical complexity to a manageable level. The physical design problem is usually decomposed into the following subproblems: *partitioning*, *placement*, *routing* and *compaction*.

Partitioning is the task of dividing a circuit into smaller parts in order to reduce the problem size. The circuit is often divided into portions that are implemented separately. The goal is to partition the circuit such that the sizes of the parts are within prescribed ranges and the complexity of the interconnections between these parts is minimized.

Placement assigns the cells of the circuit to their geometrical locations on the chip. (A cell may be a single transistor, an adder or subcircuit, etc.) The objective of placement depends on the design style. In *standard cell design* (where all cells have the same width and are placed in rows) and in *macro cell design* (where cells have different sizes and are placed irregularly), the goal is to minimize the total layout area of the chip. In *gate-matrix design* (where all cells are placed in a matrix pattern) the objective of placement is to ensure routability and to minimize congestion of the interconnections between the cells.

Routing follows the placement phase. It determines the paths of the interconnections between the cells laid out during the placement procedure. The goal is to connect all pins that belong to the same net, subject to certain quality constraints (such as minimizing the lengths of interconnections, and so on) and routing constraints (interconnections must not short-circuit or cross one another, etc.).

Compaction is often the final step in the physical layout design. It transforms the symbolic layout (produced by the preceding steps) into a mask layout, the geometric mask features on the silicon. The objective of compaction is to minimize the size of the resulting circuit layout.

An emerging design style uses *field-programmable gate arrays* (FPGAs) [1] which is similar to gate-matrix design. The overall design process for FPGAs is corresponding to the traditional VLSI design process above, consisting of technology mapping (similar to fine-grained partitioning), placement and routing (without the compaction phase).

In the following, we will give a brief overview of genetic algorithms that have been successfully applied to the major steps of the physical design of VLSI circuits.

3 Application of Genetic Algorithms to the VLSI Physical Design

3.1 Partitioning

To our knowledge, the first evolution-based algorithm for solving the partitioning problem was published in [29]. In contrast to previous heuristic algorithms that usually optimize on only one constraint, this approach is capable of handling both a number of constraints and a number of objectives. The algorithm, which does not include a crossover operator, yields multi-way partitions with fairly balanced sizes and a small number of pins for each part. The presented strategy has a reasonable execution speed that is similar to other published heuristic approaches.

In [13] and [14], different coding schemes for the problem of circuit partitioning are investigated to find the most suitable coding. The proposed genetic algorithm is specifically tailored for the partitioning of circuits with complex bit-slice components using a special two-step coding of partitions. The algorithm consists of a crossover and a mutation operator and a deterministic improvement strategy. The runtime of the algorithm is not competitive.

The genetic algorithm in [5] is based on a population structure that involves subpopulations which have their isolated evolution occasionally interrupted by inter-population communication. Although the investigated problems are from actual VLSI design efforts, neither comparisons with other approaches nor runtimes are presented.

A hybrid genetic algorithm for the ratio-cut partitioning problem is presented in [2]. Here the problem is formulated in terms of a hypergraph. The genetic encoding is a binary string, where each subset of the circuit's components has a corresponding location on the string. Before the genetic algorithm is executed, the ordering of these genes is determined by a depth-first search to improve the performance of the genetic algorithm. Traditional crossover and mutation operators are combined with a fast partitioning heuristic applied to each offspring as an improvement operator. The performance of the algorithm is compared with two other partitioning approaches, using benchmark data sets. Averaged over all benchmarks, the presented algorithm achieves better results than the other approaches, while having a similar amount of runtime for smaller graphs and less runtime for the largest graphs.

Another hybrid approach is published in [34]. It combines a simulated annealing method with a genetic algorithm. The main motivation for this approach is the parallelization of the simulated annealing strategy by replacing its single solution search process with a population-based approach using a genetic algorithm.

3.2 Placement

As mentioned in Section 2, the placement procedure is responsible for the assignment of the circuit's cells to their locations on the chip. According to the variation in size and location of these cells, placement algorithms can be divided into algorithms for standard cell design, macro cell design and gate-matrix design.

After the pioneering work of [4], further applications of genetic algorithms [31], [32] and evolution strategies [15], [16] for standard cell placement have been presented. These approaches produce high-quality placements of real-world VLSI circuits that can compete with sophisticated simulated annealing-based placement strategies. The published runtimes are up to 6 hours [15] and up to 12 hours [32], respectively.

In [21], the runtime has been reduced significantly by using a parallel implementation of a genetic algorithm that runs on a distributed network of workstations. The total population is split over different processors and a migration mechanism is used to exchange genetic material between them. While the placement results are similar to a serial genetic algorithm, an almost linear speedup can be achieved with this method.

We next discuss three investigations that use genetic algorithms for macro cell placement [3], [6], [7]. The approach in [3] is based on a two-dimensional bitmap representation of the macro cell placement problem. Another representation scheme, a binary tree, is applied in [6]. In [7], a combination of a genetic algorithm with a simulated annealing-based optimization strategy is presented. The experimental results suggest that a mixed strategy performs better than a pure genetic algorithm for the macro cell placement problem. The results are better or comparable to previously published results of placement benchmarks. However, the runtime is not as competitive.

An application of a genetic algorithm for the placement of gate-matrix design has been published in [33]. The approach uses the Genesis package [12] as the basic genetic algorithm. This package is modified with a special algorithm for constructing permutations that considers only a small subset of the solution space. The results are compared with only one previously published algorithm. The runtime is in the order of minutes (up to 1 hour).

3.3 Routing

Routing is the process of connecting pins subject to a set of routing constraints. VLSI routing is usually divided into *global routing* (to assign nets into certain routing regions) and *detailed routing* (to assign nets to exact positions inside a routing region).

To our knowledge, only one genetic algorithm for global routing has been reported [8]. The algorithm is based on a two-phase router. In the first phase, a genetic algorithm for the Steiner problem in a graph is used to generate a number of distinct, alternative routes for each net. Then, in a second phase, another genetic algorithm selects a specific route for each net (among the alternatives given from phase one), such that the overall layout area is minimized. The router is superior to TimberWolfMC [30], a state-of-the-art global router, with respect to solution quality, while being inferior with respect to runtime.

According to the position of the pins, detailed routing can be separated into *channel routing* (pins are only located on two parallel sides of the routing area) and *switchbox routing* (pins are placed on all four sides of the routing area).

In [20], a rip-up-and-rerouter is presented which is based on a probabilistic rerouting of nets of one routing result. However, the routing is done by a deterministic algorithm and main components of genetic algorithms, such as the crossover of different individuals, are not applied. Results are presented for channel and switchbox routing benchmarks.

The router in [10] combines the steepest descent method with features of genetic algorithms. The crossover operator is restricted to the exchange of entire nets and the mutation procedure performs only the creation of new individuals. The presented results are limited to simple VLSI problems, and no runtime remarks are made.

The algorithm proposed in [26] is limited to the restrictive channel routing problem. Here, all vertical net segments are located on one layer and all horizontal segments are placed on a second layer. This and other restrictions make this approach unusable for real VLSI channel routing problems.

A parallel genetic algorithm for the channel routing problem is presented in [27], [28]. A root processor executes a conventional genetic algorithm with global selection in the total population. The remaining processors execute the same genetic algorithm with their selection limited to subpopulations. After a certain number of generations, the total population of the root processor and the subpopulations of the remaining processors are interchanged. Benchmark applications are not presented.

The genetic algorithm for channel routing published in [17] is based on a problem-specific representation scheme, i.e. individuals are coded in three-dimensional chromosomes with integer representation. The genetic operators are also specifically developed for the channel routing problem. The results are either qualitatively similar to or better than the best published results for channel routing benchmarks. The runtime of the algorithm (in the range of 1...50 minutes) is not as competitive.

A genetic algorithm for the channel routing problem, which includes problem specific heuristics, is presented in [11]. The authors report results similar to [17] with (slightly) better runtimes.

A genetic algorithm for switchbox routing is presented in [18]. Similar to [17], the genotype is essentially a lattice corresponding the coordinate points of the layout. Crossover and mutation are performed in terms of interconnection segments. The algorithm assumes that the switchbox is extendable in both directions. Subsequently, these extensions are reduced with the goal to reach the fixed size of the switchbox. While more costly in runtime, on numerous benchmark examples the genetic algorithm produces solutions with equal or better routing characteristics than the previously best published results.

A parallel genetic algorithm (based on the theory of punctuated equilibria) for the channel and switchbox routing problem is presented in [19]. The algorithm runs on a distributed network of workstations. It is shown that the parallel approach outperforms a sequential genetic algorithm regarding solution quality and robustness. An extensive investigation of the parameters of a parallel genetic algorithm (number of migrants, epoch length, migrant selection strategies, etc.) is performed.

3.4 Compaction

As mentioned in Section 2, compaction transforms the symbolic layout to a mask layout with the goal of minimizing the size of the resulting circuit layout.

To the best of our knowledge, the only application of a genetic algorithm for compaction has been advanced by Fourman [9]. He describes two prototypes of genetic algorithms that perform compaction of a symbolic circuit layout. Although his results are limited to very simple layout structures, he does propose a new problem-specific representation for layout design that includes constraints of the compaction process. Neither runtimes nor real VLSI applications are discussed.

4 What Makes Genetic Algorithms Successful in the VLSI Community?

The algorithms presented in the previous section vary widely in their impact on the VLSI community. Despite the fact that most of them are interesting approaches from the viewpoint of a genetic algorithm developer, many are not applicable in real-world VLSI design systems.

After having investigated the main characteristics of the surveyed algorithms and their competitiveness, we believe that the following guidelines should be followed in developing a genetic algorithm for the VLSI design problem.

Robustness Since genetic algorithms are probabilistic approaches, it is very important to investigate the influence of the random seed on the solution quality. A VLSI designer will always hesitate to use an algorithm he/she has to run several times in order to achieve a usable and competitive result. Furthermore, the parameters used for running the genetic algorithm should be limited such that they can be easily adjusted to the specific design problem without extensive experimentation.

The probabilistic nature of the algorithm should be discussed whenever solutions of genetic algorithms are presented. In other words, it is necessary to clearly express how the presented results have been obtained. The randomness of the results also has to be taken into account when comparing the runtime of a genetic algorithm with another approach that needs to be executed only once to achieve its result.

Fair comparison with state-of-the-art algorithms Whenever possible, the presented approach should be compared with state-of-the-art algorithms regarding solution quality *and* runtime. Many of the surveyed genetic algorithms are competitive with respect to the solution quality only. However, to be of interest in the VLSI design area, a measure of running time must also be included. Less desireable is the number of recombinations, points visited in the search space, and so on.

Constraints of other algorithms have to be taken into account when comparing with their results. For example, it is not a fair comparison when the routing quality of a genetic algorithm is expressed only in terms of the number of vias [10] and then compared with the results of other approaches that minimize the netlength concurrently.

Using real-world benchmarks Due to the large number of CAD tools in VLSI design, benchmark data are available for all major design steps (e.g., [23]). A genetic algorithm developed for VLSI design will not create any interest within the VLSI community unless its performance is tested with the appropriate benchmarks. It is only by examining the results of these benchmarks that we can compare a particular genetic algorithm with any other given approach. The test examples should be large, reflecting real-world VLSI design problems.

The genetic algorithm should be used with the same set of parameters for all test examples. Problem-specific tuning does not allow a fair comparison, nor does it encourage the usage of the proposed algorithm in real design applications with their wide range of different design requirements.

5 Conclusions

Since the problems encountered in the physical design of VLSI circuits are very complex, genetic algorithms have a considerable potential in this field. Accordingly, there has been a significant increase in applications of genetic algorithms in this area in recent years. In investigating this development, the following conclusions have been reached.

- Successful genetic algorithms in VLSI design differ widely from the "traditional genetic algorithm concept" because they incorporate problem-specific knowledge into their operators. Furthermore, universal fixed-length binary implementations are often replaced by problem-specific representation schemes.
- Combinations of genetic algorithms with other optimization strategies, e.g. simulated annealing or fast deterministic algorithms, are no longer an exception. Their incorporation is often the only way to obtain an approach that is runtime competitive.
- Powerful parallel implementations of genetic algorithms have emerged in VLSI design. The increasing availability of high-speed local computer networks and inexpensive parallel computers encourages the implementation of parallel genetic algorithms with improved solution quality and runtime characteristics.
- To be successful in the area of VLSI design, the genetic algorithm has to be as robust as possible. Its results have to be compared with state-of-the-art design algorithms by using widely recognized benchmark data sets.

We have presented a survey of genetic algorithms that have been applied in VLSI physical design. We have also provided guidelines to make genetic algorithms more competitive among physical design algorithms for VLSI layout. We believe that such an approach is an important and necessary part of the continued growth of this field.

References

1. S. D. Brown, et al., *Field-Programmable Gate Arrays*, Boston, MA: Kluwer Academic Publishers, 1992.
2. T. N. Bui and B. R. Moon, "A Fast and Stable Hybrid Genetic Algorithm for the Ratio-Cut Partitioning Problem on Hypergraphs", *Proc. of the ACM-IEEE Design Automation Conference*, pp. 664-669, 1994.
3. H. Chan, P. Mazumder and K. Shahookar, "Macro-Cell and Module Placement by Genetic Adaptive Search with Bitmap-Represented Chromosome," *Integration, The VLSI Journal*, vol. 12, no. 1, pp. 49-77, Nov. 1991.
4. J. P. Cohoon and W. D. Paris, "Genetic Placement," *IEEE Trans. on Computer-Aided Design*, vol. 6, no. 6, pp. 956-964, Nov. 1987.
5. J. P. Cohoon, W. N. Martin, and D. S. Richards, "Genetic Algorithms and Punctuated Equilibria in VLSI," *Parallel Problem Solving from Nature,* H. P. Schwefel and R. Männer, eds., Lecture Notes in Computer Science, vol. 496, Berlin: Springer Verlag, pp. 134-144, 1991.
6. H. Esbensen, "A Genetic Algorithm for Macro Cell Placement," *Proc. of the European Design Automation Conference*, pp. 52-57, Sept. 1992.
7. H. Esbensen and P. Mazumder, "SAGA: A Unification of the Genetic Algorithm with Simulated Annealing and its Application to Macro-Cell Placement," *Proc. of the 7th International Conference on VLSI Design*, pp. 211-214, Jan. 1994.

8. H. Esbensen, "A Macro-Cell Global Router Based on Two Genetic Algorithms" *Proc. of the European Design Automation Conference*, pp. 428-433, Sept. 1994.

9. M. P. Fourman, "Compaction of Symbolic Layout using Genetic Algorithms," *Proc. of the First International Conference on Genetic Algorithms*, pp. 141-153, 1985.

10. M. Geraci, P. Orlando, F. Sorbello and G. Vasallo, "A Genetic Algorithm for the Routing of VLSI Circuits," *Euro Asic '91*, Parigi 27-31 Maggio, Los Alamitos, CA: IEEE Computer Society Press, pp. 218-223, 1991.

11. N. Göckel, G. Pudelko, R. Drechsler, B. Becker, "A Hybrid Genetic Algorithm for the Channel Routing Problem," *Proc. of the International Symposium on Circuits and Systems*, pp. 675-678, 1996.

12. J. J. Grefenstette and N. N. Schraudolph, *A User's Guide to GENESIS 1.2 UCSC*, CSE Dept., University of California, San Diego, 1987.

13. M. Hulin, "Analysis of Schema Distributions," *Proc. of the Fourth International Conference on Genetic Algorithms*, pp. 204-209, 1991.

14. M. Hulin, "Circuit Partitioning with Genetic Algorithms Using a Coding Scheme to Preserve the Structure of a Circuit," *Parallel Problem Solving from Nature*, H. P. Schwefel and R. Männer, eds., Lecture Notes in Computer Science, vol. 496, Berlin: Springer Verlag, pp. 75-79, 1991.

15. R. M. King and P. Banerjee, "ESP: Placement by Simulated Evolution," *IEEE Trans. on Computer-Aided Design*, vol. 8, no. 3, pp. 245-256, March 1989.

16. R. M. King and P. Banerjee, "Optimization by Simulated Evolution with Applications to Standard Cell Placement," *Proc. of the 27th ACM-IEEE Design Automation Conference*, pp. 20-25, 1990.

17. J. Lienig and K. Thulasiraman, "A Genetic Algorithm for Channel Routing in VLSI Circuits," *Evolutionary Computation*, vol. 1, no. 4, pp. 293-311, 1994.

18. J. Lienig and K. Thulasiraman, "GASBOR: A Genetic Algorithm for Switchbox Routing in Integrated Circuits," *Progress in Evolutionary Computation*, X. Yao, ed., Lecture Notes in Artificial Intelligence, vol. 956, Berlin: Springer Verlag, pp. 187-200, 1995.

19. J. Lienig, "A Parallel Genetic Algorithm for Two Detailed Routing Problems," *Proc. of the International Symposium on Circuits and Systems*, pp. 508-511, 1996.

20. Y.-L. Lin, Y.-C. Hsu and F.-S. Tsai, "SILK: A Simulated Evolution Router," *IEEE Trans. on Computer-Aided Design*, vol. 8, no. 10, pp. 1108-1114, Oct. 1989.

21. S. Mohan and P. Mazumder, "Wolverines: Standard Cell Placement on a Network of Workstations," *IEEE Trans. on Computer-Aided Design*, vol. 12, no. 9, pp. 1312-1326, Sept. 1993.

22. B. T. Preas and M. J. Lorenzetti, *Physical Design Automation of VLSI Systems*, Benjamin/Cummings, Menlo Park, CA, 1988.

23. B. T. Preas, "Benchmarks for Cell-based Layout Systems," *Proc. of the ACM-IEEE Design Automation Conference*, pp. 319-320, 1987.

24. *Proc. of the ACM-IEEE Design Automation Conference*, 1984.

25. *Proc. of the ACM-IEEE Design Automation Conference*, 1987.

26. A. T. Rahmani and N. Ono, "A Genetic Algorithm for Channel Routing Problem," *Proc. of the Fifth International Conference on Genetic Algorithms*, pp. 494-498, July 1993.

27. B. B. P. Rao, L. M. Patnaik and R. C. Hansdah, "Parallel Genetic Algorithm for Channel Routing Problem," *Proc. of the IEEE Third Great Lakes Symposium on VLSI Design*, pp. 69-70, March 1993.

28. B. B. P. Rao and R. C. Hansdah, "Extended Distributed Genetic Algorithm for Channel Routing," *Proc. of the IEEE Symposium on Parallel and Distributed Processing*, pp. 726-733, 1993.

29. Y. Saab and V. Rao, "An Evolution-Based Approach to Partitioning ASIC Systems," *Proc. of the ACM-IEEE Design Automation Conference*, pp. 767-770, 1989.

30. C. Sechen, *VLSI Placement and Global Routing Using Simulated Annealing*, Boston, MA: Kluwer Academic Publishers, 1988.

31. K. Shahookar and P. Mazumder, "GASP - A Genetic Algorithm for Standard Cell Placement," *Proc. of the European Design Automation Conference*, pp. 660-664, 1990.

32. K. Shahookar and P. Mazumder, "A Genetic Approach to Standard Cell Placement using Meta-Genetic Parameter Optimization", *IEEE Trans. on Computer-Aided Design*, vol. 9, no. 5, pp. 500-511, May 1990.

33. K. Shahookar, W. Khamisani, P. Mazumder and S. M. Reddy, "Genetic Beam Search for Gate Matrix Layout," *Proc. of the 6th International Conference on VLSI Design*, pp. 208-213, Jan. 1993.

34. J. M. Varanelli and J. P. Cohoon, "Population-Oriented Simulated Annealing: A Genetic/Thermodynamic Hybrid Approach to Optimization," *Proc. of the Sixth International Conference on Genetic Algorithms*, pp. 174-181, 1995.

Stochastic Methods for Transistor Size Optimization of CMOS VLSI Circuits

Robert Rogenmoser[1], Hubert Kaeslin[1], and Tobias Blickle[2]

[1] Integrated Systems Laboratory
[2] Computer Engineering and Networks Laboratory
ETH Zürich, Gloriastr. 35, 8092 Zürich, Switzerland

Abstract. The performance of a CMOS circuit depends heavily on its transistor sizes. We have tested a standard optimizer, a Monte Carlo scheme and a method based on Genetic Algorithms combined with very accurate SPICE simulations to automatically optimize transistor sizes of three different digital CMOS circuits. While the standard optimizer and the Monte Carlo scheme are advantageous for small circuits, the method based on Genetic Algorithms was found to be more stable for larger circuits.

1 Introduction

Transistor size optimization is a traditional obligation in VLSI (Very Large Scale Integration) design. It is used to improve the performance of a circuit to achieve a design goal in a specific technology. This design goal can either be boosting operating speed, lowering power consumption, or lowering area requirements. In this context the netlist of the circuit is already determined, only the width and the length of the MOS (Metal Oxide Semiconductor) transistors can be adjusted.

The figures of merit depend in a complex way on the individual sizes of the transistors. Changing transistor sizes in a circuit often leads to surprising results, which are not easily predicted.

It is hard to optimize digital CMOS circuits because their operation can only be modeled by distinguishing between different operating regions for each transistor depending on its terminal voltages (large signal behavior). In contrast, analog circuits can be expressed using small signal equivalents of the transistors, which are linearized in the operating point.

Even for a two transistor digital circuit such as an inverter (see Fig. 1) it is very hard to get accurate design equations. For example, a step input to a single inverter results in two operating regions with two differential equations (using level 2 models [Sah64]). If the step input is changed to a more plausible but still not entirely realistic linear rising ramp, the circuit traverses five regions of operation, each of which is described by its own differential equation.

In general, circuit designers manually optimize circuits by trial and error using an accurate circuit simulator such as SPICE. A good intuition and the designer's understanding of the transistors are important. Still, it is a tedious work of assigning sizes (i.e. width and length of the channel of the MOS) to all

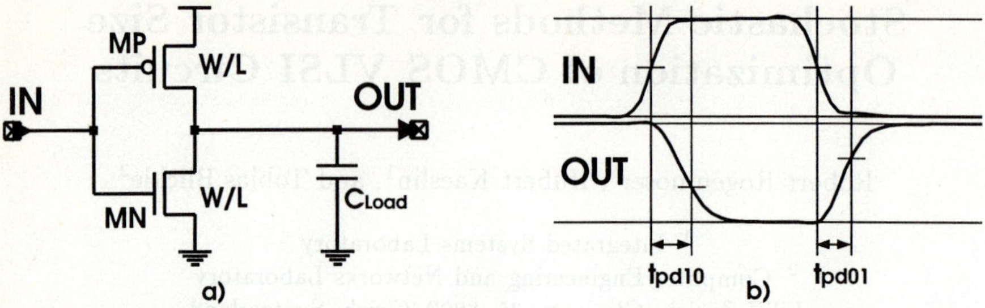

Fig. 1. CMOS Inverter: a) Transistor Diagram, b) Input and Output Waveforms

transistors, verifying the performance by simulation, and starting this process over again by reassigning new transistor sizes. An experienced designer may obtain acceptable results after a few iterations, while less trained designers may spend much more time optimizing even a small circuit. Automated tools are therefore a welcome alternative.

Some automated transistor sizing tools model transistors as switched RC-elements [Heu90]. The linearized netlist of a circuit can then be optimized using standard optimizers because such netlists consist of relatively simple equations, which are easy to differentiate. The results may be satisfactory for a first approximation but due to the simplified model they are often not sufficient.

A commercially available transistor sizing tool has been incorporated in the circuit simulator HSPICE [Hsp]. It performs iterative simulations using accurate transistor models; however, nothing has been published about the algorithms used internally.

While the optimization of very small circuits using this tool delivered reasonable results after a few iterations it was more difficult to obtain results for larger circuits. Optimization was often terminated before even mediocre termination criteria had been achieved.

Therefore, we have investigated new ways based on stochastic optimization methods to automatically optimize transistor sizes of circuits. Two different methods will be described: (1) Guided random search using a single solution and (2) using probabilistic optimization based on genetic algorithms (GA).

Method (1) has been published in [Wur93] and was originally used for sizing (scaling) Domino CMOS circuits. We applied this method to entire digital CMOS circuits and added an adaptive scheme. We will refer to it as Monte Carlo (MC) scheme.

Both methods use highly accurate SPICE simulation for the evaluation of the objective function and have been applied to combinational circuits but also to storage elements with internal feedbacks (e.g. flip-flops). All transistor in a circuit are sized by the GA or MC except predefined minimum sized transistors like, for example, for pull-up or pull-down function.

In [HK94] also a CMOS VLSI circuit optimization tool based on genetic algorithms was presented. In contrast to our work, simplified linear models for the transistors were used. These models require much lower computation times but the accuracy declines. To further reduce complexity only the output transistor pair of each gate of combinational blocks have been optimized.

In the next section we will introduce the three digital CMOS circuits with their optimization criteria and objective functions. Then we will look at the optimization methods in Sect. 3. In Sect. 4 the results are presented and discussed before drawing conclusions in the last section.

2 CMOS Circuits and Objective Functions

The functionality of a CMOS circuit is determined by its transistor network topology. However, the individual sizes of the transistors determine the final performance of the circuit and, if scaled wrongly, may even prevent the circuit from functioning correctly (e.g. in dynamic logic). For example, the p-channel transistor MP (PMOS) and the n-channel transistor MN (NMOS) in the inverter in Fig. 1a have different electrical characteristics. Therefore their sizes have to be scaled to equalize signal propagation for high and low inputs ($t_{pd10} \stackrel{!}{=} t_{pd01}$, see Fig. 1b). Moreover, they have to be adjusted for the load presented at the output.

In the simple case of an inverter most designers can optimize the transistor sizes using an accurate circuit simulator combined with extracted transistor models from fabricated devices. Typically, the PMOS is sized 1.5 to 3 times larger than the NFET from experience and after a few simulation runs the final size of the two is fixed. Because the current through a MOS transistor is proportional to W/L (W: width, L: length of the channel) only W is adjusted and L is kept minimal.

While the optimization is straightforward for an inverter, it becomes more complex for larger circuits where more input and output signals and propagation paths have to be watched. In our analysis, we looked at the optimization of three different CMOS circuits having increasing complexity: (1) a 3-input NAND gate (NAND3), (2) a dynamic edge-triggered D-flip-flop (DFF), and (3) a complementary pass gate full adder (CPLFA), see Table 1. In contrast to [HK94] we used highly accurate SPICE simulations to calculate the fitness function in spite of the relatively large calculation time for one objective function.

Table 1. Specification of optimized CMOS circuits

Circuit	Technology	# MOS total	# MOS optimized	1 Evaluation real	CPU
NAND3	1.0 μm	6	6	10.1 s	3.0 s
DFF	1.0 μm	16	14	11.6 s	5.8 s
CPLFA	0.6 μm	34	26	46.5 s	36.7 s

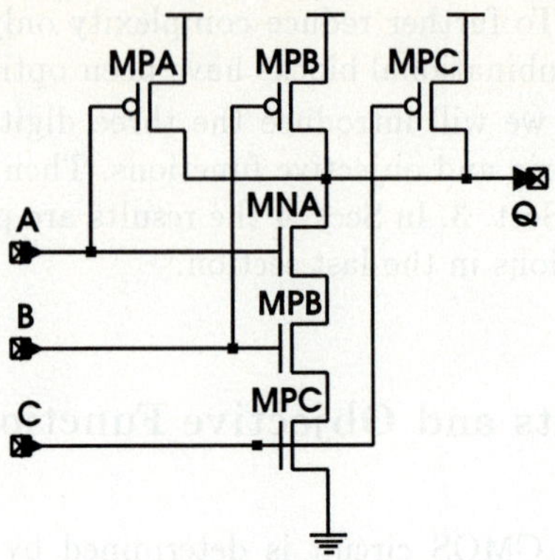

Fig. 2. 3-input CMOS NAND gate (NAND3)

2.1 Objective Functions

The most important optimization goal for these circuits was to minimize the propagation delay for all inputs to the output for both, the high to low (01) and the low to high (10) transitions with limited increase in power consumption. The objective function for the NAND3 was therefore:

$$f = \left(0.9 \times \frac{t_{del}}{t_0} + 0.1 \times \frac{P}{P_0}\right)^2$$

$$\text{with:}$$

$$t_{del} = \max(t_{A01}, t_{A10}, t_{B01}, t_{B10}, t_{C01}, t_{C10})$$

$$P = \sum_i W_i$$

The values for t_{del} and P were adjusted to ensure that power consumption has a weight of about 10 %. The value for t_{del} was determined by performing a SPICE simulation and measuring all propagation delays for each input combination and extracting the largest value. Power consumption was determined by summation of all transistor widths W (for CMOS circuits: $P = f \cdot C \cdot V^2, C \propto \sum W$).

A similar objective function was used for the DFF. However, in a flip-flop not only propagation delay t_{pd} but also other parameters such as setup time t_{su} are important design parameters. Moreover, in the case of the present dynamic D-flip-flop internal timings such as the precharge time t_{ch} has to be taken into consideration. Fig. 3 shows such a dynamic flip-flop which was used for high-speed designs [RH96, RH95].

Hence, t_{del} has to be specified in more detail as:

$$t_{del} = \max(t_{suM} + t_{pdM}, 2 \times t_{ch})$$

$$\text{with:}$$

$$t_{suM} = \max(t_{su0}, t_{su1})$$

$$t_{pdM} = \max(t_{pdQ0}, t_{pdQ1}, t_{pdQB0}, t_{pdQB1})$$

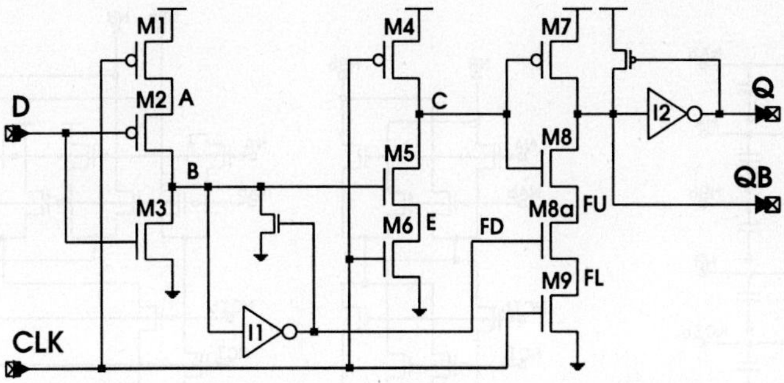

Fig. 3. Dynamic edge-triggered D-flip-flop (DFF)

For both circuits, NAND3 and DFF, the timings depend very much on the capacitive load on the outputs. This load has been adjusted so that it corresponds to twice the load that the circuit presents itself at the input (i.e. consecutive identical gates with fanout two).

For the third circuit, the CPLFA (see Fig. 4), a slightly different objective function was chosen:

$$f = P \times t_{del}$$

Both values can easily be extracted from SPICE simulations. In this circuit all 24 transistor of the network have been optimized together with 2 transistors of an inverter at the output, which were then applied to all four output drivers (S to COb). For the six input drivers (A to CIb) the same sizes have been assigned to reflect the drive capability of the optimized circuit. The six capacitors on these drivers represent additional wiring capacitance.

3 Optimization Methods

3.1 Monte Carlo

The first stochastic optimization method is based on [Wur93], where transistors of Domino CMOS circuits were sized in an incremental way. The procedure looks as follows:

1. Assign a set of random sizes for each transistor
2. Evaluate the solution (calculate the fitness function)
3. Increase, decrease each sizes of the set by a fixed step (minimum feature size) or do not change it at all (with equal probability)
4. Evaluate the solution; if this set has a better fitness continue with this set, otherwise use the previous one.
5. If maximum number of evaluations is reached stop, else goto 3.

We used this Monte Carlo (MC) for all three circuits and incorporated an adaptive scheme. The step size is first set to four times minimum feature size.

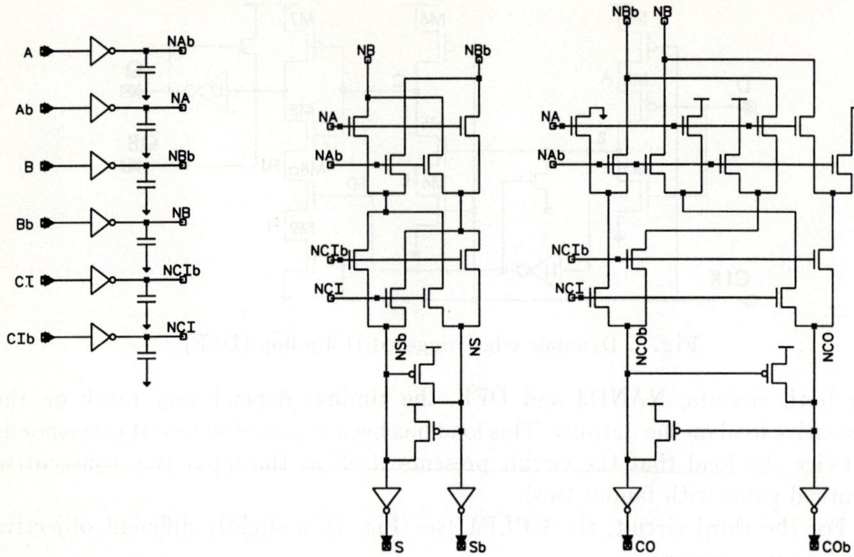

Fig. 4. Complementary Pass Gate Full Adder (CPLFA). For simplicity not all wires are drawn; nodes with same node are connected

After the first third of the optimization it is reduced to twice the minimum feature size and to the minimum for the last third. Duration of the optimization was limited by the number of function evaluations.

3.2 Genetic Algorithms

Three different variants of a genetic algorithm have been used and are summarized in Table 2. These parameters have been used to optimize the three circuits. The number of computations per evaluation was set to 400 for the NAND3, to 1000 for the DFF, and to 3000 for the CPLFA. All experiments were performed using the GENEsYs package [Bäc92].

The first setup (PT) is the standard setup provided by this package. It uses fitness proportional selection and two-point crossover. The second setup (RU) reflects empirical knowledge of optimal parameter settings. In particular, the following changes have been made:

- ranking selection, as this is known to overcome some serious disadvantages of proportional selection [Whi89, MSV93a],
- uniform crossover that has shown its superiority in several investigations (see, e.g., [Sys89]),
- the optimal mutation rate of 1/n, where n is the length of the individual in bits [MSV93b].

The third setup (ES) is based on evolution strategies [Sch81] and uses no recombination but the adaptive mutation scheme AMEM (adaptive mutation excluding mutation rates) (see, e.g. [Bäc94]).

Table 2. The parameters used in the three different setups

	PT	RU	ES
Population size	20	20	20
Selection method	proportional (elitism)	Ranking (elitism) $\eta_{max} = 1.1$	Truncation $T = 50\%$
Crossover method	two-point	uniform	none
Crossover probability	0.6	0.6	-
Mutation rate	0.03	0.008	AMEM

4 Results and Discussion

In order to compare the performance of the different optimizers, the maximum number of individuals (or simulations) was set equal for all approaches. Each experiment was performed 10 times. The overall best solutions found for the different circuits are shown in Table 3. The MC method seems to be well suited for all three problems. However, looking at the results of several simulations reveals a slightly different picture.

Table 3. Best Fitness Value for Different Optimization Methods

	Monte Carlo	Genetic Algorithm		
Circuit	MC	PT	RU	ES
NAND3	0.345	0.361	0.373	0.350
DFF	0.977	1.094	1.086	1.009
CPLFA	1.321	1.562	1.425	1.791

Figures 5a–c show the statistics for the three problems and the four optimizers at the end of each run. The line through the box marks the data's median, while the upper and lower edge of the box mark the upper and lower quartile of the data. The box encloses the interquartile range (IQR), that is the range of half of the data that clusters around the middle of the data. The tails reach to upper and lower adjacent values, where the adjacent values are the largest (smallest) datum that is not more than $1.5 \times$ IQR above or below the upper and lower quartile. All other data points are plotted beyond the ends of the tails as dots.

For the two small circuits (NAND3 and DFF) the MC outperforms the three genetic algorithms in both performance and accuracy. For the large example however, the MC has a much larger variance. The most stable optimizer for the large problem is the RU genetic algorithm.

For the CPFLA circuit the performance of the three genetic algorithms are compared in Fig. 6. Here, the average of the 10 best individuals in each generation is shown as a function of the generation number. The graph shows the superiority of the RU setup. The performance of the MC is also added to this graph, however only every 20th solution has been incorporated.

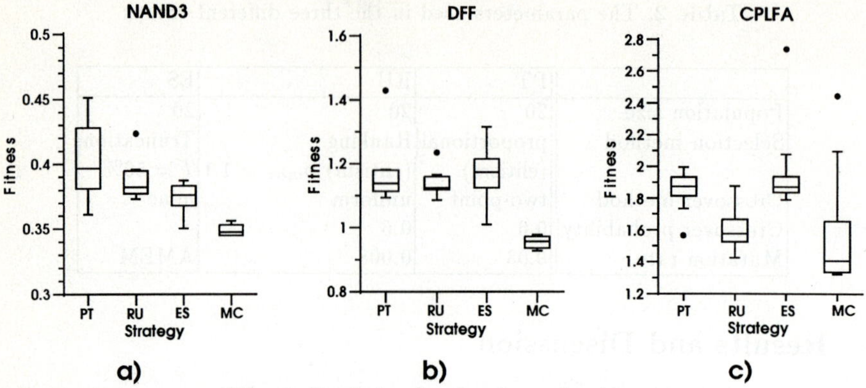

Fig. 5. Statistics for the three circuits

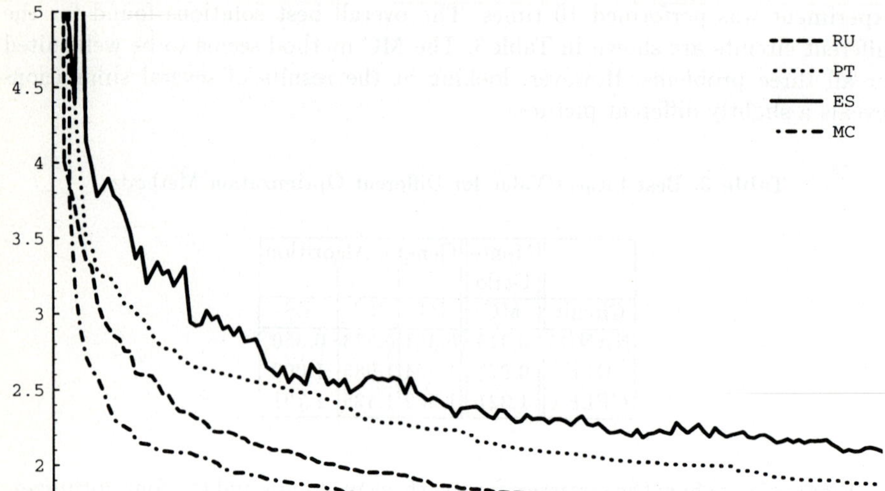

Fig. 6. The optimization processes in dependence of the generations for the three GA setups and the MC used. The graph shows the average of the best individuals for CPLFA.

Also, further computation time might have lead to better results as the objective function values continue to decline.

Some of the results were surprising, as for example the resulting transistor sizes of a 2-input NAND gate depicted on Fig. 7. In this NAND gate, the NMOS are tapered as one might expect, but the PMOS have different sizes, which seems to be wrong at first glance and are unlikely to be assigned even by an experienced VLSI designer. Simulation of this NAND gate results in equal rise and fall times for any input combination. The sizing therefore must be correct.

Analyzing the circuit in more detail reveals the reason. If node Q has to be

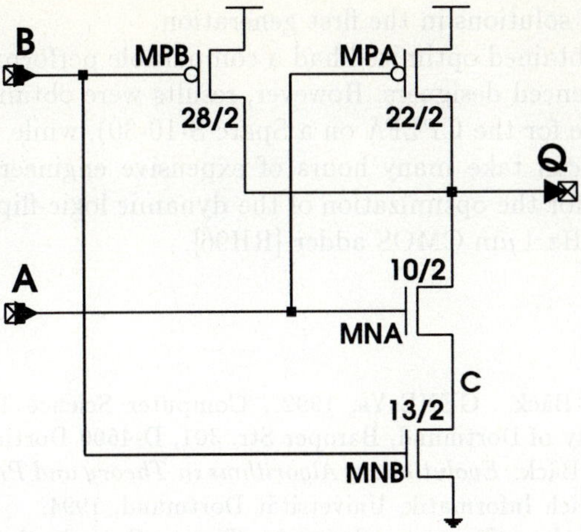

Fig. 7. 1 μm CMOS NAND gate with transistor sizes optimized by GA

charged by transistor *MPB*, input *B* is low and transistor *MNB* is off. In the worst case input *A* is high and transistor *MPB* has to charge not only the output *Q*, but also the internal node *C*. On the other hand, if the transistor *MPA* has to charge the output *Q*, input *A* is low, transistor *MNA* is turning off, and no internal capacitance has to be charged.

The difference between the sizes of the two PFETs may appear insignificant, but any additional transistor width translates straight to a higher power consumption. Furthermore, the capacitance of input *A* is more than 20 % smaller, which may appear insignificant for standard designs. However, in high-speed designs this may just be the critical quantity to maximize performance.

5 Conclusion

In this paper we have shown that the important but tedious work of manually optimizing transistor sizes of VLSI circuits can be accurately performed by stochastic optimization.

We have compared four stochastic optimization methods on three CMOS subcircuits of different complexity (6, 16, 34 MOSFETs). On the smaller two subcircuits the Monte Carlo method has been found to yield better results than the three genetic algorithms investigated. On the largest of the three subcircuits, in contrast, the genetic algorithms were found to yield significantly smaller variances provided they were allowed to run for a sufficient number of generations, which suggests that the Monte Carlo methods tends to end up in a suboptimal solution more frequently as problem size increases. Among the genetic algorithms, the most consistent results were obtained by using ranking selection and uniform crossover.

All our experiments started from a random seed - no initial guess was submitted. An advantage using genetic algorithms is the opportunity to include a set of good initial solutions in the first generation.

The circuits obtained optimized had a comparable performance as those optimized by experienced designers. However, results were obtained automatically (e.g. 8h CPU time for the CPLFA on a Sparc S-10-30), while manual optimization of a circuit can take many hours of expensive engineer's time. The GA has been applied for the optimization of the dynamic logic-flip-flops used in the design of a 800 MHz 1 μm CMOS adder [RH96].

References

[Bäc92] Thomas Bäck. GENEsYs, 1992. Computer Science Department, LSXI, University of Dortmund, Baroper Str. 301, D-4600 Dortmund 50, Germany.

[Bäc94] Thomas Bäck. *Evolutionary Algorithms in Theory and Practice.* PhD thesis, Fachbereich Informatik, Universität Dortmund, 1994.

[Heu90] L. S. Heusler. *Transistor Sizing for Timing Optimization of Combinational Digital CMOS Circuits.* PhD thesis, ETH Zürich, 1990.

[HK94] A. M. Hill and S-M. Kang. Genetic Algorithm Based Design Optimization of CMOS VLSI Circuits. In *Proceedings of the Third International Conference on Parallel Problem Solving from Nature - PPSN III*, pages 546–555, October 1994.

[Hsp] HSPICE - Circuit Simulator, Metasoft.

[MSV93a] Heinz Mühlenbein and Dirk Schlierkamp-Voosen. Predictive models for the breeder genetic algorithm. *Evolutionary Computation*, 1(1), 1993.

[MSV93b] Heinz Mühlenbein and Dirk Schlierkamp-Voosen. The science of breeding and its application to the breeder genetic algorithm. *Evolutionary Computation*, 1(4), 1993.

[RH95] R. Rogenmoser and Q. Huang. A 375 MHz 1-μm CMOS 8-Bit Multiplier. In *Proceedings of the 1995 Symposium on VLSI Circuits*, pages 13–14, June 1995.

[RH96] R. Rogenmoser and Q. Huang. An 800-MHz 1-μm CMOS Pipelined 8-bit Adder using True Single-Phase Clocked Logic-Flip-Flops. *IEEE Journal of Solid-State Circuits*, 31(3):401–409, March 1996.

[Sah64] C. T. Sah. Characteristics of the Metal-Oxide-Semiconductor Transistors. *IEEE Transactions on Electron Devices*, ED-11:324–345, July 1964.

[Sch81] H.-P. Schwefel. *Numerical Optimization of Computer Models.* Wiley, Chichester, 1981.

[Sys89] Gilbert Syswerda. Uniform crossover in genetic algorithms. In J. David Schaffer, editor, *Proceedings of the Third International Conference on Genetic Algorithms*, pages 2–9, San Mateo, CA, 1989. Morgan Kaufmann Publishers.

[Whi89] Darrell Whitley. The GENITOR algorithm and selection pressure: Why rank-based allocation of reproductive trials is best. In J. David Schaffer, editor, *Proceedings of the Third International Conference on Genetic Algorithms*, pages 116 - 121, San Mateo, CA, 1989. Morgan Kaufmann Publishers.

[Wur93] L. T. Wurtz. An Efficient Scaling Procedure for Domino CMOS Logic. *IEEE Journal of Solid-State Circuits*, 28(9):979–982, September 1993.

An Adaptive Parallel Genetic Algorithm for VLSI-Layout Optimization

Volker Schnecke and Oliver Vornberger

University of Osnabrück, Dept. of Math./Computer Science
D-49069 Osnabrück, Germany

Abstract. The generation of a high quality layout during the design of a VLSI microchip is a very complex combinatorial optimization problem. Components of a circuit have to be placed, and signal nets have to be routed on an overall minimal area. In this paper a parallel Genetic Algorithm for the combined optimization of placement and routing is presented. The main focus is on the self-adaptation of the search process: Several islands execute a sequential GA with different strategies. At fixed intervals these strategies are ranked and each strategy is adjusted to the next better one by assimilating its characteristical parameters.

1 Introduction

One strength of Genetic Algorithms (GAs) is their robustness, which mainly is caused by the fact that they deal with a sample of candidate solutions to an optimization problem at a time, and that these solutions are encoded in a problem independent representation. In most cases this *genotype* coding is a string *(chromosome)* of elementary data-types, preferably bits or floats. During the optimization process, new candidate solutions are composed using more or less standard mutation and crossover operators. When solving discrete real-world optimization problems by a GA, it is often necessary to use a complex (non string) genotype representation and operators which only generate admissible solutions. Problem-specific knowledge is often used for hillclimbing during the search.

After finding a feasible coding and implementing the operators, the 'only' work to do is to find a set of control parameters, that enable the GA to reach a global optimum and to minimize the time needed for convergence. Because these parameters depend on the representation and on the specific application, and might be changed during the evolution process, it is useful to add a self-adaptation mechanism for the values of these parameters.

In this paper, a parallel GA for a combinatorial optimization problem arising during the computer aided design of microchips is presented. The main feature of this algorithm is a tree-structured genotype representation with problem-specific operators. The paper is organized as follows: It starts with a description of the application and the chosen representation. After the outline of the genetic operators, the strategy adaptation is explained and results for real-world circuits are presented.

2 The Design of Macro-Cell Layouts

The layout generation is one of the most time consuming tasks in the design cycle for VLSI- (very large scale integrated) microchips [13, 17]. The input to this problem is a partitioned circuit, i. e. the elementary components of the circuit are grouped to build up to 50 *macro-cells* (modules). On the borders of these cells, *terminals* are located which have to be connected by *signal nets*.

The output of this design process is a layout for the circuit (fig. 1). The layout describes the *placement* of the cells and the routes for the interconnection wires between them. The main objective in layout optimization is to find an arrangement with a minimal overall area. Cells are not allowed to overlap each other, and the routing has to meet the technical constraints: space between parallel wires has to be added to prevent short circuits and for some critical nets the delay has to stay below a given threshold, which results in maximal admissible wirelengths for these nets.

Due to the complexity of the single tasks, *placement* of the cells is usually optimized separately from the computation of the *routing* for the interconnection nets. During placement an estimated amount of routing space is added, which restricts the maximal number of nets to be routed inside a *channel* between two cells. The following routing is two-phase: in the *global routing* the 'loose' (global) routes for all interconnection nets are determined, whereas during the *detailed routing* the exact ways for the wires in the channels between the modules are fixed. Due to an overestimation of the needed routing space during placement, the layout has to be *compacted* after completion. In case of fault estimation, the routing cannot be completed inside the reserved routing area. This is either realized during the computation of the global routes, or during channel routing. In the latter case, the process has to backtrack and different global routes for some nets have to be chosen. If even global routing is impossible, the modules have to be rearranged, i. e. the process has to backtrack to the placement task.

The splitting of the layout design process results from the fact that the combined optimization of both tasks is too complex to be managed by most optimization techniques. Nevertheless, because of the interdependencies between placement and routing, it is wise to combine both tasks.

3 Genetic Layout Optimization

The classical work on layout generation with GAs is done by Cohoon *et al.*[3, 4]. They encode a placement by a polish notation of a binary slicing tree, thus having a chromosome represented by a string. They use different recombination operators, which work either directly on this string, or take the tree structure into consideration by decoding the chromosome. Chan *et al.* [2] represent a placement in a bit-matrix. The layout area is divided into discrete regions and each row in the matrix describes the orientation and the position for a single cell. Recombination is done by mixing two matrices. During the optimization incorrect placements with overlapping cells are allowed and are handled by adding a

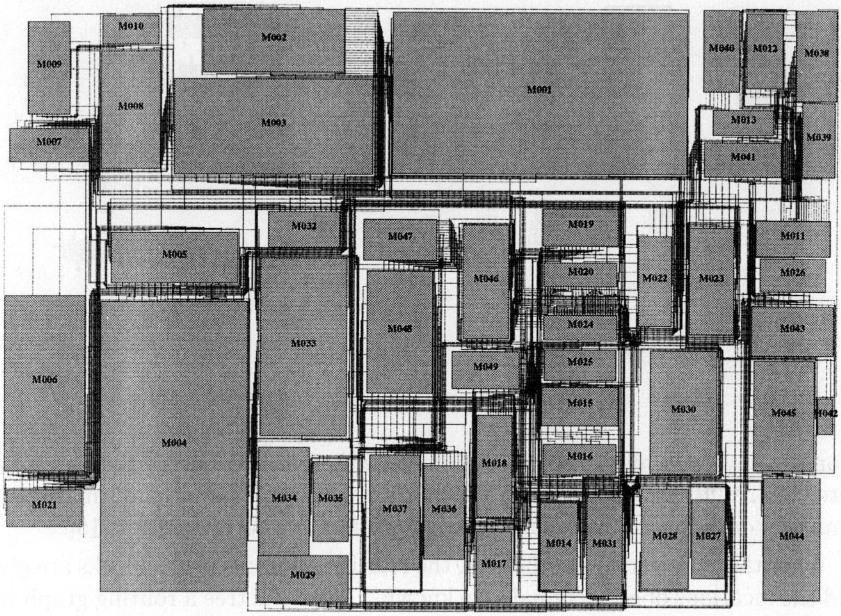

Fig. 1. A layout for the circuit *ami*49 with 49 macro-cells and 408 nets

penalty term when computing the fitness. Esbensen [6] describes a GA for macro cell placement where the genotype representation is a binary tree. In contrast to the approach of Cohoon *et al.*, this tree does not directly characterize a placement, but it can be generated by decoding the tree in a traversal due to a given order. His operators directly work on the tree structure.

The major drawback of the previously mentioned approaches is the fact, that they only optimize the placement without considering the routes to be chosen for the interconnection wirings. The approach described in this paper also uses a genotype representation as a binary tree and non-standard genetic operators, but here the global routes for the signal nets are computed before fixing the positions of the cells. Due to this, routing is not restricted by any limited capacities arising from wrong estimates for the need of routing space.

3.1 Genotype Representation

The genotype is encoded as a binary slicing tree, which defines the relative placement of the cells (fig. 2, left). It is composed in a bottom-up fashion. In each inner node two *blocks* (in the lowest level these are single cells) are joined to a *meta-block* (partial placement). In each meta-block the orientations of the combined blocks are fixed (fig. 2, right). If the blocks represent flexible macro-cells, which are cells with variable aspect ratios, different shapes are stored for the meta-block. Therefore every tree describes several possible shapes for the corre-

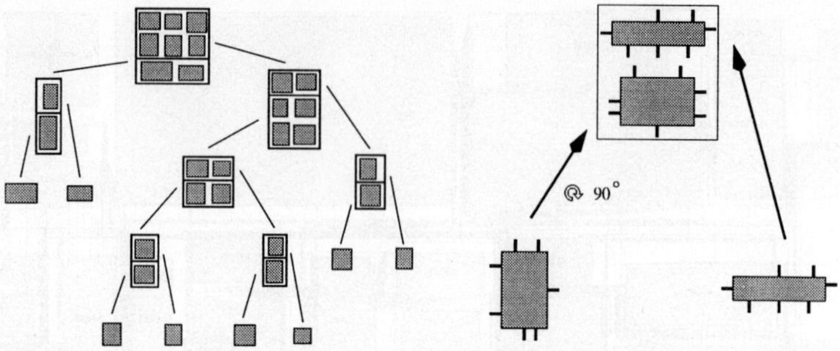

Fig. 2. The genotype (left), and the composition of a meta-block (right)

sponding layout, which enormously improves the performance of the GA. While here only results for circuits with fixed cells are presented, more information and empirical data for the flexible case can be found in a former paper [15].

After the construction of the tree, the relative positions of the blocks are given and the locations of all terminals are known. Out of the tree a routing graph (fig. 3, (II)) is constructed. The edges in this graph represent routing regions, which are parts of a channel, the vertices describe connections between two channels. For each net the shortest paths between its terminals in the routing graph are computed. Thus afterwards, the number of all nets routed through each region is known. For each channel inside a meta-block, routing space is added depending on the widest region within this channel (fig. 3, (III)).

During the construction of the initial individuals a special heuristic, the *iterated matching* introduced by Fritsch and Vornberger [10], is used to take care that highly connected cells are placed next to each other. For that purpose, out of all possible combinations those pairings of blocks are chosen which yield a maximal global quality with respect to the number of common nets. For further details on this point see [16].

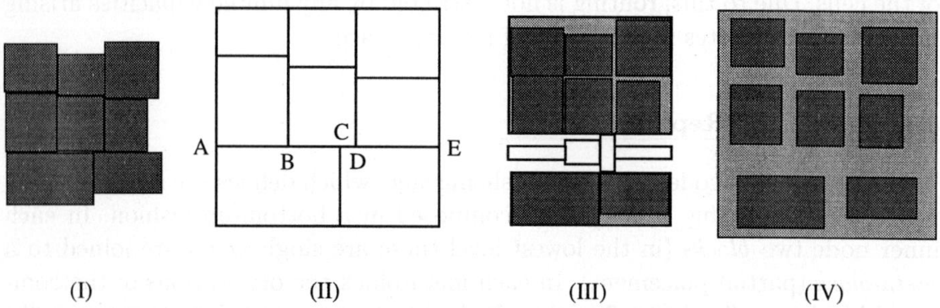

Fig. 3. A placement (I), the routing graph (II), the width for channel [A,E] is established by its widest region [C,D] (III), and the layout with added routing space (IV)

3.2 Genetic Operators

During the optimization process the placement of the blocks has to be changed and the routing has to be updated. The genetic operators directly work on the tree-structure by combining subtrees of different individuals (crossover) and modifying the tree of an individual (mutation).

The crossover operator takes two individuals out of which one offspring is composed by combining two disjunct subtrees of both parents. Unfortunately, these parts usually do not add up to a complete layout. After the combination of the two subtrees, the missing blocks have to be added to the tree to ensure that the offspring finally represents a correct layout. Here the iterated matching is used again to ensure that inside the added part of the layout highly connected cells are located near together.

A set of different mutation operators is used. The simplest operator changes the orientation of a block or a meta-block. Another operator exchanges subtrees inside the tree of the mutated individual. A distinction is made between exchanging simple blocks, a block (leaf) with a meta-block (subtree), and exchanging two meta-blocks. These cases represent the exchange of two cells, a cell with a partial layout, and the exchange of two partial layouts on the layout surface. Another mutation operator modifies the structure of the slicing tree by removing a subtree or a single block from the tree and inserting it at a different position. This corresponds to moving partial layouts or cells on the layout surface.

4 Strategy Adaptation

The performance of each GA depends on a set of control parameters like population size, crossover and mutation rates, and on the selection strategy. While there was a lot of work done in determining a globally optimal set of control parameters for a wide range of applications, in the nearer past some work on self-adapting GAs has been published. Here no static parameter set is determined, but an adaptation of the parameters during the optimization process takes place. This can be done by externally changing the mutation-rate in a predefined manner like Fogarty describes [8], or controlling the parameters of the GA by a simulated annealing like 'cooling-schedule', which is done by Esbensen and Mazumder in their GA for macro-cell placement [7]. Adaptation can be controlled by the evolution process itself by using a (meta-) GA for the optimization of the parameters like Bäck [1] or Freisleben and Härtfeler [9] have done. Wang *et al.* [18] introduce a hierarchy of GAs and suggest even to adapt the representation. The concept of *competing subpopulations* by Schlierkamp-Voosen and Mühlenbein [14] is a self adapting approach, where the sizes of subpopulations, which pursue different strategies, are adapted. Successful strategies are used by larger populations, while the size of less productive populations decreases.

The adaptation in this application also takes place on the subpopulation level, but here the population sizes are fixed, while the strategies are flexible. A strategy is characterized by a parameter set for the GA. The parameter set consists of the mutation rate, the crossover rate and the threshold for the truncation selection. Further a strategy fixes the frequency of the different mutation operators.

Due to the fact that the power of the crossover operator to create new individuals is limited to the combination of two subtrees of both parents, within this application mutation is more important than in common GAs with simple encoding. The crossover operator only combines meta-blocks, but never creates a small meta-block, because in both parents always 'real' subtrees (with more than one leaf) are chosen. Hence there are several mutation operators, and every offspring is created either by crossover or by mutation. In all generations the total number of created offspring is constant.

After a fixed interval all strategies are ranked, and the parameters of each strategy are adapted to the values of the next better strategy. The best strategy is expanded, i. e. its characteristical parameters are strengthened. For example, if the best strategy is distinguished by a low crossover rate, then this value will be decreased.

If the optimization on an island gets stuck, i. e. if no progress has been realized since the last adaptation, the strategy of this island is reset. Therefore the parameters are set back to one of the initial settings. This ensures that a strategy which has got lost in the beginning, but might be helpful at this time, is reactivated to boost the optimization.

The most important point in the implementation of an adaptation is to fix the quality criterion, regarding to which the strategies are ranked. In [14], the progress of the islands is measured based on the fitness of the best individuals observed over a period of time. Because of the small subpopulation size in this application, a fitness based quality criterion turned out to be not useful. This value is very much influenced by migrating individuals. A better criterion to describe the progress during the optimization process is the *response to selection* used in Mühlenbeins BGA [11]. This response is defined by the difference between the average fitness of a (sub-) population in two succeeding generations.

5 Results

The GA has been tested with real-world circuits. These are taken from a suite of benchmarks made available for design workshops in the early 90's, and are mostly cited in the literature as the MCNC-benchmarks[1]. It is still the most referenced benchmark suite for macro-cell layout generation, and includes partitioned circuits with 10 to 49 cells, and up to 408 nets.

In fig. 4 the effect of the strategy adaptation for a sample optimization run is visualized. The circuit is *ami*33, which consists of 33 cells and 123 nets. The

[1] The name has been historically established. These benchmarks were originally maintained by 'North Carolina's Microelectronics, Computing and Networking Center' (MCNC), but are now located at the CAD Benchmarking Laboratory, North Carolina State University.

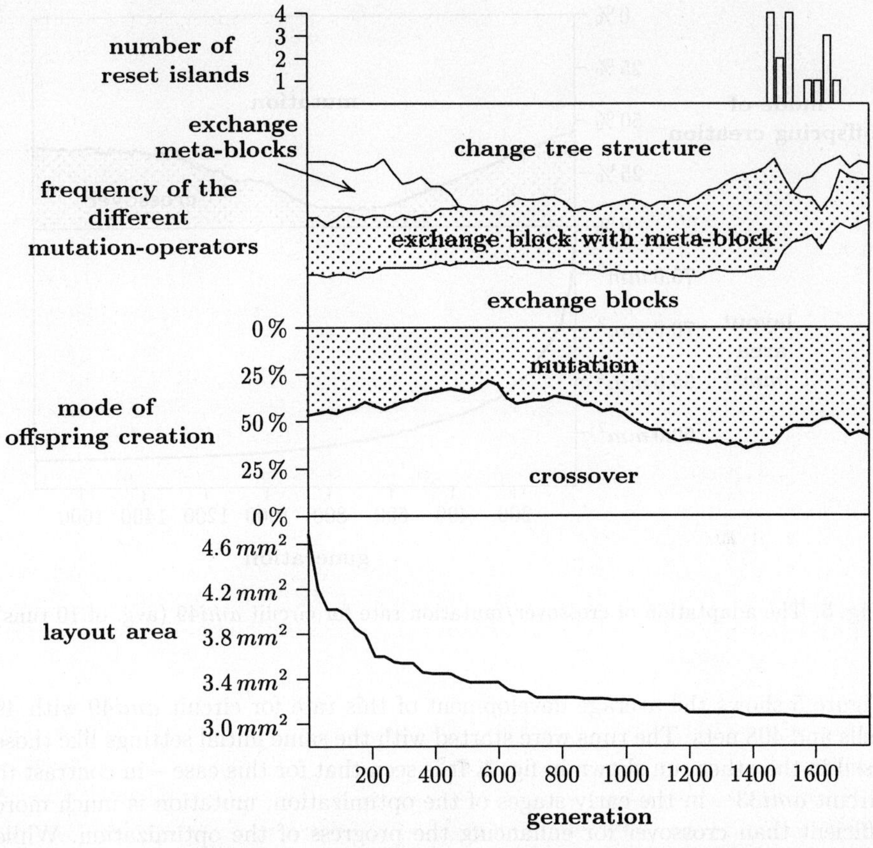

Fig. 4. The effect of the adaptation for a sample optimization run

results were achieved on a Parsytec GC/PP machine using a 12 processor network. Each island held a population of 20 individuals, the migration interval was 6 generations, and adaptation took place every 30 generations. An average of all values was taken over the 12 subpopulations except for the layout area (bottom), which describes the fitness of the best individual in the whole system. At the beginning of the optimization process, the crossover rate, i. e. the quota of offspring created using crossover rose up to 75 % around the 500th generation. After that point, with decreasing variation in the population, mutation replaced crossover as the favourite offspring creation method. At the end ($\approx$ after 1500 generations), some strategies were reset, which yielded in balancing out the crossover/mutation rate. The part of the figure which represents the frequency of the four tree-modifying mutation operators shows that the operator, which exchanges two meta-blocks might be useless, and that the changing of the tree structure seems to be more important, but this differs on single runs. Nevertheless, the shown progress of the mutation/crossover rate is typical for this circuit.

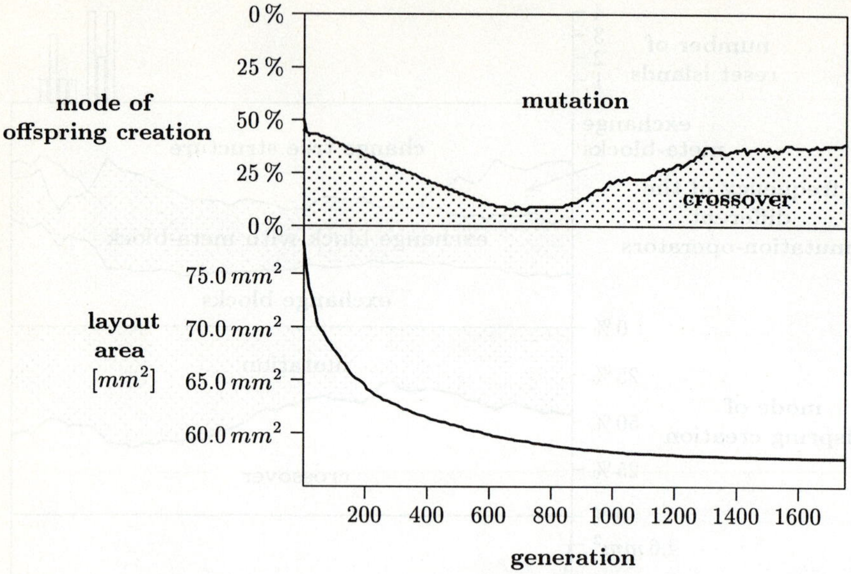

Fig. 5. The adaptation of crossover/mutation rate for circuit *ami*49 (avg. of 10 runs)

Figure 5 shows the average development of this rate for circuit *ami*49 with 49 cells and 408 nets. The runs were started with the same initial settings like those used in the other run shown in fig. 4. It is seen that for this case – in contrast to circuit *ami*33 – in the early stages of the optimization, mutation is much more efficient than crossover for enhancing the progress of the optimization. While both circuits differ in the number of cells and nets, the main difference is in the connectivity: each net in circuit *ami*33 connects an average of 3.7 terminals, whereas in circuit most nets only connect two terminals (avg. 2.3).

Figure 6 presents the effect of the adaptation on the performance, again for circuit *ami*33. The values are taken from runs on 16 processors with a subpopulation size of 10 individuals, an average of 20 runs is shown. The upper curve describes the performance resulting from experiments with the parameters set to the average values of the initial strategies of the general case. Thus all islands are pursuing the same strategy. The middle curve shows that the performance can be enhanced considerably, if the islands use different strategies. Note that in both cases no adaptation takes place. As it can be gathered from the lowest curve, the best performance is reached if the islands start with different strategies which are adapted during the search.

6 Conclusions and Future Work

The presented parallel GA computes densely packed placements for the modules of a circuit with short wirings for the signal nets. The main reasons for enabling

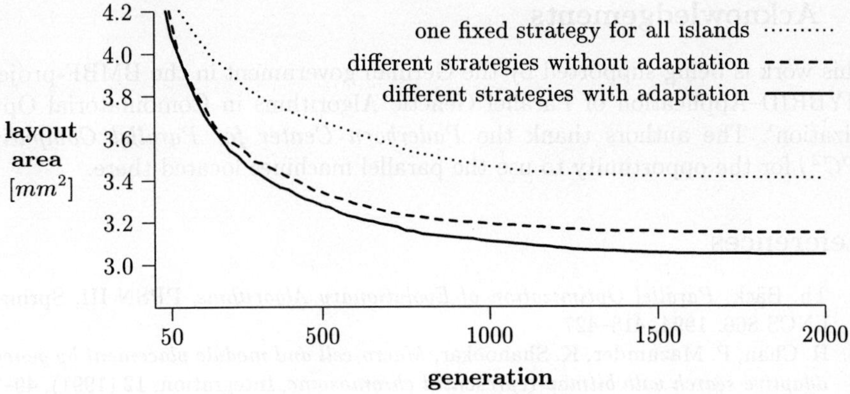

Fig. 6. The performance of the parallel GA depending on the use of different strategies and adaptation (avg. of 20 runs each)

the optimization of this real-world combinatorial problem by a GA are

- the use of a tree structured genotype encoding
- the integration of the routing in the placement process
- the application of problem-specific operators
- the strategy adaptation

Strategy adaptation returns to the GA some of its robustness, which may have been lost due to the inclusion of problem specific knowledge in the operators. It has been shown that especially the development of the crossover/mutation rate differs for the presented problems. Without adapting this parameter during the optimization, search would be less efficient.

After computing the global routes in the current implementation, the width chosen for a channel is too high in most cases, because one track is added for each net inside a routing region. This leads to layouts with an about 10 % larger area than the best results published in literature. Including a sophisticated detailed routing procedure before fixing the widths of the routing regions would avoid this drawback. Nevertheless, the main strength of GA described in this paper is the integration of the routing into the placement, which are usually separated tasks in other (genetic and non-genetic) approaches. Here the exact positions for the modules are fixed not until the computation of all global routes.

Further work in this project will be the implementation of a different recombination operator. Generating an offspring out of the trees of two parent individuals is not very efficient. On the one hand two **disjunct** subtrees have to be chosen, which decreases the number of potential pairings, and on the other hand a third part has to be added to produce a complete layout. Multi-parent crossover like it is used by Eiben *et al.* [5] or even implementing a gene-pool recombination operator like it is analysed in the work of Mühlenbein and Voigt [12] might improve the performance of the GA.

7 Acknowledgements

This work is being supported by the German government in the BMBF-project 'HYBRID–Application of Parallel Genetic Algorithms in Combinatorial Optimization'. The authors thank the *Paderborn Center for Parallel Computing (PC^2)* for the opportunity to use the parallel machines located there.

References

1. Th. Bäck, *Parallel Optimization of Evolutionary Algorithms*, PPSN III, Springer LNCS 866, 1994, 418–427
2. H. Chan, P. Mazumder, K. Shahookar, *Macro-cell and module placement by genetic adaptive search with bitmap-represented chromosome*, Integration, 12 (1991), 49–77
3. J. P. Cohoon, W. D. Paris, *Genetic Placement*, Proc. of IEEE Int. Conf. on CAD 1986, 422–425
4. J. P. Cohoon, S. U. Hegde, W. N. Martin, D. S. Richards, *Distributed Genetic Algorithms for the Floorplan Design Problem*, IEEE Trans. on CAD, Vol. 10 (4), April 1991, 483–492
5. A. E. Eiben, P.-E. Raué, Z. Ruttkay, *Genetic algorithms with multi-parent recombination*, PPSN III, Springer LNCS 866, 1994, 78–87
6. H. Esbensen, *A Genetic Algorithm for Macro Cell Placement*, Procs. of the European Design Automation Conference, 1992, 52–57
7. H. Esbensen, P. Mazumder, *SAGA: A Unification of the Genetic Algorithm with Simulated Annealing and its Application to Macro-Cell Placement*, Procs. of the 7th Int. Conf. on VLSI Design, 1994, 211–214
8. T. C. Fogarty, *Varying the Probability of Mutation in the Genetic Algorithm*, Procs. 3rd ICGA, J. D. Schaffer (ed), Morgan Kaufmann Publ., 1989, 104–109
9. B. Freisleben, M. Härtfelder, *Optimization of Genetic Algorithms by Genetic Algorithms*, Artificial Neural Nets and Genetic Algorithms, R. F. Albrecht, C. R. Reeves, N. C. Steele (eds.), Springer Verlag, 1993, 392–399
10. A. Fritsch, O. Vornberger, *Cutting Stock by Iterated Matching*, Operations Research Proceedings, U. Derigs, A. Bachem, A. Drexl (eds), Springer Verlag, 1995, 92–97
11. H. Mühlenbein, D. Schlierkamp-Voosen, *The science of breeding and its application to the breeder genetic algorithm BGA*, Evolutionary Comp., 1(4), 1994, 335–360
12. H. Mühlenbein, H.-M. Voigt, *Gene Pool Recombination in Genetic Algorithms*, Procs. of the Metaheuristics Int. Conf., I. H. Osman, J. P. Kelly (eds.), Kluwer Academic Publishers, Norwell, 1995
13. S. M. Sait, H. Youssef, *VLSI Physical Design Automation: Theory and Practice*, McGraw-Hill (1995)
14. D. Schlierkamp-Voosen, H. Mühlenbein, *Strategy Adaptation by Competing Subpopulations*, PPSN III, Springer LNCS 866, 1994, 199–208
15. V. Schnecke, O. Vornberger, *Genetic Design of VLSI-Layouts*, Procs. GALESIA '95, IEE Conference Publication No. 414, 1995, 430–435
16. V. Schnecke, O. Vornberger, *A Genetic Algorithm for VLSI Physical Design Automation*, Procs. ACEDC '96, University of Plymouth, UK, 1996, 53–58
17. N. Sherwani, *Algorithms for VLSI Physical Design Automation*, Kluwer Academic Publishers, 1993
18. G. Wang, E. D. Goodman, W. F. Punch, *Simultaneous Multi-Level Evolution*, Technical Report 96-03-01, MSU GARAGe, 1996

Evolutionary Computation in Computer Science and Operations Research

Genetic Algorithms for Protocol Validation

Enrique Alba and José M. Troya

Dpto. de Lenguajes y Ciencias de la Computación, Univ. de Málaga
Campus de Teatinos (2.2.A.6), 29071- MÁLAGA, España
{alba, troya}@tecma1.ctima.uma.es

Abstract. We present a first attempt in applying a genetic algorithm for checking the correctness of communication protocols (expressed as a pair of communicating FSMs). The GA measures the fitness of a given string by making use of a protocol simulator. Every string in the population is a trace of the execution of the protocol. The simulator evaluates the trace by running it, provoking changes and messages exchanges in the states of every FSM. The fitness of a string (trace) is high if the string detects a deadlock or if useless states or transitions are encountered. We are interested in testing the suitness of the GA search in such a domain. We have tested this genetic validation on a hand-made protocol and on the Transmission Control Protocol (TCP).

1 Introduction

The validation of a newly developed protocol is a major issue in the field of communication protocols. The existing work in this field always begins with a first phase of unambiguous specification of the protocol with a formal technique: Finite State Machines (FSMs), Petri Nets or specification languages as DRL[4], LOTOS[7] or STELLE[8] in order to facilitate the second phase, namely validation. Since the space of all possible system states is very large, recent works are shifting to the application of heuristics as an alternative to exhaustive or other existing search procedures. The applications of GAs [3][5] on different domains [1][2] are growing. In this work we want to study how a GA (GAVOR v3.0) can validate protocols.

In order to reach this goal we must define the genotype representation for any partial solution and the kind of fitness computations for characterising it. The magnitude of the search for a medium sized protocol is very high. When a communicating entity resides in a given state of its FSM, the set of possible states the other entity could reside, the contents of its (remote) messages queue and the local messages queue conform a very large search space. We are not evolving FSMs as in [6], but instead we are validating the protocol they represent.

In the design of truly working protocols (videoconferencing, multimedia, etc.) it is very important the validation of the protocol, that is, the formal warranty that the protocol does not hang up in deadlock, no messages between the PPEs are ignored or lost, and that all the devised states and transitions of the FSMs are useful. We want to complain with all these goals with the exception of lost messages (for the moment). It is very frequent that the protocol can be modelled as a FSM that is executed by the client and the server nodes. Stated in a more formal way, the communicating Peer Protocol Entities (PPEs) residing in a given level of the hierarchy of layers being developed are exchanging messages. This exchange is driven by the user actions or by the actual FSM state and input message. Of course every PPE can be in a different state of its underlying FSM. Fig. 1 depicts the whole scenario.

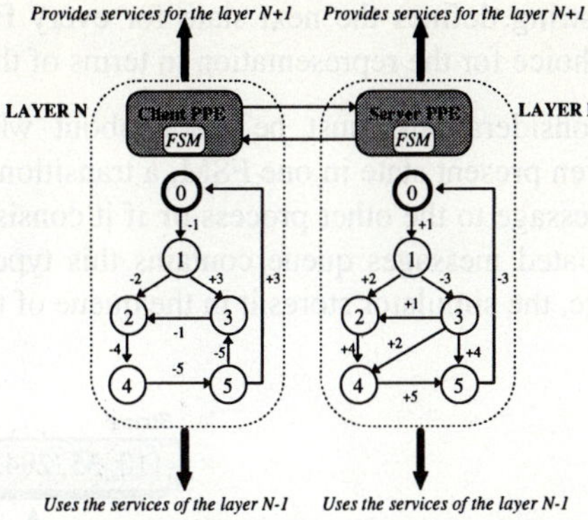

Fig. 1. *Architecture of a sample communication protocol (EXP protocol) with 2 FSMs representing both the client and the server ends. Positive values represent input messages and negative values are output messages.*

Fig. 1 shows the two PPEs each one executing its own FSM. In the most simple situation every transition is an input (positive) or output (negative) reception/transmission of a message. Messages of the same type share the same absolute value. In the rest of the paper we first state the meaning of the genotype and how crossover works. We then present the details of our measurement of the fitness and finally we expose the results and some considerations on the future work.

2 Genotype and Crossover

The first stage we face is to devise a chromosomal representation of a solution to our validation problem. Since we are interested in detecting deadlock, non-visited states and non-fired transitions, we define the strings in the population as encoding a trace of the execution of the system. This means that we will have to manage variable-length strings in the same population. Every gene in the chromosome (string position) is coded as a byte (values ranging from 0 to 255). If a gene has value `x` then the `x`-th firable transition of the actual state in the FSM will be fired. In this way the chromosome represents a sequence of system transitions.

Two problems arise from this gene interpretation. The former is concerned with its numeric value, because if a gene indicates, for example, that 56-th transition must fire, and the actual state has only 2 or 3 firable transitions (or even 0!) some mapping from the string to the actual value is needed. We make a kind of fixed remapping [3] by means of which we take `(x mod ft)` as the transition to fire, where `x` is the string value and `ft` is the *number of firable transitions* for the present state in the FSM (Fig. 2a).

The later problem with this encoding is related to the number of processes. At present we consider only two communicating processes in the system, thus we should need two different traces. One possible solution could have been to use diploid genomes and a dominance operator like in [5]. But we have decided to utilise the same haploid string as representing the two traces, because the two FSMs will be in general in different states and will have different sets of firable transitions. In this way the same gene of the string defines the next state for every FSM (Fig. 2b). This is thought to be a better choice for the representation in terms of the BBs hypothesis.

Some final considerations must be made about what we call a **firable transition**. For any given present state in one FSM, a transition is *firable* if it consists in sending an output message to the other process **or** if it consists in receiving a given message **and** its associated messages queue contains this type of message. When a process sends a message, the simulator stores it in the queue of the other process.

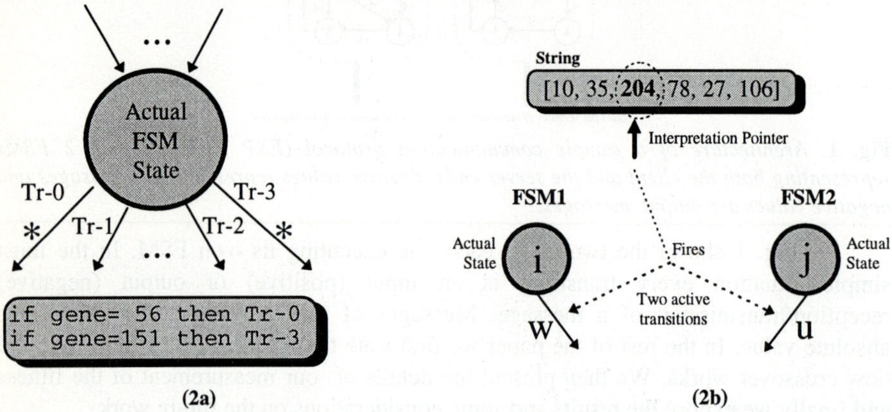

Fig. 2. *Genotype representation for genetic validation.* **(2a)** *Every gene is a positive integer. We take the* **mod** *value with respect to the number of firable transitions. The transitions with the * symbol are active. So if the current gene in the string is an even number then transition 0 will fire and if it is an odd number transition 3 will fire. In* **(2b)** *the interpretation of a string is showed. The pointer moves from left to right firing different transitions in the two FSMs.*

If we want to validate more complicated protocols then we need also to devise a more elaborated conception of a transition. We need, in every transition, an input and output parts. The FSM proceeds from a state to another one only if the input message specified in the transition is also present in its messages queue. When the transition fires the message in the output part is sent to the other process. In order to model user commands or messages from an upper layer of the protocol family, we define an **event** to be a special input message that can be always considered firable.

v2.0

```
2 //Nr. of processes
process 0:            process 1:
8 //Nr. of transits.  9
0 1 -1                0 1 +1
1 2 -2                1 2 +2
1 3 +3                1 3 -3
2 4 -4                2 4 +4
3 2 -1                3 2 +1
4 5 -5                3 4 +2
5 3 -5                3 5 +4
5 0 +3                4 5 +5
//ist-ost-iomsg       5 0 -3
```

v3.0

```
2 //Nr. of processes
process 0:            process 1:
8 //Nr. of transits.  9
0 1 ^0 -1             0 1 +1 -0
1 2 ^0 -2             1 2 +2 -0
1 3 +3 -0             1 3 ^0 -3
2 4 ^0 -4             2 4 +4 -0
3 2 ^0 -1             3 2 +1 -0
4 5 ^0 -5             3 4 +2 -0
5 3 ^0 -5             3 5 +4 -0
5 0 +3 -0             4 5 +5 -0
//ist-ost-imsg-omsg   5 0 ^0 -3
```

Fig. 3. *Two versions of files representing the FSMs in the fig. 1. The files contain the number of processes, the number of transitions per process and the transitions themselves. Every line is composed of the actual state, the next state and the transition (v2.0 in/out as a single message and v3.0 in-out as two separate messages). The first version (v2.0, left) considers transitions as input or output exchanges of messages. The later version (v3.0, right) introduces the event ^0 as the input part of an output transition. For input transitions we output a NULL (-0) message.*

We have developed a version of GAVOR for every kind of transition. In the above figure two input protocol files with the FSMs of Fig. 1 are showed. The two files represent the same sample protocol but in different versions of our GAVOR package. You can see that transitions with only output messages (always firable) in version 2 are encoded in version 3 with NULL input events (also always firable). With our coding we have tried double point crossover (DPX) because of its easy application to this domain and its widely recognised benefits. In the crossover implementation we encourage the creation of new traces.

3 Fitness Computations

For the computation of fitness values we need a complete simulator of the protocol being validated. For every trace (string) we run the simulator module and add a `D_FITNESS` quantity if a deadlock is encountered. For every non-visited state and every non-fired transition (it is not the same) we add the values `NV_FITNESS` and `NF_FITNESS` respectively.

With this evaluation scheme we need a value for `D_FITNESS` much larger than the other two values, because a deadlock detection is far more important than a useless state or transition.. One straightforward drawback is that if several enough states and transitions are not visited/fired by the trace the computed fitness can be larger than for traces that detect deadlock. This situation can be avoided if we choose `D_FITNESS>>NV_FITNESS>NF_FITNESS`. The GA maximises this fitness.

Fitness = D_FITNESS*deadlock_present + NV_FITNESS*number_nv_states + NF_FITNESS*number_nf_transitions

We have tried another kind of fitness computation consisting in penalising bad strings (the inverse of the above function but removing first the deadlock term). The results have been bad (we need a refinement) and are not reported here.

We also need to impose lower and upper limits to the initial length of the traces created for the initial population, since a too short trace will fail in representing a good tour over the FSM states and transitions while a very long trace will spent a great deal of computational resources unnecessarily. At runtime we promote (the crossover operator does it) traces of short length but do not impose limits on length.

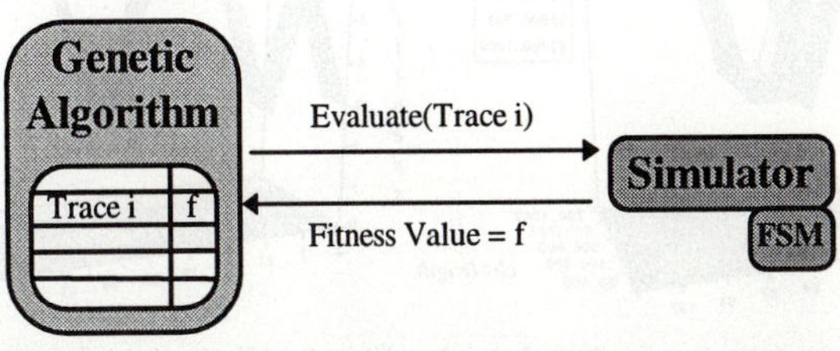

Fig. 4. *Interaction between the GA and the Simulator. The GA terminates execution when a user given number of steps has been reached. The best string stands for the maximum number of protocol violations. If the best final fitness is 0 then the GA has validated the protocol.*

4 Analysis of Results

In this section we study the efficacy and efficiency of the devised GA for the validation of two different protocols. The first protocol is the example protocol (EXP) depicted in Fig. 1 and the second one is the well-known TCP from the TCP/IP protocol family. We will perturb the original protocol by introducing deadlocks and by disabling some states and transitions in order to study the efficacy of the GA in detecting such specification errors. The EXP considers two different FSMs while the TCP protocol has a unique FSM that is run at both ends. Also the complexity of the TCP protocol is considerably greater, thus we only will use the EXP for a detailed study. TCP will be used for testing the bounds of the applicability in GA validation.

4.1 The EXP Protocol

Despite the small number of states (6+6 in total) in the EXP protocol it presents the main characteristics of a general protocol, with the added interest of using two different finite state machines (for the client and server ends).

Validating The Correct EXP Protocol.

First we want to validate the correct version of this protocol (GA parameters shown in the Table 1). Although the protocol is correct at a first glance (for a human) the GA validator had some troubles with respect to the initial length of the traces. With a value of between 20 and 100 for the initial length of strings we have always got some non-fired transitions and 1 or 2 non-visited states (typically the state 2 of FSM_1). Fig. 5 shows the results for different ranges of length.

Table 1.- *Basic Parameters for the tests with GAVOR v3.0*

Selection:	Roulette Wheel and Random Parents
Replacement:	Steady-State
Crossover:	Double Point with P_c=1.0
Mutation:	Random Transition with P_m=0.1
PopSize:	50 individuals
Nrecombin.:	100
Seeds:	{3, 7, 11, 17, 19, 23, 34, 57, 93, 137}
D_FITNESS=10	**NV_FITNESS=2 NF_FITNESS=1**

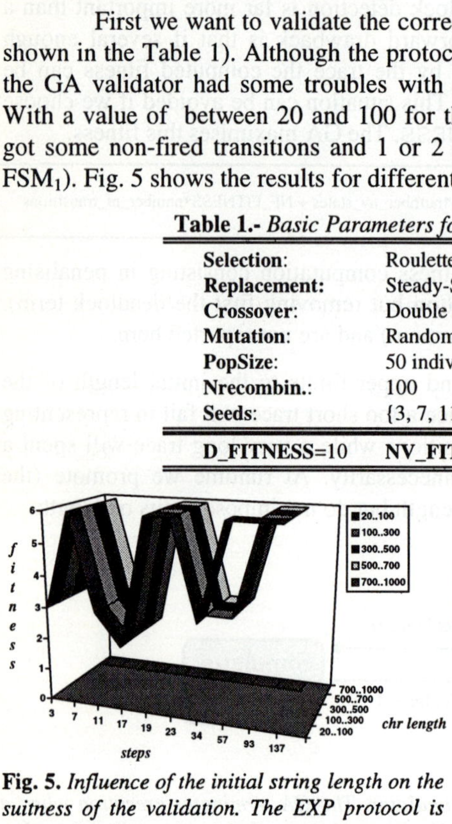

Fig. 5. *Influence of the initial string length on the suitness of the validation. The EXP protocol is correct but low string lengths make some states and transitions to appear as useless. Only 700..1000 validates.*

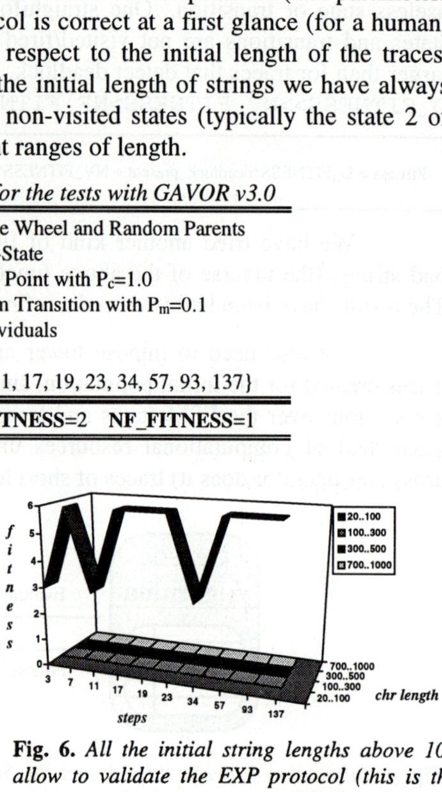

Fig. 6. *All the initial string lengths above 100 allow to validate the EXP protocol (this is the correct result since we are validating a correct protocol) when a population of 100 individuals is used.*

Since we suspected that length from 700 to 1000 was a somewhat excessive value for this relatively small protocol we enlarged the population size up to use 100 individuals and then we got a perfect validation for any initial string length greater than 100 (Fig. 6). Only the traces with lengths between 20 and 100 failed in recognising that the protocol was correct albeit the significance of their final error values is minor (two non-fired transitions and one non-visited state).

Disturbing the Correct EXP Protocol.

In these tests we want to show that GAVOR performs different levels of validation. First we have changed in FSM_0 the transition from the states 1 to 2 by removing the -2 output message and by adding a +2 input message (Fig. 7). In all the 10 runs GAVOR found that this transition was now non-firable. But also it concluded that the transitions 1-2 and 3-4 from the FSM_1 had also became non-firable because our disruption in FSM_0 had eliminated all the sources of the -2 messages and therefore any transition with a +2 condition was non-firable. This means a fitness of 3 (1+1+1).

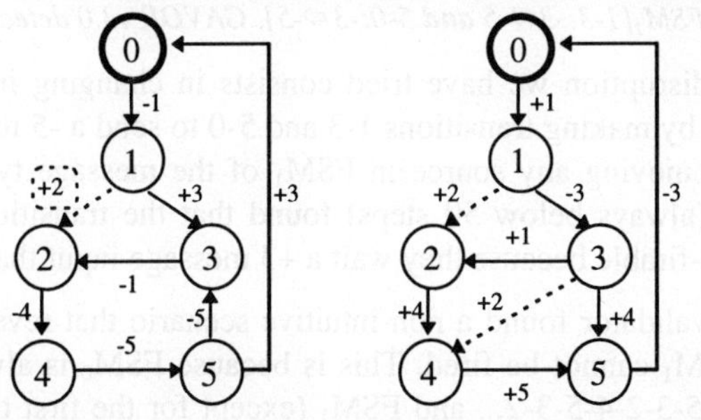

Fig. 7. *Useless Transition: FSM_0[1-2:-2⇨+2]. GAVOR v3.0 found it.*

The second kind of disruption we have introduced in the original EXP is to change in FSM_0 the transition 1-2 from -2 to +2 and also the transition 2-4 from -4 to +4 (Fig. 8). These changes are known to introduce a deadlock in the system. We want GAVOR to discover this deadlock. The runs perform very consistently in computing traces of fitness 29 (11 non-fired transitions plus 4 non-visited states plus deadlock fitness ⇨ 11*1 +2*4+10=29). We have tried initial lengths of 2..10, 5..10, 10..20 and 20..100 with 10 and with 50 individuals in the population and for every one of the 10 different seeds. The most usual trace do not visit the states 4 and 5 in any of the FSMs. In fact this is true because it is impossible to visit them!

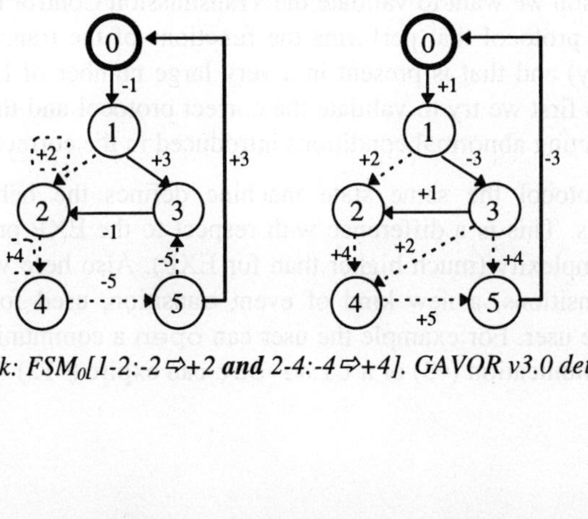

Fig. 8. *Deadlock: FSM_0[1-2:-2⇨+2* ***and*** *2-4:-4⇨+4]. GAVOR v3.0 detected this deadlock.*

In these runs we have also detected an interesting side-effect of the implementation in that when the actual state in the first FSM has two firable transitions, (O and I messages), it always fires the one with the output message. This is because we always simulate FSM_0 first and then FSM_1. With a random selection of the first FSM to simulate for every transition fire, this problem has been removed.

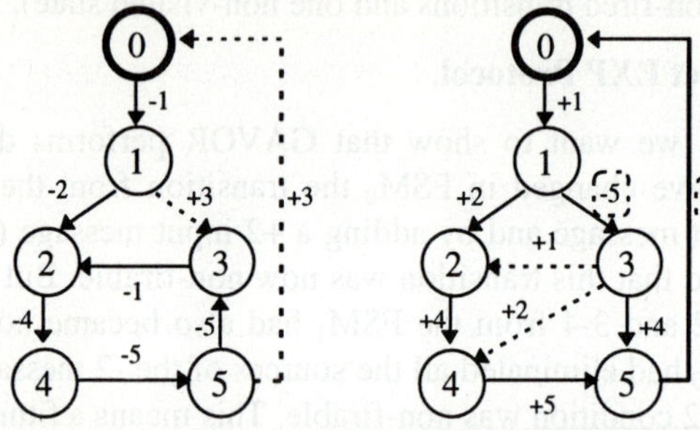

Fig. 9. *Livelock: FSM_1[1-3:-3⇨-5 and 5-0:-3⇨-5]. GAVOR v3.0 detected this condition.*

The last disruption we have tried consists in changing in the original EXP protocol the FSM_1 by making transitions 1-3 and 5-0 to send a -5 message instead of a -3 message thus removing any source in FSM_1 of the message type 3 (Fig. 9). Our validator quickly (always below 50 steps) found that the transitions 1-3 and 5-0 of FSM_0 are now non-firable because they wait a +3 message input that never arrives.

Also the validator found a non-intuitive scenario that reveals that transitions 3-2 and 3-4 in FSM_1 cannot be fired. This is because FSM_0 is always looping in its internal cycle 2-4-5-3-2-4-5-3-2... and FSM_1 (except for the first time in that it visits 0-1-2-4-5-0) is always making the same (its only permissible) loop: 0-1-3-5-0-1-3... consuming the -1 message from FSM_0 in its 0-1 transition and not in its 3-2 transition.

This kind of hidden synchronisation can make some transitions useless. In our example, FSM_1 receives messages of type 1 but they are never consumed in the 3-2 transition, but always in the 0-1 transition. Known or not, this scenario provokes a sort of *livelock* in that there exists at least one possible infinite execution that makes transition 3-2 non-firable although messages of type 1 are being received. Livelocks are typically undesired factors in any parallel system and GAVOR can detect them.

4.2 Validating The TCP

In this section we want to validate the Transmission Control Protocol. This is a broadly extended protocol that performs the functions of the transport layer (after the OSI terminology) and that is present in a very large number of LANs and in the Internet. In the tests first we try to validate the correct protocol and then we study the GA efficacy in detecting abnormal conditions introduced in the correct protocol.

In this protocol the same state machine defines the behaviour of both communication ends. This is a difference with respect to the EXP protocol. Another difference is its complexity (much higher than for EXP). Also here we have, besides the I/O normal transitions, a new kind of event transition, used for modelling the interactions with the user. For example the user can `open` a communication path (^2) or `close` the communication (^3) or a `time-out` can expire (^12) -see Fig. 10-.

Validating The Correct TCP.

In this section we want to validate the original TCP. Due to the magnitude of the search for this protocol, we consider a hit if we approach near enough to a perfect genetic validation (fitness 30 or so). Fig. 10 depicts the basic TCP finite state machine we are using. Of course a trace of fitness 0 only indicates that, at least, there exists a given good execution. If we do not find deadlock we are not absolutely sure that it does not exist, but when averaged on all the runs, if no trace finds deadlock we are reasonably sure it doesn't exist (if we find deadlock we only know it is invalid).

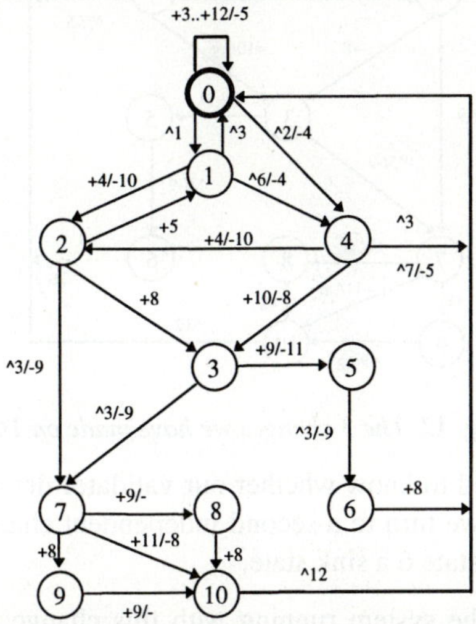

MEANING OF THE STATES

0	CLOSED
1	LISTEN
2	SYN RECVD
3	ESTABLISHED
4	SYN SENT
5	CLOSE WAIT
6	LAST ACK
7	FIN WAIT-1
8	CLOSING
9	FIN WAIT-2
10	TIMED WAIT

MEANING OF THE I/O MESSAGES

1	passive_open	7	time-out
2	active_open	8	ack
3	close	9	fin
4	syn	10	syn+ack
5	reset	11	fin+ack
6	send	12	wait

Fig. 10. *Finite State Machine forTCP. Since GAVOR v3.0 doesn't allow more than 1 transition between a given couple of states we have considered for the transitions 0➔0 only the +8/-5 (ack/reset). The same holds for the two transitions 4➔0 in that we only consider the ^3 (close).*

The conclusions about the results are somewhat difficult because we have not elaborated more complete statistics on the whole execution of the GA. We still need to consider the quantitative value for the probability of making good interpretations of the results. For example, if we detect a deadlock we are sure (Pr=1) that deadlock exists. If we do not detect deadlock, which is the probability (Pr=?) that deadlock is not really present in the protocol?. We are still developing a numeric interpretation.

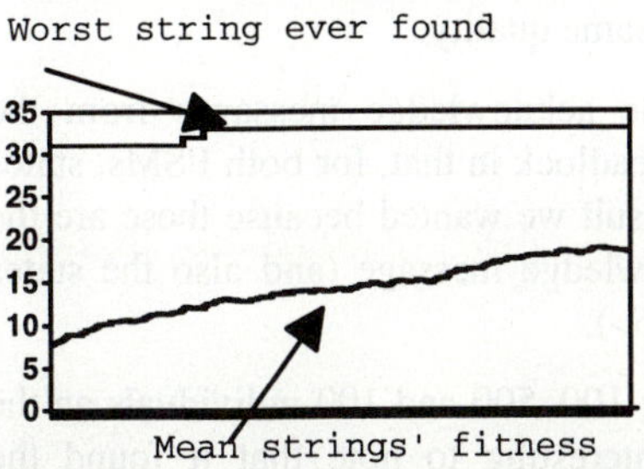

-*-*-VISITS TO STATES IN PROCESS #0-*-*-

ST0	ST1	ST2	ST3	ST4	ST5	ST6	ST7	ST8	ST9	ST10
29	14	5	5	18	2	1	7	5	2	7

-*-*-VISITS TO STATES IN PROCESS #1-*-*-

ST0	ST1	ST2	ST3	ST4	ST5	ST6	ST7	ST8	ST9	ST10
20	9	6	4	14	1	1	8	4	3	7

Fig. 11. *Genetic validation of TCP. The graphic shows the worst and mean search that strings perform for 500 recombinations of 100 strings with between 500 and 700 of initial length. The GA cannot find any deadlock or other errors (this protocol is error free).*

Disturbing the Correct TCP.

We have tried to validate three independent and incorrect versions of the original TCP. First we have changed the event ^6 from the states 1 to 4 to a new +6 (never-firable) message reception. The second disruption consists in inducing a deadlock by eliminating the only output transition (+8) from the state 6. The last disruption removes the -8 messages from the FSMs (`ack`'s won't be sent).

For the change ^6⇨+6 all the computed traces report that transition 1-4 is always inactive. We have used the parameters in Table 1 and also we have tried initial lengths of 100..500 and 100 individuals instead of only 50. The execution is slower (10 minutes) but the traces worked out more accurate results.

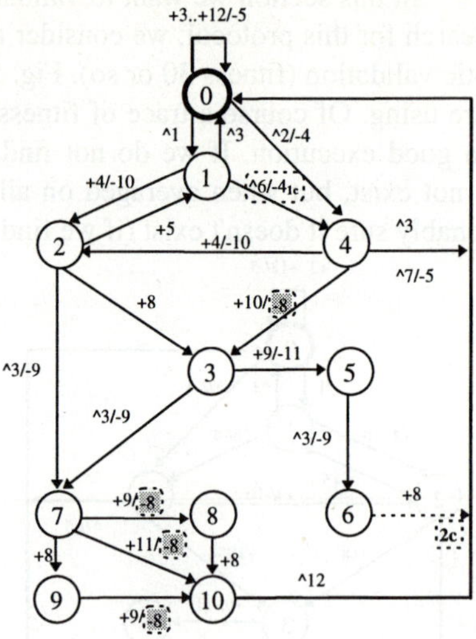

Fig. 12. *The 3 changes we have made on TCP.*

With the ^6⇨+6 disruption we wanted to know whether our validator detects useless transitions. Once we know that it do, we turn to a second independent change on the original TCP, consisting in making the state 6 a sink state.

Despite many working traces keep the system running with this change (in practice TCP can work properly with this sink state) many traces converge to the detection of deadlocks. For example, a trace with fitness 26 (10+6+10) present the final conclusion of deadlock and informs that in the client end the transitions 0-0, 2-1, 3-5 and 5-6 have not been fired, and in the server, 0-0, 1-4, 2-1, 7-9, 7-10 and 9-10 are also non-fired transitions.

With regard to the visited states in the client end, 5, 6 and 9 have not been visited while in the server process all the states have been visited (the last of them being number 6). This represents a deadlock in which the server stuck in state 6 and the client wait a never arriving message from the server. We have also tried 100..500 and 100 individuals but the results remain of the same quality.

Our last test consists in removing the acknowledge messages from the protocol. The genetic validator always found a deadlock in that, for both FSMs, states 3, 5, 6, 9 and 10 are never visited. This is the result we wanted because these are the states to which evolve after receiving an acknowledge message (and also the states only accessible by passing through them <5 and 6>).

We have extended this last test by using 100..500 and 100 individuals an the results always conclude this situation. It is interesting to note that it found the solutions quickly (10 runs in 4 minutes): the detection of deadlock is very evident.

5 Conclusions and Future Work

In this work we have attempted the validation of two communication protocols (EXP and TCP) by means of a genetic algorithm (GAVOR v3.0 package). The genotype we have used is a variable-length string (initially generated with bounded length) representing a trace (for the 2 FSMs) that defines the dynamic behaviour of the protocol. The fitness of every trace is measured by simulating the trace on the FSMs and by adding some reward value depending on how many non-visited states, non-fired transitions and deadlocks are detected.

Our results in the genetic validation are very promising and robust. This approach has proved to be good in detecting useless states and transitions in the protocol specification that represent common errors in the designer's work. Deadlocks are also detected with efficiency and livelocks are (indirectly) reported.

The technique does need some refinements with respect to the fitness computation, a different remapping from genotype to phenotype and the parameterization of the GA. Finally, the genetic search presents some problems in refining the results for large protocols. We are testing several improvements on this approach: to count for the loss of messages, to decide on how to manage the messages that remain in queue when simulation ends and studying the degree of confidence. Also a global and continued interpretation (statistics and runtime decisions) of every string worked out could allow a best validation (at present we are trying this).

References

[1] Alba, E., Aldana, J. F. and Troya, J. M., **Genetic Algorithms as Heuristics for Optimising ANN Design**. R.F. Albrecht, C.R. Reeves and N.C. Steele (eds), Artificial Neural Nets and Genetic Algorithms, Innsbruck. Springer-Verlag, pp 683-690. (1993)

[2] Alba, E., Aldana, J. F. and Troya, J. M., **Load Balancing and Query Optimisation in Dataflow Parallel Evaluation of Datalog Programs**. Lionel M. Ni (ed), Proceedings of the International Conference on Parallel and Distributed Systems, Taiwan. IEEE Computer Society Press, pp 682-688. (1994)

[3] Beasley, D., Bull, D. R. and Martin, R. R., **An Overview of Genetic Algorithms: Part 1 (Fundamentals) and Part 2 (Research Topics)**. University Computing, pp 58-69 15(2) and 15(4) pp 170-181. (1993)

[4] Díaz, M. and Troya, J.M., **A Parlog Based Real-Time Distributed Environment**. Future Generation Computer Systems 9, pp 201-218, North-Holland. (1993)

[5] Goldberg, D. E., **Genetic Algorithms, in Search, Optimization and Machine Learning**. Addison-Wesley. (1989)

[6] Fogel, L. J., Owens, A. J. and Walsh, M. J., **Artificial Intelligence Through Simulated Evolution**. New York, John Wiley. (1966)

[7] ISO, **LOTOS-A Formal Description Technique Based on the Temporal Ordering of Observational Behaviour**. ISO IS 8807. (1989)

[8] ISO, **ESTELLE-A Formal Description Technique Based on State Transition Model**. ISO 9074. (1989)

Constraint Handling for the Fault Coverage Code Generation Problem: An Inductive Evolutionary Approach

George Bilchev* and Ian Parmee*

*Plymouth Engineering Design Centre, University of Plymouth, PL4 8AA, UK
GBilchev@plymouth.ac.uk

Abstract. Real world problems quite often are constrained and their successful solution requires the application of an appropriate constraint handling technique. The lack of a uniform methodology for handling nonfeasible points largely predetermines the current best practice – the investigation of some problem-specific operators which search (within) the feasibility boundary in an efficient way. In this paper we apply this approach to a real world problem provided by Rolls Royce and Associates Ltd., and show how to design feasibility preserving operators that map the feasibility region onto itself. Some of our results provoke new ideas of how to modify real-time test and monitoring systems so as to increase their reliability.

1. Introduction

Various constraint handling techniques have recently emerged [1]. However, there is still no uniform methodology for handling unfeasible points. Current best practice involves the investigation of some problem-specific operators, which search the feasibility boundary in an efficient way [2]. This idea is based on the seemingly reasonable assumption that in real world problems the constraints and the objective functions are conflicting and therefore, the constraint global solution lies on the boundary of the feasible region.

In this paper we use a real world problem (section 2) to demonstrate a very efficient constraint handling technique. It consists of defining the feasible region in terms of the independent variables and designing feasibility preserving operators (i.e. operators that map the feasible region onto itself) (section 3). The existence of such a closed form description of the feasible space leads to a minimal redundancy problem representation [3] and could significantly reduce the search space. Currently the feasibility preserving constraint handling technique is being applied successfully to the optimization of real valued functions and linear constraints [4], and for combinatorial problems. In this paper we extend the applicability of the approach to include the fault coverage test code generation problem [5] with additional constraint requirements imposed by the designers of the circuit's logic.

We consider the reduction of a search space to be one of the most efficient approaches for solving any search problem. This idea has been fundamental for many of the existing search methodologies, including branch-and-bound, clustering, etc. In this paper we also propose to integrate the search space reduction approach with an evolutionary search engine (section 4). The idea has already produced successful results when applied to optimization of real valued continuous functions [6][7].

2. The Fault Coverage Test Code Generation Problem

Test and Monitoring Systems (TAMS) are widely used for real-time testing of the functionality of electronic circuits (fig. 1). Basically they operate by regularly initiating a test cycle on the circuit and monitoring the fault status. An integral part of the TAMS is a fault coverage test code consisting of a set of input test vectors and a set of expected output vectors. New circuits cannot be used until the fault coverage code is updated with a new set of comprehensive test vectors (fig. 2).

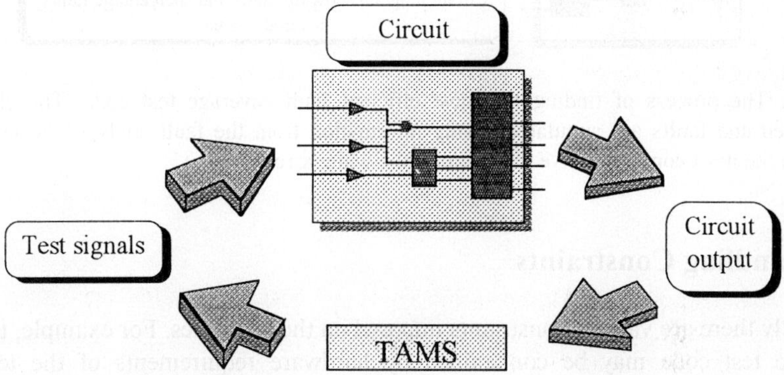

Fig. 1. Overview of test and monitoring system (TAMS)

Fault analysis is the process used to determine the fault detection coverage of a particular design. The fault analysis process for a design involves the optimization of the input stimulus to fully exercise all components to increase the testability, while logic simulation involves the optimization of the functionality of the design. These tasks are very different processes, and both tasks are necessary within the design development process. The fault analysis process fits within the product development cycle after the initial functional verification of the design and before the physical hardware testing of the product.

The amount of fault coverage within a design depends on the following two factors: (1) comprehensiveness of the test code, and (2) inherent testability of the logic design. In this paper we concentrate on the first factor and formulate the problem of finding an effective set of input test vectors as a *search problem*.

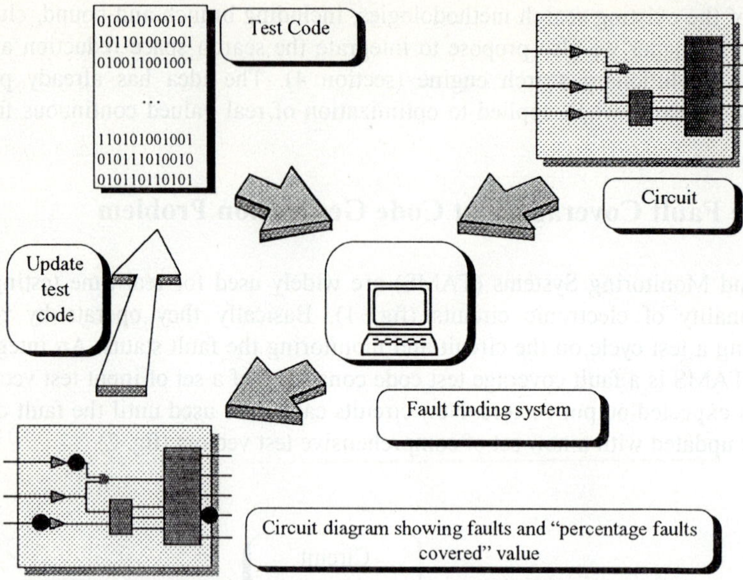

Fig.2. The process of finding the most efficient fault coverage test code: The circuit is modeled and faults are simulated. Using information from the fault analysis the task is to design the most comprehensive test vectors (the white arrow).

3. Handling Constraints

Usually there are various constraints imposed on the test codes. For example, the size of the test code may be constrained by hardware requirements of the test and monitoring system. There may also be a number of constraints concerning the possible combinations of input signals. The task is to automate the process of finding the most effective test code, i.e. the code maximizing the fault coverage (fig. 2).

The requirement that the number of test vectors must be exactly N is represented directly by the coding scheme of the problem. A sample from the associated fitness landscape of the search problem would consist of N vectors each of length m bits.

The second type of constraints impose strict requirements on the possible combinations of values within each individual test vector. The designers of the circuit define the set of legal combinations in terms of the legal states of a number of channels (fig. 3). Each channel is a logical grouping of input bits (for example, bits No. 2, 5, and 7 could form logical channel 1). Collectively the legal states of all channels define a set of legal (*supporting*) templates of the form:

```
1*0**1011***
```

where * is a don't care symbol. Each template could be viewed as a generator of a particular fraction (subspace) of the original search space. Therefore, the set of all legal templates defines the feasible region. The existence of a such closed form description of the feasible region greatly influences the selection of a constraint handling technique. In our case, it seems appropriate to maintain a population of legal samples by designing feasibility preserving search operators.

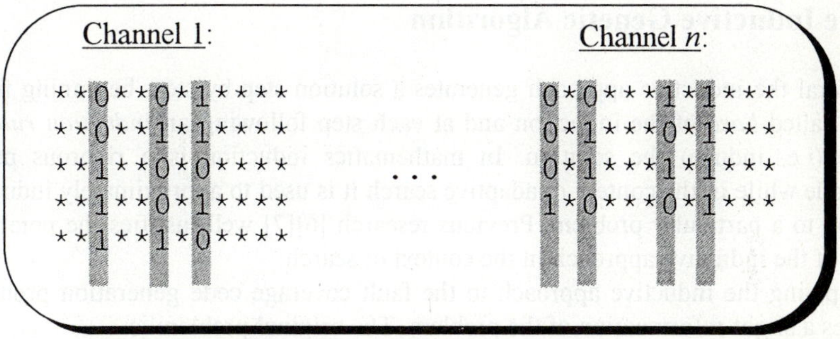

Fig. 3. A set of legal test codes is defined by the legal states of a number of logical channels.

When applied to a feasible point(s), a feasibility preserving operator always produces another feasible point(s). For the test code generation problem we have designed two versions of mutation and one of crossover which comply with the selected constraint handling technique.

`mutation 1`: (*i*) find the supporting template of the parent chromosome, and (*ii*) apply uniform mutation to the values of the don't care bits.

`100101011011`	*parent chromosome*
`1*0**1011***`	*parent's supporting template*
`110111011001`	*offspring*

`mutation 2`: (*i*) find the supporting template of the parent chromosome, (*ii*) change it randomly by another supporting template while keeping the values of the don't care symbols.

`100101011011`	*parent chromosome*
`1*0**1011***`	*parent's supporting template*
`0*1**0011***`	*new supporting template*
`001100011011`	*offspring*

`crossover`: (*i*) find the supporting template of both parents and (*ii*) apply uniform crossover to the don't care bits.

parents	100101011011	011010011001
templates	1*0**1011***	0*1**0011***
offspring 1	110111011001	001000011011

4 The Inductive Genetic Algorithm

In general the inductive approach generates a solution step by step, beginning from the so called *base* of the induction and at each step following an *induction rule* to update (i.e. induce) the solution. In mathematics induction is a rigorous proof technique while in the context of adaptive search it is used to approximately induce a solution to a particular problem. Previous research [6][7] well justifies the potential power of the inductive approach in the context of search.

Applying the inductive approach to the fault coverage code generation problem requires a slight reformuation of the problem. The original problem is:

> `Given a number` *N* `(the maximum number of fault coverage test vectors) find a sequence of` *N* `test vectors that maximizes the fault coverage.`

It can be easily reformulated as:

> `For each` *k* `= 1 to` *N* `find a sequence of` *k* `test vectors that maximizes the fault coverage.`

In this case the inductive formulation also gives meaning to intermediate solutions. Suppose for example that for some k, $1<k<N$, we know a sequence of test vectors which gives *satisfactory* fault coverage. The term satisfactory means that with k test vectors we couldn't expect to cover more faults than those already discovered by the sequence. This is a relative judgement regarding the particular circuit and can serve as an efficient stopping condition instead of the usual maximum number of generations (refer to step 6 of the algorithm). Now if for k test vectors we have already achieved a satisfactory level of fault coverage the task is to find a satisfactory fault coverage level for k+1 test vectors. The main power in the inductive approach is the assumption that the satisfactory fault coverage level for k+1 test vectors could be derived from the satisfactory level of the k test vectors. If this assumption is true then it produces an efficient search engine with computational complexity determined only by the computational complexity of the inductive step.

The Inductive Genetic Algorithm (IGA) combines the evolutionary search engine with an inductive fitness function. The overall structure of the IGA is as follows:

1. Initialize a partial solution for N = 1 (i.e. a sequence of one test vector only)

   100101011011

2. For k = 2 to N do (search for the best k*th* vector that complements the already existing partial solution)

3. Initialize a population of test vectors

   011001001110 ... 010010111010

4. Append each test vector to the partial solution, evaluate it and assign fitness

   100101011011 ... 100101011011
   011001001110 ... 010010111010

5. Reproduce according to the fitness obtained in 4. Typical operators include versions of mutation and crossover. Update the population.

6. If not end of generation, goto 4

7. Update the partial solution, increment k, goto 2

Steps 3, 4, 5, and 6 constitute a genetic algorithm. Steps 1, 2 and 7 implement the inductive approach. The overall algorithm could also be viewed as a genetic algorithm with dynamic fitness function, i.e. the fitness function changes at each generation.

5. Experiments

The associated fitness function with our model is $f = \frac{n}{N} \cdot 100\%$, where n is the number of covered faults and N is the number of all faults in the fault population.

Fig. 4 shows the performance of the Inductive Genetic Algorithm (IGA) on a fault coverage problem consisting of 200 possible faults. The number of input test vectors is 24. The search effort at each inductive step controls the trade-off between the computational complexity and the expected quality of results. The family of all possible trade-off points define the *performance trade-off* front. It is a measure of the expected gain of the quality of results as a function of the computational expense.

The fault coverage achieved for 9,000 fitness function calls is 71.5%. Previous experiments done at Rolls Royce and Associates Ltd. involved a classical genetic algorithm in which the chromosome coded all the 24 input test vectors each of length 12 bits. The best produced fault coverage for 9,000 fitness function calls was 57%.

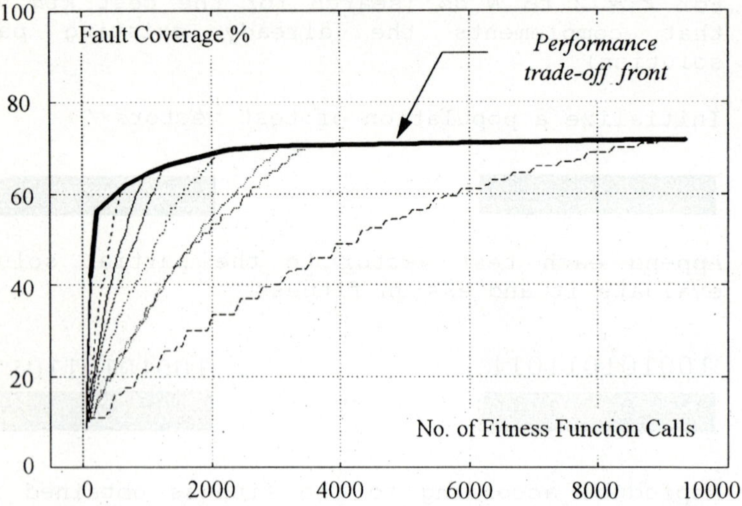

Fig 4. Runs of the Inductive Genetic Algorithm for eight different control parameter settings (population size, mutation rate, crossover rate, number of generations per inductive step). The family of all possible control parameter settings define the *performance trade-off front*, which is a measure of the trade-off between computational complexity and quality of results. The number of input test vectors is 24.

Fig. 5 shows the performance of the IGA as a function of the number of input test vectors. The same fault population of 200 faults as in the previous experiments is used. The IGA is able to find a set of 67 input test vectors that cover 100% of the fault population. If the hardware requirements allow the TAMS to use 67 test vectors then 100% fault coverage is achieved. However, in real world problems there are hard constraints imposed on the design task. For example, in our particular TAMS test code generation problem the number of input test vectors must be 24. Therefore, our objective is to design maximally comprehensive set of 24 test vectors (the design of the logic of the circuit is already fixed, so we regard the test coverage code generation problem as a search problem and do not address the inherent testability properties of the logic design). However, the availability of an algorithm that produces a population (of minimal size) covering 100% faults could be used to implement a test and monitoring system which uses several sets of 24 test vectors and applies them during different discrete time steps (interleaving).

Fig. 6 shows the effect of the constraints on the performance of the search engine. There are two graphs, each corresponding to a particular set of constraints. Each set of constraints is determined by a table of legal states as explained in section 4. Legal table 2 is derived from legal table 1 by reducing the number of legal states in channel 1. Therefore, legal table 2 corresponds to a more constrained instance of the fault coverage test code generation problem. Imposing constraints on the problem is equivalent to introducing *inherent untestability* in the circuit design. Legal identifying fault patterns could no longer be allowed and therefore, the corresponding faults would never be detected. As can be seen from fig. 6 this fact significantly influences the achieved fault coverage.

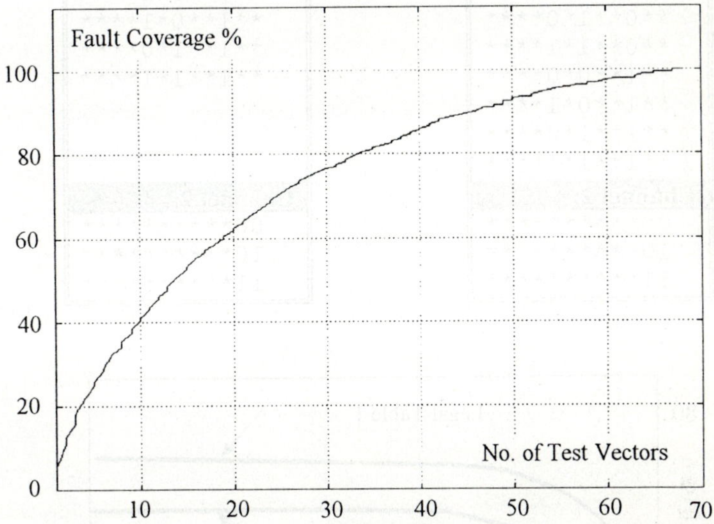

Fig. 5. The fault coverage as a function of the number of input test vectors. There are 200 faults in the fault population. An Inductive Genetic Algorithm is used to find the best set of test vectors. The number of fitness function calls in order to cover 100 percent of the fault population is approximately 10,000 and required sixty seven input test vectors.

6. Conclusions

In this paper we have described the development and application of an efficient constraint handling technique to a real world problem. As compared to previous experiments at Rolls Royce and Associates Ltd. our system has considerably improved the performance and the reliability of the test and monitoring system (TAMS). Also, some of our results suggest how to modify TAMS so as to increase real-time fault coverage.

Currently, there is no general way to find a closed form description of the feasible region. Our experience shows that it may prove to be worthy to spend some time analysing the problem before resorting to the selection of the constraint handling technique. Several existing evolutionary search systems already comply with the above conclusions [2][4] and show improved performance as compared to previous constraint handling methods. Currently such systems are applicable only to particular classes of constraints (e.g. linear constraints) and future research may involve the extension of these classes.

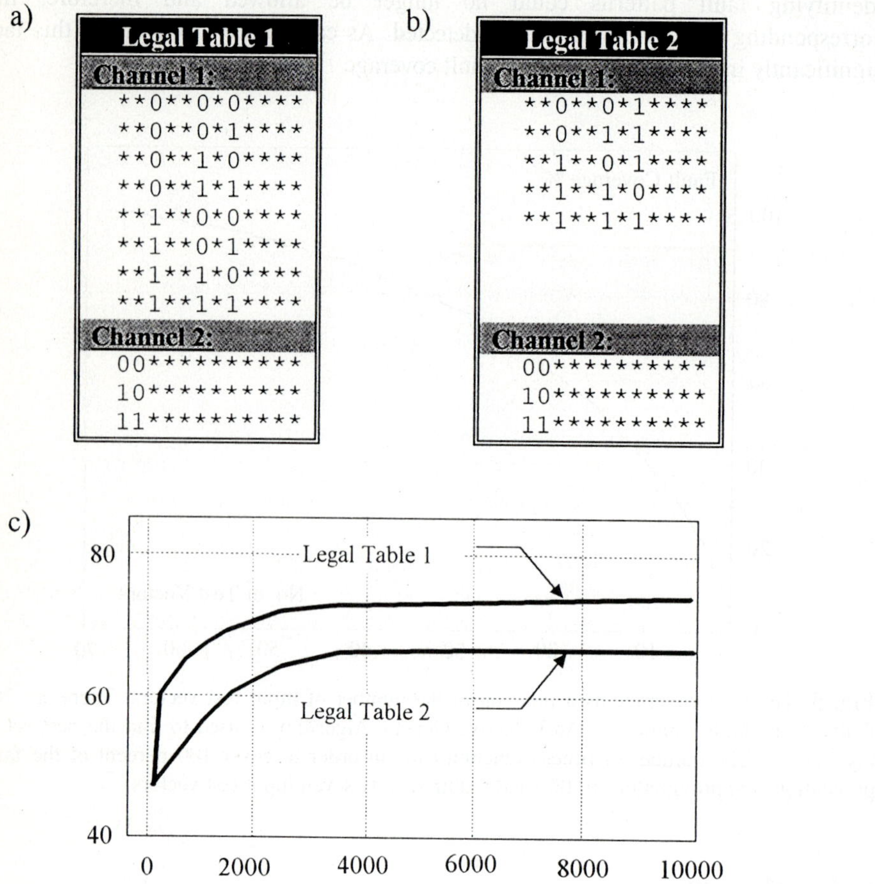

Fig. 6. Effects of constraints on the performance trade-off front of the IGA. The effect of imposing of constraints on the fault coverage problem (Legal Table 2) is equivalent to introducing inherent untestability in the circuit.

References

[1] Michalewicz Z., A Survey of Constraint Handling Techniques in Evolutionary Computation Methods, *The 4th Annual Conference on Evolutionary Programming' 95*, March 1-3, San Diego, USA

[2] Michalewicz Z., Nazhiyath, and Michalewicz M, A Note on Usefulness of Geometrical Crossover for Numerical Optimization problems, *the 5th Annual Conference on Evolutionary Programming' 96*, San Diego, USA

[3] Radcliffe N., Forma Analysis and Random Respectful Recombination, *Procs. of the 4th ICGA*, San Diego, 1991

[4] Michalewicz Z., Genetic Algorithms + data Structures = Evolutionary Programs, Springer-Verlag, 1992

[5] Bilchev, G., and Parmee I., The Inductive Genetic Algorithm with Applications to the Fault Coverage Test Code Generation Problem, *submitted to EUFIT'96*, Aachen, Germany

[6] G. Bilchev, and I. Parmee, "Learning the 'Next' Dimension", *Artificial Intelligence and Simulation of Behaviour'96*, Brighton, UK, April 1996

[7] G. Bilchev, and I. Parmee, "Inductive Search", *First International Contest on Evolutionary Optimization to be held during the 1996 IEEE Conference on Evolutionary Computation*, May 20-22, Nagoya, Japan, 1996

New Genetic Local Search Operators for the Traveling Salesman Problem

Bernd Freisleben and Peter Merz

Department of Electrical Engineering and Computer Science (FB 12)
University of Siegen
Hölderlinstr. 3, D–57068 Siegen, Germany
E-Mail: {freisleb,pmerz}@informatik.uni-siegen.de

Abstract. In this paper, an approach is presented to incorporate problem specific knowledge into a genetic algorithm which is used to compute near-optimum solutions to traveling salesman problems (TSP). The approach is based on using a tour construction heuristic for generating the initial population, a tour improvement heuristic for finding local optima in a given TSP search space, and new genetic operators for effectively searching the space of local optima in order to find the global optimum. The quality and efficiency of solutions obtained for a set of TSP instances containing between 318 and 1400 cities are presented.

1 Introduction

The *traveling salesman problem* (TSP) is a well-known NP-hard combinatorial optimization problem [15] in which a salesman tries to find the shortest closed tour to visit a set of N cities under the condition that each city is visited exactly once. Since the computation times for finding optimal solutions grow exponentially with N, many heuristic approaches have been proposed in order to compute near-optimum solutions in reasonable time. Among these are special purpose heuristics applicable only to the TSP and general methods useful in a variety of optimization problems, such as *simulated annealing* [14], *threshold accepting* [3] and *genetic algorithms* [5]. In many cases, the search efficiency of the general methods is strongly increased when some form of domain knowledge about the TSP is provided to them.

In this paper, we present means of incorporating TSP domain knowledge into a genetic algorithm (GA) and propose an approach in which *local search* (also called *local hill-climbing*) techniques and GAs are combined. The basic idea of the approach is to let the GA perform its search in the space of local minima rather than in the search space of all feasible tours. New genetic operators which are adapted to the properties of the local minima search space and which are thus different from commonly known genetic operators for the TSP, will be presented to realize the approach.

The paper is organized as follows. Section 2 reviews proposals for integrating TSP domain knowledge into a GA. Section 3 presents the new GA approach for solving the TSP. Section 4 presents computational results. Section 5 concludes the paper and outlines areas for future research.

2 Incorporating TSP Domain Knowledge into GAs

Many studies have indicated that pure GA approaches are outperformed by the conventional heuristics developed for the TSP, particularly when the problem size increases. The desire to improve the performance of GAs in TSP applications has motivated several researchers to build additional heuristic elements into GAs [21, 27]. The main possibilities to augment GAs with such heuristics are as follows:

- Instead of generating random tours which form the individuals of the initial population of a GA, it is possible to use a tour construction heuristic, such as the *nearest neighbor* (NN) heuristic or various *insertion* heuristics [15, 24]. Since an entire population has to be created, the heuristic in use must be able to produce different tours. For example, the nearest neighbor heuristic allows to construct N different tours, where N is the number of cities; each city can act as the starting point for the heuristic.
- Genetic recombination offers a large potential for using heuristic elements. For example, instead of determining new edges for producing a valid offspring in the crossover operator on a purely random basis, it might be desirable to prefer short edges. It is also possible to replace mutation by one of the well-known tour improvement heuristics such as *2-opt*, *3-opt* [16] or the *Lin-Kernighan* (LK) heuristic [17]. Independent of mutation, tour improvement heuristics may alternatively be applied to some or all individuals of the current population.
- Tour improvement heuristics can also be used for postprocessing: the resulting population or just the best individual may be the target of an additional run of a tour improvement algorithm.

Fig. 1 summarizes the possibilities of incorporating TSP heuristics into a GA by showing a general "template" for constructing such a *heuristic GA*.

Step 1:	create the initial population by a tour construction heuristic.
Step 2:	apply a tour improvement heuristic to initial population.
Step 3:	selection: select parents for mating.
Step 4:	recombination: perform heuristic crossover.
Step 5:	apply a tour improvement heuristic to offspring.
Step 6:	mutation: mutate individuals with a given probability.
Step 7:	replacement: replace some parents with new offsprings.
Step 8:	if not converged go to Step 3.
Step 9:	perform postprocessing by applying a tour improvement heuristic

Fig. 1. A heuristic GA template

Although the integration of TSP domain knowledge into GAs according to Fig. 1 seems to be a promising approach, several previous attempts to use TSP heuristics at particular steps of the template were rather discouraging. For example, Grefenstette [9] used a heuristic crossover and got solutions as far as 25%

above the optimum for a 50-cities TSP. In [8] he reports results of experiments with tour construction heuristics for generating the initial population as well as using a heuristic crossover and local hill-climbing as the mutation operator. These results were better than corresponding ones obtained with "blind" genetic search, but still worse than those produced by a simple 2-opt tour improvement heuristic. Suh and van Gucht [25] have applied 2-opt to some individuals of a GA population and reached a quality of 1.73% above the optimum for a 100-cities problem. In [11], Jog, Suh and van Gucht present better solutions for the same 100-cities problem: using 2-opt and *Or*-opt [15] as the tour improvement operator leads to a quality of 1.37% above the optimum on the average. However, the results obtained with these heuristic GA approaches are still rather poor when compared to conventional heuristics. For example, a nearest neighbor heuristic combined with a 2-opt improvement algorithm (implemented as part of our work) applied to same 100-cities instance as the one mentioned above is able to find a tour with a better quality (0.50% above the optimum) than the average quality of all heuristic GA approaches mentioned.

In [29], Whitley et al. show that their *edge recombination crossover* allows to solve a 30-cities problem to optimality and is superior to other "blind" recombination operators such as *PMX*, *cycle* and *order crossover*. The edge recombination operator has subsequently been improved by Mathias and Whitley [18] who called their enhanced versions *edge-2* and *edge-3*; edge-3 is superior to edge-2 and designed for larger TSP instances. The value obtained by using edge-3 in the 532-cities problem of Padberg and Rinaldi [22] has been reported to be 28979 (4.67%) on the average and 28752 (3.85%) as the best solution [18]. A modified version of edge-2, called *edge-NN*, has been shown by Tang and Leung [26] to be slightly superior to edge-3. Edge-NN incorporates greedy choices into the recombination step and additionally improves individuals by 2– and 3-changes. The tour lengths that have been achieved by edge-NN for the 532-cities problem are 27949 (0.95%) as the shortest tour and 28255 (2.06%) as the average value.

Mühlenbein [19, 21] has developed a parallel GA which is quite different to the ones described above. In this GA, each individual can be seen as an active entity which chooses itself a partner for mating and improves during its lifetime (i.e. local hill-climbing is performed). A new crossover operator, called MPX (*maximum preservative crossover*), has been proposed for recombination. The population structure also differs from the one of a traditional GA, as described by Gorges-Schleuter [6, 7]. In this approach, the improvement rate is set to 1, hence all individuals are local minima; the tour improvement operator is 2-opt. Compared to the above results, the solutions are much better: for the 532-cities problem a best tour length of 0.10% and an average tour length of 0.19% above the optimum has been obtained [6]. Mathias and Whitley [18] have shown that MPX is the most suitable crossover for the TSP, since it outperforms edge-3 and several others. Ulder et al. [27] have modified the parallel GA of Mühlenbein by replacing 2-opt with the LK heuristic, which is known to be the best improvement heuristic for the TSP. Not surprisingly, the results are better than those obtained using 2-opt. For the 532-cities instance an average tour length of

0.17% above the optimum has been found.

Homaifar et al. [10] recently developed another crossover for the TSP, called *matrix crossover*. Using 2-opt as the improvement operator, their GA is able to find tours up to 1.96% above the optimum in case of a 318-cities problem.

The probably most effective approach to the TSP is the one proposed by Johnson [12, 13]. His *Iterated Lin-Kernighan* heuristic (ILK) works as follows: a locally optimal solution produced by LK is slightly mutated by a random non-sequential 4-change [17] and LK is applied again to the modified solution. This is repeated until the results are satisfactory. Although ILK has recently been regarded by Johnson as a "genetic" approach [13], we do not refer to ILK as a GA since the key concepts of GAs, a population of individuals and recombination of (parts of) several individuals, are missing. In ILK, a single individual rather than a population of individuals is considered at each iteration step. Nevertheless, the results obtained by ILK for many TSP instances are truly impressive.

3 A New Approach

The above results indicate that the use of improvement operators within a GA seems to be the only way to obtain results comparable to conventional local search techniques. In [20], Mühlenbein justifies his genetic local search approach by a configuration space analysis of the TSP. From his observations he concludes that edges of best 2-opt tours are most likely also contained in other 2-opt tours and that by combining two good tours the probability of obtaining a still better tour is higher than by combining two arbitrary 2-opt tours. We believe that this also holds for tours produced by other improvement heuristics, such as 3-opt or LK. In support of this claim, Boese [1, 2] argues that the cost surfaces of TSPs exhibit a "big valley" structure, i.e. the optimum lies near the center of a single valley of near-optimal solutions.

A GA which is specifically designed to search within the space of local optima instead of the set of feasible solutions differs in some respects from a standard GA. In a standard GA, the crossover is aimed at preserving most of the information contained in the parents. Since in a local search GA the offspring produced by the crossover operator is subsequently modified by an improvement heuristic, this aim may be disadvantageous. If the two parents are too similar, the GA may fail to produce a new offspring, since after local improvement the offspring may become identical to one of the parents. The probability of getting an identical offspring increases for more effective local search methods like 3-opt or LK.

To estimate the similarity of two individuals, we need a metric for defining distances between tours. Most operations on tours are performed on the edges of the tour, so it is straightforward to define the distance between two tours as the number of edges in which the two tours differ. If this distance between two individuals is zero, then these two individuals are said to be identical, because all edges of the first can be found in the second. This distance is also used in [1, 2, 20]. It can be seen as a counterpart to the Hamming distance for bitstrings.

It is easy to see that the smaller the distance between two parents, the higher the probability of falling back in one of the two local minima. Therefore, the new crossover operator presented in the following produces an offspring by preserving the distance between tours rather keeping the number of newly introduced edges to a minimum. The proposed operator, called *DPX* (*distance preserving crossover*), tries to generate an offspring that has equal distance to both of its parents, i.e. its aim is to achieve that the three distances between offspring and parent 1, offspring and parent 2, and parent 1 and parent 2 are identical. It works as follows: the content of the first parent is copied to the offspring and all edges that are not in common with the other parent are deleted. The resulting parts of the broken tour are reconnected without using the non-shared edges of the parents. A greedy reconnection procedure is employed to achieve this: if the edge (i, j) has been destroyed, the nearest available neighbor k of i among the remaining tour fragments is taken and the edge (i, k) is added to the tour, provided that (i, k) is not contained in the two parents. In order to illustrate the DPX operator, let us consider an example.

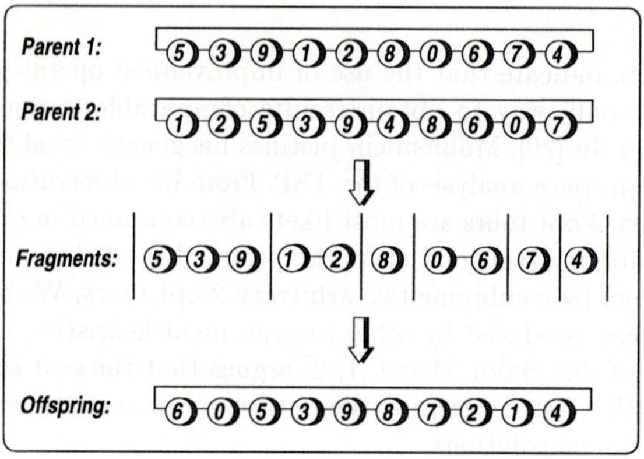

Fig. 2. The DPX crossover

Suppose that the two parents shown in Fig. 2 are given, then copying parent 1 to the offspring and deleting the edges not contained in both parents leads to the tour fragments 5 3 9 - 1 2 - 8 - 0 6 - 7 - 4. The greedy reconnection procedure fixes the broken connections by producing the offspring shown in Fig. 2 as follows. First, a city is chosen randomly as the starting point for the reconnection. Let us assume that the city to begin with is city 6, then the other endpoint (city 0) of the fragment containing city 6 is considered and its nearest neighbor in the set of available cities, {5,9,1,2,4}, is determined. The set of available cities only contains the start and endpoints of not yet visited tour fragments. City 8 and city 7 are not contained in this set, because it is not desirable to reinsert edge $(0, 8)$ or edge $(0, 7)$, since they are contained in parent 1 or parent 2, respectively. Let us assume that in the example the nearest neighbor to city 0 is city 5, so city 0 is connected to city 5, and the end of the connected fragment (city 9) is considered. At this point the set of available cities is {2,8,7}. The procedure is repeated until all fragments have been reconnected. Note that the distance d between the offspring and both parent 1 and parent 2 is identical to the distance between the two parents ($d = 6$), hence the name distance preserving crossover. The entire GA using the DPX crossover is shown in Fig. 3.

```
procedure TSP-GA;
  begin
    initialize population with nearest-neighbor heuristic;
    foreach individual do Lin-Kernighan-Opt(individual);
    repeat
      for i:=0 to # of crossovers do
        select two individuals randomly;
        DPXcrossover(mom, dad);
        Lin-Kernighan-Opt(child);
        with predefined probability do mutation(child);
        replace an individual in population by mutated child;
      end;
    until converged;
  end;
```

Fig. 3. The GA

The initial population of tours is generated by a simple nearest-neighbor tour construction heuristic, applied to P different (randomly chosen) starting points. Each individual of the initial population is then locally optimized by the LK tour improvement heuristic. The recombination process starts with randomly selecting two individuals, performing the DPX crossover as described above, and applying the LK heuristic to the produced offspring to again obtain a locally optimal tour. With a predefined probability, this tour is then mutated by a random non-sequential 4-change [17], followed by a run of the LK heuristic to transform the mutated tour into a local minimum. The resulting tour finally replaces an individual of the current population before the next iteration of the algorithm is executed.

The non-sequential 4-change as the mutation operator can be seen as a random transformation of a tour T into a tour T' with the property that the distance between T and T' is 4. The 4-change has been selected, because it is the smallest possible non-sequential change and it does not go too far away from a good solution; LK performs only sequential changes, i.e. the endpoint of a removed edge is the startpoint of a newly inserted edge, and the chance to eliminate the effect of the 4-change by two or more LK runs is low.

The replacement scheme is important to maintain a sufficient degree of diversity within the population, which in turn is required to avoid premature convergence of the GA. In an environment where the search space of local optima is investigated, the problem of premature convergence is even more severe. Our replacement scheme to maintain population diversity works as follows. First, the individual of the current population which is most similar (in terms of the distance) to the offspring to be included is identified. If the distance between them is below a predefined small threshold, that individual is replaced by the new offspring, unless that individual is the currently best individual in which case it is only replaced when the new offspring has a higher fitness; otherwise the individual with the worst fitness in the current population will be replaced.

The motivation for the individual actions performed by our approach shown in Fig. 3 can be explained as follows. The GA investigates the search space of local optima by "jumping" from one local optimum to another, with the hope to find still better local minima until the global minimum is reached. The difficulty is to jump far enough away to leave the basin of attraction of the current local minimum, but not too far to possibly miss the optimum which is expected to be somewhere near the current local minimum (see Fig. 4).

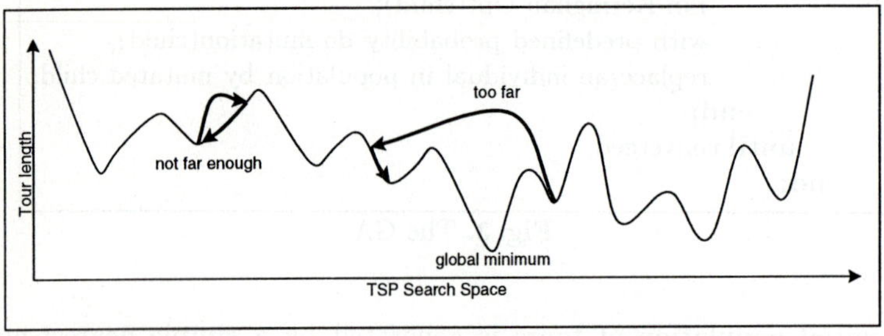

Fig. 4. Illustration of jumps within the search space of local minima

In our approach, the two entities responsible for providing the GA with the "jumping" capability are the DPX crossover and the mutation operator. Since the direction of a jump is determined by the particular edges removed/reinserted, our mutation operator performs a jump with constant distance and random direction, while the DPX performs a jump with variable distance and guided direction. The direction of a jump performed by the DPX is guided in the sense that it removes edges that most probably are not part of the optimal tour, and it selects edges for reinsertion that are not contained in the two near-optimum individuals acting as the parents.

4 Implementation and Results

The proposed approach has been implemented in C++ on a DEC-Alphastation 3000/300X (175 MHz) under OSF/1. Our implementation of the GA operators is based on Wall's GALIB library (Version 2.3.2) [28]. In Table 1 the results obtained in our experiments are shown. The TSP instances investigated were taken from the TSPLIB [23] (the numbers in the abbreviations indicate the number of cities). The shortest tours are known for all of them, thus the third and the fourth columns indicate the deviation from the optimum in percent. For each of the problem instances, 10 independent runs were performed. In the experiments, the following parameters were used: (a) population size: 20, (b) crossover rate: 0.5 (i.e. 10 new offsprings per generation), and (c) mutation rate: 0.3 (i.e. 30% of the population per generation are mutated). The experiments were stopped after 200 (lin318: 100) generations.

Results				
instance	optimum	best(quality)	average(quality)	t(hh:mm:ss)
lin318	42029	42029 (0.00%)	42029.0 (0.00%)	00:34:14
att532	27686	27686 (0.00%)	27693.7 (0.03%)	03:16:20
rat783	8806	8806 (0.00%)	8807.3 (0.01%)	05:53:30
pcb1173	56892	56893 (0.00%)	56894.7 (0.01%)	20:05:20
fl1400	20127	20127 (0.00%)	20129.5 (0.01%)	57:53:39

Table 1. The results of the proposed GA

The results shown in Table 1 demonstrate that the proposed approach is capable of producing high quality solutions for each of the TSP instances investigated. Our results are qualitatively superior to any of the results obtained by all other GA approaches known to us and comparable to the best non-GA approaches such as ILK; for example, the average quality produced by ILK for att532 [13] is slighly worse, but its runtimes are significantly better than ours. Actually, ILK may be regarded as a special case of our approach, since it is obtained by setting the population size and the mutation rate to 1 and the crossover rate to 0.

For all the instances the optimal solutions have been found with the proposed approach, except for the instance pcb1173. In this case, the best obtained tour was only slightly longer than the optimum (56893 vs. 56892); the percentage value given in the third column of Table 1 has been rounded. The average quality shows for all instances that the best solutions were found in the majority of runs.

In addition to the information shown in Table 1, it is interesting to consider the increase of quality when executing the individual steps of the proposed GA. The length of the best tour generated by the nearest neighbor tour construction heuristic is usually around 20% above the optimum and takes up to 12 seconds (for fl1400) to compute. The subsequent use of the LK improvement heuristic yields solutions which are at best between 2% and 3% above the optimum, with computation times ranging between 1 second (for lin318) and 68 seconds (for fl1400). Thus, the GA is responsible for the smallest but hardest part of the optimization process, namely contributing the remaining quality improvements to reach the values shown in Table 1.

5 Conclusions

In this paper, an approach has been presented to incorporate domain knowledge into a genetic algorithm which is supposed to compute near-optimum solutions to the traveling salesman problem (TSP). The approach is based on the use of a tour construction heuristic for generating the initial population of the GA, a tour improvement heuristic for finding local optima in the TSP search space, and new genetic operators for efficiently searching the space of local optima in order to find the global optimum. The feasibility of the proposed approach has been demonstrated by presenting performance results for a number of TSP instances containing between 318 and 1400 cities. The results are superior to those produced by other GA approaches described in the literature and comparable to the best non-GA approaches.

There are several issues for future research. For example, the efficiency of the implementation must be increased to reduce the computation times; in particular our implementation of the Lin-Kernighan heuristic is a target for improvement, and a parallel version of the whole approach would be desirable. The results of Johnson [13] indicate that additional implementation optimizations can reduce the runtimes drastically. Furthermore, additional tests of the proposed algorithm on other possibly more complex or asymmetric TSP instances [4] and comprehensive comparisons with other (possibly non-GA) approaches, in particular the ILK heuristic, are required to provide a detailed assessment of the merits of the proposed approach.

References

1. K. Boese, "Cost versus Distance in the Traveling Salesman Problem," Tech. Rep. TR-950018, UCLA CS Department, 1995.
2. K.D. Boese and S. Muddu, "A New Adaptive Multi-Start Technique for Combinatorial Global Optimizations," *Operations Research Letters 16*, pp. 101–113, 1994.
3. B. Freisleben and M. Schulte, "Combinatorial Optimization with Parallel Adaptive Threshold Accepting," in *Proceedings of the 1992 European Workshop on Parallel Computing*, Barcelona, pp. 176–179. IOS Press, 1992.
4. B. Freisleben and P. Merz, "A Genetic Local Search Algorithm for Solving Symmetric and Asymmetric Traveling Salesman Problems," in *Proc. 1996 IEEE Int. Conf. on Evolutionary Computation*, Nagoya, Japan, pp. 616–621, 1996.
5. D. E. Goldberg, *Genetic Algorithms in Search, Optimization and Machine Learning.* Addison-Wesley, 1989.
6. M. Gorges-Schleuter, "ASPARAGOS: An Asynchronous Parallel Genetic Optimization Strategy," in *Proc. of the 3rd Int. Conf. on Genetic Algorithms*, Morgan Kaufmann, 1989.
7. M. Gorges-Schleuter, "Explicit Parallelism of Genetic Algorithms through Population Structures," in *Parallel Problem Solving from Nature*, (H. Schwefel and R. Männer, Eds.), pp. 150–159, Springer-Verlag, 1991.
8. J. J. Grefenstette, "Incorporating Problem Specific Knowledge into Genetic Algorithms," in *Genetic Algorithms and Simulated Annealing*, (L. Davis, ed.), pp. 42–60, Morgan Kaufmann, 1987.
9. J. Grefenstette, R. Gopal, B. Rosimaita, and D. van Gucht, " Genetic Algorithms for the Traveling Salesman Problem," in *Proc. of an Int. Conf. on Genetic Algorithms and their Applications*, pp. 160–168, 1985.
10. L. Homaifar, C. Guan, and G. Liepins, "A New Approach to the Traveling Salesman Problem by Genetic Algorithms," in *Proc. of the 5th Int. Conf. on Genetic Algorithms*, pp. 460–466, Morgan Kaufmann, 1993.

11. P. Jog, J. Y. Suh, and D. van Gucht, "The Effects of Population Size, Heuristic Crossover and Local Improvement on a Genetic Algorithm for the Travelling Salesman Problem," in *Proc. of the 3rd Int. Conf. on Genetic Algorithms*, pp. 110–115, Morgan Kaufmann, 1989.
12. D. S. Johnson, "Local Optimization and the Traveling Salesman Problem," in *Annual Int. Colloquium on Automata, Languages and Programming*, 1990.
13. D. S. Johnson and L. A. McGeoch , "The Traveling Salesman Problem: A Case Study in Local Optimization," in (E. H. L. Aarts and J. K. Lenstra, eds.) *Local Search in Combinatorial Optimization*, Wiley & Sons, New York, to appear.
14. P. van Laarhoven and E. H. L. Aarts, *Simulated Annealing: Theory and Applications*. Kluwer Academic Publ., 1987.
15. E. L. Lawler, J. K. Lenstra and D. B. Shmoys, *The Traveling Salesman Problem: A Guided Tour of Combinatorial Optimization*. Wiley and Sons, New York, 1985.
16. S. Lin, "Computer Solutions of the Travelling Salesman Problem," *Bell System Tech. Journal*, Vol. 44, pp. 2245–2269, 1965.
17. S. Lin and B. Kernighan, "An Effective Heuristic Algorithm for the Traveling Salesman Problem," *Operations Research*, Vol. 21, pp. 498–516, 1973.
18. K. Mathias and D. Whitley, "Genetic Operators, the Fitness Landscape and the Traveling Salesman Problem," in *Parallel Problem Solving from Nature*, (R. Männer and B. Manderick, Eds.), pp. 219–228, Elsevier, 1992.
19. H. Mühlenbein, "Parallel Genetic Algorithms, Population Genetics and Combinatorial Optimization," in *Proc. of the 3rd Int. Conf. on Genetic Algorithms*, (J. D. Schaffer, ed.), pp. 416–421, Morgan Kaufmann, 1989.
20. H. Mühlenbein, "Evolution in Time and Space – The Parallel Genetic Algorithm," in *Foundations of Genetic Algorithms*, (G. J. E. Rawlins, ed.), M. Kaufmann, 1991.
21. H. Mühlenbein, M. Gorges-Schleuter, and O. Krämer, "Evolution Algorithms in Combinatorial Optimization," *Parallel Computing*, Vol. 7, pp. 65–88, 1988.
22. M. Padberg and G. Rinaldi, "Optimization of a 532-city Symmetric Traveling Salesman Problem by Branch & Cut," *Operations Research Lett. 6*, pp. 1–7, 1987.
23. G. Reinelt, "TSPLIB — A Traveling Salesman Problem Library," *ORSA Journal on Computing*, Vol. 3, No. 4, pp. 376–384, 1991.
24. G. Reinelt, *The Traveling Salesman: Computational Solutions for TSP Applications*. Vol. 840 of *Lecture Notes in Computer Science*, Springer-Verlag, 1994.
25. J. Y. Suh and D. van Gucht, "Incorporating Heuristic Information into Genetic Search," in *Proc. of the 2nd Int. Conf. on Genetic Algorithms*, pp. 100–107, Lawrence Erlbaum, 1987.
26. A. Y. C. Tang and K. S. Leung, "A Modified Edge Recombination Operator for the Travelling Salesman Problem," in *Parallel Problem Solving from Nature*, (H.-P. Schwefel and R. Männer, Eds.), pp. 180–188, Springer-Verlag, 1994.
27. N. L. J. Ulder, E. H. L. Aarts, H. J. Bandelt, P. J. M. van Laarhoven, and E. Pesch, "Genetic Local Search Algorithms for the Traveling Salesman Problem," in *Parallel Problem Solving from Nature*, (H. P. Schwefel and R. Männer, Eds.), pp. 109–116, Springer-Verlag, 1991.
28. M. Wall, "GALIB 2.3.2," http://lancet.mit.edu/ga, 1995.
29. D. Whitley, T. Starkweather, and D. Fuquay, "Scheduling Problems and Traveling Salesman: The Genetic Edge Recombination Operator," in *Proc. of the 3rd Int. Conf. on Genetic Algorithms*, pp. 133–140, Morgan Kaufmann, 1989.

An Evolutionary Approach to Hardware/Software Partitioning

Xiaobo (Sharon) Hu[1]*, Garrison Greenwood[1]* Joseph G. D'Ambrosio[2]

[1] Western Michigan University Kalamazoo MI 49008, USA
[2] General Motors R&D Center, Warren MI 48090, USA

Abstract. In this paper, we present an approach to hardware/software codesign of real-time embedded systems. Two of the difficulties associated with codesign are handling tradeoffs among multiple attributes and exploring a large design space. We use a combination of techniques from the evolutionary computation and utility theory fields to address these problem areas. A real-time microcontroller-based design example is presented to illustrate our approach.

1 Introduction

The objective of Hardware/software codesign is to produce computer systems that have a balance of hardware and software components which work together to satisfy a requirements specification. This balance between hardware and software implementations is referred to as the *partitioning problem*. Developing efficient means of performing hardware/software partitioning is key to the automatic design of complex computer systems.

A number of hardware/software partitioning approaches have been presented (*e.g.*, see [1, 2]). Most of these partitioning approaches start with a pure software or hardware specification at the behavioral level and then attempt to find a hardware/software implementation which meets the overall constraints and optimize certain attributes. Such fine-grained approaches have difficulty in exploring a large design space consisting of multiple choices of different microprocessors or microcontrollers. Additionally, these approaches have a limited means of handling tradeoffs among multiple attributes such as cost, power consumption and design time.

The exponential size of the search space for the hardware/software partitioning problem establishes the need for some type of heuristic search technique. This paper describes the combination of an *evolutionary algorithm* (EA) with *Imprecisely Specified, Multiple Attribute Utility theory* (ISMAUT) to develop real-time embedded systems. Our use of imprecise value functions based upon a designer's preferences for establishing a survival criteria is what differentiates our approach from conventional Pareto optimal searches that use EAs. The goal in most other approaches is to enumerate the entire Pareto optimal set [3]. While certainly

* Research supported in part by an External Research Program Grant from Hewlett-Packard Laboratories, Bristol, England.

laudable, this assumes that all Pareto optimal solutions are equally preferable which is often not the case. Using preferences to influence the probability of survival allows the designer to drive the search process of the EA. This helps to prevent the EA from conducting a simple blind exploration of the tradeoff space. A design example is presented to illustrate our approach.

2 Definitions & Preliminaries

Optimization problems are essentially search problems. Each individual in the population of an EA constitutes a potential solution or *alternative* within the problem space of an optimization problem. *Objectives* define desirable properties of a good alternative and *attributes* are used to determine the degree to which a specific objective is met. An objective is normally formulated as an *objective function* with the attributes as the function's arguments. The class of such problems are called *Multipleobjective Optimization Problems* (MOPs).

The hardware/software partitioning problem is an instance of a MOP. All system specifications can be modeled as a set of functions where each function has one or more performance constraints (*e.g.*, timing). Functions can be implemented in either hardware or software. Software implemented functions acquire attributes such as the number of instructions required for execution on a specific processor. Conversely, a function implemented in hardware affects the cost and power consumption of the system. The objective is to have a designer select components from a hardware library (containing microprocessors, application specific integrated circuits (ASICs), etc.) and then assign the functions as hardware or software implementations in some optimal way. The decision of whether functions in a real-time embedded system should be implemented in hardware or software forms a tradeoff between cost and performance.

In the terminology of EAs, attribute levels (dollar cost, computational power in MIPs, etc.) are used to quantify the fitness of an alternative and the objective function is equivalent to a fitness function. The goal of the EA is to find an alternative which optimizes the fitness. More formally, suppose we are given a MOP with $\mathcal{X}$ representing the set of all feasible alternatives. Further, let $\mathcal{A}$ represent the set of n attributes. Each alternative $x \in \mathcal{X}$ has an assigned level for each $a_i \in \mathcal{A}$. We let $\mathcal{A}_x$ denote the set of attribute levels associated with the alternative x. We would like to represent the fitness of x by defining an appropriate objective function $f : \mathcal{A}_x \rightarrow \Re_+$ where $\Re_+ \in [0, \infty)$.

An intuitive metric for the optimality of MOPs would be a weighted sum of attributes. Specifically,

$$f = \sum_k w_k \, a_k \tag{1}$$

where a_k is the k-th attribute and $w_k > 0$ is its associated weight. (The weights must satisfy $\sum_k w_k = 1$. Higher weight values reflect greater importance.) Unfortunately, this format for a fitness function is a bit naive and has a number of problems. For example, there often exists conflicting goals between optimizing attributes; some attributes should be maximized while others should be minimized. These factors make direct summation inappropriate. Also, there is the difficulty in specifying a precise weight of each attribute. Intuitively, it will be difficult to assign meaningful weights for more than 3 or 4 attributes.

The first problem above can be handled by *scaling* the attribute levels which maps the raw attribute levels to a convenient subset of $\Re_+$ (normally $0 \rightarrow 1$). Mapping all attribute levels to the same scale also facilitates an attribute trade-off analysis. As before, let $\mathcal{A}_x = \{a_1, a_2, \cdots, a_n\}$ represent the set of n attributes associated with the alternative x. Suppose there exists a set of real-valued functions $\{v_1, v_2, ..., v_n\}$ on $\mathcal{A}$ such that $v_i : a_i \rightarrow [0,1]$ where $v_i \rightarrow 1$ as the attribute level of a_i improves[3]. The set of real-valued functions are referred to as *attribute value functions.* These functions should (as the attribute value increases) monotonically increase for a "more-is-better" attribute and monotonically decrease for a "less-is-better" attribute. Let $\tilde{a}_i$ and $\hat{a}_i$ denote the maximum and minimum levels, respectively, of the attribute a_i. Then for a "more-is-better" attribute

$$v_i(a_i) = \frac{a_i - \hat{a}_i}{\tilde{a}_i - \hat{a}_i} \tag{2}$$

and for a "less-is-better" attribute

$$v_i(a_i) = \frac{a_i - \tilde{a}_i}{\hat{a}_i - \tilde{a}_i} \tag{3}$$

Replacing each a_k in equation (1) with the corresponding $v_k(a_k)$ and assuming $\sum_k w_k = 1$; $w_k > 0$, the fitness function is now well defined.

To handle the difficulty of assigning precise weights, we resort to techniques from utility theory (which will be discussed shortly). Here we introduce the important concepts of dominance and preference. Let x and x' be two alternatives from $\mathcal{X}$ with their associated attribute level sets $\mathcal{A}_x = \{a_1, ..., a_n\}$ and $\mathcal{A}_{x'} = \{a'_1, ..., a'_n\}$, respectively. We say x *dominates* x' if $\forall i$ a_i is better than or equal to a'_i and, in addition, there exists at least one a_j such that a_j is strictly better than a'_j. The set of non-dominated alternatives lies on a surface in attribute space known as the *Pareto optimal frontier*[4]. In each generation of an EA there exists a set of non-dominated alternatives. We call this set of alternatives the *phenotypical Pareto front*.

Given two non-dominated alternatives, a designer may still prefer one over the other. This concept is expressed with the following two relationships:

R1: $x \succ x'$ (read as "x is preferred-to x'")

R2: $x \sim x'$ (read as "x is indifferent-to x'")

x and x' are indifferent when $x \not\succ x'$ and $x' \not\succ x$ indicating that there is no clear preference between them. Relationships **R1** and **R2** together establish a *partial order* on $\mathcal{X}$. If relationship **R2** does not exist (*i.e.*, $\forall\, x, x' \in \mathcal{X}$, either $x \succ x'$ or $x' \succ x$), then a *total order* on $\mathcal{X}$ is established. Preference is purely subjective and thus is different from dominance (which is purely objective). It is easily shown that our preference relationship does not violate dominance relationships [4].

[3] Some authors in this context will refer to v_i as a "utility function".

[4] Some authors refer to this as the Pareto optimal set.

3 Overview of the Design Approach

The level of abstraction that we have adopted for modeling hardware and software components is called the *configuration level* [2]. At the configuration level, hardware is modeled as resources with no detailed functionality and software is modeled as tasks utilizing the resources. At this high level of abstraction, we are able to evaluate various partitioning schemes up front, which, in turn, guides lower level design efforts. The goal of configuration-level design is to determine which functions should be implemented in dedicated hardware circuits and which should be in software, what processors and ASICs should be used, and which software components should be executed by which processor. Our

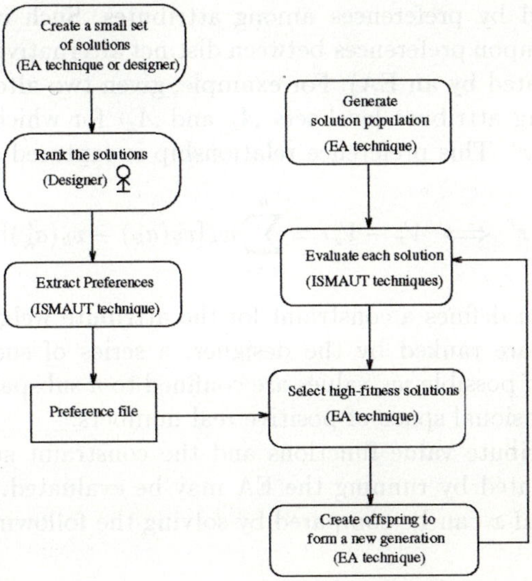

Fig. 1. Hardware/Software Partitioning System

approach to performing hardware/software partitioning (shown in Figure 1) can be summarized as follows. Initially, we obtain a small set of alternatives which can be either extracted from the initial population of an EA or which can be given by the designer. The designer then qualitatively ranks these alternatives. ISMAUT can then be used to define a set of designer's preferences which are stored into a file. (The reader is referred to [5] for details on ISMAUT.)

The EA works in a conventional manner of using genetic operators to generate new potential solutions. ISMAUT returns the dominant solutions (*i.e.*, solutions which are at least as good as any other solutions) which the EA uses to determine which individuals survive. This process continues until a satisfactory solution has been found or a fixed number of generations have been produced and evaluated. We have implemented this approach as a software package called **EvoC** (Evolutionary Codesign).

4 Evaluating Alternatives

To reflect the designer's preferences in the tradeoff of different attributes, we make use of imprecise value functions which are taken from the field of utility theory [6]. An imprecise multi-attribute value function corresponding to the alternative x has the following form:

$$V_x = \sum_k w_k \; v_k(a_k) \tag{4}$$

where $w_k \in \Re_+$ is the weight and $v_k(a_k)$ is the attribute value function for attribute a_k. All weights must satisfy $\sum_k w_k = 1$; $w_k > 0$.

V_x is imprecise in the sense that each w_k does not have a specific assignment, but is constrained by preferences among attributes. Such constraints can be formulated based upon preferences between distinct alternatives (provided by the designer or generated by an EA). For example, given two alternatives $x, x' \in \mathcal{X}$ with corresponding attribute level sets $\mathcal{A}_x$ and $\mathcal{A}_{x'}$ for which the designer has decided that $x \succ x'$. This preference relationship is captured as follows [4]:

$$x \succ x' \iff V_x - V_{x'} = \sum_{k=1}^{n} w_k[v_k(a_k) - v_k(a'_k)] > 0. \tag{5}$$

Such an expression defines a constraint for the attribute weights. When several alternative pairs are ranked by the designer, a series of such constraints are defined. The set of possible w_k values are confined to a subspace $W \subset \Re^n_+$ where $\Re^n_+$ is the n-dimensional space of positive real numbers.

Using the attribute value functions and the constraint subspace W, other configurations created by running the EA may be evaluated. More specifically, alternatives x'' and x can be compared by solving the following linear programming problem:

$$\begin{array}{ll} \text{Minimize (w.r.t. } w_k\text{):} & \sum_k w_k[v_k(a''_k) - v_k(a_k)] \\ \text{Subject to:} & w_k \in W \end{array} \tag{6}$$

Then x'' is preferred to x if Equation (7) is true.

$$z = \min \sum_k w_k[v_k(a''_k) \; - \; v_k(a_k)] > 0 \tag{7}$$

However, knowing that $z \leq 0$ is not sufficient to determine preference. We must reverse the terms in Equation (7) as shown below.

$$\overline{z} = \min \sum_k w_k[v_k(a_k) \; - \; v_k(a''_k)] > 0 \tag{8}$$

Now, if Equation (7) is false and Equation (8) is true, then $x \succ x''$. If both equations are false, then x and x'' are pairwise indifferent. More detailed information on these concepts can be found in [4].

It is important to emphasize that the initial ranking of the selected alternatives is done merely to obtain the constraint subspace W. W is then used in the series of linear programming problems that must be solved to conduct pairwise comparisons between alternatives.

5 Evolutionary Algorithms for Partitioning

For the partitioning problem, individuals in the search space are design alternatives. The data structure for each individual consists of a binary vector with a bit position allocated to each function. A logic 0 (1) in a bit position indicates that the respective function is implemented in software (hardware). There is also an integer which indicates the selected processor. In some cases there are several choices for a hardware implementation (*e.g.*, coprocessor or ASIC). The binary vector is then appended with additional bits to account for these different choices. Of course appended bits are ignored if a software implementation is selected.

The EA terminates after a fixed number of generations (Γ) have been produced and evaluated or earlier if an acceptable assignment has been found. The EA algorithm is implemented as follows:

1. Create an initial population of μ design alternatives by randomly assigning functions as either hardware or software implementations.
2. Conduct a tournament to select alternatives for reproduction. Each selected alternative generates one offspring by applying mutation operators (described below). This creates a population with a total of 2μ alternatives.
3. Rank all alternatives according to their fitness.
4. Deterministically select the μ alternatives with the highest fitness.
5. Proceed to step 2 unless an acceptable solution has been found or Γ generations have been evaluated.

Offspring are created by applying one of three mutation operators. M_1 randomly selects one bit in the binary vector and complements it. The associated function is then reassigned from a hardware (software) implementation to a software (hardware) implementation. M_2 modifies hardware assignments which are identified by bits appended onto the binary vector. A third mutation operator M_3 modifies the integer field in the data structure to select a different processor. Operator M_i is applied to a parent with probability p_i where $\sum_k p_k = 1.0$.

We use the preference relationship discussed in Section 2 to assign fitness to each alternative. Alternative x is said to have a higher fitness over alternative x' if $x \succ x'$. However, this will typically establish only a partial order. A total ranking of the alternatives (based upon a technique described by Goldberg [8]) can be done as follows. Using ISMAUT, identify all preferred alternatives, assign them rank 1 and then remove them from further contention. A new set of preferred alternatives can then be found, ranked 2, and so on until all alternatives have been ranked. Note that any alternatives which violate constraints (*e.g.*, failure to meet a deadline) will not be preferred and thus ISMAUT will assign these a high numerical rank. Note that fitness assignments based upon preference relationships preserves existing dominance relationships [4]. Therefore, the alternatives with rank 1 constitute the phenotypical Pareto optimal front. Tournament selection is used to select alternatives for the reproduction in the next generation [7]. Two distinct candidate alternatives are randomly selected from the current population and three additional distinct alternatives are randomly selected as a comparison set. If one candidate has a lower ranking than some alternative in the comparison set, and the other candidate does not, then the latter is selected for reproduction. If neither (or both) candidates have a lower ranking than some alternative in the comparison set, then a candidate is randomly chosen. (Equivalence class sharing [7] will be used in future **EvoC** versions.)

Name	Number	Activation	Deadline	Period
DigitalFilter1 (DF1)	1	0.00	46.00	104.17
DigitalFilter2 (DF2)	2	9895.83	10000.00	10000.00
DecodeSPUB (DSB)	3	0.00	83.00	208.33
DecodeSPUA (DSA)	4	83.00	138.00	208.33
ReadCAM (RC)	5	0.00	416.67	10000.00
ServiceRoutine (SR)	6	0.00	208.33	416.67
FuelCalc (FC)	7	833.33	1333.33	2500.00
SparkCalc (SC)	8	1666.67	2500.00	2500.00
ReadMAP (RM)	9	0.00	312.50	416.67

Table 1. Primary set of functions. Activation, deadline and period are in μs.

Name	Function Implemented	Instructions Executed	RAM Required	ROM Required
DF1-S	DF1	64	100	100
DF2-S	DF2	32	100	100
DSB-S	DSB	30	200	300
DSA-S	DSA	30	200	300
RC-S	RC	30	100	100
SR-S	SR	20	200	200
FC-S	FC	480	500	400
SC-S	SC	100	400	300
RM-S	RM	40	100	100

Table 2. Software modules to implement functions. RAM and ROM are measured in bytes.

Name	Functions Implemented	Cost	MIPS Available
MC1-H	CPU, RAM(2K), ROM(2K), DF1,DF2,DSB,DSA	3.50	1.30
MC2-H	CPU, RAM(2K), ROM(2K), TC(32)	3.25	1.50
MC3a-H	CPU, RAM(4K), TC(16)	5.25	2.50
MC3b-H	CPU, RAM(4K), DF1,DF2, DSB,DSA	6.25	2.50
MC4a-H	CPU, RAM(2K), DF1, DF2, DSB, DSA, TC(14)	3.75	1.70
MC4b-H	CPU, RAM(2K), DF1, DF2, DSB, DSA, TC(14)	3.25	1.35
MC4c-H	CPU, RAM(2K),TC(16)	2.50	1.70
P1-H	CPU, RAM(2K), ROM(2K)	2.00	1.43
P2-H	CPU	13.00	13.50
ASIC1-H	DF1,DF2,DSB,DSA	2.50	-
PIO1-H	TC(16)	1.00	-
RAM1-H	RAM(2K)	2.00	-
ROM1-H	ROM(2K)	1.00	-

Table 3. Hardware modules to implement functions.

6 Design Example and Discussions

The example embedded system we used is similar to the one discussed in [2]. Table 1 gives the system specification which has nine functions with real-time constraints. Activation time indicates the earliest start time for the first execution while deadline is the time by which the function must be completed after this first activation. Period indicates how often the function is required to execute. The system's attributes are component cost, critical excess MIPS ($\triangle_c$), and feasibility factor (λ). Critical MIPs indicates the amount of computational power yet available for future expansion [2]. Feasibility factor reflects the ability of an implementation to meet all temporal requirements. λ is dependent on the scheduling algorithm used and indicates the probability that the target processor has sufficient computational power to meet all of the timing requirements of the tasks assigned to it. A methodology for calculating λ can be found in [2].

Modules in the software library are listed in Table 2. For this example, we assume the software characterization given are valid for every processor. The first 4 functions may be implemented in hardware. Table 3 lists some of the hardware modules available for this system. The modules include: microcontrollers (MC), processors (P), ASICs, standard peripherals (PIO), timing channels (TC), RAM, and ROM.

Number	Part Set	Cost	Feasibility Factor (λ)	Critical Excess Req. Ratio (Δ_c)
1	DF1toTC, DF2toTC, DSB-S, DSA-S, P1-H, PIO1-H	3.00	0.013	0.011
2	DF1toTC, DF2toTC, DSB-S, DSA-S, MC2-H	3.25	0.094	0.081
3	MC1-H	3.50	0.706	0.183
4	DF1toTC, DF2toTC, DSB-S, DSA-S, MC4c-H, ROM1-H	3.50	0.325	0.281
5	MC4b-H, ROM1-H	4.25	0.899	0.233
6	P1-H, ASIC1-H	4.50	1.000	0.313
7	MC4a-H, ROM1-H	4.75	1.000	0.583
8	DF1toTC, DF2toTC, DSB-S, DSA-S, MC3a-H, ROM1-H	6.25	1.000	1.081
9	MC3b-H ROM1-H	7.25	1.000	1.383
10	DF1-S, DF2-S, DSB-S, DSA-S, P2-H, RAM1-H, ROM1-H	16.00	1.000	11.460
11	DF1toTC, DF2toTC, DSB-S, DSA-S, P2-H, PIO1-H, RAM1-H, ROM1-H	17.00	1.000	12.080
12	P2-H, ASIC1-H, RAM1-H, ROM1-H	18.50	1.000	12.380

Table 4. Pareto-optimal set of alternatives found by exhaustive search. Note that all alternatives also include: RM-S,SC-S, FC-S, SR-S, RC-S.

The only constraint used for this problem is that λ must be greater than zero which insures the design will meet real-time constraints. In most real-world problems additional constraints may be required to guarantee compatibility between the hardware modules (*e.g.*, coprocessors can only be interfaced to microprocessors from the same manufacturer). This size problem is small enough so that exhaustive search can be used to enumerate the Pareto optimal set within a reasonable amount of computational time. There are a total of 12 Pareto optimal alternatives which are identified in Table 4. Two tests were conducted using an EA with a population size of μ=20. (This example was small enough so that $\mu = 20$ was sufficient. For more complex problems μ should be several times larger.) The EA was run for Γ=50 generations with mutation probabilities of $p_1 = 0.8$, $p_2 = 0.05$, and $p_3 = 0.15$. After Γ generations had been processed, alternatives with rank 1 were output.

The first test ranked the three given alternatives according to cost (lower cost implies higher ranking). **EvoC** correctly identified alternatives 2 and 4 from Table 4. The second test ranked the three given alternatives according to Δ_c(higher value implies higher ranking). The EA consistently identified alternatives 10, 11, and 12 from Table 4. The significant aspect of these results is not simply that the EA can find *any* Pareto optimal solution, but rather that *specific* Pareto optimal solutions which correspond to a designer's preferences can be found.

7 Final Remarks

Complete enumeration of the Pareto optimal frontier $\mathcal{P}$ is rarely possible due to the high dimensionality of the tradeoff surface. Such a level of enumeration is often not even necessary as a designer's preferences really only demand enumeration of $\mathcal{P}' \subset \mathcal{P}$. This means that the progression of the phenotypical Pareto front should hopefully be towards $\mathcal{P}'$ rather than to some arbitrary subset of $\mathcal{P}$.

So how do we achieve this progression of the phenotypical Pareto front? Recall that in each generation the alternatives are ranked according to the designer's preferences. It can be shown that this preference relationship preserves Pareto optimality. *Then, if we choose the most preferred alternatives for reproduction, we are letting a designer's preferences drive the search process of the EA*. Our example has shown that we can achieve this goal with the combination of EAs and ISMAUT.

References

1. Special editions on hardware/software codesign appearing in *IEEE Design & Test of Computers*, vol.10, no.3 & no. 4, 1993
2. J.G. D'Ambrosio and X. Hu, "Configuration-level hardware/software partition for real-time embedded systems," *Proceedings of the Third International Workshop on Hardware-Software Co-Design*, 34-41, 1994
3. C. Fonseca and P. Fleming, "An Overview of Evolutionary Algorithms in Multiobjective Optimization", *Evolutionary Computation*, Vol. 3, No. 1, 1-17, 1995
4. G. Greenwood, X. Hu, and J. D'Ambrosio, "Fitness Functions for Multipleobjective Optimization Problems: Combining Preferences With Pareto Rankings", *FOGA4* (to appear)
5. C. White, A. Sage, and S. Dozono, "A Model of Multiattribute Decisionmaking and Tradeoff Weight Determination Under Uncertainty", *IEEE Trans. Syst., Man, Cybern.*", Vol SMC-14, 223-229, 1984
6. R.L. Keeney and H. Raiffa, *Decisions with Multiple Objectives: Preferences and Value Tradeoffs*, John Wiley & Sons, NY, 1976
7. J. Horn and N. Nafpliotis, " Multiobjective Optimization using the Niched Pareto Genetic Algorithm", IlliGAL Report 93005, University of Illinois at Urbana-Champaign
8. D. Goldberg, *Genetic Algorithms in Search, Optimization, and Machine Learning*, Addison-Wesley Pub. Co., 1989

Evolutionary Air Traffic Flow Management for Large 3D-problems

[1]C.H.M. van Kemenade [2]J.M. van den Akker [3]J.N. Kok
kemenade@cwi.nl vdakker@nlr.nl joost@cs.leidenuniv.nl

[1]CWI, Department of Software Technology,
P.O. Box 94079, 1090 GB Amsterdam, The Netherlands
[2]National Aerospace Laboratory NLR, Informatics Division,
Anthony Fokkkerweg 2, 1059 CM Amsterdam, The Netherlands
[3]Leiden University, Department of Computer Science
P.O. Box 9512, 2300 RA Leiden, The Netherlands

Abstract. We present an evolutionary tool to solve free-route Air Traffic Flow Management problems within a three-dimensional air space [4]. This is the first evolutionary tool which solves free-route planning problems involving a few hundred aircraft. We observe that the importance of the recombination operator increases as we scale to larger problem instances. The evolutionary algorithm is based on a variant of the elitist recombination algorithm. We show a theoretical analysis of the problem, and present the results of experiments.

1 Introduction

Previous work on application of Evolutionary Algorithms (EA's) to the Air Traffic Flow Management (ATFM) problem [1, 2, 7] handles only small problems involving few aircraft within a two-dimensional air space. We develop an evolutionary tool that can handle three-dimensional ATFM planning problems involving a few hundred of aircraft.

For smaller 2D-problem instances we obtained good results with a mutation based EA [7]. This system solves problems involving up to 20 aircraft within a square 2D sector of size 200×200 km. Using these problem instances it appeared to be impossible to define a good recombination operator. All aircraft are relatively close to one another, and as a result of the small size of the 2D sector the probability that a combination of trajectories from different plans resulted in good offspring is small. When making the transition to the large scale problems we are studying currently, involving up to 800 aircraft within a 3D-sector of size 2000×2000 km, there are more aircraft which do not get into each others proximity. As a result different conflicts can be resolved in parallel, and a recombination operator can bring the solutions together in a single plan. So by scaling the size of the problem instances, the recombination operation changed from a virtually useless operator to an important operator.

There is no reason for abandoning the use of a probabilistic algorithm, as deterministic algorithms can not be guaranteed to give a solution within a reasonable amount of time either on the ATFM problem. This problem, which will be defined formally in section 2, is assumed to be NP-hard. Hence we have to rely on effective (probabilistic) approximation methods. The plans are created before the aircraft departs. Real-time planning is only used when aircraft deviate from the original plan, and should involve only a subset of all aircraft trajectories. On the ATFM problem a probabilistic method can be as good as any deterministic method, when designed carefully. Deterministic methods can also end up in deadlock situations, or encounter problems which can not be solved by that method. Our method has been designed in such a way that it searches a broad class of possible solutions, and it is not biased toward specific solutions in this class. This helps in preventing deadlock situations, and improves global search.

In section 2 we discuss air traffic flow management problems, in section 3 we show a theoretical analysis, in section 4 we introduce the evolutionary algorithm, section 5 gives the experimental set-up and the results, and finally we draw conclusions and discuss further work in section 6.

2 Air Traffic Flow Management Problem

Air Traffic Flow Management (ATFM) is involved in planning the movements of aircraft. A complete plan describes the trajectories of all involved aircraft. A trajectory defines the exact position of an aircraft as a function of time, so it corresponds to a path with additional temporal information. Two trajectories are conflicting when at a certain time the separation between these trajectories is too small. The minimal required separation between trajectories is 16 nautical miles in the horizontal plane (1 nautical mile = 1,852 meters), or 2000 ft vertical separation (1 foot = 0.3048 meters). Usually a plan is created for a sector of limited size. A sector contains a number of layers, called flight-levels. The altitudes of different flight-levels are chosen in such a way that aircraft flying in different flight-levels are never in conflict. An ATFM plan assigns a single trajectory to each aircraft. These trajectories should be chosen in such a way that there are no conflicts between aircraft. Furthermore the length of all trajectories and the number of maneuvers should be kept low. There is also a fairness requirement that states that the additional distances and maneuvers should be divided among all the aircraft (i.e. it should not be the case that only a few aircraft do all the maneuvering and do all the extra flying). The primary target of a planning is to let all aircraft move from their entry to their exit location in such a way that none of the trajectories are conflicting. As a secondary target, one can minimize the number of maneuvers, the additional distance, and try to satisfy the fairness requirement. Maneuvers are usually uncomfortable for the passengers, and too much additional distance may lead to a delayed arrival of the aircraft. Currently ATFM is based on a restricted model of the air space, the so called network model. This model assumes a fixed network of corridors within the air space, each containing a number of flight-levels. An aircraft is assumed to fly through a corridor from beacon to beacon. Intersections of corridors are always marked by beacons. Only near those beacons, an aircraft is allowed to switch to a different corridor. So this model introduces a kind of three dimensional highway network. The main difference compared to a highway network is that flight control within this ATFM network is more strict. Aircraft are assumed to follow the trajectory which is agreed upon in advance, and pilots have to ask for clearance when they want to deviate from the planned trajectory. The network model restricts the number of possible trajectories. As a result the network model does not use the full capacity of the air space. Due to the increasing amount of air traffic, the air space above Europe is almost saturated. Increased accuracy of navigation equipment and the availability of better computers allows for less restricted air space models. One such model is the free-route model which allows arbitrary shaped trajectories, has a larger degree of flexibility, but it results in a completely different planning problem. In this paper we propose an evolutionary algorithm to create such a planning, and we study how this algorithm scales with respect to the size of the problem instances.

3 Theoretical Analysis of the ATFM problem

We assume that a planning has to be created for a square sector of size $s \times s$, containing l separate flight-levels. The source and the destination of the aircraft are 2D-locations, chosen at random within the sector, using a uniform distribution. The flight-level of the aircraft at the entry- and exit-location can be chosen freely. The entry and exit locations of flights in a planning do not have to correspond to actual locations of airports. When aircraft are departing or approaching an airport their trajectory is managed by the controllers at the corresponding airport. Such a local Air Traffic Control center at an airport usually manages lower regions of the airspace that do not overlap with the high altitude sector we are considering here. We may hence assume that the aircraft enter the airspace at some distance from the airport. We assume that all the aircraft have the same velocity v. The flights are to be planned within the interval $[0, t_{hor}]$. The time of entry is selected at random within this interval. This time of entry is accepted if the aircraft can reach its exit location within the interval $[0, t_{hor}]$, when flying in a straight line.

In order to predict the number of conflicts we can use physical models describing the number of collisions between a set of gas molecules in a box per unit of time [5]. When translating such a model to our case we get the following formula,

$$E[\#Conf] = \alpha \frac{t_{hor}\, d_{sep}\, v}{s^2 l} n^2.$$

Here v is the average velocity. The constant α is introduced to account for the non-uniform distribution of aircraft over the sector. The density of aircraft will be highest near the center of the sector, and lowest near its borders. Within the gas model this constant is one as the gas molecules are distributed uniformly over the complete volume. The complexity of a problem instance scales quadratically with the number of aircraft involved. This is tested as follows. We have varied the number of aircraft from 100 to 800. For each number of aircraft 25 random

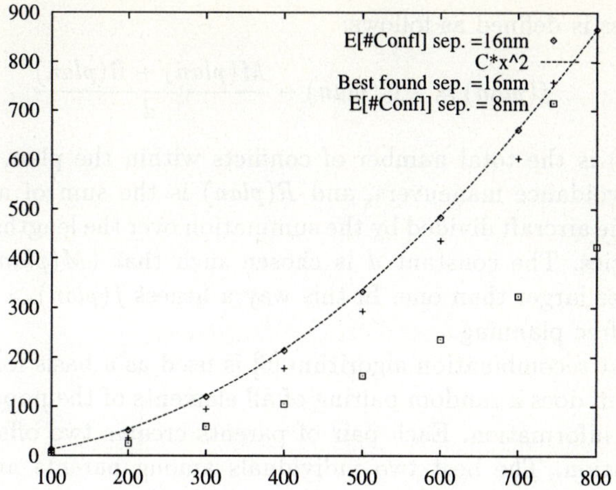

Fig. 1. $E[\#conf]$ as a function of n for a horizontal separation of 8 nm and 16 nm.

problem instances are created. For each problem instance 1000 random plans, containing only straight-line trajectories, were generated. Figure 1 shows the average number of conflicts detected as a function of the number of aircraft, and a fitted curve showing a quadratic scaling in the number of aircraft. Observe the close match between the fitted curve and the simulation results. Figure 1 also contains the average number of conflicts of the best plan $E[\#\textit{Conflicts best}]$ which is estimated by taking an average over 25 independent problem instances (for each instance the #conflicts in the best plan out of 1000 random plans is used). When comparing the result for a horizontal separation d_{sep} of 16 nm to those for a separation of 8 nm we observe the linear scaling in this parameter. This is in accordance with the gas model.

4 Evolutionary Algorithm

The elements of the population are plans. A plan is a set of trajectories, one for each flight to be scheduled. The plans in the initial population involve only straight-line trajectories from the entry to the exit location at a fixed flight-level. If we consider a problem with three flight-levels, then this yields already 3^n possible flight plans (n is the number of flights). It seems to be a reasonable choice to consider only trajectories with a small number of maneuvers. We do this by starting from an initial population containing straight-line trajectories only, and use the recombination operator to search for non-conflicting combinations of trajectories. Trajectories containing many additional maneuvers are not likely to be good due to the fairness requirement: a solution with only straight-line trajectories is an optimal solution, according to our fitness measure. As evolution proceeds, more complex trajectories arise due to the application of a mutation operator.

The fitness is defined as follows:

$$f(plan) = -C(plan) - \frac{M(plan) + R(plan)}{d}$$

Here $C(plan)$ is the total number of conflicts within the plan, $M(plan)$ is the number of avoidance maneuvers, and $R(plan)$ is the sum of all the distances traveled by the aircraft divided by the summation over the lengths of the straight-line trajectories. The constant d is chosen such that $(M(plan) + R(plan))/d$ never becomes larger than one. In this way a fitness $f(plan) > -1$ corresponds to a conflict free planning.

The Elitist recombination algorithm [6] is used as a basis for our algorithm. This algorithm does a random pairing of all elements of the population, without using fitness information. Each pair of parents creates two offspring by means of recombination. The best two individuals among parents and offspring are propagated to the next generation. This competition between parents and offspring prevents rapid duplication of relatively fit individuals, and as a result decreases the probability of premature convergence. Within our implementation each offspring competes with only one of its parents. This scheme has a lower selective pressure than the standard elitist recombination scheme. This competition with one parent is also used in the deterministic crowding scheme [3]. But deterministic crowding lets offspring compete with the most similar parent. The Elitist recombination algorithm is chosen as it does not deteriorate the average fitness when inferior offspring is produced due to the (population) elitism, and it prevents too rapid convergence of the population (the offspring always has to compete against its parents).

The main operator in our algorithm is the recombination operator. If two conflicts involve two disjoint sets of aircraft, then often it is possible to resolve these conflicts independently. A good recombination operator should be able to merge separate resolutions. The recombination operator creates one offspring using two parents. It starts with an empty plan for the offspring. Then it iteratively selects an aircraft and takes the corresponding trajectory from one of its parents. This parent is selected as follows. One of the parents is selected at random, and it is checked whether the corresponding trajectory would introduce new conflicts within the child. If it does not introduce conflicts this parent is selected, otherwise the other parent is selected. The trajectory of the selected parent is added to the child. So aircraft are selected in a random order, and for each flight the primary parent is selected at random. This selection procedure results in a preference for non-conflicting trajectories. This bias helps the recombination operator to scale-up well with the size of the problem instances. When a (purely random) uniform recombination operator is applied it likely results in offspring performing worse than the parents, when a few hundred of aircraft are involved.

The mutation operator is the only operator that introduces new trajectories within our algorithm. A new trajectory is created by making a copy of one of the existing trajectories and adding some additional maneuvers to it. Two different mutation operators have been defined:

```
while ¬ready do
  /* apply Elitist recombination for N_gen generations */
  for i ← 1 to N_gen do
    elitist recombine Population
  /* introduce new trajectories by means of mutation */
  for i ← 1 to (F_mut × #conflicts best) do
    pl ← random plan from Population
    fl ← random conflicting trajectory from pl
    k ← 0
    repeat
      k ← k + 1
      if k < N_try then
        ntr ← mutate(fl)
      else
        ntr ← random straight(fl)
    until nconflicts(pl\fl, ntr) < nconflicts(pl\fl, fl) ∨ k ≥ N_try
    if nconflicts(pl\fl, ntr) < nconflicts(pl\fl, fl) then
      pl ← ntr ∪ pl\fl
```

Fig. 2. Pseudo-code of main loop of Evolutionary ATFM

level-mutation: modifies an existing trajectory by adding a random change of flight-level at a random time.

detour-mutation: introduces a detour by changing its heading by $\pm 45^o$, flying for a random duration in this new direction, and then changes its heading towards the exit-location again.

Note that the detour mutation can cancel previously inserted maneuvers. Although these mutation operators are relatively easy to implement one can not guarantee that a single application of these operators will produce a good trajectory. New trajectories that do not resolve any conflicts will rapidly be filtered out of the population by the EA (such trajectories only introduce a penalty and no benefit for the fitness). If the probability that good trajectories are produced becomes small, premature convergence becomes likely. In order to prevent this have taken the mutation out of the selection-production cycle. We run the EA for a few generations and then we apply mutation to the plans present within the population. A mutation is only accepted if the produced trajectory increases fitness when replacing the original trajectory. Using this scheme we get a more constant production of well-performing trajectories.

Figure 2 summarizes the main loop of the evolutionary ATFM in pseudocode. The ready-predicate becomes true when a conflict-free solution is obtained, or when the maximal number of function evaluations is reached, and nconflicts(*pl*, *tr*) counts the number of between trajectory *tr* and the trajectories with plan *pl*.

Our evolutionary algorithm is designed in such a way that we get a good balance between exploration and exploitation. Good exploration is obtained because two independent applications of the recombination operator to the same pair of parents are still likely to result in different offspring and from the bias towards better trajectories within the mutation operator. Good exploitation comes from the bias towards preserving better combinations in the recombination operator, and from Elitist recombination algorithm with low selective pressure.

Our experience is that incorporation of problem specific knowledge is usually necessary when solving large problems. In this case we have introduced knowledge in several ways. We start with a population containing only straight-line trajectories. Within acceptable plans the trajectories usually do not contain many maneuvers, so this is a reasonable starting point. A single application of the mutation operator can only introduce a small number of additional maneuvers. Furthermore knowledge is incorporated in the recombination operator as it makes a biased decision when it has to decide which parent will provide the trajectory for a certain aircraft. Using this knowledge the probability that a well-performing offspring is created is increased, especially for problems involving many aircraft. Designing biased operators is not a trivial task. One has to introduce a bias to enhance the probability that an operator produces reasonable offspring, but introducing too much bias might easily lead to premature convergence. An important guideline we used is that independent operator application should likely result in different offspring, even when using the same pair of parents.

An aspect of our algorithm is that it does not rely too much on local search methods. Instead it uses a kind of random generation of trajectories by means of the mutation operator. The primary goal of the EA is to find those trajectories that perform well and combine these trajectories to a complete planning. Such a probabilistic approach does not use a explicit local search method. As a result it does not easily get trapped in a kind of deadlock situation where no enhancements are possible.

5 Experiments and Results

During the experiments we varied the number of aircraft to be planned, and as a result the expected number of conflicts in the sector. The parameters shown in Table 1 were used during all the experiments. A single application of the current mutation operators introduces one avoidance maneuver. Such an avoidance maneuver contains several elementary maneuvers. For example an application of the detour-mutation introduces two additional maneuvers, the first is a change of heading by $\pm 45^o$, and the second is a curve to move the heading of the aircraft towards the exit location.

The first set of results is obtained using straight-line trajectories only. Mutation is only used to (re)introduce straight-line trajectories that got lost. It does not introduce new trajectories. Even for this (restricted) subset of possible trajectories, l for each flight, the search space already is large. The number of possible plans is proportional to l^n. The other experiments use level-mutation, detour-mutation and mixed mutation. The mixed mutation operator first tries

Parameter		Value
plannings horizon	t_{hor}	4 hours
number of aircraft	n	100-600 aircraft
velocity	v	900 km/hour
separation	d_{sep}	16 nautical miles
size of sector	s	2000 km
#levels	l	3
population size		16
#function evaluations		2500 maximum
#independent runs		25
#avoidance man. per ac.		4
#generation inner loop	N_{gen}	2
rel. #mutations in outer loop	F_{mut}	0.5
#tries for a mutation	N_{try}	10

Table 1. Parameters used during the experiments

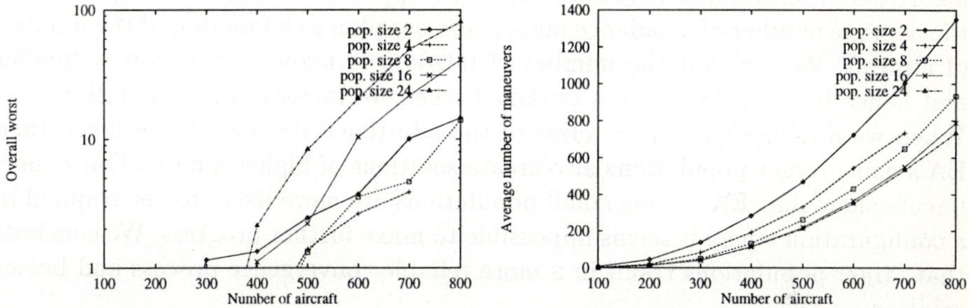

Fig. 3. overall worst solution over 25 independent problems (left) and number of avoidance maneuvers (right) for different population sizes

to find a better trajectory by applying detour-mutation, if this fails the level-mutation is applied once. The detour-mutation is applied first because it has better convergence properties. During the experiments we varied the number of aircraft. For each problem instance 25 random plans were created. All graphs show the negated fitness. A run is terminated when its negated fitness drops below one, this corresponds to a conflict-free planning. We recall that the fitness measure has been chosen in such a way that $\lfloor -f(plan) \rfloor$ corresponds to the number of conflicts within the plan. Only detour mutation is used, unless stated otherwise.

Figure 3 (left) shows the overall worst solution over all 25 independent problem instances. Different curves correspond to different population sizes. This graph suggests that the worst case behavior gets better when the population size gets smaller. The only exception is in the experiment using the extremely

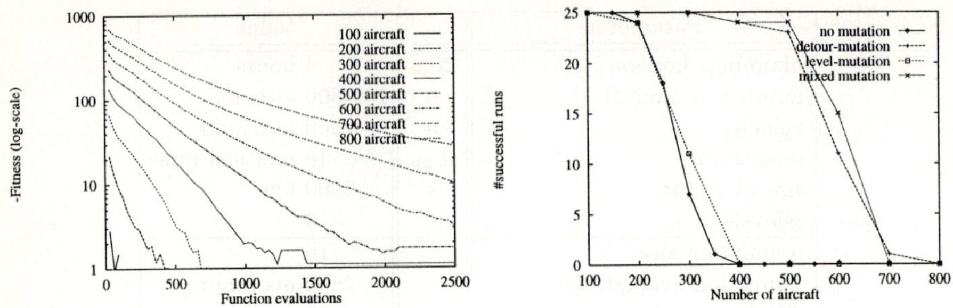

Fig. 4. Convergence curves for different problem sizes (left) and number of successful runs for different types of mutation (right)

small population size 2, which gets trapped easily. The good performance of small populations is mainly due to the upper limit on the number of function evaluations. The larger the population size, the higher the probability that the algorithm is terminated because it hits this upper limit. Figure 3 (right) shows the average number of avoidance maneuvers per plan as a function of the number of aircraft. We see that the number of introduced maneuvers becomes smaller and hence better solutions are obtained when we increase the population size. When we measure quality in terms of the additional distance to be flown then EA's using larger populations also create solutions of higher quality. Our experiments show that EA's using small populations are more likely to get trapped in a configuration where it seems impossible to make further progress. We conclude that larger populations result in a more reliable convergence process and better solutions.

Figure 4 (left) shows the average negated fitness of the best solution as a function of the number of function evaluations for a population size 16. The small bulbs in most curves are due to the fact that fitness is calculated over the non-terminated runs, so if a run terminates successfully, the shown average fitness can increase. We see that the speed of convergence is dependent upon the problem size. The failure of the algorithm to solve our largest problem instances is probably due to the limit on the number of function evaluations. On the 800 aircraft problem instances the method still obtains a 30-fold reduction in the number of conflicts on average.

Figure 4 (right) shows the number of successful runs out of the 25 independent runs, for the different types of mutation operators. When allowing no mutation, the problem rapidly becomes unsolvable as the number of aircraft increases. Without mutation only solutions involving straight-line trajectories are considered. When mutation is allowed the probability of finding a conflict-free solution is much larger, and the scaling properties are better. The method using level-mutation performs slightly better than the method without specialized mutation operators. This is probably due to the fact that a level-change takes quite some time, and that during a level-change an aircraft claims space within a number of flight-levels. A single level change can also easily introduce dependencies between aircraft.

6 Conclusions

The free-route planning problem has a search space that grows exponentially when the number of aircraft increases. To be able to handle large scale problems of this type it is required to incorporate knowledge regarding the problem domain. We have done so by means of a non-uniform seeding of the initial population and by designing problem specific evolutionary operators. Introduction of such operators has to be done carefully in order to prevent that certain good solutions are ignored and to prevent premature convergence. The choice of the evolutionary algorithm and the way mutations are introduced also have a strong influence on the balance between exploration and exploitation. A proper balance is necessary to obtain good solutions using only a limited amount of computation. The designed algorithm performs well and requires only small populations.

Given the fact that the airspace above Europe contains at least 9 separate flight levels, the our current tool can route approximately $(3 \times 4 \times 500 =)$ 6000 aircraft within a time span of 12 hours, using a horizontal separation of 16 nautical mile.

Further research will be devoted to real-time replanning. Due to weather conditions, or delays at airports it is likely that some aircraft do not fly according to their planning. Under such circumstances it is important to have rapid replanning tools, which use the current planning as their starting point.

References

1. J. Alliot, H. Gruber, G. Joly, and M. Schoenauer. Genetic algorithms for solving air traffic control conflicts. In *Ninth conference on Artificial Intelligence for Applications*, pages 338–344. IEEE Computer Society press, 1993.
2. I.S. Gerdes. Application of genetic algorithms to the problem of free-routing for aircraft. In *First IEEE conference on Evolutionary Computation*, pages 536–541, 1994.
3. S.W. Mahfoud. Crowding and preselection revisited. In *Parallel Problem Solving from Nature - 2*, pages 27–36. Springer, 1992.
4. Arnold Field Obe. *International Air Traffic Control; Management of the World's Airspace.* Pergamon Press, Oxford, 1985.
5. Princeton University, Department of Civil Engeneering. *Proceedings of the Conference on Safety Issues in Air Traffic Syustems Planning and Design*, 1983.
6. D. Thierens and D.E. Goldberg. Elitist recombination: an integrated selection recombination GA. In *First IEEE conference on Evolutionary Computation.* IEEE Press, 1994.
7. C.H.M. van Kemenade, C.F.W. Hendriks, H.H. Hesselink, and J.N. Kok. Evolutionary computation in air traffic control planning. In S. Forrest, editor, *Sixth International Conference on Genetic Algorithms*, pages 611–616. Morgan Kaufmann, 1995.

Genetic-Based Dynamic Load Balancing: Implementation and Evaluation

Masaharu Munetomo[1], Yoshiaki Takai[2], and Yoshiharu Sato[1]

[1] Information and Data Analysis, Faculty of Engineering,
[2] Division of Research and Development, Computing Center,
Hokkaido University, Sapporo 060, Japan.

Abstract. This paper presents an adaptive dynamic load balancing scheme employing a genetic algorithm which includes an evaluation mechanism of fitness values in stochastic environments. A sender-initiative task migration algorithm continues to send unnecessary requests for a task migration while the system load is heavy, which brings much overhead before the migration finishes. In a genetic-based dynamic load balancing scheme we propose, a small subset of computers to which the requests are sent off is adaptively determined by a learning procedure to reduce unnecessary requests. The learning procedure consists of stochastic learning automata and genetic operators applied to a population of strings each of which stands for a subset of computers to which task migration requests are sent off. We implement the proposed algorithm on an actual distributed system which consists of UNIX workstations. We show the effectiveness of our approach through empirical investigations on the distributed system.

1 Introduction

A distributed system consists of autonomous computers loosely connected via a communicating network. For high utilization of system facilities and quick response of tasks from users, it is essential to balance loads among computers. A dynamic load balancing algorithm equalizes each computer's load by migrating tasks from heavily-loaded computers to lightly-loaded ones.

In this paper, we present a dynamic load balancing scheme which evolves strategy for determining a destination computer to migrate a task. Basically our approach is an extended version of sender-initiative algorithms[2, 7]. In sender-initiative algorithms, a heavily-loaded computer sends task migration requests to find a lightly-loaded computers as a task receiver. While overall system load remains light, the sender-initiative algorithm performs well because a heavily-loaded computer usually succeeds in finding a lightly-loaded computer to migrate a task. When the system load is heavy, it becomes difficult to find a lightly-loaded computer because most computers cannot afford to receive additional tasks. Therefore, many request and reject messages are repeatedly sent, which needs much communication overhead and a lot of time is consumed before execution.

We employ multicast message exchanging in which a combination of the request messages issued for a task migration is determined through a learning procedure carried out within each computer. The objective of the learning is to improve the acceptance rate of the request messages in a heavy system load, which ensures effective load balancing that decreases mean response time of all the tasks processed in a distributed system. We develop a learning mechanism which consists of stochastic learning automata(SLA) and genetic algorithms(GA) applied to the population of strings each of which stands for a combination of computers to which request messages should be sent off. The learning algorithm is called *a stochastic genetic algorithm* (StGA)[5]. This algorithm employs SLA in its fitness evaluations in order to adapt to stochastic environments.

2 StGA: GA for stochastic environments

2.1 Stochastic Learning Automata

A stochastic environment generates a binary *payoff* (reward or penalty) in a probabilistic way whenever it receives an *action* as its input. The objective of reinforcement learning algorithms such as the SLA is to maximize the probability to have reward payoffs.

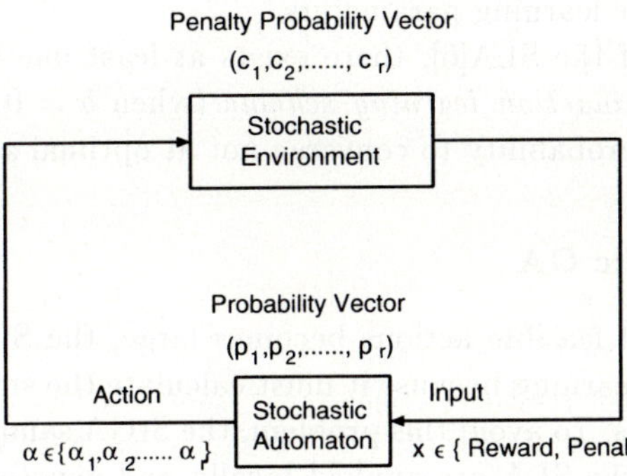

Fig. 1. Stochastic learning automata

Figure 1 illustrates an environment-automaton interaction. We have a set of feasible actions $\{\alpha_1, \cdots, \alpha_r\}$ (r : the number of feasible actions) for the automaton. A stochastic environment is formulated into an r-dimensional penalty probability vector $\mathbf{c} = (c_1, \cdots, c_r)$, where c_i stands for the probability to get penalty (failure) when an action α_i is done in the environment. The purpose of the learning is to find an optimal action α_k which minimizes the probability for the penalties ($c_k = \min_i c_i$).

We have a probability vector $\mathbf{p}(t) = (p_1(t), \cdots, p_r(t))$ for the automaton, where $p_i(t)$ is the probability for the action α_i to be selected at time t. When we have $p_k(t) = 1$, the stochastic automaton is said to reach an optimal probability vector. The probability vector at time $t+1$ is obtained by the following equation based on the result of the selected action at time t.

$$\begin{aligned} p_i(t+1) &= p_i(t) + \sum_{i \neq j}^{r} f_j(\mathbf{p}(t)), \\ p_j(t+1) &= p_j(t) - f_j(\mathbf{p}(t)) \quad (\forall j \neq i), \\ &\qquad \text{if succeeded (Reward).} \end{aligned} \tag{1}$$

$$\begin{aligned} p_i(t+1) &= p_i(t) - \sum_{i \neq j}^{r} g_j(\mathbf{p}(t)), \\ p_j(t+1) &= p_j(t) + g_j(\mathbf{p}(t)) \quad (\forall j \neq i), \\ &\qquad \text{if failed (Penalty).} \end{aligned} \tag{2}$$

In the linear learning schemes, f_j and g_j are obtained by the following linear functions:

$$\begin{aligned} f_j(\mathbf{p}) &= ap_j \ (j = 1, \cdots, r), \\ g_j(\mathbf{p}) &= b/(r-1) - bp_j, \end{aligned} \tag{3}$$

where a and b are the learning parameters.

In ε-optimality of the SLA[6], there exists at least one learning parameter of the *linear reward-inaction learning scheme* (when $b = 0$) for an arbitrarily smaller error ε (the probability to converge not at optimal actions).

2.2 The Stochastic GA

When the number of feasible actions becomes large, the SLA show extremely slow convergence in learning because it must calculate the state probabilities for all the feasible actions. To avoid this problem, the StGA samples a small number of actions to which the SLA are applied locally and genetic operators such as crossover and mutation[3] are applied to generate new actions. Each sampled action is encoded into a string each of which has its fitness value. The fitness value specifies the probability for the string to be selected when an action is applied to the environment. These values are the same as the probability vector in the SLA. So the sum of fitness values in the population becomes 1. The initial fitness is set to be $1/n$ where n is the number of strings in the population.

Figure 2 shows an overview of the StGA. The algorithm proceeds as follows: (1) A string (action) is selected according to the probability which equals to its fitness value. (2) the selected action is applied to the environment. (3) The environment returns a payoff for the action. (4) Based on the payoff, a *linear learning scheme* of the SLA is applied to the population of strings in order to

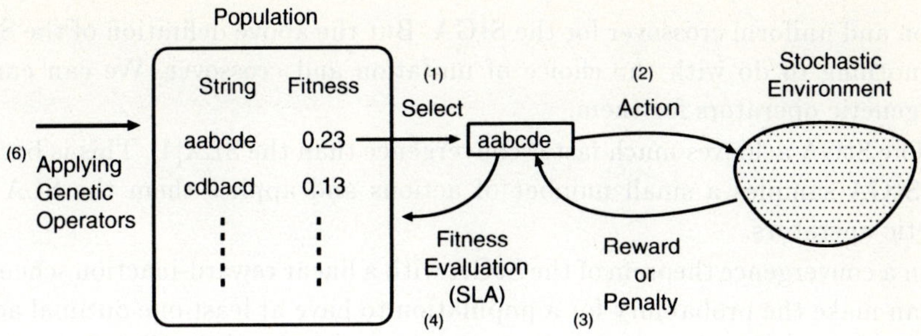

Fig. 2. Overview of the StGA

evaluate fitness values. (5) We repeat (1)—(4) n times, and (6) we apply genetic operators such as crossover and mutation. (7) We repeat (1)—(6) m times until a termination criterion is satisfied. We summarize the algorithm in Figure 3.

```
algorithm  StGA ( m, n );

Initialization;
for  i = 1  to  m  do
   for j = 1  to  n do
      Select  a  string;
      Do  an  action;
      Evaluation;
   endfor;
   Crossover;
   Mutation;
endfor;
```

Fig. 3. StGA: the algorithm

In fitness evaluations, we employ a linear learning scheme. So the fitness values in a population are recalculated by the equations (2) and (3) based on the result of the performed action.

The fitness value of the offspring after applying a mutation is directly inherited from its parent. In crossover, its fitness becomes the mean value of those of its parents. We employ a ranking selection for the StGA which replaces the worst string by the offspring.

Concerning mutation and crossover, the earlier work[4] employs simple mutation and uniform crossover for the StGA. But the above definition of the StGA has nothing to do with the choice of mutation and crossover. We can employ any genetic operators for them.

The StGA achieves much faster convergence than the SLA[4]. This is because the StGA samples a small number of actions and applies them the SLA and genetic operators.

In a convergence theorem of the StGA with a linear reward-inaction scheme[5], we can make the probability for a population to have at least one optimal action be any closer to one by adjusting a learning parameter of the SLA in its fitness evaluations.

3 Dynamic Load Balancing by Using the StGA

3.1 Sender-initiative Algorithms

A dynamic load balancing algorithm equalizes each computer's load in a distributed system by migrating tasks from heavily-loaded computers to lightly-loaded ones. The load status of a computer is usually determined by the length of its task waiting queue. When the length exceeds a limit, the computer is judged to be heavily-loaded, and otherwise, it is lightly-loaded. In sender-initiative dynamic load balancing algorithms[7], a heavily-loaded computer sends request messages for task migration to find a destination computer which is lightly-loaded. A *Request* message for the task migration is initially issued from a heavily loaded computer to another computer randomly selected. If the selected computer is lightly loaded, it returns an *Accept* message and is ready for receiving the migrated task. Otherwise, it returns a *Reject* message and the heavily loaded computer tries for others until an accept message is received or the number of requests exceeds a limit. If all the requests are rejected, no task migration takes place.

Conventional approaches employ unicast or broadcast messages to find a destination. Using unicast which sends one message at a time, we always fail to find a destination when almost all computers are heavily-loaded, which leads to many *Request* messages repeatedly issued in vain. On the other hand, when we use broadcast messages which are sent to all the computers in a distributed system, a destination is found without fail, but we need huge communication cost when the system size becomes large.

From the viewpoints above, we employ a multicast approach in which multiple messages are sent to a limited number of computers at the same time. If the sending set of the task migration request is appropriately selected, we can find a destination at high probability with small communication overhead. We apply the StGA to construct the sending set of the migration requests. We consider the sending set as a string of the StGA.

3.2 Overview of the Dynamic Load Balancing Algorithm

Figure 4 shows an overview of the dynamic load balancing by using the StGA. An action of the StGA in this application is a series of request messages for a task migration. If we receive at least one *Accept* message and can transfer an excessive task, the action succeeds, and otherwise, it fails.

Each computer has a list of all computers in the distributed system and its own population of strings for the task migration requests. Each string consists of computers' IDs to which messages for task migration requests are sent. This representation is identical to a binary representation $\{b_i\}$ where we set $b_i = 1$ if P_i is included in the list and $b_i = 0$ otherwise.

The initial string is generated by picking up randomly a specified number of computer IDs from the computer list of the system. The initial fitness is set to be $1/n$ where n is the number of strings in the population. We use the StGA to select appropriate sending sets of request messages for task migration. The objective of the learning is to maximize the probability to find lightly-loaded computers.

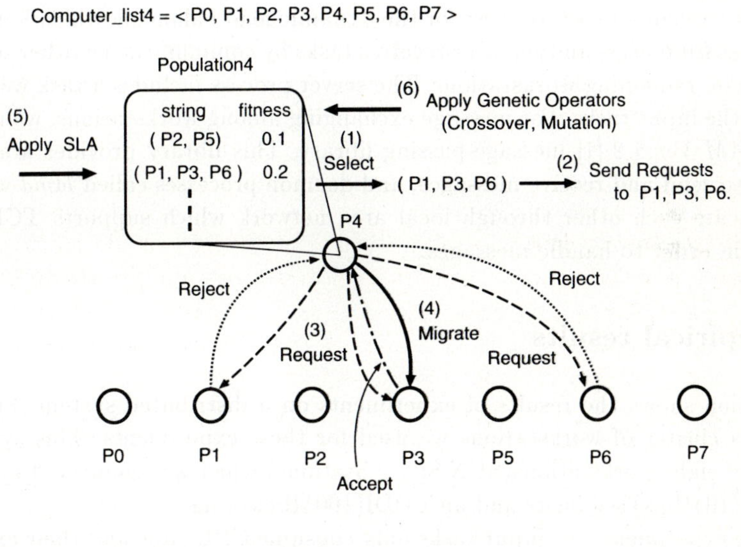

Fig. 4. Dynamic load balancing by using the StGA

When a computer, say $P4$, becomes heavily-loaded, it starts the following task migration process: (1) $P4$ selects a string from its own population. (2) By using multicast, $P4$ sends a set of task migration requests based on the selected string. In the figure, a string $(P1, P3, P6)$ is selected and *Request* messages are multicasted to $P1$, $P3$, and $P6$. (3) The results of the requests are sent back to $P4$. In this case, $P3$ is lightly-loaded and returns an *Accept* message, and other computers return *Reject* messages because they are not lightly-loaded. (4) When $P4$ receives at least one *Accept* message, $P4$ succeeds in finding a lightly-loaded computer and sends a task to be migrated with the message *Migrate* to the computer $P3$. If the received messages are all *Reject*, $P4$ fails in finding a destination. (5) Based on the results of requests, we apply linear learning scheme to the population of strings. (6) After we repeat (1)—(5) n times, we apply genetic operators such as crossover and mutation to the population.

On the above algorithm, the processes from (1) to (5) of the dynamic load balancing corresponds to the processes from (1) to (4) of the StGA, and the process (6) of the dynamic load balancing corresponds to the process (6) of the StGA. The action of the StGA in this application is to send *Request* messages of task migrations and a success of the action means that we find at least one lightly-loaded computer.

3.3 Implementation

We have implemented the proposed dynamic load balancing algorithm on a cluster of UNIX workstations connected by a local area network. On each workstation, we assign a server process for the dynamic load balancing which handles input tasks from users and sends or receives tasks by communicating other server processes on remaining workstations. The server process includes a task waiting queue of the input tasks. For message exchanging among workstations, we make use of *LAM Ver.5.2* [1] message-passing library. This library provides a set of routines to send and receive messages, and daemon processes called *lamd* which communicate each other through local area network which supports TCP/IP protocol in order to handle messages.

4 Empirical results

This section shows the results of experiments on a distributed system. Figure 5 shows a cluster of workstations we used for these experiments. This system consists of eight workstations(SUN Sparc Stations) which are connected by two Ethernet(10Mbps) segments and an FDDI(100Mbps) ring.

In the experiment, the input tasks only consume CPU time and their execution time is exponentially distributed whose mean value is 1000 milliseconds. We employ uniform crossover and simple mutations invoked at every 10 requests. The learning parameters are $a = 0.15$ and $b = 0.25$ (appeared in equations (2) and (3)), and the population size is 10.

Figure 6 shows a comparison of mean response time of the input tasks. In this figure, the x axis is the mean arrival interval time of the tasks. When the value of arrival interval becomes small, tasks arrive frequently and the computers become heavily-loaded. In terms of mean response time of the tasks, we compare dynamic

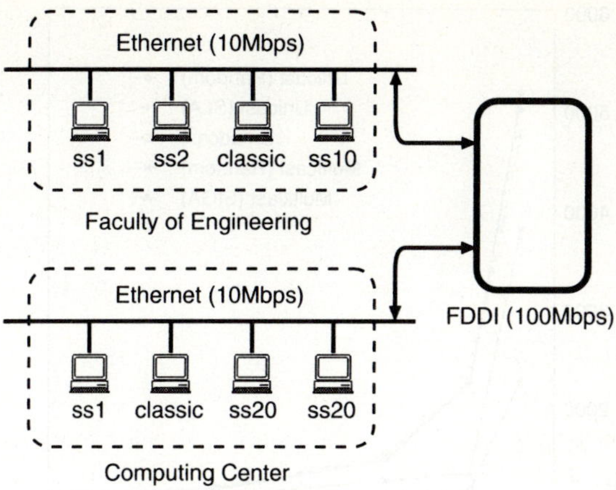

Fig. 5. A cluster of UNIX workstations

load balancing algorithms employing (1) unicast message exchanging without learning, (2) unicast with learning by the SLA, (3) broadcast, (4) multicast without learning, and (5) multicast with learning by the StGA.

The proposed algorithm which uses multicast message exchanging with the StGA achieves the best performance(the smallest mean response time) among the five algorithms. In heavy system loads(most of the computers become heavily-loaded), unicast message exchanging almost fails to find lightly loaded computers and unicast messages are repeatedly sent until a lightly-loaded computer has found. By using a reinforcement learning algorithms such as SLA, we can increase the probability to find lightly-loaded computers, which avoids unnecessary request messages. Using broadcast message exchanging, we can find a lightly-loaded computer without fail by a broadcast message, but even in a broadcast network such as the *Ethernet*, we need much communication overhead in receiving the results of the broadcast from all the computers in a distributed system. Multicast message exchanging reduces communication overhead and improves mean response time. Learning by the StGA in selecting the destination of the multicast maximizes the probability to find lightly-loaded computers with less communication overhead, which leads to smaller value of mean response time in the distributed system.

Figure 7 shows transitions of mean queue length. The x axis shows simulation time and the y axis shows mean queue length of computers in the distributed systems. Input tasks are given only from $t = 0$(s) through $t = 200$(s) and from $t = 400$(s) through $t = 600$(s), which creates periodically heavy system load.

The StGA achieves the smallest mean queue length, which ensures rapid response of the input tasks. In addition, the mean queue length rapidly decreases

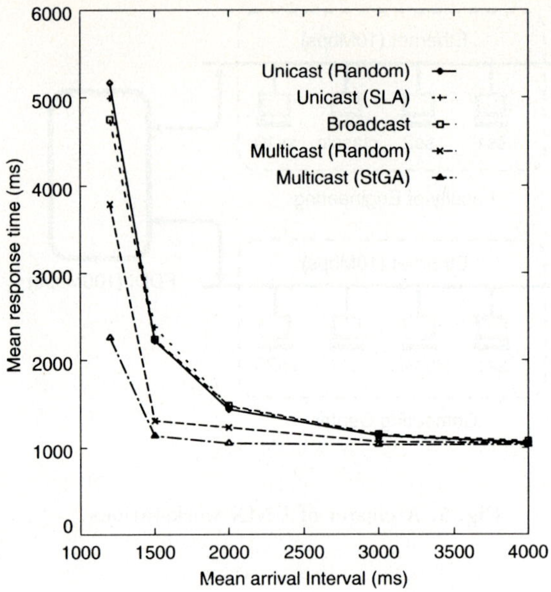

Fig. 6. Comparison of mean response time

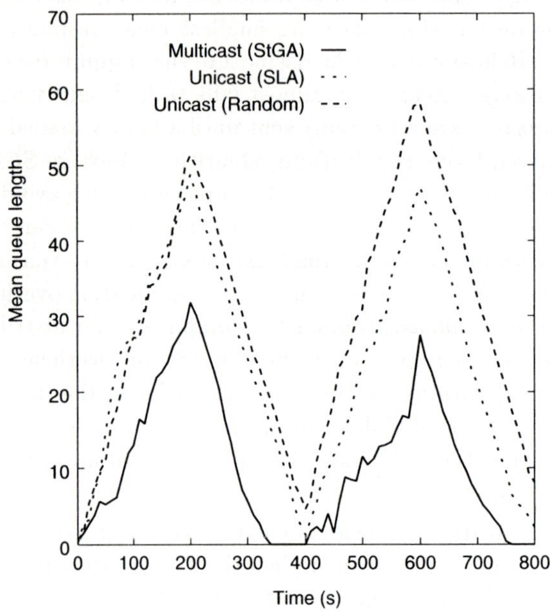

Fig. 7. Comparison of mean queue length for cyclic load changes

in the proposed algorithm after we cease to input tasks. This result shows that heavily-loaded computers effectively migrate tasks by the proposed algorithm employing the StGA, which leads to lower peak and rapid decrease of the queue length.

5 Conclusions

In this paper, we have proposed a dynamic load balancing algorithm which employs multicast message exchanging with learning capability supported by the StGA, a genetic algorithm which has an evaluation mechanism of fitness values for stochastic environments. We have implemented and evaluated the proposed dynamic load balancing algorithm on a distributed system which consists of UNIX workstations. The empirical results show the effectiveness of our algorithm compared with those employing unicast with the SLA, broadcast, and multicast without learning.

References

1. *Ohio LAM 5.2: LAM for C Programmers.* The Ohio State University, 1994.
2. Derek L. Eager, Edward D. Lazowska, and John Zahorjan. Adaptive load sharing in homogeneous distributed systems. *IEEE Transactions on Software Engineering*, 12(5):662–675, May 1986.
3. David E. Goldberg. *Genetic Algorithms in Search, Optimization and Machine Learning.* Addison Wesley, 1989.
4. Masaharu Munetomo, Yoshiaki Takai, and Yoshiharu Sato. A stochastic genetic algorithm for dynamic load balancing in distributed systems. In *Proceedings of the 1995 IEEE Conference on Systems, Man and Cybernetics*, pages 3795–3799, 1995.
5. Masaharu Munetomo, Yoshiaki Takai, and Yoshiharu Sato. An application of genetic algorithm to stochastic learning. *Trans. of the IEICE*, J79-D-II(2), 1996.
6. Kumpati S. Narendra and M. A. L. Thathachar. Learning automata — a survey. *IEEE Transactions on System, Man, and Cybernetics*, 4(4):323–334, July 1974.
7. Niranjan G. Shivaratri, Phillip Krueger, and Mukesh Singhal. Load distributing for locally distributed systems. *IEEE COMPUTER*, 25(12):33–44, December 1992.

Production Scheduling with Genetic Algorithms and Simulation

Gerhard Niemeyer and Patricia Shiroma

University of Regensburg, Chair for Business Informatics
Universitätsstr. 31, 93040 REGENSBURG, Germany

Abstract. A real-world application which develops daily production plans for a large manufacturing company is presented. It is a hybrid system, which combines a genetic algorithm with simulation. Because of the time constraints involved when generating daily schedules, a number of modifications to the standard genetic algorithm were required. A real-valued chromosome representation stored in a hierarchical, dynamic data structure is proposed. Steady-state, rank-based selection, a two-point order crossover and a simple, order-based mutation were implemented. An adaptive feedback controller was introduced to vary the mutation rate as a function of population convergence. Integration of a tabu list minimizes time wasted reevaluating known solutions. A rank-based fitness function is proposed to handle multiple, competing objectives.

1 Introduction

Although genetic algorithms have proven successful in engineering applications, there have been relatively few implementations in the business world [1]. A number of authors have investigated the use of genetic algorithms to solve job-shop problems [2] [3] [4] [5], but most of these studies have been limited to small prototypes or standard benchmark problems. While benchmark problems such as Beasley's OR-testbed [6] provide a simplified means of comparing different optimization methods, they are not very representative of the detail encountered in industrial applications. Because of the simplifications and size limitations of previous studies, a thorough investigation of the suitability of genetic algorithms for production scheduling in real-world applications is needed. This paper explores the possibility of combining genetic algorithms with simulation to generate daily schedules for an actual manufacturing company.

2 Problem Definition

A multinational manufacturing company outsources its production to a number of factories in geographically dispersed locations. The goal of this study is to generate efficient production schedules for any one of these factories. On a given day, an average of 20 jobs are to be processed in each factory. Each job is subdivided into numerous individual processing steps, called tasks here. Most jobs have an average of between 20-50 tasks. Each factory has an average of 30 employees and 10 machines. Each resource can only be assigned to one task at a time. Some parts of the production process can be performed in parallel. Tasks which do not compete for the same resources and are not predecessors of one another can be processed concurrently.

For this particular problem domain, computer processing time is a critical factor. Unlike design problems, the algorithm cannot be allowed to run for weeks in order to develop a truly optimal schedule. Daily schedules need to be generated overnight. As a result, the company is willing to forsake the goal of true optimality in favor of generating the best possible schedules in the amount of time available.

Because it is difficult to calculate the total costs associated with each production schedule, minimization of production time is often used as an approximation for the minimization of costs. In reality, however, minimizing production time usually results in higher costs due to the utilization of additional, or more efficient and therefore more expensive resources. Alternatively, the production plan which incurs the lowest costs often requires extra time to complete, because either fewer, or less efficient and therefore less expensive resources are utilized [7]. Desirable production schedules should achieve an acceptable trade-off between minimum processing costs and time.

With nonlinear production processes, the use of standardized wait times (e.g. 25% of processing time) can lead to errors. Empirical observations in the factory have shown that resource bottlenecks occur at different points in the production process, depending on the daily load and mix of jobs. Although the absolute capacities of the individual resources may appear sufficient, a specific combination of resources required by one job may not be available at the same time. For nonlinear production processes, accurate calculation of wait times requires a complete simulation of each schedule.

3 Hybridization

This paper presents a hybrid application which integrates three subsystems: the DISYS (**DI**sposition **SYS**tem) data management and logistics system, the AMTOS (**A**utomaton-based **M**odeling and **T**ask **O**perating **S**ystem) simulation software [8] and a genetic algorithm. These subsystems work together as follows. The genetic algorithm reads the list of jobs to be scheduled for one day from DISYS. The genetic algorithm generates an initial, random population of legal schedules and inputs each of these into the AMTOS simulation model, which then calculates the time and costs required to complete each schedule. The genetic algorithm uses these data to calculate the fitness function for one schedule. It then attempts to produce better schedules by performing selection, crossover and mutation on the population. The cycle repeats until the maximum number of generations is reached. The best schedule generated is then fed back into DISYS as a suggested production plan. Each of these subsystems will be described briefly.

Because of the large amount of data involved, an object-oriented data management system was utilized. The DISYS class library for object-oriented data management and logistics control was developed at the Chair for Business Informatics at the University of Regensburg under the direction of Prof. Dr. G. Niemeyer. DISYS also features a telecommunications module which enables data acquisition and distribution via modem to each of the geographically dispersed factories.

The AMTOS simulation environment has proven to be an effective tool for modeling nonlinear, asynchronous production systems [8]. For NP-complete problems

[10] such as job shop scheduling, constraints on the amount of processing time available make it practically impossible to find a truly optimal solution. In such situations, simulation studies can be of aid because they attempt to find the best possible solution in the amount of time available. A further advantage of simulation is that it focuses on the time aspect of dynamical systems. Because AMTOS updates the state of all tasks and resources in each time step, the exact wait times, setup times and costs for each task and resource can be determined. The AMTOS simulation model contains the domain specific information which is unique to the current application. Therefore, the genetic algorithm remains robust and can be adapted to several different production processes.

4 Genetic Algorithm

The challenge in this investigation was to find an efficient means of combining genetic algorithms with simulation. The amount of time necessary for each simulation run can be significant for highly complex simulation models. Because a genetic algorithm requires many generations to develop good schedules, the total amount of processing time appears prohibitive at first. In order to reduce the number of simulation runs needed, the first step is obvious: evaluate only valid schedules. In a valid schedule, each job is processed exactly once. A number of modifications to the standard genetic algorithm were required to achieve this goal. Each of these methods will be discussed.

Both the number of jobs and the number of tasks required to complete each job can vary significantly in this application. Therefore, the chromosome representation utilizes multi-hierarchical, linked lists. A dynamic data structure was chosen over a fixed-length string because it can accommodate production schedules of various sizes without wasting excess memory. On the top level of the data structure, the entire population is stored as a linked list. Each member of the population has its own linked list made up of its job sequence. All of the tasks for one job are stored in an additional linked list on the third level of the hierarchy. The chromosome representation is real-valued rather than binary. This facilitates the identification of valid schedules. In addition, direct chromosome representation makes possible the use of modified genetic operators which generate solely legal schedules.

The selection mechanism for the genetic algorithm presented here is based on Whitley's Genitor algorithm [11]. Instead of replacing the entire population at one time, a single individual is deleted: the one with the worst fitness. The two best individuals are chosen as parents, and one child is generated to replace the deleted individual. Because selection is carried out after each individual reproduction, rather than after reproducing the entire population, the fitness should improve faster after fewer iterations. Replacing the worst member of the population results in a much higher selective pressure than that found in traditional genetic algorithms [12].

Davis' two-point OX Order Crossover algorithm [13] was implemented to assure that all offspring would contain valid job sequences. The OX order crossover tends to preserve relative rather than absolute sequences [14]. For scheduling problems, the relative order of the items has been shown to be more important than adjacency [15].

The OX order crossover functions as follows:

1. Generate two random cut points on the parent chromosomes.
2. Copy the genes between the two cut points from the first parent to the child.
3. Starting from the second cut point, copy the genes from the second parent to the child. Skip any genes which were already copied from the first parent.
4. When the end of the chromosome for parent 2 is reached, start copying genes from the beginning of the chromosome for parent 2. When the end of the child's chromosome is reached, start placing genes at the beginning of the child chromosome. Continue until the chromosome for the child is complete.

In traditional, binary-coded genetic algorithms, mutation occurs by randomly flipping one bit. This tends to result in illegal schedules. In order to guarantee that only legal schedules are generated, the mutation operator here is kept simple. Two genes (jobs) are selected randomly, and their positions in the schedule are swapped.

The optimal mutation rate has been shown to be heavily dependent on the choice of chromosome representation. Applications which implement a binary encoding have been shown to benefit from a low mutation rate [16]. In contrast, applications which implement non-binary, direct chromosome representations have been shown to perform better with higher mutation rates [17].

The population size was kept fixed at 100 in order to maximize the amount of historical information available while minimizing the amount of processing time necessary. The disadvantage of relatively small populations is that they quickly converge to the point where the same strings are more or less reproduced. Furthermore, the steady-state, rank-based selection implemented in this study results in a very constant, aggressive search. This is combined with a relatively conservative two-point order crossover which has low levels of disruption. The effect of both of these operators taken together tends to result in high levels of schema construction, but low levels of exploration. In order to compensate for this effect, an adaptive mutation mechanism is proposed.

Adaptive mutation may significantly improve the performance of genetic algorithms. Initially, when the population diversity is high, a low mutation rate is desirable. After many generations, the population becomes more homogenous and starts to converge. Increasing the mutation rate where the population variance is low broadens the search and helps the algorithm to escape a local optimum [18]. To achieve this goal, an adaptive feedback controller is introduced. Adaptive feedback controllers have been shown to help stabilize values in dynamic environments [19]. In each generation, the controller compares the current population diversity with the desired level of diversity. The feedback controller gradually raises or lowers the mutation rate as a function of population convergence.

To reduce the number of simulation runs needed, the application of a simple form of tabu search to the genetic algorithm is introduced. Tabu Search [20] is an iterative search technique which keeps track of previously generated solutions in a tabu list. It is a meta-level heuristic which is designed to improve the performance of other optimization methods by guiding them away from the trap of local optimality. In every generation, the genetic algorithm updates the population with historical information about the best solutions found. The population is therefore ideally suited to utilization as a tabu list. In this application, all newly generated solutions are checked against known solutions stored in the tabu list. If a newly generated solution is identical to an existing solution already in the tabu list, then this new member is immediately deleted from the population. Granted, the deletion of duplicate members prevents the genetic algorithm from converging. The hypothesis posed in this paper is that complete convergence of a genetic algorithm is not necessary to find good solutions. Furthermore, by sacrificing convergence, the algorithm is forced to examine a wider search space, which should deliver better solutions in a shorter amount of time.

The genetic algorithm's fitness function reflects the suitability of an individual member of the population to its environment. In this study, the fitness function has multiple, competing objectives which need to be fulfilled simultaneously. The primary hard constraint which must be fulfilled in order for a job sequence to be valid is that each job must be processed exactly once. This absolute constraint is encoded into the chromosome representation of the genetic algorithm presented here. Each chromosome contains exactly one gene for each job to be processed. The next step is to ensure that all detailed schedules generated from these job sequences do not violate resource constraints. Resource requirements for each job, as well as the capacity, availability and efficiency levels of all personnel, machines and materials are stored in DISYS and checked by AMTOS during each simulation run. AMTOS supervises the resource allocation to each task in every time step and thereby ensures that resource constraints are not violated. Other hard constraints, such as predecessor relationships between individual tasks, are also explicitly handled by AMTOS. Before a task can start, AMTOS tests whether all of its predecessors have been completed.

Promised delivery dates are soft constraints, which should be fulfilled, but which are not always possible to achieve. In a highly constrained problem, it is sometimes impossible to generate a production plan which meets all promised delivery dates because the supply of resources available is insufficient. It is still, however, desirable to develop a schedule which minimizes the number and length of schedule overruns. Furthermore, it is often desirable to accelerate urgent jobs at the expense of less urgent jobs.

In this study, soft constraints are taken into account by the introduction of a penalty function. Penalty functions have been shown to be of great help in attempting to solve overly constrained optimization problems, where it is difficult to find any feasible solution [21]. Richardson [22] recommends using penalties which are functions of the distance from feasibility rather than simply functions of the number of constraints violated. In this application, this would mean taking into account the length and severity of each schedule overrun, rather than just summing the total number of overruns. The penalty function for schedule overruns is implemented as follows: For each day that a job is late, penalty points are added to the time component of the fitness value. The number of penalty points assigned is based on the job's user-defined priority level. This priority level takes into account important customers, rush orders, etc. Thus, jobs with higher priorities incur more penalty points for each day of delay, and schedules which give preference to more urgent jobs receive a higher fitness value.

Minimization of time and minimization of costs are competing objectives which are usually inversely correlated. Rather than randomly assigning one goal as the primary goal and the other goal as the secondary goal, the fitness function incorporates a user-defined preference priority for each subgoal. A further problem in defining the fitness function is that time and costs represent entirely different units of measure. As a result, the weighted values for time and costs cannot simply be added together. Substitute goals are often used to convert one unit of measure (time) into another unit of measure (costs) [23]. This leads to errors when time and costs are inversely related. Therefore, a rank-based, weighted fitness function is proposed, where each subgoal is evaluated separately. First, all members of the population are ranked according to the total production times including setup times, wait times and penalties. The algorithm keeps track of the best ($Time_{Best\ Found}$) and worst times ($Time_{Worst\ Found}$) found so far in previous generations. The rank-based fitness value for the time goal is defined as:

$$Fitness_{Time} = \frac{(Time_{Current\ Member} - Time_{Best\ Found})}{(Time_{Worst\ Found} - Time_{Best\ Found})} \quad (1)$$

Next, the rank-based fitness value is defined for the costs goal in the same manner:

$$Fitness_{Costs} = \frac{(Costs_{Current\ Member} - Costs_{Best\ Found})}{(Costs_{Worst\ Found} - Costs_{Best\ Found})} \quad (2)$$

Now that each of the partial goals have been defined according to rank and no longer according to different units of measure, they can be weighted with the user-defined preferences and added together to calculate the total fitness:

$$Fitness_{Total} = (Fitness_{Time} * Weight_{Time}) + (Fitness_{Costs} * Weight_{Costs}) \quad (3)$$

An additional advantage of the rank-based fitness function presented here is the built-in learning function. The best and worst times and costs found so far make use of historical data gathered in each generation. In early generations, little is known about the size of the problem space. The span between the best values and the worst values found so far is relatively small. As the algorithm progresses, it generates and evaluates new schedules and thereby amasses more information about the size of the problem space. In the event that the difference between best and worst times is large in comparison to the difference between best and worst costs, then this sensitivity is reflected in the calculation of the fitness function.

5 Tests

Five different algorithms were implemented to separately measure the individual advantages of selection, crossover, mutation and the tabu list:

- a Monte Carlo random search,
- a simplified form of tabu search,
- an iterative mutation algorithm with cumulative selection,
- a genetic algorithm 'type 1' (without a tabu list)
- a genetic algorithm 'type 2' (with a tabu list).

A Monte Carlo algorithm was implemented to test whether the genetic algorithm performed better than an algorithm with randomly generated solutions. The Monte

Carlo algorithm used here produces new solutions using a random number generator. Because the algorithm does not store a population, information from previous schedules is not considered when generating new schedules. There is no possibility for incremental improvement based on the exploitation of previous knowledge. The algorithm employs a primitive selection mechanism, in that each newly generated schedule is compared to the best schedule found so far. The sole purpose of this selection is to keep track of the best schedule yet generated; it has no effect whatsoever on the generation of subsequent schedules.

The second algorithm tested here is a simple form of tabu search [20], combined with the Monte Carlo algorithm described above. The best 100 schedules found so far are stored in a tabu list. Randomly generated solutions are compared to known solutions stored in the tabu list. If a new solution is identical to an existing solution, the new solution is deleted immediately without running a simulation to evaluate its fitness function. The resulting algorithm is similar to a random search without replacement, but the memory component focuses on the best solutions. It is expected that the tabu search should be more efficient than the Monte Carlo algorithm, because the tabu list prevents the algorithm from wasting time in running simulations for known solutions.

An iterative mutation algorithm was implemented for the same data set. The algorithm utilizes neither a crossover operator nor a population, so that the effectiveness of the mutation operator could be tested separately. In each iteration, the best schedule found so far is randomly modified. The fitness function of each new schedule is calculated and the best schedule is selected for the next iteration. The purpose of this comparison is to test whether the crossover operator in combination with mutation is truly superior to mutation alone.

The genetic algorithm type 1 was implemented using:

- a direct chromosome representation stored in hierarchical linked lists,
- a steady-state, rank-based selection with individual replacement [11],
- a two-point order-crossover algorithm [13],
- and a simple order-based mutation with an adaptive feedback controller which adjusts the mutation rate as a function of population convergence.

Each of these algorithms is described in Sect. 4.

The genetic algorithm type 2, is identical to the one described above in almost all respects, but with one important difference: the population is not allowed to converge. Instead, as described in Sect. 4, the population itself serves as a tabu list. he purpose of this comparison is to test whether convergence of the population is truly necessary. The hypothesis proposed here is that in the time saved by not rerunning simulations for known solutions, the genetic algorithm will be able to find better schedules faster.

6 Results

Each algorithm was tested for sample runs of 500 generations. Average processing time for 500 generations was approximately 8 hours when run on a PC with a Pentium 90 processor and 16 megabytes of RAM. For the tabu search and the genetic algorithms, the population size was held constant at 100. The Monte Carlo search and the iterative mutation algorithm each had a population of 1. Because all of the algorithms compared are stochastic, multiple runs of each algorithm were necessary. 5 different sample data sets were tested, in order to simulate one week of production time in the factory. A total of 150 test runs were performed, 30 runs for each of the 5 algorithms tested. The user-defined preferences for each subgoal were also varied: 50 runs where time optimization was the primary goal, 50 runs where minimization of costs was the primary goal, and 50 runs where time and costs were each weighted equally.

Optimization of time and minimization of costs do appear to be inversely correlated for this particular case study. When time alone was optimized, better production times were achieved, but only at the expensive of higher costs. Conversely, the schedules with the lowest costs had much longer processing times. Optimization of both time and costs resulted in a compromise between the two competing goals. The best schedules had production times which were somewhat longer than when time alone was optimized, but shorter than when costs alone were optimized. Costs incurred by the best schedules also were somewhat higher that when costs alone were optimized, but lower than when time alone was optimized.

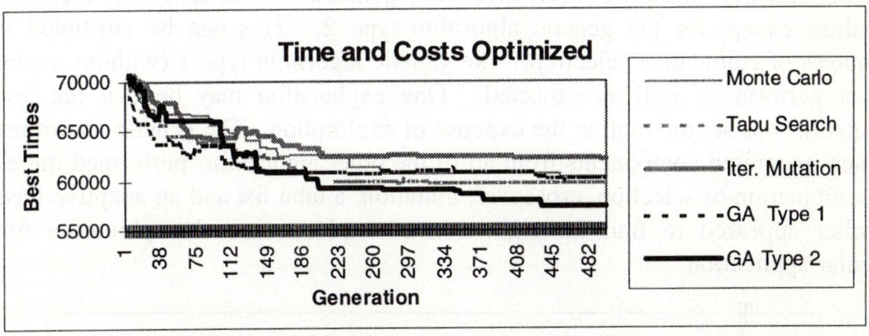

Fig. 1 Best times found when both time and costs optimized

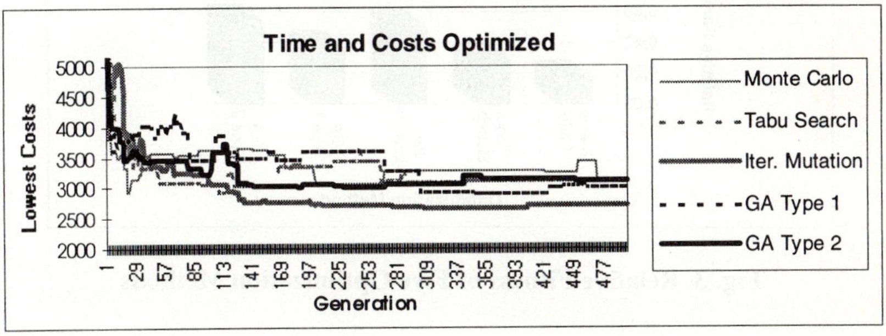

Fig. 2 Best costs found when both time and costs optimized

In order to judge overall performance of the algorithms when both time and costs were optimized simultaneously, a neutral unit of overall fitness had to be established. First, for each algorithm, the rank-based, partial fitness for each subgoal was calculated separately, based on its performance in comparison with the other methods:

$$\text{Time Fitness}_{\text{for this Algorithm}} = \frac{\text{Best Time}_{\text{for this Algorithm}} - \text{Best Time}_{\text{for all Algorithms}}}{\text{Worst Time}_{\text{for all Algorithms}} - \text{Best Time}_{\text{for all Algorithms}}} \quad (4)$$

$$\text{Costs Fitness}_{\text{for this Algorithm}} = \frac{\text{Best Costs}_{\text{for this Algorithm}} - \text{Best Costs}_{\text{for all Algorithms}}}{\text{Worst Costs}_{\text{for all Algorithms}} - \text{Best Costs}_{\text{for all Algorithms}}} \quad (5)$$

The total fitness for each optimization method is defined as:

$$\text{Total Fitness} = 1 - (\text{Time Fitness} * \text{Weight}_{\text{Time}}) + (\text{Costs Fitness} * \text{Weight}_{\text{Costs}}) \quad (6)$$

The overall performance indicator presented here is defined according to maximum total relative fitness. A score of 1.00 would correspond to an algorithm which found both the lowest absolute time and costs. Most scores fall somewhere between 0.00 and 1.00, because schedules with the lowest costs often have longer processing times and vice versa. The Monte Carlo search occasionally found good schedules by chance. Its overall performance was relatively poor, however. Due to its high level of exploitation, the tabu search rapidly found good solutions. In the long run, however, it did not perform as well because new solutions were generated randomly. The iterative mutation, although initially slower, eventually generated better schedules than all other algorithms except for the genetic algorithm type 2. This can be attributed to the advantages of cumulative selection. The genetic algorithm type 1 (without a tabu list) did not perform as well as expected. One explanation may be that the level of exploitation was set too high at the expense of exploration. The genetic algorithm type 2, which integrated components from all of the other algorithms, performed quite well. The combination of selection, crossover, mutation, a tabu list and an adaptive feedback controller appeared to find the right mix of exploration and exploitation for this particular application.

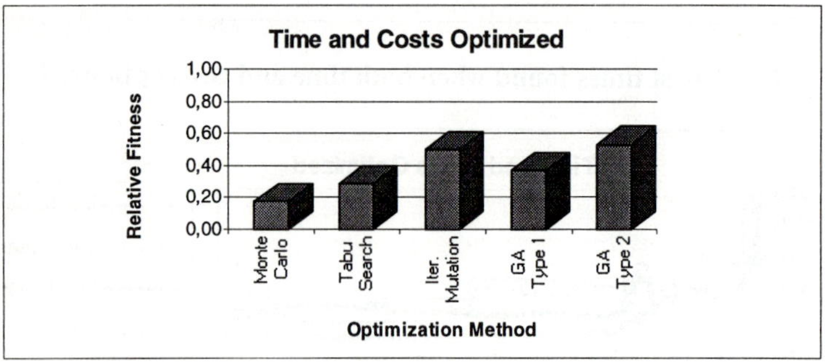

Fig. 3 Relative Fitness of Five Optimization Methods

7 Future Research

The current genetic algorithm improves daily production schedules for a single factory. In reality, the DISYS logistics system receives data via modem from multiple factories in different cities. The ultimate goal is to generate an optimal distribution of jobs among these factories and at the same time to develop efficient schedules for the jobs assigned to each factory. The main difficulty involved is that reassigning a job from one factory to another requires reoptimization of the schedules for both factories. Because the amount of computer processing time required is expected to expand exponentially, utilization of a parallel genetic algorithm will be investigated.

References

1. Nissen, V., Evolutionäre Algorithmen in der Betriebswirtschaft. *Tagungs-bericht zum Workshop: 'Evolutionäre Algorithmen in Management-Anwendungen'* (1995).
2. Davis, L., Job Shop Scheduling with Genetic Algorithms. *Proc. of the 1st Intl. Conf. on GA's*, J.G. Grefenstette, ed. (1985).
3. Kanet, J., Sridharan, V. PROGENITOR: A genetic algorithm for production scheduling. *Wirtschaftsinformatik*, 33. Jahrgang, Heft 4, August (1991).
4. Bagachi, S., Uckun, S., Miyabe, Y., Kawamura, K., Exploring Problem-Specific Recombination Operators for Job Shop Scheduling. *Proc. of the 4th Intl. Conf. on GA's*, R. Belew & L. Booker eds. (1991).
5. Yamada, T., Nakano, R., A Genetic Algorithm Applicable to Large-Scale Job-Shop Problems. *PPSN 2*, R. Männer and B. Manderick, eds., (1992).
6. Beasley, J., OR-Library: Distributing test problems by electronic mail. *Journal of the Operational Research Society*, Vol. 41 (1990).
7. Michalewicz, Z.,*Genetic Algorithms+Data Structures=Evolution Programs* (1992,1994).
8. Niemeyer, G., AMTOS - Ein universelles Werkzeug zur Modellierung, Simulation, Planung und Steuerung komplexer Prozesse. *Entscheidungsunterstützende Systeme im Unternehmen*, M. Wolff, ed. (1988).
10. Gary, M., and Johnson, D., *Computers and Intractability - a Guide to the Theory of NP-Completeness* (1979).
11. Whitley, D., The GENITOR Algorithm and Selection Pressure: Why Rank-based Allocation of Reproductive Trials is Best. *Proc. of the 3rd Intl. Conf. on GA's*, J.D. Schaffer, ed., (1989).
12. Goldberg, D. and Deb, K., A Comparative Analysis of Selection Schemes Used in Genetic Algorithms. *Foundations of Genetic Algorithms*, G. Rawlins, ed. (1991).
13. Davis, L., Applying Adaptive Algorithms to Epistatic Domains. *Proc. of the 9th Intl. Joint Conf. on Artificial Intelligence* (1985).
14. Fox, B., McMahon, M., Genetic Operators for Sequencing Problems. *Foundations of Genetic Algorithms*, G. Rawlins, ed. (1991).
15. Starkweather, T., et al., A Comparison of Genetic Sequencing Operators. *Proc. of the 4th Intl. Conf. on GA's*, R. Belew & L. Booker, eds., (1991).
16. Goldberg, D. E., *Genetic Algorithms in Search, Optimization and Machine Learning* (1989).
17. Tate, D., Smith, A., Expected Allele Coverage and the Role of Mutation in Genetic Algorithms. *Proc. of the 5th Intl. Conf. on GA's*, S. Forrest ed., (1993).
18. Fang, H., Ross, P., Corne, D., A promising genetic algorithm approach to job-shop scheduling, rescheduling and open-shop scheduling problems. *Proceceedings of the 5th Intl. Conf. on GA's,* S. Forrest, ed., (1993).
19. Niemeyer, G. *Kybernetische System- und Modelltheorie* (1977).
20. Glover, F., Tabu Search: A Tutorial. In: *Interfaces* Vol. July - August, (1990).
21. Smith, A., Tate, D., Genetic Optimization Using a Penalty Function. In *Proceceedings of the 5th Intl. Conf. on GA's,* S. Forrest, ed. (1993).
22. Richardson, J.T., et al., Some Guidelines for Genetic Algorithms with Penalty Functions. *Proc. of the 3rd Intl. Conf. on GA's*, J. D. Schaffer, ed. (1989).
23. Dorniger, C., Janscheck, O., Olearczick, E., Röhrenbacher, H., *Produktionsplanung - und Steuerung* (1990).

Network Optimization Using Evolutionary Strategies

F. Schweitzer, W. Ebeling, H. Rosé, O. Weiss

Institute of Physics, Humboldt University
Invalidenstr. 110, 10115 Berlin, Germany

Abstract. Network optimization which has to consider both the connection distance (detour) between different nodes and the total length (costs) of the network, belongs to the class of frustrated optimization problems. Here, evolutionary strategies which include both thermodynamic and biological elements, are used to find different optimized solutions (graphs of varying density) for the network in dependence on the degree of frustration. We show, that the optimization process occurs on two different time scales, and that in the asymptotic limit a a fixed relation between the mean connection distance (detour) and the total lenght (costs) of the network exist.

1 Introduction

The optimization of networks which connect a given set of nodes is of common interest in many different areas, among them electrical engineering (e.g. for electronic platines), telecommunication, or road construction and trade-logistics.

Usually, the optimization has to consider different demands, e.g. (i) to minimize the total costs of establishing the network, which should be proportional to the total length of the links between the different nodes, (ii) to minimize the time to reach any given node from any other node, which should be proportional to the length of the links along the shortest path between the two nodes. Considering only the first demand, the solution is given by a network where every node is connected to the net by just one (the possible shortest) link, which leads to the *minimal link system*, also known as *minimal spanning tree*. Contrary, considering only the second demand, the solution is given by a network where every node is connected to every other node by a direct link, which leads to the *direct link system* (compare also Fig. 1).

Compared to these two idealized limiting cases, in most real applications a network has to be established which minimizes the total length of the connections *as well* as the connection distance between any two nodes. Since both demands could not be satisfied at the same time, we have to find a compromise. Optimization problems like this are known as *frustrated problems* and are characterized by a tremendous number of nearly evenly matched solutions which have to be found in a very rugged landscape of the related optimization function. In order to find some of these matched solutions, evolutionary algorithms are applied (Rechenberg, 1994, Holland, 1975, Schwefel, 1981, Goldberg, 1989, Fogel, 1995).

These algorithms are a special class of stochastic search strategies in an ensemble of searchers which adapt certain features from natural evolution. The examples discussed here, are the Boltzmann- and the Darwin strategy, as well as a mix of both of them (Ebeling, Engel, 1986, Ebeling, 1990, Boseniuk *et al.*, 1987, 1991).

With respect to the optimization of networks, we investigate (i) the evolution of the network and the related fitness function during the optimization process, (ii) different optimized solutions (graphs of varying density) for the network in dependence on the degree of frustration.

2 Evaluation of Networks

In order to optimize networks, we first have to define a potential function (or a *fitness function*) which evaluates a given network. Let us consider a set of nodes which shall be connected by straight lines representing the links. The number of possible graphs g to connect a given set of nodes $p_1 ... p_N$ is of the order $2^{N(N-1)/2}$. Each graph should be evaluated due to the following potential function:

$$U(g) = (1 - \lambda)D(g) + \lambda C(g) \; ; \quad 0 \leq \lambda \leq 1 \tag{1}$$

Here, $D(g)$ represents the mean detour to reach different nodes on the existing network, whereas $C(g)$ represents the total costs for establishing the network, which should be proportional to the total length of the links.

In order to minimize the potential $U(g)$, both terms should be minimized. The demand for a minimized detour between every two points represents a *local constraint* to the network, whereas the demand of a minimized total length of the network means a *global constraint* (Schweitzer *et al.*, 1995). The parameter λ is introduced to weight between the two contradicting demands. The case $\lambda \to 0$ leads to a potential function, which only minimizes the detour regardless of the costs of the network, and finally results in the *direct link system* (Fig. 1a). In the opposite case, $\lambda \to 1$, only the costs of the network will be minimized, which finally leads to the *minimal link system* (Fig 1b). (We note, that in the node system considered here, the minimal link system will be different from the known Steiner tree (Fig.1c), since we assume that any link between nodes should be a straight line and no additional sub-nodes should be constructed to connect given nodes.) If λ is different from 0 or 1, it should be a measure for the *degree of frustration* of the problem.

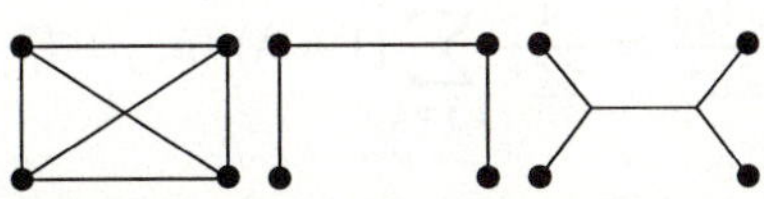

(a) *(b)* *(c)*

Fig. 1. (a) direct link system, (b) minimal link system, (c) Steiner tree for a set of 4 nodes

In this paper, the direct link system will be used as a reference state, indicated by the symbol $\star$. The detour $D(g^\star)$ is zero and the total length of the network gets its maximum value $L^\star$:

$$L^\star = \frac{1}{2}\sum_{i,j=1}^{N} \sqrt{(x_i - x_j)^2 + (y_i - y_j)^2} = \frac{1}{2}\sum_{i,j=1}^{N} l^\star_{i,j} \quad ; \; D(g^\star) = 0 \tag{2}$$

x_i, y_i are the coordinates of node i in a two-dimensional plane. For values of $0 \leq \lambda \leq 1$, the mean detour $D(g)$ is defined as follows:

$$D(g) = \frac{1}{2}\sum_{i,j=1}^{N} h_{i,j} - l^\star_{i,j} \tag{3}$$

where $l^\star_{i,j}$ means the direct (metric) distance between the nodes i and j (eq. 2) and $h_{i,j}$ is the length of the *shortest route* which connects nodes i and j *on the existing graph*. Obviously, $h_{i,j} = l^\star_{i,j}$ yields for a graph representing the direct link system.

The expression $D(g)$ can be normalized by the total length of the direct link system, which is a known constant for a given set of nodes,

$$d(g) = \frac{D(g)}{L^\star} = \frac{1}{2}\sum_{i,j=1}^{N} \frac{h_{i,j} - l^\star_{i,j}}{L^\star} \tag{4}$$

In order to specify the term representing the costs, we assume the costs simply proportional to the total length of the graph

$$C(g) = \frac{1}{2}\sum_{i,j=1}^{N} l_{i,j} \tag{5}$$

where $l_{i,j}$ is the length of the direct connection between nodes i and j, *if there is any on the existing graph*.

After a normalization of $C(g)$ similar to eq. (4), the potential function describing the network reads finally

$$u(g) = \frac{U(g)}{2L^\star} = \frac{1}{2L^\star}\sum_{i,j=1}^{N} (1-\lambda)\,(h_{i,j} - l^\star_{i,j}) + \lambda\, l_{ij} \tag{6}$$

For the reference state (direct link system), the values are $d(g^\star) = d_{min} = 0$ for the mean detour, $c(g^\star) = c_{max} = 1$ for the costs, and $u(g^\star) = \lambda$ for the potential. Based on eq. (6), a hypothetic network will be optimized with respect to the mean detour and the total length of the network.

3 Boltzmann and Darwin Strategies

An optimization process can be described as a special search for minima of a related potential in the configuration space. In the considered case, the configuration space is defined by the number of all possible graphs g to connect the given set of nodes $p_1 ... p_N$, and the potential is given by $u(g)$ (eq. 6).

Let us consider a numbered set of states $i = 1, ..., s$ in the configuration space, each of them characterized by a scalar U_i (the potential energy). Further, we assume a total number of N searchers participating in the search for potential minima. Then, $N_i(t)$ gives the actual number of searchers occupying the state i at time t. This occupation number should be an integer, but in the limit $N \to \infty$ the occupation fraction $N_i(t)/N$ may be replaced by a probability of occupation at time t, denoted by $p_i(t)$.

The optimization process has to ensure that the occupation probability for the minima of the potential will increase during the search. However, since due to the frustration of the problem a large quantity of suitable minima exist, the search strategy should also avoid a total locking of the searchers in the minima found so far in order to guarantee further search.

There are different optimization routines, like the Metropolis algorithm or the *simulated annealing* approach which fulfill these criteria. A dynamics which finds the minimum among the set of scalars (the minimum potential energy) is given by

$$\frac{dp_i(t)}{dt} = \sum_{i \neq j} A_{ij}\, p_j(t) - A_{ji}\, p_i(t) \tag{7}$$

A_{ij} denotes the transition probability for the searcher to move from state i to state j and is defined as follows:

$$A_{ij} = A^0_{ij} * \begin{cases} 1 & \text{if } U_i < U_j \\ \exp\left(-(U_i - U_j)/T(t)\right) & \text{if } U_i \geq U_j \end{cases} \tag{8}$$

This means that transitions towards a deeper minimum in U are always accepted, but transitions which lead to a deterioration are accepted only with a probability related to the difference in the potential. Thus, due to the motion along the gradients the steepest local descent of the potential will be reached; however, due to thermal fluctuations locking in those local minima will be avoided.

The prefactor A^0_{ij} is symmetric ($A^0_{ij} = A^0_{ji}$), it defines a set of possible states j which can be reached from state i. The simplest definition might be

$$A^0_{ij} = \begin{cases} 1 \text{ if } & i \text{ is adjacent to } j \\ 0 \text{ if } & i \text{ is not adjacent to } j \end{cases} \tag{9}$$

The term *adjacent* means here that state j results only from a single elementary mutation of state i, in other words, a change between the different states can only occur in small steps.

Similar to *simulated annealing*, the temperature $T(t)$ decreases during the search, with the consequence that first the larger basins of the potential minima are explored ("coarse grained search") and later on a "fine grained" search occurs within these minimum regions.

For constant temperatures, the stationary solution of eq. 7, $p_i^0 = \lim_{t\to\infty} p_i(t)$, is known to be the canonical or Boltzmann distribution

$$p_i^0 \sim \exp\left(-U_i/T\right) \tag{10}$$

therefore we call this optimization strategy Boltzmann strategy. The Boltzmann process asymptotically finds the minimum in a given set of scalars U_i; it optimized certain thermodynamic functions during the cosmic evolution.

In biological evolution, some new elements occured in the optimization process, namely (i) mutation processes due to error reproduction, and (ii) self-reproduction of species with a fitness above the average fitness, which increases precision in the course of evolution. We adapt these elements for our search strategy, which is then called Darwin strategy because it includes some biological elements known from population dynamics (Ebeling, Feistel, 1982, Boseniuk *et al.*, 1987, Ebeling *et al.*, 1994).

Let us consider again the population of N searchers, which are now distributed in different subpopulations $x_i = N_i/N$; $(i = 1, ..., N)$, each characterized by a replication rate E_i which might be proportional to the fitness. Then the average replication rate $\langle E \rangle$ is given by

$$\langle E \rangle = \frac{1}{N} \sum_{i=1}^{N} E_i x_i(t), \qquad N = \sum_{i=1}^{N} x_i(t) \tag{11}$$

Due to the Eigen – Fischer dynamics, the evolution of the subpopulations is given by the equation:

$$\frac{dx_i}{dt} = \left(E_i - \langle E \rangle\right) x_i + \sum_{j \neq i} [A_{ij}^0\, x_j - A_{ji}^0\, x_i] \tag{12}$$

Here the transition rates A_{ij} are assumed to be symmetric, since there are no directed mutations. The effect of an increasing precision in self-reproduction can be considered again by a temperature dependence of the transition rates, where a decreasing temperature leads to a smaller probability of mutation. For $A_{ij}^0 \to 0$, this evolutionary dynamics is known to approach asymptotically a final state where the average fitness $\langle E \rangle$ is equal to the maximal fitness, which means that only the (one) subpopulation with the best fitness value will survive. For finite mutation rates, $A_{ij}^0 > 0$, the target of the search is the eigenvector of eq. (12) corresponding to the highest eigenvalue, which for small mutations rates is close to the maximal value E_{max}.

To compare both strategies (Ebeling, Engel, 1986, Boseniuk *et al.*, 1987) we note that the Boltzmann strategy is able to detect the appropiate potential minima even in a unknown, rugged landscape as long as the potential barriers between local minima are not too high, which forces the locking in side minima. On the other hand, the DARWIN strategy is able to cross high barriers by tunneling if the next minimum is close enough.

In order to combine the advantages of both stragegies, a *mixed Boltzmann–Darwin strategy* has been introduced (Ebeling, Engel, 1986) Here, the asymmmetric transition probabilities (eq. 8) are adopted which favor the transition towards the minimum. On the other hand, the fitness E_i of the subspecies i is chosen to be the negative of the potential U_i indicating that the subspecies which has found the better minimum in the potential landscape, also has the higher reprodution rate. Due to the comparison with the mean value $\langle U \rangle$, there exist a global coupling between the different subpopulations.

It has been shown recently (Boseniuk *et al.*, 1987, Asselmeyer, Ebeling, 1996) that a *mixed Boltzmann–Darwin strategy* will be more successful in solving frustrated problems than both of the strategies. The basic equation for the mixed strategy which is appropriate to solve the optimization problem of minimizing U_i reads

$$\frac{dx_i}{dt} = \kappa(\langle U \rangle - U_i)\, x_i + \sum_{j \neq i} [A_{ij}\, x_j - A_{ji}\, x_i] \tag{13}$$

with the transition matrices A_{ij} obtained from eq. (8). By changing the parameters κ and T in the range $0 \leq \kappa \leq 1, \quad 0 < T \leq \infty$; we may interpolate between the two limit cases

$$\kappa = 0,\ T > 0 \ \text{Boltzmann strategy}$$
$$\kappa = 1, T \to \infty \ \text{Darwin strategy}$$

In the discussions above, the discrete numbers of searchers, $N_i(t)$, have been replaced by occupation probabilities $p_i(t)$ or population densities $x_i(t)$. We note that for small numbers N_i the stochastic search process could be also reformulated in terms of a master equation (Feistel, Ebeling, 1989; Schweitzer *et al.*, 1995).

4 Results of Computer Simulations

In order to show the evolution of the network during the optimization process (Fig. 2), we start the computer simulations with an initial graph of 39 nodes close to a direct link system (λ =0.975). During every time step, in both the Boltzmann and the mixed strategy, the graph is first mutated by adding or removing one link between nodes, and then evaluated. The decrease of the temperature is due to $T(t+1) = T_0/(1+at)$, where $T_0 = 0.01$ is the initial temperature, and $a = 0.002$ is the annealing rate. In Figs. 2-5, the Boltzmann strategy is used for the optimization.

Starting with a direct link system, the optimization process occurs in two stages (Fig. 3). During the first stage the network is strictly thined out. However, as Fig. 3a shows, this does not mean a considerable decrease in the potential, unless a remarkable increase of the mean detour is reached, related to a decrease of the costs. During the second stage, the links between the different nodes are balanced with respect to the costs and the mean detour, resulting in a slowly

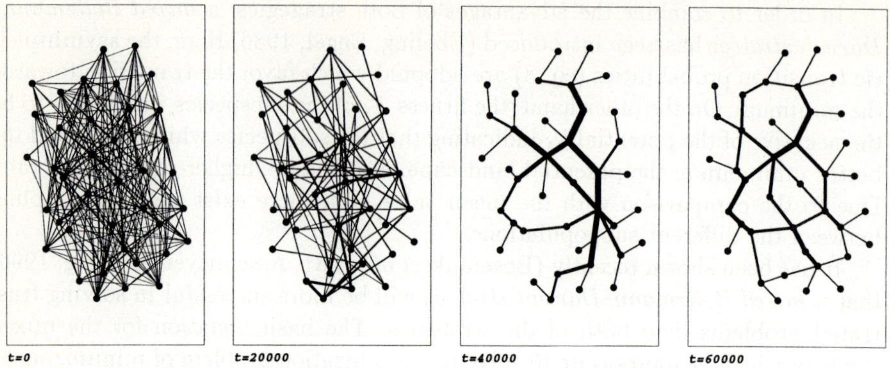

Fig. 2. Optimization of a network of 39 nodes ($\lambda = 0.975$) The graph is shown after different time steps. The thickness of the lines indicates how much a given link is used for the shortest possible connection of any node to any other.

decrease of both detour and costs. In Fig. 3b, the transition between both stages is marked by the maximum region of the curve.

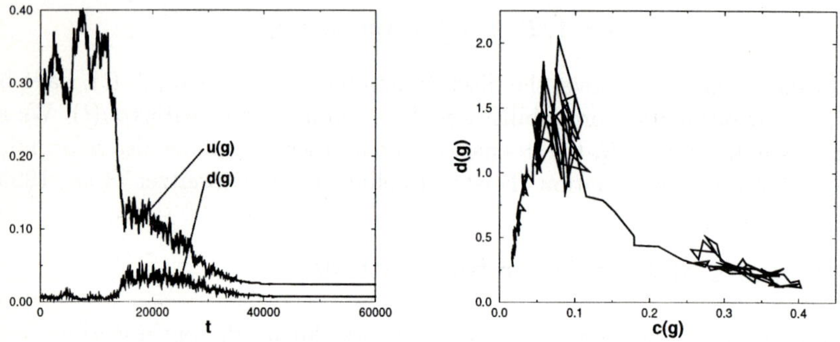

Fig. 3. (a) Time dependence of the potential $u(g)$ and the mean detour $d(g)$, (b) mean detour $d(g)$ versus costs $c(g)$ during the optimization of the network. With respect to the time, the left curve starts in the lower right corner and ends in the lower left corner. The data points are picked from a single run every 200 time steps. ($\lambda = 0.975$).

Fig. 4 presents results for the optimized network in dependence on the frustration parameter λ, which influences the final density of the graph as discussed above.

In Fig. 5 the potential values for the optimized network, u^{opt}, obtained asymptotically are plotted versus the frustration parameter λ. Surprisingly, the potential minimum in the asymptotic regime is a 4th order power function of λ:

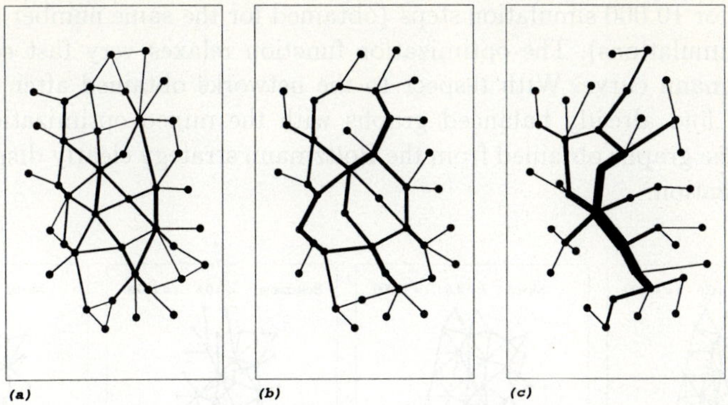

Fig. 4. Optimized networks after t=60.000 simulation steps for different values of of the frustration parameter λ: (a)$\lambda = 0.900$, (b)$\lambda = 0.975$, (c)$\lambda = 0.990$

$$u^{opt}(\lambda) = \lambda\{-0.3395\lambda^3 + 0.6380\lambda^2 - 0.4949\lambda + 0.2155\} \tag{14}$$

which is also drawn in Fig. 5. This indicates a fixed relation between the asymptotic values of $d(g)$ and $c(g)$ which allows a prediction of the best possible cost and the best affordable detour of the network in dependence on λ.

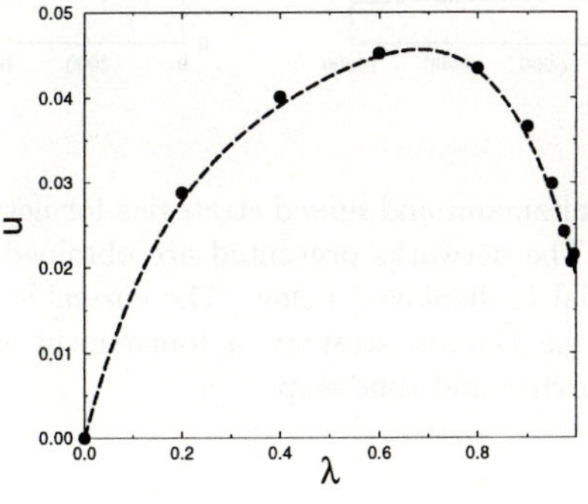

Fig. 5. Dependence of the asymptotic potential minimum on the frustration parameter λ. Dots mark the results of the simulations, averaged over 50 runs; the dashed line is given by eq. (14)

Finally, we would like to compare the results of the Boltzmann strategy and the mixed strategy which also includes Darwinian elements. As shown in the simulations above, the Boltzmann strategy finds suitable results in the asymptotic limit (about 60.000 simulation steps). However, the mixed Boltzmann-Darwin strategy already finds optimal graphs in a much shorter simulation time, as shown in Fig. 6 for 10.000 simulation steps (obtained for the same number of searchers in both simulations). The optimization function relaxes very fast compared to the Boltzmann curve. With respect to the networks obtained after 10.000 time steps, we find already balanced graphs with the mixed optimization strategy, whereas the graphs obtained from the Boltzmann strategy clearly display failures in optimization.

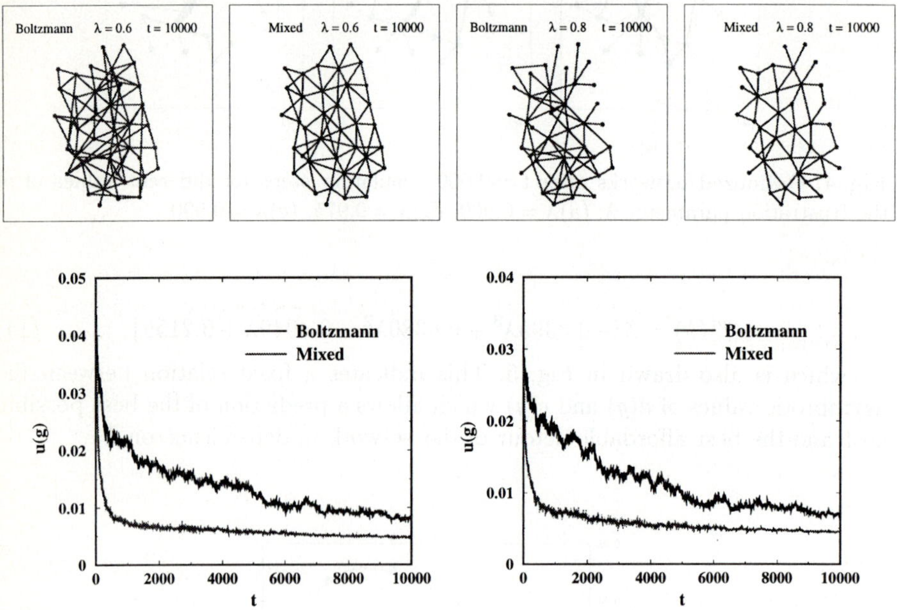

Fig. 6. Comparison of Boltzmann and mixed strategies for network optimization. (left) $\lambda = 0.6$ (right) $\lambda = 0.8$ The networks presented are obtained after 10.000 simulation steps, the related potential is displayed below. The ensemble consists of 16 searchers for both strategies. For the Darwin strategy, a tournament selection is used, with a probability of 0.3 per searcher and time step.

5 Conclusions

In order to summarize the results presented we want to conclude:

1. Network optimization which has to consider both the connection distance (detour) between different nodes and the total length (costs) of the network, belongs to the class of frustrated optimization problems, where numerous evenly matched solutions exist
2. Evolutionary optimization strategies which include both thermodynamic and biological elements (mixed strategies of simulated annealing, ensemble search,

mutation, selection and recombination) provide a suitable tool for finding optimized solutions in relatively short time (preferable in comparison to Boltzmann–like strategies)

3. Starting with a direct link system, the optimization of networks occurs on two different time scales: (a) thin-out of the network (short time scale), (b) balancing of detour compared to costs (long time scale)
4. In the asymptotic limit the potential (fitness) of the optimized network can be described by a power function, which defines a fixed relation between the mean connection distance (detour) and the total lenght (costs) of the network

Acknowledgments

This work has been supported by the Deutsche Forschungsgemeinschaft via SFB 230 "Natural Constructions" (Stuttgart, Germany).

References

Asselmeyer, T., Ebeling, W.: Mixing of Thermodynamic and Biological Strategies in Optimization, in: F. Schweitzer (ed.): *Self-Organization of Complex Structures: From Individual to Collective Dynamics*, vol. I, London: Gordon and Breach, 1996, in press.

Boseniuk, T., Ebeling, W., Engel, A.: Boltzmann and Darwin Strategies in Complex Optimization, Physics Letters **125** (1987) 307-310.

Ebeling, W.: Applications of Evolutionary Stragegies, Syst. Anal. Model. Simul. **7** (1990) 3–16.

Ebeling, W., Engel, A.: Models of Evolutionary Systems and Their Application to Optimization Problems, Syst. Anal. Model. Simul. **3** (1986) 377-385.

Ebeling, W., Feistel, R.: Models of Darwin Proceses and Evolutionary Principles, BioSystems **15** (1982) 291.

Ebeling, W., Rosé, H., Schuchhardt, J.: Evolutionary Strategies for Solving Frustrated Problems, Proc. 1st IEEE Conf. Evolutionary Computation, WCCI Orlando, pp. 79-81, 1994.

Feistel, R.; Ebeling, W.: *Evolution of Complex Systems*, Dordrecht: Kluwer, 1989

Fogel, D.B.: *Evolutionary Computation – Towards a new Philosophy of Machine Intelligence*, Piscataway: IEEE Press, 1995.

Goldberg, D.E.: *Genetic Algorithms in Search, Optimization and Machine Learning*, Reading: Addison-Wesley, 1989.

Holland, J.H.: *Adaptation in Natural and Artificial Sytstems*, Ann Arbor: University of Michigan Press, 1975.

Rechenberg, I.: *Evolutionsstrategie '94*, Stuttgart: Frommann-Holzboog, 1994.

Schweitzer, F., Ebeling, W., Rosé, H., Weiss, O.: Optimization of Road Networks Using Evolutionary Strategies (Preprint, to be published), 1995.

Schwefel, H.-P.: *Numerical Optimization of Computer Models*, New York: Wiley, 1981.

Co-evolving Parallel Random Number Generators

Moshe Sipper[1] and Marco Tomassini[2]

[1] Logic Systems Laboratory, Swiss Federal Institute of Technology, IN-Ecublens, CH-1015 Lausanne, Switzerland. E-mail: Moshe.Sipper@di.epfl.ch

[2] Swiss Scientific Computing Center, Manno, and Logic Systems Laboratory, Swiss Federal Institute of Technology, IN-Ecublens, CH-1015 Lausanne, Switzerland. E-mail: Marco.Tomassini@di.epfl.ch

Abstract. Random numbers are needed in a variety of applications, yet finding good random number generators is a difficult task. In the last decade cellular automata (CA) have been used to generate random numbers. In this paper *non-uniform* CAs are studied, where each cell may contain a *different* rule, in contrast to the original, uniform model. We present the *cellular programming* algorithm for co-evolving non-uniform CAs to perform computations, and apply it to the evolution of random number generators. Our results suggest that good generators can be evolved; these exhibit behavior at least as good as that of previously described CAs, with notable advantages arising from the existence of a "tunable" algorithm for obtaining random number generators.

Keywords: non-uniform cellular automata, random number generators, cellular programming, evolution, co-evolution, parallel computation, artificial life, complex systems.

1 Introduction

Random numbers are needed in a variety of scientific, mathematical, engineering, and industrial applications, including Monte Carlo simulations, sampling, decision theory, game theory, and the imitation of stochastic natural processes. To generate a random sequence on a digital computer, one starts with a fixed length seed, then iteratively applies some transformation to it, progressively extracting as long as possible a random sequence. Such numbers are usually referred to as *pseudo*-random, as distinguished from true random numbers resulting from some natural physical process. In order to demonstrate the efficiency of a proposed generator, it is usually subjected to a battery of empirical and theoretical tests, among which the most well known are those described by [5].

Good random number generators, or randomizers, are hard to come by; indeed, a number of generators which had gained prominence over the years, were ultimately found to be unsatisfactory, some displaying particularly "bad", non-random behavior [11]. In the last decade certain cellular automata (CA) have been shown to act as good random number generators. CAs are dynamical system in which space and time are discrete. They consist of an array of cells, each of which can be in one of a finite number of possible states, updated synchronously in discrete time steps according to a local, identical interaction rule. The state of a cell is determined by the previous states of a surrounding neighborhood of cells [20]. CAs exhibit three notable features, namely massive parallelism, locality of cellular interactions, and simplicity of basic components (cells), thus lending themselves naturally to fast, efficient hardware implementation.

The model investigated by us is an extension of the CA model, termed *non-uniform cellular automata* [12]. Such automata function in the same way as uniform ones, the only difference being in the cellular rules that need not be identical for all cells. Our main focus is on the *evolution* of non-uniform CAs to perform computational tasks, employing a local, co-evolutionary algorithm, an approach referred to as *cellular programming* [16].

In this paper we apply the cellular programming algorithm to the evolution of random number generators. While a more extensive suite of tests should be conducted, our results suggest that good randomizers can be evolved; these exhibit behavior at least as good as that of previously described CAs, with notable advantages arising from the existence of a "tunable" algorithm for the generation of randomizers (see also [18]). In Section 2 we survey previous work on randomizers and on evolving CAs. The cellular programming algorithm is delineated in Section 3, and applied to the co-evolution of random number generators in Section 4. Finally, our conclusions are presented in Section 5.

2 Previous work

The first work examining the application of CAs to random number generation is that of [21], in which rule 30 is extensively studied for its ability to produce random, temporal bit sequences[3]. Such sequences are obtained by sampling the values that a particular cell attains as a function of time. The cellular space under question is one-dimensional with $k = 2$ and $r = 1$, where k denotes the number of possible states per cell and r denotes the radius of a cell, i.e., the number of neighbors on either side (thus each cell has $2r + 1$ neighbors, including itself). A common method of examining the behavior of one-dimensional CAs is to display a two-dimensional space-time diagram, where the horizontal axis depicts the configuration at a certain time t and the vertical axis depicts successive time steps (e.g., Figure 2). The term 'configuration' refers to an assignment of 1 states to several cells, and 0s otherwise.

In [21], the uniform rule 30 CA is initialized with a configuration consisting of a single cell in state 1, with all other cells being in state 0; the initially non-zero cell is the site at which the random temporal sequence is generated. Wolfram studied this particular rule extensively, demonstrating its suitability as a high-performance randomizer which can be efficiently implemented in parallel; indeed, this CA is one of the standard generators of the massively parallel Connection Machine CM2. A non-uniform CA randomizer was presented by [3, 4], consisting of two rules, 90 and 150, arranged in a specific order in the grid. The performance of this CA in terms of random number generation was found to be at least as good as that of rule 30, with the added benefit of less costly hardware implementation.

[3] Rule numbers are given in accordance with Wolfram's convention [20], representing the decimal equivalent of the binary number encoding the rule table.

It is interesting in that it combines two rules, both of which are simple linear rules that do not comprise good randomizers, to form an efficient, high-performance generator.

The application of genetic algorithms to the *evolution* of *uniform* cellular automata was initially studied by [10] and recently undertaken by the EVCA (evolving CA) group [9, 8, 7, 2, 1]. They carried out experiments involving one-dimensional CAs with $k = 2$ and $r = 3$; spatially periodic boundary conditions were used, resulting in a circular grid. Mitchell *et al.* studied two computational tasks, namely density and synchronization, employing a genetic algorithm to evolve uniform CAs to perform these tasks. The algorithm uses a randomly generated initial population of CAs with $k = 2$, $r = 3$. Each CA is represented by a bit string, delineating its rule table, containing the output bits for all possible neighborhood configurations (i.e., the bit at position 0 is the state to which neighborhood configuration 0000000 is mapped to and so on until bit 127 corresponding to neighborhood configuration 1111111). The bit string, known as the "genome", is of size $2^{2r+1} = 128$, resulting in a huge search space of size 2^{128}. Each CA in the population was run for a maximum number of M time steps, after which its fitness was evaluated, defined as the fraction of cells in the correct state at the last time step. Using the genetic algorithm highly successful CA rules were found for both the density and the synchronization tasks.

An evolutionary approach for obtaining random number generators was taken by Koza [6], who used genetic programming to evolve a symbolic LISP expression that acts as a rule for a uniform CA (i.e., the expression is inserted into each CA cell, thereby comprising the function according to which the cell's next state is computed). He demonstrated evolved expressions that are equivalent to Wolfram's rule 30. The fitness measure used by Koza is the *entropy* E_h: let k be the number of possible values per sequence position (in our case CA states) and h a subsequence length. E_h (measured in bits) for the set of k^h probabilities of the k^h possible subsequences of length h is given by:

$$E_h = -\sum_{j=1}^{k^h} p_{h_j} \log_2 p_{h_j}$$

where $h_1, h_2, \ldots, h_{k^h}$ are all the possible subsequences of length h (by convention, $\log_2 0 = 0$ when computing entropy). The entropy attains its maximal value when the probabilities of all k^h possible subsequences of length h are equal to $1/k^h$; in our case $k = 2$ and the maximal entropy is $E_h = h$. Koza evolved LISP expressions which act as rules for uniform, one-dimensional CAs. The CAs were run for 4096 time steps and the entropy of the resulting temporal sequence of a designated cell (usually the central one) was taken as the fitness of the particular rule (i.e., LISP expression). In his experiments Koza used a subsequence length of $h = 4$, obtaining rules with an entropy of 3.996. The best rule of each run was re-tested over 65536 time steps, some of which exhibited the maximal entropy value of 4.0.

The model investigated in this paper is that of non-uniform CAs, where cellular rules need not be identical for all cells. We have previously applied this model to the study of artificial life issues, presenting multi-cellular "organisms" that display several interesting behaviors, including reproduction, growth and mobility [12, 15, 13]. In [14, 17] we demonstrated that universal computation can be attained in non-uniform, two-dimensional, 2-state, 5-neighbor CAs, which are not computation-universal in the uniform case. The universal systems we presented are simpler than previous ones and are *quasi*-uniform, meaning that the number of distinct rules is extremely small with respect to rule space size; furthermore, the rules are distributed such that a subset of dominant rules occupies most of the grid. The co-evolution of non-uniform, one-dimensional CAs to perform computations was undertaken in [16, 17], where the cellular programming algorithm was presented; we showed that high performance, non-uniform CAs can be co-evolved not only with radius $r = 3$, as studied by Mitchell *et al.*, but also for smaller radiuses, most notably $r = 1$ which is minimal. It was also found that evolved systems exhibiting high performance are quasi-uniform.

The above account leads us to ask whether good CA randomizers can be co-evolved using cellular programming; the results reported below suggest that indeed this is the case.

3 Cellular programming

We study one-dimensional, 2-state, $r = 1$ non-uniform CAs, in which each cell may contain a different rule; spatially periodic boundary conditions are used, resulting in a circular grid. A cell's rule table is encoded as a bit string, known as the "genome", containing the output bits for all possible neighborhood configurations (see Section 2). Rather than employ a *population* of evolving, uniform CAs, as with genetic algorithm approaches, our algorithm involves a *single*, non-uniform CA of size N, with cell rules initialized at random. Initial configurations are then randomly generated and for each one the CA is run for $M = 4096$ time steps.[4] Each cell's *fitness*, f_i, is accumulated over $C = 300$ initial configurations, where a single run's score equals the entropy E_h of the temporal sequence of cell i. Note that we do not restrict ourselves to one designated cell, but consider all grid cells, thus obtaining N random sequences in parallel, rather than a single one. After every C configurations evolution of rules occurs by applying the genetic operators of crossover and mutation in a completely *local* manner, driven by $nf_i(c)$, the number of fitter neighbors of cell i after c configurations. The pseudo-code of our algorithm is delineated in Figure 1. Crossover between two rules is performed by selecting at random (with uniform probability) a single crossover point and creating a new rule by combining the first rule's bit string before the crossover point with the second rule's bit string from this point onward. Mutation is applied to the bit string of a rule with probability 0.001 per bit.

There are two main differences between our evolutionary algorithm and a standard genetic algorithm: (a) A standard genetic algorithm involves a popu-

[4] A standard, 48-bit, linear congruential algorithm proved sufficient for the generation of random initial configurations.

```
for each cell i in CA do in parallel
   initialize rule table of cell i
   f_i = 0 { fitness value }
end parallel for
c = 0 { initial configurations counter }
while not done do
   generate a random initial configuration
   run CA on initial configuration for M time steps
   for each cell i do in parallel
      f_i = f_i+ entropy E_h of the temporal sequence of cell i
   end parallel for
   c = c + 1
   if c mod C = 0 then { evolve every C configurations}
      for each cell i do in parallel
         compute nf_i(c) { number of fitter neighbors }
         if nf_i(c) = 0 then rule i is left unchanged
         else if nf_i(c) = 1 then replace rule i with the fitter neighboring rule,
                                  followed by mutation
         else if nf_i(c) = 2 then replace rule i with the crossover of the two fitter
                                  neighboring rules, followed by mutation
         else if nf_i(c) > 2 then replace rule i with the crossover of two randomly
                                  chosen fitter neighboring rules, followed by mutation
                                  (this case can occur if the cellular radius, r, > 1)
         end if
         f_i = 0
      end parallel for
   end if
end while
```

Fig. 1. Pseudo-code of the cellular programming algorithm.

lation of evolving, uniform CAs; all CAs are *ranked* according to fitness, with crossover occurring between *any* two CA rules. Thus, while the CA runs in accordance with a local rule, evolution proceeds in a *global* manner. In contrast, our algorithm proceeds *locally* in the sense that each cell has access only to its locale, not only during the run but also during the evolutionary phase, and no global fitness ranking is performed. (b) The standard genetic algorithm involves a population of *independent* problem solutions; each CA is run independently, after which genetic operators are applied to produce a new population. In contrast, our CA *co-evolves* since each cell's fitness depends upon its evolving neighbors. This latter point comprises a prime difference between our algorithm and parallel genetic algorithms, which have attracted attention over the past few years [19]. Some of the proposed models resemble our system in that they are massively parallel and local; however, the co-evolutionary aspect is missing.

4 Results

In this section we describe results of applying the cellular programming algorithm to the evolution of random number generators. In our simulations we observed that the average cellular entropy taken over all grid cells is initially low (usually in the range [0.2, 0.5]), ultimately evolving to a maximum of 3.997, when using a subsequence size of $h = 4$ (i.e., the entropy is computed by considering the occurrence probabilities of 16 possible subsequences, using a "sliding window" of length 4).

We performed several such experiments using $h = 4$ and $h = 7$; the evolved, non-uniform CAs attained average fitness values (entropy) of 3.997 and 6.978, respectively. We then re-tested our best CAs over $M = 65536$ times steps (as in [6]), obtaining entropy values of 3.9998 and 6.999, respectively. Interestingly, when we performed this test with $h = 7$ for CAs which were evolved using $h = 4$, high entropy was displayed as for CAs which were originally evolved with $h = 7$. The entropy results are comparable to those of [6] as well as to the rule 30 CA of [21] and the non-uniform, rules $\{90, 150\}$ CA of [3, 4]. Note that while our fitness measure is local, the evolved entropy results reported above represent the average of *all* grid cells; thus, we obtain N random sequences rather than a single one. Figure 2 demonstrates the operation of three CAs discussed above: rule 30, rules $\{90, 150\}$, and a co-evolved CA. Note that the co-evolved CA is quasi-uniform (Section 2), as evident by observing the rules map; this map depicts the distribution of rules by assigning a unique color to each distinct rule.

We next subjected our evolved CAs to a number of additional tests, including chi-square (χ^2), serial correlation coefficient and a Monte Carlo simulation for calculating the value of π; these are well known tests described in detail in [5]. In order to apply the tests we generated sequences of 100,000 random bytes in the following manner: the CA of size $N = 50$ is run for 500 time steps, thus generating 50 random temporal bit sequences of length 500. These are concatenated to form one long sequence of length 25,000 bits; this procedure is then repeated 32 times, thus obtaining a sequence of length 800,000 bits, which are grouped into 100,000 bytes.

Table 1 shows the test results of four random number generators[5]: two co-evolved CAs (one of which is that demonstrated in Figure 2c), rule 30 CA, and the rules $\{90, 150\}$ CA. We note that for all generators the entropy, serial correlation coefficient and simulated π values are satisfactory. However, the chi-square test, which is one of the most significant ones [5], reveals a different picture. Knuth suggests that at least three sequences from a generator be subjected to the chi-square test and if a majority (i.e., at least two out of three) pass then the generator is considered to have passed (with respect to chi-square). We note that the two co-evolved CAs attain good results for the chi-square test, with the other two CAs trailing behind. It is noteworthy that our co-evolved CAs attain good results on a number of tests, while the fitness measure used during

[5] The tests were conducted using a public domain software written by J. Walker, available at `http://www.fourmilab.ch/random/`.

Fig. 2. One-dimensional random number generators: Operation of three CAs. Grid size is $N = 50$, radius is $r = 1$. White squares represent cells in state 0, black squares represent cells in state 1. The pattern of configurations is shown through time (which increases down the page); the initial configurations were generated by randomly setting the state of each grid cell to 0 or 1 with uniform probability. Top figures depict space-time diagrams, bottom figures depict rule maps. (a) Rule 30 CA. (b) Rules $\{90, 150\}$ CA. Rules map: light gray represents rule 90, black represents rule 150. (c) A co-evolved, non-uniform CA, consisting of three rules: rule 165 (22 cells), rule 90 (22 cells), rule 150 (6 cells). Rules map: black represents rule 165, dark gray represents rule 90, light gray represents rule 150.

Test	co-evolved CA (1)	co-evolved CA (2)	rule 30 CA	rules {90,150} CA
Chi-square	50.00%	50.00%	90.00%	50.00%
	50.00%	75.00%	10.00%	5.00%
	90.00%	95.00%	97.50%	10.00%
	25.00%	50.00%	0.01%	75.00%
	50.00%	75.00%	95.00%	97.50%
	25.00%	75.00%	97.50%	25.00%
	75.00%	75.00%	50.00%	25.00%
	10.00%	25.00%	5.00%	25.00%
	50.00%	50.00%	25.00%	95.00%
	90.00%	90.00%	25.00%	75.00%
(% success)	100%	90%	50%	70%
Serial correlation coefficient	0.001849	-0.003904	0.000523	0.006464
	-0.003855	0.002275	-0.001752	-0.000714
	0.001923	0.000480	0.001561	0.002054
	-0.000111	-0.002366	0.004775	-0.004812
	-0.000596	0.001942	0.002137	-0.000751
Entropy	7.998185	7.998074	7.998406	7.998209
	7.998214	7.998352	7.997887	7.997877
	7.998376	7.998446	7.998487	7.997928
	7.997998	7.998060	7.997329	7.998422
	7.998079	7.998293	7.998444	7.998507
Monte Carlo π	3.12448 (0.54%)	3.12832 (0.42%)	3.13488 (0.21%)	3.12512 (0.52%)
	3.14080 (0.03%)	3.13120 (0.33%)	3.14816 (0.21%)	3.14016 (0.05%)
	3.13584 (0.18%)	3.12208 (0.62%)	3.15168 (0.32%)	3.14992 (0.27%)
	3.12752 (0.45%)	3.12640 (0.48%)	3.13008 (0.37%)	3.15392 (0.39%)
	3.14672 (0.16%)	3.13776 (0.12%)	3.12912 (0.40%)	3.11696 (0.78%)

Table 1. Results of tests. Each entry represents the test result for a sequence of $100,000$ bytes generated by the corresponding randomizer (see text). 10 sequences were generated by each randomizer; the table lists the chi-square test results for all 10 sequences and the first 5 results for the other tests. CA Grid size is $N = 50$. Co-evolved CA (1) consists of three rules: rule 165 (22 cells), rule 90 (22 cells), and rule 150 (6 cells); co-evolved CA (2) consists of two rules: rule 165 (45 cells) and rule 225 (5 cells). Interpretation of the listed values is as follows (for a full explanation see [5]): (i) For the chi-square test "good" results are between 10% – 90%, with extremities on both sides (i.e., < 10% and > 90%) representing non-satisfactory random sequences. The percentage of sequences passing the chi-square test is also listed in the table. (ii) The serial correlation coefficient should be close to zero. (iii) Entropy should be close to 8. (iv) The random number sequence is used in a Monte Carlo computation of the value of π; the final value is shown along with the error percentage in parenthesis.

evolution is entropy alone. The relatively low result obtained by the rule 30 CA may be due to the fact that we considered N random sequences generated in parallel, rather than the single one considered by Wolfram (see Section 2). The rules {90,150} CA results may probably be somewhat improved (as perhaps our own results) by using "site spacing" and "time spacing" [3, 4].

5 Conclusions

We presented the cellular programming algorithm for co-evolving non-uniform CAs, and applied it to the problem of generating random number generators. While a more extensive suite of tests should be conducted, it seems safe to say at this point that our co-evolved generators are at least as good as the best available CA randomizers (see also [18]).

The evolved CAs are quasi-uniform, involving only $2-3$ rules; while rules 90 and 150 have been observed (e.g., Figure 2c), other rules have also emerged[6]. This can be advantageous from a hardware point of view since some rules lend themselves more easily to implementation using basic logic gates [3, 4]. It might also be possible to add restrictions to the evolutionary process, e.g., by pre-specifying rules for some cells, in order to further facilitate hardware implementation. Another possible modification of the evolutionary process is the incorporation of statistical measures of randomness into the fitness function (and not just as an aftermath benchmark). These possible extensions could lead to the automatic generation of high-performance, random number generators meeting specific user demands.

Evolving, non-uniform CAs hold potential for studying phenomena of interest in areas such as complex systems, artificial life and parallel computation. This work has shed light on the possibility of using such CAs as random number generators, and demonstrated the feasibility of their evolution.

References

1. R. Das, J. P. Crutchfield, M. Mitchell, and J. E. Hanson. Evolving globally synchronized cellular automata. In L. J. Eshelman, editor, *Proceedings of the Sixth International Conference on Genetic Algorithms*, pages 336–343, San Francisco, CA, 1995. Morgan Kaufmann.
2. R. Das, M. Mitchell, and J. P. Crutchfield. A genetic algorithm discovers particle-based computation in cellular automata. In Y. Davidor, H. -P. Schwefel, and R. Männer, editors, *Parallel Problem Solving from Nature- PPSN III*, volume 866 of *Lecture Notes in Computer Science*, pages 344–353, Berlin, 1994. Springer-Verlag.
3. P. D. Hortensius, R. D. McLeod, and H. C. Card. Parallel random number generation for VLSI systems using cellular automata. *IEEE Transactions on Computers*, 38(10):1466–1473, October 1989.

[6] One common feature of all evolved rules is the fraction of output 1 bits in the rule tables, which is exactly 0.5.

4. P. D. Hortensius, R. D. McLeod, W. Pries, D. M. Miller, and H. C. Card. Cellular automata-based pseudorandom number generators for built-in self-test. *IEEE Transactions on Computer-Aided Design*, 8(8):842–859, August 1989.
5. D. E. Knuth. *The Art of Computer Programming: Volume 2, Seminumerical Algorithms.* Addison-Wesley, Reading, MA, second edition, 1981.
6. J. R. Koza. *Genetic Programming.* The MIT Press, Cambridge, Massachusetts, 1992.
7. M. Mitchell, J. P. Crutchfield, and P. T. Hraber. Dynamics, computation, and the "edge of chaos": A re-examination. In G. Cowan, D. Pines, and D. Melzner, editors, *Complexity: Metaphors, Models and Reality*, pages 491–513. Addison-Wesley, Reading, MA, 1994.
8. M. Mitchell, J. P. Crutchfield, and P. T. Hraber. Evolving cellular automata to perform computations: Mechanisms and impediments. *Physica D*, 75:361–391, 1994.
9. M. Mitchell, P. T. Hraber, and J. P. Crutchfield. Revisiting the edge of chaos: Evolving cellular automata to perform computations. *Complex Systems*, 7:89–130, 1993.
10. N. H. Packard. Adaptation toward the edge of chaos. In J. A. S. Kelso, A. J. Mandell, and M. F. Shlesinger, editors, *Dynamic Patterns in Complex Systems*, pages 293–301. World Scientific, Singapore, 1988.
11. S. K. Park and K. W. Miller. Random number generators: Good ones are hard to find. *Communications of the ACM*, 31(10):1192–1201, October 1988.
12. M. Sipper. Non-uniform cellular automata: Evolution in rule space and formation of complex structures. In R. A. Brooks and P. Maes, editors, *Artificial Life IV*, pages 394–399, Cambridge, Massachusetts, 1994. The MIT Press.
13. M. Sipper. An introduction to artificial life. *Explorations in Artificial Life (special issue of AI Expert)*, pages 4–8, September 1995. Miller Freeman, San Francisco, CA.
14. M. Sipper. Quasi-uniform computation-universal cellular automata. In F. Morán, A. Moreno, J. J. Merelo, and P. Chacón, editors, *ECAL'95: Third European Conference on Artificial Life*, volume 929 of *Lecture Notes in Computer Science*, pages 544–554, Berlin, 1995. Springer-Verlag.
15. M. Sipper. Studying artificial life using a simple, general cellular model. *Artificial Life Journal*, 2(1):1–35, 1995. The MIT Press, Cambridge, MA.
16. M. Sipper. Co-evolving non-uniform cellular automata to perform computations. *Physica D*, 92:193–208, 1996.
17. M. Sipper. Complex computation in non-uniform cellular automata, 1996. (submitted).
18. M. Sipper and M. Tomassini. Generating parallel random number generators by cellular programming. *International Journal of Modern Physics C*, 1996. (to appear).
19. M. Tomassini. A survey of genetic algorithms. In D. Stauffer, editor, *Annual Reviews of Computational Physics*, volume III, pages 87–118. World Scientific, 1995. Also available as: Technical Report 95/137, Department of Computer Science, Swiss Federal Institute of Technology, Lausanne, Switzerland, July, 1995.
20. S. Wolfram. Statistical mechanics of cellular automata. *Reviews of Modern Physics*, 55(3):601–644, July 1983.
21. S. Wolfram. Random sequence generation by cellular automata. *Advances in Applied Mathematics*, 7:123–169, June 1986.

Scheduling by Genetic Local Search with Multi-Step Crossover

Takeshi Yamada and Ryohei Nakano

NTT Communication Science Laboratories,
2 Hikaridai, Seika-cho, Soraku-gun, Kyoto 619-02, Japan

Abstract. In this paper, multi-step crossover (MSX) and a local search method are unified as a single operator called MSXF. MSX and MSXF utilize a neighborhood structure and a distance measure in the search space. In MSXF, a solution, initially set to be one of the parents, is stochastically replaced by a relatively good solution in the neighborhood, where the replacement is biased toward the other parent. After a certain number of iterations of this process, the best solution from those generated is selected as an offspring. Using job-shop scheduling problem benchmarks, MSXF was evaluated in a GA framework as a high-level crossover working on the critical path of a schedule. Experiments showed promising performance for the proposed method.

1 Introduction

It is well known that GAs are not well suited for fine-tuning structures which are very close to optimal solutions and that it is essential to incorporate local search methods, such as neighborhood search, into GAs. The result of such incorporation is often called *Genetic Local Search (GLS)* [1]. In this framework, an offspring obtained by a recombination operator, such as a crossover, is not included in the next generation directly but is used as a "seed" for the subsequent local search. The local search moves the offspring from its initial point to the nearest locally optimal point, which is included in the next generation.

In solving combinatorial optimization problems such as job-shop scheduling problems (JSSP), it is often more difficult to define a crossover operator which recombines solutions and make global changes to them than a transition operator of a neighborhood search which only modifies a solution locally. In fact, it is rather easy to construct an example of neighborhood search for JSSP by using naturally introduced job permutations and it can even be enhanced by limiting the permutations on the critical path. Unfortunately the same method cannot help build an effective crossover operator, which prevents us from applying GAs. Recently, MSX [2] was proposed as one such high-level crossover.

Given a local search method with the appropriate neighborhood structure, MSX can be defined using the same neighborhood structure in the problem space. Using the same information as the local search uses, it can locate a good, new starting point for the subsequent local search. MSX can be defined in a problem-independent manner and can be implemented easily even if the problem to be solved is complicated.

In this paper, *Multi-Step Crossover Fusion (MSXF)*, originating from MSX, is proposed as a new high-level crossover which is fused with a local search. In MSXF, a solution, initially set to be one of the parents, is stochastically replaced by a relatively good solution from the neighborhood, where the replacement is biased toward the other parent. The biased stochastic replacement is described briefly as follows:

1. All the members in the neighborhood are indexed in ascending order according to the distance from the other parent.
2. A member is selected from the neighborhood randomly, but a smaller index is preferred. It is then probabilistically accepted according to its evaluation value.
3. If it is rejected, its index is changed to the biggest one in the neighborhood and process returns to step 2.
4. Otherwise the current solution is replaced by the selected one.

After a certain number of iterations of this process, the best one among the generated solutions is selected as an offspring. MSXF can be viewed as a recombination operator in which local search functionality is built in. In other words, it acts as a single operator unifying MSX and a local search.

MSXF has been applied to JSSP, employing a critical path-based neighborhood called the CB neighborhood. The CB neighborhood has been proved to be one of the most powerful neighborhoods for JSSP through extensive experimental studies [3]. A GA with such a tailored high-level MSXF (GA/MSXF) was evaluated with well-known benchmark problems of Muth and Thompson [4].

2 Background

2.1 Neighborhood Search

Neighborhood search is a widely used local search technique to solve combinatorial optimization problems. A solution x is represented as a point in the search space, and a set of solutions associated with x is defined as neighborhood $N(x)$. $N(x)$ is a set of feasible solutions capable of being reached from x by exactly one transition, a single perturbation of x.

The outline of a neighborhood search for minimizing $V(x)$ is described in Algorithm 1, where x denotes a point in the search space and $V(x)$ denotes its evaluation value. The criterion used in Step 1 of Algorithm 1 is called the *choice criterion* by which the neighborhood search can be categorized [5]. For example, a descent method selects a point $y \in N(x)$ such that $V(y) < V(x)$. A stochastic method probabilistically selects a point according to the Metropolis Criterion, i.e., $y \in N(x)$ is selected with probability 1 if $V(y) < V(x)$; otherwise, with probability:

$$P(y) = exp(-\Delta V/T), \quad \text{where } \Delta V = V(y) - V(x) . \tag{1}$$

Algorithm 1. Neighborhood search
• Select a starting point: $x = x_0 = x_{best}$.
do

1. Select a point $y \in N(x)$ according to the given criterion based on the value $V(y)$. Set $x = y$.
2. If $V(x) < V(x_{best})$ then set $x_{best} = x$.

until some termination condition is satisfied.

Here P is called the acceptance probability. Simulated Annealing (SA) is a method in which parameter T (called the temperature) decreases to zero following an annealing schedule as the iteration step increases. It is therefore very simple and easy to implement neighborhood search, although an extremely long time is taken to find the global optima. This time requirement prevents the search process from being trapped in a deep local optimum.

2.2 Multi-step Crossover

In a simple GA framework, the main role of the crossover operator is to function as a search engine; by piling up good *building-blocks*, better strings can be constructed. But in GLS, local search plays the leading role and the crossover, together with the selection operator, works as a navigation engine and helps find new starting points for the subsequent local search. Multi-step crossover (MSX) is designed to be successful under such a GLS framework [2].

MSX is constructed by using the distance measure and the neighborhood structure in the search space. Let the parent solutions be p_1 and p_2, and let $N(p)$ be the neighborhood of p. Set $x = p_1$. MSX modifies x in the direction of p_2 as follows: first each point $y \in N(x)$ is ranked by the distance $d(y, p_2)$ between y and p_2; the smaller the distance, the higher the rank. Then x is replaced by y with a relatively high rank, i.e., a small $d(y, p_2)$. Repeating this step modifies x in a step-by-step manner and brings x close to p_2. In the process, x loses the characteristics of p_1 and gradually obtains those of p_2. After a certain number of iterations, the resulting new solutions contain elements of both p_1 and p_2 although in different ratios.

In combinatorial optimization problems, it is computationally effective to limit the search to a subspace of the solution space without excluding a global optimum. In a neighborhood search, this can be done by limiting the size of the neighborhood to a fraction of the total available moves, while keeping the connectivity property. The subspace is called a higher-level solution space. MSX can be viewed as a high-level crossover in GLS in the sense that a new solution generated by MSX necessarily resides in the same higher-level space as the local search uses.

3 Multi-Step Crossover Fusion

Although preliminary experiments in [2] using JSSP benchmarks demonstrated the good performance of a GA with the MSX (GA/MSX), some computational drawbacks were found. Firstly the descent method which is used as a local search method in GA/MSX is too simplistic. Secondly, a lot of individuals are generated and evaluated during the MSX steps without contributing directly toward improving the solution quality. To reduce the computational time and improve the solution quality, MSX's functionality is incorporated into a neighborhood search algorithm and these two separate operators are fused together into a single unified operator called MSXF. The neighborhood search algorithm used for the base algorithm of MSXF is not a simple decent method this time, but a more efficient stochastic one. Although SA is one of the well-known stochastic methods and has been successfully applied to many problems as well as to JSSP, it would be unrealistic to use a full SA for our purpose, because it is too time consuming to run SA many times in a GA run. A restricted method with a fixed temperature parameter $T = c$ might be a good alternative. Then the acceptance probability used in Algorithm 1 is rewritten as:

$$P_c(y) = exp\left(-\frac{\Delta V}{c}\right), \quad \text{where } \Delta V = V(y) - V(x) \quad (c : \text{constant}) . \qquad (2)$$

MSX's functionality can be incorporated into Algorithm 1 by adding more acceptance bias in favor of $y \in N(x)$ with a small $d(y, p_2)$. The acceptance bias in MSXF is controlled by sorting $N(x)$ members in ascending order of $d(y_i, p_2)$ so that y_i with a smaller index i has a smaller distance $d(y_i, p_2)$. Here $d(y_i, p_2)$ can be estimated easily if $d(x, p_2)$ and the direction of the transition from x to y_i are known, and it is not necessary to generate and evaluate y_i. Then y_i is selected from $N(x)$ randomly, but with a bias in favor of y_i with a small index i. The outline of MSXF is described in Algorithm 2.

In place of $d(y_i, p_2)$, one can also use $\sigma(d(y_i, p_2) - d(x, p_2)) + r_\epsilon$ to sort $N(x)$ members in Algorithm 2. Here $\sigma(x)$ denotes the sign of x: $\sigma(x) = 1$ if $x > 0$, $\sigma(x) = 0$ if $x = 0$, $\sigma(x) = -1$ otherwise. A small random fraction r_ϵ is added to randomize the order of members with the same sign.

The termination condition can be given, for example, as the fixed number of iterations in the outer loop. MSXF is not applicable if the distance between p_1 and p_2 is too small compared to the number of iterations. In such a case, a mutation operator called *Multi-Step Mutation Fusion* (MSMF) is applied instead. MSMF can be defined in the same manner as MSXF except for one point: the bias is reversed, i.e., sort the $N(x)$ members in descending order of $d(y_i, p_2)$ in Algorithm 2.

4 Job-shop Scheduling and GA/MSXF

4.1 Job-shop Scheduling Problem

The $n \times m$ *minimum-makespan* general job-shop scheduling problem can be described by a set of n jobs that is to be processed on a set of m machines.

Algorithm 2. Multi-Step Crossover Fusion (MSXF)
• Let p_1, p_2 be parent solutions.
• Set $x = p_1 = q$.
do • For each member $y_i \in N(x)$, calculate $d(y_i, p_2)$.
• Sort $y_i \in N(x)$ in ascending order of $d(y_i, p_2)$.
do 1. Select y_i from $N(x)$ randomly, but with a bias in favor of y_i with a small index i.
2. Calculate $V(y_i)$ if y_i has not yet been visited.
3. Accept y_i with probability one if $V(y_i) \leq V(x)$, and with $P_c(y_i)$ otherwise.
4. Change the index of y_i from i to n, and those of y_k $(k \in \{i+1, i+2, \ldots, n\})$ from k to $k-1$.
until y_i is accepted.
• Set $x = y_i$.
• If $V(x) < V(q)$ then set $q = x$.
until some termination condition is satisfied.
• q is used for the next generation.

Each job has a technological sequence of the machines to be processed. Each *operation* requires the exclusive use of each machine for an uninterrupted duration called *processing time.* The time required to complete all jobs is called *makespan.* The objective when solving or optimizing this general problem is to determine the processing order of the operations for each machine that minimizes the makespan.

Job-shop scheduling problems are not only $\mathcal{NP}$-hard , but are extremely difficult to solve optimally. To solve JSSP, exhaustive search algorithms based on branch and bound methods have been studied. Recently, approximation algorithms such as simulated annealing (SA), genetic algorithms (GAs) and tabu search have also been applied with good success [6, 7, 8, 3, 9].

Job-shop scheduling problems are often described by a disjunctive graph $G = (V, C \cup D)$, where

- V is a set of nodes representing the operations of all jobs together with two special nodes, a *source* (0) and a *sink* $\star$, representing the beginning and end of the schedule, respectively.
- C is a set of conjunctive arcs representing the technological sequences of operations.
- D is a set of disjunctive arcs representing pairs of operations that must be performed on the same machines.

The processing time for each operation is the weighted value attached to the corresponding nodes.

Scheduling defines the ordering between all operations that must be processed on the same machine, i.e., to fix precedences between operations. In the

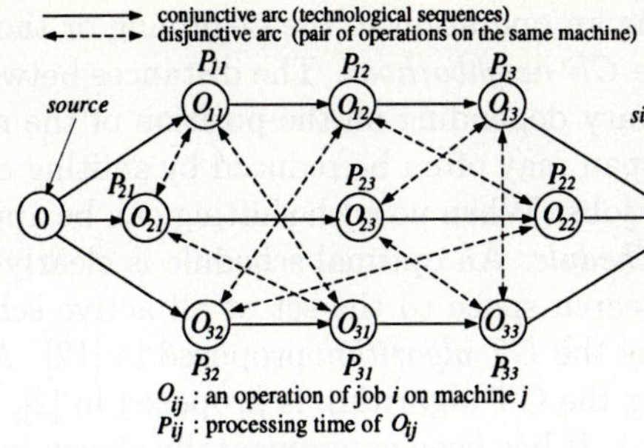

Figure 1. Disjunctive graph G of a 3×3 problem

disjunctive graph model, this is done by turning all undirected (disjunctive) arcs into directed ones. The set of all directed arcs selected from disjunctive arcs is called a *selection.*

A selection S defines a feasible schedule if and only if the resulting directed graph is acyclic. In such a case, S is called a *complete selection.* A complete selection and its corresponding feasible schedule can be used interchangeably and represented by the same symbol S.

Makespan is given by the length of the longest weighted path from source to sink in this graph. This path $\mathcal{P}$ is called the *critical path* and is composed of a sequence of *critical operations.* A sequence of consecutive critical operations on the same machine is called a *critical block.*

The distance between two schedules S and T can be measured by the number of differences in the processing orders of operations on each machine [7]. In other words, it can be calculated by summing the disjunctive arcs whose directions are different between S and T. We call this distance the *disjunctive graph* (DG) *distance.*

4.2 Neighborhood Structures for JSSP

A set of solutions of JSSP can be mapped to the space of bit-strings by marking each disjunctive arc as 1 or 0 according to its direction [7]. The DG distance and the Hamming distance in the mapped space are equivalent, and the neighborhood of a schedule S is a set of all (possibly infeasible) schedules whose DG distances from S are exactly one. This approach is simple and straightforward but not very efficient.

More efficient methods can be obtained by introducing a transition operator that exchanges a pair of consecutive operations only on the critical path and forms a neighborhood [10]. We call this the *adjacent swapping* (AS) neighborhood. DG distances between a schedule and members of its AS neighborhood are always one, so the AS neighborhood can be considered a subset of the bit-string neighborhood described above.

Another neighborhood using a transition operator on the critical path is proposed in [11]. The transition operator permutes the order of operations in a critical block by moving an operation to the beginning or the end of the critical block, thus forming the *CB neighborhood.* The distances between a schedule and its CB neighbors can vary depending on the position of the moving operation.

A schedule's makespan may often be reduced by shifting an operation to left without delaying other jobs. When no such shifting can be applied to a schedule, it is called an *active schedule.* An optimal schedule is clearly active so it is safe and efficient to limit search space to the set of all active schedules. An active schedule is generated by the *GT algorithm* proposed in [12]. An extension of the CB neighborhood using the GT algorithm is proposed in [2], which is called the active CB neighborhood. It has been experimentally shown in [13] that SA using the active CB neighborhood is very powerful. Thus, the active CB neighborhood may as well be investigated in the context of GA.

4.3 GA/MSXF for Job-shop Scheduling

The MSXF is applied to JSSP using the active CB neighborhood and the DG distance previously defined. Algorithm 3 describes the outline of the GA/MSXF routine for JSSP using the steady state model proposed in [14, 15]. To avoid premature convergence even under a small-population condition, an individual whose fitness value is equal to someone in the population is not inserted to the population in step 4.

Algorithm 3. GA/MSXF for JSSP

- Initialize population: generate a set of randomly generated schedules and apply the local search to each member of the set.

do
1. Select two schedules p_1, p_2 from the population randomly with some bias depending on their makespan values.
2. **If** the DG distance between p_1, p_2 is shorter than some predefined small value, apply MSMF to p_1 and generate q.
3. **Otherwise**, apply MSXF to p_1, p_2 using the active CB neighborhood $N(p_1)$ and the DG distance, and generate a new schedule q.
4. If q's makespan is shorter than the worst in the population, and no one in the population has the same fitness value as q, replace the worst individual with q.

until some termination condition is satisfied.

- Output the best schedule in the population.

A given problem of JSSP can be converted to another problem by reversing all the technological sequences. The new problem is equivalent to the old one in the sense that, reversing the job sequences of any feasible solution from the original problem results in a feasible solution for the reversed problem with the same critical path and makespan. It can be seen, however, that an active schedule from the original problem is not necessarily active in the reversed problem. we call a schedule *left active* if it is an active schedule for the original problem and *right active* if it is for the reversed problem. Using only the left (or right) active schedules may bias the search toward the wrong direction, therefore a mechanism to search in the space of both left and right active schedules is introduced in the GA/MSXF as follows. First, there are equal number of left and right active schedules in the initial population. The schedule q generated from p_1 and p_2 by MSXF ought to be left (or right) active if p_1 is left (or right) active, but with some probability (0.1 for example) this property is reversed.

5 Experimental Results

The performance of GA/MSXF was tested by running several simulation trials with well-known benchmark problems originated by Muth and Thompson (MT) [4].

Table 1. Performance comparisons using MT benchmark problems

Prob	Method	Best	Avg	Var	Pop	cpu time	machine	runs
MT10×10	CBSA	930	930.8	2.4	–	44m36s	SS2	10
	GA/GT+ECO	930	963	14	2025	5m	SS2	200
Opt. 930	PGA+SBP	930	947	8.2	100	2.3m	SS10	200
	GVOT	949	977	?	500	25m	SUN4	?
	GA/MSX	930	934.5	5.1	500	11m39s	SS10	10
	GA/MSXF	930	930	0	10	1m28s	DECα	10
MT20×5	CBSA	1178	1178	0	–	38m18s	SS2	5
	GA/GT+ECO	1181	1213	16	5041	30m	SS2	200
Opt. 1165	PGA+SBP	1165	1188	10.3	100	2.3m	SS10	200
	GVOT	1189	1215	?	500	25m	SUN4	?
	GA/MSX	1165	1177.3	4.2	100	10m54s	SS10	10
	GA/MSXF	1165	1165	0	10	1m22s	DECα	10

Pop: population size, cpu time: average cpu time, machine: the machine used for the experiments, runs: number of runs, SS2(SS10): SUN SPARC Station 2(10), DECα: DEC Alpha 600 5/266

Table 1 summarizes the makespan performance of the GA/MSXF method together with our previous GA/MSX method, a simulated annealing method using the CB neighborhood structure (CBSA) [3], and other GA methods published so far in literature for MT10×10 and MT20×5 problems. The GA methods include GA/GT+ECO [16], PGA+SBP [17] and GVOT [18]. For GA/MSXF, population size = 10, constant temperature $c = 10$ and the number of iterations for each MSXF = 1000 are used. The GA/MSXF experiments were performed on a DEC Alpha 600 5/226 which is about 4 times faster than a Sparc Station 10, and the programs were written in the C language. It should be noted that all of the GA/MSXF experiments successfully found optimal solutions in about one and a half minutes for both problems.

Figure 2 shows all of the solutions (in small dots) generated by an application of (a) MSXF and (b) a stochastic local search computationally equivalent to (a) for comparison. Both (a) and (b) started from the same solution (the same parent p_1), but in (a), transitions were biased toward the other solution p_2. The x-axis represents the number of disjunctive arcs whose directions are different from those of p_2 on machines with odd numbers, i.e., the DG distance was restricted to the odd machines. Similarly the y-axis representing the DG distance was restricted to the even machines.

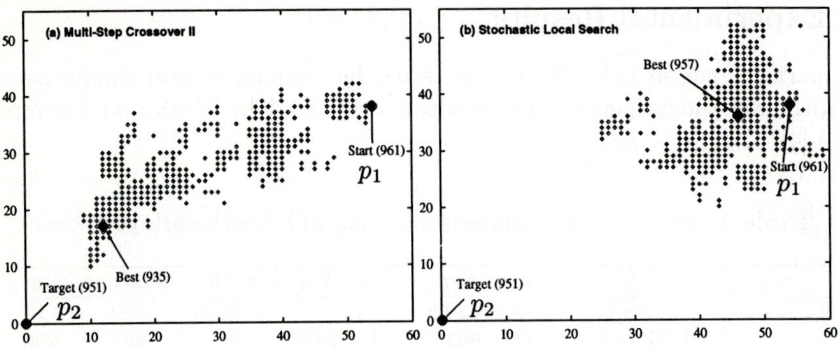

Figure 2. Distribution of solutions generated by an application of (a) MSXF and (b) a short-term stochastic local search

6 Conclusion

The multi-step crossover fusion (MSXF) has been proposed as a unified operator of a local search method and a recombination operator in GLS. MSXF uses a neighborhood structure and a measure of distance in the problem space. Starting from one parent, MSXF carries out a local neighborhood search with a limited number of iterations, where the search direction is navigated by the other parent. MSXF searches for a good solution in the problem space by concentrating its attention on the area between the parents.

We applied GA/MSXF to the job-shop scheduling problem, one of the most difficult $\mathcal{NP}$-hard combinatorial optimization problems. Preliminary experiments demonstrated that GA/MSXF outperforms GA/MSX which has been proved to be superior to other GA methods. Further research including the application of GA/MSXF to more difficult JSSP benchmark problems or to other kinds of combinatorial problems is necessary to show the full capabilities of MSXF.

Acknowledgment

Thanks to Dirk Mattfeld for his useful comments.

References

1. Ulder, N., Pesch, E., Laarhoven, P., Bandelt, H, J. and Aarts, E.: Genetic local search algorithm for the traveling salesman problem, *Proc. of 1st Problem Solving from Nature Conference (PPSN)*, pp. 109–116 (1991).
2. Yamada, T. and Nakano, R.: A GA with multi-step crossover for job-shop scheduling problems, *Proc. of Int. Conf. on GAs in Engneering Systems: Innovations and Applications (GALESIA) '95*, pp. 146–151 (1995).
3. Yamada, T., Rosen, B. and Nakano, R.: A Simulated Annealing Approach to Job Shop Scheduling using Critical Block Transition Operators, *Proc. IEEE Int. Conf. on Neural Networks (ICNN)*, pp. 4687–4692 (1994).
4. Muth, J. and Thompson, G.: *Industrial Scheduling*, Prentice-Hall, Englewood Cliffs, N.J. (1963).
5. Reeves, C. R.: Genetic Algorithms and Neighbourhood Search, *Evolutionary Computing, AISB Workshop*, pp. 115–130 (1994).
6. Aarts, E., Laarhoven, P., Lenstra, J. and Ulder, N.: A computational study of local search algorithms for job shop scheduling, *ORSA J. on Comput.*, Vol. 6, No. 2, pp. 118–125 (1994).
7. Nakano, R. and Yamada, T.: Conventional genetic algorithm for job shop problems, *Proc. of 4th Int. Conf. of Genetic Algorithms (ICGA)*, pp. 474–479 (1991).
8. Yamada, T. and Nakano, R.: A Genetic Algorithm Applicable to Large-Scale Job-Shop Problems, *2nd PPSN*, pp. 281–290 (1992).
9. Taillard, E.: Parallel taboo search techniques for the job-shop scheduling problem, *ORSA J. on Comput.*, Vol. 6, No. 2, pp. 108–117 (1994).
10. Laarhoven, P., Aarts, E. and Lenstra, J.: Job Shop Scheduling by Simulated Annealing, *Oper. Res.*, Vol. 40, No. 1, pp. 113–125 (1992).
11. Brucker, P., Jurisch, B. and Sievers, B.: A Branch & Bound Algorithm for the Job-Shop Scheduling Problem, *Discrete Applied Mathematics*, Vol. 49, pp. 107–127 (1994).
12. Giffler, B. and Thompson, G.: Algorithms for solving production scheduling problems, *Oper. Res.*, Vol. 8, pp. 487–503 (1960).
13. Yamada, T. and Nakano, R.: Job-Shop Scheduling by Simulated Annealing Combined with Deterministic Local Search, *Meta-heuristics: theory & applications*, Kluwer academic publishers, MA, USA., pp. 237–248 (1996).
14. Whitley, D.: The genitor algorithm and selection pressure: why rank-based allocation of reproductive trials is best, *3rd ICGA*, pp. 116–121 (1989).
15. Syswerda, G.: Uniform crossover in genetic algorithms, *3rd ICGA*, pp. 2–9 (1989).
16. Davidor, Y., Yamada, T. and Nakano, R.: The ECOlogical Framework II: Improving GA Performance At Virtually Zero Cost, *5th ICGA*, pp. 171–176 (1993).
17. D.C. Mattfeld, H. K. and Bierwirth, C.: Control of Parallel population dynamics by social-like behavior of ga-individuals, *3rd PPSN* (1994).
18. Fang, H.L., P. R. and Corne, D.: A Promising Genetic Algorithm Approach to Job-Shop Scheduling, Rescheduling, and Open-Shop Scheduling Problems, *5th ICGA*, pp. 375–382 (1993).

Evolutionary Computation in Mechanical, Chemical, Biological, and Optical Engineering

Finding the Conformation of Organic Molecules with Genetic Algorithms

Susanne Beiersdörfer[2], Jens Schmitt[2], Markus Sauer[1], Andreas Schulz[1], Stefan Siebert[1], Jürgen Hesser[2], Reinhard Männer[2], Jürgen Wolfrum[1]

[1]Universität Heidelberg, Physikalisch-Chemisches Institut, Im Neuenheimer Feld 253, D-69120 Heidelberg, Germany
[2]Universität Mannheim, Lehrstuhl für Informatik V, B6, D-68131 Mannheim, Germany

Abstract. Finding the optimal conformation for fluorescent labeled nucleosides is difficult for standard GAs. We investigated the structure of molecule and of the resulting search space itself and concluded that the problem is of the "needle in the haystack" type.
Using niching and island models and a crossover operator adapted to the underlying problem, the GA was able to find the global optimum. Each of these improvements increased the probability to find the global optimum from 0% (standard GA) to ~30%. The combination of either niching + island model, or graph crossover + island model, increased the probability up to 80%; the combination of all three methods up to 90%.

1 Introduction

Conformational analysis [7], i.e. the prediction of the three-dimensional structure of molecules, has become an increasingly important task in theoretical chemistry over the last few years. Important practical applications are the protein folding problem and drug design, among others. Based on the assumption that the molecules have the structure with the lowest energy level, this analysis can be done by a minimization of the conformational energy.
The standard approaches to solve this problem are Montecarlo methods [13]. In the last years Genetic Algorithms (GAs) have also been applied increasingly often [13][5]. Le Grand and Merz [1] found low energy conformations of polypeptides with a GENITOR based GA. Here an interesting way for choosing the best crossover method was used. At the beginning, three methods —twopoint, twopoint wrap around and

uniform crossover— were chosen with the same probability. During the run these probabilities were changed according to the improvements obtained by each crossover type. This method, though very time consuming (one week of CPU time), was successfully applied to the 46 amino acid protein crambin.

Besides, GAs have only very recently been applied to larger molecules and proteins. Only a few statements have been made about the detection of global minimum solutions by GAs. One reason is that sometimes, e.g. in the application mentioned above, it is difficult to prove the optimality of the determined solution. Another probably more important reason is that standard GAs hardly find the global optimum solution if the energy function has many local optima. In these cases they do not reach the robustness of Montecarlo methods, i.e., Montecarlo methods have a higher probability to locate the global optimum.

Judson et al. [2] used a GA with niching and boxcar (λ-) selection where the structure of the molecule was required for simulating the docking of ligands into proteins. Using 4 niches and a migration interval of 20 generations they succeeded to find the global optimal solution in 5 of 8 attempts.

Our experiments described below confirm the effectiveness of Judson´s niching approach. In contrast to Judson we also investigated the search space of the problem and could explain why niching is necessary. Furthermore we used a problem-specific crossover operator that improved considerably the efficiency of the niching GA on finding the global optimal solution.

2 Problem Setting

The chemical and spectroscopic properties of a flexible molecule are often influenced by its conformation. A conformation of a given molecule is classically defined as the set of arrangements of its atoms in space, which can be obtained solely by rotation about single bonds. The potential energy of a molecule can be calculated using force fields from molecular mechanics. The goal of a conformational search is to find the structure with the lowest energy on a complex hypersurface. In our implementation we used the MM2 force field [4] as fitness function. Generally the search is restricted to variations of flexible torsion angles [7] that are represented as a vector ω.

The fitness function is mainly a function of the distance between pairs of non-bonded atoms. Considering one such pair of atoms, it has an energy minimum that describes the equilibrium state and the energy increases exponentially with smaller distances between both non-bonded atoms.

3 Fluorescent Labeled Nucleoside

It has been shown that Genetic Algorithms (GAs) can efficiently solve the multiple minima problem for a class of organic molecules, namely for n-alcanes. We can explain the success of the GA by the observation that in the first generations better-than-average schemata combine to form the global minimum. In this section we show

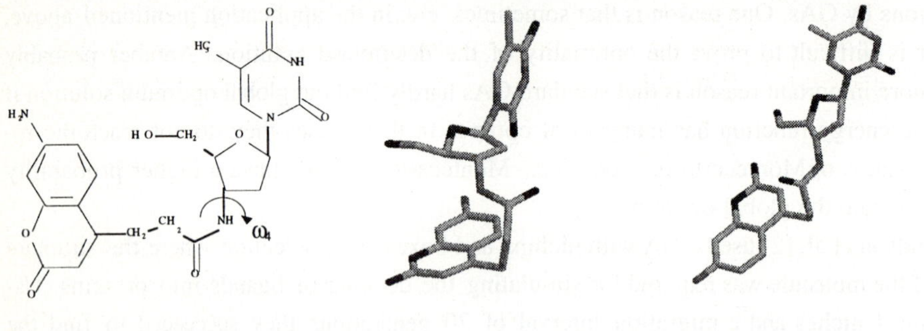

Fig. 1: Left: Chemical structure of 3C3-coumarin120-thymidine conjugate [3]. Bold bonds mark the position of flexible bonds (torsion angles). Middle: Conformation of the global optimal solution (2.7 kcal). Right: Conformation of the next-to-best cluster of solutions (3.4 kcal).

that this cannot be expected for more complicated molecules. As an example we used 3'-(7-aminocoumarine-4-propanoyl)amino-thymidine, a fluorescence labeled nucleoside for bioanalytical applications [8]. The global minimum structure is known from extensive Montecarlo searches using a "usage direct" sampling scheme.

The chemical structure and the various torsion angles are shown in fig. 1 (left). Fig. 1 (middle) shows structure representing the currently best known minimum. Fig. 1 (right) represents a typical next-to-best structure. The main characteristics are determined by the angle ω_4. The global minimum structure consists of an angle of about 45° resulting in an overall folded geometry. In contrast, the higher energy structures have an ω_4 of about 135°.

In nearly all cases the standard Genetic Algorithm —that has been successfully used for finding the correct conformation for alcanes— has found only the next-to-best solution with ω_4 = 135°.

3.1 Investigation of the Search Space

In order to understand this result we investigated the search space. We considered both torsion angles as schemata, ω_4 =45° as schema S_1, and ω_4 = 135° as schema S_2. Fig. 2 shows the difference of the relative frequency of individuals containing schemata S_1 and S_2 in the initial population in a randomly chosen start population.

The diagram shows that individuals containing schema S_2 occur more frequent at lower energy scales in the initial population than those containing S_1. This is the reason why it turned out that individuals with schema S_2 have, on average, a lower energy than those with schema S_1.

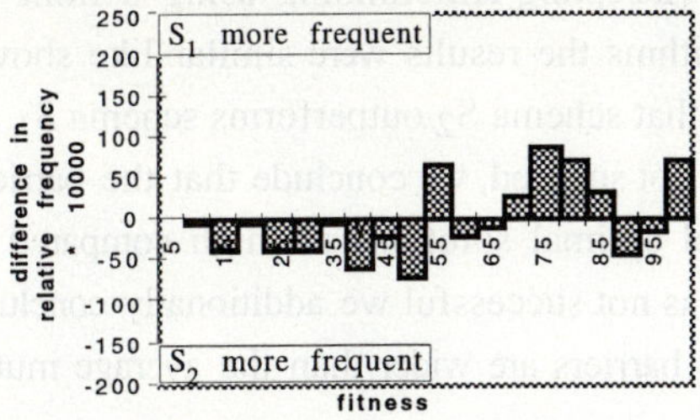

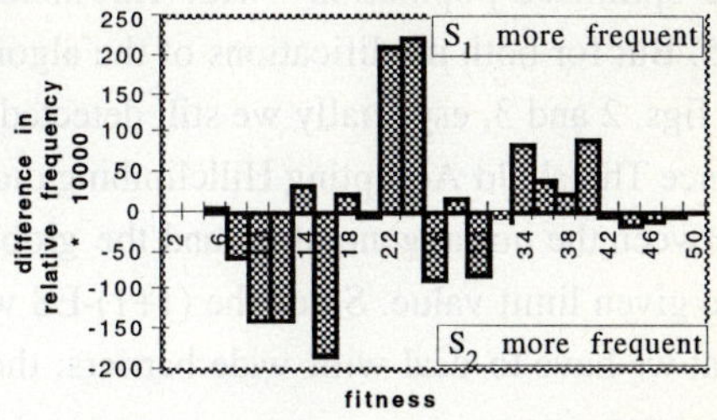

Fig. 2: Difference of the relative frequency of individuals containing schemata S_1 and S_2 in the initial population.

Fig. 3: Difference of the relative frequency of individuals containing schemata S_1 and S_2 in the population of the 5th generation.

Fig. 3 shows the same type of diagram using individuals of the 5th generation. Qualitatively we see the same situation as in fig. 2. On average schema S_2 more often occurs at lower energy levels than schema S_1 and they are again fitter as before. This explains the observed behavior of the GA. Schema S_2 is better than schema S_1 for many generations. According to the schema theorem [9] the frequency of occurrence of schema S_2 increases exponentially compared to schema S_1. Only a few generations are necessary until schema S_1 vanishes from the population.

In order to test whether local optimization of the other torsion angles could mitigate this problem we investigated the following two local optimization schemes:

Our first approach was modeled after the hillclimbing approach (Threshold Accepting Hillclimbing). A binary chromosome is modified by a single bit flip. If the newly created chromosome has a better fitness or if its fitness is worse but within a certain limit it replaces the original chromosome. As possible limits we tested fixed values in [0,1] as well as limits that decreased with increasing fitness. The modification and replacement step was repeated for all bits on the chromosome until no further improvements were made. Threshold Accepting Hillclimbing was applied to each individual in the initial population.

Our second approach was an (1+1)-Evolution Strategy ((1+1)-ES) [10] on each individual in the initial population. The angle ω was modified by the (1+1)-ES mutation as follows (non-uniform mutation from Michalewicz [11] with t=0). We chose two uniformly distributed random values $r_1, r_2 \in [0,1]$ and computed the new value of ω using the formula $\omega+(360°-\omega)\cdot(1-r_2)$ if $r_1<0.5$ and $\omega+\omega\cdot(1-r_2)$ otherwise. We ran the (1+1)-ES 30 times on each individual of the initial population.

We were interested in the influence of these local optimization schemes on both schemata. Hence, we applied both methods on populations which contained randomly chosen elements of S_1 and S_2 in equal shares and kept the angle ω_4 fixed during the optimization process. We achieved the best result —in respect to the average fitness of the optimized population—with Threshold Accepting Hillclimbing using a limit of 0.5. But for both modifications of the algorithms the results were similar like shown in figs. 2 and 3, especially we still detected that schema S_2 outperforms schema S_1.
Since Threshold Accepting Hillclimbing did not succeed, we conclude that the barriers between the initial generation and the global optimal solutions are high compared to the given limit value. Since the (1+1)-ES was not successful we additionally conclude that we have to deal with wide barriers; the barriers are wider than the average mutation step size.
All these observations led us to the assumption that we are dealing an isolated global optimum is surrounded by much worse solutions. This conclusion can be drawn from the structure of both solutions as well: For the 135° case we have an unfolded molecule. Small variations in the other torsion angles have only minor effects on the energy of the structure. For the 45° case the situation, however, is different. Here, almost all other torsion angles must nearly have their correct, optimal value since small variations lead to overlaps in the molecule. These overlaps mean that some atoms have a small respective distance to each other which leads to high repulsion energies in the van der Waals energy term.
It seems that a remedy to these problems is to prevent schema S_1 from dying out until at least one individual is in the attraction zone of the global optimum. This behavior is achieved by using e.g. niching methods. We have tested two different niche building approaches, deterministic crowding [6] and island models.

3.2 Niching

By the use of deterministic crowding [6] two properties can be achieved: the diversity of the population's individuals is promoted and high energy individuals are discarded from the population by the elitist strategy. SUS selection in combination with deterministic crowding (crossover rate 1.0) and small population sizes (20 or 40 individuals) results in the presence of up to 20% of schema S_1 in the final population. The energy distribution is widespread and the global solution is not found in spite of the presence of schema S_1. Enlarging the population size (80, 160 or 320 individuals) leads to a sharp energy distribution of low energy structures in which schema S_1 is not included. All final structures include schema S_2 and correspond to the cluster of the next-to-best solution, the unfolded structure.

3.3 Island Models

To improve the quality of the solutions we used two island models. The first was the standard island model where during each generation two islands are selected randomly for an exchange of individuals with a certain migration probability.

The second was the parallel island model where migration occurs in migration phases. parallel island model uses the following parameters:

Migration interval	Number of generations between migration phases.
Migration rate	Percentage of deme size that migrates (the best individuals of the source island replace the worst individuals in the destination island).
Migration neighborhood	The relationship between source islands and possible destination islands; source and destination islands are randomly selected in our case.
Deme size	Population size divided by number of islands.

Table 1 shows the effect of using the parallel island model instead of a panmictic population. While for the panmictic model the global optimum has never been found, the island model succeeded in 35% of all cases.

Tab. 1: Comparison of different population structures, panmictic and island models. Population size: 800, number of trials: 20, mutation rate: 0.001, crossover: twopoint, crossover rate: 0.5, migration interval: 5, number of migrants: 5% of deme size, sigma-scaling (parameter -0.15), SUS selection.

population structure	frequency of finding the global optimum	mean of best fitness found	spread of best fitness found
panmictic	0	4.30	0.68
parallel island	7	3.43	0.61

3.4 Niching + Standard Island Model

To improve the algorithm the standard island model was included in the GA with niching. Generally sharp energy distributions of the final population with low energy structures were found. After parameter optimization we were able to find the global solution with schema S_1 in up to 80% of all trials.

Tab. 2: Comparison of niching + island models; population size: 400, number of trials: 20, mutation rate: 0.01, crossover: twopoint, crossover rate: 1.0, SUS selection, 10 islands.

migration rate	frequency of finding the global optimum	frequency of finding the global optimum
10%	16	11
8%	11	14
6%	10	11
4%	7	15

3.5 Graph Crossover

To increase the frequency that the global optimum is found, denoted as robustness of our implementation in the following, we adapted the crossover operator to the structure of the given problem. We used the bonding relationships between the atoms of the molecule to reduce the probability that building blocks are disrupted by crossover. The molecule is considered as a graph with the atoms being the set of nodes V and the bonds being the set of edges E.

The new crossover operator, called graph crossover, builds a graph G'=(V',E'), where V' are the atoms of the molecule and E' reflects the bonding relationships between them. G' is then transformed to a graph G=(V,E) by considering only the nodes V of V' which are located at a rotatable bond. E' is reduced to E by replacing certain paths in G' by new edges. These graphs connect two nodes of V and the internal nodes belong to V\V'. The reduced graph of 3C3-coumarin120-thymidine is shown in fig. 4.

The crossover operator first chooses a random node of the reduced graph and deletes randomly neighboring edges until the graph is separated into two disconnected subgraphs. Subgraphs between two randomly chosen individuals are exchanged and after joining the subgraphs a repair algorithm is applied to the resulting children. The last step is necessary if the two subgraphs are misaligned.

The repair algorithm modifies the disrupted torsion angle by twisting it left and right by a small angle. The best structure of the three offspring, the unmodified, that with a left and that with a right twist, is used as the final offspring.

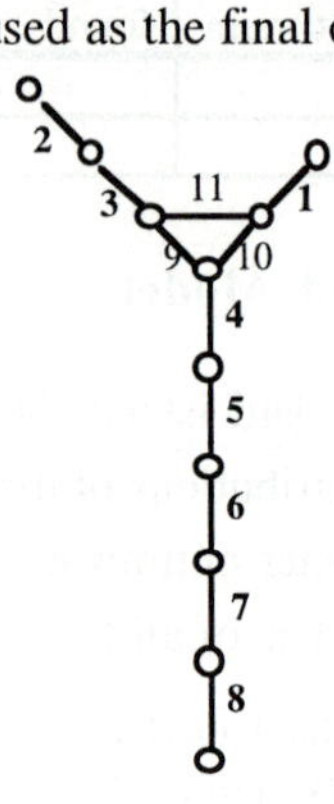

Fig. 4: Reduced graph of 3C3-coumarin120-thymidine conjugate [3]. Bold numbers identify the torsion angles that are represented in the chromosome. The other numbers belong to edges that are not connected to non-flexible torsion angles.

The graph crossover differs from the onepoint crossover in two aspects. First it can generate subgraphs which the onepoint crossover cannot produce. For example (see fig. 4) a cut at the locations 9 and 11 (note that a single cut of the graph crossover can dissect both edges) yields the subgraphs with edges *(2,3)* and *(1,10,4,5,6,7,8)* that correspond to torsion angles (2,3) and (1,4,5,6,7,8). This cut is not possible with the onepoint crossover due to the representation of the nodes (see fig. 5). Second, the probability of disruption is smaller than for onepoint crossover. When onepoint crossover cuts e.g. in between torsion angles 2 and 3 it exchanges two subgraphs *(1)* and *(2)*. The graph crossover, however, exchanges only subgraph *(2)* and has thus a smaller number of cuts and therefore a lower probability to disrupt schemata that are connected parts of the graph.

1	2	3	4	5	6	7	8

Fig. 5: Alignment of the torsion angles on the linear chromosome.

Tab. 3: Comparison of different crossover operators; population size: 1024, number of trials: 10, mutation rate: 0.01, crossover rate: 0.5, panmictic population, sigma-scaling (parameter -0.15), SUS-selection.

crossover operator	frequency of finding the global optimum	mean of best fitness found	spread of best fitness found
onepoint	1	4.53	0.63
G-Crossover	3	3.54	0.60

The efficiency of the graph crossover for this problem was compared with the onepoint crossover. Table 3 shows the result for 10 trials. It demonstrates that the robustness of the GA has increased considerably. It reaches the global optimum with 30%.

3.6 Graph Crossover + Parallel Island Model

Tab. 4: Comparison of different island sizes; population size: 1024, number of trials: 10, mutation rate: 0.01, crossover rate: 0.5, migration interval: 5, number of migrants: 5% of deme size, sigma-scaling (parameter -0.15), SUS selection.

number of islands	frequency of finding the global optimum	mean of best fitness found	spread of best fitness found
1	3	3.54	0.60
2	6	3.43	0.81
4	7	3.23	0.43
8	5	3.20	0.49
16	8	2.96	0.23

Since both the graph crossover and the parallel island model were superior to panmictic populations with standard crossover, we combined them to exploit their beneficial effects on the robustness of the GA. Table 4 shows that the best results for a fixed population size (= number of islands times the deme size) were obtained by using 16 islands. The combined algorithm found the global optimum in 80% of all tests.

3.7 Graph Crossover + Parallel/Standard Island Model + Niching

Finally we tested the combination of niching, graph crossover, and both island models. The probability to locate the global optimum increased up to 90% for the combination of graph crossover, parallel island model, and niching. Although we achieved the same maximal success rate as with graph crossover, the results were less sensitive to the parameter settings (Table 5). Moreover, the results were much closer to the global optimal solution compared to the same configuration using twopoint crossover. We consider the repair step in graph crossover as mainly responsible for this improvement.

Tab. 5: Comparison of niching + island models; population size: 400, number of trials: 20, mutation rate: 0.01, crossover: twopoint, crossover rate: 1.0, SUS-selection.

migration rate	frequency of finding the global optimum for 10 islands	frequency of finding the global optimum for 20 islands
10%	12	15
8%	12	13
6%	14	16
4%	8	14

4 Conclusions

We have demonstrated that island models and niching as well as a problem specific crossover improve the success rate from 0% to 90% of finding the global optimum for the conformation of 3'-(7-aminocoumarine-4-propanoyl)amino-thymidine.

Further investigations in adapting the parameters and examining other crossover operators increase this probability additionally. We used next a poly-peptide (met-enkephaline) as application problem; which allowed us to compare directly with the best Montecarlo methods mentioned in literature. Here we found a better result than reported in literature using an ECEPP-2 energy function. A corresponding paper is forthcoming.

5 Acknowledgment

This work has been supported by the Deutsche Forschungsgemeinschaft under grant Ma 1150/21, Wo 175/26. We additionally thank S. Lorentzen for many fruitful discussions and ideas.

References

1. Le Grand, S.M., Merz jr., K.M. The Application of the Genetic Algorithm to the Minimization of Potential Energy Functions. J. of glob. Opt., Vol. 3, 1993, pp. 49-66.
2. Judson, R.S., Tan, Y.T., Mori, E., Melius, C., Jaeger, E.P., Treasurywala, A.M., Mathiowetz, A. Docking Flexible Molecules: A Case of Three Proteins. J. of Comp. Chemistry, Vol. 16, No. 11, 1995, pp. 1405-1419.
3. Schulz, A. Untersuchung der Donor-Akzeptor Wechselwirkungsgeometrie von Cumarin 120-Thymidin Konjugaten. PhD. Thesis, University of Heidelberg, 1995.
4. Allinger, N.L. Comformational Analysis. 130. MM2. A Hydrogen Force Field Utilizing V_1 and V_2 Torsion Terms. J. Am. Chem. Soc., Vol. 99, 1977, pp. 8127-8134.
5. Brodmeier, T., Pretsch E. Application of Genetic Algorithms in Molecular Modelling. J. of Comp. Chemistry, Vol. 15, 1994, pp. 588-595.
6. Mahfoud, S.W. Niching Methods for Genetic Algorithms. Ph.D. Thesis, Illigal Report No 95001, Univ. of Illinois at Urbana-Champaign, 1995.
7. Leach, A.R. A Survey of Methods for Searching the Conformational Space of Small and Medium-Sized Molecules. In: Rev. in Comp. Chemistry, Vol. 2, 1991, pp. 1-55.
8. Han, K.-T., Sauer, M., Schulz, A., Seeger, S., Wolfrum, J. Time-Resolved Fluorescence Studies of Labeled Nucleosides. Ber. Bunsenges. Phys. Chem., Vol. 97, 1992, pp. 1728-1730.
9. Goldberg, D.E. Genetic Algorithms in Search, Optimization, and Machine Learning. Add. Wesley, Reading, 1989.
10. Rechenberg, I. Evolutionsstrategie '94. Fromman-Holzboog, Stuttgart, 1994.
11. Michaliewicz, Z. Genetic Algorithms + Data Structures = Evolution Programs. 2nd ed., Springer, Berlin, 1994.
12. Elofsson, A; Le Grand, S.M.; Eisenberg, D. Local moves: Efficient algorithm for simulation of protein folding. Proteins: Structure, Function, and Genetics, 1995, Vol. 23, pp. 73-82.

Investigating a Parallel Breeder Genetic Algorithm on the Inverse Aerodynamic Design

I. De Falco, A. Della Cioppa, R. Del Balio and E. Tarantino

Research Institute on Parallel Information Systems (IRSIP)
National Research Council of Italy (CNR)
Via P. Castellino, 111
80131 Naples - Italy

Abstract. Breeder Genetic Algorithms represent a class of random optimisation techniques gleaned from the science of population genetics, which have proved their ability to solve hard optimisation problems with continuous parameters. In this paper we test a parallel version of this technique against a sequential Breeder Genetic Algorithm on a typical inverse design problem in Aerodynamics, the problem of an aerofoil geometry recover starting from a target pressure distribution. Our results show that Parallel Breeder Genetic Algorithms are well suited for applications in Aerodynamics.

Keywords: Breeder Genetic Algorithms, Aerodynamic Design, Parallel Genetic Algorithms.

1 Introduction

There are two problems in Aerodynamics: the *analysis* and the *design* [1, 2]. The former (**direct problem**) consists in describing a flow field given the geometry of the object, whereas the latter (**inverse problem**) requires to find the geometry of the object causing the given flow field. As an example of the second class of problems, we may be asked to determine the shape of an aerofoil when we are assigned a given surface pressure distribution. Furthermore, the design may be subject to constraints allowing the aerodynamic shape to achieve some extremely important features: the aerofoil is sometimes imposed to be compatible with entirely shock–free transonic flow fields or to produce flow fields with minimum entropy generation, minimum noise generation or uniform surface heat flux, and so on. There are some mathematical models used for the shape design which are based on partial differential, integral and algebraic equations. It may sometimes happen, however, that the result of an inverse design based on the above models is a shape which is mathematically acceptable yet it is not physically meaningful and cannot be manufactured; this is, for example, if the lower and the upper surfaces of the aerofoil cross over ('fish tail shapes') or never meet (open trailing edge shapes). Another keypoint in the inverse design methodologies is that an aerofoil obtained even by mathematical models has the desired characteristics only at the design conditions, but if just one of them (angle of attack, free stream Mach number, ...) changes then the shape will have to be changed. Furthermore, in some case, the result of the design may be a mildly concave shape, partially covered by the supersonic flow. In this case ('hanging shock') even at the project operating point the aerodynamic efficiency will not be satisfactory, though all the mathematical conditions are perfectly satisfied. As a consequence of all of the above, it is well known to people working in aerodynamic field that it is more appropriate to draw an almost shock–free shape even at the design conditions, provided that this shock does not increase significantly at off–design conditions. Although skilful engineers are capable of producing successful shapes when considering one operating condition, difficulties arise especially when the problem consists in more operating conditions. In such a case the problem shows all its difficulty, so optimisation methods are needed to help the designer. Many optimisation techniques have been proposed and used by researchers [3, 4]. A basic feature for a numerical optimisation algorithm to be considered of interest is its robustness, because only in this case it may be a key factor for the development of aerodynamic optimisation methods.

During last years Genetic Algorithms (GAs) [5, 6] have been more and more widely applied in many and very different application fields, ranging from the scientific to the commercial and the industrial ones, and they have proved their ability in efficiently solving very different problems. Therefore they are being applied also in the inverse design problem. Some features of the GAs (the use of objective function rather than derivatives or any auxiliary knowledge, the use of probabilistic transition rules instead of deterministic ones, the search from a population of points rather than a single point) make them very robust and therefore attractive for aerodynamic applications. Good results have been obtained by applying GAs to the aerodynamic design problem [7, 8], much better than those achieved by using gradient–based techniques. Nonetheless, the current state of the art is not fully satisfactory. In fact, two problems are to be faced. The first is represented by the huge computation times required by all techniques (GAs included) to find good solutions, due to the need of performing lots, say thousands, of evaluations each one is, in this field, very time–consuming. The second is given by the huge width of the search space. For typical real problems, even not too difficult, at least about twenty variables are to be taken into account, many of them being real variables varying in large admissible ranges, so the search algorithm has to choose among billions of billions of possible solutions. Because of this, new heuristic optimisation techniques are welcome capable of performing efficient searches and reducing the execution times. One more point to be focussed is that such a technique should, if possible, be easily parallelisable, so as to take advantage of the nowadays widely available parallel computers, with the aim to further reduce the search time.

In the last years Mühlenbein and Schlierkamp–Voosen proposed an approach called Breeder Genetic Algorithms (BGAs) [9, 10, 11] which can be seen as a recombination between Evolution Strategies (ESs) [12] and GAs. In fact BGAs use truncation selection which is very similar to the (μ, λ)–strategy in ESs and the search process is mainly driven by recombination making BGAs very similar to GAs. It has been proved that BGAs can solve problems more efficiently than GAs due to the theoretical faster convergence to the optimum [10] and they can, like GAs, be easily written in a parallel form, so we wish to test them on the inverse design.

The paper is organised as follows. Section 2 describes the BGAs. In section 3 the problem faced is described in detail and in section 4 the Parallel BGA (PBGA) is depicted. Section 5 reports our experimental results with the comparison of a sequential and a parallel version of BGAs on the above problem. Finally, section 6 contains our conclusions and foreseen future work in this area.

2 Breeder Genetic Algorithms

The BGAs are based on the concepts of evolution of species and selection typical of GAs; however they differ in the fact that the evolution of the population is 'driven' by the breeding mechanism. This consists in the selection, at each generation, of the $\mathcal{T}\%$ best elements within the current population of $\mathcal{N}$ elements ($\mathcal{T}\%$ is called *truncation rate* and its typical values are within the range 10% to 50%). These elements are let free to mate randomly, without roulette wheel selection, so that they generate a new population of $\mathcal{N}-1$ elements. The former best element is then inserted in this new population, and the cycle of life continues. By doing so, the best elements are treated as 'super-individuals' and mated together, hoping that this can lead to a fitter population. These concepts are taken from other sciences and mimic animal breeding. Another feature of BGAs is the fact that they represent solutions as sequences of real numbers, rather than sequences of bits or integers, so they allow a representation of a phenomenon much closer to the reality than discrete GAs.

A BGA can be formally described by:

$$\mathrm{BGA} = (\mathcal{P}_0, \mathcal{N}, \mathcal{T}, \Gamma, \Delta, \mathcal{A}, \Theta) \tag{1}$$

where $\mathcal{P}_0$ is the initial random population, $\mathcal{N}$ the population size, $\mathcal{T}$ the truncation threshold, Γ the recombination operator, Δ the mutation operator, $\mathcal{A}$ the fitness function and Θ a termination criterion.

Typical recombination operators are the Discrete Recombination (DR), the Extended Line Recombination (ELR) and the Extended Intermediate Recombination (EIR) [10]. DR mixes the alleles in the sequences and can only generate corners in the hypercube defined by the sequences, whereas ELR and EIR generate a new allele by means of a linear combination of the corresponding alleles and can generate respectively any point on the lines connecting the corresponding vertices and in the volume of the hypercube defined by the sequences. Typical mutation operators are discrete and continuous BGA mutation schemes. A wider explanation of these operators can be found in [10].

3 The test problem faced

We have chosen a typical inverse design problem, known in literature as *Europt T4* problem, as a test for our technique. Given a surface pressure distribution *Cp*, at a prefixed operating condition, the inverse problem faced consists in reaching the aerofoil configuration with the fixed *Cp* distribution at the same operating condition. The closer we get to this goal configuration, the better the technique. In this work, the BGAs technique has been employed for the reconstruction of the Korn Aerofoil for subsonic inviscid flow starting from the NACA64A410 aerofoil (Fig. 1). The operating conditions considered for the design task are the following: $\mathcal{M} = 0.75$ and angle of attack[1] equal to zero, where $\mathcal{M}$ is the Mach number[2].

The objective function used for our inverse problem is the classical referred to in literature for this kind of problems defined as follows:

$$Obj\,(\mathbf{x}) = \oint_{\gamma} \left(Cp(\mathbf{x}, s) - Cp_t(s)\right)^2 ds \tag{2}$$

where Cp and Cp_t are respectively the current and the target pressure distribution at the operating condition and s is the arc length along the Cp shape γ. The fitness function of a generated aerofoil is proportional to the inverse of the objective function (2) so the problem becomes a typical maximisation problem and a fitness of infinite value would mean that the two Cp shapes are absolutely identical.

3.1 Aerofoil geometric representation

The representation of the aerofoil geometry is a very important issue for these problems. Usually, researchers working in the field of the aerodynamic design use either a representation given in points modifying the geometry by means of a set of *ad hoc* modification functions or a B-spline representation [13] consisting in a set of points which control the curve (the aerofoil) geometry. The latter representation seems better because it allows to generate curves in a general way and, if it is needed, permits to fix some control points and move the remaining ones allowing a local optimisation. This is the reason why we have used it defining a closed curve with a set of m control points. Such a curve varies as a function of a parameter called degree of the curve (the higher the degree the softer the curve, without spikes, and the farther the shape from the control points). If we let these control points slightly move within given ranges, we will obtain new curves, so new aerofoils. The parameters to be optimised are, thus, the positions of these control points.

[1] The angle of attack is the angle between the segment connecting the Trailing with Leading Edges and the direction of the freestream.

[2] The Mach number is defined as the ratio between the flow velocity V and the sound velocity c at the same point.

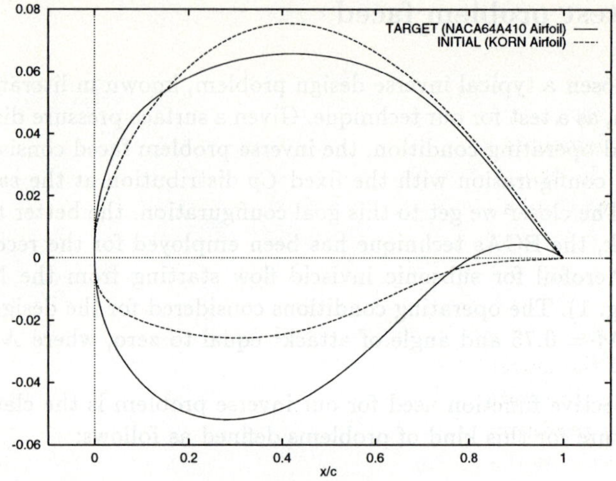

Fig. 1. The initial and target airfoil.

For our problem we have defined a set of control points both for the upper and the lower aerofoil shape $\mathcal{B}^0 = \{\mathcal{B}_1^0, \ldots, \mathcal{B}_m^0\}$ and the following variation has been allowed $\mathcal{W} = \{\mathcal{W}_1, \ldots, \mathcal{W}_m\}$. Hence, the variation law that has been defined for each control point is the following:

$$\mathcal{B}_{i_x} = \mathcal{B}_{i_x}^0 + \mathcal{W}_{i_x}, \quad \mathcal{B}_{i_y} = \mathcal{B}_{i_y}^0 + \mathcal{W}_{i_y} \tag{3}$$

The aerofoil shape has been defined using two open B-spline curves of degree 4 with 9 control points for both the upper and lower surface. The initial and final points, i.e. $\mathcal{B}_1^0 = (0.0, 0.0)$ and $\mathcal{B}_9^0 = (1.0, 0.0)$, have been fixed on both the curves for closing the aerofoil and the remaining ones are let free to move. So, we have 14 control points corresponding to 28 coordinates to be optimised. The variations $\mathcal{W}_{i_x}$ and $\mathcal{W}_{i_y}$ of each control point are in the range $[-0.04, 0.04]$. This is a very general approach because no specific knowledge of the desired final shape has been used, differently from other approaches which allow a different range for each point. Hence, we have computed the vertices of the polygon which defines the NACA64A410 aerofoil geometry using it as the initial polygon for the genetic optimisation.

4 A parallel BGA version

The high computation time, required by both the flow field solver for the evaluation of the goodness of each profile and the high number of evaluations needed by classical GAs or BGAs to explore huge search spaces, leads to exploit explicit parallelism.

Many researches have been effected on GAs with the aim to design effective parallel approaches [14, 15, 16]. The motivation behind the studies of parallel versions is twofold. The first goal is to reduce the processing time necessary to reach an acceptable solution and the second is to find better solutions with respect to the sequential version.

Among the parallel approaches introduced, the coarse–grained model [17], usually implemented on distributed MIMD computers, seems to be the most interesting. In this approach, the population should be divided into a few subpopulations and a migration process is used to send some individuals from one subpopulation to another. In this context we have implemented a simple parallel version which consists of a set of four classical BGAs, running in parallel, each assigned to a different processing element in a completely connected topology, thus the local searches are linked together allowing, in each generation, an exchange of the current best individuals among all processes.

From the Computer Science point of view, there is not a unique definition to measure the performance of parallel algorithms, so researchers adopt different criteria to evaluate the goodness of their algorithms. The performance evaluation becomes even more difficult for the probabilistic search strategies. Since in a previous paper [18] we have tested the BGA on the same problem and we have found the best sequential version in terms of the optimal set of the genetic parameters (population size $\mathcal{N}$, truncation rate $\mathcal{T}, \ldots$), in this work the approach adopted consists in designing a parallel version starting from the optimal set of values found. Consequently, a set of $\mathcal{N}_{Proc}$ processes with a population size $\mathcal{N}_p$ equal to $\mathcal{N}/\mathcal{N}_{Proc}$ is allocated on the parallel system. We will adopt two criteria for the performance evaluation: at parity of the final solution and of the number of evaluations.

The pseudo–code of a generic local search process is delineated in the following:

Procedure **Breeder Genetic Algorithm**
begin
  randomly generate an initial population of $\mathcal{N}_p$ individuals;
  evaluate goodness of each individual;
  while (termination criterion not fulfilled) **do**
    save the best individual in the new population;
    select the best $\mathcal{T}$% individuals;
    for $i = 1$ **to** $\mathcal{N}_p - 1$ **do**
      randomly select two elements among the $\mathcal{T}$%;
      recombine them so as to obtain one offspring;
      perform mutation on the offspring;
      evaluate goodness of the offspring;
    od
    send the current best individual to the *master* process;
    broadcast the current best individual;
    exploit the received solutions;
    update variables for termination;
  od
end

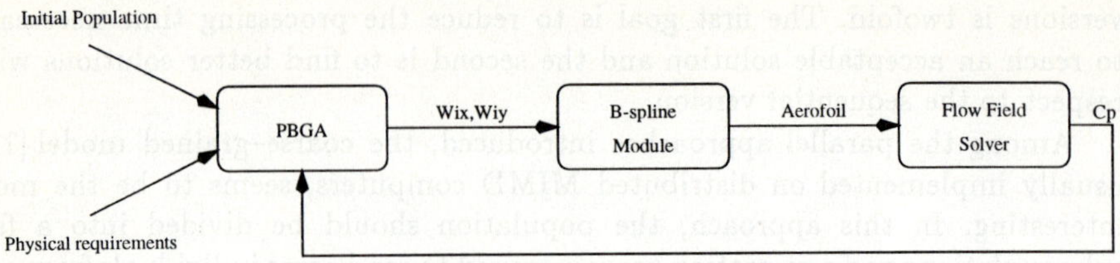

Fig. 2. The cascade of the systems employed.

The *master* process is simply a collector of the current local best solutions of the 'slave' processes and saves the best element at each generation. As regards the exploitation of the received solutions, these replace the worst elements (in our case 3 elements) in each local population.

The overall system is illustrated in Fig. 2.

5 Experimental results

We have made preliminary sets of experiments for the sequential BGA in order to find the best values for the control parameters and the best combination for the genetic operators [18]. The results have led to a BGA version with EIR and continuous mutation operators, δ which defines the recombination interval $[-\delta, 1+\delta]$ equal to 0.25 and a which specifies the mutation interval equal to 0.5. The population size is $\mathcal{N} = 120$ and the truncation rate $\mathcal{T} = 10\%$. All the tests have been performed on a parallel machine, the *Meiko Computing Surface 2*. It is a distributed global memory architecture in which every processing element has more CPUs, and its own local memory system. We have used for the parallel implementation the Parallel Virtual Machine (PVM) as message–passing paradigm among the nodes. It should be pointed out that a float representation has been chosen for the variables involved and, as a consequence, the resulting possible configurations of the search space are $\simeq 10^{163}$. BGA codes have been written in ANSI C programming language, while the aerodynamic analysis code is an inviscid full potential flow field solver written in FORTRAN 77.

A decomposition of the population size $\mathcal{N}$ has been effected, so each process has $\mathcal{N}_p = 30$ with the same truncation percentage, so 3 elements are selected for mating. Due to the approximations, a fitness values of about 100,000 has been fixed as stop criterium. This value represents the minimum fitness value representative of shapes satisfying the problem. In Fig. 3(a), the evolution process in terms of maximum and average fitness over 10 runs is depicted.

Comparing the BGA and the PBGA at parity of the final solution, the speedup in terms of ratio of sequential and parallel convergence time is equal to 6.15. This value has been computed neglecting the time due to the message passing because the time consumed by the BGA and by the flow field solver is much higher. On the other hand, the ratio between the total number of evaluations performed by the BGA and by the PBGA is equal to 1.54. These

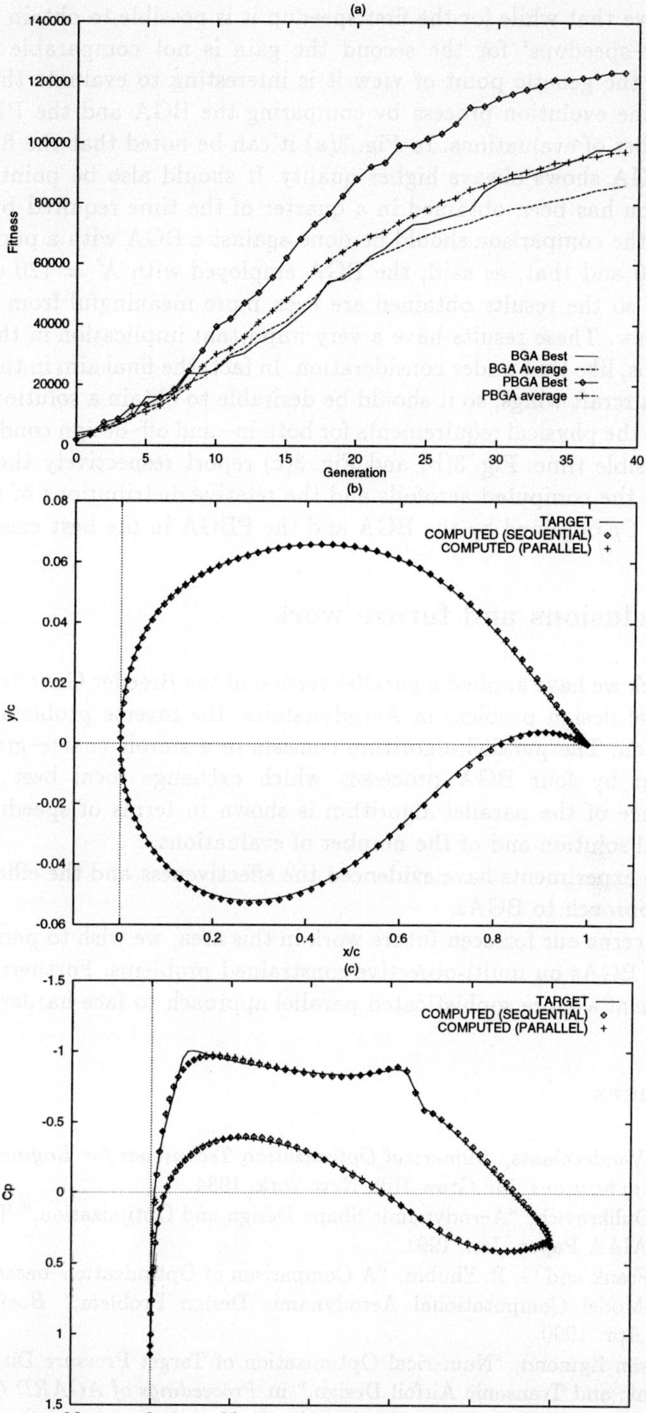

Fig. 3. The results obtained by means of the BGA and the PBGA.

results prove that while for the first speedup it is possible to obtain good values and 'super–speedups' for the second the gain is not comparable to the first one. From the genetic point of view it is interesting to evaluate the migration effects in the evolution process by comparing the BGA and the PBGA at the same number of evaluations. In Fig. 3(a) it can be noted that the final solution of the PBGA shows always higher quality. It should also be pointed out that this solution has been obtained in a quarter of the time required by the BGA. Note that the comparison should be done against a BGA with a population size equal to 30 and that, as said, the BGA employed with $\mathcal{N} = 120$ outperforms the above, so the results obtained are even more meaningful from the parallel point of view. These results have a very important implication in the industrial applications, like that under consideration. In fact, the final aim in this context is to design aircraft wings, so it should be desirable to obtain a solution as close as possible to the physical requirements for both in– and off–design conditions in the lowest possible time. Fig. 3(b) and Fig. 3(c) report respectively the initial, the target and the computed aerofoils and the relative distributions of the pressure coefficient *Cp* obtained by the BGA and the PBGA in the best execution.

6 Conclusions and future work

In this work we have applied a parallel version of the Breeder Genetic Algorithms to a typical design problem in Aerodynamics, the inverse problem for aerofoil optimisation. The parallel algorithm consists in a simple coarse–grained model constituted by four BGA processes which exchange local best individuals. Performance of the parallel algorithm is shown in terms of speedup at parity of the final solution and of the number of evaluations.

All the experiments have evidenced the effectiveness and the efficiency of the parallel approach to BGAs.

As concerns our foreseen future work in this area, we wish to perform further tests with BGAs on multi-objective constrained problems. Furthermore we aim to implement a more sophisticated parallel approach to face harder problems.

References

1. G. N. Vanderplaats, *Numerical Optimization Techniques for Engineering Design: with Applications.* Mc Graw Hill, New York, 1984.
2. G. S. Dulikravich, "Aerodynamic Shape Design and Optimization," Tech. Rep. 91-0476, AIAA Paper, Jan. 1991.
3. P. D. Frank and G. R. Shubin, "A Comparison of Optimization–based Approaches for a Model Computational Aerodynamic Design Problem," *Boeing Computer Serv.*, Apr. 1990.
4. J. A. van Egmond, "Numerical Optimization of Target Pressure Distributions for Subsonic and Transonic Airfoil Design," in *Proceedings of AGARD Conference on Computational Methods for Aerodynamic Design (Inverse) and Optimization*, no. 463, ref. 17, Mar. 1990.

5. J. H. Holland, *Adaptation in Natural and Artificial Systems.* MIT Press, 1975.
6. D. E. Goldberg, *Genetic Algorithms in Search, Optimization and Machine Learning.* Addison-Wesley, Reading, Mass., 1989.
7. S. Obayashi and S. Takanashi, "Genetic Optimization of Target Pressure Distributions for Inverse Design Methods," in *Proceedings of the 12th AIAA Computational Fluid Dynamics Conference*, San Diego, CA, Jun 19-22 1995.
8. I. De Falco, R. Del Balio, A. Della Cioppa and E. Tarantino, "A Parallel Genetic Algorithm for Transonic Airfoil Optimisation," in *Proceedings of the IEEE International Conference on Evolutionary Computing*, Perth, University of Western Australia, Australia, pp. 429–434, 1995.
9. H. Mühlenbein and D. Schlierkamp-Voosen, "Analysis of Selection, Mutation and Recombination in Genetic Algorithms," *Neural Network World*, vol. 3, pp. 907–933, 1993.
10. H. Mühlenbein and D. Schlierkamp-Voosen, "Predictive Models for the breeder Genetic Algorithm I. Continuous Parameter Optimization," *Evolutionary Computation*, vol. 1, no. 1, pp. 25–49, 1993.
11. H. Mühlenbein and D. Schlierkamp-Voosen, "The Science of Breeding and its Application to the Breeder Genetic Algorithm," *Evolutionary Computation*, vol. 1, pp. 335–360, 1994.
12. T. Bäck, F. Hoffmeister and H. Schwefel, "A Survey of Evolution Strategies," in *Proceedings of the 4th International Conference on Genetic Algorithms*, (R. K. Belew, L. B. Booker, eds.), pp. 2–12, M. Kaufmann Publisher, 1991.
13. D. E. Rogers, *Mathematical Elements for Computer Graphics.* Addison-Wesley, Reading, Mass., 1989.
14. R. Tanese, "Distributed Genetic Algorithms," in *Proceedings of the 3rd International Conference on Genetic Algorithms*, (J. D. Schaffer, ed.), pp. 434–439, M. Kaufmann Publisher, 1989.
15. B. Manderick and P. Spiessens, "Fine–grained Parallel Genetic Algorithms," in *Proceedings of the 3rd International Conference on Genetic Algorithms*, (J. D. Schaffer, ed.), pp. 428–433, M. Kaufmann Publisher, 1989.
16. H. Mühlenbein, M. Schomisch and J. Born, "The Parallel Genetic Algorithm as Function Optimizer," *Parallel Computing*, vol. 17, pp. 619–632, 1991.
17. E. Cantú–Paz, "A Summary of Research on Parallel Genetic Algorithms" *IlliGAL Report*, no. 95007, University of Illinois at Urbana–Champaign, USA, July 1995.
18. I. De Falco, R. Del Balio, A. Della Cioppa and E. Tarantino, "Breeder Genetic Algorithm for Airfoil Design Optimisation," in *Proceedings of the IEEE International Conference on Evolutionary Computing*, Nagoya, Japan, pp. 71–75, 1996.

An Evolutionary Design for f-θ Lenses

Yoshiji Fujimoto[1], Masato Nishiguchi[1], Kenichi Nomoto[1], Kensuke Takahashi[1] and Shigeyoshi Tsutsui[2]

[1] Department of Applied Mathematics and Informatics, Ryukoku University
Seta, Ohtsu, Shiga 520-21 Japan (fujimoto@math.ryukoku.ac.jp)

[2] Department of Management and Information Science, Hannan University
5-4-33 Amamihigashi, Matsubara, Osaka 580 Japan (tsutsui@hannan-u.ac.jp)

Abstract. In this paper, we tried evolutionary designs of f–θ lenses for a laser printer or a digital copier with a real-valued GA (NDX: Normal Distributed Crossover) and a genotype GA with high mutation. The f-θ lens represented by a B-Spline curve refract a laser beam reflected from rotating mirror to scan a photo sensitive drum with a constant velocity. Fitness is evaluated by accumulated errors between destinations of ray traces and given targets. We compared the performances of two evolutionary methods. Empirical results show that the real-valued GA has converged faster with better accuracy than the genotype GA for the f–θ lens design problem with strong epistasis.

1 Introduction

In the paper "Evolution Strategy" [1] by Rechenberg, the evolutionary development of an Eye Lens was presented as one of the applications of ES (Evolutionary Strategy) . However, we can hardly find any application of evolutionary methods to optical lens design, although lens design problems are formulated as optimization problems of evaluation factors such as 5 aberrations, the point spread function and the optical transfer function [2].

We tried to design an f-θ lens normally implemented in a commercial Laser Beam Printer by two evolutionary methods. The f-θ lens refract a laser beam reflected by a rotating mirror to scan an OPC (Organic Photo Conductor) drum with a constant velocity. In this paper, we like to show the possibility to design special lenses by using the ray tracing method [2] and evolutionary methods , although we are not experts of optical design. Two evolutionary methods, the real-valued GA with NDX (Normal Distributed Crossover) and the genotype GA with high mutation, are implemented and experiments for lens design are conducted. The f-θ lenses are described by B-Spline curves and fitness is evaluated by accumulation of errors between destinations of ray traces and given targets.

Our objectives are to design an f-θ lens consisting of one lens for a rotating polygon mirror and to design a special f-θ lens for a vibrating mirror that may be produced by micro-machining techniques in the near future.

2 Design of an f-θ lens

2. 1 Optical System of a Laser Printer

Fig. 1 shows the optical system of a commercial laser beam printer. A semiconductor laser unit emits a pulse modulated laser beam onto a rotating polygon mirror. The polygon mirror is rotating with a constant angular velocity and reflect the laser beam for scanning the surface of an OPC drum. If the laser beam directly scan the surface of it, the laser spot doesn't scan the surface with a constant speed. That is, the laser spot scans faster around both the side of the drum than around the center. An f-θ lens refract the path of the laser beam so that the laser spot scan the surface of the OPC drum with a constant speed. The modulated laser spot discharges the positive charges distributed uniformly on the OPC surface to draw a negatively charged pattern. The negative charges attracts the positively charged toners on the OPC drum. The attracted toners are transferred on a paper with the same pattern as the negatively charged pattern on the surface of OPC drum and is fixed on the paper by a heat roller.

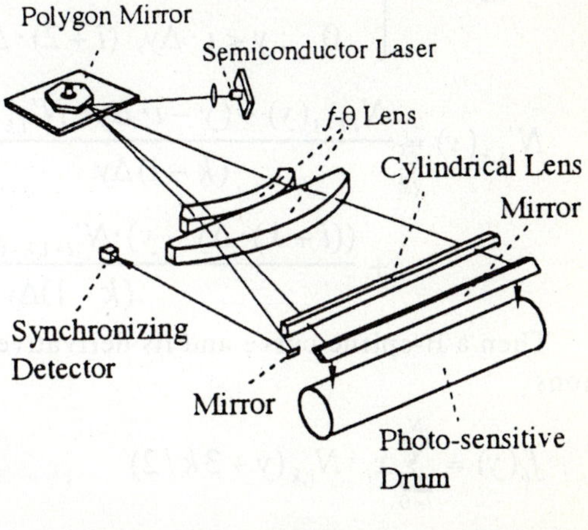

Fig.1 The optical system of a Laser Printer

2. 2 Representation of lens shape

A commercial laser printer uses the f-θ lens which consists of the combination of two or three lenses [3] as shown in Fig 1. However, in this paper we try to design an f-θ lens which consists of a single lens. Moreover, one side of the lens is flat plane and the shape of other side is represented by the two dimensional B-spline curve that is well known as an expression of an arbitrary curve. A single lens with a single plane simplifies the problem of lens design by reducing the number of parameters to apply evolutionary methods and cuts costs of the optical system down.

The B-spline curve is defined by the positions (x_i, y_i) ($i=1,\cdots,N$) of the N guide points. For simplicity, the y-coordinates of these guide points may be kept at equal intervals for the representation of the lens shape as shown in Fig. 3. By equating them, the rank k basis functions $N_{i,k}(y)$ of the B-spline curve are defined recursively as follows.

$$N_{i,1}(y) = \begin{cases} 1 & : i \cdot \Delta y \le y < (i+1) \cdot \Delta y \\ 0 & : y < i \cdot \Delta y,\ (i+1) \cdot \Delta y < y \end{cases} \quad ; \tag{1}$$

$$N_{i,k}(y) = \frac{(y - i \cdot \Delta y)\, N_{i,k-1}(y)}{(k-1)\Delta y} + \frac{((i+k) \cdot \Delta y - y)\, N_{i+1,k-1}(y)}{(k-1)\Delta y} . \tag{2}$$

Also the derivatives of the rank k basis functions are defined in the same way by the following equations.

$$N'_{i,2}(y) = \begin{cases} 1 & : i \cdot \Delta y \le y < (i+1) \cdot \Delta y \\ -1 & : (i+1) \cdot \Delta y \le y < (i+2) \cdot \Delta y \\ 0 & : y < i \cdot \Delta y,\ (i+2) \cdot \Delta y < y \end{cases} \quad ; \tag{3}$$

$$N'_{i,k}(y) = \frac{N_{i,k-1}(y) + (y - i \cdot \Delta y) \cdot N'_{i,k-1}(y)}{(k-1)\Delta y} + \frac{((i+k) \cdot \Delta y - y) \cdot N'_{i+1,k-1}(y) - N_{i+1,k-1}(y)}{(k-1)\Delta y} . \tag{4}$$

Then a B-spline curve and its derivative are given by the following equations.

$$f_l(y) = \sum_{i=0}^{N} x_i \cdot N_{i,k}(y + 3k/2) \quad ; \tag{5}$$

$$f_l'(y) = \sum_{i=0}^{N} x_i \cdot N'_{i,k}(y + 3k/2) \ . \tag{6}$$

These equations show that the functional value at a point x is depend on the positions of k guide points. When a series of x coordinates (parameters) of the guide points is used as a chromosome of an individual in a GA, each parameter has strong epistasis [4] with other parameters like the f_2 function given by De Jong [5]. Therefore, it is conjectured that the convergence to the solution by evolutionary methods may be considerably slow.

2. 3 Ray tracing

The optical system with the f-θ lens represented by a B-spline curve that is simulated in a computer is illustrated in Fig. 2 and the details around the rotating mirror and the f-θ lens is shown in Fig. 3. For simplicity, the polygon mirror is replaced by a rotating mirror in this model. In order to evaluate the performance of an f-θ lens, we have to calculate ray traces as shown in Figs. 2 and 3. When we calculate the refraction points along the ray traces, it becomes cumbersome, as it involves calculations for cross points of the laser beam re-

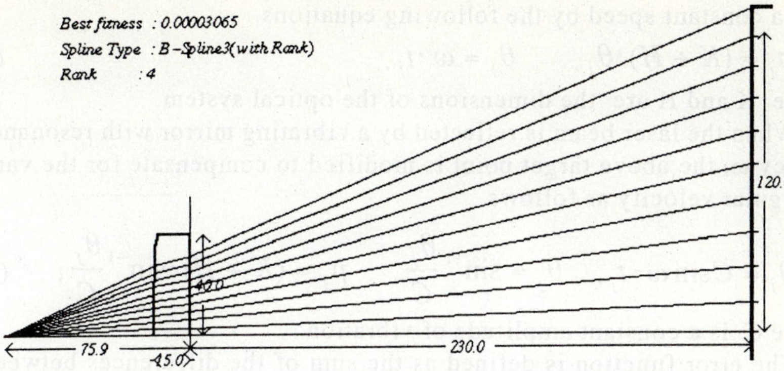

Fig. 2 Optical system for the f-θ lens design

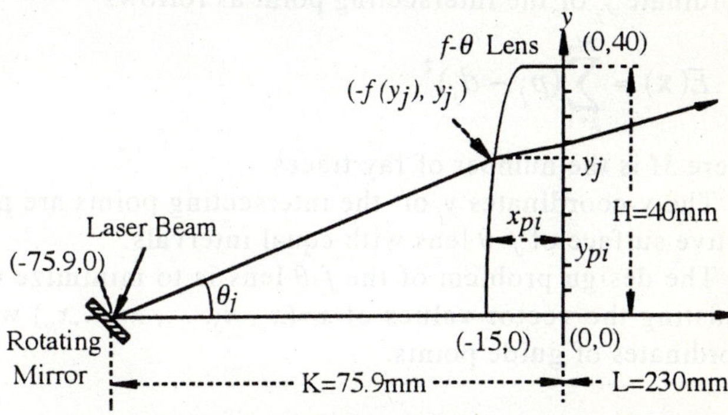

Fig. 3 Detailed optical system for the f-θ lens design

flected from the rotating mirror with angle θ_j and the surface of the f-θ lens which must be determined by solving the simultaneous equations that represent cross-point of the straight line and the B-spline curve. However, if the y-coordinate y_j of a cross-point is given, it would be easy to calculate the cross-point, the derivative at this point and the beam reflecting angle θ_j by Eqs. (1) ~ (6). The other refraction points and the destination d_j of the beam on the surface of the OPC drum can be calculated by using trigonometric functions as a routine process.

The dimensions for the f-θ lens design are as follows.

- The distance K from the reflecting point on the mirror to the y axis (flat plane of lens) : 75.9 mm.
- The distance H from the y axis to the surface of the OPC drum : 230.0 mm.
- The height of the lens : 40.0 mm (half part of lens).
- The width of the OPC drum : 110.0 mm (half width for A4 size and letter size papers)
- The maximum reflecting angle : 21.5 degree (half swing).
- The index of refraction of the lens glass : 1.52 (Spectacle Crown).

2. 4 Design problem of an f-θ lens

The target point p_j of the j-th laser beam which is reflected with an angle θ_j from the mirror rotating with a constant angular velocity ω is defined proportional to elapsed time from a start of scanning to scan the drum surface with a constant speed by the following equations.

$$p_j = (K + H)\cdot\theta_j, \qquad \theta_j = \omega \cdot t_j, \tag{7}$$

where K and H are the dimensions of the optical system.

When the laser beam is reflected by a vibrating mirror with resonance frequency ω, the above target point is modified to compensate for the variation of angular velocity as follows.

$$\theta'_j = C\sin\omega\cdot t_j, \quad \theta_j = \sin^{-1}\frac{\theta'_j}{C}, \quad p_j = (K + H)\cdot\sin^{-1}\frac{\theta'_j}{C}; \tag{8}$$

where C is a constant amplitude of vibration.

The error function is defined as the sum of the differences between this target point p_j and the destination d_j of j-th ray trace determined by the y-coordinate y_j of the intersecting point as follows.

$$E(\mathbf{x}) = \sum_{j=1}^{M}(p_j - d_j)^2 \tag{9}$$

where M is the number of ray traces.

The y-coordinates y_j of the intersecting points are placed to cover the effective surface of f-θ lens with equal intervals.

The design problem of the f-θ lens is to minimize this error function by adjusting the vector values of $\boldsymbol{x}=(x_1, x_2, \ldots, x_i,\ldots,x_N)$ which is a series of x-coordinates of guide points.

3 Evolutionary methods

We implemented two types of evolutionary methods for the lens design problems. They are the genotype GA with high mutation that is the basic part of f-GA [6] and the real-valued GA with the NDX (Normal Distribution Crossover)[7][8].

3. 1 The genotype GA with high mutation

This GA was developed as a mixed version of the generational and the steady state evolutions in which parents and offspring compete together. The f-GA introduced the concept of selective crossover and high mutation. The normalized hamming distance H between a pair of parents is calculated and 2-point crossover is executed with probability H^α ($0<\alpha<1.0$) and high mutation is performed with probability ($1-H^\alpha$) to the parent that has lower fitness. The high mutation has considerably higher probability of mutation than that of normal mutation. In this application, forking [6] is not performed.

3. 2 The real-valued GA with the NDX

The real-valued GA with the NDX [7] [8] was proposed for optimization in real vector space. This method has only one genetic operator NDX that generates two offspring C_1, C_2 from a pair of parents P_1, P_2 by adding random numbers with normal distribution to parameters of both the parents. The standard deviation σ_i of the normal distribution $\mathrm{Nrnd}(\sigma_i)$ is chosen proportional to the distance between the parents.

$$x_i(C_k) = x_i(P_k) + \mathrm{Nrnd}(\sigma_i) \qquad i = 1,2,\cdots,N \quad k = 1,2\,; \tag{10}$$

$$\sigma_i = \beta \times |x_i(P_1) - x_i(P_2)|\,; \tag{11}$$

where $x_i(P_k)$, $x_i(C_k)$ are parameters of a parent and an offspring respectively and β is a constant.

Selection is done in the same way as the genotype GA and there is no mutation.

3. 3 Representation of chromosome

The chromosome of each individual p is the vector $\boldsymbol{x}(\mathrm{p})=(x_1(\mathrm{p}), x_2(\mathrm{p}), \ldots, x_i(\mathrm{p}),\ldots,x_N(\mathrm{p}))$ where the components are x-coordinates of guide points that represent the surface curve of the f-θ lens. The number of components in the vector is 10 and y-coordinates of 10 guide points are positioned at equal intervals over 40 mm lens height. Each element is coded by a double floating number in the real-valued GA and by 19 bits Gray code in the genotype GA. As the f-θ lens is symmetric against the x axis, the vector is copied to represent the other side of the lens and the center is fixed to a constant value that determine the width of the lens.

3.4 Fitness Function

The fitness function of evolutionary methods for the f-θ lens design is defined by Eq. (9). This is accumulated distance between the target point and the destination of the corresponding ray trace. We arrange the 100 points y_i over 62% of lens height (40 mm) with equal intervals as the points in this range are affected by the guide points out side of this range. The error function is calculated by accumulating the differences between the destinations of 100 ray traces and their corresponding targets.

4 Empirical Results

4. 1 Experiments

We have carried out 8 experiments with combinations of the following three alternative cases to compare the evolutionary methods. The first alternative is the real-valued GA (RGA) or the genotype GA with high mutations (GGA). The second alternative is the design for rotating mirror or for vibrating mirror. The third choice is the number of rank for a B-spline curve. Higher rank gives smoother curve, but higher rank requires exponential increase of computation. We took 4 and 5 as ranks.

The width of the f-θ lens at the center is set to 15 mm and the range of each of the 10 parameters which represent the lens curve is set from 11.5 mm to 16.74287 mm in both the evolutionary methods. The range of the parameters was chosen by preparatory experiments with rough precision and wide range.

For the experiments of the genotype GA with high mutation, population size, normal and high permutation rates are set to 80, 0.006 and 0.06 respectively, and α is set to 0.02. In the experiments of the real-valued GA, β is set to 0.707 to make the total distribution of offspring close to normal distribution as shown in Fig. 4.

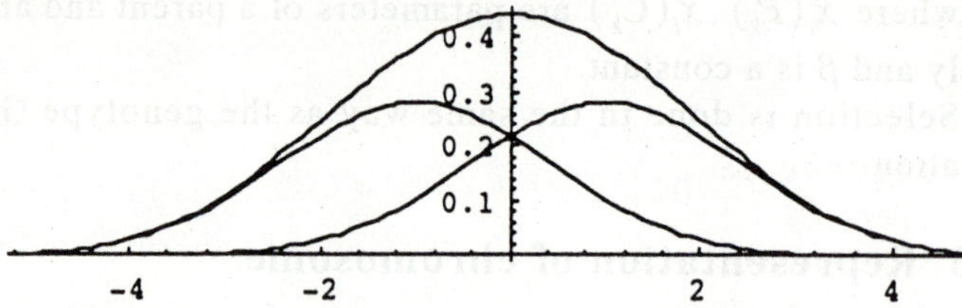

Fig.4 Total distribution of offspring (β = 0.707)

4. 2 Results and Discussions

Results of the 8 experiments are shown in Table 1. Each experiment with 300,000 trials is repeated 30 times for different random seeds. In Table 1, the *Best* shows the minimum error value among 30 repetitions and the *Min Trials* and *Max Trials* show the minimum and maximum number of trials (evaluations) until the best value is found, respectively. Fig. 5 and Fig. 6 show the process of error convergence versus trials for rotating mirror and vibrating mirror, respectively. For example, Fig. 7, Fig. 8 and Fig. 2 show the ray tracings of the best individuals so far at 80, 2,000 and 164,000 trials, respectively. We show the curve of the f-θ lens obtained by the real-valued GA for the rotating mirror and for the vibrating mirror with rank 5 in Fig. 9 and Fig. 10, respectively.

Table 1 shows that the RGA converges faster with smaller error than the GGA and reaches the same solution in each repetition with more or less the same number of trial numbers. This means that the evaluation function is conjectured to be almost unimodal. Although the GGA could attain the same or-

Table 1 Results of 8 experiments for f-θ lens design

Rank	Performance	Rotating Mirror		Vibrating Mirror	
		RGA(NDX)	GGA	RGA(NDX)	GGA
4	Best(Error)	3.0652×10^{-5}	3.1621×10^{-5}	4.9169×10^{-6}	7.3548×10^{-6}
	MinTrials	145,040	285,015	125,040	230,024
	MaxTrials	180,000	300,000	185,040	300,000
5	Best(Error)	1.0732×10^{-6}	2.2403×10^{-6}	2.4050×10^{-7}	5.7294×10^{-7}
	MinTrials	165,000	300,000	140,000	275,017
	MaxTrials	190,000	300,000	210,000	300,000

RGA : Real-valued GA with NDX GGA : Genotype GA with High mutation der of small error as the RGA, the time required for the convergence to the best value by the GGA is considerably longer and has larger variance than the RGA. The reason of bad convergence is supposed to be epistasis between parameters of the lens surface that is regarded as a weak point of GA. On the RGA, it is conjectured that the NDX crossover works successfully to change many parameters of an individual with strong correlations simultaneously.

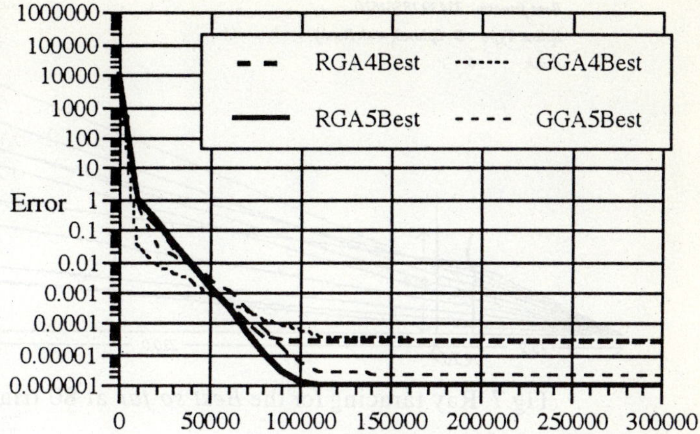

Fig.5 Error versus trials for the rotating mirror

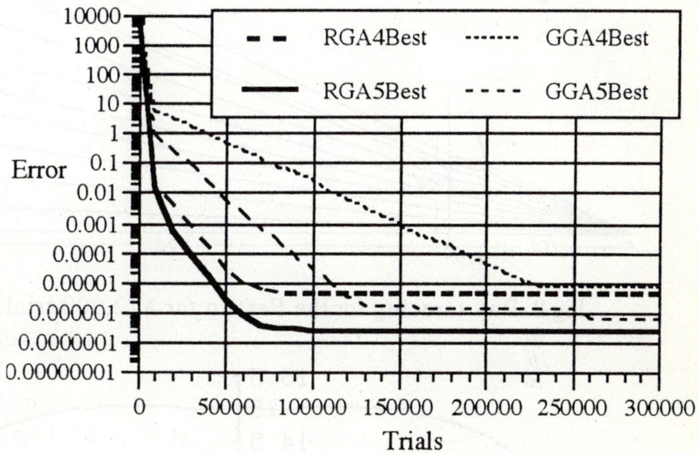

Fig.6 Error versus trials for the vibrating mirror

A comparison between rank 4 and 5 shows that the B-spline curve with rank 5 has better approximation for the f-θ lens than that with rank 4. The error values obtained by the RGA with rank 5 show that the error of one ray trace from a target is smaller than 0.0011 mm for rotating mirror and smaller than 0.0005 mm for vibrating mirror and is small enough for practical use.

5 Conclusions

In this paper, we have tried successfully to design two kinds of f-θ lenses for rotating mirror and for vibrating mirror with two evolutionary methods : the real-valued GA and the genotype GA with high mutation. The real-valued GA has shown faster convergence and better accuracy than the genotype GA for the lens design problem. From experiments, it is evident that the RGA is

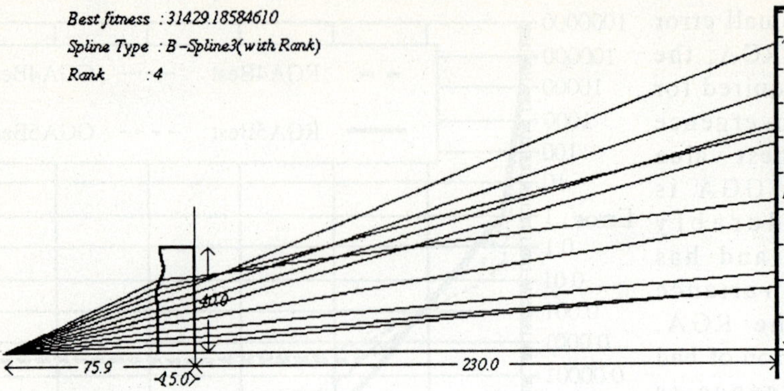

Fig.7 Ray taracing for the *Best so far* at 80 trials

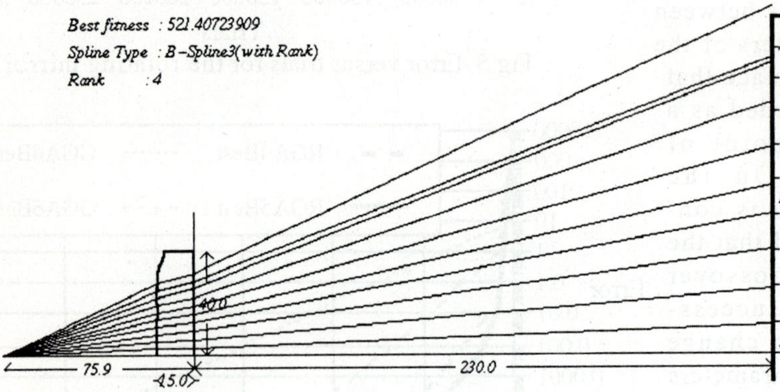

Fig.8 Ray taracing for the *Best so far* at 2,000 trials

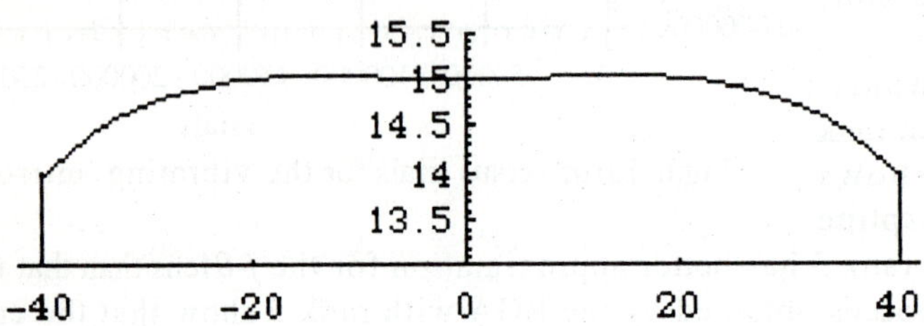

Fig.9 The curve of the f-θ lens for the rorating mirror (rank=5)

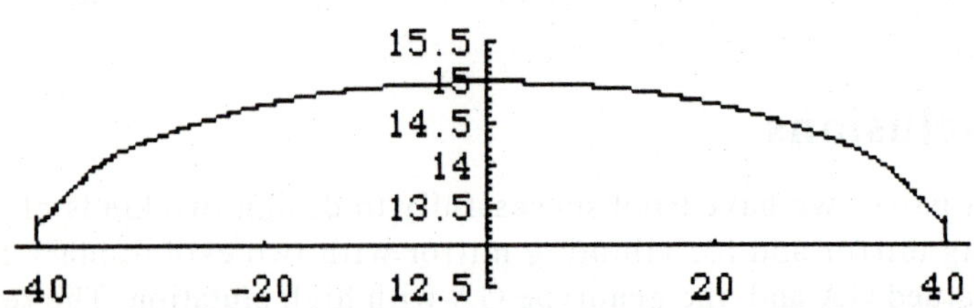

Fig.10 The curve of the f-θ lens for the vibrating mirror (rank=5)

effective for the problems that are almost unimodal and have strong epistasis between parameters. We also have a firm belief that it is possible to use the evolutionary methods with ray tracing methods for practical lens design problems.

Future works of evolutionary lens design are to design three dimensional f-θ lens with two curve surfaces that has the function focusing the laser beam reflected from polygon mirror and to improve the performance of these GAs for problems with strong epistasis. Furthermore, a challenging work is to search directly equations that define the surface of the f-θ lens by the Genetic Programming.

6 Acknowledgments

This research is partially supported by the Ministry of Education, Science, Sports and Culture under Grant-in-Aid for Scientific Research (C) (No. 08680417) and for Scientific Research on Priority Areas (No. 08233105) .

References

1. Ingo Rechenberg: Evolution Strategy; *Computational Intelligent Imitating Life*. pp.147-159, IEEE Press, (1994)
2. Jurgen R. Meyer-Arendt: *Introduction to Classical & Modern Optics Third Edition*. Prentice-Hall, (1989).
3. W. J. Smith: *Modern Lens Design; A Resource Manual*. pp. 411-430, Genesee Optics Software, Inc. (1992)
4. Yuval Davidor: Epistasis Variance: A viewpoint on GA-Hardness; *Foundations of Genetic Algorithms*. edited by Gregory J. E. Rawlins, pp. 23-35, Morgan Koufmann, (1991).
5. D.E. Goldberg: *Genetic Algorithms in Search, Optimization and Machine Learning*. pp. 106-120, Addison-Wesley Publishing Company, Inc., 1989.
6. S. Tsutsui and Y. Fujimoto: Forking Genetic Algorithm with Blocking and Shrinking Modes (fGA); ICGA-93, pp. 206-213, (1993).
7. Alden H. Wright: Genetic Algorithms for Real Parameter Optimization; *Foundations of Genetic Algorithms*. edited by Gregory J. E. Rawlins, pp. 205-218, Morgan Koufmann, (1991).
8. A. Kamiya, I. Ono, M. Yamamura and S. Kobayashi: Thermal Power Plant Start-up Scheduling with Evolutionary Computation by Using an Enforcement Operator; IEEE International Conference on Systems, Man and Cybernetics, pp. 1372-1379, (1995)

Optimization of Heat Exchanger Networks by Means of Evolution Strategies

Bernd Groß[1], Ulrich Hammel[2], Peter Maldaner[2], Andreas Meyer[2], Peter Roosen[1] and Martin Schütz[2]

[1] RWTH Aachen
Department of Chemical Engineering
Technical Thermodynamics Group
52062 Aachen
E-Mail: {gross,roosen}@milenka.ltt.rwth-aachen.de

[2] University of Dortmund
Department of Computer Science
Systems Analysis Group
44221 Dortmund
E-Mail:{hammel,maldaner,meyer,schuetz}@ls11.informatik.uni-dortmund.de

Abstract. This paper describes the adaptation of Evolution Strategies (ESs) for simulation based heat exchanger network synthesis. Due to space limitations the presentation is restricted to a brief overview of the application domain, the problems and pitfalls we encountered during the project and hints to solutions. Some of these problems are of general relevance for the application of Evolutionary Algorithms in cases where the objective function is based on a simulation model and are therefore discussed in more detail. The emphasis lies on the design of a suitable genetic representation.

1 Introduction

The problem of heat exchanger network synthesis (HENS) has caused a significant amount of research within the last 25 years. Heat exchanger networks (HENs) are of great practical importance in chemical engineering problems due to large cost saving potentials, and their synthesis is known as a mathematically non-trivial mixed-integer non-linear programming (MINLP) problem.

Heat exchangers (HEs) serve to transfer heat between streams of fluids of different temperatures. Consider a chemical plant with dozens or hundreds of streams connecting different process units. Heat exchanger networks (see section 2) are usually implemented in order to minimize the overall energy consumption of the plant. But due to the fact, that the network itself introduces additional investment costs an economical optimum is sought for.

Since modern simulation tools allow for the prediction of the system's behavior with high accuracy, the design of chemical plants is nowadays based on exhaustive simulation studies. The identification of a cost-optimal solution among the set of feasible ones (e.g. restricted by the second law of thermodynamics) is still a challenging task, though. The reasons are manifold, and we will just mention a few. The following problems are typical in cases where the objective function is based on a simulation model. Therefore the discussion is kept rather general.

Most often, the simulation tool at hand does not allow to access its internal representation of the model, which in turn requires the separation of the simulator and the optimizer. Consequently, the optimizer needs a separate representation of those elements of the model which are relevant to the optimization process. This may be trivial as long as those objects which are subject to variation are simple, e.g., in the case of parameter optimization. But the design of the representation might turn out to be a non-trivial task if the optimizer has to handle complex objects. We will discuss this issue in section 3.3. Additionally, the interfacing of the optimizer and simulator might raise severe technical problems. In this project the simulator ASPEN PLUS™ is used for the calculation of the thermodynamical steady state on which the objective function is based on, but we omit a description of the technical details.

The black-box nature of the simulation model does not allow to derive analytical information about the objective function. In practice either direct search strategies have to be applied or the input/output behavior of the simulation model is approximated by a closed function, which serves as a substitute for the model during the optimization process. Approximations usually lead to suboptimal solutions which are improved manually in a second step based on simulation studies (see section 2.3). Additionally, it is often difficult to handle constraint violations because the simulation process will simply fail for non-feasible parameter settings (see section 3.5).

Finally, most simulation studies are expensive with respect to time and space consumption. Though, reasonable run times may be achieved through parallel optimization strategies. We come back to this issue in section 3.2.

This paper briefly describes the goals and the current state of a project aiming at the optimal design of chemical processes, supported by the German Volkswagen-Stiftung. In the following we concentrate on those issues, which we believe are of general relevance for the tackling of real-world problems beyond the scope of this particular application. Because of limited space we had to decide between an in-depth discussion of one special aspect of our work and a brief overview only touching the most relevant topics. We decided for the latter, mainly because of the lack of literature necessary to understand the whole picture before going into detail.

2 Heat Exchanger Networks (HENs)

HENS can be seen as a subproblem of process synthesis in general. In every chemical process there are a number of streams which are to be heated (*cold streams*), and ones to be cooled (*hot streams*). The expressions *cold* and *hot* do not describe the temperature levels, they only indicate if heat is to be supplied to or removed from the stream in question.

As an example consider Figure 1 depicting a four-stream HEN (the special problem statement is designated as 4SP1 (4 Streams, Problem 1) in the literature [8]). The figure shows two hot streams H_1, H_2 and two cold streams C_1, C_2. The streams are represented by arrows which also indicate the direction of the flow. Numbers at both ends represent the incoming and target temperatures (given as $[^\circ F]$) respectively. Bracketed numbers denote the heat-capacity flowrates of the streams (given as $[\frac{Btu}{h^\circ F}]$). Gray shaded circles labeled C and H represent heaters and coolers, whereas the numbered circles denote heat exchangers (HEs). The enthalpy transfer is given below each circle as $[\frac{Btu}{h}] \cdot 10^6$.

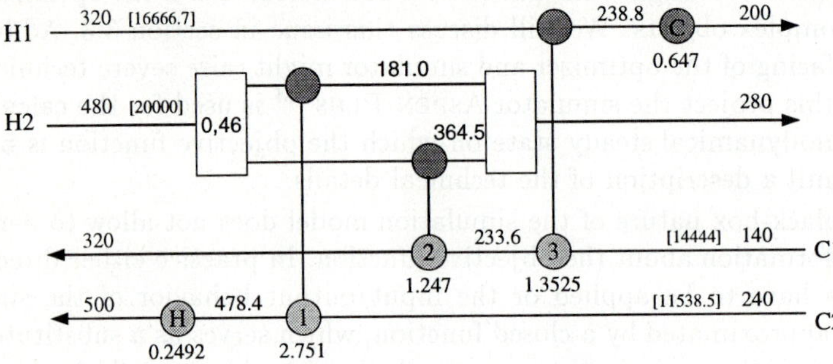

Fig. 1.: Example HEN with stream splitting (ratio 0.46).

Aiming at an internal recovery of energy, called energy integration, the heat from the hot streams should be transferred to the cold streams as far as possible. Only the remaining needs must be supplied by utilities like saturated steam at different pressure levels, furnaces, or by cooling water, brine, etc. Accordingly the streams are matched in a network of heat exchangers. In general, it will not be possible to exchange the complete energy between the process streams due to two restrictions: The sum of energy demand of the cold streams is usually not equal to the cooling demand of the hot streams. Even more important is the fact, that heat can only be transferred from a medium with higher temperature to one with lower temperature. This seems to be trivial, but in the problem of HENS this second law of thermodynamics often limits the amount of transferred heat. Therefore both hot and cold utilities may be required.

Several different networks can be found, which achieve the maximum internal heat exchange [10]. Such *energy optimal* solutions correspond to minimal utility costs. The practical application of optimization techniques in chemical engineering strongly focuses on *cost minimization*, though, including both investment costs and energy costs.

2.1 Problem definition

The objective function can be described as $f = min\{K_{tot}\}$ (K_{tot} denote the total costs of a HEN) with:

$$K_{tot} = \delta a\left(\sum_{i=1}^{N_{HX}} A^b_{HX,i} + \sum_{i=1}^{N_C} A^b_{C,i} + \sum_{i=1}^{N_H} A^b_{H,i}\right) + z\left(\sum_{i=1}^{N_H} c_{H,i}\dot{Q}_{H,i} + \sum_{i=1}^{N_C} c_{C,i}\dot{Q}_{C,i}\right) \quad (1)$$

where

$$A_{x,i} = \frac{\dot{Q}_{x,i}}{U_{x,i} \Delta T_{ln,x,i}} \tag{2}$$

given the following definitions

δ:	annual rate of return of the investment
a, b:	cost coefficient and cost exponent (e.g. b = 0.6)
$A_{x,i}, x \in \{C, H, HX\}$:	area of coolers, heaters and heat exchangers
N_C, N_H, N_{HX}:	number of coolers, heaters and heat exchangers
z:	Equipment availability [h/yr]
$c_{H,i}, c_{C,i}$:	specific utility price [$/Btu]
$\dot{Q}_{H,i}, \dot{Q}_{C,i}$:	heat supplied by utilities
$\dot{Q}_{x,i}$:	heat transferred in the *i*th exchanger
$U_{x,i}$:	average overall heat transfer coefficient of the match
$\Delta T_{ln,x,i}$:	logarithmic mean temperature difference

For more details like assumptions and concrete problem data please consult the literature, e.g. [3].

2.2 General characteristics of the objective function

In equation 2 the area (and thus the costs) of a heat exchanger connecting the hot stream i and the cold stream j may be described as a function of the enthalpy transfer $\dot{Q}_{ij}$:

$$A_{ij}(\dot{Q}_{ij}) = \frac{1}{U_{ij}} \cdot \frac{C^*_{p_i} C^*_{p_j}}{C^*_{p_j} - C^*_{p_i}} \cdot$$

$$\left(\ln \left(\frac{C^*_{p_i}}{C^*_{p_j}} \right) + \ln \left(C^*_{p_j} (T'_i - T'_j) - \dot{Q}_{ij} \right) - \ln \left(C^*_{p_i} (T'_i - T'_j) - \dot{Q}_{ij} \right) \right). \tag{3}$$

where the heat-capacity flowrates $C^*_{p_i}$ and $C^*_{p_j}$ of both streams and both incoming temperatures T'_i and T'_j of the HE are given. (When making things more precise a numbering of the HEs, as used in eqn. 2 is not sufficient. Instead the numbers of the streams connected with each other have to be specified; see eqn. 3.)

Equation 3 shows that each HE produces one singularity, i.e. the size of the HE goes to infinity whenever the enthalpy $\dot{Q}_{ij}$ approximates $C^*_{p_i}(T'_i - T'_j)$. (Negative values $C^*_{p_j}(T'_i - T'_j)$ are omitted here.) Stated another way, the area of the HE grows superlinear with the enthalpies. Indicated by formula 1, this behaviour is balanced by the sublinear cost exponent $b = 0.6$ for wide regions of the parameter space.

Thus, the response surface is dominated by wide smooth regions inside the valid parameter space and exponential growth near the restrictions. The minima are located close to the singularities, i.e. close to the border.

The problem complexity increases dramatically, if more than two exchangers are varied and arbitrary splitting ratios are introduced. Furthermore, the goal of this research is the optimization of the overall structure of the network, i.e. the positions and sequences of matches (i.e. link between two streams established by a HE) are not fixed.

Equations 1 and 3 have also been used to derive a substitute function which approximates the behavior of the simulation model. It differs from the original simulation model in the fact, that it is restricted to fixed splitting ratios, whereas the simulator ASPEN PLUS™ is able to optimize splitting ratios internally. Thus the domain of the substitute function is a subset of that of the original model. Because of its runtime advantage compared to a simulation run, this substitute function was intensely used for numerical experimentation and evaluation of strategy variants.

2.3 Common optimization techniques

Several techniques have been developed for HEN optimization. Some of them utilize thermodynamic knowledge like the *Pinch Point Analysis* developed by Linnhoff [9] and the exergo-economic optimization [5, 7]. Others are based on the combination of mixed-integer linear programming and non-linear programming techniques.

Each of these methods has its special drawbacks. Some of them impose simplifications on the model, eventually excluding good solutions from the search space. Others have to be classified as local search methods yielding only suboptimal solutions.

3 Evolving HEN-models by means of Evolution Strategies

3.1 Basic ES-notation and experimental framework

For a detailed description of Evolution Strategies and Evolutionary Computation in general see [1, 16, 4]. Throughout this article we use the standard notation $(\mu \overset{+}{,} \lambda)$-ES. If not otherwise stated we apply mutation with n step sizes and local discrete recombination on object variables and local intermediate recombination on strategy variables.

3.2 Evaluating models of parallelism

Exploiting the inherent parallelism of Evolution Strategies may reduce optimization runtimes significantly, which is especially helpful if the evaluation of the merit function is expensive. Usually, like in our case, the simulator is not available for any given hardware architecture. Thus, we are restricted to workstation clusters. Beside some technical problems, (e.g., licensing, machine workloading) which have to be solved, a decision has to be made which model of parallelism to apply. In order to make efficient use of parallel processes the strict synchronization introduced through the global selection mechanism must be released. This in turn may influence convergence probability and velocity of the search process.

Different models of parallelism have been proposed in the literature. We compared three common approaches, the simple master-slave approach with steady-state selection [2], a migration model [15] and a special diffusion model, the linear-neighborhood ES(LNES) [17] with respect to convergence velocity and reliability. As test functions we utilized the so called sphere model as well as Rastrigin's function [1].

Because of limited space we just summarize the two main results: The (24+1)-steady-state approach outperformed all other variants with respect to convergence velocity, whereas the (128,768)-LNES (using a torus topology) showed the best reliability, while still preserving reasonable convergence speed.

First application of parallel variants to the optimization of HENs showed encouraging results. Future investigations will concentrate on variants of the diffusion model, especially LNES.

3.3 Representations

The genetic representation has great influence on the performance of an Evolutionary Algorithm. The basic components of a HEN are streams, splitters, mixers and heat exchangers. Besides some real-valued parameters (enthalpy transfer, splitting ratios) the structure of the network (positions of splits and matches) has to be encoded, too, if the structure is subject to the evolution process as well.

In general, the components of the network can be enumerated and thus considered as an ordered set. The structural parameters may then be coded as positional parameters, i.e., integer values. Following the traditional Genetic Algorithm approach all these parameters would be coded down to a binary representation. But there can be found lots of hints in the literature, that this is at least not suitable for real valued parameters [1].

A more promising approach is to recode the problem as a pure parameter optimization problem. Figure 2 (left) shows a representation of the HEN illustrated in figure 1 which is based on a matrix, consisting of $n_h \times n_c$ submatrices where n_h and n_c denote the number of hot and cold streams. The matches of each stream are numbered in increasing order according to the direction of the flow. Each cell represents a potential heat exchanger (more precisely the enthalpy transfer between the corresponding streams). E.g., the entry in the first cell means that the first match of stream H_1 is established with the first match of stream C_1. For values below a certain threshold the heat exchanger is considered to be not active. This way arbitrary matches can be realized. Two entries in one row or column indicate a split.

This representation was initially chosen for its simplicity. The variable-dimensional mixed-integer problem is now reduced to a parameter optimization problem with fixed dimensions. Genetic operators are easily defined (see section 3.4). The approach performs well for small problems. For larger problems the representation turned out to be not suitable, due to the fact, that the size of the matrix increases proportional to $n_h^2 * n_c^2$, resulting in a very bad performance of the search process (see section 4).

		stream C1		stream C2		cooling water	Σ
		Pos1	Pos2	Pos1	Pos2		
stream H1	Pos1	$1.353 \cdot 10^6$				$0.647 \cdot 10^6$	$2.0 \cdot 10^6$
	Pos2						
stream H2	Pos1		$1.247 \cdot 10^6$	$2.751 \cdot 10^6$			$3.998 \cdot 10^6$
	Pos2						
heating steam				$0.249 \cdot 10^6$			
Σ		2.6^6		$3.0 \cdot 10^6$			

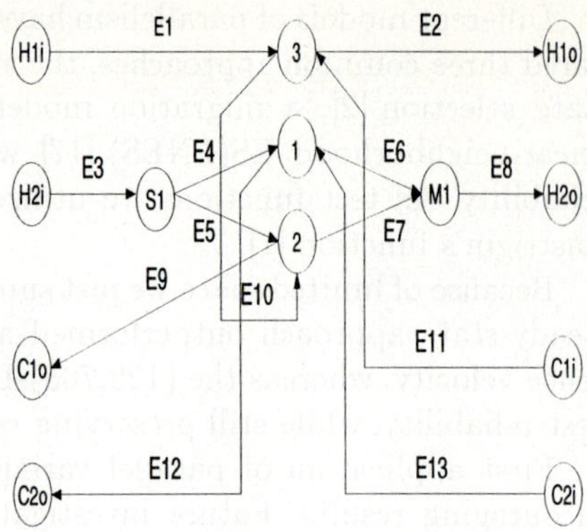

Fig. 2.: Matrix representation of the HEN shown in figure 1 (left) and the corresponding graph representation (right).

Rechenberg [14] argues that structural problems can easily be coded as mixed-integer representations and he suggests a multi-level approach separating the optimization of the integer and real parts. But this representation does not reflect the connectivity of the structural components, which to our experience is essential in order to define well behaving genetic operators.

But what are the basic requirements for a suitable representation? First of all, every feasible solution should be representable – which is not true for the matrix representation above. It is, e.g., not possible to have two matches on one branch of a split. This might exclude an important set of solutions. Furthermore, the representation should not complicate the search process, e.g., by introducing additional nonlinearities or extra dimensions. Again, the matrix does not fulfill this requirement, since it allows for a lot of different representations of the same network. The representation of non-feasible solutions should be avoided. This is not always possible. E.g., most of the instances of the matrix will violate the second law of thermodynamics and these instances can not be easily repaired. Of course, the representation should be general enough to serve for a large problem domain and it should ease the definition of genetic operators. Finally, but most important, the representation should preserve a strong causality [14]. Small changes of the genotype should have a small impact on the phenotype.

In order to find a representation which fulfills most of the requirements above, we developed the general graph representation depicted in figure 2 (right), where each node represents a component of the network and an edge represents a physical or logical link. Nodes and edges are attributed with the corresponding physical data (e.g. heat-capacity flowrates, splitting ratio). Input and output nodes are labeled $H_{1,i}, H_{2,i}, C_{1,i}, C_{2,i}$ and $H_{1,o}, H_{2,o}, C_{1,o}, C_{2,o}$ respectively. The HEs are numbered from 1 to 3. The splitter and mixer are named S_1 and M_1. Note that the graph representation is still general in the sense that it allows for the coding of arbitrary structures.

3.4 Genetic operators

The matrix representation

In order to avoid too many lethal individuals in the initial population the initialization operator prefers sparse matrices. Mutation is performed as usual for the standard ES (see [16]). All experiments based on the matrix representation were performed with a (15,100)–ES with n step-sizes. The standard recombination operators of ESs performed very bad applied to the linearized matrix. Thus we utilized an adopted version of the one-point crossover operator common in standard GAs which showed much better results. This is due to the fact, that the latter mostly preserves the "neighborhood-relationship" among the HEs.

The graph representation

The initial population completely consists of empty HENs, i.e. networks in which heating and cooling is completely realized by external sources.

The mutation operator is much more complex than that used for the matrix representation, since it consists of two parts. The first one modifies the real-valued parameters (enthalpies and splitting ratios) equal to the standard operator and the other one accomplishes structural changes on the graph. For reasons of simplification a fixed maximum number of nodes is assumed, keeping the number of dimensions constant. E.g., in the case of the 4SP1-problem we limit the number of units to 10 HEs and 5 splitters and mixers respectively.

The basic mutation scheme is to switch a node from an active state to a passive state or vice versa with low uniform probability. Whenever a node is chosen for being active/non-active the corresponding connections have to be set. Recombination is not yet implemented. Again all experiments were performed with a standard (15,100)–ES and n step-sizes for the real-valued parameters.

3.5 Constraint handling

First of all, well designed representations and genetic operators may help to avoid the generation of infeasible individuals. E.g., the matrix representation described above tends to produce much more violations of the second law of thermodynamics compared to the graph representation. To handle the remaining constraint violations different techniques can be found in the literature [16, 13, 12]. Here we made use of penalty terms mostly known from GAs. One peculiarity of the given heat exchanger problem is that the simulator is not able to compute networks with physically impossible parameters, e.g. crossing temperatures. As a crude estimator we use the costs for a network with no heat exchangers. Which of course is not very satisfying.

4 Results

The numerical results for some benchmark problems taken from literature are summarized in table 1. Due to space limitations the corresponding problem definitions are not given here; the optimal costs are taken from [6]. Only the best known solution for the 10SP1-problem is taken from [11]. The results clearly demonstrate that well adapted evolution strategies are able to solve complex structural optimization problems, such as the synthesis of heat-exchanger networks.

Please note that those values derived from literature are found by making intense use of knowledge about the special problem at hand. It follows that these procedures are not applicable if the problem is changed, e.g. if other processing units than heat-exchangers are introduced. In contrast, the ES-variants presented here only apply general knowledge, which should be reusable for different tasks. The surprising result that the best known value for the 4SP1-problem was easily surpassed stems from the fact that most authors introduce minimum temperature differences between matching streams in order to derive a minimum energy network by analytical means. This restriction is released in our approach, since it is not needed for the strategy to work.

Finally, it should be mentioned that both representations are well suited for non-complex problems, such as the 4SP1-problem, whereas only the graph representation is able to come close to the best results, known from literature, in other cases.

Problem	Literature $[\frac{\$}{year}]$	ES $[\frac{\$}{year}]$	Difference [%]
4SP1	13587	10710	−21,3
5SP1	38268	40570	6,0
6SP1	35010	36970	5,6
7SP1	30172	32260	6,9
7SP2	28260	30820	9,1
8SP1	41228	45570	10,5
10SP1	43857	45840	3,9
20SP1	23482	26540	13,0

Table 1.: Expenses of the best found HENs to several problem instances known from Literature. The column "Difference" represents the procentual costs difference between the best solution found by evolution strategies (ES) and the best literature solution.

5 Outlook

The numerical results demonstrate the suitability of Evolutionary Algorithms for HEN synthesis. Future research will aim at the solution of more complex process synthesis problems. The representation will be generalized in order to ease the incorporation of problem knowledge. Further investigations are intended to improve the gain from parallel algorithms and more sophisticated techniques will be tested for constraint handling.

Acknowledgments

The authors gratefully acknowledge support by the VW foundation, grant I/69 253 (Bernd Groß) and grant I/69 254 (Martin Schütz)

References

1. Th. Bäck. *Evolutionary Algorithms in Theory and Practice.* Oxford University Press, New York, 1996.
2. Th. Bäck, Th. Beielstein, B. Naujoks, and J. Heistermann. Evolutionary Algorithms for the Optimization of Simulation Models Using PVM. In J. Dongarra, M. Gengler, B. Tourancheau, and X. Vigouroux, editors, *EuroPVM '95: Second European PVM Users' Group Meeting,* pages 277–282. Hermes, Paris, 1995.
3. C.A. Floudas and A.R. Ciric. Strategies for overcoming uncertainties in heat exchanger network synthesis. *Comp. chem. Engng.,* 13(10):1133–1152, 1989.
4. D. B. Fogel. *Evolutionary Computation: Toward a New Philosophy of Machine Intelligence.* IEEE Press, Piscataway, NJ, 1995.
5. K. Hesselmann. Optimization of Heat Exchanger Networks. *22nd National Heat Transfer Conference, Niagara Falls,* 496, 1984.
6. Klaus Hesselmann. *Wärmeaustauscher-Netzwerke: Eine exergoökonomische Betrachtung.* Dissertation, Rheinisch-Westfälische Technische Hochschule Aachen, 1985.
7. K. Hesselmann K.-F. Knoche. Exergoökonomische Bewertung einer Luftzerlegungs-Anlage. *Chem.-Ing.-Tech.,* 57(7):602–609, 1985.
8. K. F. Lee, A. H. Masso, and D. F. Rudd. Branch and Bound Synthesis of Integrated Process Designs. *I&EC Fundamentals,* 9(1):48–58, 1970.
9. B. Linnhoff. Pinch Analysis — a state-of-the-art overview. *Trans IChemE,* 71A:503–523, 1993.
10. B. Linnhoff and J.R. Flower. Pinch Analysis — a state-of-the-art overview. *AIChE Journal,* 24(4):642–654, 1978.
11. B. Linnhoff, D. R. Mason, and I. Wardle. Understanding Heat-Exchanger Networks. *Computers and Chemical Engineering,* 3:295–302, 1979.
12. Z. Michalewicz. A Hierarchy of Evolution Programms: An Experimental Study. *Evolutionary Computation,* 1(1):51–76, 1993.
13. Z. Michalewicz and C. Z. Janikow. Handling Constraints in Genetic Algorithms. In *Proceedings of the 4th International Conference on Genetic Algorithms,* pages 151–157, San Mateo, CA, 1991. Morgan Kaufmann Publishers.
14. I. Rechenberg. *Evolutionsstrategie '94,* volume 1 of *Werkstatt Bionik und Evolutionstechnik.* frommann–holzboog, Stuttgart, 1994.
15. G. Rudolph. Globale Optimierung mit parallelen Evolutionsstrategien. Diploma thesis, University of Dortmund, Department of Computer Science, 1990.
16. H.-P. Schwefel. *Evolution and Optimum Seeking.* Sixth-Generation Computer Technology Series. Wiley, New York, 1995.
17. J. Sprave. Linear Neighborhood Evolution Strategy. In *Proceedings of the 3rd Annual Conference on Evolutionary Programming,* pages 42–51, San Diego, CA, Feb 1994. World Scientific.

Industrial Plant Pipe-Route Optimisation with Genetic Algorithms

Dae Gyu Kim[1], David Corne[2], Peter Ross[3]

[1] School of Cognitive and Computing Sciences,
University of Sussex at Brighton, Falmer, Brighton, BN1 9QH, UK
Email: dgkim@cogs.susx.ac.uk
[2] Parallel, Emergent, and Distributed Architectures Laboratory (PEDAL),
Department of Computer Science, University of Reading,
Whiteknights, Reading RG6 2AY, UK. Email: D.W.Corne@reading.ac.uk
[3] Department of Artificial Intelligence, University of Edinburgh,
80 South Bridge, Edin. EH1 1HN, UK. Email: peter@aisb.ed.ac.uk

Abstract. The pipe-route design problem for heavy industrial plant concerns minimising pipe material cost while satisfying constraints on required interconnections and obstacle avoidance. This process is invariably done by human experts, but modern stochastic iterative search techniques allow the opportunity to automate this process. This study explores the possibility of automated industrial pipe-route design on three test problems, using stochastic hillclimbing, simulated annealing, and genetic algorithms. The representation strategy is explained and discussed, and results are presented which show great promise for genetic algorithms in particular in this application area.

1 Introduction

Hard pipe route design problems arise when equipment (such as pumps, boilers, and so on) need to be multiply interconnected by fluid or gas-carrying pipes in such a way as to satisfy various constraints and objectives, such as to avoid obstacles, avoid undue pressure variations, enable easy maintenance, and minimise material cost, while of course satisfying the required interconnections. Pipe route design is one of the most important steps involved in the design of large-scale engineering plant such as ships, power plants, chemical plants, and so on. In practice, the process mainly relies on human experts and their associated experience, since the range and complexity of the constraints tends to dissuade attempts at automation.

In most industrial design practice, the locations of the various pieces of equipment involved are determined in advance. Given these locations, a Piping and Instrumentation Diagram (P&ID) is prepared, which specifies the connections which must be made. For example, figure 1, in combination with a list of required connections (such as E1-nozzle1 connects to E2-nozzle7, E4-nozzle5 connects to E4nozzle7, and so on ...), constitutes a P&ID.

A designer is then given the job of laying out the pipe routes in accordance with the P&ID, while meeting several other constraints and objectives as men-

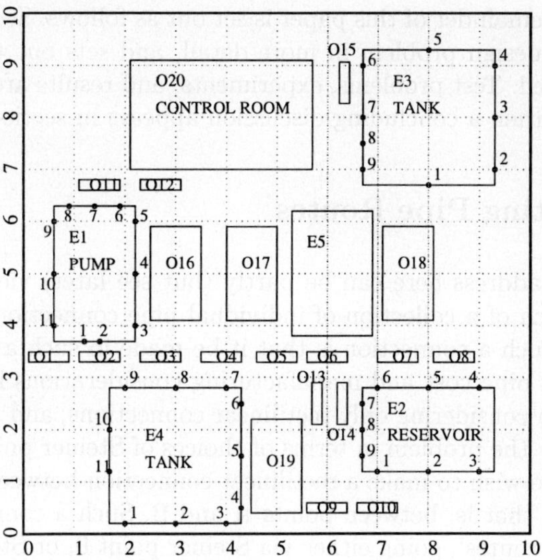

Fig. 1. A Piping & Instrumentation Diagram

tioned above. Designers' skill and experience tends to lead to routing designs which generally work well, but the greatly time-consuming nature of the design process [1] makes it practically impossible to explore alternatives or seriously attempt to optimise the design. Modern methods for tackling awkward problems, such as genetic algorithms (GAs) and simulated annealing (SA), introduce the opportunity to greatly speed up and perhaps improve design practice and quality in this area. The work reported here hence explored the potential for GAs and other stochastic methods on this problem.

Many routing problems have been addressed with GAs . For example, [2] use a GA to optimise the routing between chips on multi-chip modules, while [3] describe three forms of pipe-network optimisation problem: pipe-sizing, layout design, and pressure-regulation. The problem described here, however, differs in certain key respects from others we have so far found in the literature. For example, pipe-layout problems studied tend to concern finding the best way to arrange connections between multiple demand and supply stations, however in our case the interconnections are all pre-specified and the problem is instead to minimise overall pipe-length taking obstacles into account. Connections which need to be made are also pre-specified in electrical routing examples such as [2], however, unlike in our case, such cases also typically involve designing the relative layout of the items being interconnected, while having no analogue of the potential to merge connections (see below).

Overview The remainder of this paper is set out as follows. Section 2 describes the pipe routing design problem in more detail, and sets out the chromosome representation used. Test problems, experiments, and results are then presented in section 3, and then a concluding discussion appears in section 4.

2 Representing Pipe Routes

The problem we address here can be partly (but see later) viewed as optimising separately each of a collection of individual pipe connections. The essential requirement for such a connection is that it be made in such a way as to avoid obstacles. Taking pipe cost and manufacturing considerations into account, we can be justified in considering only rectilinear connections, and we therefore can conveniently view the problem in terms of choices of Steiner points [4]. Figure 2 illustrates this; we wish to make a rectilinear connection between the pump and the storage tank, that is, between points A and B. Such a connection can take one of two 'basic routes', going either via Steiner point 0, or Steiner point 1.

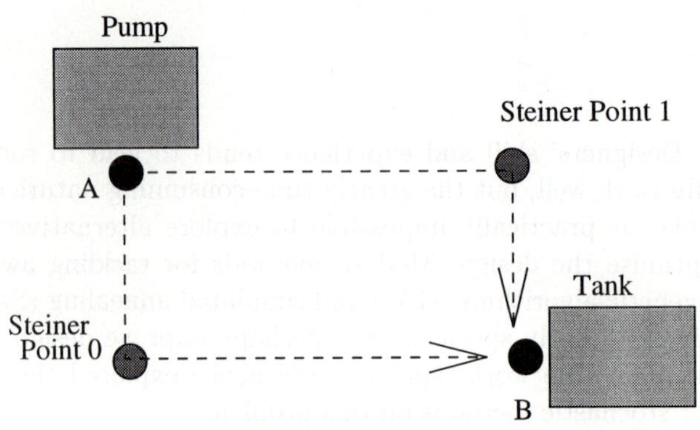

Fig. 2. Illustrating Steiner Points

In order to avoid obstacles, however, the basic routes must be diverted somehow. There are essentially two possible diversions, termed 'escape graphs' [5], around each obstacle. This is illustrated in figure 3. Hence, a single basic route (ie: a route involving a particular choice of Steiner point) gives rise to 2^k different possible routes when there are k obstacles in the way.

Associated with every connection which has to be made, then, is a collection of potential routes derived from the two (in two dimensions) possible Steiner points, and the appropriate obstacles in the P&ID. Figure 4 illustrates a general case, in which the connection between 'Start' and 'End' must be made around three obstacles (left hand side of the figure), giving rise to 6 possible routes as

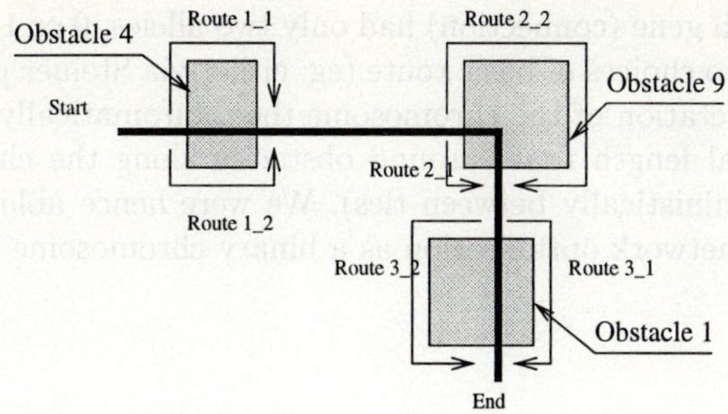

Fig. 3. The construction of possible routes around obstacles

detailed in the right hand side of the figure. As can be seen, Routes A and B are the two that arise from the first basic route (involving Steiner point 0) and the single obstacle. The two obstacles obstructing the second basic route (involving Steiner point 1) give rise to the four potential routes C,D,E and F.

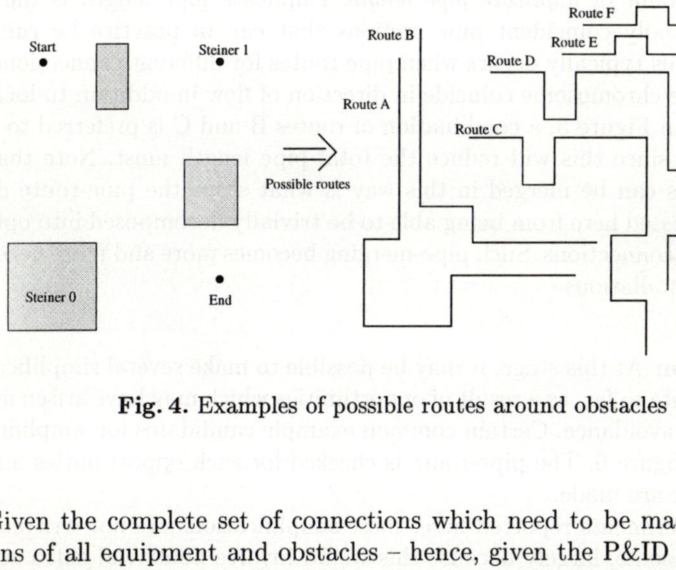

Fig. 4. Examples of possible routes around obstacles

Given the complete set of connections which need to be made and the locations of all equipment and obstacles – hence, given the P&ID – our strategy is to preprocess the information to produce the choice of all possible routes for each individual connection (Eg: as illustrated for the single example connection in figure 4). A simple chromosome representation strategy is then to provide a gene for each connection, alleles of each gene indexing the set of possible routes for that particular connection.

Following preliminary experimentation on small test cases, the representation strategy we chose as most promising for the main work reported here was one in which each gene (connection) had only two alleles, 0 or 1, representing respectively the two choices of basic route (eg: either via Steiner point 0 or Steiner point 1). Interpretation of the chromosome then automatically determined and used the minimal length route around obstacles along the chosen basic route (choosing deterministically between ties). We were hence able to represent 2D rectilinear pipe-network optimisation as a binary chromosome problem.

Evaluation

The first step in interpreting a chromosome simply uses preprocessed information to determine which potential route is represented in the chromosome for each gene. That is, if gene i displays allele 0 (1), then the route to be taken for the ith connection is the one via Steiner point 0 (1) which, taking obstacle avoidance into account, has minimal length.

Three operations are now applied in order to interpret the chromosome as a complete pipe route. These are: *Merging*, *Simplification*, and *Equivalent-length calculation*. Each is discussed briefly next.

Merging Total pipe length is calculated as the sum of each pipe connection minus the amount of *duplicate pipe length.* Duplicate pipe length is the total length of spatially coincident pipe sections that can in practice be run as a single pipe. This typically occurs when pipe routes for different connections represented in the chromosome coincide in direction of flow in addition to location. For example, in Figure 5, a combination of routes B and C is preferred to other combinations, since this will reduce the total pipe length most. Note that the fact that pipes can be merged in this way is what stops the pipe-route design problem addressed here from being able to be trivially decomposed into optimising individual connections. Such pipe-merging becomes more and more necessary with larger installations.

Simplification At this stage, it may be possible to make several simplifications in the pipe route so far, as a result of opportunities which may have arisen mainly from obstacle avoidance. Certain common example candidates for simplification are shown in figure 6. The pipe-route is checked for such opportunities and the simplifications are made.

In the experiments reported here, these simplifications are not written back to the chromosome, largely because this would involve nontrivial extra computational expense.

Equivalent-Length Calculation Finally, each corner in the pipe network is converted into its *equivalent length.* This is a way of taking corners into consideration, whereby each corner is converted into a straight pipe with a certain length which gives the same fluid pressure drop as the corner [6], and the amount is added to the total pipe length of the system.

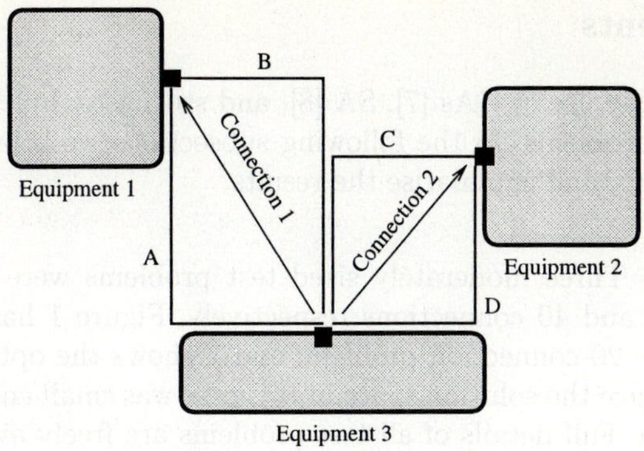

Fig. 5. Merging duplicate pipe routes

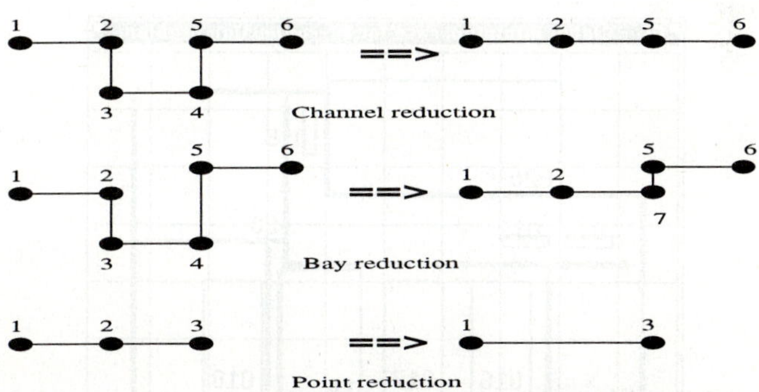

Fig. 6. Cases for pipe-route simplification

Remarks Mainly owing to the merging and simplification processes, pipe-route interpretation gives rise to a complex and time-consuming evaluation function. To avoid undue complexity, the interpretation process as described above is therefore 'incomplete' in certain respects – for example, simplification may lead to new opportunities for merging, but there is no extra merging step following the simplification step. Also, simplification should ideally be iterated until no more opportunities exist, but this would be particularly time-consuming. Also, of course, it is built in to the interpretation function that, for each of the two (or occasionally one) Steiner points relevant to a connection, only one of the several choices for potential routes around obstacles is allowed to be chosen. Allowing more possible routes to be encoded may of course lead to better opportunity for merging and simplification, leading to better overall solutions. This is yet to be investigated fully, but preliminary experiments suggested that the representation employed here struck a generally more robust balance between time complexity and solution quality.

3 Experiments

We investigated the use of GAs [7], SA [8], and stochastic hillclimbing (SH) on each of the test problems. In the following subsections we briefly overview the experimental setup, and summarise the results.

Test Problems Three moderately sized test problems were developed, consisting of 20, 30, and 40 connections respectively. Figure 1 has already shown the layout for the 20-connection problem, and 7 shows the optimal pipe route, which we know since the solution space in this case was small enough to allow an exhaustive search. Full details of all test problems are freely available from the authors, and a web-site is currently being prepared to disseminate these details more accessibly.

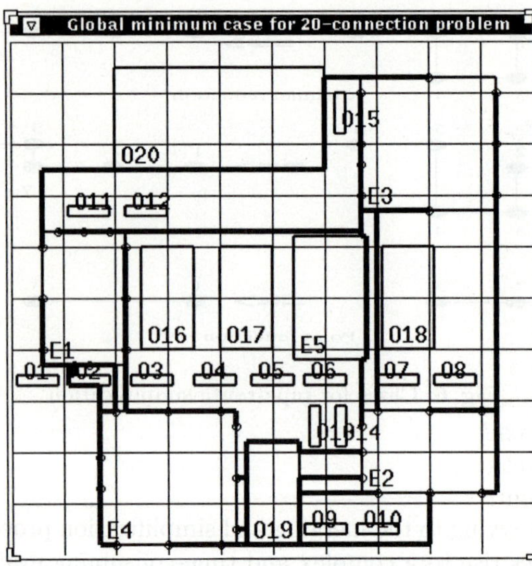

Fig. 7. The global minimum case with the 20-connection problem

Exhaustive search of the 20-connections problem results in the landscape displayed in figure 8. The horizontal axis represents the numerical value of the binary chromosome (in millions), from chromosome 0000... on the left-hand side to chromosome 1111... on the far right, while the vertical axis displays total pipe length for each chromosome. Though fine structure is essentially hidden, the figure suggests that the landscape is deeply infected with local optima. For example, one can imagine a hillclimber, perhaps being trapped in the far left region of the landscape (mainly 0's) unable to escape to the global optimum far towards the right (rather Hamming distant from it, in a mainly 1's area).

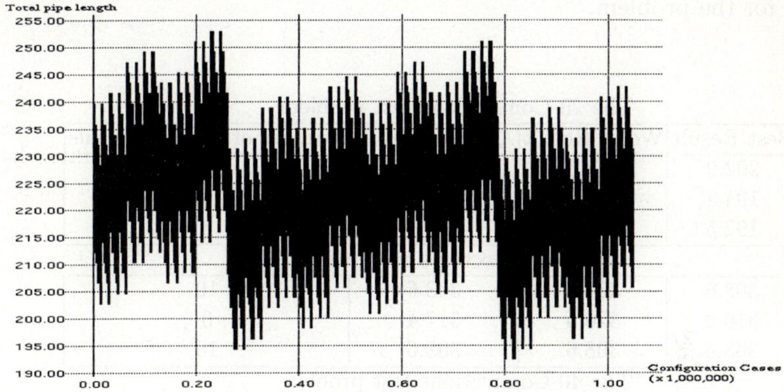

Fig. 8. Solution space for the 20-connection problem

Search space size for the 30 and 40 connection problems was more realistic with respect to real problem cases, and also (of course) not feasibly amenable to exhaustive search.

Experimental Setup Unless otherwise stated, each individual trial of an algorithm ran for a maximum of 5,000 evaluations. This is a rather modest figure, but we felt it important to seek good performance in such a relatively small space of time since pipe-route design optimisation problems can necessitate rather complex evaluation functions, as noted in section 2.

Standard SH was employed (random starting point; continually seek new mutants, replace current with new only if new is better or equal to current), using simple single-gene mutation as the neighbourhood operator. That is, a mutation step consisted of choosing a gene at random, and flipping its value.

SA used the same neighbourhood operator, and a simple geometric cooling schedule with starting temperature, number of iterations per temperature step, and final temperature set respectively at 30× the number of connections in the problem, 50, and 0.001. These parameters arose as a fairly robust set following much time consuming preliminary experimentation with different SA setups.

The GA used steady-sate reproduction, rank-based selection (as in [9], uniform crossover, a population size of 50, and the same mutation operator as SH and SA.

Results Table 1 summarises results for trials on the 20, 30, and 40 connections test problems. 10 trials each were made with each method, and the table records, in column order, the best (minimum) result over the 10 trials, the worst result, the mean result over the trials, and the number of trials (out of 10) in which an optimal (known, in the 20-connections case) pipe-route design was found. In the 30 and 40 connections cases, number of optimal trials refers to the best-known result for the problem.

	Best Result	Worst Result	Average Result	Number of Optimal Trials
		The 20-Connections test problem		
SH	202.0	218.6	207.4	0
SA	194.4	195.7	195.2	0
GA	192.5	194.4	192.6	8
		The 30-Connections test problem		
SH	308.6	308.6	308.6	10
SA	316.2	320.5	317.4	0
GA	308.6	308.6	308.6	10
		The 40-Connections test problem		
SH	392.9	402.3	396.2	0
SA	397.9	406.8	404.9	0
GA	354.3	354.3	354.3	10

Table 1. Summary of Results on test problems

On the 20-connections problem, SH performance was rather poor in relation to both SA and GA, with SH and GA competing relatively closely, although the GA seems clearly superior.

In the 30-connections case, SA seemed to have trouble, losing out to SH and GA, both of which found the same best-known result in every trial. We can only conjecture that this example may have sported a fitness landscape with few or no hard-to-escape local optima, enabling SH and GA to be steered quickly to a result, leaving SA to unwisely, in this case, explore less promising avenues.

In the 40-connections case, the GA is clearly far superior to the other methods, with SH second-best, and SA a close third.

In each case, T-tests report the GA superior to SA with 95% confidence. In the 20-connections and 40-connections case, T-tests also find GA superior to SH with 95% confidence.

4 Discussion

Initial indications are that use of GAs on pipe-route design problems appears very promising. Commercial security considerations unfortunately made it prohibitively hard to compare with human expert results on real problem examples.

However, we can at least report that a GA was able to fairly reliably find the global optimum solution where this was known (the 20-connections case), and that the GA appears superior to either SA or SH on this problem in larger test cases.

Further work therefore seems warranted, in particular extending the technique to three-dimensional pipe-route design. In 3D, for example, there are typically 6 Steiner points giving rise to 6 basic routes, with 4 main potential escape routes around any obstacle. This leads to a straightforward extension of our representation. Choosing pipe-route diameters in conjunction with other aspects of the problem is a further necessary extension towards real-world examples. There is also much scope to design problem specific operators.

In summary, this study has suggested that industrial plant pipe-route optimisation can be feasibly done using GAs. We present a natural and effective representation for the problem, and results that suggest GAs are superior to either SH or SA on these problems (at least with the representation and standard operators used here). Results point towards the potential success of extending the technique to deal with real industrial plant pipe-route design, supporting the work of human experts in this area.

References

1. Kang Soo Kim. Personal communication with Kang Soo Kim, Executive director in the DAEWOO Heavy Industry Co., Seoul, Korea, August 1994.
2. Jens Lienig and Holder Brandt. An evolutionary algorithm for the routing of multichip modules. In Manner Davidor, Schwefel, editor, *Parallel Problem Solving from Nature - PPSN III*, pages 588–597. Springer-Verlag, 1994.
3. Dragan A. Savic and Godfrey A. Walters. Genetic operations and constraint handling for pipe network optimization. In *Proceedings of the AISB workshop*. AISB, 1994.
4. J. Hesser, R. Maenner, and O. Stucky. Optimization of Steiner trees using Genetic Algorithms. In D. Schaffer, editor, *Proceedings of the Third International Conference on Genetic Algorithms*, pages 231–236. International Conference on Genetic Algorithms, 1989.
5. Josep L. Ganley and James P. Cohoon. Optimal Rectilinear Steiner Tree Routing in the Presence of Obstacles. *IEEE Transactions of Computer-Aided Design of Integrated Circuits and Systems*, 1993.
6. Frank M. White. *Fluid Mechanics*. McGraw-Hill Book Company, second edition, 1986.
7. David E. Goldberg. *Genetic Algorithms: in Search, Optimization & Machine Learning*. Addison Wesley, 1989.
8. P. J. M. van Laarhoven and E. H. L. Aarts. *Simulated Annealing: Theory and Applications*. D. Reidel Publishing Company, 1987.
9. Darrell Whitley. The genitor algorithm and selection pressure: Why rank-based allocation of reproductive trial is best. In D. Schaffer, editor, *Proceedings of the Third International Conference on Genetic Algorithms*. International Conference on Genetic Algorithms, 1989.

An Evolutionary Algorithm for Design Optimization of Microsystems

M. Gorges-Schleuter, W. Jakob, S. Meinzer, A. Quinte, W. Süß, H. Eggert

Forschungszentrum Karlsruhe, Institut für Angewandte Informatik,
Postfach 3640, D-76021 Karlsruhe, Germany

Abstract. The concept of an evolutionary algorithm for improving the design optimization process is presented. A first application, the design optimization of a micropump, is used for both, the description of the concept being especially tailored for multicriteria applications and the presentation of very promising results.

The behavior of the micropump is formulated as an analog model including the various domains as there are electrical, thermal, and pneumatic phenomena. The parameters of this model are modified with the proposed evolutionary algorithm until a satisfactory behavior of the system is reached. The quality of the optimization depends highly on the quality of the simulation model at hand, therefore we give in addition an outlook of an evolutionary algorithm for improving the analog simulation model by using FEM results.

1 Introduction

The innovative field of microsystem technology is an interdisciplinary research area. An intelligent microsystem consists of a combination of microcomponents, e.g. micro-actuators and microsensors, microelectronic devices, assembling and bonding, and information technology for data processing.

Industrial application of microsystems requires short development times as well as reliable designs comparable to the state of the art in micro electronics. To achieve this goal CAD based design techniques and simulation are necessary but not sufficient as outlined below. During the design process the engineer is faced with an extremely large search space of possible design solutions and parameterizations. Although a great percentage of the design directions can be dismissed based on the available knowledge and the experience gained from previous designs in most cases the remaining search space will be far too large to be systematically investigated. Thus a trial-and-error process is started which can be described as *poking in the fog* rather than a systematic search. It is mainly based on three properties: the experience and the knowledge of the engineer, his attitude, and on good luck. To overcome this unsatisfactory situation a more systematic exploration of the search space is necessary.

The overall idea of the concept presented in this paper is to substitute the human of Fig. 1 by an automated explorer and to involve the engineer in high level decision making only. The task of the explorer is to implement an "intelligent" search focusing on promising areas of the search space, avoiding suboptima and adapting itself to the search landscape on hand. The proposed explorer is based on the GLEAM concept

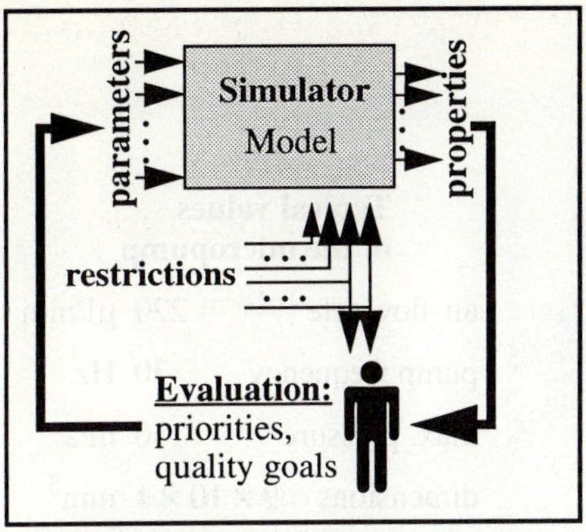

Fig. 1. Conventional Design Process

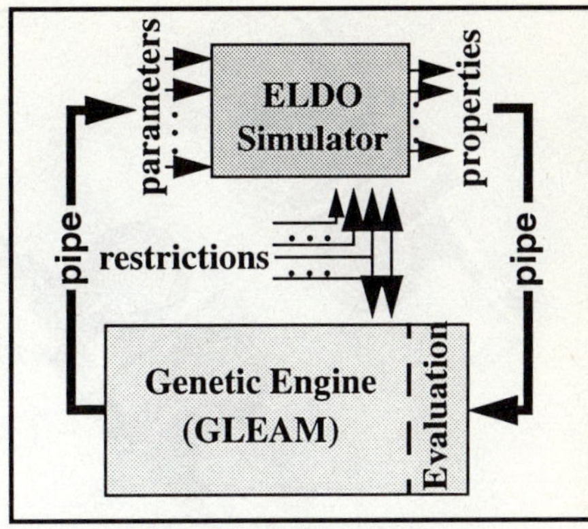

Fig. 2. Part of SIMOT

(Genetic Learning Algorithms and Methods) [1]. GLEAM is a Genetic Algorithm [2] which utilizes a hierarchical list-like data structure of genes, representation specific genetic operators [4], and a geographical distributed population structure with local selection only [4,5,6].

The application presented in this paper focuses on the evolutionary optimization of microcomponents. We have chosen a micropump developed at the FZK as a specific case study. The design of the micropump is complex enough, a model description is available, and we do have real data of micropumps already build. In addition, the results of our simulations will be part of future design cycles.

The further contents of this paper starts with the description of the specific application, a microfluidic component. Then we present our general concept for using an evolutionary algorithm for design optimization tasks and describe the features of our evolutionary algorithm. Next, we introduce the model of the micropump, specify the optimization task, and present first optimization results. Finally, we give an outlook to further work including the use of EAs for improved simulation modeling and models, speed-up by parallelization, and propositions under consideration for an improved behavior of the evolutionary search itself.

2 The Application: A micropump

Our first application was the optimization of the behavior of a thermo-pneumatic-driven micropump which was developed at the IMT (Institut for Microstructural Engineering), another institute of our research centre [7]. Fig. 3 shows a module of four of these micropumps. The pumps are assembled with a cable for the power supply. A schematic overview of the micropump together with an analog model is shown in Fig. 4. The micropump has been manufactured by combining thermoplastic molding with membrane techniques. The pump case consists of two pieces with a polyimide membrane of 1.5 μm thickness in-between. The inlet and outlet valves are formed by orifices in the membrane over a valve seat, which is part of the case. The membrane is driven by an integrated thermopneumatic actuator, a heating coil attached on top of the membrane in the actuator chamber. The gold wire is heated by an electrical current, this warms up the gas in the closed actuator chamber and the resulting expansion of the gas causes an elas-

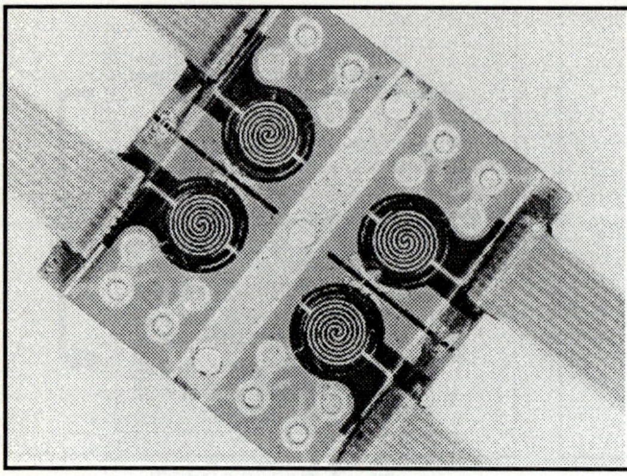

Typical values of the micropump

air-flow rate	220 µl/min
pump frequency	30 Hz
max. pressure	130 hPa
dimensions	$9 \times 10 \times 1$ mm^3

Fig. 3. A module of four micropumps

tic deformation of the membrane, which presses the gas in the channel of the pump through the outlet valve. This is the phase shown in Fig. 4. Switching off the current cools down the gas in the actuator chamber, the pressure drops, and the membrane moves back. The passive outlet valve closes, the inlet valves opens and new gas streams into the pump channel.

3 SIMOT - The General Concept

The evaluation of a given design will in many cases be done by simulation. The result of a simulation run consists of values for the system properties of interest. Using these values the design engineer constructs a quality measure either in his mind or more explicitly by calculating some reference numbers which can be weighted and summed up in order to form a single quality value. Thus a multi-criteria evaluation can be done which is the base for a multicriteria optimization by ranking the designs suggested so far. The quality value is used to direct the search process by the automated explorer. The task of the engineer is now focused on the definition of appropriate global designs, both the constraints and the parameters, and the associated evaluation functions and weights. The latter means to define the design goals and the lines of compromise. Based on the results of some optimization runs these global terms and figures have to be readjusted in order to achieve a satisfactory solution. This scenario still reflects an iterative design process but the work of the human concentrates on much higher levels of abstraction and the evolutionary algorithm now investigates the space of possible solutions which is done much more thoroughly as the strategy is not limited by the human way of thinking. The achieved results are in general of higher quality and provided that enough computer power is available also be obtained in reasonable times.

SIMOT, our **SIM**ulation and **O**ptimization **T**ool environment, consists at the present stage of implementation of two parts, a genetic engine based on GLEAM and tailored for the needs of multicriteria parameter optimization and a powerful simulation tool ELDO®[1] as shown in Fig. 2. Both software components are linked via pipes in

1 ELDO is a trademark of ANACAD EES, Ltd.

order to achieve a fast communication. Restrictions are as far as possible already taken into account by the genetic engine.

3.1 The Evolutionary Algorithm

The search space our automated explorer is faced with will be in general multimodal, highly non-linear, more or less high dimensional, restricted and discontinuous. Thus it is a suitable application area for an adaptive search technique. The GLEAM [1] concept combines the traditional approaches of Genetic Algorithms [2] and Evolution Strategies [3] with modern computer science and data modeling. It has approved its performance in such different areas of application as machine learning [4], robot path planning [8], resource planning and job shop scheduling [9].

GLEAM uses a list-like hierarchical data structure. The elements of the data structure depend on the actual application. The hierarchy may be used to treat parts of the data structure as a unit and thus prevent them from being separated by the crossover operators or to hide them completely thus prevent them from being modified by the genetic operators.

The mutation operator is inspired from its counterpart in evolution strategies in the sense that small variations of genetic values are more likely than larger variations. GLEAM allows the usage of any arbitrary alphabet for the internal representation being mostly naturally induced by the application considered. As a consequence mutations can neither be realized as bit-flipping operations as used with binary alphabets in Genetic Algorithms nor by use of a normal-distributed variation as in the real-valued representation used in Evolution Strategies. Assuming that the elements of the underlying alphabet (i.e. the values a certain gene can take) are sorted by some criteria, we create before any mutation a division of the range of values into classes. By mutation a change of the current gene value to a random value within the nearby classes is very likely and this probability shortens with the distance of a class as defined by a prespecified step function.

There are various crossover operators implementing traditional n-point crossover, uniform crossover, and crossover operators respecting the relative positioning, the absolute positioning, or the order of the elements in the parents. Each crossover operator may be activated on a percentage basis. Each time a crossover operator is chosen, a new offspring is generated. Thus if several crossover operators have a percentage of choice greater than zero, there will be a chance that more than one offspring will be generated. The resulting set of offsprings will be evaluated and only the best will be considered to be included into the population.

The population is distributed geographically. A linear ring structure has been chosen and the selection process is limited to nearby individuals. The size of the neighborhood of any individual is chosen to be 9. Each individual and its partner being chosen by local linear ranking produce offsprings by means of mutation and crossover. These are evaluated and the best of them is compared with the individual and replaces it immediately, but only if the offspring is better than the weakest in the neighborhood and with the exception of those individuals being the local best, then the offspring must be better than the individual itself (local elitism) [4,5,6]. This process is continued until a termination criterion like elapsed time or the already achieved quality is reached.

The high amount of computing time consumed by each simulation , varying between 3 and 4 minutes, limits the practical possible size of the population. The experiments reported in this paper use a population size of 60. The linear population structure and the small neighborhood size limit the speed of the information flow by the diffusion process. This together with a strong survival rule of offsprings permit the observation of the effects of the isolation-by-distance, despite of the relatively small population size. So, we observe as the result of an optimization run a set of in most cases different solutions of more or less high quality. The resulting quality depends on the details of the evaluation formulas, the degrees of freedom for the search process itself and on the time or amount of generations spend in the search process.

The usage of a geographical population structure and local-only selection and replacement makes GLEAM explicit parallel. This allows a "natural" parallelization with an observed linear speed-up [5,9].

3.2 The Simulation Part

An important property of microsystems is the existence of various physical domains such as microelectronic, micromechanic, microfluidic and others. For each of these domains various simulators exist. The small dimension of microsystems induce a strong interaction between the domains and thus a separate modeling of these domains is not sufficient. ELDO is a tool for analog and mixed signal simulation. Analog models are usually derived analytically and their simulation can be done in short times. For circuit simulators like SPICE it is necessary to build the model with electrical devices as resistors and capacities. This can be done because the behavior of a system can be described with a mathematical equation which can often be alternately described by an electrical network where only the parameters are different. For those components, which cannot be described in analogy to an electrical network, it is necessary to prepare tables or to use controlled sources. In contrast to that the analog hardware description language (HDL-A) of ELDO allows mathematical equations to be used explicitly [9]. Thus various physical domains for example electrical, mechanical, thermal or fluidic can be described with one common description language. This is important in those cases, like ours, where heterogeneous systems have to be simulated.

4 The Application

4.1 The Model of the Micropump

The first model of the micropump was an analog model (Fig. 4). Resistors, capacities and sources (lump elements) are the devices with which the heat flow and the volume flow are described. The electrical, the thermal, and the pneumatic domain are included in this model. In the thermal system the voltage represents the temperature and the current the heat flow rate. In the pneumatic system the pressure is the analogy to the voltage and the volume flow rate that to the current. The behavior of the valves, of the gas and also of the membrane is nonlinear and so controlled sources with tables are needed to describe their behavior.

To build such an analytical model usually some simplifications have to be done. On the other hand that type of model satisfies the requirements for an optimization: the

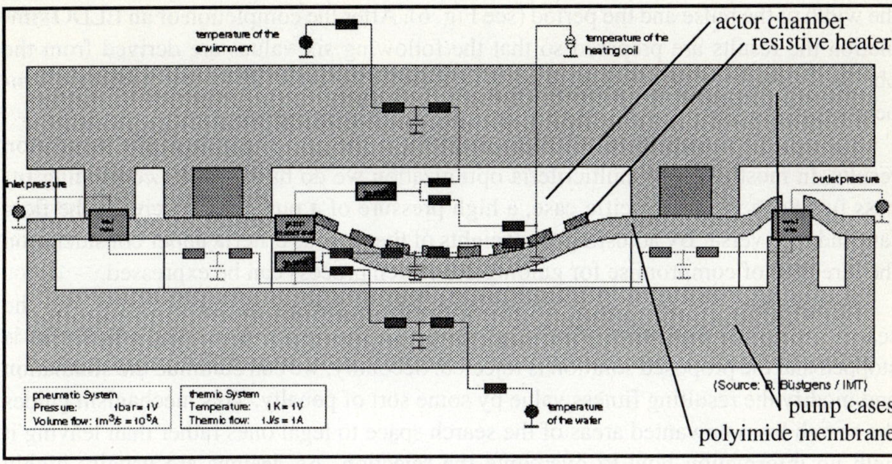

Fig. 4. Schematic view and electrical analog model of the micropump

models are parameterizable and the simulation is considerable fast. We used this rough model for our first runs. For validation five manufactured micropumps are compared with the result of the simulation model. Fig. 5 shows the air flow rate as a function of the pressure drop at the inlet. We see, that the simulation approximates the behavior of the real micropump rather conservative.

4.2 The Optimization Task

The goals of the optimization of the micropump design are a high flow rate and efficiency coupled with a low temperature of the micropump by parameter variation of geometry, production process (e.g. membrane tension), and power supply.

Our first optimization task was the variation of the form of the heating impulses. The heating impulse depends on five parameters: the magnitude, the rise time, the fall time,

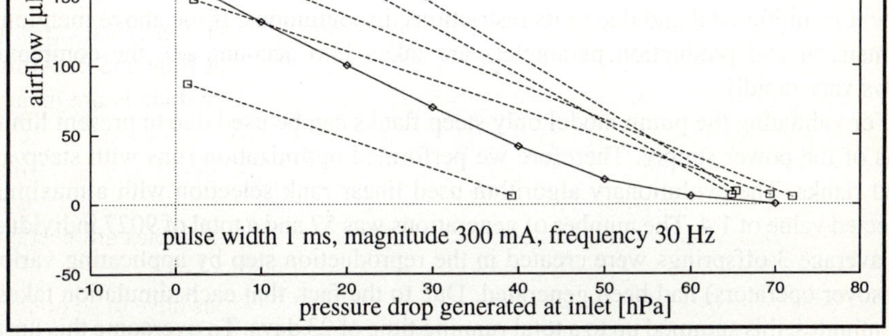

Fig. 5. Comparison of micropump simulation data and real data

the width of the pulse and the period (see Fig. 6). After the completion of an ELDO simulation the results are prepared so that the following six values are derived from the obtained waves: the rate of fluid flow, the pressure over both valves, the maximum temperature of the heating coil, the electrical power and the efficiency.

The genetic search process is very sensitive to the interpretation of the simulation results. In most cases of multicriteria optimization we do have several conflicting fitness functions. In our specific case, a high pressure of a pump will decrease the flow rate and vice versa. By adjusting the weights of the various criteria under consideration the direction of compromise for guiding the search process can be expressed.

Restrictions, like the pump temperature, can in general be incorporated into the search process in two ways. Firstly, as soon as a restriction is met the simulation is stopped and the proposed solution is rejected. Secondly, we can continue the simulation and modify the resulting fitness value by some sort of penalty. This mechanism guides the search from unwanted areas of the search space to legal ones rather than leaving it with no information how to overcome the rejection. As designs are usually highly restricted this is an important technique to meet these restrictions.

As an example, we describe the consideration of the heater temperature of our pump. If the heater gets too hot it will burn through, so this restriction has to be fulfilled under all circumstances. Nevertheless, we allow during simulation the excess of the given limit (850 Kelvin) and apply an exponential penalty function, so that the overall fitness is drastically dropped with increased violation of the temperature limit. The search is quasi pushed to legal parts of the search space. Additionally, we can affect the fitness contribution of a specific criteria directly. In our application, a low temperature of about 600 Kelvin is wanted. So, the increase of the fitness is significantly lowered when the desired value is reached.

4.3 The Optimization Results

Originally the micropump was actuated with a short heating impulse with high magnitude (Fig. 7a). The result of our optimization run gave an improved form of the heating impulse as follows: medium magnitude, long rise time and long fall time, but a short width of the pulse itself. Fig. 7b shows the result of first optimization runs. With this power supply the air flow rate is significantly improved and the pump will get not too hot.

Although these first optimizations consider only five control parameters of the power supply the search space has already a size of about 10^{22}. As first experiments show it is multimodal and due to its restrictions discontinuous. If the above mentioned geometrical and production parameters are taken into account too, the complexity grows very rapidly.

For validating the pump model only steep flanks can be used due to present limitations of the power supply. Therefore we performed optimization runs with steep and fixed flanks. The evolutionary algorithm used linear rank selection with a maximum expected value of 1.4. The number of generations was 57 and a total of 9027 individuals (on average 3 offsprings were created in the reproduction step by applicating various crossover operators) had been generated. Due to the fact, that each simulation takes 3 to 4 minutes, this summed up to a total running time of 23 days. To overcome this unsat-

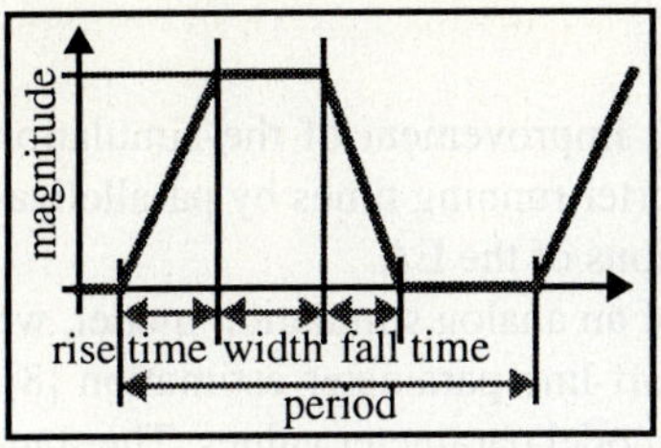

Fig. 6. Pulse modulated power supply

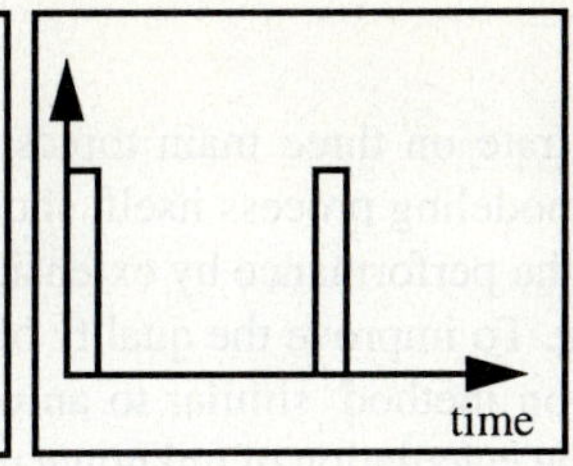

Fig. 7a. Original pulse

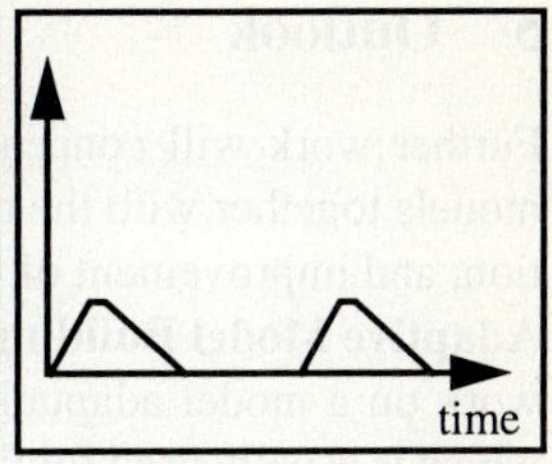

Fig. 7b. Improved pulse

isfactory situation, a parallel PVM-based version of the system, which utilizes the net of SUN workstations of the institute, is currently under development. The concept of parallelization can be found in [4,5].

Next we investigate the parameter space of 7 evolutionary solutions found in the same run and compare these to the measurement data. Fig. 8 shows how the solutions are placed in the parameter space if we consider the values of pulse width vs. frequency found. We observe three niches of different characteristics being established in the population. Medium frequency is either combined with very low or high pulse width or a high frequency with medium pulse width is found. Of course the magnitude is different to prevent a burn through of the micropump, i.e. a small pulse width is combined with a high magnitude of 1200 mA and a high pulse width is combined with only 275 mA. Comparing the optimization values with the measurement values (the nine values within the ellipse in the lower left corner) we realize that the latter have been taken in a small subspace only.

Fig. 9 visualizes the behavior of the micropump in terms of the air flow rate and maximal heater temperature of both, the behavior of the standard pump (stnd) and the seven solutions found with improved behavior (1-7). The optimization results are sorted by the maximal temperature of the heater.

These results demonstrate that the efficiency of the micropump model may easily be quadrupled. We realized that the way of human thinking is often too restrictive compared to the space of promising solutions. But, it shows too that our simulation model needs verification for a much larger parameter space.

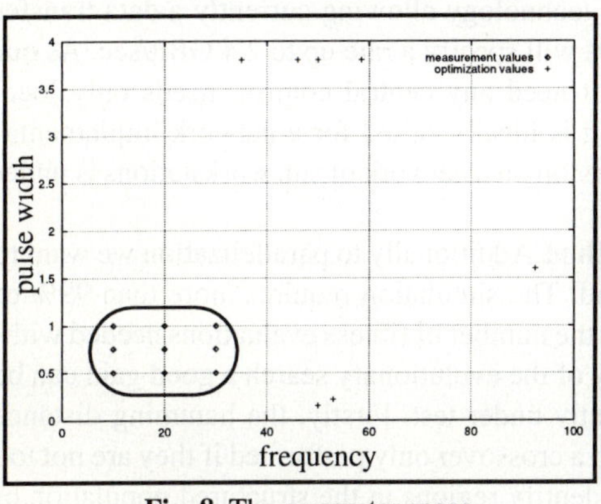

Fig. 8. The parameter space

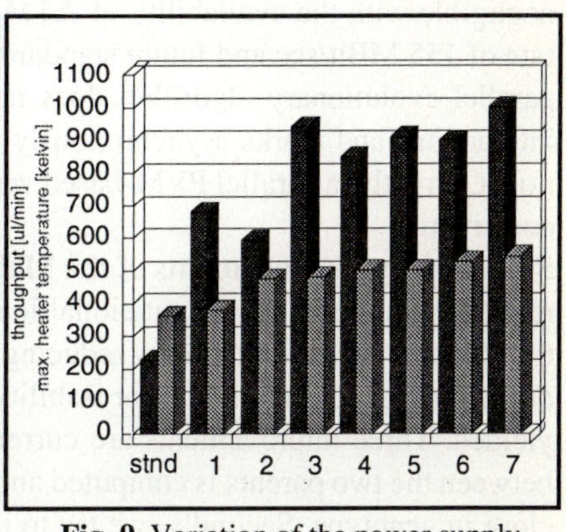

Fig. 9. Variation of the power supply

5 Outlook

Further work will concentrate on three main topics: improvement of the simulation models together with the modeling process itself, shorter running times by parallelization, and improvement of the performance by extensions of the EA.

Adaptive Model Building. To improve the quality of an analog simulation model, we work on a model adaptation method, similar to an off-line parameter estimation [8], which is usually used for the calculation of unknown model parameter values. The standard off-line parameter estimation method is based on the variation of unknown parameter values of an analog simulation model until the desired coincidence of the model behavior with a behavior reference, for example a measuring series of a real system, is obtained. Using this procedure we want to improve the analog simulation models with support of Finite Element Method (FEM) [11] analysis as the reference and GLEAM for the parameter tuning.

Especially in system components with a complex geometry like a micro valve in which the fluid resistance cannot be determined analytically with the necessary precision, the FEM can be used successfully for the determination of such items in an analog simulation model. This advantage of our approach is that we can obtain now parameterizable analog simulation models. This means that also functional dependencies of design parameters like geometry or material constants can be taken into account, which is an important assumption for their application in the area of design optimization. The creation of behavior references with FEM, which reflects the behavior of the system in the complete design parameter range, requires a lot of additional computing power. But, this has to be done only once and the resulting analog simulation model or parts of it can be reused later.

Speed-up by Parallelization. For practical applications "short" turn around times, this means one night might be sufficient, are necessary. To achieve this the parallel nature of our evolutionary search process is used for parallelization. Earlier investigations using a transputer cluster [5,6,9] have shown a linear speed-up of an EA with a geographically structured population and local rules only. The fast technological development especially in the internetworking area offers the opportunity of an efficient parallelization in a network of workstations. Delays due to communication overhead will be negligible with the availability of ATM technology allowing currently a data transfer rate of 155 MBit/sec and future standards will specify a rate up to 2.4 GBit/sec. As our parallel evolutionary algorithm does not need any central control, needs only local interactions and works asynchronously it is ideally suited for a network implementation. Currently, a parallel PVM-based version on a network of sun workstations is under construction.

Speed-up by Improvements of the Method. Additionally to parallelization we want to reduce the amount of computational load. The simulation requires more than 99% of the computing time and thus by reducing the number of fitness evaluations needed without lowering the performance or stability of the evolutionary search a good gain can be yielded. Three improvements are currently under test. Firstly, the hamming distance between the two parents is computed and a crossover only performed if they are not too close in genotype. Secondly, we try to identify regions in the structured population of (nearly) identical individuals. We claim, that these regions have already been converged. Our new partial reinitialization operator keeps some of the individuals including the local best if specified and initializes the remaining individuals to add new genetic material. These two techniques are of a general nature and their application concerns the later stages of an optimization run, when some convergence has occurred.

The third technique incorporates some domain specific knowledge and operates during the entire optimization run. It reflects the fact that a human being would restrict the search space by eliminating those parts of the parameter space which can safely be ignored. In our application this can be done e.g. for an heating impulse consuming too much power and thus will surely burn the heater. We do not know whether the form of the impulse should be like a needle or a brick, but, we do know that both a high magnitude and a long duration will destroy the pump. So, we build a filter which calculates the energy of the impulse and rejects the trial if the value is too high. As this threshold value is not known a priori it is adjusted adaptively during a run.

Acknowledgments. The authors want to thank Burkhard Büstgens (IMT), who developed the micropump prototypes and a first SPICE model of his pumps and Werner Schomburg (IMT), the responsible engineer for the development of microfluidic components, for his valuable cooperation.

References

1. Blume, C.: GLEAM - A System for "Intuitive Learning". Proc. 1st Int. Workshop on Parallel Problem Solving from Nature, LNCS 496, Springer Verlag (1990)
2. Holland, J.: Adaptation in Natural and Artificial Systems. The University of Michigan Press, Ann Arbor. (1975)
3. Schwefel, H.-P.: Numerical Optimization of Computer Models. Wiley, Chichester (1981)
4. Jakob, W., Gorges-Schleuter, M., Blume, C.: Application of Genetic Algorithms to Task Planning and Learning. Proc. 2nd Int. Conf. PPSN, North-Holland (1992), 291-300
5. Gorges-Schleuter, M.: Explicit Parallelism of GAs through Population Structures. Proc. 1st Parallel Problem Solving from Nature, LNCS 496, Springer Verlag (1990), 150-159
6. Gorges-Schleuter, M.: Parallel Evolutionary Algorithms and the Concept of Population Structures. In: Plantamura, V., Soucek, B., Visaggio,G. (Eds.): Frontier Decision Support Concepts. Wiley, New York (1994), 261-319
7. B. Büstgens, W. Bacher, W. Bier, R. Ehnes, L. Keydel, D. Maas, R. Ruprecht, W. Schomburg: Micromembrane Pump Manufactured by Molding. Proc. 4th Int. Conf. On New Actuators, Actuator '94, Bremen, 86, (1994)
8. Blume, C., Krisch, S., Jakob, W.: Robot Trajectory Planning with Collision Avoidance Using Genetic Algorithms. Proc. 25th Int. Symp. on Industrial Robots, Hannover, FRG (1994)
9. Jakob,W., Blume,C.: Verbesserte Planung und Optimierung mit Hilfe eines erweiterten Genetischen Algorithmus (in german). Proc. TAT 93. Springer Verlag, Heidelberg (1994)
10. Fischer-Binder, J.-O.: Analog Extensions to VHDL. Firma Bosch (1993). ftp: nestor.epfl.ch
11. Zienkiewicz, O.C.: The Finite Element Method. McGraw-Hill Company, London (1977)

A Learning Classifier System for Three-Dimensional Shape Optimization

Robert A. Richards and Sheri D. Sheppard

Stanford University, PO Box 9723
Stanford, CA 94309-9723, USA

Abstract. A learning classifier system complex is developed in order to accomplish the broader goal of developing a methodology to perform generalized zeroth-order two- and three-dimensional shape optimization. Specifically, the methodology has the objective of determining the optimal boundary to minimize mass while satisfying constraints on stress and geometry. Even with the enormous advances in shape optimization no method has proven to be satisfactory across the broad spectrum of optimization problems facing the modern engineer. Similarly the available software in the field of learning classifier systems is so embryonic that a new software package had to be developed for this application. The shape optimization via hypothesizing inductive classifier system complex (SPHINcsX) instantiates the methodology in a software package overcoming many of the limitations of today's conventional shape optimization techniques, while advancing the state-of-the-art in classifier system software tools.

1 Introduction

This paper surveys the Shape oPtimization via Hypothesizing Inductive classifier system compleX (SPHINcsX, pronounced *s f ĭ n k s*). The complex is a software package which embodies advances in classifier system software design as well as the novel methodology for performing zeroth-order stress constrained shape optimization via the classifier system. The complex starts with a design component and modifies boundaries to optimize the shape (minimizing its mass) while meeting all design constraints.

The broadest objectives of the research, which drive the development of SPHINcsX, are:

- to develop a general scaleable methodology for component design optimization, from simple two-dimensional sizing designs to three-dimensional shape designs,
- to investigate the classifier system's applicability as a tool for satisfying the above objective.

To couple the disparate realms of mechanical engineering shape optimization and classifier systems, another objective became:

- to advance the software instantiation of the classifier system to the point of providing visual feedback of its workings and visual presentation of its results. That is, de-mystify the internal workings and simplify the interpretation of the output.

Some of SPHINcsX's sub-objectives, to make it *general*, include:

- perform without the benefit of derivatives of the objective function and constraints with respect to the design variables, that is; a zeroth order method,
- be independent of the analysis tool and boundary representation.

The scope of SPHINcsX is limited as follows:

- optimization occurs on isotropic components acted upon by loads, and in static equilibrium due to constraints,
- the design modifications occur by modifying the boundaries of the component; no new boundaries, such as voids, are introduced,
- the objective is to minimize the component's mass,
- constraints are placed on the maximum stress allowed.

The overall approach is to take the problem of shape optimization (see Zienkiewicz & Campbell [1973] and Haftka & Grandhi [1986]) and interface it with a classifier system. The resulting complex takes an initial design, calculates the stress properties and applies a set of rules (classifiers) to generate a new design. This iterative process continues until an optimum design is created. The evolving design's changes in merit are used as feedback to the complex and its underlying classifier system. Utilizing the feedback and a genetic algorithm, better classifiers gain strength and breed with other good rules in an attempt to evolve better rules.

There are three distinct classes of shape optimization problems. In order of complexity, these are: size, shape, and topological optimization. The current investigation considers shape optimization, which subsumes size optimization, but does not deal with topological optimization

The objective is to minimize the mass of the design by manipulation of non-constrained boundaries. The explicit constraints consist of the bounds placed on the design variables, if any. The design points defining the boundary are the design variables. Since the optimization performed in this study is relative to stress, the major implicit constraint is the maximum allowable von Mises stress. The design is assumed optimized when all the design's stresses are within a certain percentage of the maximum allowable, or the incremental improvement falls below a threshold.

2 Process of Shape Optimization

The initial condition starts with a (normally feasible) design. A *feasible design* is one where none of the constraints are violated. Figure 1 shows that there are four major modules in the shape optimization process: *boundary representation*, *analysis*, *optimization*, *termination*.

The boundary representation must be defined as a part of the design's initial condition. The optimal shape depends on the boundary representation and the design variables selected to represent the modifiable boundaries. SPHINcsX attempts to treat the boundary representation module as a black box; but since the optimization module must interface with the boundary representation module it must be cognizant of the representation used. Boundary representations used with SPHINcsX are restricted so that the design variables are actually on the design boundary. This restriction still allows for most boundary representations, including lines, arcs, circles, ellipses, cubic splines, and surface patches.

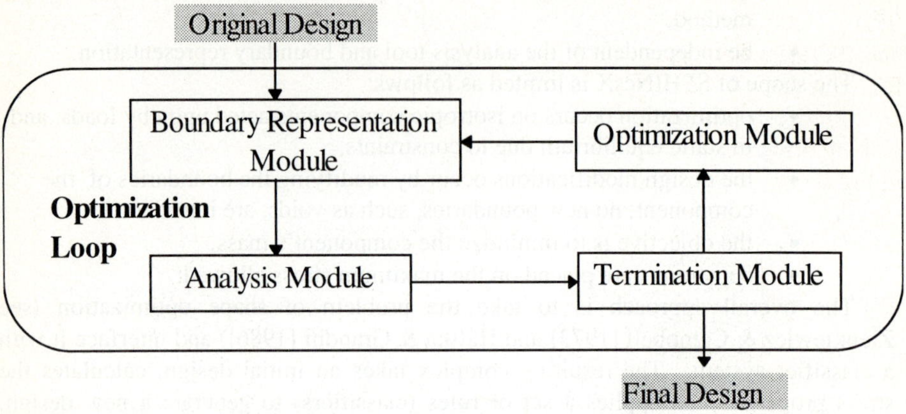

Fig. 1. Shape Optimization Process Overview

The analysis module's purpose is to determine the values of the: *objective function*, *implicit constraints*, *auxiliary information* (needed by the optimization module). The analysis module utilized in conjunction with SPHINcsX is envisioned as a black box which will provide the stress and mass information to the optimization module allowing for analysis technique independence. There is no auxiliary information (such as derivatives) needed by the SPHINcsX optimization module.

The termination module checks to see if any of the termination criteria are met. From here the system branches, stopping if the termination module determines the termination branch should be taken, otherwise the branch is made to the optimization module.

The optimization module determines which design variables to modify and the magnitude of the modifications. The optimization module then changes the design variable values. These new design variable values are subsequently passed to the boundary representation module, completing the optimization loop (iteration).

3 Classifier System & Genetic Algorithm

The classifier system (CS) utilized in this research has internal functionality similar to the Michigan style classifier systems described in the founding work by Holland and Reitman [1978], and in later works by Riolo [1988], Goldberg [1989], Dorigo & Sirtori [1991], and Wilson [1994]. The classifier system is stimulus-response and utilizes both a genetic algorithm and a covering operator. The major difference between SPHINcsX and earlier classifier system software packages is in the realm of visualization. Graphical enhancements have been integrated to better understand the processes that occur during learning and better understand the output of the learning process. SPHINcsX is designed in modules to provide for easier integration with other environments besides shape optimization and to permit operation without all the modules being present.

The following describes some of the visualization tools included with SPHINcsX. The interfaces (detector, effector, feedback) between the environment and the classifier system are not detailed here, however, they are summarized in Richards [1996] and in further detail in Richards [1995].

SPHINcsX provides a graphical user interface for setting up classifier system and environment specific parameters. The opening screen for SPHINcsX is shown in Figure 2.

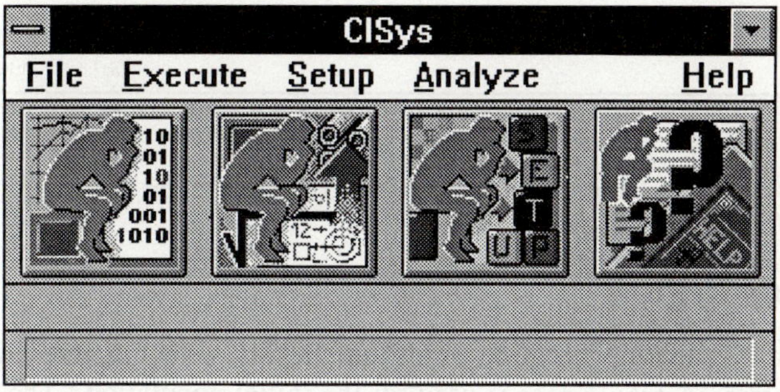

Fig. 2 Main Window for SPHINcsX Application.

In the main window SPHINcsX provides buttons for commencing or continuing the learning process; applying the classifiers with learning disabled (application mode); setting up the classifier system and environment parameters via forms; and accessing on-line help. The parameter settings can be saved to a text file for later retrieval.

Runtime options are also available, these include having textual output as well as graphical. The graphical output includes performance results being created dynamically, such as those shown below for the performance metrics P2, P3, described below. Plots showing a strength histogram and default hierarchy plots can be output after each application of the genetic algorithm (epoch). A default hierarchy plot is shown in Figure 3. Other options include showing strength versus iteration number plots for the active classifiers during the past epoch. The system also saves its state as it learns so that if the learning is interrupted for any reason it can be continued from the last complete iteration. This proved valuable for research with SPHINcsX included learning sessions which took weeks to complete.

When learning is complete many aspects of the learning process can be recalled (if the user selected this option), including population snapshots. A graphical population viewer is also available to convert the tertiary alphabet of classifiers into a more human readable format. These tools permitted the feedback necessary to first; find errors in the software, second; to optimize the myriad of settings required by the classifier system and its underlying genetic algorithm, third; to monitor the learning process and fourth; to verify the intelligence of the learned classifier system.

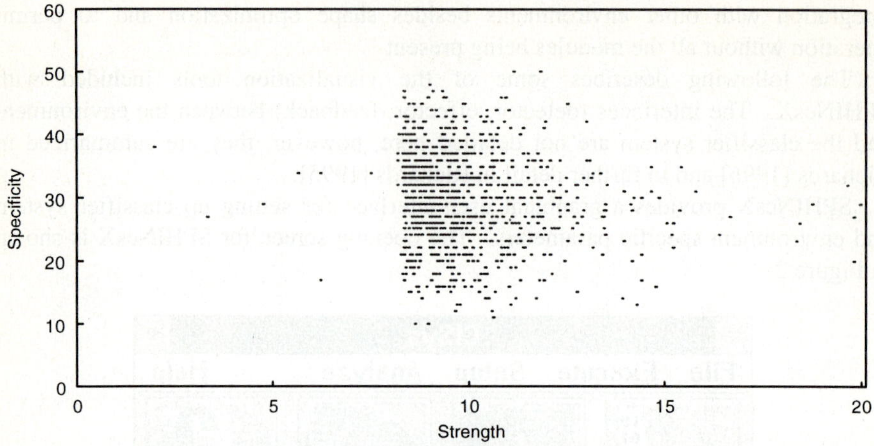

Fig. 3. Sample Default Hierarchy Plot

4 Learning Regime

The SPHINcsX's learning regime algorithm begins with the initialization of the classifier system. A *tabula rasa* is used for the initial population. The population is created by randomly picking a *0*, *1*, or # for each position for each classifier's antecedent. The probability of picking a # for each position is determined by the, # *probability parameter* (0.6). All the classifier system parameter settings used in SPHINcsX may be found in Richards [1995].

In order to teach SPHINcsX in learning mode, a suite of design optimization problems is needed. The educational process consists of a progression through a learning suite of designs on which optimization is attempted. The learning suite contains a range of designs covering the spectrum from simple, one variable sizing optimization designs to multiple variable sizing optimization designs.

The learning suite is broken down into *clusters*; *clusters* are groups of similar designs, that have a common unique characteristic. The design *clusters* composing the learning suite are named as follows ranging from simple to more complex: *Tension Rod (TRg)*, *Pressure Vessel (PV)*, *Torsion Solid Rod (TSR)*, *Cantilever Beam (CB)*, *Torsion Elliptical Solid Rod (TESR)*, and *Torsion Elliptical Hollow Rod (TEHR)*.

Next, the initialization of the design to be optimized occurs. A list of the necessary design initializations consists of setting up the parameters defined by the learning suite. The educational process consists of a progression through a learning suite of designs on which optimization is attempted. The selected design has its design variables stochastically set to their initial values, the resulting initial design is then used in the SPHINcsX algorithm where an attempted optimization proceeds. After the attempted optimization, the process continues with the selection of another initial design. *Attempted* is used because a maximum of 100 iterations is set, so that if 100 iterations occur and the optimum has not been reached, the optimization is ceased and a new design is stochastically generated.

The progress of the learning regime is evaluated by monitoring the performance metrics, *P1*, *P2*, *P3*. *P1* is the ratio of the number of correct responses to the total number of responses. *P2* is the total number of correct responses during an epoch to the epoch length. *P3* is the number of iterations needed to optimize the design. The performance metrics, *P1* and *P2* should show asymptotic improvement with increasing learning iterations, and thus reveal not only the learning progress but also a point where the diminishing returns are so small that continued learning is not justified. The genetic algorithm's purpose is exploration, so the populace after the GA application will most likely initially perform worse because some new members will be provided with artificially high strengths. Therefore, the asymptotic improvements in *P1* and *P2* may not be monotonic.

The learning iterations, t_I, t_{II}, t_{III}, t_{IV}, t_V, and t_{VI}, when each of the design clusters are introduced into the learning regime are not set *a priori*, but are determined via the monitoring of the performance metrics. Each introduction of a new design cluster is expected to cause an initial decrease in all the performance metrics.

Learning commences by selecting a design from the general tension rod cluster, TRg. The information provided by the performance metrics must be examined in tandem to assess when learning has occurred to the level where continued learning with the same cluster of designs is inefficient.

After 5,000 learning iterations, the initial design selection scheme had progressed through the TRg cluster, PV cluster, TSR cluster, CB cluster, TESR cluster, and TEHR cluster.

Figure 4 and Figure 5 depict *P2* and *P3* performance respectively, throughout the learning regime. In Figure 4 the vertical lines denote transitions from one cluster to the next. Note in Figure 5 blank regions of more than 100 iterations occur when SPHINcsX failed to converge within the maximum allowed 100 iterations. Recall also that *P3* was not expected to decrease monotonically through a design cluster because the initial design was set stochastically.

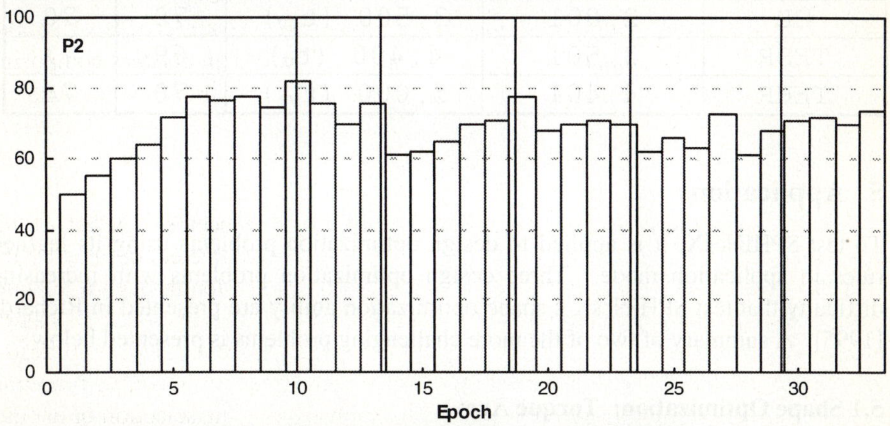

Fig. 4. Correct Response Rate per Epoch (P2)

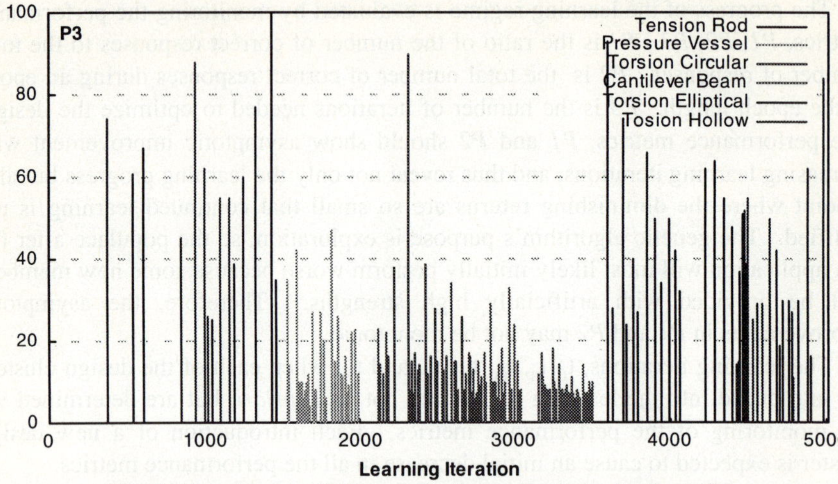

Fig. 5. Iterations to Optimum for Learning Suite Designs (P3)

Table 1 summarizes some of the aspects of the learning process, showing the ranges of learning iterations (defined empirically, as stated above) applied to each design cluster as well as presenting the level of the performance metrics *P1* and *P2* at the end of each cluster's learning phase.

Table 1. Learning Summary

Design Cluster	Iteration (Start)	Iteration (End)	P1	P2
TRg	1	1,500 (t_I)	69	82
PV	1,501	2,000 (t_{II})	70	76
TSR	2,001	2,800 (t_{III})	69	71
CB	2,801	3,500 (t_{IV})	70	70
TESR	3,501	4,400 (t_V)	69	71
TEHR	4,401	5,000 (t_{VI})	70	74

5 Applications

To test SPHINcsX, it is applied to design optimization problems using its learned rules in application mode. Three design optimization problems with increasing difficulty that test SPHINcsX's shape optimization ability are presented in Richards [1995]. A summary of two of the more challenging problems is presented below.

5.1 Shape Optimization: Torque Arm

The goal of the torque arm design problem is to find the shape that minimizes the mass of the torque arm by varying only the shape of the boundary between points A and B as shown in Figure 6, without exceeding the maximum allowable von Mises stress. The torque arm's shape is invariant through its thickness, t, and is loaded by both a transverse load, F_b, and a tensile load, F_t, on the inside of the small hole. In addition, the torque arm is constrained around the circumference of the larger hole. Figure 6 depicts the initial design.

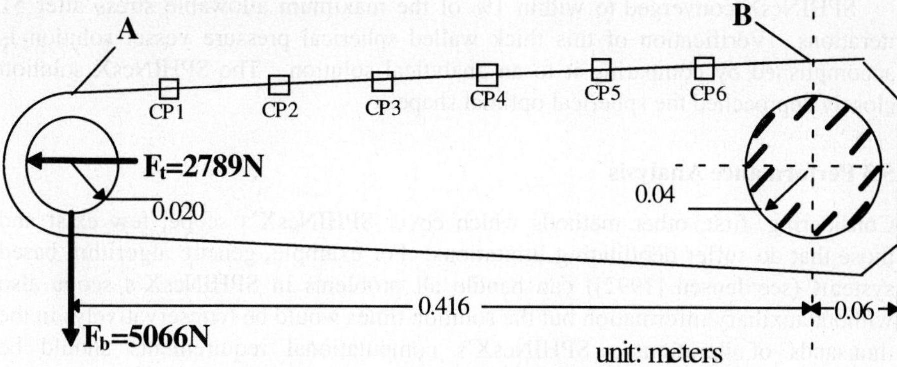

Fig. 6. Initial Configuration and Loading Conditions of the Torque Arm

SPHINcsX converged to within 2% of a fully stressed boundary after 36 iterations. Only one finite element analysis was required in each iteration. The initial mass was, 0.824 kg. The mass of the final design was 0.540 kg, a 34.5% decrease in mass. This example demonstrates the capability of SPHINcsX in solving a realistic design problem. Figure 7 depicts the shape of the optimized design.

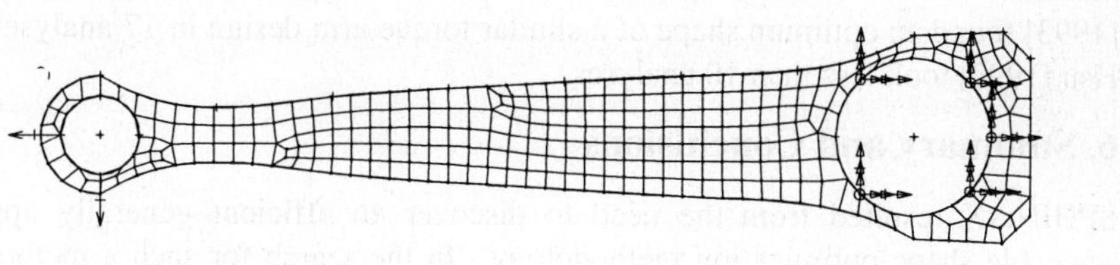

Fig. 7. Optimized Analysis Model of the Torque Arm

5.2 Three Dimensional Shape Optimization: Pressure Vessel

The prominent straddle point definition included provisions to seamlessly allow for three-dimensional boundaries. Thus, the structure of the individual classifiers remains the same, as does all of the internal operations of SPHINcsX.

This application utilizes a spherical pressure vessel, with a fixed spherical exterior loaded by a constant pressure. The initial interior cavity is an irregular non-optimal void. The goal of this problem is to find the shape of the cavity that minimizes the mass of the pressure vessel without exceeding the maximum allowable von Mises stress. There are a total of 22 design variables

The initial design has both under stressed regions and over-stressed regions. Note that no supplemental education is provided before attempting to apply SPHINcsX to a three dimensional problem. The classifier population that learned via a suite of two-dimensional problems is expected to handle this challenge.

SPHINcsX converged to within 1% of the maximum allowable stress after 51 iterations. Verification of this thick walled spherical pressure vessel solution is accomplished by comparing it to an analytical solution. The SPHINcsX solution closely approached the spherical optimal shape.

5.3 Performance Analysis

Considering, first, other methods which cover SPHINcsX's scope, few exist and those that do suffer debilitating limitations. For example, genetic algorithm based systems (see Jensen [1992]) can handle all problems in SPHINcsX's scope also without auxiliary information but the solution times would be (conservatively) in the thousands of iterations. SPHINcsX's computational requirements should be drastically less in 3-D than techniques which depend on derivative information, but successful applications in the literature are scarce (Kodiyalam et al. [1992]). An illustration of the considerable cost of performing 3-D optimization utilizing derivatives is provided by Chargin et al. [1991] where, with 23 design variables, the derivative calculation per analysis required over six times the computational overhead as the underlying analysis.

Modern optimization methods provide more competition to SPHINcsX in the realm of two-dimensional shape optimization. Recall that for the torque arm SPHINcsX determined the optimum in 36 iterations, this is competitive with other methods, however, many specialized methods can perform better. Belegundu [1993] found an optimum shape of a similar torque arm design in 17 analyses, while Hsu [1992] took less than 10 analyses.

6. Summary and Conclusions

SPHINcsX resulted from the need to discover an efficient generally applicable scaleable shape optimization methodology. In the search for such a methodology, non-calculus-based search and optimization techniques were explored to determine if any could provide results superior to the state of the art. Machine learning in general and the classifier system in particular appeared to possess the desired features.

SPHINcsX learned to perform general shape optimization and did so without the benefit of derivative information or any other auxiliary information. Furthermore, *generalized learning was achieved via sizing design problems only.* It is a further credit to the methodology that it learned without knowing anything about the initial shape, the representation of the curve under modification, the concept of stress and strain or optimization. Essentially, SPHINcsX learned to recognize patterns of stress and execute appropriate action. That is, the mapping between a control point's stress pattern and beneficial control point modification has been discovered.

The results illustrate the computational efficiency of SPHINcsX. The computational effort, after learning, is small relative to that of methods using derivatives. The pressure vessel application demonstrated how the computational effort increased less than linearly with the increase in design variables. SPHINcsX demonstrates that the classifier system indeed can be a valuable tool in helping to solve shape optimization problems.

Bibliography

Belegundu, Ashok D., "Optimizing the Shapes of Mechanical Components", Mechanical Engineering, January 1993, pp. 46-48.

Chargin, Mladin K., Ingo Raasch, Ralph Bruns, and Dawson Deuermeyer. "General Shape Optimization Capability", *Finite Elements in Analysis and Design*, Vol. 7, 1991, pp. 343-354.

Dorigo, Marco and Enrico Sirtori, "Alecsys: A Parallel Laboratory for Learning Classifier Systems", *Proceedings of Fourth International Conference on Genetic Algorithms* - July 13-16, 1991 - San Diego - California, Morgan Kaufmann , San Mateo, CA.

Goldberg, D.D., *Genetic Algorithms in Search, Optimization & Machine Learning*, Addison-Wesley, NY, 1989.

Haftka, R.T., and R.V. Grandhi, "Structural Shape Optimization - A Survey", *Computer Methods in Applied Mechanics and Engineering*, Elsevier Science Publishers B.V., North-Holland, 1986, pp. 91-106.

Holland, J.H. and J.S. Reitman, "Cognitive Systems Based on Adaptive Algorithms", in *D.A. Waterman and F. Hayes-Roth (eds.), Pattern-Directed Inference Systems*, Academic Press, NY, 1978.

Hsu, Y.L, *Zeroth Order Optimization Methods of Two Dimensional Shape Optimization*, Ph.D. Dissertation, Department of Mechanical Engineering , Stanford University, 1992.

Jensen, Eric Dean, *Topological Structural Design Using Genetic Algorithms*, Ph.D. Dissertation, Purdue University, Lafayette, IN, 1992.

Kodiyalam, Srinivas, Virendra Kumar and Peter M. Finnigan, "Constructive Solid Geometry Approach to Three-Dimensional Structural Shape Optimization", *AIAA Journal*, Vol. 30, No. 5, May 1992, pp. 1408-1415.

Richards, Robert A., Three-dimensional Shape Optimization Utilizing a Learning Classifier System. In Koza, John R., Goldberg, David E., Fogel, David B., and Riolo, Rick L. (editors). Genetic Programming 1996: Proceedints of the First Annual Conference, July 28-31, 1996, Stanford University. Cambridge, MA: The MIT Press. 1996. Pages 539-546.

Richards, Robert A., *Zeroth-Order Shape Optimization Utilizing a Learning Classifier System*, Ph.D. Dissertation, Stanford University, Stanford, CA, 1995.

Riolo, Rick L., *Empirical Studies of Default Hierarchies and Sequences of Rules in Learning Classifier Systems*, Ph.D. Dissertation, Computer Science and Engineering Department, University of Michigan, 1988.

Wilson, Stewart W., "ZCS: A Zeroth Level Classifier System", *Evolutionary Computation*, Vol. 2, No. 1, Spring 1994, pp. 1-18.

Zienkiewicz, O. C., and J.S. Campbell, "Shape Optimization and Sequential Linear Programming", Gallagher, R.H. and Zienkiewicz, O.C. (eds.), *Optimal Structural Design*, Wiley, NY, 1973.

Author Index

Subject Index

Springer-Verlag and the Environment

We at Springer-Verlag firmly believe that an international science publisher has a special obligation to the environment, and our corporate policies consistently reflect this conviction.

We also expect our business partners – paper mills, printers, packaging manufacturers, etc. – to commit themselves to using environmentally friendly materials and production processes.

The paper in this book is made from low- or no-chlorine pulp and is acid free, in conformance with international standards for paper permanency.

Lecture Notes in Computer Science

For information about Vols. 1–1071

please contact your bookseller or Springer-Verlag

Vol. 1072: R. Kasturi, K. Tombre (Eds.), Graphics Recognition. Proceedings, 1995. X, 308 pages. 1996.

Vol. 1073: J. Cuny, H. Ehrig, G. Engels, G. Rozenberg (Eds.), Graph Grammars and Their Application to Computer Science. Proceedings, 1994. X, 565 pages. 1996.

Vol. 1074: G. Dowek, J. Heering, K. Meinke, B. Möller (Eds.), Higher-Order Algebra, Logic, and Term Rewriting. Proceedings, 1995. VII, 287 pages. 1996.

Vol. 1075: D. Hirschberg, G. Myers (Eds.), Combinatorial Pattern Matching. Proceedings, 1996. VIII, 392 pages. 1996.

Vol. 1076: N. Shadbolt, K. O'Hara, G. Schreiber (Eds.), Advances in Knowledge Acquisition. Proceedings, 1996. XII, 371 pages. 1996. (Subseries LNAI).

Vol. 1077: P. Brusilovsky, P. Kommers, N. Streitz (Eds.), Mulimedia, Hypermedia, and Virtual Reality. Proceedings, 1994. IX, 311 pages. 1996.

Vol. 1078: D.A. Lamb (Ed.), Studies of Software Design. Proceedings, 1993. VI, 188 pages. 1996.

Vol. 1079: Z.W. Raś, M. Michalewicz (Eds.), Foundations of Intelligent Systems. Proceedings, 1996. XI, 664 pages. 1996. (Subseries LNAI).

Vol. 1080: P. Constantopoulos, J. Mylopoulos, Y. Vassiliou (Eds.), Advanced Information Systems Engineering. Proceedings, 1996. XI, 582 pages. 1996.

Vol. 1081: G. McCalla (Ed.), Advances in Artificial Intelligence. Proceedings, 1996. XII, 459 pages. 1996. (Subseries LNAI).

Vol. 1082: N.R. Adam, B.K. Bhargava, M. Halem, Y. Yesha (Eds.), Digital Libraries. Proceedings, 1995. Approx. 310 pages. 1996.

Vol. 1083: K. Sparck Jones, J.R. Galliers, Evaluating Natural Language Processing Systems. XV, 228 pages. 1996. (Subseries LNAI).

Vol. 1084: W.H. Cunningham, S.T. McCormick, M. Queyranne (Eds.), Integer Programming and Combinatorial Optimization. Proceedings, 1996. X, 505 pages. 1996.

Vol. 1085: D.M. Gabbay, H.J. Ohlbach (Eds.), Practical Reasoning. Proceedings, 1996. XV, 721 pages. 1996. (Subseries LNAI).

Vol. 1086: C. Frasson, G. Gauthier, A. Lesgold (Eds.), Intelligent Tutoring Systems. Proceedings, 1996. XVII, 688 pages. 1996.

Vol. 1087: C. Zhang, D. Lukose (Eds.), Distributed Artificial Intelliegence. Proceedings, 1995. VIII, 232 pages. 1996. (Subseries LNAI).

Vol. 1088: A. Strohmeier (Ed.), Reliable Software Technologies – Ada-Europe '96. Proceedings, 1996. XI, 513 pages. 1996.

Vol. 1089: G. Ramalingam, Bounded Incremental Computation. XI, 190 pages. 1996.

Vol. 1090: J.-Y. Cai, C.K. Wong (Eds.), Computing and Combinatorics. Proceedings, 1996. X, 421 pages. 1996.

Vol. 1091: J. Billington, W. Reisig (Eds.), Application and Theory of Petri Nets 1996. Proceedings, 1996. VIII, 549 pages. 1996.

Vol. 1092: H. Kleine Büning (Ed.), Computer Science Logic. Proceedings, 1995. VIII, 487 pages. 1996.

Vol. 1093: L. Dorst, M. van Lambalgen, F. Voorbraak (Eds.), Reasoning with Uncertainty in Robotics. Proceedings, 1995. VIII, 387 pages. 1996. (Subseries LNAI).

Vol. 1094: R. Morrison, J. Kennedy (Eds.), Advances in Databases. Proceedings, 1996. XI, 234 pages. 1996.

Vol. 1095: W. McCune, R. Padmanabhan, Automated Deduction in Equational Logic and Cubic Curves. X, 231 pages. 1996. (Subseries LNAI).

Vol. 1096: T. Schäl, Workflow Management Systems for Process Organisations. XII, 200 pages. 1996.

Vol. 1097: R. Karlsson, A. Lingas (Eds.), Algorithm Theory – SWAT '96. Proceedings, 1996. IX, 453 pages. 1996.

Vol. 1098: P. Cointe (Ed.), ECOOP '96 – Object-Oriented Programming. Proceedings, 1996. XI, 502 pages. 1996.

Vol. 1099: F. Meyer auf der Heide, B. Monien (Eds.), Automata, Languages and Programming. Proceedings, 1996. XII, 681 pages. 1996.

Vol. 1100: B. Pfitzmann, Digital Signature Schemes. XVI, 396 pages. 1996.

Vol. 1101: M. Wirsing, M. Nivat (Eds.), Algebraic Methodology and Software Technology. Proceedings, 1996. XII, 641 pages. 1996.

Vol. 1102: R. Alur, T.A. Henzinger (Eds.), Computer Aided Verification. Proceedings, 1996. XII, 472 pages. 1996.

Vol. 1103: H. Ganzinger (Ed.), Rewriting Techniques and Applications. Proceedings, 1996. XI, 437 pages. 1996.

Vol. 1104: M.A. McRobbie, J.K. Slaney (Eds.), Automated Deduction – CADE-13. Proceedings, 1996. XV, 764 pages. 1996. (Subseries LNAI).

Vol. 1105: T.I. Ören, G.J. Klir (Eds.), Computer Aided Systems Theory – CAST '94. Proceedings, 1994. IX, 439 pages. 1996.

Vol. 1106: M. Jampel, E. Freuder, M. Maher (Eds.), Over-Constrained Systems. X, 309 pages. 1996.

Vol. 1107: J.-P. Briot, J.-M. Geib, A. Yonezawa (Eds.), Object-Based Parallel and Distributed Computation. Proceedings, 1995. X, 349 pages. 1996.

Vol. 1108: A. Díaz de Ilarraza Sánchez, I. Fernández de Castro (Eds.), Computer Aided Learning and Instruction in Science and Engineering. Proceedings, 1996. XIV, 480 pages. 1996.

Vol. 1109: N. Koblitz (Ed.), Advances in Cryptology – Crypto '96. Proceedings, 1996. XII, 417 pages. 1996.

Vol. 1110: O. Danvy, R. Glück, P. Thiemann (Eds.), Partial Evaluation. Proceedings, 1996. XII, 514 pages. 1996.

Vol. 1111: J.J. Alferes, L. Moniz Pereira, Reasoning with Logic Programming. XXI, 326 pages. 1996. (Subseries LNAI).

Vol. 1112: C. von der Malsburg, W. von Seelen, J.C. Vorbrüggen, B. Sendhoff (Eds.), Artificial Neural Networks – ICANN 96. Proceedings, 1996. XXV, 922 pages. 1996.

Vol. 1113: W. Penczek, A. Szałas (Eds.), Mathematical Foundations of Computer Science 1996. Proceedings, 1996. X, 592 pages. 1996.

Vol. 1114: N. Foo, R. Goebel (Eds.), PRICAI'96: Topics in Artificial Intelligence. Proceedings, 1996. XXI, 658 pages. 1996. (Subseries LNAI).

Vol. 1115: P.W. Eklund, G. Ellis, G. Mann (Eds.), Conceptual Structures: Knowledge Representation as Interlingua. Proceedings, 1996. XIII, 321 pages. 1996. (Subseries LNAI).

Vol. 1116: J. Hall (Ed.), Management of Telecommunication Systems and Services. XXI, 229 pages. 1996.

Vol. 1117: A. Ferreira, J. Rolim, Y. Saad, T. Yang (Eds.), Parallel Algorithms for Irregularly Structured Problems. Proceedings, 1996. IX, 358 pages. 1996.

Vol. 1118: E.C. Freuder (Ed.), Principles and Practice of Constraint Programming — CP 96. Proceedings, 1996. XIX, 574 pages. 1996.

Vol. 1119: U. Montanari, V. Sassone (Eds.), CONCUR '96: Concurrency Theory. Proceedings, 1996. XII, 751 pages. 1996.

Vol. 1120: M. Deza. R. Euler, I. Manoussakis (Eds.), Combinatorics and Computer Science. Proceedings, 1995. IX, 415 pages. 1996.

Vol. 1121: P. Perner, P. Wang, A. Rosenfeld (Eds.), Advances in Structural and Syntactical Pattern Recognition. Proceedings, 1996. X, 393 pages. 1996.

Vol. 1122: H. Cohen (Ed.), Algorithmic Number Theory. Proceedings, 1996. IX, 405 pages. 1996.

Vol. 1123: L. Bougé, P. Fraigniaud, A. Mignotte, Y. Robert (Eds.), Euro-Par'96. Parallel Processing. Proceedings, 1996, Vol. I. XXXIII, 842 pages. 1996.

Vol. 1124: L. Bougé, P. Fraigniaud, A. Mignotte, Y. Robert (Eds.), Euro-Par'96. Parallel Processing. Proceedings, 1996, Vol. II. XXXIII, 926 pages. 1996.

Vol. 1125: J. von Wright, J. Grundy, J. Harrison (Eds.), Theorem Proving in Higher Order Logics. Proceedings, 1996. VIII, 447 pages. 1996.

Vol. 1126: J.J. Alferes, L. Moniz Pereira, E. Orlowska (Eds.), Logics in Artificial Intelligence. Proceedings, 1996. IX, 417 pages. 1996. (Subseries LNAI).

Vol. 1127: L. Böszörményi (Ed.), Parallel Computation. Proceedings, 1996. XI, 235 pages. 1996.

Vol. 1128: J. Calmet, C. Limongelli (Eds.), Design and Implementation of Symbolic Computation Systems. Proceedings, 1996. IX, 356 pages. 1996.

Vol. 1129: J. Launchbury, E. Meijer, T. Sheard (Eds.), Advanced Functional Programming. Proceedings, 1996. VII, 238 pages. 1996.

Vol. 1130: M. Haveraaen, O. Owe, O.-J. Dahl (Eds.), Recent Trends in Data Type Specification. Proceedings, 1995. VIII, 551 pages. 1996.

Vol. 1131: K.H. Höhne, R. Kikinis (Eds.), Visualization in Biomedical Computing. Proceedings, 1996. XII, 610 pages. 1996.

Vol. 1132: G.-R. Perrin, A. Darte (Eds.), The Data Parallel Programming Model. XV, 284 pages. 1996.

Vol. 1133: J.-Y. Chouinard, P. Fortier, T.A. Gulliver (Eds.), Information Theory and Applications. Proceedings, 1995. XII, 309 pages. 1996.

Vol. 1134: R. Wagner, H. Thoma (Eds.), Database and Expert Systems Applications. Proceedings, 1996. XV, 921 pages. 1996.

Vol. 1135: B. Jonsson, J. Parrow (Eds.), Formal Techniques in Real-Time and Fault-Tolerant Systems. Proceedings, 1996. X, 479 pages. 1996.

Vol. 1136: J. Diaz, M. Serna (Eds.), Algorithms - ESA '96. Proceedings, 1996. XII, 566 pages. 1996.

Vol. 1137: G. Görz, S. Hölldobler (Eds.), KI-96: Advances in Artificial Intelligence. Proceedings, 1996. XI, 387 pages. 1996. (Subseries LNAI).

Vol. 1138: J. Calmet, J.A. Campbell, J. Pfalzgraf (Eds.), Artificial Intelligence and Symbolic Mathematical Computation. Proceedings, 1996. VIII, 381 pages. 1996.

Vol. 1139: M. Hanus, M. Rogriguez-Artalejo (Eds.), Algebraic and Logic Programming. Proceedings, 1996. VIII, 345 pages. 1996.

Vol. 1140: H. R. Kuchen, S. Doaitse Swierstra (Eds.), Programming Languages: Implementations, Logics, and Programs. Proceedings, 1996. XI, 479 pages. 1996.

Vol. 1141: H.-M. Voigt, W. Ebeling, I. Rechenberg, H.-P. Schwefel (Eds.), Parallel Problem Solving from Nature – PPSN IV. Proceedings, 1996. XVII, 1.050 pages. 1996.

Vol. 1142: R.W. Hartenstein, M. Glesner (Eds.), Field-Programmable Logic. Proceedings, 1996. X, 432 pages. 1996.

Vol. 1143: T.C. Fogarty (Ed.), Evolutionary Computing. Proceedings, 1996. VIII, 305 pages. 1996.

Vol. 1144: J. Ponce, A. Zisserman, M. Hebert (Eds.), Object Representation in Computer Vision. Proceedings, 1996. VIII, 403 pages. 1996.

Vol. 1145: R. Cousot, D.A. Schmidt (Eds.), Static Analysis. Proceedings, 1996. IX, 389 pages. 1996.